The European Philosophers

FROM DESCARTES
TO NIETZSCHE

THE EUROPEAN PHILOSOPHERS

FROM DESCARTES
TO NIETZSCHE

EDITED AND WITH AN INTRODUCTION BY
MONROE C. BEARDSLEY

THE MODERN LIBRARY

NEW YORK

Library of Congress Cataloging-in-Publication Data

The European philosophers from Descartes to Nietzsche / edited by Monroe C. Beardsley ; with an updated bibliography.—Modern Library pbk. ed.
p.   cm.
Originally published: New York: Modern Library, 1992, in series: Modern library of the world's best books. With an updated bibliography.
Includes bibliographical references.
ISBN 0-375-75804-6
1. Philosophy, Modern. 2. Philosophy, European.
3. Philosophers—Europe. I. Beardsley, Monroe C.

B790 .E97   2002
190—dc21   2002070263

Modern Library website address: www.modernlibrary.com

Printed in the United States of America

2 4 6 8 9 7 5 3 1

CONTENTS

BARUCH SPINOZA

GOTTFRIED WILHELM VON LEIBNIZ

JEAN-JACQUES ROUSSEAU

Contents

FRIEDRICH NIETZSCHE

INTRODUCTION

by Monroe C. Beardsley

A MASTER of ceremonies assigned to introduce the twelve philosophers represented in this book will do well to keep his voice low and his speeches short. For they are eminently capable of speaking for themselves. Indeed, there is some danger of obscuring the variety and individuality of their thought by too facile a summary or survey. Between the earliest and the latest of the works included here, we have two hundred and fifty years of vigorous and adventurous philosophizing. And what a range of styles and outlooks! When we set Spinoza beside Nietzsche, for example, or Leibniz beside Mach, or Pascal beside Kant, we get some notion of how far apart on basic philosophical questions—on the nature of man, his place in the scheme of things, the sort of life he ought to lead—different thinkers can be.

And that is perhaps the first thing to be noticed and borne in mind: that each of these philosophers is thinking for himself, and trying to make his own way toward the truth. They start with very different equipment, and from different launching platforms of experience. And so, since truth (though one) is many-sided, they have grasped different aspects and different measures of it. No doubt, too, all of them have accepted some false propositions, which—not without reason—they took to be true; for philosophic truth is sometimes hard as well as complicated. Each of these philosophers is, in certain ways, unique. To read him well, to get what he has to give, we must enter inside his system, learn his technical language, follow with attention the peculiar pattern in which his argument develops. Rousseau does not think like Fichte, nor Descartes like Schopenhauer, yet each *is* thinking, and the record of his thought—its successes and failures—is here for us to learn from.

Nevertheless, individuality and difference are not the whole story of modern European philosophy. For on a closer look, we find connections and interrelations among these philosophers that give them much more the appearance of taking part in a common enterprise, even when they are reacting against each other. We recall, for example, with what uncontainable excitement Kant read Rousseau's *Émile* when it was first published, and how strongly Rousseau influenced his ethical theory; and the

deep mark left by Schopenhauer's philosophy on Nietzsche's, though his
ethical theory was passionately repudiated by the latter. We must be careful not to read back into the past all the connections that we can now see
from our later vantage point; for example, though Leibniz's metaphysics
was a dominant influence in the eighteenth century, some of his most important ideas were hidden away in papers and not published until late in
the nineteenth century; and again, Spinoza was not much more than a
symbol of a heretical pantheism, abhorred but unread until rediscovered
by the German romantics. Yet we can point out affinities among even apparently disparate thinkers, as when we see how much of Leibniz's analytical method is still preserved in Mach, of Pascal's mistrust of reason in
Nietzsche, of Spinoza's concern with freedom in Fichte.

In this Introduction, then, we shall look for a moment at the period—if
it may be called a period—as a whole. It would be hazardous, of course, to
attempt to date the beginning of modern Western philosophy from the
publication of Descartes' *Discourse on Method* (1637), though probably this
book has a better claim than any other, even that of its chief rival, Bacon's
Novum Organum (1620). And it would be hopeless to plead for a date to
mark the end of this philosophical epoch, at, say, Nietzsche's *Beyond Good
and Evil* (1886) or the death of Mach (1916). We are too sharply aware,
when we read Nietzsche and Mach, of the extent to which many of the
concerns, and many of the programs, of philosophers today derive directly
from their thought. Yet, if the modern period can be only vaguely or arbitrarily bounded, it can at least be studied, and we can ask whether any
dominant themes, overall patterns of movement, or notable achievements
can be found within it. This question is one that is best asked by the reader
after he has read, or read around in, these works. The present Introduction
is not a retrospective review; it is only a preparation of the stage.

One parenthetical note is best inserted here. Though I refer primarily
to the philosophers on the continent of Europe, it will not always be possible, or necessary, to keep them sharply segregated from the philosophers who were working at the same time in Great Britain. Some broad
and pervasive differences between the Continental European and the
British philosophers have often been noted and described—differences
in the problems that struck them as most in need of study, or most interesting to tackle, and differences in style of philosophizing. But the period
we are dealing with was, throughout most of its duration, a period of true
internationality so far as the republic of letters was concerned. There
were national predilections, but there was no intellectual isolationism.
Hobbes and Hume lived for a time in France, Leibniz and Rousseau
visited England, but this moving about was not the main source of mutual

stimulation. The period was one of extensive correspondence and exchange of books, so that even comparative stay-at-homes such as Spinoza, Locke, and Kant, were fully in touch with their leading contemporaries. Therefore much of what can be said about the Continental European philosophers can also be said about the British, though perhaps with qualifications. This applies particularly to what is said below.

When we consider European philosophy in the seventeenth, eighteenth, and nineteenth centuries, we have a choice among three very different approaches.

The first might be called the *expressionistic,* or symptomatic, *approach.* Its essence is to consider philosophies, like other forms of cultural behavior, as manifestations of the minds or the societies that gave them birth. Many philosophers have been interesting in themselves simply as personalities or psychological cases, for example Pascal, Rousseau, Schopenhauer, and Nietzsche. We may treat their philosophies, like their dreams, as indications of mental peculiarities or unconscious wishes. On a larger scale, if we take the Age of Reason, the Enlightenment, or the Romantic Period (appropriately capitalized) as organic entities of some sort, then we may try the "physiognomic" method of Spengler and Egon Friedell, and read the spirit of the age from its philosophical products, with the help of cross references to its wars, its mathematics, its sculpture, its music, its laws, its technology, and so on.

For those who conceive of works of art primarily as vehicles of self-expression, this approach to philosophies turns them into objects of aesthetic contemplation—a form of poetry, though perhaps bad poetry, as Santayana suggested. Then a book like the present one becomes a guided tour (pleasant if the guide is not too chatty) through a gallery of self-portraits in prose—some of which are more beautiful than others, of course, but all of which are revelations of the thinkers or the age that produced them. As the visitors pass along, from Descartes to Nietzsche, we hear appropriate comments: "How insecure Spinoza must have been, to construct a metaphysics in which nothing is left to chance! How completely the seventeenth century's pride in its intellect, and absolute worship of rationality, is expressed in the dry propositions of Leibniz's *Monadology*! How much of the spirit of Beethoven's *Eroica* can also be found in the philosophy of Fichte—in the self-positing of the Ego, and his calling of the German people to a new destiny!"

This aesthetic reaction to philosophical works cannot, of course, be prohibited. It remains open to any reader who is inclined that way. But in my opinion it is a questionable reaction, and if it is the only or even the chief reaction it is absurdly inappropriate. It is questionable because such psychoanalytic "interpretations" and insights into the *Zeitgeist* are very difficult to verify, and are therefore very likely to rest on loose and rather subjective associations. It is inappropriate because a philosophical work is a venture in knowledge, and therefore claims to deserve predicates that go beyond the aesthetic predicates "beautiful" and "expressive"—namely, the predicates "true" and "false." If it does not succeed in deserving either of these predicates—if, somehow, it turns out not to be making a genuine and arguable assertion about reality—then at least it deserves an explanation of why it fails. There is nothing wrong, of course, in our responding to the eloquence of some passages (such as the Appendix to Book I) of Spinoza's *Ethics,* or to the architectural order of the *Critique of Pure Reason,* or to the sharp and telling irony of Nietzsche's apothegms. But the *Ethics,* the *Critique of Pure Reason,* and *Beyond Good and Evil* are not poems; they are statements about man and the world, and to ignore their cognitive, or truth-claiming, aspect is to lose a rare opportunity to increase the range and depth of our own philosophical knowledge.

The second approach to modern philosophy sometimes encompasses the first, but goes beyond it, and is finally different. It is the *historical approach.* If we consider philosophies as events in the history of man, then they will have connections with other events. They will have causes and effects which the historian can set himself to track down.

Now this second approach has two main subdivisions, which might be called *external* and *internal.* Something can be said in favor of both of them.

By the *external historical* approach, I mean the search for causal connections between philosophical ideas and other elements found in their cultural contexts. Perhaps a psychologist could show that Rousseau's concept of the General Will, or Neitzsche's concept of the Superman, or even Leibniz's concept of the "windowless" monad, were derived from unconscious leanings or yearnings. But a cultural historian might consider that a trivial truth, for suppose he could give his own evidence that these concepts were inevitable consequences of other developments—social, scientific, religious, economic—occurring at the same time, so that if these philosophers had not thought of them someone else would have. Given the social conditions attending the decline of the French monarchy, perhaps someone would have had to consider the possibility that a community is more than an aggregate of individuals and has a psychological being of its own on which a theory of rights can be based. Given Victorian economic conditions and the Darwinian theory of evolution, perhaps someone would have had to draw the moral that man's future lies in a further development of those competitive qualities thought to be decisive in his past evolution. Once the infinitesimal calculus had been invented, perhaps someone would have had to inquire whether the problem of the relation between mind and body, as Descartes left it, couldn't be solved by conceiving of all reality as a continuum of extensionless spirit-points.

So the cultural historian might claim. And speculative as these hypotheses may be, they suggest some fruitful lines of inquiry. Here historians will differ according to the factors they consider most effective.

For example, a good case can be made for interpreting the major trends in modern philosophy as responses to developments in *physical science*. Descartes' dualism of primary and secondary qualities is anticipated in Galileo, and his whole task might be understood as one of working out a metaphysical system that would take account of seventeenth century physics—not primarily its results, which were still far from being completely seen when he was writing, but its new concepts, its method of scientific inquiry, its new combination of mathematics and experiment. And Kant, the other great revolutionary figure in this group, certainly considered it to be a major part of his task to answer the question, "How is a science of nature possible?" Indeed it was this question that gave rise to perhaps the most original and influential part of his thought. Leibniz was concerned with a metaphysics of physics, just as Mach was two centuries later. There is no major philosopher, not even Pascal and Nietzsche, whose thinking did not in some degree confront the fact of the rise of modern science, surely one of the most portentous facts in the modern world.

In these systems we also see a widespread concern with the demands of *religion,* especially in relation to science. Descartes and Pascal, contemporaneously, mark out almost the extreme bounds of response, at least in some respects. Yet each, in his own special way, was trying to make the knowledge of God's existence the absolutely independent groundwork of the whole of man's knowledge and life. In this they were as "God-intoxicated" as Spinoza. So, too, Hegel, and Comte, and Nietzsche, again in very different ways, were preoccupied with religion and were dedicated to the purification of religious truths. Leibniz's major work was a theodicy. One of the high points of Rousseau's *Émile* was the "Confession of Faith of the Savoyard Vicar," which caused such a scandal at the time. And the basic division in Kant's philosophy, between the Practical and the Theoretical (or Speculative) Reason, is over the three problems of God, Freedom, and Immortality.

Many of the philosophical ideas in this volume were in part responses to the great *social and political issues* of their day. This becomes more often evident as the period moves on. Leibniz was much interested in problems of statecraft and diplomacy, but we do not feel that his conclusions are part and parcel of his philosophy. With Spinoza the connection is closer, but still not inevitable, for a liberal political view very similar to that in his two political treatises would be equally consistent with a very different metaphysics. Rousseau's *Social Contract* is, of course, a direct grappling with great social problems; and we see similar responses in Kant and Fichte to the period of the Revolution, in Hegel and Comte to the post-revolutionary period of reorganization in Europe, and in Nietzsche to the basic trends during the latter part of the century: empire, widening suffrage, the rise of labor, militarism and nationalism.

Or we could look for the effects, as well as the causes, of philosophical ideas—though here the search might be even more difficult. It takes little effort to observe Rousseau's powerful effect on the French Revolution, or Fichte's on the unification of Germany after the Napoleonic wars. Other connections, equally apparent at a hasty glance, may be much more doubtful. At least they are not to be accepted before a skeptical examination. For example, there is Nietzsche and the rise of Nazism. Certainly there is a similarity between some of Nietzsche's ideas and some of Hitler's, and the apologists of National Socialism were happy to quote Nietzsche on their own behalf. But it is not easy to discover to just what extent there was genuine influence, or what features, if any, of Hitler's fantastic Third Reich would have been different if it had not been for Nietzsche. Again, it is fashionable to attribute various unfortunate tendencies in our own time to the rise of positivism in the nineteenth century—to Comte and Mach. But it takes a good deal more evidence to justify this accusation than to make it fashionable.

The deeper and more lasting philosophical influences are quite likely to be underground and hard to trace. Some of the conceptual forces set in motion by Descartes bore fruit right away, some of them not until the French Revolution, and then only by way of other minds, such as Voltaire's and the Encyclopedists'. Hegel's thinking about Absolute Spirit, history, the state, the law, and the family had a long-range impact, and still does, but much of it through the theorems and corollaries drawn by his followers and interpreters and applied by them to later conditions. Witness, for example, the transmigration of Hegelian dialectic through Marx, Engels, and Lenin.

There is, of course, a great deal more to be said about the interactions between philosophy and other areas of culture. I have pointed out but a few of the directions in which to look. This sort of inquiry is important, but like the first approach, it sometimes leads to the view that we can look at these philosophers only as units in a causal process. Just as a historian of the fine arts can, if he tries, write a whole history of the development of Mannerist and Baroque painting, considering influences and derivations, techniques and styles, without ever once saying whether any of the paintings is good or bad, so the external historian of philosophical ideas might run through the history of modern philosophy without ever using the words "true" and "false." And to forget that Descartes' *Meditations,* Hegel's *Logic,* and Comte's *System of Positive Polity* are addressed to our rational belief is to miss what is distinctively philosophical about them.

The *internal historical* approach takes us closer to the heart of the matter. Though from the cultural historian's point of view it represents a considerable abstraction, it covers a good deal of important ground. Here our interest is still historical, but we are concerned with the development of philosophy in itself; we aim to grasp the challenge and response of one philosophy to another. Just as an expert chess player, coming upon a chess match broken off in the middle, can hardly help thinking what the next move might be, so philosophers have often found their first problems and their first intellectual tools in the legacies of their predecessors. Not that philosophical thinking is exactly like playing chess, or that the history of philosophy should be regarded as an endless game. But there is an analogy. The philosopher comes upon the scene at a certain point, as others have left it, and he takes up his problems, his philosophical tasks, in the form in which he finds them. Even so original a mind as Kant's later proved to be began with the situation as it existed: with the threat that Hume's kind of skepticism seemed to raise, not only against the rationalistic Leibnizian metaphysics Kant studied as a youth, but against the very basis of human knowledge.

The philosophers represented here provide excellent material for study of this inner causation of philosophical ideas. For we have two great phases or epochs of philosophical history, marked by the two peaks, Descartes and Kant. These two philosophers, surely among the very greatest of all time, are strikingly similar, not in their ideas but in their roles in the history of modern philosophy. Each became convinced that philosophical development had reached an impasse in his time, from which only a radical stroke would break it loose; each was determined to effect a revolution; each undertook a thorough reexamination of the foundations of knowledge; each tried to carry out his principles into a ramified system that would serve as a suitable basis for future philosophical work. And most of all, each produced a system that was at once vitally original, brilliantly reasoned out, full of fruitful new ideas, and inherently unstable. A combination like this is irresistible in philosophy:

no philosopher after Descartes could fail to reckon with him in some degree (even Pascal, who recoiled from his whole mode of philosophizing); and few of the great minds could wholly keep from being drawn into the work of trying to repair the deep gaps and apparent inconsistencies in the system he left.

The great philosophers make part of their contribution in the form of distinctions which they are the first to devise or to clarify. In Descartes' case it was that between the mental and the physical realms. When such a distinction proves its great value by doing away with some unnecessary problems and helping to solve others, it may acquire a different status and become a dualism, as this distinction did in the metaphysics of Descartes. And then it may generate new problems of its own. The distinction may be one that is not easy to dispense with, and yet is seemingly impossible to resolve because the parts once put asunder resist reassembling. So Descartes, having divided mind from body, as two essentially distinct substances, left the mind-body problem, which is just the problem of explaining—as he never succeeded in doing despite a somewhat half-hearted attempt at a theory of interaction—how they can intelligibly be related. The logical possibilities are not numerous and they all had to be investigated. The materialistic hypothesis, reducing minds to material objects, was tried by Hobbes and Gassendi; the idealistic one, going the other way, was tried by Leibniz and Berkeley. Malebranche proposed a more sophisticated solution, called Occasionalism, according to which God constantly regulates the two substances in such a way that whenever a change originates in one, the appropriate "effect"—which is therefore not really an effect at all—occurs in the other. Spinoza's proposal was perhaps the most sophisticated of all: that mental and physical events are really identical but are conceived under different aspects. The development of phenomenalism, in Hartley and Hume, and further reflections by Kant and Mach, later made possible a still different theory: that each sense-datum or element of experience can be part of either a mind or a body, depending on the way it is related to others.

The philosophy that followed Descartes, then, was in no trivial or tautological sense post-Cartesian, at least so far as its metaphysics and epistemology were concerned. To decide how far other branches of philosophy—aesthetics, political philosophy, ethics, philosophy of history, for example—were shaped by the Cartesian principles and concepts would be a lengthy task. There is no doubt, for instance, that Descartes' distinction between clear and obscure, and between distinct and confused, ideas, given redefinition by Leibniz, played an important part in eighteenth century theories of sensuous beauty and poetry, as can be seen in Baumgarten's *Reflections on Poetry* (1735). And his theory of innate ideas helped to bolster the doctrine of natural rights that was so fundamental in seventeenth and eighteenth century political theory up to Bentham. These are just two samples out of a large field.

Kant, too, was deeply convinced of the coherence and completeness of his system, and he never doubted—as his *Opus Postumum* shows—that the cracks that were beginning to appear could be mended. Still, his ultimate distinction between the phenomenal and the noumenal world, between the world of appearance and the Thing in Itself, was an endless puzzle and a nagging thorn to his successors. The relation between the theoretical and the practical reason, between the categories of the one and the postulates of the other, Kant left in delicate balance, but the questions that were soon to arise led to painful decisions. Whenever one took from Kant something as sound and established, it seemed that something else equally dear to him would have to be given up if consistency were to be preserved. And thus we have a number of roads leading out from the Kantian fountain, many of them well-travelled, all worthy of exploration, and some of them still with many miles lying ahead of us. One could take seriously Kant's words about the meaninglessness of cosmological speculation, abandon the noumenal world as nonsense, and adopt a revived but more critical Humeanism; this was the road taken by Ernst Mach, which led to the logical empiricism, or logical positivism, of the twentieth century. If the Thing in Itself seemed indispensable, there were various possibilities. Perhaps there was another way—an immediate, intuitive form of knowledge—by which it could be known; this was the way of Schopenhauer, who transformed the Thing in Itself into the Will to Life. Perhaps the two worlds could be gotten together by following Kant's own clue of the "primacy of the practical reason"—making the world of appearance itself a product of the self's will to selfhood; that, or something like it, was what Fichte had in mind. Or perhaps within the structure of an all-embracing Absolute Spirit, unfolding itself in history and in thought, the two realms might once more be brought into reconciliation; that was Hegel's idea. Each of these roads, in turn, was later to develop its own forks and side-branches. But nearly all of the most fruitful and vigorous philosophies of our own time—logical empiricism, analytical philosophy, the process-philosophies of Bergson and Whitehead, monistic and pluralistic idealisms, instrumentalism or pragmatic contextualism—owe a great deal, directly or indirectly, to the philosophy of Kant. Nor is this only in respect to their epistemological theses. It would indeed take a considerable essay even to summarize the long-range effects of Kant's reflections about religious belief, aesthetic value, and moral obligation.

I have not lost count of the third approach that I promised above. One further reflection on the *internal historical* approach will provide a transition to it. When we look at the history of philosophy as a continuing interplay of ideas that are directed to the solution of specifically philosophical problems, we see crises and climaxes, periods of bold assertion and of mopping up. We see new starts and the rebirth of old ideas in new forms. But that is not all we see. For, at least in the history of Western philosophy from the Greeks to the present, we also see progress.

Some philosophers believe it is a mistake, or at least very odd, to speak of philosophic progress, especially since problems (such as those that concerned the thirteenth-century theologians) may seem to be as often bypassed as solved by later philosophers. There is a complicated historical issue here, which we shall not take time to discuss: what actually happens when problems die without being disposed of. But the view I have in mind at the moment is that the history of philosophy is like the history of art, or more like it than it is like the history of science. One scientific discovery builds upon another, and later scientific theories are better, come nearer to truth, or are more probable, than earlier ones. But modern poetry or painting or music is not necessarily better than the earlier—it is just different. Perhaps it is good, perhaps bad, in its own way, but it does not necessarily reflect progress.

How progress should be understood in the arts is an interesting question. In one sense it surely takes place, as it takes place in geographical (or interplanetary) exploration. The areas the explorer discovers and maps for the first time may be no better than those already known, but his discoveries enlarge the boundaries of our experience and thus increase our knowledge or our opportunities for knowledge. So too the painter, composer, or poet opens up new modes of experience, calls our attention to new forms and new qualities. He is an explorer of aesthetic values, of which there may be worlds yet unknown, and he makes his contribution to civilization when he creates new objects that are of aesthetic worth, whether or not they are greater than others that have already been made. Indeed, he may open up territories that later artists will mine with brilliant, unforeseeable success.

So it seems to me that the philosopher explores possible lines of thought, which must be explored even if sometimes only to show (whether the philosopher knows it or not) that they are dead ends. That will not in itself make him a great philosopher, though if he carries out his work with care and persistence, with rigor and with imagination, he will be of great service. If even with all his effort and skill he fails to solve his problems—say the mind-body problem, or the problem of free will, or the problem of justifying induction—we can be pretty sure that the method he tried is not the right one. If along the way he forges some new and significant concepts, distinctions, terms, methodological principles, then he will be making a lasting contribution, just as timelessly valid—so long as there are philosophers at work—as any knowledge. And finally, of course, he may turn up and establish with reasonable arguments some important truths that his successors can use, even though they cannot help rejecting some of his other propositions.

The modern period, from Descartes to Nietzsche, illustrates this generalization very fully. And the period itself is one of permanent achievement, in many respects, despite all the disagreements it exhibits. If the philosophers of ancient Greece showed the way to philosophy (in its Western form) by asking many of the right questions for the first time, it is the philosophers of the modern world who have taught us to think hard about the methods that might yield satisfactory answers to those questions. Compared with Greek philosophy and medieval philosophy, modern philosophy is on the whole man-centered, self-conscious, and epistemological. The opening blasts of Descartes and Bacon made a deliberate break with the past, and called not first for more knowledge but for an examination of knowledge itself. And though our twelve philosophers were concerned, among them, with all the basic problems of metaphysics, and with theories of value as well as with epistemology, they tended, on the whole, to regard the epistemological problems as the most basic. Kant was the first philosopher who thought of making a whole philosophy out of a critique, but all of the greatest modern philosophers began with some sort of critique.

It is dangerous to generalize in such simple terms, of course, and indeed modern philosophy has too often been oversimplified. The most familiar pattern is that which divides the Continental rationalists from the British empiricists, and outlines the development in the seventeenth and eighteenth centuries as a conflict between the two schools, reconciled at last by Kant. These terms "rationalism" and "empiricism" are so widely used that they deserve a brief comment here, or at least a warning. For they are of variable meaning. If we wish to sort the British and Continental European philosophers into separate camps, we have to give these labels a very loose meaning. Thus we might say that the empiricists (the British) lay a greater stress on sense-experience in the acquisition of knowledge—or something equally rough. It is not very helpful to say this; it doesn't take us very far in understanding these philosophers. On the other hand, we can take the terms in a more recent sense, where they are fairly clear: the rationalist is one who believes in synthetic *a priori* knowledge, or in *a priori* concepts. In this definition we use terms that Kant was the first to introduce in just these meanings. So we do not find it easy to apply the definition to the pre-Kantian philosophers. But it may be clarifying to see where Spinoza and Locke, for example, stand in relation to the later distinction—to ask what they would say if forced to choose. Then our simple clash of schools will have to be abandoned, for some of the British philosophers (Locke and Berkeley, for example) will turn out to have rationalistic elements in their thinking.

But what is perhaps even more interesting is to notice how these basic distinctions were gradually forged in the thinking of these philosophers as they worked on each other's ideas. We see, for example, how Leibniz's concept of analyticity, Descartes' principle that God can separate distinct substances, Locke's discussion of "trivial truths," Berkeley's criticism of "abstract ideas," and Hume's principle that "whatever is distinguishable is separable," all lie behind, and lead up to, Kant's distinction between analytic and synthetic judgments. This is only one example. And it is, in my opinion, an example of philosophic progress. Some philosophers of our day have objected to the analytic-synthetic distinction; others, while not rejecting it, believe that its application to everyday statements is restricted. But even if it should yield in the end to more ultimate distinctions, its role in the history of philosophy is secure. It will have served an important purpose.

This sketchy discussion of philosophic progress brings us around to the third and final approach. For if we can think of these philosophers in some such way as I have just suggested, then we can also regard them in a perspective that is neither expressionistic nor historical, but simply *philosophical*. To ask whether their works exhibit progress is to compare them with a standard that is outside history itself. We take them out of time, not asking who wrote them, when or why or to what end, but what truth is there in them that we can understand and keep. In all these systems there are things that are living and things that are dead. The dead may interest the historian; the living is for anyone. For we are not all historians, but we are all human beings. And in so far as we reflect upon ourselves, and our world, and what we are doing in it, we are all philosophers.

What, then, do these thinkers have to say to us, to help us build our own philosophy and to think things out in our own way? When we read their works in this spirit we are looking for important propositions and for good reasons for those propositions. Sometimes we recognize a proposition to be true because our own experience supports it, as did the experience of the philosopher himself. Then we must find room in our own philosophy for that truth. Where we conclude that a proposition is false, it may still be well reasoned—and then we have learned, not that proposition, but the logical connection between that proposition and some other propositions which must also be rejected if that one is. Where we suspect that the philosopher, in a particular place, is talking neither truth nor falsity but nonsense—and there may be some of that, too—then we may still learn from him. For one thing we can be sure of: that if one of these philosophers talks nonsense, it is no simple and obvious form of nonsense, but subtle and elusive, and if we can figure out why it is nonsense we shall have understood something of the highest usefulness to our own thinking.

Some philosophical problems are always with us because they turn up in different forms from age to age and have to be thought about again and again. Others arise from special crises in science or religion or society, and may be resolved. But in either case, the issues that we face today are partly determined by the work of thinkers of the last generation and of earlier ones. To read the modern philosophers, then, is in part to discover how things got (philosophically speaking) to where they are today. And if there are some problems that seem insoluble or highly resistent to rational attack, we can sometimes get new ideas for dealing with them by turning back in the history of philosophy to see how and where the problems got started, and whether perhaps they might have been avoided in the first place if the course of thought had taken a different turn. Thus, for example, there is the present-day problem of whether there are such things as sense-data, and incorrigible statements about them; we might go back to Descartes, who first opened up this line of thought, and try to find out whether a different road, if taken then, might have avoided the difficulties. Again, there is the problem of understanding the logical relation between value-judgments and factual statements—the "is" and the "ought." We might restudy the ethics of Hume and Kant, who did so much to make this distinction definite, in search of clues for another way of getting at the matter.

This may make philosophical inquiry look like a long and arduous task, and one that we can never be sure of having completed. That is so. But the acceptance of this human lot—to which man is doomed the moment he begins to philosophize—is the common spiritual core of all these philosophers despite their differences of conclusion and of method. The length and the difficulty of the knowledge-task that man has set himself does not discourage them, for they do not expect high and precious truths to be easy of attainment. Their attitude is poles apart from the demand for unearned "belief" that is so highly prized by many—the swallowing of slogans, the unreflecting reliance upon handy authority or custom or prevailing opinion. And perhaps it is in catching and carrying away a portion of that noble and dedicated spirit that we find what is of greatest worth to our own efforts to know the truth.

PREFACE

I have aimed to exhibit the range of problems that occupied the attention of modern philosophers on the continent of Europe during nearly three centuries, and at the same time to represent the major philosophers fully enough to show their most significant ideas. Therefore I have resorted to a double device of choosing major works, or large selections from them, and adding to some of them other short passages to clarify and amplify important points. My hope has been that this book will be found capable of standing as a companion volume to the well-known collection edited by Professor Edwin A. Burtt, *The English Philosophers from Bacon to Mill.*

I should like to thank two of my colleagues at Swarthmore College: Professor Susan Cobbs, to whom I appealed for help with the classical quotations, and Professor Jerome Shaffer, who gave me generous time and excellent advice about my selections from four of the philosophers.

Swarthmore, Pa.   M. C. BEARDSLEY
November, 1959

THE EUROPEAN PHILOSOPHERS

FROM DESCARTES

TO NIETZSCHE

RENÉ DESCARTES

Discourse on Method, Parts I-III

Meditations on First Philosophy

SUPPLEMENTARY PASSAGES

Intuition and Deduction
Metaphysical Doubt and Certainty
The *Cogito*
The Clearness and Distinctness Criterion
Infinity and the Idea of God
Innate Ideas
Eternal Truths
Is Descartes' Argument Circular?
Substance
Modes
Space and Bodies
The Pineal Gland
The Automatism of Brutes

RENÉ DESCARTES

RENÉ DESCARTES (1596–1650) was educated according to the higher standards of his time, and showed his abilities early, at the Jesuit College of La Flèche and at Poitiers. Much of his thinking during the following years consisted of a fundamental reexamination of that education. Indeed, as we see in Part I of the *Discourse on Method,* this was in a way the beginning of his philosophy. At the age of twenty-two he joined the army of Prince Maurice of Nassau, then at peace, and began a period of wide travel about Europe, combined with study and reading, conversation and correspondence. He settled in Holland in 1629 and remained for twenty years, carrying on his scientific and philosophical work. He died in Sweden, where he had gone to be philosophical instructor to Queen Christina.

Besides his two best known works, the *Discourse* and the *Meditations* (see below; see also *The Philosophical Works of Descartes,* trans. and ed. Elizabeth S. Haldane and G. R. T. Ross, Cambridge: Cambridge University Press: rep. 1969; trans. Donald A. Cress, Indianapolis: Hackett Publishing Co., 1980), Descartes' philosophical writings include the unfinished *Rules for the Guidance of Our Native Powers* (or *for the Direction of Understanding*), written by about 1630, in which he attempted to draw up in detail his complete method for obtaining certainty of knowledge in any field, whether in mathematics (as in his creation of the new mathematical field of analytic geometry) natural science, or philosophy; *The Principles of Philosophy* (published in 1644), in which the argument of the *Meditations* is set out with fuller attention to some difficult points, and some of his physical and psychological theories are expounded; and *The Passions of the Soul* (published in 1649), a systematic analysis of the emotions. Other works include: *Descartes: Philosophical Letters* (trans. and ed. Anthony Kenny, Oxford: Clarendon Press, 1970); *The Discourse on Method; Optics, Geometry and Meteorology* (trans. Paul J. Olscamp, Indianapolis: Bobbs-Merrill, 1965).

It would be hard to overstate the historical fruitfulness of Descartes' thought, which dominated modern philosophy at least until the appearance of Kant and the effects of which, for good or ill, are still with us. Though the strikingly original ideas and apparently revolutionary movements in philosophy often seem more continuous with the past, less new and surprising, as we examine their historical conditions in detail, Descartes' philosophy is a turning point if ever there is one. And he meant it to be; he aimed to make a clean sweep and build all over again. He worked out the first thoroughgoing metaphysical solution to the great intellectual problems of his age, which centered around the conflicts between traditional Christianity and the new physical and mathematical sciences—problems about God, immortality, the nature of man, the importance of reason. In his attempt to give a rational reconstruction of knowledge, he was able to formulate in the clearest way certain concepts and principles—for example, of substance as that which requires nothing other than itself to exist, of the separability in principle of whatever is distinguishable, of analysis into ultimately simple and clear ideas—that struck his contemporaries and successors with the force of liberating discoveries. His ideas were extraordinarily persuasive to modern philosophers yet at the same time were found to have serious internal incompatibilities; and the challenge of reconciling them helped to generate a period of intense and brilliant philosophical activity in England and on the Continent, one that led to many important discoveries.

Thus Descartes was the first modern philosopher to tackle the problem of the method of philosophizing itself: how can we know that the method of knowing which we use is justified? And to raise this question as he did was important in leading to a deeper grasp of the philosopher's problems, even if it should turn out that to pose it in his fashion is to set an impossible task. Descartes formulated in modern terms the problem of the existence of the external physical world—a problem that many have wrestled with—and he did this by discovering, in effect, what are now called incorrigible propositions, or basic propositions about sense-data that involve no inference but are mere reports of immediate experience. He examined the possibility of making a sharp distinction between mental and physical behavior, by postulating two substances underlying them, and his work helped to show up the difficulties in such a conception of man as well as in the less fundamental dualism of the Aristotelian-Thomistic system. He worked out a very clear and complete mechanistic conception of the physical world, including the world of organic creatures, and his thinking along this line has helped to give direction and impetus to the scientific study of nature every since. A new note was struck by his confidence in reason—as in the famous opening words of the *Discourse*—that is, in the individual person's ability to strike out for himself and make his basic beliefs about reality reasonable. This was highly contagious and was instantly inspiriting to his age. And indeed Descartes invented a whole new style of philosophizing, the analysis of the meaning and grounds of everyday beliefs with familiar examples mulled over in the study—a style alive in Locke, in Hume, in Wittgenstein.

Discourse on the Method of Rightly Conducting the Reason and Seeking for Truth in the Sciences*

If this Discourse appears too long to be read all at once, it may be separated into six portions. And in the first there will be found various considerations respecting the sciences; in the second, the principal rules regarding the Method which the author has sought out; while in the third are some of the rules of morality which he has derived from this Method. In the fourth are the reasons by which he proves the existence of God and of the human soul, which form the foundation of his Metaphysics. In the fifth, the order of the questions regarding physics which he has investigated, and particularly the explanation of the movement of the heart, and of some other difficulties which pertain to medicine, as also the difference between the soul of man and that of the brutes. And in the last part the questions raised relate to those matters which the author believes to be requisite in order to advance further in the investigation of nature, in addition to the reasons that caused him to write.

PART I

Good sense is of all things in the world the most equally distributed, for everybody thinks himself so abundantly provided with it, that even those most difficult to please in all other matters do not commonly desire more of it than they already possess. It is unlikely that this is an error on their part; it seems rather to be evidence in support of the view that the power of forming a good judgment and of distinguishing the true from the false, which is properly speaking what is called Good Sense or Reason, is by nature equal in all men. Hence

* Translated by Elizabeth S. Haldane and G. R. T. Ross, in *The Philosophical Works of Descartes,* Cambridge: Cambridge University Press, 1911, 2 vols., with some modification by the present editor. Reprinted by permission. *Discours de la Methode pour bien conduire sa raison, & chercher la verité dans les sciences* was first published at Leyden in 1637, as a general introduction to three long essays, on Dioptrics, Meteors, and Geometry, which were intended as further illustrations of the Method.

too, it will show that the diversity of our opinions does not proceed from some men being more rational than others, but solely from the fact that our thoughts pass through diverse channels and the same objects are not considered by all. For to be possessed of good mental powers is not sufficient; the principal matter is to apply them well. The greatest minds are capable of the greatest vices as well as of the greatest virtues, and those who proceed very slowly may, provided they always follow the straight road, really advance much faster than those who, though they run, forsake it.

For myself, I have never ventured to presume that my mind was in any way more perfect than that of the ordinary man; I have even longed to possess thought as quick, or an imagination as accurate and distinct, or a memory as comprehensive or ready, as some others. And besides these I do not know any other qualities that make for the perfection of the human mind. For as to Reason or Sense, inasmuch as it is the only thing that constitutes us men and distinguishes us from the brutes, I would fain believe that it is to be found complete in each individual, and in this I follow the common opinion of the philosophers, who say that the question of more or less occurs only in the sphere of the *accidents* and does not affect the *forms* or natures of the *individuals* in the same *species*.

But I shall not hesitate to say that I have had great good fortune from my youth up, in lighting upon and pursuing certain paths that have conducted me to considerations and maxims from which I have formed a Method, by whose assistance it appears to me I have the means of gradually increasing my knowledge and of little by little raising it to the highest possible point that the mediocrity of my talents and the brief duration of my life permit me to reach. For I have already reaped from it fruits of such a nature that, even though I always try in the judgments I make on myself to lean to the side of self-depreciation rather than to that of arrogance, and though, looking with the eye of a philosopher on the diverse actions and enterprises of all mankind, I find scarcely any that do not seem to me vain and useless, I do not cease to receive extreme satisfaction in the progress I seem already to have made in the search after truth, and to form such hopes for the future as to venture to believe that, if amongst the occupations of men, simply as men, there is some one in particular that is excellent and important, that is the one I have selected.

It must always be recollected, however, that possibly I deceive myself, and that what I take to be gold and diamonds is perhaps no more than copper and glass. I know how subject we are to delusion in whatever touches ourselves, and also how much the judgments of our friends ought to be suspected when they are in our favor. But in this Discourse I shall be very happy to show the paths I have followed, and to set forth my life as in a picture, so that everyone may judge of it for himself; and thus in learning from common talk what opinions are held of it, I shall obtain a new means of self-instruction to add to those which I have been in the habit of using.

Thus my design is not here to teach the Method which everyone should follow in order to promote the good conduct of his Reason, but only to show in what manner I have endeavored to conduct my own. Those who set about giving precepts must esteem themselves more skilful than those to whom they advance them, and if they fall short in the smallest matter they must, of course, take the blame for it. But regarding this Treatise simply as a history, or, if you prefer it, a fable in which, amongst certain things which may be imitated, there are possibly others also which it would not be right to follow, I hope that it will be of use to some without being hurtful to any, and that all will thank me for my frankness.

I have been nourished on letters since my childhood, and since I was given to believe that by their means a clear and certain knowledge could be obtained of all that is useful in life, I had an extreme desire to acquire instruction. But as soon as I had achieved the entire course of study at the close of which one is usually received into the ranks of the learned, I entirely changed my opinion. For I found myself embarrassed with so many doubts and errors that it seemed to me that the effort to instruct myself had no effect other than the increasing discovery of my own ignorance. And yet I was studying at one of the most celebrated Schools in Europe, where I thought that there must be men of learning if they were to be found anywhere in the world. I learned there all that others learned; and not being satisfied with the sciences that we were taught, I even read through all the books which fell into my hands, treating of what is considered most curious and rare. Along with this I knew the judgments that others had formed of me, and I did not feel that I was esteemed inferior to my fellow-students, although there were amongst them some destined to fill the places of our masters. And finally our century seemed to me as flourishing, and as fertile in great minds, as any that had preceded. And this made me take the liberty of judging all others by myself and of coming to the conclusion that there was no learning in the world such as I was formerly led to believe it to be.

I did not omit, however, always to hold in esteem those exercises which are the occupation of the Schools. I knew that the Languages which one learns there are essential for the understanding of all ancient literature; that Fables with their charm stimulate the mind and Histories of memorable deeds exalt it; and that, when read with discretion, these books assist in forming a sound judgment. I was aware that the reading of all good books is indeed like a conversation with the noblest men of past centuries who were the authors of them, nay a carefully studied conversation, in which they reveal to us none but the best of their thoughts. I deemed Eloquence to have a power and beauty beyond compare; that Poesy has most ravishing delicacy and sweetness; that in Mathematics there are the subtlest discoveries and inventions which may accomplish much, both in satisfying the curious, and in furthering all the arts, and in diminishing man's labor; that those writings which deal with Morals contain much that is instructive, and many exhortations to virtue that are most useful; that Theology points out the way to Heaven; that Philosophy teaches us to speak with an appearance of truth on all things, and causes us to be admired by the less learned; that Jurisprudence, Medicine and all other sciences bring honor and riches to those who cultivate them; and finally that [it is good to have examined all things, even those most full of superstition and falsehood, in order that we may know their just value, and avoid being deceived by them.]

But I considered that I had already given sufficient time to Languages and likewise even to the reading of the literature of the ancients, both their Histories and their Fables. For to converse with those of other centuries is almost the same thing as to travel. It is good to know something of the customs of different people in order to judge more sanely of our own, and [not to think that everything of a fashion not ours is absurd and contrary to reason, as do those who have seen nothing] But when one employs too much time in travelling, one becomes a stranger in one's own country, and when one is too curious about things which were practiced in past centuries, one is usually very ignorant about those which are practiced in our own time. Besides, Fables make one imagine many events possible which in reality are not so, and even the most accurate of Histories, if they do not exactly misrepresent or exaggerate the value of things in order to render them more worthy of being read, at least omit in them all the circumstances that are basest and least notable; and from this fact it follows that what is retained is not portrayed as it really is, and that those who regulate their conduct by examples derived from such a source, are liable to fall into the extravagances of the knights-errant of Romance, and form projects beyond their power of performance.

I esteemed Eloquence most highly and I was enamored of Poesy, but I thought that both were gifts of the mind rather than fruits of study. Those who have the strongest power of reasoning, and who most skilfully arrange their thoughts in order to render them clear and intelligible, have the best power of persuasion even if they can but speak the language of Lower Brittany and have never learned rhetoric. And those who have the most delightful original ideas and who know how to express them with the maximum of style and suavity, would not fail to be the best poets even if the art of Poetry were unknown to them.

Most of all was I delighted with Mathematics because of the certainty of its demonstrations and the evidence of its reasoning; but I did not yet understand its true use, and, believing that it was of service only in the mechanical arts, I was astonished that, seeing how firm and solid was its basis, no loftier edifice had been reared thereupon. On the other hand I compared the works of the ancient pagans which deal with Morals to palaces most superb and magnificent, which are yet built on sand and mud alone. They praise the virtues most highly and show them to be more worthy of being prized than anything else in the world, but they do not sufficiently teach us to become acquainted with them, and [often what is called by a fine name is nothing but insensibility, or pride, or despair, or parricide.]

I honored our Theology and aspired as much as anyone to reach to heaven, but having learned to regard it as a most highly assured fact that the road is not less open to the most ignorant than to the most learned, and that the revealed truths which conduct thither are quite above our intelligence, I should not have dared to submit them to the feebleness of my reasonings; and I thought that, in order to undertake to examine them and succeed in so doing, it was necessary to have some extraordinary assistance from above and to be more than a mere man.

I shall not say anything about Philosophy but that, seeing that it has been cultivated for many centuries by the best minds that have ever lived, and that nevertheless no single thing is to be found in it that is not subject of dispute, and consequently dubious, I had not enough presumption to hope to fare better there than other men had done. And also, considering how many conflicting opinions there may be regarding the self-same matter, all supported by learned people, while there can never be more than one that is true, I esteemed as well-nigh false all that only went as far as being probable.

Then as to the other sciences, inasmuch as they derive their principles from Philosophy, I judged that one could have built nothing solid on foundations so far from firm. And neither the honor nor the promised gain was sufficient to persuade me to cultivate them, for, thanks be to God, I did not find myself in a condition that obliged me to make a merchandise of science for the improvement of my fortune; and, although I did not pretend to scorn all glory like the Cynics, I yet had very small esteem for what I could not hope to acquire, excepting through fictitious titles. And, finally, as to false doctrines, I thought that I already knew well enough what they were worth to be subject to deception neither by the promises of an alchemist, the predictions of an astrologer, the impostures of a magician, the artifices or the empty boastings of any of those who make a profession of knowing that of which they are ignorant.

This is why, as soon as age permitted me to emerge from the control of my tutors, I entirely quitted the study of letters. And resolving to seek no other science than that which could be found in myself, or at least in the great book of the world, I employed the rest of my youth in travel, in seeing courts and armies, in intercourse with men of diverse temperaments and conditions, in collecting varied experiences, in proving myself in the various predicaments in which I was placed by fortune, and under all circumstances bringing my mind to bear on the things which came before it, so that I might derive some profit from my experience. (For it seemed to me that I might meet with much more truth in the reasonings that each man makes on the matters that specially concern him, and the issue of which would very soon punish him if he made a wrong judgment, than in the case of (those made by a man of letters in his study touching speculations that lead to no result, and that bring about no other consequences to himself excepting that he will be all the more vain) the more they are removed from common sense, since in this case it proves him to have employed so much the more ingenuity and skill in trying to make them seem probable. And I always had an excessive desire to learn to distinguish the true from the false, in order to see clearly in my actions and to walk with confidence in this life.

It is true that while I only considered the manners of other men I found in them nothing to give me settled convictions; and I remarked in them almost as much diversity as I had formerly seen in the opin-

empiricism

ions of philosophers. So much was this the case that the greatest profit I derived from their study was that, in seeing many things which, although they seem to us very extravagant and ridiculous, were yet commonly received and approved by other great nations, [I learned to believe nothing too certainly of which I had only been convinced by example and custom.] Thus little by little I was delivered from many errors which can obscure the light of nature and render us less capable of listening to Reason. But after I had employed several years in thus studying the book of the world and trying to acquire some experience, I one day formed the resolution of also making myself an object of study and of employing all the strength of my mind in choosing the road I should follow. This succeeded much better, it appeared to me, than if I had never departed from my country or my books.

PART II

I was then in Germany, to which country I had been attracted by the wars which are not yet at an end. And as I was returning from the coronation of the Emperor to join the army, the setting in of winter detained me in a quarter where, since I found no society to divert me, while fortunately I had also no cares or passions to trouble me, I remained the whole day shut up alone in a stove-heated room, where I had complete leisure to occupy myself with my own thoughts. One of the first of the considerations that occurred to me was that there is very often less perfection in works composed of several portions, and carried out by the hands of various masters, than in those on which one individual alone has worked. Thus we see that buildings planned and carried out by one architect alone are usually more beautiful and better proportioned than those which many have tried to put in order and improve, making use of old walls that were built with other ends in view. In the same way also, those ancient cities which, originally mere villages, have become in the process of time great towns, are usually badly constructed in comparison with those which are regularly laid out on a plain by a surveyor who is free to follow his own ideas. Even though, considering their buildings each one apart, there is often as much or more display of skill in the one case than in the other, the former have large buildings and small buildings indiscriminately placed together, thus rendering the streets crooked and irregular, so that it might be said that it was chance rather than the will of men guided by reason that led to such an arrangement. And if we consider that this happens despite the fact that from all time there have been certain officials who have had the special duty of looking after the buildings of private individuals in order that they may be public ornaments, we shall understand how difficult it is to bring about much that is satisfactory in operating only upon the works of others. Thus I imagined that those people who were once half-savage, and who have become civilized only by slow degrees, merely forming their laws as the disagreeable necessities of their crimes and quarrels constrained them, could not succeed in establishing so good a system of government as those who, from the time they first came together as communities, carried into effect the constitution laid down by some prudent legislator. Thus it is quite certain that the constitution of the true Religion whose ordinances are of God alone is incomparably better regulated than any other. And to come down to human affairs, I believe that if Sparta was very flourishing in former times, this was not because of the excellence of each and every one of its laws, seeing that many were very strange and even contrary to good morals, but because, [being drawn up by one individual, they all tended towards the same end.] And similarly I thought that the sciences found in books—in those at least whose reasonings are only probable and which have no demonstrations, composed as they are of the gradually accumulated opinions of many different individuals—do not approach so near to the truth as the simple reasoning that a man of common sense can quite naturally carry out respecting the things which come immediately before him. Again I thought that since we have all been children before being men, and since it has for long fallen to us to be governed by our appetites and by our teachers (who often enough contradicted one another, and none of whom perhaps counselled us always for the best), it is almost impossible that our judgments should be so excellent or solid as they would have been had we had complete use of our Reason since our birth, and had we been guided by it alone.

It is true that we do not find that all the houses in a town are razed to the ground for the sole reason that the town is to be rebuilt in another fashion, with streets made more beautiful; but at the same time we see that many people cause their own houses to be knocked down in order to rebuild them, and that sometimes they are forced to do so where there is danger of the houses falling of themselves, and when the foundations are not secure. From such examples I argued to myself that there was no plausibility in the claim of any private individual to reform a state by altering everything, and by overturning it throughout, in order to set it right again. Nor is it likewise probable that the whole body of the Sciences, or the order of teaching established by the Schools, should be reformed. But as regards all the opinions which up to this time I had embraced, I thought I could not do better than endeavor once for all to sweep them completely away, so that they might later on be replaced, either by others that were better, or by the same, when I had made them conform to the uniformity of a rational scheme. And I firmly believed that by this means I should succeed in directing my life much better than if I had only built on old foundations, and relied on principles of which I allowed myself to be in youth persuaded without having inquired into their truth. For although in so doing I recognized various difficulties, these were at the same time not unsurmountable, nor comparable to those which are found in reformation of the most insignificant kind in matters which concern the public. In the case of great bodies it is too difficult a task to raise them again when they are once thrown down, or even to keep them in their places when once thoroughly shaken; and their fall cannot be otherwise than very violent. Then as to any imperfections they may possess (and the very diversity that is found between them is sufficient to tell us that these in many cases exist) custom has doubtless greatly mitigated them, while it has also helped us to avoid, or insensibly corrected, a number against which mere foresight would have found it difficult to guard. And finally the imperfections are almost always more supportable than would be the process of removing them, just as the great roads which wind about amongst the mountains become, because of being frequented, little by little so well-beaten and easy that it is much better to follow them than to try to go more directly by climbing over rocks and descending to the foot of precipices.

This is the reason why I cannot in any way approve of those turbulent and unrestful spirits who, being called neither by birth nor fortune to the management of public affairs, never fail to have always in their minds some new reforms. And if I thought that in this Treatise there was contained the smallest justification for this folly, I should be very sorry to allow it to be published. My design has never extended beyond trying to reform my own opinion and to build on a foundation that is entirely my own. If my work has given me a certain satisfaction, so that I here present to you a draft of it, I do not so do because I wish to advise anybody to imitate it. Those to whom God has been most beneficent in the bestowal of His grace will perhaps form designs that are more elevated; but I fear much that this particular one will seem too venturesome for many. The simple resolve to strip oneself of all opinions and beliefs formerly received is not to be regarded as an example that each man should follow, and the world may be said to be mainly composed of two classes of minds neither of which could prudently adopt it. There are those who, believing themselves to be cleverer than they are, cannot restrain themselves from being precipitate in judgment and have not sufficient patience to arrange their thoughts in proper order; hence, once a man of this description had taken the liberty of doubting the principles he formerly accepted, and had deviated from the beaten track, he would never be able to maintain the path which must be followed to reach the appointed end more quickly, and he would hence remain wandering astray all through his life. Secondly, there are those who having reason or modesty enough to judge that they are less capable of distinguishing truth from falsehood than some others from whom instruction might be obtained, are right in contenting themselves with following the opinions of these others rather than in searching better ones for themselves.

For myself I should doubtless have been of these last if I had never had more than a single master, or had I never known the diversities that have from all time existed between the opinions of men of the greatest learning. But I had been taught, even in my College days, that there is nothing imaginable so strange or so little credible that it has not been maintained by one philosopher or other, and I further recognized in the course of my travels that all those whose sentiments are very contrary to ours are yet not necessarily barbarians or savages, but may be possessed of Reason in as great or even a greater degree than ourselves. I also considered how very different the self-same man, identical in mind and spirit, may become, according as he is brought up from childhood amongst the French or Germans, or has passed his whole life amongst Chinese or cannibals. I likewise noticed how even in the fashions of one's clothing the same thing that pleased us ten years ago, and that will perhaps please us once again before ten years are passed, seems at the present time extravagant and ridiculous. I thus concluded that it is much more custom and example that persuade us than any certain knowledge, and yet in spite of this the voice of the majority is valueless as a proof of any truths that are a little difficult to discover, because such truths are much more likely to have been discovered by one man than by a nation. I could not, however, put my finger on a single person whose opinions seemed preferable to those of others, and I found that I was, so to speak, constrained myself to undertake the direction of my procedure.

But like one who walks alone and in the twilight I resolved to go so slowly, and to use so much circumspection in all things, that if my advance was but very small, at least I guarded myself well from falling. I did not wish to set about the final rejection of any single opinion which might formerly have crept into my beliefs without having been introduced there by means of Reason, until I had first of all employed sufficient time in planning out the task which I had undertaken, and in seeking the true Method of arriving at a knowledge of all the things of which my mind was capable.

Among the different branches of Philosophy, I had in my younger days to a certain extent studied Logic; and in those of Mathematics, Geometrical Analysis and Algebra—three arts or sciences which seemed as though they ought to contribute something to the design I had in view. But in examining them I observed in respect to Logic that the syllogisms and the greater part of the other teaching served better in explaining to others those things that one knows (or like the art of Lully, in enabling one to speak without judgment of those things of which one is ignorant) than in learning what is new. And although in reality Logic contains many precepts that are very true and very good, there are at the same time mingled with them so many others that are hurtful or superfluous, that it is almost as difficult to separate the two as to draw a Diana or a Minerva out of a block of marble that is not yet roughly hewn. And as to the Analysis of the ancients and the Algebra of the moderns, besides the fact that they embrace only matters the most abstract, such as appear to have no actual use, the former is always so restricted to the consideration of symbols that it cannot exercise the Understanding without greatly fatiguing the Imagination; and in the latter one is so subjected to certain rules and formulas that the result is the construction of an art that is confused and obscure, and that embarrasses the mind, instead of a science that contributes to its cultivation. This made me feel that some other Method must be found, which, comprising the advantages of the three, is yet exempt from their faults. And as a multiplicity of laws often furnishes excuses for evil-doing, and as a State is hence much better ruled when, having but very few laws, these are most strictly observed; so, instead of the great number of precepts of which Logic is composed, I believed that I should find the four which I shall state quite sufficient, provided that I adhered to a firm and constant resolve never on any single occasion to fail in their observance.

The first of these was to accept nothing as true which I did not clearly recognize to be so: that is to say, carefully to avoid precipitation and prejudice in judgments, and to accept in them nothing more than what was presented to my mind so clearly and distinctly that I could have no occasion to doubt it.

The second was to divide up each of the difficulties that I examined into as many parts as possible, and as seemed requisite in order that it might be resolved in the best manner possible.

The third was to carry on my reflections in due order, commencing with objects that were the most simple and easy to understand, in order to rise little by little, or by degrees, to knowledge of the most complex, assuming an order, even if a fictitious one, among those which do not follow a natural sequence relatively to one another.

The last was in all cases to make enumerations so complete and reviews so general that I should be certain of having omitted nothing.

Those long chains of reasoning, simple and easy as they are, of which geometricians make use in order to arrive at the most difficult demonstrations, had caused me to imagine that all those things which fall under the cognizance of man might very likely be mutually related in the same fashion; and that, provided only that we abstain from receiving anything as true that is not so, and always retain the order that is necessary in order to deduce the one conclusion from the other, there can be nothing so remote that we cannot reach to it, nor so recondite that we cannot discover it. And I had not much trouble in discovering which objects it was necessary to begin with, for I already knew that I must begin with the most simple and most easy to apprehend. Considering also that of all those who have hitherto sought for the truth in the Sciences, it has been the mathematicians alone who have been able to succeed in making any demonstrations, that is to say producing reasons that are evident and certain, I did not doubt that it had been by means of a similar kind that they carried on their investigations. I did not at the same time hope for any practical result in so doing, except that my mind would become accustomed to the nourishment of truth and would not content itself with false reasoning. But for all that I had no intention of trying to master all those particular sciences that receive in common the name of Mathematics; but observing that, although their objects are different, they do not fail to agree in this, that they take nothing under consideration but the various relationships or proportions that are present in these objects, I thought it would be better if I only examined these proportions in their general aspect, and without viewing them otherwise than in the objects that would serve most to facilitate a knowledge of them. Not that I should in any way restrict them to these objects, for I might later on all the more easily apply them to all other objects to which they were applicable. Then, having carefully noted that in order to comprehend the proportions I should sometimes require to consider each one in particular, and sometimes merely keep them in mind, or take them in groups, I thought that, in order the better to consider them in detail, I should picture them in the form of lines, because I could find no method more simple nor more capable of being distinctly represented to my imagination and senses. I considered, however, that in order to keep them in my memory or to embrace several at once, it would be essential that I should explain them by means of certain formulas, the shorter the better. And for this purpose it was requisite that I should borrow all that is best in Geometrical Analysis and Algebra, and correct the errors of the one by the other.

As a matter of fact, I can venture to say that the exact observation of the few precepts which I had chosen gave me so much facility in sifting out all the questions embraced in these two sciences, that in the two or three months I employed in examining them—commencing with the most simple and general, and making each truth that I discovered a rule for helping me to find others—not only did I arrive at the solution of many questions that I had hitherto regarded as most difficult, but, towards the end, it seemed to me that I was able to determine in the case of those of which I was still ignorant, by what means, and how far, it was possible to solve them. In this I might perhaps appear to you to be very vain if you did not remember that having but one truth to discover in respect to each matter, whoever succeeds in finding it knows in its regard as much as can be known. It is the same as with a child, for instance, who has been instructed in Arithmetic and has made an addition according to the rule prescribed; he may be sure of having found as regards the sum of figures given to him all that the human mind can know. For, in conclusion, the Method that teaches us to follow the true order and enumerate exactly every term in the matter under investigation contains everything which gives certainty to the rules of Arithmetic.

But what pleased me most in this Method was that I was certain by its means of exercising my reason in all things, if not perfectly, at least as well as was in my power. And besides this, I felt in making use of it that my mind gradually accustomed itself to conceive of its objects more accurately and distinctly; and not having restricted this Method to any particular matter, I promised myself to apply it as usefully to the difficulties of other sciences as I had done to those of Algebra. Not that on this account I dared undertake to examine just at once all those which might present themselves; for that would itself have been contrary to the order that the Method prescribes. But having noticed that the knowledge of these difficulties must be dependent on principles derived from Philosophy in which I yet found nothing to be certain, I thought that it was requisite above all to try to establish certainty in it. I considered also that since this endeavor is the most important in all the world, and that in which precipitation and prejudice were most to be feared, I should not try to grapple with it till I had attained to a much riper age than that of three and twenty, which was the age I had reached. I thought, too, that I should first of all employ much time in preparing myself for the work by eradicating from my mind all the wrong opinions that I had up to this time accepted, and accumulating a variety of experiences fitted later on to afford matter for my reasonings, and by ever exercising myself in the Method I had prescribed, in order more and more to fortify myself in the power of using it.

PART III

And finally, as it is not sufficient, before commencing to rebuild the house which we inhabit, to pull it down and provide materials and an architect (or to act in this capacity ourselves, and make a careful drawing of its design), unless we have also provided ourselves with some other house where we can be comfortably lodged during the time of rebuilding, so in order that I should not remain irresolute in my actions while reason obliged me to be so in my judgments, and that I might not omit to carry on my life as happily as I could, I formed for myself a code of morals for the time being, which did not consist of more than three or four maxims, which maxims I should like to enumerate to you.

The first was to obey the laws and customs of my country, adhering constantly to the religion in which by God's grace I had been instructed since my childhood, and in all other things directing my conduct by opinions the most moderate in nature, and the farthest removed from excess in all those which are commonly received and acted on by the most judicious of those with whom I might come in contact. For since I began to count my own opinions as nought. because I desired to place all under examination, I was convinced that I could not do better than follow those held by people on whose judgment reliance could be placed. And although such persons may possibly exist amongst the Persians and Chinese as well as amongst ourselves, it seemed to me that it was most expedient to bring my conduct into harmony with the ideas of those with whom I should have to live; and that, in order to ascertain that these were their real opinions, I should observe what they did rather than what they said, not only because in the corrupt state of our manners there are few people who desire to say all that they believe, but also because many are themselves ignorant of their beliefs. For since the act of thought by which we believe a thing is different from that by which we know that we believe it, the one often exists without the other. And amongst many opinions all equally received, I chose only the most moderate, both because these are always most suited for putting into practice, and probably the best (for all excess has a tendency to be bad), and also because I would have in a less degree turned aside from the right path, supposing that I was wrong, than if, having chosen an extreme course, I found that I had chosen amiss. I also made a point of counting as excess all the engagements by means of which we limit in some degree our liberty. Not that I hold in low esteem those laws which, in order to remedy the inconstancy of feeble souls, permit, when we have a good object in our view, that certain vows be taken, or contracts made, which oblige us to carry out that object. This sanction is even given for security in commerce where designs are wholly indifferent. But because I saw nothing in all the world remaining constant, and because for my own part I promised myself gradually to get my judgments to grow better and never to grow worse, I should have thought that I had committed a serious sin against commonsense if, because I approved of something at one time, I was obliged to regard it similarly at a later time, after it had possibly ceased to meet my approval, or after I had ceased to regard it in a favorable light.

My second maxim was that of being as firm and resolute in my actions as I could be, and not to follow less faithfully opinions the most dubious, when my mind was once made up regarding them, than if these had been beyond doubt. In this I should be following the example of travellers, who, finding themselves lost in a forest, know that they ought not to wander first to one side and then to the other, nor, still less, to stop in one place, but understand that they should continue to walk as straight as they can in one direction, not diverging for any slight reason, even though it was possibly chance alone that first determined them in their choice. By this means if they do not go exactly where they wish, they will at least arrive somewhere at the end, where probably they will be better off than in the middle of a forest. And thus since often enough in the actions of life no delay is permissible, it is very certain that, when it is beyond our power to discern the opinions which carry most truth, we should follow the most probable; and even though we notice no greater probability in the one opinion than in the other, we at least should make up our minds to follow a particular one and afterwards consider it as no longer doubtful in its relationship to practice, but as very true and very certain, inasmuch as the reason that caused us to determine upon it is known to be good. And henceforward this principle was sufficient to deliver me from all the penitence and remorse that usually affect the mind and agitate the conscience of those weak and vacillating creatures who allow themselves to keep changing their procedure, and practice as good those things which they afterwards judge to be evil.

My third maxim was to try always to conquer myself rather than fortune, and to alter my desires rather than change the order of the world, and generally to accustom myself to believe that there is nothing entirely within our power but our own thoughts: so that after we have done our best in regard to the things that are external to us, our ill-success cannot possibly be failure on our part. And this alone seemed to me sufficient to prevent my desiring anything in the future beyond what I could actually obtain, hence rendering me content; for since our will does not naturally induce us to desire anything but what our understanding represents to it as in some way possible of attainment, it is certain that if we consider all good things that are external to us as equally beyond our power, we should not have more regret in resigning those goods which appear to pertain to our birth, when we are deprived of them for no fault of our own, than we have in not possessing the kingdoms of China or Mexico. In the same way, making what is called a virtue of a necessity, we should no more desire to be well if ill, or free if in prison, than we now do to have our bodies formed of a substance as little corruptible as diamonds, or to have wings to fly like birds. I allow, however, that to accustom oneself to regard all things from this point of view requires long exercise and meditation often repeated; and I believe that it is principally in this that is to be found the secret of those philosophers who, in ancient times, were able to free themselves from the empire of fortune, or, despite suffering or poverty, to rival their gods in their happiness. For, ceaselessly occupying themselves in considering the limits prescribed to them by nature, they persuaded themselves so completely that nothing was within their own power but their thoughts, that this conviction alone was sufficient to prevent their having any longing for other things. And they had so absolute a mastery over their thoughts that they had some reason for esteeming themselves as more rich and more powerful, and more free and more happy, than other men who, however favored by nature or fortune they might be, if devoid of this philosophy, never could achieve all they wanted.

And last of all, to conclude this moral code, I felt it incumbent on me to make a review of the various occupations of men in this life in order to try to choose the best; and, without wishing to say anything of the employment of others, I thought that I could not do better than continue in the one in which I found myself engaged, that is to say, in occupying my whole life in cultivating my Reason, and in advancing myself as much as possible in the knowledge of the truth in accordance with the method I had prescribed to myself. I had experienced so much satisfaction since beginning to use this method, that I did not believe that any sweeter or more innocent could in this life be found,—every day discovering by its means some truths that seemed to me sufficiently important, although commonly ignored by other men. The satisfaction I had so filled my mind that all else seemed of no account. And, besides, the three preceding maxims were founded solely on the plan that I had formed of continuing to instruct myself. For, since God has given to each of us some light with which to distinguish truth from error, I could not believe that I ought for a single moment to content myself with accepting the opinions held by others unless I had in view the employment of my own judgment in examining them at the proper time; and I could not have held myself free of scruple in following such opinions, if nevertheless I had not intended to lose no occasion of finding superior opinions, supposing them to exist; and finally, I should not have been able to restrain my desires nor to remain content, if I had not followed a road by which, thinking that I should be certain to be able to acquire all the knowledge of which I was capable, I also thought I should likewise be certain of obtaining all the best things that could ever come within my power. And inasmuch as our will impels us neither to follow after nor to flee from anything, excepting as our understanding represents it as good or evil, it is sufficient to judge wisely in order to act well, and the best judgment brings the best action—that is to say, the acquisition of all the virtues and all the other good things that it is possible to obtain. When one is certain that this point is reached, one cannot fail to be contented.

Having thus assured myself of these maxims, and having set them on one side along with the truths of religion, which have always taken the first place in my creed, I judged that as far as the rest of my opinions were concerned, I could safely undertake to rid myself of them. And inasmuch as I hoped to be able to reach my end more successfully in converse with man than in living longer shut up in the warm room where these reflections had come to me, I hardly awaited the end of winter before I once more set myself to travel. And in all the nine following years I did nought but roam hither and thither, trying to be a spectator rather than an actor in all the comedies the world displays. More especially did I reflect in each matter that came before me as to anything that could make it subject to suspicion of doubt, and give occasion for mistake, and I rooted out of my mind all the errors that might have formerly crept in. Not that indeed I imitated the skeptics, who only doubt for the sake of doubting, and pretend to be always uncertain; for, on the contrary, my design was only to provide myself with good ground for assurance, and to reject the quicksand and mud in order to find the rock or clay. In this task it seems to me I succeeded pretty well, since in trying to discover the error or uncertainty of the propositions I examined, not by feeble conjectures, but by clear and assured reasonings, I encountered nothing so dubious that I could not draw from it some conclusion that was tolerably secure, if this were no more than the inference that it contained in it nothing that was certain. And just as in pulling down an old house we usually preserve the debris to serve in building up another, so in destroying all those opinions which I considered to be ill-founded, I made various observations and acquired many experiences that have since been of use to me in establishing those which are more certain. And more than this, I continued to exercise myself in the method I had laid down for my use; for besides the fact that I was careful as a rule to conduct all my thoughts according to its maxims, I set aside, from time to time, some hours that I more especially employed in practicing myself in the solution of mathematical problems according to the Method, or in the solution of other problems which though pertaining to other sciences, I was able to make almost similar to those of mathematics, by detaching them from all principles of other sciences which I found to be not sufficiently secure. You will see the result in many examples which are expounded in this volume. And hence, without living to all appearance in any way differently from those who, having no occupation beyond spending their lives in ease and innocence, study to separate pleasure from vice, and who, in order to enjoy their leisure without weariness, make use of all distractions that are innocent and good, I did not cease to prosecute my design, and to profit perhaps even more in my study of Truth than if I had done nothing but read books or associate with literary people.

These nine years thus passed away before I had taken any definite part in regard to the difficulties as to which the learned are in the habit of disputing, or had commenced to seek the foundation of any philosophy more certain than the vulgar. And the example of many excellent men who had tried to do the same before me, but, as it appears to me, without success, made me imagine it to be so hard that possibly I would not have dared to undertake the task, had I not discovered that someone had spread abroad the report that I had already reached its conclusion. I cannot tell on what they based this opinion; if my conversation has contributed anything to it, this must have arisen from my confessing my ignorance more ingenuously than those who have studied a little usually do. And perhaps it was also due to my having shown forth my reasons for doubting many things which were held by others to be certain, rather than from having boasted of any special philosophic system. But being at heart honest enough not to desire to be esteemed as different from what I am, I thought that I must try by every means in my power to render myself worthy of the reputation I had gained. And it is just eight years ago that this desire made me resolve to remove myself from all places where any acquaintances were possible, and to retire to a country such as this, where the long-continued war has caused such order to be established that the armies which are maintained seem only to be of use in allowing the inhabitants to enjoy the fruits of peace with so much the more security; and where, in the crowded throng of a great and very active nation, which is more concerned with its own affairs than curious about those of others, without missing any of the conveniences of the most populous towns, I can live as solitary and retired as in deserts the most remote.

[Descartes concluded the *Discourse* with this apology and resolution:]

If I write in French which is the language of my country, rather than in Latin which is that of my teachers, that is because I hope that those who avail themselves only of their natural reason in its purity may be better judges of my opinions than those who believe only in the writings of the ancients; and as to those who unite good sense with study, whom alone I crave for my judges, they will not, I feel sure, be so partial to Latin as to refuse to follow my reasoning because I expound it in a vulgar tongue.

For the rest, I do not desire to speak here more particularly of the progress which I hope in the future to make in the sciences, nor to bind myself as regards the public with any promise which I shall not with certainty be able to fulfill. But I will just say that I have resolved not to employ the time which remains to me in life in any other matter than in endeavoring to acquire some knowledge of nature, which shall be of such a kind that it will enable us to arrive at rules for Medicine more assured than those which have as yet been attained; and my inclination is so strongly opposed to any other kind of pursuit, more especially to those which can only be useful to some by being harmful to others, that if certain circumstances had constrained me to employ them, I do not think that I should have been capable of succeeding. In so saying I make a declaration that I know very well cannot help me to make myself of consideration in the world, but to this end I have no desire to attain; and I shall always hold myself to be more indebted to those by whose favor I may enjoy my leisure without hindrance, than I shall be to any who may offer me the most honorable position in all the world.

Meditations on First Philosophy*

In which the Existence of God and the Distinction in Man of Soul and Body are Demonstrated

SYNOPSIS OF THE SIX FOLLOWING MEDITATIONS

In the first meditation I set forth the grounds on which all things, and especially material things, can be doubted—so long, that is to say, as we have no other foundations for the sciences than those on which we have hitherto relied. Although the utility of a doubt so general may not, on first suggestion, be apparent, it is none the less very great. It frees us from all prejudices; it opens to us the easiest way of detaching the mind from the senses; and lastly, it secures us against further doubting of what we shall conclude to be true.

In the second meditation the mind, on making use of the freedom proper to it, finds that it can suppose to be non-existent all those things the existence of which can in any wise be doubted, but while so doing it has perforce to recognize that it must itself exist. This is a point of the greatest importance; it is in this way that the mind is enabled to distinguish easily between the things which pertain to itself, that is, to its intellectual nature, and the things which pertain to the body. Some may, perhaps, be led to expect to find at this stage in my argument a statement of grounds in proof of the immortality of the soul, and I therefore think it proper to give warning that, since it has been my endeavor to write in this treatise nothing of which I cannot give exact demonstration, I have found myself obliged to adopt an order similar to that used by geometers, viz., to state all the premises on which the proposition in question depends, before coming to any conclusion regarding it. Now the first and chief prerequisite for knowledge of the immortality of the soul is our being able to form as perspicuous an

---

* Translated by Norman Kemp Smith in *Descartes: Philosophical Writings*, N. Y.: Modern Library, 1958. Reprinted by permission of Macmillan & Company, Ltd., St. Martin's Press, and Professor Kemp Smith's representatives. The words added in square brackets are explanations by the translator. The *Meditationes de Prima Philosophia* were first published in 1641 (2d ed., 1642; first French edition, revised by Descartes, 1647). The manuscript had been circulated among a number of philosophers and theologians, whose detailed objections, along with Descartes' replies, were published along with the *Meditations* themselves.

25

apprehension of it as possible, an apprehension completely distinct from all apprehension of body; and this is what has been done in this second meditation. In addition we have to be assured (1) that all the things we judge clearly and distinctly are true in that very mode in which we are judging them, and this could not be proved at any point prior to the fourth meditation; (2) that we have a distinct apprehension of the corporeal, and this I give partly in the second and partly in the fifth and sixth meditations; and (3) that on these grounds we have to conclude that whatever things are clearly and distinctly apprehended as being diverse substances, as are mind and body, are indeed distinct each from the other, a conclusion drawn in the sixth meditation. This is further confirmed in that same meditation, where it is pointed out that we cannot apprehend body save as divisible, nor, on the other hand, the mind save as indivisible. For we cannot think of the half of a mind as we can of the half of any body, however small; so that, as we thus see, not only are their natures diverse but also in some measure contraries. I have not, however, pursued the matter further in this present treatise, not only for the reason that these considerations suffice to show that the extinction of the mind does not follow from the corruption of the body, thus affording men the hope of a life after death, but also because the premises which enable us to infer the immortality of the mind call for an exposition of the whole science of physics. We should have to establish (1) that all substances whatsoever, all things that is to say, which owe their existence to God's creation of them, are by their very nature incorruptible, and that they can never cease to be, unless through God's withdrawing from them His concurrence they are thereby reduced to nothing; (2) that whereas body, taken generally [i.e., taking body collectively, as meaning matter], is a substance, and therefore can never perish, the human body, in so far as it differs from other bodies [i.e., taking "bodies" in the plural, thereby meaning material things], is composed entirely of a certain configuration of members, and other similar accidents, while the human mind is not constituted of accidents of any kind whatever, but is a pure substance. For though all the accidents of the mind suffer change, though, for instance, it thinks of other things, wills others, and senses others, it is yet always the same mind. The human body, on the contrary, is no longer the same, if a change takes place in the structure of some of its parts. Thus it follows, that while the body may, indeed, easily enough perish, the mind is in its own nature immortal.

In the third meditation I have, as it seems to me, developed at sufficient length my chief argument in proof of the existence of God. None the less, being anxious to withdraw the minds of my readers from the senses, I was unwilling to make use in that section of any comparisons drawn from corporeal things, and there may perhaps have remained many obscurities which, as I hope, may later be entirely removed by my replies to objections. Thus, to take one instance [and to employ one such comparison], the reader may wonder how it can be that the idea of a being supremely perfect (an idea that is in fact in us) contains so much objective reality, that is to say participates by representation in so many degrees of being and of perfection, that it cannot but proceed from a cause supremely perfect. In replying to objections, I have illustrated my argument by use of a comparison, that of an ingeniously perfect machine, the idea of which exists in the mind of some workman. The objective [i.e., representative] perfection of this idea must have some cause, viz., either the science of the workman, or that of some other person from whom he has received the idea: so likewise, the idea of God, which is in us, must have God as its cause.

In the fourth meditation it is shown that whatever we judge clearly and distinctly is true; and also at the same time it is explained in what the nature of error consists. Knowledge of these conclusions is required not only for the confirming of the preceding truths but also for the understanding of those that follow. (In passing, I may remark that I do not here treat of sin, that is, of error committed in the pursuit of good and evil, but solely of that which arises in deciding between the true and the false. Nor do I dwell on matters bearing on faith or on the conduct of life, but only on those speculative truths which can be known by way of the natural light.)

In the fifth meditation, in addition to a general account of corporeal nature, a new proof is given of the existence of God, a proof not perhaps free any more than the former from certain difficulties. The countering of these difficulties has again to await my reply to objections. I further show in what sense it is true that the certainty even of geometrical demonstrations is dependent on our knowledge of there being a God.

Finally, in the sixth meditation I distinguish the action of the understanding from that of the imagination; their distinguishing characters are described; the mind is proved to be really distinct from the body, and yet to be so closely conjoined with it as to form with it one single thing. All the errors which are wont to originate in the senses are then brought under review, and the manner of avoiding them indicated.

Then in conclusion I give an account of all the grounds enabling us to
be assured of the existence of material things; not that I consider them
to be of great utility in establishing what they prove, viz., that a world
does indeed exist, that men have bodies and the like, things which no
one of sound mind has ever doubted; but because, on viewing them
closely, we come to discern that they are neither so strong nor so
evident as those through which we gain knowledge of our mind and
of God, so that these latter are, of all the things which can be known
through our human powers, the most certain and the most evident.
The establishing of this conclusion has been my prime aim in these
meditations; and that is why, in this synopsis, I have omitted mention
of the many other issues on which I have dwelt only incidentally.

MEDITATION I

Concerning the Things of which we may doubt

It is now several years since I first became aware how many false
opinions I had from my childhood been admitting as true, and how
doubtful was everything I have subsequently based on them. Accordingly I have ever since been convinced that if I am to establish
anything firm and lasting in the sciences, I must once for all, and by
a deliberate effort, rid myself of all those opinions to which I have
hitherto given credence, starting entirely anew, and building from the
foundations up. But as this enterprise was evidently one of great magnitude, I waited until I had attained an age so mature that I could no
longer expect that I should at any later date be better able to execute
my design. This is what has made me delay so long; and I should now
be failing in my duty, were I to continue consuming in deliberation
such time for action as still remains to me.

Today, then, as I have suitably freed my mind from all cares, and
have secured for myself an assured leisure in peaceful solitude, I shall
at last apply myself earnestly and freely to the general overthrow of all
my former opinions. In doing so, it will not be necessary for me to show
that they are one and all false; that is perhaps more than can be done.
But since reason has already persuaded me that I ought to withhold
belief no less carefully from things not entirely certain and indubitable
than from those which appear to me manifestly false, I shall be
justified in setting all of them aside, if in each case I can find any
ground whatsoever for regarding them as dubitable. Nor in so doing
shall I be investigating each belief separately—that, like inquiry into

their falsity, would be an endless labor. The withdrawal of foundations involves the downfall of whatever rests on these foundations, and what I shall therefore begin by examining are the principles on which my former beliefs rested.

Whatever, up to the present, I have accepted as possessed of the highest truth and certainty I have learned either from the senses or through the senses. Now these senses I have sometimes found to be deceptive; and it is only prudent never to place complete confidence in that by which we have even once been deceived.

But, it may be said, although the senses sometimes deceive us regarding minute objects, or such as are at a great distance from us, there are yet many other things which, though known by way of sense, are too evident to be doubted; as, for instance, that I am in this place, seated by the fire, attired in a dressing-gown, having this paper in my hands, and other similar seeming certainties. Can I deny that these hands and this body are mine, save perhaps by comparing myself to those who are insane, and whose brains are so disturbed and clouded by dark bilious vapors that they persist in assuring us that they are kings, when in fact they are in extreme poverty; or that they are clothed in gold and purple when they are in fact destitute of any covering; or that their head is made of clay and their body of glass, or that they are pumpkins. They are mad; and I should be no less insane were I to follow examples so extravagant.

None the less I must bear in mind that I am a man, and am therefore in the habit of sleeping, and that what the insane represent to themselves in their waking moments I represent to myself, with other things even less probable, in my dreams. How often, indeed, have I dreamt of myself being in this place, dressed and seated by the fire, whilst all the time I was lying undressed in bed! At the present moment it certainly seems that in looking at this paper I do so with open eyes, that the head which I move is not asleep, that it is deliberately and of set purpose that I extend this hand, and that I am sensing the hand. The things which happen to the sleeper are not so clear nor so distinct as all of these are. I cannot, however, but remind myself that on many occasions I have in sleep been deceived by similar illusions; and on more careful study of them I see that there are no certain marks distinguishing waking from sleep; and I see this so manifestly that, lost in amazement, I am almost persuaded that I am now dreaming.

Let us, then, suppose ourselves to be asleep, and that all these particulars—namely, that we open our eyes, move the head, extend the hands—are false and illusory; and let us reflect that our hands perhaps, and the whole body, are not what we see them as being. Nevertheless we must at least agree that the things seen by us in sleep are as it were like painted images, and cannot have been formed save in the likeness of what is real and true. The types of things depicted, eyes, head, hands, etc.—these at least are not imaginary, but true and existent. For in truth when painters endeavor with all possible artifice to represent sirens and satyrs by forms the most fantastic and unusual, they cannot assign them natures which are entirely new, but only make a certain selection of limbs from different animals. Even should they excogitate something so novel that nothing similar has ever before been seen, and that their work represents to us a thing entirely fictitious and false, the colors used in depicting them cannot be similarly fictitious; they at least must truly exist. And by this same reasoning, even should those general things, viz., a body, eyes, a head, hands and such like, be imaginary, we are yet bound to admit that there are things simpler and more universal which are real existents and by the intermixture of which, as in the case of the colors, all the images of things of which we have any awareness be they true and real or false and fantastic, are formed. To this class of things belong corporeal nature in general and its extension, the shape of extended things, their quantity or magnitude, and their number, as also the location in which they are, the time through which they endure, and other similar things.

This, perhaps, is why we not unreasonably conclude that physics, astronomy, medicine, and all other disciplines treating of composite things are of doubtful character, and that arithmetic, geometry, etc., treating only of the simplest and most general things and but little concerned as to whether or not they are actual existents, have a content that is certain and indubitable. For whether I am awake or dreaming, 2 and 3 are 5, a square has no more than four sides; and it does not seem possible that truths so evident can ever be suspected of falsity.

Yet even these truths can be questioned. That God exists, that He is all-powerful and has created me such as I am, has long been my settled opinion. How, then, do I know that He has not arranged that there be no Earth, no heavens, no extended thing, no shape, no magnitude, no location, while at the same time securing that all these things appear to me to exist precisely as they now do? Others, as I sometimes think, deceive themselves in the things which they believe they know best. How do I know that I am not myself deceived every time I add 2 and 3, or count the sides of a square, or judge of things yet simpler, if anything simpler can be suggested? But perhaps God has not been willing that I should be thus deceived, for He is said to be supremely good. If, however, it be repugnant to the goodness of God to have created me such that I am constantly subject to deception, it would also appear to be contrary to His goodness to permit me to be sometimes deceived, and that He does permit this is not in doubt.

There may be those who might prefer to deny the existence of a God so powerful, rather than to believe that all other things are uncertain. Let us, for the present, not oppose them; let us allow, in the manner of their view, that all which has been said regarding God is a fable. Even so we shall not have met and answered the doubts suggested above regarding the reliability of our mental faculties; instead we shall have given added force to them. For in whatever way it be supposed that I have come to be what I am, whether by fate or by chance, or by a continual succession and connection of things, or by some other means, since to be deceived and to err is an imperfection, the likelihood of my being so imperfect as to be the constant victim of deception will be increased in proportion as the power to which they assign my origin is lessened. To such argument I have assuredly nothing to reply; and thus at last I am constrained to confess that there is no one of all my former opinions which is not open to doubt, and this not merely owing to want of thought on my part, or through levity, but from cogent and maturely considered reasons. Henceforth, therefore, should I desire to discover something certain, I ought to refrain from assenting to these opinions no less scrupulously than in respect of what is manifestly false.

But it is not sufficient to have taken note of these conclusions; we must also be careful to keep them in mind. For long-established customary opinions perpetually recur in thought, long and familiar usage having given them the right to occupy my mind, even almost against my will, and to be masters of my belief. Nor shall I ever lose this habit of assenting to and of confiding in them, not at least so long as I consider them as in truth they are, namely, as opinions which, though in some fashion doubtful (as I have just shown), are still, none the less, highly probable and such as it is much more reasonable to believe than to deny. This is why I shall, as I think, be acting prudently if, taking a directly contrary line, I of set purpose employ

every available device for the deceiving of myself, feigning that all
these opinions are entirely false and imaginary. Then, in due course,
having so balanced my old-time prejudices by this new prejudice that
I cease to incline to one side more than to another, my judgment, no
longer dominated by misleading usages, will not be hindered by them
in the apprehension of things. In this course there can, I am convinced, be neither danger nor error. What I have under consideration
is a question solely of knowledge, not of action, so that I cannot for
the present be at fault as being over-ready to adopt a questioning
attitude.

Accordingly I shall now suppose, not that a true God, who as such
must be supremely good and the fountain of truth, but that some
malignant genius exceedingly powerful and cunning has devoted all
his powers in the deceiving of me; I shall suppose that the sky, the
earth, colors, shapes, sounds and all external things are illusions and
impostures of which this evil genius has availed himself for the abuse
of my credulity; I shall consider myself as having no hands, no eyes,
no flesh, no blood, nor any senses, but as falsely opining myself to
possess all these things. Further, I shall obstinately persist in this way
of thinking; and even if, while so doing, it may not be within my
power to arrive at the knowledge of any truth, there is one thing I
have it in me to do, viz., to suspend judgment, refusing assent to
what is false. Thereby, thanks to this resolved firmness of mind, I
shall be effectively guarding myself against being imposed upon by
this deceiver, no matter how powerful or how craftily deceptive he
may be.

This undertaking is, however, irksome and laborious, and a certain
indolence drags me back into the course of my customary life. Just as
a captive who has been enjoying in sleep an imaginary liberty, should
he begin to suspect that his liberty is a dream, dreads awakening, and
conspires with the agreeable illusions for the prolonging of the deception, so in similar fashion I gladly lapse back into my accustomed
opinions. I dread to be wakened, in fear lest the wakefulness may
have to be laboriously spent, not in the tranquilizing light of truth,
but in the extreme darkness of the above-suggested questionings.

MEDITATION II   - *Start*

Concerning the Nature of the Human Mind, and how it is more easily known than the Body

So disquieting are the doubts in which yesterday's meditation has involved me that it is no longer in my power to forget them. Nor do I yet see how they are to be resolved. It is as if I had all of a sudden fallen into very deep water, and am so disconcerted that I can neither plant my feet securely on the bottom nor maintain myself by swimming on the surface. I shall, however, brace myself for a great effort, entering anew on the path which I was yesterday exploring; that is, I shall proceed by setting aside all that admits even of the very slightest doubt, just as if I had convicted it of being absolutely false; and I shall persist in following this path, until I have come upon something certain, or, failing in that, until at least I know, and know with certainty, that in the world there is nothing certain.

Archimedes, that he might displace the whole earth, required only that there might be some one point, fixed and immovable, to serve in leverage; so likewise I shall be entitled to entertain high hopes if I am fortunate enough to find some one thing that is certain and indubitable.

I am supposing, then, that all the things I see are false; that of all the happenings my memory has ever suggested to me, none has ever so existed; that I have no senses; that body, shape, extension, movement and location are but mental fictions. What is there, then, which can be esteemed true? Perhaps this only, that nothing whatsoever is certain.

But how do I know that there is not something different from all the things I have thus far enumerated and in regard to which there is not the least occasion for doubt? Is there not some God, or other being by whatever name we call Him, who puts these thoughts into my mind? Yet why suppose such a being? May it not be that I am myself capable of being their author? Am I not myself at least a something? But already I have denied that I have a body and senses. This indeed raises awkward questions. But what is it that thereupon follows? Am I so dependent on the body and senses that without them I cannot exist? Having persuaded myself that outside me there is nothing, that there is no heaven, no Earth, that there are no minds, no bodies, am I thereby committed to the view that I also do not exist? By no means. If I am persuading myself of something, in so doing I assuredly do exist. But what if, unknown to me, there be some deceiver, very powerful and very cunning, who is constantly employing his ingenuity in deceiving me? Again, as before, without doubt, if he is deceiving me, I exist. Let him deceive me as much as he will, he can never cause me to be nothing so long as I shall be thinking that I am something. And thus, having reflected well, and carefully examined all things, we have finally to conclude that this declaration, *Ego sum, ego existo,*[1] is necessarily true every time I propound it or mentally apprehend it.

But I do not yet know in any adequate manner what I am, I who am certain that I am; and I must be careful not to substitute some other thing in place of myself, and so go astray in this knowledge which I am holding to be the most certain and evident of all that is knowable by me. This is why I shall now meditate anew on what, prior to my venturing on these questionings, I believed myself to be. I shall withdraw those beliefs which can, even in the least degree, be invalidated by the reasons cited, in order that at length, of all my previous beliefs, there may remain only what is certain and indubitable.

What then did I formerly believe myself to be? Undoubtedly I thought myself to be a man. But what is a man? Shall I say a rational animal? No, for then I should have to inquire what is "animal," what "rational"; and thus from the one question I should be drawn on into several others yet more difficult. I have not, at present, the leisure for any such subtle inquiries. Instead, I prefer to meditate on the thoughts which of themselves sprang up in my mind on my applying myself to the consideration of what I am, considerations suggested by my own proper nature. I thought that I possessed a face, hands, arms, and that whole structure to which I was giving the title "body," composed as it is of the limbs discernible in a corpse. In addition, I took notice that I was nourished, that I walked, that I sensed, that I thought, all of which actions I ascribed to the soul. But what the soul might be I did not stop to consider; or if I did, I imaged it as being something extremely rare and subtle, like a wind, a flame or an ether, and as diffused throughout my grosser parts. As to the nature of "body," no doubts whatsoever disturbed me. I had, as I thought, quite distinct knowledge of it; and had I been called upon to explain the manner in which I then conceived it, I should have explained myself somewhat thus: by "body" I understand whatever can be determined by a certain shape, and comprised in a certain location, whatever so fills a

---

[1] [I am; I exist.—M.C.B.]

certain space as to exclude from it every other body, whatever can be apprehended by touch, sight, hearing, taste or smell, and whatever can be moved in various ways, not indeed of itself but something foreign to it by which it is touched and impressed. For I nowise conceived the power of self-movement, of sensing or knowing, as pertaining to the nature of body: on the contrary I was somewhat astonished on finding in certain bodies faculties such as these.

But what am I now to say that I am, now that I am supposing that there exists a very powerful, and if I may so speak, malignant being, who employs all his powers and skill in deceiving me? Can I affirm that I possess any one of those things which I have been speaking of as pertaining to the nature of body? On stopping to consider them with closer attention, and on reviewing all of them, I find none of which I can say that it belongs to me; to enumerate them again would be idle and tedious. What then, of those things which I have been attributing not to body, but to the soul? What of nutrition or of walking? If it be that I have no body, it cannot be that I take nourishment or that I walk. Sensing? There can be no sensing in the absence of body; and besides I have seemed during sleep to apprehend things which, as I afterwards noted, had not been sensed. Thinking? Here I find what does belong to me: it alone cannot be separated from me. *I am, I exist.* This is certain. How often? As often as I think. For it might indeed be that if I entirely ceased to think, I should thereupon altogether cease to exist. I am not at present admitting anything which is not necessarily true; and, accurately speaking, I am therefore [taking myself to be] only a thinking thing, that is to say, a mind, an understanding or reason—terms the significance of which has hitherto been unknown to me. I am, then, a real thing, and really existent. What thing? I have said it, a thinking thing.

And what more am I? I look for aid to the imagination. [But how mistakenly!] I am not that assemblage of limbs we call the human body; I am not a subtle penetrating air distributed throughout all these members; I am not a wind, a fire, a vapor, a breath or anything at all that I can image. I am supposing all these things to be nothing. Yet I find, while so doing, that I am still assured that I am a something.

But may it not be that those very things which, not being known to me, I have been supposing non-existent, are not really different from the self that I know? As to that I cannot say, and am not now discussing it. I can judge only of things that are known to me. Having come to know that I exist, I am inquiring as to what I am, this I that

I thus know to exist. Now quite certainly this knowledge, taken in the precise manner as above, is not dependent on things the existence of which is not yet known to me; consequently and still more evidently it does not depend on any of the things which are feigned by the imagination. Indeed this word *feigning* warns me of my error; for I should in truth be feigning were I to *image* myself to be a something; since imaging is in no respect distinguishable from the contemplating of the shape or image of a *corporeal* thing. Already I know with certainty that I exist, and that all these imaged things, and in general whatever relates to the nature of body, may possibly be dreams merely or deceptions. Accordingly, I see clearly that it is no more reasonable to say, "I will resort to my imagination in order to learn more distinctly what I am," than if I were to say, "I am awake and apprehend something that is real, true; but as I do not yet apprehend it sufficiently well, I will of express purpose go to sleep, that my dreams may represent it to me with greater truth and evidence." I know therefore that nothing of all I can comprehend by way of the imagination pertains to this knowledge I [already] have of myself, and that if the mind is to determine the nature of the self with perfect distinctness, I must be careful to restrain it, diverting it from all such imaginative modes of apprehension.

What then is it that I am? A thinking thing. What is a thinking thing? It is a thing that doubts, understands, affirms, denies, wills, abstains from willing, that also can be aware of images and sensations.

Assuredly if all these things pertain to me, I am indeed a something. And how could it be they should not pertain to me? Am I not that very being who doubts of almost everything, who none the less also apprehends certain things, who affirms that one thing only is true, while denying all the rest, who yet desires to know more, who is averse to being deceived, who images many things, sometimes even despite his will, and who likewise apprehends many things which seem to come by way of the senses? Even though I should be always dreaming, and though he who has created me employs all his ingenuity in deceiving me, is there any one of the above assertions which is not as true as that I am and that I exist? Any one of them which can be distinguished from my thinking? Any one of them which can be said to be separate from the self? So manifest is it that it is I who doubt, I who apprehend, I who desire, that there is here no need to add anything by way of rendering it more evident. It is no less certain that I can apprehend images. For although it may happen (as I have been supposing) that none of the things imaged are true, the imaging, *quâ* active power, is none the less really in me, as forming part of my thinking. Again, I am the being who senses, that is to say, who apprehends corporeal things, as if by the organs of sense, since I do in truth see light, hear noise, feel heat. These things, it will be said, are false, and I am only dreaming. Even so, it is none the less certain that it seems to me that I see, that I hear, and that I am warmed. This is what in me is rightly called sensing, and as used in this precise manner is nowise other than thinking.

From all this I begin to know what I am somewhat better than heretofore. But it still seems to me—for I am unable to prevent myself continuing in this way of thinking—that corporeal things, which are reconnoitered by the senses, and whose images inform thought, are known with much greater distinctness than that part of myself (whatever it be) which is not imageable—strange though it may be to be thus saying that I know and comprehend more distinctly those things which I am supposing to be doubtful and unknown, and as not belonging to me, than others which are known to me, which appertain to my proper nature and of the truth of which I am convinced—in short are known more distinctly than I know myself. But I can see how this comes about: my mind delights to wander and will not yet suffer itself to be restrained within the limits of truth.

Let us, therefore, once again allow the mind the freest reign, so that when afterwards we bring it, more opportunely, under due constraint, it may be the more easily controlled. Let us begin by considering the things which are commonly thought to be the most distinctly known, viz., the bodies which we touch and see; not, indeed, bodies in general, for such general notions are usually somewhat confused, but one particular body. Take, for example, this piece of wax; it has been but recently taken from the hive; it has not yet lost the sweetness of the honey it contained; it still retains something of the odor of the flowers from which it has been gathered; its color, its shape, its size, are manifest to us; it is hard, cold, easily handled, and when struck upon with the finger emits a sound. In short, all that is required to make a body known with the greatest possible distinctness is present in the one now before us. But behold! While I am speaking let it be moved toward the fire. What remains of the taste exhales, the odor evaporates, the color changes, the shape is destroyed, its size increases, it becomes liquid, it becomes hot and can no longer be handled, and when struck upon emits no sound. Does the wax, notwithstanding these changes, still remain the same wax? We must admit that it does; no one doubts that it does, no one judges otherwise.

What, then, was it I comprehended so distinctly in knowing the piece of wax? Certainly, it could be nothing of all that I was aware of by way of the senses, since all the things that came by way of taste, smell, sight, touch and hearing, are changed, and the wax none the less remains.

Perhaps it has all along been as I am now thinking, viz., that the wax was not that sweetness of honey, nor that pleasing scent of flowers, nor that whiteness, that shape, that sound, but a body which a little while ago appeared to me decked out with those modes, and now appears decked out with others. But what precisely is it that I am here imaging? Let us attentively consider the wax, withdrawing from it all that does not belong to it, that we may see what remains. As we find, what then alone remains is a something extended, flexible and movable. But what is this "flexible," this "movable"? What am I then imaging? That the piece of wax from being round in shape can become square, or from being square can become triangular? Assuredly not. For I am apprehending that it admits of an infinity of similar shapes, and am not able to compass this infinity by way of images. Consequently this comprehension of it cannot be the product of the faculty of imagination.

What, we may next ask, is its extension? Is it also not known [by way of the imagination]? It becomes greater when the wax is melted, greater when the wax is made to boil, and ever greater as the heat increases; and I should not be apprehending what the wax truly is, if I did not think that this piece of wax we are considering allows of a greater variety of extensions than I have ever imaged. I must, therefore, admit that I cannot by way of images comprehend what this wax is, and that it is by the mind alone that I [adequately] apprehend it. I say this particular wax, for as to wax in general that is yet more evident. Now what is this wax which cannot be [adequately] apprehended save by the mind? Certainly the same that I see, touch, image, and in short, the very body that from the start I have been supposing it to be. And what has especially to be noted is that our [adequate] apprehension of it is not a seeing, nor a touching, nor an imaging, and has never been such, although it may formerly have seemed so, but is solely an inspection of the mind which may be imperfect and confused, as it formerly was, or clear and distinct, as it now is, according as my attention is directed less or more to the constituents composing the body.

I am indeed amazed when I consider how weak my mind is and how prone to error. For although I can, dispensing with words, [directly] apprehend all this in myself, none the less words have a hampering hold upon me, and the accepted usages of ordinary speech tend to mislead me. Thus when the wax is before us we say that we see it to be the same wax as that previously seen, and not that we judge it to be the same from its retaining the same color and shape. From this I should straightway conclude that the wax is known by ocular vision, independently of a strictly mental inspection, were it not that perchance I recall how when looking from a window at beings passing by on the street below, I similarly say that it is men I am seeing, just as I say that I am seeing the wax. What do I see from the window beyond hats and cloaks, which might cover automatic machines? Yet I judge those to be men. In analogous fashion, what I have been supposing myself to see with the eyes I am comprehending solely with the faculty of judgment, a faculty proper not to my eyes but to my mind.

But aiming as I do at knowledge superior to the common, I should be ashamed to draw grounds for doubt from the forms and terms of ordinary speech. I prefer therefore to pass on, and to ask whether I apprehended the wax on my first seeing it, and while I was still believing that I knew it by way of the external senses, or at least by the *sensus communis,* as they call it, that is to say by the imaginative faculty, more perfectly and more evidently than I now apprehend it after having examined with greater care what it is and in what way it can be known. It would indeed be foolish to have doubts as to the answer to this question. Was there anything in that first apprehension which was distinct? What did I apprehend that any animal might not have seen? When, however, I distinguish the wax from its external forms; when stripped as it were of its vestments I consider it in complete nakedness, it is certain that though there may still be error in my judgment, I could not be thus apprehending it without a mind that is human.

What now shall I say of the mind itself, i.e., of myself? For as yet I do not admit in myself anything but mind. What am I to say in regard to this I which seems to apprehend this piece of wax so distinctly? Do I not know myself much more truly and much more certainly, and also much more distinctly and evidently, than I do the wax? For if I judge that the wax is or exists because I see it, evidently it follows, with yet greater evidence that I myself am or exist, inasmuch as I am thus seeing it. For though it may be that what I see is not in truth wax, and that I do not even possess eyes with which to see anything, yet assuredly when I see, or (for I no longer allow the distinction) when I think I see, it cannot be that I myself who think am not a something. So likewise, if I judge that the wax exists because I touch it, it will follow that I am; and if I judge that the imagination, or some other cause whatever it be, persuades me that the wax exists, the same conclusion follows [viz., that I am *thinking* by way of an image and *thinking* what I thus image to be independently existing]. And what I have here said regarding the piece of wax may be said in respect of all other things which are external to me.

And yet a further point: if the apprehension of the wax has seemed to me more determinate and distinct when sight and touch, and many causes besides, have rendered it manifest to me, how much more evidently and distinctly must I now know myself, since all the reasons which can aid in the apprehension of wax, or of any body whatsoever, afford yet better evidence of the nature of my mind. Besides, in the mind itself there are so many more things which can contribute to the more distinct knowledge of it, that those which come to it by way of the body scarcely merit being taken into account.

Thus, then, I have been brought step by step to the conclusion I set out to establish. For I now know that, properly speaking, bodies are cognized not by the senses or by the imagination, but by the understanding alone. They are not thus cognized because seen or touched, but only in so far as they are apprehended understandingly. Thus, as I now recognize, nothing is more easily or more evidently apprehended by me than my mind. Difficult, however, as it is to rid oneself of a way of thinking to which the mind has been so long accustomed, it is well that I should halt for some time at this point, that by prolonged meditation I may more deeply impress upon myself this new knowledge.

MEDITATION III

Concerning God: that He exists

I shall now close my eyes, stop my ears, withdraw all my senses, I shall even efface from my thinking all images of corporeal things; or since that can hardly be done, I shall at least view them as empty and false. In this manner, holding converse only with myself and closely examining my nature, I shall endeavor to obtain, little by little, better and more familiar knowledge of myself. I am a thinking thing, i.e., a thing that doubts, affirms, denies, knows some few things, is ignorant of many, that loves, that hates, that wills, that refuses, that images also and senses. For as I before remarked, although the things which I sense or image are perhaps, apart from me, nothing at all, I am nevertheless certain that those ways of thinking, which I call sensings and imagings, in so far as they are no more than ways of thinking, pertain to me. In those few words I have summed up all that I truly know, or at least all that I have thus far been aware of knowing.

I shall now endeavor to discover whether, on closer attention, there may not perhaps pertain to me other things which I have not yet considered. I am certain that I am a thinking thing. But do I thereby know also what is required to render me thus certain of anything? In this first knowledge there is indeed nothing save the clear and distinct apprehension of what I am affirming; yet this would not suffice to render me certain of its truth, if it could ever happen that anything which I apprehend thus clearly and distinctly should yet prove false; and accordingly I would now seem to be able to adopt as a general rule that everything I apprehend in a genuinely clear and distinct manner is true.

I have, however, been receiving and admitting as altogether certain and manifest several other things which yet I have afterwards found to be altogether doubtful. What were those things? They were the Earth, the sky, the stars, and all the other things I was apprehending by way of the senses. But what was there that I clearly apprehended in them? Nothing save that the ideas or thoughts of such things presented themselves to my mind. And even now I do not deny that those ideas are to be met with in me. There was, however, another thing which I was affirming, and which, being habituated to belief in it, I supposed myself to be apprehending clearly, although in truth I was not so apprehending it, namely that there were things outside me, from which these proceed and to which they are altogether similar. It was in this that I was mistaken; or if I was perhaps judging correctly, assuredly this was not due to any knowledge conveyed to me by way of direct apprehension.

But when I considered something very simple and easy, bearing on arithmetic or geometry, for instance that 2 and 3 together make 5, and other things of this sort, was I not, then at least, intuiting them sufficiently perspicuously to justify me in affirming their truth? If afterwards I entertained doubts regarding them, this was indeed for no other reason than that it occurred to me that a God might perhaps have endowed me with a nature such that I may be deceived even in respect of the things which seem to me the most manifest of all. For whenever this supposition of God's omnipotence comes up in my mind, I cannot but confess that it is easy for Him, if He so wishes, to cause me to err, even in those matters which I regard myself as intuiting with the eyes of the mind in the most evident manner. None the less, when I direct my attention to the things which I believe myself to be apprehending quite clearly, I am so persuaded of their truth that I cannot but break into protestations such as these: Let who will deceive me, he will never be able to bring it about that in the very time during which I shall be thinking that I am a something, I shall yet be nothing; or that, at some future time, it will be true that I have never been, it now being true to say that I am; or that 2 and 3 could make more or less than 5; or any other such things which I clearly see cannot be other than I apprehend them as being. And certainly since I have no reason to believe that there is a God who is a deceiver (and indeed have not yet even considered the grounds for supposing that a God of any kind exists), the ground of my doubts, entirely dependent as it is on this supposition, is but slight, and so to speak metaphysical. But to be able to eliminate it, I must at the earliest possible opportunity inquire whether there is indeed a God; and should I find there is a God, I must also inquire whether He can be a deceiver. For without the knowledge of these two truths I do not see how I can be certain of anything.

Now in order that I may be enabled to conduct this inquiry without interrupting the order of meditation I have proposed to myself— namely to pass step by step from the first notions I discover in my mind to those which I can afterwards find to be there—I must here divide all my thoughts into certain kinds, and consider in which of these kinds truth and error, in the strict sense, are to be found. Some of my thoughts are, as it were, images of things; and to them alone strictly belongs the title "idea," e.g., when I represent to myself a man, or a chimera, or the sky, or an angel, or even God. Other thoughts have in addition other forms; for instance when I will, fear, affirm, deny, while in so doing I am always indeed apprehending something as the subject of my thought, I am also embracing in thought something more than the similitude of this thing; and of the thoughts of this kind some are called volitions or affections, whereas others are called judgments. If ideas are considered only in themselves, and not as referred to some other thing, they cannot, strictly speaking, be false. For whether I image a goat or a chimera, that I am imaging the latter is no less true than that I am imaging the former. Nor need I fear there may be falsity in the will or in the affections. For though I am able to desire things that are evil, or even what has never existed, it is yet none the less true that I so desire them. There thus remain only our judgments; and it is in respect of them that I must take diligent heed lest I be deceived. And assuredly the chief and most usual error to be met with in them consists in judging that the ideas which are in me are similar to, conformed to, the things which are outside me; if I considered them as being only certain modes or ways in which I think, without referring them to anything beyond, they would hardly afford any material for error.

To consider now the ideas [that are strictly so called], some appear to me to be innate, others to be adventitious, that is to say foreign to me and coming from without, and others to be made or invented by me. When I apprehend what a thing is, what a truth is, or what a thought is, I would seem to be holding the power of so doing from no other source than my own nature. On the other hand, when I hear a sound, see the Sun, or sense fire, I have hitherto judged these to proceed from certain things situated outside me. Lastly it appears to me that sirens, hippogriffs and other similar chimeras are my own mental inventions. But perhaps I may yet come to hold that all of these ideas are of the kind I call adventitious, coming to me from without, or that they are all innate, or are all made by me; for I have not yet clearly discerned their true origin.

Here my chief task must be to inquire, in respect of those ideas which seem to me to come from things existing outside me, what grounds there are obliging me to believe they are similar to the outside things. The first of those grounds is that I seem to be so taught by nature; and the second, that I experience in myself that these ideas are not in any wise dependent on my will, nor therefore on myself. Often they present themselves to me in spite of myself, as, for instance, at the present moment, whether I will or not, I feel heat; and because of this I am persuaded that this sensation or idea is produced in me by a thing that is different from me, viz., by the heat of the fire near which I am sitting. And as it has seemed to me, nothing is more obvious than that I may therefore judge that what this external thing is impressing on me is not anything different from itself, but its similitude.

Next, I must consider whether these grounds are sufficiently strong and convincing. When I here say that I am so taught by nature I understand by the word "nature" only a certain spontaneous impulse which constrains me to this belief, and not a natural light enabling me to know that the belief is true. These two things are widely different; for what the natural light shows me to be true (e.g., that inasmuch as

I doubt, it follows that I am, and the like), I cannot anywise call in doubt, since I have in me no other faculty or power whereby to distinguish the true from the false, none as trustworthy as the natural light, and none that can teach me the falsity of what the natural light shows me to be true. As I have often observed, when this question relates to the choice between right and wrong in action, the natural impulses have frequently misled me; and I do not see that I have any better ground for following them in questions of truth and error.

As to the other ground, that these ideas, as not being dependent on my will, must necessarily proceed from things situated outside me, I do not find it any more convincing than that of which I have been speaking. For just as the natural impulses, notwithstanding the fact that they are not always in accordance with my will, are none the less in me, so likewise it may be that I have in me, though indeed unknown to me, some faculty or power capable of producing the ideas, and of doing so without the aid of any external things. That, as I have hitherto thought, is precisely what I am doing when I dream.

And lastly, even should the ideas proceed from things other than myself, it does not therefore follow that they must be similar to those things. On the contrary, I have observed in a number of instances how greatly a thing can differ from our ideas of it. For example, I find present to me two completely diverse ideas of the Sun; the one in which the Sun appears to me as extremely small is, it would seem, derived from the senses, and to be counted as belonging to the class of adventitious ideas; the other, in which the Sun is taken by me to be many times larger than the whole Earth, has been arrived at by way of astronomical reasonings, that is to say, elicited from certain notions innate in me, or formed by me in some other manner. Certainly, these two ideas of the Sun cannot both resemble the same Sun; and reason constrains me to believe that the one which seems to have emanated from it in a direct manner is the more unlike.

These various considerations convince me that hitherto it has not been by any assured judgment, but only from a sort of blind impulse, that I have believed in the existence of things outside me and different from me, things which by way of the sense-organs or by whatever means they employ, have conveyed to me their ideas or images, and have thus impressed on me their similitudes.

But there is yet another way of inquiring whether any of those things, the ideas of which are in me, exist outside me. If ideas are taken in so far only as they are certain ways of thinking, I recognize among them no differences or inequality; they all appear to me to proceed from me in the same manner. When, however, they are viewed as images, of which one represents one thing and another some other thing, it is evident that they differ greatly one from another. Those which represent substances are without doubt something more, and contain in themselves, so to speak, more objective reality (that is to say participate by representation in a higher degree of being or of perfection) than those which represent only modes or accidents; and again, the idea by which I apprehend a supreme God, eternal, infinite, immutable, omniscient, omnipotent, and the creator of all things which are in addition to Himself, has certainly in it more objective reality than those ideas by which finite substances are represented.

Now it is manifest by the natural light that there must be at least as much reality in the efficient and total cause as in its effect. For whence can the effect draw its reality if not from its cause? How could this cause communicate to it this reality if it did not itself have it? And hence it follows, not only that something cannot proceed from nothing; but also that what is more perfect, i.e., contains more reality, cannot proceed from what is less perfect. And this is not only evidently true of those effects the reality of which philosophers term actual or formal, but also of the ideas the reality of which is viewed only as being what they term objective [i.e., representational]. Thus, for example, a stone which has not yet existed cannot now begin to be unless it be produced by some thing which possesses in itself, either formally or eminently, all that enters into the composition of the stone (i.e., which contains in itself the same things or others more excellent than those which are in the stone). Thus heat cannot be produced in a subject previously devoid of it save by a cause of an order or degree or kind at least as perfect as the heat, and so in all other cases. But neither can the idea of the heat or of the stone exist in me unless it too has been placed in me by a cause which contains in itself at least as much reality as I am ascribing to the heat or the stone. For although this cause may not communicate to the idea anything of its formal, i.e., of its actual reality, we ought not on that account to view this cause as less real. As we have to recognize, it is the very nature of an idea to require for itself no other formal [i.e., actual] reality save that which it receives and borrows from the thought or mind of which it is a mode, i.e., a manner or way of thinking. But nevertheless, if an idea is to contain one [particular] objective reality rather than some other, it must undoubtedly derive it from some cause in which there is to be found at least as much formal [i.e., actual] reality as in the idea there is objective [i.e., representational] reality. For if anything [of that kind] be allowed as being met with in the idea and yet not in the cause of the idea, it must have derived its origin from nothing. But however imperfect that mode of being—the mode of being objectively in the understanding by way of representation through its idea—we certainly cannot, for all that, declare it to be in itself nothing, nor consequently that the idea owes its origin to nothing.

Nor may I, on the ground that the reality which I ascribe to my ideas is only objective [i.e., representational], suspect it of not being also formally [i.e., actually] present in their causes, and so hold it to be sufficient if in them also it exists only objectively. Just as the objective mode of existence belongs to ideas by their very nature, so the formal mode of existence appertains to the causes of these ideas, at least to the first and chief of their causes, by the very nature of those causes. For although, it may be, one idea gives birth to another, the series of the ideas cannot be carried back *in infinitum*; we must in the end reach a first idea, the cause of which is, as it were, the archetype in which all the reality or perfection that is in the idea only objectively, by way of representation, is contained formally [i.e., actually]. In this way the natural light makes it evident to me that the ideas are in me in the manner of images, which may indeed fall short of the perfection of the things from which they have been derived, but can never contain anything greater or more perfect.

The longer and more carefully I examine all these things, the more clearly and distinctly do I recognize their truth. What then am I to conclude from it all? This, namely, that if the objective reality of any one of my ideas be so great that I am certain it cannot be in me either formally or eminently, and that consequently I cannot myself be the cause of it, it necessarily follows that I am not alone in the world and that there is likewise existing some other thing, which is the cause of this idea. Were no idea of this kind to be met with in me, I should have no argument sufficient to render me certain of the existence of anything different from me. For after careful inquiry in every possible quarter, I have up to the present failed to discover any other.

Now among my ideas in addition to the idea which exhibits me to myself—an idea as to which there can here be no difficulty—there is another which represents God, others representing corporeal and inanimate things, others representing angels, others representing animals, and again others representing to me men similar to myself. As regards the ideas which represent other men, or animals, or angels, I can easily understand that they may have been compounded from those which I have of myself, of corporeal things, and of God, even although there may be, outside myself, neither men, animals nor angels. As regards the ideas of corporeal things, there is nothing in them so great or so excellent that it might not possibly have proceeded from myself, and on considering them closely and examining each separately in the way in which I yesterday examined the idea of wax, I find that there is but little in them which is clearly and distinctly apprehended, viz., magnitude or extension in length, breadth and depth, shape which results from the limitation of extension, the location which bodies have in relation to one another, and motion or change of location, to which may be added substance, duration and number. As to other things such as light and the colors, sounds, odors, tastes, heat and cold and the other tactual qualities, they present themselves to me so confusedly and obscurely that I cannot tell whether they are true or false, i.e., whether the ideas I have of them are ideas of real things or whether they present only chimerical beings which are incapable of [independent] existence. For though, as I have before remarked, it is only in judgments that formal falsity, falsity properly so called, can be met with, there can yet in ideas be a certain material falsity, namely when the ideas represent what is nothing as if it were something. For example, so far are the ideas I have of heat and cold from being clear and distinct, that I cannot learn from them whether cold is only a privation of heat or heat a privation of cold, or indeed whether either or neither is a real quality. And inasmuch as ideas are taken as being images [i.e., as standing for something], there cannot be any that do not seem to us to represent something; and accordingly, if it be indeed true that cold is nothing but a privation of heat, the idea which represents it to me as something real and positive may quite properly be termed false; and so in other cases. Ideas of this kind I need not indeed assign to any author other than myself. For, if they are false, i.e., if they represent what is not a thing, then by the light of reason it is known to me that they proceed from nothing, i.e., that they are in me only because of some lack of perfection in my nature. On the other hand, even supposing them to be true, if what they exhibit to me has such little reality—so little that I cannot even distinguish the thing thus represented from not-being—I do not see why they may not have been produced by myself.

As to the clear and distinct ideas I have of corporeal things, there are some which, as it seems to me, I can have obtained from the idea [i.e., the immediate awareness] I have of myself, e.g., those of substance, duration. number and the like. For when I think a stone to be a substance or to be a thing capable of existing by itself, and in like manner think myself to be a substance, though I am then indeed apprehending myself to be a thinking non-extended thing, and the stone, on the contrary, to be an extended non-thinking thing, and though there is accordingly a notable difference between the two, none the less they appear to agree in this, that they represent substances. In the same way, when I apprehend myself as now existing and re-collect that I have existed at other times, and when I have thoughts of which I apprehend the number, I acquire the ideas of duration and number, which I can thereafter freely transfer to other things. As to the other qualities composing the ideas of corporeal things, extension, shape, location and motion, it is true that they are not indeed formally [i.e., actually] in me, since I am nothing other than a thinking thing; but as they are merely certain modes of substance—and as it were the vestments under which corporeal substance appears to us— whereas I am myself a substance, it would seem that they may be contained in me eminently.

The only idea that remains for consideration, therefore, is the idea of God. Is there in that idea anything which cannot be regarded as proceeding from myself? By the name "God" I mean a substance that is infinite, immutable, independent, all-knowing, all-powerful, and by which I myself and everything else, if any such other things there be, have been created. All those attributes are so great and so eminent, that the more attentively I consider them the less does it seem possible that they can have proceeded from myself alone; and thus, in the light of all that has been said, we have no option save to conclude that God exists. For though the idea of substance may be in me in so far as I am myself a substance, yet, being as I am a finite entity, it would not be the idea of an *infinite* substance; it can be this only as having proceeded from some substance which is in itself infinite.

The argument cannot be met by supposing that I apprehend the infinite not through a true idea but only by negation of that which is finite, in the manner in which I apprehend rest and darkness by the negation of motion and light. On the contrary there is manifestly more reality in the infinite substance than in the finite substance, and my awareness of the infinite must therefore be in some way prior to my awareness of the finite, that is to say, my awareness of God must be prior to that of myself. For how could I know that I doubt and desire, i.e., know that something is lacking to me and that I am not wholly perfect, save by having in me the idea of a being more perfect than myself, by comparison with which I may recognize my deficiencies.

Nor can our argument be evaded by declaring that this idea of God is perhaps materially false, and that consequently, as in the already mentioned ideas of heat and cold, it may have nothing as its source, i.e., that its existence may be due to my imperfection. On the contrary, since this idea is completely clear and distinct, and contains within itself more objective reality than any other, there can be none which is of itself more true or less open to the suspicion of falsity. This idea of a being supremely perfect and infinite is, I maintain, entirely true, for although we may perhaps entertain the supposition that no such being exists, we yet cannot suppose, as I have been supposing in the case of cold, that the idea of it exhibits to me nothing real. The idea is also completely clear and distinct for the further reason that whatsoever I apprehend clearly and distinctly of the real and of the true, and of what purports some perfection, is in its entirety contained in it. This holds true, even though it be that I do not comprehend the infinite, and that in God there is an infinitude of things which I cannot comprehend, or even reach in any way by thought. For it is of the nature of the infinite that I, finite as I am and limited, cannot comprehend it. It suffices that I understand this, and that I judge that whatever I apprehend clearly, and which I know to purport some perfection, and perchance also an infinitude of yet other perfections of which I am ignorant, is in God formally or eminently. Consequently, the idea I have of Him is the most completely true, the most completely clear and distinct, of all the ideas that are in me.

But perhaps I am something more than I am supposing myself to be; perhaps all those perfections which I am attributing to God are in some fashion potentially in me, although they do not yet show themselves or issue in action. Indeed I am already aware that my knowledge increases, perfecting itself little by little; and I see nothing to prevent its thus increasing more and more *in infinitum,* nor any reason why on its being thus increased and perfected I may not in this way be able to acquire all the other perfections of the Divine nature, nor finally, why the power I have of acquiring these perfections, if the power be indeed thus already in me, may not suffice to provide the idea of them.

But on closer examination I recognize that this cannot be allowed. For, in the first place, even should it be true that my knowledge, little by little, daily increases, and that many things potentially mine are not yet actual, none the less these powers do not pertain to, or make the least approach to, the idea I have of God in whom nothing is merely potential, and all is actual and operative. There can indeed be no

more convincing evidence of the imperfection of my knowledge than
that it gradually increases. Again, although my knowledge can be
ever more and more increased, I may not, for this reason, suppose
that it can ever be actually infinite; for it can never be so increased as
not still to allow of yet further increase. But when I judge God to be
actually infinite, I do so as judging that nothing can be added to His
sovereign perfection. And lastly, I comprehend that what is objective
in an idea cannot be produced by a being that exists potentially only
—which properly speaking is nothing—but only by a being that is
formal, that is to say, actual.

Assuredly, in all that I have been saying there is nothing which is
not, on attentive consideration, manifest by the natural light. When,
however, my attention is divided, and my mind is, as it were, blinded
by the images of sensible things, I do not so readily recollect why the
idea of a being more perfect than I, must necessarily have proceeded
from a being which is indeed more perfect; and this is why I am concerned to continue the inquiry as to whether I myself, who have this
idea of God, could exist, if no such being exists.

I ask, therefore, from what do I derive my existence? Perhaps from
myself, or from my parents or from some other causes less perfect
than God: for I can think or conjecture nothing more perfect than
God, or even equal to God.

But were I independent of everything else, and myself the author of
my being, I should not be anywise in doubt or entertain desires for
what is other than myself; in short, nothing would be lacking to me. I
should have given myself all those perfections of which I had any
idea, and should thus be God. Nor should it be imagined that what is
lacking to me is more difficult to acquire than what I already possess.
On the contrary, it is manifestly much more difficult to bring it to pass
that I, i.e., a thing, a substance that thinks, should emerge out of
nothing, than it would be to obtain knowledge of many things of which
I am ignorant, such knowledge being only an accident of this thinking
substance. If I had this greater perfection, that is to say were capable
of being myself the author of my existence, I would not have denied
myself what is more easy of acquisition, viz., the knowledge in which
I am lacking. Nor would I have deprived myself of any of the things
which I apprehend as being contained in the idea of God, none of
which seems to me more difficult to acquire. Were any one of them
more difficult, it would certainly appear to me as being such (supposing I were myself the author of all the other things I possess), because in it I should thereby be experiencing a limit to my power.

Even if I suppose that I have always existed as I now am, I cannot evade the force of this reasoning, on the plea that there will then be no need to seek for any author of my existence. The course of my life can be divided into innumerable parts, none of which is in any way dependent on the others. Accordingly it does not follow that because I was in existence a short time ago I must be in existence now, unless there be some cause which produces me, creates me as it were anew at this very instant, that is to say, conserves me. To all those who consider with attention the nature of time it is indeed evident that a thing in order to be conserved at each of the moments in which it endures has need of the same power and action as would be required to produce and create it anew, if it did not yet exist. That the difference between creation and conservation is a difference solely in our way of thinking is one of the many things which the natural light manifests to us.

What, therefore, is now required is that I interrogate myself as to whether there be in me some power by which I can secure that I who now am shall still be in the time that follows. Since I am nothing but a thinking thing—this at least is the only part of myself which thus far has been definitely in question—if such a power resided in me, I should undoubtedly be conscious of it. But I experience no such power; and thereby I quite evidently know that I am dependent on some being other than myself.

Perhaps, however, the being on which I am dependent is not the being I call God, and I am produced either by my parents or by some other causes less perfect than God. But this cannot be. As I said before, manifestly there must be at least as much reality in the cause as in the effect. Accordingly, inasmuch as I am a thinking thing and have in me an idea of God, whatever the cause be to which my nature has finally to be traced, it too must be allowed to be a thinking thing, and to possess the idea of all the perfections I attribute to God. We may then inquire whether this cause derives its origin and its existence from itself or from some other thing. If self-existent, it follows from the reasons above cited that it must itself be God; as having the power of self-existence, it must, beyond doubt, likewise have the power of actually possessing all the perfections of which it has in itself the idea, that is, all those which I apprehend as being in God. Should it, however, hold its existence from some cause other than itself, we shall again ask, in the same manner, respecting this other cause, whether it exists of itself or through some other, until we at length reach an ultimate cause, which will be God.

Here, as is evident, there can be no regression *in infinitum*; for the question we are asking is not only as to the cause which has in past time produced me, but more especially as to what it is that is conserving me at the present moment.

Nor may we suppose that several partial causes have concurred in the producing of me; that from one I have received the idea of some one of the perfections I attribute to God; from another the idea of some other, so that while all these perfections exist somewhere in the universe, they are not to be found conjoined together in one entity which is God. On the contrary, the unity, the simplicity, that is the inseparability of all the things which are in God, is one of the chief perfections I apprehend to be in Him; and assuredly this idea of the unity of all God's perfections could not have been placed in me by any cause from which I did not also have the ideas of His other perfections. For how could it have made me understand them to be at once conjoined and inseparable, without at the same time making me know what they are?

Finally, as regards my parents, even though all that I have ever held concerning them were true, it would not follow that it is they who conserve me, nor that they have brought me into being in so far as I am a thinking thing, since what they did was merely to implant certain dispositions in that matter in which I judge that I (that is to say, my mind, which alone at present I identify with myself) reside. Here, therefore, there can be no further question in their regard, and from this alone, viz., that I exist, and have in me the idea of a Being sovereignly perfect, that is to say, God, I have forthwith to conclude that His existence is demonstrated in the most evident manner.

It only remains to me to examine how I have obtained this idea. I have not acquired it through the senses, and it is never presented to me unexpectedly, as sensible things are wont to be, when these act, or seem to act, on the external sense-organs. Nor is it a product or fiction of my mind; for it is not in my power to take from or add anything to it. Consequently the only alternative is to allow that it is innate in me, just as is the idea of myself.

Certainly I ought not to find it strange that God, in creating me, has placed this in me, to be, as it were, the mark of the workman imprinted on his work. Nor need the mark be something different from the work itself. From this alone, that God has created me, it is highly likely that He has in some fashion made me in His image and similitude, and that I apprehend this similitude by means of the same faculty by which I apprehend myself—that is to say, when my mind is attentively directed upon myself, not only do I know that I am a thing imperfect, incomplete and dependent on what is other than myself, ever aspiring after something better and greater than myself, but I also know that He on whom I depend possesses in Himself all the great things to which I aspire, and this not indefinitely or potentially only, but really, i.e., actually and infinitely, and that He is thus God. The whole force of this argument, as thus used to prove the existence of God, consists in this, that I recognize that it is not possible that my nature should be what it is, viz., that I should have in me the idea of God, if God did not veritably exist—a God, I say, the idea of whom is in me, who possesses all those high perfections which, however they may transcend my powers of comprehension, I am yet in some fashion able to reach in thought, and who is subject to no defects. And from all this it is sufficiently evident that He cannot be a deceiver, it being manifest by the natural light that all fraud and deception proceed from defect.

But before I examine this conclusion with more care, and before passing to the consideration of other truths which can be obtained by way of it, it seems to me right to linger for a while on the contemplation of this all-perfect God, to ponder at leisure His marvelous attributes, to intuit, to admire, to adore, the incomparable beauty of this inexhaustible light, so far at least as the powers of my mind may permit, dazzled as they are by what they are endeavoring to see. For just as by faith we believe that the supreme felicity of the life to come consists in the contemplation of the Divine majesty, so do we now experience that a similar meditation, though one so much less perfect, can enable us to enjoy the highest contentment of which we are capable in this present life.

MEDITATION IV

Concerning the True and the False

In these past days I have become so accustomed to detaching my mind from the senses, and have so convincingly noted how very little we can apprehend with certainty regarding things corporeal, how we can know much more regarding the human mind, and even more regarding God, that I shall no longer have difficulty in diverting my thought from things imageable to what, in distinction from all that is material, is purely intelligible. Certainly the idea I have of the human mind, in so far as it is a thinking thing, not extended in length

breadth or depth, and not characterized by anything that appertains
to body, is incomparably more distinct than the idea of any corporeal
thing. And when I consider that I doubt, that is to say that I am an
incomplete and dependent thing, the idea of a being complete and
independent, that is to say, of God, then presents itself to my mind
with such clearness and distinctness that I can be confident that nothing more evident or more certain can be known by way of our human
faculties. I am so confident, owing to this alone, that the idea of God
is in me, i.e., that I exist and have the idea, that I can conclude with
certainty that God exists, and that my existence depends entirely on
Him at every moment of my life. Already, therefore, I here seem to
find a path that will lead us from this contemplation of the true God,
in whom all the treasures of the sciences and of wisdom are contained,
to the knowledge of the other things in the universe.

For, in the first place, I recognize that it is impossible that He
should ever deceive me, since in all fraud and deception there is some
element of imperfection. The power of deception may indeed seem
to be evidence of subtlety or power; yet unquestionably the will to
deceive testifies to malice and feebleness, and accordingly cannot be
found in God.

Further, I experience in myself a certain power of judging, which
undoubtedly I have received from God along with all the other
things I possess; and since He does not will to deceive me, it is certain
that this God-given faculty cannot, if I use it aright, ever lead me
astray.

As to this, no question would remain, did it not seem to follow
that I can never err. For if I hold from God all that I possess, and
if He has given me no faculty which is deceitful, it seems that I can
never be betrayed into error. It is indeed true that when I think only
of God, I am aware of nothing which can cause error or falsity. But
on reverting to myself, experience at once shows that I am indeed
subject to an infinity of errors, and on examining the cause of these
more closely, I note that in addition to the real and positive idea of
God, that is, of a Being of sovereign perfection, there is also present to
me a certain negative idea, so to speak, of nothing, i.e., of what is
infinitely far removed from every kind of perfection, and that I am a
something intermediate between God and nothingness, that is to say,
placed between sovereign Being and not-being in such fashion that
while there is in truth nothing in me, in so far as I have been created
by sovereign Being, which can deceive me or lead me into error, yet
none the less, in so far as I likewise participate in nothingness, i.e.,

in not-being, in other words, in so far as I am not myself the sovereign Being, I find myself subject to innumerable imperfections, and ought not therefore to be surprised that I should be liable to error. Thus also I come to know that error, in so far as it is error, is not something real depending on God, but only a defect. To incur an error I have therefore no need of any special power assigned me by God, enabling me to do so. I fall into error because the power which God has given me of distinguishing the true from the false is not in me an infinite power.

This does not, however, entirely satisfy me. Error is not a pure negation; it is a privation, i.e., the absence of some knowledge that I ought to possess; and on considering the nature of God, it does not seem possible that He should have given me any faculty which is not perfect of its kind, that is to say which is anywise wanting in the perfection proper to it. For if it be true that the more skilled the artisan the more perfectly accomplished is the work of his hands, how can we allow that anything produced by this sovereign Creator of all things can be other than absolutely perfect in all respects. Certainly God could have created me such that I could never be liable to error; and no less certain is it that He invariably wills what is best. Is it then better that I should be liable to error than that I should not?

On considering this more closely, what first occurs to me is that I need not be surprised if I fail to understand why God acts as He does. Nor may I doubt His existence because of my perhaps finding that there are several other things respecting which I can understand neither for what reason nor how He has created them. Already knowing, as I do, that my nature is extremely weak and limited, and that the nature of God is immense, incomprehensible and infinite, I have no difficulty in recognizing that there is an infinity of things in His power, the causes of which transcend my powers of understanding. This consideration is alone sufficient to convince me that the species of cause which we term final is not applicable in respect of physical things; for, as it seems to me, we cannot without foolhardiness inquire into and profess to discover God's inscrutable ends.

I also bethink myself that in inquiring as to whether the works of God are perfect, we should not consider any one creature separately, but the universe of things as a whole. For what, regarded by itself, might perhaps with some semblance of reason appear to be very imperfect, may none the less, when regarded as but a part of the universe, prove to be quite perfect in nature. Thus far, since my resolve has been to doubt of all things, I have as yet known with certainty only my own existence and that of God. But having also thereby come to know the infinite power of God, I am in no position to deny that He may have produced many other things, or at least that He has the power of producing them, so that the existence He has assigned me is no more than that of being a part only in the totality of things.

Consequently, on regarding myself more closely, and on examining what are my errors (for they alone testify to there being imperfection in me), I find that they depend on two concurrent causes, on my power of knowing and on the power of choice, that is, of free will— in other words, on the co-operation of the understanding and the will. For by the understanding alone, I neither affirm nor deny anything, but merely apprehend the ideas of things I can affirm or deny. Viewing the understanding thus precisely, we can say that no error is ever to be found in it. And although there may be an infinity of things in the world of which I have in my understanding no ideas, we cannot on this account say that it is deprived of those ideas as of something which its nature requires, but only that it does not have them, there being indeed no sufficient proof that God ought to have given me a greater power of knowing than He has given me. However skilled an artificer I represent Him to be, I have no reason to think of Him as bound to place in each of His works all the perfections which He can place in some of them. Nor again can I complain that God has not given me a will ample and perfect, that is, a free will. I am conscious of a will so extended as to be subject to no limits. What here, as it seems to me, is truly noteworthy, is that of all the other things which are in me, no one is so perfect and so extensive that I do not recognize it as allowing of being yet greater and more perfect. To take, for example, my faculty of understanding, I at once recognize it as being in me of small extent and extremely limited; and at the same time I frame the idea of another faculty, much more extended and even infinite; and from this alone, that I can represent the latter idea in this way [i.e., as being a faculty that is infinite], I have no difficulty in likewise recognizing that it pertains to the nature of God. If in the same way I examine my memory, my imagination, or any other of my faculties, I do not find any which is not in me small and circumscribed, and in God infinite. Free will alone, that is liberty of choice, do I find to be so great in me that I can entertain no idea of any such power possibly greater, so that it is chiefly my will which enables me to know that I bear a certain image and similitude of God. The power of will is indeed incomparably greater in God than in man; the knowledge and the potency which in God are conjoined with it, render it more constant and more efficacious, and in respect of its object extend it to a greater number of things; nevertheless it does not seem to be greater, considered formally and precisely in itself [i.e., as a faculty]. The power of will consists solely in this, that we have the power to do a thing or not to do it (that is to say, to affirm or to deny, to pursue or to shun it), or rather in this alone, that in affirming or denying, pursuing or shunning, what is proposed to us by the understanding, we so act that we have no feeling of being constrained to it by any external force. For in order to be free it is not necessary that I should be indifferent in the choice between alternatives; on the contrary, the more I am inclined toward one of them, whether because I approve it as evidently good and true, or because God in this inward manner determines my inward thinking, the more freely do I choose and embrace it. Divine grace and natural knowledge, so far from diminishing liberty, augment and confirm it. The indifference of which I am aware when for want of a reason I am not carried to one side rather than to another, is the lowest grade of liberty, testifying to a lack of knowledge, i.e., to a certain negation, not to a perfection in the will. Were the true and the good always clear to me, I should never need to deliberate as to what I ought to judge or choose, and I should thus be entirely free, without ever being indifferent.

All this enables me to recognize that the power of will which I have received from God is not of itself the cause of my errors; in its kind it is altogether ample and perfect. Nor is the cause of my errors traceable to my power of understanding or thinking; for since I understand nothing save by the power of understanding which God has given me, undoubtedly all that I apprehend I apprehend rightly, and it is impossible that I should be deceived regarding it. What then is the source of my errors? This alone, that the will is of wider range than the understanding, and that I do not restrain it within the same limits as the understanding, but extend it to things which I do not understand; and as the will is of itself, in respect of such things, indifferent, it is easily deflected from the true and the good, and readily falls into error and sin, choosing the evil in place of the good, or the false in place of the true.

For example, in our recent inquiry as to whether there is any existing world, finding that inasmuch as this inquiry is being made by me it manifestly follows that I myself exist, I could not but judge to be true what I thus clearly apprehend—not that I was forced to do so by any external power, but simply because the strong light of understanding was followed by a strong inclination of the will. My act of belief was thus the more spontaneous and free in proportion as I was the less indifferent in the matter. But not only do I know that I exist inasmuch as I am a thinking thing; there is likewise present to my mind a certain idea of corporeal nature, and I thereupon find myself doubting whether this thinking nature which is in me, or rather by which I am what I am, differs from this corporeal nature, or whether both are not one and the same thing. In so doing I am supposing that I do not as yet know of any reason which should persuade me to give preference to one view over the other. Certainly, in such circumstances, it is a matter of indifference to me which of the two I affirm or deny, or even as to whether I form any judgment at all on this issue.

Moreover this indifference extends not only to things regarding which the understanding has no knowledge, but in general to all those which are not known quite perspicuously at the moment when the will is deliberating upon them; for however probable the conjectures which dispose me to judge in a particular manner, the very awareness that they are only conjectures, and not certain and indubitable reasons, is sufficient to impel me to judge them in the directly opposite manner. I have of late had considerable experience of this, setting aside as false all that I had hitherto unquestioningly held, and doing so for no other reason than that I had come to be aware that they could in some degree be doubted.

Now if I abstain from all judging of a thing which I do not apprehend sufficiently clearly and distinctly, it is evident that I am acting rightly and am not deceived. Should I, on the other hand, decide to deny or affirm, I am not in that case making a right use of my free will, and should I in so deciding choose the wrong alternative, it is evident that I am deceived. Even should I decide for what is true, it is by chance only that I shall be doing so, and still shall not be free from the fault of misusing my freedom. The natural light teaches us that knowledge, by way of the understanding, ought always to precede the determination of the will; and it is in the failure to do so that the privation, which constitutes the form of error, consists. Privation is then, I say, there in the act, in so far as it proceeds from me; it is not to be found in the faculty as I have it from God, nor even in the act in so far as it depends on Him [through His continued upholding of me in existence].

Nor have I any ground for complaint that God has not given me a greater power of understanding or a natural light stronger than that which He has actually given, since it is of the very nature of a finite understanding not to apprehend all things, and of a created understanding to be finite. Having every reason to render thanks to God who owes me nothing, and who has yet given me all the perfections I possess, I should be far from thinking Him to have been unjust in depriving me of, or in keeping back, the other perfections which He has not given me.

Nor have I ground to complain in that He has given me a will more ample than my understanding. Since the will consists entire in one single thing, and is, so to speak, indivisible, it would appear that its nature is such that nothing can be taken from it without destroying it; and certainly the more ample it is, the more reason I have to be grateful.

Nor, finally, ought I to complain that God concurs with me in framing those [wrongful] acts of the will, that is to say, the judgments in which I suffer deception. In so far as they depend on God they are entirely true and good and my ability to form them is, in its own way, a greater perfection in me than if I were unable to do so. The privation in which alone the formal [i.e., actual] reason of error or sin consists has no need of concurrence from God since it is not a thing; and if referred to God as to its cause, it ought (in conformity with the usage of the Schools) to be entitled negation, not privation. For it is not in truth an imperfection in God that He has given me the freedom of assenting or not assenting to things of which He has not placed a clear and distinct knowledge in my understanding. On the other hand, unquestionably, it is an imperfection in me that I do not use this freedom aright, rashly passing judgment on things which I apprehend only obscurely and confusedly. I recognize, indeed, that God could easily have so created me that, while still remaining free and while still with only limited knowledge, I should yet not err, viz., by endowing my understanding with a clear and distinct knowledge of all the things upon which I shall ever have to deliberate, or simply by so deeply engraving on my memory the resolution never to pass judgment on anything of which I have no clear and distinct understanding, that I shall never lose hold on that resolution. And I easily understand that in so far as I consider myself alone, as if in the world there were only myself, I should have been much more perfect than I now am, had God created me in that fashion. But this does not justify me in refusing to recognize that in respect of the universe as a whole it is a greater perfection that certain of its parts should not

be exempt from defect than that they should all be exactly alike. And
I have, therefore, no right to complain because God, in placing me
in the world, has not willed to assign me the nobler, more perfect
rôle. If He has not done so by the first of the means above noted,
that which would depend on my having a clear and evident knowledge
of all the things upon which I may have to deliberate, at least He has
left within my power the other means, viz., that of firmly adhering to
the resolution never to pass judgment on things not clearly known to
me. For although I am aware of a certain weakness in my nature
which prevents me from continuously concentrating my mind on any
one thought, I can yet by attentive and oft-repeated meditation so
imprint it on my memory that I shall never fail to recall it as often
as I have need of it, and so can acquire the habit of not erring.

Inasmuch as it is in this habit that the highest and chief perfection
of man consists, I have, I consider, gained not a little by this day's
meditation, discovering, as I have done, the cause of error and
falsity. Certainly there can be no other cause than that which I have
now explained; for so long as I so restrain my will within the limits
of my knowledge that it frames no judgment save on things which are
clearly and distinctly apprehended by the understanding, I can never
be deceived. Since all clear and distinct awareness is undoubtedly
something, it cannot owe its origin to nothing, and must of necessity
have God as its author—God, I say, who being supremely perfect,
cannot be the cause of any error. Consequently, as we have to conclude, all such awareness is true. Nor have I today learned merely
what, to escape error, I should avoid, but also what I must do to
arrive at knowledge of the truth. Such knowledge is assured to me
provided I direct my attention sufficiently to those things which I
perfectly understand, separating them from those which I apprehend
only confusedly and obscurely. To this task I shall, from now on,
give diligent heed.

MEDITATION V

*Concerning the Essence of Material Things; and again,
concerning God, that He exists*

Many other questions respecting the attributes of God, and respecting my own proper nature, that is to say, respecting my mind, remain
for investigation; and perhaps, on some future occasion, I shall return

to them. Meanwhile, having discovered what must be done, and what avoided, in order to arrive at the knowledge of truth, what I have now chiefly to do is to endeavor to emerge from the state of doubt into which I fell in the preceding days respecting material things, and to determine whether, with certainty, anything can be known of them.

But before inquiring as to whether any material things exist outside me, I have first to examine the ideas of them in so far as these are in my thought, and to determine which of them are distinct and which confused.

Beyond question, I image distinctly that quantity which philosophers commonly term continuous, the extension in length, breadth and depth that is in this quantity, or rather in the quantified thing to which it is attributed. Further, I can number in it many diverse parts, and attribute to each of them all sorts of sizes, shapes, locations and local motions, and to each of these motions all degrees of duration.

Not only do I know these things distinctly when considering them in general, I can also, on giving attention to them, apprehend innumerable particulars respecting shapes, number, motion and other such things, which are so evidently true and so accordant with my nature, that on beginning to discover them it does not seem to me that I am learning something new, but rather that I am recollecting what I already knew, i.e., that I am for the first time taking note of things that were already in my mind but to which I had not hitherto directed my attention.

What here seems to me especially noteworthy is that I find in my mind innumerable ideas of things which, even if they do not perhaps exist anywhere outside my thought, yet cannot be said to be in themselves nothing. Though it may be in my power to think or not to think them, they are not framed by me, and possess true and immutable natures of their own. For instance, when I image a triangle, although there is not perhaps and never has been anywhere in the world apart from my thought any such shape, it has yet a certain determinate nature or essence or form which is immutable and eternal, not framed by me, and in no wise dependent on my mind, as appears from the fact that diverse properties can be demonstrated as belonging to the triangle, viz., that its three angles are equal to two right angles, that its greatest side is subtended by its greatest angle and the like, which, whether I will or not, I now clearly recognize as proper to it, although I had no thought whatsoever of them when for the first time I imaged a triangle. It cannot, therefore, be said that they have been framed and invented by me.

Nor does the objection hold that perhaps this idea of the triangle has come into my mind from external things by way of the sense-organs, through my having seen bodies triangularly shaped. I am in a position to think of innumerable other shapes which cannot be suspected of ever having been objects of sense, and of which, no less than of the triangle, I can demonstrate diverse properties, all of them clearly apprehended and therefore assuredly true. Each of these shapes is therefore a something, not a mere nothing; for it is evident that everything true is something; and as I have already shown, all those things which I know clearly and distinctly are true. And even if I had not proved this to be so, the nature of my mind is such that I cannot but assent to what I clearly apprehend, at least while I am so apprehending it. Always, as I recall, even while my mind was chiefly preoccupied with the objects of sense, I recognized as being the most certain of all truths those which relate to shapes and numbers, and all else that pertains to arithmetic and geometry, and in general to pure and abstract mathematics.

Now if, directly on my being able to find an idea of something in my thought, it at once follows that whatever I clearly and distinctly apprehend as pertaining to the thing does in truth belong to it, may I not derive from this an argument for the existence of God? Certainly the idea of God, that is of a being sovereignly perfect, is no less present to me than is that of any shape or number; and I know that an actual and external existence pertains to His nature no less clearly and distinctly than I know that whatever is demonstrable of a shape or number belongs to the nature of the shape or number. Even, therefore, were it the case that not all of what I have been meditating in these preceding days is true, this at least holds, that the existence of God ought not to have for me a lesser degree of certainty than I have hitherto been ascribing to mathematical truths.

This, on first hearing, is not immediately evident, seeming to be a sophism. Being accustomed in all other things to distinguish between existence and essence, I readily believe that existence can also be disjoined from the essence of God, and that God can therefore be conceived as not actually existing. But on closer study, it becomes manifest to me that it is no more possible to separate existence from the essence of God than the equality of its three angles to two right angles from the essence of a triangle or the idea of a mountain from that of a valley; so that to think of God (that is, of a being completely perfect) as without existence (that is, as lacking a certain perfection) is as impossible as to think of a mountain without a valley.

[Here we encounter another objection.] Though I cannot think of God save as existing, any more than I can think of a mountain without a valley, yet just as it does not follow that because I cannot think of a mountain without a valley, a mountain exists anywhere in the world, so likewise it does not follow that because I think of God as existing that He does in fact exist. My thinking imposes no necessity on things. I can image a winged horse, though there is no existing horse that has wings. May I not in similar fashion be attributing existence to God although there is no God who is existent?

This objection rests on a fallacy. Because I cannot think of a mountain without a valley, it does not indeed follow that there is any mountain or valley in existence, but only that mountain and valley, be they existent or non-existent, are inseparably conjoined each with the other. In the case of God, however, I cannot think Him save as existing; and it therefore follows that existence is inseparable from Him, and that He therefore really exists. It is not that this necessity is brought about by my thought, or that my thought is imposing any necessity on things; on the contrary, the necessity which lies in the thing itself, that is the necessity of God's existence, determines me to think in this way. It is not in my power to think God as lacking existence (i.e., to think of this sovereignly perfect being as devoid of complete perfection) in the manner in which I am free to image a horse with wings or without wings.

Nor may it be objected that though it is indeed necessary to grant that God exists, provided the supposition has antecedently been made that God possesses all perfections and that existence is itself one of these perfections, the supposition is not in fact itself necessary. If we start by supposing that all quadrilateral shapes are inscribable in the circle, we have to grant that the rhombus can be so inscribed, a conclusion manifestly false. [But the two suppositions are very different in character.] It is not indeed necessary that I should at any time be dwelling on the idea of God. None the less, as often as I may be concerned to entertain the thought of first and sovereign being, summoning this idea from the treasure-house of my mind, I must necessarily attribute all perfections to Him, although I may not then enumerate all of them, nor direct my attention to any one of them separately. And as soon as I take notice that existence is a perfection, I am thereby constrained to conclude that this first sovereign being truly exists—just as while it is not at any time necessary for me to be imaging a triangle, yet whenever I wish to consider a rectilinear figure having only three sides, I have no option save to attribute to it all those properties from which it is rightly concluded that its three angles are not greater than two right angles, even although I may not then be taking note of this particular consequence. Now this does not hold in the case of the rhombus-assumption above cited. For when I consider which shapes are capable of being inscribed in the circle, it is in no wise necessary to hold that all quadrilateral shapes are of this number; on the contrary, I cannot even pretend this to be the case, so long as I decline to accept anything save what I clearly and distinctly apprehend. Consequently there is a great difference between false suppositions of this kind and the true ideas which are born with me, the first and chief of which is the idea of God. For, as I note, there are many respects in which this idea is not fictitious, as depending merely on my thought, but is the image of a true and immutable nature; first, in that I cannot think of anything, save God alone, to the very essence of which existence pertains; secondly, in that I cannot entertain the thought of there being two or more Gods of this kind, and that, granted one such God exists, it is evident to me that He must necessarily have existed from all eternity and will exist to all eternity; and finally, in that I apprehend many other properties in God, no one of which I can either diminish or change.

Thus, whatever proof or mode of argument I may adopt, it always comes back to this, that it is only the things I apprehend clearly and distinctly which have the power to convince me. And although among the things which I apprehend in this manner some are indeed obvious to everyone, others are manifest only to those who consider them more closely, scrutinizing them earnestly. Once they have been discovered, they are, however, not esteemed any less certain than those others. To take, as an example, the right-angled triangle: that the square of the base is equal to the squares of the other two sides is not at first as manifest to us as that the base lies opposite the greatest angle; yet once it has been apprehended we are not less certain of its truth. As regards God, if my mind were not overlaid by so many prejudices, and beset on all sides by the images of sensible things, I should know nothing prior to knowing Him and nothing more easily. For is there anything more evident than that there is a God, that is to say, a sovereign being, and that of all beings He alone has existence as appertaining to His essence? For a proper grasp of this truth close attention has indeed been required. Now, however, I am as completely assured of it as of all that I hold most certain; and now also I have come to recognize that so absolutely dependent on it are all those other certainties, that save through knowledge of it nothing whatsoever can be perfectly known.

But while my nature is such that I cannot but accept as true all that I apprehend in a really clear and distinct manner, it is also such that I am unable to keep my mind always fixed on one and the same object. Often I have occasion to recall having judged a thing to be true without at the same time being aware of the reasons that determined me in so doing; and it may happen meanwhile that other reasons are presented to me—such as would readily cause me to change my opinion, were I ignorant that there is a God. I should then have no true and certain knowledge of anything; but only vague and vacillating opinions. When for instance I consider the nature of the triangle, instructed, as I have been, in the principles of geometry, it is quite evident to me that its three angles are equal to two right angles; and so long as I attend to the demonstrations I cannot but believe this to be true. None the less, as soon as I cease to attend to the demonstration, and although I may still recollect having had a clear comprehension of it, I may readily come to doubt its truth, if I do not know that there is a God. For I can then persuade myself of being so constituted by nature as to be easily deceived even in those things which I believe myself to apprehend in the most evident manner, especially when I recollect that frequently I have held to be true and certain what afterwards other reasons have constrained me to reckon as false.

But once I have recognized that there is a God, and that all things depend on Him and that He is not a deceiver, and from this, in turn, have inferred that all things which I clearly and distinctly apprehend are of necessity true, then, even though I may no longer be attending to the reasons on account of which I have judged this to be so (provided only I bear in mind that I once recognized them clearly and distinctly), no contrary reason can be brought forward sufficient to lead me to doubt it; and the knowledge I have of it is thus true and certain. Such knowledge extends, in similar fashion, to all the other things I remember as having been at any time demonstrated, the truths of geometry and the like. For what can now be brought against them, to lead me to doubt them? Will it be urged that in the past my nature was such as often to be deceived? But I now know that I cannot be deceived in the things which I know in a perspicuous manner. Will it be said that I have formerly held as true and certain what afterwards I have discovered to be false? But I was then having no clear and distinct apprehension of them, and having as yet no knowledge of the rule by following which I am assured of truth, I readily yielded assent on grounds which I have since discovered to be less strong than I then supposed them to be. What further objection is there? Will it be said that perhaps I am dreaming (an objection I myself raised a little while ago), that is, that all the thoughts I am now entertaining are no more true than those which come to me in dreams? Even so, what difference would that make? For even should I be asleep and dreaming, whatever is present to my understanding in an evident manner is indisputably true.

Thus, in this evident manner, I see that the certainty and truth of all knowledge depends on knowledge of the true God, and that before I knew Him I could have no perfect knowledge of any other thing. And now that I know Him, I have the means of acquiring a perfect knowledge of innumerable things, not only in respect of God Himself and other intelligible things, but also in respect of that corporeal nature which is the object of pure mathematics.

MEDITATION VI   *— End*

Concerning the Existence of Material Things and the Real Distinction between the Mind and Body of Man

There now remains only the inquiry as to whether material things exist. This at least I already know, that in so far as they are dealt with by pure mathematics, they are possible existents, since, as there treated, they are apprehended clearly and distinctly. Indubitably God possesses the power of producing everything that I am capable of apprehending distinctly; and I have never considered anything to be impossible to Him save what I found to be impossible of distinct apprehension. Further, the faculty of imagination, of which, as experience tells me, I make use when I apply myself to the consideration of material things, is able to persuade me of their existence; for when I attentively consider what imagination is, I find that it is nothing but a certain application of the cognitive faculty to a body which is immediately present to it and therefore existent.

To make this plain, I shall first dwell on the difference there is between the imagination and pure intellection. For instance, when I image a triangle I not only apprehend it to be a shape bounded by three lines, but also by concentrating my attention on these three lines I intuit them as present, this being what I term imaging. When, however, I wish to think of a chiliagon, I do indeed apprehend it to be a shape composed of a thousand sides, and do so just as easily as in apprehending a triangle to be composed of three sides only. I cannot, however, image the thousand sides of a chiliagon as I do the three sides of a triangle, nor intuit them as present, as it were, with the eyes of the mind. And although in accordance with the habit I have of always imaging something when I think of corporeal things, it may happen that I confusedly represent to myself some shape, it is yet evident that this shape is not a chiliagon, since it in no wise differs from what I represent to myself when I think of a myriagon or any other shape of many sides, nor would it be of any use in determining the properties distinguishing a chiliagon from those other polygons. If, however, it be a pentagon which is under question, while I can indeed, as in the case of the chiliagon, apprehend its shape without the aid of the imagination, I am able also to image it, applying my mind attentively to each of its five sides and the area they enclose. Now in thus imaging its shape, I am plainly aware of having to make a certain special effort of the mind, an effort not required in merely thinking of it; and this special effort of the mind makes clear to me the difference there is between imagination and pure intellection.

Therewith I also note that this power of imaging which is in me, in so far as it differs from the power of understanding, is no wise necessary to my essential being, that is to say, to the essence of my mind. For even if I did not have it, I should undoubtedly none the less remain the same as I now am; and from this, it seems, we may conclude that my power of imaging depends on something different from me, i.e., from my mind. And I easily understand that if there exists some body to which the mind is so united that it is able, when it pleases, to apply itself to it, i.e., as it were, to contemplate it, it may in this way be able to image corporeal things. If this be so, this mode of thinking differs from pure intellection solely in this, that the mind, in intellection, is turning in some way in upon itself, taking note of some one of the ideas which it possesses in itself, whereas when imaging it is turning itself toward the body and is intuiting in it something conformed to the idea which it has formed for itself or has apprehended by way of the senses. Now if it be the case that body exists, I can, I say, easily understand that the imaging may be carried out in this manner. There is indeed no other way equally convincing of accounting for it; and for this reason I conjecture that body probably does exist. The conjecture [as thus arrived at] is, however, probable only. For however careful and comprehensive my inquiries may be, I nevertheless do not find that even from what is distinct in the idea I have of corporeal nature by way of these imagings, any argument can be obtained which justifies my concluding, in a necessary manner, the existence of any body.

Now I am accustomed to image many other things besides that corporeal nature which is the object of pure mathematics, viz., colors, sounds, tastes, pain and the like, though none of them so distinctly. And inasmuch as I apprehend them much better by way of the senses (by the mediation of which and of memory they seem to have reached the imagination), it is proper that, for the more convenient examination of them, I should likewise examine the nature of sense and inquire whether from those ideas which are apprehended by this mode of thinking—the mode which I entitle sensing—I can obtain any certain proof of the existence of corporeal things.

First, I shall recall to mind the things which, as having been sensed, I have hitherto held to be true, and what my grounds were for so regarding them. Secondly, I shall then examine the reasons which afterwards led me to doubt of them. And finally, I shall consider what I ought now to believe in regard to them.

From the start, then, I have sensed myself as having a head, hands, feet and the other members of which this body—a body I considered to be part of myself, and possibly even the whole of myself—is composed. I also sensed this body as being located among other bodies by which it could be affected in many ways, beneficial or harmful, being made aware of what was beneficial by a certain sensation of pleasure and of what was harmful by a sensation of pain. In addition to pleasure and pain, I was aware in myself of hunger, thirst, and other such appetites, as also of certain corporeal inclinations to joy, sorrow, anger, and other such affections. On the other hand, as foreign to myself, I sensed, besides the extension, shapes and movements of bodies, also their hardness, heat and other tactual qualities, and in addition, light, colors, odors, tastes and sounds, the variety of which enabled me to distinguish from one another the sky, the Earth, the sea, and all the other bodies.

Assuredly, since the ideas of all these qualities were claiming my attention, and since it was they alone that I properly and immediately sensed, it was not without reason that I thought I was sensing certain things plainly different from my thinking, namely, bodies from which those ideas proceeded. For as experience showed me, they presented themselves to me without my consent being required, and in such fashion that I could not sense any object, however I might wish to do so, save on its being present to the sense-organ, and was unable not to sense it when it was present.

Further, since the ideas I received by way of the senses were much more lively, better defined, and even in their way more distinct, than any of those which I could deliberately and knowingly frame for myself, it seemed impossible that they could have proceeded from myself; and it followed, therefore, that they must have been caused in me by other things. Having no information regarding these things beyond what these same ideas gave me, the only supposition that could then commend itself to me was that they resemble the ideas. And because I likewise recalled that formerly I had relied more on the senses than on reason, and had observed that the ideas which I framed for myself were not so well defined as those which I apprehended by way of sense, and were for the most part composed of parts of those latter, I was readily persuaded that I had not in my understanding any idea not previously sensed.

Nor was it without reason that I regarded the body, which by a certain special right I called my own, as belonging to me more closely than any other. I could never, indeed, be separated from it as from other bodies; I felt in it, and on account of it, all my passions and all my affections; I was aware of pain and the titillation of pleasure in its parts, and not in the parts of the other bodies located outside it.

When, however, I inquired why from some—I know not what— sensing of pain a certain sadness of mind follows, and a certain joy on the sensing of pleasure, or why that strange twitching of the stomach which I call hunger should put me in mind of taking food, and dryness of throat of drinking, I could, as in other experiences of this kind, give no reason, save that I am so taught by nature. For assuredly there is no affinity, none at least that I can understand, between this twitching of the stomach and the desire to eat, any more than between the sensing of a thing which causes pain and the thought of sadness which springs from this sensing. And in the same way, it seemed to me, all the other judgments which I was accustomed to pass on the objects of sense had been taught me by nature. For I observed that they were formed in me before I had the leisure to weigh and consider any reasons which might oblige me to make them.

In due course, however, numerous experiences by degrees sapped the faith I had thus reposed in the senses. As I from time to time observed, towers which from afar seemed round on closer view appeared square, colossal statues erected on the summits of these towers appeared small when similarly viewed from below. In innumerable other instances I similarly found the judgments which concerned the things of the external senses to be erroneous: nor indeed only those based on the external senses, but those also which are based on the internal senses. What can be more internal than pain? Yet I have been assured by men whose arm or leg has been amputated, that it still seemed to them that they occasionally felt pain in the limb they had lost—thus giving me ground to think that I could not be quite certain that a pain I endured was indeed due to the limb in which I seemed to feel it.

To these grounds of doubt I have lately added two others of the widest generality. The first of these was that there is nothing of all that I believed myself to be sensing when awake which I cannot think of as being also sometimes sensed during sleep; and since I do not believe that the things I seem to sense in dreams come to me from things located outside me, I no longer found any ground for believing this of the things I seem to sense while awake. Secondly, since I was still ignorant of the Author of my being, or rather was feigning myself to be so, I saw nothing to prevent my being so constituted by nature that I might be deceived even in those things which appeared to me to be unquestionably true.

As to the grounds on which I had before been persuaded of the truth of these things, I had no difficulty in countering them. For inasmuch as I seem to be inclined by nature to many things from which reason was dissuading me, I considered that I ought not to place much confidence in its teaching; and though my sensuous apprehensions do not depend on my will, I did not think that I ought on this ground to conclude that they proceed from things other than myself. There can perhaps exist in me some faculty hitherto unknown to me, which produces them.

Now that I begin to know myself better and to discover the Author of my being, I do not in truth think that I ought rashly to admit all the things which the senses may seem to teach; but neither do I think that they should all be called in doubt.

In the first place, since I know that all the things I clearly and distinctly apprehend can be created by God exactly as I apprehend them, my being able to apprehend one thing apart from another is, in itself, sufficient to make me certain that the one is different from the other, or at least that it is within God's power to posit them separately; and even though I do not comprehend by what power this separation comes about, I shall have no option but to view them as different. Accordingly, simply from knowing that I exist, and that, meantime, I do not observe any other thing as evidently pertaining to my nature, i.e., to my essence, except this only, that I am a thinking thing, I rightly conclude that my essence consists in this alone, that I am a thinking thing (i.e., a substance, the whole nature or essence of which consists in thinking). And although possibly (or rather certainly, as I shall shortly be declaring) I have a body with which I am very closely conjoined, yet since on the one hand I have a clear and distinct idea of myself, in so far as I am only a thinking unextended thing, and on the other hand a distinct idea of the body, in so far as it is only an extended unthinking thing, it is certain that I am truly distinct from my body, and can exist without it.

I further find in myself faculties of thinking which are quite special modes of thinking, distinct from myself, viz., the faculties of imaging and sensing; I can clearly and distinctly apprehend myself as complete without them, but not them without the self, i.e., without an intelligent substance in which they reside. For in the notion we have of them, or (to use the terms of the Schools) in their formal concept, they include some sort of intellection, and I am thereby enabled to recognize that they are at once related to, and distinguished from, the self, as being its modes (just as shapes, movements, and the other modes and accidents of bodies are in respect of the bodies which uphold them).

I am also aware in me of certain faculties, such as the power of changing location, of assuming diverse postures, and the like, which cannot be thought, and cannot therefore exist, any more than can the preceding, apart from some substance in which they reside. But evidently, since the clear and distinct apprehension of these faculties involves the feature of extension, but not any intellection, they must, if they indeed exist, belong to some substance which is corporeal, i.e., extended and unthinking. Now there is, indeed, a certain passive faculty of sense, i.e., of receiving and knowing the ideas of sensible things, but this would be useless to me if there did not also exist in me, or in some other being, an active faculty capable of producing or effecting these ideas. This active faculty cannot, however, be in me—not at least in so far as I am only a thinking thing—since it does not presuppose intellection, and since the ideas present themselves to me without my contributing in any way to their so doing, and often even against my will. This faculty must therefore exist in some substance different from me—a substance that, as already noted, contains, either formally or eminently, all the reality which is objectively [i.e., by way of representation] in the ideas produced by the faculty, and this substance is either body, i.e., corporeal nature, in which there is contained formally, i.e., actually, all that is objectively, i.e., by representation, in those ideas; or it is God Himself, or some creature nobler than body, in which all of it is eminently contained.

But since God is no deceiver, it is evident that He does not of Himself, and immediately, communicate those ideas to me. Nor does He do so by way of some creature in which their objective reality is not contained formally [i.e., actually], but only eminently. For as He has given me no faculty whereby I could discover this to be the case, but on the contrary a very strong inclination to believe that those ideas are conveyed to me by corporeal things, I do not see how He could be defended against the charge of deception, were the ideas produced otherwise than by corporeal things. We have, therefore, no option save to conclude that corporeal things do indeed exist.

Yet they are not perhaps exactly such as we apprehend by way of the senses; in many instances they are apprehended only obscurely and confusedly. But we must at least admit that whatever I there clearly and distinctly apprehend, i.e., generally speaking, everything comprised in the object of pure mathematics, is to be found in them. As regards those other things which are only particular, such as that the Sun is of this or that magnitude and shape, and the like, or as regards those things which are apprehended less clearly, such as light, sound, pain and the like, however dubious and uncertain all of these may be, yet inasmuch as God is no deceiver and that there cannot therefore, in the opinions I form, be any falsity for the correction of which He has not given me some faculty sufficient thereto, I may, I believe, confidently conclude that in regard to these things also the means of avoiding error are at my disposal.

Thus there can be no question that all those things in which I am instructed by nature contain some truth; for by nature, considered in general, I now understand no other than either God Himself or the order of created things as instituted by Him, and by my nature in particular I understand the totality of all those things which God has given me.

Now there is nothing which nature teaches me more expressly, or more sensibly, than that I have a body which is adversely affected when I sense pain, and stands in need of food and drink when I suffer hunger or thirst, etc.; and consequently I ought not to doubt there being some truth in all this.

Nature also teaches me by these sensings of pain, hunger, thirst, etc., that I am not lodged in my body merely as a pilot in a ship, but so intimately conjoined, and as it were intermingled with it, that with it I form a unitary whole. Were not this the case, I should not sense pain when my body is hurt, being, as I should then be, merely a thinking thing, but should apprehend the wound in a purely cognitive manner, just as a sailor apprehends by sight any damage to his ship; and when my body has need of food and drink I should apprehend this expressly, and not be made aware of it by confused sensings of hunger, thirst, pain, etc. For these sensings of hunger, thirst, pain, etc., are in truth merely confused modes of thinking, arising from and dependent on the union, and, as it were, the intermingling of mind and body.

Besides this, nature teaches me that my body exists as one among other bodies, some of which are to be sought after and others shunned. And certainly on sensing colors, sounds, odors, tastes, heat, hardness and the like, I rightly conclude that in the bodies from which these various sensory apprehensions proceed, there are variations corresponding to them, though not perhaps resembling them; and since among these sense-apprehensions some are pleasing to me, and others displeasing, there can be no doubt that my body, or rather my entire self, inasmuch as I am composed of body and mind, can be variously affected, beneficially or harmfully, by surrounding bodies.

Many other things, however, that may seem to have been taught me by nature, are not learned from her, but have gained a footing in my mind only through a certain habit I have of judging inconsiderately. Consequently, as easily happens, the judgments I pass are erroneous: for example in the judgment that all space in which there is nothing capable of affecting my senses is a vacuum, that in a hot body there is something similar to the idea of heat which is in my mind, that in a white or green body there is the very whiteness or greenness which I am sensing, that in a bitter or sweet body there are these very tastes, and so in other like instances; that the stars, towers and other distant objects are of the sizes and shapes they exhibit to my eyes, etc.

In order, however, that there may in this regard be no lack of distinctness of apprehension, I must define more accurately what I ought to mean, when I speak of being taught by nature. Nature I am here taking in a more restricted sense than when it signifies the totality of all that God has given me. Many things included in that totality belong to the mind alone, e.g., the notion I have of the truth that what has once taken place can no longer not have taken place, and all those other truths which are known by the natural light, without the aid of the body; of these latter I am not here speaking. The term "nature" likewise extends to many things which pertain only to body, such as its having weight, and the like, and with these also I am not here dealing, but only with what God has given me as a being composed of body as well as of mind. Nature, taken in this special [restricted] sense, does indeed teach me to shun whatever causes me to sense pain, or to pursue what causes me to sense pleasure, and other things of that sort; but I do not find that it teaches me, by way of sensory apprehensions, that we should, without previous careful and mature mental examination of them, likewise draw conclusions regarding things located in the world outside us; for, as would seem, it is the task of the mind alone, not of the composite mind-body, to discern truth in questions of this kind.

Thus, although the impression a star makes on my eye is no larger than that made by the flame of a small candle, there is yet in me no real or positive power determining me to believe that the star is no larger than the flame; it is merely that, without reason, I have so judged from my earliest years. And though on approaching fire I sense heat, and on approaching it too closely I sense pain, this is no ground for concluding that something resembling the heat is in the fire and also something resembling the pain, but only that in it there is something, whatever it be, which produces in me these sensations of heat and pain.

So also, although there are spaces in which I find nothing to affect my senses, it does not follow that in them there is no body, for in this, as in many other matters, I have been accustomed to pervert the order of nature. These sensuous apprehensions have been given me by nature only as testifying to my mind what things are beneficial or harmful to the composite whole of which it is a part. For this they are indeed sufficiently clear and distinct. But what I have done is to use them as rules sufficiently reliable to be employed in the immediate determination of the *essence* of bodies external to me; and, as so employed, their testimony cannot be other than obscure and confused.

I have already sufficiently examined how it happens that, notwithstanding the sovereign goodness of God, falsity has to be recognized as occurring in judgments of this kind. Here, however, a difficulty presents itself respecting the things which I am taught by nature to seek or to avoid, and also respecting the internal sensations in which

I seem sometimes to have detected error. Thus, for instance, the agreeable taste of some food into which poison has been introduced may induce me to swallow the poison, and so serve to deceive me. In this instance, however, nature is impelling me to seek only that which is sweet-tasting, not the poison which is unknown to me; and all I can conclude from this is that I am not omniscient—in which there is no reason for surprise. Man's nature is finite, and his knowledge is therefore correspondingly limited.

But even in that to which nature itself directly impels us, we not infrequently err, as when the sick desire to drink and eat what would prove harmful to them. It will perhaps be said that the reason of the error is that their nature has been corrupted. That, however, does not remove the difficulty: the sick man is no less truly God's creature than when in health; and it is therefore no less repugnant to God's goodness that the sick man's nature should be thus deceptive. A clock composed of wheels and counterweights observes all the laws of nature no less accurately when it is ill-constructed and shows the hours incorrectly, than when it fulfills the purposes of its maker in every respect. In similar fashion, if the body of a man be considered as a kind of machine, so built and composed of bones, nerves, muscles, veins, blood and skin, that even were there in it no mind, it would still have all the motions it now has, with the exception only of those which, as being exercised by order of the will, depend on the mind, I readily recognize that it would be as natural to this body, supposing it to be, for example, dropsical, to suffer that dryness of the throat which is wont to suggest to the mind the sensation of thirst, and so to be disposed by this dryness to move the nerves and other parts in the way that leads to the drinking and thereby to the worsening of its malady, and to do so no less naturally than when, there being no such malady, it is by a similar dryness of the throat moved to drink in furtherance of its well-being. In view of the use for which the clock was designed by its maker, I can indeed say that it is deflected from its proper nature when it thus shows the hours incorrectly; and in the same manner, if I view the machine of the human body as having been framed by God for the motions which ordinarily occur in it, I may recognize that it, too, is departing from its nature when, though the throat be dry, drinking is yet not contributory to its well-being. None the less I recognize that this last manner of understanding the term "nature" is very different from the other; it is a merely external denomination, depending on my manner of mentally comparing a sick man and an ill-constructed clock with the idea I have of a healthy man and a well-made clock, which signifies nothing to be found in the things of which it speaks; whereas the term "nature," according to the other manner of understanding, signifies something veritably found in the things, and which is therefore not without some truth.

But although in respect of a body suffering from dropsy, it is indeed only in this conventional manner that we can speak of its nature as being corrupt (not being in any need of drink, and the throat being yet parched), none the less in respect of the composite whole, i.e., of the mind in its union with such a body, we have here what is more than merely a manner of speaking; it is a veritable error of [our] nature that it should thus thirst when drink would be harmful to it. And accordingly we have still to inquire why it is that the goodness of God does not prevent [our] nature, i.e., nature as understood in this latter manner, from being deceptive.

In this inquiry, what I first note is the great difference between mind and body, in that body, from its very nature, is always divisible, and mind altogether indivisible. For truly, when I consider the mind, that is to say, my self in so far only as I am a thinking thing, I can distinguish in myself no parts; I apprehend myself to be a thing single and entire. Although the whole mind may seem to be united to the whole body, yet if a foot, an arm, or any other part of the body, is cut off, I know that my mind is not thereby diminished. Nor can its faculties of willing, sensing, understanding, etc., be spoken of as being its parts; it is one and the same mind which wills, which senses, which understands. The opposite holds in respect of a corporeal, i.e., of an extended, thing. I cannot think of it save as readily divisible into parts, and therefore recognize it as being divisible. This, of itself, would suffice to convince me that the mind is altogether different from the body, even if I had not already so decided on other grounds.

In the next place, I take note that the mind is immediately affected, not by all parts of the body, but only by the brain, or rather perhaps only by one small part of it, viz., by that part in which the *sensus communis* is said to be. This part, as often as it is affected in the same way, exhibits always one and the same impression to the mind, although the other parts of the body may meantime have become otherwise disposed, as is proved by innumerable experiences on which there is here no need to dwell.

I further note that the nature of body is such that no one of its parts can be moved by another a little way distant from it which cannot be moved in the same manner by any one of the parts that lie between those two, even though the more remote part be not then acting. As, for instance, if the cord, A, B, C, D, be held taut, and its last part, D, be pulled, its first part will not be moved in a different way from how it would be were one of the intermediate parts, B or C, pulled—the last part, D, meanwhile remaining unmoved. So, too, on my sensing pain in my foot; the science of physics teaches me that this sensation is generated by way of nerves dispersed over the foot and extending, like cords, from it to the brain, and that when they are pulled in the foot, they pull those inmost parts of the brain in which they terminate, thereby exciting in them a certain motion which nature has instituted to enable the mind to sense pain as if it were in the foot. But since these nerves, in order to reach from the foot to the brain, have to pass through the tibia, the leg, the loins, the back and neck, it may happen that, although their extremities in the foot are not affected, but only certain of their intermediate parts, in the loins or neck, the motion excited in the brain will be the same as would have been caused by an injury to the foot, and the mind will then necessarily sense pain in the foot just as if the foot had indeed been hurt. This also holds in respect of all our other senses.

Finally, I note that each of the motions that occur in the part of the brain by which the mind is immediately affected gives rise always to one and the same sensation, and likewise note that we cannot wish for or imagine any better arrangement. The sensation which is thus caused is, of all the sensations which the motion might conceivably cause, the one best fitted and most generally useful for the conservation of the human body when in full health. Now experience shows that all our senses are thus constituted; and in them, therefore, there is nothing which does not testify to the power and goodness of God.

When, for example, the nerves of the foot are violently moved, in an unusual manner, the motion, passing through the medulla of the spine to the innermost parts of the brain, gives a sign to it as to what it should sense, viz., pain as though in the foot, whereby the mind is incited to do all it can to avert what is causing the injury.

God could indeed have so constituted the nature of man that this same motion in the brain should have exhibited to the mind something different; there might, for example, have been exhibited to us the motion itself, in the mode in which it exists in the brain, or in so far as it is in the foot or in some intermediate place between them— in short, something, whatever it be, other than that which we do experience. But of all these [conceivable] alternatives, there is none which would have more effectively contributed to the conservation of the body.

Similarly, when we have need of drink, there is a certain dryness of the throat which moves the nerves of the throat and by way of this the internal parts of the brain, and this motion, in turn, affects the mind with the sensation of thirst, there being nothing in all these happenings which it is more useful for us to know than that we have need of drink for the preservation of our health; and so in other like instances.

In view of these considerations, it is manifest that, notwithstanding the sovereign goodness of God, the nature of man, in so far as it is a composite of mind and body, must sometimes be at fault and deceptive. For should some cause, not in the foot, but in another part of the nerves that extend from the foot to the brain, or even in the brain itself, give rise to the motion ordinarily excited when the foot is injuriously affected, pain will be felt just as though it were in the foot, and thus naturally the sense will be deceived; for since the same motion in the brain cannot but give rise in the mind always to the same sensation, and since this sensation is much more frequently due to a cause that is injurious to the foot than by one acting in another quarter, it is reasonable that it should convey to the mind pain as in the foot, rather than as in any other part. And if it sometimes happens that dryness of the throat is not due to this being required for the health of the body but to a quite different cause, as in the case of the dropsical, it is much better that it should then be deceptive than that it should, while the body is well-disposed, be all the time failing us; and so likewise in other cases.

And certainly, this consideration is of the greatest help in enabling me not only to recognize all the errors to which my nature is subject, but also in making it easier for me to avoid or to amend them. For in knowing that in respect of those things which concern the well-being of the body, all my senses more frequently indicate the true than the false, and being able almost always to avail myself of more than one sense in the examining of any one thing, and being able also to make use of my memory for the connecting of the present with the past, and of my understanding for the reviewing (as already done) of all the causes of error, I ought no longer to fear that the things ordinarily exhibited to me by sense are false. I ought indeed to reject as hyperbolical and ridiculous all the doubts of these past days, more especially that regarding sleep, as being indistinguishable from the waking state. How marked, I now find, is the difference between them! Our memory can never connect our dreams with one another and with the whole course of our lives, in the manner in which we are wont to connect the things which happen to us while awake. If, while I am awake, someone should all of a sudden appear to me, and as suddenly disappear, as happens in dreams, and in such fashion that I could not know whence he came or whither he went, quite certainly it would not be unreasonable to esteem it a specter, that is, a phantom formed in my brain, rather than a real man. When, on the other hand, in apprehending things, I know the place whence they have come, and that in which they are, and the time at which they present themselves to me, and while doing so can connect them, uninterruptedly, with the course of my life as a whole, I am completely certain that what I thus experience is taking place while I am awake, and not in dreams. And if after having summoned to my aid all my senses, my memory and my understanding, in scrutiny of these occurrences, I find that none of them presents me with what is at variance with any other, I ought no longer to entertain the least doubt as to their truth. God being no deceiver, it cannot be that I am here being misled.

But since the necessities of active living do not always allow of the delay required for so accurate a scrutiny, it must be confessed that the life of man is, in respect of this and that particular, frequently subject to error, and that we have thus to acknowledge the weakness of our nature.

Supplementary Passages

1

Intuition and Deduction (see *Discourse*, Part II)

By intuition I understand, not the fluctuating testimony of the senses, nor the misleading judgment of a wrongly combining imagination, but the apprehension which the mind, pure and attentive, gives us so easily and so distinctly that we are thereby freed from all doubt as to what it is that we are apprehending. In other words, intuition is that non-dubious apprehension of a pure and attentive mind which is born in the sole light of reason; and it is surer than deduction (though, as we have already noted, deduction also can never be wrongly performed by us) in virtue of its being simpler. Thus each of us can see by intuition that he exists, that he thinks, that the triangle is bounded by three lines only, the sphere by a single surface, and the like. Such intuitions are more numerous than most people are prepared to recognize, disdaining, as they do, to occupy their minds with things so simple.

As readers may perhaps be troubled by this novel use of the term "intuition," and of other terms which I am constrained in similar fashion to dissociate from their current meaning, I here give a general warning that I have no thought of keeping to the meaning with which those terms have of late been employed in the Schools. For it would have been difficult for me so to employ them, while still maintaining my own differing standpoint. When appropriate terms are lacking, I convert to my own use those which seem to me most suitable. I shall pay no attention save to the meaning proper to the Latin of each word.

To proceed, this evidence and certitude, proper to intuition, is required not only in single affirmations but also in all discourse. Consider, for example, this consequence: 2 and 2 amount to the same as 3 and 1. Not only do we have to intuit that 2 and 2 amount to 4 and that 3 and 1 also amount to 4, but also that the first-mentioned proposition is a necessary conclusion from these two.

The question may therefore be raised, why do we place alongside intuition this other mode of knowing, viz., by way of *deduction*—by which we understand all that is necessarily concluded from other certainly known data. Could we, however, have done otherwise? Many things are known with certainty, though not by themselves evident, but only as they are deduced from true and known primary data by a continuous and uninterrupted movement of thought in the perspicuous intuiting of the several items. This is how we are in a position to know that the last link in a long chain is connected with its first link, even though we cannot include all the intermediate links, on which that connection depends, in one and the same intuitive glance, and instead have to survey them successively, and thereby to obtain assurance that each link, from the first to the last, connects with that which is next to it. We therefore distinguish intuition from the certitude yielded by deduction in this respect, that we have to conceive deduction as calling for a certain movement or succession not required in the case of intuition; and also, therefore, in this further respect, that inasmuch as immediately present evidence, such as is required for intuition, is not indispensably required by deduction, its certitude rests in some way on memory. To sum up, we can therefore say that those propositions which are immediately gathered from primary data are, according to our differing manner of arriving at them, known sometimes by intuition and sometimes by deduction— the primary data themselves by intuition alone, the remote conclusions not otherwise than by deduction.

These two paths are the most certain of the paths to knowledge, and in respect of powers native to us no others should be admitted. All other paths should be regarded as dangerous and liable to error. This does not, however, hinder us from believing that what has been divinely revealed to us is more certain than all we otherwise know, inasmuch as this faith of ours, like all faith that bears on things obscure, is an act not of our cognitive powers but of the will. In so far, however, as our beliefs rest on intellectual foundations, they can and ought to be, more than all things else, reached by one or other of the two above-mentioned paths, as we may perhaps elsewhere find opportunity to explain more at length.

[FROM *Rules for the Guidance of Our Native Powers,* trans. Norman Kemp Smith, in *Descartes: Philosophical Writings. ibid.;* Rule III]

2

Metaphysical Doubt and Certainty (see *Meditation* I)

If there are finally any persons who are not sufficiently persuaded of the existence of God and of their soul by the reasons which I have brought forward, I wish that they should know that all other things of which they perhaps think themselves more assured (such as possessing a body, and that there are stars and an earth and so on) are less certain. For, although we have a moral assurance of these things which is such that it seems that it would be extravagant in us to doubt them, at the same time no one, unless he is devoid of reason, can deny, when a metaphysical certainty is in question, that there is sufficient cause for our not having complete assurance, by observing the fact that when asleep we may similarly imagine that we have another body, and that we see other stars and another earth, without there being anything of the kind. For how do we know that the thoughts that come in dreams are more false than those that we have when we are awake, seeing that often enough the former are not less lively and vivid than the latter? And though the wisest minds may study the matter as much as they will, I do not believe that they will be able to give any sufficient reason for removing this doubt, unless they presuppose the existence of God.

> [FROM the *Discourse on Method,* Part IV, trans. by Elizabeth S. Haldane and G. R. T. Ross, in *The Philosophical Works of Descartes,* Cambridge: Cambridge University Press, 1911, 2 vols.]

(3)
— Start

The Cogito (see *Meditation* II)

What grounds have you for saying that "there was no need of such an elaborate mechanism in order to prove that I exist"? Really these very words of yours give me the best grounds for believing that my labors have not yet been sufficiently great, since I have as yet failed to make you understand the matter rightly. When you say that "I could have inferred the same conclusions from any of my other actions," you wander far from the truth, because there is none of my activities of which I am wholly certain (in the sense of having metaphysical certitude, which alone is here involved), save thinking alone. For example, you have no right to make the inference: *I walk, hence I exist,* except in so far as our awareness of walking is a thought; it is of this alone that the inference holds good, not of the motion of the body, which sometimes does not exist, as in dreams, when nevertheless I appear to walk. Hence from the fact that I think that I walk I can very well infer the existence of the mind which so thinks, but not that of the body which walks. So it is also in all other cases.

> [FROM Descartes' reply to the Fifth Set of Objections, by Gassendi; trans. Haldane and Ross, *ibid.*]

— End

4

The Clearness and Distinctness Criterion (see *Meditation* III)

There are even a number of people who throughout all their lives perceive nothing so correctly as to be capable of judging of it properly. For the knowledge upon which a certain and incontrovertible judgment can be formed, should not alone be clear but also distinct. I term that clear which is present and apparent to an attentive mind, in the same way as we assert that we see objects clearly when, being present to the regarding eye, they operate upon it with sufficient strength. But the distinct is that which is so precise and different from all other objects that it contains within itself nothing but what is clear.

When, for instance, a severe pain is felt, the perception of this pain may be very clear, and yet for all that not distinct, because it is usually confused by the sufferers with the obscure judgment that they form upon its nature, assuming as they do that something exists in the part affected, similar to the sensation of pain of which they are alone clearly conscious. In this way perception may be clear without being distinct, but cannot be distinct without being also clear.

> [FROM Principles XLV and XLVI of the First Part of *The Principles of Philosophy*, trans. Haldane and Ross, *ibid.*]

5

— Start

Infinity and the Idea of God (see *Meditation* III)

[A] The objection you subjoin, that "the idea of God can be constructed out of a previous survey of corporeal things," seems to be no nearer the truth than if you should say that we have no faculty of hearing, but have attained to a knowledge of sound from seeing colors alone; you can imagine a greater analogy and parity between colors and sounds than between corporeal things and God. . . .

There is no drawback in the fact that in that [Second] Meditation I dealt only with the human mind; most readily and gladly do I admit that the idea we have, e.g., of the Divine intellect, does not differ from that we have of our own, except merely as the idea of an infinite number differs from that of a number of the second or third power; and the same holds good of the various attributes of God, of which we find some trace in ourselves.

But, besides this, we have in the notion of God absolute immensity, simplicity, and a unity that embraces all other attributes; and of this idea we find no example in us: it is, as I have said before, "like the mark of the workman imprinted on his work." By means of this, too, we recognize that none of the particular attributes which we, owing to the limitations of our minds, assign piecemeal to God, just as we find them in ourselves, belong to Him and to us in precisely the same sense. Also we recognize that of various particular indefinite attributes of which we have ideas, as e.g., knowledge whether indefinite or infinite, likewise power, number, length, etc., and of various infinite attributes also, some are contained formally in the idea of God, e.g., knowledge and power, others only eminently, as number and length; and this would certainly not be so if that idea were nothing else than a figment in our minds.

> [FROM Descartes' reply to the Second Set of Objections, collected by Father Mersenne; trans. Haldane and Ross, *ibid.*]

[B] We will thus never hamper ourselves with disputes about the infinite, since it would be absurd that we who are finite should undertake to decide anything regarding it, and by this means, in trying to comprehend it, so to speak regard it as finite. That is why we do not care to reply to those who demand whether the half of an infinite line is infinite, and whether an infinite number is even or odd and so on, because it is only those who imagine their mind to be infinite who appear to find it necessary to investigate such questions. And for our part, while we regard things in which, in a certain sense, we observe no limits, we shall not for all that state that they are infinite, but merely hold them to be indefinite. Thus because we cannot imagine an extension so great that we cannot at the same time conceive that there may be one yet greater, we shall say that the magnitude of possible things is indefinite. And because we cannot divide a body into parts which are so small that each part cannot be divided into others yet smaller, we shall consider that the quantity may be divided into parts whose number is indefinite. And because we cannot imagine so many stars that it is impossible for God to create more, we shall suppose the number to be indefinite, and so in other cases.

And we shall name these things "indefinite" rather than "infinite" in order to reserve to God alone the name of infinite, first of all because in Him alone we observe no limitation whatever, and because we are quite certain that He can have none, and in the second place in regard to other things, because we do not in the same way positively understand them to be in every part unlimited, but merely negatively admit that their limits, if they exist, cannot be discovered by us.

> [FROM Principles XXVI and XXVII of the First Part of *The Principles of Philosophy,* trans. Haldane and Ross, *ibid.*]

6

Innate Ideas (see *Meditation* III)

[A] [In reply to the objection of Hobbes: "I should like to know whether the minds of those who are in a profound and dreamless sleep yet think. If not, they have at that time no ideas. Whence no idea is innate, for what is innate is always present."] When I say that an idea is innate in us [or imprinted in our souls by nature], I do not mean that it is always present in us. That would make no idea innate. I mean merely that we possess the faculty of summoning up this idea.

> [FROM Descartes' reply to the Third Set of Objections by Thomas Hobbes, trans. Haldane and Ross, *ibid.*]

[B] In article twelve he appears to dissent from me only in words, for when he says that "the mind has no need of innate ideas, or notions, or axioms," and at the same time allows it the faculty of thinking (to be considered natural or innate), he makes an affirmation in effect identical with mine, but denies it in words. For I never wrote or concluded that the mind required innate ideas which were in some sort different from its faculty of thinking; but when I observed the existence in me of certain thoughts which proceeded, not from extraneous objects nor from the determination of my will, but solely from the faculty of thinking which is within me, then, that I might distinguish the ideas or notions (which are the forms of these thoughts) from other thoughts *adventitious* or *factitious,* I termed the former "innate." In the same sense we say that in some families generosity is innate, in others certain diseases like gout or gravel, not that on this account the babes of these families suffer from these diseases in their mother's womb, but because they are born with a certain disposition or propensity for contracting them.

> [FROM *Notes Directed Against a Certain Program*, 1747, a critique of an anti-Cartesian manifesto by a former disciple, Regius or Le Bloy; trans. Haldane and Ross, *ibid.*]

7

Eternal Truths (see *Meditation* III)

You ask me what kind of cause God is of the eternal truths he has established. I answer: the same kind of cause of them, as of all things he has created: namely, the efficient and the total cause. For he is certainly Author of the essence of creatures, as well as of their existence; now this essence is nothing other than the eternal truths. I do not conceive of them as emanating from God, like rays from the Sun; but I know that God is Author of all things, and these truths are something; and consequently, that God is their Author. I say that I know this, but not that I conceive or comprehend it; for we can know that God is infinite and almighty, even though our soul, being finite, cannot comprehend or conceive him. This is like our being able to touch a mountain with our hands, although we cannot embrace it as we could a tree or any other object not too big for our arms; for comprehension means that our thought embraces a thing, but for knowledge it is enough that our thought touches the thing.

Again, you ask what made it necessary for God to create these truths. What I say is that God was just as much free to make it untrue that all straight lines drawn from center to circumference are equal, as he was not to create the world. And certainly these truths are not necessarily conjoined with God's essence any more than other creatures are.

You ask what God did in order to produce them; I say that in the very act of willing them and understanding them from eternity, He created them; or, if you confine the word "created" to the existence of things, He established and made them. For in God's will, understanding and creation are one and the same thing; none is prior to another even conceptually.

> [FROM a letter to Father Mersenne, May 27, 1631, trans. Elizabeth Anscombe and Peter T. Geach, in *Descartes: Philosophical Writings*, London: Nelson, 1954. By permission of Thomas Nelson and Sons Ltd., Edinburgh.]

8

Is Descartes' Argument Circular? (see *Meditations* IV and V)

[A] Thirdly, when I said that "we could know nothing with certainty unless we were first aware that God existed," I announced in express terms that I referred only to the science apprehending such conclusions "as can recur in memory without attending further to the proofs which led me to make them." Further, knowledge of first principles is not usually called science by dialecticians. But when we become aware that we are thinking beings, this is a primitive act of knowledge derived from no syllogistic reasoning. He who says, *"I think, hence I am, or exist,"* does not deduce existence from thought by a syllogism, but, by a simple act of mental vision, recognizes it as if it were a thing that is known *per se*. This is evident from the fact that if it were syllogistically deduced, the major premise, *that everything that thinks is, or exists,* would have to be known previously; but yet that has rather been learned from the experience of the individual —that unless he exists he cannot think. For our mind is so constituted by nature that general propositions are formed out of the knowledge of particulars.

That "an atheist can know clearly that the three angles of a triangle are equal to two right angles," I do not deny, I merely affirm that, on the other hand, such knowledge on his part cannot constitute true science, because no knowledge that can be rendered doubtful should be called science. Since he is, as supposed, an atheist, he cannot be sure that he is not deceived in the things that seem most evident to him, as has been sufficiently shown; and though perchance the doubt does not occur to him, nevertheless it may come up, if he examine the matter, or if another suggests it; he can never be safe from it unless he first recognizes the existence of a God.

> [FROM Descartes' Reply to the Second Set of Objections, collected by Father Mersenne; trans. Haldane and Ross, *op. cit.*]

[B] Finally, to prove that I have not argued in a circle in saying, that "the only secure reason we have for believing that what we clearly and distinctly perceive is true, is the fact that God exists; but that clearly we can be sure that God exists only because we perceive that," I may cite the explanations that I have already given at sufficient length in my reply to the second set of Objections, numbers 3 and 4. There I distinguished those matters that in actual truth we clearly perceive from those we remember to have formerly perceived. For first, we are sure that God exists because we have attended to the proofs that established this fact; but afterwards it is enough for us to remember that we have perceived something clearly, in order to be sure that it is true; but this would not suffice, unless we knew that God existed and that he did not deceive us.

> [FROM Descartes' Reply to the Fourth Set of Objections, by Antoine Arnauld; trans. Haldane and Ross, *ibid.*]

9

Substance (see *Meditation* VI)

As regards these matters which we consider as being things or modes of things, it is necessary that we should examine them here one by one. And when we conceive of substance, we merely conceive an existent thing which requires nothing but itself in order to exist. To speak truth, nothing but God answers to this description as being that which is absolutely self-sustaining, for we perceive that there is no other created thing which can exist without being sustained by His power. That is why the word substance does not pertain *univoce*[1] to God and to other things, as they say in the Schools, that is, no common signification for this appellation which will apply equally to God and to them can be distinctly understood.

Created substances, however, whether corporeal or thinking, may be conceived under this common concept; for they are things which need only the concurrence of God in order to exist. But yet substance cannot be first discovered merely from the fact that it is a thing that exists, for that fact alone is not observed by us. We may, however, easily discover it by means of any one of its attributes because it is a common notion that nothing is possessed of no attributes, properties, or qualities. For this reason, when we perceive any attribute, we therefore conclude that some existing thing or substance to which it may be attributed, is necessarily present.

But although any one attribute is sufficient to give us a knowledge of substance, there is always one principal property of substance which constitutes its nature and essence, and on which all the others depend. Thus extension in length, breadth and depth, constitutes the nature of corporeal substance; and thought constitutes the nature of

---

[1] [In the same sense.—M.C.B.]

thinking substance. For all else that may be attributed to body pre-supposes extension, and is but a mode of this extended thing; as everything that we find in mind is but so many diverse forms of think-ing. Thus, for example, we cannot conceive figure but as an extended thing, nor movement but as in an extended space; so imagination, feel-ing, and will, only exist in a thinking thing. But, on the other hand, we can conceive extension without figure or action, and thinking without imagination or sensation, and so on with the rest; as is quite clear to anyone who attends to the matter.

> [FROM Principles LI, LII, and LIII of the First Part of *The Principles of Philosophy,* trans. Haldane and Ross, *ibid.*]

10

Modes (see *Meditation* VI)

And, indeed, when we here speak of modes we mean nothing more than what elsewhere is termed *attribute* or *quality.* But when we con-sider substance as modified or diversified by them, I avail myself of the word *mode*; and when from the disposition or variation it can be named as of such and such a kind, we shall use the word *qualities* [to designate the different modes which cause it to be so termed]; and finally when we more generally consider that these modes or qualities are in substance we term them *attributes.* And because in God any variableness is incomprehensible, we cannot ascribe to Him modes or qualities; but simply attributes. And even in created things that which never exists in them in any diverse way, like existence and duration in the existing and enduring thing, should be called not qualities or modes, but attributes.

Some of the attributes are in things themselves and others are only in our thought. Thus time, for example, which we distinguish from duration taken in its general sense and which we describe as the measure of movement, is only a mode of thinking; for we do not in-deed apprehend that the duration of things which are moved is different from that of the things which are not moved, as is evident from the fact that if two bodies are moved for the space of an hour, the one quickly, the other slowly, we do not count the time longer in one case than in the other, although there is much more movement in one of the two bodies than in the other. But in order to comprehend the duration of all things under the same measure, we usually compare their duration with the duration of the greatest and most regular motions, which are those that create years and days, and these we term time. Hence this adds nothing to the notion of duration, generally taken, but a mode of thinking.

Similarly number when we consider it abstractly or generally and not in created things, is but a mode of thinking; and the same is true of all that which [in the schools] is named *universals*. . . .

But as to the number in things themselves, this proceeds from the distinction which exists between them; and *distinction* is of three sorts, viz. *real, modal,* and *of reason*. The *real* is properly speaking found between two or more substances; and we can conclude that two substances are really distinct one from the other from the sole fact that we can conceive the one clearly and distinctly without the other. For in accordance with the knowledge which we have of God, we are certain that He can carry into effect all that of which we have a distinct idea. . . .

There are two sorts of *modal distinctions,* i.e. the one between the mode properly speaking, and the substance of which it is the mode, and the other between two modes of the same substance. The former we recognize by the fact that we can clearly conceive substance without the mode which we say differs from it, while we cannot reciprocally have a perception of this mode without perceiving the substance. There is, for example, a modal distinction between figure or movement and the corporeal substance in which both exist; there is also a distinction between affirming or recollecting and the mind. As to the other kind of distinction, its characteristic is that we are able to recognize the one mode without the other and *vice versa,* but we can conceive neither the one nor the other without recognizing that both subsist in one common substance. If, for example, a stone is moved and along with that is square, we are able to conceive the square figure without knowing that it is moved, and reciprocally, we may be aware that it is moved without knowing that it is square; but we cannot have a conception of this movement and figure unless we have a conception of the substance of the stone. As for the distinction whereby the mode of one substance is different from another substance, or from the mode of another substance, as the movement of one body is different from another body or from mind, or else as movement is different from duration; it appears to me that we shall call it real rather than modal; because we cannot clearly conceive these modes apart from the substances of which they are the modes and which are really distinct.

Finally the *distinction of reason* is between substance and some one of its attributes without which it is not possible that we should have a distinct knowledge of it, or between two such attributes of the same substance. This distinction is made manifest from the fact that we cannot have a clear and distinct idea of such a substance if we exclude from it such an attribute; or we cannot have a clear idea of the one of the two attributes if we separate from it the other. For example, because there is no substance which does not cease to exist when it ceases to endure, duration is only distinct from substance by thought, and all the modes of thinking which we consider as though they existed in the objects, differ only in thought both from the objects of which they are the thought and from each other in a common object. . . .

> [FROM Principles LVI, LVII, LVIII, LX, LXI, and LXII of the First Part of *The Principles of Philosophy*, trans. Haldane and Ross, *ibid.*]

11

Space and Bodies (see *Meditation* VI)

Space or internal place and the corporeal substance which is contained in it, are not different otherwise than in the mode in which they are conceived of by us. For, in truth, the same extension in length, breadth, and depth, which constitutes space, constitutes body; and the difference between them consists only in the fact that in body we consider extension as particular and conceive it to change just as body changes; in space, on the contrary, we attribute to extension a generic unity, so that after having removed from a certain space the body which occupied it, we do not suppose that we have also removed the extension of that space, because it appears to us that the same extension remains so long as it is of the same magnitude and figure, and preserves the same position in relation to certain other bodies, whereby we determine this space.

And it will be easy for us to recognize that the same extension which constitutes the nature of body likewise constitutes the nature of space, nor do the two mutually differ, excepting as the nature of the genus or species differs from the nature of the individual, provided that, in order to discern the idea that we have of any body, such as stone, we reject from it all that is not essential to the nature of body. In the first place, then, we may reject hardness, because if the stone were liquefied or reduced to powder, it would no longer possess hardness, and yet would not cease to be a body; let us in the next place reject color, because we have often seen stones so transparent that they had no color; again we reject weight, because we see that fire although very light is yet body; and finally we may reject cold, heat, and all the other qualities of the kind either because they are not considered as in the stone, or else because with the change of their qualities the stone is not for that reason considered to have lost its nature as body. After examination we shall find that there is nothing remaining in the idea of body excepting that it is extended in length, breadth, and depth; and this is comprised in our idea of space, not only of that which is full of body, but also of that which is called a vacuum. . . .

As regards a vacuum in the philosophic sense of the word, i.e. a space in which there is no substance, it is evident that such cannot exist, because the extension of space or internal place, is not different from that of body. For, from the mere fact that a body is extended in length, breadth, or depth, we have reason to conclude that it is a substance, because it is absolutely inconceivable that nothing should possess extension; we ought to conclude also that the same is true of the space which is supposed to be void, i.e. that since there is in it extension, there is necessarily also substance.

And when we take this word vacuum in its ordinary sense, we do not mean a place or space in which there is absolutely nothing, but only a place in which there are none of those things which we expected to find there. Thus because a pitcher is made to hold water, we say that it is empty when it contains nothing but air; or if there are no fish in a fish-pond, we say there is nothing in it, even though it be full of water. . . .

. . . And therefore, if it is asked what would happen if God removed all the body contained in a vessel without permitting its place being occupied by another body, we shall answer that the sides of the vessel will thereby come into immediate contiguity with one another. For two bodies must touch when there is nothing between them, because it is manifestly contradictory for these two bodies to be apart from one another, or that there should be a distance between them, and yet that this distance should be nothing; for distance is a mode of extension, and without extended substance it cannot therefore exist.

There is therefore but one matter in the whole universe, and we know this by the simple fact of its being extended. All the properties which we clearly perceive in it may be reduced to the one, viz. that it can be divided, or moved according to its parts, and consequently is capable of all these affections which we perceive can arise from the motion of its parts. For its partition by thought alone makes no difference to it; but all the variation in matter, or diversity in its forms, depends on motion. . . .

> [FROM Principles X, XI, XVI, XVII, XVIII, and XXIII of the Second Part of *The Principles of Philosophy,* trans. Haldane and Ross, *ibid.*]

12

The Pineal Gland (see *Meditation* VI)

It is likewise necessary to know that although the soul is joined to the whole body, there is yet in that a certain part in which it exercises its functions more particularly than in all the others; and it is usually believed that this part is the brain, or possibly the heart: the brain, because it is with it that the organs of sense are connected, and the heart because it is apparently in it that we experience the passions. But, in examining the matter with care, it seems as though I had clearly ascertained that the part of the body in which the soul exercises its functions immediately is in nowise the heart, nor the whole of the brain, but merely the most inward of all its parts, to wit, a certain very small gland which is situated in the middle of its substance and so suspended above the duct whereby the animal spirits in its anterior cavities have communication with those in the posterior, that the slightest movements which take place in it may alter very greatly the course of these spirits; and reciprocally that the smallest changes which occur in the course of the spirits may do much to change the movements of this gland. . . .

Let us then conceive here that the soul has its principal seat in the little gland which exists in the middle of the brain, from whence it radiates forth through all the remainder of the body by means of the animal spirits, nerves, and even the blood, which, participating in the impressions of the spirits, can carry them by the arteries into all the members. And recollecting what has been said above about the machine of our body, i.e., that the little filaments of our nerves are so distributed in all its parts, that on the occasion of the diverse movements which are there excited by sensible objects, they open in diverse ways the pores of the brain, which causes the animal spirits contained in these cavities to enter in diverse ways into the muscles, by which means they can move the members in all the different ways in which they are capable of being moved; and also that all the other causes which are capable of moving the spirits in diverse ways suffice to conduct them into diverse muscles; let us here add that the small gland which is the main seat of the soul is so suspended between the cavities which contain the spirits that it can be moved by them in as many different ways as may also be moved in diverse ways by the soul, whose nature is such that it receives in itself as many diverse impressions, that is to say, that it possesses as many diverse perceptions as there are diverse movements in this gland. Reciprocally, likewise, the machine of the body is so formed that from the simple fact that this gland is diversely moved by the soul, or by such other cause, whatever it is, it thrusts the spirits which surround it towards the pores of the brain, which conduct them by the nerves into the muscles, by which means it causes them to move the limbs.

> [FROM Articles XXXI and XXXIV of the First Part of *The Passions of the Soul*, trans. Haldane and Ross, *ibid*.]

13

The Automatism of Brutes (see *Meditation* VI)

. . . As for the understanding or thought attributed by Montaigne and others to brutes, I cannot hold their opinion; not, however, because I am doubtful of the truth of what is commonly said, that men have absolute dominion over all the other animals; for while I allow that there are some which are stronger than we are, and I believe there may be some, also, which have natural cunning capable of deceiving the most sagacious men; yet I consider that they imitate or surpass us only in those of our actions which are not directed by thought; for it often happens that we walk and that we eat without thinking at all upon what we are doing; and it is so much without the use of our reason that we repel things which harm us, and ward off blows struck at us, that, although we might fully determine not to put our hands before our heads when falling, we could not help doing so. I believe, also, that we should eat as the brutes do, without having learned how, if we had no power of thought at all; and it is said that those who walk in their sleep sometimes swim across rivers, where, had they been awake, they would have been drowned.

As for the movements of our passions, although in ourselves they are accompanied with thought, because we possess that faculty, it is, nevertheless, very evident that they do not depend upon it, because they often arise in spite of us, and, consequently, they may exist in brutes, and even be more violent than they are in the men, without warranting the conclusion that brutes can think; in fine there is no one of our external actions which can assure those who examine them that our body is anything more than a machine which moves of itself, but which also has in it a mind which thinks—excepting words, or other signs made in regard to whatever subjects present themselves, without reference to any passion. I say words, or other signs, because mutes make use of signs in the same way as we do of the voice, and these signs are pertinent; but I exclude the talking of parrots, but not that of the insane, which may be apropos to the case in hand, although it is irrational; and I add that these words or signs are not to relate to any passion, in order to exclude, not only cries of joy or pain and the like, but, also, all that can be taught to any animal by art; for if a magpie be taught to say "good-morning" to its mistress when it sees her coming, it may be that the utterance of these words is associated with the excitement of some one of its passions; for instance, there will be a stir of expectation of something to eat, if it has been the custom of the mistress to give it some dainty bit when it spoke those words; and in like manner all those things which dogs, horses, and monkeys are made to do are merely motions of their fear, their hope, or their joy, so that they might do them without any thought at all.

Now, it seems to me very remarkable that language, as thus defined, belongs to man alone; for although Montaigne and Charron have said that there is more difference between one man and another than between a man and a brute, nevertheless there has never yet been found a brute so perfect that it has made use of a sign to inform other animals of something which had no relation to their passions; while there is no man so imperfect as not to use such signs; so that the deaf and dumb invent particular signs by which they express their thoughts, which seems to me a very strong argument to prove that the reason why brutes do not talk as we do is that they have no faculty of thought, and not at all that the organs for it are wanting. And it cannot be said that they talk among themselves, but we do not understand them; for, as dogs and other animals express to us their passions, they would express to us as well their thoughts, if they had them. I know, indeed, that brutes do many things better than we do, but I am not surprised at it; for that, also, goes to prove that they act by force of nature and by springs, like a clock, which tells better what the hour is than our judgment can inform us. And, doubtless, when swallows come in the spring, they act in that like clocks. All that honey-bees do is of the same nature; and the order that cranes keep in flying, or monkeys drawn up for battle, if it be true that they do observe any order, and, finally, the instinct of burying their dead is no more surprising than that of dogs and cats, which scratch the ground to bury their excrements, although they almost never do bury them, which shows that they do it by instinct only, and not by thought. It can only be said that, although the brutes do nothing which can convince us that they think, nevertheless, because their bodily organs are not very different from ours, we might conjecture that there was some faculty of thought joined to these organs, as we experience in ourselves, although theirs be much less perfect, to which I have nothing to reply, except that, if they could think as we do, they would have an immortal soul as well as we, which is not likely, because there is no reason for believing it of some animals without believing it of all, and there are many of them too imperfect to make it possible to believe it of them, such as oysters, sponges, etc.

[FROM a letter to the Marquis of Newcastle, trans. Henry A. P. Torrey, in *The Philosophy of Descartes in Extracts from his Writings,* N. Y.: Holt, 1892.]

BLAISE PASCAL

Thoughts (abridged)

BLAISE PASCAL

BLAISE PASCAL (1623–1662) was born at Clermont in Auvergne, the son of an able and respected government official, who was a member of Father Mersenne's group of *savants.* Pascal was educated by his father, broadly and along progressive lines, and was trained especially in experimental science. His short life, during most of which he suffered from painful and debilitating illness, was crammed with achievements, including his brilliant pioneering work in mathematics on conic sections (his method, partly borrowed, anticipated modern projective geometry), on the cycloid (his results suggested to Leibniz the infinitesimal calculus), and on probability; his contributions to physics on the nature of the vacuum and the pressure of liquids, including original and extremely well-executed experiments with Torricellian tubes; various inventions and practical suggestions such as the first mechanical calculating machine, a method of teaching children to read, and the idea for the first regular bus line in Paris. In his writings, both scientific and theological, he evolved a new prose style, direct, clear, and flexible, which had a powerful and lasting influence on the course of French literature.

His deepest concern, however, especially in the later years of his life, was with religion. In his youth he was converted to Jansenism, a theological perspective unusual in Catholicism, being notable for its Calvinistic emphasis on the importance of God's free grace and on the individual moral conscience. His sister entered the convent at Port-Royal-des-Champs, in the valley of the Chevreuse, and his closest friends were among the group of scholars and others who were close to that religious community and who supported and advanced the Jansenist cause. Pascal himself had an overwhelming mystical experience in 1654. His eighteen *Letters to a Provincial,* which appeared pseudonymously during 1656, were written in defense of Antoine Arnauld, Professor at the Sorbonne and defender of Jansenism, who was brought before the Sorbonne Theological Faculty for heresy. But a more profound and subtle conception of Pascal's religion is to be seen in those notes toward a great apology for Christianity that he left behind at his death, and that are now known as the *Thoughts* (see below).

Even though, as some propose, Pascal were to be denied the strict title of "philosopher," it would have to be granted that he thought deeply about the philosophy of religion, raised philosophical questions, and gave some striking and influential answers. Calling attention to the importance of religious experience for epistemology, he approached the problem of religious knowledge in a way that was remarkably original for his century. Indeed, some aspects of his thought have not been fully understood or appreciated until our own time, when the reflections of the Existentialists and Neo-orthodox theologians have prepared us to see how much meaning there is in Pascal's analysis of the paradoxical character of man and of the human predicament. With his view of the "heart" as a source of knowledge—a very different sort of intuition from Descartes'—Pascal believed he could mark the limits of reason better than his rationalist contemporaries. His attempt to justify belief in God even in the absence of reasons for saying that the belief is true—the argument of his famous "wager"—opened out some new lines of thought in the "ethics of belief," and set a fundamental challenge to modern philosophers.

Thoughts* (*abridged*)

4. *Mathematics, intuition.* True eloquence makes light of eloquence, true morality makes light of morality; that is to say, the morality of the judgment, which has no rules, makes light of the morality of the intellect.

For it is to judgment that perception belongs, as science belongs to intellect. Intuition is the part of judgment, mathematics of intellect.

To make light of philosophy is to be a true philosopher.

72. *Man's disproportion.* [This is where our innate knowledge leads us. If it be not true, there is no truth in man; and if it be true, he finds therein great cause for humiliation, being compelled to abase himself in one way or another. And since he cannot exist without this knowledge, I wish that, before entering on deeper researches into nature, he would consider her both seriously and at leisure, that he would reflect upon himself also, and knowing what proportion there is . . .] Let man then contemplate the whole of nature in her full and grand majesty, and turn his vision from the low objects which surround him. Let him gaze on that brilliant light, set like an eternal lamp to illumine the universe; let the earth appear to him a point in comparison with the vast circle described by the sun; and let him wonder at the fact that this vast circle is itself but a very fine point in comparison with that described by the stars in their revolution round the firmament. But if our view be arrested there, let our imagination pass beyond; it will sooner exhaust the power of conception than nature that of supplying material for conception. The whole visible world is only an imperceptible atom in the ample bosom of nature. No idea approaches it. We may enlarge our conceptions beyond all imaginable space; we only produce atoms in comparison with the reality of things. It is an infinite sphere, the center of which is everywhere, the circum-

* From *Pensées,* translated by William Finlayson Trotter (1904), from the edition of Léon Brunschvicg (1897). Dutton Everyman Paperback edition. Reprinted by permission of E. P. Dutton & Co., New York, and J. M. Dent & Sons, London. The present selection includes about one-eighth of the original, the parts of greatest philosophical interest. The *Pensées* (the title was given by the group who edited the first, or "Port-Royal," edition, in 1670) are notes for Pascal's projected defense of Christianity, which was to have been his crowning achievement. Sentences in square brackets were erased by Pascal and restored by his French editor.

ference nowhere. In short it is the greatest sensible mark of the almighty power of God, that imagination loses itself in that thought.

Returning to himself, let man consider what he is in comparison with all existence; let him regard himself as lost in this remote corner of nature; and from the little cell in which he finds himself lodged, I mean the universe, let him estimate at their true value the earth, kingdoms, cities, and himself. What is a man in the Infinite?

But to show him another prodigy equally astonishing, let him examine the most delicate things he knows. Let a mite be given him, with its minute body and parts incomparably more minute, limbs with their joints, veins in the limbs, blood in the veins, humors in the blood, drops in the humors, vapors in the drops. Dividing these last things again, let him exhaust his powers of conception, and let the last object at which he can arrive be now that of our discourse. Perhaps he will think that here is the smallest point in nature. I will let him see therein a new abyss. I will paint for him not only the visible universe, but all that he can conceive of nature's immensity in the womb of this abridged atom. Let him see therein an infinity of universes, each of which has its firmament, its planets, its earth, in the same proportion as in the visible world; in each earth animals, and in the last mites, in which he will find again all that the first had, finding still in these others the same thing without end and without cessation. Let him lose himself in wonders as amazing in their littleness as the others in their vastness. For who will not be astounded at the fact that our body, which a little while ago was imperceptible in the universe, itself imperceptible in the bosom of the whole, is now a colossus, a world, or rather a whole, in respect of the nothingness which we cannot reach? He who regards himself in this light will be afraid of himself, and observing himself sustained in the body given him by nature between those two abysses of the Infinite and Nothing, will tremble at the sight of these marvels; and I think that, as his curiosity changes into admiration, he will be more disposed to contemplate them in silence than to examine them with presumption.

For in fact what is man in nature? A Nothing in comparison with the Infinite, an All in comparison with the Nothing, a mean between nothing and everything. Since he is infinitely removed from comprehending the extremes, the end of things and their beginning are hopelessly hidden from him in an impenetrable secret; he is equally incapable of seeing the Nothing from which he was made, and the Infinite in which he is swallowed up.

What will he do then, but perceive the appearance of the middle of things, in an eternal despair of knowing either their beginning or their end. All things proceed from the Nothing, and are borne towards the Infinite. Who will follow these marvelous processes? The Author of these wonders understands them. None others can do so.

Through failure to contemplate these Infinites, men have rashly rushed into the examination of nature, as though they bore some proportion to her. It is strange that they have wished to understand the beginnings of things, and thence to arrive at the knowledge of the whole, with a presumption as infinite as their object. For surely this design cannot be formed without presumption or without a capacity infinite like nature.

If we are well informed, we understand that, as nature has graven her image and that of her Author on all things, they almost all partake of her double infinity. Thus we see that all the sciences are infinite in the extent of their researches. For who doubts that geometry, for instance, has an infinite infinity of problems to solve? They are also infinite in the multitude and fineness of their premises; for it is clear that those which are put forward as ultimate are not self-supporting, but are based on others which, again having others for their support, do not permit of finality. But we represent some as ultimate for reason, in the same way as in regard to material objects we call that an indivisible point beyond which our senses can no longer perceive anything, although by its nature it is infinitely divisible.

Of these two Infinites of science, that of greatness is the most palpable, and hence a few persons have pretended to know all things. "I will speak of the whole," said Democritus.

But the infinitely little is the least obvious. Philosophers have much oftener claimed to have reached it, and it is here they have all stumbled. This has given rise to such common titles as *First Principles, Principles of Philosophy,* and the like, as ostentatious in fact, though not in appearance, as that one which blinds us, *De omni scibili.*[1]

We naturally believe ourselves far more capable of reaching the center of things than of embracing their circumference. The visible extent of the world visibly exceeds us; but as we exceed little things, we think ourselves more capable of knowing them. And yet we need no less capacity for attaining the Nothing than the All. Infinite capacity is required for both, and it seems to me that whoever shall have understood the ultimate principles of being might also attain to the knowledge of the Infinite. The one depends on the other, and one

---

[1] [Concerning everything that can be known.—M.C.B.]

leads to the other. These extremes meet and reunite by force of distance, and find each other in God, and in God alone.

Let us then take our compass; we are something, and we are not everything. The nature of our existence hides from us the knowledge of first beginnings which are born of the Nothing; and the littleness of our being conceals from us the sight of the Infinite.

Our intellect holds the same position in the world of thought as our body occupies in the expanse of nature.

Limited as we are in every way, this state which holds the mean between two extremes is present in all our impotence. Our senses perceive no extreme. Too much sound deafens us; too much light dazzles us; too great distance or proximity hinders our view. Too great length and too great brevity of discourse tends to obscurity; too much truth is paralyzing (I know some who cannot understand that to take four from nothing leaves nothing). First principles are too self-evident for us; too much pleasure disagrees with us. Too many concords are annoying in music; too many benefits irritate us; we wish to have the wherewithal to over-pay our debts. *Beneficia eo usque læta sunt dum videntur exsolvi posse; ubi multum antevenere, pro gratia odium redditur.*[1] We feel neither extreme heat nor extreme cold. Excessive qualities are prejudicial to us and not perceptible by the senses; we do not feel but suffer them. Extreme youth and extreme age hinder the mind, as also too much and too little education. In short, extremes are for us as though they were not, and we are not within their notice. They escape us, or we them.

This is our true state; this is what makes us incapable of certain knowledge and of absolute ignorance. We sail within a vast sphere, ever drifting in uncertainty, driven from end to end. When we think to attach ourselves to any point and to fasten to it, it wavers and leaves us; and if we follow it, it eludes our grasp, slips past us, and vanishes for ever. Nothing stays for us. This is our natural condition, and yet most contrary to our inclination; we burn with desire to find solid ground and an ultimate sure foundation whereon to build a tower reaching to the Infinite. But our whole groundwork cracks, and the earth opens to abysses.

Let us therefore not look for certainty and stability. Our reason is always deceived by fickle shadows; nothing can fix the finite between the two Infinites, which both enclose and fly from it.

---

[1] [Benefits are pleasurable as long as it seems possible to repay them. When they go beyond that, hatred instead of gratitude is returned.—Tacitus, *Annals*, IV, 18.—M.C.B.]

If this be well understood, I think that we shall remain at rest, each in the state wherein nature has placed him. As this sphere which has fallen to us as our lot is always distant from either extreme, what matters it that man should have a little more knowledge of the universe? If he has it, he but gets a little higher. Is he not always infinitely removed from the end, and is not the duration of our life equally removed from eternity, even if it lasts ten years longer?

In comparison with these Infinites all finites are equal, and I see no reason for fixing our imagination on one more than on another. The only comparison which we make of ourselves to the finite is painful to us.

If man made himself the first object of study, he would see how incapable he is of going further. How can a part know the whole? But he may perhaps aspire to know at least the parts to which he bears some proportion. But the parts of the world are all so related and linked to one another, that I believe it impossible to know one without the other and without the whole.

Man, for instance, is related to all he knows. He needs a place wherein to abide, time through which to live, motion in order to live, elements to compose him, warmth and food to nourish him, air to breathe. He sees light; he feels bodies; in short, he is in a dependent alliance with everything. To know man, then, it is necessary to know how it happens that he needs air to live, and, to know the air, we must know how it is thus related to the life of man, etc. Flame cannot exist without air; therefore to understand the one, we must understand the other.

Since everything then is cause and effect, dependent and supporting, mediate and immediate, and all is held together by a natural though imperceptible chain, which binds together things most distant and most different, I hold it equally impossible to know the parts without knowing the whole, and to know the whole without knowing the parts in detail.

[The eternity of things in itself or in God must also astonish our brief duration. The fixed and constant immobility of nature, in comparison with the continual change which goes on within us, must have the same effect.]

And what completes our incapability of knowing things, is the fact that they are simple, and that we are composed of two opposite natures, different in kind, soul and body. For it is impossible that our rational part should be other than spiritual; and if any one maintain that we are simply corporeal, this would far more exclude us from the knowledge of things, there being nothing so inconceivable as to say that matter knows itself. It is impossible to imagine how it should know itself.

So if we are simply material, we can know nothing at all; and if we are composed of mind and matter, we cannot know perfectly things which are simple, whether spiritual or corporeal. Hence it comes that almost all philosophers have confused ideas of things, and speak of material things in spiritual terms, and of spiritual things in material terms. For they say boldly that bodies have a tendency to fall, that they seek after their center, that they fly from destruction, that they fear the void, that they have inclinations, sympathies, antipathies, all of which attributes pertain only to mind. And in speaking of minds, they consider them as in a place, and attribute to them movement from one place to another; and these are qualities which belong only to bodies.

Instead of receiving the ideas of these things in their purity, we color them with our own qualities, and stamp with our composite being all the simple things which we contemplate.

Who would not think, seeing us compose all things of mind and body, but that this mixture would be quite intelligible to us? Yet it is the very thing we least understand. Man is to himself the most wonderful object in nature; for he cannot conceive what the body is, still less what the mind is, and least of all how a body should be united to a mind. This is the consummation of his difficulties, and yet it is his very being. *Modus quo corporibus adhærent spiritus comprehendi ab hominibus non potest, et hoc tamen homo est.*[1] Finally, to complete the proof of our weakness, I shall conclude with these two considerations. . . .

76. To write against those who made too profound a study of science: Descartes.

77. I cannot forgive Descartes. In all his philosophy he would have been quite willing to dispense with God. But he had to make Him give a fillip to set the world in motion; beyond this, he has no further need of God.

---

[1] [The way by which minds cling to bodies cannot be understood by men; nevertheless, this is man.—St. Augustine, *The City of God*, XXI, 10.—M.C.B.]

78.   Descartes useless and uncertain.

79.   [*Descartes.*—We must say summarily: "This is made by figure
and motion," for it is true. But to say what these are, and to compose
the machine, is ridiculous. For it is useless, uncertain, and painful.
And were it true, we do not think all philosophy is worth one hour
of pain.]

82.   *Imagination.*   It is that deceitful part in man, that mistress of
error and falsity, the more deceptive that she is not always so; for she
would be an infallible rule of truth, if she were an infallible rule of
falsehood. But being most generally false, she gives no sign of her
nature, impressing the same character on the true and the false.

I do not speak of fools, I speak of the wisest men; and it is among
them that the imagination has the great gift of persuasion. Reason
protests in vain; it cannot set a true value on things.

This arrogant power, the enemy of reason, who likes to rule and
dominate it, has established in man a second nature to show how all-
powerful she is. She makes men happy and sad, healthy and sick, rich
and poor; she compels reason to believe, doubt, and deny; she blunts
the senses, or quickens them; she has her fools and sages; and nothing
vexes us more than to see that she fills her devotees with a satisfaction far more full and entire than does reason. Those who have a
lively imagination are a great deal more pleased with themselves than
the wise can reasonably be. They look down upon men with haughti-
ness; they argue with boldness and confidence, others with fear and
diffidence; and this gaiety of countenance often gives them the advantage in the opinion of the hearers, such favor have the imaginary
wise in the eyes of judges of like nature. Imagination cannot make
fools wise; but she can make them happy, to the envy of reason which
can only make its friends miserable; the one covers them with glory,
the other with shame.

What but this faculty of imagination dispenses reputation, awards
respect and veneration to persons, works, laws, and the great? How
insufficient are all the riches of the earth without her consent!

Would you not say that this magistrate, whose venerable age commands the respect of a whole people, is governed by pure and lofty
reason, and that he judges causes according to their true nature without considering those mere trifles which only affect the imagination of
the weak? See him go to sermon, full of devout zeal, strengthening his

reason with the ardor of his love. He is ready to listen with exemplary respect. Let the preacher appear, and let nature have given him a hoarse voice or a comical cast of countenance, or let his barber have given him a bad shave, or let by chance his dress be more dirtied than usual, then however great the truths he announces, I wager our senator loses his gravity.

If the greatest philosopher in the world find himself upon a plank wider than actually necessary, but hanging over a precipice, his imagination will prevail, though his reason convince him of his safety. Many cannot bear the thought without a cold sweat. I will not state all its effects.

Every one knows that the sight of cats or rats, the crushing of a coal, etc., may unhinge the reason. The tone of voice affects the wisest, and changes the force of a discourse or a poem.

Love or hate alters the aspect of justice. How much greater confidence has an advocate, retained with a large fee, in the justice of his cause! How much better does his bold manner make his case appear to the judges, deceived as they are by appearances! How ludicrous is reason, blown with a breath in every direction!

I should have to enumerate almost every action of men who scarce waver save under her assaults. For reason has been obliged to yield, and the wisest reason takes as her own principles those which the imagination of man has everywhere rashly introduced. [He who would follow reason only would be deemed foolish by the generality of men. We must judge by the opinion of the majority of mankind. Because it has pleased them, we must work all day for pleasures seen to be imaginary; and after sleep has refreshed our tired reason, we must forthwith start up and rush after phantoms, and suffer the impressions of this mistress of the world. This is one of the sources of error, but it is not the only one.]

Our magistrates have known well this mystery. Their red robes, the ermine in which they wrap themselves like furry cats, the courts in which they administer justice, the *fleurs-de-lis,* and all such august apparel were necessary; if the physicians had not their cassocks and their mules, if the doctors had not their square caps and their robes four times too wide, they would never have duped the world, which cannot resist so original an appearance. If magistrates had true justice, and if physicians had the true art of healing, they would have no occasion for square caps; the majesty of these sciences would of itself be venerable enough. But having only imaginary knowledge, they must employ those silly tools that strike the imagination with which they have to deal; and thereby in fact they inspire respect. Soldiers alone are not disguised in this manner, because indeed their part is the most essential; they establish themselves by force, the others by show.

Therefore our kings seek out no disguises. They do not mask themselves in extraordinary costumes to appear such; but they are accompanied by guards and halberdiers. Those armed and red-faced puppets who have hands and power for them alone, those trumpets and drums which go before them, and those legions round about them, make the stoutest tremble. They have not dress only, they have might. A very refined reason is required to regard as an ordinary man the Grand Turk, in his superb seraglio, surrounded by forty thousand janissaries.

We cannot even see an advocate in his robe and with his cap on his head, without a favorable opinion of his ability. The imagination disposes of everything; it makes beauty, justice, and happiness, which is everything in the world. I should much like to see an Italian work, of which I only know the title, which alone is worth many books, *Della opinione regina del mondo*. I approve of the book without knowing it, save the evil in it, if any. These are pretty much the effects of that deceptive faculty, which seems to have been expressly given us to lead us into necessary error. We have, however, many other sources of error.

Not only are old impressions capable of misleading us; the charms of novelty have the same power. Hence arise all the disputes of men, who taunt each other either with following the false impressions of childhood or with running rashly after the new. Who keeps the due mean? Let him appear and prove it. There is no principle, however natural to us from infancy, which may not be made to pass for a false impression either of education or of sense.

"Because," say some, "you have believed from childhood that a box was empty when you saw nothing in it, you have believed in the possibility of a vacuum. This is an illusion of your senses, strengthened by custom, which science must correct." "Because," say others, "you have been taught at school that there is no vacuum, you have perverted your common sense which clearly comprehended it, and you must correct this by returning to your first state." Which has deceived you, your senses or your education?

We have another source of error in diseases. They spoil the judgment and the senses; and if the more serious produce a sensible change, I do not doubt that slighter ills produce a proportionate impression.

Our own interest is again a marvelous instrument for nicely putting out our eyes. The justest man in the world is not allowed to be judge in his own cause; I know some who, in order not to fall into this self-love, have been perfectly unjust out of opposition. The sure way of losing a just cause has been to get it recommended to these men by their near relatives.

Justice and truth are two such· subtle points, that our tools are too blunt to touch them accurately. If they reach the point, they either crush it, or lean all round, more on the false than on the true. . . .

194.   . . . Let them at least learn what is the religion they attack, before attacking it. If this religion boasted of having a clear view of God, and of possessing it open and unveiled, it would be attacking it to say that we see nothing in the world which shows it with this clearness. But since, on the contrary, it says that men are in darkness and estranged from God, that He has hidden Himself from their knowledge, that this is in fact the name which He gives Himself in the Scriptures, *Deus absconditus*;[1] and finally, if it endeavors equally to establish these two things: that God has set up in the Church visible signs to make Himself known to those who should seek Him sincerely, and that He has nevertheless so disguised them that He will only be perceived by those who seek Him with all their heart; what advantage can they obtain, when, in the negligence with which they make profession of being in search of the truth, they cry out that nothing reveals it to them; and since that darkness in which they are, and with which they upbraid the Church, establishes only one of the things which she affirms, without touching the other, and, very far from destroying, proves her doctrine?

In order to attack it, they should have protested that they had made every effort to seek Him everywhere, and even in that which the Church proposes for their instruction, but without satisfaction. If they talked in this manner, they would in truth be attacking one of her pretensions. But I hope here to show that no reasonable person can speak thus, and I venture even to say that no one has ever done so. We know well enough how those who are of this mind behave. They believe they have made great efforts for their instruction, when they

---

[1] [Hidden God.—M.C.B.]

have spent a few hours in reading some book of Scripture, and have questioned some priest on the truths of the faith. After that, they boast of having made vain search in books and among men. But, verily, I will tell them what I have often said, that this negligence is insufferable. We are not here concerned with the trifling interests of some stranger, that we should treat it in this fashion; the matter concerns ourselves and our all.

The immortality of the soul is a matter which is of so great consequence to us, and which touches us so profoundly, that we must have lost all feeling to be indifferent as to knowing what it is. All our actions and thoughts must take such different courses, according as there are or are not eternal joys to hope for, that it is impossible to take one step with sense and judgment, unless we regulate our course by our view of this point which ought to be our ultimate end.

Thus our first interest and our first duty is to enlighten ourselves on this subject, whereon depends all our conduct. Therefore among those who do not believe, I make a vast difference between those who strive with all their power to inform themselves, and those who live without troubling or thinking about it.

I can have only compassion for those who sincerely bewail their doubt, who regard it as the greatest of misfortunes, and who, sparing no effort to escape it, make of this inquiry their principal and most serious occupation.

But as for those who pass their life without thinking of this ultimate end of life, and who, for this sole reason that they do not find within themselves the lights which convince them of it, neglect to seek them elsewhere, and to examine thoroughly whether this opinion is one of those which people receive with credulous simplicity, or one of those which, although obscure in themselves, have nevertheless a solid and immovable foundation, I look upon them in a manner quite different.

This carelessness in a matter which concerns themselves, their eternity, their all, moves me more to anger than pity; it astonishes and shocks me; it is to me monstrous. I do not say this out of the pious zeal of a spiritual devotion. I expect, on the contrary, that we ought to have this feeling from principles of human interest and self-love; for this we need only see what the least enlightened persons see.

We do not require great education of the mind to understand that there is no real and lasting satisfaction; that our pleasures are only vanity; that our evils are infinite; and, lastly, that death, which threatens us every moment, must infallibly place us within a few years under the dreadful necessity of being for ever either annihilated or unhappy.

There is nothing more real than this, nothing more terrible. Be we as heroic as we like, that is the end which awaits the noblest life in the world. Let us reflect on this, and then say whether it is not beyond doubt that there is no good in this life but in the hope of another; that we are happy only in proportion as we draw near it; and that, as there are no more woes for those who have complete assurance of eternity, so there is no more happiness for those who have no insight into it.

Surely then it is a great evil thus to be in doubt, but it is at least an indispensable duty to seek when we are in such doubt; and thus the doubter who does not seek is altogether completely unhappy and completely wrong. And if besides this he is easy and content, professes to be so, and indeed boasts of it; if it is this state itself which is the subject of his joy and vanity, I have no words to describe so silly a creature.

How can people hold these opinions? What joy can we find in the expectation of nothing but hopeless misery? What reason for boasting that we are in impenetrable darkness? And how can it happen that the following argument occurs to a reasonable man?

"I know not who put me into the world, nor what the world is, nor what I myself am. I am in terrible ignorance of everything. I know not what my body is, nor my senses, nor my soul, not even that part of me which thinks what I say, which reflects on all and on itself, and knows itself no more than the rest. I see those frightful spaces of the universe which surround me, and I find myself tied to one corner of this vast expanse, without knowing why I am put in this place rather than in another, nor why the short time which is given me to live is assigned to me at this point rather than at another of the whole eternity which was before me or which shall come after me. I see nothing but infinites on all sides, which surround me as an atom, and as a shadow which endures only for an instant and returns no more. All I know is that I must soon die, but what I know least is this very death which I cannot escape.

"As I know not whence I come, so I know not whither I go. I know only that, in leaving this world, I fall for ever either into annihilation or into the hands of an angry God, without knowing to which of these two states I shall be for ever assigned. Such is my state, full of weakness and uncertainty. And from all this I conclude that I ought to spend all the days of my life without caring to inquire into what must happen to me. Perhaps I might find some solution to my doubts, but I will not take the trouble, nor take a step to seek it; and after treating with scorn those who are concerned with this care, I will go without foresight and without fear to try the great event, and let myself be led carelessly to death, uncertain of the eternity of my future state."

Who would desire to have for a friend a man who talks in this fashion? Who would choose him out from others to tell him of his affairs? Who would have recourse to him in affliction? And indeed to what use in life could one put him?

In truth, it is the glory of religion to have for enemies men so unreasonable; and their opposition to it is so little dangerous that it serves on the contrary to establish its truths. For the Christian faith goes mainly to establish these two facts: the corruption of nature, and redemption by Jesus Christ. Now I contend that if these men do not serve to prove the truth of the redemption by the holiness of their behavior, they at least serve admirably to show the corruption of nature by sentiments so unnatural.

Nothing is so important to man as his own state, nothing is so formidable to him as eternity; and thus it is not natural that there should be men indifferent to the loss of their existence, and to the perils of everlasting suffering. They are quite different with regard to all other things. They are afraid of mere trifles; they foresee them; they feel them. And this same man who spends so many days and nights in rage and despair for the loss of office, or for some imaginary insult to his honor, is the very one who knows without anxiety and without emotion that he will lose all by death. It is a monstrous thing to see in the same heart and at the same time this sensibility to trifles and this strange insensibility to the greatest objects. It is an incomprehensible enchantment, and a supernatural slumber, which indicates as its cause an all-powerful force.

There must be a strange confusion in the nature of man, that he should boast of being in that state in which it seems incredible that a single individual should be. However, experience has shown me so great a number of such persons that the fact would be surprising, if we did not know that the greater part of those who trouble themselves about the matter are disingenuous, and not in fact what they say. They are people who have heard it said that it is the fashion to be thus daring. It is what they call shaking off the yoke, and they try to imitate this. But it would not be difficult to make them understand how greatly they deceive themselves in thus seeking esteem. This is not the way to gain it, even I say among those men of the world who take a healthy view of things, and who know that the only way to succeed in this life is to make ourselves appear honorable, faithful, judicious, and capable of useful service to a friend; because naturally men love only what may be useful to them. Now, what do we gain by hearing it said of a man that he has now thrown off the yoke, that he does not believe there is a God who watches our actions, that he considers himself the sole master of his conduct, and that he thinks he is accountable for it only to himself? Does he think that he has thus brought us to have henceforth complete confidence in him, and to look to him for consolation, advice, and help in every need of life? Do they profess to have delighted us by telling us that they hold our soul to be only a little wind and smoke, especially by telling us this in a haughty and self-satisfied tone of voice? Is this a thing to say gaily? Is it not, on the contrary, a thing to say sadly, as the saddest thing in the world?

If they thought of it seriously, they would see that this is so bad a mistake, so contrary to good sense, so opposed to decency, and so removed in every respect from that good breeding which they seek, that they would be more likely to correct than to pervert those who had an inclination to follow them. And indeed, make them give an account of their opinions, and of the reasons which they have for doubting religion, and they will say to you things so feeble and so petty, that they will persuade you of the contrary. The following is what a person one day said to such a one very appositely: "If you continue to talk in this manner, you will really make me religious." And he was right, for who would not have a horror of holding opinions in which he would have such contemptible persons as companions!

Thus those who only feign these opinions would be very unhappy, if they restrained their natural feelings in order to make themselves the most conceited of men. If, at the bottom of their heart, they are troubled at not having more light, let them not disguise the fact; this avowal will not be shameful. The only shame is to have none. Nothing reveals more an extreme weakness of mind than not to know the misery of a godless man. Nothing is more indicative of a bad disposition of heart than not to desire the truth of eternal promises. Nothing is more dastardly than to act with bravado before God. Let them then leave these impieties to those who are sufficiently ill-bred to be really capable of them. Let them at least be honest men, if they cannot be Christians. Finally, let them recognize that there are two kinds of people one can call reasonable; those who serve God with all their heart because they know Him, and those who seek Him with all their heart because they do not know Him.

But as for those who live without knowing Him and without seeking Him, they judge themselves so little worthy of their own care, that they are not worthy of the care of others; and it needs all the charity of the religion which they despise, not to despise them even to the point of leaving them to their folly. But because this religion obliges us always to regard them, so long as they are in this life, as capable of the grace which can enlighten them, and to believe that they may, in a little time, be more replenished with faith than we are, and that, on the other hand, we may fall into the blindness wherein they are, we must do for them what we would they should do for us if we were in their place, and call upon them to have pity upon themselves, and to take at least some steps in the endeavor to find light. Let them give to reading this some of the hours which they otherwise employ so uselessly; whatever aversion they may bring to the task, they will perhaps gain something, and at least will not lose much. But as for those who bring to the task perfect sincerity and a real desire to meet with truth, those I hope will be satisfied and convinced of the proofs of a religion so divine, which I have here collected, and in which I have followed somewhat after this order . . .

228.   Objection of atheists: "But we have no light."

229.   This is what I see and what troubles me. I look on all sides, and I see only darkness everywhere. Nature presents to me nothing which is not matter of doubt and concern. If I saw nothing there which revealed a Divinity, I would come to a negative conclusion; if I saw everywhere the signs of a Creator, I would remain peacefully in faith. But, seeing too much to deny and too little to be sure, I am in a state to be pitied; wherefore I have a hundred times wished that if a God maintains nature, she should testify to Him unequivocally, and that, if the signs she gives are deceptive, she should suppress them altogether; that she should say everything or nothing, that I might see which cause I ought to follow. Whereas in my present state, ignorant of what I am or of what I ought to do, I know neither my condition nor my duty. My heart inclines wholly to know where is

the true good, in order to follow it; nothing would be too dear to me for eternity.

I envy those whom I see living in the faith with such carelessness, and who make such a bad use of a gift of which it seems to me I would make such a different use.

230. It is incomprehensible that God should exist, and it is incomprehensible that He should not exist; that the soul should be joined to the body, and that we should have no soul; that the world should be created, and that it should not be created, etc.; that original sin should be, and that it should not be.

231. Do you believe it to be impossible that God is infinite, without parts?—Yes. I wish therefore to show you an infinite and indivisible thing. It is a point moving everywhere with an infinite velocity; for it is one in all places, and is all totality in every place.

Let this effect of nature, which previously seemed to you impossible, make you know that there may be others of which you are still ignorant. Do not draw this conclusion from your experiment, that there remains nothing for you to know; but rather that there remains an infinity for you to know.

232. Infinite movement, the point which fills everything, the moment of rest; infinite without quantity, indivisible and infinite.

233. *Infinite—nothing.* Our soul is cast into a body, where it finds number, time, dimension. Thereupon it reasons, and calls this nature necessity, and can believe nothing else.

Unity joined to infinity adds nothing to it, no more than one foot to an infinite measure. The finite is annihilated in the presence of the infinite, and becomes a pure nothing. So our spirit before God, so our justice before divine justice. There is not so great a disproportion between our justice and that of God, as between unity and infinity.

The justice of God must be vast like His compassion. Now justice to the outcast is less vast, and ought less to offend our feelings than mercy towards the elect.

We know that there is an infinite, and are ignorant of its nature. As we know it to be false that numbers are finite, it is therefore true that there is an infinity in number. But we do not know what it is. It is false that it is even, it is false that it is odd; for the addition of a unit can make no change in its nature. Yet it is a number, and every number is odd or even (this is certainly true of every finite number). So we may well know that there is a God without knowing what He is. Is there not one substantial truth, seeing there are so many things which are not the truth itself?

We know then the existence and nature of the finite, because we also are finite and have extension. We know the existence of the infinite, and are ignorant of its nature, because it has extension like us, but not limits like us. But we know neither the existence nor the nature of God, because He has neither extension nor limits.

But by faith we know His existence; in glory we shall know His nature. Now, I have already shown that we may well know the existence of a thing, without knowing its nature.

Let us now speak according to natural lights.

If there is a God, He is infinitely incomprehensible, since, having neither parts nor limits, He has no affinity to us. We are then incapable of knowing either what He is or if He is. This being so, who will dare to undertake the decision of the question? Not we, who have no affinity to Him.

Who then will blame Christians for not being able to give a reason for their belief, since they profess a religion for which they cannot give a reason? They declare, in expounding it to the world, that it is a foolishness, *stultitiam*; and then you complain that they do not prove it! If they proved it, they would not keep their word; it is in lacking proofs, that they are not lacking in sense. "Yes, but although this excuses those who offer it as such, and takes away from them the blame of putting it forward without reason, it does not excuse those who receive it." Let us then examine this point, and say, "God is, or He is not." But to which side shall we incline? Reason can decide nothing here. There is an infinite chaos which separates us. A game is being played at the extremity of this infinite distance where heads or tails will turn up. What will you wager? According to reason, you can do neither the one thing nor the other; according to reason, you can defend neither of the propositions.

Do not then reprove for error those who have made a choice; for you know nothing about it. "No, but I blame them for having made, not this choice, but a choice; for again both he who chooses heads and he who chooses tails are equally at fault, they are both in the wrong. The true course is not to wager at all."

Yes; but you must wager. It is not optional. You are embarked. Which will you choose then? Let us see. Since you must choose, let us see which interests you least. You have two things to lose, the true and the good; and two things to stake, your reason and your will, your knowledge and your happiness; and your nature has two things to shun, error and misery. Your reason is no more shocked in choosing one rather than the other, since you must of necessity choose. This is one point settled. But your happiness? Let us weigh the gain and the loss in wagering that God is. Let us estimate these two chances. If you gain, you gain all; if you lose, you lose nothing. Wager, then, without hesitation that He is.—"That is very fine. Yes, I must wager; but I may perhaps wager too much."—Let us see. Since there is an equal risk of gain and of loss, if you had only to gain two lives, instead of one, you might still wager. But if there were three lives to gain, you would have to play (since you are under the necessity of playing), and you would be imprudent, when you are forced to play, not to chance your life to gain three at a game where there is an equal risk of loss and gain. But there is an eternity of life and happiness. And this being so, if there were an infinity of chances, of which one only would be for you, you would still be right in wagering one to win two, and you would act stupidly, being obliged to play, by refusing to stake one life against three at a game in which out of an infinity of chances there is one for you, if there were an infinity of an infinitely happy life to gain. But there is here an infinity of an infinitely happy life to gain, a chance of gain against a finite number of chances of loss, and what you stake is finite. It is all divided; wherever the infinite is and there is not an infinity of chances of loss against that of gain, there is no time to hesitate, you must give all. And thus, when one is forced to play, he must renounce reason to preserve his life, rather than risk it for infinite gain, as likely to happen as the loss of nothingness.

For it is no use to say it is uncertain if we will gain, and it is certain that we risk, and that the infinite distance between the *certainty* of what is staked and the *uncertainty* of what will be gained, equals the finite good which is certainly staked against the uncertain infinite. It is not so, as every player stakes a certainty to gain an uncertainty, and yet he stakes a finite certainty to gain a finite uncertainty, without transgressing against reason. There is not an infinite distance between the certainty staked and the uncertainty of the gain; that is untrue. In truth, there is an infinity between the certainty of gain and the certainty of loss. But the uncertainty of the gain is proportioned to the certainty of the stake according to the proportion of the chances of gain and loss. Hence it comes that, if there are as many risks on one side as on the other, the course is to play even; and then the certainty of the stake is equal to the uncertainty of the gain, so far is it from fact that there is an infinite distance between them. And so our proposition is of infinite force, when there is the finite to stake in a game where there are equal risks of gain and of loss, and the infinite to gain. This is demonstrable; and if men are capable of any truths, this is one.

"I confess it, I admit it. But, still, is there no means of seeing the faces of the cards?"—Yes, Scripture and the rest, etc. "Yes, but I have my hands tied and my mouth closed; I am forced to wager, and am not free. I am not released, and am so made that I cannot believe. What, then, would you have me do?"

True. But at least learn your inability to believe, since reason brings you to this, and yet you cannot believe. Endeavor then to convince yourself, not by increase of proofs of God, but by the abatement of your passions. You would like to attain faith, and do not know the way; you would like to cure yourself of unbelief, and ask the remedy for it. Learn of those who have been bound like you, and who now stake all their possessions. These are people who know the way which you would follow, and who are cured of an ill of which you would be cured. Follow the way by which they began; by acting as if they believed, taking the holy water, having masses said, etc. Even this will naturally make you believe, and deaden your acuteness.—"But this is what I am afraid of."—And why? What have you to lose?

But to show you that this leads you there, it is this which will lessen the passions, which are your stumbling-blocks.

The end of this discourse.—Now, what harm will befall you in taking this side? You will be faithful, honest, humble, grateful, generous, a sincere friend, truthful. Certainly you will not have those poisonous pleasures, glory and luxury; but will you not have others? I will tell you that you will thereby gain in this life, and that, at each step you take on this road, you will see so great certainty of gain, so much nothingness in what you risk, that you will at last recognize that you have wagered for something certain and infinite, for which you have given nothing.

"Ah! This discourse transports me, charms me," etc.

If this discourse pleases you and seems impressive, know that it is made by a man who has knelt, both before and after it, in prayer to that Being, infinite and without parts, before whom he lays all he has, for you also to lay before Him all you have for your own good and for His glory, that so strength may be given to lowliness.

234.   If we must not act save on a certainty, we ought not to act on religion, for it is not certain. But how many things we do on an uncertainty, sea voyages, battles! I say then we must do nothing at all, for nothing is certain, and that there is more certainty in religion than there is as to whether we may see to-morrow; for it is not certain that we may see to-morrow, and it is certainly possible that we may not see it. We cannot say as much about religion. It is not certain that it is; but who will venture to say that it is certainly possible that it is not? Now when we work for to-morrow, and so on an uncertainty, we act reasonably; for we ought to work for an uncertainty according to the doctrine of chance which was demonstrated above.

Saint Augustine has seen that we work for an uncertainty, on sea, in battle, etc. But he has not seen the doctrine of chance which proves that we should do so. Montaigne has seen that we are shocked at a fool, and that habit is all-powerful; but he has not seen the reason of this effect.

All these persons have seen the effects, but they have not seen the causes. They are, in comparison with those who have discovered the causes, as those who have only eyes are in comparison with those who have intellect. For the effects are perceptible by sense, and the causes are visible only to the intellect. And although these effects are seen by the mind, this mind is, in comparison with the mind which sees the causes, as the bodily senses are in comparison with the intellect.

239. *Objection.*   Those who hope for salvation are so far happy; but they have as a counterpoise the fear of hell.

Reply.   Who has most reason to fear hell: he who is in ignorance whether there is a hell, and who is certain of damnation if there is; or he who certainly believes there is a hell, and hopes to be saved if there is?

241. *Order.*   I would have far more fear of being mistaken, and of finding that the Christian religion was true, than of not being mistaken in believing it true.

242. *Preface to the second part.* To speak of those who have treated of this matter.

I admire the boldness with which these persons undertake to speak of God. In addressing their argument to infidels, their first chapter is to prove Divinity from the works of nature. I should not be astonished at their enterprise, if they were addressing their argument to the faithful; for it is certain that those who have the living faith in their heart see at once that all existence is none other than the work of the God whom they adore. But for those in whom this light is extinguished, and in whom we purpose to rekindle it, persons destitute of faith and grace, who, seeking with all their light whatever they see in nature that can bring them to this knowledge, find only obscurity and darkness; to tell them that they have only to look at the smallest things which surround them, and they will see God openly, to give them, as a complete proof of this great and important matter, the course of the moon and planets, and to claim to have concluded the proof with such an argument, is to give them ground for believing that the proofs of our religion are very weak. And I see by reason and experience that nothing is more calculated to arouse their contempt.

It is not after this manner that Scripture speaks, which has a better knowledge of the things that are of God. It says, on the contrary, that God is a hidden God, and that, since the corruption of nature, He has left men in a darkness from which they can escape only through Jesus Christ, without whom all communion with God is cut off. *Nemo novit Patrem, nisi Filius, et cui voluerit Filius revelare.*[1]

This is what Scripture points out to us, when it says in so many places that those who seek God find Him. It is not of the light, "like the noonday sun," that this is said. We do not say that those who seek the noonday sun, or water in the sea, shall find them; and hence the evidence of God must not be of this nature. So it tells us elsewhere: *Vere tu es Deus absconditus.*[2]

243. It is an astounding fact that no canonical writer has ever made use of nature to prove God. They all strive to make us believe in Him. David, Solomon, etc., have never said, "There is no void, therefore there is a God." They must have had more knowledge than

---

[1] [No one knows the Father except the Son, and the man to whom the Son would wish to reveal him.—Matthew xi, 27.—M.C.B.]

[2] [In truth, thou art a hidden God.—Isaiah, xlv, 15.—M.C.B.]

the most learned people who came after them, and who have all made use of this argument. This is worthy of attention.

244. "Why! Do you not say yourself that the heavens and birds prove God?" No. "And does your religion not say so?" No. For although it is true in a sense for some souls to whom God gives this light, yet it is false with respect to the majority of men.

245. There are three sources of belief: reason, custom, inspiration. The Christian religion, which alone has reason, does not acknowledge as her true children those who believe without inspiration. It is not that she excludes reason and custom. On the contrary, the mind must be opened to proofs, must be confirmed by custom, and offer itself in humbleness to inspirations, which alone can produce a true and saving effect. *Ne evacuetur crux Christi.*[1]

252. For we must not misunderstand ourselves; we are as much automatic as intellectual; and hence it comes that the instrument by which conviction is attained is not demonstrated alone. How few things are demonstrated! Proofs only convince the mind. Custom is the source of our strongest and most believed proofs. It bends the automaton, which persuades the mind without its thinking about the matter. Who has demonstrated that there will be a to-morrow, and that we shall die? And what is more believed? It is, then, custom which persuades us of it; it is custom that makes so many men Christians; custom that makes them Turks, heathens, artisans, soldiers, etc. (Faith in baptism is more received among Christians than among Turks.) Finally, we must have recourse to it when once the mind has seen where the truth is, in order to quench our thirst, and steep ourselves in that belief, which escapes us at every hour; for always to have proofs ready is too much trouble. We must get an easier belief, which is that of custom, which, without violence, without art, without argument, makes us believe things, and inclines all our powers to this belief, so that our soul falls naturally into it. It is not enough to believe only by force of conviction, when the automaton is inclined to believe the contrary. Both our parts must be made to believe, the mind by reasons which it is sufficient to have seen

---

[1] [Let not the cross of Christ be made of no effect.—I Corinthians, i, 17.—M.C.B.]

once in a lifetime, and the automaton by custom, and by not allowing
it to incline to the contrary. *Inclina cor meum, Deus.*[1]

The reason acts slowly, with so many examinations, and on so
many principles, which must be always present, that at every hour it
falls asleep, or wanders, through want of having all its principles
present. Feeling does not act thus; it acts in a moment, and is always
ready to act. We must then put our faith in feeling; otherwise it will
be always vacillating.

253.　Two extremes: to exclude reason, to admit reason only.

260.　They hide themselves in the press, and call numbers to their
rescue. Tumult.

Authority.　So far from making it a rule to believe a thing because
you have heard it, you ought to believe nothing without putting yourself into the position as if you had never heard it.

It is your own assent to yourself, and the constant voice of your
own reason, and not of others, that should make you believe.

Belief is so important! A hundred contradictions might be true.
If antiquity were the rule of belief, men of ancient time would then
be without rule. If general consent, if men had perished?

False humanity, pride.

Lift the curtain. You try in vain; if you must either believe, or
deny, or doubt. Shall we then have no rule? We judge that animals
do well what they do. Is there no rule whereby to judge men?

To deny, to believe, and to doubt well, are to a man what the race
is to a horse.

Punishment of those who sin, error.

267.　The last proceeding of reason is to recognize that there is
an infinity of things which are beyond it. It is but feeble if it does not
see so far as to know this. But if natural things are beyond it, what
will be said of supernatural?

268. *Submission.*　We must know where to doubt, where to feel
certain, where to submit. He who does not do so, understands not
the force of reason. There are some who offend against these three
rules, either by affirming everything as demonstrative, from want of

---

[1] [Incline my heart, O God.—M.C.B.]

knowing what demonstration is; or by doubting everything, from want of knowing where to submit; or by submitting in everything, from want of knowing where they must judge.

269.   Submission is the use of reason in which consists true Christianity.

270. *Saint Augustine.*   Reason would never submit, if it did not judge that there are some occasions on which it ought to submit. It is then right for it to submit, when it judges that it ought to submit.

271.   Wisdom sends us to childhood. *Nisi efficiamini sicut parvuli.*[1]

272.   There is nothing so conformable to reason as this disavowal of reason.

273.   If we submit everything to reason, our religion will have no mysterious and supernatural element. If we offend the principles of reason, our religion will be absurd and ridiculous.

274.   All our reasoning reduces itself to yielding to feeling.
But fancy is like, though contrary to feeling, so that we cannot distinguish between these contraries. One person says that my feeling is fancy, another that his fancy is feeling. We should have a rule. Reason offers itself; but it is pliable in every sense; and thus there is no rule.

275.   Men often take their imagination for their heart; and they believe they are converted as soon as they think of being converted.

276.   M. de Roannez said: "Reasons come to me afterwards, but at first a thing pleases or shocks me without my knowing the reason, and yet it shocks me for that reason which I only discover afterwards." But I believe, not that it shocked him for the reasons which were found afterwards, but that these reasons were only found because it shocks him.

---

[1] [Unless we became as little children.—Matthew, xviii, 3.—M.C.B.]

277.   The heart has its reasons, which reason does not know. We feel it in a thousand things. I say that the heart naturally loves the Universal Being, and also itself naturally, according as it gives itself to them; and it hardens itself against one or the other at its will. You have rejected the one, and kept the other. Is it by reason that you love yourself?

282.   We know truth, not only by the reason, but also by the heart, and it is in this last way that we know first principles; and reason, which has no part in it, tries in vain to impugn them. The skeptics, who have only this for their object, labor to no purpose. We know that we do not dream, and however impossible it is for us to prove it by reason, this inability demonstrates only the weakness of our reason, but not, as they affirm, the uncertainty of all our knowledge. For the knowledge of first principles, as space, time, motion, number, is as sure as any of those which we get from reasoning. And reason must trust these intuitions of the heart, and must base them on every argument. (We have intuitive knowledge of the tri-dimensional nature of space, and of the infinity of number, and reason then shows that there are no two square numbers one of which is double of the other. Principles are intuited, propositions are inferred, all with certainty, though in different ways.) And it is as useless and absurd for reason to demand from the heart proofs of her first principles, before admitting them, as it would be for the heart to demand from reason an intuition of all demonstrated propositions before accepting them.

This inability ought, then, to serve only to humble reason, which would judge all, but not to impugn our certainty, as if only reason were capable of instructing us. Would to God, on the contrary, that we had never need of it, and that we knew everything by instinct and intuition! But nature has refused us this boon. On the contrary, she has given us but very little knowledge of this kind; and all the rest can be acquired only by reasoning.

Therefore, those to whom God has imparted religion by intuition are very fortunate, and justly convinced. But to those who do not have it, we can give it only by reasoning, waiting for God to give them spiritual insight, without which faith is only human, and useless for salvation.

283. *Order. Against the objection that Scripture has no order.* The heart has its own order; the intellect has its own, which is by

principle and demonstration. The heart has another. We do not prove that we ought to be loved by enumerating in order the causes of love; that would be ridiculous.

284.   Jesus Christ and Saint Paul employ the rule of love, not of intellect; for they would warm, not instruct. It is the same with Saint Augustine. This order consists chiefly in digressions on each point to indicate the end, and keep it always in sight.

294.   On what shall man found the order of the world which he would govern? Shall it be on the caprice of each individual? What confusion! Shall it be on justice? Man is ignorant of it.

Certainly had he known it, he would not have established this maxim, the most general of all that obtain among men, that each should follow the custom of his own country. The glory of true equity would have brought all nations under subjection, and legislators would not have taken as their model the fancies and caprice of Persians and Germans instead of this unchanging justice. We would have seen it set up in all the States on earth and in all times; whereas we see neither justice nor injustice which does not change its nature with change in climate. Three degrees of latitude reverse all jurisprudence; a meridian decides the truth. Fundamental laws change after a few years of possession; right has its epochs; the entry of Saturn into the Lion marks to us the origin of such and such a crime. A strange justice that is bounded by a river! Truth on this side of the Pyrenees, error on the other side.

Men admit that justice does not consist in these customs but that it resides in natural laws, common to every country. They would certainly maintain it obstinately, if reckless chance which has distributed human laws had encountered even one which was universal; but the farce is that the caprice of men has so many vagaries that there is no such law.

Theft, incest, infanticide, parricide, have all had a place among virtuous actions. Can anything be more ridiculous than that a man should have the right to kill me because he lives on the other side of the water, and because his ruler has a quarrel with mine, though I have none with him?

Doubtless there are natural laws; but good reason once corrupted has corrupted all. *Nihil amplius nostrum est; quod nostrum dicimus, artis est. Ex senatus consultis et plebiscitis crimina exercentur. Ut olim vitiis, sic nunc legibus laboramus.*[1]

The result of this confusion is that one affirms the essence of justice to be the authority of the legislator; another, the interest of the sovereign; another, present custom, and this is the most sure. Nothing, according to reason alone, is just in itself; all changes with time. Custom creates the whole of equity, for the simple reason that it is accepted. It is the mystical foundation of its authority; whoever carries it back to first principle destroys it. Nothing is so faulty as those laws which correct faults. He who obeys them because they are just, obeys a justice which is imaginary, and not the essence of law; it is quite self-contained, it is law and nothing more. He who will examine its motive will find it so feeble and so trifling that if he be not accustomed to contemplate the wonders of human imagination, he will marvel that one century has gained for it so much pomp and reverence. The art of opposition and of revolution is to unsettle established customs, sounding them even to their source, to point out their want of authority and justice. We must, it is said, get back to the natural and fundamental laws of the State, which an unjust custom has abolished. It is a game certain to result in the loss of all; nothing will be just on the balance. Yet people readily lend their ear to such arguments. They shake off the yoke as soon as they recognize it; and the great profit by their ruin, and by that of these curious investigators of accepted customs. But from a contrary mistake men sometimes think they can justly do everything which is not without an example. That is why the wisest of legislators said that it was necessary to deceive men for their own good; and another, a good politician, *Cum veritatem qua liberetur ignoret, expedit quod fallatur.*[2] We must not see the fact of usurpation; law was once introduced without reason, and has become reasonable. We must make it be regarded as authoritative, eternal, and conceal its origin, if we do not wish that it should soon come to an end.

---

[1] [Nothing is ours completely; what we call ours belongs to art. From decrees of the Senate and from ordinances of the people, crimes are practiced. As formerly we suffered from our vices, so now we suffer from our laws.—The three sentences are all from different authors: Cicero, *De Finibus*, V, 21; Seneca, *Letters*, 95; Tacitus, *Annals*, III, 25.—M.C.B.]

[2] [When he ignores the truth by which he is made free, it is expedient that he be deceived.—An inaccurate quotation from St. Augustine, *City of God*, IV, 27.—M.C.B.]

319.   How rightly do we distinguish men by external appearances rather than by internal qualities! Which of us two shall have precedence? Who will give place to the other? The least clever. But I am as clever as he. We should have to fight over this. He has four lackeys, and I have only one. This can be seen; we have only to count. It falls to me to yield, and I am a fool if I contest the matter. By this means we are at peace, which is the greatest of boons.

320.   The most unreasonable things in the world become most reasonable, because of the unruliness of men. What is less reasonable than to choose the eldest son of a queen to rule a State? We do not choose as captain of a ship the passenger who is of the best family.

This law would be absurd and unjust; but because men are so themselves, and always will be so, it becomes reasonable and just. For whom will men choose, as the most virtuous and able? We at once come to blows, as each claims to be the most virtuous and able. Let us then attach this quality to something indisputable. This is the king's eldest son. That is clear, and there is no dispute. Reason can do no better, for civil war is the greatest of evils.

331.   We can only think of Plato and Aristotle in grand academic robes. They were honest men, like others, laughing with their friends, and when they diverted themselves with writing their *Laws* and the *Politics,* they did it as an amusement. That part of their life was the least philosophic and the least serious; the most philosophic was to live simply and quietly. If they wrote on politics, it was as if laying down rules for a lunatic asylum; and if they presented the appearance of speaking of a great matter, it was because they knew that the madmen, to whom they spoke, thought they were kings and emperors. They entered into their principles in order to make their madness as little harmful as possible.

339.   I can well conceive a man without hands, feet, head (for it is only experience which teaches us that the head is more necessary than feet). But I cannot conceive man without thought; he would be a stone or a brute.

340.   The arithmetical machine produces effects which approach nearer to thought than all the actions of animals. But it does nothing which would enable us to attribute will to it, as to the animals.

346.   Thought constitutes the greatness of man.

347.   Man is but a reed, the most feeble thing in nature; but he
is a thinking reed. The entire universe need not arm itself to crush
him. A vapor, a drop of water suffices to kill him. But, if the universe
were to crush him, man would still be more noble than that which
killed him, because he knows that he dies and the advantage which
the universe has over him; the universe knows nothing of this.

All our dignity consists, then, in thought. By it we must elevate
ourselves, and not by space and time which we cannot fill. Let us
endeavor, then, to think well; this is the principle of morality.

348.   *A thinking reed.*   It is not from space that I must seek my
dignity, but from the government of my thought. I shall have no more
if I possess worlds. By space the universe encompasses and swallows
me up like an atom; by thought I comprehend the world.

385.   *Skepticism.*   Each thing here is partly true and partly false.
Essential truth is not so; it is altogether pure and altogether true.
This mixture dishonors and annihilates it. Nothing is purely true,
and thus nothing is true, meaning by that pure truth. You will say it
is true that homicide is wrong. Yes; for we know well the wrong and
the false. But what will you say is good? Chastity? I say no; for the
world would come to an end. Marriage? No; continence is better. Not
to kill? No; for lawlessness would be horrible, and the wicked would
kill all the good. To kill? No; for that destroys nature. We possess
truth and goodness only in part, and mingled with falsehood and evil.

386.   If we dreamt the same thing every night, it would affect us
as much as the objects we see every day. And if an artisan were sure
to dream every night for twelve hours' duration that he was a king I
believe he would be almost as happy as a king who should dream
every night for twelve hours on end that he was an artisan.

If we were to dream every night that we were pursued by enemies,
and harassed by these painful phantoms, or that we passed every day
in different occupations, as in making a voyage, we should suffer
almost as much as if it were real, and should fear to sleep, as we fear
to wake when we dread in fact to enter on such mishaps. And, indeed,
it would cause pretty nearly the same discomforts as the reality.

But since dreams are all different, and each single one is diversified,
what is seen in them affects us much less than what we see when

awake, because of its continuity, which is not, however, so continuous and level as not to change too; but it changes less abruptly, except rarely, as when we travel, and then we say, "It seems to me I am dreaming." For life is a dream a little less inconstant.

387. [It may be that there are true demonstrations; but this is not certain. Thus, this proves nothing else but that it is not certain that all is uncertain, to the glory of skepticism.]

397. The greatness of man is great in that he knows himself to be miserable. A tree does not know itself to be miserable. It is then being miserable to know oneself to be miserable; but it is also being great to know that one is miserable.

398. All these same miseries prove man's greatness. They are the miseries of a great lord, of a deposed king.

414. Men are so necessarily mad that not to be mad would amount to another form of madness.

417. This twofold nature of man is so evident that some have thought that we had two souls. A single subject seemed to them incapable of such sudden variations from unmeasured presumption to a dreadful dejection of heart.

418. It is dangerous to make man see too clearly his equality with the brutes without showing him his greatness. It is also dangerous to make him see his greatness too clearly, apart from his vileness. It is still more dangerous to leave him in ignorance of both. But it is very advantageous to show him both. Man must not think that he is on a level either with the brutes or with the angels, nor must he be ignorant of both sides of his nature; but he must know both.

419. I will not allow man to depend upon himself, or upon another, to the end that being without a resting-place and without repose . . .

420. If he exalt himself, I humble him; if he humble himself, I exalt him; and I always contradict him, till he understands that he is an incomprehensible monster.

434.   The chief arguments of the skeptics—I pass over the lesser ones—are that we have no certainty of the truth of these principles apart from faith and revelation, except in so far as we naturally perceive them in ourselves. Now this natural intuition is not a convincing proof of their truth; since, having no certainty, apart from faith, whether man was created by a good God, or by a wicked demon, or by chance, it is doubtful whether these principles given to us are true, or false, or uncertain, according to our origin. Again, no person is certain, apart from faith, whether he is awake or sleeps, seeing that during sleep we believe that we are awake as firmly as we do when we *are* awake; we believe that we see space, figure, and motion; we are aware of the passage of time, we measure it; and in fact we act as if we were awake. So that half of our life being passed in sleep, we have on our own admission no idea of truth, whatever we may imagine. As all our intuitions are then illusions, who knows whether the other half of our life, in which we think we are awake, is not another sleep a little different from the former, from which we awake when we suppose ourselves asleep?

[And who doubts that, if we dreamt in company, and the dreams chanced to agree, which is common enough, and if we were always alone when awake, we should believe that matters were reversed? In short, as we often dream that we dream, heaping dream upon dream, may it not be that this half of our life, wherein we think ourselves awake, is itself only a dream on which the others are grafted, from which we wake at death, during which we have as few principles of truth and good as during natural sleep, these different thoughts which disturb us being perhaps only illusions like the flight of time and the vain fancies of our dreams?]

These are the chief arguments on one side and the other.

I omit minor ones, such as the skeptical talk against the impressions of custom, education, manners, country, and the like. Though these influence the majority of common folk, who dogmatize only on shallow foundations, they are upset by the least breath of the skeptics. We have only to see their books if we are not sufficiently convinced of this, and we shall very quickly become so, perhaps too much.

I notice the only strong point of the dogmatists, namely, that, speaking in good faith and sincerely, we cannot doubt natural principles. Against this the skeptics set up in one word the uncertainty of our origin, which includes that of our nature. The dogmatists have been trying to answer this objection ever since the world began.

So there is open war among men, in which each must take a part, and side either with dogmatism or skepticism. For he who thinks to remain neutral is above all a skeptic. The neutrality is the essence of the sect; he who is not against them is essentially for them. [In this appears their advantage.] They are not for themselves; they are neutral, indifferent, in suspense as to all things, even themselves being no exception.

What then shall man do in this state? Shall he doubt everything? Shall he doubt whether he is awake, whether he is being pinched, or whether he is being burned? Shall he doubt whether he doubts? Shall he doubt whether he exists? We cannot go so far as that; and I lay it down as a fact that there never has been a real complete skeptic. Nature sustains our feeble reason, and prevents it raving to this extent.

Shall he then say, on the contrary, that he certainly possesses truth—he who, when pressed ever so little, can show no title to it, and is forced to let go his hold?

What a chimera then is man! What a novelty! What a monster, what a chaos, what a contradiction, what a prodigy! Judge of all things, imbecile worm of the earth; depositary of truth, a sink of uncertainty and error; the pride and refuse of the universe!

Who will unravel this tangle? Nature confutes the skeptics, and reason confutes the dogmatists. What then will you become, O men! who try to find out by your natural reason what is your true condition? You cannot avoid one of these sects, nor adhere to one of them.

Know then, proud man, what a paradox you are to yourself. Humble yourself, weak reason; be silent, foolish nature; learn that man infinitely transcends man, and learn from your Master your true condition, of which you are ignorant. Hear God.

For in fact, if man had never been corrupt, he would enjoy in his innocence both truth and happiness with assurance; and if man had always been corrupt, he would have no idea of truth or bliss. But, wretched as we are, and more so than if there were no greatness in our condition, we have an idea of happiness, and cannot reach it. We perceive an image of truth, and possess only a lie. Incapable of absolute ignorance and of certain knowledge, we have thus been manifestly in a degree of perfection from which we have unhappily fallen.

It is, however, an astonishing thing that the mystery furthest removed from our knowledge, namely, that of the transmission of sin, should be a fact without which we can have no knowledge of ourselves. For it is beyond doubt that there is nothing which more shocks our reason than to say that the sin of the first man has rendered guilty those, who, being so removed from this source, seem incapable of participation in it. This transmission does not only seem to us impossible, it seems also very unjust. For what is more contrary to the rules of our miserable justice than to damn eternally an infant incapable of will, for a sin wherein he seems to have so little a share, that it was committed six thousand years before he was in existence? Certainly nothing offends us more rudely than this doctrine; and yet, without this mystery, the most incomprehensible of all, we are incomprehensible to ourselves. The knot of our condition takes its twists and turns in this abyss, so that man is more inconceivable without this mystery than this mystery is inconceivable to man.

[Whence it seems that God, willing to render the difficulty of our existence unintelligible to ourselves, has concealed the knot so high, or, better speaking, so low, that we are quite incapable of reaching it; so that it is not by the proud exertions of our reason, but by the simple submissions of reason, that we can truly know ourselves.

These foundations, solidly established on the inviolable authority of religion, make us know that there are two truths of faith equally certain: the one, that man, in the state of creation, or in that of grace, is raised above all nature, made like unto God and sharing in His divinity; the other, that in the state of corruption and sin, he is fallen from this state and made like unto the beasts. . . .]

542. *Preface.* The metaphysical proofs of God are so remote from the reasoning of men, and so complicated, that they make little impression; and if they should be of service to some, it would be only during the moment that they see such demonstration; but an hour afterwards they fear they have been mistaken.

Quod curiositate cognoverunt superbia amiserunt.[1]

This is the result of the knowledge of God obtained without Jesus Christ; it is communion without a mediator with the God whom they have known without a mediator. Whereas those who have known God by a mediator know their own wretchedness.

792.   The infinite distance between body and mind is a symbol of the infinitely more infinite distance between mind and charity; for charity is supernatural.

---

[1] [What they learned through their eager desire for knowledge, they lost through pride.—St. Augustine, Sermon CXLI.—M.C.B.]

All the glory of greatness has no luster for people who are in search of understanding.

The greatness of clever men is invisible to kings, to the right, to chiefs, and to all the worldly great.

The greatness of wisdom, which is nothing if not of God, is invisible to the carnal-minded and to the clever. These are three orders differing in kind.

Great geniuses have their power, their glory, their greatness, their victory, their luster, and have no need of worldly greatness, with which they are not in keeping. They are seen, not by the eye, but by the mind; this is sufficient.

The saints have their power, their glory, their victory, their luster, and need no worldly or intellectual greatness, with which they have no affinity; for these neither add anything to them, nor take away anything from them. They are seen of God and the angels, and not of the body, nor of the curious mind. God is enough for them.

Archimedes, apart from his rank, would have the same veneration. He fought no battles for the eyes to feast upon; but he has given his discoveries to all men. Oh! how brilliant he was to the mind!

Jesus Christ, without riches, and without any external exhibition of knowledge, is in His own order of holiness. He did not invent; He did not reign. But He was humble, patient, holy, holy to God, terrible to devils, without any sin. Oh! in what great pomp and in what wonderful splendor, He is come to the eyes of the heart, which perceive wisdom!

It would have been useless for Archimedes to have acted the prince in his books on geometry, although he was a prince.

It would have been useless for our Lord Jesus Christ to come like a king, in order to shine forth in His kingdom of holiness. But He came there appropriately in the glory of His own order.

It is most absurd to take offense at the lowliness of Jesus Christ, as if His lowliness were in the same order as the greatness which He came to manifest. If we consider this greatness in His life, in His passion, in His obscurity, in His death, in the choice of His disciples, in their desertion, in His secret resurrection, and the rest, we shall see it to be so immense, that we shall have no reason for being offended a a lowliness which is not of that order.

But there are some who can only admire worldly greatness, a though there were no intellectual greatness; and others who only admire intellectual greatness, as though there were not infinitely higher things in wisdom.

All bodies, the firmament, the stars, the earth and its kingdoms, are not equal to the lowest mind; for mind knows all these and itself; and these bodies nothing.

All bodies together, and all minds together, and all their products, are not equal to the least feeling of charity. This is of an order infinitely more exalted.

From all bodies together, we cannot obtain one little thought; this is impossible, and of another order. From all bodies and minds, we cannot produce a feeling of true charity; this is impossible, and of another and supernatural order.

816. *Title: How it happens that men believe so many liars who say that they have seen miracles, and do not believe any of those who say that they have secrets to make men immortal, or restore youth to them.* Having considered how it happens that so great credence is given to so many impostors, who say they have remedies, often to the length of men putting their lives into their hands, it has appeared to me that the true cause is that there are true remedies. For it would not be possible that there should be so many false remedies, and that so much faith should be placed in them, if there were none true. If there had never been any remedy for any ill, and all ills had been incurable, it is impossible that men should have imagined that they could give remedies, and still more impossible that so many others should have believed those who boasted of having remedies; in the same way as did a man boast of preventing death, no one would believe him, because there is no example of this. But as there were a number of remedies found to be true by the very knowledge of the greatest men, the belief of men is thereby induced; and, this being known to be possible, it has been therefore concluded that it was. For people commonly reason thus: "A thing is possible, therefore it is"; because the thing cannot be denied generally, since there are particular effects which are true, the people, who cannot distinguish which among these particular effects are true, believe them all. In the same way, the reason why so many false effects are credited to the moon, is that there are some true, as the tide.

It is the same with prophecies, miracles, divination by dreams, sorceries, etc. For if there had been nothing true in all this, men would have believed nothing of them; and thus, instead of concluding that there are no true miracles because there are so many false, we must, on the contrary, say that there certainly are true miracles, since there are false, and that there are false miracles only because some are true. We must reason in the same way about religion; for it would not be possible that men should have imagined so many false religions, if there had not been a true one. The objection to this is that savages have a religion; but the answer is that they have heard the true spoken of, as appears by the deluge, circumcision, the cross of Saint Andrew, etc.

BARUCH SPINOZA

Ethics Demonstrated in Geometrical Order (*abridged*)

Theologico-Political Treatise

Chapter XX

SUPPLEMENTARY PASSAGES

Experience and Definition
Substance and Attribute
Natura Naturata
Man's Dependence upon God
Method
Excusability
The Nature of Evil

BARUCH SPINOZA

BARUCH (or BENEDICT) SPINOZA (1632–1677) was born into a well-to-do family of Portuguese Jews who had moved to Amsterdam seeking refuge from religious persecution. Educated at a Jewish school, he came to have doubts about some principles of orthodox Judaism and was excommunicated from the Synagogue at the age of twenty-four. From that time on, cut off from most of the Jewish community in Holland, he lived for the most part in quiet, supporting himself by the craft of polishing optical lenses, which he had learned as a youth, with modest financial help from a small circle of devoted friends. Through his considerable correspondence he kept in touch with philosophical, scientific, political, and theological developments throughout Europe, and became widely known as an original metaphysician, a freethinker in religion, and a liberal in politics.

During his lifetime Spinoza published two books: one an analysis of the philosophy of Descartes (see *Earlier Philosophical Writings: The Cartesian Principles and Thoughts on Metaphysics,* trans. Frank A. Hayes, Indianapolis: Bobbs-Merrill, 1963), the other the *Theologico-Political Treatise* (1670); see trans. by R. H. Elwes, *Works of Spinoza,* New York: Dover, Vol. II, 1955, a pioneering work in the critical study of the Bible. His major work, the *Ethics,* though largely written by 1666, was not published until some months after his death, in 1677, along with other works, including the unfinished *Political Treatise* and the unfinished *Treatise on the Correction* (or *Improvement*) *of the Understanding.* His *Short Treatise Concerning God, Man and His Wellbeing* was first discovered in manuscript, and published, in 1852 (see trans. by Abraham Wolf, New York: Russell & Russell, 1963). Several fundamental points in Spinoza's philosophy are further clarified in his *Letters,* translated and edited by A. Wolf, London: Allen and Unwin, 1928 (also trans. by Elwes, Vol. I, and trans. by Samuel Shirley, Indianapolis: Hackett, 1982).

Spinoza's achievement in philosophy was great, though he founded no school of close followers, as did Descartes and Leibniz, and was indeed not much read with sympathy or understanding until long after his death, for "Spinozist" became a familiar abusive synonym for "wicked pantheist." In his patient, rigorous, and determined thinking-out of his system, he presents the example of a man fully in touch with the main currents of thought in his own time and yet amazingly independent of some of them. For he was able to contemplate fearlessly the logical consequences his most brilliant contemporaries could not bring themselves to draw from basic principles they all accepted. His sharp and bold examination of the religious ideas of his age helped pave the way for the less trammelled and inhibited religious thinking of the Enlightenment and more recent times. He showed how certain spiritual attitudes toward the universe could be made independent of belief in a personal God. Spinoza explored more thoroughly than anyone before him the implications and difficulties of a completely monistic metaphysics. He was the first to conceive and to undertake a program for the objective scientific study of man and of human behavior in a spirit of truth-seeking without self-deception, and his psychological methods and principles in the *Ethics* foreshadow twentieth-century psychology and psychiatry. Spinoza emphasized the role of intelligence in ethics in a way not paralleled until John Dewey; the line of thought he initiated remains one of the fruitful possibilities for solving the problem of the relation between factual and normative elements (what *is* and what *ought to be*) in ethical decision.

Ethics Demonstrated in Geometrical Order* (*abridged*)

PART I: OF GOD

Definitions

I. By *cause of itself* I understand that whose essence involves existence, or that whose nature cannot be conceived except as existing.

II. That thing is called *finite in its own kind* which can be limited by another thing of the same nature. For example, a body is called finite because we always conceive another which is greater. So a thought is limited by another thought; but a body is not limited by a thought, nor a thought by a body.

III. By *substance* I understand that which is in itself and is conceived through itself; in other words, that the conception of which does not need the conception of another thing from which it must be formed.

IV. By *attribute* I understand that which the intellect perceives of substance as constituting its essence.

V. By *mode* I understand the modifications of substance, or that which is in another thing through which also it is conceived.

VI. By *God* I understand Being absolutely infinite, that is to say, substance consisting of infinite attributes, each one of which expresses eternal and infinite essence.

Explanation. I say "absolutely infinite" but not "infinite in its own kind," for of whatever is infinite only in its own kind we can deny infinite attributes; but to the essence of that which is absolutely infinite pertains whatever expresses essence and involves no negation.

VII. That thing is called free which exists from the necessity of its own nature alone and is determined to action by itself alone. That thing, on the other hand, is called necessary or rather compelled

---

* Translated by William Hale White (1883), revised by Amelia Hutchison Stirling (1884, 1899; 4th ed. London: Oxford University Press, 1930); with some modifications by James Gutman (N. Y.: Hafner, 1957) and by the present editor. Reprinted by permission of the Oxford University Press and the Hafner Publishing Co. *Ethica, ordine geometrico demonstrata* first appeared in the *Opera Posthuma* (1677). The version presented here is approximately one-third of the original—it omits many theorems, especially in the later Parts, and it omits the proofs of some of the theorems that are given. There are some parenthetical citations to omitted theorems, but in each case the relevant content has been summarized where the theorems are cited.

which by another is determined to existence and action in a fixed and prescribed manner.

VIII. By *eternity* I understand existence itself, so far as it is conceived necessarily to follow from the definition alone of the eternal thing.

Explanation. For such existence, like the essence of the thing, is conceived as an eternal truth. It cannot therefore be explained by duration or time, even if the duration be conceived without beginning or end.

Axioms

I. Everything which is, is either in itself or in another.

II. That which cannot be conceived through another must be conceived through itself.

III. From a given determinate cause an effect necessarily follows; and, on the other hand, if no determinate cause be given it is impossible that an effect can follow.

IV. The knowledge of an effect depends upon and involves the knowledge of the cause.

V. Those things which have nothing in common with one another cannot through one another be mutually understood, that is to say, the conception of the one does not involve the conception of the other.

VI. A true idea must agree with that of which it is the idea.

VII. The essence of that thing which can be conceived as not existing does not involve existence.

Propositions

PROPOSITION 1. *Substance is by its nature prior to its modifications.*

Demonstration. This is evident from Defs. III and V.

PROPOSITION 2. *Two substances having different attributes have nothing in common with one another.*

Demonstration. This is also evident from Def. III. For each substance must be in itself and must be conceived through itself, that is to say, the conception of one does not involve the conception of the other.—Q.E.D.

PROPOSITION 3. *If two things have nothing in common with one another, one cannot be the cause of the other.*

Demonstration. If they have nothing in common with one another, they cannot (Ax. V) through one another be mutually understood, and therefore (Ax. IV) one cannot be the cause of the other. —Q.E.D.

PROPOSITION 4. *Two or more distinct things are distinguished from one another, either by the difference of the attributes of the substances or by the difference of their modifications.*

Demonstration. Everything which is, is either in itself or in another (Ax. I), that is to say (Defs. III and V), outside the intellect there is nothing but substances and their modifications. There is nothing therefore outside the intellect by which a number of things can be distinguished one from another, but substance or (which is the same thing by Def. IV) their attributes and their modifications. —Q.E.D.

PROPOSITION 5. *In nature there cannot be two or more substances of the same nature or attribute.*

Demonstration. If there were two or more distinct substances, they would have to be distinguished from one another by difference of attributes or difference of modifications (Prop. 4). If they are distinguished only by difference of attributes, it will be granted that there is but one substance of the same attribute. But if they are distinguished by difference of modifications, since substance is prior by nature to its modifications (Prop. 2), the modifications therefore being placed on one side, and the substance being considered in itself, or, in other words (Def. III and Ax. VI), truly considered, it cannot be conceived as distinguished from another substance, that is to say (Prop. 4), there cannot be two or more substances, but only one possessing the same nature or attribute.—Q.E.D.

PROPOSITION 6. *One substance cannot be produced by another substance.*

Demonstration. There cannot in nature be two substances of the same attribute (Prop. 5), that is to say (Prop. 2), two which have anything in common with one another. And therefore (Prop. 3), one cannot be the cause of the other, that is to say, one cannot be produced by the other.—Q.E.D.

Corollary. Hence it follows that there is nothing by which substance can be produced, for in Nature there is nothing but substances and their modifications (as is evident from Ax. I and Defs. III and V). But substance cannot be produced by substance (Prop. 6). Therefore absolutely there is nothing by which substance can be produced.—Q.E.D.

Another Demonstration. This corollary is demonstrated more easily by the *reductio ad absurdum*. For if there were anything by which substance could be produced, the knowledge of substance would be dependent upon the knowledge of its cause (Ax. IV), and therefore (Def. III) it would not be substance.

PROPOSITION 7. *It pertains to the nature of substance to exist.*

Demonstration. There is nothing by which substance can be produced (Prop. 6, Corol.). It will therefore be the cause of itself, that is to say (Def. I), its essence necessarily involves existence, or, in other words, it pertains to its nature to exist.—Q.E.D.

PROPOSITION 8. *Every substance is necessarily infinite.*

Demonstration. Substance which has only one attribute cannot exist except as one substance (Prop. 5), and to the nature of this one substance it pertains to exist (Prop. 7). It must therefore from its nature exist as finite or infinite. But it cannot exist as finite substance, for (Def. II) it must (if finite) be limited by another substance of the same nature, which also must necessarily exist (Prop. 7), and therefore there would be two substances of the same attribute, which is absurd (Prop. 5). It exists therefore as infinite substance.—Q.E.D.

. . . *Note 2.* I fully expect that those who judge things confusedly, and who have not been accustomed to cognize things through their first causes, will find it difficult to comprehend the demonstration of the seventh Proposition, since they do not distinguish between the

modifications of substances and substances themselves, and are ignorant of the manner in which things are produced. Hence it comes to
pass that they erroneously ascribe to substances a beginning like that
which they see belongs to natural things; for those who are ignorant
of the true causes of things confound everything, and without any
mental repugnance represent trees speaking like men, or imagine that
men are made out of stones as well as begotten from seed, and that
all forms can be changed into one another. So also those who confound human nature with the divine readily attribute to God human
emotions, especially so long as they are ignorant of the manner in
which emotions are produced in the mind. But if men would attend to
the nature of substance, they could not entertain a single doubt of
the truth of Proposition 7; indeed this proposition would be considered by all to be axiomatic, and reckoned amongst common notions.
For by "substance" would be understood that which is in itself and is
conceived through itself, or, in other words, that the knowledge of
which does not need the knowledge of another thing. But by "modifications" would be understood those things which are in another
thing—those things the conception of which is formed from the
conception of the thing in which they are. Hence we can have true
ideas of non-existent modifications, since, although they may not
actually exist outside the intellect, their essence nevertheless is so
comprehended in something else that they may be conceived through
it. But the truth of substances is not outside the intellect unless in the
substances themselves, because they are conceived through themselves. If anyone, therefore, were to say that he possessed a clear and
distinct, that is to say, a true idea of substance, and that he nevertheless doubted whether such a substance exists, he would forsooth be in
the same position as if he were to say that he had a true idea and
nevertheless doubted whether or not it was false (as is evident to
anyone who pays a little attention). Similarly if anyone were to affirm
that substance is created, he would affirm at the same time that a
false idea had become true, and this is a greater absurdity than can
be conceived. It is therefore necessary to admit that the existence of
substance, like its essence, is an eternal truth. Hence a demonstration
(which I have thought worth while to append) by a different method
is possible, showing that there are not two substances possessing the
same nature. But in order to prove this methodically it is to be noted,
first, that the true definition of any one thing neither involves nor
expresses anything except the nature of the thing defined. From

which it follows, secondly, that a definition does not involve or express any certain number of individuals, since it expresses nothing but the nature of the thing defined. For example, the definition of a triangle expresses nothing but the simple nature of a triangle, and not any certain number of triangles. Thirdly, it is to be observed that of every existing thing there is some certain cause by reason of which it exists. Fourthly and finally, it is to be observed that this cause by reason of which a thing exists must either be contained in the nature itself and definition of the existing thing (simply because it pertains to the nature of the thing to exist), or it must exist outside the thing. This being granted, it follows that if a certain number of individuals exist in nature there must necessarily be a cause why those individuals, and neither more nor fewer, exist. If, for example, there are twenty men in existence (whom, for the sake of greater clearness, I suppose existing at the same time, and that no others existed before them), it will not be sufficient, in order that we may give a reason why twenty men exist, to give a cause for human nature generally; but it will be necessary, in addition, to give a reason why neither more nor fewer than twenty exist, since, as we have already observed under the third head, there must necessarily be a cause why each exists. But this cause (as we have shown under the second and third heads) cannot be contained in human nature itself, since the true definition of a man does not involve the number twenty, and therefore (by the fourth head) the cause why these twenty men exist, and consequently the cause why each exists, must necessarily lie outside each one; and therefore we must conclude generally that whenever it is possible for several individuals of the same nature to exist, there must necessarily be an external cause for their existence.

Since now it pertains to the nature of substance to exist (as we have shown in this note), its definition must involve necessary existence, and consequently from its definition alone its existence must be concluded. But from its definition (as we have already shown under the second and third heads) the existence of more substances than one cannot be deduced. It follows, therefore, from this definition that there cannot be two substances possessing the same nature.

PROPOSITION 9. *The more reality or being a thing possesses, the more attributes belong to it.*

Demonstration. This is evident from Def. IV.

PROPOSITION 10. *Each attribute of a substance must be conceived through itself.*

Demonstration. For an attribute is that which the intellect perceives of substance, as constituting its essence (Def. IV), and therefore (Def. III) it must be conceived through itself.—Q.E.D.

Note. From this it is apparent that although two attributes may be conceived as really distinct—that is to say, one without the assistance of the other—we cannot nevertheless thence conclude that they constitute two beings or two different substances; for this is the nature of substance that each of its attributes is conceived through itself, since all the attributes which substance possesses were always in it together, nor could one be produced by another; but each expresses the reality or being of substance. It is very far from being absurd, therefore, to ascribe to one substance a number of attributes, since nothing in Nature is clearer than that each being must be conceived under some attribute, and the more reality or being it has, the more attributes it possesses expressing necessity or eternity and infinity. Nothing consequently is clearer than that Being absolutely infinite is necessarily defined, as we have shown (Def. VI), as Being which consists of infinite attributes, each one of which expresses a certain essence, eternal and infinite. But if anyone now asks by what sign, therefore, we may distinguish between substances, let him read the following propositions, which show that in Nature only one substance exists, and that it is absolutely infinite. For this reason that sign would be sought for in vain.

PROPOSITION 11. *God or substance consisting of infinite attributes, each one of which expresses eternal and infinite essence, necessarily exists.*

Demonstration. If this be denied, conceive, if it be possible, that God does not exist. Then it follows (Ax. VII) that His essence does not involve existence. But this (Prop. 7) is absurd. Therefore God necessarily exists.—Q.E.D.

Another demonstration. For the existence or non-existence of everything there must be a reason or cause. For example, if a triangle exists there must be a reason or cause why it exists; and if it does not exist there must be a reason or cause which hinders its existence or which negates it. But this reason or cause must either be contained in the nature of the thing or lie outside it. For example, the nature of the thing itself shows the reason why a square circle does not exist, the reason being that a square circle involves a contradiction. And the reason, on the other hand, why substance exists follows from its nature alone, which involves existence (see Prop. 7). But the reason why a circle or triangle exists or does not exist is not drawn from their nature, but from the order of corporeal nature generally; for from that it must follow either that a triangle necessarily exists or that it is impossible for it to exist. But this is self-evident. It follows that if there is no cause or reason which hinders a thing from existing, it exists necessarily. If, therefore, there is no reason or cause which hinders God from existing or which negates His existence, we must conclude absolutely that He necessarily exists. But if there is such a reason or cause it must be either in the nature itself of God or must lie outside it, that is to say, in another substance of another nature. For if the reason lay in a substance of the same nature, the existence of God would be by this very fact admitted. But substance possessing another nature could have nothing in common with God (Prop. 2), and therefore could not give Him existence nor negate it. Since, therefore, the reason or cause which could negate the divine existence cannot be outside the divine nature, it will necessarily, supposing that the divine nature does not exist, be in His nature itself, which would therefore involve a contradiction. But to affirm this of the Being absolutely infinite and consummately perfect is absurd. Therefore, neither in God nor outside God is there any cause or reason which can negate His existence, and therefore God necessarily exists.—Q.E.D.

Another demonstration. Inability to exist is impotence, and, on the other hand, ability to exist is power, as is self-evident. If, therefore, there is nothing which necessarily exists except things finite, it follows that things finite are more powerful than the absolutely infinite Being, and this (as is self-evident) is absurd; therefore, either nothing exists or Being absolutely infinite also necessarily exists. But we ourselves exist, either in ourselves or in something else which necessarily exists (Ax. I and Prop. 7). Therefore, the Being absolutely infinite—that is to say (Def. VI), God—necessarily exists.—Q.E.D.

Note. In this last demonstration I wished to prove the existence of God *a posteriori,* in order that the demonstration might be the more easily understood, and not because the existence of God does not follow *a priori* from the same grounds. For since ability to exist is power, it follows that the more reality belongs to the nature of anything, the greater is the power for existence it derives from itself; and it also follows, therefore, that the Being absolutely infinite, or God, has from Himself an absolutely infinite power of existence, and that He therefore necessarily exists. Many persons, nevertheless, will perhaps not be able easily to see the force of this demonstration, because they have been accustomed to contemplate those things alone which flow from external causes, and they see also that those things which are quickly produced from these causes, that is to say, which easily exist, easily perish, whilst, on the other hand, they adjudge those things to be more difficult to produce, that is to say, not so easy to bring into existence, to which they conceive more properties pertain. In order that these prejudices may be removed I do not need here to show in what respect this saying, "What is quickly made quickly perishes," is true, nor to inquire whether, looking at the whole of Nature, all things are or are not equally easy. But this only it will be sufficient for me to observe: that I do not speak of things which are produced by external causes, but that I speak of substances alone which (Prop. 6) can be produced by no external cause. For whatever perfection or reality those things may have which are produced by external causes, whether they consist of many parts or of few, they owe it all to the virtue of an external cause, and therefore their existence springs from the perfection of an external cause alone and not from their own. On the other hand, whatever perfection substance has is due to no external cause. Therefore, its existence must follow from its nature alone, and is, therefore, nothing else but its essence. Perfection consequently does not prevent the existence of a thing but establishes it; imperfection, on the other hand, prevents existence, and so of no existence can we be more sure than of the existence of the Being absolutely infinite or perfect, that is to say, God. For since His essence shuts out all imperfection and involves absolute perfection, for this very reason all cause of doubt concerning His existence is taken away, and the highest certainty concerning it is given—a truth which I trust will be evident to anyone who bestows only moderate attention.

PROPOSITION 13. *Substance absolutely infinite is indivisible.*

Demonstration. For if it were divisible, the parts into which it would be divided will or will not retain the nature of substance absolutely infinite. If they retain it there will be a plurality of substances possessing the same nature, which (Prop. 5) is absurd. If the second case be supposed, then (as above) substance absolutely infinite can cease to be, which (Prop. 11) is also absurd.

Corollary.   Hence it follows that no substance, and consequently no bodily substance in so far as it is substance, is divisible.

Note.   That substance is indivisible is more easily to be understood from this consideration alone—that the nature of substance cannot be conceived unless as infinite, and that by a part of substance nothing else can be understood than finite substance, which (Prop. 8) involves a manifest contradiction.

PROPOSITION 14.   *Besides God no substance can be nor can be conceived.*

Demonstration.   Since God is Being absolutely infinite, of whom no attribute can be denied which expresses the essence of substance (Def. VI), and since He necessarily exists (Prop. 11), it follows that if there were any substance besides God, it would have to be explained by some attribute of God, and thus two substances would exist possessing the same attribute, which (Prop. 5) is absurd; and therefore there cannot be any substance except God, and consequently none other can be conceived. For if any other could be conceived, it would necessarily be conceived as existing, and this (by the first part of this demonstration) is absurd. Therefore, besides God no substance can be nor can be conceived.—Q.E.D.

Corollary 1.   Hence it follows with the greatest clearness, firstly, that God is one, that is to say (Def. VI), in Nature there is but one substance, and it is absolutely infinite, as (Note to Prop. 10) we have already intimated.

Corollary 2.   It follows, secondly, that the thing extended and the thing thinking are either attributes of God or (Ax. I) modifications of the attributes of God.

PROPOSITION 15.   *Whatever is, is in God, and nothing can either be or be conceived without God.*

Demonstration. Besides God there is no substance, nor can any be conceived (Prop. 14), that is to say (Def. III), nothing which is in itself and is conceived through itself. But modes (Def. V) can neither be nor be conceived without substance; therefore they can exist only in the divine nature and through it alone can they be conceived. But besides substances and modes nothing is assumed (Ax. I). Therefore, nothing can be or be conceived without God.—Q.E.D.

Note. There are those who imagine God to be like a man, composed of body and soul and subject to passions; but it is clear enough from what has already been demonstrated how far off men who believe this are from the true knowledge of God. But these I dismiss, for all men who have in any way looked into the divine nature deny that God is corporeal. That He cannot be so they conclusively prove by showing that by "body" we understand a certain quantity possessing length, breadth, and depth, limited by some fixed form; and that to attribute these to God, a being absolutely infinite, is the greatest absurdity. But yet at the same time, from other arguments by which they endeavor to confirm their proof, they clearly show that they remove altogether from the divine nature substance itself corporeal or extended, affirming that it was created by God. By what divine power, however, it could have been created they are altogether ignorant, so that it is clear they do not understand what they themselves say. But I have demonstrated, at least in my own opinion, with sufficient clearness (see Prop. 6, Corol., and Prop. 8, Note 2), that no substance can be produced or created by another being. Moreover (Prop. 14), we have shown that besides God no substance can be nor can be conceived; and hence we have concluded that extended substance is one of the infinite attributes of God. But for the sake of a fuller explanation I will refute my adversaries' arguments, which, taken altogether, come to this: first, that corporeal substance, in so far as it is substance, consists, as they suppose, of parts, and therefore they deny that it can be infinite, and consequently that it can pertain to God. This they illustrate by many examples, one or two of which I will adduce. If corporeal substance, they say, be infinite, let us conceive it to be divided into two parts; each part, therefore, will be either finite or infinite. If each part be finite, then the infinite is composed of two finite parts, which is absurd. If each part be infinite, there is then an infinite twice as great as another infinite, which is also absurd. Again, if infinite quantity be measured by equal parts of a foot each, it must contain an infinite number of such parts, and

similarly if it be measured by equal parts of an inch each; and therefore one infinite number will be twelve times greater than another
infinite number. Lastly, if from one point of any infinite quantity it
be imagined that two lines, AB, AC, which at first are at a certain
and determinate distance from one another, be infinitely extended, it

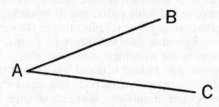

is plain that the distance between B and C will be continually increased, and at length from being determinate will be indeterminable.
Since therefore these absurdities follow, as they think, from supposing quantity to be infinite, they conclude that corporeal substance
must be finite, and consequently cannot pertain to the essence of God.
A second argument is assumed from the absolute perfection of God.
For God, they say, since He is a being absolutely perfect, cannot
suffer; but corporeal substance, since it is divisible, can suffer; it
follows, therefore, that it does not pertain to God's essence. These
are the arguments which I find in authors, by which they endeavor
to show that corporeal substance is unworthy of the divine nature
and cannot pertain to it. But anyone who will properly attend will
discover that I have already answered these arguments, since the
sole foundation of them is the supposition that bodily substance consists of parts—a supposition which (Prop. 13, Corol.) I have shown to
be absurd. Moreover, if anyone will rightly consider the matter, he
will see that all these absurdities (supposing that they are all absurdities—a point which I will now take for granted), from which these
authors attempt to draw the conclusion that substance extended is finite, do not by any means follow from the supposition that quantity is
infinite, but from the supposition that infinite quantity is measurable,
and that it is made up of finite parts. Therefore, from the absurdities
to which this leads nothing can be concluded except that infinite quantity is not measurable, and that it cannot be composed of finite parts.
But this is what we have already demonstrated (Prop. 13), and the
shaft therefore which is aimed at us turns against those who cast it. If,
therefore, from these absurdities anyone should attempt to conclude

that substance extended must be finite, he would, forsooth, be in the position of the man who supposes a circle to have the properties of a square, and then concludes that it has no center, such that all the lines drawn from it to the circumference are equal. For corporeal substance, which cannot be conceived except as infinite, one and indivisible (Props. 8, 5, and 13), is conceived by those against whom I argue to be composed of finite parts, and to be multiplex and divisible, in order that they may prove it finite. Just in the same way others, after they have imagined a line to consist of points, know how to discover many arguments by which they show that a line cannot be divided *ad infinitum*; and indeed it is not less absurd to suppose that corporeal substance is composed of bodies or parts than to suppose that a body is composed of surfaces, surfaces of lines, and that lines, finally, are composed of points. Every one who knows that clear reason is infallible ought to admit this, and especially those who deny that a vacuum can exist. For if corporeal substance could be so divided that its parts could be really distinct, why could not one part be annihilated, the rest remaining, as before, connected with one another? And why must all be so fitted together that there can be no vacuum? For of things which are really distinct the one from the other, one can be and remain in its own position without the other Since, therefore, it is supposed that there is no vacuum in Nature (about which I will speak at another time), but that all the parts must be united so that no vacuum can exist, it follows that they cannot be really separated, that is to say, that corporeal substance, in so far as it is substance, cannot be divided. If, nevertheless, anyone should now ask why there is a natural tendency to consider quantity as capable of division, I reply that quantity is conceived by us in two ways: either abstractly or superficially, that is to say, as we imagine it, or else as substance, in which way it is conceived by the intellect alone. If, therefore, we regard quantity (as we do very often and easily) as it exists in the imagination, we find it to be finite, divisible, and composed of parts; but if we regard it as it exists in the intellect, and conceive it in so far as it is substance, which is very difficult, then, as we have already sufficiently demonstrated, we find it to be infinite, one, and indivisible. This will be plain enough to all who know how to distinguish between the imagination and the intellect, and more especially if we remember that matter is everywhere the same, and that, except in so far as we regard it as affected in different ways, parts are not distinguished in it, that is to say, they are distinguished with regard to mode, but not with regard to reality. For example, we conceive water as being divided, in so far as it is water, and that its parts are separated from one another; but in so far as it is corporeal substance we cannot thus conceive it, for as such it is neither separated nor divided. Moreover, water, in so far as it is water, is originated and destroyed; but in so far as it is substance, it is neither originated nor destroyed. By this reasoning I think that I have also answered the second argument, since that, too, is based upon the assumption that matter, considered as substance, is divisible and composed of parts. And even if what I have urged were not true, I do not know why matter should be unworthy of the divine nature, since (Prop. 14) outside God no substance can exist from which the divine nature could suffer. All things, I say, are in God, and everything which takes place takes place by the laws alone of the infinite nature of God, and follows (as I shall presently show) from the necessity of His essence. Therefore, in no way whatever can it be asserted that God suffers from anything, or that substance extended, even if it be supposed divisible, is unworthy of the divine nature, provided only it be allowed that it is eternal and infinite. But enough on this point for the present.

PROPOSITION 16. *From the necessity of the divine nature infinite numbers of things in infinite ways (that is to say, all things which can be conceived by the infinite intellect) must follow.*

Demonstration. This proposition must be plain to every one who considers that from the given definition of anything a number of properties necessarily following from it (that is to say, following from the essence of the thing itself) are inferred by the intellect, and just in proportion as the definition of the thing expresses a greater reality, that is to say, just in proportion as the essence of the thing defined involves a greater reality, will more properties be inferred. But the divine nature possesses absolutely infinite attributes (Def. VI), each one of which expresses infinite essence in its own kind and therefore, from the necessity of the divine nature, infinite numbers of things in infinite ways (that is to say, all things which can be conceived by the infinite intellect) must necessarily follow.—Q.E.D.

Corollary 1. Hence it follows that God is the efficient cause of all things which can fall under the infinite intellect.

Corollary 2. It follows, secondly, that God is cause through Himself, and not through that which is contingent.

Corollary 3. It follows, thirdly, that God is absolutely the first cause.

PROPOSITION 17. *God acts from the laws of His own nature only, and is compelled by no one.*

Demonstration. We have just shown (Prop. 16) that from the necessity, or (which is the same thing) from the laws only of the divine nature, infinite numbers of things absolutely follow; and we have demonstrated (Prop. 15) that nothing can be nor can be conceived without God, but that all things are in God. Therefore, outside Himself, there can be nothing by which He may be determined or compelled to act; and therefore He acts from the laws of His own nature only, and is compelled by no one.—Q.E.D.

Corollary 1. Hence it follows, firstly, that there is no cause, either external to God or within Him, which can excite Him to act except the perfection of His own nature.

Corollary 2. It follows, secondly, that God alone is a free cause; for God alone exists from the necessity alone of His own nature (Prop. 11, and Prop. 14, Corol. 1), and acts from the necessity alone of His own nature (Prop. 17). Therefore (Def. VII), He alone is a free cause.—Q.E.D.

Note. There are some who think that God is a free cause because He can, as they think, bring about that those things which we have said follow from His nature—that is to say, those things which are in His power—should not be or should not be produced by Him. But this is simply saying that God could bring about that it should not follow from the nature of a triangle that its three angles should be equal to two right angles, or that from a given cause an effect should not follow, which is absurd. But I shall show further on, without the help of this proposition, that neither intellect nor will pertain to the nature of God.

I know, indeed, that there are many who think themselves able to demonstrate that intellect of the highest order and freedom of will both pertain to the nature of God, for they say that they know nothing more perfect which they can attribute to Him than that which is the chief perfection in ourselves. But although they conceive God as actually possessing the highest intellect, they nevertheless do not believe that He can bring about that all those things should exist which are actually in His intellect, for they think that by such a supposition they would destroy His power. If He had created, they say, all things which are in His intellect, He could have created nothing more, and this, they believe, does not accord with God's omnipotence; so then they prefer to consider God as indifferent to all things, and creating nothing except that which He has decreed to create by a certain absolute will. But I think that I have shown with sufficient clearness (Prop. 16) that from the supreme power of God, or from His infinite nature, infinite things in infinite ways, that is to say, all things, have necessarily flowed, or continually follow by the same necessity, in the same way as it follows from the nature of a triangle, from eternity and to eternity, that its three angles are equal to two right angles. The omnipotence of God has therefore been actual from eternity, and in the same actuality will remain to eternity. In this way the omnipotence of God, in my opinion, is far more firmly established. My adversaries, indeed (if I may be permitted to speak plainly), seem to deny the omnipotence of God, inasmuch as they are forced to admit that He has in His mind an infinite number of things which might be created, but which, nevertheless, He will never be able to create, for if He were to create all things which He has in His mind, He would, according to them, exhaust His omnipotence and make Himself imperfect. Therefore, in order to make a perfect God, they are compelled to make Him incapable of doing all those things to which His power extends, and anything more absurd than this, or more opposed to God's omnipotence, I do not think can be imagined. Moreover—to say a word, too, here about the intellect and will which we commonly attribute to God—if intellect and will pertain to His eternal essence, these attributes cannot be understood in the sense in which men generally use them, for the intellect and will which could constitute His essence would have to differ entirely from our intellect and will, and could resemble ours in nothing except in name. There could be no further likeness than that between the celestial constellation of the Dog and the animal which barks. This I will demonstrate as follows. If intellect pertains to the divine nature, it cannot, like our intellect, follow the things which are its object (as many suppose), nor can it be simultaneous in its nature with them, since God is prior to all things in causality (Prop. 16, Corol. 1); but, on the contrary, the truth and formal essence of things is what it is, because as such it exists objectively in God's intellect. Therefore, the intellect of God, in so far as it is conceived to constitute His essence, is in truth the cause of things, both of their essence and of their existence—a truth which seems to have been understood by those who have maintained that God's intellect, will, and power are one and the same thing. Since, therefore, God's intellect is the sole cause of things, both of their essence and of their existence (as we have already shown), it must necessarily differ from them with regard both to its essence and existence; for an effect differs from its cause precisely in that which it has from its cause. For example, one man is the cause of the existence but not of the essence of another, for the essence is an eternal truth; and therefore, with regard to essence, the two men may exactly resemble one another, but, with regard to existence, they must differ. Consequently, if the existence of one should perish, that of the other will not therefore perish; but if the essence of one could be destroyed and become false, the essence of the other would be likewise destroyed. Therefore a thing which is the cause both of the essence and of the existence of any effect must differ from that effect both with regard to its essence and with regard to its existence. But the intellect of God is the cause both of the essence and existence of our intellect; therefore the intellect of God, so far as it is conceived to constitute the divine essence, differs from our intellect both with regard to its essence and its existence, nor can it coincide with our intellect in anything except the name, which is what we essayed to prove. The same demonstration may be applied to the will, as anyone may easily see for himself.

PROPOSITION 18. *God is the immanent and not the transient cause of all things.*

Demonstration. All things which are, are in God and must be conceived through Him (Prop. 15), and therefore (Prop. 16, Corol. 1) He is the cause of the things which are in Himself. This is the first thing which was to be proved. Moreover, outside God there can be no substance (Prop. 14), that is to say (Def. III), outside Him nothing can exist which is in itself. This was the second thing to be proved. God, therefore, is the immanent, but not the transient, cause of all things.—Q.E.D.

PROPOSITION 19. *God is eternal, or, in other words, all His attributes are eternal.*

Demonstration. For God (Def. VI) is substance which (Prop. 11) necessarily exists, that is to say (Prop. 7), a substance to whose nature it pertains to exist, or (which is the same thing) a substance from the definition of which it follows that it exists, and therefore (Def. VIII) He is eternal.—Q.E.D.

PROPOSITION 20. *The existence of God and His essence are one and the same thing.*

Demonstration. God (Prop. 19) and all His attributes are eternal, that is to say (Def. VIII), each one of His attributes expresses existence. The same attributes of God, therefore, which (Def. IV) manifest the eternal essence of God, at the same time manifest His eternal existence, that is to say, the very same thing which constitutes the essence of God constitutes at the same time His existence, and therefore His existence and His essence are one and the same thing.— Q.E.D.

Corollary 1. Hence it follows, first, that the existence of God, like His essence, is an eternal truth.

Corollary 2. It follows, secondly, that God is immutable, or (which is the same thing) all His attributes are immutable; for if they were changed as regards their existence, they must be changed also as regards their essence (Prop. 20), that is to say (as is self-evident), from being true, they would become false, which is absurd.

PROPOSITION 21. *All things which follow from the absolute nature of any attribute of God must forever exist, and must be infinite, that is to say, through that same attribute they are eternal and infinite.*

Demonstration. Conceive, if possible (supposing that the truth of the proposition is denied), that in some attribute of God something which is finite and has a determinate existence or duration follows from the absolute nature of that attribute—for example, one of God's ideas. But thought, since it is admitted to be an attribute of God, is necessarily (Prop. 11) in its nature infinite. But so far as it has God's idea it is by supposition finite. But (Def. II) it cannot be conceived as finite unless it be determined by thought itself. But it cannot be determined by thought itself so far as it constitutes God's idea, for so far by supposition it is finite. Therefore it must be determined by thought so far as it does not constitute God's idea, but which, nevertheless (Prop. 11), necessarily exists. Thought, therefore, exists which does not form God's idea, and therefore from its nature, in so far as it is absolute thought, God's idea does not necessarily follow (for it is conceived as forming and as not forming God's idea), which is contrary to the hypothesis. Therefore, if one of God's ideas, in the attribute of thought or anything else in any attribute of God follow from the necessity of the absolute nature of that attribute (for the demonstration being universal will apply in every case), that thing must necessarily be infinite, which was the first thing to be proved.

Again, that which thus follows from the necessity of the nature of any attribute cannot have a determinate duration. For, if the truth of this be denied, let it be supposed that in some attribute of God a thing exists which follows from the necessity of the nature of the attribute—for example, one of God's ideas in the attribute of thought —and let it be supposed that at some time it has either not existed or will not exist. But since thought is supposed to be an attribute of God, it must exist both necessarily and unchangeably (Prop. 11, and Prop. 20, Corol. 2). Therefore, beyond the limits of the duration of God's idea (for it is supposed that at some time it has either not existed or will not exist), thought must exist without God's idea; but this is contrary to hypothesis, for the supposition is that thought being given, the idea necessarily follows. Therefore, neither one of God's ideas in the attribute of thought, nor anything else which necessarily follows from the absolute nature of any attribute of God, can have a determinate duration, but through the same attribute is eternal; which was the second thing to be proved. Observe that what we have affirmed here is true of everything which in any attribute of God necessarily follows from the absolute nature of God.—Q.E.D.

[There follows a series of proofs of the absolute dependence of all things upon God: He is the cause of their existence, of their continuing in existence—since their essence (Prop. 24) does not involve existence—of their essence (Prop. 25), and of their actions (Prop. 26), nor can they free themselves from God's causality (Prop. 27). The infinite modes follow necessarily from God's attributes or from other infinite modes (Props. 22, 23); the finite modes are the result of finite causes, and these in turn of other finite causes, *ad infinitum* (Prop. 28).]

PROPOSITION 29. *In Nature there is nothing contingent, but all things are determined from the necessity of the divine nature to exist and act in a certain manner.*

Demonstration. **Whatever is, is in God (Prop. 15); but God** cannot be called a contingent thing, for (Prop. 11) He exists necessarily and not contingently. Moreover, the modes of the divine nature have followed from it necessarily and not contingently (Prop. 16), and that, too, whether it be considered absolutely (Prop. 21), or as determined to action in a certain manner (Prop. 27). But God is the cause of these modes, not only in so far as they simply exist (Prop. 24, Corol.), but also (Prop. 26) in so far as they are considered as determined to any action. And if they are not determined by God (by the same proposition), it is an impossibility and not a contingency that they should determine themselves; and, on the other hand (Prop. 27), if they are determined by God, it is an impossibility and not a contingency that they should render themselves indeterminate. Wherefore all things are determined from a necessity of the divine nature, not only to exist, but to exist and act in a certain manner, and there is nothing contingent.—Q.E.D.

Note. Before I go any further, I wish here to explain or rather to recall to recollection what is meant by *natura naturans* and what by *natura naturata*. For, from what has gone before, I think it is plain that by *natura naturans* we are to understand that which is in itself and is conceived through itself, or those attributes of substance which express eternal and infinite essence, that is to say (Corol. 1, Prop. 14, and Prop. 17, Corol. 2), God in so far as He is considered as a free cause. But by *natura naturata* I understand everything which follows from the necessity of the nature of God or of any one of God's attributes, that is to say, all the modes of God's attributes in so far as they are considered as things which are in God, and which without God can neither be nor can be conceived.

PROPOSITION 32. *The will cannot be called a free cause, but can only be called necessary.*

Demonstration. The will is only a certain mode of thought, like the intellect, and therefore (Prop. 28) no volition can exist or be determined to action unless it be determined by another cause, and this again by another, and so on *ad infinitum*. And if the will be supposed infinite, it must be determined to existence and action by God, not in so far as He is substance absolutely infinite, but in so far as He possesses an attribute which expresses the infinite and eternal essence of thought (Prop. 23). In whatever way, therefore, the will be conceived, whether as finite or infinite, it requires a cause by which it may

be determined to existence and action, and therefore (Def. VII) it
cannot be called a free cause, but only necessary or compelled.—
Q.E.D.

Corollary 1. Hence it follows, first, that God does not act from
freedom of the will.

Corollary 2. It follows, secondly, that will and intellect are
related to the nature of God as motion and rest, and absolutely as all
natural things, which (Prop. 29) must be determined by God to existence and action in a certain manner. For the will, like all other
things, needs a cause by which it may be determined to existence and
action in a certain manner, and although from a given will or intellect
infinite things may follow, God cannot on this account be said to act
from freedom of will, any more than He can be said to act from freedom of motion and rest by reason of the things which follow from
motion and rest (for from motion and rest infinite numbers of things
follow). Therefore, will does not appertain to the nature of God
more than other natural things, but is related to it as motion and rest
and all other things are related to it—these all following, as we have
shown, from the necessity of the divine nature, and being determined
to existence and action in a certain manner.

PROPOSITION 33. *Things could have been produced by God in
no other manner and in no other order than that in which they have
been produced.*

Demonstration. All things have necessarily followed from the
given nature of God (Prop. 16), and from the necessity of His nature
have been determined to existence and action in a certain manner
(Prop. 29). If, therefore, things could have been of another nature or
could have been determined in another manner to action, so that the
order of nature would have been different, the nature of God might
then be different to that which it now is, and hence (Prop. 11) that
different nature would necessarily exist, and there might consequently
be two or more Gods, which (Prop. 14, Corol. 1) is absurd. Therefore, things could be produced by God in no other manner and in no
other order than that in which they have been produced.—Q.E.D.

Note 1. Since I have thus shown, with greater clearness than that
of noonday light, that in things there is absolutely nothing by virtue
of which they can be called contingent, I wish now to explain in a

few words what is to be understood by "contingent," but firstly, what
is to be understood by "necessary" and "impossible." A thing is called
necessary either in reference to its essence or its cause. For the existence of a thing necessarily follows either from the essence and definition of the thing itself or from a given efficient cause. In the same way
a thing is said to be impossible either because the essence of the thing
itself or its definition involves a contradiction, or because no external
cause exists determinate to the production of such a thing. But a thing
cannot be called contingent unless with reference to a deficiency in
our knowledge. For if we do not know that the essence of a thing involves a contradiction, or if we actually know that it involves no contradiction, and nevertheless we can affirm nothing with certainty
about its existence because the order of causes is concealed from us,
that thing can never appear to us either as necessary or impossible,
and therefore we call it either contingent or possible.

Note 2.   From what has gone before it clearly follows that things
have been produced by God in the highest degree of perfection, since
they have necessarily followed from the existence of a most perfect
nature. Nor does this doctrine accuse God of any imperfection, but, on
the contrary, His perfection has compelled us to affirm it. Indeed,
from its contrary would clearly follow, as I have shown above, that
God is not absolutely perfect, since, if things had been produced in
any other fashion, another nature would have had to be assigned to
Him, different from that which the consideration of the most perfect
Being compels us to assign to Him. I do not doubt that many will
reject this opinion as ridiculous, nor will they care to apply themselves
to its consideration, and this from no other reason than that they have
been in the habit of assigning to God another liberty widely different
from that absolute will which (Def. VII) we have taught. On the other
hand, I do not doubt, if they were willing to study the matter and
properly to consider the series of our demonstrations, that they would
altogether reject this liberty which they now assign to God, not only
as of no value, but as a great obstacle to knowledge. Neither is there
any need that I should here repeat those things which are said in the
Note to Prop. 17. But for the sake of those who differ from me, I
will here show that, although it be granted that will pertains to God's
essence, it follows nevertheless from His perfection that things could
be created in no other mode or order by Him. This it will be easy to
show if we first consider that which my opponents themselves admit—
that it depends upon the decree and will of God alone that each thing

should be what it is, for otherwise God would not be the cause of all things. It is also admitted that all God's decrees were decreed by God Himself from all eternity, for otherwise imperfection and inconstancy would be proved against Him. But since in eternity there is no *when* nor *before* nor *after,* it follows from the perfection of God alone that He neither can decree nor could ever have decreed anything else than that which He has decreed, that is to say, God has not existed before His decrees, and can never exist without them. But it is said that although it be supposed that God had made the nature of things different from that which it is, or that from eternity He had decreed something else about Nature and her order, it would not thence follow that any imperfection exists in God. But if this be said, it must at the same time be allowed that God can change His decrees. For if God had decreed something about Nature and her order other than that which He has decreed—that is to say, if He had willed and conceived something else about Nature—He would necessarily have had an intellect and a will different from those which He now has. And if it be allowed to assign to God another intellect and another will without any change of His essence and of His perfections, what is the reason why He cannot now change His decrees about creation and nevertheless remain equally perfect? For His intellect and will regarding created things and their order remain the same in relationship to His essence and perfection in whatever manner His intellect and will are conceived. Moreover, all the philosophers whom I have seen admit that there is no such thing as an intellect existing potentially in God, but only an intellect existing actually. But since His intellect and His will are not distinguishable from His essence, as all admit, it follows from this also that if God had had another intellect actually and another will, His essence would have been necessarily different, and hence, as I showed at the beginning, if things had been produced by God in a manner different from that in which they now exist, God's intellect and will, that is to say, His essence (as has been granted), must have been different, which is absurd.

Since, therefore, things could have been produced by God in no other manner or order, this being a truth which follows from His absolute perfection, there is no sound reasoning which can persuade us to believe that God was unwilling to create all things which are in His intellect with the same perfection as that in which they exist in His intellect. But we shall be told that there is no perfection nor imperfection in things, but that that which is in them by reason of which they are perfect or imperfect and are said to be good or evil depends upon the will of God alone, and therefore, if God had willed he could have effected that that which is now perfection should have been the extreme of imperfection, and *vice versa*. But what else would this be than openly to affirm that God, who necessarily understands what He wills, is able by His will to understand things in a manner different from that in which He understands them, which, as I have just shown, is a great absurdity? I can therefore turn the argument on my opponents in this way: all things depend upon the power of God. In order that things may be differently constituted, it would be necessary that God's will should be differently constituted; but God's will cannot be other than it is, as we have lately most clearly deduced from His perfection. Things therefore cannot be differently constituted. I confess that this opinion, which subjects all things to a certain indifferent God's will, and affirms that all things depend upon God's good pleasure, is at a less distance from the truth than the opinion of those who affirm that God does everything for the sake of the Good. For these seem to place something outside of God which is independent of Him, to which He looks while He is at work as to a model, or at which He aims as if at a certain mark. This is indeed nothing else than to subject God to fate, the most absurd thing which can be affirmed of Him whom we have shown to be the first and only free cause of the essence of all things as well as of their existence. Therefore it is not worth while that I should waste time in refuting this absurdity.

PROPOSITION 34. *The power of God is His essence itself.*

PROPOSITION 35. *Whatever we conceive to be in God's power necessarily exists.*

Appendix

I have now explained the nature of God and its properties. I have shown that He necessarily exists; that He is one God; that from the necessity alone of His own nature He is and acts; that He is, and in what way He is, the free cause of all things; that all things are in Him, and so depend upon Him that without Him they can neither be nor can be conceived; and, finally, that all things have been predetermined by Him, not indeed from freedom of will or from absolute good pleasure, but from His absolute nature or infinite power.

Moreover, wherever an opportunity was afforded, I have endeavored to remove prejudices which might hinder the perception of the truth of what I have demonstrated; but because not a few still remain which have been and are now sufficient to prove a very great hindrance to the comprehension of the connection of things in the manner in which I have explained it, I have thought it worth while to call them up to be examined by reason. But all these prejudices which I here undertake to point out depend upon this solely: that it is commonly supposed that all things in Nature, like men, work to some end; and, indeed, it is thought to be certain that God Himself directs all things to some sure end, for it is said that God has made all things for man, and man that he may worship God. This, therefore, I will first investigate by inquiring, first, why so many rest in this prejudice, and why all are so naturally inclined to embrace it. I shall then show its falsity, and, finally, the manner in which there have arisen from it prejudices concerning *good* and *evil, merit* and *sin, praise* and *blame, order* and *disorder, beauty* and *deformity,* and so forth. This, however, is not the place to deduce these things from the nature of the human mind. It will be sufficient if I here take as an axiom that which no one ought to dispute, namely, that man is born ignorant of the causes of things, and that he has a desire, of which he is conscious, to seek that which is profitable to him. From this it follows, first, that he thinks himself free because he is conscious of his wishes and appetites, whilst at the same time he is ignorant of the causes by which he is led to wish and desire, not dreaming what they are; and, secondly, it follows that man does everything for an end, namely, for that which is profitable to him, which is what he seeks. Hence it happens that he attempts to discover merely the final causes of that which has happened; and when he has heard them he is satisfied, because there is no longer any cause for further uncertainty. But if he cannot hear from another what these final causes are, nothing remains but to turn to himself and reflect upon the ends which usually determine him to the like actions, and thus by his own mind he necessarily judges that of another. Moreover, since he discovers, both within and without himself, a multitude of means which contribute not a little to the attainment of what is profitable to himself—for example, the eyes, which are useful for seeing, the teeth for mastication, plants and animals for nourishment, the sun for giving light, the sea for feeding fish, etc.—it comes to pass that all natural objects are considered as means for obtaining what is profitable. These, too, being evidently discovered and not created by man, hence he has a cause for believing that some other person exists who has prepared them for man's use. For having considered them as means it was impossible to believe that they had created themselves, and so he was obliged to infer from the means which he was in the habit of providing for himself that some ruler or rulers of Nature exist, endowed with human liberty, who have taken care of all things for him, and have made all things for his use. Since he never heard anything about the mind of these rulers, he was compelled to judge of it from his own, and hence he affirmed that the gods direct everything for his advantage in order that he may be bound to them and hold them in the highest honor. This is the reason why each man has devised for himself, out of his own brain, a different mode of worshipping God, so that God might love him above others, and direct all Nature to the service of his blind cupidity and insatiable avarice.

Thus has this prejudice been turned into a superstition and has driven deep roots into the mind—a prejudice which was the reason why everyone has so eagerly tried to discover and explain the final causes of things. The attempt, however, to show that Nature does nothing in vain (that is to say, nothing which is not profitable to man) seems to end in showing that Nature, the gods, and man are alike mad.

Do but see, I pray, to what all this has led. Amidst so much in Nature that is beneficial, not a few things must have been observed which are injurious, such as storms, earthquakes, diseases, and it was affirmed that these things happened either because the gods were angry because of wrongs which had been inflicted on them by man, or because of sins committed in the method of worshipping them; and although experience daily contradicted this, and showed by an infinity of examples that both the beneficial and the injurious were indiscriminately bestowed on the pious and the impious, the inveterate prejudices on this point have not therefore been abandoned. For it was much easier for a man to place these things aside with others of the use of which he was ignorant, and thus retain his present and inborn state of ignorance, than to destroy the whole superstructure and think out a new one. Hence it was looked upon as indisputable that the judgments of the gods far surpass our comprehensions; and this opinion alone would have been sufficient to keep the human race in darkness to all eternity if mathematics, which does not deal with ends but with the essences and properties of forms, had not placed before us another rule of truth. In addition to mathematics, other causes also might be assigned, which it is superfluous here to enumerate, tending to make men reflect upon these universal prejudices, and leading them to a true knowledge of things.

I have thus sufficiently explained what I promised in the first place to explain. There will now be no need of many words to show that Nature has set no end before herself, and that all final causes are nothing but human fictions. For I believe that this is sufficiently evident both from the foundations and causes of this prejudice, and from Prop. 16 and Prop. 32, Corol., as well as from all those propositions in which I have shown that all things are begotten by a certain eternal necessity of Nature and in absolute perfection. This much, nevertheless, I will add, that this doctrine concerning an end altogether overturns Nature. For that which is in truth the cause it considers as the effect, and *vice versa*. Again, that which is first in Nature it puts last; and, finally, that which is supreme and most perfect it makes the most imperfect. For (passing by the first two assertions as self-evident) it is plain from Props. 21, 22, and 23, that that effect is the most perfect which is immediately produced by God, and in proportion as intermediate causes are necessary for the production of a thing is it imperfect. But if things which are immediately produced by God were made in order that He might obtain the end He had in view, then the last things for the sake of which the first exist must be the most perfect of all. Again, this doctrine does away with God's perfection. For if God works to obtain an end, He necessarily seeks something of which He stands in need. And although theologians and metaphysicians distinguish between the end of want and the end of assimilation, they confess that God has done all things for His own sake, and not for the sake of the things to be created, because before the creation they can assign nothing except God for the sake of which God could do anything, and, therefore, they are necessarily compelled to admit that God stood in need of and desired those things for which He determined to prepare means. This is self-evident. Nor is it here to be overlooked that the adherents of this doctrine, who have found a pleasure in displaying their ingenuity in assigning the ends of things, have introduced a new species of argument, not the *reductio ad impossibile,* but the *reductio ad ignorantiam,* to prove their position, which shows that it had no other method of defense left. For, by way of example, if a stone has fallen from some roof on somebody's head and killed him, they will demonstrate in this manner that the stone has fallen in order to kill the man. For if it did not fall for that purpose by the will of God, how could so many circumstances concur through chance (and a number often simultaneously do concur)? You will answer, perhaps, that the event happened because the wind blew and the man was passing that way. But, they will urge, why did the wind blow at that time, and why did the man pass that way precisely at the same moment? If you again reply that the wind rose then because the sea on the preceding day began to be stormy, the weather hitherto having been calm, and that the man had been invited by a friend, they will urge again—because there is no end of questioning—But why was the sea agitated, why was the man invited at that time? And so they will not cease from asking the causes of causes until at last you fly to the will of God—the refuge for ignorance.

So, also, when they behold the structure of the human body, they are amazed; and because they are ignorant of the causes of such art, they conclude that the body was made not by mechanical but by a supernatural or divine art, and has been designed so that one part may not injure another. Hence it happens that the man who endeavors to find out the true causes of miracles, and who desires as a wise man to understand Nature, and not to gape at it like a fool, is generally considered and proclaimed to be a heretic and impious by those whom the vulgar worship as the interpreters both of Nature and the gods. For these know that when ignorance is removed, amazed stupidity—the sole ground on which they rely in arguing or in defending their authority—is taken away also. But these things I leave and pass on to that which I determined to do in the third place.

After man has persuaded himself that all things which exist are made for him, he must in everything adjudge that to be of the greatest importance which is most useful to him, and he must esteem that to be of surpassing worth by which he is most beneficially affected. In this way he is compelled to form those notions by which he explains Nature, such, for instance, as *good, evil, order, confusion, heat, cold, beauty,* and *deformity*; and because he supposes himself to be free, notions like those of *praise* and *blame, sin* and *merit,* have arisen. These latter I shall hereafter explain when I have treated of human nature; the former I will here briefly unfold.

It is to be observed that man has given the name "good" to everything which leads to health and the worship of God; on the contrary, everything which does not lead thereto he calls "evil." But because those who do not understand Nature affirm nothing about things themselves, but only imagine them and take the imagination to be understanding, they therefore, ignorant of things and their nature, firmly believe an *order* to be in things; for when things are so placed that, if they are represented to us through the senses, we can easily imagine them and, consequently, easily remember them, we call them well arranged; but if they are not placed so that we can imagine and remember them, we call them badly arranged or "confused." Moreover, since those things are more especially pleasing to us which we can easily imagine, men therefore prefer order to confusion, as if order were something in Nature apart from our own imagination; and they say that God has created everything in order, and in this manner they ignorantly attribute imagination to God unless they mean perhaps that God, out of consideration for the human imagination, has disposed things in the manner in which they can most easily be imagined. No hesitation either seems to be caused by the fact that an infinite number of things are discovered which far surpass our imagination, and very many which confound it through its weakness. But enough of this. The other notions which I have mentioned are nothing but modes in which the imagination is affected in different ways, and, nevertheless, they are regarded by the ignorant as being specially attributes of things because, as we have remarked, men consider all things as made for themselves, and call the nature of a thing good, evil, sound, putrid, or corrupt, just as they are affected by it. For example, if the motion by which the nerves are affected by means of objects represented to the eye conduces to well-being, the objects by which it is caused are called "beautiful"; while those exciting a contrary motion are called "deformed." Those things, too, which stimulate the senses through the nostrils are called sweet-smelling or stinking; those which act through the taste are called sweet or bitter, full-flavored or insipid; those which act through the touch, hard or soft, heavy or light; those, lastly, which act through the ears are said to make a noise, sound, or harmony, the last having caused men to lose their senses to such a degree that they have believed that God even is delighted with it. Indeed, philosophers may be found who have persuaded themselves that the celestial motions beget a harmony. All these things sufficiently show that everyone judges things by the constitution of his brain, or rather accepts the modifications of his imagination in the place of things. It is not, therefore, to be wondered at, as we may observe in passing, that all those controversies which we see have arisen amongst men, so that at last skepticism has been the result. For although human bodies agree in many things, they differ in more, and therefore that which to one person is good will appear to another evil, that which to one is well arranged to another is confused, that which pleases one will displease another, and so on in other cases which I pass by both because we cannot notice them at length here, and because they are within the experience of everyone. For everyone has heard the expressions: So many heads, so many ways of thinking; everyone is satisfied with his own way of thinking; differences of brains are not less common than differences of taste—all which maxims show that men decide upon matters according to the constitution of their brains, and imagine rather than understand things. If men understood things, they would, as mathematics proves, at least be all alike convinced if they were not all alike attracted. We see, therefore, that all those methods by which the common people are in the habit of explaining Nature are only different sorts of imaginations, and do not reveal the nature of anything in itself, but only the constitution of the imagination; and because they have names as if they were entities existing apart from the imagination, I call them entities not of the reason but of the imagination. All argument, therefore, urged against us based upon such notions can be easily refuted. Many people, for instance, are accustomed to argue thus: If all things have followed from the necessity of the most perfect nature of God, how is it that so many imperfections have arisen in Nature—corruption, for instance, of things till they stink; deformity, exciting disgust; confusion, evil, crime? But, as I have just observed, all this is easily answered. For the perfection of things is to be judged by their nature and power alone; nor are they more or less perfect because they delight or offend the human senses, or because they are beneficial or prejudicial to human nature. But to those who ask why God has not created all men in such a manner that they might be controlled by the dictates of reason alone, I give but this answer: because to Him material was not wanting for the creation of everything, from the highest down to the very lowest grade of perfection; or, to speak more properly, because the laws of His nature were so ample that they sufficed for the production of everything which can be conceived by an infinite intellect, as I have demonstrated in Prop. 16.

These are the prejudices which I undertook to notice here. If any others of a similar character remain, they can easily be rectified with a little thought by anyone.

PART II: OF THE NATURE AND ORIGIN OF THE MIND

I pass on now to explain those things which must necessarily follow from the essence of God or the Being eternal and infinite—not, indeed, to explain all these things, for we have demonstrated (Part I, Prop. 16) that an infinitude of things must follow in an infinite number of ways, but to consider those things only which may conduct us, as it were by the hand, to a knowledge of the human mind and its highest happiness.

Definitions

I. By *body* I understand a mode which expresses in a certain and determinate manner the essence of God in so far as He is considered as the thing extended. (See Part I, Prop. 25, Corol.)

II. I say that to the *essence* of anything pertains that, which being given, the thing itself is necessarily posited, and, being taken away, the thing is necessarily taken; or, in other words, that without which the thing can neither be nor be conceived, and which in its turn cannot be nor be conceived without the thing.

III. By *idea* I understand a conception of the mind which the mind forms because it is a thinking thing.

Explanation. I use the word "conception" rather than "perception" because the name perception seems to indicate that the mind is passive in its relation to the object, but the word "conception" seems to express the action of the mind.

IV. By *adequate* idea I understand an idea which, in so far as it is considered in itself, without reference to the object, has all the properties or internal signs of a true idea.

Explanation. I say internal, so as to exclude that which is external, the agreement, namely, of the idea with its object.

V. *Duration* is the indefinite continuation of existence.

Explanation. I call it indefinite because it cannot be determined by the nature itself of the existing thing nor by the efficient cause, which necessarily posits the existence of the thing but does not take it away.

VI. By *reality* and *perfection* I understand the same thing.

VII. By *individual things* I understand things which are finite and which have a determinate existence; and if a number of individuals so unite in one action that they are all simultaneously the cause of one effect, I consider them all, so far, as a one individual thing.

Axioms

I. The essence of man does not involve necessary existence; that is to say, the existence as well as the non-existence of this or that man may or may not follow from the order of nature.

II. Man thinks.

III. Modes of thought, such as love, desire, or the emotions of the mind, by whatever name they may be called, do not exist unless in the same individual exists the idea of a thing loved, desired, etc. But the idea may exist although no other mode of thinking exist.

IV. We perceive that a certain body is affected in many ways.

V. No individual things are felt or perceived by us except bodies and modes of thought.

Propositions

PROPOSITION 1. *Thought is an attribute of God, or God is a thinking thing.*

Demonstration. Individual thoughts, or this and that thought, are modes which express the nature of God in a certain and determinate manner (Part I, Prop. 25, Corol.). God therefore possesses an attribute (Part I, Def. V) the conception of which is involved in all individual thoughts, and through which they are conceived. Thought, therefore, is one of the infinite attributes of God which expresses the eternal and infinite essence of God (Part I, Def. VI), or, in other words, God is a thinking thing.—Q.E.D.

Note. This proposition is plain from the fact that we can conceive an infinite thinking Being. For the more things a thinking being can think, the more reality or perfection we conceive it to possess, and therefore the being which can think an infinitude of things in infinite ways is necessarily infinite by his power of thinking. Since, therefore, we can conceive an infinite Being by attending to thought alone, thought is necessarily one of the infinite attributes of God (Part I, Defs. IV and VI), which is the proposition we wished to prove.

PROPOSITION 2. *Extension is an attribute of God, or God is an extended thing.*

Demonstration. The demonstration of this proposition is of the same character as that of the last.

PROPOSITION 3. *In God there necessarily exists the idea of His essence and of all things which necessarily follow from His essence.*

Demonstration. For God (Part I, Prop. 1) can think an infinitude of things in infinite ways, or (which is the same thing, by Prop. 16 of Part I) can form an idea of His essence and of all the things which necessarily follow from it. But everything which is in the power of God is necessary (Part I, Prop. 35), and therefore this idea necessarily exists, and (Part I, Prop. 15) it cannot exist unless in God.— Q.E.D.

PROPOSITION 4. *God's idea, from which infinite numbers of things follow in infinite ways, can be one only.*

Demonstration. The infinite intellect comprehends nothing but the attributes of God and His modifications (Part I, Prop. 30). But God is one (Part I, Prop. 14, Corol.). Therefore God's idea, from which infinite numbers of things follow in infinite ways, can be one only.— Q.E.D.

PROPOSITION 6. *The modes of any attribute have God for a cause only in so far as He is considered under that attribute of which they are modes, and not in so far as He is considered under any other attribute.*

Demonstration. Each attribute is conceived by itself and independently of any other (Part I, Prop. 10). Therefore the modes of any attribute involve the conception of that attribute and of no other, and therefore (Part I, Ax. IV) have God for a cause in so far as He is considered under that attribute of which they are modes, and not in so far as He is considered under any other attribute.—Q.E.D.

PROPOSITION 7. *The order and connection of ideas is the same as the order and connection of things.*

This is evident from Ax. IV of Part I. For the idea of anything caused depends upon a knowledge of the cause of which the thing caused is the effect.

Corollary. Hence it follows that God's power of thinking is equal to His actual power of acting, that is to say, whatever follows *formally* from the infinite nature of God, follows from God's idea, in the same order and in the same connection *objectively* in God.

Note. Before we go any further, we must here recall to our memory what we have already demonstrated—that everything which can be perceived by the infinite intellect as constituting the essence of substance pertains entirely to the one sole substance only, and consequently that substance thinking and substance extended are one and the same substance, which is now comprehended under this attribute and now under that. Thus, also, a mode of extension and the idea of that mode are one and the same thing expressed in two different ways —a truth which some of the Hebrews appear to have seen as if through a cloud, since they say that God, the intellect of God, and the things which are the objects of that intellect are one and the same thing. For example, the circle existing in Nature and the idea that is in God of an existing circle are one and the same thing which is manifested through different attributes; and, therefore, whether we think of Nature under the attribute of extension or under the attribute of thought or under any other attribute whatever, we shall discover one and the same order or one and the same connection of causes, that is to say, in every case the same sequence of things. Nor have I had any other reason for saying that God is the cause of the idea, for example, of the circle in so far only as He is a thinking thing, and of the circle itself in so far as He is an extended thing, but this, that the formal being of the idea of a circle can only be perceived through another mode of thought, as its proximate cause, and this again must be perceived through another, and so on *ad infinitum*. So that when things are considered as modes of thought we must explain the order of the whole of Nature or the connection of causes by the attribute of thought alone, and when things are considered as modes of extension, the order of the whole of Nature must be explained through the attribute of extension alone, and so with other attributes. Therefore, God is in truth the cause of things as they are in themselves, in so far as He consists of infinite attributes, nor for the present can I explain the matter more clearly.

PROPOSITION 10. *The being of substance does not pertain to the essence of man, or, in other words, substance does not constitute the form of man.*

Corollary. Hence it follows that the essence of man consists of certain modifications of the attributes of God; for the being of substance does not pertain to the essence of man (Part II, Prop. 10). It is therefore something (Part I, Prop. 15) which is in God, and which without God can neither be nor be conceived, or (Part I, Prop. 25, Corol.) a modification or mode which expresses the nature of God in a certain and determinate manner.

PROPOSITION 11. *The first thing which forms the actual being of the human mind is nothing else but the idea of an individual thing actually existing.*

Corollary. Hence it follows that the human mind is a part of the infinite intellect of God, and therefore, when we say that the human mind perceives this or that thing, we say nothing else than that God has this or that idea; not indeed in so far as He is infinite, but in so far as He is manifested through the nature of the human mind, or in so far as He forms the essence of the human mind; and when we say that God has this or that idea, not merely in so far as He forms the nature of the human mind, but in so far as He has at the same time with the human mind the idea also of another thing, then we say that the human mind perceives the thing partially or inadequately.

Note. At this point many of my readers will no doubt stick fast, and will think of many things which will cause delay; and I therefore beg of them to advance slowly, step by step, with me, and not to pronounce judgment until they shall have read everything which I have to say.

PROPOSITION 13. *The object of the idea constituting the human mind is a body, or a certain mode of extension actually existing, and nothing else.*

Corollary. Hence it follows that man is composed of mind and body, and that the human body exists as we perceive it.

Note. Hence we see not only that the human mind is united to the body, but also what is to be understood by the union of the mind and body. But no one can understand it adequately or distinctly without knowing adequately beforehand the nature of our body; for those things which we have proved hitherto are altogether general, nor do they refer more to man than to other individuals, all of which are animate, although in different degrees. For of everything there necessarily exists in God an idea of which He is the cause, in the same way as the idea of the human body exists in Him; and therefore everything that we have said of the idea of the human body is necessarily true of the idea of any other thing. We cannot, however, deny that ideas, like objects themselves, differ from one another, and that one is more excellent and contains more reality than another, just as the object of one idea is more excellent and contains more reality than another. Therefore, in order to determine the difference between the human mind and other things and its superiority over them, we must first know, as we have said, the nature of its object, that is to say, the nature of the human body. I am not able to explain it here, nor is such an explanation necessary for what I wish to demonstrate.

[Spinoza introduces at this point a short section on the fundamental properties of bodies, or physical objects, their motions and parts. The section ends with six postulates, or assumptions, about the human body, which are used in proving the next series of theorems about the relation between mind and body. When the body is affected by an external object (by sound-waves or falling bricks), the mind simultaneously forms an idea of that interaction, and this idea involves both the nature of the body and that of the external object (Prop. 16). This idea, or modification of the mind, will remain until excluded by an incompatible idea (Prop. 17); whence arise the persistence of images and the mind's capability of contemplating things that do not exist as if they were actually present (such as images of people long dead, or of mythological monsters that never existed). This makes error possible (Note to Prop. 17). Spinoza also explains the association of ideas (Prop. 18).

The next dozen propositions concern the limitations of human knowledge: the mind, in the ordinary course of life, does not have adequate knowledge of itself, of the body, or of external objects, but only confused knowledge of them (Prop. 29, Corol. and Note). Yet there is a basis for the possibility of such adequate knowledge in the fact that God possesses a perfectly adequate idea of the human mind, which in Him is united to his adequate idea of the human body (Props. 20, 21).]

PROPOSITION 32. *All ideas, in so far as they are related to God, are true.*

Demonstration. All the ideas which are in God always agree with those things of which they are the ideas (Part II, Prop. 7, Corol.), and therefore (Part I, Ax. VI) they are all true.—Q.E.D.

PROPOSITION 33. *In ideas there is nothing positive on account of which they are called false.*

Demonstration. If the contrary be asserted, conceive, if it be possible, a positive mode of thought which shall constitute the form or error of falsity. This mode of thought cannot be in God (Part II, Prop. 32), but outside God it can neither be nor be conceived (Part I, Prop. 15), and therefore in ideas there is nothing positive on account of which they are called false.—Q.E.D.

PROPOSITION 34. *Every idea which in us is absolute, that is to say, adequate and perfect, is true.*

Demonstration. When we say that an adequate and perfect idea is in us, we say nothing else than (Part II, Prop. 11, Corol.) that an adequate and perfect idea exists in God in so far as He constitutes the essence of the human mind, and consequently (Part II, Prop. 32) we say nothing else than that this idea is true.—Q.E.D.

PROPOSITION 35. *Falsity consists in the privation of knowledge, which inadequate, that is to say, mutilated and confused ideas involve.*

Demonstration. There is nothing positive in ideas which can constitute a form of falsity (Part II, Prop. 33). But falsity cannot consist in absolute privation (for we say that minds and not bodies err and are mistaken); nor can it consist in absolute ignorance, for to be ignorant and to be in error are different. Falsehood, therefore, consists in the privation of knowledge which is involved by inadequate knowledge of things or by inadequate and confused ideas.—Q.E.D.

Note. In Part II, Prop. 17, Note, I have explained how error consists in the privation of knowledge; but for the sake of fuller explanation I will give an example. For instance, men are deceived because they think themselves free, and the sole reason for thinking so is that they are conscious of their own actions, and ignorant of the causes by which those actions are determined. Their idea of liberty therefore is this—that they know no cause for their own actions; for as to saying that their actions depend upon their will, these are words to which no idea is attached. What the will is, and in what manner it moves the body, everyone is ignorant, for those who pretend otherwise, and devise seats and dwelling-places of the soul, usually excite our laughter or disgust. Just in the same manner, when we look at the sun, we imagine his distance from us to be about 200 feet; the error not consisting solely in the imagination, but arising from our not knowing what the true distance is when we imagine, and what are the causes of our imagination. For although we may afterwards know that the sun is more than 600 diameters of the earth distant from us, we still imagine it near us, since we imagine it to be so near, not because we are ignorant of its true distance, but because a modification of our body involves the essence of the sun in so far as our body itself is affected by it.

PROPOSITION 36. *Inadequate and confused ideas follow by the same necessity as adequate or clear and distinct ideas.*

PROPOSITION 38. *Those things which are common to everything, and which are equally in the part and in the whole, can only be adequately conceived.*

Corollary. Hence it follows that some ideas or notions exist which are common to all men, for (Lem. 2)[1] all bodies agree in some things, which (Part II, Prop. 38) must be adequately, that is to say, clearly and distinctly, perceived by all.

PROPOSITION 40. *Those ideas are also adequate which follow in the mind from ideas which are adequate in it.*

Note 1. Not to omit anything which is necessary for us to know, I will briefly give the causes from which terms called *transcendental*, such as *being, thing, something,* have taken their origin. These terms have arisen because the human body, inasmuch as it is limited, can form distinctly in itself only a certain number of images at once. (For the explanation of the word *image* see Part II, Prop. 17, Note.)

---

[1] [Lemma 2 (here omitted) is proved from Def. I of Part II.—M.C.B.]

If this number be exceeded, the images will become confused; and if the number of images which the body is able to form distinctly be greatly exceeded, they will all run one into another. Since this is so, it is clear (Part II, Props. 17, Corol., and 18) that in proportion to the number of images which can be formed at the same time in the body will be the number of bodies which the human mind can imagine at the same time. If the images in the body, therefore, are all confused, the mind will confusedly imagine all the bodies without distinguishing the one from the other, and will include them all, as it were, under one attribute—that of "being" or "thing." The same confusion may also be caused by lack of uniform force in the images and from other analogous causes, which there is no need to discuss here, the consideration of one cause being sufficient for the purpose we have in view. For it all comes to this, that these terms signify ideas in the highest degree confused. It is in this way that those notions have arisen which are called *universal,* such as, *man, horse, dog*; that is to say, so many images of men, for instance, are formed in the human body at once that they exceed the power of the imagination, not entirely, but to such a degree that the mind has no power to imagine the determinate number of men and the small differences of each, such as color and size. It will therefore distinctly imagine only that in which all of them agree in so far as the body is affected by them, for by that the body was chiefly affected, that is to say, by each individual, and this it will express by the name "man," covering thereby an infinite number of individuals; to imagine a determinate number of individuals being out of its power. But we must observe that these notions are not formed by all persons in the same way, but that they vary in each case according to the thing by which the body is more frequently affected, and which the mind more easily imagines or recollects. For example, those who have more frequently looked with admiration upon the stature of men, by the name "man" will understand an animal of erect stature, while those who have been in the habit of fixing their thoughts on something else will form another common image of men, describing man, for instance, as an animal capable of laughter, a biped without feathers, a rational animal, and so on—each person forming universal images of things according to the temperament of his own body. It is not, therefore, to be wondered at that so many controversies have arisen among those philosophers who have endeavored to explain natural objects by the images of things alone.

Note 2. From what has been already said, it clearly appears that we perceive many things and form universal ideas:

1a. From individual things, represented by the senses to us in a mutilated and confused manner and without order to the intellect (Part II, Prop. 29, Corol.). These perceptions I have therefore been in the habit of calling knowledge from vague experience.

1b. From signs; as, for example, when we hear or read certain words, we recollect things and form certain ideas of them similar to them, through which ideas we imagine things (Part II, Prop. 18, Note).

These two ways of looking at things I shall hereafter call knowledge of the first kind, opinion, or imagination.

2. From our possessing common notions and adequate ideas of the properties of things (Part II, Props. 38, Corol., 39, with Corol., and 40). This I shall call reason and knowledge of the second kind.

Besides these two kinds of knowledge, there is a third, as I shall hereafter show, which we shall call intuitive science. This kind of knowing advances from an adequate idea of the formal essence of certain attributes of God to the adequate knowledge of the essence of things. All this I will explain by one example. Let there be three numbers given through which it is required to discover a fourth which shall be to the third as the second is to the first. A merchant does not hesitate to multiply the second and third together and divide the product by the first, either because he has not yet forgotten the things which he heard without any demonstration from his schoolmaster, or because he has seen the truth of the rule with the more simple numbers, or because from the 19th Prop. in the 7th book of Euclid he understands the common property of all proportionals.

But with the simplest numbers there is no need of all this. If the numbers 1, 2, 3, for instance, be given, everyone can see, much more clearly than by any demonstration that the fourth proportional is 6, because from the ratio in which we see by one intuition that the first stands to the second we conclude the fourth.

PROPOSITION 41. *Knowledge of the first kind alone is the cause of falsity; knowledge of the second and third orders is necessarily true.*

PROPOSITION 43. *He who has a true idea knows at the same time that he has a true idea, nor can he doubt the truth of the thing.*

Note. . . . Then, again, what can be clearer or more certain than a true idea as the standard of truth? Just as light reveals both itself and the darkness, so truth is the standard of itself and of the false. I consider what has been said to be a sufficient answer to the objection that if a true idea is distinguished from a false idea only in so far as it is said to agree with that of which it is the idea, the true idea therefore has no reality or perfection above the false idea (since they are distinguished by an external sign only), and consequently the man who has true ideas will have no greater reality or perfection than he who has false ideas only. I consider, too, that I have already replied to those who inquire why men have false ideas, and how a man can certainly know that he has ideas that agree with those things of which they are the ideas. . . . .

PROPOSITION 44. *It is not of the nature of reason to consider things as contingent but as necessary.*

Corollary 1. Hence it follows that it is through the imagination alone that we look upon things as contingent both with reference to the past and the future.

Corollary 2. It is of the nature of reason to perceive things under a certain form of eternity.

PROPOSITION 45. *Every idea of any body or actually existing individual thing necessarily involves the eternal and infinite essence of God.*

PROPOSITION 47. *The human mind possesses an adequate knowledge of the eternal and infinite essence of God.*

PROPOSITION 48. *In the mind there is no absolute or free will, but the mind is determined to this or that volition by a cause which is also determined by another cause, and this again by another, and so on* ad infinitum.

Demonstration. The mind is a certain and determinate mode of thought (Part II, Prop. 11), and therefore (Part I, Prop. 17, Corol. 2) it cannot be the free cause of its own actions or have an absolute faculty of willing or not willing, but must be determined to this or that volition (Part I, Prop. 28) by a cause which is also determined by another cause, and this again by another, and so on *ad infinitum.* —Q.E.D.

Note. In the same manner it is demonstrated that in the mind there exists no absolute faculty of understanding, desiring, loving, etc. These and the like faculties, therefore, are either altogether fictitious or else are nothing but metaphysical or universal entities which we are in the habit of forming from individual cases. The intellect and will, therefore, are related to this or that idea or volition as rockiness is related to this or that rock, or as man is related to Peter or Paul. The reason why men imagine themselves to be free we have explained in the Appendix to the First Part. Before, however, I advance any further, I must observe that by the "will" I understand a faculty of affirming or denying, but not a desire—a faculty, I say, by which the mind affirms or denies that which is true or false, and not a desire by which the mind seeks a thing or turns away from it. But now that we have demonstrated that these faculties are universal notions which are not distinguishable from the individual notions from which they are formed, we must now inquire whether the volitions themselves are anything more than the ideas of things. We must inquire, in other words, whether in the mind there exists any other affirmation or negation than that which the idea involves in so far as it is an idea. For this purpose see the following proposition, together with Def. III of Part II, so that thought may not fall into pictures. For by "ideas" I do not understand the images which are formed at the back of the eye, or, if you please, in the middle of the brain, but rather the conceptions of thought.

PROPOSITION 49. *In the mind there is no volition or affirmation and negation except that which the idea, in so far as it is an idea, involves.*

Demonstration. In the mind there exists (Part II, Prop. 48) no absolute faculty of willing or not willing. Only individual volitions exist, that is to say, this and that affirmation and this and that negation. Let us conceive, therefore, any individual volition, that is, any mode of thought, by which the mind affirms that the three angles of a triangle are equal to two right angles. This affirmation involves the conception or idea of the triangle, that is to say, without it the affirmation cannot be conceived. For to say that A must involve the conception B is the same as saying that A cannot be conceived without B. Moreover, without the idea of the triangle this affirmation (Part II, Ax. III) cannot be, and it can therefore neither be nor be conceived without that idea. But this idea of the triangle must involve this same affirmation that its three angles are equal to two right angles. Therefore also, *vice versa,* this idea of the triangle without this affirmation can neither be nor be conceived. Therefore (Part II, Def. II) this affirmation pertains to the essence of the idea of the triangle, nor is it anything else besides this. Whatever, too, we have said of this volition (since it has been taken arbitrarily) applies to all other volitions, that is to say, they are nothing but ideas.—Q.E.D.

Corollary. The will and the intellect are one and the same.

Demonstration. The will and the intellect are nothing but the individual volitions and ideas themselves (Part II, Prop. 48, and Note). But the individual volition and idea (Part II, Prop. 49) are one and the same. Therefore the will and the intellect are one and the same.—Q.E.D.

Note. I have thus removed what is commonly thought to be the cause of error. It has been proved above that falsity consists solely in the privation which mutilated and confused ideas involve. A false idea, therefore, in so far as it is false, does not involve certitude. Consequently, when we say that a man assents to what is false and does not doubt it, we do not say that he is certain, but merely that he does not doubt, that is to say, that he assents to what is false because there are no causes sufficient to make his imagination waver (Part II, Prop. 44, Note). Although, therefore, a man may be supposed to adhere to what is false, we shall never on that account say that he is certain. For by "certitude" we understand something positive (Part II, Prop. 43, and Note), and not the privation of doubt; but by the privation of certitude we understand falsity. If the preceding proposition, however, is to be more clearly comprehended, a word or two must be added; it yet remains also that I should answer the objections which may be brought against our doctrine, and finally, in order to remove all scruples, I have thought it worth while to indicate some of its advantages. I say some, as the principal advantages will be better understood when we come to the Fifth Part. I begin, therefore, with the first, and I warn my readers carefully to distinguish between an idea or conception of the mind and the images of things formed by our imagination. Secondly, it is necessary that we should distinguish between ideas and the words by which things are signified. For it is because these three things, images, words, and ideas, are by many people either altogether confounded or not distinguished with sufficient accuracy and care that such ignorance exists about this doctrine of the will, so necessary to be known both for the purposes of speculation and for the wise government of life. Those who think that ideas consist of images which are formed in us by meeting with external bodies persuade themselves that those ideas of things of which we can form no similar image are not ideas, but mere fancies constructed by the free power of the will. They look upon ideas, therefore, as dumb pictures on a tablet and, being prepossessed with this prejudice, they do not see that an idea, in so far as it is an idea, involves affirmation or negation. Again, those who confound words with the idea or with the affirmation itself which the idea involves, think that they can will contrary to their perception because they affirm or deny something in words alone contrary to their perception. It will be easy for us, however, to divest ourselves of these prejudices if we attend to the nature of thought, which in no way involves the conception of extension, and by doing this we clearly see that an idea, since it is a mode of thought, is not an image of anything, nor does it consist of words. For the essence of words and images is formed of bodily motions alone, which involve in no way whatever the conception of thought.

Let this much suffice under this head. I pass on now to the objections to which I have already alluded.

The first is that it is supposed to be certain that the will extends itself more widely than the intellect, and is therefore different from it. The reason why men suppose that the will extends itself more widely than the intellect is because they say they have discovered that they do not need a larger faculty of assent—that is to say, of affirmation —and denial than that which they now have for the purpose of assenting to an infinite number of other things which we do not perceive, but that they do need a greater faculty for understanding them. The will, therefore, is distinguished from the intellect, the latter being finite, the former infinite. The second objection which can be made is that there is nothing which experience seems to teach more clearly than the possibility of suspending our judgment, so as not to assent to the things we perceive; and we are strengthened in this opinion because no one is said to be deceived in so far as he perceives a thing, but only in so far as he assents to it or dissents from it. For example, a man who imagines a winged horse does not therefore admit the existence of a winged horse, that is to say, he is not necessarily deceived unless he grants at the same time that a winged horse exists. Experience, therefore, seems to show nothing more plainly than that the will or faculty of assent is free and different from the faculty of the intellect.

Thirdly, it may be objected that one affirmation does not seem to contain more reality than another, that is to say, it does not appear that we need a greater power for affirming a thing to be true which is true than for affirming a thing to be true which is false. Nevertheless, we observe that one idea contains more reality or perfection than another, for as some objects are nobler than others, in the same proportion are their ideas more perfect. It appears indisputable, therefore, that there is a difference between the will and the intellect.

Fourthly, it may be objected that if a man does not act from freedom of the will, what would he do if he were in a state of equilibrium, like the ass of Buridan? Would he not perish from hunger and thirst? And if this be granted, do we not seem to conceive him as a statue of a man or as an ass? If I deny that he would thus perish, he will consequently determine himself and possess the power of going where he likes and doing what he likes.

There may be other objections besides these, but as I am not bound to discuss what every one may dream, I shall therefore make it my business to answer as briefly as possible only those which I have mentioned. In reply to the first objection, I grant that the will extends itself more widely than the intellect if by the intellect we understand only clear and distinct ideas, but I deny that the will extends itself more widely than the perceptions or the faculty of conception, nor, indeed, do I see why the faculty of will should be said to be infinite any more than the faculty of feeling; for as by the same faculty of will we can affirm an infinite number of things (one after the other, for we cannot affirm an infinite number of things at once), so also by the same faculty of feeling we can feel or perceive (one after another) an infinite number of bodies. If it be said that there are an infinite number of things which we cannot perceive, I reply that such things as these we can reach by no thought, and consequently by no faculty of will. But it is said that if God wished us to perceive those things, it would be necessary for Him to give us a larger faculty of perception, but not a larger faculty of will than He has already given us, which is the same thing as saying that if God wished us to understand an infinite number of other beings, it would be necessary for Him to give us a greater intellect, but not a more universal idea of being (in order to embrace that infinite number of beings) than He has given us. For we have shown that the will is a *universal* or the idea by which we explain all individual volitions, that is to say, that which is common to them all. It is not to be wondered at, therefore, that those who believe this common or universal idea of all the volitions to be a faculty should say that it extends itself infinitely beyond the limits of the intellect. For the universal is predicated of one or of many, or of an infinite number of individuals.

The second objection I answer by denying that we have free power of suspending judgment. For when we say that a person suspends judgment, we only say in other words that he sees that he does not perceive the thing adequately. The suspension of the judgment, therefore, is in truth a perception and not free will. In order that this may be clearly understood, let us take the case of a boy who imagines a horse and perceives nothing else. Since this imagination involves the existence of the horse (Part II, Prop. 17, Corol.), and the boy does not perceive anything which negates its existence, he will necessarily contemplate it as present, nor will he be able to doubt its existence although he may not be certain of it. This is a thing which we daily experience in dreams, nor do I believe that there is any one who thinks that he has the free power during dreams of suspending his judgment upon those things which he dreams, and of causing himself not to dream those things which he dreams that he sees; and yet in dreams it nevertheless happens that we suspend our judgment, for we dream that we dream.

I grant, it is true, that no man is deceived in so far as he perceives, that is to say, I grant that mental images, considered in themselves, involve no error (Part II, Prop. 17, Note), but I deny that a man in so far as he perceives affirms nothing. For what else is it to perceive a winged horse than to affirm of the horse that it has wings? For if the mind perceived nothing else but this winged horse, it would regard it as present, nor would it have any reason for doubting its existence, nor any power of refusing assent to it, unless the image of the winged horse be joined to an idea which negates its existence, or the mind perceives that the idea of the winged horse which it has is inadequate. In either of the two latter cases it will necessarily deny or doubt the existence of the horse.

With regard to the third objection, what has been said will perhaps be a sufficient answer—namely, that the will is something universal, which is predicated of all ideas, and that it signifies that only which is common to them all, that is to say, affirmation. Its adequate essence, therefore, in so far as it is thus considered in the abstract, must be in every idea, and in this sense only must it be the same in all; but not in so far as it is considered as constituting the essence of an idea, for, so far, the individual affirmations differ just as the ideas differ. For example, the affirmation which the idea of a circle involves differs from that which the idea of a triangle involves, just as the idea of a circle differs from the idea of a triangle. Again, I absolutely deny that we need a power of thinking in order to affirm that to be true which is true, equal to that which we need in order to affirm that to be true which is false. For these two affirmations, if we look to the mind, are related to one another as being and non-being, for there is nothing positive in ideas which constitutes a form of falsity (Part II, Prop. 35, and Note, and Prop. 47, Note).

Here, therefore, particularly is it to be observed how easily we are deceived when we confuse universals with individuals, and the entities of reason and abstractions with realities.

With regard to the fourth objection, I say that I entirely grant that if a man were placed in such a state of equilibrium he would perish of hunger and thirst, supposing he perceived nothing but hunger and thirst, and the food and drink which were equidistant from him. If you ask me whether such a man would not be thought an ass rather than a man, I reply that I do not know; nor do I know what ought to be thought of a man who hangs himself, or of children, fools, and madmen.

It remains for me now to show what service to our own lives a knowledge of this doctrine is. This we shall easily understand from the remarks which follow. Notice:

1. It is of service in so far as it teaches us that we do everything by the will of God alone, and that we are partakers of the divine nature in proportion as our actions become more and more perfect and we more and more understand God. This doctrine, therefore, besides giving repose in every way to the soul, has also this advantage that it teaches us in what our highest happiness or blessedness consists, namely, in the knowledge of God alone, by which we are drawn to do those things only which love and piety persuade. Hence we clearly see how greatly those stray from the true estimation of virtue

who expect to be distinguished by God with the highest rewards for virtue and the noblest actions as if for the completest servitude, just as if virtue itself and the service of God were not happiness itself and the highest liberty.

2. It is of service to us in so far as it teaches us how we ought to behave with regard to the things of fortune, or those which are not in our power, that is to say, which do not follow from our own nature; for it teaches us with equal mind to wait for and bear each form of fortune because we know that all things follow from the eternal decree of God, according to that same necessity by which it follows from the essence of a triangle that its three angles are equal to two right angles.

3. This doctrine contributes to the welfare of our social existence, since it teaches us to hate no one, to despise no one, to mock no one, to be angry with no one, and to envy no one. It teaches every one, moreover, to be content with his own, and to be helpful to his neighbor, not from any womanish pity, from partiality, or superstition, but by the guidance of reason alone, according to the demand of time and circumstance, as I shall show in the Third Part.

4. This doctrine contributes not a little to the advantage of common society, in so far as it teaches us by what means citizens are to be governed and led, not in order that they may be slaves, but that they may freely do those things which are best.

Thus I have discharged the obligation laid upon me in this Note, and with it I make an end of the Second Part, in which I think that I have explained the nature of the human mind and its properties at sufficient length, and, considering the difficulties of the subject, with sufficient clearness. I think, too, that certain truths have been established, from which much that is noble, most useful, and necessary to be known, can be deduced, as we shall partly see from what follows.

PART III: ON THE ORIGIN AND NATURE OF THE EMOTIONS

Most persons who have written about the emotions and man's conduct of life seem to discuss, not the natural things which follow the common laws of Nature, but things which are outside her. They seem indeed to consider man in Nature as a kingdom within a kingdom. For they believe that man disturbs rather than follows her order, that he has an absolute power over his own actions, and that he is altogether self-determined. They then proceed to attribute the cause of human weakness and changeableness, not to the common power of Nature, but to some vice of human nature which they therefore bewail, laugh at, mock, or, as is more generally the case, detest; whilst he who knows how to revile most eloquently or subtly the weakness of the mind is looked upon as divine. It is true that very eminent men have not been wanting, to whose labor and industry we confess ourselves much indebted, who have written many excellent things about the right conduct of life, and who have given to mortals counsels full of prudence, but no one, so far as I know, has determined the nature and strength of the emotions, and what the mind is able to do toward controlling them. I remember, indeed, that the celebrated Descartes, although he believed that the mind is absolute master over its own actions, tried nevertheless to explain by their first causes human emotions, and at the same time to show the way by which the mind could obtain absolute power over them; but in my opinion he has shown nothing but the acuteness of his great intellect, as I shall make evident in the proper place, for I wish to return to those who prefer to detest and scoff at human emotions and actions than understand them. To such as these it will doubtless seem a marvelous thing for me to endeavor to treat by a geometrical method the vices and follies of men, and to desire by a sure method to demonstrate those things which these people cry out against as being opposed to reason, or as being vanities, absurdities, and monstrosities. The following is my reason for so doing. Nothing happens in Nature which can be attributed to any vice of Nature, for she is always the same and everywhere one. Her virtue is the same, and her power of acting, that is to say, her laws and rules, according to which all things are and are changed from form to form, are everywhere and always the same, so that there must also be one and the same method of understanding the nature of all things whatsoever, that is to say, by the universal laws and rules of Nature. The emotions, therefore, of hatred, anger, envy, considered in themselves, follow from the same necessity and virtue of Nature as other individual things; they have therefore certain causes through which they are to be understood, and certain properties which are just as worthy of being known as the properties of any other thing in the contemplation alone of which we delight. I shall, therefore, pursue the same method in considering the nature and strength of the emotions and the power of the mind over them which I pursued in our previous discussion of God and the mind, and I shall consider human actions and appetites just as if I were considering lines, planes, or bodies.

Definitions and Postulates

DEF. I.   I call that an *adequate* cause whose effect can be clearly and distinctly perceived by means of the cause. I call that an *inade-quate* or partial cause whose effect cannot be understood by means of the cause alone.

DEF. II.   I say that we *act* when anything is done, either within us or without us, of which we are the adequate cause, that is to say (by the preceding Def.), when from our nature anything follows. either within us or without us, which by that nature alone can be clearly and distinctly understood. On the other hand, I say that we *suffer* when anything is done within us, or when anything follows from our nature of which we are not the cause except partially.

DEF. III.   By *emotion* I understand the modifications of the body by which the power of acting of the body itself is increased, diminished, helped, or hindered, together with the ideas of these modifications.

If, therefore, we can be the adequate cause of any of these modifications, I understand the emotion to be an action, otherwise it is a passive state.

POST. I.   The human body can be affected in many ways by which its power of acting is increased or diminished, and also in other ways which make its power of acting neither greater nor less.

This postulate or axiom is based upon Post. I and Lemmas 5 and 7, in Part II following Prop. 13.

POST. II.   The human body is capable of suffering many changes, and, nevertheless, can retain the impressions or traces of objects (Part II, Post. 5), and consequently the same images of things. (For the definition of images see Part II, Prop. 17, Note.)

Propositions

PROPOSITION 1.   *Our mind acts at times and at times suffers: in so far as it has adequate ideas, it necessarily acts; and in so far as it has inadequate ideas, it necessarily suffers.*

Demonstration.   In every human mind some ideas are adequate, and others mutilated and confused (Part II, Prop. 40, Note). But the ideas which in any mind are adequate are adequate in God in so far as He forms the essence of that mind (Part II, Prop. 11, Note), while those again which are inadequate in the mind are also adequate in God (by the same Corol.), not in so far as He contains the essence of that mind only, but in so far as He contains the ideas of other things at the same time in Himself. Again, from any given idea some effect must necessarily follow (Part I, Prop. 36), of which God is the adequate cause (Part III, Def. I), not in so far as He is infinite, but in so far as He is considered as affected with the given idea (Part II, Prop. 9). But of that effect of which God is the cause, in so far as He is affected by an idea which is adequate in any mind, that same mind is the adequate cause (Part II, Prop. 11, Corol.). Our mind, therefore (Part III, Def. II), in so far as it has adequate ideas, necessarily at times acts, which is the first thing we had to prove. Again, if there be anything which necessarily follows from an idea which is adequate in God, not in so far as He contains within Himself the mind of one man only, but also, together with this, the ideas of other things, then the mind of that man (Part II, Prop. 11, Corol.) is not the adequate cause of that thing, but is only its partial cause, and therefore (Part II, Def. II), in so far as the mind has inadequate ideas, it necessarily at times suffers. This was the second thing to be proved. Therefore our mind, etc.—Q.E.D.

Corollary. Hence it follows that the mind is subject to passions in proportion to the number of inadequate ideas which it has, and that it acts in proportion to the number of adequate ideas which it has.

PROPOSITION 2. *The body cannot determine the mind to thought, neither can the mind determine the body to motion nor rest, nor to anything else if there be anything else.*

Demonstration. All modes of thought have God for a cause in so far as He is a thinking thing, and not in so far as He is manifested by any other attribute (Part II, Prop. 6). That which determines the mind to thought, therefore, is a mode of thought and not of extension, that is to say (Part II, Def. I), it is not the body. This is the first thing which was to be proved. Again, the motion and rest of the body must be derived from some other body, which has also been determined to motion or rest by another, and, absolutely, whatever arises in the body must arise from God, in so far as He is considered as affected by some mode of extension, and not in so far as He is considered as affected by any mode of thought (Part II, Prop. 6), that is to say, whatever arises in the body cannot arise from the mind, which is a mode of thought (Part II, Prop. 11). This is the second thing which was to be proved. Therefore, the body cannot determine, etc.—Q.E.D.

Note. This proposition will be better understood from what has been said in the Note to Prop. 7 of Part II, that is to say, that the mind and the body are one and the same thing, conceived at one time under the attribute of thought, and at another under that of extension. For this reason, the order or concatenation of things is one, whether Nature be conceived under this or under that attribute, and consequently the order of the state of activity and passivity of our body is coincident in Nature with the order of the state of activity and passivity of the mind. This is also plain from the manner in which we have demonstrated Prop. 12 of Part II.

Although these things are so, and no ground for doubting remains, I scarcely believe, nevertheless, that, without a proof derived from experience, men will be induced calmly to weigh what has been said, so firmly are they persuaded that, solely at the bidding of the mind, the body moves or rests, and does a number of things which depend upon the will of the mind alone, and upon the power of thought. For what the body can do no one has hitherto determined, that is to say, experience has taught no one hitherto what the body, without being determined by the mind, can do and what it cannot do from the laws of Nature alone, in so far as nature is considered merely as corporeal. For no one as yet has understood the structure of the body so accurately as to be able to explain all its functions, not to mention the fact that many things are observed in brutes which far surpass human sagacity, and that sleepwalkers in their sleep do very many things which they dare not do when awake—all this showing that the body itself can do many things, from the laws of its own nature alone, at which the mind belonging to that body is amazed. Again, nobody knows by what means or by what method the mind moves the body, nor how many degrees of motion it can communicate to the body, nor with what speed it can move the body. So that it follows that, when men say that this or that action of the body springs from the mind which has command over the body, they do not know what they say, and they do nothing but confess with pretentious words that they know nothing about the cause of the action and see nothing in it to wonder at. But they will say that, whether they know or do not know by what means the mind moves the body, it is nevertheless in their experience that if the mind were not fit for thinking the body would be inert. They say, again, it is in their experience that the mind alone has power both to speak and be silent, and to do many other things which they therefore think to be dependent on a decree of the mind. But with regard to the first assertion, I ask them if experience does not also teach that if the body be sluggish the mind at the same time is not fit for thinking? When the body is asleep, the mind slumbers with it and has not the power to think, as it has when the body is awake. Again, I believe that all have discovered that the mind is not always equally fitted for thinking about the same subject, but in proportion to the fitness of the body for this or that image to be excited in it will the mind be better fitted to contemplate this or that object. But my opponents will say that from the laws of Nature alone, in so far as it is considered to be corporeal merely, it cannot be that the causes of architecture, painting, and things of this sort, which are the results of human art alone, could be deduced, and that the human body, unless it were determined and guided by the mind, would not be able to build a temple. I have already shown, however, that they do not know what the body can do, nor what can be deduced from the consideration of its nature alone, and that they find that many things are done merely by the laws of Nature which they would never have believed to be possible without the direction of the mind, as, for example, those things which sleepwalkers do in their sleep, and at which they themselves are astonished when they wake. I adduce also here the structure itself of the human body, which so greatly surpasses in workmanship all those things which are constructed by human art, not to mention, what I have already proved, that an infinitude of things follows from Nature under whatever attribute it may be considered.

With regard to the second point, I should say that human affairs would be much more happily conducted if it were equally in the power of men to be silent and to speak; but experience shows over and over again that there is nothing which men have less power over than the tongue, and that there is nothing which they are less able to do than to govern their appetites, so that many persons believe that we do those things only with freedom which we seek indifferently, as the desire for such things can easily be lessened by the recollection of another thing which we frequently call to mind; it being impossible, on the other hand, to do those things with freedom which we seek with such ardor that the recollection of another thing is unable to mitigate it. But if, however, we had not found out that we do many things which we afterwards repent, and that when agitated by conflicting emotions we see that which is better and follow that which is worse, nothing would hinder us from believing that we do everything with freedom. Thus the infant believes that it is by free will that it seeks the breast; the angry boy believes that by free will he wishes vengeance; the timid man thinks it is with free will he seeks flight; the drunkard believes that by a free command of his mind he speaks the things which when sober he wishes he had left unsaid. Thus the madman, the chatterer, the boy, and others of the same kind, all believe that they speak by a free command of the mind, whilst, in truth, they have no power to restrain the impulse which they have to speak, so that experience itself, no less than reason, clearly teaches that men believe themselves to be free simply because they are conscious of their own actions, knowing nothing of the causes by which they are determined; it teaches, too, that the decrees of the mind are nothing but the appetites themselves, which differ, therefore, according to the different temper of the body. For every man determines all things from his emotion; those who are agitated by contrary emotions do not know what they want, whilst those who are agitated by no emotion are easily driven hither and thither. All this plainly shows that the decree of the mind, the appetite, and determination of the body are coincident in Nature, or rather that they are one and the same thing which, when it is considered under the attribute of thought and manifested by that, is called a "decree," and when it is considered under the attribute of extension and is deduced from the laws of motion and rest is called a "determination." This, however, will be better understood as we go on, for there is another thing which I wish to be observed here—that we cannot by a mental decree do a thing unless we recollect it. We cannot speak a word, for instance, unless we recollect it. But it is not in the free power of the mind either to recollect a thing or to forget it. It is believed, therefore, that the power of the mind extends only thus far—that from a mental decree we can speak or be silent about a thing only when we recollect it. But when we dream that we speak, we believe that we do so from a free decree of the mind, and yet we do not speak, or, if we do, it is the result of a spontaneous motion of the body. We dream, again, that we are concealing things, and that we do this by virtue of a decree of the mind like that by which, when awake, we are silent about things we know. We dream, again, that, from a decree of the mind, we do some things which we should not dare to do when awake. And I should like to know, therefore, whether there are two kinds of decrees in the mind—one belonging to dreams and the other free. If this be too great nonsense, we must necessarily grant that this decree of the mind which is believed to be free is not distinguishable from the imagination or memory, and is nothing but the affirmation which the idea necessarily involves in so far as it is an idea (Part II, Prop. 49). These decrees of the mind, therefore, arise in the mind by the same necessity as the ideas of things actually existing. Consequently, those who believe that they speak or are silent or do anything else from a free decree of the mind dream with their eyes open.

PROPOSITION 3. *The actions of the mind arise from adequate ideas alone, but the passive states depend upon those alone which are inadequate.*

PROPOSITION 4. *A thing cannot be destroyed except by an external cause.*

PROPOSITION 5. *In so far as one thing is able to destroy another are they of contrary natures, that is to say, they cannot exist in the same subject.*

PROPOSITION 6. *Each thing, in so far as it is in itself, endeavors to persevere in its being.*

Demonstration. Individual things are modes by which the attributes of God are expressed in a certain and determinate manner (Part I, Prop. 25, Corol. 7), that is to say (Part I, Prop. 34), they are things which express in a certain and determinate manner the power of God by which He is and acts. A thing, too, has nothing in itself through which it can be destroyed, or which can negate its existence (Part III, Prop. 4), but, on the contrary, it is opposed to everything which could negate its existence (Part III, Prop. 5). Therefore, in so far as it can, and in so far as it is in itself, it endeavors to persevere in its own being.—Q.E.D.

PROPOSITION 7. *The effort by which each thing endeavors to persevere in its own being is nothing but the actual essence of the thing itself.*

PROPOSITION 9. *The mind, both in so far as it has clear and distinct ideas and in so far as it has confused ideas, endeavors to persevere in its being for an indefinite time, and is conscious of this effort.*

Note. This effort, when it is related to the mind alone, is called "will," but when it is related at the same time both to the mind and the body is called "appetite," which is therefore nothing but the very essence of man, from the nature of which necessarily follow those things which promote his preservation, and thus he is determined to do those things. Hence there is no difference between appetite and desire, unless in this particular that desire is generally related to men in so far as they are conscious of their appetites, and it may therefore be defined as appetite of which we are conscious. From what has been said it is plain, therefore, that we neither strive for, wish, seek, nor desire anything because we think it to be good, but, on the contrary, we adjudge a thing to be good because we strive for, wish, seek, or desire it.

PROPOSITION 11. *If anything increases, diminishes, helps, or limits our body's power of action, the idea of that thing increases, diminishes, helps, or limits our mind's power of thought.*

Note. We thus see that the mind can suffer great changes, and can pass now to a greater and now to a lesser perfection; these passive states explaining to us the emotions of joy and sorrow. By "joy," therefore, in what follows, I shall understand the passive states through which the mind passes to a greater perfection; by "sorrow," on the other hand, the passive states through which it passes to a less perfection. The emotion of joy, related at the same time both to the mind and the body, I call "pleasurable excitement" (*titillatio*) or "cheerfulness"; that of sorrow I call "pain" or "melancholy." It is, however, to be observed that pleasurable excitement and pain are related to a man when one of his parts is affected more than the others; cheerfulness and melancholy, on the other hand, when all parts are equally affected. What the nature of desire is I have explained in the Note to Prop. 9 of Part III; and besides these three—joy, sorrow, and desire—I know of no other primary emotion; the others springing from these, as I shall show in what follows.

PROPOSITION 13. *Whenever the mind imagines those things which lessen or limit the body's power of action, it endeavors as* much as possible to recollect what excludes the existence of these things.

Note. From what has been said we can clearly see what love is and what hatred is. *Love* is nothing but joy accompanied with the idea of an external cause, and *hatred* is nothing but sorrow with the accompanying idea of an external cause. We see, too, that he who loves a thing necessarily endeavors to keep it before him and to preserve it, and, on the other hand, he who hates a thing necessarily endeavors to remove and destroy it. But we shall speak at greater length upon these points in what follows.

PROPOSITION 16. *If we imagine a certain thing to possess something which resembles an object which usually affects the mind with joy or sorrow, although the quality in which the thing resembles the object is not the efficient cause of these emotions, we shall nevertheless, by virtue of the resemblance alone, love or hate the thing.*

PROPOSITION 17. *If we imagine that a thing that usually affects us with the emotion of sorrow has any resemblance to an object which usually affects us equally with a great emotion of joy, we shall at the same time hate the thing and love it.*

Note. This state of mind which arises from two contrary emotions is called "vacillation of the mind." It is related to emotion as doubt is related to the imagination (Part II, Prop. 44, Note).

PROPOSITION 18. *A man is affected by the image of a past or future thing with the same emotion of joy or sorrow as that with which he is affected by the image of a present thing.*

Note 2. From what has now been said we understand the nature of Hope, Fear, Confidence, Despair, Gladness, Remorse. *Hope* is nothing but unsteady joy, arising from the image of a future or past thing about whose issue we are in doubt. *Fear,* on the other hand, is an unsteady sorrow, arising from the image of a doubtful thing. If the doubt be removed from these emotions, then hope and fear become *confidence* and *despair,* that is to say, joy or sorrow, arising from the image of a thing for which we have hoped or which we have feared. *Gladness,* again, is joy arising from the image of a past thing whose

issues we have doubted. *Remorse* is the sorrow which is opposed to gladness.

PROPOSITION 27. *Although we may not have been moved toward a thing by any emotion, yet if it is like ourselves, whenever we imagine it to be affected by any emotion, we are affected by the same.*

Note to Prop. 29. This effort to do some things and omit doing others, solely because we wish to please men, is called "ambition," especially if our desire to please the common people is so strong that our actions or omissions to act are accompanied with injury to ourselves or to others. Otherwise this endeavor is usually called "humanity." Again, the joy with which we imagine another person's action, the purpose of which is to delight us, I call "praise," and the sorrow with which we turn away from an action of a contrary kind I call "blame."

PROPOSITION 30. *If a person has done anything which he imagines will affect others with joy, he also will be affected with joy, accompanied with an idea of himself as its cause, that is to say, he will look upon himself with joy. If, on the other hand, he has done anything which he imagines will affect others with sorrow, he will look upon himself with sorrow.*

Demonstration. He who imagines that he affects others with joy or sorrow will necessarily be affected with joy or sorrow (Part III, Prop. 27). But since man is conscious of himself (Part II, Props. 19 and 23) by means of the modifications by which he is determined to act, therefore he who has done anything which he imagines will affect others with joy will be affected with joy accompanied with a consciousness of himself as its cause, that is to say, he will look upon himself with joy, and, on the other hand, etc.—Q.E.D.

Note. Since love (Part III, Prop. 13, Note) is joy attended with the idea of an external cause, and hatred is sorrow attended with the idea of an external cause, the joy and sorrow spoken of in this proposition will be a kind of love and hatred. But because love and hatred are related to external objects, we will therefore give a different name to the emotions which are the subject of this proposition, and we will call this kind of joy which is attended with the idea of an external

cause "self-exaltation," and the sorrow opposed to it we will call "shame."

PROPOSITION 39. *If a man hates another he will endeavor to do him evil unless he fears a greater evil will therefore arise to himself; and, on the other hand, he who loves another will endeavor to do him good by the same rule.*

Note. By "good" I understand here every kind of joy and everything that conduces to it, chiefly, however, anything that satisfies longing, whatever that thing may be. By "evil" I understand every kind of sorrow, and chiefly whatever thwarts longing. For we have shown above (Part III, Prop. 9, Note) that we do not desire a thing because we adjudge it to be good, but, on the contrary, we call it good because we desire it, and, consequently, everything to which we are averse we call evil. Each person, therefore, according to his emotion judges or estimates what is good and what is evil, what is better and what is worse, and what is the best and what is the worst. Thus the covetous man thinks plenty of money to be the best thing and poverty the worst. The ambitious man desires nothing like glory, and on the other hand dreads nothing like shame. To the envious person, again, nothing is more pleasant than the misfortune of another, and nothing more disagreeable than the prosperity of another. And so each person according to his emotion judges a thing to be good or evil, useful or useless.

PROPOSITION 43. *Hatred is increased through return of hatred, but may be destroyed by love.*

Demonstration. If we imagine that the person we hate is affected with hatred toward us, a new hatred is thereby produced (Part III, Prop. 40), the old hatred still remaining (by hypothesis). If, on the other hand, we imagine him to be affected with love toward us, in so far as we imagine it (Part III, Prop. 30) shall we look upon ourselves with joy and endeavor (Part III, Prop. 29) to please him, that is to say (Part III, Prop. 41), in so far shall we endeavor not to hate him nor to affect him with sorrow. This effort (Part III, Prop. 37) will be greater or less as the emotion from which it arises is greater or less, and, therefore, should it be greater than that which springs from hatred, and by which (Part III, Prop. 26) we endeavor to affect with

sorrow the object we hate, then it will prevail and banish hatred from the mind.—Q.E.D.

PROPOSITION 46. *If we have been affected with joy or sorrow by any one who belongs to a class or nation different from our own, and if our joy or sorrow is accompanied with the idea of this person as its cause, under the common name of his class or nation, we shall not love or hate him merely, but the whole of the class or nation to which he belongs.*

Demonstration. This proposition is demonstrated in the same way as Prop. 16 of Part III.

PROPOSITION 49. *For the same reason, love or hatred toward an object we imagine to be free must be greater than toward an object which is under necessity.*

Demonstration. An object which we imagine to be free must (Part I, Def. VII) be perceived through itself and without others. If, therefore, we imagine it to be the cause of joy or sorrow, we shall for that reason alone love or hate it (Part III, Prop. 13, Note), and that, too, with the greatest love or the greatest hatred which can spring from the given emotion (Part III, Prop. 48). But if we imagine that the object which is the cause of that emotion is necessary, then (by the same Def. VII) we shall imagine it as the cause of that emotion, not alone, but together with other causes, and so (Part III, Prop. 48) our love or hatred toward it will be less.—Q.E.D.

Note. Hence it follows that our hatred or love toward one another is greater than toward other things because we think we are free. We must take into account also the imitation of emotions which we have discussed in Part III, Props. 27, 34, 40, and 43.

PROPOSITION 56. *Of joy, sorrow, and desire, and consequently of every emotion which either, like vacillation of mind, is compounded of these or, like love, hatred, hope, and fear, is derived from them, there are just as many kinds as there are kinds of objects by which we are affected.*

Demonstration. Joy and sorrow, and consequently the emotions which are compounded of these or derived from them, are passive states (Part III, Prop. 11, Note). But (Part III, Prop. 1) we necessarily suffer in so far as we have inadequate ideas, and (Part III, Prop. 3) only in so far as we have them; that is to say (see Part II, Prop. 40, Note), we necessarily suffer only in so far as we imagine, or (see Part II, Prop. 17, and Note) in so far as we are affected with an emotion which involves the nature of our body and that of an external body. The nature, therefore, of each passive state must necessarily be explained in such a manner that the nature of the object by which we are affected is expressed. The joy, for example, which springs from an object A involves the nature of that object A, and the joy which springs from B involves the nature of that object B and therefore these two emotions of joy are of a different nature because they arise from causes of a different nature. In like manner the emotion of sorrow which arises from one object is of a different kind from that which arises from another cause, and the same thing is to be understood of love, hatred, hope, fear, vacillation of mind, etc., so that there are necessarily just as many kinds of joy, sorrow, love, hatred, etc., as there are kinds of objects by which we are affected. But desire is the essence itself or nature of a person in so far as this nature is conceived from its given constitution as determined toward any action (Part III, Prop. 9, Note), and, therefore, as a person is affected by external causes with this or that kind of joy, sorrow, love, hatred, etc., that is to say, as his nature is constituted in this or that way, so must his desire vary and the nature of one desire differ from that of another, just as the emotions from which each desire arises differ. There are as many kinds of desires, therefore, as there are kinds of joy, sorrow, love, etc., and, consequently (as we have just shown), as there are kinds of objects by which we are affected.—Q.E.D.

PROPOSITION 57. *The emotion of one person differs from the corresponding emotion of another as much as the essence of the one person differs from that of the other.*

[In the theorems of Part III, of which only a sample of the most important have been given here, Spinoza aims to prove exactly how the mind behaves emotionally. He regards an understanding of these laws as essential for the next step, which is to discover (in Parts IV and V) what can be done with this understanding. Part III concludes with an elaborate set of "Definitions of the Emotions," in which many emotions are analyzed with subtlety. Spinoza then gives his "general definition of the emotions": An emotion is a "confused idea by which the mind affirms of its body, or any part of it, a greater or less power of existence than before; and this increase of power being given, the mind itself is determined to one particular thought rather than to another." This definition is clarified in the following passage.]

Explanation. I say, in the first place, that an emotion or passion of the mind *is a confused idea.* For we have shown (Part III, Prop. 3), that the mind suffers only in so far as it has inadequate or confused ideas. I say again, *by which the mind affirms of its body, or any part of it, a greater or less power of existence than before.* For all ideas which we possess of bodies indicate the actual constitution of our body rather than the nature of the external body (Part II, Prop. 16, Corol. 2); but this idea which constitutes the reality of an emotion must indicate or express the constitution of the body or of some part of it; which constitution the body or any part of it possesses from the fact that its power of action or force of existence is increased or diminished, helped or limited. But it is to be observed that when I say "a greater or less power of existence than before," I do not mean that the mind compares the present with the past constitution of the body, but that the idea which constitutes the reality of an emotion affirms something of the body which actually involves more or less reality than before. Moreover, since the essence of the mind (Part II, Props. 11 and 13) consists in its affirmation of the actual existence of its body, and since we understand by perfection the essence itself of the thing, it follows that the mind passes to a greater or less perfection when it is able to affirm of its body, or some part of it, something which involves a greater or less reality than before. When, therefore, I have said that the mind's power of thought is increased or diminished, I have wished to be understood as meaning nothing else but that the mind has formed an idea of its body, or some part of its body, which expresses more or less reality than it had hitherto affirmed of the body. For the value of ideas and the actual power of thought are measured by the value of the object. Finally, I added, *which being given, the mind itself is determined to one particular thought rather than to another,* that I might also express the nature of desire in addition to that of joy and sorrow, which is explained by the first part of the definition.

PART IV: OF HUMAN BONDAGE;
OR OF THE STRENGTH OF THE EMOTIONS

Preface

The impotence of man to govern or restrain the emotions I call "bond·
age," for a man who is under their control is not his own master,
but is mastered by fortune, in whose power he is, so that he is often
forced to follow the worse, although he sees the better before him. I
propose in this part to demonstrate why this is, and also to show
what of good and evil the emotions possess. But before I begin I
should like to say a few words about perfection and imperfection, and
about good and evil. If a man has proposed to do a thing and has
accomplished it, he calls it perfect, and not only he, but every one
else who has really known or has believed that he has known the
mind and intention of the author of that work will call it perfect too.
For example, having seen some work (which I suppose to be as yet
not finished), if we know that the intention of the author of that work
is to build a house, we shall call the house imperfect; while, on the
other hand, we shall call it perfect as soon as we see the work has
been brought to the end which the author had determined for it. But
if we see any work such as we have never seen before, and if we do
not know the mind of the workman, we shall then not be able to say
whether the work is perfect or imperfect. This seems to have been the
first signification of these words; but afterwards men began to form
universal ideas—to think out for themselves types of houses, buildings, castles, and to prefer some types of things to others; and so it
happened that each person called a thing perfect which seemed to
agree with the universal idea which he had formed of that thing, and,
on the other hand, he called a thing imperfect which seemed to agree
less with his typal conception, although, according to the intention of
the workman, it had been entirely completed. This appears to be the
only reason why the words "perfect" and "imperfect" are commonly
applied to natural objects which are not made with human hands; for
men are in the habit of forming, both of natural as well as of artificial
objects, universal ideas which they regard as types of things, and
which they think Nature has in view, setting them before herself as
types, too; it being the common opinion that she does nothing except for the sake of some end. When, therefore, men see something

done by Nature which does not altogether answer to that typal conception which they have of the thing, they think that Nature herself has failed or committed an error, and that she has left the thing imperfect. Thus we see that the custom of applying the words "perfect" and "imperfect" to natural objects has arisen rather from prejudice than from true knowledge of them. For we have shown in the Appendix to the First Part of this work that Nature does nothing for the sake of an end, for that eternal and infinite Being whom we call God or Nature acts by the same necessity by which He exists; for we have shown that He acts by the same necessity of Nature as that by which He exists (Part I, Prop. 16). The reason or cause, therefore, why God or Nature acts and the reason why He exists are one and the same. Since, therefore, He exists for no end, He acts for no end; and since He has no principle or end of existence, He has no principle or end of action. A final cause, as it is called, is nothing, therefore, but human desire, in so far as this is considered as the principle or primary cause of anything. For example, when we say that having a house to live in was the final cause of this or that house, we merely mean that a man, because he imagined the advantages of a domestic life, desired to build a house. Therefore, having a house to live in, in so far as it is considered as a final cause, is merely this particular desire, which is really an efficient cause, and is considered as primary because men are usually ignorant of the causes of their desires; for, as I have often said, we are conscious of our actions and desires, but ignorant of the causes by which we are determined to desire anything. As for the vulgar opinion that Nature sometimes fails or commits an error, or produces imperfect things, I class it amongst those fictions mentioned in the Appendix to the First Part.

Perfection, therefore, and imperfection are really only modes of thought, that is to say, notions which we are in the habit of forming from the comparison with one another of individuals of the same species or genus, and this is the reason why I have said, in Part II, Def. VI, that I understand reality and perfection to be the same thing; for we are in the habit of referring all individuals in Nature to one genus which is called the most general, that is to say, to the notion of being, which embraces absolutely all the individual objects in Nature. In so far, therefore, as we refer the individual objects in Nature to this genus and compare them one with another, and discover that some possess more being or reality than others, in so far do we call some more perfect than others; and in so far as we assign to the latter anything which, like limitation, termination, impotence, etc., involves negation, shall we call them imperfect because they do not affect our minds so strongly as those we call perfect, but not because anything which really belongs to them is wanting, or because Nature has committed an error. For nothing belongs to the nature of anything except that which follows from the necessity of the nature of the efficient cause, and whatever follows from the necessity of the nature of the efficient cause necessarily happens.

With regard to good and evil, these terms indicate nothing positive in things, considered in themselves, nor are they anything more than modes of thought, or notions which we form from the comparison of one thing with another. For one and the same thing may at the same time be both good and evil or indifferent. Music, for example, is good to a melancholy person, bad to one mourning, while to a deaf man it is neither good nor bad. But although things are so, we must retain these words. For since we desire to form for ourselves an idea of man upon which we may look as a model of human nature, it will be of service to us to retain these expressions in the sense I have mentioned. By "good," therefore, I understand in the following pages everything which we are certain is a means by which we may approach nearer and nearer to the model of human nature we set before us. By "evil," on the contrary, I understand everything which we are certain hinders us from reaching that model. Again, I shall call men more or less perfect or imperfect in so far as they approach more or less nearly to this same model. For it is to be carefully observed that when I say that an individual passes from a less to a greater perfection and *vice versa,* I do not understand that from one essence or form he is changed into another (for a horse, for instance, would be as much destroyed if it were changed into a man as if it were changed into an insect), but rather we conceive that his power of action, in so far as it is understood by his own nature, is increased or diminished. Finally, by "perfection" generally, I understand as I have said, reality, that is to say, the essence of any object in so far as it exists and acts in a certain manner, no regard being paid to its duration. For no individual thing can be said to be more perfect because for a longer time it has persevered in existence; inasmuch as the duration of things cannot be determined by their essence, the essence of things involving no fixed or determined period of existence; any object, whether it be more or less perfect, always being able to persevere in existence with the same force as that with which it commenced existence. All things, therefore, are equal in this respect.

Definitions

I. By *good* I understand that which we certainly know is useful to us.

II. By *evil,* on the contrary, I understand that which we certainly know hinders us from possessing anything that is good.

With regard to these two definitions, see the close of the preceding preface.

III. I call individual things *contingent* in so far as we discover nothing whilst we attend to their essence alone, which necessarily posits their existence or which necessarily excludes it.

IV. I call these individual things *possible,* in so far as we are ignorant, whilst we attend to the causes from which they must be produced, whether these causes are determined to the production of these things. In Part I, Prop. 33, Note 1, I made no distinction between possible and contingent because there was no occasion there to distinguish them accurately.

V. By *contrary emotions* I understand in the following pages those which, although they may be of the same kind, draw a man in different directions; such as voluptuousness and avarice, which are both a species of love, and are not contrary to one another by nature, but only by accident.

VI. What I understand by emotion felt toward a thing future, present, and past, I have explained in Part III, Prop. 18, Notes 1 and 2, to which the reader is referred.

Here, however, it is to be observed that it is the same with time as it is with place; for as beyond a certain limit we can form no distinct imagination of distance, that is to say, as we usually imagine all objects to be equally distant from us, and as if they were on the same plane, if their distance from us exceeds 200 feet, or if their distance from the position we occupy is greater than we can distinctly imagine —so we imagine all objects to be equally distant from the present time, and refer them as if to one moment, if the period to which their existence belongs is separated from the present by a longer interval than we can usually imagine distinctly.

VII. By *end* for the sake of which we do anything, I understand appetite.

VIII. By *virtue* and *power* I understand the same thing, that is to say (Part III. Prop. 7). virtue, in so far as it is related to man, is the essence itself or nature of the man in so far as it has the power of effecting certain things which can be understood through the laws of that nature alone.

Axiom

There is no individual thing in Nature which is not surpassed in strength and power by some other thing, but any individual thing being given, another and a stronger is also given by which the former can be destroyed.

Propositions

PROPOSITION 2. *We suffer in so far as we are a part of Nature, which part cannot be conceived by itself nor without the other parts.*

PROPOSITION 3. *The force by which man perseveres in existence is limited, and infinitely surpassed by the power of external causes.*

PROPOSITION 8. *Knowledge of good or evil is nothing but an emotion of joy or sorrow in so far as we are conscious of it.*

Note to Prop. 17. In these propositions I consider that I have explained why men are more strongly influenced by an opinion than by true reason, and why the true knowledge of good and evil causes disturbance in the mind, and often gives way to every kind of lust, whence the saying of the poet, *"Video meliora proboque, deteriora sequor."* [1] The same thought appears to have been in the mind of the Preacher when he said, "He that increaseth knowledge increaseth sorrow." [2] I say these things not because I would be understood to conclude, therefore, that it is better to be ignorant than to be wise, or that the wise man in governing his passions is nothing better than the fool, but I say them because it is necessary for us to know both the strength and weakness of our nature, so that we may determine what reason can do and what it cannot do in governing our emotions. This moreover, let it be remembered, is the Part in which I meant to treat of human weakness alone, all consideration of the power of reason over the passions being reserved for a future portion of the book.

PROPOSITION 18. *The desire which springs from joy, other things being equal, is stronger than that which springs from sorrow.*

---

[1] [I see a better course, and I approve; yet follow I the worse. Ovid, *Metamorphoses,* Bk. VIII (Jason and Medea), I.20.—M.C.B.]
[2] [Ecclesiastes I:18.—M.C.B.]

Note. I have thus briefly explained the causes of human impotence and want of stability, and why men do not obey the dictates of reason. It remains for me now to show what it is which reason prescribes to us, which emotions agree with the rules of human reason, and which, on the contrary, are opposed to these rules. Before, however, I begin to demonstrate these things by our full geometrical method, I should like briefly to set forth here these dictates of reason in order that what I have in my mind about them may be easily comprehended by all. Since reason demands nothing which is opposed to nature, it demands, therefore, that every person should love himself, should seek his own profit—what is truly profitable to him—should desire everything that really leads man to greater perfection, and absolutely that every one should endeavor, as far as in him lies, to preserve his own being. This is all true as necessarily as that the whole is greater than its part (Part III, Prop. 6). Again, since virtue (Part IV, Def. VIII) means nothing but acting according to the laws of our own nature, and since no one endeavors to preserve his being (Part III, Prop. 7) except in accordance with the laws of his own nature, it follows: *First,* that the foundation of virtue is that endeavor itself to preserve our own being, and that happiness consists in this—that a man can preserve his own being. *Secondly,* it follows that virtue is to be desired for its own sake, nor is there anything more excellent or more useful to us than virtue, for the sake of which virtue ought to be desired. *Thirdly,* it follows that all persons who kill themselves are impotent in mind, and have been thoroughly overcome by external causes opposed to their nature. Again, from Part II, Post. IV, it follows that we can never free ourselves from the need of something outside us for the preservation of our being, and that we can never live in such a manner as to have no intercourse with objects which are outside us. Indeed, so far as the mind is concerned, our intellect would be less perfect if the mind were alone and understood nothing but itself. There are many things, therefore, outside us which are useful to us, and which, therefore, are to be sought. Of all these, none more excellent can be discovered than those which exactly agree with our nature. If, for example, two individuals of exactly the same nature are joined together, they make up a single individual, doubly stronger than each alone. Nothing, therefore, is more useful to man than man. Men can desire, I say, nothing more excellent for the preservation of their being than that all should so agree at every point that the minds and bodies of all should form, as it were, one mind and one body; that all should together endeavor as much as possible to preserve their being, and that all should together seek the common good of all. From this it follows that men who are governed by reason, that is to say, men who, under the guidance of reason, seek their own profit, desire nothing for themselves which they do not desire for other men, and that, therefore, they are just, faithful, and honorable.

These are those dictates of reason which I purposed briefly to set forth before commencing their demonstration by a fuller method, in order that, if possible, I might win the attention of those who believe that this principle—that every one is bound to seek his own profit—is the foundation of impiety, and not of virtue and piety. Having now briefly shown that this belief of theirs is the contrary of the truth, I proceed, by the same method as that which we have hitherto pursued, to demonstrate what I have said.

PROPOSITION 19.   *According to the laws of his own nature each person necessarily desires that which he considers to be good, and avoids that which he considers to be evil.*

PROPOSITION 20.   *The more each person strives and is able to seek his own profit, that is to say, to preserve his being, the more virtue does he possess; on the other hand, in so far as each person neglects his own profit, that is to say, neglects to preserve his own being, is he impotent.*

PROPOSITION 23.   *A man cannot be absolutely said to act in conformity with virtue, in so far as he is determined to any action because he has inadequate ideas, but only in so far as he is determined because he understands.*

PROPOSITION 24.   *To act absolutely in conformity with virtue is, in us, nothing but acting, living, and preserving our being (these three things have the same meaning) as reason directs, from the ground of seeking our own profit.*

PROPOSITION 28.   *The highest good of the mind is the knowledge of God, and the highest virtue of the mind is to know God.*

PROPOSITION 32.   *In so far as men are subject to passions, they cannot be said to agree in nature.*

PROPOSITION 35. *So far as men live in conformity with the guidance of reason, in so far only do they always necessarily agree in nature.*

PROPOSITION 36. *The highest good of those who follow after virtue is common to all, and all may equally enjoy it.*

PROPOSITION 37. *The good which every one who follows after virtue seeks for himself he will desire for other men; and his desire on their behalf will be greater in proportion as he has a greater knowledge of God.*

Note 2. In the Appendix to the First Part I promised I would explain what are praise and blame, merit and crime, justice and injustice. I have already shown what is the meaning of praise and blame in Part III, Prop. 29, Note, and this will be a fitting place for the explanation of the rest. A few words must, however, first be said about the natural and civil state of man.

It is by the highest right of Nature that each person exists, and consequently it is by the highest right of Nature that each person does those things which follow from the necessity of his nature; and therefore it is by the highest right of Nature that each person judges what is good and what is evil, consults his own advantage as he thinks best (Part IV, Props. 19 and 20), avenges himself (Part III, Prop. 40, Corol. 2), and endeavors to preserve what he loves and to destroy what he hates (Part III, Prop. 28). If men lived according to the guidance of reason, everyone would enjoy this right without injuring any one else (Part IV, Prop. 35, Corol. 1). But because men are subject to emotions (Part IV, Prop. 4, Corol.), which far surpass human power or virtue (Part IV, Prop. 6), they are often drawn in different directions (Part IV, Prop. 33), and are contrary to one another (Part IV, Prop. 34), although they need one another's help (Part IV, Prop. 35, Note).

In order, then, that men may be able to live in harmony and be a help to one another, it is necessary for them to cede their natural right, and beget confidence in one another that they will do nothing by which one can injure the other. In what manner this can be done, so that men who are necessarily subject to emotions (Part IV, Prop. 4, Corol.), and are uncertain and changeable (Part IV, Prop. 33), can beget confidence in one another and have faith in one another, is evident from Part IV, Prop. 7 and Part III, Prop. 39. It is there shown that no emotion can be restrained unless by a stronger and contrary emotion, and that every one abstains from doing an injury through fear of a greater injury. By this law, therefore, can society be strengthened, if only it claims for itself the right which every individual possesses of avenging himself and deciding what is good and what is evil, and provided, therefore, that it possess the power of prescribing a common rule of life, of promulgating laws and supporting them, not by reason, which cannot restrain the emotions (Part IV, Prop. 17, Note), but by penalties.

This society, firmly established by law and with a power of self-preservation, is called a "State," and those who are protected by its right are called "citizens." We can now easily see that in the natural state there is nothing which by universal consent is good or evil, since everyone in a natural state consults only his own profit, deciding according to his own way of thinking what is good and what is evil with reference only to his own profit, and is not bound by any law to obey anyone but himself. Hence in a natural state sin cannot be conceived, but only in a civil state where it is decided by universal consent what is good and what is evil, and where everyone is bound to obey the State. "Sin," therefore, is nothing but disobedience, which is punished by the law of the State alone; obedience, on the other hand, being regarded as a *merit* in a citizen, because on account of it he is considered worthy to enjoy the privileges of the State. Again, in a natural state no one by common consent is the owner of anything, nor is there anything in Nature which can be said to be the rightful property of this and not of that man, but all things belong to all, so that in a natural state it is impossible to conceive a desire of rendering to each man his own or taking from another that which is his; that is to say, in a natural state there is nothing which can be called just or unjust, but only in a civil state, in which it is decided by universal consent what is one person's and what is another's. Justice and injustice, therefore, sin and merit, are external notions, and not attributes, which manifest the nature of the mind. But enough of these matters.

PROPOSITION 40. *Whatever conduces to the universal fellowship of men, that is to say, whatever causes men to live in harmony with one another, is profitable, and, on the contrary, whatever brings discord into the State is evil.*

PROPOSITION 45. *Hatred can never be good.*

PROPOSITION 46. *He who lives according to the guidance of reason strives as much as possible to repay the hatred, anger, or contempt of others toward himself with love or generosity.*

PROPOSITION 64. *The knowledge of evil is inadequate knowledge.*

Corollary. Hence it follows that if the human mind had none but adequate ideas it would form no notion of evil.

PROPOSITION 67. *A free man thinks of nothing less than of death, and his wisdom is not a meditation upon death but upon life.*

Appendix

My observations in this part concerning the true method of life have not been arranged so that they could be seen at a glance, but have been demonstrated here and there according as I could more easily deduce one from another. I have determined, therefore, here to collect them, and reduce them under principal heads.

I. All our efforts or desires follow from the necessity of our nature in such a manner that they can be understood either through it alone as their proximate cause, or in so far as we are a part of Nature, which part cannot be adequately conceived through itself and without the other individuals.

II. The desires which follow from our nature in such a manner that they can be understood through it alone are those which are related to the mind, in so far as it is conceived to consist of adequate ideas. The remaining desires are not related to the mind, except in so far as it conceives things inadequately, whose power and increase cannot be determined by human power, but by the power of objects which are without us. The first kind of desires, therefore, are properly called actions, but the latter passive states, for the first always indicate our power, and the latter, on the contrary, indicate our impotence and imperfect knowledge.

III. Our actions, that is to say, those desires which are determined by man's power or reason, are always good; the others may be good as well as evil.

IV. It is therefore most profitable to us in life to make perfect the intellect or reason as far as possible, and in this one thing consists the highest happiness or blessedness of man; for blessedness is nothing but the peace of mind which springs from the intuitive knowledge of God, and to perfect the intellect is nothing but to understand God, together with the attributes and actions of God which flow from the necessity of His nature. The final aim, therefore, of a man who is guided by reason, that is to say, the chief desire by which he strives to govern all his other desires, is that by which he is led adequately to conceive himself and all things which can be conceived by his intelligence.

V. There is no rational life therefore, without intelligence, and things are good only in so far as they assist man to enjoy that life of the mind which is determined by intelligence. Those things alone, on the other hand, we call evil which hinder man from perfecting his reason and enjoying a rational life.

VI. But because all those things of which man is the efficient cause are necessarily good, it follows that no evil can happen to man except from external causes, that is to say, except in so far as he is a part of the whole of Nature, whose laws human nature is compelled to obey —compelled also to accommodate himself to this whole of Nature in almost an infinite number of ways.

VII. It is impossible that a man should not be a part of Nature and follow her common order; but if he be placed amongst individuals who agree with his nature, his power of action will by that very fact be assisted and supported. But if, on the contrary, he be placed amongst individuals who do not in the least agree with his nature, he will scarcely be able without great change on his part to accommodate himself to them.

VIII. Anything that exists in Nature which we judge to be evil or ble to hinder us from existing and enjoying a rational life, we are lowed to remove from us in that way which seems the safest; and hatever, on the other hand, we judge to be good or to be profitable ⁀ the preservation of our being or the enjoyment of a rational life, are permitted to take for our use and use in any way we may think per; and absolutely, everyone is allowed by the highest right of ure to do that which he believes contributes to his own profit.

X. Nothing, therefore, can agree better with the nature of any ᶜct than other individuals of the same kind, and so (see §7) there is thing more profitable to man for the preservation of his being an the enjoyment of a rational life than a man who is guided by reᵃn. Again, since there is no single thing we know which is more excent than a man who is guided by reason, it follows that there is nothg by which a person can better show how much skill and talent he possesses than by so educating men that at last they will live under the direct authority of reason.

X. In so far as men are carried away by envy or any emotion of hatred toward one another, so far are they contrary to one another, and, consequently, so much the more are they to be feared, as they have more power than other individual parts of Nature.

XI. Minds, nevertheless, are not conquered by arms, but by love and generosity.

XII. Above all things it is profitable to men to form communities and to unite themselves to one another by bonds which may make all of them as one man; and, absolutely, it is profitable for them to do whatever may tend to strengthen their friendships.

XIII. But to accomplish this, skill and watchfulness are required; for men are changeable (those being very few who live according to the laws of reason), and nevertheless generally envious and more inclined to vengeance than pity. To bear with each, therefore, according to his disposition and to refrain from imitating his emotions requires a singular power of mind. But those, on the contrary, who know how to revile men, to denounce vices rather than teach virtues, and not to strengthen men's minds but to weaken them, are injurious both to themselves and others, so that many of them, through an excess of impatience and a false zeal for religion, prefer living with brutes rather than amongst men; just as boys or youths, unable to endure with equanimity the rebukes of their parents, fly to the army, choosing the discomforts of war and the rule of a tyrant rather than the comforts of home and the admonitions of a father, suffering all kinds of burdens to be imposed upon them in order that they may revenge themselves upon their parents.

XIV. Although, therefore, men generally determine everything by their pleasure, many more advantages than disadvantages arise from their common union. It is better, therefore, to endure with equanimity the injuries inflicted by them, and to apply our minds to those things which subserve concord and the establishment of friendship.

XV. The things which beget concord are those which are related to justice, integrity, and honor; for besides that which is unjust and injurious, men take ill also anything which is esteemed base, or that anyone should despise the received customs of the State. But in order to win love, those things are chiefly necessary which have reference to religion and piety. (See Part IV, Prop. 37, Notes 1 and 2; Prop. 46, Note, and Prop. 73, Note.)

XVI. Concord, moreover, is often produced by fear, but it is without good faith. It is to be observed, too, that fear arises from impotence of mind, and therefore is of no service to reason; nor is pity, although it seems to present an appearance of piety.

XVII. Men also are conquered by liberality, especially those who have not the means wherewith to procure what is necessary for the support of life. But to assist every one who is needy far surpasses the strength or profit of a private person, for the wealth of a private person is altogether insufficient to supply such wants. Besides, the power of any one man is too limited for him to be able to unite every one with himself in friendship. The care, therefore, of the poor is incumbent on the whole of society and concerns only the general profit.

XVIII. In the receipt of benefits and in returning thanks, care altogether different must be taken—concerning which see Part IV, Prop. 70, Note, and Prop. 71, Note.

XIX. The love of a harlot, that is to say, the lust of sexual intercourse, which arises from mere external form; and absolutely all love which recognizes any other cause than the freedom of the mind, easily passes into hatred unless, which is worse, it becomes a species of delirium, and thereby discord is cherished rather than concord (Part III, Prop. 31, Corol.).

XX. With regard to marriage, it is plain that it is in accordance with reason if the desire to connection is engendered not merely by external form, but by a love of begetting children and wisely educating them; and if, in addition, the love both of the husband and wife has for its cause not external form merely, but chiefly liberty of mind.

XXI. Flattery, too, produces concord, but only by means of the disgraceful crime of slavery or perfidy; for there are none who are more taken by flattery than the proud, who wish to be first and are not so.

XXII. There is a false appearance of piety and religion in dejection; and although dejection is the opposite of pride, the humble, dejected man is very near akin to the proud (Part IV, Prop. 57, Note).

XXIII. Shame also contributes to concord, but only with regard to those matters which cannot be concealed. Shame, too, inasmuch as it is a kind of sorrow, does not belong to the service of reason.

XXIV. The remaining emotions of sorrow which have man for their object are directly opposed to justice, integrity, honor, piety, and religion; and although indignation may seem to present an appearance of equity, yet there is no law where it is allowed to everyone to judge the deeds of another, and to vindicate his own or another's right.

XXV. Affability, that is to say, the desire of pleasing men, which is determined by reason, is related to piety (Part IV, Prop. 37, Note). But if affability arise from an emotion, it is ambition or desire, by which men, generally under a false pretense of piety, excite discords and seditions. For he who desires to assist other people, either by advice or by deed, in order that they may together enjoy the highest good, will strive, above all things, to win their love, and not to draw them into admiration, so that a doctrine may be named after him, nor absolutely to give any occasion for envy. In common conversation, too, he will avoid referring to the vices of men, and will take care only sparingly to speak of human impotence, while he will talk largely of human virtue or power, and of the way by which it may be made perfect, so that men, being moved not by fear or aversion but solely by the emotion of joy, may endeavor as much as they can to live under the rule of reason.

XXVI. Except man, we know no individual thing in Nature in whose mind we can take pleasure, nor anything which we can unite with ourselves by friendship or any kind of intercourse, and therefore regard to our own profit does not demand that we should preserve anything which exists in Nature except men, but teaches us to preserve it or destroy it in accordance with its varied uses, or to adapt it to our own service in any way whatever.

XXVII. The profit which we derive from objects without us, over and above the experience and knowledge which we obtain because we observe them and change them from their existing forms into others, is chiefly the preservation of the body, and for this reason those objects are the most profitable to us which can feed and nourish the body, so that all its parts are able properly to perform their functions. For the more capable the body is of being affected in many ways, and affecting external bodies in many ways, the more capable of thinking is the mind (Part IV, Props. 38 and 39). But there seem to be very few things in Nature of this kind, and it is consequently necessary for the requisite nourishment of the body to use many different kinds of food, for the human body is composed of a great number of parts of different nature, which need constant and varied food in order that the whole of the body may be equally adapted for all those things which can follow from its nature, and consequently that the mind also may be equally adapted to conceive many things.

XXVIII. The strength of one man would scarcely suffice to obtain these things if men did not mutually assist one another. As money has presented us with an abstract of everything, it has come to pass that its image above every other usually occupies the mind of the multitude because they can imagine hardly any kind of joy without the accompanying idea of money as its cause.

XXIX. This, however, is a vice only in those who seek money not from poverty or necessity, but because they have learned the arts of gain by which they keep up a grand appearance. As for the body itself, they feed it in accordance with custom, but sparingly because they believe that they lose so much of their goods as they spend upon the preservation of their body. Those, however, who know the true use of money, and regulate the measure of wealth according to their needs, live contented with few things.

XXX. Since, therefore, those things are good which help the parts of the body to perform their functions, and since joy consists in this that the power of man, in so far as he is made up of mind and body, is helped or increased, it follows that all those things which bring joy are good. But inasmuch as things do not work to this end—that they may affect us with joy—nor is their power of action guided in accordance with our profit, and finally, since joy is generally related chiefly to some one part of the body, it follows that generally the emotions of joy (unless reason and watchfulness be present), and consequently the desires which are begotten from them, are excessive. It is to be added that an emotion causes us to put that thing first which is sweet to us in the present, and that we are not able to judge the future with an equal emotion (Part IV, Prop. 44, Note; Prop. 60, Note).

XXXI. Superstition, on the contrary, seems to affirm that what brings sorrow is good, and, on the contrary, that what brings joy is evil. But, as we have already said (Part IV, Prop. 45, Note), no one except an envious man is delighted at my impotence or disadvantage, for the greater the joy with which we are affected, the greater the perfection to which we pass, and consequently the more do we participate in the divine nature; nor can joy ever be evil which is controlled by a true consideration for our own profit. On the other hand, the man who is led by fear and does what is good that he may avoid what is evil, is not guided by reason.

XXXII. But human power is very limited and is infinitely surpassed by the power of external causes, so that we do not possess an absolute power to adapt to our service the things which are without us. Nevertheless we shall bear with equanimity those things which happen to us contrary to what a consideration of our own profit demands if we are conscious that we have performed our duty, that the power we have could not reach so far as to enable us to avoid those things, and that we are a part of the whole of Nature, whose order we follow. If we clearly and distinctly understand this, the part of us which is determined by intelligence, that is to say, the better part of us, will be entirely satisfied therewith, and in that satisfaction will endeavor to persevere; for, in so far as we understand, we cannot desire anything except what is necessary, nor, absolutely, can we be satisfied with anything but the truth. Therefore, in so far as we understand these things properly, will the efforts of the better part of us agree with the order of the whole of Nature.

PART V: OF THE POWER OF THE INTELLECT; OR OF HUMAN FREEDOM

Preface

I pass at length to the other part of Ethics which concerns the method or way which leads to freedom. In this part, therefore, I shall treat of the power of reason, showing how much reason itself can control the emotions, and then what is freedom of mind or blessedness. Thence we shall see how much stronger the wise man is than the ignorant. In what manner and in what way the intellect should be rendered perfect, and with what art the body is to be cared for in order that it may properly perform its functions, I have nothing to do with here; for the former belongs to logic, the latter to medicine. I shall occupy myself here, as I have said, solely with the power of the mind or of reason, first of all showing the extent and nature of the authority which it has over the emotions in restraining them and governing them; for that we have not absolute authority over them we have already demonstrated. The Stoics indeed thought that the emotions depend absolutely on our will, and that we are absolutely masters over them; but they were driven, by the contradiction of experience, though not by their own principles, to confess that not a little practice and study are required in order to restrain and govern the emotions. This one of them attempted to illustrate, if I remember rightly, by the example of two dogs, one of a domestic and the other of a hunting breed; for he was able by habit to make the house-dog hunt, and the hunting dog, on the contrary, to desist from running after hares. To the Stoical opinion Descartes much inclines. He affirms that the soul or mind is united specially to a certain part of the brain called the pineal gland, which the mind by the mere exercise of the will is able to move in different ways, and by whose help the mind perceives all the movements which are excited in the body and external objects. This gland he affirms is suspended in the middle of the brain in such a manner that it can be moved by the least motion of the animal spirits. Again, he affirms that any variation in the manner in which the animal spirits impinge upon this gland is followed by a variation in the manner in which it is suspended in the middle of the brain, and moreover that the number of different impressions on the gland is the same as that of the different external objects which propel the animal spirits towards it. Hence it comes to pass that if the gland, by the will of the soul moving it in different directions, be afterwards suspended in this or that way in which it had once been suspended by the spirits agitated in this or that way, then the gland itself will propel and determine the animal spirits themselves in the same way as that in which they had before been repelled by a similar suspension of the gland. Moreover, he affirmed that each volition of the mind is united in nature to a certain motion of the gland. For example, if a person wishes to behold a remote object, this volition will cause the pupil of the eye to dilate, but if he thinks merely of the dilation of the pupil, to have that volition will profit him nothing because Nature has not connected a motion of the gland which serves to impel the animal spirits toward the optic nerve in a way suitable for dilation or contraction of the pupil with the volition of dilation or contraction, but only with the volition of beholding objects afar off or close at hand. Finally, he maintained that, although each motion of this gland appears to be connected by Nature from the commencement of our life with an individual thought, these motions can nevertheless be connected by habit with other thoughts—a proposition which he attempts to demonstrate in his *Passions of the Soul,* Part I, Art. 50.

From this he concludes that there is no mind so feeble that it cannot, when properly directed, acquire absolute power over its passions; for passions, as defined by him, are "perceptions or sensations, or emotions of the soul which are related to it specially, and which (N.B.) are produced, preserved, and strengthened by some motion of the spirits." (See the *Passions of the Soul,* Part I, Art. 27.) But since it is possible to join to a certain volition any motion of the gland and, consequently, of the spirits, and since the determination of the will depends solely on our power, we shall be able to acquire absolute mastery over our passions provided only we determine our will by fixed and firm decisions by which we desire to direct our actions and

bind with these decisions the movements of the passions we wish to
have. So far as I can gather from his own words, this is the opinion of
that distinguished man, and I could scarcely have believed it possible
for one so great to have put it forward if it had been less subtle. I can
hardly wonder enough that a philosopher who firmly resolved to make
no deduction except from self-evident principles, and to affirm nothing
but what he clearly and distinctly perceived, and who blamed all the
schoolmen because they desired to explain obscure matters by occult
qualities, should accept a hypothesis more occult than any occult
quality. What does he understand, I ask, by the union of the mind and
body? What clear and distinct conception has he of thought intimately connected with a certain small portion of matter? I wish that
he had explained this union by its proximate cause. But he conceived
the mind to be so distinct from the body that he was able to assign no
single cause of this union, nor of the mind itself, but was obliged to
have recourse to the cause of the whole universe, that is to say, to
God. Again, I should like to know how many degrees of motion the
mind can give to that pineal gland, and with how great a power the
mind can hold it suspended. For I do not understand whether this
gland is acted on by the mind more slowly or more quickly than by the
animal spirits, and whether the movements of the passions, which we
have so closely bound with firm decisions, might not be separated
from them again by bodily causes, from which it would follow that
although the mind had firmly determined to meet danger, and had
joined to this decision the motion of boldness, the sight of the danger
might cause the gland to be suspended in such a manner that the
mind could think of nothing but flight. Indeed, since there is no relation between the will and motion, so there is no comparison between
the power or strength of the body and that of the mind, and consequently the strength of the body can never be determined by the
strength of the mind. It is to be remembered also that this gland is not
found to be so situated in the middle of the brain that it can be driven
about so easily and in so many ways, and that all the nerves are not
extended to the cavities of the brain. Lastly, I omit all that Descartes
asserts concerning the will and the freedom of the will, since I have
shown over and over again that it is false. Therefore, inasmuch as the
power of the mind, as I have shown above, is determined by intelligence alone, we shall determine by the knowledge of the mind alone
the remedies against the emotions—remedies which every one, I believe, has experienced, although there may not have been any accurate

observation or distinct perception of them, and from this knowledge of the mind alone shall we deduce everything which relates to its blessedness.

Axioms

I. If two contrary actions be excited in the same subject, a change must necessarily take place in both, or in one alone, until they cease to be contrary.

II. The power of an emotion is limited by the power of its cause, in so far as the essence of the emotion is manifested or limited by the essence of the cause itself.

This axiom is evident from Part III, Prop. 7.

Propositions

PROPOSITION 2. *If we detach a perturbation of the mind or an emotion from the thought of an external cause and connect it with other thoughts, then the love or hatred toward the external cause and the fluctuations of the mind which arise from these emotions will be destroyed.*

PROPOSITION 3. *An emotion which is a passion ceases to be a passion as soon as we form a clear and distinct idea of it.*

Demonstration. An emotion which is a passion is a confused idea (by the general definition of the emotions). If, therefore, we form a clear and distinct idea of this emotion, the idea will not be distinguished—except by reason—from this emotion, in so far as the emotion is related to the mind alone (Part II, Prop. 21, and Note), and therefore (Part III, Prop. 3) the emotion will cease to be a passion.—Q.E.D.

Corollary. In proportion, then, as we know an emotion better is it more within our control, and the less does the mind suffer from it.

PROPOSITION 4. *There is no modification of the body of which we cannot form some clear and distinct conception.*

Corollary. Hence it follows that there is no emotion of which we cannot form some clear and distinct conception. For an emotion is an idea of a modification of the body (by the general definition of the emotions), and this idea therefore (Part V, Prop. 4) must involve some clear and distinct conception.

PROPOSITION 6. *In so far as the mind understands all things as necessary, so far has it greater power over the emotions, or suffers less from them.*

Note. The more this knowledge that things are necessary is applied to individual things which we imagine more distinctly and more vividly, the greater is this power of the mind over the emotions—a fact to which experience also testifies. For we see that sorrow for the loss of anything good is diminished if the person who has lost it considers that it could not by any possibility have been preserved. So also we see that nobody pities an infant because it does not know how to speak, walk, or reason, and lives so many years not conscious, as it were, of itself; but if a number of human beings were born adult, and only a few here and there were born infants, everyone would pity the infants because we should then consider infancy not as a thing natural and necessary, but as a defect or fault of Nature. Many other facts of a similar kind we might observe.

PROPOSITION 14. *The mind can cause all the modification of the body or the images of things to be related to the idea of God.*

Demonstration. There is no modification of the body of which the mind cannot form some clear and distinct conception (Part V, Prop. 4), and therefore (Part I, Prop. 15) it can cause all the modifications of the body to be related to the idea of God.—Q.E.D.

PROPOSITION 15. *He who clearly and distinctly understands himself and his emotions loves God, and loves Him better the better he understands himself and his emotions.*

Demonstration. He who clearly and distinctly understands himself and his emotions rejoices (Part III, Prop. 53), and his joy is attended with the idea of God (Part V, Prop. 14), therefore (Def. VI of the emotions) he loves God, and (by the same reasoning) loves Him better the better he understands himself and his emotions.—Q.E.D.

PROPOSITION 16. *This love of God above everything else ought to occupy the mind.*

Demonstration. For this love is connected with all the modifica-tions of the body (Part V, Prop. 14), by all of which it is cherished (Part V, Prop. 15), and therefore (Part V, Prop. 11) above every-thing else ought to occupy the mind.—Q.E.D.

PROPOSITION 17. *God is free from passions, nor is He affected with any emotion of joy or sorrow.*

Demonstration. All ideas, in so far as they are related to God, are true (Part II, Prop. 32), that is to say (Part II, Def. IV), are ade-quate, and therefore (by the general definition of the emotions) God is free from passions. Again, God can neither pass to a greater nor to a less perfection (Part I, Prop. 20, Corol. 2), and therefore (Defs. II and III of the emotions) He cannot be affected with any emotion of joy or sorrow.—Q.E.D.

Corollary. Properly speaking, God loves no one and hates no one; for God (Part V, Prop. 17) is not affected with any emotion of joy or sorrow, and consequently (Defs. VI and VII of the emotions) He neither loves nor hates anyone.

PROPOSITION 18. *No one can hate God.*

Demonstration. The idea of God which is in us is adequate and perfect (Part II, Props. 46 and 47), and, therefore, in so far as we contemplate God do we act (Part III, Prop. 3), and consequently (Part III, Prop. 59), no sorrow can exist with the accompanying idea of God, that is to say (Def. VII of the emotions), no one can hate God.—Q.E.D.

Corollary. Love of God cannot be turned into hatred.

Note. But some may object that, if we understand God to be the cause of all things, we do for that very reason consider Him to be the cause of sorrow. But I reply that in so far as we understand the causes of sorrow it ceases to be a passion (Part V, Prop. 3), that is to say (Part III, Prop. 59), it ceases to be sorrow; and, therefore, in so far as we understand God to be the cause of sorrow do we rejoice.

PROPOSITION 19. *He who loves God cannot strive that God should love him in return.*

PROPOSITION 20. *This love of God cannot be defiled either by the emotion of envy or jealousy, but is the more strengthened, the more people we imagine to be connected with God by the same bond of love.*

Note. It is possible to show in the same manner that there is no emotion directly contrary to this love and able to destroy it, and so we may conclude that this love of God is the most constant of all the emotions, and that, in so far as it is related to the body, it cannot be destroyed unless with the body itself. What its nature is, in so far as it is related to the mind alone, we shall see hereafter.

I have, in what has preceded, included all the remedies for the emotions, that is to say, everything which the mind, considered in itself alone, can do against them. It appears therefrom that the power of the mind over the emotions consists:

1. In the knowledge itself of the emotions. (See Part V, Prop. 4, Note.)

2. In the separation by the mind of the emotions from the thought of an external cause, which we imagine confusedly. (See Part V, Prop. 2, and Part V, Prop. 4, Note.)

3. In the duration, in which the modifications which are related to objects we understand surpass those related to objects conceived in a mutilated or confused manner (Part V, Prop. 7).

4. In the multitude of causes by which the modifications which are related to the common properties of things or to God are nourished (Part V, Props. 9 and 11).

5. In the order in which the mind can arrange its emotions and connect them one with the other (Part V, Prop. 10, Note; Part V, Props. 12, 13, and 14). . . .

From all this we easily conceive what is the power which clear and distinct knowledge, and especially that third kind of knowledge (see Part II, Prop. 47, Note) whose foundation is the knowledge itself of God possesses over the emotions—the power, namely, by which it is able, in so far as they are passions, if not actually to destroy them (see Part V, Prop. 3 with the Note to Prop. 4), at least to make them constitute the smallest part of the mind (see Part V, Prop. 14). Moreover, it begets a love toward an immutable and eternal object (see Part V, Prop. 15) of which we are really partakers (see Part II, Prop. 45)—a love which therefore cannot be vitiated by the defects which are in common love, but which can always become greater and greater (Part V, Prop. 15), occupy the largest part of the mind (Part V, Prop. 16) and thoroughly affect it.

I have now concluded all that I had to say relating to this present life. For any one who will attend to what has been urged in this Note, and to the definition of the mind and its emotions, and to Part III, Props. 1 and 3, will easily be able to see the truth of what I said in the beginning of the Note—that in these few words all the remedies for the emotions are comprehended. It is time, therefore, that I should now pass to the consideration of those matters which appertain to the duration of the mind without relation to the body.

PROPOSITION 21.   *The mind can imagine nothing, nor can it recollect anything that is past, except while the body exists.*

PROPOSITION 22.   *In God, nevertheless, there necessarily exists an idea which expresses the essence of this or that human body under the form of eternity.*

PROPOSITION 23.   *The human mind cannot be absolutely destroyed with the body, but something of it remains which is eternal.*

PROPOSITION 24.   *The more we understand individual objects, the more we understand God.*

PROPOSITION 25.   *The highest effort of the mind and its highest virtue is to understand things by the third kind of knowledge.*

PROPOSITION 27.   *From this third kind of knowledge arises the highest possible peace of mind.*

PROPOSITION 30.   *Our mind, in so far as it knows itself and the body under the form of eternity, necessarily has a knowledge of God, and knows that it is in God and is conceived through Him.*

PROPOSITION 36.   *The intellectual love of the mind toward God is the very love with which He loves Himself, not in so far as He is infinite, but in so far as He can be manifested through the essence of the human mind, considered under the form of eternity; that is to say, the intellectual love of the mind toward God is part of the infinite love with which God loves Himself.*

Demonstration. This love of the mind must be related to the actions of the mind (Part V, Prop. 32, Corol., and Part III, Prop. 3), and it is therefore an action by which the mind contemplates itself; and which is accompanied with the idea of God as cause (Part V, Prop. 32, with the Corol.), that is to say (Part I, Prop. 25, Corol., and Part II, Prop. 11, Corol.), it is an action by which God, in so far as He can be manifested through the human mind, contemplates Himself, the action being accompanied with the idea of Himself; and therefore (Part V, Prop. 35), this love of the mind is part of the infinite love with which God loves Himself.—Q.E.D.

Corollary. Hence it follows that God, in so far as He loves Himself, loves men, and consequently that the love of God toward men and the intellectual love of the mind toward God are one and the same thing.

PROPOSITION 38. *The more objects the mind understands by the second and third kinds of knowledge, the less it suffers from those emotions which are evil, and the less it fears death.*

PROPOSITION 40. *The more perfection a thing possesses, the more it acts and the less it suffers; and conversely the more it acts, the more perfect it is.*

PROPOSITION 42. *Blessedness is not the reward of virtue but is virtue itself; nor do we delight in blessedness because we restrain our lusts, but, on the contrary, because we delight in it, therefore are we able to restrain them.*

Demonstration. Blessedness consists in love toward God (Part V, Prop. 36, and Note) which arises from the third kind of knowledge (Part V, Prop. 32, Corol.), and this love, therefore (Part III, Props. 59 and 3), must be related to the mind in so far as it acts. Blessedness, therefore (Part IV, Def. VIII), is virtue itself, which was the first thing to be proved. Again, the more the mind delights in this divine love or blessedness, the more it understands (Part V, Prop. 32), that is to say (Part V, Prop. 3, Corol.), the greater is the power it has over its emotions, and (Part V, Prop. 38) the less it suffers from emotions which are evil. Therefore, it is because the mind delights in this divine love or blessedness that it possesses the power of restraining the lusts; and because the power of man to restrain the emotions is in the intellect alone, no one, therefore, delights in blessedness because he has restrained his emotions, but, on the contrary, the power of restraining his lusts springs from blessedness itself.—Q.E.D.

Note. I have finished everything I wished to explain concerning the power of the mind over the emotions and concerning its freedom. From what has been said we see what is the strength of the wise man, and how much he surpasses the ignorant who is driven forward by lust alone. For the ignorant man is not only agitated by external causes in many ways, and never enjoys true peace of soul, but lives also ignorant, as it were, both of God and of things, and as soon as he ceases to suffer ceases also to be. On the other hand, the wise man, in so far as he is considered as such, is scarcely ever moved in his mind, but, being conscious by a certain eternal necessity of himself, of God, and of things, never ceases to be, and always enjoys true peace of soul. If the way which, as I have shown, leads hither seems very difficult, it can nevertheless be found. It must indeed be difficult since it is so seldom discovered, for if salvation lay ready to hand and could be discovered without great labor, how could it be possible that it should be neglected almost by everybody? But all noble things are as difficult as they are rare.

Theologico-Political Treatise*

Chapter XX

FREEDOM OF THOUGHT AND SPEECH

If men's minds were as easily controlled as their tongues, every king would sit safely on his throne, and government by compulsion would cease; for every subject would shape his life according to the intentions of his rulers, and would esteem a thing true or false, good or evil, just or unjust, in obedience to their dictates. However, . . . no man's mind can possibly lie wholly at the disposition of another, for no one can willingly transfer his natural right of free reason and judgment, or be compelled so to do. For this reason government which attempts to control minds is accounted tyrannical, and it is considered an abuse of sovereignty and a usurpation of the rights of subjects to seek to prescribe what shall be accepted as true, or rejected as false, or what opinions should actuate men in their worship of God. All these questions fall within a man's natural right, which he cannot abdicate even with his own consent.

I admit that the judgment can be biased in many ways, and to an almost incredible degree, so that while exempt from direct external control it may be so dependent on another man's words, that it may fitly be said to be ruled by him; but although this influence is carried to great lengths, it has never gone so far as to invalidate the statement that every man's understanding is his own, and that brains are as diverse as palates.

Moses, not by fraud, but by Divine virtue, gained such a hold over the popular judgment that he was accounted superhuman, and believed to speak and act through the inspiration of the Deity; nevertheless, even he could not escape murmurs and evil interpretations. How much less then can other monarchs avoid them! Yet such unlimited power, if it exists at all, must belong to a monarch, and least of all to a democracy, where the whole or a great part of the people wield authority collectively. This is a fact which I think every one can explain for himself.

However unlimited, therefore, the power of a sovereign may be,

---

* Translated by R. H. M. Elwes, in *The Chief Works of Spinoza,* London: George Bell (Bohn's Philosophical Library), 2 vols., 1883-84; rev. ed. 1906. A few sentences have been omitted. The *Tractatus Theologico-Politicus* was first published in 1670.

however implicitly it is trusted as the exponent of law and religion, it can never prevent men from forming judgments according to their intellect, or being influenced by any given emotion. It is true that it has the right to treat as enemies all men whose opinions do not, on all subjects, entirely coincide with its own; but we are not discussing its strict rights, but its proper course of action. I grant that it has the right to rule in the most violent manner, and to put citizens to death for very trivial causes, but no one supposes it can do this with the approval of sound judgment. Nay, inasmuch as such things cannot be done without extreme peril to itself, we may even deny that it has the absolute power to do them, or, consequently, the absolute right; for the rights of the sovereign are limited by his power.

Since, therefore, no one can abdicate his freedom of judgment and feeling; since every man is by indefeasible natural right the master of his own thoughts, it follows that men, thinking in diverse and contradictory fashions, cannot, without disastrous results, be compelled to speak only according to the dictates of the supreme power. Not even the most experienced, to say nothing of the multitude, know how to keep silence. Men's common failing is to confide their plans to others, though there be need for secrecy, so that a government would be most harsh which deprived the individual of his freedom of saying and teaching what he thought; and would be moderate if such freedom were granted. Still we cannot deny that authority may be as much injured by words as by actions. Hence, although the freedom we are discussing cannot be entirely denied to subjects, its unlimited concession would be most baneful; we must, therefore, now inquire, how far such freedom can and ought to be conceded without danger to the peace of the state, or the power of the rulers.

It follows, plainly, from the explanation given above, of the foundations of a state, that the ultimate aim of government is not to rule, or restrain by fear, nor to exact obedience, but, contrariwise, to free every man from fear that he may live in all possible security; in other words, to strengthen his natural right to exist and work without injury to himself or others.

No, the object of government is not to change men from rational beings into beasts or puppets, but to enable them to develop their minds and bodies in security, and to employ their reason unshackled; neither showing hatred, anger or deceit, nor watched with the eyes of jealousy and injustice. In fact, the true aim of government is liberty.

Now we have seen that in forming a state the power of making laws must either be vested in the body of the citizens, or in a portion of them, or in one man. For, although men's free judgments are very diverse, each one thinking that he alone knows everything, and although complete unanimity of feeling and speech is out of the question, it is impossible to preserve peace unless individuals abdicate their right of acting entirely on their own judgment. Therefore, the individual justly cedes the right of free action, though not of free reason and judgment; no one can act against the authorities without danger to the state, though his feelings and judgment may be at variance therewith; he may even speak against them, provided that he does so from rational conviction, not from fraud, anger or hatred, and provided that he does not attempt to introduce any change on his private authority.

For instance, supposing a man shows that a law is repugnant to sound reason, and should therefore be repealed; if he submits his opinion to the judgment of the authorities (who alone have the right of making and repealing laws), and meanwhile acts in nowise contrary to that law, he has deserved well of the state, and has behaved as a good citizen should; but if he accuses the authorities of injustice, and stirs up the people against them, or if he seditiously strives to abrogate the law without their consent, he is a mere agitator and rebel.

Thus we see how an individual may declare and teach what he believes, without injury to the authority of his rulers, or to the public peace; namely, by leaving in their hands the entire power of legislation as it affects action, and by doing nothing against their laws, though he be compelled often to act in contradiction to what he believes, and openly feels, to be best.

Such a course can be taken without detriment to justice and dutifulness, nay, it is the one which a just and dutiful man would adopt. We have shown that justice is dependent on the laws of the authorities, so that no one who contravenes their accepted decrees can be just, while the highest regard for duty, as we have pointed out, is exercised in maintaining public peace and tranquillity. These could not be preserved if every man were to live as he pleased. Therefore it is no less than undutiful for a man to act contrary to his country's laws, for if the practice became universal the ruin of states would necessarily follow.

Hence, so long as a man acts in obedience to the laws of his rulers, he in nowise contravenes his reason, for in obedience to reason he transferred the right of controlling his actions from his own hands to theirs. This doctrine we can confirm from actual custom, for in a conference of great and small powers, schemes are seldom carried unanimously, yet all unite in carrying out what is decided on, whether they voted for or against. But I return to my proposition.

From the fundamental notions of a state, we have discovered how a man may exercise free judgment without detriment to the supreme power: from the same premises we can no less easily determine what opinions would be seditious. Evidently those which by their very nature nullify the compact by which the right of free action was ceded. For instance, a man who holds that the supreme power has no rights over him, or that promises ought not to be kept, or that every one should live as he pleases, or other doctrines of this nature in direct opposition to the above-mentioned contract, is seditious, not so much from his actual opinions and judgment, as from the deeds which they involve; for he who maintains such theories abrogates the contract which tacitly, or openly, he made with his rulers. Other opinions which do not involve acts violating the contract, such as revenge, anger, and the like, are not seditious, unless it be in some corrupt state, where superstitious and ambitious persons, unable to endure men of learning, are so popular with the multitude that their word is more valued than the law.

However, I do not deny that there are some doctrines which, while they are apparently only concerned with abstract truths and falsehoods, are yet propounded and published with unworthy motives. . . . Reason should nevertheless remain unshackled. If we hold to the principle that a man's loyalty to the state should be judged, like his loyalty to God, from his actions only—namely, from his charity towards his neighbors—we cannot doubt that the best government will allow freedom of philosophical speculation no less than of religious belief. I confess that from such freedom inconveniences may sometimes arise, but what question was ever settled so wisely that no abuses could possibly spring therefrom? He who seeks to regulate everything by law is more likely to arouse vices than to reform them. It is best to grant what cannot be abolished, even though it be in itself harmful. How many evils spring from luxury, envy, avarice, drunkenness and the like, yet these are tolerated—vices as they are—because they cannot be prevented by legal enactments. How much more, then, should free thought be granted, seeing that it is in itself a virtue and that it cannot be crushed! Besides, the evil results can easily be checked, as I will show, by the secular authorities, not to mention that such freedom is absolutely necessary for progress in science and the liberal arts: for no man follows such pursuits to advantage unless his judgment be entirely free and unhampered.

But let it be granted that freedom may be crushed, and men be so bound down that they do not dare to utter a whisper, save at the bidding of their rulers; nevertheless this can never be carried to the pitch of making them think according to authority, so that the necessary consequences would be that men would daily be thinking one thing and saying another, to the corruption of good faith, that mainstay of government, and to the fostering of hateful flattery and perfidy, whence spring stratagems, and the corruption of every good art.

It is far from possible to impose uniformity of speech, for the more rulers strive to curtail freedom of speech the more obstinately are they resisted; not indeed by the avaricious, the flatterers, and other numskulls, who think supreme salvation consists in filling their stomachs and gloating over their money-bags, but by those whom good education, sound morality, and virtue have rendered more free. Men, as generally constituted, are most prone to resent the branding as criminal of opinions which they believe to be true, and the proscription as wicked of that which inspires them with piety towards God and man; hence they are ready to forswear the laws and conspire against the authorities, thinking it not shameful but honorable to stir up seditions and perpetuate any sort of crime with this end in view. Such being the constitution of human nature, we see that laws directed against opinions affect the generous minded rather than the wicked, and are adapted less for coercing criminals than for irritating the upright; so that they cannot be maintained without great peril to the state.

Moreover, such laws are almost always useless, for those who hold that the opinions proscribed are sound, cannot possibly obey the law; whereas those who already reject them as false, accept the law as a kind of privilege, and make such boast of it, that authority is powerless to repeal it, even if such a course be subsequently desired.

. . . And, lastly, how many schisms have arisen in the Church from the attempt of the authorities to decide by law the intricacies of theological controversy! If men were not allured by the hope of getting the law and the authorities on their side, of triumphing over their adversaries in the sight of an applauding multitude, and of acquiring honorable distinctions, they would not strive so maliciously, nor would such fury sway their minds. This is taught not only by reason but by daily examples, for laws of this kind prescribing what every man shall believe and forbidding any one to speak or write to the contrary, have often been passed as sops or concessions to the anger of those who cannot tolerate men of enlightenment, and who, by such harsh and crooked enactments, can easily turn the devotion of the masses into fury and direct it against whom they will.

How much better would it be to restrain popular anger and fury, instead of passing useless laws, which can only be broken by those who love virtue and the liberal arts, thus paring down the state till it is too small to harbor men of talent. What greater misfortune for a state can be conceived than that honorable men should be sent like criminals into exile, because they hold diverse opinions which they cannot disguise? What, I say, can be more hurtful than that men who have committed no crime or wickedness should, simply because they are enlightened, be treated as enemies and put to death, and that the scaffold, the terror of evil-doers, should become the arena where the highest examples of tolerance and virtue are displayed to the people with all the marks of ignominy that authority can devise?

He that knows himself to be upright does not fear the death of a criminal, and shrinks from no punishment. His mind is not wrung with remorse for any disgraceful deed. He holds that death in a good cause is no punishment, but an honor, and that death for freedom is glory.

What purpose, then, is served by the death of such men, what example is proclaimed? The cause for which they die is unknown to the idle and the foolish, hateful to the turbulent, loved by the upright. The only lesson we can draw from such scenes is to flatter the persecutor, or else to imitate the victim.

If formal assent is not to be esteemed above conviction, and if governments are to retain a firm hold of authority and not be compelled to yield to agitators, it is imperative that freedom of judgment should be granted, so that men may live together in harmony, however diverse, or even openly contradictory their opinions may be. We cannot doubt that such is the best system of government and open to the fewest objections, since it is the one most in harmony with human nature. In a democracy (the most natural form of government) every one submits to the control of authority over his actions, but not over his judgment and reason; that is, seeing that all cannot think alike, the voice of the majority has the force of law, subject to repeal if circumstances bring about a change of opinion. In proportion as the power of free judgment is withheld we depart from the natural condition of mankind, and consequently the government becomes more tyrannical.

In order to prove that from such freedom no inconvenience arises which cannot easily be checked by the exercise of the sovereign power, and that men's actions can easily be kept in bounds, though their opinions be at open variance, it will be well to cite an example. Such an one is not very far to seek. The city of Amsterdam reaps the fruit of this freedom in its own great prosperity and in the admiration of all other people. For in this most flourishing state, and most splendid city, men of every nation and religion live together in the greatest harmony, and ask no questions before trusting their goods to a fellow-citizen, save whether he be rich or poor, and whether he generally acts honestly, or the reverse. His religion and sect is considered of no importance: for it has no effect before the judges in gaining or losing a cause, and there is no sect so despised that its followers, provided that they harm no one, pay every man his due, and live uprightly, are deprived of the protection of the magisterial authority.

On the other hand, when the religious controversy between Remonstrants and Counter-Remonstrants began to be taken up by politicians and the States, it grew into a schism, and abundantly showed that laws dealing with religion and seeking to settle its controversies are much more calculated to irritate than to reform, and that they give rise to extreme license. Further, it was seen that schisms do not originate in a love of truth, which is a source of courtesy and gentleness, but rather in an inordinate desire for supremacy. From all these considerations it is clearer than the sun at noonday, that the true schismatics are those who condemn other men's writings, and seditiously stir up the quarrelsome masses against their authors, rather than those authors themselves, who generally write only for the learned, and appeal solely to reason. In fact, the real disturbers of the peace are those who, in a free state, seek to curtail the liberty of judgment which they are unable to tyrannize over.

I have thus shown:—I. That it is impossible to deprive men of the liberty of saying what they think. II. That such liberty can be conceded to every man without injury to the rights and authority of the sovereign power, and that every man may retain it without injury to such rights, provided that he does not presume upon it to the extent of introducing any new rights into the state, or acting in any way contrary to the existing laws. III. That every man may enjoy this liberty without detriment to the public peace, and that no inconveniences arise therefrom which cannot easily be checked. IV. That every man may enjoy it without injury to his allegiance. V. That laws dealing with speculative problems are entirely useless. VI. Lastly, that not only may such liberty be granted without prejudice to the public peace, to loyalty, and to the rights of rulers, but that it is even necessary for their preservation. For when people try to take it away, and bring to trial, not only the acts which alone are capable of offending, but also the opinions of mankind, they only succeed in surrounding their victims with an appearance of martyrdom, and raise feelings of pity and revenge rather than of terror. Uprightness and good faith are thus corrupted, flatterers and traitors are encouraged, and sectarians triumph, inasmuch as concessions have been made to their animosity, and they have gained the state sanction for the doctrines of which they are the interpreters. Hence they arrogate to themselves the state authority and rights, and do not scruple to assert that they have been directly chosen by God, and that their laws are Divine, whereas the laws of the state are human, and should therefore yield obedience to the laws of God—in other words, to their own laws. Every one must see that this is not a state of affairs conducive to public welfare. Wherefore, . . . the safest way for a state is to lay down the rule that religion is comprised solely in the exercise of charity and justice, and that the rights of rulers in sacred, no less than in secular, matters should merely have to do with actions, but that every man should think what he likes and say what he thinks.

Supplementary Passages

1

Experience and Definition (see *Ethics,* Part I, Defs.)

You ask me whether we need experience to know whether the Definition of some Attribute is true. To this I reply, that we only need Experience in the case of whatever cannot be deduced from the definition of a thing, as, for instance, the existence of Modes: for this cannot be deduced from the definition of a thing. But we do not need experience in the case of those things whose existence is not distinguished from their essence, and therefore follows from their definition. Indeed, no experience will ever be able to teach us this: for experience does not teach us the essence of things; the utmost which it can effect is to determine our mind so that it only thinks of certain essences of things. Therefore, since the existence of attributes does not differ from their essence, we shall not be able to apprehend it by any kind of experience.

[FROM Letter X, to Simon De Vries, ca. March, 1663; trans. A. Wolf. Reprinted by permission from *The Correspondence of Spinoza,* London: George Allen & Unwin, 1928]

2

Substance and Attribute (see *Ethics,* Part I, Defs. III, IV)

But I do not yet see . . . why it [the third definition] should cause difficulty. For the definition as I gave it you, unless I am mistaken, reads as follows: *By substance I mean that which is in itself and is conceived through itself, that is, whose conception does not involve the conception of some other thing. I mean the same by attribute, except that it is called attribute with respect to the intellect, which attributes such and such a nature to substance.* This definition, I say, explains clearly enough what I wish you to understand by substance or attribute. You however wish me to explain by means of an example, which it is very easy to do, how one and the same thing can be called by two names. But, not to seem niggardly, I will supply two examples. First, I say that by the name Israel I mean the third Patriarch, I also mean the same Patriarch by the name Jacob, since the name Jacob was given to him because he had seized his brother's heel. Secondly by plane I mean that which reflects all the rays of light without any change; I mean the same by white, except that it is called white in relation to a man who is looking at the plane [surface].

[FROM Letter IX, to Simon De Vries, March, 1663; trans. A. Wolf, *ibid.*]

3

Natura Naturata (see *Ethics,* Part I, Prop. 29)

Now as regards the general *Natura naturata,* or the modes or creations which depend on or have been created by God immediately, of these we know no more than two, namely, *Motion* in matter, and the *Understanding* in the thinking being. These, then, we say, have been from all eternity, and to all eternity will remain immutable. A work truly as great as becomes the greatness of the work-master.

All that specially concerns Motion, such as that it has been from all eternity, and to all eternity will remain immutable; that it is infinite in its kind; that it can neither be, nor be understood, through itself, but only by means of Extension—all this, I say, since it more properly belongs to a treatise on Natural Science rather than here, we shall not consider in this place; but we shall only say this about it, that it is a Son, Product, or Effect created immediately by God.

As regards the Understanding in the thinking being, this, like the first, is also a Son, Product, or immediate Creation of God, also created by him from all eternity, and remaining immutable to all eternity. It has but one function, namely, to understand clearly and distinctly all things at all times . . .

[FROM Chapter IX of the First Part of the *Short Treatise on God, Man, and His Well-being,* trans. A. Wolf, London: A. and C. Black, 1910]

4

Man's Dependence upon God (see *Ethics,* Part I, Prop. 33; Part IV, Prop. 2)

As to what you say, that I make men so dependent on God that I make them like the elements, plants and stones, this shows sufficiently that you most perversely misunderstand my opinion, and confuse things which concern the understanding with imagination. For if you had grasped with your pure understanding what dependence upon God is, you would certainly not think that things in so far as they depend on God, are dead, corporeal and imperfect (who ever dared to speak in so vile a fashion of the most perfect Being?). On the contrary, you would understand that for that reason, and in so far as they depend on God, they are perfect—so much so, that we best understand this dependence and necessary operation through God's decree when we consider not logs and plants, but the most intelligible and most perfect created things.

[FROM Letter XXI, to William van Blyenbergh, January 28, 1675; trans. A. Wolf, *The Correspondence of Spinoza, op. cit.*]

5

Method (see *Ethics,* Part II, Prop. 43)

Now that we know what kind of knowledge is necessary for us, we must indicate the way and the method whereby we may gain the said knowledge concerning the things needful to be known. In order to accomplish this, we must first take care not to commit ourselves to a search going back to infinity—that is, in order to discover the best method for finding out the truth, there is no need of another method to discover such method; nor of a third method for discovering the second, and so on to infinity. By such proceedings, we should never arrive at the knowledge of the truth, or, indeed, at any knowledge at all. The matter stands on the same footing as the making of material tools, which might be argued about in a similar way. For, in order to work iron, a hammer is needed, and the hammer cannot be forthcoming unless it has been made; but, in order to make it, there was need of another hammer and other tools, and so on to infinity. We might thus vainly endeavor to prove that men have no power of working iron. But as men at first made use of the instruments supplied by nature to accomplish very easy pieces of workmanship, laboriously and imperfectly, and then, when these were finished, wrought other things more difficult with less labor and greater perfection; and so gradually mounted from the simplest operations to the making of tools, and from the making of tools to the making of more complex tools, and fresh feats of workmanship, till they arrived at making, with small expenditure of labor, the vast number of complicated mechanisms which they now possess—so, in like manner, the intellect, by its native strength,[1] makes for itself intellectual instru-

---

[1] By native strength, I mean that not bestowed on us by external causes, as I shall afterwards explain in my philosophy.

ments, whereby it acquires strength for performing other intellectual operations, and from these operations gets again fresh instruments, or the power of pushing its investigations further, and thus gradually proceeds till it reaches the summit of wisdom.

> [FROM *On the Improvement of the Understanding*, from Volume II of Spinoza's *Chief Works*, trans. R. H. M. Elwes, London: George Bell (Bohn's Philosophical Library), 1884]

6

Excusability (see *Ethics*, Part III, Introductory section; Part IV, Prop. 73)

What I said in my previous letter, that we are inexcusable because we are in the power of God as clay in the hand of the potter, I wanted to be understood in this sense, namely, that no one can blame God because He has given him an infirm nature or an impotent mind. For it would be just as absurd for a circle to complain that God has not given it the properties of a sphere, or a child who is tortured by a stone, that He has not given him a healthy body, as for a weak-minded man to complain that God has denied him strength and the true knowledge and love of God, and that He has given him a nature so weak that he cannot restrain or moderate his desires. For to the nature of each thing there belongs no more than necessarily follows from its given cause. But that it does not belong to the nature of each man to be strong-minded and that it is no more in our power to have a sound body than a sound Mind, no one can deny, unless he wishes to contradict both experience and reason. But you will insist that if men sin from the necessity of their nature, they are excusable: but you do not explain what you want to conclude from this, whether, namely, you want to conclude that God is unable to be angry with them or that they are worthy of blessedness, that is, of the knowledge and love of God. Now if you mean the former, I fully admit that God is not angry, and that all things come to pass according to His decision; but I deny that they ought therefore all to be blessed: for men can be excusable and nevertheless lack blessedness, and be tormented in many ways. For a horse is excusable for being a horse and not a man; nevertheless it must be a horse and not a man. He who goes mad from the bite of a dog is, indeed, to be excused and yet is rightly suffocated, and, lastly, he who is unable to control his desires, and to restrain them through fear of the laws, although he must be excused for his weakness, is nevertheless unable to enjoy peace of mind, and the knowledge and love of God, but necessarily perishes.

[FROM Letter LXXVIII, to Henry Oldenburg, February 7, 1676; trans. A. Wolf, *The Correspondence of Spinoza, op. cit.*]

7

The Nature of Evil (see *Ethics,* Part IV, Preface and Prop. 64)

I say, then, in the first place, that Privation is not an act of depriving, but only a simple and mere lack, which in itself is nothing: for it is only a thing of Reason, or a way of thinking, which we form when we compare things with each other. We say, for example, that a blind man is deprived of sight because we easily imagine him as seeing. This imagination comes about either because we compare him with others who see, or because we compare his present state with a past state when he did see. And when we consider this man in this way, that is by comparing his nature with that of others or with a former nature of his own, we affirm that sight belongs to his nature and therefore we say that he is deprived of it. But when the decree of God and His nature are considered, we cannot say of that man any more than of a stone, that he is deprived of sight, for at that time sight pertains to that man no less inconsistently than to a stone; *for to that man there pertains and belongs nothing more than the Divine understanding and will attributed to him.* And therefore God is no more the cause of his not seeing than of the stone's not seeing, which is mere Negation. *So also when we consider the nature of the man who is led by his desire for pleasure, and when we compare his present desire with that which is felt by the upright, or with that which he himself had on another occasion, we assert that the man is deprived of a better desire, because we judge that the desire of virtue then pertains to him. This we cannot do if we consider the nature of God's decree and His understanding. For in this respect the better desire belongs no more to that man's nature at that time than it does to the Nature of a Devil or of a stone,* and therefore in this respect the better desire is not Privation but Negation. So that Privation is nothing else but denying of a thing something which we judge to pertain to its nature, and Negation is nothing else but denying something of a thing because it does not belong to its nature. Hence it is clear why the desire of Adam for earthly things was evil only in relation to our understanding and not in relation to that of God. *For although God knew both the past and the present state of Adam He did not therefore conceive Adam as deprived of a past state, that is, conceive the past state as pertaining to his nature.* For then God would conceive something contrary to His will, that is, contrary to His own understanding.

[FROM Letter XXI, to William van Blyenbergh, January 28, 1675; trans. A. Wolf, *ibid.*]

GOTTFRIED WILHELM von LEIBNIZ

First Truths

Discourse on Metaphysics

Monadology

SUPPLEMENTARY PASSAGES

Necessary and Contingent Truths

Space and Time

Expression

The Ontological Argument

The Relation between Soul and Body

Progress

Possibility and Existence

Matter

Monads

The Pre-established Harmony

GOTTFRIED WILHELM
VON LEIBNIZ

IN AN AGE abounding with brilliant men, many of whom made important contributions in several fields of inquiry, Gottfried Wilhelm von Leibniz (1646–1716) was perhaps the most wide-ranging in his intellectual interests and in his intellectual achievements. Yet he combined his active thinking about problems in philosophy, theology, mathematics, natural science, law, history, and literature, with equally intensive work on various diplomatic and technological problems.

Leibniz studied law at Leipzig University, where he was refused a degree in 1666 because of his youth. He entered the service of the Elector and Archbishop of Mainz, a leader in the Holy Roman Empire whose ambition was to create a lasting European peace after the devastating Thirty Years' War. Leibniz worked out a number of plans— among them a detailed plan for the invasion of Egypt, which was designed to tempt Louis XIV into undertaking an expedition there instead of against the Low Countries. Leibniz went to Paris in connection with his plan. (Louis did not follow it, but judging from its similarity to that adopted by Napoleon in his successful invasion of Egypt, it was militarily sound.) He remained for four years, and he came into contact with scholars in various fields. On a visit to London (1673), he was made a member of the Royal Society. When the Elector died, he accepted the post of Librarian to the Duke of Brunswick at Hanover (1676), where he remained till his death, except for travels to do research for a history of the House of Brunswick.

Though most famous for his discovery (independent of Newton's, but at about the same time) of the infinitesimal calculus, including the notation that is used today, Leibniz was also concerned with problems of dynamics, and he laid the foundations for the first system of symbolic logic. He made substantial improvements on Pascal's calculating machine, and invented a device for drawing all sorts of geometrical figures. He worked for a long time, without success, on the problem of keeping the ducal mines (which were under his charge) free of water. He founded the Berlin Academy. And meanwhile, throughout most of his life, he appears to have read nearly everything printed in most of his fields of interest.

In philosophy Leibniz wrote two long books, many essays, and a very large number of fragmentary pieces. These are still in the library at Hanover, and many of them are as yet unpublished. He also engaged in incredibly extensive correspondence, much of which has been preserved.

Of the two books, the *Theodicy* (trans. E. M. Huggard, New Haven: Yale University Press, 1952)—a vindication of God's justice to man (Leibniz invented the term "theodicy")—was published in 1710, and became the chief foundation of Leibniz's philosophical reputation in the eighteenth century. The other, *New Essays on Human Understanding* (trans. Peter Remnant and Jonathan Bennett, Cambridge: Cambridge University Press, 1982), was a point-by-point discussion of Locke's great *Essay;* but after Locke's death in 1704 Leibniz decided not to publish it.

The essays include several important expositions of his philosophy besides those included in the present volume for example: *Meditations on Knowledge, Truth, and Ideas* (1684), *A New System of the Nature and the Communication of Substances* (1695), *On the Radical Origination of Things* (1697), *The Principles of Nature and of Grace, Based on Reason* (1714), which are all included in the most extensive collection of English translations of Leibniz's works, that of Leroy E. Loemker, *Gottfried Wilhelm Leibniz: Philosophical Papers and Letters,* 2nd ed., Boston: D. Reidel Publishing Co., 1969; and in Philip Wiener, ed., *Leibniz Selections,* New York: Scribner (Modern Student's Library), 1951. The political essays are included in the volume *Leibniz: Political Writings* (trans. and ed. Patrick Riley, Cambridge: Cambridge University Press, 2d ed., 1972).

Leibniz was a tireless correspondent; he took advantage of every opportunity to learn from his contemporaries, scientists, theologians, and others, and he was constantly explaining, clarifying, and defending his philosophy against counter-arguments. His letters contain some of his best statements on various points in his philosophy. Among the notable correspondences are those with Samuel Clarke (ed. H. G. Alexander, Manchester: Manchester University Press, 1956), Arnauld (trans. George H. Montgomery, Chicago: Open Court, 1931), Des Bosses, and De Volder (selections from all these are in Loemker, *op. cit.*).

Leibniz's contribution to the development of modern philosophy is important, over and above his considerable historical influence. (His

system was a major force on the Continent until the appearance of
Kant's critical philosophy.) He developed the methods of exact logical
analysis in philosophy beyond those of his predecessors; his precise
and terse mode of argument set a high standard of care and rigor. By
bringing together his knowledge of various fields—he was always
making apt analogies with number theory, or ancient history, or legal
principles, or politics, or biology—he contributed greatly to the clarification of several philosophical concepts that have proved extremely
important to our thinking: identity, necessity, analyticity, spatial and
temporal relation. He explored the grounds and consequences of several fundamental and significant principles, and thereby helped later
philosophers to determine whether these principles are true: the principle of the identity of indiscernibles, of sufficient reason, of the analyticity of truth, of continuity, of simplicity or economy in the
construction of explanatory hypotheses. And his vigorous and ingenious debate over the problems of theodicy, for decades with numerous
correspondents and periodical writers, helped people to think much
more effectively about these problems by bringing to bear the methods
and conclusions of his metaphysics.

First Truths*

First truths are those which predicate something of themselves or deny the opposite of their opposites. For example, A is A, or A is not non-A; if it is true that A is B, it is false that A is not B or that A is non-B. Likewise, everything is what it is; everything is similar or equal to itself; nothing is greater or less than itself. These and other truths of this kind, though they may have various degrees of priority, can nevertheless all be grouped under the one name of *identities*.

All other truths are reduced to first truths with the aid of definitions or by the analysis of concepts; in this consists *proof* a priori, which is independent of experience. I shall give as example this proposition which is accepted as an axiom by mathematicians and all other people alike: the whole is greater than its part, or the part is less than the whole. This is very easily demonstrated from the definition of less or greater, with the addition of a primitive axiom or identity. For that is *less* which is equal to a part of another thing (the *greater*). This definition is very easily understood and is consistent with the general practice of men, when they compare things with each other and measure the excess by subtracting an amount equal to the smaller from the greater. Hence one may reason as follows. A part is equal to a part of the whole (namely, to itself, by the axiom of identity, according to which each thing is equal to itself). But what is equal to a part of a whole is less than the whole (by the definition of less). Therefore the part is less than the whole.

The predicate or consequent therefore always inheres in the subject or antecedent. And as Aristotle, too, observed, the nature of truth in general or the connection between the terms of a proposition consists in this fact. In identities this connection and the inclusion of the predicate in the subject are explicit; in all other propositions they are implied and must be revealed through the analysis of the concepts, which constitutes a demonstration a priori.

This is true, moreover, in every affirmative truth, universal or singular, necessary or contingent, whether its terms are intrinsic or

* Reprinted from *Gottfried Wilhelm Leibniz: Philosophical Papers and Letters*, trans. Leroy E. Loemker, 2 vols., 1956. Copyright ©1956 by the University of Chicago. Reprinted by permission of Katharine Kokomoor. This paper was probably written sometime during the period 1680-84; its title derives from the first two words, "*primae veritates*."

extrinsic denominations. Here lies hidden a wonderful secret which contains the nature of contingency or the essential distinction between necessary and contingent truths and which removes the difficulty involved in a fatal necessity determining even free things.

These matters have not been adequately considered because they are too easy, but there follow from them many things of great importance. At once they give rise to the accepted axiom that *there is nothing without a reason, or no effect without a cause.* Otherwise there would be truth which could not be proved a priori or resolved into identities—contrary to the nature of truth, which is always either expressly or implicitly identical. It follows also that, if there is a correspondence between two data in a determining series, then there will also be a correspondence of the same kind in the series sought for and determined by the former. For no difference can be accounted for unless its reason is found in the data. A corollary, or, better, an example, of this is the postulate of Archimedes stated at the beginning of his book on the balance—that if the arms of a balance and its weights are supposed equal, everything will be in equilibrium. This also gives a *reason for eternal things.* If it be assumed that the world has existed from eternity and has contained only spheres, a reason should have to be given why it contains spheres rather than cubes.

It follows also that *there are no two individual things in nature which differ only numerically.* For surely it must be possible to give a reason why they are different, and this must be sought in some differences within themselves. Thus the observation of Thomas Aquinas about separate intelligences, which he declared never differ in number alone, must be applied to other things also. Never are two eggs, two leaves, or two blades of grass in a garden to be found exactly similar to each other. So perfect similarity occurs only in incomplete and abstract concepts, where matters are conceived, not in their totality but according to a certain single viewpoint, as when we consider only figures and neglect the figured matter. So geometry is right in studying similar triangles, even though two perfectly similar material triangles are never found. And, although gold or some other metal, or salt, and many liquids, may be taken for homogeneous of the predicate. Likewise, whenever the denomination of a thing is changed, some variation has to occur in the thing itself.

The complete or perfect concept of an individual substance involves all its predicates, past, present, and future. For certainly it is already true now that a future predicate will be a predicate in the future, and so it is contained in the concept of the thing. Therefore there is contained in the perfect individual concepts of Peter or Judas, considered as merely possible concepts and setting aside the divine decree to create them, everything that will happen to them, whether necessarily or freely. And all this is known by God. Thus it is obvious that God elects from an infinity of possible individuals those whom he judges best suited to the supreme and secret ends of his wisdom. In an exact sense, he does not decree that Peter should sin or Judas be damned but only that, in preference to other possible individuals, Peter, who will sin—certainly, indeed, yet not necessarily but freely— and Judas, who will suffer damnation—under the same condition— shall come into existence, or that the possible concept shall become actual. And although the eternal possible concept of Peter also contains his future salvation, the cooperation of grace is not yet absent from it, for this same perfect concept of this possible Peter also contains as a possibility the help of divine grace which will be granted to him.

Every individual substance involves the whole universe in its perfect concept, and all that exists in the universe has existed or will exist. For there is no thing upon which some true denomination, at least of comparison or relation, cannot be imposed by another thing. Yet there is no purely extrinsic denomination. I have shown the same thing in many other ways which are in harmony with each other.

All individual created substances, indeed, are different expressions of the same universe and of the same universal cause, God. But these expressions vary in perfection as do different representations or perspectives of the same city seen from different points.

Every created individual substance exerts physical action and passion on all others. For if a change occurs in one, some corresponding change results in all others, because their denomination is changed. This is confirmed by our experience of nature, for we observe that in a vessel full of liquid (the whole universe is such a vessel) a motion made in the middle is propagated to the edges, though it may become more and more insensible as it recedes farther from its origin.

It can be said that, speaking with metaphysical rigor, *no created substance exerts a metaphysical action or influence upon another.* For to say nothing of the fact that it cannot be explained how anything can pass over from one thing into the substance of another, it has already been shown that all the future states of each thing follow from its own concept. What we call causes are in metaphysical rigor only concomitant requisites. This is illustrated by our experiences of nature, for bodies in fact recede from other bodies by force of their own elasticity and not by any alien force, although another body has been required to set the elasticity (which arises from something inn͏ sic to the body itself) working.

If the diversity of soul and body be assumed, their union can be explained from this without the common hypothesis of an *influx,* which is unintelligible, and without the hypothesis of occasional causes, which calls upon a God *ex machina.* For God has equipped both soul and body from the beginning with such great wisdom and workmanship that, through the original constitution and essence of each, everything which happens in one corresponds perfectly and automatically to whatever happens in the other, just as if something had passed over from the one into the other. I call this the *hypothesis of concomitance.* This is true of all the substances in the whole universe but is not perceptible in all as it is in the soul and body.

There is no vacuum. For the different parts of empty space would be perfectly similar and congruent with each other and could not by themselves be distinguished. So they would differ in number alone, which is absurd. Time too may be proved not to be a thing, in the same way as space.

There is no corporeal substance in which there is nothing but extension, or magnitude, figure, and their variations. For otherwise there could exist two corporeal substances perfectly similar to each other, which is absurd. Hence it follows that there is something in corporeal substances analogous to the soul, which is commonly called form.

There are no atoms; indeed, there is no body so small that it is not actually subdivided. By this very fact, since it is affected by all other things in the entire world, and receives some effect from all which must cause a change in the body, it has even preserved all past impressions and anticipates the future ones. If anyone says that this effect is contained in the motions impressed on the atom, which receives the effect *in toto* without any division in it, it can be replied that not only must an effect in the atom result from all the impressions of the universe but, conversely, the entire state of the universe can be gathered from the atom. Thus the cause can be inferred from the effect. But, from the figure and motion of the atom alone, we cannot by regression infer what impressions have produced the given effect on it, since the same motion can be caused by different impressions, not to mention the fact that we cannot explain why bodies of a definite smallness should not be further divisible.

Hence it follows that *every small part of the universe contains a world with an infinite number of creatures.* But a continuum is not divisible into points, nor is it divisible in all possible ways. It is not divisible into points, because points are not parts but limits. It is not divisible in all possible ways, because not all creatures are in the same part; yet it is certain that the parts are infinitely divisible. Thus, if you bisect a straight line and then any part of it, you will set up different divisions than if you trisect it.

There is no actual determinate figure in things, for none can satisfy the infinity of impressions. So neither a circle nor an ellipse nor any other line is definable by us except in our intellect, or, if you prefer, before the lines are drawn or their parts distinguished.

Space, time, extension, and motion are not things but well-founded modes of our consideration.

Extension, motion, and bodies themselves, insofar as they consist in extension and motion alone, are not substances but true phenomena, like rainbows and parhelia. For figures do not define things, and, if only their extension is considered, bodies are not one substance but many.

For the substance of bodies there is required something which lacks extension; otherwise there would be no principle to account for the reality of the phenomena or for true unity. There would always be a plurality of bodies, never one body alone; and therefore there could not, in truth, be many. By a similar argument Cordemoi proved the existence of atoms. But, since these have been excluded, there remains only something that lacks extension, something like the soul, which was once called a form or species.

Corporeal substance can neither come into being nor perish except through creation or annihilation. For, once it does last, it will last always, for there is no reason for a change. Nor does the dissolution of a body have anything in common with its destruction. *Therefore ensouled beings neither begin nor perish; they are only transformed.*

Discourse on Metaphysics*

I. *Concerning the divine perfection and that God does everything in the most desirable way.* The conception of God which is the most common and the most full of meaning is expressed well enough in the words: God is an absolutely perfect being. The implications, however, of these words fail to receive sufficient consideration. For instance, there are many different kinds of perfection, all of which God possesses, and each one of them pertains to him in the highest degree.

We must also know what perfection is. One thing which can surely be affirmed about it is that those forms or natures which are not susceptible of it to the highest degree, say the nature of numbers or of figures, do not permit of perfection. This is because the number which is the greatest of all (that is, the sum of all the numbers), and likewise the greatest of all figures, imply contradictions. The greatest knowledge, however, and omnipotence contain no impossibility. Consequently power and knowledge do admit of perfection, and in so far as they pertain to God they have no limits.

Whence it follows that God who possesses supreme and infinite wisdom acts in the most perfect manner not only metaphysically, but also from the moral standpoint. And with respect to ourselves it can be said that the more we are enlightened and informed in regard to the works of God the more will we be disposed to find them excellent and conforming entirely to that which we might desire.

II. *Against those who hold that there is in the works of God no goodness, or that the principles of goodness and beauty are arbitrary.* Therefore I am far removed from the opinion of those who maintain that there are no principles of goodness or perfection in the nature of things, or in the ideas which God has about them, and who say that the works of God are good only through the formal reason that God has made them. If this position were true, God, knowing that he is

* From *Leibniz: Discourse on Metaphysics,* trans. George R. Montgomery, revised by Albert R. Chandler, Chicago: Open Court, 1924, with some corrections by the present editor. This essay was written in 1686 and gets its name from a letter to the Landgrave Ernest of Hesse-Rheinfels, February 1/11, 1686, in which Leibniz referred to it as *"un petit discours de la métaphysique,"* and enclosed a list of the section headings, to be forwarded to Arnauld.

the author of things, would not have to regard them afterwards and find them good, as the Holy Scripture witnesses. Such anthropomorphic expressions are used only to let us know that excellence is recognized in regarding the works themselves, even if we do not consider their evident dependence on their author. This is confirmed by the fact that it is in reflecting upon the works that we are able to discover the one who wrought. They must therefore bear in themselves his character. I confess that the contrary opinion seems to me extremely dangerous and closely approaches that of recent innovators who hold that the beauty of the universe and the goodness which we attribute to the works of God are chimeras of human beings who think of God in human terms. In saying, therefore, that things are not good according to any standard of goodness, but simply by the will of God, it seems to me that one destroys, without realizing it, all the love of God and all his glory; for why praise him for what he has done, if he would be equally praiseworthy in doing the contrary? Where will be his justice and his wisdom if he has only a certain despotic power, if arbitrary will takes the place of reasonableness, and if in accord with the definition of tyrants, justice consists in that which is pleasing to the most powerful? Besides it seems that every act of willing supposes some reason for the willing and this reason, of course, must precede the act. This is why, accordingly, I find so strange those expressions of certain philosophers who say that the eternal truths of metaphysics and Geometry, and consequently the principles of goodness, of justice, and of perfection, are only effects of the will of God. To me it seems that all these follow from his understanding, which does not depend upon his will any more than does his essence.

III. *Against those who think that God might have made things better than he has.* Neither am I able to approve of the opinion of certain modern writers who boldly maintain that what God has made is not perfect in the highest degree, and that he might have done better. It seems to me that the consequences of such an opinion are wholly inconsistent with the glory of God. *Uti minus malum habet rationem boni, ita minus bonum habet rationem mali*[1] I think that one acts imperfectly if he acts with less perfection than he is capable of. To show that an architect could have done better is to find fault

---

[1] [As the lesser evil contains an element of good, so the lesser good contains an element of evil.—M.C.B.]

with his work. Furthermore this opinion is contrary to the Holy Scriptures when they assure us of the goodness of God's work. For if comparative perfection were sufficient, then in whatever way God had accomplished his work, since there is an infinitude of possible imperfections, it would always have been good in comparison with the less perfect; but a thing is little praiseworthy when it can be praised only in this way.

I believe that a great many passages from the divine writings and from the holy fathers will be found favoring my position, while hardly any will be found in favor of that of these modern thinkers. Their opinion is, in my judgment, foreign to the writers of antiquity and is a deduction based upon our too slight acquaintance with the general harmony of the universe and with the hidden reasons for God's conduct. In our ignorance, therefore, we are tempted to decide audaciously that many things might have been done better.

These modern thinkers insist upon certain hardly tenable subtleties, for they imagine that nothing is so perfect that there might not have been something more perfect. This is an error. They think, indeed, that they are thus safeguarding the liberty of God. As if it were not the highest liberty to act in perfection according to the sovereign reason. For to think that God acts in anything without having any reason for his willing, even if we overlook the fact that such action seems impossible, is an opinion which conforms little to God's glory. For example, let us suppose that God chooses between A and B, and that he takes A without any reason for preferring it to B. I say that this action on the part of God is at least not praiseworthy, for all praise ought to be founded upon reason which *ex hypothesi* is not present here. My opinion is that God does nothing for which he does not deserve to be glorified.

IV. *That love for God demands on our part complete satisfaction with and acquiescence in that which he has done.* The general knowledge of this great truth that God acts always in the most perfect and most desirable manner possible, is in my opinion the basis of the love which we owe to God in all things; for he who loves seeks his satisfaction in the felicity or perfection of the object loved and in the perfection of his actions. *Idem velle et idem nolle vera amicitia est.*[1] I believe that it is difficult to love God truly when one, having the power to change his disposition, is not disposed to wish for

---

[1] [To wish the same and to reject the same is true friendship.—M.C.B.]

that which God desires. In fact those who are not satisfied with what God does seem to me like dissatisfied subjects whose attitude is not very different from that of rebels. I hold, therefore, that on these principles, to act conformably to the love of God it is not sufficient to force oneself to be patient, we must be really satisfied with all that comes to us according to his will. I mean this acqui-escence in regard to the past; for as regards the future one should not be a quietist with arms folded, open to ridicule, awaiting that which God will do; according to the sophism which the ancients called λόγον ἄεργον, the lazy reason. It is necessary to act conformably to the presumptive will of God as far as we are able to judge of it, trying with all our might to contribute to the general welfare and particularly to the ornamentation and the perfection of that which touches us, or of that which is nigh and, so to speak, at hand. For if the future shall perhaps show that God did not wish our good intention to have its way, it does not follow that he did not wish us to act as we have; on the contrary, since he is the best of all masters, he always demands only the right intentions, and it is for him to know the hour and the proper place to let good designs succeed.

V. *In what the principles of the divine perfection consist, and that the simplicity of the means counterbalances the richness of the effects.* It is sufficient, therefore, to have this confidence in God, that he has done everything for the best and that nothing will be able to injure those who love him. To know in particular, however, the reasons which have moved him to choose this order of the universe, to permit sin, to dispense his salutary grace in a certain man-ner—this passes the capacity of a finite mind, above all when such a mind has not come into the joy of the vision of God. Yet it is possible to make some general remarks touching the course of providence in the government of things. One is able to say, there-fore, that he who acts perfectly is like an excellent Geometer who knows how to find the best construction for a problem; like a good architect who utilizes his location and the funds destined for the building in the most advantageous manner, leaving nothing which shocks or which does not display that beauty of which it is capable; like a good householder who employs his property in such a way that there shall be nothing uncultivated or sterile; like a skillful engineer who makes his production in the least difficult way possible; and like an intelligent author who encloses the most of reality in the least possible compass.

Of all beings those which are the most perfect and occupy the least possible space, that is to say those which interfere with one another the least, are spirits, whose perfections are the virtues. That is why we may not doubt that the felicity of the spirits is the principal aim of God and that he puts this purpose into execution, as far as the general harmony will permit. We will recur to this subject again.

When the simplicity of God's way is spoken of, reference is specially made to the means which he employs, and on the other hand when the variety, richness and abundance are mentioned, it is the ends or effects that are referred to. Thus one ought to be proportioned to the other, just as the cost of a building should balance the beauty and grandeur which is expected. It is true that nothing costs God anything, just as there is no cost for a philosopher who makes hypotheses in constructing his imaginary world, because God has only to make decrees in order that a real world come into being; but in matters of wisdom the decrees or hypotheses count as expenditure in proportion as they are more independent of one another. Reason wishes to avoid multiplicity in hypotheses or principles very much as the simplest system is preferred in Astronomy.

VI. *That God does nothing which is not orderly, and that it is not even possible to conceive of events which are not regular.* The activities or the acts of will of God are commonly divided into ordinary and extraordinary. But it is well to bear in mind that God does nothing out of order. Therefore, that which passes for extraordinary is so only with regard to a particular order established among the created things, for as regards the universal order, everything conforms to it. This is so true that not only does nothing occur in this world which is absolutely irregular, but it is even impossible to conceive of such an occurrence. Because, let us suppose for example that some one jots down a quantity of points upon a sheet of paper helter skelter, as do those who exercise the ridiculous art of Geomancy; now I say that it is possible to find a geometrical line whose concept shall be uniform and constant, that is, in accordance with a certain formula, and which line at the same time shall pass through all of those points, and in the same order in which the hand jotted them down. Moreover, if a continuous line be traced, which is now straight, now circular, and now of any other description, it is possible to find a mental equivalent, a formula or an equation common to all the points of this line by virtue of which formula the changes in the direction of the line must occur. There is no instance of a face whose contour does not form part of a geometric line and which can not be traced entire by a certain mathematical motion. But when the formula is very complex, that which conforms to it passes for irregular. Thus we may say that in whatever manner God might have created the world, it would always have been regular and in a certain order. God, however, has chosen the most perfect, that is to say the one which is at the same time the simplest in hypotheses and the richest in phenomena, as might be the case with a geometric line, whose construction was easy, but whose properties and effects were extremely remarkable and of great significance. I use these comparisons to picture a certain imperfect resemblance to the divine wisdom, and to point out that which may at least raise our minds to conceive in some sort what cannot otherwise be expressed. I do not pretend at all to explain thus the great mystery upon which the whole universe depends.

VII. *That miracles conform to the regular order although they go against the subordinate regulations; concerning that which God desires or permits and concerning general and particular intentions.* Now since nothing is done which is not orderly, we may say that miracles are quite within the order of natural operations. We use the term "natural" of these operations because they conform to certain subordinate regulations which we call the nature of things. For it can be said that this nature is only a custom of God's which he can change on the occasion of a stronger reason than that which moved him to use these regulations. As regards general and particular intentions, according to the way in which we understand the matter, it may be said on the one hand that everything is in accordance with his most general intention, or that which best conforms to the most perfect order he has chosen; on the other hand, however, it is also possible to say that he has particular intentions which are exceptions to the subordinate regulations above mentioned. Of God's laws, however, the most universal, i.e., that which rules the whole course of the universe, is without exceptions.

It is possible to say that God desires everything which is an object of his particular intention. When we consider the objects of his general intentions, however, such as are the modes of activities of created things and especially of the reasoning creatures with

whom God wishes to co-operate, we must make a distinction; for if
the action is good in itself, we may say that God wishes it and at
times commands it, even though it does not take place; but if it is
bad in itself and becomes good only by accident when the course
of events, and especially chastisement and satisfaction, has corrected its malignity and rewarded the ill with interest in such a way
that more perfection results in the whole train of circumstances than
would have come if that ill had not occurred—if all this takes
place we must say that God permits the evil, and not that he desired
it, although he has co-operated by means of the laws of nature which
he has established. He knows how to produce the greatest good
from it.

VIII. *In order to distinguish between the activities of God and
the activities of created things we must explain the conception of an
individual substance.*   It is quite difficult to distinguish God's actions
from those of his creatures. Some think that God does everything;
others imagine that he only conserves the force that he has given
to created things. How far can we say either of these opinions is
right?

In the first place since activity and passivity pertain properly to
individual substances (*actiones sunt suppositorum*) it will be necessary to explain what such a substance is. It is indeed true that when
several predicates are attributes of a single subject and this subject
is not an attribute of another, we speak of it as an individual substance, but this is not enough, and such an explanation is merely
nominal. We must therefore inquire what it is to be an attribute in
reality of a certain subject. Now it is evident that every true predica-
tion has some basis in the nature of things, and even when a proposition is not identical, that is, when the predicate is not expressly
contained in the subject, it is still necessary that it be virtually contained in it, and this is what the philosophers call *in-esse,* saying
thereby that the predicate is in the subject. Thus the content of the
subject must always include that of the predicate in such a way that
if one understands perfectly the concept of the subject, he will know
that the predicate appertains to it also. This being so, we are able
to say that this is the nature of an individual substance or of a
complete being, namely, to afford a conception so complete that the
concept shall be sufficient for the understanding of it and for the
deduction of all the predicates of which the substance is or may
become the subject. But an accident is something the conception of

which does not include all that can be attributed to the subject of which it is predicated. Thus the quality of king, which belonged to Alexander the Great, an abstraction from the subject, is not sufficiently determined to constitute an individual, and does not contain the other qualities of the same subject, nor everything which the idea of this prince includes. God, however, seeing the individual concept, or hæcceity, of Alexander, sees there at the same time the basis and the reason of all the predicates which can be truly uttered regarding him; for instance that he will conquer Darius and Porus, even to the point of knowing *a priori* (and not by experience) whether he died a natural death or by poison—facts which we can learn only through history. When we carefully consider the connection of things we see also the possibility of saying that there was always in the soul of Alexander marks of all that had happened to him and evidences of all that would happen to him and traces even of everything which occurs in the universe, although God alone could recognize them all.

IX. *That every individual substance expresses the whole universe in its own manner and that in its full concept are included all its experiences together with all the attendant circumstances and the whole sequence of exterior events.* There follow from these considerations several notable paradoxes; among others that it is not true that two substances may be exactly alike and differ only numerically, *solo numero,* and that what St. Thomas says on this point regarding angels and intelligences—*quod ibi omne individuum sit species infima*[1]—is true of all substances, provided that the specific difference is understood as Geometers understand it in the case of figures; again that a substance will be able to commence only through creation and perish only through annihilation; that a substance cannot be divided into two nor can one be made out of two, and that thus the number of substances neither augments nor diminishes through natural means, although they are frequently transformed. Furthermore every substance is like an entire world and like a mirror of God, or indeed of the whole world which it portrays, each one in its own fashion; almost as the same city is variously represented according to the various viewpoints from which it is regarded. Thus the universe is multiplied in some sort as many times as there are substances, and the glory of God is multiplied in the same way by as many wholly different representations of his works. It can indeed

---

[1] [That with them every individual is a species with only one member.—M.C.B.]

be said that every substance bears in some sort the character of God's infinite wisdom and omnipotence, and imitates him as much as it is able to; for it expresses, although confusedly, all that happens in the universe, past, present and future, deriving thus a certain resemblance to an infinite perception or power of knowing. And since all other substances express this particular substance and accommodate themselves to it, we can say that it exerts its power upon all the others in imitation of the omnipotence of the creator.

X. *That the belief in substantial forms has a certain basis in fact, but that these forms effect no changes in the phenomena and must not be employed for the explanation of particular events.* It seems that the ancients, and able men who were accustomed to profound meditations and taught theology and philosophy centuries ago, some of whom recommend themselves to us on account of their piety, had some knowledge of that which we have just said and this is why they introduced and maintained the substantial forms so much decried to-day. But they were not so far from the truth nor so open to ridicule as the common run of our new philosophers imagine. I grant that the consideration of these forms is of no service in the details of physics and ought not to be employed in the explanation of particular phenomena. In regard to this last point, the schoolmen were at fault, as were also the physicists of times past who followed their example, thinking they had given the reason for the properties of a body in mentioning the forms and qualities without going to the trouble of examining the manner of operation; as if one should be content to say that a clock had a certain amount of clockness derived from its form, and should not inquire in what that clockness consisted. This is indeed enough for the man who buys it, provided he surrenders the care of it to someone else. The fact, however, that there was this misunderstanding and misuse of the substantial forms should not bring us to throw away something whose recognition is so necessary in metaphysics, since without these we will not be able, I hold, to know the ultimate principles nor to lift our minds to the knowledge of the incorporeal natures and of the marvels of God. Yet as the geometer does not need to encumber his mind with the famous puzzle of the composition of the continuum, and as no moralist, and still less a jurist or a statesman has need to trouble himself with the great difficulties which arise in conciliating free will with the providential activity of God (since the geometer is able to make all his demonstrations and the statesman can complete all his deliberations without entering into these discussions which are so necessary and important in Philosophy and Theology), so in the same way the physicist can explain his experiments, now using simpler experiments already made, now employing geometrical and mechanical demonstrations without any need of the general considerations which belong to another sphere, and if he employs the cooperation of God, or perhaps of some soul or animating force, or something else of a similar nature, he goes out of his path quite as much as that man who, when facing an important practical question, would wish to enter into profound argumentations regarding the nature of destiny and of our liberty; a fault which men quite frequently commit without realizing it when they cumber their minds with considerations regarding fate, and thus they are even sometimes turned from a good resolution or from some necessary provision.

XI. *That the opinions of the theologians and of the so-called scholastic philosophers are not to be wholly despised.* I know that I am advancing a great paradox in pretending to resuscitate in some sort the ancient philosophy, and to recall *postliminio* the substantial forms almost banished from our modern thought. But perhaps I will not be condemned lightly when it is known that I have long meditated over the modern philosophy and that I have devoted much time to experiments in physics and to the demonstrations of geometry and that I, too, for a long time was persuaded of the baselessness of those "beings" which, however, I was finally obliged to take up again in spite of myself and as though by force. The many investigations which I carried on compelled me to recognize that our moderns do not do sufficient justice to Saint Thomas and to the other great men of that period and that there is in the theories of the scholastic philosophers and theologians far more solidity than is imagined, provided that these theories are employed relevantly and in their place. I am persuaded that if some careful and meditative mind were to take the trouble to clarify and direct their thoughts in the manner of analytic geometers, he would find a great treasure of very important truths, wholly demonstrable.

XII. *That the conception of the extension of a body is in a way imaginary and does not constitute the substance of the body.* But to resume the thread of our discussion, I believe that he who will meditate upon the nature of substance, as I have explained it above, will find that the whole nature of bodies is not exhausted in their extension, that is to say, in their size, figure and motion, but that we must recognize something which corresponds to soul, something which is commonly called substantial form, although these forms effect no change in the phenomena, any more than do the souls of beasts, that is if they have souls. It is even possible to demonstrate that the ideas of size, figure and motion are not so distinct as is imagined, and that they include something imaginary relative to our perceptions as do, although to a greater extent, the ideas of color, heat, and the other similar qualities in regard to which we may doubt whether they are actually to be found in the nature of the things outside of us. This is why these latter qualities are unable to constitute substance and if there were no other principle of identity in bodies than that which has just been referred to a body would not subsist more than for a moment.

The souls and the substantial forms of other bodies are entirely different from intelligent souls, which alone know their actions, and not only do not perish through natural means but indeed always retain the knowledge of what they are; a fact which makes them alone open to chastisement or recompense, and makes them citizens of the republic of the universe whose monarch is God. Hence it follows that all the other creatures should serve them, a point which we shall discuss more amply later.

XIII. *As the individual concept of each person includes once for all everything which can ever happen to him, in it can be seen the a priori evidences or the reasons for the reality of each event, and why one has happened rather than another. But these events, however certain, are nevertheless contingent, being based on the free choice of God and of his creatures. It is true that their choices always have their reasons, but they incline to the choices under no compulsion of necessity.* But before going further it is necessary to meet a difficulty which may arise regarding the principles which we have set forth in the preceding. We have said that the concept of an individual substance includes once for all everything which can ever happen to it and that in considering this concept one will be able to see everything which can truly be said concerning the individual, just as we are able to see in the nature of a circle all the properties which can be derived from it. But does it not seem that in this way the difference between contingent and necessary truths will be destroyed, that there will be no place for human liberty, and that an absolute fatality will rule as well over all our actions as over all the rest of the events of the world? To this I reply that a distinction must be made between that which is certain and that which is necessary. Every one grants that future contingencies are assured since God foresees them, but we do not say just because of that that they are necessary. But it will be objected, that if any conclusion can be deduced infallibly from some definition or concept, it is necessary; and now since we have maintained that everything which is to happen to any one is already virtually included in his nature or concept, as all the properties are contained in the definition of a circle, therefore, the difficulty still remains. In order to meet the objection completely, I say that the connection or sequence is of two kinds: the one, absolutely necessary, whose contrary implies contradiction, occurs in the eternal verities like the truths of geometry; the other is necessary only *ex hypothesi,* and so to speak by accident, and in itself it is contingent since the contrary is not implied. This latter sequence is not founded upon ideas wholly pure and upon the pure understanding of God, but upon his free decrees and upon the processes of the universe. Let us give an example. Since Julius Caesar will become perpetual Dictator and master of the Republic and will overthrow the liberty of Rome, this action is contained in his concept, for we have supposed that it is the nature of such a perfect concept of a subject to involve everything, in fact so that the predicate may be included in the subject (*ut possit inesse subjecto*). We may say that it is not in virtue of this concept or idea that he is obliged to perform this action, since it pertains to him only because God knows everything. But it will be insisted in reply that his nature or form responds to this concept, and since God imposes upon him this personality, he is compelled henceforth to live up to it. I could reply by instancing the similar case of the future contingencies which as yet have no reality save in the understanding and will of God, and which, because God has given them in advance this form, must needs correspond to it. But I prefer to overcome a difficulty rather than to excuse it by instancing other difficulties, and what I am about to say will serve to clear up the one as well as the other. It is here that must be applied the distinction in the kind of relation, and I say that that which happens conformably to these decrees is assured, but that it is not therefore necessary, and if anyone did the contrary, he would do nothing impossible in itself, although it is impossible *ex hypothesi* that that other happen. For if anyone were capable of carrying out a complete demonstration by virtue of which he could prove this connection of the subject, which is Caesar, with the predicate, which is his successful enterprise, he would bring us to see in fact that the future dictatorship of Caesar had its basis in his concept or nature, so that one would see there a reason why he resolved to cross the Rubicon rather than to stop, and why he won instead of losing the day at Pharsalus, and that it was reasonable and by consequence assured that this would occur, but one would not prove that it was necessary in itself, nor that the contrary implied a contradiction, almost in the same way in which it is reasonable and assured that God will always do what is best although that which is less perfect is not thereby implied. For it would be found that this demonstration of this predicate as belonging to Caesar is not as absolute as are those of numbers or of geometry, but that this predicate supposes a sequence of things which God has chosen by his free will. This sequence is based on the first free decree of God which was to do always that which is the most perfect and upon the decree which God made following the first one, regarding human nature, which is that men should always do, although freely, that which appears to them best. Now every truth which is founded upon this kind of decree is contingent, although certain, for the decrees of God do not change the possibilities of things and, as I have already said, although God assuredly chooses the best, this does not prevent that which is less perfect from being possible in itself. Although it will never happen, it is not its impossibility but its imperfection which causes him to reject it. Now nothing is necessitated whose opposite is possible. One will then be in a position to satisfy these kinds of difficulties, however great they may appear (and in fact they have not been less vexing to all other thinkers who have ever treated this matter), provided that he considers well that all contingent propositions have reasons why they are thus, rather than otherwise, or indeed (what is the same thing) that they have *a priori* proofs of their truth, which render them certain and show that the connection of the subject and predicate in these propositions has its basis in the nature of the one and of the other, but he must further remember that such contingent propositions have not the demonstrations of necessity, since their reasons are founded only on the principle of contingency or of the existence of things, that is to say, upon that which is, or which appears to be, the best among several things equally possible. Necessary truths, on the other hand, are founded upon the principle of contradiction, and upon the possibility or impossibility of the essences themselves, without regard here to the free will of God or of creatures.

XIV. *God produces different substances according to the different views which he has of the world, and by the intervention of God, the appropriate nature of each substance brings it about that what happens to one corresponds to what happens to all the others, without, however, their acting upon one another directly.* After having seen, to a certain extent, in what the nature of substances consists, we must try to explain the dependence they have upon one another and their actions and passions. Now it is first of all very evident that created substances depend upon God who preserves them and can produce them continually by a kind of emanation just as we produce our thoughts, for when God turns, so to say, on all sides and in all fashions, the general system of phenomena which he finds it good to produce for the sake of manifesting his glory, and when he regards all the aspects of the world in all possible manners, since there is no relation which escapes his omniscience, the result of each view of the universe as seen from a different position is a substance which expresses the universe conformably to this view, provided God sees fit to render his thought effective and to produce the substance, and since God's vision is always true, our perceptions are always true and that which deceives us are our judgments, which are of us. Now we have said before, and it follows from what we have just said that each substance is a world by itself, independent of everything else excepting God; therefore, all our phenomena, that is all things which are ever able to happen to us, are only consequences of our being. Now as the phenomena maintain a certain order conformably to our nature, or so to speak to the world which is in us (from whence it follows that we can, for the regulation of our conduct, make useful observations which are justified by the outcome of the future phenomena) and as we are thus able often to judge the future by the past without deceiving ourselves, we have sufficient grounds for saying that these phenomena are true and we will not be put to the task of inquiring whether they are outside of us, and whether others perceive them also.

Nevertheless it is most true that the perceptions and expressions of all substances intercorrespond, so that each one following independently certain reasons or laws which he has noticed meets others which are doing the same, as when several people, having agreed to meet together in a certain place on a set day, are able to carry out the plan if they wish. Now although all express the same phenomena, this does not bring it about that their expressions are exactly alike. It is sufficient if they are proportional. As when several spectators think they see the same thing and are agreed about it, although each one sees or speaks according to the measure of his vision. It is God alone (from whom all individuals emanate continually, and who sees the universe not only as they see it, but besides in a very different way from them) who is the cause of this correspondence in their phenomena and who brings it about that that which is particular to one, is also common to all, otherwise there would be no relation. In a way, then, we might properly say, although it seems strange, that a particular substance never acts upon another particular substance nor is it acted upon by it. That which happens to each one is only the consequence of its complete idea or concept, since this idea already includes all the predicates and expresses the whole universe. In fact nothing can happen to us except thoughts and perceptions, and all our thoughts and perceptions are but the consequence, contingent it is true, of our precedent thoughts and perceptions, in such a way that were I able to consider directly all that happens or appears to me at the present time, I should be able to see all that will happen to me or that will ever appear to me. This future will not fail me, and will surely appear to me even if all that which is outside of me were destroyed, save only that God and myself were left.

Since, however, we ordinarily attribute to other things an action upon us which brings us to perceive things in a certain manner, it is necessary to consider the basis of this judgment and to inquire what there is of truth in it.

XV. *The action of one finite substance upon another consists only in the increase in the degrees of the expression of the first combined with a decrease in that of the second, in so far as God has in advance fashioned them so that they shall act in accord.* Without entering into a long discussion it is sufficient for reconciling the language of metaphysics with that of practical life to remark that we preferably attribute to ourselves, and with reason, the phenomena which we express the most perfectly, and that we attribute to other substances those phenomena which each one expresses the best. Thus a substance, which is of an infinite extension in so far as it expresses all, becomes limited in proportion to its more or less perfect manner of expression. It is thus then that we may conceive of substances as interfering with and limiting one another, and hence we are able to say that in this sense they act upon one another, and that they, so to speak, accommodate themselves to one another. For it can happen that a single change which augments the expression of the one may diminish that of the other. Now the virtue of a particular substance is to express well the glory of God, and the better it expresses it, the less is it limited. Everything when it expresses its virtue or power, that is to say, when it acts, changes to better, and expands just in so far as it acts. When therefore a change occurs by which several substances are affected (in fact every change affects them all) I think we may say that those substances which by this change pass immediately to a greater degree of perfection, or to a more perfect expression, exert power and act while those which pass to a lesser degree disclose their weakness and suffer. I also hold that every activity of a substance which has perception implies some pleasure, and every passion some pain, except that it may very well happen that a present advantage will be eventually destroyed by a greater evil, whence it comes that one may sin in acting or exerting his power and in finding pleasure.

XVI. *The extraordinary intervention of God is not excluded from that which our particular essences express, because their expression includes everything. Such intervention, however, goes beyond the power of our natural being or of our distinct expression, because these are finite, and follow certain subordinate regulations.* There remains for us at present only to explain how it is possible that God has influence at times upon men or upon other substances by an extraordinary or miraculous intervention, since it seems that nothing is able to happen which is extraordinary or supernatural in as much as all the events which occur to the other substances are only the consequences of their natures. We must recall what was said above in regard to the miracles in the universe. These always conform to the universal law of the general order, although they may contravene the subordinate regulations, and since every person or substance is like a little world which expresses the great world, we can say that this extraordinary action of God upon this substance is nevertheless miraculous, although it is comprised in the general order of the universe in so far as it is expressed by the individual essence or concept of this substance. This is why, if we understand in our natures all that they express, nothing is supernatural in them, because they reach out to everything, an effect always expressing its cause, and God being the veritable cause of the substances. But as that which our natures express the most perfectly pertains to them in a particular manner, that being their special power, and since they are limited, as I have just explained, there are many things which surpass the powers of our natures and even of all limited natures. As a consequence, to speak more clearly, I say that the miracles and the extraordinary interventions of God have this peculiarity that they cannot be foreseen by any created mind however enlightened. This is because the distinct comprehension of the fundamental order surpasses them all, while on the other hand, that which is called natural depends upon less fundamental regulations which the creatures are able to understand. In order then that my words may be as irreprehensible as the meaning I am trying to convey, it will be well to associate certain words with certain significations. We may call that which includes everything that we express and which expresses our union with God himself, nothing going beyond it, our essence. But that which is limited in us may be designated as our nature or our power, and in accordance with this terminology that which goes beyond the natures of all created substances is supernatural.

XVII. *An example of a subordinate regulation, or law of nature, which demonstrates that God always preserves the same amount of force[1] but not the same quantity of motion[2]:—against the Cartesians and many others.* I have frequently spoken of subordinate regulations, or laws of nature, and it seems that it will be well to give an example. Our new philosophers are unanimous in employing that famous law that God always preserves the same amount of motion in the universe. In fact it is a very plausible law, and in times past I held it as indubitable. But since then I have learned in what its fault consists. Descartes and many other clever mathematicians have thought that the quantity of motion, that is to say the velocity multiplied by the bulk of the moving body, is exactly equivalent to the moving force, or to speak in mathematical terms that the force varies as the velocity multiplied by the bulk. Now it is reasonable that the same force is always preserved in the universe. So also, looking to phenomena, it will be readily seen that a mechanical perpetual motion is impossible, because the force in such a machine, being always diminished a little by friction and so ultimately destined to be entirely spent, would necessarily have to recoup its losses, and consequently would keep on increasing of itself without any new

---

[1] [In modern terms, mv^2, or kinetic energy.—M.C.B.]
[2] [In modern terms, mv, or momentum.—M.C.B.]

impulsion from without; and we see furthermore that the force of a body is diminished only in proportion as it gives up force, either to a contiguous body or to its own parts, in so far as they have a separate movement. The mathematicians to whom I have referred think that what can be said of force can be said of the quantity of motion. In order, however, to show the difference I make two suppositions: in the first place, that a body falling from a certain height acquires a force enabling it to remount to the same height, provided that its direction is turned that way, and provided that there are no hindrances. For instance, a pendulum will rise exactly to the height from which it has fallen, provided the resistance of the air and of certain other small particles do not diminish a little its acquired force.

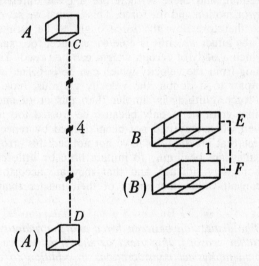

I suppose in the second place that it will take as much force to lift a body A weighing one pound to the height CD, four feet, as to raise a body B weighing four pounds to the height EF, one foot. These two suppositions are granted by our new philosophers. It is therefore manifest that the body A falling from the height CD acquires exactly as much force as the body B falling from the height EF, for the body B at F, having by the first supposition sufficient force to return to E, has therefore the force to carry a body of four pounds to the distance of one foot, EF. And likewise the body A at D, having the force to return to C, has also the force required to carry a body weighing one pound, its own weight, back to C, a distance of four feet. Now by the second supposition the force of these two bodies is equal. Let us now see if the quantity of motion is the same in each case. It is here that we will be surprised to find a very great difference, for it has been proved by Galileo that the velocity acquired by the fall CD is double the velocity acquired by the fall EF, although the height is four times as great. Multiplying, therefore, the body A, whose bulk is 1, by its velocity, which is 2, the product or the quantity of movement will be 2, and on the other hand, if we multiply the body B, whose bulk is 4, by its velocity, which is 1, the product or quantity of motion will be 4. Hence the quantity of the motion of the body A at the point D is half the quantity of motion of the body B at the point F, yet their forces are equal, and there is therefore a great difference between the quantity of motion and the force. This is what we set out to show. We can see therefore how the force ought to be estimated by the quantity of the effect which it is able to produce, for example by the height to which a body of certain weight can be raised. This is a very different thing from the velocity which can be imparted to it, and in order to impart to it double the velocity we must have more than double the force. Nothing is simpler than this proof and Descartes has fallen into error here, only because he trusted too much to his thoughts even when they had not been ripened by reflection. But it astonishes me that his disciples have not noticed this error, and I am afraid that they are beginning to imitate little by little certain Peripatetics whom they ridicule, and that they are accustoming themselves to consult rather the books of their master than reason or nature.

XVIII. *The distinction between force and the quantity of motion is, among other reasons, important as showing that we must have recourse to metaphysical considerations in addition to extension if we wish to explain the phenomena of matter.* This consideration of the force, distinguished from the quantity of motion, is of importance, not only in physics and mechanics for finding the real laws of nature and the principles of motion, and even for correcting many practical errors which have crept into the writings of certain able mathematicians, but also in metaphysics it is of importance for the better understanding of principles. Because motion, if we regard only its exact and formal meaning, that is, change of place, is not something really absolute, and when several bodies change their places reciprocally, it is not possible to determine, by considering the bodies alone, to which among them movement or repose is to be attributed, as I could demonstrate geometrically, if I wished to stop for it now. But the force, or the proximate cause of these changes is something more real, and there are sufficient grounds for attributing it to one body rather than to another, and it is only through this latter investigation that we can determine to which one the movement must appertain. Now this force is something different from size, shape and motion, and it can be seen from this consideration that the whole meaning of a body is not exhausted in its extension together with its modifications, as our moderns persuade themselves. We are therefore obliged to restore certain beings or forms which they have banished. It appears more and more clear that although all the particular phenomena of nature can be explained mathematically or mechanically by those who understand them, yet nevertheless the general principles of corporeal nature and even of mechanics are metaphysical rather than geometrical, and belong rather to certain indivisible forms or natures as the causes of the appearances, than to the corporeal mass or to extension. In this way we are able to reconcile the mechanical philosophy of the moderns with the circumspection of those intelligent and well-meaning persons who, with a certain justice, fear that we are becoming too far removed from immaterial beings and that we are thus prejudicing piety.

XIX. *The utility of final causes in Physics.* As I do not wish to judge people in ill part I bring no accusation against our new philosophers who pretend to banish final causes from physics, but I am nevertheless obliged to avow that the consequences of such a banishment appear to me dangerous, especially when joined to that position which I refuted at the beginning of this treatise. That position seemed to go the length of discarding final causes entirely, as though God proposed no end and no good in his activity, or as if good were not the object of his will. I hold on the contrary that it is just in this that the principle of all existences and of the laws of nature must be sought, since God always proposes the best and most perfect. I am quite willing to grant that we are liable to err when we wish to determine the purposes or councils of God, but this is the case only when we try to limit them to some particular design, thinking that he has had in view only a single thing, while in fact he regards everything at once. As for instance, if we think that God has made the world only for us, it is a great blunder, although it is quite true that he has made it entirely for us, and that there is nothing in the universe which does not touch us and which does not accommodate itself to the regard which he has for us according to the principle laid down above. Therefore when we see some good effect or some perfection which happens or which follows from the works of God we are able to say assuredly that God has purposed it, for he does nothing by chance, and is not like us who sometimes fail to do well. Therefore, far from being able to fall into error in this respect as do the extreme statesmen who postulate too much foresight in the designs of Princes, or as do commentators who seek for too much erudition in their authors, it will be impossible to attribute too much reflection to God's infinite wisdom, and there is no matter in which error is less to be feared provided we confine ourselves to affirmations and provided we avoid negative statements which limit the designs of God. All those who see the admirable structure of animals find themselves led to recognize the wisdom of the author of things and I advise those who have any sentiment of piety and indeed of true philosophy to hold aloof from the expressions of certain pretentious minds who instead of saying that eyes were made for seeing, say that we see because we find ourselves having eyes. When one seriously holds such opinions which hand everything over to material necessity or to a kind of chance (although either alternative ought to appear ridiculous to those who understand what we have explained above) it is difficult to recognize an intelligent author of nature. The effect should correspond to its cause and indeed it is best known through the recognition of its cause, so that it is reasonable to introduce a sovereign intelligence ordering things, and in place of making use of the wisdom of this sovereign being, to employ only the properties of matter to explain phenomena. As if in order to account for the capture of an important place by a prince, the historian should say it was because the particles of powder in the cannon having been touched by a spark of fire expanded with a rapidity capable of pushing a hard solid body against the walls of the place, while the little particles which composed the brass of the cannon were so well interlaced that they did not separate under this impact—as if he should account for it in this way instead of making us see how the foresight of the conqueror brought him to choose the right time and means and how his ability surmounted all obstacles.

XX. *A noteworthy disquisition in Plato's Phaedo against the philosophers who were too materialistic.* This reminds me of a fine disquisition by Socrates in Plato's *Phaedo,* which agrees perfectly with my opinion on this subject and seems to have been uttered expressly for our too materialistic philosophers. This agreement has led me to a desire to translate it although it is a little long. Perhaps this example will give some of us an incentive to share in many of the other beautiful and well balanced thoughts which are found in the writings of this famous author.[1]

XXI. *If the mechanical laws depended upon Geometry alone without metaphysical influences, the phenomena would be very different from what they are.* Now since the wisdom of God has always been recognized in the details of the mechanical structures of certain particular bodies, it should also be shown in the general economy of the world and in the constitution of the laws of nature. This is so true that even in the laws of motion in general, the plans of this wisdom have been noticed. For if bodies were only extended masses, and motion were only a change of place, and if everything ought to be and could be deduced by geometric necessity from these two definitions alone, it would follow, as I have shown elsewhere, that the smallest body on contact with a very large one at rest would impart to it its own velocity, yet without losing any of the velocity that it had. A quantity of other rules wholly contrary to the formation of a system would also have to be admitted. But the decree of the divine wisdom in preserving always the same force and the same total direction has provided for a system. I find indeed that many of the effects of nature can be accounted for in a twofold way, that is to say by a consideration of efficient causes, and again independently by a consideration of final causes. An example of the latter is God's decree always to carry out his plan by the easiest and most determined way. I have shown this elsewhere in accounting for the catoptric and dioptric laws, and I will speak more at length about it in what follows.

XXII. *Reconciliation of the two methods of explanation, the one using final causes, and the other efficient causes, thus satisfying both those who explain nature mechanically and those who have recourse to incorporeal natures.* It is worth while to make the preceding remark in order to reconcile those who hope to explain mechanically the formation of the first tissue of an animal and all the interrelation of the parts, with those who account for the same structure by referring to final causes. Both explanations are good; both are useful,

---

[1] [*Phaedo* 97^b-99^c (here omitted) contains Socrates' account of reading Anaxagoras, and finding that his explanation of the world was not teleological, but mechanistic.—M.C.B.]

not only for the admiring of the work of a great artificer, but also for the discovery of useful facts in physics and medicine. And writers who take these diverse routes should not speak ill of each other. For I see that those who attempt to explain the beauty of the divine anatomy ridicule those who imagine that the apparently fortuitous flow of certain fluids has been able to produce such a beautiful variety and that they regard them as overbold and irreverent. These others on the contrary treat the former as simple and superstitious, and compare them to those ancients who regarded the physicists as impious when they maintained that not Jupiter thundered but some material which is found in the clouds. The best plan would be to join the two ways of thinking. To use a practical comparison, we recognize and praise the ability of a workman not only when we show what designs he had in making the parts of his machine, but also when we explain the instruments which he employed in making each part, especially if these instruments are simple and ingeniously contrived. God is also a workman able enough to produce a machine still a thousand times more ingenious than our bodies, by employing only certain quite simple fluids purposely composed in such a way that ordinary laws of nature alone are required to develop them so as to produce such a marvelous effect. But it is also true that this development would not take place if God were not the author of nature. Yet I find that the method of efficient causes, which goes much deeper and is in a measure more immediate and *a priori,* is also more difficult when we come to details, and I think that our philosophers are still very frequently far removed from making the most of this method. The method of final causes, however, is easier and can be frequently employed to find out important and useful truths which we should have to seek for a long time, if we were confined to that other more physical method of which anatomy is able to furnish many examples. It seems to me that Snell, who was the first discoverer of the laws of refraction, would have waited a long time before finding them if he had tried to seek out first how light was formed. But he apparently followed that method which the ancients employed for Catoptrics, that is, the method of final causes. Because, while seeking for the easiest way in which to conduct a ray of light from one given point to another given point by reflection from a given plane (supposing that that was the design of nature) they discovered the equality of the angles of incidence and reflection, as can be seen from a little treatise by Heliodorus of Larissa and also elsewhere. This principle Snell, I believe, and afterwards independently of him, Fermat, applied most ingeniously to refraction. For since the rays while in the same media always maintain the same proportion of sines, which in turn corresponds to the resistance of the media, it appears that they follow the easiest way, or at least that way which is the most determinate for passing from a given point in one medium to a given point in another medium. That demonstration of this same theorem which Descartes has given, using efficient causes, is much less satisfactory. At least we have grounds to think that he would never have found the principle by that means if he had not learned in Holland of Snell's discovery.

XXIII. *Returning to immaterial substances we explain how God acts upon the understanding of spirits and ask whether one always keeps the idea of what he thinks about.* I have thought it well to insist a little upon final causes, upon incorporeal natures and upon an intelligent cause with respect to bodies so as to show the use of these conceptions in physics and in mathematics. This for two reasons, first, to purge from mechanical philosophy the impiety that is imputed to it, second, to elevate to nobler lines of thought the thinking of our philosophers who incline to materialistic considerations alone. Now, however, it will be well to return from bodies to the consideration of immaterial natures and particularly of spirits, and to speak of the methods which God uses to enlighten them and to act upon them. Although we must not forget that there are here at the same time certain laws of nature in regard to which I can speak more amply elsewhere. It will be enough for now to touch upon ideas and to inquire if we see everything in God and how God is our light. First of all it will be in place to remark that the wrong use of ideas occasions many errors. For when one reasons in regard to anything, he imagines that he has an idea of it and this is the foundation upon which certain philosophers, ancient and modern, have constructed a demonstration of God that is extremely imperfect. It must be, they say, that I have an idea of God, or of a perfect being, since I think of him and we cannot think without having ideas; now the idea of this being includes all perfections and since existence is one of these perfections, it follows that he exists. But I reply, inasmuch as we often think of impossible chimeras, for example of the highest degree of swiftness, of the greatest number, of the meeting of the conchoid with its base or determinant, such reasoning is not sufficient. It is therefore in this sense that we can say that there are true and false ideas according as the thing which is in question is possible or not. And it is when he is assured of the possibility of a thing, that one can boast of having an idea of it. Therefore, the aforesaid argument proves that God exists, if he is possible. This is in fact an excellent privilege of the divine nature, to have need only of a possibility or an essence in order to actually exist, and it is just this which is called self-sufficient being, *ens a se*.

XXIV. *What clear and obscure, distinct and confused, adequate and inadequate, intuitive and suppositive knowledge is, and nominal, real, causal and essential definition.* In order to understand better the nature of ideas it is necessary to touch somewhat upon the various kinds of knowledge. When I am able to recognize a thing among others, without being able to say in what its differences or characteristics consist, the knowledge is *confused*. Sometimes indeed we may know clearly, that is without being in the slightest doubt, that a poem or a picture is well or badly done because there is in it an "I know not what" which satisfies or shocks us. Such knowledge is not yet distinct. It is when I am able to explain the peculiarities which a thing has, that the knowledge is called *distinct*. Such is the knowledge of an assayer who discerns the true gold from the false by means of certain tests or marks which make up the definition of gold. But distinct knowledge has degrees, because ordinarily the conceptions which enter into the definitions will themselves be in need of definition, and are only known confusedly. When at length everything which enters into a definition or into distinct knowledge is known distinctly, even back to the primitive conception, I call that knowledge *adequate*. When my mind understands at once and distinctly all the primitive ingredients of a conception, then we have *intuitive* knowledge. This is extremely rare, as most human knowledge is only confused or suppositive. It is well also to distinguish nominal from real definition. I call a definition *nominal* when there can be doubt whether the concept is possible; as for instance, when I say that an endless screw is a line in three dimensional space whose parts are congruent or fall one upon another. Now although this is one of the reciprocal properties of an endless screw, he who did not know by other means what an endless screw was could doubt if such a line were possible, because the other lines whose parts are congruent (there are only two: the circumference of a circle and the straight line) are plane figures, that is to say they can be described *in plano*. This instance enables us to see that any reciprocal property can serve as a nominal definition, but when the property brings us to see the possibility of a thing it makes the definition *real*, and as long as one has only a nominal definition he cannot be sure of the consequences which he draws, because if it conceals a contradiction or an impossibility he would be able to draw the opposite conclusions. That is why truths do not depend upon names and are not arbitrary, as some of our new philosophers think. There is also a considerable difference among real definitions, for when the possibility is proved only by experience, as in the definition of quicksilver, whose possibility we know because such a body, which is both an extremely heavy fluid and quite volatile, actually exists, the definition is merely real and nothing more. If, however, the proof of the possibility is *a priori,* the definition is not only real but also *causal,* as for instance when it contains the possible generation of a thing. Finally, when the definition, without assuming anything which requires a proof *a priori* of its possibility, carries the analysis clear to the primitive concepts, the definition is perfect or *essential.*

XXV. *In what cases knowledge is added to mere contemplation of the idea.* Now it is manifest that we have no idea of a concept when it is impossible. And in the case of suppositive knowledge, even if we have an idea, we do not fully grasp it, because such a concept is known only in the same manner as concepts that are covertly impossible. And even if it is in fact possible, it is not by this kind of knowledge that we learn its possibility. For instance, when I am thinking of a thousand or of a chiliagon, I frequently do it without contemplating the idea. Even if I say a thousand is ten times a hundred, I frequently do not trouble to think what ten and a hundred are, because I assume that I know, and I do not consider it necessary to stop just at present to conceive of them. Therefore it may well happen, as it in fact does happen often enough, that I am mistaken in regard to a concept which I assume that I understand, although it is an impossible truth or at least is incompatible with others with which I join it, and whether I am mistaken or not, this suppositive sort of knowledge remains the same. It is, then, only when our knowledge is clear in regard to confused conceptions, and when it is intuitive in regard to those which are distinct, that we see its entire idea.

XXVI. *Ideas are all stored up within us. Plato's doctrine of reminiscence.* In order to see clearly what an idea is, we must guard ourselves against a misunderstanding. Many regard the idea as the form or the differentiation of our thinking, and according to this opinion we have the idea in our mind only in so far as we are thinking of it, and each separate time that we think of it anew we have another idea although similar to the preceding one. Some, however, take the idea as the immediate object of thought, or as a permanent form which remains even when we are no longer contemplating it. As a matter of fact our soul has the power of representing to itself any form or nature whenever the occasion comes for thinking about it, and I think that this activity of our soul is, so far as it expresses some nature, form or essence, properly the idea of the thing. This is in us, and is always in us, whether we are thinking of it or no. (Our soul expresses God and the universe and all essences as well as all existences.) This position is in accord with my principles that nothing enters naturally into our minds from outside.

It is a bad habit we have of thinking as though our minds receive certain messengers, as it were, or as if they had doors or windows. We have in our minds all those forms for all periods of time because the mind at every moment expresses all its future thoughts and already thinks confusedly everything that it will ever think distinctly. Nothing can be taught us of which we have not already in our minds the idea. This idea is as it were the material out of which the thought will form itself. This is what Plato has excellently brought out in his doctrine of reminiscence, a doctrine which contains a great deal of truth, provided that it is properly understood and purged of the error of pre-existence, and provided that one does not conceive of the soul as having already known and thought at some other time what it learns and thinks now. Plato has also confirmed his position by a beautiful experiment. He introduces [*Meno*] a boy whom he leads, by short steps, to extremely difficult truths of geometry bearing on incommensurables, all this without teaching the boy anything, merely drawing out replies by a well-arranged series of questions. This shows that the soul virtually knows those things, and needs only to turn its attention to them to recognize the truth. Consequently it possesses at least the idea upon which those truths depend. We may say even that it already possesses those truths, if we consider them as the relations of the ideas.

XXVII. *In what respect our souls can be compared to blank tablets and how conceptions are derived from the senses.* Aristotle preferred to compare our souls to blank tablets prepared for writing, and he maintained that nothing is in the understanding which does not come through the senses. This position is in accord with the popular conceptions, as Aristotle's approach usually is. Plato thinks more profoundly. Such tenets or practicologies are nevertheless allowable in ordinary use somewhat in the same way as those who accept the Copernican theory still continue to speak of the rising and setting of the sun. I find indeed that these usages can be given a real meaning containing no error, quite in the same way as I have already pointed out that we may truly say particular substances act upon one another. In this same sense we may say that knowledge is received from without through the medium of the senses because certain exterior things contain or express more particularly the causes which determine us to certain thoughts. When, however, we are dealing with the exactness of metaphysical truths, it is important to recognize the powers and independence of the soul which extend infinitely further than is commonly supposed. In the ordinary uses of life we attribute to the soul only that which belongs to it most manifestly and particularly, and there is no advantage in going further. In order, therefore, to avoid misunderstandings it would be well to choose separate terms for the two. These expressions which are in the soul whether one is conceiving of them or not may be called *ideas,* while those which one conceives of or constructs may be called *conceptions.* But whatever terms are used, it is always false to say that all our conceptions come from the so-called external senses, because those conceptions which I have of myself and of my thoughts, and consequently of being, of substance, of action, of identity, and of many others come from an inner experience.

XXVIII. *The only immediate object of our perceptions which exists outside of us is God, and in him alone is our light.* In the strictly metaphysical sense no external cause acts upon us except God and he alone is in immediate relation with us only by virtue of our continual dependence upon him. Whence it follows that there is absolutely no other external object which comes into contact with our souls and directly excites perceptions in us. We have in our souls ideas of everything only because of the continual action of God upon us, that is to say, because every effect expresses its cause and therefore the essences of our souls are certain expressions, imitations or images of the divine essence, divine thought and divine will, including all the ideas which are there contained. We may say, therefore, that God is for us the only immediate external object, and that we see things through him. For example, when we see the sun or the stars, it is God who gives to us and preserves in us the ideas, and whenever our senses are affected according to his own laws in a certain manner, it is he, who by his continual concurrence, determines our thinking.

God is the sun and the light of souls, *lumen illuminans omnem hominem venientem in hunc mundum*,[1] and this is by no means a novel conception. I think I have already remarked that during the scholastic period many believed God to be the light of the soul, *intellectus agens animæ rationalis*,[2] following in this the Holy Scriptures and the fathers who were always more Platonic than Aristotelian in their mode of thinking. The Averroists misused this conception, but others, among whom were several mystic theologians, and William of Saint Amour also, I think, understood this conception in a manner which assured the dignity of God and was able to raise the soul to a knowledge of its welfare.

XXIX. *Yet we think directly by means of our own ideas and not through God's.* Nevertheless I cannot approve of the position of certain able philosophers who seem to hold that our ideas themselves are in God and not at all in us. I think that in taking this position they have neither sufficiently considered the nature of substance, which we have just explained, nor the complete purview and independence of the soul, which includes all that happens to it and expresses God, and with him all possible and actual beings, in the same way that an effect expresses its cause. It is indeed inconceivable that the soul should think using the ideas of something else. The soul when it thinks of anything must be affected dynamically in a certain manner, and it must have in itself in advance not only the passive capacity of being thus affected, a capacity already wholly determined, but it must have also an active power by virtue of which it has always had in its nature the marks of the future production of this thought, and the disposition to produce it at its proper time. All of this shows that the soul already includes the idea which is comprised in any particular thought.

XXX. *How God inclines our souls without necessitating them; that there are no grounds for complaint; that we must not ask why Judas sinned because this free act is contained in his concept, the only question being why Judas the sinner is admitted to existence in preference to other possible persons; concerning the original imperfection or limitation before the fall and concerning the different degrees of grace.* Regarding the action of God upon the human will

---

[1] [The light lighting every man who comes into this world. John I, 9.— M.C.B.]

[2] [The active intellect of the rational soul.—M.C.B.]

there are many quite difficult considerations which it would take too long to investigate here. Nevertheless the following is what can be said in general. God in cooperating with ordinary actions only follows the laws which he has established, that is to say, he continually preserves and produces our being so that the ideas come to us spontaneously or with freedom in that order which the concept of our individual substance carries with itself. In this concept they can be foreseen for all eternity. Furthermore, by virtue of the decree which God has made that the will shall always seek the apparent good expressing or imigrating God's will in certain particular conditions (in regard to which this apparent good always has in it something of reality), he, without at all necessitating our choice, determines it by that which appears most desirable. For, absolutely speaking, our will as contrasted with necessity, is in a state of indifference, being able to act otherwise, or wholly to suspend its action, either alternative being and remaining possible. It therefore devolves upon the soul to be on guard against appearances, by means of a firm will, to reflect and to refuse to act or decide in certain circumstances, except after mature deliberation. It is, however, true and has been assured from all eternity that certain souls will not employ their power upon certain occasions.

But who could do more than God has done, and can such a soul complain of anything except itself? All these complaints after the deed are unjust, inasmuch as they would have been unjust before the deed. Would this soul shortly before committing the sin have had the right to complain of God as though he had determined the sin? Since the determinations of God in these matters cannot be foreseen, how would the soul know that it was preordained to sin unless it had already committed the sin? It is merely a question of willing or not willing, and God could not have set an easier or juster condition. Therefore all judges, without asking the reasons which have disposed a man to have an evil will, consider only how far this will is wrong. But, you object, perhaps it is ordained from all eternity that I will sin. Find your own answer. Perhaps it has not been. Now then, without asking for what you are unable to know and in regard to which you can have no light, act according to your duty as you know it. But, some one will object; whence comes it then that this man will assuredly do this sin? The reply is easy. It is that otherwise he would not be this man. For God foresees from all time that there will be a certain Judas, and in the concept or idea of him which God has, is contained this future free act. The only question, therefore, which remains is why this certain Judas, the betrayer, who is only a possibility in the idea of God, actually exists. To this question, however, we can expect no answer here on earth, excepting to say in general that it is because God has found it good that he should exist notwithstanding that sin which he foresaw. This evil will be more than overbalanced. God will derive a greater good from it, and it will finally turn out that this series of events in which is included the existence of this sinner, is the most perfect among all the possible series of events. An explanation in every case of the admirable economy of this choice cannot be given while we are sojourners on earth. It is enough to know the excellence without understanding it. It is here that we must recognize the unfathomable depth of the divine wisdom, without hesitating at a detail which involves an infinite number of considerations. It is clear, however, that God is not the cause of ill. For not only after the loss of innocence by men, has original sin possessed the soul, but even before that there was an original limitation or imperfection in the very nature of all creatures, which rendered them open to sin and able to fall. There is, therefore, no more difficulty in the supralapsarian view than there is in the other views of sin. To this also, it seems to me, can be reduced the opinion of Saint Augustine and of other authors: that the root of evil is in the privation, that is to say, in the lack or limitation of creatures, which God graciously remedies by whatever degree of perfection it pleases him to give. This grace of God, whether ordinary or extraordinary, has its degrees and its measures. It is always efficacious in itself to produce a certain proportionate effect and furthermore it is always sufficient not only to keep one from sin but even to effect his salvation, provided that the man co-operates with that which is in him. It has not always, however, sufficient power to overcome the inclination, for, if it did, man would no longer have obstacles to overcome and this power is reserved to that absolutely efficacious grace which is always victorious, whether through its own self or through the congruity of circumstances.

XXXI. *Concerning the grounds of election; concerning faith foreseen and the absolute decree and that it all reduces to the question why God has chosen and resolved to admit to existence just such a possible person, whose concept includes just such a sequence of free acts and of free gifts of grace. This at once puts an end to all difficulties.* Finally, the grace of God is wholly unprejudiced and creatures have no claim upon it. Just as it is not sufficient in accounting for God's choice in his dispensations of grace to refer to his absolute or conditional prevision of men's future actions, so it is also wrong to imagine his decrees as absolute with no reasonable motive. As concerns foreseen faith and good works, it is very true that God has elected none but those whose faith and charity he foresees, *quos se fide donaturum praescivit.*[1] The same question, however, arises again as to why God gives to some rather than to others the grace of faith or of good works. As concerns God's ability to foresee, not the faith and good deeds, but their material and predisposition, or that which a man on his part contributes to them (since there are as truly diversities on the part of men as on the part of grace, and a man although he needs to be aroused to good and needs to become converted, yet must continue to act that way)—as regards his ability to foresee there are many who say that God, knowing what a particular man will do without grace, that is without his extraordinary assistance, or knowing at least what will be the human contribution, resolves to give grace to those whose natural dispositions are the best, or at any rate are the least imperfect and evil. But if this were the case then the natural dispositions in so far as they were good would be like gifts of grace, since God would have given advantages to some over others; and therefore, since he would well know that the natural advantages which he had given would serve as motives for his grace or for his extraordinary assistance, would not everything be reduced to his mercy? I think, therefore, that since we do not know how much and in what way God takes account of natural dispositions in the dispensations of his grace, it would be safest and most exact to say, in accordance with our principles and as I have already remarked, that there must needs be among possible beings the person Peter or John whose concept or idea contains all that particular sequence of ordinary and extraordinary manifestations of grace together with the rest of the accompanying events and circumstances, and that it has pleased God to choose him from among an infinite number of persons equally possible for actual existence. When we have said this there seems nothing left to ask, and all difficulties vanish. For in regard to that great and ultimate question why it has pleased God to choose him from among so great a number of possible persons, it is surely unreasonable to demand more than the general reasons which we have given. The reasons in detail surpass our ken. Therefore, instead of postulating an absolute decree, which being without reason would be unreasonable, and instead of postulating reasons which do not suc-

---

[1] [To whom he foresaw that he would grant faith.—M.C.B.]

ceed in solving the difficulties and in turn have need themselves of reasons, it will be best to say with St. Paul that there are for God's choice certain great reasons of wisdom and congruity which he follows, which reasons, however, are unknown to mortals and are founded upon the general order, whose goal is the greatest perfection of the world. This is what is meant when the motives of God's glory and of the manifestation of his justice are spoken of, as well as when men speak of his mercy, and his perfection in general; that immense vastness of riches, in fine, with which the soul of the same St. Paul was transported.

XXXII. *Usefulness of these principles in matters of piety and of religion.* In addition it seems that the thoughts which we have just explained, and particularly the great principle of the perfection of God's operations and the concept of substance which includes all its changes with all its accompanying circumstances, far from injuring, serve rather to confirm religion, serve to dissipate great difficulties, to inflame souls with a divine love, and to raise the mind to a knowledge of incorporeal substances, much more than the present-day hypotheses. For it appears clearly that all other substances depend upon God just as our thoughts emanate from our own substances; that God is all in all and that he is intimately united to all created things, in proportion, however, to their perfection; that it is he alone who determines them from without by his influence, and if to act is to determine directly, it may be said in metaphysical language that God alone acts upon me and he alone can cause me good or ill, other substances contributing only because of his determinations; because God, who takes all things into consideration, distributes his bounties and compels created beings to accommodate themselves to one another. Thus God alone constitutes the liaison or communication between substances. It is through him that the phenomena of the one meet and accord with the phenomena of the others, so that there may be reality in our perceptions. In common parlance, however, an action is attributed to particular causes in the sense that I have explained above, because it is not necessary to make continual mention of the universal cause when speaking of particular cases. It can be seen also that every substance has a perfect spontaneity (which becomes liberty in intelligent substances). Everything that happens to it is a consequence of its idea or its being and nothing determines it except God. It is for this reason that a person of exalted mind and revered saintliness used to say that the soul ought often to think as if there were only God and itself in the world. Nothing can make us grasp immortality more firmly than this independence and vastness of the soul which protects it completely against exterior things, since it alone constitutes our universe and together with God is sufficient for itself. It is as impossible for it to perish save through annihilation as it is impossible for the universe to destroy itself, the universe whose perpetual animate expression it is. Furthermore, the changes in this extended mass which is called our body cannot possibly affect the soul nor can the dissipation of the body destroy that which is indivisible.

XXXIII. *Explanation of the relation between the soul and the body, a matter which has been regarded as inexplicable or else as miraculous; concerning the origin of confused perceptions.* We can also see the explanation of that great mystery of the union of the soul and the body, that is to say how it comes about that the passions and actions of the one are accompanied by the actions and passions or else the appropriate phenomena of the other. For it is not possible to conceive how one can have an influence upon the other and it is unreasonable to have recourse at once to the extraordinary intervention of the universal cause in an ordinary and particular case. The following, however, is the true explanation. We have said that everything which happens to a soul or to any substance is a consequence of its concept; hence the idea itself or the essence of the soul brings it about that all of its appearances or perceptions should be born out of its nature and precisely in such a way that they correspond of themselves to that which happens in the universe at large, but more particularly and more perfectly to that which happens in the body associated with it, because it is in a particular way and only for a certain time that, according to the relation of other bodies to its own body, the soul expresses the state of the universe. This last fact enables us to see how our body belongs to us, without, however, being attached to our essence. I believe that those who are careful thinkers will decide favorably for our principles because of this single reason, viz., that they are able to see in what consists the relation between the soul and the body, which appears inexplicable in any other way. We can also see that the perceptions of our senses, even when they are clear, must necessarily contain certain confused elements, for as all the bodies in the universe are in sympathy, ours receives the impressions of all the others, and while our senses respond to everything, our soul cannot pay attention to every particular. That is why our confused sensations are the result of a variety of perceptions. This variety is infinite. It is almost like the confused murmuring which is heard by those who approach the shore of a sea. It comes from the continual beatings of innumerable waves. If now, out of many perceptions which do not fit together to make one, no particular one perception surpasses the others, and if they make impressions about equally strong or equally capable of holding the attention of the soul, they can be perceived only confusedly.

XXXIV. *Concerning the difference between spirits and other substances, souls or substantial forms; that the immortality which men desire includes memory.* Supposing that the bodies which constitute a *unum per se,* as human bodies do, are substances, and have substantial forms, and supposing that animals have souls, we are obliged to grant that these souls and these substantial forms cannot entirely perish, any more than can the atoms or the ultimate elements of matter, according to the position of other philosophers; for no substance perishes, although it may become very different. Such substances also express the whole universe, although more imperfectly than do spirits. The principal difference, however, is that they do not know what they are, nor what they do. Consequently, not being able to reason, they are unable to discover necessary and universal truths. It is also because they do not reflect upon themselves that they have no moral qualities, whence it follows that when they undergo myriad transformations—as when a caterpillar changes into a butterfly—the result from a moral or practical standpoint is the same as if we said that they perished in each case, and we can indeed say it from the physical standpoint in the same way that we say bodies perish in their dissolution. But the intelligent soul, knowing that it exists, having the ability to say that word "I" so full of meaning, not only continues and exists metaphysically far more certainly than do the others, but it remains the same from the moral standpoint, and constitutes the same personality, for it is its memory or knowledge of this "I" which renders it open to punishment and reward. Also the immortality which is required in morals and in religion does not consist merely in this perpetual existence, which pertains to all substances, for if in addition there were no remembrance of what one had been, immortality would not be at all desirable. Suppose that some individual could suddenly become King of China on condition, however, of forgetting what he had been, as though being born again, would it not amount to the same practically, or as far as the effects could be perceived, as if the individual were annihilated, and a king of China were the same instant created in his place? The individual would have no reason to desire this.

XXXV. *The excellence of spirits; that God considers them preferable to other creatures.* In order, however, to prove by natural reasons that God will preserve forever not only our substance, but also our personality, that is to say the recollection and knowledge of what we are (although the distinct knowledge is sometimes suspended during sleep and in swoons) it is necessary to join moral to metaphysical considerations. God must be considered not only as the principle and the cause of all substances and of all existing things, but also as the chief of all persons or intelligent substances, as the absolute monarch of the most perfect city or republic, such as is constituted by all the spirits together in the universe, God being the most complete of all spirits at the same time that he is greatest of all beings. For assuredly the spirits are the most perfect of substances and best express the divinity. Since all the nature, purpose, virtue and function of substance is, as has been sufficiently explained, to express God and the universe, there is no room for doubting that those substances which give the expression, knowing what they are doing and which are able to understand the great truths about God and the universe, do express God and the universe incomparably better than do those natures which are either brutish and incapable of recognizing truths, or are wholly destitute of sensation and knowledge. The difference between intelligent substances and those which are not intelligent is quite as great as between a mirror and one who sees. As God is himself the greatest and wisest of spirits, it is easy to understand that the spirits with which he can, so to speak, enter into conversation and even into social relations by communicating to them in particular ways his feelings and his will, so that they are able to know and love their benefactor, must be much nearer to him than the rest of created things which may be regarded as the instruments of spirits. In the same way we see that all wise persons regard a man as of greater worth than anything else, however precious it may be; and it seems that the greatest satisfaction which a soul, satisfied in other respects, can have is to see itself loved by others. However, with respect to God there is this difference, that his glory and our worship can add nothing to his satisfaction, the recognition of creatures being nothing but a consequence of his sovereign and perfect felicity, far from contributing to it or from causing it even in part. Nevertheless, that which is reasonable in finite spirits is found eminently in him, and as we praise a king who prefers to preserve the life of a man before that of the most precious and rare of his animals, we should not doubt that the most enlightened and most just of all monarchs has the same preference.

XXXVI. *God is the monarch of the most perfect republic composed of all the spirits, and the happiness of this city of God is his principal purpose. That spirits express God rather than the world, but that the other substances express the world rather than God.* Spirits are of all substances the most capable of perfection, and their perfections are different in this, that they interfere with one another the least, or rather they aid one another the most, for only the most virtuous can be the most perfect friends. Hence it follows that God, who always aims at the greatest perfection, will have the greatest care for spirits and will give not only to all of them in general, but even to each one in particular the highest perfection which the universal harmony will permit. We can even say that it is because he is a spirit that God is the originator of existences, for if he had lacked the power of will to choose what is best, there would have been no reason why one possible being should exist rather than any other. Therefore God's being a spirit himself dominates all the considerations which he may have toward created things. Spirits alone are made in his image, being as it were of his blood or as children in the family, since they alone are able to serve him of free will, and to act consciously imitating the divine nature. A single spirit is worth a whole world, because it not only expresses the whole world, but it also knows it and governs itself as does God. In this way we may say that though every substance expresses the whole universe, yet the other substances express the world rather than God, while spirits express God rather than the world. This nature of spirits, so noble that it enables them to approach divinity as much as is possible for created things, has as a result that God derives infinitely more glory from them than from the other beings, or rather the other beings furnish to spirits the material for glorifying him. This moral quality of God which constitutes him Lord and Monarch of spirits influences him, so to speak, personally and in a unique way. It is through this that he humanizes himself, that he is willing to suffer anthropomorphisms, and that he enters into social relations with us as a Prince with his subjects; and this consideration is so dear to him that the happy and prosperous condition of his empire, which consists in the greatest possible felicity of its inhabitants, becomes supreme among his laws. Happiness is to persons what perfection is to beings. And if the dominant principle in the existence of the physical world is the decree to give it the greatest possible perfection, the primary purpose in the moral world, or in the city of God which constitutes the noblest part of the universe, ought to be to extend the greatest happiness possible. We must not therefore doubt that God has so ordained everything that spirits not only shall live forever, because this is unavoidable, but that they shall also preserve forever their moral quality, so that his city may never lose a person, quite in the same way that the world never loses a substance. Consequently they will always be conscious of their being, otherwise they would be open to neither reward nor punishment, a condition which is the essence of a republic, and above all of the most perfect republic where nothing can be neglected. In fine, God being at the same time the most just and the most benevolent of monarchs, and requiring only a good will on the part of men, provided that it be sincere and serious, his subjects cannot desire a better condition. To render them perfectly happy he desires only that they love him.

XXXVII. *Jesus Christ has revealed to men the mystery and the admirable laws of the kingdom of heaven, and the greatness of the supreme happiness which God has prepared for those who love him.* The ancient philosophers knew very little of these important truths. Jesus Christ alone has expressed them divinely well, and in a way so clear and simple that the dullest minds have understood them. His gospel has entirely changed the face of human affairs. It has brought us to know the kingdom of heaven, or that perfect republic of spirits which deserves to be called the city of God. He it is who has discovered to us its wonderful laws. He alone has made us see how much God loves us and with what care everything that concerns us has been provided for; how God, inasmuch as he cares for the sparrows, will not neglect reasoning beings, who are infinitely more dear to him; how all the hairs of our heads are numbered; how heaven and earth may pass away but the word of God and that which belongs to the means of our salvation will not pass away; how God has more regard for the least among intelligent souls than for the whole machinery of the world; how we ought not to fear those who are able to destroy the body but are unable to destroy the soul, since God alone can render the soul happy or unhappy; and how the souls of the righteous are protected by his hand against all the upheavals of the universe, since God alone is able to act upon them; how none of our acts are forgotten; how everything is to be accounted for, even careless words, and even a spoonful of water which is well used; in fact how everything must result in the greatest welfare of the good, for the righteous shall become like suns, and neither our sense nor our minds have ever tasted of anything approaching the joys which God has laid up for those that love him.

Monadology*

1. The *monad* of which we shall here speak is merely a simple substance, which enters into composites; *simple,* that is to say, without parts.

2. And there must be simple substances, since there are composites; for the composite is only a collection or aggregate of simple substances.

3. Now where there are no parts, neither extension, nor figure, nor divisibility is possible. And these monads are the true atoms of nature, and, in a word, the elements of all things.

4. Their dissolution also is not at all to be feared, and there is no conceivable way in which a simple substance can perish naturally.

5. For the same reason there is no conceivable way in which a simple substance can begin naturally, since it cannot be formed by composition.

6. Thus it may be said that the monads can only begin or end all at once, that is to say, they can only begin by creation and end by annihilation; whereas that which is composite begins or ends by parts.

7. There is also no way of explaining how a monad can be altered or changed in its inner being by any other creature, for nothing can be transposed within it, nor can we conceive in it any internal movement that can be excited, directed, augmented or diminished within it, as we can in composites, where there may be change among the parts. The monads have no windows through which anything can enter or depart. The accidents cannot detach themselves nor go about outside of substances, as did formerly the sensible species of the Schoolmen. Thus neither substance nor accident can enter a monad from outside.

8. Nevertheless, the monads must have some qualities, otherwise they would not even be entities. And if simple substances did not differ at all in their qualities there would be no way of perceiving any

---

* Trans. George Martin Duncan, in *The Philosophical Works of Leibniz,* New Haven: Tuttle, Morehouse & Taylor, 2d ed., 1908, with some revisions by the present editor. The *Monadology,* written in 1714, is the most famous succinct statement of Leibniz's developed metaphysics; its title was supplied by the editor of the first German translation, 1720. The present edition omits the cross-references to parallel passages in the *Theodicy* which Leibniz added to many of the sections.

change in things, since what is in the compound can only come from the simple ingredients, and the monads, if they had no qualities, would be indistinguishable from one another, seeing also they do not differ in quantity. Consequently, a plenum being supposed, each place would always receive, in any motion, only the equivalent of what it had had before, and one state of things would be indistinguishable from another.

9. It is necessary, indeed, that each monad be different from every other. For there are never in nature two beings which are exactly alike and in which it is not possible to find an internal difference, or one founded upon an intrinsic quality.

10. I take it also for granted that every created being, and consequently the created monad also, is subject to change, and even that this change is continuous in each.

11. It follows from what has just been said, that the natural changes of the monads proceed from an *internal principle,* since an external cause could not influence their inner being.

12. But, besides the principle of change, there must be an individuating *detail of changes,* which forms, so to speak, the specification and variety of the simple substances.

13. This detail must involve a multitude in the unity or in that which is simple. For since every natural change takes place by degrees, something changes and something remains; and consequently, there must be in the simple substance a plurality of affections and of relations, although it has no parts.

14. The passing state, which involves and represents a multitude in unity or in the simple substances, is nothing else than what is called *perception,* which must be distinguished from apperception or consciousness, as will appear in what follows. Here it is that the Cartesians especially failed, for they took no account of the perceptions of which we are not conscious. It is this also which made them believe that only spirits are monads and that there are no souls in animals or other entelechies. They, along with most people, have failed to distinguish between a prolonged state of unconsciousness and death strictly speaking, and have therefore agreed with the old scholastic prejudice of entirely separate souls, and have even confirmed ill-balanced minds in the belief in the mortality of the soul.

15. The action of the internal principle which causes the change or the passage from one perception to another, may be called *appetition*; it is true that desire cannot always completely attain to the whole

perception for which it strives, but it always attains something of it and reaches new perceptions.

16. We experience in ourselves a multiplicity in a simple substance, when we find that the most trifling thought of which we are conscious involves a variety in the object. Thus all those who admit that the soul is a simple substance ought to admit this multiplicity in the monad, and M. Bayle ought not to have found any difficulty in it, as he has done in his *Dictionary* (article "Rorarius").

17. It must be confessed, moreover, that perception and that which depends on it are *inexplicable by mechanical causes,* that is, by figures and motions. And, supposing that there were a machine so constructed as to think, feel and have perception, we could conceive of it as enlarged and yet preserving the same proportions, so that we might enter it as we do a mill. And this granted, we should find, on visiting it, only pieces that push against one another, but never anything by which to explain a perception. This must be sought for, therefore, in the simple substance and not in the composite or in the machine. Furthermore, nothing but this (namely, perceptions and their changes) can be found in the simple substance. It is also in this alone that all the *internal activities* of simple substances can consist.

18. The name of *entelechies* might be given to all simple substances or created monads, for they have within themselves a certain perfection (ἔχουσι τὸ ἐντελές); there is a certain sufficiency (αὐτάρκεια) which makes them the sources of their internal activities, and so to speak, incorporeal automata.

19. If we choose to give the name "soul" to everything that has perceptions and appetitions in the general sense which I have just explained, all simple substances or created monads may be called souls, but as feeling is something more than a simple perception, I am willing that the general name of "monads" or "entelechies" shall suffice for those simple substances which have only perception, and that only those substances shall be called "souls" whose perception is more distinct and is accompanied by memory.

20. For we experience in ourselves a state in which we remember nothing and have no distinguishable perception, as when we fall into a swoon or when we are overpowered by a profound and dreamless sleep. In this state the soul does not differ sensibly from a simple monad; but as this state is not continuous and as the soul comes out of it, the soul is something more than a mere monad.

21. And it does not at all follow that in such a state the simple substance is without any perception. This is indeed impossible, for

the reasons mentioned above; for it cannot perish, nor can it subsist without some affection, which is nothing but its perception; but when there is a great number of minute perceptions, in which nothing is distinct, we are stunned; as when we turn continually in the same direction many times in succession, whence arises a dizziness that may make us faint and that does not let us distinguish anything. And death may produce for a time this condition in animals.

22. And as every present state of a simple substance is naturally the consequence of its preceding state, so its present is big with its future.

23. Therefore, since on being awakened from a stupor, we are *aware* of our perceptions, we must have had them immediately before, although we were unconscious of them; for one perception can come in a natural way only from another perception, as a motion can come in a natural way only from a motion.

24. From this we see that if there were nothing distinct, nothing, so to speak, in relief and of a higher flavor in our perceptions, we should always be in a dazed state. This is the condition of simply bare monads.

25. We also see that nature has given to animals heightened perceptions, by the pains she has taken to furnish them with organs that collect many rays of light or many undulations of air, in order to render these more efficacious by uniting them. There is something of the same kind in odor, in taste, in touch and perhaps in a multitude of other senses that are unknown to us. And I shall presently explain how what occurs in the soul represents what occurs in the organs.

26. Memory furnishes souls with a sort of *consecutiveness* which imitates reason, but which ought to be distinguished from it. We observe that animals, having the perception of something which strikes them and of which they have had a similar perception before, expect, through the representation in their memory, that which was associated with it in the preceding perception, and experience feelings similar to those which they had had at that time. For instance, if we show dogs a stick, they remember the pain it has caused them and whine and run.

27. And the strong imagination which impresses and moves them, arises either from the magnitude or the multitude of preceding perceptions. For often a strong impression produces all at once the effect of a long-continued *habit,* or of many oft-repeated moderate perceptions.

28. Men act like the brutes, in so far as the order of their perceptions results from the principle of memory alone, resembling the

empirical physicians who practice without theory; and we are simple empirics in three-fourths of our actions. For example, when we expect that there will be daylight to-morrow, we are acting as empirics, because that has always happened up to this time. It is only the astronomer who judges of this by reason.

29. But the knowledge of necessary and eternal truths is what distinguishes us from mere animals and furnishes us with *reason* and the sciences, raising us to a knowledge of ourselves and of God. This is what we call the rational soul or *spirit*.

30. It is also by the knowledge of necessary truths, and by their abstractions, that we rise to *acts of reflection*, which make us think of that which calls itself *"I,"* and to observe that this or that is within *us*: and it is thus that, in thinking of ourselves, we think of being, of substance, simple or composite, of the immaterial and of God Himself, conceiving that what is limited in us is in Him without limits. And these reflective acts furnish the principal objects of our reasonings.

31. Our reasonings are founded on two great principles, that of *contradiction*, in virtue of which we judge that to be *false* which involves contradiction, and that *true* which is opposed or contradictory to the false.

32. And that of *sufficient reason*, in virtue of which we hold that no fact can be real or existent, no statement true, unless there be a sufficient reason why it is so and not otherwise, although usually these reasons cannot be known to us.

33. There are also two kinds of truths, those of *reasoning* and those of *fact*. Truths of reasoning are necessary, and their opposite is impossible; those of *fact* are contingent, and their opposite is possible. When a truth is necessary its reason can be found by analysis, resolving it into more simple ideas and truths until we reach those which are primitive.

34. It is thus that mathematicians by analysis reduce speculative *theorems* and practical *canons* to *definitions, axioms* and *postulates*.

35. And there are finally simple ideas, definitions of which cannot be given; there are also axioms and postulates, in a word, *primary principles*, which cannot be proved, and indeed need no proof; and these are *identical propositions,* whose opposite involves an explicit contradiction.

36. But there must also be a *sufficient reason* for *contingent truths,* or *truths of fact*—that is, for the sequence of things spread through the universe of created objects—where the resolution into

particular reasons might run into endless detail, on account of the immence variety of the things in nature and the division of bodies *ad infinitum*. There is an infinity of shapes and movements, present and past, that enter into the efficient cause of my present writing, and there is an infinity of slight inclinations and dispositions, past and present, of my soul, which enter into its final cause.

37. And as all this *detail* involves other contingents, anterior or more detailed, each one of which requires a like analysis for its explanation, we make no advance: and the sufficient or final reason must be outside of the sequence or *series* of this detail of contingents, however infinite it may be.

38. And thus it is that the final reason of things must be found in a necessary substance, in which the detail of changes exists only eminently, as in their source; and this is what we call God.

39. Now this substance being a sufficient reason of all this detail, which also is linked together throughout, *there is but one God, and this God is sufficient*.

40. We may also conclude that this supreme substance, which is unique, universal and necessary, having nothing outside of itself that is independent of it, and being a pure consequence of possible being, must be incapable of limitation and must contain as much reality as is possible.

41. Whence it follows that God is absolutely perfect, *perfection* being only the magnitude of positive reality taken in its strictest meaning, setting aside the limits or bounds in things that have them. And where there are no limits, that is, in God, perfection is absolutely infinite.

42. It follows also that the creatures have their perfections from the influence of God, but that their imperfections arise from their own nature, incapable of existing without limits. For it is by this that they are distinguished from God.

43. It is also true that in God is the source not only of existences but also of essences, so far as they are real, or of that which is real in the possible. This is because the understanding of God is the region of eternal truths, or of the ideas on which they depend, and because, without Him, there would be nothing real in the possibilities, and not only nothing existing but also nothing possible.

44. For if there is a reality in essences or possibilities, or indeed in the eternal truths, this reality must be founded in something existing and actual. and consequently in the existence of the necessary be-

ing, in whom essence involves existence, or with whom it is sufficient to be possible in order to be actual.

45. Hence God alone (or the necessary being) has this prerogative, that He must exist if He is possible. And since nothing can hinder the possibility of that which possesses no limitation, no negation, and, consequently, no contradiction, this alone is sufficient to establish the existence of God *a priori*. We have thus proved it by the reality of the eternal truths. But a little while ago (§§36-39) we also proved it *a posteriori*, since contingent beings exist, and they can only have their final or sufficient reason in a necessary being that has its reason for existence in itself.

46. Yet we must not imagine, as some do, that the eternal truths, being dependent upon God, are arbitrary and depend upon His will, as Descartes seems to have held, and afterwards M. Poiret. This is true only of contingent truths, the principle of which is *fitness*, or the choice of the *best*, whereas necessary truths depend solely on His understanding and are its internal object.

47. Thus God alone is the primitive unity or the original simple substance, of which all created or derived monads are the products, and are generated, so to speak, by continual fulgurations of the Divinity, from moment to moment, limited by the receptivity of the creature, to whom limitation is essential.

48. In God is *Power*, which is the source of all; then *Knowledge*, which contains the detail of ideas; and finally *Will*, which effects changes or products according to the principle of the best. These correspond to what in created monads form the subject or basis, the perceptive faculty, and the appetitive faculty. But in God these attributes are absolutely infinite or perfect; and in the created monads or in the *entelechies* (or *perfectihabies*, as Hermolaus Barbarus translated the word), they are only imitations proportioned to the perfection of the monads.

49. The creature is said to *act* externally in so far as it has perfection, and to *undergo* the actions of another in so far as it is imperfect. Thus *action* is attributed to the monad in so far as it has distinct perceptions, and *passivity* in so far as it has confused perceptions.

50. And one creature is more perfect than another, in that there is found in it that which serves to account *a priori* for what takes place in the other, and it is in this way that it is said to act upon the other.

51. But in simple substances the influence of one monad upon another is purely *ideal*, and it can have its effect only through the in-

tervention of God, inasmuch as in the ideas of God a monad may reasonably demand that God, in regulating the others from the commencement of things, have regard to it. For since a created monad can have no physical influence upon the inner being of another, it is only in this way that one can be dependent upon another.

52. And hence it is that the actions and undergoings of creatures are mutual. For God, in comparing two simple substances, finds in each one reasons that compel Him to adjust the other to it, and consequently that which in certain respects is active, is according to another point of view, passive: *active* in so far as what is known distinctly in it serves to account for what occurs in another; and *passive* in so far as the reason for what occurs in it is found in what is distinctly known in another.

53. Now, as there is an infinity of possible universes in the ideas of God, and as only one of them can exist, there must be a sufficient reason for God's choice, which determines Him to select one rather than another.

54. And this reason can only be found in the *fitness,* or in the degrees of perfection, which these worlds contain, each possible world having a right to claim existence according to the measure of perfection which it possesses.

55. And this is the cause of the existence of the Best: namely, that His wisdom makes it known to God, His goodness makes Him choose it, and His power makes Him produce it.

56. Now this *connection,* or this adaptation, of all created things to each and of each to all, brings it about that each simple substance has relations which express all the others, and that, consequently, it is a perpetual living mirror of the universe.

57. And as the same city viewed from different sides appears entirely different, and is as if multiplied *perspectively,* so also it happens that, because of the infinite multitude of simple substances, there are as it were so many different universes, which are nevertheless only the perspectives of a single one, according to the different *points of view* of each monad.

58. And this is the way to obtain as great a variety as possible, but with the greatest possible order; that is, it is the way to obtain as much perfection as possible.

59. Moreover, this hypothesis (which I dare to call demonstrated) is the only one that brings into relief the grandeur of God. M. Bayle recognized this, when in his *Dictionary* (Art. "Rorarius") he raised objections to it; in which indeed he was disposed to think that I

attributed too much to God and more than is possible. But he can state no reason why this universal harmony, which brings it about that each substance expresses exactly all the others through its relations to them, is impossible.

60. Besides, we can see, in what I have just said, the *a priori* reasons why things could not be otherwise than they are. Because God, in regulating all, has had regard to each part, and particularly to each monad, whose nature being representative, nothing can limit it to representing only a part of things; although it is true that this representation is but confused as regards the detail of the whole universe, and can be distinct only in the case of a small part of things, that is to say, in the case of those which are nearest or greatest in relation to each of the monads; otherwise each monad would be a divinity. It is not as regards the object but only as regards the modification of the knowledge of the object, that monads are limited. They tend confusedly toward the infinite, toward the whole; but they are limited and differentiated by the degrees of their distinct perceptions.

61. And composite substances are analogous in this respect to simple substances. For since the world is a *plenum,* rendering all matter connected, and since in a plenum every motion has some effect on distant bodies in proportion to their distance, so that each body is affected not only by those in contact with it, and feels in some way all that happens to them, but also by their means is affected by those which are in contact with the former, with which it itself is in immediate contact, it follows that this intercommunication extends to any distance whatever. And consequently, each body feels all that happens in the universe, so that he who sees all could read in each what happens everywhere, and even what has been or shall be, discovering in the present what is removed in time as well as in space; σύμπνοια πάντα,[1] said Hippocrates. But a soul can read in itself only what is distinctly represented in it. It cannot develop all its potentialities at once, for they reach into the infinite.

62. Thus, although each created monad represents the entire universe, it represents more distinctly the body which is particularly connected with it, and of which it forms the entelechy; and as this body expresses the whole universe through the connection of all matter in the plenum, the soul also represents the whole universe in representing the body that belongs to it in a particular way.

63. The body belonging to a monad that is its entelechy or soul

---

[1] [All things agree together.—M.C.B.]

constitutes, together with the entelechy, what may be called a *living being,* and, together with a soul, what may be called an *animal*. Now this body of a living being or of an animal is always organic, for since every monad is in its way a mirror of the universe, and since the universe is regulated in a perfect order, there must also be an order in the representative, that is, in perceptions of the soul, and hence in the body, through which the universe is represented in the soul.

64. Thus each organic body of a living being is a kind of divine machine or natural automaton, which infinitely surpasses all artificial automata. For a machine made by man's art is not a machine in each one of its parts; for example, the teeth of a brass wheel have parts or fragments which to us are no longer artificial and have nothing in themselves to show the special use in the machine for which the wheel was designed. But nature's machines, that is, living bodies, are machines even in their smallest parts *ad infinitum.* Herein lies the difference between nature and art, that is, between the divine art and ours.

65. And the author of nature has been able to employ this divine and infinitely marvelous artifice because each portion of matter is not only divisible *ad infinitum,* as the ancients recognized, but also is actually subdivided into infinite parts, each of which has some motion of its own: otherwise it would be impossible for each portion of matter to express the whole universe.

66. Whence we see that there is a world of creatures, of living beings, of animals, of entelechies, of souls, in the smallest particle of matter.

67. Each portion of matter may be conceived of as a garden full of plants, and as a pond full of fish. But each branch of the plant, each member of the animal, each drop of its humors is also such a garden or such a pond.

68. And although the earth and air that lies between the plants of the garden, and the water between the fish of the pond, are neither plant nor fish, yet they also contain them, but for the most part so tiny as to be imperceptible to us.

69. Therefore there is nothing fallow, nothing sterile, nothing dead in the universe, no chaos, no confusion except in appearance; somewhat as a pond would appear from a distance, in which we might see the confused movement and swarming, so to speak, of the fishes in the pond, without discerning the fish themselves.

70. We see thus that each living body has a ruling entelechy, which in the animal is the soul; but the members of this living body are full

of other living beings, plants, animals, each of which has also its entelechy or governing soul.

71. But it must not be imagined, as has been done by some people who have misunderstood my thought, that each soul has a mass or portion of matter belonging to it or attached to it forever, and that consequently it possesses other inferior living beings, destined to its service forever. For all bodies are, like rivers, in a perpetual flux, and parts are entering into them and departing from them continually.

72. Thus the soul changes its body only gradually and by degrees, so that it is never deprived of all its organs at once. There is often a metamorphosis in animals, but never metempsychosis or transmigration of souls. There are also no entirely *separate* souls, nor *genii* without bodies. God alone is wholly without body.

73. For which reason also, it happens that there is, strictly speaking, neither absolute birth nor complete death, consisting in the separation of the soul from the body. What we call *birth* is development or growth, as what we call *death* is envelopment and diminution.

74. Philosophers have been greatly puzzled over the origin of forms, entelechies, or souls; but to-day, when we know by exact investigations upon plants, insects and animals that the organic bodies of nature are never products of chaos or putrefaction, but always come from seeds, in which there was undoubtedly some *preformation,* it has been thought that not only the organic body was already there before conception, but also a soul in this body, and, in a word, the animal itself; and that by means of conception this animal has merely been prepared for a great transformation, in order to become an animal of another kind. Something similar is seen outside of birth, as when worms become flies, and caterpillars become butterflies.

75. The *animals,* some of which are raised by conception to the grade of larger animals, may be called *spermatic*; but those among them that remain in their class (that is, the most part) are born, multiply, and are destroyed like the large animals, and it is only a small number of chosen ones that pass to a larger theater.

76. But this is only half the truth. I have, therefore, held that if the animal never commences by natural means, neither does it end by natural means; and that not only will there be no birth, but also no utter destruction or death, strictly speaking. And these reasonings, made *a posteriori* and drawn from experience, harmonize perfectly with my principles deduced *a priori,* as above (cf. §§ 3, 4, 5).

77. Thus it may be said that not only the soul (mirror of an in-

destructible universe) is indestructible, but also the animal itself, although its mechanism often perishes in part and takes on or puts off organic coatings.

78. These principles have given me the means of explaining naturally the union or rather the conformity of the soul and the organic body. The soul follows its own peculiar laws and the body also follows its own laws, and they agree in virtue of the *pre-established harmony* between all substances, since they are all representations of one and the same universe.

79. Souls act according to the laws of final causes, by appetitions, ends and means. Bodies act in accordance with the laws of efficient causes or of motion. And the two realms, that of efficient causes and that of final causes, are in harmony with each other.

80. Descartes recognized that souls cannot impart any force to bodies, because there is always the same quantity of force in matter. Nevertheless he believed that the soul could change the direction of bodies. But this was because, in his day, the law of nature that affirms also the conservation of the same total direction in matter, was not known. If he had known this, he would have lighted upon my system of pre-established harmony.

81. According to this system, bodies act as if (what is impossible) there were no souls, and souls act as if there were no bodies, and both act as if each influenced the other.

82. As to *spirits* or rational souls, although I find that the same thing which I have stated (namely, that animals and souls begin only with the world and end only with the world) holds good at bottom with regard to all living beings and animals, yet there is this peculiarity in rational animals, that their spermatic animalcules, as long as they remain such, have only ordinary or sensitive souls; but as soon as those that are, so to speak, elected, attain by actual conception to human nature, their sensitive souls are elevated to the rank of reason and to the prerogative of spirits.

83. Among other differences between ordinary souls and spirits, some of which I have already mentioned, there is also this, that souls in general are the living mirrors or images of the universe of creatures, but minds or spirits are in addition images of Divinity itself, or of the author of nature, able to know the system of the universe and to imitate something of it by architectonic samples, each spirit being like a little divinity in its own department.

84. Hence it is that spirits are capable of entering into a sort of society with God, and that He is, in relation to them, not only what

an inventor is to his machine (as God is in relation to the other creatures), but also what a prince is to his subjects, and even a father to his children.

85. Whence it is easy to conclude that the assembly of all spirits must compose the City of God, that is, the most perfect state possible, under the most perfect of monarchs.

86. This City of God, this truly universal monarchy, is a moral world within the natural world, and the highest and most divine of the works of God; it is in this that the glory of God truly consists, for He would have none if His greatness and goodness were not known and admired by spirits. It is also in relation to this divine city that He properly has goodness, whereas His wisdom and His power are everywhere manifest.

87. As we have above established a perfect harmony between two natural kingdoms, the one of efficient, the other of final causes, we should also notice here another harmony between the physical kingdom of nature and the moral kingdom of grace; that is, between God considered as the architect of the mechanism of the universe and God considered as monarch of the divine city of spirits.

88. This harmony makes things progress toward grace by natural means. This globe, for example, must be destroyed and repaired by natural means, at such times as the government of spirits may demand it, for the punishment of some and the reward of others.

89. It may be said, farther, that God as architect satisfies in every respect God as legislator, and that therefore sins, by the order of nature and even by the mechanical structure of things, must carry their punishment with them; and that in the same way, good actions will obtain their rewards by mechanical ways through their relations to bodies, although this cannot and should not always happen immediately.

90. Finally, under this perfect government, there will be no good action unrewarded, no bad action unpunished; and everything must result in the well-being of the good, that is, of those who are not disaffected in this great State, who, after having done their duty, trust in providence, and who love and imitate, as is meet, the author of all good, taking pleasure in the contemplation of his perfections, according to the nature of truly *pure love,* which takes pleasure in the happiness of the beloved. This is what causes wise and virtuous persons to work for all that seems in harmony with the divine will, presumptive or antecedent, and nevertheless to content themselves with that which God in reality brings to pass by his secret, consequent and

decisive will, recognizing that if we could sufficiently understand the order of the universe, we should find that it surpasses all the wishes of the wisest, and that it is impossible to render it better than it is, not only for all in general, but also for ourselves in particular, if we are attached, as we should be, to the author of all, not only as to the architect and efficient cause of our being, but also as to our master and final cause, who ought to be the whole aim of our will, and who, alone, can make our happiness.

Supplementary Passages

1

Necessary and Contingent Truths (see *First Truths,* fourth paragraph)

A true affirmation is one the predicate of which is present in the subject. Thus in every true affirmative proposition, necessary or contingent, universal or singular, the concept of the predicate is in some way contained in the concept of the subject, so that he who perfectly understood each concept as God understands it, would by that very fact perceive that the predicate is present in the subject. . . .

An absolutely necessary proposition is one which can be resolved into identical propositions, or the opposite of which implies a contradiction. Let me show this by an example in numbers. I shall call binary every number which can be exactly divided by two, and ternary or quaternary every number that can be exactly divided by three or four, and so on. . . . I say therefore that this proposition, "Every duodenary number is quaternary," is absolutely necessary, since it can be resolved into identical propositions in the following way. A duodenary number is binary-senary (by definition); senary is binary-ternary (by definition). Therefore a duodenary number is binary-binary-ternary. Further, binary-binary is quaternary (by definition). Therefore a duodenary number is quaternary-ternary. Therefore a duodenary number is quaternary. Q.E.D. But even if other definitions had been given, it could always have been shown that it comes to the same thing. Therefore I call this necessity metaphysical or geometrical. What lacks such necessity, I call contingent. . . . In contingent truth, even though the predicate is really present in the subject, nevertheless by whatever resolution you please of either term, indefinitely continued, you will never arrive at demonstration or identity. And it is for God alone, comprehending the infinite all at once, to perceive how one is present in the other, and to understand *a priori* the perfect reason of contingency, which in creatures is furnished (*a posteriori*) by experience. Thus contingent truths are related to necessary as surd roots, i.e., the roots of incommensurable numbers, to the expressible roots of commensurable numbers. For just as it can be shown that a small number is present in another greater number, by reducing both to the greatest common measure, so too essential propositions or truths are demonstrated: i.e., a resolution

302

is carried on until it arrives at terms which it is established by the definitions are common to either term. But as a greater number contains a certain other incommensurable number, and let whatever resolution you please be continued to infinity, it never arrives at a common measure—so in contingent truth, it never arrives at demonstration however much you may resolve the concepts. There is only this difference, that in surd roots we can nevertheless carry out demonstrations, by showing that the error is less than any assignable number, but in contingent truths not even this is conceded to a created mind. And so I consider that I have unfolded something secret, which has long perplexed even myself—while I did not understand how the predicate could be in the subject, and yet the proposition not be necessary. But the knowledge of things geometrical and the analysis of infinities kindled this light for me, so that I understood that concepts too are resoluble to infinity.

Hence we now learn that propositions which pertain to the essences and those which pertain to the existences of things are different. Essential surely are those which can be demonstrated from the resolution of terms, that is, which are necessary, or virtually identical, and the opposite of which, moreover, is impossible or virtually contradictory. And these are the eternal truths. They did not obtain only while the world existed, but they would also obtain if God had created a world with a different plan. But from these, existential or contingent truths differ entirely. Their truth is understood *a priori* by the infinite mind alone, and they cannot be demonstrated by any resolution. They are of the sort that are true at a certain time, and they do not only express what pertains to the possibility of things, but also what actually does exist, or would exist contingently if certain things were supposed. For example, take the proposition, I am now living, the sun is shining. For suppose I say that the sun is shining in our hemisphere at this hour, because up to now its motion has been such that, granted its continuation, this certainly follows. Even then (not to mention the non-necessary obligation of its continuing) that its motion even before this was so much and of this kind is similarly a contingent truth, for which again the reason should be inquired—nor could it be fully produced except from the perfect knowledge of all parts of the universe. This, however, exceeds all created powers. For there is no portion of matter which is not actually subdivided into other parts; hence the parts of any body whatsoever are actually infinite. Thus neither the sun nor any other body can be perfectly known by a creature. Much less can we arrive at the end of the analysis if we search for the mover causing the motion of any body whatsoever and again for the mover of this; for we shall always arrive at smaller bodies without end. But God is not in need of that transition from one contingent to another earlier or simpler contingent—a transition which can never have an end (as also one contingent is in fact not the cause of another, even though it may seem so to us). But he perceives in any individual substance from its very concept the truth of all its accidents, calling in nothing extrinsic, since any one at all involves in its way all the others and the whole universe. Hence into all propositions into which existence and time enter, by that very fact the whole series of things enters, nor can the now or here be understood except in relation to other things. For this reason such propositions do not allow of a demonstration or terminable resolution by which their truth might appear. And the same holds of all accidents of individual created substances. Indeed even though some one were able to know the whole series of the universe, he still could not state the reason of it, except by having undertaken the comparison of it with all other possible universes. From this it is clear why a demonstration of no contingent proposition can be found, however far the resolution of concepts be continued.

[FROM *Necessary and Contingent Truths,* in T. V. Smith and Marjorie Grene, eds., *From Descartes to Kant,* by permission of the University of Chicago Press. Copyright, 1940, by the University of Chicago.]

2

Space and Time (see *First Truths,* near end)

4. As for my own opinion, I have said more than once, that I hold space to be something merely relative, as time is; that I hold it to be an order of coexistences, as time is an order of successions. For space denotes, in terms of possibility, an order of things which exist at the same time, considered as existing together; without enquiring into their manner of existing. And when many things are seen together, one perceives that order of things among themselves.

5. I have many demonstrations, to confute the fancy of those who take space to be a substance, or at least an absolute being. But I shall only use, at the present, one demonstration, which the author here gives me occasion to insist upon. I say then, that if space were an absolute being, there would something happen for which it would be impossible there should be a sufficient reason. Which is against

my axiom. And I prove it thus. Space is something absolutely uniform; and, without the things placed in it, one point of space does not absolutely differ in any respect whatsoever from another point of space. Now from hence it follows (supposing space to be something in itself, besides the order of bodies among themselves), that 'tis impossible there should be a reason why God, preserving the same situations of bodies among themselves, should have placed them in space after one certain particular manner, and not otherwise; why every thing was not placed the quite contrary way, for instance, by changing East into West. But if space is nothing else, but that order or relation; and is nothing at all without bodies, but the possibility of placing them; then those two states, the one such as it now is, the other supposed to be the quite contrary way, would not at all differ from one another. Their difference therefore is only to be found in our chimerical supposition of the reality of space in itself. But in truth the one would exactly be the same thing as the other, they being absolutely indiscernible; and consequently there is no room to enquire after a reason of the preference of the one to the other.

6. The case is the same with respect to time. Supposing any one should ask, why God did not create every thing a year sooner; and the same person should infer from thence, that God has done something, concerning which 'tis not possible there should be a reason, why he did it so, and not otherwise: the answer is, that his inference would be right, if time was any thing distinct from things existing in time. For it would be impossible there should be any reason, why things should be applied to such particular instants, rather than to others, their succession continuing the same. But then the same argument proves that instants, consider'd without the things, are nothing at all; and that they consist only in the successive order of things: which order remaining the same, one of the two states, viz., that of a supposed anticipation, would not at all differ, nor could be discerned from, the other which now is.

> [FROM Leibniz's Third Paper in *The Leibniz-Clarke Correspondence,* ed. H. G. Alexander, 1956; published by Manchester University Press in their series of Philosophical Classics]

3

Expression (see *Discourse,* § IX; *Monadology,* §§ 58-62)

One thing expresses another, in my usage, when there is a constant and regular relation between what can be said about one and about the other. It is in this way that a projection in perspective expresses a geometric figure. Expression is common to all the forms and is a genus of which natural perception, animal feeling, and intellectual knowledge are species. In natural perception and feeling it suffices that what is divisible and material and is found dispersed among several beings should be expressed or represented in a single indivisible being or in a substance which is endowed with a true unity. The possibility of such a representation of several things in one cannot be doubted, since our soul provides us with an example of it. But in the reasonable soul this representation is accompanied by consciousness, and it is then that it is called thought. Now this expression takes place everywhere, because every substance sympathizes with all the others and receives a proportional change corresponding to the slightest change which occurs in the whole world, although this change will be more or less noticeable as other bodies or their actions have more or less relationship with ours. With this I believe Descartes would himself have agreed, for he would undoubtedly grant that, because of the continuity and divisibility of all matter, the slightest movement exerts its effect upon near-by bodies, and so from body to body to infinity, but in diminishing proportion. So our body must be affected in some way by the changes of all the rest. Now to all the motions of our body there correspond certain perceptions or thoughts of the soul, more or less confused; thus the soul will also have some thought of all the motions of the universe, and in my opinion every other soul or substance will have some perception or expression of it.

[FROM a letter to Antoine Arnauld, October 9, 1687, trans. Leroy M. Loemker, *Gottfried Wilhelm Leibniz: Philosophical Papers and Letters, op. cit.*]

4

The Ontological Argument (see *Discourse,* § XXIII)

[A.] It often happens that we falsely believe ourselves to have ideas of things in our minds, when we assume wrongly that we have already explained certain terms which we are using. It is not true, or at least it is ambiguous, to say, as some do, that we cannot speak of anything and understand what we say, without having an idea of it. For often we understand perfectly each single word or remember to have understood it earlier; yet, because we are content with this blind knowledge and do not sufficiently press the analysis of the concepts, we overlook a contradiction which the composite concept may involve. I was led to examine this point more distinctly by an argument which was famous among the Scholastics long ago and was revived by Descartes. It is an argument for the existence of God and is stated as follows. Whatever follows from the idea or definition of a thing can be predicated of the thing itself. Existence follows from the idea of God, or the most perfect being, or that than which no greater can be thought. For a most perfect being involves all perfections, among which existence is one. Therefore existence can be predicated of God.

It should be noticed, however, that the most you can draw out of this argument is that, if God is possible, it follows that he exists; for we cannot safely infer from definitions until we know that they are real or that they involve no contradiction. The reason for this is that from concepts which involve a contradiction, contradictory conclusions can be drawn simultaneously, and this is absurd. To explain this I usually make use of the example of the most rapid motion, which involves an absurdity. Suppose that a wheel turns at a most rapid rate. Then anyone can see that, if a spoke of the wheel is extended beyond its rim, its extremity will move more rapidly than will a nail in the rim itself. The motion of the nail is therefore not the most rapid, contrary to hypothesis. Yet, at first glance we may seem to have an idea of the most rapid motion, for we understand perfectly what we are saying. But we cannot have any idea of the impossible. Likewise it is not enough to think of a most perfect being in order to assert that we have an idea of it, and in the demonstration which I referred to above we must either prove or assume the possibility of a most perfect being in order to reason rightly. However, there is nothing truer than that we have an idea of God and that the most perfect being is possible and, indeed, necessary. But the above argument is not conclusive and has already been rejected by Thomas Aquinas.

[FROM *Meditations on Knowledge, Truth, and Ideas,* published 1684; trans. Leroy E. Loemker, *ibid.*]

[B.] I call every simple quality which is positive and absolute, or expresses whatever it expresses without any limits, a *perfection.*

But a quality of this sort, because it is simple, is therefore irresolvable or indefinable, for otherwise, either it will not be a simple quality but an aggregate of many, or, if it is one, it will be circumscribed by limits and so be known through negations of further progress, contrary to the hypothesis, for a purely positive quality was assumed.

From these considerations it is not difficult to show that *all perfections are compatible with each other,* or can exist in the same subject. For let the proposition be of this kind:

A and B are incompatible

(understanding by A and B two simple forms of this kind, or perfections; it is the same if more are assumed like them); it is evident that it cannot be demonstrated without the resolution of the terms A and B, of each or both; for otherwise their nature would not enter into the ratiocination and the incompatibility could be demonstrated as well from any other as from themselves. But now (by hypothesis) they are irresolvable. Therefore this proposition cannot be demonstrated from these forms.

But it might certainly be demonstrated by these if it were true, because it is not true *per se,* for all propositions necessarily true are either demonstrable or known *per se.* Therefore, this proposition is not necessarily true. Or if it is not necessary that A and B exist in the same subject, they cannot therefore exist in the same subject, and since the reasoning is the same as regards any other assumed qualities of this kind, therefore all perfections are compatible.

It is granted, therefore, that either a subject of all perfections or the most perfect being can be known.

Whence it is evident that it also exists, since existence is contained in the number of the perfections.

> [FROM a fragment in Latin, which Leibniz showed to Spinoza at The Hague in November, 1676; trans. Alfred Gideon Langley, in the appendix to his translation of Leibniz's *New Essays,* Chicago: Open Court, 2d ed., 1916]

5

The Relation between Soul and Body (see *Discourse,* § XXXIII; *Monadology,* § 80)

M. Descartes wished to compromise and to make a part of the body's action dependent upon the soul. He believed in the existence of a rule of Nature to the effect, according to him, that the same quantity of movement is conserved in bodies. He deemed it not possible that the influence of the soul should violate this law of bodies, but he believed that the soul notwithstanding might have power to change the direction of the movements that are made in the body; much as a rider, though giving no force to the horse he mounts, nevertheless controls it by guiding that force in any direction he pleases. But as that is done by means of the bridle, the bit, the spurs and other material aids, it is conceivable how that can be; there are, however, no instruments such as the soul may employ for this result, nothing indeed either in the soul or in the body, that is, either in thought or in the mass, which may serve to explain this change of the one by the other. In a word, that the soul should change the quantity of force and that it should change the line of direction, both these things are equally inexplicable. . . .

Being on other considerations already convinced of the principle of Harmony in general, I was in consequence convinced likewise of the *preformation* and the Pre-established Harmony of all things amongst themselves. . . .

Far from its being prejudicial, nothing can be more favorable to freedom than that system. And M. Jacquelot has demonstrated well in his book on the *Conformity of Faith with Reason,* that it is just as if he who knows all that I shall order a servant to do the whole day long on the morrow made an automaton entirely resembling this servant, to carry out to-morrow at the right moment all that I should order; and yet that would not prevent me from ordering freely all that I should please, although the action of the automaton that would serve me would not be in the least free.

One may however give a true and philosophic sense to this *mutual dependence* which we suppose between the soul and the body. It is that the one of these two substances depends upon the other ideally, in so far as the reason of that which is done in the one can be furnished by that which is in the other. This had already happened when God ordered beforehand the harmony that there would be between them. Even so would that automaton, that should fulfil the servant's function, depend upon me *ideally,* in virtue of the knowledge of him who, foreseeing my future orders, would have rendered it capable of serving me at the right moment all through the morrow. The knowledge of my future intentions would have actuated this great craftsman, who would accordingly have fashioned the automaton: my influence would be objective, and his physical. For in so far as the soul has perfection and distinct thoughts, God has accommodated the body to the soul, and has arranged beforehand that the body is impelled to execute its orders. And in so far as the soul is imperfect and as its perceptions are confused, God has accommodated the soul to the body, in such sort that the soul is swayed by the passions arising out of corporeal representations. This produces the same effect and the same appearance as if the one depended immediately upon the other, and by the agency of a physical influence. Properly speaking, it is by its confused thoughts that the soul represents the bodies which encompass it.

> [FROM §§ 60-66 of the *Theodicy*, trans. E. M. Huggard, New Haven: Yale University Press, and London: Routledge & Kegan Paul, 1952]

6

Progress (see *Discourse*, § XXXVI)

As for the nature of succession, where you seem to hold that we must think of a first, fundamental instant, just as unity is the foundation of numbers and the point is the foundation of extension, I could reply to this that the instant is indeed the foundation of time but that, since there is no one point whatsoever in nature which is fundamental with respect to all other points and which is therefore the seat of God, so to speak, I likewise see no necessity whatever of conceiving a primary instant. I admit, however, that there is this difference between instants and points—one point of the universe has no advantage of priority over another, while a preceding instant always has the advantage of priority, not merely in time but in nature, over following instants. But this does not make it necessary for there to be a first instant. There is involved here the difference between the analysis of necessities and the analysis of contingents. The analysis of necessities, which is that of essences, proceeds *from the posterior by nature to the prior by nature,* and it is in this sense that numbers are analyzed into unities. But in contingents or existents, this analysis *from the posterior by nature to the prior by nature* proceeds to infinity without ever being reduced to primitive elements. Thus the analogy of numbers to instants does not at all apply here. It is true that the concept of numbers is finally resolvable into the concept of unity, which is not further analyzable and can be considered the primitive number. But it does not follow that the concepts of different instants can be resolved finally into a primitive instant. Yet I do not venture to deny that there may be a first instant. Two hypotheses can be formed—one that nature is always equally perfect, the other that it always increases in perfection. If it is always equally perfect, though in variable ways, it is more probable that it had no beginning. But if it always increases in perfection (assuming that it is impossible to give it its whole perfection at once), there would still be two ways of explaining the matter, namely, by the ordinates of the hyperbola B or by that of the triangle C. According to the hypothesis of the hyperbola, there would be no beginning, and the instants or states of the world would have been increasing in perfection from all eternity. But, according to the hypothesis of the triangle, there would have been a beginning. The hypothesis of equal perfection would be that of rectangle A. I

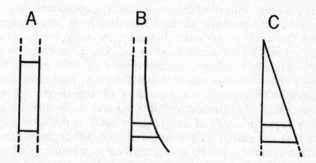

do not yet see any way of demonstrating which of these we should choose by pure reason. But though the state of the world could never be absolutely perfect at any particular instant whatever according to the hypothesis of increase, nevertheless the whole actual sequence would always be the most perfect of all possible sequences, because God always chooses the best possible.

[FROM a letter to Louis Bourguet, August 5, 1715, trans. Leroy M. Loemker, *op. cit.*]

7

Possibility and Existence (see *Monadology*, §§ 53-55)

But in order to explain a little more clearly how, from eternal or essential or metaphysical truths, temporary, contingent or physical truths arise, we ought first to recognize that from the very fact that something exists rather than nothing, there is in possible things, that is, in the very possibility or essence, a certain need of existence, and, so to speak, some claim to existence; in a word, that essence tends in itself towards existence. Whence it further follows that all possible things, whether expressing essence or possible reality, tend by equal right toward existence, according to their quantity of essence or reality, or according to the degree of perfection which they contain, for perfection is nothing but quantity of essence.

Hence it is most clearly understood that among the infinite combinations of possibles and possible series, that one actually exists by which the most of essence or of possibility is brought into existence. And indeed there is always in things a principle of determination which involves a maximum and minimum, such that the greatest effect is obtained with the least, so to speak, expenditure. . . .

And thus we now have physical necessity from metaphysical; for although the world be not metaphysically necessary, in the sense that its contrary implies a contradiction or a logical absurdity, it is nevertheless physically necessary, or determined in such a way that its contrary implies imperfection or moral absurdity. And as possibility is the principle of essence, so perfection or the degree of essence (through which the greatest possible number is at the same time possible) is the principle of existence. Whence at the same time it is evident that the author of the world is free, although he makes all things determinately; for he acts according to a principle of wisdom or of perfection. Indeed indifference arises from ignorance, and the wiser one is, the more determined one is to the highest degree of perfection.

[FROM *On the Radical Origination* (or *Ultimate Origin*) *of Things*, 1697, trans. George Martin Duncan in *The Philosophical Works of Leibnitz, op. cit.,* and slightly revised]

8

Matter (see *Monadology,* § 62)

As for the first point, it follows from the very fact that a mathematical body cannot be analyzed into primary constituents that it is also not real but something mental and designates nothing but the possibility of parts, not something actual. A mathematical line, namely, is in this respect like arithmetical unity; in both cases the parts are only possible and completely indefinite. A line is no more the aggregate of the lines into which it can be cut than unity is the aggregate of the fractions into which it can be split up. And, as in counting, the number is not a substance without the things counted, so neither is a mathematical body or extension without active and passive entities or motion. But in real things, that is, bodies, the parts are not indefinite—as they are in space, which is a mental thing— but actually specified in a fixed way according to the divisions and subdivisions which nature actually introduces through the varieties of motion. And granted that these divisions proceed to infinity, they are nonetheless all the results of fixed primary constituents or real unities, though infinite in number. Accurately speaking, however, matter is not composed of these constitutive unities but results from them, since matter or extended mass is nothing but a phenomenon grounded in things, like the rainbow or the mock-sun, and all reality belongs only to unities.

[FROM a letter to Burcher de Volder, June 30, 1704, trans. Leroy M. Loemker, *op. cit.*]

9

Monads (see *Monadology,* § 63)

I consider the explanation of all phenomena solely through the perceptions of monads functioning in harmony with each other, with corporeal substances rejected, to be useful for a fundamental investigation of things. In this way of explaining things, space is the order of coexisting phenomena, as time is the order of successive phenomena, and there is no spatial or absolute nearness or distance between monads. And to say that they are crowded together in a point or disseminated in space is to use certain fictions of our mind when we seek to visualize freely what can only be understood. In this conception, also, there is involved no extension or composition of the continuum, and all difficulties about points disappear. It is this that I tried to say somewhere in my *Theodicy*—that the difficulties in the composition of a continuum ought to warn us that we must think far differently of things. We must see then what must be superadded to monads if we add a substantial union or assume that there is a corporeal, and therefore a material, substance; whether it be necessary in that case to return to a mathematical body. Certainly monads cannot properly be in an absolute space, since they are not really ingredients but merely requisites of matter. It will not be necessary on this ground, therefore, to set up certain indivisible localities, which throw us into such difficulties. It is enough that corporeal substance is something that reifies phenomena outside of souls, but I should not wish to conceive actual parts in it except those made by actual division, nor indivisible parts, except as an extreme measure.

I believe the monads always have full existence and that we cannot conceive of parts being said to be potentially in the whole. Nor do I see what a dominant monad would detract from the existence of other monads, since there is really no intercourse between them but merely an agreement. The unity of corporeal substance in a horse does not arise from any "refraction" of monads but from a superadded substantial chain through which nothing else is changed in the monads themselves. Some worm can be a part of my body and subject to my dominant monad, and the same worm can have other animalcules in its body subject to its dominant monads. But, considered in the monads themselves, domination and subordination consists only in degrees of perfection. . . .

> [FROM a letter to Bartholomew Des Bosses, June 16, 1712, trans. Leroy M. Loemker, *ibid.*]

10

The Pre-established Harmony (see *Monadology*, §§ 78-83)

Some wise and penetrating friends, having considered my novel hypothesis concerning the great question of the union of soul and body, and having found it of importance, have besought me to give some explanations of the difficulties which have been raised and which come from the fact that it has not been well understood.

I have thought that the matter might be rendered intelligible to every sort of mind by the following comparison:

Imagine two clocks or two watches which agree perfectly. Now this may happen in *three ways*. The first consists in the mutual influence of one clock on the other; the second, in the care of a man who attends thereto; the third, in their own accuracy.

The *first way,* which is that of influence, has been experimented on by the late M. Huygens, to his great astonishment. He had two large pendulums attached to the same piece of wood; the continual beats of these pendulums communicated similar vibrations to the particles of wood; but these different vibrations not being able to subsist very well in their order and without interfering with each other, unless the pendulums agreed, it happened by a kind of marvel that even when their beats had been purposely disturbed they soon came again to beat together, almost like two chords which are in unison.

The *second way* of making two clocks, even although poor ones, always accord, would be to have a skillful workman who should see to it that they are kept in constant agreement. This is what I call the way of assistance.

Finally, the *third way* would be to make at the start these two clocks with such art and accuracy that we could be assured of their future accordance. This is the way of preëstablished agreement.

Put now the soul and the body in the place of these two clocks Their harmony or sympathy will arise in one of these three ways *The way of influence* is that of the common philosophy; but as we cannot conceive of material particles or properties, or immaterial qualities, which can pass from one of these substances into the other, we are obliged to abandon this view. *The way of assistance* is that of the system of occasional causes; but I hold that this is making a *Deus ex Machina* intervene in a natural and ordinary matter, when. according to reason, he ought not to intervene except in the manner in which he coöperates in all the other affairs of nature.

Thus, there remains only my hypothesis; that is, *the way of the harmony preëstablished* by a prevenient divine contrivance, which from the beginning has formed each of these substances in a way so perfect, and regulated with so much accuracy, that merely by following laws of its own, received with its being, it nevertheless agrees with the other, just as if there were mutual influence, or as if God in addition to his general coöperation constantly put his hand thereto.

After this I do not think I need to prove anything, unless it be that you wish me to prove that God has everything necessary to making use of this prevenient contrivance, semblances of which we see even among men, according to their skill. And supposing that he can do it, you see well that this is the most admirable way and the one most worthy of him.

It is true that I have yet other proofs but they are more profound, and it is not necessary to state them here.

[The *Third Explanation* of the *New System of the Nature and of the Interaction of Substances* (1690), trans. George Martin Duncan, in *The Philosophical Works of Leibnitz, op. cit.*]

JEAN JACQUES ROUSSEAU

JEAN JACQUES ROUSSEAU (1712–1778) was born a "citizen" of Geneva—that is, a member of the highest of the five classes in the Republic of Switzerland—and he took pride in this status until Geneva condemned and burned his two greatest works, at which time he renounced his citizenship. His father, a watchmaker, brought him up until he was ten, chiefly on fiction and history, then left him in the care of others. Apprenticed to an engraver, he ran away from harsh treatment in 1728. After accepting conversion to Catholicism (he became a Protestant again in 1754), he was taken in by the brilliant and elegant Madame de Warens at Annecy. There followed a period of wandering and a succession of jobs: travelling musician, assistant to a surveyor, music teacher, student of philosophy and science, tutor, secretary to the Ambassador to Venice, clerk in the revenue office. From 1741 to 1756 he lived mostly in Paris, associated with the Encyclopedists and enjoying considerable fame, and after that, until 1762, in the country near Paris. Serious danger of arrest for his religious and political views, and continual persecution, kept him again on the move; to Neuchâtel in Switzerland under the protection of Frederick the Great, to England under the wing of David Hume, and finally back to Paris and the country nearby, where he died.

Rousseau's impact upon his age and the following one is probably greater than that of any other single writer, and in more than one direction. His fresh way of looking at man and nature and the human community, the eloquence and fascination of his style, his passionate yearning for reform in government and the social order, made him the inspiration—and to many the saint—of the Revolution. His novel *La Nouvelle Héloise* (1761) was one of the key works that launched the Romantic Movement in literature, with its celebration of the "natural" man, the man of good sentiment. His *Confessions* (published posthumously, 1782–89; New York: Modern LIbrary, 1945), and other autobiographical writings, were a new and astonishing kind of intro-

JEAN JACQUES ROUSSEAU

The Social Contract (*abridged*)

spective self-analysis, full of psychological penetration as well as unconscious self-revelation. He also wrote on music (as in Diderot's *Encyclopedia*) and composed it—one of his Christmas songs is still sung.

Rousseau's more philosophical works cannot be sharply divided into separate categories, for his principal preoccupations are found to some extent in all of them. He began with his prize essay, the *Discourse on Moral Effects of the Arts and Sciences* (1750), in which he enthusiastically attacked civilization as a corruption of nature. This thesis he turned in a more political direction in his second essay, the *Discourse on the Origin and Foundation of Inequality Among Men* (1775), which, while celebrating the "state of nature," recognized and examined the necessity of social order. The *Discourse on Political Economy*, written for the *Encyclopedia* (1775), foreshadowed parts of the *Social Contract* (1762), his major work in political philosophy (see below). (The three *Discourses*, trans. by G. D. H. Cole, are published by Everyman's Library, London: J. M. Dent, 1913, and New York: E. P. Dutton, 1950; *The First and Second Discourses*, trans. Roger D. and Judith R. Masters, New York: St. Martin's Press, 1964.) In the same year as the *Social Contract* appeared *Emile* (trans. A. Bloom, New York: Basic Books, 1979), his long work on the philosophy of education, in which he undertook to develop the educational methods suitable for raising children, in the light of his theory of man: The child must be helped to unfold its own nature, to mature at its own pace, and childhood has a right to happiness. This book has an important place in the history of educational theory, and its influence throughout Europe has been immense.

For all the obscurities and vacillations of viewpoint in his major works, which have enabled disciples of various points of view (democratic and totalitarian) to claim him as their master, important achievements, especially in the realm of social and political philosophy, can probably be claimed for Rousseau. He contributed to the clarification of certain fundamental terms, such as "right," "liberty," and "law"; his grasp of the element of universality in law was one of his most fruitful bequests to his successors, such as Kant. He understood better than his predecessors the distinction between factual and normative questions in social philosophy. He saw more clearly, too, that the problem of the "social contract" was not a historical but a logical one. He explored more profoundly the real nature of that bond that creates the unity of the state; he had the originality to reject the Natural Law theory, interpreted in the usual way, and to look for a new foundation of rights. Perhaps his most important achievement was his insistence that the sort of society we live in is up to us, for we are responsible, we choose; and he offered those who would accept this challenge a new and inspiring conception of man.

The Social Contract, or Principles of Political Right* (*abridged*)

BOOK I

I mean to inquire if, in the civil order, there can be any sure and legitimate rule of administration, men being taken as they are and laws as they might be. In this inquiry I shall endeavor always to unite what right sanctions with what is prescribed by interest, in order that justice and utility may in no case be divided.

I enter upon my task without proving the importance of the subject. I shall be asked if I am a prince or a legislator, to write on politics. I answer that I am neither, and that is why I do so. If I were a prince or a legislator, I should not waste time in saying what wants doing; I should do it, or hold my peace.

As I was born a citizen of a free State, and a member of the Sovereign, I feel that, however feeble the influence my voice can have on public affairs, the right of voting on them makes it my duty to study them: and I am happy, when I reflect upon governments, to find my inquiries always furnish me with new reasons for loving that of my own country.

Chapter I

Subject of the First Book

Man is born free; and everywhere he is in chains. One thinks himself the master of others, and still remains a greater slave than they. How did this change come about? I do not know. What can make it legitimate? That question I think I can answer.

If I took into account only force, and the effects derived from it, I should say: "As long as a people is compelled to obey, and obeys, it does well; as soon as it can shake off the yoke, and shakes it off, it does still better; for, regaining its liberty by the same right as took it away, either it is justified in resuming it, or there was no justification

---

* From *The Social Contract and Other Discourses,* trans. G. D. H. Cole (1913). Everyman's Library edition. Reprinted by permission of E. P. Dutton & Co., New York, and J. M. Dent & Sons Ltd., London. *Du Contrat social, ou Principes du Droit politique,* was first published in 1762; the present selection consists of about two-fifths of the original.

for those who took it away." But the social order is a sacred right which is the basis of all rights. Nevertheless, this right does not come from nature, and must therefore be founded on conventions. Before coming to that, I have to prove what I have just asserted.

Chapter II

The First Societies

The most ancient of all societies, and the only one that is natural, is the family: and even so the children remain attached to the father only so long as they need him for their preservation. As soon as this need ceases, the natural bond is dissolved. The children, released from the obedience they owed to the father, and the father, released from the care he owed his children, return equally to independence. If they remain united, they continue so no longer naturally, but voluntarily; and the family itself is then maintained only by convention.

This common liberty results from the nature of man. His first law is to provide for his own preservation, his first cares are those which he owes to himself; and, as soon as he reaches years of discretion, he is the sole judge of the proper means of preserving himself, and consequently becomes his own master.

The family then may be called the first model of political societies: the ruler corresponds to the father, and the people to the children; and all, being born free and equal, alienate their liberty only for their own advantage. The whole difference is that, in the family, the love of the father for his children repays him for the care he takes of them, while, in the State, the pleasure of commanding takes the place of the love which the chief cannot have for the peoples under him.

Grotius denies that all human power is established in favor of the governed, and quotes slavery as an example. His usual method of reasoning is constantly to establish right by fact.[1] It would be possible to employ a more logical method, but none could be more favorable to tyrants.

It is then, according to Grotius, doubtful whether the human race belongs to a hundred men, or that hundred men to the human race: and, throughout his book, he seems to incline to the former alterna-

---

[1] "Learned inquiries into public right are often only the history of past abuses; and troubling to study them too deeply is a profitless infatuation" (*Essay on the Interests of France in Relation to its Neighbors,* by the Marquis d'Argenson). This is exactly what Grotius has done.

tive, which is also the view of Hobbes. On this showing, the human species is divided into so many herds of cattle, each with its ruler, who keeps guard over them for the purpose of devouring them.

As a shepherd is of a nature superior to that of his flock, the shepherds of men, i.e. their rulers, are of a nature superior to that of the peoples under them. Thus, Philo tells us, the Emperor Caligula reasoned, concluding equally well either that kings were gods, or that men were beasts.

The reasoning of Caligula agrees with that of Hobbes and Grotius. Aristotle, before any of them, had said that men are by no means equal naturally, but that some are born for slavery, and others for dominion.

Aristotle was right; but he took the effect for the cause. Nothing can be more certain than that every man born in slavery is born for slavery. Slaves lose everything in their chains, even the desire of escaping from them: they love their servitude, as the comrades of Ulysses loved their brutish condition.[1] If then there are slaves by nature, it is because there have been slaves against nature. Force made the first slaves, and their cowardice perpetuated the condition.

I have said nothing of King Adam, or Emperor Noah, father of the three great monarchs who shared out the universe, like the children of Saturn, whom some scholars have recognized in them. I trust to getting due thanks for my moderation; for, being a direct descendant of one of these princes, perhaps of the eldest branch, how do I know that a verification of titles might not leave me the legitimate king of the human race? In any case, there can be no doubt that Adam was sovereign of the world, as Robinson Crusoe was of his island, as long as he was its only inhabitant; and this empire had the advantage that the monarch, safe on his throne, had no rebellions, wars, or conspirators to fear.

Chapter III

The Right of the Strongest

The strongest is never strong enough to be always the master, unless he transforms strength into right, and obedience into duty. Hence the right of the strongest, which, though to all seeming meant ironically, is really laid down as a fundamental principle. But are we never

---

[1] See a short treatise of Plutarch's entitled "That Animals Reason."

to have an explanation of this phrase? Force is a physical power, and I fail to see what moral effect it can have. To yield to force is an act of necessity, not of will—at the most, an act of prudence. In what sense can it be a duty?

Suppose for a moment that this so-called "right" exists. I maintain that the sole result is a mass of inexplicable nonsense. For, if force creates right, the effect changes with the cause: every force that is greater than the first succeeds to its right. As soon as it is possible to disobey with impunity, disobedience is legitimate; and, the strongest being always in the right, the only thing that matters is to act so as to become the strongest. But what kind of right is that which perishes when force fails? If we must obey perforce, there is no need to obey because we ought; and if we are not forced to obey, we are under no obligation to do so. Clearly, the word "right" adds nothing to force: in this connection, it means absolutely nothing.

Obey the powers that be. If this means yield to force, it is a good precept, but superfluous: I can answer for its never being violated. All power comes from God, I admit; but so does all sickness: does that mean that we are forbidden to call in the doctor? A brigand surprises me at the edge of a wood: must I not merely surrender my purse on compulsion; but, even if I could withhold it, am I in conscience bound to give it up? For certainly the pistol he holds is also a power.

Let us then admit that force does not create right, and that we are obliged to obey only legitimate powers. In that case, my original question recurs.

Chapter IV

Slavery

Since no man has a natural authority over his fellow, and force creates no right, we must conclude that conventions form the basis of all legitimate authority among men.

If an individual, says Grotius, can alienate his liberty and make himself the slave of a master, why could not a whole people do the same and make itself subject to a king? There are in this passage plenty of ambiguous words which would need explaining; but let us confine ourselves to the word *alienate*. To alienate is to give or to sell. Now, a man who becomes the slave of another does not give himself; he sells himself, at the least for his subsistence: but for what does a people sell itself? A king is so far from furnishing his subjects with their subsistence that he gets his own only from them; and, according to Rabelais, kings do not live on nothing. Do subjects then give their persons on condition that the king take their goods also? I fail to see what they have left to preserve.

It will be said that the despot assures his subjects civil tranquillity. Granted; but what do they gain, if the wars his ambition brings down upon them, his insatiable avidity, and the vexatious conduct of his ministers press harder on them than their own dissensions would have done? What do they gain, if the very tranquillity they enjoy is one of their miseries? Tranquillity is found also in dungeons; but is that enough to make them desirable places to live in? The Greeks imprisoned in the cave of the Cyclops lived there very tranquilly, while they were awaiting their turn to be devoured.

To say that a man gives himself gratuitously, is to say what is absurd and inconceivable; such an act is null and illegitimate, from the mere fact that he who does it is out of his mind. To say the same of a whole people is to suppose a people of madmen; and madness creates no right.

Even if each man could alienate himself, he could not alienate his children: they are born men and free; their liberty belongs to them, and no one but they has the right to dispose of it. Before they come to years of discretion, the father can, in their name, lay down conditions for their preservation and well-being, but he cannot give them irrevocably and without conditions: such a gift is contrary to the ends of nature, and exceeds the rights of paternity. It would therefore be necessary, in order to legitimize an arbitrary government, that in every generation the people should be in a position to accept or reject it; but, were this so, the government would be no longer arbitrary.

To renounce liberty is to renounce being a man, to surrender the rights of humanity and even its duties. For him who renounces everything no indemnity is possible. Such a renunciation is incompatible with man's nature; to remove all liberty from his will is to remove all morality from his acts. Finally, it is an empty and contradictory convention that sets up, on the one side, absolute authority, and, on the other, unlimited obedience. Is it not clear that we can be under no obligation to a person from whom we have the right to exact everything? Does not this condition alone, in the absence of equivalence or exchange, in itself involve the nullity of the act? For what right can my slave have against me, when all that he has belongs to me, and, his right being mine, this right of mine against myself is a phrase devoid of meaning?

Grotius and the rest find in war another origin for the so-called right of slavery. The victor having, as they hold, the right of killing the vanquished, the latter can buy back his life at the price of his liberty; and this convention is the more legitimate because it is to the advantage of both parties.

But it is clear that this supposed right to kill the conquered is by no means deducible from the state of war. Men, from the mere fact that, while they are living in their primitive independence, they have no mutual relations stable enough to constitute either the state of peace or the state of war, cannot be naturally enemies. War is constituted by a relation between things, and not between persons; and, as the state of war cannot arise out of simple personal relations, but only out of real relations, private war, or war of man with man, can exist neither in the state of nature, where there is no constant property, nor in the social state, where everything is under the authority of the laws.

Individual combats, duels, and encounters, are acts which cannot constitute a state; while the private wars, authorized by the Establishments of Louis IX, King of France, and suspended by the Peace of God, are abuses of feudalism, in itself an absurd system if ever there was one, and contrary to the principles of natural right and to all good polity.

War then is a relation, not between man and man, but between State and State, and individuals are enemies only accidentally, not as men, nor even as citizens,[1] but as soldiers; not as members of their country, but as its defenders. Finally, each State can have for enemies

---

[1] The Romans, who understood and respected the right of war more than any other nation on earth, carried their scruples on this head so far that a citizen was not allowed to serve as a volunteer without engaging himself expressly against the enemy, and against such and such an enemy by name. A legion in which the younger Cato was seeing his first service under Popilius having been reconstructed, the elder Cato wrote to Popilius that, if he wished his son to continue serving under him, he must administer to him a new military oath, because, the first having been annulled, he was no longer able to bear arms against the enemy. The same Cato wrote to his son telling him to take great care not to go into battle before taking this new oath. I know that the siege of Clusium and other isolated events can be quoted against me; but I am citing laws and customs. The Romans are the people that least often transgressed its laws; and no other people has had such good ones.

only other States, and not men; for between things disparate in nature there can be no real relation.

Furthermore, this principle is in conformity with the established rules of all times and the constant practice of all civilized peoples. Declarations of war are intimations less to powers than to their subjects. The foreigner, whether king, individual, or people, who robs, kills, or detains the subjects, without declaring war on the prince, is not an enemy, but a brigand. Even in real war, a just prince, while laying hands, in the enemy's country, on all that belongs to the public, respects the lives and goods of individuals: he respects rights on which his own are founded. The object of the war being the destruction of the hostile State, the other side has a right to kill its defenders, while they are bearing arms; but as soon as they lay them down and surrender, they cease to be enemies or instruments of the enemy, and become once more merely men, whose life no one has any right to take. Sometimes it is possible to kill the State without killing a single one of its members; and war gives no right which is not necessary to the gaining of its object. These principles are not those of Grotius: they are not based on the authority of poets, but derived from the nature of reality and based on reason.

The right of conquest has no foundation other than the right of the strongest. If war does not give the conqueror the right to massacre the conquered peoples, the right to enslave them cannot be based upon a right which does not exist. No one has a right to kill an enemy except when he cannot make him a slave, and the right to enslave him cannot therefore be derived from the right to kill him. It is accordingly an unfair exchange to make him buy at the price of his liberty his life, over which the victor holds no right. Is it not clear that there is a vicious circle in founding the right of life and death on the right of slavery, and the right of slavery on the right of life and death?

Even if we assume this terrible right to kill everybody, I maintain that a slave made in war, or a conquered people, is under no obligation to a master, except to obey him as far as he is compelled to do so. By taking an equivalent for his life, the victor has not done him a favor; instead of killing him without profit, he has killed him usefully. So far then is he from acquiring over him any authority in addition to that of force, that the state of war continues to subsist between them: their mutual relation is the effect of it, and the usage of the right of war does not imply a treaty of peace. A convention has indeed been made; but this convention, so far from destroying the state of war, presupposes its continuance.

So, from whatever aspect we regard the question, the right of slavery is null and void, not only as being illegitimate, but also because it is absurd and meaningless. The words *slave* and *right* contradict each other, and are mutually exclusive. It will always be equally foolish for a man to say to a man or to a people: "I make with you a convention wholly at your expense and wholly to my advantage; I shall keep it as long as I like, and you will keep it as long as I like."

Chapter V

That We Must Always Go Back to a First Convention

Even if I granted all that I have been refuting, the friends of despotism would be no better off. There will always be a great difference between subduing a multitude and ruling a society. Even if scattered individuals were successively enslaved by one man, however numerous they might be, I still see no more than a master and his slaves, and certainly not a people and its ruler; I see what may be termed an aggregation, but not an association; there is as yet neither public good nor body politic. The man in question, even if he has enslaved half the world, is still only an individual; his interest, apart from that of others, is still a purely private interest. If this same man comes to die, his empire, after him, remains scattered and without unity, as an oak falls and dissolves into a heap of ashes when the fire has consumed it.

A people, says Grotius, can give itself to a king. Then according to Grotius, a people is a people before it gives itself. The gift is itself a civil act, and implies public deliberation. It would be better, before examining the act by which a people gives itself to a king, to examine that by which it has become a people; for this act, being necessarily prior to the other, is the true foundation of society.

Indeed, if there were no prior convention, where, unless the election were unanimous, would be the obligation on the minority to submit to the choice of the majority? How have a hundred men who wish for a master the right to vote on behalf of ten who do not? The law of majority voting is itself something established by convention, and presupposes unanimity, on one occasion at least.

Chapter VI

The Social Compact

I suppose men to have reached the point at which the obstacles in the way of their preservation in the state of nature show their power of resistance to be greater than the resources at the disposal of each individual for his maintenance in that state. That primitive condition can then subsist no longer; and the human race would perish unless it changed its manner of existence.

But, as men cannot engender new forces, but only unite and direct existing ones, they have no other means of preserving themselves than the formation, by aggregation, of a sum of forces great enough to overcome the resistance. These they have to bring into play by means of a single motive power, and cause to act in concert.

This sum of forces can arise only where several persons come together: but, as the force and liberty of each man are the chief instruments of his self-preservation, how can he pledge them without harming his own interests, and neglecting the care he owes to himself? This difficulty, in its bearing on my present subject, may be stated in the following terms:

"The problem is to find a form of association which will defend and protect with the whole common force the person and goods of each associate, and in which each, while uniting himself with all, may still obey himself alone, and remain as free as before." This is the fundamental problem of which the *Social Contract* provides the solution.

The clauses of this contract are so determined by the nature of the act that the slightest modification would make them vain and ineffective; so that, although they have perhaps never been formally set forth, they are everywhere the same and everywhere tacitly admitted and recognized, until, on the violation of the social compact, each regains his original rights and resumes his natural liberty, while losing the conventional liberty in favor of which he renounced it.

These clauses, properly understood, may be reduced to one—the total alienation of each associate, together with all his rights, to the whole community; for, in the first place, as each gives himself absolutely, the conditions are the same for all; and, this being so, no one has any interest in making them burdensome to others.

Moreover, the alienation being without reserve, the union is as perfect as it can be, and no associate has anything more to demand: for, if the individuals retained certain rights, as there would be no common superior to decide between them and the public, each, being on one point his own judge, would ask to be so on all; the state of nature would thus continue, and the association would necessarily become inoperative or tyrannical.

Finally, each man, in giving himself to all, gives himself to nobody; and as there is no associate over which he does not acquire the same right as he yields others over himself, he gains an equivalent for everything he loses, and an increase of force for the preservation of what he has.

If then we discard from the social compact what is not of its essence, we shall find that it reduces itself to the following terms:

"Each of us puts his person and all his power in common under the supreme direction of the general will, and, in our corporate capacity, we receive each member as an indivisible part of the whole."

At once, in place of the individual personality of each contracting party, this act of association creates a moral and collective body, composed of as many members as the assembly contains voters, and receiving from this act its unity, its common identity, its life, and its will. This public person, so formed by the union of all other persons, formerly took the name of *city,*[1] and now takes that of *Republic* or *body politic;* it is called by its members *State* when passive, *Sovereign* when active, and *Power* when compared with others like itself. Those who are associated in it take collectively the name of *people,* and severally are called *citizens,* as sharing in the sovereign power, and *subjects,* as being under the laws of the State. But these terms are

---

[1] The real meaning of this word has been almost wholly lost in modern times; most people mistake a town for a city, and a townsman for a citizen. They do not know that houses make a town, but citizens a city. The same mistake long ago cost the Carthaginians dear. I have never read of the title of citizens being given to the subjects of any prince, not even the ancient Macedonians or the English of to-day, though they are nearer liberty than any one else. The French alone everywhere familiarly adopt the name of citizens, because, as can be seen from their dictionaries, they have no idea of its meaning; otherwise they would be guilty in usurping it, of the crime of *lèse-majesté:* among them, the name expresses a virtue, and not a right. When Bodin spoke of our citizens and townsmen, he fell into a bad blunder in taking the one class for the other. M. d'Alembert has avoided the error, and, in his article on Geneva, has clearly distinguished the four orders of men (or even five, counting mere foreigners) who dwell in our town, of which two only compose the Republic. No other French writer, to my knowledge, has understood the real meaning of the word "citizen."

often confused and taken one for another: it is enough to know how to distinguish them when they are being used with precision.

Chapter VII

The Sovereign

This formula shows us that the act of association comprises a mutual undertaking between the public and the individuals, and that each individual, in making a contract, as we may say, with himself, is bound in a double capacity; as a member of the Sovereign he is bound to the individuals, and as a member of the State to the Sovereign. But the maxim of civil right, that no one is bound by undertakings made to himself, does not apply in this case; for there is a great difference between incurring an obligation to yourself and incurring one to a whole of which you form a part.

Attention must further be called to the fact that public deliberation, while competent to bind all the subjects to the Sovereign, because of the two different capacities in which each of them may be regarded, cannot, for the opposite reason, bind the Sovereign to itself; and that it is consequently against the nature of the body politic for the Sovereign to impose on itself a law which it cannot infringe. Being able to regard itself in only one capacity, it is in the position of an individual who makes a contract with himself; and this makes it clear that there neither is nor can be any kind of fundamental law binding on the body of the people—not even the social contract itself. This does not mean that the body politic cannot enter into undertakings with others, provided the contract is not infringed by them; for in relation to what is external to it, it becomes a simple being, an individual.

But the body politic or the Sovereign, drawing its being wholly from the sanctity of the contract, can never bind itself, even to an outsider, to do anything derogatory to the original act, for instance, to alienate any part of itself, or to submit to another Sovereign. Violation of the act by which it exists would be self-annihilation; and that which is itself nothing can create nothing.

As soon as this multitude is so united in one body, it is impossible to offend against one of the members without attacking the body, and still more to offend against the body without the members resenting it. Duty and interest therefore equally oblige the two contracting parties to give each other help; and the same men should seek to combine, in their double capacity, all the advantages dependent upon that capacity.

Again, the Sovereign, being formed wholly of the individuals who compose it, neither has nor can have any interest contrary to theirs; and consequently the sovereign power need give no guarantee to its subjects, because it is impossible for the body to wish to hurt all its members. We shall also see later on that it cannot hurt any in particular. The Sovereign, merely by virtue of what it is, is always what it should be.

This, however, is not the case with the relation of the subjects to the Sovereign, which, despite the common interest, would have no security that they would fulfil their undertakings, unless it found means to assure itself of their fidelity.

In fact, each individual, as a man, may have a particular will contrary or dissimilar to the general will which he has as a citizen. His particular interest may speak to him quite differently from the common interest: his absolute and naturally independent existence may make him look upon what he owes to the common cause as a gratuitous contribution, the loss of which will do less harm to others than the payment of it is burdensome to himself; and, regarding the moral person which constitutes the State as a *persona ficta,* because not a man, he may wish to enjoy the rights of citizenship without being ready to fulfil the duties of a subject. The continuance of such an injustice could not but prove the undoing of the body politic.

In order then that the social compact may not be an empty formula, it tacitly includes the undertaking, which alone can give force to the rest, that whoever refuses to obey the general will shall be compelled to do so by the whole body. This means nothing less than that he will be forced to be free; for this is the condition which, by giving each citizen to his country, secures him against all personal dependence. In this lies the key to the working of the political machine; this alone legitimizes civil undertakings, which, without it, would be absurd, tyrannical, and liable to the most frightful abuses.

Chapter VIII

The Civil State

The passage from the state of nature to the civil state produces a very remarkable change in man, by substituing justice for instinct in his conduct, and giving his actions the morality they had formerly lacked.

Then only, when the voice of duty takes the place of physical impulses and right of appetite, does man, who so far had considered only himself, find that he is forced to act on different principles, and to consult his reason before listening to his inclinations. Although, in this state, he deprives himself of some advantages which he got from nature, he gains in return others so great, his faculties are so stimulated and developed, his ideas so extended, his feelings so ennobled, and his whole soul so uplifted, that, did not the abuses of this new condition often degrade him below that which he left, he would be bound to bless continually the happy moment which took him from it for ever, and, instead of a stupid and unimaginative animal, made him an intelligent being and a man.

Let us draw up the whole account in terms easily commensurable. What man loses by the social contract is his natural liberty and an unlimited right to everything he tries to get and succeeds in getting; what he gains is civil liberty and the proprietorship of all he possesses. If we are to avoid mistake in weighing one against the other, we must clearly distinguish natural liberty, which is bounded only by the strength of the individual, from civil liberty, which is limited by the general will; and possession, which is merely the effect of force or the right of the first occupier, from property, which can be founded only on a positive title.

We might, over and above all this, add, to what man acquires in the civil state, moral liberty, which alone makes him truly master of himself; for the mere impulse of appetite is slavery, while obedience to a law which we prescribe to ourselves is liberty. But I have already said too much on this head, and the philosophical meaning of the word "liberty" does not now concern us.

Chapter IX

Real Property

Each member of the community gives himself to it, at the moment of its foundation, just as he is, with all the resources at his command, including the goods he possesses. This act does not make possession, in changing hands, change its nature, and become property in the hands of the Sovereign; but, as the forces of the city are incomparably greater than those of an individual, public possession is also, in fact, stronger and more irrevocable, without being any more legitimate, at any rate from the point of view of foreigners. For the State, in relation to its members, is master of all their goods by the social contract, which, within the State, is the basis of all rights; but, in relation to other powers, it is so only by the right of the first occupier, which it holds from its members.

The right of the first occupier, though more real than the right of the strongest, becomes a real right only when the right of property has already been established. Every man has naturally a right to everything he needs; but the positive act which makes him proprietor of one thing excludes him from everything else. Having his share, he ought to keep to it, and can have no further right against the community. This is why the right of the first occupier, which in the state of nature is so weak, claims the respect of every man in civil society. In this right we are respecting not so much what belongs to another as what does not belong to ourselves.

In general, to establish the right of the first occupier over a plot of ground, the following conditions are necessary: first, the land must not yet be inhabited; secondly, a man must occupy only the amount he needs for his subsistence; and, in the third place, possession must be taken, not by an empty ceremony, but by labor and cultivation, the only sign of proprietorship that should be respected by others, in default of a legal title.

In granting the right of first occupancy to necessity and labor, are we not really stretching it as far as it can go? Is it possible to leave such a right unlimited? Is it to be enough to set foot on a plot of common ground, in order to be able to call yourself at once the master of it? Is it to be enough that a man has the strength to expel others for a moment, in order to establish his right to prevent them from ever returning? How can a man or a people seize an immense territory and keep it from the rest of the world except by a punishable usurpation, since all others are being robbed, by such an act, of the place of habitation and the means of subsistence which nature gave them in common? When Nuñez Balboa, standing on the seashore, took possession of the South Seas and the whole of South America in the name of the crown of Castille, was that enough to dispossess all their actual inhabitants, and to shut out from them all the princes of the world? On such a showing, these ceremonies are idly multiplied, and the Catholic King need only take possession all at once, from his apartment, of the whole universe, merely making a subsequent reservation about what was already in the possession of other princes.

We can imagine how the lands of individuals, where they were contiguous and came to be united, became the public territory, and how the right of Sovereignty, extending from the subjects over the lands they held, became at once real and personal. The possessors were thus made more dependent, and the forces at their command used to guarantee their fidelity. The advantage of this does not seem to have been felt by ancient monarchs, who called themselves King of the Persians, Scythians, or Macedonians, and seemed to regard themselves more as rulers of men than as masters of a country. Those of the present day more cleverly call themselves Kings of France, Spain, England, etc.: thus holding the land, they are quite confident of holding the inhabitants.

The peculiar fact about this alienation is that, in taking over the goods of individuals, the community, so far from despoiling them, only assures them legitimate possession, and changes usurpation into a true right and enjoyment into proprietorship. Thus the possessors, being regarded as depositaries of the public good, and having their rights respected by all the members of the State and maintained against foreign aggression by all its forces, have, by a cession which benefits both the public and still more themselves, acquired, so to speak, all that they gave up. This paradox may easily be explained by the distinction between the rights which the Sovereign and the proprietor have over the same estate, as we shall see later on.

It may also happen that men begin to unite one with another before they possess anything, and that, subsequently occupying a tract of country which is enough for all, they enjoy it in common, or share it out among themselves, either equally or according to a scale fixed by the Sovereign. However the acquisition be made, the right which each individual has to his own estate is always subordinate to the right which the community has over all: without this, there would be neither stability in the social tie, nor real force in the exercise of Sovereignty.

I shall end this chapter and this book by remarking on a fact on which the whole social system should rest: i.e. that, instead of destroying natural inequality, the fundamental compact substitutes, for such physical inequality as nature may have set up between men, an equality that is moral and legitimate, and that men, who may be unequal in strength or intelligence, become every one equal by convention and legal right.[1]

---

[1] Under bad governments, this equality is only apparent and illusory; it serves only to keep the pauper in his poverty and the rich man in the position he has usurped. In fact, laws are always of use to those who possess and harmful to those who have nothing: from which it follows that the social state is advantageous to men only when all have something and none too much.

BOOK II

Chapter I

That Sovereignty is Inalienable

The first and most important deduction from the principles we have
so far laid down is that the general will alone can direct the State
according to the object for which it was instituted, i.e. the common
good: for if the clashing of particular interests made the establishment of societies necessary, the agreement of these very interests
made it possible. The common element in these different interests is
what forms the social tie; and, were there no point of agreement between them all, no society could exist. It is solely on the basis of this
common interest that every society should be governed.

I hold then that Sovereignty, being nothing less than the exercise
of the general will, can never be alienated, and that the Sovereign,
who is no less than a collective being, cannot be represented except
by himself: the power indeed may be transmitted, but not the will.

In reality, if it is not impossible for a particular will to agree on
some point with the general will, it is at least impossible for the agreement to be lasting and constant; for the particular will tends, by its
very nature, to partiality, while the general will tends to equality. It
is even more impossible to have any guarantee of this agreement; for
even if it should always exist, it would be the effect not of art, but of
chance. The Sovereign may indeed say: "I now will actually what
this man wills, or at least what he says he wills"; but it cannot say:
"What he wills to-morrow, I too shall will" because it is absurd for
the will to bind itself for the future, nor is it incumbent on any will
to consent to anything that is not for the good of the being who wills.
If then the people promises simply to obey, by that very act it dissolves itself and loses what makes it a people; the moment a master
exists, there is no longer a Sovereign, and from that moment the body
politic has ceased to exist.

This does not mean that the commands of the rulers cannot pass
for general wills, so long as the Sovereign, being free to oppose them,
offers no opposition. In such a case. universal silence is taken to
imply the consent of the people. This will be explained later on.

Chapter II

That Sovereignty is Indivisible

Sovereignty, for the same reason as makes it inalienable, is indivisible; for will either is, or is not, general;[1] it is the will either of the body of the people, or only of a part of it. In the first case, the will, when declared, is an act of Sovereignty and constitutes law: in the second, it is merely a particular will, or act of magistracy—at the most a decree.

But our political theorists, unable to divide Sovereignty in principle, divide it according to its object: into force and will; into legislative power and executive power; into rights of taxation, justice, and war; into internal administration and power of foreign treaty. Sometimes they confuse all these sections, and sometimes they distinguish them; they turn the Sovereign into a fantastic being composed of several connected pieces: it is as if they were making man of several bodies, one with eyes, one with arms, another with feet, and each with nothing besides. We are told that the jugglers of Japan dismember a child before the eyes of the spectators; then they throw all the members into the air one after another, and the child falls down alive and whole. The conjuring tricks of our political theorists are very like that; they first dismember the body politic by an illusion worthy of a fair, and then join it together again we know not how.

This error is due to a lack of exact notions concerning the Sovereign authority, and to taking for parts of it what are only emanations from it. Thus, for example, the acts of declaring war and making peace have been regarded as acts of Sovereignty; but this is not the case, as these acts do not constitute law, but merely the application of a law, a particular act which decides how the law applies, as we shall see clearly when the idea attached to the word "law" has been defined.

If we examined the other divisions in the same manner, we should find that, whenever Sovereignty seems to be divided, there is an illusion: the rights which are taken as being part of Sovereignty are really all subordinate, and always imply supreme wills of which they only sanction the execution.

It would be impossible to estimate the obscurity this lack of exactness has thrown over the decisions of writers who have dealt with

---

[1] To be general, a will need not always be unanimous; but every vote must be counted: any exclusion is a breach of generality.

political right, when they have used the principles laid down by them to pass judgment on the respective rights of kings and peoples. Every one can see, in Chapters III and IV of the first book of Grotius, how the learned man and his translator, Barbeyrac, entangle and tie themselves up in their own sophistries, for fear of saying too little or too much of what they think, and so offending the interests they have to conciliate. Grotius, a refugee in France, ill content with his own country, and desirous of paying his court to Louis XIII, to whom his book is dedicated, spares no pains to rob the peoples of all their rights and invest kings with them by every conceivable artifice. This would also have been much to the taste of Barbeyrac, who dedicated his translation to George I of England. But unfortunately the expulsion of James II, which he called his "abdication," compelled him to use all reserve, to shuffle and to tergiversate, in order to avoid making William out a usurper. If these two writers had adopted the true principles, all difficulties would have been removed, and they would have been always consistent; but it would have been a sad truth for them to tell, and would have paid court for them to no one save the people. Moreover, truth is no road to fortune, and the people dispenses neither ambassadorships, nor professorships, nor pensions.

Chapter III

Whether the General Will is Fallible

It follows from what has gone before that the general will is always right and tends to the public advantage; but it does not follow that the deliberations of the people are always equally correct. Our will is always for our own good, but we do not always see what that is; the people is never corrupted, but it is often deceived, and on such occasions only does it seem to will what is bad.

There is often a great deal of difference between the will of all and the general will; the latter considers only the common interest, while the former takes private interest into account, and is no more than a sum of particular wills: but take away from these same wills the pluses and minuses that cancel one another,[1] and the general will remains as the sum of the differences.

---

[1] "Every interest," says the Marquis d'Argenson, "has different principles. The agreement of two particular interests is formed by opposition to a third."

If, when the people, being furnished with adequate information, held its deliberations, the citizens had no communication one with another, the grand total of the small differences would always give the general will, and the decision would always be good. But when factions arise, and partial associations are formed at the expense of the great association, the will of each of these associations becomes general in relation to its members, while it remains particular in relation to the State: it may then be said that there are no longer as many votes as there are men, but only as many as there are associations. The differences become less numerous and give a less general result. Lastly, when one of these associations is so great as to prevail over all the rest, the result is no longer a sum of small differences, but a single difference; in this case there is no longer a general will, and the opinion which prevails is purely particular.

It is therefore essential, if the general will is to be able to express itself, that there should be no partial society within the State, and that each citizen should think only his own thoughts:[2] which was indeed the sublime and unique system established by the great Lycurgus. But if there are partial societies, it is best to have as many as possible and to prevent them from being unequal, as was done by Solon, Numa, and Servius. These precautions are the only ones that can guarantee that the general will shall be always enlightened, and that the people shall in no way deceive itself.

Chapter IV

The Limits of the Sovereign Power

If the State is a moral person whose life is in the union of its members, and if the most important of its cares is the care for its own preservation, it must have a universal and compelling force, in order

---

He might have added that the agreement of all interests is formed by opposition to that of each. If there were no different interests, the common interest would be barely felt, as it would encounter no obstacle; all would go on of its own accord, and politics would cease to be an art.

[2] "In fact," says Machiavelli, "there are some divisions that are harmful to a Republic and some that are advantageous. Those which stir up sects and parties are harmful; those attended by neither are advantageous. Since, then, the founder of a Republic cannot help enmities arising, he ought at least to prevent them from growing into sects." (*History of Florence*, Book VII).

to move and dispose each part as may be most advantageous to the whole. As nature gives each man absolute power over all his members, the social compact gives the body politic absolute power over all its members also; and it is this power which, under the direction of the general will, bears, as I have said, the name of Sovereignty.

But, besides the public person, we have to consider the private persons composing it, whose life and liberty are naturally independent of it. We are bound then to distinguish clearly between the respective rights of the citizens and the Sovereign,[1] and between the duties the former have to fulfil as subjects, and the natural rights they should enjoy as men.

Each man alienates, I admit, by the social compact, only such part of his powers, goods, and liberty as it is important for the community to control; but it must also be granted that the Sovereign is sole judge of what is important.

Every service a citizen can render the State he ought to render as soon as the Sovereign demands it; but the Sovereign, for its part, cannot impose upon its subjects any fetters that are useless to the community, nor can it even wish to do so; for no more by the law of reason than by the law of nature can anything occur without a cause.

The undertakings which bind us to the social body are obligatory only because they are mutual; and their nature is such that in fulfilling them we cannot work for others without working for ourselves. Why is it that the general will is always in the right, and that all continually will the happiness of each one, unless it is because there is not a man who does not think of "each" as meaning him, and consider himself in voting for all? This proves that equality of rights and the idea of justice which such equality creates originate in the preference each man gives to himself, and accordingly in the very nature of man. It proves that the general will, to be really such, must be general in its object as well as its essence; that it must both come from all and apply to all; and that it loses its natural rectitude when it is directed to some particular and determinate object, because in such a case we are judging of something foreign to us, and have no true principle of equity to guide us.

Indeed, as soon as a question of particular fact or right arises on a point not previously regulated by a general convention, the matter becomes contentious. It is a case in which the individuals concerned

---

[1] Attentive readers, do not, I pray, be in a hurry to charge me with contradicting myself. The terminology made it unavoidable, considering the poverty of the language; but wait and see.

are one party, and the public the other, but in which I can see neither the law that ought to be followed nor the judge who ought to give the decision. In such a case, it would be absurd to propose to refer the question to an express decision of the general will, which can be only the conclusion reached by one of the parties and in consequence will be, for the other party, merely an external and particular will, inclined on this occasion to injustice and subject to error. Thus, just as a particular will cannot stand for the general will, the general will, in turn, changes its nature, when its object is particular, and, as general, cannot pronounce on a man or a fact. When, for instance, the people of Athens nominated or displaced its rulers, decreed honors to one, and imposed penalties on another, and, by a multitude of particular decrees, exercised all the functions of government indiscriminately, it had in such cases no longer a general will in the strict sense; it was acting no longer as Sovereign, but as magistrate. This will seem contrary to current views; but I must be given time to expound my own.

It should be seen from the foregoing that what makes the will general is less the number of voters than the common interest uniting them; for, under this system, each necessarily submits to the conditions he imposes on others: and this admirable agreement between interest and justice gives to the common deliberations an equitable character which at once vanishes when any particular question is discussed, in the absence of a common interest to unite and identify the ruling of the judge with that of the party.

From whatever side we approach our principle, we reach the same conclusion, that the social compact sets up among the citizens an equality of such a kind, that they all bind themselves to observe the same conditions and should therefore all enjoy the same rights. Thus, from the very nature of the compact, every act of Sovereignty, i.e. every authentic act of the general will, binds or favors all the citizens equally; so that the Sovereign recognizes only the body of the nation, and draws no distinctions between those of whom it is made up. What, then, strictly speaking, is an act of Sovereignty? It is not a convention between a superior and an inferior, but a convention between the body and each of its members. It is legitimate, because based on the social contract, and equitable, because common to all; useful, because it can have no other object than the general good, and stable, because guaranteed by the public force and the supreme power. So long as the subjects have to submit only to conventions of this sort, they obey no one but their own will; and to ask how far the respective rights of the Sovereign and the citizens extend, is to ask up to what point the latter can enter into undertakings with themselves, each with all, and all with each.

We can see from this that the sovereign power, absolute, sacred, and inviolable as it is, does not and cannot exceed the limits of general conventions, and that every man may dispose at will of such goods and liberty as these conventions leave him; so that the Sovereign never has a right to lay more charges on one subject than on another, because, in that case, the question becomes particular, and ceases to be within its competency.

When these distinctions have once been admitted, it is seen to be so untrue that there is, in the social contract, any real renunciation on the part of the individuals, that the position in which they find themselves as a result of the contract is really preferable to that in which they were before. Instead of a renunciation, they have made an advantageous exchange: instead of an uncertain and precarious way of living they have got one that is better and more secure; instead of natural independence they have got liberty; instead of the power to harm others, security for themselves; and instead of their strength, which others might overcome, a right which social union makes invincible. Their very life, which they have devoted to the State, is by it constantly protected; and when they risk it in the State's defense, what more are they doing than giving back what they have received from it? What are they doing that they would not do more often and with greater danger in the state of nature, in which they would inevitably have to fight battles at the peril of their lives in defense of that which is the means of their preservation? All have indeed to fight when their country needs them; but then no one has ever to fight for himself. Do we not gain something by running, on behalf of what gives us our security, only some of the risks we should have to run for ourselves, as soon as we lose it?

Chapter V

The Right of Life and Death

The question is often asked how individuals, having no right to dispose of their own lives, can transfer to the Sovereign a right which they do not possess. The difficulty of answering this question seems to me to lie in its being wrongly stated. Every man has a right to risk his own life in order to preserve it. Has it ever been said that a man who throws himself out of the window to escape from a fire is guilty of suicide? Has such a crime ever been laid to the charge of him who perishes in a storm because, when he went on board, he knew of the danger?

The social treaty has for its end the preservation of the contracting parties. He who wills the end wills the means also, and the means must involve some risks, and even some losses. He who wishes to preserve his life at others' expense should also, when it is necessary, be ready to give it up for their sake. Furthermore, the citizen is no longer the judge of the dangers to which the law desires him to expose himself; and when the prince says to him: "It is expedient for the State that you should die," he ought to die, because it is only on that condition that he has been living in security up to the present, and because his life is no longer a mere bounty of nature, but a gift made conditionally by the State.

The death-penalty inflicted upon criminals may be looked on in much the same light: it is in order that we may not fall victims to an assassin that we consent to die if we ourselves turn assassins. In this treaty, so far from disposing of our own lives, we think only of securing them, and it is not to be assumed that any of the parties then expects to get hanged.

Again, every malefactor, by attacking social rights, becomes on forfeit a rebel and a traitor to his country; by violating its laws he ceases to be a member of it; he even makes war upon it. In such a case the preservation of the State is inconsistent with his own, and one or the other must perish; in putting the guilty to death, we slay not so much the citizen as an enemy. The trial and the judgment are the proofs that he has broken the social treaty, and is in consequence no longer a member of the State. Since, then, he has recognized himself to be such by living there, he must be removed by exile as a violator of the compact, or by death as a public enemy; for such an enemy is not a moral person, but merely a man; and in such a case the right of war is to kill the vanquished.

But, it will be said, the condemnation of a criminal is a particular act. I admit it: but such condemnation is not a function of the Sovereign; it is a right the Sovereign can confer without being able itself to exert it. All my ideas are consistent, but I cannot expound them all at once.

We may add that frequent punishments are always a sign of weakness or remissness on the part of the government. There is not a single ill-doer who could not be turned to some good. The State has no right to put to death, even for the sake of making an example, any one whom it can leave alive without danger.

The right of pardoning or exempting the guilty from a penalty imposed by the law and pronounced by the judge belongs only to the authority which is superior to both judge and law, i.e. the Sovereign; even its right in this matter is far from clear, and the cases for exercising it are extremely rare. In a well-governed State, there are few punishments, not because there are many pardons, but because criminals are rare; it is when a State is in decay that the multitude of crimes is a guarantee of impunity. Under the Roman Republic, neither the senate nor the consuls ever attempted to pardon; even the people never did so, though it sometimes revoked its own decision. Frequent pardons mean that crime will soon need them no longer, and no one can help seeing whither that leads. But I feel my heart protesting and restraining my pen; let us leave these questions to the just man who has never offended, and would himself stand in no need of pardon.

Chapter VI

Law

By the social compact we have given the body politic existence and life; we have now by legislation to give it movement and will. For the original act by which the body is formed and united still in no respect determines what it ought to do for its preservation.

What is well and in conformity with order is so by the nature of things and independently of human conventions. All justice comes from God, who is its sole source; but if we knew how to receive so high an inspiration, we should need neither government nor laws. Doubtless, there is a universal justice emanating from reason alone; but this justice, to be admitted among us, must be mutual. Humanly speaking, in default of natural sanctions, the laws of justice are ineffective among men: they merely make for the good of the wicked and the undoing of the just, when the just man observes them towards everybody and nobody observes them towards him. Conventions and laws are therefore needed to join rights to duties and refer justice to its object. In the state of nature, where everything is common, I owe nothing to him whom I have promised nothing; I recognize as belonging to others only what is of no use to me. In the state of society all rights are fixed by law, and the case becomes different.

But what, after all, is a law? As long as we remain satisfied with attaching purely metaphysical ideas to the word, we shall go on arguing without arriving at an understanding; and when we have defined a law of nature, we shall be no nearer the definition of a law of the State.

I have already said that there can be no general will directed to a particular object. Such an object must be either within or outside the State. If outside, a will which is alien to it, cannot be, in relation to it, general; if within, it is part of the State, and in that case there arises a relation between whole and part which makes them two separate beings, of which the part is one, and the whole minus the part of the other. But the whole minus a part cannot be the whole; and while this relation persists, there can be no whole, but only two unequal parts; and it follows that the will of one is no longer in any respect general in relation to the other.

But when the whole people decrees for the whole people, it is considering only itself; and if a relation is then formed, it is between two aspects of the entire object, without there being any division of the whole. In that case the matter about which the decree is made is, like the decreeing will, general. This act is what I call a law.

When I say that the object of laws is always general, I mean that law considers subjects *en masse* and actions in the abstract, and never a particular person or action. Thus the law may indeed decree that there shall be privileges, but cannot confer them on anybody by name. It may set up several classes of citizens, and even lay down the qualifications for membership of these classes, but it cannot nominate such and such persons as belonging to them; it may establish a monarchical government and hereditary succession, but it cannot choose a king, or nominate a royal family. In a word, no function which has a particular object belongs to the legislative power.

On this view, we at once see that it can no longer be asked whose business it is to make laws, since they are acts of the general will; nor whether the prince is above the law, since he is a member of the State; nor whether the law can be unjust, since no one is unjust to himself; nor how we can be both free and subject to the laws, since they are but registers of our wills.

We see further that, as the law unites universality of will with universality of object, what a man, whoever he be, commands of his own motion cannot be a law; and even what the Sovereign commands with regard to a particular matter is no nearer being a law, but is a decree, an act, not of sovereignty, but of magistracy.

I therefore give the name "Republic" to every State that is governed by laws, no matter what the form of its administration may be: for only in such a case does the public interest govern, and the *res publica* rank as a *reality*. Every legitimate government is republican;[1] what government is I will explain later on.

Laws are, properly speaking, only the conditions of civil association. The people, being subject to the laws, ought to be their author: the conditions of the society ought to be regulated solely by those who come together to form it. But how are they to regulate them? Is it to be by common agreement, by a sudden inspiration? Has the body politic an organ to declare its will? Who can give it the foresight to formulate and announce its acts in advance? Or how is it to announce them in the hour of need? How can a blind multitude, which often does not know what it wills, because it rarely knows what is good for it, carry out for itself so great and difficult an enterprise as a system of legislation? Of itself the people wills always the good, but of itself it by no means always sees it. The general will is always in the right, but the judgment which guides it is not always enlightened. It must be got to see objects as they are, and sometimes as they ought to appear to it; it must be shown the good road it is in search of, secured from the seductive influences of individual wills, taught to see times and spaces as a series, and made to weigh the attractions of present and sensible advantages against the danger of distant and hidden evils. The individuals see the good they reject; the public wills the good it does not see. All stand equally in need of guidance. The former must be compelled to bring their wills into conformity with their reason; the latter must be taught to know what it wills. If that is done, public enlightenment leads to the union of understanding and will in the social body: the parts are made to work exactly together and the whole is raised to its highest power. This makes a legislator necessary.

---

[1] I understand by this word, not merely an aristocracy or a democracy, but generally any government directed by the general will, which is the law. To be legitimate, the government must be, not one with the Sovereign, but its minister. In such a case even a monarchy is a Republic. This will be made clearer in the following book.

Chapter VII

The Legislator

In order to discover the rules of society best suited to nations, a superior intelligence beholding all the passions of men without experiencing any of them would be needed. This intelligence would have to be wholly unrelated to our nature, while knowing it through and through; its happiness would have to be independent of us, and yet ready to occupy itself with ours; and lastly, it would have, in the march of time, to look forward to a distant glory, and, working in one century, to be able to enjoy in the next.[1] It would take gods to give men laws.

What Caligula argued from the facts, Plato, in the dialogue called the *Politicus,* argued in defining the civil or kingly man, on the basis of right. But if great princes are rare, how much more so are great legislators! The former have only to follow the pattern which the latter have to lay down. The legislator is the engineer who invents the machine, the prince merely the mechanic who sets it up and makes it go. "At the birth of societies," says Montesquieu, "the rulers of Republics establish institutions, and afterwards the institutions mold the rulers." [2]

He who dares to undertake the making of a people's institutions ought to feel himself capable, so to speak, of changing human nature, of transforming each individual, who is by himself a complete and solitary whole, into part of a greater whole from which he in a manner receives his life and being; of altering man's constitution for the purpose of strengthening it; and of substituting a partial and moral existence for the physical and independent existence nature has conferred on us all. He must, in a word, take away from man his own resources and give him instead new ones alien to him, and incapable of being made use of without the help of other men. The more completely these natural resources are annihilated, the greater and the more lasting are those which he acquires, and the more stable and perfect the new institutions; so that if each citizen is nothing and can do nothing without the rest, and the resources acquired by the

---

[1] A people becomes famous only when its legislation begins to decline. We do not know for how many centuries the system of Lycurgus made the Spartans happy before the rest of Greece took any notice of it.

[2] Montesquieu, *The Greatness and Decadence of the Romans,* ch. i.

whole are equal or superior to the aggregate of the resources of all
the individuals, it may be said that legislation is at the highest possible
point of perfection.

The legislator occupies in every respect an extraordinary position
in the State. If he should do so by reason of his genius, he does so no
less by reason of his office, which is neither magistracy, nor Sovereignty. This office, which sets up the Republic, nowhere enters into
its constitution; it is an individual and superior function, which has
nothing in common with human empire; for if he who holds command over men ought not to have command over the laws, he who
has command over the laws ought not any more to have it over men;
or else his laws would be the ministers of his passions and would
often merely serve to perpetuate his injustices: his private aims would
inevitably mar the sanctity of his work.

When Lycurgus gave laws to his country, he began by resigning
the throne. It was the custom of most Greek towns to entrust the
establishment of their laws to foreigners. The Republics of modern
Italy in many cases followed this example; Geneva did the same and
profited by it.[1] Rome, when it was most prosperous, suffered a revival
of all the crimes of tyranny, and was brought to the verge of destruction, because it put the legislative authority and the sovereign power
into the same hands.

Nevertheless, the decemvirs themselves never claimed the right to
pass any law merely on their own authority. "Nothing we propose to
you," they said to the people, "can pass into law without your consent. Romans, be yourselves the authors of the laws which are to
make you happy."

He, therefore, who draws up the laws has, or should have, no right
of legislation, and the people cannot, even if it wishes, deprive itself
of this incommunicable right, because, according to the fundamental
compact, only the general will can bind the individuals, and there can
be no assurance that a particular will is in conformity with the general
will, until it has been put to the free vote of the people. This I have
said already; but it is worth while to repeat it.

Thus in the task of legislation we find together two things which

---

[1] Those who know Calvin only as a theologian much underestimate the
extent of his genius. The codification of our wise edicts, in which he played a
large part, does him no less honor than his *Institute*. Whatever revolution time
may bring in our religion, so long as the spirit of patriotism and liberty still
lives among us, the memory of this great man will be forever blessed.

appear to be incompatible: an enterprise too difficult for human powers, and, for its execution, an authority that is no authority.

There is a further difficulty that deserves attention. Wise men, if they try to speak their language to the common herd instead of its own, cannot possibly make themselves understood. There are a thousand kinds of ideas which it is impossible to translate into popular language. Conceptions that are too general and objects that are too remote are equally out of its range: each individual, having no taste for any other plan of government than that which suits his particular interest, finds it difficult to realize the advantages he might hope to draw from the continual privations good laws impose. For a young people to be able to relish sound principles of political theory and follow the fundamental rules of statecraft, the effect would have to become the cause; the social spirit, which should be created by these institutions, would have to preside over their very foundation; and men would have to be before law what they should become by means of law. The legislator therefore, being unable to appeal to either force or reason, must have recourse to an authority of a different order, capable of constraining without violence and persuading without convincing.

This is what has, in all ages, compelled the fathers of nations to have recourse to divine intervention and credit the gods with their own wisdom, in order that the peoples, submitting to the laws of the State as to those of nature, and recognizing the same power in the formation of the city as in that of man, might obey freely, and bear with docility the yoke of the public happiness.

This sublime reason, far above the range of the common herd, is that whose decisions the legislator puts into the mouth of the immortals, in order to constrain by divine authority those whom human prudence could not move.[1] But it is not anybody who can make the gods speak, or get himself believed when he proclaims himself their interpreter. The great soul of the legislator is the only miracle that can prove his mission. Any man may grave tablets of stone, or buy an oracle, or feign secret intercourse with some divinity, or train a bird

---

[1] "In truth," says Machiavelli, "there has never been, in any country, an extraordinary legislator who has not had recourse to God; for otherwise his laws would not have been accepted: there are, in fact, many useful truths of which a wise man may have knowledge without their having in themselves such clear reasons for their being so as to be able to convince others." (*Discourses on Livy,* Bk. V, ch. xi).

to whisper in his ear, or find other vulgar ways of imposing on the people. He whose knowledge goes no further may perhaps gather round him a band of fools; but he will never found an empire, and his extravagances will quickly perish with him. Idle tricks form a passing tie; only wisdom can make it lasting. The Judaic law, which still subsists, and that of the child of Ishmael, which, for ten centuries has ruled half the world, still proclaim the great men who laid them down; and, while the pride of philosophy or the blind spirit of faction sees in them no more than lucky impostures, the true political theorist admires, in the institutions they set up, the great and powerful genius which presides over things made to endure.

We should not, with Warburton, conclude from this that politics and religion have among us a common object, but that, in the first periods of nations, the one is used as an instrument for the other.

BOOK III

Before speaking of the different forms of government, let us try to fix the exact sense of the word, which has not yet been very clearly explained.

Chapter I

Government in General

I warn the reader that this chapter requires careful reading, and that I am unable to make myself clear to those who refuse to be attentive.

Every free action is produced by the concurrence of two causes; one moral, i.e. the will which determines the act; the other physical, i.e. the power which executes it. When I walk towards an object, it is necessary first that I should will to go there, and, in the second place, that my feet should carry me. If a paralytic wills to run and an active man wills not to, they will both stay where they are. The body politic has the same motive powers; here too force and will are distinguished, will under the name of legislative power and force under that of executive power. Without their concurrence, nothing is, or should be, done.

We have seen that the legislative power belongs to the people, and can belong to it alone. It may, on the other hand, readily be seen, from the principles laid down above, that the executive power cannot belong to the generality as legislature or Sovereign, because it consists wholly of particular acts which fall outside the competency of the law, and consequently of the Sovereign, whose acts must always be laws.

The public force therefore needs an agent of its own to bind it together and set it to work under the direction of the general will, to serve as a means of communication between the State and the Sovereign, and to do for the collective person more or less what the union of soul and body does for man. Here we have what is, in the State, the basis of government, often wrongly confused with the Sovereign, whose minister it is.

What then is government? An intermediate body set up between the subjects and the Sovereign, to secure their mutual correspondence, charged with the execution of the laws and the maintenance of liberty, both civil and political.

The members of this body are called magistrates or *kings,* that is to say *governors,* and the whole body bears the name *prince.*[1] Thus those who hold that the act by which a people puts itself under a prince is not a contract, are certainly right. It is simply and solely a commission, an employment, in which the rulers, mere officials of the Sovereign, exercise in their own name the power of which it makes them depositaries. This power it can limit, modify, or recover at pleasure; for the alienation of such a right is incompatible with the nature of the social body, and contrary to the end of association.

I call then *government,* or supreme administration, the legitimate exercise of the executive power, and prince or magistrate the man or the body entrusted with that administration.

In government reside the intermediate forces whose relations make up that of the whole to the whole, or of the Sovereign to the State. This last relation may be represented as that between the extreme terms of a continuous proportion, which has government as its mean proportional. The government gets from the Sovereign the orders it gives the people, and, for the State to be properly balanced, there must, when everything is reckoned in, be equality between the product or power of the government taken in itself, and the product or power of the citizens, who are on the one hand sovereign and on the other subject.

Furthermore, none of these three terms can be altered without the equality being instantly destroyed. If the Sovereign desires to govern,

---

[1] Thus at Venice the College, even in the absence of the Doge, is called "Most Serene Prince."

or the magistrate to give laws, or if the subjects refuse to obey, dis-order takes the place of regularity, force and will no longer act together, and the State is dissolved and falls into despotism or anarchy. Lastly, as there is also only one mean proportional between each relation, there is also only one good government possible for a State. But, as countless events may change the relations of a people, not only may different governments be good for different peoples, but also for the same people at different times.

In attempting to give some idea of the various relations that may hold between these two extreme terms, I shall take as an example the number of a people, which is the most easily expressible.

Suppose the State is composed of ten thousand citizens. The Sov-ereign can only be considered collectively and as a body; but each member, as being a subject, is regarded as an individual: thus the Sovereign is to the subject as ten thousand to one, i.e. each member of the State has as his share only a ten-thousandth part of the sover-eign authority, although he is wholly under its control. If the people numbers a hundred thousand, the condition of the subject undergoes no change, and each equally is under the whole authority of the laws, while his vote, being reduced to one hundred thousandth part, has ten times less influence in drawing them up. The subject therefore remaining always a unit, the relation between him and the Sovereign increases with the number of the citizens. From this it follows that, the larger the State, the less the liberty.

When I say the relation increases, I mean that it grows more un-equal. Thus the greater it is in the geometrical sense, the less relation there is in the ordinary sense of the word. In the former sense, the relation, considered according to quantity, is expressed by the quo-tient; in the latter, considered according to identity, it is reckoned by similarity.

Now, the less relation the particular wills have to the general will, that is, morals and manners to laws, the more should the repressive force be increased. The government, then, to be good, should be pro-portionately stronger as the people is more numerous.

On the other hand, as the growth of the State gives the depositaries of the public authority more temptations and chances of abusing their power, the greater the force with which the government ought to be endowed for keeping the people in hand, the greater too should be the force at the disposal of the Sovereign for keeping the government in hand. I am speaking, not of absolute force, but of the relative force of the different parts of the State.

It follows from this double relation that the continuous proportion between the Sovereign, the prince, and the people, is by no means an arbitrary idea, but a necessary consequence of the nature of the body politic. It follows further that, one of the extreme terms, viz., the people, as subject, being fixed and represented by unity, whenever the duplicate ratio increases or diminishes, the simple ratio does the same, and is changed accordingly. From this we see that there is not a single unique and absolute form of government, but as many governments differing in nature as there are States differing in size.

If, ridiculing this system, any one were to say that, in order to find the mean proportional and give form to the body of the government, it is only necessary, according to me, to find the square root of the number of the people, I should answer that I am here taking this number only as an instance; that the relations of which I am speaking are not measured by the number of men alone, but generally by the amount of action, which is a combination of a multitude of causes; and that, further, if, to save words, I borrow for a moment the terms of geometry, I am none the less well aware that moral quantities do not allow of geometrical accuracy.

The government is on a small scale what the body politic which includes it is on a great one. It is a moral person endowed with certain faculties, active like the Sovereign and passive like the State, and capable of being resolved into other similar relations. This accordingly gives rise to a new proportion, within which there is yet another, according to the arrangement of the magistracies, till an indivisible middle term is reached, i.e. a single ruler or supreme magistrate, who may be represented, in the midst of this progression, as the unity between the fractional and the ordinal series.

Without encumbering ourselves with this multiplication of terms, let us rest content with regarding government as a new body within the State, distinct from the people and the Sovereign, and intermediate between them.

There is between these two bodies this essential difference, that the State exists by itself, and the government only through the Sovereign. Thus the dominant will of the prince is, or should be, nothing but the general will or the law; his force is only the public force concentrated in his hands, and, as soon as he tries to base any absolute and independent act on his own authority, the tie that binds the whole together begins to be loosened. If finally the prince should come to have a particular will more active than the will of the Sovereign, and should employ the public force in his hands in obedience to this particular will, there would be, so to speak, two Sovereigns, one rightful and the other actual, the social union would evaporate instantly, and the body politic would be dissolved.

However, in order that the government may have a true existence and a real life distinguishing it from the body of the State, and in order that all its members may be able to act in concert and fulfil the end for which it was set up, it must have a particular personality, a sensibility common to its members, and a force and will of its own making for its preservation. This particular existence implies assemblies, councils, power of deliberation and decision, rights, titles, and privileges belonging exclusively to the prince and making the office of magistrate more honorable in proportion as it is more troublesome. The difficulties lie in the manner of so ordering this subordinate whole within the whole, that it in no way alters the general constitution by affirmation of its own, and always distinguishes the particular force it possesses, which is destined to aid in its preservation, from the public force, which is destined to the preservation of the State; and, in a word, is always ready to sacrifice the government to the people, and never to sacrifice the people to the government.

Furthermore, although the artificial body of the government is the work of another artificial body, and has, we may say, only a borrowed and subordinate life, this does not prevent it from being able to act with more or less vigor or promptitude, or from being, so to speak, in more or less robust health. Finally, without departing directly from the end for which it was instituted, it may deviate more or less from it, according to the manner of its constitution.

From all these differences arise the various relations which the government ought to bear to the body of the State, according to the accidental and particular relations by which the State itself is modified, for often the government that is best in itself will become the most pernicious, if the relations in which it stands have altered according to the defects of the body politic to which it belongs.

Chapter II

The Constituent Principle in the Various Forms of Government

To set forth the general cause of the above differences, we must here distinguish between government and its principle, as we did before between the State and the Sovereign.

The body of the magistrates may be composed of a greater or a less number of members. We said that the relation of the Sovereign to the subjects was greater in proportion as the people was more numerous, and, by a clear analogy, we may say the same of the relation of the government to the magistrates.

But the total force of the government, being always that of the State, is invariable; so that, the more of this force it expends on its own members, the less it has left to employ on the whole people.

The more numerous the magistrates, therefore, the weaker the government. This principle being fundamental, we must do our best to make it clear.

In the person of the magistrate we can distinguish three essentially different wills: first, the private will of the individual, tending only to his personal advantage; secondly, the common will of the magistrates, which is relative solely to the advantage of the prince, and may be called corporate will, being general in relation to the government, and particular in relation to the State, of which the government forms part; and, in the third place, the will of the people or the sovereign will, which is general both in relation to the State regarded as the whole, and to the government regarded as a part of the whole.

In a perfect act of legislation, the individual or particular will should be at zero; the corporate will belonging to the government should occupy a very subordinate position; and, consequently, the general or sovereign will should always predominate and should be the sole guide of all the rest.

According to the natural order, on the other hand, these different wills become more active in proportion as they are concentrated. Thus, the general will is always the weakest, the corporate will second, and the individual will strongest of all: so that, in the government, each member is first of all himself, then a magistrate, and then a citizen—in an order exactly the reverse of what the social system requires.

This granted, if the whole government is in the hands of one man, the particular and the corporate will are wholly united, and consequently the latter is at its highest possible degree of intensity. But, as the use to which the force is put depends on the degree reached by the will, and as the absolute force of the government is invariable, it follows that the most active government is that of one man.

Suppose, on the other hand, we unite the government with the legislative authority, and make the Sovereign prince also, and all the citizens so many magistrates: then the corporate will, being confounded with the general will, can possess no greater activity than that will, and must leave the particular will as strong as it can possibly be. Thus, the government, having always the same absolute force, will be at the lowest point of its relative force or activity.

These relations are incontestable, and there are other considerations which still further confirm them. We can see, for instance, that each magistrate is more active in the body to which he belongs than each citizen in that to which he belongs, and that consequently the particular will has much more influence on the acts of the government than on those of the Sovereign; for each magistrate is almost always charged with some governmental function, while each citizen, taken singly, exercises no function of Sovereignty. Furthermore, the bigger the State grows, the more its real force increases, though not in direct proportion to its growth; but, the State remaining the same, the number of magistrates may increase to any extent, without the government gaining any greater real force; for its force is that of the State, the dimension of which remains equal. Thus the relative force or activity of the government decreases, while its absolute or real force cannot increase.

Moreover, it is a certainty that promptitude in execution diminishes as more people are put in charge of it: where prudence is made too much of, not enough is made of fortune; opportunity is let slip, and deliberation results in the loss of its object.

I have just proved that the government grows remiss in proportion as the number of the magistrates increases; and I previously proved that, the more numerous the people, the greater should be the repressive force. From this it follows that the relation of the magistrates to the government should vary inversely to the relation of the subjects to the Sovereign; that is to say, the larger the State, the more should the government be tightened, so that the number of the rulers diminish in proportion to the increase of that of the people.

It should be added that I am here speaking of the relative strength of the government, and not of its rectitude: for, on the other hand, the more numerous the magistracy, the nearer the corporate will comes to the general will; while under a single magistrate, the corporate will is, as I said, merely a particular will. Thus, what may be gained on one side is lost on the other, and the art of the legislator is to know how to fix the point at which the force and the will of the government, which are always in inverse proportion, meet in the relation that is most to the advantage of the State.

Chapter IX

The Marks of a Good Government

The question "What absolutely is the best government?" is un-answerable as well as indeterminate; or rather, there are as many good answers as there are possible combinations in the absolute and relative situations of all nations.

But if it is asked by what sign we may know that a given people is well or ill governed, that is another matter, and the question, being one of fact, admits of an answer.

It is not, however, answered, because every one wants to answer it in his own way. Subjects extol public tranquillity, citizens individual liberty; the one class prefers security of possessions, the other that of person; the one regards as the best government that which is most severe, the other maintains that the mildest is the best; the one wants crimes punished, the other wants them prevented; the one wants the State to be feared by its neighbors, the other prefers that it should be ignored; the one is content if money circulates, the other demands that the people shall have bread. Even if an agreement were come to on these and similar points, should we have got any further? As moral qualities do not admit of exact measurement, agreement about the mark does not mean agreement about the valuation.

For my part, I am continually astonished that a mark so simple is not recognized, or that men are of so bad faith as not to admit it. What is the end of political association? The preservation and prosperity of its members. And what is the surest mark of their preservation and prosperity? Their numbers and population. Seek then nowhere else this mark that is in dispute. The rest being equal, the government under which, without external aids, without naturalization or colonies, the citizens increase and multiply most is beyond question the best. The government under which a people wanes and diminishes is the worst. Calculators, it is left for you to count, to measure, to compare.[1]

---

[1] On the same principle it should be judged what centuries deserve the preference for human prosperity. Those in which letters and arts have flourished have been too much admired, because the hidden object of their culture has not been fathomed, and their fatal effects not taken into account. "Idque apud imperitos humanitas vocabatur, cum pars servitutis esset." ["Fools called 'humanity' what was a part of slavery." Tacitus, *Agricola,* 31.] Shall we never see the maxims books lay down the vulgar interest that makes their writers speak? No, whatever they may say, when, despite its renown, a country is de-

Chapter XV
Deputies or Representatives

As soon as public service ceases to be the chief business of the citizens and they would rather serve with their money than with their persons, the State is not far from its fall. When it is necessary to march out to war, they pay troops and stay at home: when it is necessary to meet in council, they name deputies and stay at home. By reason of idleness and money, they end by having soldiers to enslave their country and representatives to sell it.

It is through the hustle of commerce and the arts, through the greedy self-interest of profit, and through softness and love of amenities that personal services are replaced by money payments. Men surrender a part of their profits in order to have time to increase them at leisure. Make gifts of money, and you will not be long without chains. The word "finance" is a slavish word, unknown in the city-state. In a country that is truly free, the citizens do everything with their own arms and nothing by means of money; so far from paying to be exempted from their duties, they would even pay for the privilege of fulfilling them themselves. I am far from taking the common

---

populated, it is not true that all is well, and it is not enough that a poet should have an income of 100,000 francs to make his age the best of all. Less attention should be paid to the apparent repose and tranquillity of the rulers than to the well-being of their nations as wholes, and above all of the most numerous States. A hail-storm lays several cantons waste, but it rarely makes a famine. Outbreaks and civil wars give rulers rude shocks, but they are not the real ills of peoples, who may even get a respite, while there is a dispute as to who shall tyrannize over them. Their true prosperity and calamities come from their permanent condition: it is when the whole remains crushed beneath the yoke, that decay sets in, and that the rulers destroy them at will, and "ubi solitudinem faciunt, pacem appellant." ["Where they create solitude, they call it peace." Tacitus, *Agricola,* 31.] When the bickerings of the great disturbed the kingdom of France, and the Coadjutor of Paris took a dagger in his pocket to the Parliament, these things did not prevent the people of France from prospering and multiplying in dignity, ease, and freedom. Long ago Greece flourished in the midst of the most savage wars; blood ran in torrents, and yet the whole country was covered with inhabitants. It appeared, says Machiavelli, that in the midst of murder, proscription, and civil war, our republic only throve: the virtue, morality, and independence of the citizens did more to strengthen it than all their dissensions had done to enfeeble it. A little disturbance gives the soul elasticity; what makes the race truly prosperous is not so much peace as liberty.

view: I hold enforced labor to be less opposed to liberty than taxes.

The better the constitution of a State is, the more do public affairs encroach on private in the minds of the citizens. Private affairs are even of much less importance, because the aggregate of the common happiness furnishes a greater proportion of that of each individual, so that there is less for him to seek in particular cares. In a well-ordered city every man flies to the assemblies: under a bad government no one cares to stir a step to get to them, because no one is interested in what happens there, because it is foreseen that the general will will not prevail, and lastly because domestic cares are all-absorbing. Good laws lead to the making of better ones; bad ones bring about worse. As soon as any man says of the affairs of the State *What does it matter to me?* the State may be given up for lost.

The lukewarmness of patriotism, the activity of private interests, the vastness of States, conquest, and the abuse of government suggested the method of having deputies or representatives of the people in the national assemblies. These are what, in some countries, men have presumed to call the Third Estate. Thus the individual interest of two orders is put first and second; the public interest occupies only the third place.

Sovereignty, for the same reason as makes it inalienable, cannot be represented; it lies essentially in the general will, and will does not admit of representation: it is either the same, or other; there is no intermediate possibility. The deputies of the people, therefore, are not and cannot be its representatives: they are merely its stewards, and can carry through no definitive acts. Every law the people has not ratified in person is null and void—is, in fact, not a law. The people of England regards itself as free: but it is grossly mistaken: it is free only during the election of members of parliament. As soon as they are elected, slavery overtakes it, and it is nothing. The use it makes of the short moments of liberty it enjoys shows indeed that it deserves to lose them.

The idea of representation is modern; it comes to us from feudal government, from that iniquitous and absurd system which degrades humanity and dishonors the name of man. In ancient republics and even in monarchies, the people never had representatives; the word itself was unknown. It is very singular that in Rome, where the tribunes were so sacrosanct, it was never even imagined that they could usurp the functions of the people, and that in the midst of so great a multitude they never attempted to pass on their own authority a single *plebiscitum.* We can, however, form an idea of the difficulties caused sometimes by the people being so numerous, from what happened in the time of the Gracchi, when some of the citizens had to cast their votes from the roofs of buildings.

Where right and liberty are everything, disadvantages count for nothing. Among this wise people everything was given its just value, its lictors were allowed to do what its tribunes would never have dared to attempt; for it had no fear that its lictors would try to represent it.

To explain, however, in what way the tribunes did sometimes represent it, it is enough to conceive how the government represents the Sovereign. Law being purely the declaration of the general will, it is clear that, in the exercise of the legislative power, the people cannot be represented; but in that of the executive power, which is only the force that is applied to give the law effect, it both can and should be represented. We thus see that if we looked closely into the matter we should find that very few nations have any Laws. However that may be, it is certain that the tribunes, possessing no executive power, could never represent the Roman people by right of the powers entrusted to them, but only by usurping those of the senate.

In Greece, all that the people had to do, it did for itself; it was constantly assembled in the public square. The Greeks lived in a mild climate; they had no natural greed; slaves did their work for them; their great concern was with liberty. Lacking the same advantages, how can you preserve the same rights? Your severer climates add to your needs; for half the year your public squares are uninhabitable; the flatness of your languages unfits them for being heard in the open air; you sacrifice more for profit than for liberty, and fear slavery less than poverty.

What then? Is liberty maintained only by the help of slavery? It may be so. Extremes meet. Everything that is not in the course of nature has its disadvantages, civil society most of all. There are some unhappy circumstances in which we can only keep our liberty at others' expense, and where the citizen can be perfectly free only when the slave is most a slave. Such was the case with Sparta. As for you, modern peoples, you have no slaves, but you are slaves yourselves; you pay for their liberty with your own. It is in vain that you boast of this preference; I find in it more cowardice than humanity.

I do not mean by all this that it is necessary to have slaves, or that the right of slavery is legitimate: I am merely giving the reasons why modern peoples, believing themselves to be free, have representatives, while ancient peoples had none. In any case, the moment a people allows itself to be represented, it is no longer free: it no longer exists.

All things considered, I do not see that it is possible henceforth for the Sovereign to preserve among us the exercise of its rights, unless the city is very small. But if it is very small, it will be conquered? No. I will show later on how the external strength of a great people[1] may be combined with the convenient polity and good order of a small State.

Chapter XVI

That the Institution of Government Is Not a Contract

The legislative power once well established, the next thing is to establish similarly the executive power; for this latter, which operates only by particular acts, not being of the essence of the former, is naturally separate from it. Were it possible for the Sovereign, as such, to possess the executive power, right and fact would be so confounded that no one could tell what was law and what was not; and the body politic, thus disfigured, would soon fall a prey to the violence it was instituted to prevent.

As the citizens, by the social contract, are all equal, all can prescribe what all should do, but no one has a right to demand that another shall do what he does not do himself. It is strictly this right, which is indispensable for giving the body politic life and movement, that the Sovereign, in instituting the government, confers upon the prince.

It has been held that this act of establishment was a contract between the people and the rulers it sets over itself—a contract in which conditions were laid down between the two parties binding the one to command and the other to obey. It will be admitted, I am sure, that this is an odd kind of contract to enter into. But let us see if this view can be upheld.

First, the supreme authority can no more be modified than it can be alienated; to limit it is to destroy it. It is absurd and contradictory for the Sovereign to set a superior over itself; to bind itself to obey a master would be to return to absolute liberty.

Moreover, it is clear that this contract between the people and such

---

[1] I had intended to do this in the sequel to this work, when in dealing with external relations I came to the subject of confederations. The subject is quite new, and its principles have still to be laid down.

and such persons would be a particular act; and from this it follows that it can be neither a law nor an act of Sovereignty, and that consequently it would be illegitimate.

It is plain too that the contracting parties in relation to each other would be under the law of nature alone and wholly without guarantees of their mutual undertakings, a position wholly at variance with the civil state. He who has force at his command being always in a position to control execution, it would come to the same thing if the name "contract" were given to the act of one man who said to another: "I give you all my goods, on condition that you give me back as much of them as you please."

There is only one contract in the State, and that is the act of association, which in itself excludes the existence of a second. It is impossible to conceive of any public contract that would not be a violation of the first.

BOOK IV

Chapter I
That the General Will Is Indestructible

As long as several men in assembly regard themselves as a single body, they have only a single will which is concerned with their common preservation and general well-being. In this case, all the springs of the State are vigorous and simple and its rules clear and luminous; there are no embroilments or conflicts of interests; the common good is everywhere clearly apparent, and only good sense is needed to perceive it. Peace, unity, and equality are the enemies of political subtleties. Men who are upright and simple are difficult to deceive because of their simplicity; lures and ingenious pretexts fail to impose upon them, and they are not even subtle enough to be dupes. When, among the happiest people in the world, bands of peasants are seen regulating affairs of State under an oak, and always acting wisely, can we help scorning the ingenious methods of other nations, which make themselves illustrious and wretched with so much art and mystery?

A State so governed needs very few laws; and, as it becomes necessary to issue new ones, the necessity is universally seen. The first man to propose them merely says what all have already felt, and there is no question of factions or intrigues or eloquence in order to secure the passage into law of what every one has already decided to do, as soon as he is sure that the rest will act with him.

Theorists are led into error because, seeing only States that have been from the beginning wrongly constituted, they are struck by the impossibility of applying such a policy to them. They make great game of all the absurdities a clever rascal or an insinuating speaker might get the people of Paris or London to believe. They do not know that Cromwell would have been put to "the bells" by the people of Berne, and the Duc de Beaufort on the treadmill by the Genevese.

But when the social bond begins to be relaxed and the State to grow weak, when particular interests begin to make themselves felt and the smaller societies to exercise an influence over the larger, the common interest changes and finds opponents: opinion is no longer unanimous; the general will ceases to be the will of all; contradictory views and debates arise; and the best advice is not taken without question.

Finally, when the State, on the eve of ruin, maintains only a vain, illusory, and formal existence, when in every heart the social bond is broken, and the meanest interest brazenly lays hold of the sacred name of "public good," the general will becomes mute: all men, guided by secret motives, no more give their views as citizens than if the State had never been; and iniquitous decrees directed solely to private interest get passed under the name of laws.

Does it follow from this that the general will is exterminated or corrupted? Not at all: it is always constant, unalterable, and pure; but it is subordinated to other wills which encroach upon its sphere. Each man, in detaching his interest from the common interest, sees clearly that he cannot entirely separate them; but his share in the public mishaps seems to him negligible beside the exclusive good he aims at making his own. Apart from this particular good, he wills the general good in his own interest, as strongly as any one else. Even in selling his vote for money, he does not extinguish in himself the general will, but only eludes it. The fault he commits is that of changing the state of the question, and answering something different from what he is asked. Instead of saying, by his vote, "It is to the advantage of the State," he says, "It is of advantage to this or that man or party that this or that view should prevail." Thus the law of public order in assemblies is not so much to maintain in them the general will as to secure that the question be always put to it, and the answer always given by it.

I could here set down many reflections on the simple right of voting

in every act of Sovereignty—a right which no one can take from the
citizens—and also on the right of stating views, making proposals,
dividing and discussing, which the government is always most careful
to leave solely to its members; but this important subject would need
a treatise to itself, and it is impossible to say everything in a single
work.

IMMANUEL KANT

Critique of Pure Reason (*abridged*)

SUPPLEMENTARY PASSAGES

The Good Will and the Categorical Imperative
The Postulates of Practical Reason
Taste and the Aesthetic Judgment

IMMANUEL KANT

IMMANUEL KANT (1724–1804), the son of a saddle-maker, was born and died in Königsberg in East Prussia. During his entire life he was never away from that city except between 1746 when he left the University of Königsberg and 1755 when he returned there to teach. During those years he supported himself as a private tutor in nearby parts of East Prussia. But though Kant did not travel, and though he spent the remaining years of his life as a university teacher (he became Professor of Logic and Metaphysics in 1770), his town was a crossroads of trade, visited by many travellers with whom he was very sociable, and his constant curiosity about developments in science, politics, and numerous other subjects was well supplied by frequent conversations and enormous reading. Kant was one of the great teachers, admired and recalled with affection by university students as well as by those who attended his clear, stimulating, and witty public lectures. His productivity was remarkable, especially during the period after 1770, when his new Critical Philosophy began to take shape and occupy his mind.

Kant's major work (if one may call it one work rather than three) is the set of *Critiques* for which he is most famous. The *Critique of Pure Reason* (trans. Max Müller, London: Macmillan, 1881; trans. Norman Kemp-Smith, London: Macmillan, 1929; reprinted, New York: St. Martin's Press, 1966), is the first, greatest, and most fundamental; it presents his epistemology and his new conception of metaphysics. Its argument, in a less exact form, is also in his *Prolegomena to Any Future Metaphysics* (1783; trans. by P. G. Lucas, Manchester: University of Manchester, 1953). The *Critique of Practical Reason and Other Writings in Moral Philosophy* (1788; trans. and ed. Lewis White Beck, Chicago: University of Chicago Press, 1949; reprinted, New York: Liberal Arts Press, 1956) presents his ethical theory; its argument in a different order, is also in his *Foundations of the Metaphysic of Morals* (1785; trans. Beck, Indianapolis: Bobbs-Merrill, 1959; trans. H. J. Paton, New York: Harper & Row, 1964). The *Critique of Judgement*

(1790; trans. by J. H. Bernard, London: Macmillan, 2d ed., 1914; and by J. C. Meredith in two volumes, *Kant's Critique of Aesthetic Judgement,* Oxford: Clarendon Press, 1911, and *Kant's Critique of Teleological Judgement,* Oxford: Clarendon Press, 1928) deals with judgments involving the idea of purposiveness, or appropriateness to ends, both aesthetic judgments and teleological propositions in natural science. Among Kant's many other works, including scientific essays and essays on history and culture, two should be noted here: *Religion Within the Limits of Reason Alone* (1793; translated by T. M. Greene and H. H. Hudson, Chicago: Open Court, 1954) and *Eternal* [or *Perpetual*] *Peace* (1795; trans. Beck, *op. cit.*). The former contains Kant's mature philosophy of religion; the latter is a remarkable plan for European unity (both are translated by Carl Friedrich in *The Philosophy of Kant,* New York: Modern Library, 1949). For other translations of Kant's works see W. Hastie, *Kant's Principles of Politics,* Edinburg: T. and T. Clark, 1891; T. K. Abbott, *Kant's Critique of Practical Reason and Other Works on the Theory of Ethics,* London: Longmans, Green, 1909.

It was almost universally agreed that Kant's philosophical achievement was very great, though of course it will depend on one's own point of view which of his ideas one singles out as most significant. There is such a wealth of original thoughts, in such a wide range of philosophical fields, that a brief summary cannot come close to doing justice to Kant; but certain of his ideas must be acknowledged by any philosopher as important contributions. He did more than anyone else to construct the distinction between analytic and synthetic propositions, which has proved so fruitful in twentieth-century philosophy. With the help of this distinction he invented a wholly new sort of philosophical question—How is it possible for us to know synthetic *a priori* propositions? And he invented a new sort of philosophical argument—the transcendental argument, which aims to prove the truth of one proposition as a necessary presupposition of another. Even if, as present-day empiricists hold, the basic enterprise was mistaken, there is no question that it was well worth trying, and in following it out with all his supreme care, imagination, and systematic order, Kant gave a new direction and a new stimulus to the thinking of philosophers ever since. Indeed, we owe to him, in large part, our present-day conception of philosophy as clearly distinct from empirical science.

Kant called attention to the importance of examining the categories of thinking in every field by showing how these basic concepts play a fundamental role in experience and knowledge. He carried certain traditional problems—about substance, causality, space and time—to deeper levels and forced a reexamination of assumptions long held on inadequate grounds. He made profound criticisms of certain traditional metaphysical arguments, such as those concerning God and the world. He concluded that questions reaching beyond the bounds of possible experience are not only unanswerable, but unaskable, and thereby launched a radically empirical movement that has gathered strength to our own time. In the field of ethics, or moral philosophy, he introduced the sharpest cleavage ever made between ethics and all factual knowledge; and he brilliantly explored the possibility of basic ethical principles that would—like the maxim of universalizability—owe nothing to empirical knowledge or feeling or intuition. At the same time it was Kant who created the whole subject of aesthetics and established it as a distinct field. He formulated the essential problems about the logical justifiability of aesthetic judgments and he was the first clearly to distinguish aesthetic experience from other forms of experience. Moreover, he did so in terms of concepts ("satisfaction without interest" and "purposiveness without purpose") that are still recognized to be an important part of the truth.

Critique of Pure Reason* (*abridged*)

[The structure of this work is very complex, and the selections below constitute less than one-seventh of it. Missing parts of the argument are summarized, but to keep in mind the relations among the selections and their place in the whole argument it is helpful to refer to a complete Table of Contents, which is therefore given here. Those sections which are represented as a whole or in part below are named in italics.]

TABLE OF CONTENTS

---

* Translated by Norman Kemp Smith, London: Macmillan, 1929 (abridged edition, N. Y.: Modern Library, 1958). Reprinted by permission of Macmillan & Company, Ltd., St. Martin's Press, and the representatives of Professor Kemp Smith. *Kritik der reinen Vernunft* was first published in 1781; the second edition, with important changes, was published in 1787.

II. TRANSCENDENTAL DOCTRINE OF METHOD

Preface to Second Edition

. . . Hitherto it has been assumed that all our knowledge must conform to objects. But all attempts to extend our knowledge of objects by establishing something in regard to them *a priori,* by means of concepts, have, on this assumption, ended in failure. We must therefore make trial whether we may not have more success in the tasks of metaphysics, if we suppose that objects must conform to our knowledge. This would agree better with what is desired, namely, that it should be possible to have knowledge of objects *a priori,* determining something in regard to them prior to their being given. We should then be proceeding precisely on the lines of Copernicus' primary hypothesis. Failing of satisfactory progress in explaining the movements of the heavenly bodies on the supposition that they all revolved round the spectator, he tried whether he might not have better success if he made the spectator to revolve and the stars to remain at rest. . . .

Introduction

I. The Distinction between Pure and Empirical Knowledge

There can be no doubt that all our knowledge begins with experience. For how should our faculty of knowledge be awakened into action did not objects affecting our senses partly of themselves produce representations, partly arouse the activity of our understanding to compare these representations, and, by combining or separating them, work up the raw material of the sensible impressions into that knowledge of objects which is entitled experience? In the order of time, therefore, we have no knowledge antecedent to experience, and with experience all our knowledge begins.

But though all our knowledge begins with experience, it does not follow that it all arises out of experience. For it may well be that even our empirical knowledge is made up of what we receive through impressions and of what our own faculty of knowledge (sensible impressions serving merely as the occasion) supplies from itself. If our faculty of knowledge makes any such addition, it may be that we are not in a position to distinguish it from the raw material, until with long practice of attention we have become skilled in separating it.

This, then, is a question which at least calls for closer examination, and does not allow of any off-hand answer:—whether there is any knowledge that is thus independent of experience and even of all impressions of the senses. Such knowledge is entitled *a priori*, and distinguished from the *empirical*, which has its sources *a posteriori*, that is, in experience.

The expression *"a priori"* does not, however, indicate with sufficient precision the full meaning of our question. For it has been customary to say, even of much knowledge that is derived from empirical sources, that we have it or are capable of having it *a priori*, meaning thereby that we do not derive it immediately from experience, but from a universal rule—a rule which is itself, however, borrowed by us from experience. Thus we would say of a man who undermined the foundations of his house, that he might have known *a priori* that it would fall, that is, that he need not have waited for the experience of its actual falling. But still he could not know this completely *a priori*. For he had first to learn through experience that bodies are heavy, and therefore fall when their supports are withdrawn.

In what follows, therefore, we shall understand by *a priori* knowledge, not knowledge independent of this or that experience, but knowledge absolutely independent of all experience. Opposed to it is empirical knowledge, which is knowledge possible only *a posteriori*, that is, through experience. *A priori* modes of knowledge are entitled pure when there is no admixture of anything empirical. Thus, for instance, the proposition, "every alteration has its cause," while an *a priori* proposition, is not a pure proposition, because alteration is a concept which can be derived only from experience.

II. *We are in Possession of certain Modes of* a priori *Knowledge, and even the Common Understanding is never without them*

What we here require is a criterion by which to distinguish with certainty between pure and empirical knowledge. Experience teaches us that a thing is so and so, but not that it cannot be otherwise. First, then, if we have a proposition which in being thought is thought as *necessary*, it is an *a priori* judgment; and if, besides, it is not derived from any proposition except one which also has the validity of a necessary judgment, it is an absolutely *a priori* judgment. Secondly, experience never confers on its judgments true or strict, but only assumed and comparative *universality*, through induction. We can properly only say, therefore, that, so far as we have hitherto observed, there is no exception to this or that rule. When, on the other hand, strict universality is essential to a judgment, this indicates a special source of knowledge, namely, a faculty of *a priori* knowledge. Necessity and strict universality are thus sure criteria of *a priori* knowledge, and are inseparable from one another.

Now it is easy to show that there actually are in human knowledge judgments which are necessary and in the strictest sense universal, and which are therefore pure *a priori* judgments. If an example from the sciences be desired, we have only to look to any of the propositions of mathematics; if we seek an example from the understanding in its quite ordinary employment, the proposition, "every alteration must have a cause," will serve our purpose. In the latter case, indeed, the very concept of a cause so manifestly contains the concept of a necessity of connection with an effect and of the strict universality of the rule, that the concept would be altogether lost if we attempted to derive it, as Hume has done, from a repeated association of that which happens with that which precedes, and from a custom of connecting representations, a custom originating in this repeated association, and constituting therefore a merely subjective necessity.

Such *a priori* origin is manifest in certain concepts, no less than in judgments. If we remove from our empirical concept of a body, one by one, every feature in it which is [merely] empirical, the color, the hardness or softness, the weight, even the impenetrability, there still remains the space which the body (now entirely vanished) occupied, and this cannot be removed. Again, if we remove from our empirical concept of any object, corporeal or incorporeal, all properties which experience has taught us, we yet cannot take away that property through which the object is thought as substance or as inhering in a substance (although this concept of substance is more determinate than that of an object in general). Owing, therefore, to the necessity with which this concept of substance forces itself upon us, we have no option save to admit that it has its seat in our faculty of *a priori* knowledge.

III. *Philosophy stands in Need of a Science which shall determine the Possibility, the Principles, and the Extent of all* a priori *Knowledge*

But what is still more extraordinary than all the preceding is this, that certain modes of knowledge leave the field of all possible experi-

ences and have the appearance of extending the scope of our judgments beyond all limits of experience, and this by means of concepts
to which no corresponding object can ever be given in experience.

It is precisely by means of the latter modes of knowledge, in a
realm beyond the world of the senses, where experience can yield
neither guidance nor correction, that our reason carries on those
enquiries which owing to their importance we consider to be far more
excellent, and in their purpose far more lofty, than all that the understanding can learn in the field of appearances. Indeed we prefer to run
every risk of error rather than desist from such urgent enquiries, on
the ground of their dubious character, or from disdain and indifference. These unavoidable problems set by pure reason itself are *God,
freedom,* and *immortality.* The science which, with all its preparations,
is in its final intention directed solely to their solution is metaphysics;
and its procedure is at first dogmatic, that is, it confidently sets itself
to this task without any previous examination of the capacity or
incapacity of reason for so great an undertaking.

Now it does indeed seem natural that, as soon as we have left the
ground of experience, we should, through careful enquiries, assure
ourselves as to the foundations of any building that we propose to
erect, not making use of any knowledge that we possess without first
determining whence it has come, and not trusting to principles without
knowing their origin. It is natural, that is to say, that the question
should first be considered, how the understanding can arrive at all
this knowledge *a priori,* and what extent, validity, and worth it may
have. Nothing, indeed, could be more natural, if by the term "natural"
we signify what fittingly and reasonably ought to happen. But if we
mean by "natural" what ordinarily happens, then on the contrary nothing is more natural and more intelligible than the fact that this enquiry
has been so long neglected. For one part of this knowledge, the
mathematical, has long been of established reliability, and so gives
rise to a favorable presumption as regards the other part, which may
yet be of quite different nature. Besides, once we are outside the
circle of experience, we can be sure of not being *contradicted* by
experience. The charm of extending our knowledge is so great that
nothing short of encountering a direct contradiction can suffice to
arrest us in our course; and this can be avoided, if we are careful in
our fabrications—which none the less will still remain fabrications.
Mathematics gives us a shining example of how far, independently of
experience, we can progress in *a priori* knowledge. It does, indeed,
occupy itself with objects and with knowledge solely in so far as they

allow of being exhibited in intuition. But this circumstance is easily overlooked, since this intuition can itself be given *a priori,* and is therefore hardly to be distinguished from a bare and pure concept. Misled by such a proof of the power of reason, the demand for the extension of knowledge recognizes no limits. The light dove, cleaving the air in her free flight, and feeling its resistance, might imagine that its flight would be still easier in empty space. It was thus that Plato left the world of the senses, as setting too narrow limits to the understanding, and ventured out beyond it on the wings of the ideas, in the empty space of the pure understanding. He did not observe that with all his efforts he made no advance—meeting no resistance that might, as it were, serve as a support upon which he could take a stand, to which he could apply his powers, and so set his understanding in motion. It is, indeed, the common fate of human reason to complete its speculative structures as speedily as may be, and only afterwards to enquire whether the foundations are reliable. What keeps us, during the actual building, free from all apprehension and suspicion, and flatters us with a seeming thoroughness, is this other circumstance, namely, that a great, perhaps the greatest, part of the business of our reason consists in analysis of the concepts which we already have of objects. This analysis supplies us with a considerable body of knowledge, which, while nothing but explanation or elucidation of what has already been thought in our concepts, though in a confused manner, is yet prized as being, at least as regards its form, new insight. But so far as the matter or content is concerned, there has been no extension of our previously possessed concepts, but only an analysis of them. Since this procedure yields real knowledge *a priori,* which progresses in an assured and useful fashion, reason is so far misled as surreptitiously to introduce, without itself being aware of so doing, assertions of an entirely different order, in which it attaches to given concepts others completely foreign to them, and moreover attaches them *a priori.* And yet it is not known how reason can be in position to do this. Such a question is never so much as thought of. I shall therefore at once proceed to deal with the difference between these two kinds of knowledge.

IV. The Distinction between Analytic and Synthetic Judgments

In all judgments in which the relation of a subject to the predicate is thought (I take into consideration affirmative judgments only, the subsequent application to negative judgments being easily made), this relation is possible in two different ways. Either the predicate B belongs to the subject A, as something which is (covertly) contained in this concept A; or B lies outside the concept A, although it does indeed stand in connection with it. In the one case I entitle the judgment analytic, in the other synthetic. Analytic judgments (affirmative) are therefore those in which the connection of the predicate with the subject is thought through identity; those in which this connection is thought without identity should be entitled synthetic. The former, as adding nothing through the predicate to the concept of the subject, but merely breaking it up into those constituent concepts that have all along been thought in it, although confusedly, can also be entitled explicative. The latter, on the other hand, add to the concept of the subject a predicate which has not been in any wise thought in it, and which no analysis could possibly extract from it; and they may therefore be entitled ampliative.

Judgments of experience, as such, are one and all synthetic. For it would be absurd to found an analytic judgment on experience. Since, in framing the judgment, I must not go outside my concept, there is no need to appeal to the testimony of experience in its support. That a body is extended is a proposition that holds *a priori* and is not empirical. For, before appealing to experience, I have already in the concept of body all the conditions required for my judgment. I have only to extract from it, in accordance with the principle of contradiction, the required predicate, and in so doing can at the same time become conscious of the necessity of the judgment—and that is what experience could never have taught me. On the other hand, though I do not include in the concept of a body in general the predicate "weight," none the less this concept indicates an object of experience through one of its parts, and I can add to that part other parts of this same experience, as in this way belonging together with the concept. From the start I can apprehend the concept of body analytically through the characters of extension, impenetrability, figure, etc., all of which are thought in the concept. Now, however, looking back on the experience from which I have derived this concept of body, and finding weight to be invariably connected with the above characters, I attach it as a predicate to the concept; and in doing so I attach it synthetically, and am therefore extending my knowledge. The possibility of the synthesis of the predicate "weight" with the concept of "body" thus rests upon experience. While the one concept is not contained in the other, they yet belong to one another, though only contingently, as parts of a whole, namely, of an experience which is itself a synthetic combination of intuitions.

But in *a priori* synthetic judgments this help is entirely lacking. [I do not here have the advantage of looking around in the field of experience.] Upon what, then, am I to rely, when I seek to go beyond the concept A, and to know that another concept B is connected with it? Through what is the synthesis made possible? Let us take the proposition, "Everything which happens has its cause." In the concept of "something which happens," I do indeed think an existence which is preceded by a time, etc., and from this concept analytic judgments may be obtained. But the concept of a "cause" lies entirely outside the other concept, and signifies something different from "that which happens," and is not therefore in any way contained in this latter representation. How come I then to predicate of that which happens something quite different, and to apprehend that the concept of cause, though not contained in it, yet belongs, and indeed necessarily belongs, to it? What is here the unknown = X which gives support to the understanding when it believes that it can discover outside the concept A a predicate B foreign to this concept, which it yet at the same time considers to be connected with it? It cannot be experience, because the suggested principle has connected the second representation with the first, not only with greater universality, but also with the character of necessity, and therefore completely *a priori* and on the basis of mere concepts. Upon such synthetic, that is, ampliative principles, all our *a priori* speculative knowledge must ultimately rest; analytic judgments are very important, and indeed necessary, but only for obtaining that clearness in the concepts which is requisite for such a sure and wide synthesis as will lead to a genuinely new addition to all previous knowledge.

V. In all Theoretical Sciences of Reason Synthetic a priori Judgments are contained as Principles

1. *All mathematical judgments, without exception, are synthetic.* This fact, though incontestably certain and in its consequences very important, has hitherto escaped the notice of those who are engaged in the analysis of human reason, and is, indeed, directly opposed to all their conjectures. For as it was found that all mathematical inferences proceed in accordance with the principle of contradiction (which the nature of all apodeictic certainty requires), it was supposed that the fundamental propositions of the science can themselves

be known to be true through that principle. This is an erroneous view. For though a synthetic proposition can indeed be discerned in accordance with the principle of contradiction, this can only be if another synthetic proposition is presupposed, and if it can then be apprehended as following from this other proposition; it can never be so discerned in and by itself.

First of all, it has to be noted that mathematical propositions, strictly so called, are always judgments *a priori*, not empirical; because they carry with them necessity, which cannot be derived from experience. If this be demurred to, I am willing to limit my statement to *pure* mathematics, the very concept of which implies that it does not contain empirical, but only pure *a priori* knowledge.

We might, indeed, at first suppose that the proposition $7 + 5 = 12$ is a merely analytic proposition, and follows by the principle of contradiction from the concept of a sum of 7 and 5. But if we look more closely we find that the concept of the sum of 7 and 5 contains nothing save the union of the two numbers into one, and in this no thought is being taken as to what that single number may be which combines both. The concept of 12 is by no means already thought in merely thinking this union of 7 and 5; and I may analyze my concept of such a possible sum as long as I please, still I shall never find the 12 in it. We have to go outside these concepts, and call in the aid of the intuition which corresponds to one of them, our five fingers, for instance, or, as Segner does in his *Arithmetic,* five points, adding to the concept of 7, unit by unit, the five given in intuition. For starting with the number 7, and for the concept of 5 calling in the aid of the fingers of my hand as intuition, I now add one by one to the number 7 the units which I previously took together to form the number 5, and with the aid of that figure [the hand] see the number 12 come into being. That 5 should be added to 7, I have indeed already thought in the concept of a sum $= 7 + 5$, but not that this sum is equivalent to the number 12. Arithmetical propositions are therefore always synthetic. This is still more evident if we take larger numbers. For it is then obvious that, however we might turn and twist our concepts, we could never, by the mere analysis of them, and without the aid of intuition, discover what [the number is that] is the sum.

Just as little is any fundamental proposition of pure geometry analytic. That the straight line between two points is the shortest, is a synthetic proposition. For my concept of *straight* contains nothing of quantity, but only of quality. The concept of the shortest is wholly an addition, and cannot be derived, through any process of analysis, from the concept of the straight line. Intuition, therefore, must here be called in; only by its aid is the synthesis possible.

Some few fundamental propositions, presupposed by the geometrician, are, indeed, really analytic, and rest on the principle of contradiction. But, as identical propositions, they serve only as links in the chain of method and not as principles; for instance, $a = a$; the whole is equal to itself; or $(a + b) > a$, that is, the whole is greater than its part. And even these propositions, though they are valid according to pure concepts, are only admitted in mathematics because they can be exhibited in intuition.

2. *Natural science (physics) contains* a priori *synthetic judgments as principles.* I need cite only two such judgments: that in all changes of the material world the quantity of matter remains unchanged; and that in all communication of motion, action and reaction must always be equal. Both propositions, it is evident, are not only necessary, and therefore in their origin *a priori,* but also synthetic. For in the concept of matter I do not think its permanence, but only its presence in the space which it occupies. I go outside and beyond the concept of matter, joining to it *a priori* in thought something which I have not thought *in* it. The proposition is not, therefore, analytic, but synthetic, and yet is thought *a priori;* and so likewise are the other propositions of the pure part of natural science.

3. *Metaphysics,* even if we look upon it as having hitherto failed in all its endeavors, is yet, owing to the nature of human reason, a quite indispensable science, and *ought to contain* a priori *synthetic knowledge.* For its business is not merely to analyze concepts which we make for ourselves *a priori* of things, and thereby to clarify them analytically, but to extend our *a priori* knowledge. And for this purpose we must employ principles which add to the given concept something that was not contained in it, and through *a priori* synthetic judgments venture out so far that experience is quite unable to follow us, as, for instance, in the proposition, that the world must have a first beginning, and such like. Thus metaphysics consists, at least *in intention,* entirely of *a priori* synthetic propositions.

VI. *The General Problem of Pure Reason*

Much is already gained if we can bring a number of investigations under the formula of a single problem. For we not only lighten our own task, by defining it accurately, but make it easier for others, who would test our results, to judge whether or not we have succeeded in what we set out to do. Now the proper problem of pure reason is contained in the question: How are *a priori* synthetic judgments possible?

That metaphysics has hitherto remained in so vacillating a state of uncertainty and contradiction, is entirely due to the fact that this problem, and perhaps even the distinction between analytic and synthetic judgments, has never previously been considered. Upon the solution of this problem, or upon a sufficient proof that the possibility which it desires to have explained does in fact not exist at all, depends the success or failure of metaphysics. Among philosophers, David Hume came nearest to envisaging this problem, but still was very far from conceiving it with sufficient definiteness and universality. He occupied himself exclusively with the synthetic proposition regarding the connection of an effect with its cause (*principium causalitatis*), and he believed himself to have shown that such an *a priori* proposition is entirely impossible. If we accept his conclusions, then all that we call metaphysics is a mere delusion whereby we fancy ourselves to have rational insight into what, in actual fact, is borrowed solely from experience, and under the influence of custom has taken the illusory semblance of necessity. If he had envisaged our problem in all its universality, he would never have been guilty of this statement, so destructive of all pure philosophy. For he would then have recognised that, according to his own argument, pure mathematics, as certainly containing *a priori* synthetic propositions, would also not be possible; and from such an assertion his good sense would have saved him.

In the solution of the above problem, we are at the same time deciding as to the possibility of the employment of pure reason in establishing and developing all those sciences which contain a theoretical *a priori* knowledge of objects, and have therefore to answer the questions:

How is pure mathematics possible?
How is pure science of nature possible?

Since these sciences actually exist, it is quite proper to ask *how* they are possible; for that they must be possible is proved by the fact that they exist. But the poor progress which has hitherto been made in metaphysics, and the fact that no system yet propounded can, in view of the essential purpose of metaphysics, be said really to exist, leaves everyone sufficient ground for doubting as to its possibility.

Yet, in a certain sense, this *kind of knowledge* is to be looked upon as given; that is to say, metaphysics actually exists, if not as a science, yet still as natural disposition (*metaphysica naturalis*). For human reason, without being moved merely by the idle desire for extent and variety of knowledge, proceeds impetuously, driven on by an inward need, to questions such as cannot be answered by any empirical employment of reason, or by principles thence derived. Thus in all men, as soon as their reason has become ripe for speculation, there has always existed and will always continue to exist some kind of metaphysics. And so we have the question:

How is metaphysics, as natural disposition, possible?

that is, how from the nature of universal human reason do those questions arise which pure reason propounds to itself, and which it is impelled by its own need to answer as best it can?

But since all attempts which have hitherto been made to answer these natural questions—for instance, whether the world has a beginning or is from eternity—have always met with unavoidable contradictions, we cannot rest satisfied with the mere natural disposition to metaphysics, that is, with the pure faculty of reason itself, from which, indeed, some sort of metaphysics (be it what it may) always arises. It must be possible for reason to attain to certainty whether we know or do not know the objects of metaphysics, that is, to come to a decision either in regard to the objects of its enquiries or in regard to the capacity or incapacity of reason to pass any judgment upon them, so that we may neither with confidence extend our pure reason or set to it sure and determinate limits. This last question, which arises out of the previous general problem, may, rightly stated, take the form:

How is metaphysics, as science, possible? . . .

We may, then, and indeed we must, regard as abortive all attempts, hitherto made, to establish a metaphysic *dogmatically*. For the analytic part in any such attempted system, namely, the mere analysis of the concepts that inhere in our reason *a priori,* is by no means the aim of, but only a preparation for, metaphysics proper, that is, the extension of its *a priori* synthetic knowledge. For such a purpose, the analysis of concepts is useless, since it merely shows what is contained in these concepts, not how we arrive at them *a priori*. A solution of this latter problem is required, that we may be able to determine the valid employment of such concepts in regard to the objects of all knowledge in general. Nor is much self-denial needed to give up these claims, seeing that the undeniable, and in the dogmatic procedure of reason also unavoidable, contradictions of reason with itself have long since undermined the authority of every metaphysical system yet propounded. Greater firmness will be required if we are not to be deterred by inward difficulties and outward opposition from endeavoring, through application of a method entirely different from any hitherto employed, at last to bring to a prosperous and fruitful growth a science indispensable to human reason—a science whose every branch may be cut away but whose root cannot be destroyed.

VII. The Idea and Division of a Special Science, under the Title "Critique of Pure Reason"

In view of all these considerations, we arrive at the idea of a special science which can be entitled the Critique of Pure Reason. For reason is the faculty which supplies the principles of *a priori* knowledge. Pure reason is, therefore, that which contains the principles whereby we know anything absolutely *a priori*. . . .

I entitle *transcendental* all knowledge which is occupied not so much with objects as with the mode of our knowledge of objects in so far as this mode of knowledge is to be possible *a priori*. . . . We have to carry the analysis so far only as is indispensably necessary in order to comprehend, in their whole extent, the principles of *a priori* synthesis, with which alone we are called upon to deal. It is upon this enquiry, which should be entitled not a doctrine, but only a transcendental critique, that we are now engaged. . . .

By way of introduction or anticipation we need only say that there are two stems of human knowledge, namely, *sensibility* and *understanding*, which perhaps spring from a common, but to us unknown, root. Through the former, objects are given to us; through the latter, they are thought. Now in so far as sensibility may be found to contain *a priori* representations constituting the condition under which objects are given to us, it will belong to transcendental philosophy. And since the conditions under which alone the objects of human knowledge are given must precede those under which they are thought, the transcendental doctrine of sensibility will constitute the first part of the science of the elements.

I. TRANSCENDENTAL DOCTRINE
OF ELEMENTS

FIRST PART: Transcendental Aesthetic

In whatever manner and by whatever means a mode of knowledge may relate to objects, *intuition* is that through which it is in immediate relation to them, and to which all thought as a means is directed. But intuition takes place only in so far as the object is given to us. This again is only possible, to man at least, in so far as the mind is affected in a certain way. The capacity (receptivity) for receiving representations through the mode in which we are affected by objects, is entitled *sensibility*. Objects are *given* to us by means of sensibility, and it alone yields us *intuitions*; they are *thought* through the understanding, and from the understanding arise *concepts*. But all thought must, directly or indirectly, by way of certain characters, relate ultimately to intuitions, and therefore, with us, to sensibility, because in no other way can an object be given to us.

The effect of an object upon the faculty of representation, so far as we are affected by it, is *sensation*. That intuition which is in relation to the object through sensation, is entitled *empirical*. The undetermined object of an empirical intuition is entitled *appearance*.

That in the appearance which corresponds to sensation I term its *matter*; but that which so determines the manifold of appearance that it allows of being ordered in certain relations, I term the *form* of appearance. That in which alone the sensations can be posited and ordered in a certain form, cannot itself be sensation; and therefore, while the matter of all appearance is given to us *a posteriori* only, its form must lie ready for the sensations *a priori* in the mind, and so must allow of being considered apart from all sensation.

I term all representations *pure* (in the transcendental sense) in which there is nothing that belongs to sensation. The pure form of sensible intuitions in general, in which all the manifold of intuition is intuited in certain relations, must be found in the mind *a priori*. This pure form of sensibility may also itself be called *pure intuition*. Thus, if I take away from the representation of a body that which the understanding thinks in regard to it, substance, force, divisibility, etc., and likewise what belongs to sensation, impenetrability, hardness, color, etc., something still remains over from this empirical intuition, namely, extension and figure. These belong to pure intuition, which, even without any actual object of the senses or of sensation, exists in the mind *a priori* as a mere form of sensibility.

The science of all principles of *a priori* sensibility I call *transcendental aesthetic*. There must be such a science, forming the first part of the transcendental doctrine of elements, in distinction from that part which deals with the principles of pure thought, and which is called transcendental logic.

In the transcendental aesthetic we shall, therefore, first *isolate* sensibility, by taking away from it everything which the understanding thinks through its concepts, so that nothing may be left save empirical intuition. Secondly, we shall also separate off from it everything which belongs to sensation, so that nothing may remain save pure intuition and the mere form of appearances, which is all that sensibility can supply *a priori*. In the course of this investigation it will be found that there are two pure forms of sensible intuition, serving as principles of *a priori* knowledge, namely, space and time. To the consideration of these we shall now proceed.

Section 1: Space

Close Reading

Metaphysical Exposition of this Concept

By means of outer sense, a property of our mind, we represent to ourselves objects as outside us, and all without exception in space. In space their shape, magnitude, and relation to one another are determined or determinable. Inner sense, by means of which the mind intuits itself or its inner state, yields indeed no intuition of the soul itself as an object; but there is nevertheless a determinate form [namely, time] in which alone the intuition of inner states is possible, and everything which belongs to inner determinations is therefore represented in relations of time. Time cannot be outwardly intuited, any more than space can be intuited as something in us. What, then, are space and time? Are they real existences? Are they only determinations or relations of things, yet such as would belong to things even if they were not intuited? Or are space and time such that they belong only to the form of intuition, and therefore to the subjective constitution of our mind, apart from which they could not be ascribed to anything whatsoever? In order to obtain light upon these questions, let us first give an exposition of the concept of space. By *exposition* (*expositio*) I mean the clear, though not necessarily exhaustive, representation of that which belongs to a concept: the exposition is *metaphysical* when it contains that which exhibits the concept *as given a priori.*

1. Space is not an empirical concept which has been derived from outer experiences. For in order that certain sensations be referred to something outside me (that is, to something in another region of space from that in which I find myself), and similarly in order that I may be able to represent them as outside and alongside one another, and accordingly as not only different but as in different places, the representation of space must be presupposed. The representation of space cannot, therefore, be empirically obtained from the relations of outer appearance. On the contrary, this outer experience is itself possible at all only through that representation.

2. Space is a necessary *a priori* representation, which underlies all outer intuitions. We can never represent to ourselves the absence of space, though we can quite well think it as empty of objects. It must therefore be regarded as the condition of the possibility of appearances, and not as a determination dependent upon them. It is an *a priori* representation, which necessarily underlies outer appearances.

3. Space is not a discursive or, as we say, general concept of relations of things in general, but a pure intuition. For, in the first place, we can represent to ourselves only one space; and if we speak of diverse spaces, we mean thereby only parts of one and the same unique space. Secondly, these parts cannot precede the one all-embracing space, as being, as it were, constituents out of which it can be composed; on the contrary, they can be thought only as *in* it. Space is essentially one; the manifold in it, and therefore the general concept of spaces, depends solely on [the introduction of] limitations. Hence it follows that an *a priori,* and not an empirical, intuition underlies all concepts of space. For kindred reasons, geometrical propositions, that, for instance, in a triangle two sides together are greater than the third, can never be derived from the general concepts of line and triangle, but only from intuition, and this indeed *a priori,* with apodeictic certainty.

4. Space is represented as an infinite *given* magnitude. Now every concept must be thought as a representation which is contained in an infinite number of different possible representations (as their common character), and which therefore contains these *under* itself; but no concept, as such, can be thought as containing an infinite number of representations *within* itself. It is in this latter way, however, that space is thought; for all the parts of space coexist *ad infinitum.*

Consequently, the original representation of space is an *a priori* intuition, not a concept.

The Transcendental Exposition of the Concept of Space

I understand by a transcendental exposition the explanation of a concept, as a principle from which the possibility of other *a priori* synthetic knowledge can be understood. For this purpose it is required (1) that such knowledge does really flow from the given concept, (2) that this knowledge is possible only on the assumption of a given mode of explaining the concept.

Geometry is a science which determines the properties of space synthetically, and yet *a priori*. What, then, must be our representation of space, in order that such knowledge of it may be possible? It must in its origin be intuition; for from a mere concept no propositions can be obtained which go beyond the concept—as happens in geometry (Introduction, V). Further, this intuition must be *a priori*, that is, it must therefore be pure, not empirical, intuition. For geometrical propositions are one and all apodeictic, that is, are bound up with the consciousness of their necessity; for instance, that space has only three dimensions. Such propositions cannot be empirical or, in other words, judgments of experience, nor can they be derived from any such judgments (Introduction, II).

How, then, can there exist in the mind an outer intuition which precedes the objects themselves, and in which the concept of these objects can be determined *a priori*? Manifestly, not otherwise than in so far as the intuition has its seat in the subject only, as the formal character of the subject, in virtue of which, in being affected by objects, it obtains *immediate representation,* that is, *intuition,* of them; and only in so far, therefore, as it is merely the form of outer *sense* in general.

Our explanation is thus the only explanation that makes intelligible the *possibility* of geometry, as a body of *a priori* synthetic knowledge. Any mode of explanation which fails to do this, although it may otherwise seem to be somewhat similar, can by this criterion be distinguished from it with the greatest certainty.

Conclusions from the above Concepts

(a) Space does not represent any property of things in themselves, nor does it represent them in their relation to one another. That is to say, space does not represent any determination that attaches to the objects themselves, and which remains even when abstraction has been made of all the subjective conditions of intuition. For no determinations, whether absolute or relative, can be intuited prior to the existence of the things to which they belong, and none, therefore, can be intuited *a priori*.

(*b*) Space is nothing but the form of all appearances of outer sense. It is the subjective condition of sensibility, under which alone outer intuition is possible for us. Since, then, the receptivity of the subject, its capacity to be affected by objects, must necessarily precede all intuitions of these objects, it can readily be understood how the form of all appearances can be given prior to all actual perceptions, and so exist in the mind *a priori*, and how, as a pure intuition, in which all objects must be determined, it can contain, prior to all experience, principles which determine the relations of these objects.

It is, therefore, solely from the human standpoint that we can speak of space, of extended things, etc. If we depart from the subjective condition under which alone we can have outer intuition, namely, liability to be affected by objects, the representation of space stands for nothing whatsoever. This predicate can be ascribed to things only in so far as they appear to us, that is, only to objects of sensibility. The constant form of this receptivity, which we term sensibility, is a necessary condition of all the relations in which objects can be intuited as outside us; and if we abstract from these objects, it is a pure intuition, and bears the name of space. Since we cannot treat the special conditions of sensibility as conditions of the possibility of things, but only of their appearances, we can indeed say that space comprehends all things that appear to us as external, but not all things in themselves, by whatever subject they are intuited, or whether they be intuited or not. For we cannot judge in regard to the intuitions of other thinking beings, whether they are bound by the same conditions as those which limit our intuition and which for us are universally valid. . . . Our exposition therefore establishes the *reality*, that is, the objective validity, of space in respect of whatever can be presented to us outwardly as object, but also at the same time the *ideality* of space in respect of things when they are considered in themselves through reason, that is, without regard to the constitution of our sensibility. We assert, then, the *empirical reality* of space, as regards all possible outer experience; and yet at the same time we assert its *transcendental ideality*—in other words, that it is nothing at all, immediately we withdraw the above condition, namely, its limitation to possible experience, and so look upon it as something that underlies things in themselves . . .

[The argument in SECTION 2, which deals with Time, parallels that of SECTION 1: Time is also a form of intuition, and this is what makes possible our *a priori* knowledge of certain temporal axioms (such as that if event E_3 is later than E_2, and E_2 later than E_1, then E_3 is later than E_1), of the nature and properties of motion, and of arithmetic, which depends upon counting, and therefore on Time. But Time is in one respect more fundamental than Space, for it is the "formal *a priori* condition of all appearances whatsoever," that is, both inner, introspected experience, as well as outer.]

close Reading

General Observations on the Transcendental Aesthetic

. . . The concepts of sensibility and of appearance would be falsified, and our whole teaching in regard to them would be rendered empty and useless, if we were to accept the view that our entire sensibility is nothing but a confused representation of things, containing only what belongs to them in themselves, but doing so under an aggregation of characters and partial representations that we do not consciously distinguish. . . .

The philosophy of Leibniz and Wolff, in thus treating the difference between the sensible and the intelligible as merely logical, has given a completely wrong direction to all investigations into the nature and origin of our knowledge. This difference is quite evidently transcendental. It does not merely concern their [logical] form, as being either clear or confused. It concerns their origin and content. It is not that by our sensibility we cannot know the nature of things in themselves in any save a confused fashion; we do not apprehend them in any fashion whatsoever. If our subjective constitution be removed, the represented object, with the qualities which sensible intuition bestows upon it, is nowhere to be found, and cannot possibly be found. For it is this subjective constitution which determines its form as appearance.

We commonly distinguish in appearances that which is essentially inherent in their intuition and holds for sense in all human beings, from that which belongs to their intuition accidentally only, and is valid not in relation to sensibility in general but only in relation to a particular standpoint or to a peculiarity of structure in this or that sense. The former kind of knowledge is then declared to represent the object in itself, the latter its appearance only. But this distinction is merely empirical. If, as generally happens, we stop short at this point, and do not proceed, as we ought, to treat the empirical intuition as itself mere appearance, in which nothing that belongs to a thing in itself can be found, our transcendental distinction is lost. We then believe that we know things in themselves, and this in spite of the fact that in the world of sense, however deeply we enquire into its objects, we have to do with nothing but appearances. The rainbow in a sunny shower may be called a mere appearance, and the rain the thing in itself. This is correct, if the latter concept be taken in a merely physical sense. Rain will then be viewed only as that which, in all experience and in all its various positions relative to the senses, is determined thus, and not otherwise, in our intuition. But if we take this empirical object in its general character, and ask, without considering whether or not it is the same for all human sense, whether it represents an object in itself (and by that we cannot mean the drops of rain, for these are already, as appearances, empirical objects), the question as to the relation of the representation to the object at once becomes transcendental. We then realize that not only are the drops of rain mere appearances, but that even their round shape, nay even the space in which they fall, are nothing in themselves, but merely modifications or fundamental forms of our sensible intuition, and that the transcendental object remains unknown to us. . . .

When I say that the intuition of outer objects and the self-intuition of the mind alike represent the objects and the mind, in space and in time, as they affect our senses, that is, as they appear, I do not mean to say that these objects are a mere *illusion*. For in an appearance the objects, nay even the properties that we ascribe to them, are always regarded as something actually given. Since, however, in the relation of the given object to the subject, such properties depend upon the mode of intuition of the subject, this object as *appearance* is to be distinguished from itself as object *in itself*. Thus when I maintain that the quality of space and of time, in conformity with which, as a condition of their existence, I posit both bodies and my own soul, lies in my mode of intuition and not in those objects in themselves, I am not saying that bodies merely *seem* to be outside me, or that my soul only *seems* to be given in my self-consciousness. It would be my own fault, if out of that which I ought to reckon as appearance, I made mere illusion. That does not follow as a consequence of our principle of the ideality of all our sensible intuitions—quite the contrary. It is only if we ascribe *objective reality* to these forms of representation, that it becomes impossible for us to prevent everything being thereby transformed into mere *illusion*. For if we regard space and time as properties which, if they are to be possible at all, must be found in things in themselves, and if we reflect on the absurdities in which we are then involved, in that two infinite things, which are not substances, nor anything actually inhering in substances, must yet have existence, nay, must be the necessary condition of the existence of all things, and moreover must continue to exist, even although all existing things be removed—we cannot blame the good Berkeley for degrading bodies to mere illusion. Nay, even our own existence, in being made thus dependent upon the self-subsistent reality of a non-entity, such as time, would necessarily be changed with it into sheer illusion—an absurdity of which no one has yet been guilty. . . .

SECOND PART: Transcendental Logic

Introduction: The Idea of a Transcendental Logic

I. Logic in General

If the *receptivity* of our mind, its power of receiving representations in so far as it is in any wise affected, is to be entitled sensibility, then the mind's power of producing representations from itself, the *spontaneity* of knowledge, should be called the understanding. Our nature is so constituted that our *intuition* can never be other than sensible; that is, it contains only the mode in which we are affected by objects. The faculty, on the other hand, which enables us to *think* the object of sensible intuition is the understanding. To neither of these powers may a preference be given over the other. Without sensibility no object would be given to us, without understanding no object would be thought. Thoughts without content are empty, intuitions without concepts are blind. It is, therefore, just as necessary to make our concepts sensible, that is, to add the object to them in intuition, as to make our intuitions intelligible, that is, to bring them under concepts. These two powers or capacities cannot exchange their functions. The understanding can intuit nothing, the senses can think nothing. Only through their union can knowledge arise. . . .

["Pure *general* logic," the science of the rules of understanding, abstracts from thought all its empirical content, and deals with its form alone: for example, with the forms of arguments in virtue of which they are valid. Transcendental Logic, on the other hand, while it also sets aside everything that is empirical in origin, is not purely formal, for it is concerned with the *a priori* content of our concepts of objects: it aims to make explicit whatever the understanding can think *a priori* of objects, and to discover the origin, scope, and validity of whatever the understanding can know *a priori* of objects.

Transcendental Logic is divided into Transcendental Analytic and Transcendental Dialectic. The former "deals with the elements of the pure knowledge yielded by understanding, and the principles without which no object can be thought. . . . It is a logic of truth." The latter is a critique of the "dialectical illusions" that arise when the concepts and principles of the understanding are illegitimately extended.]

FIRST DIVISION: Transcendental Analytic

BOOK I: Analytic of Concepts

CHAPTER I

The Transcendental Clue to the Discovery of All Pure Concepts of the Understanding

[There are two parts to the Analytic. The Analytic of Concepts (Book I) must list the *a priori* concepts of the understanding, and prove that this list is both a complete set (there are other, derived concepts, but no other fundamental ones) and a necessary set. The Analytic of Principles (Book II) must list the *a priori* propositions that arise from the application of the *a priori* concepts to experience, and prove that these propositions are necessarily true of all possible experience of objects.

The understanding is discursive; it knows by means of concepts, which involve "the act of bringing various representations under one common representation." Concepts are combined into judgments (the understanding is essentially "the faculty of judgment"), and every judgment has a logical form. Thus a table exhibiting all the basic logical forms of judgments that the understanding can make will reveal the *a priori* capacities of understanding—its logical *repertoire*.]

TABLE OF JUDGMENTS

I
Quantity of Judgments
Universal - Tigers
Particular - White tigers
Singular - White tigers named Fluffy

II
Quality
Affirmative
Negative
Infinite

III
Relation
Categorical
Hypothetical
Disjunctive

IV
Modality
Problematic
Assertoric
Apodeictic

[This list of the forms of judgment shows all the possible (fundamental) ways in which the understanding can relate concepts, and hence the ways in which it can connect objects in knowledge. Each form of judgment employs an *a priori* concept through which the elements of the judgment are synthesized, and so from the Table of Judgments we can derive a table of all the pure concepts of the understanding (or categories) that can be applied *a priori* to objects.]

TABLE OF CATEGORIES

I
Of Quantity
Unity
Plurality
Totality

II
Of Quality
Reality
Negation
Limitation

III
Of Relation
Of Inherence and Subsistence
(*substantia et accidens*)
Of Causality and Dependence
(*cause and effect*)
Of Community (reciprocity
between agent and patient)

IV
Of Modality
Possibility—Impossibility
Existence—Non-existence
Necessity—Contingency

CHAPTER II

The Deduction of the Pure Concepts of the Understanding

[The Transcendental Deduction of the Categories, the knottiest part of Kant's *Critique,* is omitted here, but its general line of argument must be summarized. To explain, as Locke did, how a certain concept was acquired through experience is to give an "empirical deduction," or derivation, of that concept. This cannot be done, of course, with the categories, since they are *a priori*; and in any case the empirical derivation would only be genetic: it would not justify the employment of those concepts. A "transcendental deduction," on the other hand, explains how the categories can relate *a priori* to objects —how, in a sense, the objects are derived from the categories, because the categories are required by the very conditions under which knowledge of objects becomes possible.

It is obvious and unchallengeable that in our experience we find ourselves confronted with persisting physical objects (such as chairs and trees), and with events in the world about us. From the Aesthetic we know that the understanding is presented with a manifold of sense-data, which have been spatially and temporally ordered by the *a priori* forms of sensibility. But how is it possible, then, for the understanding to transform this manifold into a world of objects? How, in other words, is knowledge of objects—not a mere congeries of sense data—possible? For an object is more than a collection of data, and an event is more than a series of data. "If we can prove," says Kant, "that by their means [i.e., by means of the categories] alone an object can be thought, this will be a sufficient deduction of them."

One striking feature of our experience of objects is its duality: to know an object is to distinguish between the object as something objective, something independent of us, and our own subjective experience. We are, in fact, in possession of two fundamental ideas that underlie our common experience and all our empirical sciences: there is the concept of *nature,* or the totality of all objects and events, as an enduring and independent world, in which things are related not only spatially and temporally but by means of natural laws; there is the concept of the *self,* or the totality of all one's internal experiences, which is set over against nature, since object and subject are correlative. In terms of this division, we assign certain sense-data (for example, the green leaf) to the objective world, and others (for example, the pink elephant) to the subjective self.

This self, however, is the *empirical* self, a collection or sequence of experiences; what, then, gives it its unity, makes it a single self (makes us feel that we are the same person today that we were yesterday)? Similarly, nature is a collection whose unity is imposed upon it, or wrought into it (since its lawfulness includes a necessity that is not afforded by mere regular sequences of appearances)—but how? Underlying both these unities (of the self and of nature), then, there must be a transcendental self—Kant calls it the "transcendental unity of apperception"—which, operating through understanding, synthesizes appearances in such a way as to produce objects, and at the same time the contrast between the objective and the subjective. Whatever *a priori* concepts can then be shown to be indispensable to this task, that is, necessarily used by the understanding in synthesizing objects, will necessarily apply to all objects. Thus, for example, if in uniting a collection of sensations into a chair the understanding has to use the category of substance, then it will follow that all such objects are substances. The Transcendental Deduction has thus a conditional conclusion: it remains to be shown, in the second half of the Analytic (the Analytic of Principles) that the categories already listed are precisely those required and employed by the understanding in constructing the objective world.

Another version of the argument, emphasized in the Second Edition of the *Critique* (in which this chapter was entirely rewritten) is that even to become a sense-intuition for a given individual, and thus even to be part of the manifold of intuition, spatially and temporally ordered, a datum must be taken by the self as an element in its own unified experience, and hence categorized.]

All Sensible Intuitions are subject to the Categories, as Conditions under which alone their Manifold can come together in one Consciousness.   The manifold given in a sensible intuition is necessarily subject to the original synthetic unity of apperception, because in no other way is the *unity* of intuition possible (§ 17). But that act of understanding by which the manifold of given representations (be they intuitions or concepts) is brought under one apperception, is the logical function of judgment (cf. § 19). All the manifold, therefore, so far as it is given in a single empirical intuition, is *determined* in respect of one of the logical functions of judgment, and is thereby brought into one consciousness. Now the *categories* are just these functions of judgment, in so far as they are employed in determination of the manifold of a given intuition (cf. § 13). Consequently, the manifold in a given intuition is necessarily subject to the categories.

[The conclusion is, then, twofold: we can know important propositions *a priori* about experience, and about the objects we experience; but because of the very method required to justify our belief in these propositions it follows that "there can be no *a priori* knowledge except of objects of possible experience."]

BOOK II: Analytic of Principles

CHAPTER I

The Schematism of the Pure Concepts of Understanding

[A concept can be applied to a particular only in virtue of a common feature, as the concept *chair* applies to a chair because the chair has the properties contained in that concept. Since categories are wholly different from sense-appearances, there must be, for them to be applicable, a "mediating representation," which, though *a priori,* can also be found in appearance. Such a representation Kant calls a "transcendental schema" (plural: schemata). Now, time is both an *a priori* form and also present in all appearance as its necessary condition; and it is subject to various "transcendental determinations" that can serve as schemata for the categories. Here are some examples.]

The schema of substance is permanence of the real in time, that is, the representation of the real as a substrate of empirical determination of time in general, and so as abiding while all else changes. . . .

The schema of cause, and of the causality of a thing in general, is the real upon which, whenever posited, something else always follows. It consists, therefore, in the succession of the manifold, in so far as that succession is subject to a rule. . . .

The schema of possibility is the agreement of the synthesis of different representations with the conditions of time in general. Opposites, for instance, cannot exist in the same thing at the same time, but only the one after the other. The schema is therefore the determination of the representation of a thing at some time or other.

The schema of actuality is existence in some determinate time.

The schema of necessity is existence of an object at all times.

We thus find that the schema of each category contains and makes capable of representation only a determination of time. The schema of magnitude is the generation (synthesis) of time itself in the successive apprehension of an object. The schema of quality is the synthesis of sensation or perception with the representation of time; it is the filling of time. The schema of relation is the connecting of perceptions with one another at all times according to a rule of time-determination. Finally the schema of modality and of its categories is time itself as the correlate of the determination whether and how an object belongs to time. The schemata are thus nothing but *a priori* determinations of time in accordance with rules. These rules relate in the order of the categories to the *time-series,* the *time-content,* the *time-order,* and lastly to the *scope of time* in respect of all possible objects. . . .

CHAPTER II
System of All Principles of Pure Understanding

["Every object stands under the necessary conditions of synthetic unity of the manifold of intuition in a possible experience." The necessary conditions are the categories; therefore, corresponding to the categories are synthetic *a priori* propositions, or principles, which the understanding necessarily knows because of its assurance that all experience of objects must conform to those categories. The principles are rules for the objective employment of the categories.

Corresponding to the categories of Quantity are the "Axioms of Intuition," whose central principle is: "All intuitions are extensive magnitudes." (This is what justifies the application of pure mathematics to reality.) Corresponding to the categories of Quantity are the "Anticipations of Perception," whose central principle is: "All intuitions are intensive magnitudes." (This is the principle of continuity in nature.) Corresponding to the categories of Relation are the "Analogies of Experience," so called because, like arithmetical proportions (which used to be called "analogies"), they are rules for discovery. Corresponding to the categories of Modality are the "Postulates of Empirical Thought in General," which state the conditions under which objects and events may be said to be possible, actual, or necessary.

The first two groups are called "mathematical principles," the last two "dynamical," because the former apply to sense-data in general, the latter to existence. The former are also called "constitutive," the latter "regulative," because the former enable us to construct magnitudes (intensive and extensive) mathematically, whereas the latter only guide inquiry.

Each of these principles requires a proof—in the case of the Analogies, three distinct proofs. Kant's method here can be illustrated by the two most important arguments, the proofs for the first two Analogies.]

ANALOGIES OF EXPERIENCE

The principle of the Analogies is: Experience is possible only through the representation of a necessary connection of perceptions.

Proof

Experience is an empirical knowledge, that is, a knowledge which determines an object through perceptions. It is a synthesis of perceptions, not contained in perception but itself containing in one consciousness the synthetic unity of the manifold of perceptions. This synthetic unity constitutes the essential in any knowledge of *objects* of the senses, that is, in experience as distinguished from mere intuition or sensation of the senses. In experience, however, perceptions come together only in accidental order, so that no necessity determining their connection is or can be revealed in the perceptions themselves. For apprehension is only a placing together of the manifold of empirical intuition; and we can find in it no representation of any necessity which determines the appearances thus combined to have connected existence in space and time. But since experience is a knowledge of objects through perceptions, the relation involved in the existence of the manifold has to be represented in experience, not as it comes to be constructed in time but as it exists objectively in time. Since time, however, cannot itself be perceived, the determination of the existence of objects in time can take place only through their relation in time in general, and therefore only through concepts that connect them *a priori*. Since these always carry necessity with them, it follows that experience is only possible through the representation of a necessary connection of perceptions.

The three modes of time are *duration, succession,* and *coexistence.* There will, therefore, be three rules of all relations of appearances in time, and these rules will be prior to all experience, and indeed make it possible. By means of these rules the existence of every appearance can be determined in respect of the unity of all time. . . .

A

FIRST ANALOGY: *Principles of Permanence of Substance*

In all change of appearances substance is permanent; its quantum in nature is neither increased nor diminished.

Proof

All appearances are in time; and in it alone, as substratum (as permanent form of inner intuition), can either coexistence or succession be represented. Thus the time in which all change of appearances has to be thought, remains and does not change. For it is that in which, and as determinations of which, succession or coexistence can alone be represented. Now time cannot by itself be perceived. Consequently there must be found in the objects of perception, that is, in the appearances, the substratum which represents time in general; and all change or coexistence must, in being apprehended, be perceived in this substratum, and through relation of the appearances to it. But the substratum of all that is real, that is, of all that belongs to the existence of things, is *substance;* and all that belongs to existence can be thought only as a determination of substance. Consequently the permanent, in relation to which alone all time-relations of appearances can be determined, is substance in the [field of] appearance, that is, the real in appearance, and as the substrate of all change remains ever the same. And as it is thus unchangeable in its existence, its quantity in nature can be neither increased nor diminished.

Our *apprehension* of the manifold of appearance is always successive, and is therefore always changing. Through it alone we can never determine whether this manifold, as object of experience, is coexistent or in sequence. For such determination we require an underlying ground which exists *at all times,* that is, something *abiding* and *permanent,* of which all change and coexistence are only so many ways (modes of time) in which the permanent exists. And simultaneity and succession being the only relations in time, it follows that only in the permanent are relations of time possible. In other words, the permanent is the *substratum* of the empirical representation of time itself; in it alone is any determination of time possible. Permanence, as the abiding correlate of all existence of appearances, of all change and of all concomitance, expresses time in general. For change does not affect time itself, but only appearances in time. (Coexistence is not a mode of time itself; for none of the parts of time coexist; they are all in succession to one another.) If we ascribe succession to time itself, we must think yet another time, in which the sequence would be possible. Only through the permanent does existence in different parts of the time-series acquire a magnitude which can be entitled duration. For in bare succession existence is always vanishing and recommencing, and never has the least magnitude. Without the permanent there is therefore no time-relation. Now time cannot be perceived in itself; the permanent in the appearances is therefore the substratum of all determination of time, and, as likewise follows, is also the condition of the possibility of all synthetic unity of perceptions, that is, of experience. All existence and all change in time have thus to be viewed as simply a mode of the existence of that which remains and persists. In all appearances the permanent is the object itself, that is, substance as phenomenon; everything, on the other hand, which changes or can change belongs only to the way in which substance or substances exist, and therefore to their determinations.

I find that in all ages, not only philosophers, but even the common understanding, have recognized this permanence as a substratum of all change of appearances, and always assume it to be indubitable. The only difference in this matter between the common understanding and the philosopher is that the latter expresses himself somewhat more definitely, asserting that throughout all changes in the world *substance* remains, and that only the *accidents* change. But I nowhere find even the attempt at a proof of this obviously synthetic proposition. Indeed, it is very seldom placed, where it truly belongs, at the head of those laws of nature which are pure and completely *a priori*. Certainly the proposition, that substance is permanent, is tautological. For this permanence is our sole ground for applying the category of substance to appearance; and we ought first to have proved that in all appearances there is something permanent, and that the transitory is nothing but determination of its existence. But such a proof cannot be developed dogmatically, that is, from concepts, since it concerns a synthetic *a priori* proposition. Yet as it never occurred to anyone that such propositions are valid only in relation to possible experience, and can therefore be proved only through a deduction of the possibility of experience, we need not be surprised that though the above principle is always postulated as lying at the basis of experience (for in empirical knowledge the need of it is *felt*), it has never itself been proved. . . .

B

SECOND ANALOGY: *Principle of Succession in Time, in Accordance with the Law of Causality*

All alterations take place in conformity with the law of the connection of cause and effect.

Proof

. . . The apprehension of the manifold of appearance is always successive. The representations of the parts follow upon one another. Whether they also follow one another in the object is a point which calls for further reflection, and which is not decided by the above statement. Everything, every representation even, in so far as we are

conscious of it, may be entitled object. But it is a question for deeper
enquiry what the word "object" ought to signify in respect of appearances when these are viewed not in so far as they are (as representations) objects, but only in so far as they stand for an object. The
appearances, in so far as they are objects of consciousness simply in
virtue of being representations, are not in any way distinct from their
apprehension, that is, from their reception in the synthesis of imagination; and we must therefore agree that the manifold of appearances
is always generated in the mind successively. Now if appearances were
things in themselves, then since we have to deal solely with our representations, we could never determine from the succession of the
representations how their manifold may be connected in the object.
How things may be in themselves, apart from the representations
through which they affect us, is entirely outside our sphere of knowledge. In spite, however, of the fact that the appearances are not things
in themselves, and yet are what alone can be given to us to know,
in spite also of the fact that their representation in apprehension is
always successive, I have to show what sort of a connection in time
belongs to the manifold in the appearances themselves. For instance,
the apprehension of the manifold in the appearance of a house which
stands before me is successive. The question then arises, whether
the manifold of the house is also in itself successive. This, however,
is what no one will grant. Now immediately I unfold the transcendental meaning of my concepts of an object, I realize that the house
is not a thing in itself, but only an appearance, that is, a representation, the transcendental object of which is unknown. What, then,
am I to understand by the question: how the manifold may be
connected in the appearance itself, which yet is nothing in itself?
That which lies in the successive apprehension is here viewed as representation, while the appearance which is given to me, notwithstanding
that it is nothing but the sum of these representations, is viewed as
their object; and my concept, which I derive from the representations
of apprehension, has to agree with it. Since truth consists in the agreement of knowledge with the object, it will at once be seen that we
can here enquire only regarding the formal conditions of empirical
truth, and that appearance, in contradistinction to the representations
of apprehension, can be represented as an object distinct from them
only if it stands under a rule which distinguishes it from every other
apprehension and necessitates some one particular mode of connection
of the manifold. The object is *that* in the appearance which contains
the condition of this necessary rule of apprehension.

Let us now proceed to our problem. That something happens, *i.e.* that something, or some state which did not previously exist, comes to be, cannot be perceived unless it is preceded by an appearance which does not contain in itself this state. For an event which should follow upon an empty time, that is, a coming to be preceded by no state of things, is as little capable of being apprehended as empty time itself. Every apprehension of an event is therefore a perception that follows upon another perception. But since, as I have above illustrated by reference to the appearance of a house, this likewise happens in all synthesis of apprehension, the apprehension of an event is not yet thereby distinguished from other apprehensions. But, as I also note, in an appearance which contains a happening (the preceding state of the perception we may entitle A, and the succeeding B) B can be apprehended only as following upon A; the perception A cannot follow upon B but only precede it. For instance, I see a ship move down stream. My perception of its lower position follows upon the perception of its position higher up in the stream, and it is impossible that in the apprehension of this appearance the ship should first be perceived lower down in the stream and afterwards higher up. The order in which the perceptions succeed one another in apprehension is in this instance determined, and to this order apprehension is bound down. In the previous example of a house my perceptions could begin with the apprehension of the roof and end with the basement, or could begin from below and end above; and I could similarly apprehend the manifold of the empirical intuition either from right to left or from left to right. In the series of these perceptions there was thus no determinate order specifying at what point I must begin in order to connect the manifold empirically. But in the perception of an event there is always a rule that makes the order in which the perceptions (in the apprehension of this appearance) follow upon one another a *necessary* order.

In this case, therefore, we must derive the *subjective succession* of apprehension from the *objective succession* of appearances. Otherwise the order of apprehension is entirely undetermined, and does not distinguish one appearance from another. Since the subjective succession by itself is altogether arbitrary, it does not prove anything as to the manner in which the manifold is connected in the object. The objective succession will therefore consist in that order of the manifold of appearance according to which, *in conformity with a rule,* the apprehension of that which happens follows upon the apprehension of that which precedes. Thus only can I be justified in asserting, not merely of my apprehension, but of appearance itself, that a succession is to be met with in it. This is only another way of saying that I cannot arrange the apprehension otherwise than in this very succession.

In conformity with such a rule there must lie in that which precedes an event the condition of a rule according to which this event invariably and necessarily follows. I cannot reverse this order, proceeding back from the event to determine through apprehension that which precedes. For appearance never goes back from the succeeding to the preceding point of time, though it does indeed stand in relation to *some* preceding point of time. The advance, on the other hand, from a given time to the determinate time that follows is a necessary advance. Therefore, since there certainly is something that follows [*i.e.* that is *apprehended* as following], I must refer it necessarily to something else which precedes it and upon which it follows in conformity with a rule, that is, of necessity. The event, as the conditioned, thus affords reliable evidence of some condition, and this condition is what determines the event.

Let us suppose that there is nothing antecedent to an event, upon which it must follow according to rule. All succession of perception would then be only in the apprehension, that is, would be merely subjective, and would never enable us to determine objectively which perceptions are those that really precede and which are those that follow. We should then have only a play of representations, relating to no object; that is to say, it would not be possible through our perception to distinguish one appearance from another as regards relations of time. For the succession in our apprehension would always be one and the same, and there would be nothing in the appearance which so determines it that a certain sequence is rendered objectively necessary, I could not then assert that two states follow upon one another in the [field of] appearance, but only that one apprehension follows upon the other. That is something merely subjective, determining no object; and may not, therefore, be regarded as knowledge of any object, not even of an object in the [field of] appearance.

If, then, we experience that something happens, we in so doing always presuppose that something precedes it, on which it follows according to a rule. Otherwise I should not say of the object that it follows. For mere succession in my apprehension, if there be no rule determining the succession in relation to something that precedes, does not justify me in assuming any succession in the object. I render my subjective synthesis of apprehension objective only by reference to a rule in accordance with which the appearances in their succession, that is, as they happen, are determined by the preceding state. The experience of an event [*i.e.* of anything as *happening*] is itself possible only on this assumption. . . .

If, then, it is necessary law of our sensibility, and therefore a *formal condition* of all perceptions, that the preceding time necessarily determines the succeeding (since I cannot advance to the succeeding time save through the preceding), it is also an indispensable law of *empirical representation* of the time series that the appearances of past time determine all existence in the succeeding time, and that these latter, as events, can take place only in so far as the appearances of past time determine their existence in time, that is, determine them according to a rule. *For only in appearances can we empirically apprehend this continuity in the connection of times.*

Understanding is required for all experience and for its possibility. Its primary contribution does not consist in making the representation of objects distinct, but in making the representation of an object possible at all. This it does by carrying the time-order over into the appearances and their existence. For to each of them, [viewed] as [a] consequent, it assigns, through relation to the preceding appearances, a position determined *a priori* in time. Otherwise, they would not accord with time itself, which [in] *a priori* [fashion] determines the position of all its parts. Now since absolute time is not an object of perception, this determination of position cannot be derived from the relation of appearances to it. On the contrary, the appearances must determine for one another their position in time, and make their time-order a necessary order. In other words, that which follows or happens must follow in conformity with a universal rule upon that which was contained in the preceding state. A series of appearances thus arises which, with the aid of the understanding, produces and makes necessary the same order and continuous connection in the series of possible perceptions as is met with *a priori* in time—the form of inner intuition wherein all perceptions must have a position.

That something happens is, therefore, a perception which belongs to a possible experience. This experience becomes actual when I regard the appearance as determined in its position in time, and therefore as an object that can always be found in the connection of perceptions in accordance with a rule. This rule, by which we determine something according to succession of time, is, that the condition under which an event invariably and necessarily follows is to be found in what precedes the event. The principle of sufficient reason is thus the ground of possible experience, that is, of objective knowledge of appearances in respect of their relation in the order of time. . . .

At this point a difficulty arises with which we must at once deal. The principle of the causal connection among appearances is limited in our formula to their serial succession, whereas it applies also to their coexistence, when cause and effect are simultaneous. For instance, a room is warm while the outer air is cool. I look around for the cause, and find a heated stove. Now the stove, as cause, is simultaneous with its effect, the heat of the room. Here there is no serial succession in time between cause and effect. They are simultaneous, and yet the law is valid. The great majority of efficient natural causes are simultaneous with their effects, and the sequence in time of the latter is due only to the fact that the cause cannot achieve its complete effect in one moment. But in the moment in which the effect first comes to be, it is invariably simultaneous with the causality of its cause. If the cause should have ceased to exist a moment before, the effect would never have come to be. Now we must not fail to note that it is the *order* of time, not the *lapse* of time, with which we have to reckon; the relation remains even if no time has elapsed. The time between the causality of the cause and its immediate effect may be [a] *vanishing* [quantity], and they may thus be simultaneous; but the relation of the one to the other will always still remain determinable in time. If I view as a cause a ball which impresses a hollow as it lies on a stuffed cushion, the cause is simultaneous with the effect. But I still distinguish the two through the time-relation of their dynamical connection. For if I lay the ball on the cushion, a hollow follows upon the previous flat smooth shape; but if (for any reason) there previously exists a hollow in the cushion, a leaden ball does not follow upon it. . . .

[Kant distinguishes his "transcendental idealism" from "material idealism" (for example, the system of Berkeley), which erases the distinction between the empirically objective and the empirically subjective—the very distinction for which Kant's Analytic provides an underpinning and explanation. In a section (omitted here) called "Refutation of [Material] Idealism," introduced in connection with the second Postulate of Empirical Thought, Kant argues that the consciousness of one's own existence presupposes the existence of objects in external space, and therefore that Berkeley cannot be correct in denying the existence of external objects.]

The Ground of the Distinction of All Objects in General into Phenomena and Noumena

We have now not merely explored the territory of pure understanding, and carefully surveyed every part of it, but have also measured its extent, and assigned to everything in it its rightful place. This domain is an island, enclosed by nature itself within unalterable limits. It is the land of truth—enchanting name!—surrounded by a wide and stormy ocean, the native home of illusion, where many a fog bank and many a swiftly melting iceberg give the deceptive appearance of farther shores, deluding the adventurous seafarer ever anew with empty hopes, and engaging him in enterprises which he can never abandon and yet is unable to carry to completion. Before we venture on this sea, to explore it in all directions and to obtain assurance whether there be any ground for such hopes, it will be well to begin by casting a glance upon the map of the land which we are about to leave, and to enquire, first, whether we cannot in any case be satisfied with what it contains—are not, indeed, under compulsion to be satisfied, inasmuch as there may be no other territory upon which we can settle; and, secondly, by what title we possess even this domain, and can consider ourselves as secured against all opposing claims. Although we have already given a sufficient answer to these questions in the course of the Analytic, a summary statement of its solutions may nevertheless help to strengthen our conviction, by focussing the various considerations in their bearing on the questions now before us.

We have seen that everything which the understanding derives from itself is, though not borrowed from experience, at the disposal of the understanding solely for use in experience. The principles of pure understanding, whether constitutive *a priori,* like the mathematical principles, or merely regulative, like the dynamical, contain nothing but what may be called the pure schema of possible experience. For experience obtains its unity only from the synthetic unity which the understanding originally and of itself confers upon the synthesis of imagination in its relation to apperception; and the appearances, as data for a possible knowledge, must already stand *a priori* in relation to, and in agreement with, that synthetic unity. . . .

If the assertion, that the understanding can employ its various principles and its various concepts solely in an empirical and never in a transcendental manner, is a proposition which can be known with certainty, it will yield important consequences. The transcendental employment of a concept in any principle is its application to things *in general and in themselves;* the empirical employment is its application *merely to appearances;* that is, to objects of a possible experience. That the latter application of concepts is alone feasible is evident from the following considerations. We demand in every concept, first, the logical form of a concept (of thought) in general, and secondly, the possibility of giving it an object to which it may be applied. In the absence of such object, it has no meaning and is completely lacking in content, though it may still contain the logical function which is required for making a concept out of any data that may be presented. Now the object cannot be given to a concept otherwise than in intuition; for though a pure intuition can indeed precede the object *a priori,* even this intuition can acquire its object, and therefore objective validity, only through the empirical intuition of which it is the mere form. Therefore all concepts, and with them all principles, even such as are possible *a priori,* relate to empirical intuitions, that is, to the data for a possible experience. Apart from this relation they have no objective validity, and in respect of their representations are a mere play of imagination or of understanding. . . .

That this is the case with all categories and the principles derived from them, appears from the following consideration. We cannot define any one of them in any real fashion, that is, make the possibility of their object understandable, without at once descending to the conditions of sensibility, and so to the form of appearances—to which, as their sole objects, they must consequently be limited. For if this condition be removed, all meaning, that is, relation to the object, falls away; and we cannot through any example make comprehensible to ourselves what sort of a thing is to be meant by such a concept. . . .

If I leave out permanence (which is existence in all time), nothing remains in the concept of substance save only the logical representation of a subject—a representation which I endeavor to realize by representing to myself something which can exist only as subject and never as predicate. But not only am I ignorant of any conditions under which this logical pre-eminence may belong to anything; I can neither put such a concept to any use, nor draw the least inference from it. For no object is thereby determined for its employment, and consequently we do not know whether it signifies anything whatsoever. If I omit from the concept of cause the time in which something follows upon something else in conformity with a rule, I should find in the pure category nothing further than that there is something from which we can conclude to the existence of something else. In that case not only would we be unable to distinguish cause and effect from one another, but since the power to draw such inferences requires conditions of which I know nothing, the concept would yield no indication how it applies to any object. So long as the definition of possibility, existence, and necessity is sought solely in pure understanding, they cannot be explained save through an obvious tautology. For to substitute the logical possibility of the *concept* (namely, that the concept does not contradict itself) for the transcendental possibility of *things* (namely, that an object corresponds to the concept) can deceive and leave satisfied only the simple-minded.

From all this, it undeniably follows that the pure concepts of understanding can *never* admit of *transcendental* but *always* only of *empirical* employment, and that the principles of pure understanding can apply only to objects of the senses under the universal conditions of a possible experience, never to things in general without regard to the mode in which we are able to intuit them.

Accordingly the Transcendental Analytic leads to this important conclusion, that the most the understanding can achieve *a priori* is to anticipate the form of a possible experience in general. And since that which is not appearance cannot be an object of experience, the understanding can never transcend those limits of sensibility within which alone objects can be given to us. Its principles are merely rules for the exposition of appearances; and the proud name of an Ontology that presumptuously claims to supply, in systematic doctrinal form, synthetic *a priori* knowledge of things in general (for instance, the principle of causality) must, therefore, give place to the modest title of a mere Analytic of pure understanding. . . .

At the same time, if we entitle certain objects, as appearances, sensible entities (phenomena), then since we thus distinguish the mode in which we intuit them from the nature that belongs to them in themselves, it is implied in this distinction that we place the latter, considered in their own nature, although we do not so intuit them, or that we place other possible things, which are not objects of our senses but are thought as objects merely through the understanding, in opposition to the former, and that in so doing we entitle them intelligible entities (noumena). The question then arises, whether our pure concepts of understanding have meaning in respect of these latter, and so can be a way of knowing them.

At the very outset, however, we come upon an ambiguity which may occasion serious misapprehension. The understanding, when it entitles an object in a [certain] relation mere phenomenon, at the same time forms, apart from that relation, a representation of an *object in itself,* and so comes to represent itself as also being able to form *concepts* of such objects. And since the understanding yields no concepts additional to the categories, it also supposes that the object in itself must at least be *thought* through these pure concepts, and so is misled into treating the entirely *indeterminate* concept of an intelligible entity, namely, of a something in general outside our sensibility, as being a *determinate* concept of an entity that allows of being known in a certain [purely intelligible] manner by means of the understanding.

If by 'noumenon' we mean a thing so far as it is *not an object of our sensible intuition,* and so abstract from our mode of intuiting it, this is a noumenon in the negative sense of the term. But if we understand by it an *object* of a *non-sensible intuition,* we thereby presuppose a special mode of intuition, namely, the intellectual, which is not that which we possess, and of which we cannot comprehend even the possibility. This would be 'noumenon' in the *positive* sense of the term. . . .

The possibility of a thing can never be proved merely from the fact that its concept is not self-contradictory, but only through its being supported by some corresponding intuition. If, therefore, we should attempt to apply the categories to objects which are not viewed as being appearances, we should have to postulate an intuition other than the sensible, and the object would thus be a noumenon in the *positive sense.* Since, however, such a type of intuition, intellectual intuition, forms no part whatsoever of our faculty of knowledge, it follows that the employment of the categories can never extend further than to the objects of experience. Doubtless, indeed, there are intelligible entities corresponding to the sensible entities; there may also be intelligible entities to which our sensible faculty of intuition has no relation whatsoever; but our concepts of understanding, being mere forms of thought for our sensible intuition, could not in the least apply to them. That, therefore, which we entitle 'noumenon' must be understood as being such only in a *negative* sense. . . .

If the objective reality of a concept cannot be in any way known, while yet the concept contains no contradiction and also at the same time is connected with other modes of knowledge that involve given concepts which it serves to limit, I entitle that concept problematic. The concept of a *noumenon*—that is, of a thing which is not to be thought as object of the senses but as a thing in itself, solely through a pure understanding—is not in any way contradictory. For we cannot assert of sensibility that it is the sole possible kind of intuition. Further, the concept of a noumenon is necessary, to prevent sensible intuition from being extended to things in themselves, and thus to limit the objective validity of sensible knowledge. The remaining things, to which it does not apply, are entitled noumena, in order to show that this knowledge cannot extend its domain over everything which the understanding thinks. But none the less we are unable to comprehend how such noumena can be possible, and the domain that lies out beyond the sphere of appearances is for us empty. That is to say, we have an understanding which *problematically* extends further, but we have no intuition, indeed not even the concept of a possible intuition, through which objects outside the field of sensibility can be given, and through which the understanding can be employed *assertorically* beyond that field. The concept of a noumenon is thus a merely *limiting concept,* the function of which is to curb the pretensions of sensibility; and it is therefore only of negative employment. At the same time it is no arbitrary invention; it is bound up with the limitation of sensibility, though it cannot affirm anything positive beyond the field of sensibility. . . .

SECOND DIVISION: Transcendental Dialectic

[There is a "natural and unavoidable dialectic of pure reason," by which reason is always tempted into "dialectical illusions"; these cannot be eliminated once and for all so that the temptation disappears: reason must be constantly on guard, with the help of the Critical Philosophy, which shows how such errors occur and how they can be corrected.

As the faculty of understanding was called the "faculty of rules," so reason is the "faculty of principles"; it "secures the unity of the rules of understanding under principles," just as the understanding "secures the unity of appearance by means of rules." The work of understanding issues in judgments; reason produces syllogisms (that is, arguments), and is thus a second-order faculty. A syllogism makes explicit the logical condition, or ground, of its conclusion, but each syllogistic achievement poses for reason a new task, for reason is once again constrained to ask of each premise in turn what is *its* logical ground, i.e., what premises support it. Thus reason sets itself this task: "to find for the conditioned knowledge obtained through the understanding the unconditioned whereby its unity is brought to completion." And in performing this task it *seems* to be guided by a unique assumption, a "principle of pure reason," namely that if the conditioned is given, the whole series of conditions back to

an ultimate unconditioned is also given. This principle and its subordinate ones (unlike the principles of understanding, which are
"immanent") are "transcendent," that is, they transcend all possible
experience. The problem for the Transcendental Dialectic, then, is
whether such a principle can be justified, and how it is to be understood.]

BOOK I: The Concepts of Pure Reason

[The word "idea," which Plato used for his moral and epistemological archetypes, may be used here for a special sort of representation
formed by pure reason alone.]

But though the following out of these considerations is what gives
to philosophy its peculiar dignity, we must meantime occupy ourselves with a less resplendent, but still meritorious task, namely, to
level the ground, and to render it sufficiently secure for moral edifices
of these majestic dimensions. For this ground has been honeycombed
by subterranean workings which reason, in its confident but fruitless
search for hidden treasures, has carried out in all directions, and
which threaten the security of the superstructures. Our present duty
is to obtain insight into the transcendental employment of pure reason, its principles and ideas, that we may be in a position to determine
and estimate its influence and true value. Yet, before closing these
introductory remarks, I beseech those who have the interests of philosophy at heart (which is more than is the case with most people)
that, if they find themselves convinced by these and the following
considerations, they be careful to preserve the expression "idea" in its
original meaning, that it may not become one of those expressions
which are commonly used to indicate any and every species of representation, in a happy-go-lucky confusion, to the consequent detriment
of science. There is no lack of terms suitable for each kind of representation, that we should thus needlessly encroach upon the province
of any one of them. Their serial arrangement is as follows. The genus
is *representation* in general (*repraesentatio*). Subordinate to it stands
representation with consciousness (*perceptio*). A *perception* which
relates solely to the subject as the modification of its state is *sensation*
(*sensatio*), an objective perception is *knowledge* (*cognitio*). This is
either *intuition* or *concept* (*intuitus vel conceptus*). The former relates immediately to the object and is single, the latter refers to it
mediately by means of a feature which several things may have in
common. The concept is either an *empirical* or a *pure concept*. The

pure concept, in so far as it has its origin in the understanding alone (not in the pure image of sensibility), is called a *notion*. A concept formed from notions and transcending the possibility of experience is an *idea* or concept of reason. . . .

I understand by idea a necessary concept of reason to which no corresponding object can be given in sense-experience. Thus the pure concepts of reason, now under consideration, are *transcendental ideas*. They are concepts of pure reason, in that they view all knowledge gained in experience as being determined through an absolute totality of conditions. They are not arbitrarily invented; they are imposed by the very nature of reason itself, and therefore stand in necessary relation to the whole employment of understanding. Finally, they are transcendent and overstep the limits of all experience; no object adequate to the transcendental idea can ever be found within experience. . . .

[As the forms of judgment were the clues to the categories of understanding, so the forms of the syllogism are the clues to the transcendental ideas. There are three basic syllogistic forms (in traditional Aristotelian logic), the categorical, hypothetical, and disjunctive forms, so there must be three basic ideas that reason employs in constructing arguments, that is, in connecting judgments into inferences. And, again, there must be three ways in which reason is constrained to seek for an unconditioned: "first, of the *categorical* synthesis in a *subject*; second, of the *hypothetical* synthesis of the members of a *series*; third, of the *disjunctive* synthesis of the parts in a *system*."]

All pure concepts in general are concerned with the synthetic unity of representations, but [those of them which are] concepts of pure reason (transcendental ideas) are concerned with the unconditioned synthetic unity of all conditions in general. All transcendental ideas can therefore be arranged in three classes, the *first* containing the absolute (unconditioned) *unity of the thinking subject,* the *second* the absolute *unity of the series of conditions of appearance,* the *third* the absolute *unity of the condition of all objects of thought in general.*

The thinking subject is the object of *psychology,* the sum-total of all appearances (the world) is the object of *cosmology,* and the thing which contains the highest condition of the possibility of all that can be thought (the being of all beings) the object of *theology.* Pure reason thus furnishes the idea for a transcendental doctrine of the soul (*psychologia rationalis*), for a transcendental science of the world (*cosmologia rationalis*), and, finally, for a transcendental knowledge of God (*theologia transzendentalis*). . . .

In what precise modes the pure concepts of reason come under these three headings of all transcendental ideas will be fully explained in the next chapter. They follow the guiding-thread of the categories. For pure reason never relates directly to objects, but to the concepts which understanding frames in regard to objects. Similarly it is only by the process of completing our argument that it can be shown how reason, simply by the synthetic employment of that very function of which it makes use in categorical syllogisms, is necessarily brought to the concept of the absolute unity of the *thinking subject,* how the logical procedure used in hypothetical syllogisms leads to the idea of the completely unconditioned *in a series* of given conditions, and finally how the mere form of the disjunctive syllogism must necessarily involve the highest concept of reason, that of a *being of all beings*—a thought which, at first sight, seems utterly paradoxical. . . .

BOOK II: The Dialectical Inferences of Pure Reason

CHAPTER I

The Paralogisms of Pure Reason

A logical paralogism is a syllogism which is fallacious in form, be its content what it may. A transcendental paralogism is one in which there is a transcendental ground, constraining us to draw a formally invalid conclusion. Such a fallacy is therefore grounded in the nature of human reason, and gives rise to an illusion which cannot be avoided, although it may, indeed, be rendered harmless. . . .

[Accompanying all concepts (including transcendental ones) is the consciousness of thinking them; "I think" is thus a transcendental concept, of a sort, too—though the "I" referred to here is hardly to be called a concept at all, being "in itself completely empty." However, the metaphysicians have founded a branch of metaphysics, "rational psychology," on this basis, and have tried (like Descartes) to show that by pure reason alone, starting with the "I think," it is possible to deduce a series of important propositions about the soul. To carry this through, while keeping the whole enterprise purely rational—admitting no empirical data—the "I," or ego, has to be thought of in terms of the categories, and so we have the following possibilities.]

1
The soul is *substance.*

2
As regards its quality it is *simple.*

3
As regards the different times
in which it exists, it is numerically identical, that is,
unity (not plurality)

4
It is in relation to *possible* objects in space.

All the concepts of pure psychology arise from these elements, simply by way of combination, without admission of any other principle. This substance, merely as object of inner sense, gives the concept of *immateriality,* as simple substance, that of *incorruptibility;* its identity, as intellectual substance, *personality;* all these three together, *spirituality;* while the relation to objects in space gives *commercium* with bodies, and so leads us to represent the thinking substance as the principle of life in matter, that is, as soul (*anima*), and as the ground of *animality.* This last, in turn, as limited by spirituality, gives the concept of *immortality.*

In connection with these concepts we have four paralogisms of a transcendental psychology—which is wrongly regarded as a science of pure reason—concerning the nature of our thinking being. . . .

[In the first edition version, Kant formulated four separate syllogisms, and discussed each one; in the second edition, he combined them into a single argument.]

The whole procedure of rational psychology is determined by a paralogism, which is exhibited in the following syllogism:

That which cannot be thought otherwise than as subject does not exist otherwise than as subject, and is therefore substance.
A thinking being, considered merely as such, cannot be thought otherwise than as subject.
Therefore it exists also only as subject, that is, as substance.

In the major premiss we speak of a being that can be thought in general, in every relation, and therefore also as it may be given in intuition. But in the minor premiss we speak of it only in so far as it regards itself, as subject, simply in relation to thought and the unity of consciousness, and not as likewise in relation to the intuition through which it is given as object to thought. Thus the conclusion is arrived at fallaciously, *per sophisma figurae dictionis.*[1]

That we are entirely right in resolving this famous argument into a paralogism will be clearly seen, if we call to mind what has been said in the General Note to the Systematic Representation of the Principles and in the Section on Noumena. For it has there been proved that the concept of a thing which can exist by itself as subject and never as mere predicate, carries with it no objective reality; in other words, that we cannot know whether there is any object to which the concept is applicable—as to the possibility of such a mode of existence we have no means of deciding—and that the concept therefore yields no knowledge whatsoever. If by the term "substance" be meant an object which can be given, and if it is to yield knowledge, it must be made to rest on a permanent intuition, as being that through which alone the object of our concept can be given, and as being, therefore, the indispensable condition of the objective reality of the concept. Now in inner intuition there is nothing permanent, for the "I" is merely the consciousness of my thought. So long, therefore, as we do not go beyond mere thinking, we are without the necessary condition for applying the concept of substance, that is, of a self-subsistent subject, to the self as a thinking being. And with the objective reality of the concept of substance, the allied concept of simplicity likewise vanishes; it is transformed into a merely logical qualitative unity of self-consciousness in thought in general, which has to be present whether the subject be composite or not. . . .

Rational psychology exists not as *doctrine,* furnishing an addition to our knowledge of the self, but only as *discipline.* It sets impassable limits to speculative reason in this field, and thus keeps us, on the one hand, from throwing ourselves into the arms of a soulless materialism,

---

[1] "Thought" is taken in the two premisses in totally different senses: in the major premiss, as relating to an object in general and therefore to an object as it may be given in intuition; in the minor premiss, only as it consists in relation to self-consciousness. In this latter sense, no object whatsoever is being thought; all that is being represented is simply the relation to self as subject (as the form of thought). In the former premiss we are speaking of *things* which cannot be thought otherwise than as subjects; but in the latter premiss we speak not of *things* but of *thought* (abstraction being made from all objects) in which the "I" always serves as the subject of consciousness. The conclusion cannot, therefore, be, "I cannot exist otherwise than as subject," but merely, "In thinking my existence, I cannot employ myself, save as subject of the judgment [therein involved]." This is an identical proposition, and casts no light whatsoever upon the mode of my existence.

or, on the other hand, from losing ourselves in a spiritualism which must be quite unfounded so long as we remain in this present life. But though it furnishes no positive doctrine, it reminds us that we should regard this refusal of reason to give satisfying response to our inquisitive probings into what is beyond the limits of this present life as reason's hint to divert our self-knowledge from fruitless and extravagant speculation to fruitful practical employment. Though in such practical employment it is directed always to objects of experience only, it derives its principles from a higher source, and determines us to regulate our actions as if our destiny reached infinitely far beyond experience, and therefore far beyond this present life. . . .

CHAPTER II

The Antinomy of Pure Reason

Section 1: System of Cosmological Ideas

In proceeding to enumerate cosmological ideas with systematic precision according to a principle, we must bear in mind two points. In the first place we must recognize that pure and transcendental concepts can issue only from the understanding. Reason does not really generate any concept. The most it can do is to *free* a concept of *understanding* from the unavoidable limitations of possible experience, and so to endeavor to extend it beyond the limits of the empirical, though still, indeed, in terms of its relation to the empirical. This is achieved in the following manner. For a given conditioned, reason demands on the side of the conditions—to which as the conditions of synthetic unity the understanding subjects all appearances— absolute totality, and in so doing converts the category into a transcendental idea. For only by carrying the empirical synthesis as far as the unconditioned is it enabled to render it absolutely complete; and the unconditioned is never to be met with in experience, but only in the idea. Reason makes this demand in accordance with the principle that if *the conditioned is given, the entire sum of conditions, and consequently the absolutely unconditioned* (through which alone the conditioned has been possible) *is also given*. The transcendental ideas are thus, in the *first* place, simply categories extended to the unconditioned, and can be reduced to a table arranged according to the [fourfold] headings of the latter. In the *second* place, not all categories are fitted for such employment, but only those in which the synthesis constitutes a *series* of conditions subordinated to, not coordinated with, one another, and generative of a [given] conditioned. Absolute totality is demanded by reason only in so far as the ascending series of conditions relates to a given conditioned. It is not demanded in regard to the descending line of consequences, nor in reference to the aggregate of coordinated conditions of these consequences. For in the case of the given conditioned, conditions are presupposed, and are considered as given together with it. On the other hand, since consequences do not make their conditions possible, but rather presuppose them, we are not called upon, when we advance to consequences or descend from a given condition to the conditioned, to consider whether the series does or does not cease; the question as to the totality of the series is not in any way a presupposition of reason. . . .

I propose to name the synthesis of a series which begins, on the side of the conditions, from the condition which stands nearest to the given appearance and so passes to the more remote conditions, the *regressive* synthesis; and that which advances, on the side of the conditioned, from the first consequence to the more distant, the *progressive*. The first proceeds *in antecedentia,* the second *in consequentia.* The cosmological ideas deal, therefore, with the totality of the regressive synthesis proceeding *in antecedentia,* not *in consequentia.* . . .

When we select out those categories which necessarily lead to a series in the synthesis of the manifold, we find that there are but four cosmological ideas, corresponding to the four titles of the categories:

1.   Absolute completeness
                  of the *Composition*
          of the given whole of all appearances.

2.   Absolute completeness
                  in the *Division*
    of a given whole in the [field of] appearance.

3.   Absolute completeness
                  in the *Origination*
              of an appearance.

4.   Absolute completeness
        as regards *Dependence* of *Existence*
    of the alterable in the [field of] appearance.

Section 2: Antithetic of Pure Reason

If thetic be the name for any body of dogmatic doctrines, antithetic may be taken as meaning, not dogmatic assertions of the opposite, but the conflict of the doctrines of seemingly dogmatic knowledge (*thesis cum antithesi*) in which no one assertion can establish superiority over another. The antithetic does not, therefore, deal with one-sided assertions. It treats only of the conflict of the doctrines of reason with one another and the causes of this conflict. The transcendental antithetic is an enquiry into the antinomy of pure reason, its causes and outcome. If in employing the principles of understanding we do not merely apply our reason to objects of experience, but venture to extend these principles beyond the limits of experience, there arise *pseudo-rational* doctrines which can neither hope for confirmation in experience nor fear refutation by it. Each of them is not only in itself free from contradiction, but finds conditions of its necessity in the very nature of reason—only that, unfortunately, the assertion of the opposite has, on its side, grounds that are just as valid and necessary.

A dialectical doctrine of pure reason must therefore be distinguished from all sophistical propositions in two respects. It must not refer to an arbitrary question such as may be raised for some special purpose, but to one which human reason must necessarily encounter in its progress. And secondly, both it and its opposite must involve no mere artificial illusion such as at once vanishes upon detection, but a natural and unavoidable illusion, which even after it has ceased to beguile still continues to delude though not to deceive us, and which though thus capable of being rendered harmless can never be eradicated.

Such dialectical doctrine relates not to the unity of understanding in empirical concepts, but to the unity of reason in mere ideas. Since this unity of reason involves a synthesis according to rules, it must conform to the understanding; and yet as demanding absolute unity of synthesis it must at the same time harmonize with reason. But the conditions of this unity are such that when it is adequate to reason it is too great for the understanding; and when suited to the understanding, too small for reason. There thus arises a conflict which cannot be avoided, do what we will. . . .

[Kant's method of argument in the Antinomies, and his view of the significance of his results, are well brought out in the First and Third Antinomies, which are presented here in full, together with his

"Observations" on each. The arguments in the Second and Fourth Antinomies are omitted, but their theses and antitheses are given.]

First Conflict of the Transcendental Ideas

Thesis

The world has a beginning in time, and is also limited as regards space.

Antithesis

The world has no beginning, and no limits in space; it is infinite as regards both time and space.

Proof

If we assume that the world has no beginning in time, then up to every given moment an eternity has elapsed, and there has passed away in the world an infinite series of successive states of things. Now the infinity of a series consists in the fact that it can never be completed through successive synthesis. It thus follows that it is impossible for an infinite world-series to have passed away, and that a beginning of the world is therefore a necessary condition of the world's existence. This was the first point that called for proof.

As regards the second point let us again assume the opposite, namely, that the world is an infinite given whole of coexisting things. Now the magnitude of a quantum which is not given in intuition as within certain limits can be thought only through the synthesis of its parts, and the totality of such a quantum only through a synthesis that is brought to completion through

Proof

For let us assume that it has a beginning. Since the beginning is an existence which is preceded by a time in which the thing is not, there must have been a preceding time in which the world was not, i.e. an empty time. Now no coming to be of a thing is possible in an empty time, because no part of such a time possesses, as compared with any other, a distinguishing condition of existence rather than of non-existence; and this applies whether the thing is supposed to arise of itself or through some other cause. In the world many series of things can, indeed, begin; but the world itself cannot have a beginning, and is therefore infinite in respect of past time.

As regards the second point, let us start by assuming the opposite, namely, that the world in space is finite and limited, and consequently exists in an empty space which is unlimited. Things will therefore not only be related in space but also related to space.

repeated addition of unit to unit. In order, therefore, to think, as a whole, the world which fills all spaces, the successive synthesis of the parts of an infinite world must be viewed as completed, that is, an infinite time must be viewed as having elapsed in the enumeration of all coexisting things. This, however, is impossible. An infinite aggregate of actual things cannot therefore be viewed as a given whole, nor consequently as simultaneously given. The world is, therefore, as regards extension in space, not infinite, but is enclosed within limits. This was the second point in dispute.

Now since the world is an absolute whole beyond which there is no object of intuition, and therefore no correlate with which the world stands in relation, the relation of the world to empty space would be a relation of it to no *object*. But such a relation, and consequently the limitation of the world by empty space, is nothing. The world cannot, therefore, be limited in space; that is, it is infinite in respect of extension.

OBSERVATION ON THE FIRST ANTINOMY

I. *On the Thesis*

In stating these conflicting arguments I have not sought to elaborate sophisms. That is to say, I have not resorted to the method of the special pleader who attempts to take advantage of an opponent's carelessness— freely allowing the appeal to a misunderstood law, in order that he may be in a position to establish his own unrighteous claims by the refutation of that law. Each of the above proofs arises naturally out of the matter in dispute, and no advantage has been taken of the openings afforded by erroneous conclusions arrived at by dogmatists in either party.

II. *On the Antithesis*

The proof of the infinitude of the given world-series and of the world-whole, rests upon the fact that, on the contrary assumption, an empty time and an empty space, must constitute the limit of the world. I am aware that attempts have been made to evade this conclusion by arguing that a limit of the world in time and space is quite possible without our having to make the impossible assumption of an absolute time prior to the beginning of the world, or of an absolute space extending beyond the real world. With the latter part of this doctrine, as held by the philosophers

I might have made a pretense of establishing the thesis in the usual manner of the dogmatists, by starting from a defective concept of the infinitude of a given magnitude. I might have argued that a magnitude is infinite if a greater than itself, as determined by the multiplicity of given units which it contains, is not possible. Now no multiplicity is the greatest, since one or more units can always be added to it. Consequently an infinite given magnitude, and therefore an infinite world (infinite as regards the elapsed series or as regards extension) is impossible; it must be limited in both respects. Such is the line that my proof might have followed. But the above concept is not adequate to what we mean by an infinite whole. It does not represent *how* great it is, and consequently is not the concept of a *maximum*. Through it we think only its relation to any assignable unit in respect to which it is greater than all number. According as the unit chosen is greater or smaller, the infinite would be greater or smaller. Infinitude, however, as it consists solely in the relation to the given unit, would always remain the same. The absolute magnitude of the whole would not, therefore, be known in this way; indeed, the above concept does not really deal with it.

The true transcendental con-

cept of the infinite is this, that the successive synthesis of units required for the enumeration of a quantum can never be completed. Hence it follows with complete certainty that an eternity of actual successive states leading up to a given moment cannot have elapsed, and that the world must therefore have a beginning.

of the Leibnizian school, I am entirely satisfied. Space is merely the form of outer intuition; it is not a real object which can be outwardly intuited; it is not a correlate of the appearances, but the form of the appearances themselves. And since space is thus no object but only the form of possible objects, it cannot be regarded as something absolute in itself that determines the existence of things. Things, as appearances, determine space, that is, of all its possible predicates of magnitude and relation they determine this or that particular one to belong to the real. Space, on the other hand, viewed as a self-subsistent something, is nothing real in itself; and cannot, therefore, determine the magnitude or shape of real things. Space, it further follows, whether full or empty, may be limited by appearances, but appearances cannot be limited *by an empty space* outside them. This is likewise true of time. But while all this may be granted, it yet cannot be denied that these two nonentities, empty space outside the world and empty time prior to it, have to be assumed if we are to assume a limit to the world in space and in time.

The method of argument which professes to enable us to avoid the above consequence (that of having to assume that if the world has limits in time and cept of infinitude is this, that the successive synthesis of units required for the enumeration of a quantum can never be completed. Hence it follows with complete certainty that an eternity of actual successive states leading up to a given (the present) moment cannot have elapsed, and that the world must therefore have a beginning.

In the second part of the thesis the difficulty involved in a series that is infinite and yet has elapsed does not arise, since the manifold of a world which is infinite in respect of extension is given as *coexisting*. But if we are to think the totality of such a multiplicity, and yet cannot appeal to limits that of themselves constitute it a totality in intuition, we have to account for a concept which in this case cannot proceed from the whole to the determinate multiplicity of the parts, but which must demonstrate the possibility of a whole by means of the successive synthesis of the parts. Now since this synthesis must constitute a never to be completed series, I cannot think a totality either prior to the synthesis or by means of the synthesis. For the concept of totality is in this case itself the representation of a completed synthesis of the parts. And since this completion is impossible, so likewise is the concept of it.

space, the infinite void must determine the magnitude in which actual things are to exist) consists in surreptitiously substituting for the sensible world some intelligible world of which we know nothing; for the first beginning (an existence preceded by a time of non-existence) an existence in general which presupposes no other condition whatsoever; and for the limits of extension boundaries of the world-whole—thus getting rid of time and space. But we are here treating only of the *mundus phaenomenon* and its magnitude, and cannot therefore abstract from the aforesaid conditions of sensibility without destroying the very being of that world. If the sensible world is limited, it must necessarily lie in the infinite void. If that void, and consequently space in general as *a priori* condition of the possibility of appearances, be set aside, the entire sensible world vanishes. This world is all that is given us in our problem. The *mundus intelligibilis* is nothing but the general concept of a world in general, in which abstraction is made from all conditions of its intuition, and in reference to which, therefore, no synthetic proposition, either affirmative or negative, can possibly be asserted.

Second Conflict of the Transcendental Ideas

Thesis	*Antithesis*
Every composite substance in the world is made up of simple parts, and nothing anywhere exists save the simple or what is composed of the simple.	No composite thing in the world is made up of simple parts, and there nowhere exists in the world anything simple.

Third Conflict of the Transcendental Ideas

Thesis

Causality in accordance with laws of nature is not the only causality from which the appearances of the world can one and all be derived. To explain these appearances it is necessary to assume that there is also another causality, that of freedom.

Proof

Let us assume that there is no other causality than that in accordance with laws of nature. This being so, everything which *takes place* presupposes a preceding state upon which it inevitably follows according to a rule. But the preceding state must itself be something which has taken place (having come to be in a time in which it previously was not); for if it had always existed, its consequence also would have always existed, and would not have only just arisen. The causality of the cause through which something takes place is itself, therefore, something that has *taken place,*

Antithesis

There is no freedom; everything in the world takes place solely in accordance with laws of nature.

Proof

Assume that there is freedom in the transcendental sense, as a special kind of causality in accordance with which the events in the world can have come about, namely, a power of absolutely beginning a state, and therefore also of absolutely beginning a series of consequences of that state; it then follows that not only will a series have its absolute beginning in this spontaneity, but that the very determination of this spontaneity to originate the series, that is to say, the causality itself, will have an absolute beginning; there will be no antecedent through which this which again presupposes, in accordance with the law of nature, a preceding state and its causality, and this in similar manner a still earlier state, and so on. If, therefore, everything takes place solely in accordance with laws of nature, there will always be only a relative and never a first beginning, and consequently no completeness of the series on the side of the causes that arise the one from the other. But the law of nature is just this, that nothing takes place without a cause *sufficiently* determined *a priori*. The proposition that no causality is possible save in accordance with laws of nature, when taken in unlimited universality, is therefore self-contradictory; and this cannot, therefore, be regarded as the sole kind of causality.

We must, then, assume a causality through which something takes place, the cause of which is not itself determined, in accordance with necessary laws, by another cause antecedent to it, that is to say, an *absolute spontaneity* of the cause, whereby a series of appearances, which proceeds in accordance with laws of nature, begins *of itself*. This is transcendental freedom, without which, even in the [ordinary] course of nature, the series of appearances on the side of the causes can never be complete.

act, in taking place, is determined in accordance with fixed laws. But every beginning of action presupposes a state of the not yet acting cause; and a *dynamical* beginning of the action, if it is also a first beginning, presupposes a state which has no *causal* connection with the preceding state of the cause, that is to say, in nowise follows from it. Transcendental freedom thus stands opposed to the law of causality; and the kind of connection which it assumes as holding between the successive states of the active causes renders all unity of experience impossible. It is not to be met with in any experience, and is therefore an empty thought-entity.

In nature alone, therefore, [not in freedom], must we seek for the connection and order of cosmical events. Freedom (independence) from the laws of nature is no doubt a liberation from compulsion, but also from the guidance of all rules. For it is not permissible to say that the *laws* of freedom enter into the causality exhibited in the course of nature, and so take the place of natural laws. If freedom were determined in accordance with laws, it would not be freedom; it would simply be nature under another name. Nature and transcendental freedom differ as do conformity to law and lawlessness. Nature does indeed impose upon the understanding the exacting task of always seeking the origin of events ever higher in the series of causes, their causality being always conditioned. But in compensation it holds out the promise of thorough-going unity of experience in accordance with laws. The illusion of freedom, on the other hand, offers a point of rest to the enquiring understanding in the chain of causes, conducting it to an unconditioned causality which begins to act of itself. This causality is, however, blind, and abrogates those rules through which alone a completely coherent experience is possible.

OBSERVATION ON THE THIRD ANTINOMY

I. On the Thesis

The transcendental idea of freedom does not by any means constitute the whole content of the psychological concept of that name, which is mainly empirical. The transcendental idea stands only for the absolute spontaneity of an action, as the proper ground of its imputability. This, however, is, for philosophy, the real stumbling-block; for there are insurmountable difficulties in the way of admitting any such type of unconditioned causality. What has always so greatly embarrassed speculative reason in dealing with the question of the freedom of the will, is its strictly transcendental aspect. The prob-

II. On the Antithesis

The defender of an omnipotent nature (transcendental *physiocracy*), in maintaining his position against the pseudo-rational arguments offered in support of the counter-doctrine of freedom, would argue as follows. *If you do not, as regards time, admit anything as being mathematically first in the world, there is no necessity, as regards causality, for seeking something that is dynamically first.* What authority have you for inventing an absolutely first state of the world, and therefore an absolute beginning of the everflowing series of appearances, and so of procuring a resting-place for your imagination by

lem, properly viewed, is solely this: whether we must admit a power of *spontaneously* beginning a series of successive things or states. How such a power is possible is not a question which requires to be answered in this case, any more than in regard to causality in accordance with the laws of nature. For, [as we have found], we have to remain satisfied with the *a priori* knowledge that this latter type of causality must be presupposed; we are not in the least able to comprehend how it can be possible that through one existence the existence of another is determined, and for this reason must be guided by experience alone. The necessity of a first beginning, due to freedom, of a series of appearances we have demonstrated only in so far as it is required to make an origin of the world conceivable; for all the later following states can be taken as resulting according to purely natural laws. But since the power of spontaneously beginning a series in time is thereby proved (though not understood), it is now also permissible for us to admit within the course of the world different series as capable in their causality of beginning of themselves, and so to attribute to their substances a power of acting from freedom. And we must not allow ourselves to be prevented from drawing this conclusion by a misapprehen-

setting bounds to limitless nature? Since the substances in the world have always existed—at least the unity of experience renders necessary such a supposition—there is no difficulty in assuming that change of their states, that is, a series of their alterations, has likewise existed, and therefore that a first beginning, whether mathematical or dynamical, is not to be looked for. The possibility of such an infinite derivation, without a first member to which all the rest is merely a sequel, cannot indeed, in respect of its possibility, be rendered comprehensible. But if for this reason you refuse to recognize this enigma in nature, you will find yourself compelled to reject many fundamental synthetic properties and forces, which as little admit of comprehension. The possibility even of alteration itself would have to be denied. For were you not assured by experience that alteration actually occurs, you would never be able to excogitate *a priori* the possibility of such a ceaseless sequence of being and not-being.

Even if a transcendental power of freedom be allowed, as supplying a beginning of happenings in the world, this power would in any case have to be outside the world (though any such assumption that over and above the sum of all possible intuitions there exists an object which cannot be sion, namely that, as a series occurring in the world can have only a relatively first beginning, being always preceded in the world by some other state of things, no absolute first beginning of a series is possible during the course of the world. For the absolutely first beginning of which we are here speaking is not a beginning in time, but in causality. If, for instance, I at this moment arise from my chair, in complete freedom, without being necessarily determined thereto by the influence of natural causes, a new series, with all its natural consequences *in infinitum,* has its absolute beginning in this event, although as regards time this event is only the continuation of a preceding series. For this resolution and act of mine do not form part of the succession of purely natural effects, and are not a mere continuation of them. In respect of its happening, natural causes exercise over it no determining influence whatsoever. It does indeed follow upon them, but without arising out of them; and accordingly, in respect of causality though not of time, must be entitled an absolutely first beginning of a series of appearances.

This requirement of reason, that we appeal in the series of natural causes to a first beginning, due to freedom, is amply confirmed when we observed that

given in any possible perception, is still a very bold one). But to ascribe to substances in the world itself such a power, can never be permissible; for, should this be done, that connection of appearances determining one another with necessity according to universal laws, which we entitle nature, and with it the criterion of empirical truth, whereby experience is distinguished from dreaming, would almost entirely disappear. Side by side with such a lawless faculty of freedom, nature [as an ordered system] is hardly thinkable; the influences of the former would so unceasingly alter the laws of the latter that the appearances which in their natural course are regular and uniform would be reduced to disorder and incoherence.

all the philosophers of antiquity, with the sole exception of the Epicurean School, felt themselves obliged, when explaining cosmical movements, to assume a *prime mover,* that is, a freely acting cause, which first and of itself began this series of states. They made no attempt to render a first beginning conceivable through nature's own resources.

FOURTH CONFLICT OF THE TRANSCENDENTAL IDEAS

Thesis	*Antithesis*
There belongs to the world, either as its part or as its cause, a being that is absolutely necessary.	An absolutely necessary being nowhere exists in the world, nor does it exist outside the world as its cause.

Section 3: The Interest of Reason in These Conflicts

[It is reason's proud pretension to be able to solve the four ultimate cosmological problems, which it cannot refrain from posing to itself, that gives rise to the "dialectical play of cosmological ideas." When the inevitable contradictions arise among the "pseudo-rational" solutions, reason must humbly stand back and consider what has gone wrong. But this is not easy for it to do, since its stake in the outcome is considerable, though it is divided within itself. The side of the thesis in each of the antinomies, which insists on ultimate intelligibility, is that of the *dogmatist*; the side of the antithesis, which is content with partial and limited explanations of appearances, is that of the *empiricist*. Each of these parties is concerned to uphold important interests.]

In the determination of the cosmological ideas, we find on the side of *dogmatism,* that is, of the thesis:

First, a certain *practical interest* in which every well-disposed man, if he has understanding of what truly concerns him, heartily shares. That the world has a beginning, that my thinking self is of simple and therefore indestructible nature, that it is free in its voluntary actions and raised above the compulsion of nature, and finally that all order in the things constituting the world is due to a primordial being, from which everything derives its unity and purposive connection—these are so many foundation stones of morals and religion. The antithesis robs us of all these supports, or at least appears to do so.

Secondly, reason has a *speculative interest* on the side of the thesis. When the transcendental ideas are postulated and employed in the manner prescribed by the thesis, the entire chain of conditions and the derivation of the conditioned can be grasped completely *a priori*. For we then start from the unconditioned. This is not done by the antithesis, which for this reason is at a very serious disadvantage. To the question as to the conditions of its synthesis it can give no answer which does not lead to the endless renewal of the same enquiry. According to the antithesis, every given beginning compels us to advance to one still higher; every part leads to a still smaller part; every event is preceded by another event as its cause; and the conditions of existence in general rest always again upon other conditions, without ever obtaining unconditioned footing and support in any self-subsistent thing, viewed as primordial being.

Thirdly, the thesis has also the advantage of *popularity*; and this certainly forms no small part of its claim to favor. The common understanding finds not the least difficulty in the idea of the unconditioned beginning of all synthesis. Being more accustomed to descend to consequences than to ascend to grounds, it does not puzzle over the possibility of the absolutely first; on the contrary, it finds comfort in such concepts, and at the same time a fixed point to which the thread by which it guides its movements can be attached. In the restless ascent from the conditioned to the condition, always with one foot in the air, there can be no satisfaction.

In the determination of the cosmological ideas, we find on the side of *empiricism,* that is, of the *antithesis*: first, no such practical interest (due to pure principles of reason) as is provided for the thesis by morals and religion. . . .

But, . . . in compensation, empiricism yields advantages to the speculative interest of reason, which are very attractive and far surpass those which dogmatic teaching bearing on the ideas of reason can offer. According to the principle of empiricism the understanding is always on its own proper ground, namely, the field of genuinely possible experiences, investigating their laws, and by means of these laws affording indefinite extension to the sure and comprehensible knowledge which it supplies. Here every object, both in itself and in its relations, can and ought to be represented in intuition, or at least in concepts for which the corresponding images can be clearly and distinctly provided in given similar intuitions. There is no necessity to leave the chain of the natural order and to resort to ideas, the objects of which are not known, because, as mere thought-entities, they can never be given. . . .

The empiricist will never allow, therefore, that any epoch of nature is to be taken as the absolutely first, or that any limit of his insight into the extent of nature is to be regarded as the widest possible. Nor does he permit any transition from the objects of nature—which he can analyze through observation and mathematics, and synthetically determine in intuition (the extended)—to those which neither sense nor imagination can ever represent *in concreto* (the simple). Nor will he admit the legitimacy of assuming in nature itself any power that operates independently of the laws of nature (freedom), and so of encroaching upon the business of the understanding, which is that of investigating, according to necessary rules, the origin of appearances. And, lastly, he will not grant that a cause ought ever to be sought outside nature, in an original being. We know nothing but nature, since it alone can present objects to us and instruct us in regard to their laws. . . .

Section 4: The Absolute Necessity of a Solution of the Transcendental Problems of Pure Reason

To profess to solve all problems and to answer all questions would be impudent boasting, and would argue such extravagant self-conceit as at once to forfeit all confidence. Nevertheless there are sciences the very nature of which requires that every question arising within their domain should be completely answerable in terms of what is known, inasmuch as the answer must issue from the same sources from which the question proceeds. In these sciences it is not permissible to plead unavoidable ignorance; the solution can be demanded. We must be able, in every possible case, in accordance with a rule, to know what is *right* and what is *wrong,* since this concerns our obligation, and we have no obligation to that which we cannot know. In the explanation of natural appearances, on the other hand, much must remain uncertain and many questions insoluble, because what we know of nature is by no means sufficient, in all cases, to account for what has to be explained. The question, therefore, is whether in transcendental philosophy there is any question relating to an object presented to pure reason which is unanswerable by this reason, and whether we may rightly excuse ourselves from giving a decisive answer. . . .

Now I maintain that transcendental philosophy is unique in the whole field of speculative knowledge, in that no question which concerns an object given to pure reason can be insoluble for this same human reason, and that no excuse of an unavoidable ignorance, or of the problem's unfathomable depth, can release us from the obligation to answer it thoroughly and completely. That very concept which puts us in a position to ask the question must also qualify us to answer it, since, as in the case of right and wrong, the object is not to be met with outside the concept. . . .

Section 5: Skeptical Representation of the Cosmological Questions in the Four Transcendental Ideas

[The necessity and sufficiency of the critical solution of the antinomies can also be pointed up by "the skeptical mode of dealing with the questions which pure reason puts to pure reason." A cosmological idea is "meaningful" only if it can be made to agree in some way with a conceivable object of experience generated by the successive synthesis of appearances, but the antinomies prove that the cosmological ideas "must either be too large or too small for any concept of the understanding."]

For suppose:—

First, that *the world has no beginning:* it is then *too large* for our concept, which, consisting as it does in a successive regress, can never reach the whole eternity that has elapsed. Or suppose that *the world has a beginning,* it will then, in the necessary empirical regress, be *too small* for the concept of the understanding. For since the beginning still presupposes a time which precedes it, it is still not unconditioned; and the law of the empirical employment of the understanding therefore obliges us to look for a higher temporal condition; and the world [as limited in time] is therefore obviously too *small* for this law.

This is also true of the twofold answer to the question regarding the magnitude of the world in space. If it is *infinite* and unlimited, it is too *large* for any possible empirical concept. If it is *finite* and limited, we have a right to ask what determines these limits. Empty space is no self-subsistent correlate of things, and cannot be a condition at which we could stop; still less can it be an empirical condition, forming part of a possible experience. (For how can there be any experience of the absolutely void?) And yet to obtain absolute totality in the *empirical* synthesis it is always necessary that the unconditioned be an empirical concept. Consequently, a *limited* world is too *small* for our concept. . . .

Thirdly, if we suppose that nothing happens in the world save in accordance with the laws of *nature,* the causality of the cause will always itself be something that happens, making necessary a regress to a still higher cause, and thus a continuation of the series of conditions *a parte priori* without end. Nature, as working always through efficient causes, is thus too *large* for any of the concepts which we can employ in the synthesis of cosmical events.

If, in certain cases, we admit the occurrence of self-caused events, that is, generation through *freedom,* then by an unavoidable law of nature the question 'why' still pursues us, constraining us, in accordance with the law of causality [which governs] experience, to pass beyond such events; and we thus find that such totality of connection is too *small* for our necessary empirical concept. . . .

We have said that in all these cases the cosmical idea is either too large or too small for the empirical regress, and therefore for any possible concept of the understanding. We have thus been maintaining that the fault lies with the idea, in being too large or too small for that to which it is directed, namely, possible experience. Why have we not expressed ourselves in the opposite manner, saying that in the former case the empirical concept is always too small for the idea, and in the latter too large, and that the blame therefore attaches to the empirical regress? The reason is this. Possible experience is that which can alone give reality to our concepts; in its absence a concept is a mere idea, without truth, that is, without relation to any object. The possible empirical concept is therefore the standard by which we must judge whether the idea is a mere idea and thought-entity, or whether it finds its object in the world. For we can say of anything that it is too large or too small relatively to something else, only if the former is required for the sake of the latter, and has to be adapted to it. Among the puzzles propounded in the ancient dialectical Schools was the question, whether, if a ball cannot pass through a hole, we should say that the ball is too large or the hole too small. In such a case it is a matter of indifference how we choose to express ourselves, for we do not know which exists for the sake of the other. In the case, however, of a man and his coat, we do not say that a man is too tall for his coat, but that the coat is too short for the man. . . .

Section 6: Transcendental Idealism as the Key to the Solution of the Cosmological Dialectic

We have sufficiently proved in the Transcendental Aesthetic that everything intuited in space or time, and therefore all objects of any experience possible to us, are nothing but appearances, that is, mere representations, which, in the manner in which they are represented, as extended beings, or as series of alterations, have no independent existence outside our thoughts. This doctrine I entitle *transcendental idealism.*

The objects of experience, then, are *never* given *in themselves,* but only in experience, and have no existence outside it. That there may be inhabitants in the moon, although no one has ever perceived them, must certainly be admitted. This, however, only means that in the possible advance of experience we may encounter them. For everything is real which stands in connection with a perception in accordance with the laws of empirical advance. They are therefore real if they stand in an empirical connection with my actual consciousness, although they are not for that reason real in themselves, that is, outside this advance of experience. . . .

Section 7: Critical Solution of the Cosmological Conflict of Reason with itself

The whole antinomy of pure reason rests upon the dialectical argument: If the conditioned is given, the entire series of all its conditions is likewise given; objects of the senses are given as conditioned; therefore, etc. We shall be in a better position to detect what is deceptive in this pseudo-rational argument, if we first correct and define some of the concepts employed in it.

In the first place, it is evident beyond all possibility of doubt, that if the conditioned is given, a regress in the series of all its conditions is *set* us *as a task.* For it is involved in the very concept of the conditioned that something is referred to a condition, and if this condition is again itself conditioned, to a more remote condition, and so through all the members of the series. The above proposition is thus analytic, and has nothing to fear from a transcendental criticism. It is a logical postulate of reason, that through the understanding we follow up and extend as far as possible that connection of a concept with its conditions which directly results from the concept itself.

Further, if the conditioned as well as its condition are things in themselves, then upon the former being given, the regress to the latter is not only *set as a task,* but therewith already really *given.* . . . If, however, what we are dealing with are appearances—as mere representations appearances cannot be given save in so far as I attain knowledge of them, or rather attain them in themselves, for they are

nothing but empirical modes of knowledge—I cannot say, in the same sense of the terms, that if the conditioned is given, all its conditions (as appearances) are likewise given, and therefore cannot in any way infer the absolute totality of the series of its conditions. The *appearances* are in their apprehension themselves nothing but an empirical synthesis in space and time, and are given only in *this synthesis*. It does not, therefore, follow, that if the conditioned, in the [field of] appearance, is given, the synthesis which constitutes its empirical condition is given therewith and is presupposed. This synthesis first occurs in the regress, and never exists without it. What we can say is that a *regress* to the conditions, that is, a continued empirical synthesis, on the side of the conditions, is enjoined or *set as a task,* and that *in this regress* there can be no lack of given conditions.

These considerations make it clear that the major premiss of the cosmological inference takes the conditioned in the transcendental sense of a pure category, while the minor premiss takes it in the empirical sense of a concept of the understanding applied to mere appearances. The argument thus commits that dialectical fallacy which is entitled *sophisma figurae dictionis*. This fallacy is not, however, an artificial one; a quite natural illusion of our common reason leads us, when anything is given as conditioned, thus to assume in the major premiss, as it were *without thought or question,* its conditions and their series. This assumption is indeed simply the logical requirement that we should have adequate premisses for any given conclusion. Also, there is no reference to a time-order in the connection of the conditioned with its condition; they are presupposed as given *together* with it. Further, it is no less natural, in the minor premiss, to regard appearances both as things in themselves and as objects given to the pure understanding, than to proceed as we have done in the major, in which we have [similarly] abstracted from all those conditions of intuition under which alone objects can be given. Yet in so doing we have overlooked an important distinction between the concepts. The synthesis of the conditioned with its conditions (and the whole series of the latter) does not in the major premiss carry with it any limitation through time or any concept of succession. The empirical synthesis, on the other hand, that is, the series of the conditions in appearance, as subsumed in the minor premiss, is necessarily successive, the members of the series being given only as following upon one another in time; and I have therefore, in this case, no right to assume the absolute *totality* of the synthesis and of the series thereby represented. In

the major premiss all the members of the series are given in themselves, without any condition of time, but in this minor premiss they
are possible only through the successive regress, which is given only
in the process in which it is actually carried out.

When this error has thus been shown to be involved in the argument upon which both parties alike base their cosmological assertions,
both might justly be dismissed, as being unable to offer any sufficient
title in support of their claims. But the quarrel is not thereby ended—
as if one or both of the parties had been proved to be wrong in the
actual doctrines they assert, that is, in the conclusions of their arguments. For although they have failed to support their contentions by
valid grounds of proof, nothing seems to be clearer than that since one
of them asserts that the world has a beginning and the other that it has
no beginning and is from eternity, one of the two must be in the right.
But even if this be so, none the less, since the arguments on both sides
are equally clear, it is impossible to decide between them. The parties
may be commanded to keep the peace before the tribunal of reason;
but the controversy none the less continues. There can therefore be no
way of settling it once and for all and to the satisfaction of both sides,
save by their becoming convinced that the very fact of their being able
so admirably to refute one another is evidence that they are really
quarreling about nothing, and that a certain transcendental illusion has
mocked them with a reality where none is to be found. This is the
path which we shall now proceed to follow in the settlement of a dispute that defies all attempts to come to a decision.

If we regard the two propositions, that the world is infinite in magnitude and that it is finite in magnitude, as contradictory opposites,
we are assuming that the world, the complete series of appearances,
is a thing in itself that remains even if I suspend the infinite or the
finite regress in the series of its appearances. If, however, I reject this
assumption, or rather this accompanying transcendental illusion, and
deny that the world is a thing in itself, the contradictory opposition of
the two assertions is converted into a merely dialectical opposition.
Since the world does not exist in itself, independently of the regressive
series of my representations, it exists *in itself* neither as an *infinite*
whole nor as a *finite* whole. It exists only in the empirical regress of
the series of appearances, and is not to be met with as something in
itself. If, then, this series is always conditioned, and therefore can
never be given as complete, the world is not an unconditioned whole,
and does not exist as such a whole, either of infinite or of finite
magnitude.

What we have here said of the first cosmological idea, that is, of the absolute totality of magnitude in the [field of] appearance, applies also to all the others. . . .

Thus the antinomy of pure reason in its cosmological ideas vanishes when it is shown that it is merely dialectical, and that it is a conflict due to an illusion which arises from our applying to appearances that exist only in our representations, and therefore, so far as they form a series, not otherwise than in a successive regress, that idea of absolute totality which holds only as a condition of things in themselves. From this antinomy we can, however, obtain, not indeed a dogmatic, but a critical and doctrinal advantage. It affords indirect proof of the transcendental ideality of appearances—a proof which ought to convince any who may not be satisfied by the direct proof given in the Transcendental Aesthetic. This proof would consist in the following dilemma. If the world is a whole existing in itself, it is either finite or infinite. But both alternatives are false (as shown in the proofs of the antithesis and thesis respectively). It is therefore also false that the world (the sum of all appearances) is a whole existing in itself. From this it then follows that appearances in general are nothing outside our representations—which is just what is meant by their transcendental ideality.

Section 9: The Empirical Employment of the Regulative Principle of Reason, in respect of all Cosmological Ideas

I

Solution of the Cosmological Idea of the Totality of the Composition of the Appearances of a Cosmic Whole

Here, as in the other cosmological questions, the regulative principle of reason is grounded on the proposition that in the empirical regress we can have *no experience of an absolute limit,* that is, no experience of any condition as being one that *empirically* is absolutely unconditioned. The reason is this: such an experience would have to contain a limitation of appearances by nothing, or by the void, and in the continued regress we should have to be able to encounter this limitation in a perception—which is impossible.

This proposition, which virtually states that the only conditions which we can reach in the empirical regress are conditions which must themselves again be regarded as empirically conditioned, contains the rule *in terminis,* that however far we may have advanced in the ascending series, we must always enquire for a still higher member of the series, which may or may not become known to us through experience.

For the solution, therefore, of the first cosmological problem we have only to decide whether in the regress to the unconditioned magnitude of the universe, in time and space, this never limited ascent can be called a regress to infinity, or only an indeterminately continued regress (*in indefinitum*).

The quite general representation of the series of all past states of the world, as well as of the things which coexist in cosmic space, is itself merely a possible empirical regress which I think to myself, though in an indeterminate manner. Only in this way can the concept of such a series of conditions for a given perception arise at all. Now we have the cosmic whole only in concept, never, as a whole, in intuition. We cannot, therefore, argue from the magnitude of the cosmic whole to the magnitude of the regress, determining the latter in accordance with the former; on the contrary, only by reference to the magnitude of the empirical regress am I in a position to make for myself a concept of the magnitude of the world. But of this empirical regress the most that we can ever know is that from every given member of the series of conditions we have always still to advance empirically to a higher and more remote member. This is the *regressus in indefinitum,* which, as it determines no magnitude in the object, is clearly enough distinguishable from the *regressus in infinitum.* . . .

Thus the first and negative answer to the cosmological problem regarding the magnitude of the world is that the world has no first beginning in time and no outermost limit in space.

For if we suppose the opposite, the world would be limited on the one hand by empty time and on the other by empty space. Since, however, as appearance, it cannot in itself be limited in either manner —appearance not being a thing in itself—these limits of the world would have to be given in a possible experience, that is to say, we should require to have a perception of limitation by absolutely empty time or space. But such an experience, as completely empty of content, is impossible. Consequently, an absolute limit of the world is impossible empirically, and therefore also absolutely.

The affirmative answer likewise directly follows, namely, that the regress in the series of appearances, as a determination of the magnitude of the world, proceeds *in indefinitum*. This is equivalent to saying that, although the sensible world has no absolute magnitude, the empirical regress (through which alone it can be given on the side of its conditions) has its own rule, namely, that it must always advance from every member of the series, as conditioned, to one still more remote; doing so by means either of our own experience, or of the guiding-thread of history, or of the chain of effects and causes. And as the rule further demands, our sole and constant aim must be the extension of the possible empirical employment of the understanding, this being the only proper task of reason in the application of its principles. . . . In other words, the regress does not proceed to the infinite, as if the infinite could be given, but only indeterminately far, in order [by means of the regress] to give that empirical magnitude which first becomes actual in and through this very regress.

II

Concluding Note on the Solution of the Mathematical-transcendental Ideas, and Preliminary Observation on the Solution of the Dynamical-transcendental Ideas

According to the table of categories given above, two of the classes of concepts imply a *mathematical,* the other two a *dynamical* synthesis of appearances. Hitherto it has not been necessary to take account of this distinction; for just as in the general representation of all transcendental ideas we have been conforming to conditions within the [field of] appearances, so in the two mathematical-transcendental ideas the only object we have had in mind is object as appearance. But now that we are proceeding to consider how far *dynamical* concepts of the understanding are adequate to the idea of reason, the distinction becomes of importance, and opens up to us an entirely new view of the suit in which reason is implicated. . . .

Inasmuch as the dynamical ideas allow of a condition of appearances outside the series of the appearances, that is, a condition which is not itself appearance, we arrive at a conclusion altogether different from any that was possible in the case of the mathematical antinomy. In it we were obliged to denounce both the opposed dialectical assertions as false. In the dynamical series, on the other hand, the completely conditioned, which is inseparable from the series considered as appearances, is bound up with a condition which, while indeed empirically unconditioned, is also *non-sensible.* We are thus able to obtain satisfaction for *understanding* on the one hand and for *reason* on the other. The dialectical arguments, which in one or other way sought unconditioned totality in mere appearances, fall to the ground, and the propositions of reason, when thus given this more correct interpretation, may *both* alike be *true*. This can never be the case with those cosmological ideas which refer only to a mathematically unconditioned unity; for in them no condition of the series of appearances can be found that is not itself appearance, and as appearance one of the members of the series.

III

Solution of the Cosmological Idea of Totality in the Derivation of Cosmical Events from their Causes

When we are dealing with what happens there are only two kinds of causality conceivable by us; the causality is either according to *nature* or arises from *freedom*. The former is the connection in the sensible world of one state with a preceding state on which it follows according to a rule. . . .

By freedom, on the other hand, in its cosmological meaning, I understand the power of beginning a state *spontaneously*. Such causality will not, therefore, itself stand under another cause determining it in time, as required by the law of nature. Freedom, in this sense, is a pure transcendental idea, which, in the first place, contains nothing borrowed from experience, and which, secondly, refers to an object that cannot be determined or given in any experience. . . . The difficulty which then meets us, in dealing with the question regarding nature and freedom, is whether freedom is possible at all, and if it be possible, whether it can exist along with the universality of the natural law of causality. Is it a truly disjunctive proposition to say that every effect in the world must arise *either* from nature *or* from freedom; or must we not rather say that in one and the same event, in different relations, both can be found? That all events in the sensible world stand in thoroughgoing connection in accordance with unchangeable laws of nature is an established principle of the Transcendental Analytic, and allows of no exception. The question, therefore, can only be whether freedom is completely excluded by this inviolable rule, or whether an effect, notwithstanding its being thus determined in accordance with nature, may not at the same time be grounded in freedom. The common but fallacious presupposition of the *absolute reality* of appearances here manifests its injurious influence, to the confounding of reason. For if appearances are things in themselves, freedom cannot be upheld. Nature will then be the complete and sufficient determining cause of every event. The condition of the event will be such as can be found only in the series of appearances; both it and its effect will be necessary in accordance with the law of nature. If, on the other hand, appearances are not taken for more than they actually are; if they are viewed not as things in themselves, but merely as representations, connected according to empirical laws, they must themselves have grounds which are not appearances. The effects of such an intelligible cause appear, and accordingly can be determined through other appearances, but its causality is not so determined. While the effects are to be found in the series of empirical conditions, the intelligible cause, together with its causality, is outside the series. Thus the effect may be regarded as free in respect of its intelligible cause, and at the same time in respect of appearances as resulting from them according to the necessity of nature.

Possibility of Causality through Freedom, in Harmony with the Universal Law of Natural Necessity

Whatever in an object of the senses is not itself appearance, I entitle *intelligible*. If, therefore, that which in the sensible world must be regarded as appearance has in itself a faculty which is not an object of sensible intuition, but through which it can be the cause of appearances, the *causality* of this being can be regarded from two points of view. Regarded as the causality of a thing in itself, it is *intelligible* in its *action;* regarded as the causality of an appearance in the world of sense, it is *sensible* in its *effects*. We should therefore have to form both an empirical and an intellectual concept of the causality of the faculty of such a subject, and to regard both as referring to one and the same effect. This twofold manner of conceiving the faculty possessed by an object of the senses does not contradict any of the concepts which we have to form of appearances and of a possible experience. For since they are not things in themselves, they must rest upon a transcendental object which determines them as mere representations; and consequently there is nothing to prevent us from ascribing to this transcendental object, besides the quality in terms of which it appears, a *causality* which is not appearance, although its *effect* is to be met with in appearance. Every efficient cause must have a *character,* that is, a law of its causality, without which it would not be a cause. On the above supposition, we should, therefore, in a subject belonging to the sensible world have, first, an *empirical character,* whereby its actions, as appearances, stand in thoroughgoing connection with other appearances in accordance with unvarying laws of nature. And since these actions can be derived from the other appearances, they constitute together with them a single series in the order of nature. Secondly, we should also have to allow the subject an *intelligible character,* by which it is indeed the cause of those same actions [in their quality] as appearances, but which does not itself stand under any conditions of sensibility, and is not itself appearance. We can entitle the former the character of the thing in the [field of] appearance, and the latter its character as thing in itself.

Now this acting subject would not, in its intelligible character, stand under any conditions of time; time is only a condition of appearances, not of things in themselves. In this subject no *action* would *begin* or *cease,* and it would not, therefore, have to conform to the law of the determination of all that is alterable in time, namely, that everything *which happens* must have its cause in the *appearances* which precede it. In a word, its causality, so far as it is intelligible, would not have a place in the series of those empirical conditions through which the event is rendered necessary in the world of sense. This intelligible character can never, indeed, be immediately known, for nothing can be perceived except in so far as it appears. It would have to be *thought* in accordance with the empirical character—just as we are constrained to think a transcendental object as underlying appearances, though we know nothing of what it is in itself.

In its empirical character, therefore, this subject, as appearance, would have to conform to all the laws of causal determination. To this extent it could be nothing more than a part of the world of sense, and its effects, like all other appearances, must be the inevitable outcome of nature. In proportion as outer appearances are found to influence it, and in proportion as its empirical character, that is, the law of its causality, becomes known through experience, all its actions must admit of explanation in accordance with the laws of nature. In other words, all that is required for their complete and necessary determination must be found in a possible experience.

In its intelligible character (though we can only have a general concept of that character) this same subject must be considered to be free from all influence of sensibility and from all determination through appearances. Inasmuch as it is *noumenon,* nothing *happens* in it; there can be no change requiring dynamical determination in time, and therefore no causal dependence upon appearances. And consequently, since natural necessity is to be met with only in the sensible world, this active being must in its actions be independent of, and free from all such necessity. No action begins *in* this active being itself; but we may yet quite correctly say that the active being *of itself* begins its effects in the sensible world. In so doing, we should not be asserting that the effects in the sensible world can begin of themselves; they are always predetermined through antecedent empirical conditions, though solely through their empirical character (which is no more than the appearance of the intelligible), and so are only possible as a continuation of the series of natural causes. In this way freedom and nature, in the full sense of these terms, can exist together, without any conflict, in the same actions, according as the actions are referred to their intelligible or to their sensible cause.

Explanation of the Cosmological Idea of Freedom in its Connection with Universal Natural Necessity

Admitting that in the whole series of events there is nothing but natural necessity, is it yet possible to regard one and the same event as being in one aspect merely an effect of nature and in another aspect an effect due to freedom; or is there between these two kinds of causality a direct contradiction? . . .

The principle of the causal connection of appearances is required in order that we may be able to look for and to determine the natural conditions of natural events, that is to say, their causes in the [field of] appearance. If this principle be admitted, and be not weakened through any exception, the requirements of the understanding, which in its empirical employment sees in all happenings nothing but nature, and is justified in so doing, are completely satisfied; and physical explanations may proceed on their own lines without interference. These requirements are not in any way infringed, if we assume, even though the assumption should be a mere fiction, that some among the natural causes have a faculty which is intelligible only, inasmuch as its determination to action never rests upon empirical conditions, but solely on grounds of understanding. We must, of course, at the same time be able to assume that the *action* of these causes *in the* [*field of*] *appearance* is in conformity with all the laws of empirical causality. In this way the acting subject, as *causa phaenomenon*, would be bound up with nature through the indissoluble dependence of all its actions, and only as we ascend from the empirical object to the transcendental should we find that this subject, together with all its causality in the [field of] appearance, has in its *noumenon* certain conditions which must be regarded as purely intelligible. For if in determining in what ways appearances can serve as causes we follow the rules of nature, we need not concern ourselves what kind of ground for these appearances and their connection may have to be thought as existing in the transcendental subject, which is empirically unknown to us. This intelligible ground does not have to be considered in empirical enquiries; it concerns only thought in the pure understanding; and although the effects of this thought and action of the pure understanding are to be met with in the appearances, these appearances must none the less be capable of complete causal explanation in terms of other appearances in accordance with natural laws. We have to take their strictly empirical character as the supreme ground of explanation, leaving entirely out of account their intelligible character (that is, the transcendental cause of their empirical character) as being completely unknown, save in so far as the empirical serves for its sensible sign.

Let us apply this to experience. Man is one of the appearances of the sensible world, and in so far one of the natural causes the causality of which must stand under empirical laws. Like all other things in nature, he must have an empirical character. This character we come to know through the powers and faculties which he reveals in his actions. In lifeless, or merely animal, nature we find no ground for thinking that any faculty is conditioned otherwise than in a merely sensible manner. Man, however, who knows all the rest of nature solely through the senses, knows himself also through pure apperception; and this, indeed, in acts and inner determinations which he cannot regard as impressions of the senses. He is thus to himself, on the one hand phenomenon, and on the other hand, in respect of certain faculties the action of which cannot be ascribed to the receptivity of sensibility, a purely intelligible object. We entitle these faculties understanding and reason. The latter, in particular, we distinguish in a quite peculiar and especial way from all empirically conditioned powers. For it views its objects exclusively in the light of ideas, and in accordance with them determines the understanding, which then proceeds to make an empirical use of its own similarly pure concepts.

That our reason has causality, or that we at least represent it to ourselves as having causality, is evident from the *imperatives* which in all matters of conduct we impose as rules upon our active powers. *'Ought'* expresses a kind of necessity and of connection with grounds which is found nowhere else in the whole of nature. The understanding can know in nature only what is, what has been, or what will be. We cannot say that anything in nature *ought to be* other than what in all these time-relations it actually is. When we have the course of nature alone in view, *'ought'* has no meaning whatsoever. It is just as absurd to ask what ought to happen in the natural world as to ask what properties a circle ought to have. All that we are justified in asking is: what happens in nature? what are the properties of the circle?

This *'ought'* expresses a possible action the ground of which cannot be anything but a mere concept; whereas in the case of a merely natural action the ground must always be an appearance. The action to which the *'ought'* applies must indeed be possible under natural conditions. These conditions, however, do not play any part in determining the will itself, but only in determining the effect and its consequences in the [field of] appearance. No matter how many natural grounds or how many sensuous impulses may impel me to *will,* they can never give rise to the *'ought,'* but only to a willing which, while very far from being necessary, is always conditioned; and the *'ought'* pronounced by reason confronts such willing with a limit and an end—nay more, forbids or authorizes it. Whether what is willed be an object of mere sensibility (the pleasant) or of pure reason (the good), reason will not give way to any ground which is empirically given. Reason does not here follow the order of things as they present themselves in appearance, but frames for itself with perfect spontaneity an order of its own according to ideas, to which it adapts the empirical conditions, and according to which it declares actions to be necessary, even although they have never taken place, and perhaps never will take place. And at the same time, reason also presupposes that it can have causality in regard to all these actions, since otherwise no empirical effects could be expected from its ideas. . . .

Thus the will of every man has an empirical character, which is nothing but a certain causality of his reason, so far as that causality exhibits, in its effects in the [field of] appearance, a rule from which we may gather what, in their kind and degrees, are the actions of reason and the grounds thereof, and so may form an estimate concerning the subjective principles of his will. Since this empirical character must itself be discovered from the appearances which are its effect and from the rule to which experience shows them to conform, it follows that all the actions of men in the [field of] appearance are determined in conformity with the order of nature, by their empirical character and by the other causes which cooperate with that character; and if we could exhaustively investigate all the appearances of men's wills, there would not be found a single human action which we could not predict with certainty, and recognize as proceeding necessarily from its antecedent conditions. So far, then, as regards this empirical character there is no freedom; and yet it is only in the light of this character that man can be studied—if, that is to say, we are simply *observing,* and in the manner of anthropology seeking to institute a physiological investigation into the motive causes of his actions.

But when we consider these actions in their relation to reason—I do not mean speculative reason, by which we endeavor *to explain* their coming into being, but reason in so far as it is itself the cause *producing* them—if, that is to say, we compare them with [the standards of] reason in its *practical* bearing, we find a rule and order altogether different from the order of nature. For it may be that all that *has happened* in the course of nature, and in accordance with its empirical grounds must inevitably have happened, *ought not to have happened.* Sometimes, however, we find, or at least believe that we find, that the ideas of reason have in actual fact proved their causality in respect of the actions of men, as appearances; and that these actions have taken place, not because they were determined by empirical causes, but because they were determined by grounds of reason. . . .

In order to illustrate this regulative principle of reason by an example of its empirical employment—not, however, to confirm it, for it is useless to endeavor to prove transcendental propositions by examples—let us take a voluntary action, for example, a malicious lie by which a certain confusion has been caused in society. First of all, we endeavor to discover the motives to which it has been due, and then, secondly, in the light of these, we proceed to determine how far the action and its consequences can be imputed to the offender. As regards the first question, we trace the empirical character of the action to its sources, finding these in defective education, bad company, in part also in the viciousness of a natural disposition insensitive to shame, in levity and thoughtlessness, not neglecting to take into account also the occasional causes that may have intervened. We proceed in this enquiry just as we should in ascertaining for a given natural effect the series of its determining causes. But although we believe that the action is thus determined, we none the less blame the agent, not indeed on account of his unhappy disposition, nor on account of the circumstances that have influenced him, nor even on account of his previous way of life; for we presuppose that we can leave out of consideration what this way of life may have been, that we can regard the past series of conditions as not having occurred and the act as being completely unconditioned by any preceding state, just as if the agent in and by himself began in this action an entirely new series of consequences. Our blame is based on a law of reason whereby we regard reason as a cause that irrespective of all the above-mentioned empirical conditions could have determined, and ought to have determined, the agent to act otherwise. This causality of reason we do not regard as only a cooperating agency, but as complete in itself, even when the sensuous impulses do not favor but are directly opposed to it; the action is ascribed to the agent's intelligible character; in the moment when he utters the lie, the guilt is entirely his. Reason, irrespective of all empirical conditions of the act, is completely free, and the lie is entirely due to its default.

Such imputation clearly shows that we consider reason to be unaffected by these sensible influences, and not liable to alteration. . . . When we say that in spite of his whole previous course of life the agent could have refrained from lying, this only means that the act is under the immediate power of reason, and that reason in its causality is not subject to any conditions of appearance or of time. . . .

The reader should be careful to observe that in what has been said our intention has not been to establish the *reality* of freedom as one of the faculties which contain the cause of the appearances of our sensible world. . . . What we have alone been able to show, and what we have alone been concerned to show, is that this antinomy rests on a sheer illusion, and that causality through freedom is at least *not incompatible with* nature.

CHAPTER III

The Ideal of Pure Reason

[Every concept is subject to the "principle of determinability," namely: that of every pair of contradictory predicates, only one can apply to it. This derives from the law of contradiction. Every individual thing, moreover, is "as regards its possibility" also subject to the "principle of determination," namely: that of every pair of contradictory predicates, at least one must belong to it. This principle, which derives from the law of the excluded middle, relates individual things to the "sum-total of all possibilities." Reason holds the principle that "everything which exists is completely determined," and therefore "to know a thing completely, we must know every possible [predicate], and must determine it thereby, either affirmatively or negatively." The concept of the totality of all possibility is a purely *a priori* concept, itself complete and fully determinate, and "it thus becomes the concept of an individual object which is completely determined through the mere idea, and must therefore be entitled an *ideal* of pure reason."

Since every negation is derived from the corresponding property whose absence it is, the concept of the completely determined is that of the whole store of positive predicates from which things are characterized: the idea of an *omnitudo realitas,* or *ens realissimum,* a thing in itself that possesses the positive one of every possible pair of contradictory predicates. This is the "transcendental ideal," which when thought of as a primordial being, and categorized as one, simple, all-sufficient, eternal, is the idea of God, the object of "transcendental theology."

Reason would realize the "merely fictitious," or constructed, nature of the ideal, if it were not impelled (as was seen in the antinomies) to seek a resting-place in the regress from the given conditioned to an unconditioned. Once it is caught in the conviction that the existence of contingent beings (ourselves and material objects) entails that there must be some being that exists necessarily—the argument for the thesis of the fourth antinomy—reason must look about for some way of conceiving that necessary being. "Now that which in its concept contains a therefore for every wherefore, that which is in no respect defective, that which is in every way sufficient as a condition, seems precisely the being to which absolute necessity can fittingly be ascribed. . . . The concept of an *ens realissimum* is therefore, of all concepts of possible things, that which best squares with the concept of an unconditionally necessary being; and though it may not be completely adequate to it, we have no choice in the matter, but find ourselves constrained to hold to it"—if we must have a necessary being, and therefore some candidate for that role. Hence arises the (metaphysical) doctrine of the existence of God.]

There are only three possible ways of proving the existence of God by means of speculative reason. All the paths leading to this goal begin either from determinate experience and the specific constitution of the world of sense as thereby known, and ascend from it, in accordance with laws of causality, to the supreme cause outside the world; or they start from experience which is purely indeterminate, that is from experience of existence in general; or finally they abstract from all experience, and argue completely *a priori,* from mere concepts, to the existence of a supreme cause. The first proof is the *physico-theological,* the second the *cosmological,* the third the *ontological.* There are, and there can be, no others.

I propose to show that reason is as little able to make progress on the one path, the empirical, as on the other path, the transcendental, and that it stretches its wings in vain in thus attempting to soar above the world of sense by the mere power of speculation. As regards the order in which these arguments should be dealt with, it will be exactly the reverse of that which reason takes in the progress of its own development, and therefore of that which we have ourselves followed in the above account. For it will be shown that, although experience is what first gives occasion to this enquiry, it is the *transcendental concept* which in all such endeavors marks out the goal that reason has set itself to attain, and which is indeed its sole guide in its efforts to achieve that goal. I shall therefore begin with the examination of the transcendental proof, and afterwards enquire what effect the addition of the empirical factor can have in enhancing the force of the argument.

Section 4: The Impossibility of an Ontological Proof of the Existence of God

It is evident, from what has been said, that the concept of an absolutely necessary being is a concept of pure reason, that is, a mere idea the objective reality of which is very far from being proved by the fact that reason requires it. For the idea instructs us only in regard to a certain unattainable completeness, and so serves rather to limit the understanding than to extend it to new objects. But we are here faced by what is indeed strange and perplexing, namely, that while the inference from a given existence in general to some absolutely necessary being seems to be both imperative and legitimate, all those conditions under which alone the understanding can form a concept of such a necessity are so many obstacles in the way of our doing so.

In all ages men have spoken of an *absolutely necessary* being, and in so doing have endeavored, not so much to understand whether and how a thing of this kind allows even of being thought, but rather to prove its existence. There is, of course, no difficulty in giving a verbal definition of the concept, namely, that it is something the non-existence of which is impossible. But this yields no insight into the conditions which make it necessary to regard the non-existence of a thing as absolutely unthinkable. It is precisely these conditions that we desire to know, in order that we may determine whether or not, in resorting to this concept, we are thinking anything at all. The expedient of removing all those conditions which the understanding indispensably requires in order to regard something as necessary, simply through the introduction of the word *unconditioned,* is very far from sufficing to show whether I am still thinking anything in the concept of the unconditionally necessary, or perhaps rather nothing at all.

Nay more, this concept, at first ventured upon blindly, and now become so completely familiar, has been supposed to have its meaning exhibited in a number of examples; and on this account all further enquiry into its intelligibility has seemed to be quite needless. Thus the fact that every geometrical proposition, as, for instance, that a triangle has three angles, is absolutely necessary, has been taken as justifying us in speaking of an object which lies entirely outside the sphere of our understanding as if we understood perfectly what it is that we intend to convey by the concept of that object.

All the alleged examples are, without exception, taken from *judgments,* not from *things* and their existence. But the unconditioned necessity of judgments is not the same as an absolute necessity of things. The absolute necessity of the judgment is only a conditioned necessity of the thing, or of the predicate in the judgment. The above proposition does not declare that three angles are absolutely necessary, but that, under the condition that there is a triangle (that is, that a triangle is given), three angles will necessarily be found in it. So great, indeed, is the deluding influence exercised by this logical necessity that, by the simple device of forming an *a priori* concept of a thing in such a manner as to include existence within the scope of its meaning, we have supposed ourselves to have justified the conclusion that because existence necessarily belongs to the object of this concept—always under the condition that we posit the thing as given (as existing)—we are also of necessity, in accordance with the law of identity, required to posit the existence of its object, and that this being is therefore itself absolutely necessary—and this, to repeat, for the reason that the existence of this being has already been thought in a concept which is assumed arbitrarily and on condition that we posit its object.

If, in an identical proposition, I reject the predicate while retaining the subject, contradiction results; and I therefore say that the former belongs necessarily to the latter. But if we reject subject and predicate alike, there is no contradiction; for nothing is then left that can be contradicted. To posit a triangle, and yet to reject its three angles, is self-contradictory; but there is no contradiction in rejecting the triangle together with its three angles. The same holds true of the concept of an absolutely necessary being. If its existence is rejected, we reject the thing itself with all its predicates; and no question of contradiction can then arise. There is nothing outside it that would then be contradicted, since the necessity of the thing is not supposed to be derived from anything external; nor is there anything internal that would be contradicted, since in rejecting the thing itself we have at the same time rejected all its internal properties. "God is omnipotent" is a necessary judgment. The omnipotence cannot be rejected if we posit a Deity, that is, an infinite being; for the two concepts are identical. But if we say, "There is no God," neither the omnipotence nor any other of its predicates is given; they are one and all rejected together with the subject, and there is therefore not the least contradiction in such a judgment.

We have thus seen that if the predicate of a judgment is rejected together with the subject, no internal contradiction can result, and that this holds no matter what the predicate may be. The only way of evading this conclusion is to argue that there are subjects which cannot be removed, and must always remain. That, however, would only be another way of saying that there are absolutely necessary subjects; and that is the very assumption which I have called in question, and the possibility of which the above argument professes to establish. For I cannot form the least concept of a thing which, should it be rejected with all its predicates, leaves behind a contradiction; and in the absence of contradiction I have, through pure *a priori* concepts alone, no criterion of impossibility.

Notwithstanding all these general considerations, in which every one must concur, we may be challenged with a case which is brought forward as proof that in actual fact the contrary holds, namely, that there is one concept, and indeed only one, in reference to which the not-being or rejection of its object is in itself contradictory, namely, the concept of the *ens realissimum*. It is declared that it possesses all reality, and that we are justified in assuming that such a being is possible (the fact that a concept does not contradict itself by no means proves the possibility of its object: but the contrary assertion I am for the moment willing to allow). Now [the argument proceeds] "all reality" includes existence; existence is therefore contained in the concept of a thing that is possible. If, then, this thing is rejected, the internal possibility of the thing is rejected—which is self-contradictory.

My answer is as follows. There is already a contradiction in introducing the concept of existence—no matter under what title it may be disguised—into the concept of a thing which we profess to be thinking solely in reference to its possibility. If that be allowed as legitimate, a seeming victory has been won; but in actual fact nothing at all is said: the assertion is a mere tautology. We must ask: Is the proposition that *this or that thing* (which, whatever it may be, is allowed as possible) *exists,* an analytic or a synthetic proposition? If it is analytic, the assertion of the existence of the thing adds nothing to the thought of the thing; but in that case either the thought, which is in us, is the thing itself, or we have presupposed an existence as belonging to the realm of the possible, and have then, on that pretext, inferred its existence from its internal possibility—which is nothing but a miserable tautology. The word "reality," which in the concept of the thing sounds other than the word 'existence' in the concept of the predicate, is of no avail in meeting this objection. For if all positing (no matter what it may be that is posited) is entitled reality, the thing with all its predicates is already posited in the concept of the subject, and is assumed as actual; and in the predicate this is merely repeated. But if, on the other hand, we admit, as every reasonable person must, that all existential propositions are synthetic, how can we profess to maintain that the predicate of existence cannot be rejected without contradiction? This is a feature which is found only in analytic propositions, and is indeed precisely what constitutes their analytic character.

I should have hoped to put an end to these idle and fruitless disputations in a direct manner, by an accurate determination of the concept of existence, had I not found that the illusion which is caused by the confusion of a logical with a real predicate (that is, with a predicate which determines a thing) is almost beyond correction. Anything we please can be made to serve as a logical predicate; the subject can even be predicated of itself; for logic abstracts from all content. But a *determining* predicate is a predicate which is added to the concept of the subject and enlarges it. Consequently, it must not be already contained in the concept.

Being is obviously not a real predicate; that is, it is not a concept of something which could be added to the concept of a thing. It is merely the positing of a thing, or of certain determinations, as existing in themselves. Logically, it is merely the copula of a judgment. The proposition, "God is omnipotent," contains two concepts, each of which has its object—God and omnipotence. The small word "is" adds no new predicate, but only serves to posit the predicate *in its relation* to the subject. If, now, we take the subject (God) with all its predicates (among which is omnipotence), and say "God is," or "There is a God," we attach no new predicate to the concept of God, but only posit the subject in itself with all its predicates, and indeed posit it as being an *object* that stands in relation to my *concept*. The content of both must be one and the same; nothing can have been added to the concept, which expresses merely what is possible, by my thinking its object (through the expression "it is") as given absolutely. Otherwise stated, the real contains no more than the merely possible.

A hundred real thalers do not contain the least coin more than a hundred possible thalers. For as the latter signify the concept, and the former the object and the positing of the object, should the former contain more than the latter, my concept would not, in that case, express the whole object, and would not therefore be an adequate concept of it. My financial position is, however, affected very differently by a hundred real thalers than it is by the mere concept of them (that is, of their possibility). For the object, as it actually exists, is not analytically contained in my concept, but is added to my concept (which is a determination of my state) synthetically; and yet the conceived hundred thalers are not themselves in the least increased through thus acquiring existence outside my concept.

By whatever and by however many predicates we may think a thing —even if we completely determine it—we do not make the least addition to the thing when we further declare that this thing *is*. Otherwise, it would not be exactly the same thing that exists, but something more than we had thought in the concept; and we could not, therefore, say that the exact object of my concept exists. If we think in a thing every feature of reality except one, the missing reality is not added by my saying that this defective thing exists. On the contrary, it exists with the same defect with which I have thought it, since otherwise what exists would be something different from what I thought. When, therefore, I think a being as the supreme reality, without any defect, the question still remains whether it exists or not. For though, in my concept, nothing may be lacking of the possible real content of a thing in general, something is still lacking in its relation to my whole state of thought, namely, [in so far as I am unable to assert] that knowledge of this object is also possible *a posteriori*. And here we find the source of our present difficulty. Were we dealing with an object of the senses, we could not confound the existence of the thing with the mere concept of it. For through the concept the object is thought only as conforming to the *universal conditions* of possible empirical knowledge in general, whereas through its existence it is thought as belonging to the context of experience as a whole. In being thus connected with the *content* of experience as a whole, the concept of the object is not, however, in the least enlarged; all that has happened is that our thought has thereby obtained an additional possible perception. It is not, therefore, surprising that, if we attempt to think existence through the pure category alone, we cannot specify a single mark distinguishing it from mere possibility.

Whatever, therefore, and however much our concept of an object may contain, we must go outside it, if we are to ascribe existence to the object. In the case of objects of the senses, this takes place through their connection with some one of our perceptions, in accordance with empirical laws. But in dealing with objects of pure thought, we have no means whatsoever of knowing their existence, since it would have to be known in a completely *a priori* manner. Our consciousness of all existence (whether immediately through perception, or mediately through inferences which connect something with perception) belongs exclusively to the unity of experience; any [alleged] existence outside this field, while not indeed such as we can declare to be absolutely impossible, is of the nature of an assumption which we can never be in a position to justify.

The concept of a supreme being is in many respects a very useful idea; but just because it is a mere idea, it is altogether incapable, by itself alone, of enlarging our knowledge in regard to what exists. It is not even competent to enlighten us as to the *possibility* of any existence beyond that which is known in and through experience. The analytic criterion of possibility, as consisting in the principle that bare positives (realities) give rise to no contradiction, cannot be denied to it. But since the realities are not given to us in their specific characters; since even if they were, we should still not be in a position to pass judgment; since the criterion of the possibility of synthetic knowledge is never to be looked for save in experience, to which the object of an idea cannot belong, the connection of all real properties in a thing is a synthesis, the possibility of which we are unable to determine *a priori*. And thus the celebrated Leibniz is far from having succeeded in what he plumed himself on achieving—the comprehension *a priori* of the possibility of this sublime ideal being.

The attempt to establish the existence of a supreme being by means of the famous ontological argument of Descartes is therefore merely so much labor and effort lost; we can no more extend our stock of [theoretical] insight by mere ideas, than a merchant can better his position by adding a few noughts to his cash account.

Section 5: The Impossibility of a Cosmological Proof of the Existence of God

To attempt to extract from a purely arbitrary idea the existence of an object corresponding to it is a quite unnatural procedure and a mere innovation of scholastic subtlety. Such an attempt would never have been made if there had not been antecedently, on the part of our reason, the need to assume as a basis of existence in general something necessary (in which our regress may terminate); and if, since this necessity must be unconditioned and certain *a priori,* reason had not, in consequence, been forced to seek a concept which would satisfy, if possible, such a demand, and enable us to know an existence in a completely *a priori* manner. Such a concept was supposed to have been found in the idea of an *ens realissimum;* and that idea was therefore used only for the more definite knowledge of that necessary being, of the necessary existence of which we were already convinced, or persuaded, on other grounds. This natural procedure of reason was, however, concealed from view, and instead of ending with this concept, the attempt was made to begin with it, and so to deduce from it that necessity of existence which it was only fitted to supplement. Thus arose the unfortunate ontological proof, which yields satisfaction neither to the natural and healthy understanding nor to the more academic demands of strict proof.

The *cosmological proof,* which we are now about to examine, retains the connection of absolute necessity with the highest reality, but instead of reasoning, like the former proof, from the highest reality to necessity of existence, it reasons from the previously given unconditioned necessity of some being to the unlimited reality of that being. It thus enters upon a course of reasoning which, whether rational or only pseudo-rational, is at any rate natural, and the most convincing not only for common sense but even for speculative understanding. It also sketches the first outline of all the proofs in natural theology, an outline which has always been and always will be followed, however much embellished and disguised by superfluous additions. This proof, termed by Leibniz the proof *a contingentia mundi,* we shall now proceed to expound and examine.

It runs thus: If anything exists, an absolutely necessary being must also exist. Now I, at least, exist. Therefore an absolutely necessary being exists. The minor premiss contains an experience, the major premiss the inference from there being any experience at all to the existence of the necessary. The proof therefore really begins with experience, and is not wholly *a priori* or ontological. For this reason, and because the object of all possible experience is called the world, it is entitled the *cosmological* proof. Since, in dealing with the objects of experience, the proof abstracts from all special properties through which this world may differ from any other possible world, the title also serves to distinguish it from the physico-theological proof, which is based upon observations of the particular properties of the world disclosed to us by our senses.

The proof then proceeds as follows: The necessary being can be determined in one way only, that is, by one out of each possible pair of opposed predicates. It must therefore be *completely* determined through its own concept. Now there is only one possible concept which determines a thing completely *a priori,* namely, the concept of the *ens realissimum.* The concept of the *ens realissimum* is therefore the only concept through which a necessary being can be thought. In other words, a supreme being necessarily exists.

In this cosmological argument there are combined so many pseudo-rational principles that speculative reason seems in this case to have brought to bear all the resources of its dialectical skill to produce the greatest possible transcendental illusion. The testing of the argument may meantime be postponed while we detail in order the various devices whereby an old argument is disguised as a new one, and by which appeal is made to the agreement of two witnesses, the one with credentials of pure reason and the other with those of experience. In reality the only witness is that which speaks in the name of pure reason; in the endeavor to pass as a second witness it merely changes its dress and voice. In order to lay a secure foundation for itself, this proof takes its stand on experience, and thereby makes profession of being distinct from the ontological proof, which puts its entire trust in pure *a priori* concepts. But the cosmological proof uses this experience only for a single step in the argument, namely, to conclude the existence of a necessary being. What properties this being may have, the empirical premiss cannot tell us. Reason therefore abandons experience altogether, and endeavors to discover from mere concepts what properties an absolutely necessary being must have, that is, which among all possible things contains in itself the conditions (*requisita*) essential to absolute necessity. Now these, it is supposed, are nowhere to be found save in the concept of an *ens realissimum*; and the conclusion is therefore drawn, that the *ens realissimum* is the absolutely necessary being. But it is evident that we are here presupposing that the concept of the highest reality is completely adequate to the concept of absolute necessity of existence; that is, that the latter can be inferred from the former. Now this is the proposition maintained by the ontological proof; it is here being assumed in the cosmological proof, and indeed made the basis of the proof; and yet it is an assumption with which this latter proof has professed to dispense. For absolute necessity is an existence determined from mere concepts. If I say, the concept of the *ens realissimum* is a concept, and indeed the only concept, which is appropriate and adequate to necessary existence, I must also admit that necessary existence can be inferred from this concept. Thus the so-called cosmological proof really owes any cogency which it may have to the ontological proof from mere concepts. The appeal to experience is quite superfluous; experience may perhaps lead us to the concept of absolute necessity, but is unable to demonstrate this necessity as belonging to any determinate thing. For immediately we endeavor to do so, we must abandon all experience and search among pure concepts to discover whether any one of them contains the conditions of the possibility of an absolutely necessary being. If in this way we can determine the possibility of a necessary being, we likewise establish its existence. For what we are then saying is this; that of all possible beings there is one which carries with it absolute necessity, that is, that this being exists with absolute necessity.

Fallacious and misleading arguments are most easily detected if set out in correct syllogistic form. This we now proceed to do in the instance under discussion.

If the proposition, that every absolutely necessary being is likewise the most real of all beings, is correct (and this is the *nervus probandi* of the cosmological proof), it must, like all affirmative judgments, be convertible, at least *per accidens*. It therefore follows that some *entia realissima* are likewise absolutely necessary beings. But one *ens realissimum* is in no respect different from another, and what is true of *some* under this concept is true also of *all*. In this case, therefore, I can convert the proposition *simpliciter,* not only *per accidens,* and say that every *ens realissimum* is a necessary being. But since this proposition is determined from its *a priori* concepts alone, the mere concept of the *ens realissimum* must carry with it the absolute necessity of that being; and this is precisely what the ontological proof has asserted and what the cosmological proof has refused to admit, although the conclusions of the latter are indeed covertly based on it.

Thus the second path upon which speculative reason enters in its attempt to prove the existence of a supreme being is not only as deceptive as the first, but has this additional defect, that it is guilty of an *ignoratio elenchi*. It professes to lead us by a new path, but after a short circuit brings us back to the very path which we had deserted at its bidding.

I have stated that in this cosmological argument there lies hidden a whole nest of dialectical assumptions, which the transcendental critique can easily detect and destroy. These deceptive principles I shall merely enumerate, leaving to the reader, who by this time will be sufficiently expert in these matters, the task of investigating them further, and of refuting them.

We find, for instance, (1) the transcendental principle whereby from the contingent we infer a cause. This principle is applicable only in the sensible world; outside that world it has no meaning whatsoever. For the mere intellectual concept of the contingent cannot give rise to any synthetic proposition, such as that of causality. The principle of causality has no meaning and no criterion for its application save only in the sensible world. But in the cosmological proof it is precisely in order to enable us to advance beyond the sensible world that it is employed. (2) The inference to a first cause, from the impossibility of an infinite series of causes, given one after the other, in the sensible world. The principles of the employment of reason do not justify this conclusion even within the world of experience, still less beyond this world in a realm into which this series can never be extended. (3) The unjustified self-satisfaction of reason in respect of the completion of this series. The removal of all the conditions without which no concept of necessity is possible is taken by reason to be a completion of the concept of the series, on the ground that we can then conceive nothing further. (4) The confusion between the logical possibility of a concept of all reality united into one (without inner contradiction) and the transcendental possibility of such a reality. In the case of the latter there is needed a principle to establish the practicability of such a synthesis, a principle which itself, however, can apply only to the field of possible experiences—etc. . . .

Section 6: The Impossibility of the Physico-theological Proof

If, then, neither the concept of things in general nor the experience of any *existence in general* can supply what is required, it remains only to try whether a *determinate experience,* the experience of the things of the present world, and the constitution and order of these, does not provide the basis of a proof which may help us to attain to an assured conviction of a supreme being. Such proof we propose to entitle the *physico-theological.* Should this attempt also fail, it must follow that no satisfactory proof of the existence of a being corresponding to our transcendental idea can be possible by pure speculative reason.

In view of what has already been said, it is evident that we can count upon a quite easy and conclusive answer to this enquiry. For how can any experience ever be adequate to an idea? The peculiar nature of the latter consists just in the fact that no experience can ever be equal to it. The transcendental idea of a necessary and all-sufficient original being is so overwhelmingly great, so high above everything empirical, the latter being always conditioned, that it leaves us at a loss, partly because we can never find in experience material sufficient to satisfy such a concept, and partly because it is always in the sphere of the conditioned that we carry out our search, seeking there ever vainly for the unconditioned—no law of any empirical synthesis giving us an example of any such unconditioned or providing the least guidance in its pursuit. . . .

This world presents to us so immeasurable a stage of variety, order, purposiveness, and beauty, as displayed alike in its infinite extent and in the unlimited divisibility of its parts, that even with such knowledge as our weak understanding can acquire of it, we are brought face to face with so many marvels immeasurably great, that all speech loses its force, all numbers their power to measure, our thoughts themselves all definiteness, and that our judgment of the whole resolves itself into an amazement which is speechless, and only the more eloquent on that account. Everywhere we see a chain of effects and causes, of ends and means, a regularity in origination and dissolution. Nothing has of itself come into the condition in which we find it to exist, but always points to something else as its cause, while this in turn commits us to repetition of the same enquiry. The whole universe must thus sink into the abyss of nothingness, unless, over and above this infinite chain of contingencies, we assume something to support it—something which is original and independently self-subsistent, and which as the cause of the origin of the universe secures also at the same time its continuance. What magnitude are we to ascribe to this supreme cause—admitting that it is supreme in respect of all things in the world? We are not acquainted with the whole content of the world, still less do we know how to estimate its magnitude by comparison with all that is possible. But since we cannot, as regards causality, dispense with an ultimate and supreme being, what is there to prevent us ascribing to it a degree of perfection that sets it *above everything else that is possible?* This we can easily do—though only through the slender outline of an abstract concept—by representing this being to ourselves as combining in itself all possible perfection, as in a single substance. This concept is in conformity with the demand of our reason for parsimony of principles; it is free from self-contradiction, and is never decisively contradicted by any experience; and it is likewise of such a character that it contributes to the extension of the employment of reason within experience, through the guidance which it yields in the discovery of order and purposiveness.

This proof always deserves to be mentioned with respect. It is the oldest, the clearest, and the most accordant with the common reason of mankind. It enlivens the study of nature, just as it itself derives its existence and gains ever new vigor from that source. It suggests ends and purposes, where our observation would not have detected them by itself, and extends our knowledge of nature by means of the guiding-concept of a special unity, the principle of which is outside nature. This knowledge again reacts on its cause, namely, upon the idea which has led to it, and so strengthens the belief in a supreme Author [of nature] that the belief acquires the force of an irresistible conviction.

It would therefore not only be uncomforting but utterly vain to attempt to diminish in any way the authority of this argument. Reason, constantly upheld by this ever-increasing evidence, which, though empirical, is yet so powerful, cannot be so depressed through doubts suggested by subtle and abstruse speculation, that it is not at once aroused from the indecision of all melancholy reflection, as from a dream, by one glance at the wonders of nature and the majesty of the universe—ascending from height to height up to the all-highest, from the conditioned to its conditions, up to the supreme and unconditioned Author [of all conditioned being].

But although we have nothing to bring against the rationality and utility of this procedure, but have rather to commend and to further it, we still cannot approve the claims, which this mode of argument would fain advance, to apodeictic certainty and to an assent founded on no special favor or support from other quarters. It cannot hurt the good cause, if the dogmatic language of the overweening sophist be toned down to the more moderate and humble requirements of a belief adequate to quieten our doubts, though not to command unconditional submission. I therefore maintain that the physico-theological proof can never by itself establish the existence of a supreme being, but must always fall back upon the ontological argument to make good its deficiency. It only serves as an introduction to the ontological argument; and the latter therefore contains (in so far as a speculative proof is possible at all) *the one possible ground of proof* with which human reason can never dispense.

The chief points of the physico-theological proof are as follows: (1) In the world we everywhere find clear signs of an order in accordance with a determinate purpose, carried out with great wisdom; and this in a universe which is indescribably varied in content and unlimited in extent. (2) This purposive order is quite alien to the things of the world, and only belongs to them contingently; that is to say, the diverse things could not of themselves have cooperated, by so great a combination of diverse means, to the fulfilment of determinate final purposes, had they not been chosen and designed for these purposes by an ordering rational principle in conformity with underlying ideas. (3) There exists, therefore, a sublime and wise cause (or more than one), which must be the cause of the world not merely as a blindly working all-powerful nature, by *fecundity,* but as intelligence, through *freedom.* (4) The unity of this cause may be inferred from the unity of the reciprocal relations existing between the parts of the world as members of an artfully arranged structure—inferred with certainty in so far as our observation suffices for its verification, and beyond these limits with probability, in accordance with the principles of analogy.

We need not here criticize natural reason too strictly in regard to its conclusion from the analogy between certain natural products and what our human art produces when we do violence to nature, and constrain it to proceed not according to its own ends but in conformity with ours—appealing to the similarity of these particular natural products with houses, ships, watches. Nor need we here question its conclusion that there lies at the basis of nature a causality similar to that responsible for artificial products, namely, an understanding and a will; and that the inner possibility of a self-acting nature (which is what makes all art, and even, it may be, reason itself, possible) is therefore derived from another, though superhuman, art—a mode of reasoning which could not perhaps withstand a searching transcendental criticism. But at any rate we must admit that, if we are to specify a cause at all, we cannot here proceed more securely than by analogy with those purposive productions of which alone the cause and mode of action are fully known to us. Reason could never be justified in abandoning the causality which it knows for grounds of explanation which are obscure, of which it does not have any knowledge, and which are incapable of proof.

On this method of argument, the purposiveness and harmonious adaptation of so much in nature can suffice to prove the contingency of the form merely, not of the matter, that is, not of the substance in the world. To prove the latter we should have to demonstrate that the things in the world would not of themselves be capable of such order and harmony, in accordance with universal laws, if they were not *in their substance* the product of supreme wisdom. But to prove this we should require quite other grounds of proof than those which are derived from the analogy with human art. The utmost, therefore, that the argument can prove is an *architect* of the world who is always very much hampered by the adaptability of the material in which he works, not a *creator* of the world to whose idea everything is subject. This, however, is altogether inadequate to the lofty purpose which we have before our eyes, namely, the proof of an all-sufficient primordial being. To prove the contingency of matter itself, we should have to resort to a transcendental argument, and this is precisely what we have here set out to avoid.

The inference, therefore, is that the order and purposiveness everywhere observable throughout the world may be regarded as a completely contingent arrangement, and that we may argue to the existence of a cause *proportioned* to it. But the concept of this cause must enable us to know something quite *determinate* about it, and can therefore be no other than the concept of a being who possesses all might, wisdom, etc., in a word, all the perfection which is proper to an all-sufficient being. For the predicates—"very great," "astounding," "immeasurable" in power and excellence—give no determinate concept at all, and do not really tell us what the thing is in itself. They are only relative representations of the magnitude of the object, which the observer, in contemplating the world, compares with himself and with his capacity of comprehension, and which are equally terms of eulogy whether we be magnifying the object or be depreciating the observing subject in relation to that object. Where we are concerned with the magnitude (of the perfection) of a thing, there is no determinate concept except that which comprehends all possible perfection; and in that concept only the allness (*omnitudo*) of the reality is completely determined.

Now no one, I trust, will be so bold as to profess that he comprehends the relation of the magnitude of the world as he has observed it (alike as regards both extent and content) to omnipotence, of the world order to supreme wisdom, of the world unity to the absolute unity of its Author, etc. Physico-theology is therefore unable to give any determinate concept of the supreme cause of the world, and cannot therefore serve as the foundation of a theology which is itself in turn to form the basis of religion.

To advance to absolute totality by the empirical road is utterly impossible. None the less this is what is attempted in the physico-theological proof. What, then, are the means which have been adopted to bridge this wide abyss?

The physico-theological argument can indeed lead us to the point of admiring the greatness, wisdom, power, etc., of the Author of the world, but can take us no further. Accordingly, we then abandon the argument from empirical grounds of proof, and fall back upon the contingency which, in the first steps of the argument, we had inferred from the order and purposiveness of the world. With this contingency as our sole premiss, we then advance, by means of transcendental concepts alone, to the existence of an absolutely necessary being, and [as a final step] from the concept of the absolute necessity of the first cause to the completely determinate or determinable concept of that necessary being, namely, to the concept of an all-embracing reality. Thus the physico-theological proof, failing in its undertaking, has in face of this difficulty suddenly fallen back upon the cosmological proof; and since the latter is only a disguised ontological proof, it has really achieved its purpose by pure reason alone—although at the start it disclaimed all kinship with pure reason and professed to establish its conclusions on convincing evidence derived from experience.

Those who propound the physico-theological argument have therefore no ground for being so contemptuous in their attitude to the transcendental mode of proof, posing as clear-sighted students of nature, and complacently looking down upon that proof as the artificial product of obscure speculative refinements. For were they willing to scrutinize their own procedure, they would find that, after advancing some considerable way on the solid ground of nature and experience, and finding themselves just as far distant as ever from the object which discloses itself to their reason, they suddenly leave this ground, and pass over into the realm of mere possibilities, where they hope upon the wings of ideas to draw near to the object—the object that has refused itself to all their *empirical* enquiries. For after this tremendous leap, when they have, as they think, found firm ground, they extend their concept—the *determinate* concept, into the possession of which they have now come, they know not how—over the whole sphere of creation. And the ideal, [which this reasoning thus involves, and] which is entirely a product of pure reason, they then elucidate by reference to experience, though inadequately enough, and in a manner far below the dignity of its object; and throughout they persist in refusing to admit that they have arrived at this knowledge or hypothesis by a road quite other than that of experience.

Thus the physico-theological proof of the existence of an original or supreme being rests upon the cosmological proof, and the cosmological upon the ontological. And since, besides these three, there is no other path open to speculative reason, the ontological proof from pure concepts of reason is the only possible one, if indeed any proof of a proposition so far exalted above all empirical employment of the understanding is possible at all.

APPENDIX TO THE TRANSCENDENTAL DIALECTIC
The Regulative Employment of the Ideas of Pure Reason

[Since the transcendental ideas are formed inevitably by the power of reason, they must have a function, a proper *immanent* use, as well as their *transcendent* misuse. They do not have a constitutive, but only a regulative employment, which is, indeed, indispensable: "that of directing the understanding toward a certain goal upon which the routes marked out by all its rules converge, as upon their point of intersection."]

If we consider in its whole range the knowledge obtained for us by the understanding, we find that what is peculiarly distinctive of reason in its attitude to this body of knowledge is that it prescribes and seeks to achieve its *systematization,* that is, to exhibit the connection of its parts in conformity with a single principle. This unity of reason always presupposes an idea, namely, that of the form of a whole of knowledge—a whole which is prior to the determinate knowledge of the parts and which contains the conditions that determine *a priori* for every part its position and relation to the other parts. This idea accordingly postulates a complete unity in the knowledge obtained by the understanding, by which this knowledge is to be not a mere contingent aggregate, but a system connected according to necessary laws. We may not say that this idea is a concept of the object, but only of the thoroughgoing unity of such concepts, in so far as that unity serves as a rule for the understanding. These concepts of reason are not derived from nature; on the contrary, we interrogate nature in accordance with these ideas, and consider our knowledge as defective so long as it is not adequate to them. . . .

The Final Purpose of the Natural Dialectic of Human Reason

. . . There is a great difference between something being given to my reason as an *object absolutely,* or merely as an *object in the idea.* In the former case our concepts are employed to determine the object;

in the latter case there is in fact only a schema for which no object, not even a hypothetical one, is directly given, and which only enables us to represent to ourselves other objects in an indirect manner, namely in their systematic unity, by means of their relation to this idea. Thus I say that the concept of a highest intelligence is a mere idea, that is to say, its objective reality is not to be taken as consisting in its referring directly to an object (for in that sense we should not be able to justify its objective validity). It is only a schema constructed in accordance with the conditions of the greatest possible unity of reason—the schema of the concept of a thing in general, which serves only to secure the greatest possible systematic unity in the empirical employment of our reason. We then, as it were, derive the object of experience from the supposed object of this idea, viewed as the ground or cause of the object of experience. We declare, for instance, that the things of the world must be viewed *as if* they received their existence from a highest intelligence. The idea is thus really only a heuristic, not an ostensive, concept. It does not show us how an object is constituted, but how, under its guidance, we should *seek* to determine the constitution and connection of the objects of experience. If, then, it can be shown that the three transcendental ideas (the psychological, the cosmological, and the theological), although they do not directly relate to, or determine, any object corresponding to them, none the less, as rules of the empirical employment of reason, lead us to systematic unity, under the presupposition of such an *object in the idea*; and that they thus contribute to the extension of empirical knowledge, without ever being in a position to run counter to it, we may conclude that it is a necessary maxim of reason to proceed always in accordance with such ideas. This, indeed, is the transcendental deduction of all ideas of speculative reason, not as *constitutive* principles for the extension of our knowledge to more objects than experience can give, but as *regulative* principles of the systematic unity of the manifold of empirical knowledge in general, whereby this empirical knowledge is more adequately secured within its own limits and more effectively improved than would be possible, in the absence of such ideas, through the employment merely of the principles of the understanding.

I shall endeavor to make this clearer. In conformity with these ideas as principles we shall, *first,* in psychology, under the guidance of inner experience, connect all the appearances, all the actions and receptivity of our mind, *as if* the mind were a simple substance which persists with personal identity (in this life at least), while its states, to which those of the body belong only as outer conditions, are in continual change. *Secondly,* in cosmology, we must follow up the conditions of both inner and outer natural appearances, in an enquiry which is to be regarded as never allowing of completion, just *as if* the series of appearances were in itself endless, without any first or supreme member. We need not, in so doing, deny that, outside all appearances, there are purely intelligible grounds of the appearances; but as we have no knowledge of these whatsoever, we must never attempt to make use of them in our explanations of nature. *Thirdly,* and finally, in the domain of theology, we must view everything that can belong to the context of possible experience *as if* this experience formed an absolute but at the same time completely dependent and *sensibly* conditioned unity, and yet also at the same time *as if* the sum of all appearances (the sensible world itself) had a single, highest and all-sufficient ground beyond itself, namely, a self-subsistent, original, creative reason. For it is in the light of this idea of a creative reason that we so guide the empirical employment of *our* reason as to secure its greatest possible extension—that is, by viewing all objects *as if* they drew their origin from such an archetype. In other words, we ought not to derive the inner appearances of the soul from a simple thinking substance but from one another, in accordance with the idea of a simple being; we ought not to derive the order and systematic unity of the world from a supreme intelligence, but to obtain from the idea of a supremely wise cause the rule according to which reason in connecting empirical causes and effects in the world may be employed to best advantage, and in such manner as to secure satisfaction of its own demands. . . .

[The highest concept of systematic formal unity that reason can derive from its ideas is that of *purpose,* and it is in thinking of nature as purposeful (as having been designed by a supreme intelligence) that it supplies its ultimate guiding maxim to empirical science: Search (not only for mechanical, but also) for teleological laws!]

If, in connection with a transcendental theology, we ask, *first,* whether there is anything distinct from the world, which contains the ground of the order of the world and of its connection in accordance with universal laws, the answer is that there *undoubtedly* is. . . . If, *secondly,* the question be, whether this being is substance, of the greatest reality, necessary, etc., we reply that *this question is entirely without meaning.* For all categories through which we can attempt to form a concept of such an object allow only of empirical employment, and have no meaning whatsoever when not applied to objects of possible experience, that is, to the world of sense. . . . If, *thirdly*, the question be, whether we may not at least think this being, which is distinct from the world, in *analogy* with the objects of experience, the answer is: certainly, but only as object in *idea* and not in reality, namely, only as being a substratum, to us unknown, of the systematic unity, order, and purposiveness of the arrangement of the world— an idea which reason is constrained to form as the regulative principle of its investigation of nature. . . .

But the question may still be pressed: Can we, on such grounds, assume a wise and omnipotent Author of the world? *Undoubtedly* we may; and we not only may, but *must,* do so. But do we then extend our knowledge beyond the field of possible experience? *By no means.* All that we have done is merely to presuppose a something, a merely transcendental object, of which, as it is in itself, we have no concept whatsoever. It is only in relation to the systematic and purposive ordering of the world, which, if we are to study nature, we are constrained to presuppose, that we have thought this unknown being *by analogy* with an intelligence (an empirical concept); that is, have endowed it, in respect of the ends and perfection which are to be grounded upon it, with just those properties which, in conformity with the conditions of our reason, can be regarded as containing the ground of such systematic unity. This idea is thus valid only in respect of the *employment* of our reason *in reference to the world.* . . .

But, it will still be asked, can I make any such use of the concept and of the presupposition of a supreme being in the rational consideration of the world? Yes, it is precisely for this purpose that reason has resorted to this idea. But may I then proceed to regard seemingly purposive arrangements as purposes, and so derive them from the divine will, though, of course, mediately through certain special natural means, themselves established in furtherance of that divine will? Yes, we can indeed do so; but only on condition that we regard it as a matter of indifference whether it be asserted that divine wisdom has disposed all things in accordance with its supreme ends, or that the idea of supreme wisdom is a regulative principle in the investigation of nature and a principle of its systematic and purposive unity, in accordance with universal laws, even in those cases in which we are unable to detect that unity. In other words, it must be a matter of complete indifference to us, when we perceive such unity, whether we say that God in his wisdom has willed it to be so, or that nature has wisely arranged it thus. . . .

Supplementary Passages

1

The Good Will and the Categorical Imperative

Section 1

Nothing can possibly be conceived in the world, or even out of it, which can be called good without qualification, except a GOOD WILL. Intelligence, wit, judgment, and the other *talents* of the mind, however they may be named, or courage, resolution, perseverance, as qualities of temperament, are undoubtedly good and desirable in many respects. But these gifts of nature may also become extremely bad and mischievous if the will which is to make use of these gifts, and which therefore constitutes what is called *character,* is not good. It is the same with the *gifts of fortune.* Power, riches, honor, even health, and the general well-being and contentment with one's condition which is called *happiness,* all inspire pride and often presumption if there is not a good will to correct the influence of these on the mind, and with this to rectify also the whole principle of acting and adapt it to its end. The sight of a being, not adorned with a single feature of a pure and good will, enjoying unbroken prosperity can never give pleasure to an impartial rational spectator. Thus a good will appears to constitute the indispensable condition for being even worthy of happiness. . . .

A good will is good not because of what it performs or effects, nor by its aptness for attaining some proposed end, but simply by virtue of the volition; that is, it is good in itself and when considered by itself is to be esteemed much higher than all that it can bring about in pursuing any inclination, nay even in pursuing the sum total of all inclinations. It might happen that, owing to special misfortune, or to the niggardly provision of a step-motherly nature, this will should wholly lack power to accomplish its purpose. If with its greatest efforts this will should yet achieve nothing and there should remain only good will (to be sure, not a mere wish but the summoning of all means in our power), then, like a jewel, good will would still shine by its own light as a thing having its whole value in itself.

We assume, as a fundamental principle, that no organ [designed] for any purpose will be found in the physical constitution of an organized being, except one which is also the fittest and best adapted for that purpose. Now if the proper object of nature for a being with reason and a will was its *preservation,* its *welfare,* in a word its happiness, then nature would have hit upon a very bad arrangement when it selected the reason of the creature to carry out this function. For all the actions which the creature has to perform with a view to this purpose, and the whole rule of its conduct would be far more surely prescribed by [its own] instinct, and that end [happiness] would have been attained by instinct far more certainly than it ever can be by reason. . . . Nevertheless, reason is imparted to us as a practical faculty; that is, as one which is to have influence on the *will.* Therefore, if we admit that nature generally in the distribution of natural propensities has adapted the means to the end, nature's true intention must be to produce a *will,* which is not merely good as a *means* to something else but *good in itself.* Reason is absolutely necessary for this sort of will. . . .

[The analysis of the notion of a will that is good in itself reveals the notion of duty, or moral obligation, which all rational beings possess. And we clearly distinguish actions performed *in accordance with* duty (though from a prudential or utilitarian motive) from actions performed *out of respect for* duty: that is, actions performed not only *as,* but *because,* duty requires. Kant's first main proposition, then, is that only actions performed specifically for the sake of duty possess "true moral worth."]

The second proposition is: That an action done from duty derives its moral worth, *not from the purpose* which is to be attained by it, but from the maxim by which it is determined. Therefore the action does not depend on the realization of its objective, but merely on the *principle* of volition by which the action has taken place, without regard to any object of desire. . . .

The third proposition, which is a consequence of the preceding two, I would express thus: *Duty is the necessity of an action, resulting from respect for the law.* . . .

But what sort of law can it be the conception of which must determine the will, even without our paying any attention to the effect expected from it, in order that this will may be called good absolutely and without qualification? As I have stripped the will of every impulse which could arise for it from obedience to any law, there remains nothing but the general conformity of the will's actions to law in general. Only this conformity to law is to serve the will as a principle; that is, I am never to act in any way other than *so I could*

want my maxim also to become a general law. It is the simple conformity to law in general, without assuming any particular law applicable to certain actions, that serves the will as its principle, and
must so serve it, if duty is not to be a vain delusion and a chimerical
notion. . . . It is a wholly different thing to be truthful from a sense
of duty, than to be so from apprehension of injurious consequences.
In the first case, the very conceiving of the action already implies a
law for me; in the second case, I must first look about elsewhere to
see what results may be associated with it which would affect me. For
it is beyond all doubt wicked to deviate from the principle of duty;
but to be unfaithful to my maxim of prudence may often be very
advantageous to me, although it is certainly wiser to abide by it. However, the shortest way, and an unerring one, to discover the answer to
this question of whether a lying promise is consistent with duty, is to
ask myself, "Would I be content if this maxim of extricating myself
from difficulty by a false promise held good as a general law for others
as well as for myself?" Would I care to say to myself, "Everyone
may make a deceitful promise when he finds himself in a difficulty
from which he cannot extricate himself otherwise"? Then I would
presently become aware that while I can decide in favor of the lie, I
can by no means decide that lying should be a general law. For under
such a law there would be no promises at all, since I would state my
intentions in vain in regard to my future actions to those who would
not believe my allegation, or, if they did so too hastily, they would
pay me back in my own coin. Hence, as soon as such a maxim was
made a universal law, it would necessarily destroy itself. . . .

Section 2

The concept of an objective principle, in so far as it is compulsory
for a will, is called a command of reason and the formulation of such
a command is called an IMPERATIVE.

All imperatives are expressed by the word *ought* (*or shall*) and they
indicate thereby the relation of an objective law of reason to a will,
which, because of its subjective constitution, is not necessarily determined by this [compulsion]. . . .

All *imperatives* command either *hypothetically* or *categorically*. . . .
Since every practical law represents a possible action as good, and on
this account as necessary for a subject who can determine practically
by reason, all imperatives are formulations determining an action
which is necessary according to the principle of a will in some respects

good. If the action is good only as a means *to something else,* then the imperative is *hypothetical.* If the action is conceived as good *in itself* and consequently as necessarily being the principle of a will which of itself conforms to reason then it is *categorical.*

Therefore we shall have to investigate *a priori* the possibility of a *categorical* imperative, since, in this case, we do not have the advantage that the imperative's reality is given in experience, so that the elucidation of its possibility would be needed only for explaining it, not for establishing it. It can be discerned that the categorical imperative has the purport of a practical law. All the rest may certainly be called *principles* of the will but not laws, since whatever is merely necessary for attaining some casual purpose may be considered contingent in itself, and at any time we can be free from the precept if we give up the purpose. However, the unconditional command leaves the will no liberty to choose the opposite, and consequently only the will carries with it that necessity we require in a law. . . .

When I conceive of a hypothetical imperative at all, I do not know previously what it will contain until I am given the condition. But when I conceive of a categorical imperative I know at once what it contains. In addition to the law, the imperative contains only the necessity that the maxim conform to this law. As the maxim contains no condition restricting the maxim, nothing remains but the general statement of the law to which the maxim of the action should conform, and it is only this conformity that the imperative properly represents as necessary.

Therefore there is only one categorical imperative, namely this: *Act only on a maxim by which you can will that it, at the same time, should become a general law.*

Now, if all imperatives of duty can be deduced from this one imperative as easily as from their principle, then we shall be able at least to show what we understand by it and what this concept means, although it would remain undecided whether what is called duty is not just a vain notion.

Since the universality of the law constitutes what is properly called *nature* in the most general sense [as to form]; that is, the existence of things as far as determined by general laws, the general imperative of duty may be expressed thus: *Act as if the maxim of your action were to become by your will a general law of nature.*

We will now enumerate a few duties, adopting the usual division of duties to ourselves and to others, and of perfect and imperfect duties.

1. A man, while reduced to despair by a series of misfortunes and

feeling wearied of life, is still so far in possession of his reason that he can ask himself whether it would not be contrary to his duty to himself to take his own life. Now he enquires whether the maxim of his action could become a general law of nature. His maxim is: Out of self-love I consider it a principle to shorten my life when continuing it is likely to bring more misfortune than satisfaction. The question then simply is whether this principle of self-love could become a general law of nature. Now we see at once that a system of nature, whose law would be to destroy life by the very feeling designed to compel the maintenance of life, would contradict itself, and therefore could not exist as a system of nature; hence that maxim cannot possibly be a general law of nature and consequently it would be wholly inconsistent with the supreme principle of all duty.

2. Another man finds himself forced by dire need to borrow money. He knows that he will not be able to repay it, but he also sees that nothing will be lent him unless he promises firmly to repay it within a definite time. He would like to make this promise but he still has enough conscience to ask himself: Is it not unlawful and contrary to my duty to get out of a difficulty in this way? However, suppose that he does decide to do so, the maxim of his action would then be expressed thus: When I consider myself in want of money, I shall borrow money and promise to repay it although I know that I never can. Now this principle of self-love or of one's own advantage may perhaps be agreeable to my whole future well-being; but the question is now: Is it right? Here I change the suggestion of self-love into a general law and state the question thus: How would it be if my maxim were a general law? I then realize at once that it could never hold as a general law of nature but would necessarily contradict itself. For if it were a general law that anyone considering himself to be in difficulties would be able to promise whatever he pleases intending not to keep his promise, the promise itself and its object would become impossible since no one would believe that anything was promised him, but would ridicule all such statements as vain pretenses. . . .

Now, if a supreme practical principle ought to exist, or a categorical imperative with respect to the human will, it must be one which turns the concept of what is necessarily an end for everybody because it is *an end in itself* into an *objective* principle of the will which can serve as a general practical law. The basis of this principle is that *rational nature exists as an end in itself.* Man necessarily conceives his own existence as being this rational nature, to the extent that it is a *subjective* principle of human actions. But every other rational being regards its existence similarly for the same rational reason that holds true for me, so at the same time it is an objective principle from which, as a supreme practical ground, all laws of the will must needs be deductible. Accordingly, the practical imperative will be as follows: *Act so as to treat man, in your own person as well as in that of anyone else, always as an end, never merely as a means.* We shall now enquire whether this principle can be realized.

To use the previous examples:

First: In regard to the concept of necessary duty to oneself, whoever contemplates suicide will ask himself whether his action is consistent with the idea of man as *an end in itself.* If he destroys himself to escape onerous conditions, he uses a person merely as a *means* to maintain a tolerable condition until life ends. But man is not a thing, that is to say, something which can be used *merely* as means, but in all his actions must always be considered as an end in itself. Therefore I cannot dispose in any way of man in my own person so as to mutilate, damage or kill him. (It is a matter of morals proper to define this principle more precisely to avoid all misunderstanding. Therefore I bypass such questions as that of the amputation of the limbs in order to preserve one's life, and of exposing one's life to danger with a view to preserving it, etc.)

Second: As regards necessary or obligatory duties toward others, whoever is thinking of making a lying promise to others will see at once that he would be using another man *merely as a means,* without the latter being the end in itself at the same time. The person whom I propose to use by such a promise for my own purposes cannot possibly assent to my way of acting toward him. . . . This conflict with the principle of duty toward others becomes more obvious if we consider examples of attacks on the liberty and property of others. Here it is clear that whoever transgresses the rights of men intends to use the person of others merely as means without considering that as rational beings they shall always be regarded as ends also; that is, as beings who could possibly be the end of the very same action. . . .

Section 3

The *will* is a kind of causality of living beings in so far as they are rational, and *freedom* should be that quality of this causality through which it can be an efficient cause independent of extraneous *determining* causes; just as *physical necessity* is the peculiar quality of the causality of all non-rational beings as impelled into activity by extraneous causes.

The above definition of freedom is *negative* and therefore unsuitable for understanding its essence; but it leads to a *positive* concept which is all the more ample and fruitful. Since the concept of causality implies that of law, according to which something called a cause produces something else called an effect, freedom, though not a quality of the will in so far as it depends on natural laws, is not for that reason without law, but must rather be a causality acting in accordance with immutable laws of a peculiar kind; otherwise free will would be an absurdity. Natural necessity is a heteronomy of efficient causes because every effect if possible only according to the law [of natural causality:] some [antecedent cause] determines the efficient cause to act causally. What else can freedom of the will be but autonomy; that is, the property of the will to be a law unto itself? But the proposition: the will is a law unto itself in every action, only expresses the principle of acting on no other maxim than that which can also aim to be a general law. This is precisely the formula of the categorical imperative and of the principle of ethics, so that a free will and a will subject to moral laws are one and the same. . . .

[FROM the *Metaphysical Foundation of Morals* (or the *Fundamental Principles of the Metaphysic of Morals*), 1785, trans. Carl J. Friedrich in *The Philosophy of Kant*, N. Y.: Modern Library, 1949. Copyright, 1949, by Random House, Inc. Reprinted by permission of Random House, Inc.]

2

The Postulates of Practical Reason

I. *The Antinomy of Practical Reason.* In the *summum bonum* which is practical for us, *i.e.* which to be realized by our will, virtue and happiness are thought as necessarily combined, so that the one cannot be assumed by pure practical reason without the other also being attached to it. Now this combination (like every other) is either analytic or synthetic. It has been shown that it cannot be analytic; it must then be synthetic, and, more particularly, must be conceived as the connection of cause and effect, since it concerns a practical good, i.e. one that is possible by means of action; consequently, either the desire of happiness must be the motive to maxims of virtue, or the maxim of virtue must be the efficient cause of happiness. The first is absolutely impossible, because (as was proved in the Analytic) maxims which place the determining principle of the will in the desire for personal happiness are not moral at all, and no virtue can be founded on them. But the second is also impossible, because the practical connection of causes and effects in the world, as the result of the determination of the will, does not depend upon the moral dispositions of the will, but on the knowledge of the laws of nature and the physical power to use them for one's purposes; consequently, we cannot expect in the world by the most punctilious observance of the moral laws any necessary connection of happiness with virtue adequate to the *summum bonum*. Now as the promotion of this *summum bonum,* the conception of which contains this connection, is *a priori* a necessary object of our will, and inseparably attached to the moral law, the impossibility of the former must prove the falsity of the latter. If then the supreme good is not possible by practical rules, then the moral law also which commands us to promote it is directed to vain imaginary ends, and must consequently be false.

II. *Critical Solution of the Antinomy of Practical Reason. . . .* The first of the two propositions—that the endeavor after happiness produces a virtuous mind—is absolutely false. But the second—that a virtuous mind necessarily produces happiness—is not absolutely false, but false only in so far as virtue is considered as a form of causality in the sensible world, and consequently only if I suppose existence in it to be the only sort of existence of a rational being; it is therefore only *conditionally* false. But as I am not only justified in thinking that I exist as a noumenon in a world of the understanding, but even have in the moral law a purely intellectual determining principle of my causality (in the sensible world), it is not impossible that morality of mind should have a causal connection with happiness (as an effect in the sensible world), if not immediate, then mediated by an intelligent author of nature, and moreover necessary; while in a system of nature which is merely an object of the senses this combination could never occur except contingently, and therefore could not suffice for the *summum bonum*.

Thus, notwithstanding this seeming conflict of practical reason with itself, the *summum bonum,* which is the necessary supreme end of a will morally determined, is a true object thereof; for it is practically possible, and the maxims of the will which as regards their matter refer to it have objective reality. . . .

III. *On the Primacy of Pure Practical Reason in its Union with the Speculative Reason.* . . . If practical reason could not assume or think as given anything further than what speculative reason of itself could offer it from its own insight, the latter would have primacy. But suppose that it has of itself original *a priori* principles with which certain theoretical positions are inseparably connected, but which are withdrawn from any possible insight of speculative reason (though not contradicting it); then the question is, which interest is the superior—not which must give way, for they do not necessarily conflict. The question is whether speculative reason, which knows nothing of all that the practical offers for its acceptance, should take up these propositions, and (although they transcend it) try to unite them with its own concepts as a foreign possession handed over to it, or whether it is justified in obstinately following its own separate interest and, according to the canon of Epicurus, rejecting as vain subtlety everything that cannot accredit its objective reality by manifest examples shown in experience—no matter how much it is interwoven with the interest of the practical (pure) use of reason, and in itself not incompatible with the theoretical—merely because it infringes on the interest of the speculative reason by removing the bounds that the latter has set for itself, and giving it up to every nonsense or delusion of imagination. . . .

IV. *The Immortality of the Soul as a Postulate of Pure Practical Reason.* The realization of the *summum bonum* in the world is the necessary object of a will determinable by the moral law. But in this will the perfect accordance of the mind with the moral law is the supreme condition of the *summum bonum.* This then must be possible, as well as its object, since it is contained in the command to promote the latter. Now, the perfect accordance of the will with the moral law is *holiness,* a perfection of which no rational being of the sensible world is capable at any moment of his existence. Since, nevertheless, it is required as practically necessary, it can only be found in an infinite progression toward that perfect accordance, and on the principles of pure practical reason it is necessary to assume such a practical progress as the real object of our will.

Now, this infinite progress is only possible on the supposition of an infinite duration of the existence and personality of the same rational being; this is called the immortality of the soul. The *summum bonum,* then, is practically possible only on the supposition of the immortality of the soul; consequently this immortality, being inseparably connected with the moral law, is a postulate of pure practical reason—by which I mean a theoretical proposition which is not demonstrable as such, but which is an inseparable result of an unconditional *a priori* practical law.

This principle of the moral destination of our nature, namely, that it is only in an infinite progress that we can attain perfect accordance with the moral laws, is of the greatest use, not merely for the present purpose of supplementing the impotence of speculative reason, but also with respect to religion. In default of it, either the moral law is quite degraded from its holiness, being made out to be indulgent, and conformable to our convenience, or else men strain their notions of their vocation and their expectation to an unattainable goal, hoping to acquire complete holiness of will, and so lose themselves in fantastic theosophic dreams, which wholly contradict self-knowledge. In both cases the unceasing effort to obey punctually and thoroughly a strict and inflexible command of reason, which yet is not ideal but real, is only hindered. For a rational but finite being, the only thing possible is an endless progress from the lower to higher degrees of moral perfection. The Infinite Being, to whom the condition of time is nothing, sees in this—to us—endless succession a whole that is in accordance with the moral law; and the holiness which His command inexorably requires, in order to be true to His justice in the share which He assigns to each in the *summum bonum,* is to be found in a single intellectual intuition of the whole existence of rational beings. All that can be expected of the creature in respect of the hope of this participation would be the consciousness of his tried character, by which, from the progress he has hitherto made from the worse to the morally better, and the immutability of purpose which has thus become known to him, he may hope for a further unbroken continuance of the same progress, however long his existence may last, even beyond this life; and thus he may hope, not indeed here, nor at any imaginable point of his future existence, but only in the endlessness of his duration (which God alone can survey) to be perfectly adequate to His will, without indulgence or excuse, which do not harmonize with justice.

V. *The Existence of God as a Postulate of Pure Practical Reason.* . . . Happiness is the condition of a rational being in the world with whom everything goes according to his wish and will; it rests, therefore, on the harmony of physical nature with his whole end and with the essential determining principle of his will. Now the moral law as a law of freedom commands by principles that ought to be quite independent of nature and of its harmony with our faculty of desire (as incentive). But the acting rational being in the world is not the cause both of the world and of nature itself. There is not the least ground, therefore, in the moral law for a necessary connection between morality and proportionate happiness in a being which belongs to the world as part of it, and is therefore dependent on it, and which for that reason cannot by his will be a cause of this nature, nor by his own power make it thoroughly harmonize, as far as his happiness is concerned, with his practical principles. Nevertheless, in the practical problem of pure reason, i.e. the necessary pursuit of the *summum bonum,* such a connection is postulated as necessary: we ought to endeavor to promote the *summum bonum,* which, therefore, must be possible. Accordingly, the existence of a cause of all nature, distinct from nature itself, and containing the principle of this connection—namely, of the exact harmony of happiness with morality— is also postulated. Now, this supreme cause must contain the principle of the harmony of nature, not merely with a law of the will of rational beings, but with the conception of this law, in so far as they make it the supreme determining principle of the will, and consequently not merely with the form of morality, but with its motive, that is, with moral character. Therefore, the *summum bonum* is possible in the world only on the supposition of a Supreme Being having a causality corresponding to moral character. Now a being that is capable of acting on the conception of laws is an *intelligence* (a rational being), and the causality of such a being according to this conception of laws is his *will;* therefore the supreme cause of nature, which must be presupposed as a condition of the *summum bonum* is a being which is the cause of nature by intelligence and will, and consequently its author—that is, God. It follows that the postulate of the possibility of the *highest derived good* (the best world) is likewise the postulate of the reality of a *highest original good,* that is to say, of the existence of God. Now it was seen to be a duty for us to promote the *summum bonum*; consequently it is not merely allowable, but it is a necessity connected with duty as a requisite, that we should presuppose the possibility of this *summum bonum;* and as this is possible only on condition of the existence of God, it inseparably connects this supposition with duty; that is, it is morally necessary to assume the existence of God.

It must be remarked here that this moral necessity is subjective (that is, a want), and not objective (that is, itself a duty), for there cannot be a duty to suppose the existence of anything, since this concerns only the theoretical employment of reason. Moreover, it is not meant that it is necessary to suppose the existence of God as a basis of all obligation in general, for this rests, as has been sufficiently proved, simply on the autonomy of reason itself. What belongs to duty here is only the endeavor to realize and promote the *summum bonum* in the world, the possibility of which can therefore be postulated; and as our reason finds it not conceivable except on the supposition of a supreme intelligence, the admission of this existence is therefore connected with the consciousness of our duty, although the admission itself belongs to the domain of speculative reason. Considered in respect of this alone, as a principle of explanation, it may be called a hypothesis, but in reference to the intelligibility of an object given us by the moral law (the *summum bonum*), and consequently as a requirement for practical purposes, it may be called *faith,* that is to say a pure rational faith, since pure reason (both in its theoretical and its practical use) is the sole source from which it springs. . . .

VI. *Of the Postulates of Pure Practical Reason in General.*   These postulates all proceed from the principle of morality, which is not a postulate but a law, by which reason determines the will directly— which will, because it is so determined as a pure will, requires these necessary conditions of obedience to its precept. These postulates are not theoretical dogmas but practically necessary presuppositions; while then they do not extend our speculative knowledge, they give objective reality to the ideas of speculative reason in general (by means of their reference to what is practical), and give it a right to concepts the bare possibility of which it could not otherwise venture to affirm.

These postulates are those of *immortality,* of *freedom* positively considered (as the causality of a being in so far as he belongs to the intelligible world), and of the *existence of God.* The first results from the practically necessary condition of a duration adequate to the complete fulfilment of the moral law; the second from the necessary presupposition of independence from the sensible world and of the faculty of determining one's will according to the law of an intelligible

world, that is, of freedom; the third from the necessary condition of
the existence of the *summum bonum* in such an intelligible world, by
the presupposition of the supreme independent good, that is, the
existence of God. . . .

Thus the fact that respect for the moral law necessarily makes the
summum bonum an object of our endeavors, and the consequent supposition of its objective reality, lead through the postulates of practical reason to concepts which speculative reason might indeed present
as problems, but could never solve. Thus it leads, first, to a problem—namely, that of immortality—in the solution of which speculative reason could only commit *paralogisms,* because it could not lay
hold of the character of permanence, by which to complete the
psychological concept of an ultimate subject necessarily ascribed to
the soul in self-consciousness, so as to make it the real conception of
a substance—a character that practical reason furnishes in the postulate of a duration required for accordance with the moral law in the
summum bonum, which is the whole end of practical reason. Second,
it leads to a concept that speculative reason contained only as an
antinomy, the solution of which it could base only on a notion, indeed
problematically conceivable, but whose objective reality it could not
prove or determine—namely, the cosmological idea of an intelligible
world and the consciousness of our existence in it. It leads to this by
means of the postulate of freedom, the reality of which it lays down
by virtue of the moral law, and with it likewise the law of an intelligible world, to which speculative reason could only point, but whose
concept it could not define. Third, it gives significance to what speculative reason was able to think, but was obliged to leave undetermined
as a mere transcendental *ideal,* viz. the *theological* conception of the
First Being. This significance is given in a practical view, that is, as
a condition of the possibility of the object of a will determined by that
law; it is the supreme principle of the *summum bonum* in an intelligible world, invested with sovereign power by means of moral legislation.

Is our knowledge, however, actually extended in this way by pure
practical reason, and is that immanent in practical reason which for
the speculative was only transcendent? Certainly, but only in a practical point of view. For we do not thereby take knowledge of the
nature of our souls, nor of the intelligible world, nor of the Supreme
Being, as they are in themselves, but we have merely combined the
conceptions of them in the practical concept of the *summum bonum*
as the object of our will, and this altogether *a priori,* but only by

means of the moral law, and merely in reference to it, in respect to the object which it commands. But how freedom is possible, and how we are to conceive this kind of causality theoretically and positively, is not thereby discovered; only that there is such a causality is postulated by and for the moral law. It is the same with the remaining ideas, the possibility of which no human intelligence will ever fathom, but the truth of which, on the other hand, no sophistry will ever wrest from the conviction even of the commonest man.

[FROM the Dialectic of the *Critique of Practical Reason*, 1788, trans. T. K. Abbott, London: Longmans, Green, 6th ed., 1909, with revisions by the present editor]

3

Taste and the Aesthetic Judgment

First Aspect of the Judgment of Taste (Quality).

§ 1. *The judgment of taste is aesthetic.* If we wish to discern whether anything is beautiful or not, we do not refer its image to the object by means of the intellect with a view to knowledge, but by means of the imagination, acting perhaps in conjunction with the intellect, we refer the image to the subject and its feeling of pleasure or displeasure. Therefore the judgment of taste is not an intellectual judgment and so not logical, but is aesthetic—which means that it is one whose determining ground *cannot be other than subjective. . . .*

§ 2. *The delight which determines the judgment of taste is independent of all interest.* The delight which we connect with imagining the real existence of an object is called interest. Such a delight, therefore, always involves a reference to the faculty of desire, either as its determining ground, or else as necessarily implicated with its determining ground. Now, where the question is whether something is beautiful, we do not want to know whether we or anyone else are or even could be concerned in the real existence of the thing, but rather what estimate we form of it on mere contemplation (intuition or reflection). If anyone asks me whether I consider that the palace I see before me is beautiful, I may perhaps reply that I do not care for things that are merely made to be gaped at. Or I may reply in the same strain as that Iroquois *sachem* who said that nothing in Paris pleased him better than the eating-houses. I may even go a step further and inveigh with the vigor of a Rousseau against the vanity of the great who spend the sweat of the people on such superfluous things. Or finally, I may quite easily persuade myself that if I found myself on an uninhabited island without hope of ever again coming among men and could conjure such a palace into existence by a mere wish, I should still not trouble to do so as long as I had a hut there that was comfortable enough for me. All this may be admitted and approved; only it is not the point now at issue. All one wants to know is whether the mere image of the object is to my liking, no matter how indifferent I may be to the real existence of the object of this imagining. It is quite plain that in order to say that the object *is beautiful,* and to show that I have taste, everything turns on the meaning which I can give to this representation, and not on any factor which makes me dependent on the real existence of the object. Everyone must allow that a judgment on the beautiful which is tinged with the slightest interest is very partial and not a pure judgment of taste. One must not be in the least prepossessed in favor of the real existence of the thing, but must preserve complete indifference in this respect, in order to play the part of judge in matters of taste. . . .

Second Aspect of the Judgment of Taste (Quantity):

§ 6. *The beautiful is that which, apart from concepts, is represented as the Object of a* UNIVERSAL *delight.*   This definition of the beautiful is deducible from the foregoing definition of it as an object of delight apart from any interest. For where anyone is conscious that he has delight in an object independent of interest, it is inevitable that he should look on the object as one containing a basis of delight for all men. For, since the delight is not based on any inclination of the subject (or on any other deliberate interests), but the subject feels himself completely *free* in respect to the liking which he accords to the object, he can find as reasons for his delight no personal conditions to which his own subjective self might alone be party. Hence he must regard it as resting on what he may also presuppose in every other person; and therefore he must believe that he has reason for demanding a similar delight from everyone. Accordingly he will speak of the beautiful as if beauty were a quality of the object and the judgment logical (acquiring a knowledge of the object by concepts of it); although it is only aesthetic, and contains merely a reference of the image of the object to the subject; because it still bears this resemblance to the logical judgment, that it may be presupposed to be valid for all men. But this universality cannot spring from concepts. For from concepts there is no transition to the feeling of pleasure or displeasure (save in the case of pure practical laws, which, however, carry an interest with them; and such an interest does not attach to the pure judgment of taste). The result is that the judgment of taste, with its attendant consciousness of detachment from all interest, must involve a claim to validity for all men, and must do so apart from universality attached to objects; i.e., there must be coupled with it a claim to subjective universality.

Third Aspect of the Judgment of Taste (the Relation of the Ends Brought Under Review in Such Judgments):

§ 10. *Finality in general.* Let us define the meaning of "an end" in transcendental terms (i.e. without presupposing anything empirical, such as the feeling of pleasure). An end is the object of a concept so far as this concept is regarded as the cause of the object (the real ground of its possibility); and the causality of a *concept* in respect of its *object* is finality (*forma finalis*). Then wherever, not merely the knowledge of an object, but the object itself (its form or real existence) as an effect, is thought to be possible only through a concept of it, there we imagine an end. The image of the effect is here the determining ground of its cause and takes the lead of it. The consciousness of the causality of imagining the state of the subject as one tending *to preserve a continuance* of that state, may be said here to denote in a general way what is called pleasure; whereas displeasure is that imagining which contains the ground for converting the state of the images into their opposite (for hindering or removing them). . . .

§ 11. *The sole foundation of the judgment of taste is the* FORM OF APPROPRIATENESS *of an object (or mode of imagining it).* Whenever an end is regarded as a source of delight it always imports an interest as determining ground of the judgment on the object of pleasure. Hence the judgment of taste cannot rest on any subjective end as its ground. But neither can any image of an objective end, i.e., of the possibility of the object itself on principles of final connection, determine the judgment of taste, and, furthermore, neither can any concept of the good. For the judgment of taste is an aesthetic and not a thinking judgment, and so does not deal with any *concept* of the nature or of the internal or external possibility, by this or that cause, of the object, but simply with the relative bearing of the representative powers so far as they are determined by imagination.

Now this relation is present when an object is. characterized as beautiful, coupled with the feeling of pleasure. This pleasure is by the judgment of taste pronounced valid for everyone; hence an agreeableness attending the imagining is just as incapable of containing the determining ground of the judgment as imagining the perfection of the object or the concept of the good. We are thus left with the subjective appropriateness in the imagined object, exclusive of any end (objective or subjective)—consequently the bare form of appropriateness in the image whereby an object is *given* to us, so far as we are conscious of it—as that which is alone capable of constituting the delight which, apart from any concept, we estimate as universally communicable, and so of forming the determining ground of the judgment of taste.

[FROM the Analytic of Aesthetic Judgment in the *Critique of Judgment,* 1790; trans. J. C. Meredith, Oxford, 1911. By permission of the Clarendon Press, Oxford]

JOHANN GOTTLIEB FICHTE

The Vocation of Man

BOOK III

JOHANN GOTTLIEB FICHTE

THE LIFE of Johann Gottlieb Fichte (1762–1814) was one of considerable hardship and struggle. It began at Rammenau, a village in Saxon Lusatia, where his father was a farmer and linen-maker. After studying at Leipzig for three years he lived for some years in a succession of tutoring jobs in various places, including Zurich, where he married in 1793. During this period he discovered Kant's philosophy and became a philosopher himself. His *Essay Toward a Critique of All Revelation,* which appeared after some delays in 1792, became famous as an extension of the critical philosophy, and led to an appointment at the University of Jena in 1794. Here he was extremely successful as a lecturer both to students and to the public, but he was dismissed in 1799 after a notable conflict over the limits of academic freedom, in which Fichte vigorously defended his right to expound his own philosophy (including his philosophy of religion) in his writings. There followed several years of writing and public lecturing as one of the leading figures in Berlin. He left for a time before the advance of Napoleon's army in 1806, but returned to deliver his famous *Addresses to the German Nation* (1807), in which, even during the French occupation, he tried to rouse the Germans to a sense of national unity, to moral regeneration, and political reform. Fichte was among the founders and first faculty members of the University of Berlin, which opened in 1810. He remained in that post until his death.

Much of the fundamental and difficult exposition of Fichte's philosophy is in *The Science of Knowledge* (trans. Peter Heath and John Lachs, New York: Meredith, 1970) which he developed in a number of versions. The first version (1794) was *On the Concept of the Science of Knowledge, or So-called Philosophy;* it was followed by *Fundamental Principles of the Science of Knowledge* trans. A. E. Kroeger, London: Trübner and Co., 1889. A later version, the *New Exposition of the Science of Knowledge* (trans. Kroeger, St. Louis: privately printed, 1869), was written in 1801, but first published in 1845. Fichte's moral and social philosophy is presented in his *Theory of Natural Law* (1796) and the *Theory of Morals* (1798); see translations by Kroeger, *The Science of Rights,* London: Trübner, 1889, and *The Science of Ethics Based on the Science of Knowledge,* London: Trübner, 1907.

Fichte took with the utmost seriousness Kant's conclusion that the practical, or moral, reason can obtain assurance of truth in regions where the theoretical reason cannot enter, and he went beyond Kant in concluding that the practical reason was the more fundamental in all knowledge. He made action—the self's assertion of its ideal self in freedom—the cornerstone of his system. It is his merit to have investigated the possibility of deriving the main categories of a philosophy from the basic concept of the self as an active, a normative, being. In this he led the way to important lines of thought later explored by the pragmatists and instrumentalists. His passionate conviction that ethical and political consequences of philosophical beliefs are to be put into practice—that philosophy is not only a guide of life but a critique of institutions and a stimulus to social reform—left its mark on some later philosophies; this conviction shows up in his views of international relations and his continuing defense of freedom within the state. And his inspiring conception of what man is capable of if he sets himself to make the most of his natural existence is a beacon for naturalistic philosophies of all times, even though Fichte did not regard himself as a naturalist.

The Vocation of Man*

[This introduction to Fichte's philosophy consists of three parts. In Book I, "Doubt," Fichte builds up a contrast, as he sees it, between the individual's inward conviction of his own freedom of will and the rigid determinism that his intellect finds in Nature: "In immediate consciousness, I appear to myself as free; by reflection on the whole of Nature, I discover that freedom is absolutely impossible." From the resulting despair, Fichte is roused in Book II, "Knowledge," by a visiting Spirit, who appears and conducts a dialogue with him. The point of the Spirit's argument is that everything that we are capable of knowing immediately is what is in our minds: "In all perception you perceive only your own state." Even the principle of causality itself, which is presupposed in the concept of Nature as determined, is only a projection of the self, which therefore need have no fear of being subject to it. But the Spirit's argument plunges Fichte into a new skepticism: how, then, can he have any assurance that there is a real world, with other selves in it? But you have another way of knowing this, another means, if you will only use it, says the Spirit, and disappears.]

BOOK III: FAITH

Terrible Spirit, your discourse has smitten me to the ground. But you refer me to myself, and what would I be if anything external to myself could irrecoverably cast me down? I will—yes, surely I will follow your counsel.

What do you seek, then, my complaining heart? What is it that excites you against a system to which my understanding cannot raise the slightest objection?

This it is: I demand something beyond a mere presentation or conception—something that is, has been, and will be, even if the presentation were not, and that the presentation only records, without producing it or in the smallest degree changing it. A mere presentation I now see to be a deceptive show; my presentations must have a meaning behind them, and if my entire knowledge revealed to me nothing

---

* Translated by William Smith, London: S. Chapman, 1848; revised by him for *The Popular Works of Johann Gottlieb Fichte,* ed. Smith, London: Trübner, 4th ed., 1889; revised by the present editor. *Die Bestimmung des Menschen* was published in 1800. Book III ends with a lengthy prayer, or exhortation to the Infinite Will, which is omitted here.

but knowledge, I would be defrauded of my whole life. That there is nothing whatever but my presentations or conceptions is, to the natural sense of mankind, a silly and ridiculous conceit which no man can seriously entertain, and which requires no refutation. To the better-informed judgment, which knows the deep, and, *by mere reasoning,* irrefragable grounds for this assertion, it is a prostrating, annihilating thought.

And what, then, is this something lying beyond all presentation, toward which I stretch forward with such ardent longing? What is the power with which it draws me toward it? What is the central point in my soul to which it is attached, and with which alone it can be effaced?

"Not merely TO KNOW, but according to your knowledge TO DO, is your vocation"—this is loudly proclaimed in the innermost depths of my soul, as soon as I recollect myself for a moment and turn my observation upon myself. "Not for idle contemplation of yourself, not for brooding over devout sensations—no, for action you are here; action, and action alone, determines your worth."

This voice leads me out from presentation, from mere cognition, to something that lies beyond it and is entirely opposed to it; to something greater and higher than all knowledge, containing within itself the end and object of all knowledge. When I act, I doubtless know that I act and how I act; nevertheless this knowledge is not the act itself, but only the observation of it. This voice thus announces to me precisely what I sought: a something lying beyond mere knowledge, and, in its nature, wholly independent of knowledge.

Thus it is; I know it immediately. But once I have entered the domain of speculation, the doubt that has been awakened within me will secretly endure and will continue to disturb me. Since I have placed myself in this position, I can obtain no complete satisfaction until everything I accept is justified before the tribunal of speculation. I have thus to ask myself: How is it thus? Whence arises that voice in my soul which directs me to something beyond mere presentation and knowledge?

There is within me an impulse to absolute, independent self-activity. Nothing is more unendurable to me than to be merely by another, for another, and through another; I must be something for myself and by myself alone. This impulse I feel along with the perception of my own existence, it is inseparably united to my consciousness of myself.

I explain this feeling to myself by reflection, and, as it were, add to this blind impulse the power of sight by means of thought. According to this impulse I must act as an absolutely independent being: thus I understand and translate the impulse. I must be independent. Who am I? Subject and object in one—the conscious being and that of which I am conscious, gifted with intuitive knowledge and myself revealed in that intuition, the thinking mind and myself the object of the thought, inseparable and ever present to each other. As both, I must be what I am, absolutely by myself alone—by myself originate conceptions, by myself produce a condition of things lying beyond these conceptions. But how is the latter possible? With nothing I cannot connect any being whatsoever; from nothing there can never arise something; my objective thought is necessarily mediative only. But any being that is connected with another being becomes thereby dependent; it is no longer a primary, original, and genetic, but only a secondary and derived, being. I am constrained to connect myself with something; I cannot connect myself with another being without losing that independence which is the condition of my own existence.

My conception and origination of *a purpose,* however, is, by its very nature, absolutely free—producing something out of nothing. With such a conception I must connect my activity, in order that it may be possible to regard it as free, and as proceeding absolutely from myself alone.

In the following manner, therefore, I conceive of my independence as *I.* I ascribe to myself the power of originating a conception simply because I originate it, of originating *this* conception simply because I originate *this* one—by the absolute sovereignty of myself as an intelligence. I further ascribe to myself the power of manifesting this conception beyond itself by means of an action—ascribe to myself a real, active power, capable of producing something beyond itself—a power that is entirely different from the mere power of conception. These conceptions, which are called conceptions of design, or purposes, are not, like the conceptions of mere knowledge, copies of something already existing, but rather types of something yet to be; the real power lies beyond them, and is *in itself* independent of them; it only receives from them its immediate determinations, which are apprehended by knowledge. Such an independent power it is that, in consequence of this impulse, I ascribe to myself.

Here then, it appears, is the point at which consciousness connects itself with reality; the real efficiency of my conception, and the real power of action which, in consequence of it, I am compelled to ascribe to myself, is this point. Let it be as it may with the reality of a sensible world beyond me; I possess reality and comprehend it—it lies within my own being, it is native to myself.

I conceive this, my real power of action, in thought, but I do not create it by thought. The immediate feeling of my impulse to independent activity lies at the foundation of this thought; the thought does no more than portray this feeling and accept it in its own form, the form of thought. This procedure may, I think, be vindicated before the tribunal of speculation.

What! Shall I, once more, knowingly and intentionally deceive myself? This procedure can by no means be justified before that strict tribunal.

I feel within me an impulse and an effort toward outward activity; this appears to be true, and to be the only truth belonging to the matter. Since it is I who feel this impulse, and since I cannot pass beyond myself, either with my whole consciousness, or in particular with my capacity of sensation—since this *I* itself is the last point at which I am conscious of this impulse, it certainly appears to me as an impulse founded in myself, to an activity also founded in myself. Might it not be however that this impulse, although unperceived by me, is in reality the impulse of a foreign power invisible to me, and that notion of independence merely a delusion, arising from my sphere of vision being limited to myself alone? I have no reason to assume this, but just as little reason to deny it. I must confess that I know absolutely nothing, and can know nothing, about it.

Do I then indeed *feel* that real power of free action which, strangely enough, I ascribe to myself without knowing anything of it? By no means; it is merely the *determinable* element that, by the well-known laws of thought whereby all capacities and all powers arise, we are compelled to add in imagination to the *determinate* element—the real action, which itself is, in like manner, only an assumption.

Is that procession, from the mere conception to an imaginary realization of it, anything more than the usual and well-known procedure of all objective thought, which always strives to be, not mere thought, but something more? By what dishonesty can this procedure be made of more value here than in any other case? Can it possess any deeper significance when to the conception of a thought it adds a realization of this thought, than when to the conception of this table it adds an actual and present table? "The conception of a purpose, a particular determination of events in me, appears in a double shape—partly as *subjective,* a Thought; partly as *objective,* an Action." What reason that would not unquestionably itself need a genetic deduction could I adduce against this explanation?

I say that I feel this impulse: it is therefore I myself who say so, and think so while I say it. Do I then really feel, or only think that I feel? Is not all that I call feeling only a presentation produced by my objective process of thought, and indeed the first transition point of all objectivity? And then again, do I really think, or do I merely think that I think? And do I think that I really think, or merely that I possess the idea of thinking? What can hinder speculation from raising such questions, and continuing to raise them without end? What can I answer, and where is there a point at which I can command such questionings to cease? I know, and must admit, that each definite act of consciousness may be made the subject of reflection, and a new consciousness of the first consciousness may thus be created; and that thereby the immediate consciousness is raised a step higher, and the first consciousness darkened and made doubtful; and that to this ladder there is no highest step. I know that all skepticism rests upon this process, and that the system that has so violently prostrated me is founded on the adoption and the clear consciousness of it.

I know that if I am not merely to play another perplexing game with this system, but intend really and practically to adopt it, I must refuse obedience to that voice within me. I cannot *will* to act, for according to that system I cannot *know* whether I can really act or not: I can never believe that I truly act; what seems to be my action must appear to me as entirely without meaning, as a mere delusive picture. All earnestness and all interest is withdrawn from my life; and life, as well as thought, is transformed into a mere play that proceeds from nothing and tends to nothing.

Shall I then refuse obedience to that inward voice? I will not do so. I will freely accept the vocation this impulse assigns to me, and in this resolution I will lay hold at once of thought, in all its reality and truthfulness, and on the reality of all things that are presupposed therein, I will restrict myself to the position of natural thought in which this impulse places me, and cast from me all those over-refined and subtle inquiries which alone could make me doubtful of its truth.

I understand you now, sublime Spirit! I have found the organ by which to apprehend this reality, and, with this, probably all other reality. Knowledge is not this organ: no knowledge can be its own foundation, its own proof; every knowledge presupposes another higher knowledge on which it is founded, and to this ascent there is no end. It is FAITH, that voluntary acquiescence in the view that is naturally presented to us, because only through this view can we fulfil our vocation; this it is that first lends a sanction to knowledge, and raises to certainty and conviction what without it might be mere delusion. It is not knowledge, but a resolution of the will to admit the validity of knowledge.

Let me hold fast forever by this doctrine, which is no mere verbal distinction, but a true and deep one, bearing with it the most important consequences for my whole existence and character. All my conviction is but faith, and it proceeds from the will, not from the understanding. Knowing this, I will enter upon no disputation, because I foresee that thereby nothing can be gained; I will not suffer myself to be perplexed by it, for the source of my conviction lies higher than all disputation; I will not suffer myself to entertain the desire of pressing this conviction on others by reasoning, and I will not be surprised if such an undertaking should fail. I have adopted my mode of thinking first of all for myself, not for others, and only before myself will I justify it. He who possesses the honest, upright purpose of which I am conscious will also attain a similar conviction; but without that, this conviction can in no way be attained. Now that I know this, I also know from what point all culture of myself and others must proceed—from the will, not from the understanding. If the former be only fixedly and honestly directed toward the Good, the latter will of itself apprehend the True. Should the latter only be exercised, while the former remains neglected, there can arise nothing whatever but a dexterity in groping after vain and empty refinements, throughout the absolute void inane. Now that I know this, I am able to confute all false knowledge that may rise in opposition to my faith. I know that every pretended truth produced by mere speculative thought, and not founded upon faith, is assuredly false and surreptitious; for mere knowledge, thus produced, leads only to the conviction that we can know nothing. I know that such false knowledge never can discover anything but what it has previously placed in its premises through faith, from which it probably draws conclusions that are wholly false. Now that I know this, I possess the touchstone of all truth and of all conviction. Conscience alone is the root of all truth: whatever is opposed to conscience, or stands in the way of the fulfilment of her behests, is assuredly false; and it is impossible for me to arrive at a conviction of its truth, even if I should be unable to discover the fallacies by which it is produced.

So has it been with all men who have ever seen the light of this world. Without being conscious of it, they apprehend all the reality that has an existence for them, through faith alone; and this faith forces itself on them simultaneously with their existence; it is born with them. How could it be otherwise? If in mere knowledge, in mere perception and reflection, there is no ground for regarding our mental presentations as more than mere pictures that necessarily pass before our view, why do we yet regard all of them as more than this, and assume, as their foundation, something that exists independently of all presentation? If we all possess the capacity and the instinct to proceed beyond our first natural view of things, why do so few actually go beyond it, and why do we even defend ourselves, with a sort of bitterness, from every motive by which others try to persuade us to this course? What is it that holds us confined within this first natural belief? Not inferences of reason, for there are none such; it is the interest we have in a reality that we desire to produce—the good, absolutely for its own sake, the common and sensuous, for the sake of the enjoyment they afford. No one who lives can divest himself of this interest, and just as little can he cast off the faith this interest brings with it. We are all born in faith; he who is blind, follows blindly the secret and irresistible impulse; he who sees, follows by sight, and believes because he resolves to believe.

What unity and completeness does this view present!—what dignity does it confer upon human nature! Our thought is not founded on itself alone, independently of our impulses and affections; man does not consist of two independent and separate elements; he is absolutely one. All our thought is founded on our impulses; as a man's affections are, so is his knowledge. These impulses compel us to a certain mode of thought only so long as we do not perceive the constraint; the constraint vanishes the moment it is perceived; and it is then no longer the impulse by itself, but we ourselves, according to our impulse, who form our own system of thought.

But I shall open my eyes, shall learn thoroughly to know myself, shall recognize that constraint; this is my vocation. I shall thus—and, under that supposition, I shall necessarily—form my own mode of thought. Then I shall stand absolutely independent, thoroughly equipped and perfected through my own act and deed. The primitive source of all my other thought and of my life itself, that from which everything proceeds that can have an existence in me, for me, or through me, the innermost spirit of my spirit, is no longer a foreign power, but it is, in the strictest possible sense, the product of my own will. I am wholly my own creation. I might have followed blindly the leading of my spiritual nature. But I would not be a work of Nature but of myself, and I have become so even by means of this resolution. By endless subtleties I might have made the natural conviction of my own mind dark and doubtful. But I have accepted it with freedom, simply because I resolved to accept it. I have chosen the system I have now adopted with settled purpose and deliberation from among other possible modes of thought, because I have recognized in it the only one consistent with my dignity and my vocation. With freedom and consciousness I have returned to the point at which Nature had left me. I accept what she announces—but I do not accept it because I must; I believe it because I will.

The exalted vocation of my understanding fills me with reverence. It is no longer the deceptive mirror that reflects a series of empty pictures, proceeding from nothing and tending to nothing; it is bestowed upon me for a great purpose. Its cultivation for this purpose is entrusted to me; it is placed in my hands, and at my hands it will be required. It is placed in my hands. I know immediately—and here my faith accepts the testimony of my consciousness without further criticism—I know that I am not placed under the necessity of allowing my thoughts to float about without direction or purpose, but that I can voluntarily arouse and direct my attention to one object, or turn it away again towards another, I know that it is neither a blind necessity that compels me to a certain mode of thought, nor an empty chance that runs riot with my thoughts, but that it is I who think, and that I can think of that whereof I decide to think. Thus by reflection I have discovered something more; I have discovered that I myself, by my own act alone, produce my whole system of thought and the particular view I take of truth in general, since it remains with me either by over-refinement to deprive myself of all sense of truth, or to yield myself to it with faithful obedience. My whole mode of thought, and the cultivation that my understanding receives, as well as the objects to which I direct it, depend entirely on myself. True insight is merit; the perversion of my capacity for knowledge—thoughtlessness, obscurity, error, and unbelief—is guilt.

There is but one point toward which I have unceasingly to direct all my attention—namely, what I *ought to do,* and how I may best fulfil my obligation. All my thoughts must have a bearing on my actions, and must be capable of being considered as means, however remote, to this end; otherwise they are an idle and aimless show, a mere waste of time and strength, the perversion of a noble power that is entrusted to me for a very different end.

I dare hope, I dare surely promise myself, to follow out this undertaking with good results. The Nature on which I have to act is not a foreign element called into existence without reference to me, into which I cannot penetrate. It is molded by my own laws of thought, and must be in harmony with them; it must be thoroughly transparent, knowable and penetrable to me, even to its inmost recesses. In all its phenomena it expresses nothing but the connections and relations of my own being to myself; and as surely as I may hope to know myself, so surely may I expect to comprehend it. Let me seek only what I ought to seek, and I shall find; let me ask only what I ought to ask, and I shall receive an answer.

I.

That voice within my soul in which I believe, and on account of which I believe in every other thing to which I attach credence, does not command me merely to act *in general*. This is impossible; all these general principles are formed only through my own voluntary observation and reflection, applied to many individual facts, but never in themselves express any fact whatever. This voice of my conscience announces to me precisely what I ought to do, and what to leave undone, in every particular situation of life; it accompanies me, if I will but listen to it with attention, through all the events of my life, and never refuses me its reward when I am called upon to act. It carries with it immediate conviction, and irresistibly compels my assent to its behests; it is impossible for me to contend against it.

To listen to it, to obey it honestly and unreservedly, without fear or equivocation—this is my true vocation, the whole end and purpose of my existence. My life ceases to be an empty play without truth or significance. There is something that must absolutely be done for its own sake alone; what conscience demands of me in this particular situation of life it is mine to do, for this alone am I here; to know it, I have understanding; to perform it, I have power. Through this edict of conscience alone, truth and reality are introduced into my conceptions. I cannot refuse them my attention and my obedience without thereby surrendering the very purpose of my existence.

Hence I cannot withhold my belief from the reality they announce, without at the same time renouncing my vocation. It is absolutely true, without further proof or confirmation—nay, it is the first truth, and the foundation of all other truth and certainty—that this voice must be obeyed; and therefore everything becomes to me true and certain whose truth and certainty is assumed in the possibility of such obedience.

There appear before me in space certain phenomena to which I transfer the idea of myself; I conceive of them as beings like myself. Speculation, when carried out to its last results, has indeed taught me, or would teach me, that these supposed rational beings external to myself are but the products of my own presentative power, that, according to certain laws of my thought, I am compelled to represent out of myself my conception of myself, and that, according to the same laws, I can transfer this conception only to certain definite intuitions. But the voice of my conscience thus speaks: "Whatever these beings may be in and for themselves, you shall act towards them as self-existent, free, substantive beings, wholly independent of yourself. Assume it as already known that they can give a purpose to their own being wholly by themselves, and quite independently of you; never interrupt the accomplishment of this purpose, but rather further it to the utmost of your power. Honor their freedom, lovingly take up their purposes as if they were your own." Thus ought I to act, by this course of action *ought* all my thought to be guided—nay, it *shall* and *must* necessarily be so, if I have resolved to obey the voice of my conscience. Hence I shall always regard these beings as in possession of an existence for themselves wholly independent of mine, as capable of forming and carrying out their own purposes; from this point of view, I shall never be able to conceive of them otherwise, and my previous speculations regarding them shall vanish like an empty dream. I *think* of them as beings like myself, I have said; but strictly speaking, it is not by mere thought that they are first presented to me as such. It is by the voice of my conscience, by the command: "Here set a limit to your freedom; here recognize and reverence purposes which are not your own." This it is that is first translated into the thought, "Here, certainly and truly, are beings like myself, free and independent." To view them otherwise, I must in action renounce, and in speculation disregard, the voice of my conscience.

Other phenomena present themselves before me that I do not regard as beings like myself, but as things irrational. Speculation finds no difficulty in showing how the conception of such things is developed solely from my own presentative faculty and its necessary modes of activity. But I apprehend these things, also, through want, desire, and enjoyment. Not by the mental conception, but by hunger, thirst, and their satisfaction, does anything become for me food and drink. I am necessitated to believe in the reality of that which threatens my sensuous existence, or in that which alone is able to maintain it. Conscience enters the field in order that it may at once sanctify and restrain this natural impulse. "You shall maintain, exercise, and strengthen yourself and your physical powers, for they have been taken account of in the plans of reason. But you can maintain them only by legitimate use, conformable to their nature. There are also, besides you, many other beings like yourself, whose powers have been counted upon like your own, and can be maintained only in the same way as your own. Concede to them the same privilege that has been allowed to you. Respect what belongs to them as their possession; use what belongs to you legitimately as your own." Thus ought I to act, according to this course of action must I think. I am compelled to regard these things as standing under their own natural laws, independent of, though perceivable by me, and therefore to ascribe to them an independent existence. I am compelled to believe in such laws; the task of investigating them is set before me, and that empty speculation vanishes like a mist when the genial sun appears.

In short, there is for me absolutely no such thing as an existence that has no relation to myself, and that I contemplate merely for the sake of contemplating it; whatever has an existence for me, has it only through its relation to my own being. But there is, in the highest sense, only one relation to me possible, all others are but subordinate forms of this: my vocation to moral activity. My world is the object and sphere of my duties, and absolutely nothing more; there is no other world for me, and no other qualities of my world than what are implied in this; my whole united capacity, all finite capacity, is insufficient to comprehend any other. Whatever possesses an existence for me, can bring its existence and reality into contact with me only through this relation, and only through this relation do I comprehend it; for any other existence than this I have no organ whatever.

To the question whether, in deed and in fact, such a world exists as that which I represent to myself, I can give no answer more fundamental, more secure from doubt, than this: I have, most certainly and truly, these determinate duties, which announce themselves to me as duties towards certain objects, to be fulfilled by means of certain materials—duties that I cannot otherwise conceive of, and cannot otherwise fulfil, than within such a world as I represent to myself. Even to one who has never meditated on his own moral vocation, if there could be such a one, or who, if he has given it some general consideration, has, at least, never entertained the slightest purpose of fulfilling it at any time within an indefinite futurity—even for him, his sensuous world, and his belief in its reality, arises in no other manner than from his ideas of a moral world. If he does not apprehend it by the thought of his duties, he certainly does so by the demand for his rights. What he perhaps never requires of himself, he does certainly exact from others in their conduct towards him—that they should treat him with propriety, consideration, and respect, not as an irrational thing, but as a free and independent being; and thus, by supposing in them an ability to comply with his own demands, he is compelled also to regard them as themselves considerate, free, and independent of the dominion of mere natural power. Even should he never propose to himself any other purpose in his use and enjoyment of surrounding objects but simply that of enjoying them, he at least demands this enjoyment as a right, in the possession of which he claims to be left undisturbed by others; and thus he apprehends even the irrational world of sense by means of a moral idea. These claims of respect for his rationality, independence, and preservation, no one can resign who possesses a conscious existence; and with these claims, at least, there is united in his soul earnestness, renunciation of doubt, and faith in a reality, even if they be not associated with the recognition of a moral law within him. Take the man who denies his own moral vocation, and your existence, and the existence of a material world, except as a mere futile effort in which speculation tries her strength; approach him practically, apply his own principles to life, and act as if either he had no existence at all, or were merely a portion of rude matter; he will soon lay aside his scornful indifference, and indignantly complain of you, earnestly call your attention to your conduct towards him; mantain that you ought not and dare not so to act; and thus prove to you, by deeds, that you are assuredly capable of acting upon him; that *he is,* and that *you are,* that there is a medium by which you can influence him, and that you, at least, have duties to perform towards him.

Thus, it is not the operation of supposed external objects, which indeed exist for us, and we for them, only in so far as we already know of them, and it is just as little an empty vision evoked by our own imagination and thought, the products of which must, like itself, be mere empty pictures—it is not these, but the necessary faith in our own freedom and power, in our own real activity, and in the definite laws of human action, that lies at the root of all our consciousness of a reality external to ourselves—a consciousness that is itself but faith, since it is founded on another faith, of which however it is a necessary consequence. We are compelled to believe that we act, and that we ought to act in a certain manner; we are compelled to assume a certain sphere for this action; this sphere is the real, actually present world, such as we find it, and on the other hand, the world is absolutely nothing more than, and cannot, in any way, extend itself beyond, this sphere. From this necessity of action proceeds the consciousness of the actual world; and not the reverse way, from the consciousness of the actual world the necessity of action; this, not that, is the first; the former is derived from the latter. We do not act because we know, but we know because we are called upon to act; the practical reason is the root of all reason. The laws of action for rational beings are *immediately certain*; their world is certain only through that previous certainty. We cannot deny these laws without plunging the world, and ourselves with it, into absolute annihilation; we raise ourselves from this abyss, and maintain ourselves above it, solely by our moral activity.

II.

There is something I am called upon to do, simply in order that it may be done; something to avoid doing, solely that it may be left undone. But can I act without having an end in view beyond the action itself, without directing my intention toward something that can become possible by means of my action, and only by means of it? Can I will, without having something that I will? No; this would be contradictory to the very nature of my mind. To every action there is united in my thought, immediately and by the laws of thought itself, a condition of things placed in futurity, to which my action is related as the efficient cause to the effect produced. But this purpose or end of my action must not be proposed to me for its own sake—perhaps through some necessity of Nature—and then my course of action determined according to this end; I must not have an end assigned to me, and then inquire how I must act in order to attain this end; my action must not be dependent on the end, but I must act in a certain manner simply because I ought so to act—this is the first point. That a result will follow from this course of action is proclaimed by the voice within me. This result necessarily becomes an end to me, since I am bound to perform the action that brings it, and it alone, to pass. I will that something shall come to pass, because I must act so that it may come to pass; just as I do not hunger because food is before me but a thing becomes food for me because I hunger, so I do not act as I do because a certain end is to be attained, but the end becomes an end to me because I am bound to act in the manner by which it may be attained. I have not first in view the point toward which I am to draw my line, and then, by its position, determine the direction of my line and the angle it shall make; but I draw my line absolutely in a right angle, and thereby the points are determined through which my line must pass. The end does not determine the commandment; but, on the contrary, the immediate purport of the commandment determines the end.

I say it is the law that commands me to act which of itself assigns an end to my action; the same inward power that compels me to think that I ought to act thus, compels me also to believe that from my action some result will arise; it opens to my spiritual vision a prospect into another world, which is really a world, a state, namely, and not an action, but another and better world than what is present to the physical eye; it constrains me to aspire after this better world, to embrace it with every power, to long for its realization, to live only in it, and in it alone find satisfaction. The law itself is my guarantee for the certain attainment of this end. The same resolution by which I devote my whole thought and life to the fulfilment of this law, and determine to see nothing beyond it, brings with it the indestructible conviction that the promise it implies is likewise true and certain, and renders it impossible for me even to conceive the possibility of the opposite. As I live in obedience to it, so do I live also in the contemplation of its end, in that better world it promises to me.

Even in the mere consideration of the world as it is, apart from this law, there arises within me the wish, the desire—no, not the mere desire, but the absolute demand—for a better world. I cast a glance on the present relations of men toward each other and toward Nature, on the feebleness of their powers, the strength of their desires and passions. A voice within me proclaims with irresistible conviction, "It is impossible that it can remain thus; it must become different and better."

I cannot think of the present state of humanity as that in which it is destined to remain; I am absolutely unable to conceive of this as its complete and final vocation. Then, indeed, would everything be a dream and a delusion; and it would not be worth the trouble to have lived and played out this ever-repeated game, which tends to nothing and signifies nothing. Only in so far as I can regard this state as a means toward a better, as the transition point to a higher and more perfect state, has it any value in my eyes; not for its own sake, but for the sake of that better world for which it prepares the way, can I support it, esteem it, and joyfully perform my part in it. My mind can accept no place in the present, nor rest in it even for a moment; my whole being flows onward, incessantly and irresistibly, toward that future and better state of things.

Shall I eat and drink only that I may hunger and thirst and eat and drink again, till the grave that is open beneath my feet shall swallow me up and I myself become the food of worms? Shall I beget beings like myself, that they too may eat and drink and die, and leave behind them beings like themselves to do the same as I have done? To what purpose this ever-revolving circle, this ceaseless and unvarying round, in which all things appear only to pass away, and pass away only that they may reappear as they were before——this monster continually devouring itself that it may again bring itself forth, and bringing itself forth only that it may again devour itself?

This can never be the vocation of my being, and of all being. There must be something that is, because it has come into existence, and endures, and cannot come anew, having once become such as it is. And this abiding existence must be produced amid the vicissitudes of the transitory and perishable, maintain itself there, and be borne onwards, pure and inviolate, upon the waves of time.

Our species still laboriously extorts the means of its subsistence and preservation from an opposing Nature. The larger portion of mankind is still condemned through life to severe toil, in order to supply nourishment for itself and for the smaller portion that thinks for it; immortal spirits are compelled to fix their whole thoughts and endeavors on the earth that brings forth their food. It still frequently happens that, when the laborer has finished his toil and has promised himself in return a lasting endurance both for himself and for his work, a hostile element will destroy in a moment what it has cost him years of patient industry and deliberation to accomplish, and the assiduous and careful man is undeservedly made the prey of hunger and misery; often do floods, storms, volcanoes, desolate whole countries, and works that bear the impress of a rational soul are mingled with their authors in the wild chaos of death and destruction. Disease sweeps into an untimely grave men in the pride of their strength, and children whose existence has as yet borne no fruit; pestilence stalks through blooming lands, leaves the few who escape its ravages like lonely orphans bereaved of the accustomed support of their fellows, and does all that it can do to give back to the desert those regions which the labor of man has won from it as a possession to himself. Thus it is now, but thus it cannot remain forever. No work that bears the stamp of Reason, and has been undertaken to extend her power, can ever be wholly lost in the onward progress of the ages. The sacrifices that the irregular violence of Nature extorts from Reason must at least exhaust, disarm, and appease that violence. The same power that has burst out into lawless fury cannot again commit the same excesses; it cannot be destined to renew its strength; through its own outbreak its energies must henceforth and forever be exhausted. All those outbreaks of unregulated power before which human strength vanishes into nothing, those desolating hurricanes, those earthquakes, those volcanoes, can be nothing else than the last struggles of the rude mass against the law of regular, progressive, living, and systematic activity to which it is compelled to submit in opposition to its own undirected impulses —nothing but the last shivering strokes by which the perfect formation of our globe has yet to be accomplished. That resistance must gradually become weaker and at length be exhausted, since, in the regulated progress of things, there can be nothing to renew its strength; that formation must at length be achieved, and our destined dwelling-place be made complete. Nature must gradually be resolved into a condition in which her regular action may be calculated and safely relied upon, and her power bear a fixed and definite relation to the power that is destined to govern it—that of man. In so far as this relation already exists, and the cultivation of Nature has attained a firm footing, the works of man, by their mere existence, and by an influence altogether beyond the original intent of their authors, shall again react upon Nature, and become to her a new vivifying principle. Cultivation shall quicken and ameliorate the sluggish and baleful atmosphere of primeval forests, deserts, and marshes; more regular and varied cultivation shall diffuse throughout the air new impulses to life and fertility; and the sun shall pour his most animating rays into an atmosphere breathed by healthful, industrious, and civilized nations. Science, first called into existence by the pressure of necessity, shall afterwards calmly and carefully investigate the unchangeable laws of Nature, review its powers at large, and learn to calculate their possible manifestations, and, while closely following the footsteps of Nature in the living and actual world, form for itself in thought a new ideal one. Every discovery that Reason has extorted from Nature shall be maintained throughout the ages, and become the ground of new knowledge, for the common possession of our species. Thus shall Nature ever become more and more intelligible and transparent even in her most secret depths; human power, enlightened and armed by human invention, shall rule over her without difficulty, and the conquest, once made, shall be peacefully maintained. This dominion of man over Nature shall gradually be extended, until, at length, no further expenditure of mechanical labor shall be necessary than what the human body requires for its development, cultivation, and health; and this labor shall cease to be a burden, for a reasonable being is not destined to be a bearer of burdens.

But it is not Nature, it is Freedom itself, by which the greatest and most terrible disorders incident to our species are produced; man is the cruelest enemy of man. Lawless hordes of savages still wander over vast wildernesses; they meet, and the victor devours his foe at the triumphal feast; or where culture has at length united these wild hordes under some social bond, they attack each other, as nations, with the power that law and union have given them. Defying toil and privation, their armies traverse peaceful plains and forests; they meet each other, and the sight of their brethren is the signal for slaughter. Equipped with the mightiest inventions of the human intellect, hostile fleets plough their way through the ocean; through storm and tempest man rushes to meet his fellow men upon the lonely inhospitable sea; they meet, and defy the fury of the elements that they may destroy each other with their own hands. Even in the interior of states, where men seem to be united in equality under the law, it is still for the most part only force and fraud that rule under that venerable name; and here the warfare is so much the more shameful that it is not openly declared to be war, and the party attacked is even deprived of the privilege of defending himself against unjust oppression. Combinations of the few rejoice aloud in the ignorance, the folly, the vice, and the misery in which the greater number of their fellow-men are sunk, avowedly seek to retain them in this state of degradation, and even to plunge them deeper in it in order to perpetuate their slavery— nay, would destroy any one who ventured to enlighten or improve them. No attempt at amelioration can anywhere be made without rousing up from slumber a host of selfish interests to war against it, and uniting even the most varied and opposite in a common hostility. The good cause is ever the weaker, for it is simple, and can be loved only for itself; the bad attracts each individual by the promise that is most seductive to him; and its adherents, always at war among themselves, so soon as the good makes its appearance, conclude a truce that they may unite the whole powers of their wickedness against it. Scarcely, indeed, is such an opposition needed, for even the good themselves are but too often divided by misunderstanding, error, distrust, and secret self-love, and that so much the more violently, the more earnestly each strives to propagate what he recognizes as best; and thus internal discord dissipates a power that, even when united, could scarcely hold the balance with evil. One blames the other for rushing onward with stormy impetuosity to his object, without waiting until the good result shall have been prepared; while he in turn is blamed that, through hesitation and cowardice, he accomplishes nothing, but allows all things to remain as they are, contrary to his better conviction, because for him the hour of action never arrives—and only the Omniscient can determine whether either of the parties in the dispute is in the right. Every one regards the undertaking, the necessity of which is most apparent to him, and in the prosecution of which he has acquired the greatest skill, as most important and needful, as the point from which all improvement must proceed; he requires all good men to unite their efforts with his, and to subject themselves to him for the accomplishment of his particular purpose, holding it to be treason to the good cause if they hold back; while they on the other hand make the same demands upon him, and accuse him of similar treason for a similar refusal. Thus do all good intentions among men appear to be lost in vain disputations, which leave behind them no trace of their existence; while in the meantime the world goes on as well, or as ill, as it can without human effort, by the blind mechanism of Nature—and so will go on forever.

And so go on forever? No; not so, unless the whole existence of humanity is to be an idle game, without significance and without end. It cannot be intended that those savage tribes should always remain savage; no race can be born with all the capacities of perfect humanity and yet be destined never to develop these capacities, never to become more than what a sagacious animal by its own proper nature might become. Those savages must be destined to be the progenitors of more powerful, cultivated, and virtuous generations; otherwise it is impossible to conceive of a purpose in their existence, or even of the possibility of their existence in a world ordered and arranged by reason. Savage races may become civilized, for this has already occurred; the most cultivated nations of modern times are the descendants of savages. Whether civilization is a direct and natural development of human society, or is invariably brought about through instruction and example from without, and the primary source of all human culture must be sought in a superhuman guidance, by the same way in which nations that once were savage have emerged into civilization, will those who are yet uncivilized gradually attain it. They must, no doubt, at first pass through the same dangers and corruptions of a merely sensual civilization, by which the civilized nations are still oppressed, but they will thereby be brought into union with the great whole of humanity and be made capable of taking part in its further progress.

It is the vocation of our species to unite itself into one single body, all the parts of which shall be thoroughly known to each other, and all possessed of similar culture. Nature, and even the passions and vices of men, have from the beginning tended toward this end; a great part of the way toward it is already passed, and we may surely calculate that this end, which is the condition of all further social progress, will in time be attained! Let us not ask of history if man, on the whole, has yet become purely moral! To a more extended, comprehensive, energetic freedom he has certainly attained; but hitherto it has been an almost necessary result of his position that this freedom has been applied chiefly to evil purposes. Neither let us ask whether the aesthetic and intellectual culture of the ancient world, concentrated on a few points, may not have excelled in degree that of modern times! It might happen that we would receive a humiliating answer, and that in this respect the human race has not advanced, but rather seemed to retrograde, in its riper years. But let us ask of history at what period the existing culture has been most widely diffused, and distributed among the greatest number of individuals, and we shall doubtless find that from the beginning of history down to our own day, the few light-points of civilization have spread themselves abroad from their center, that one individual after another, and one nation after another, has been embraced within their circle, and that this wider outspread of culture is proceeding under our own eyes. And this is the first point to be attained in the endless path on which humanity must advance. Until this shall have been attained, until the existing culture of every age shall have been diffused over the whole inhabited globe, and our species becomes capable of the most unlimited inter-communication with itself, one nation or one continent must pause on the great common path of progress, and wait for the advance of the others; and each must bring as an offering to the universal commonwealth, for the sake of which alone it exists, its ages of apparent immobility or retrogression. When that first point shall have been attained, when every useful discovery made at one end of the earth shall be at once made known and communicated to all the rest, then, without further interruption, without halt or regress, with united strength and equal step, humanity shall move onward to a higher culture, of which we can at present form no conception.

Within those singular associations, thrown together by unreasoning accident, which we call States, after they have subsisted for a time in peace, when the resistance excited by yet new oppression has been lulled to sleep, and the fermentation of contending forces appeased, abuse, by its continuance and by general sufferance, assumes a sort of established form, and the ruling classes, in the uncontested enjoyment of their extorted privileges, have nothing more to do but to extend them further, and to give to this extension also the same established form. Urged by their insatiable desires, they will continue from generation to generation their efforts to acquire wider and yet wider privileges, and never say, "It is enough!" until at last oppression shall reach its limit, and become wholly insupportable, and despair give back to the oppressed that power which their courage, extinguished by centuries of tyranny, could not procure for them. They will then no longer endure any among them who cannot be satisfied to be on an equality with others, and so to remain. In order to protect themselves against internal violence or new oppression, all will take on themselves the same obligations. Their deliberations—in which every man shall decide whatever he decides for himself, and not for one subject to him whose sufferings will never affect him, and in whose fate he takes no concern—deliberations according to which no one can hope that it shall be he who is to *practice* a permitted injustice, but every one must fear that he may have to *suffer* it—deliberations that alone deserve the name of legislation, which is something wholly different from the ordinances of combined lords to the countless herds of their slaves—these deliberations will necessarily be guided by justice, and will lay the foundation of a true State, in which each individual, from a regard for his own security, will be irresistibly compelled to respect the security of every other without exception, since, under the supposed legislation, every injury that he attempted to do to another would not fall upon its object, but would infallibly recoil upon himself.

By the establishment of this only true State, this firm foundation of internal peace, the possibility of foreign war, at least with other *true* States, is cut off. Even for its own advantage, even to prevent the thought of injustice, plunder and violence entering the minds of its own citizens, and to leave them no possibility of gain, except by means of industry and diligence within their legitimate sphere of activity, every true state must forbid as strictly, prevent as carefully, compensate as exactly, or punish as severely, any injury to the citizen of a neighboring state, as to one of its own. The law concerning the security of neighbors is necessarily a law in every state that is not a robber-state; and by its operation the possibility of any just complaint of one state against another, and consequently every case of self-defense among nations, is entirely prevented. There are no necessary, permanent, and immediate relations of states, as such, with each other that should be productive of strife; there are, properly speaking, only relations of the individual citizens of one state to the individual citizens of another; a state can be injured only in the person of one of its citizens; but such injury will be immediately compensated and the aggrieved state satisfied. Between such states as these, there is no rank that can be insulted, no ambition that can be offended. No officer of the one state is authorized to meddle in the internal affairs of another, nor is there any temptation for him to do so, since he could not derive the slightest personal advantage from any such influence. That a whole nation should determine, for the sake of plunder, to make war on a neighboring country, is impossible; for in a state where all are equal, the plunder could not become the booty of a few, but must be equally divided amongst all, and the share of no one individual could ever recompense him for the trouble of the war. Only where the advantage falls to the few oppressors, and the injury, the toil, the expense, to the countless herd of slaves, is a war of spoliation possible and conceivable. Not from states like themselves could such states as these entertain any fear of war, only from savages or barbarians whose lack of skill to enrich themselves by industry impels them to plunder, or from enslaved nations, driven by their masters to a war from which they themselves will reap no advantage. In the former case, each individual civilized state must already be the stronger through the arts of civilization; against the latter danger, the common advantage of all demands that they should strengthen themselves by union. No free state can reasonably suffer in its vicinity associations governed by rulers whose interests would be promoted by the subjugation of adjacent nations, and whose very existence is therefore a constant source of danger to their neighbors; a regard for their own security compels all free states to transform all around them into free states like themselves, and thus, for the sake of their own welfare, to extend the empire of culture over barbarism, of freedom over slavery. Soon will the nations civilized or enfranchised by them, find themselves placed in the same relation toward others still in the thrall of barbarism or slavery, in which the earlier free nations previously stood toward them, and they will be compelled to do the same things for these that were previously done for themselves; and thus, of necessity, by reason of the existence of some few really free states, will the empire of civilization, freedom, and with it universal peace, gradually embrace the whole world.

Thus, from the establishment of a just internal organization, and of peace between individuals, there will necessarily result integrity in the external relations of nations towards each other, and universal peace among them. But the establishment of this just internal organization, and the emancipation of the first nation that shall be truly free, arises as a necessary consequence from the ever-growing oppression exercised by the ruling classes towards their subjects, which gradually becomes insupportable—a progress that may safely be left to the passions and the blindness of those classes, even although warned of the result.

In these only true states all temptation to evil, nay, even the possibility of a man resolving upon a bad action with any reasonable hope of benefit to himself, will be entirely taken away; and the strongest possible motives will be offered to every man to make virtue the sole object of his will.

There is no man who loves evil because it is evil; it is only the advantages and enjoyments expected from it and, in the present condition of humanity, likely to result from it, that are loved. So long as this condition shall continue, so long as a premium shall be set upon vice, a fundamental improvement of mankind as a whole can scarcely be hoped for. But in a civil society constituted as it ought to be, as reason requires it to be, as the thinker may easily describe it to himself although he may nowhere find it actually existing at the present day, and as it must necessarily exist in the first nation that shall really acquire true freedom—in such a state of society, evil will present no advantages, but rather the most certain disadvantages, and self-love itself will restrain the excess of self-love when it would run out into injustice. By the unerring administration of such a state, every fraud or oppression practiced upon others, all self-aggrandizement at their expense, will be rendered not merely vain, and all labor so applied fruitless, but such attempts would even recoil upon their author, and assuredly bring home to himself the evil that he would cause to others. In his own land, outside his own land, throughout the whole world, he could find no one whom he might injure and yet go unpunished. But it is not to be expected, even of a bad man, that he would deter mine upon evil merely for the sake of such a resolution, although he had no power to carry it into effect, and nothing could arise from it but infamy to himself. The use of liberty for evil purposes is thus destroyed; man must resolve either to renounce his freedom altogether, and patiently to become a mere passive wheel in the great machine of the universe, or else to employ it for good. In soil thus prepared, good will easily prosper. When men shall no longer be divided by selfish purposes, nor their powers exhausted in struggles with each other, nothing will remain for them but to direct their united strength against the one common enemy that still remains unsubdued—resisting, uncultivated nature. No longer estranged from each other by private ends, they will necessarily combine for this common object; and thus there arises a body everywhere animated by the same spirit and the same love. Every misfortune to the individual, since it can no longer be a gain to any other individual, is a misfortune to the whole, and to each individual member of the whole, and is felt with the same pain, and remedied with the same activity, by every member; every step in advance made by one man is a step in advance made by the whole species. Here, where the petty, narrow self of mere individual personality is merged in the more comprehensive unity of the social constitution, each man truly loves every other as himself—as a member of this greater *self* that now claims all his love, and of which he himself is no more than a member, capable of participating only in a common gain or in a common loss. The strife of evil against good is here abolished, for here no evil can intrude. The strife of the good among themselves for the sake of good, disappears, now that they find it easy to love good for its own sake alone and not because they are its authors, now that it has become all-important to them that the truth should really be discovered, that the useful action should be done, but not at all important by whom this may be accomplished. Here each individual is at all times ready to join his strength to that of others, to make it subordinate to that of others; and whoever, according to the judgment of all, is most capable of accomplishing the greatest amount of good, will be supported by all, and his success rejoiced in by all with an equal joy.

This is the purpose of our earthly life, which reason sets before us, and for the infallible attainment of which she is our pledge and security. This is not an object given to us only that we may strive after it for the mere purpose of exercising our powers on something great, the real existence of which we may perhaps be compelled to abandon to doubt; it shall, it must be realized; there must be a time in which it shall be accomplished, as surely as there is a sensible world and a species of reasonable beings existent in time with respect to which nothing earnest and rational is conceivable besides this purpose, and whose existence becomes intelligible only through this purpose. Unless all human life be metamorphosed into a mere theatrical display for the gratification of some malignant spirit, who has implanted in poor humanity this inextinguishable longing for the imperishable only to amuse himself with its ceaseless pursuit of that which it can never overtake—its ever-repeated efforts, Ixion-like, to embrace that which still eludes its grasp, its restless hurrying onward in an ever-recurring circle, only to mock its earnest aspirations with an empty, insipid farce—unless the wise man, seeing through this mockery, and feeling an irrepressible disgust at continuing to play his part in it, is to cast life indignantly from him and make the moment of his awakening to reason also that of his physical death—unless these things are so, this purpose most assuredly must be attained. Yes! it is attainable *in life,* and *through life,* for Reason commands me to live: it is attainable, for I am.

III.

But when this end shall have been attained, and humanity shall at length stand at this point, what is there then to do? Upon earth there is no higher state than this; the generation that has once reached it can no more than abide there, steadfastly maintain its position, die, and leave behind it descendants who shall do the like, and who will again leave behind them descendants to follow in their footsteps. Humanity would thus stand still upon her path; and therefore her earthly end cannot be her highest end. This earthly end is conceivable, attainable, and finite. Even though we consider all preceding generations as means for the production of the last complete one, we do not thereby escape the question of earnest reason—to what end, then, is this last one? Since a human species has appeared upon earth, its existence there must certainly be in accordance with, and not contrary to, reason; and it must attain all the development it is possible for it to attain on earth. But why should such a species have an existence at all—why may it not as well have remained in the womb of chaos? Reason is not for the sake of existence, but existence for the sake of reason. An existence that does not of itself satisfy reason and solve all her questions cannot possibly be the true being.

And then, are those actions commanded by the voice of conscience

—by that voice whose dictates I never dare to criticize, but must always obey in silence—are those actions, in reality, always the means, and the only means, for the attainment of the earthly purpose of humanity? That I cannot do otherwise than refer them to this purpose, and dare not have any other object in view to be attained by means of them, is incontestible. But then are these, my intentions, always fulfilled?—is it enough that we will what is good, in order that it may happen? Alas! Many virtuous intentions are entirely lost for this world, and others appear even to hinder the purpose they were designed to promote. On the other hand, the most despicable passions of men, their vices and their crimes, often forward, more certainly, the good cause than the endeavors of the virtuous man, who will never do evil that good may come! It seems that the Highest Good of the world pursues its course of increase and prosperity quite independently of all human virtues or vices, according to its own laws, through an invisible and unknown Power, just as the heavenly bodies run their appointed course, independently of all human effort, and that this Power carries forward, in its own great plan, all human intentions, good and bad, and with overruling wisdom employs for its own purpose what was undertaken for other ends.

Thus, even if the attainment of this earthly end could be the purpose of our existence, and every doubt that reason could raise with regard to it were silenced, yet this end would not be ours, but the end of that unknown power. We do not know, even for a moment, what is conducive to this end; and nothing is left to us but to give by our actions some material, no matter what, for this power to work upon, and to leave to it the task of elaborating this material to its own purposes. It would, in that case, be our highest wisdom not to trouble ourselves about matters that do not concern us, to live according to our own fancy or inclinations, and quietly leave the consequences to that unknown power. The moral law within us would be void and superfluous, and absolutely unfitted to a being destined to nothing higher than this. In order to be at one with ourselves, we should have to refuse obedience to that law, and to suppress it as a perverse and foolish fanaticism.

No! I will not refuse obedience to the law of duty; as surely as I live and am, I will obey, absolutely because it commands. This resolution shall be first and highest in my mind, that by which everything else is determined, but which is itself determined by nothing else; this shall be the innermost principle of my spiritual life.

But, as a reasonable being, before whom a purpose must be set solely by its own will and determination, it is impossible for me to act without a motive and without an end. If this obedience is to be recognized by me as a reasonable service—if the voice that demands this obedience be really that of the creative reason within me, and not a mere fanciful enthusiasm, invented by my own imagination, or communicated to me somehow from without—this obedience must have some consequences, must serve some end. It is evident that it does not serve the purpose of the world of sense; there must, therefore, be a super-sensuous world, whose purposes it does promote.

The mist of delusion clears away from before my sight! I receive a new organ, and a new world opens before me. It is disclosed to me only by the law of reason, and answers only to that law in my spirit. I apprehend this world; limited as I am by my sensuous view, I must thus name the unnameable; I apprehend this world merely in and through the end demanded by my obedience; it is in reality nothing but this necessary end itself that reason annexes to the law of duty.

Setting aside everything else, how could I suppose that this law had reference to the world of sense, or that the whole end and object of the obedience it demands is to be found within that world, since what alone is important in this obedience serves no purpose whatever in that world, can never become a cause in it, and can never produce results. In the world of sense, which proceeds on a chain of material causes and effects, and in which whatever happens depends merely on what preceded it, it is never of any importance *how, and with what motives and intentions,* an action is performed, but only *what the action is.*

Had it been the whole purpose of our existence to produce an earthly condition of our species, there would have been required only an unerring mechanism by which our outward actions might have been determined—we would not have needed to be more than wheels well fitted to the great machine. Freedom would have been, not merely vain, but even obstructive; a virtuous will wholly superfluous. The world would, in that case, be most unskillfully directed, and attain the purposes of its existence by wasteful extravagance and circuitous byways. Had you, mighty World-Spirit! withheld from us this freedom that you are now constrained to adapt to your plans with labor and contrivance; had you rather at once compelled us to act in the way in which your plans required that we should act, you would have attained your purposes by a much shorter way, as the humblest of the dwellers in these your worlds can tell you. But I am free; and therefore such a chain of causes and effects, in which freedom is absolutely superfluous and without aim, cannot exhaust my whole nature. I must be free; for it is not the mere mechanical act, but the free determination of free will, for the sake of duty and for the ends of duty only—thus speaks the voice of conscience within us—this alone it is which constitutes our true worth. The bond with which this law of duty binds me is a bond for living spirits only; it disdains to rule over a dead mechanism, and addresses its decrees only to the living and the free. It requires of me this obedience; this obedience therefore cannot be nugatory or superfluous.

And now the Eternal World rises before me more brightly, and the fundamental law of its order stands clearly and distinctly apparent to my mental vision. In this world, *will* alone, as it lies concealed from mortal eye in the secret obscurities of the soul, is the first link in a chain of consequences that stretches through the whole invisible realms of spirit; as, in the physical world, *action*—a certain movement of matter—is the first link in a material chain that runs through the whole system of nature. The will is the efficient, living principle of the world of reason, as motion is the efficient, living principle of the world of sense. I stand in the center of two entirely opposite worlds: a visible world, in which action is the only moving power, and an invisible and absolutely incomprehensible world, in which will is the ruling principle. I am one of the primitive forces of both these worlds. My will embraces both. This will is, in itself, a constituent element of the super-sensuous world; for as I move it by my successive resolutions, I move and change something in that world, and my activity thus extends itself throughout the whole and gives birth to new and ever-enduring results that henceforward possess a real existence and need not again be produced. This will may break forth in a material act, and this act belongs to the world of sense and does there what pertains to a material act to do.

It is not necessary that I should first be severed from the terrestrial world before I can obtain admission into the celestial one; I am and live in it even now, far more truly than in the terrestrial; even now it is my only sure foundation, and the eternal life on the possession of which I have already entered is the only ground why I should still prolong this earthly one. What we call heaven does not lie beyond the grave; it is even here diffused around us, and its light arises in every pure heart. My will is mine, and it is the only thing that is wholly mine and entirely dependent on myself; and through it I have already become a citizen of the realm of freedom and of pure spiritual activity. What determination of my will—of the only thing by which I am raised from earth into this region—is best adapted to the order of the spiritual world, is proclaimed to me at every moment by my conscience, the bond that constantly unites me to it; and it depends solely on myself to give my activity the appointed direction. Thus I cultivate myself for this world, labor in it, and for it, in cultivating one of its members, in it, and only in it, pursue my purpose according to a settled plan, without doubt or hesitation, certain of the result, since here no foreign power stands opposed to my free will. That, in the world of sense, my will also becomes an action, is but the law of this sensuous world. I did not send forth the act as I did the will; only the latter was wholly and purely my work—it was all that proceeded forth from me. It was not even necessary that there should be another particular act on my part to unite the deed to the will; the deed unites itself to it according to the law of that second world with which I am connected through my will, and in which this will is likewise an original force, as it is in the first. I am indeed compelled, when I regard my will, determined according to the dictates of conscience, as a fact and an efficient cause in the world of sense, to refer it to that earthly purpose of humanity as a means to the accomplishment of an end— not as if I should first survey the plan of the world and from this knowledge calculate what I had to do, but the specific action that conscience directly enjoins me to do reveals itself to me at once as the only means by which, in my position, I can contribute to the attainment of that end. Even if it should afterwards appear as if this end had not been promoted—nay, if it should even seem to have been hindered—by my action, yet I can never regret it, nor perplex myself about it, so surely as I have truly obeyed my conscience in performing this act. Whatever consequences it may have in this world, in the other world nothing but good can result from it. And even in this world, should my action appear to have failed of its purpose, my conscience *for that very reason* commands me to repeat it in a manner that may more effectually reach its end; or, should it seem to have hindered that purpose, *for that very reason* to make good the detriment and annihilate the untoward result. I will as I ought, and the new deed follows. It may happen that the consequences of this new action, in the world of sense, may appear to me not more beneficial than those of the first; but, with respect to the other world, I retain the same calm assurance as before; and, in the present, it is again my bounden duty to make good my previous failure by new action. And thus, should it still appear that, during my whole earthly life, I have not advanced the good cause a single hair's-breadth in this world, yet I dare not cease my efforts: after every unsuccessful attempt, I must still believe that the next will be successful. But in the spiritual world no step is ever lost. In short, I do not pursue the earthly purpose for its own sake alone, or as a final aim, but only because my true final aim, obedience to the law of conscience, does not present itself to me in this world in any other shape than as the advancement of this end. I may not cease to pursue it, unless I were to deny the law of duty, or unless that law were to manifest itself to me, in this life, in some other shape than as a commandment to promote this purpose in my own place; I shall actually cease to pursue it in another life in which that commandment shall have set before me some other purpose wholly incomprehensible to me here. In this life, I must *will* to promote it, because I must obey; whether it be *actually* promoted by the deed that follows my will thus fittingly directed is not my care; I am responsible only for the will, but not for the result. Previous to the actual deed, I can never resign this purpose; the deed, when it is completed, I may resign, and repeat it, or improve it. Thus do I live and labor, even here, in my most essential nature and in my nearest purposes, only for the other world, and my activity for it is the only thing of which I am completely certain; in the world of sense I labor only for the sake of the other, and only because I cannot work for the other without at least *willing* to work for it.

I will establish myself firmly in this, to me, wholly new view of my vocation. The present life cannot be rationally regarded as the whole purpose of my existence, or of the existence of a human species in general; there is something in me, and there is something required of me, that finds in this life nothing to which it can be applied, and that is entirely superfluous and unnecessary for the attainment of the highest objects that can be attained on earth. There must therefore be a purpose in human existence that lies beyond this life. But should the present life, which is nevertheless imposed upon us, and which cannot be designed solely for the development of reason—since even awakened reason commands us to maintain it and to promote its highest purposes with all our powers—should this life not prove entirely vain and ineffectual, it must at least have relation to a future life, as means to an end. Now there is nothing in this present life whose ultimate consequences do not remain on earth—nothing whereby we could be connected with a future life—except our virtuous will, which in this world, by the fundamental laws thereof, is entirely fruitless. Only by our virtuous will can we, must we, labor for another life, and for the first and nearest objects that are there revealed to us; and it is the consequences, invisible to us, of this virtuous will through which we first acquire a firm foothold in that life, from whence we may then advance in a further course of progress.

That our virtuous will, in and for and through itself, must have consequences, we know already in this life, for reason cannot command anything that is without a purpose; but what these consequences may be—nay, how it is even possible for a mere will to produce any effect at all—as to this we can form no conception whatever, so long as we are still confined to this material world; and it is true wisdom not to undertake an inquiry in which we know beforehand that we shall be unsuccessful. With respect to the nature of these consequences, the present life is therefore, in relation to the future, *a life in faith.* In the future life, we shall possess these consequences, for we shall then proceed from them as our starting-point, and build upon them as our foundation; and this other life will thus be, in relation to the consequences of our virtuous will in the present, *a life in sight.* In that other life, we shall also have an immediate purpose set before us, as we have in the present; for our activity must not cease But we remain finite beings—and for finite beings there is but finite determinate activity, and every determinate act has a determinate end. As, in the present life, the actually existing world as we find it around us, the fitting adjustment of this world to the work we have to do in it, the degree of culture and virtue already attained by men, and our own physical powers—as these stand related to the purposes of this life, so, in the future life, the consequences of our virtuous will in the present shall stand related to the purposes of that other existence. The present is the commencement of our existence; the endowments requisite for its purpose, and a firm footing in it, have been freely bestowed on us; the future is the continuation of this existence, and in it we must acquire for ourselves a commencement, and a definite footing.

And now the present life no longer appears vain and useless; for this and this alone it is given to us—that we may acquire for ourselves a firm foundation in the future life—and only by means of this foundation is it connected with our whole external existence. It is very possible, that the immediate purpose of this second life may prove as unattainable by finite powers, with certainty and after a fixed plan, as the purpose of the present life is now, and that even there a virtuous will may appear superfluous and without result. But it can never be lost there, any more than here, for it is the eternal and unalterable command of reason. Its necessary efficacy would, in that case, direct us to a third life, in which the consequences of our virtuous will in the second life would become visible—a life that, during the second life, would again be believed in through faith, but with firmer, more unwavering confidence, since we should already have had practical experience of the truthfulness of reason, and have regained the fruits of a pure heart that had been faithfully garnered up in a previously completed life.

As in the present life it is only from the command of conscience to follow a certain course of action that there arises our conception of a certain purpose in this action, and from this our whole intuitive perception of a world of sense, so in the future, upon a similar, but now to us wholly inconceivable command, will be founded our conception of the immediate purpose of that life; and upon this, again, our intuitive perception of a world in which we shall set out from the consequences of our virtuous will in the present life. The present world exists for us only through the law of duty; the other will be revealed to us, in a similar manner, through another command of duty; for in no other manner can a world exist for any reasonable being.

This, then, is my whole sublime vocation, my true nature. I am a member of two orders: the one purely spiritual, in which I rule by my will alone; the other sensuous, in which I operate by my deed. The whole end of reason is pure activity, absolutely by itself alone, having no need of any instrument out of itself—independence of everything that is not reason, absolute freedom. The will is the living principle of reason, is itself reason, when purely and simply apprehended; that reason is active by itself alone, means that pure will, merely as such, lives and rules. It is only the Infinite Reason that lives immediately and wholly in this purely spiritual order. The finite reason—which does not of itself constitute the world of reason, but is only one of its many members—lives necessarily at the same time in a sensuous order, that is to say, in one that presents to it another object, beyond a purely spiritual activity—a material object, to be promoted by instruments and powers that indeed stand under the immediate dominion of the will, but whose activity is also conditioned by their own natural laws. Yet as surely as reason is reason, the will must operate absolutely by itself, and independently of the natural laws by which the material action is determined; and hence the sensuous life of every finite being points towards a higher, into which the will, by itself alone, may open the way, and of which it may acquire possession, a possession which indeed we must again sensuously conceive of as a state, and not as a mere will.

These two orders—the purely spiritual and the sensuous, the latter consisting possibly of an innumerable series of particular lives—have existed since the first moment of the development of an active reason within me, and still proceed parallel to each other. The latter order is only a phenomenon for myself, and for those with whom I am associated in this life; the former alone gives it significance, purpose, and value. I *am* immortal, imperishable, eternal, as soon as I form the resolution to obey the laws of reason; I do not need to *become* so. The super-sensuous world is no future world; it is now present; it can at no point of finite existence be more present than at another, not more present after an existence of myriads of lives than at this moment. My sensuous existence may, in future, assume other forms, but these are just as little the true life as its present form. By that resolution I lay hold on eternity, and cast off this earthly life and all other forms of sensuous life which may yet lie before me in futurity, and place myself far above them. I become the sole source of my own being and its phenomena, and, henceforth, unconditioned by anything external to me, I have life in myself. My will, which is directed by no foreign agency in the order of the super-sensuous world, but by myself alone, is this source of true life, and of eternity.

It is my will alone that is this source of true life and of eternity; only by recognising this will as the peculiar seat of moral goodness, and by actually raising it thereto, do I obtain the assurance and the possession of that super-sensuous world.

Without regard to any conceivable or visible object, without inquiry as to whether my will may be followed by any result other than the mere volition, I must will in accordance with the moral law. My will stands alone, apart from all that is not itself, and is its own world merely by itself and for itself, not only as being itself an absolutely *first,* primary and original power, before which there is no preceding influence by which it may be governed, but also as being followed by no conceivable or comprehensible *second* step in the series, coming after it, by which its activity may be brought under the dominion of a foreign law. If there proceeded from it any second, and from this again a third result, and so forth, in any conceivable sensuous world opposed to the spiritual world, then its strength would be broken by the resistance it would encounter from the independent elements of such a world that it would set in motion; the mode of its activity would no longer exactly correspond to the purpose expressed in the volition; and the will would no longer remain free, but be partly limited by the peculiar laws of its heterogeneous sphere of action. And so I must actually regard the will in the present sensuous world, the only one known to me. I am indeed compelled to believe, and consequently to act as if I thought, that by my mere volition my tongue, my hand, or my foot, might be set in motion; but how a mere aspiration, an impress of intelligence upon itself, such as will is, can be the principle of motion to a heavy material mass, this I not only find it impossible to conceive, but the mere assertion is, before the tribunal of the understanding, a palpable absurdity; here the movement of matter even in myself can be explained only by the internal forces of matter itself.

Such a view of my will as I have taken, can, however, be attained only through an intimate conviction that it is not merely the highest active principle for this world—which it certainly might be, without having freedom in itself, by the mere influence of the system of the universe, perchance, as we must conceive of a formative power in Nature—but that it absolutely disregards all earthly objects, and generally all objects lying out of itself, and recognizes itself, for its own sake, as its own ultimate end. But by such a view of my will I am at once directed to a super-sensuous order of things, in which the will, by itself alone and without any instrument lying out of itself, becomes an efficient cause in a sphere that, like itself, is purely spiritual, and is thoroughly accessible to it. That moral volition is demanded of us absolutely for its own sake alone—a truth I discover only as a fact in my inward consciousness, and cannot come to know in any other way—this was the first step of my thought. That this demand is reasonable, and the source and standard of all else that is reasonable, that it is not modelled upon any other thing whatever, but that all other things must, on the contrary, model themselves upon it, and be dependent upon it—another conviction I cannot arrive at from without, but can attain only by inward experience, by means of the unhesitating and immovable assent I freely accord to this demand—this was the second step of my thought. And by these two steps I have attained to faith in a super-sensuous Eternal World. If I abandon the former, the latter falls to the ground. If it were true—as many say it is, assuming it without further proof as self-evident and extolling it as the highest summit of human wisdom—that all human virtue must have before it a certain definite external object, and that it must first be assured of the possibility of attaining this object, before it can act and before it can become virtue, that, consequently, reason by no means contains within itself the principle and the standard of its own activity, but must receive this standard from without, through contemplation of an external world—if this were true, then the ultimate end of our existence might be accomplished here below, human nature might be completely developed and exhausted by our earthly vocation, and we should have no rational ground for raising our thoughts above the present life.

But every thinker who has somewhere acquired those first principles even historically, moved perhaps by a mere love of the new and unusual, and who is able to carry out a correct course of reasoning from them, might speak and teach as I have now spoken to myself. He would then present us with the thoughts of some other being, not with his own; everything would float before him empty and without significance, because he would be without the sense whereby he might apprehend its reality. He is a blind man, who, upon certain true principles concerning colors that he has learned historically, has built a perfectly correct theory of color, notwithstanding that there is in reality no color existing for him; he can tell how, under certain conditions, it *must be,* but to him it *is* not so, because he does not stand under these conditions. The faculty by which we lay hold on Eternal Life is to be attained only by actually renouncing the sensuous and its objects, and sacrificing them to that law which takes cognizance of our will only and not of our actions, renouncing them with the firmest conviction that it is reasonable for us to do so—nay, that it is the only thing reasonable for us. By this renunciation of the Earthly, faith in the Eternal first arises in our soul, and is there enshrined apart, as the only support to which we can cling after we have given up all else —as the only animating principle that can elevate our minds and inspire our lives. We must indeed, according to the figure of a sacred doctrine, first "die unto the world and be born again, before we can enter the kingdom of God."

I see—Oh I now see clearly before me the cause of my former indifference and blindness concerning spiritual things! Absorbed by mere earthly objects, lost in them with all our thoughts and efforts, moved and urged onward only by the notion of a result lying beyond ourselves—by the desire of such a result and of our enjoyment therein —insensible and dead to the pure impulse of reason, which gives a law to itself and offers to our aspirations a purely spiritual end, the immortal Psyche remains, with fettered pinions, fastened to the earth. Our philosophy becomes the history of our own heart and life; and according to what we ourselves are, we conceive of man and his vocation. Never impelled by any other motive than the desire for what can be actually realized in this world, there is for us no true freedom—no freedom that holds the ground of its determination absolutely and entirely within itself. Our freedom is, at best, that of the self-forming plant, not essentially higher in its nature, but only more artistic, in its results, not producing a mere material form with roots, leaves, and blossoms, but a mind with impulses, thoughts, and actions. We cannot have the slightest conception of true freedom, because we do not ourselves possess it; when it is spoken of, we either bring down what is said to the level of our own notions, or at once declare all such talk to be nonsense. Without the idea of freedom, we are likewise without the faculty for another world. Everything of this kind floats past before us like words that are not addressed to us; like a pale shadow, without color or meaning, which we know not how to lay hold of or retain. We leave it as we find it, without the least participation or sympathy. Or should we ever be urged by a more active zeal to consider it seriously, we then convince ourselves to our own satisfaction that all such ideas are untenable and worthless reveries, which the man of sound understanding unhesitatingly rejects; and according to the premises from which we proceed, made up as they are of our inward experiences, we are perfectly in the right and secure from either refutation or conversion so long as we remain what we are. The excellent doctrines that are taught among us with a special authority, concerning freedom, duty, and everlasting life, become to us romantic fables, like those of Tartarus and the Elysian fields, although we do not publish to the world this secret opinion, because we find it expedient, by means of these figures, to maintain an outward decorum among the populace, or, should we be less reflective, and ourselves bound in the chains of authority, then we sink to the level of the common mind, and believing what, *thus understood,* would be mere foolish fables, we find in those pure spiritual symbols only the promise of continuing throughout eternity the same miserable existence we possess here below.

In one word: only by the fundamental improvement of my will

does a new light arise within me concerning my existence and vocation; without this, however much I may speculate, and with no matter what rare intellectual gifts I may be endowed, darkness remains within me and around me. The improvement of the heart alone leads to true wisdom. Let my whole life then be unceasingly devoted to this one purpose.

IV.

My Moral Will merely as such, in and through itself, shall certainly and invariably produce consequences; every determination of my will in accordance with duty, although no action should follow it, shall operate in another, to me incomprehensible, world, in which nothing but this moral determination of the will shall possess efficient activity. What is it that is assumed in this conception?

Obviously a *Law,* a rule absolutely without exception, according to which a will determined by duty must have consequences, just as in the material world that surrounds me I assume a law according to which this ball, when thrown by my hand with this particular force, in this particular direction, necessarily moves in such a direction with a certain degree of velocity, perhaps strikes another ball with a certain amount of force, which in its turn moves on with a certain velocity, and so on. As here, in the mere direction and motion of my hand, I already perceive and apprehend all the consequent directions and movements, with the same certainty as if they were already present before me, even so do I embrace by means of my virtuous will a series of necessary and inevitable consequences in the spiritual world, as if they were already present before me—only that I cannot define them as I do those in the material world, that is, I only know *that* they must be, but not *how* they shall be; and even in knowing this I conceive of a law of the spiritual world, in which my pure will is one of the moving forces, as my hand is one of the moving forces of the material world. My own firm confidence in these results, and the conceptions of this law of the spiritual world, are one and the same; they are not two thoughts, one of which arises by means of the other, but they are entirely the same thought, just as the confidence with which I calculate on a certain motion in a material body, and the conception of a mechanical law of nature on which that motion depends, are one and the same. The conception of a law expresses nothing more than the firm, immovable confidence of reason in a principle, and the absolute impossibility of admitting its opposite.

I assume such a law of a spiritual world, not given by my will nor by the will of any finite being, nor by the will of all finite beings taken together, but to which my will, and the will of all finite beings, is subject. Neither I nor any finite and therefore sensuous being can conceive how a mere will can have consequences, nor what may be the true nature of those consequences; for herein consists the essential character of our finite nature, that we are unable to conceive this, that having indeed our will, as such, wholly within our power, we are nevertheless compelled by our sensuous nature to regard the consequences of that will as sensuous states; how then can I, or any other finite being whatever, propose as objects, and thereby give reality to, what can neither be imagined nor conceived? I cannot say that in the material world my hand, or any other body which belongs to that world and is subject to the universal law of gravity, brings this law into operation; these bodies themselves stand under this law, and are able to set another body in motion only in accordance with this law, and only in so far as that body, by virtue of this law, partakes of the universal moving power of Nature. Just as little can a finite will give a law to the super-sensuous world, which no finite spirit can embrace; but all finite wills stand under the law of that world, and can produce results therein only inasmuch as that law already exists, and inasmuch as they themselves, in accordance with the form of that law which is applicable to finite wills, bring themselves under its conditions, and within the sphere of its activity, by moral obedience—by moral obedience, I say, the only tie that unites them to that highei world, the only nerve that descends from it to them, and the only organ through which they can react upon it. As the universal power of attraction embraces all bodies, and holds them together in themselves and with each other, and the movement of each separate body is possible only on the supposition of this power, so does that super-sensuous law unite, hold together, and embrace all finite reasonable beings. My will, and the will of all finite beings, may be regarded from a double point of view: partly as a mere *volition,* an internal act directed upon itself alone, and, in so far, the will is complete in itself, concluded in this act of volition; partly as something beyond this, a *fact.* It assumes the latter form to me, as soon as I regard it as completed; but it must also become so beyond me: in the world of sense, as the moving principle, for instance, of my hand, from the movement of which, again, other movements follow; in the super-sensuous world, as the principle of a series of spiritual consequences of which I have no conception. From the former point of view, as a mere act of volition, it stands wholly within my own power; its assumption of the latter character, that of an active first principle, depends not upon me, but on a law to which I myself am subject— on the law of nature in the world of sense, on a super-sensuous law in the world of pure thought.

What, then, is this law of the spiritual world which I conceive? This idea now stands before me, in fixed and perfect shape; I cannot, and dare not add anything whatever to it; I have only to express and interpret it distinctly. It is obviously not such as I may suppose the principle of my own, or any other possible sensuous world, to be—a fixed, inert existence, from which, by the encounter of a will, some internal power may be evolved, something altogether different from a mere will. For—and this is the substance of my belief—my will, abso- lutely by itself, and without the intervention of any instrument that might weaken its expression, shall act in a perfectly congenial sphere, reason upon reason, spirit upon spirit—in a sphere to which neverthe- less it does not give the law of life, activity, and progress, but which has that law in itself; therefore, upon self-active reason. But self- active reason is will. The law of the super-sensuous world must, there- fore, be a Will—a Will that operates purely as will, by itself, and ab- solutely without any instrument or sensible material of its activity, which is, at the same time, both act and product, with whom to will is to do, to command is to execute, in which therefore the instinctive demand of reason for absolute freedom and independence is realized: a Will that in itself is law, determined by no fancy or caprice, through no previous reflection, hesitation or doubt, but eternal, unchangeable, on which we may securely and infallibly rely, as the physical man relies with certainty on the laws of his world; a Will in which the moral will of finite beings, and this alone, has sure and unfailing results, since for it all else is unavailing, all else is as if it were not.

That sublime Will thus pursues no solitary path withdrawn from the other parts of the world of reason. There is a spiritual bond be- tween Him and all finite rational beings, and He himself is this spirit- ual bond of the rational universe. Let me will, purely and decidedly, my duty, and He wills that, in the spiritual world at least, my will shall prosper. Every moral resolution of a finite being goes up before Him, and—to speak after the manner of mortals—moves and deter- mines Him, not in consequence of a momentary satisfaction, but in accordance with the eternal law of His being. With surprising clear- ness does this thought, which hitherto was surrounded with darkness, now reveal itself to my soul—the thought that my will, merely as such, and through itself, shall have results. It has results, because it is immediately and infallibly perceived by another Will to which it is related, which is its own accomplishment and the only living principle of the spiritual world; *in Him* it has its first results, and *through Him* it acquires an influence on the whole spiritual world, which throughout is but a product of that Infinite Will.

Thus do I approach—the mortal must speak in his own language —thus do I approach that Infinite Will; and the voice of conscience in my soul, which teaches me in every situation of life what I have there to do, is the channel through which again His influence descends upon me. That voice, made sensuous by my environment, and translated into my language, is the oracle of the Eternal World that announces to me how I am to perform my part in the order of the spiritual universe, or in the Infinite Will who is Himself that order. I cannot, indeed, survey or comprehend that spiritual order, and I need not do so; I am but a link in its chain, and can no more judge of the whole than a single tone of music can judge of the entire harmony of which it forms a part. But what I myself ought to be in this harmony of spirits I must know, for it is only I myself who can make me so; and this must be immediately revealed to me by a voice whose tones descend upon me from that other world. Thus do I stand connected with the ONE who alone has existence, and thus do I participate in His being. There is nothing real, lasting, imperishable in me, but these two elements: the voice of conscience, and my free obedience. By the first, the spiritual world bows down to me, and embraces me as one of its members; by the second I raise myself into this world, apprehend it, and react upon it. That Infinite Will is the mediator between it and me; for He himself is the original source both of it and me. This is the one True and Imperishable, for which my soul yearns even from its inmost depths; all else is mere appearance, ever vanishing, and ever returning in a new semblance.

This Will unites me with himself; He also unites me with all finite beings like myself, and is the common mediator between us all. This is the great mystery of the invisible world, and its fundamental law, in so far as it is a world or system of many individual wills—*the union, and direct reciprocal action, of many separate and independent wills*—a mystery that already lies clearly before every eye in the present life, without attracting the notice of any one, or being regarded as in any way wonderful. The voice of conscience, which imposes on each his particular duty, is the light-beam on which we come forth from the bosom of the Infinite, and assume our place as particular individual beings; it fixes the limits of our personality; it is thus the true original element of our nature, the foundation and material of all our life. The absolute freedom of the will, which we bring down with us from the Infinite into the world of Time, is the principle of our life. I act; and, the sensible intuition through which alone I become a personal intelligence being supposed, it is easy to conceive how I must necessarily know of my action—I know it, because it is I myself who act; it is easy to conceive how, by means of this sensible intuition, my spiritual act appears to me as a fact in a world of sense, and how, on the other hand, by the same process of becoming sensuous, the law of duty that, in itself, is a purely spiritual law, should appear to me as the command to such an action; it is easy to conceive how an actually present world should appear to me as the condition of this action, and, in part, as the consequence and product of it. Thus far I remain within myself and upon my own territory; everything here that has an existence for me unfolds itself purely and solely from myself; I see everywhere only myself, and no true existence out of myself. But in this my world I admit, also, the operations of other beings, separate and independent of me, as much as I of them. How these beings can themselves know of the influences that proceed from them may easily be conceived; they know of them in the same way I know of my own. But how *I* can know of *them* is absolutely inconceivable, just as it is inconceivable how *they* can possess that knowledge of *my* existence, and its manifestations, which nevertheless I ascribe to them. How do they come within my world, or I within theirs?—since the principle by which the consciousness of ourselves, of our operations, and of their sensuous conditions, is deduced from ourselves, *i.e.,* the principle that each individual must undoubtedly know what he himself does, is here wholly inapplicable. How have free spirits knowledge of free spirits, since we know that free spirits are the only reality, and that an independent world of sense, through which they might act on each other, is no longer to be taken into account. Or shall it be said that I perceive reasonable beings like myself by the changes they produce in the world of sense? Then I ask again: How do you perceive these changes? I comprehend very well how you can perceive changes that are brought about by the mere mechanism of nature; for the law of this mechanism is no other than the law of your own thought, according to which, this world being once assumed, it is carried out into farther developments. But the changes of which we now speak are not brought about by the mere mechanism of nature, but by a free will elevated above all nature; and only in so far as you can regard them in this character, can you infer from them the existence of free beings like yourself. Where then is the law within you, according to which you can realize the determinations of other wills absolutely independent of you? In short, this mutual recognition and reciprocal action of free beings in this world is perfectly inexplicable by the laws of nature or of thought, and can be explained only through the One in whom they are united, although to each other they are separate—through the Infinite Will who sustains and embraces them all in His own sphere. Not immediately from you to me, nor from me to you, flows the knowledge we have of each other; we are separated by an insurmountable barrier. Only through the common fountain of our spiritual being do we know of each other; only in Him do we recognize each other, and influence each other. "Here reverence the image of freedom upon the earth; here, a work that bears its impress"—thus it is proclaimed within me by the voice of that Will which speaks to me only in so far as it imposes duties upon me; and the only principle through which I recognize you and your work is the command of conscience to respect them.

Whence, then, our feelings, our sensible intuitions, our discursive laws of thought, on all of which is founded the external world we behold, in which we believe that we exert an influence on each other? With respect to the last two—our sensible intuitions and our laws of thought—to say these are laws of reason in itself is to give no satisfactory answer at all. For us, indeed, who are excluded from the pure domain of reason in itself, it may be impossible to think otherwise, or to conceive of reason under any other law. But the true law of reason in itself is the practical law, the law of the super-sensuous world, or of that sublime Will. And, leaving this for a moment undecided, whence comes our universal agreement as to feelings, which, nevertheless, are something positive, immediate, inexplicable? On this agreement in feeling, perception, and in the laws of thought, however, depends the fact that we all behold the same external world.

"It is a harmonious, although inconceivable, limitation of the infinite rational beings who compose our species; and only by means of such a harmonious limitation do they become a species"—thus answers the philosophy of mere knowledge, and here it must rest as its highest point. But what can set a limit to reason but reason itself? —what can limit all finite reason but the Infinite Reason? This universal agreement concerning a sensible world, assumed and accepted by us as the foundation of all our other life, and as the sphere of our duty—which, strictly considered, is just as incomprehensible as our unanimity concerning the products of our reciprocal freedom—this agreement is the result of the One Eternal Infinite Will. Our faith, of which we have spoken as faith in duty, is only faith in Him, in His reason, in His truth. What, then, is the peculiar and essential truth we accept in the world of sense, and believe in? Nothing less than that from our free and faithful performance of our duty in this world there will arise to us throughout eternity a life in which our freedom and morality may still continue their development. If this be true, then indeed there is truth in our world, and the only truth possible for finite beings; and it must be true, for this world is the result of the Eternal Will in us, and that Will, by the law of His own being, can have no other purpose with respect to finite beings than the one we have set forth.

That Eternal Will is thus assuredly the Creator of the World, in the only way He can be so, and in the only way it needs creation—in the finite reason. Those who regard Him as building up a world from an everlasting inert matter, which must still remain inert and lifeless, like a vessel made by human hands, not an eternal procession of His self-development—or who ascribe to Him the production of a material universe out of nothing—know neither the world nor Him. If only matter can be reality, then the world would indeed be nothing, and throughout all eternity would remain nothing. Reason alone exists: the Infinite in Himself, the finite in Him and through Him. Only in our minds has He created a world; at least that *from which* we unfold it, and that *by which* we unfold it: the voice of duty, and harmonious feelings, intuitions, and laws of thought. It is His light through which we behold the light and all that it reveals to us. In our minds He still creates this world, and acts upon it by acting upon our minds through the call of duty, as soon as another free being changes anything therein. In our minds He upholds this world, and thereby the finite existence of which alone we are capable, by continually evolving from each state of our existence other states in succession. When He shall have sufficiently proved us according to His supreme designs for our next succeeding vocation, and we shall have sufficiently cultivated ourselves for entering upon it, then, by what we call death, He will annihilate for us this life and introduce us to a new life, the product of our virtuous actions. All our life is His life. We are in His hand, and abide therein, and no one can pluck us out of His hand. We are eternal, because He is eternal. . . .

GEORG WILHELM FRIEDRICH HEGEL

Introduction to the Philosophy of History

Logic (Part I of the Encyclopedia of the
Philosophical Sciences), Chapter VII, A

SUPPLEMENTARY PASSAGES

Philosophy and the Actual World

Dialectic

Spirit

Art

Religion

GEORG WILHELM
FRIEDRICH HEGEL

BORN INTO an upper middle class family in Stuttgart, Georg Wilhelm Friedrich Hegel (1770–1831) studied in the seminary at the University of Tübingen, where his earliest reflections on the lifelong problems of his philosophy began under the stimulus of his fellow theological students, the poet Hölderlin and the philosopher Schelling. After seven years as a private tutor, he became a lecturer at Jena (1801). For a few years he edited a philosophical journal with Schelling, and was appointed to a professorship in 1805. Napoleon's victory in the battle of Jena interrupted his teaching for some years, and he spent this interval as editor of a newspaper in Bamberg and as principal of a school in Nuremberg. He married, very happily, in 1811. In 1816 he was appointed at Heidelberg, in 1818 at Berlin, where he remained till his death, the much respected and widely famous founder of a new school of philosophy.

Hegel published four books in his lifetime. The first, *The Phenomenology of the Spirit* (1807; trans. as *The Phenomenology of Mind,* by J. B. Baillie, London: Allen and Unwin, 1910; rev., 1931; trans. as *The Phenomenology of Spirit,* by A. V. Miller, Oxford: Oxford University Press, 1977) is an original and puzzling work, in which Hegel distinguishes various kinds and grades of human experience as phases through which Spirit passes on its way to complete self-consciousness. *The Science of Logic* (in two parts, 1812, 1816; trans. W. H. Johnson and L. G. Struthers, London: Allen and Unwin, 2 vols., 1929) is the fullest development of his system of categories, which is also presented in his shorter *Logic,* a selection from which is included in the present volume. This shorter *Logic* is Part I of Hegel's third published work, *The Encyclopaedia of the Philosophical Sciences (The Encyclopaedia of Logic,* trans. T. F. Geraets et al., Hackett, 1991; for Part III of *The Encyclopaedia,* see *Philosophy of Mind,* trans. A. V. Miller, Oxford: Oxford University Press, 1971). His ethical and political philosophy is presented in *The Philosophy of Right* (or *Law*) (1820; trans. T. M. Knox, Oxford: Clarendon Press, 1942).

The main branches of Hegel's philosophy were elaborated in his university lectures, of which his notes and some detailed reports by students remain. On the basis of these, four other large works were published after his death. These are: *Lectures on the Philosophy of Religion* (1832; rev. 1840; trans. E. B. Speirs and J. B. Sanderson, London: Kegan Paul, Trench & Trubner, 3 vols., 1895; trans. R. F. Brown, P. C. Hodgson, and J. M. Stewart, *The Lectures on the Philosophy of Religion of 1827,* 1 vol., Berkeley: University of California Press, 1988); *Lectures on the History of Philosophy* (1833–36; rev. 1842; trans. E. S. Haldane, London: Kegan Paul, 3 vols., 1892–96; the introduction also trans. T. M. Knox and A. V. Miller, New York: Oxford University Press, 1987); *Lectures on Aesthetics* (1835–38; rev. 1840–43; trans. F. P. B. Osmaston, London: G. Bell, 4 vols., 1920; trans. T. M. Knox, Oxford University Press, 2 vols., 1975; the Introduction and also trans. by Bernard Bosanquet, London: Kegan Paul, 1886; the Introduction and also trans. by T. M. Knox, New York: Oxford University Press, 1979); selections trans. by Anne and Henry Paolucci are in *Hegel on Tragedy,* Westport: Greenwood Press, 1962); *Lectures on the Philosophy of History* (trans. J. Sibree, London: Colonial Press, 1900); of considerable interest also are his *Early Theological Writings* (trans. T. M. Knox and Richard Kroner, Chicago: University of Chicago Press, 1948); and *The Difference Between Fichte's and Schelling's System of Philosophy* (trans. H. S. Harris and Walter Cerf, Albany: State University of New York Press, 1977).

The influences, both for good and ill, of so vast a system of thought as Hegel's philosophy cannot very safely be summed up, but in his widespread philosophical explorations he made important discoveries, and opened up new routes of inquiry even for those who are skeptical of the existence of the worlds he claimed to have found. Early in his development, Hegel sought a rational method of transcending Kant's phenomenal world, to get at a more ultimate reality, and though his thinking was substantially assisted by both Schelling and Fichte, it was he who worked out in detail a new kind of reasoning, his dialectical method, which, for all its debt to Plato and Kant, was in his hands highly original. It was an attempt worth making and, at the very least, he turned up some interesting and illuminating relations among concepts or categories that play a fundamental role, largely unnoticed, in our ordinary thinking: real and ideal, existence and actuality, something and nothing. Besides inventing his own technical terms, he, like Aristotle, often tried to clarify the use of ordinary language.

On the large scale, Hegel's thinking was an attempt—sometimes heroic—to do justice to the reality of partial truths, relative perspectives, one-sided insights, without losing track of truth itself completely. He is a relentless critic of what he calls "abstractions," and his whole system, which is temporal or historical in its basic way of moving, exhibits an incredible confidence that all antithetical ideas can in the end be given a positive and fruitful place in the complex of truth. It was this orientation that enabled him to develop one branch of philosophy, the philosophy of history, more profoundly, in the questions he raised, than anyone had ever done before, and to develop some concepts that have proved (for all their perils) highly useful to the sciences of man: cultural anthropology, sociology, political science—concepts such as culture, the state (in his sense), organism, world history, pre-history.

Introduction to the Philosophy of History*

I. The Three Kinds of History

The subject of this course of lectures is the Philosophical History of the World. And by this must be understood, not a collection of general observations respecting it, suggested by the study of its records and illustrated by its facts, but Universal History itself. To gain a clear idea at the outset of the nature of our task, it seems necessary to begin with an examination of the other methods of treating History. The various methods may be ranged under three heads:

1. Original History.
2. Reflective History.
3. Philosophical History.

(1) Of the first kind, the mention of one or two distinguished names will furnish a definite type. To this category belong Herodotus, Thucydides, and other historians of the same order, whose descriptions are for the most part limited to deeds, events, and states of society, which they had before their eyes, and whose spirit they shared. They simply transferred what was passing in the world around them to the realm of representative intellect. An external phenomenon is thus translated into an internal conception. In the same way the poet operates upon the material supplied him by his emotions, projecting it into an image for the conceptual faculty. These original historians did, it is true, find statements and narratives of other men ready to hand. One person cannot be an eye- and ear-witness of everything. But they make use of such aids only as the poet does of that heritage of an already-formed language, to which he owes so much; merely as an ingredient. Historians bind together the fleeting elements of story, and treasure them up for immortality in the Temple of Mnemosyne. Legends, Ballad-stories, Traditions must be excluded from such original history. These are but dim and hazy forms of historical ap-

* From *Lectures on the Philosophy of History,* translated by J. Sibree, London: G. Bell (Bohn's Philosophical Library), 1881, from the edition by Karl Hegel, 1840. These notes for lectures delivered during the years 1822-31, supplemented by two sets of notes by students, were first published (after Hegel's death) in 1837 as *Lectures on the Philosophy of History.* The selection given here is the general Introduction. Sibree's translation has been edited, and chapter headings added, for this edition.

prehension, and therefore belong to nations whose intelligence is but half awakened. Here, on the contrary, we have to do with people fully conscious of what they were and what they were about. The domain of reality—actually seen, or capable of being so—affords a much firmer basis than that fugitive and shadowy element in which were engendered those legends and poetic dreams whose historical prestige vanishes as soon as nations have attained a mature individuality.

Such original historians, then, change the events, the deeds and the states of society with which they are conversant, into an object for the conceptual faculty. The narratives they leave us cannot, therefore, be very comprehensive in their range. Herodotus, Thucydides, Guicciardini, may be taken as fair samples of the class in this respect. What is present and living in their environment, is their proper material. The influences that have formed the writer are identical with those which have moulded the events that constitute the matter of his story. The author's spirit, and that of the actions he narrates, are one and the same. He describes scenes in which he himself has been an actor, or at any rate an interested spectator. It is short periods of time, individual shapes of persons and occurrences, single unreflected traits, of which he makes his picture. And his aim is nothing more than the presentation to posterity of an image of events as clear as that which he himself possessed in virtue of personal observation or life-like descriptions by others. Reflections are none of his business, for he lives in the spirit of his subject; he has not attained an elevation above it. If, as in Caesar's case, he belongs to the exalted rank of generals or statesmen, it is the prosecution of his own aims that constitutes the history.

Such speeches as we find in Thucydides (for example), of which we can positively assert that they are not *bona fide* reports, would seem to contradict our statement that a historian of his kind presents us no reflected picture; that persons and people appear in his works in *propriâ personâ*. Speeches, it must be allowed, are veritable transactions in the human commonwealth; in fact, very gravely influential transactions. It is, indeed, often said, "Such and such things are only talk"; by way of demonstrating their harmlessless. That for which this excuse is brought, may be mere "talk"; and talk enjoys the important privilege of being harmless. But addresses of peoples to peoples, or orations directed to nations and to princes, are integral constituents of history. Granted that such orations as those of Pericles —that most profoundly accomplished, genuine, and noble statesman

—were elaborated by Thucydides; it must yet be maintained that they were not foreign to the character of the speaker. In the orations in question, these men proclaim the maxims adopted by their country-men, those that formed their own character; they record their views of their political relations, and of their moral and spiritual nature; and the principle of their designs and conduct. What the historian puts into their mouths is no supposititious system of ideas, but an uncorrupted transcript of their intellectual and moral traits.

Of these historians, whom we must make thoroughly our own, with whom we must linger long, if we would live with their respective nations, and enter deeply into their spirit: of these historians, to whose pages we may turn not for the purpose of erudition merely, but with a view to deep and genuine enjoyment, there are fewer than might be imagined. Herodotus, the Father, i.e. the Founder, of History, and Thucydides have already been mentioned. Xenophon's *Retreat of the Ten Thousand* is a work equally original. Caesar's *Commentaries* are the simple masterpiece of a mighty spirit. Among the ancients, these annalists were necessarily great captains and statesmen. In the Middle Ages, if we except the Bishops, who were placed in the very center of the political world, the Monks monopolize this category as naïve chroniclers who were as decidedly isolated from active life as those ancient annalists had been connected with it. In modern times the relations are entirely altered. Our culture is essentially comprehensive, and immediately changes all events into historical representations. Of this first type of history, we have vivid, simple, clear narrations—especially of military affairs—which might fairly take their place with those of Caesar. In richness of matter and fulness of detail as regards strategic techniques, and attendant circumstances, they are even more instructive. The French "Memoires" also fall under this category. In many cases these are written by men of mark, though relating to affairs of little note. They not infrequently contain a large proportion of anecdotical matter, so that the ground they occupy is narrow and trivial. Yet they are often veritable master-pieces in history; as those of Cardinal Retz, which in fact trench on a larger historical field. In Germany such masters are rare. Frederick the Great (*Histoire de mon temps*) is an illustrious exception. Writers of this order must occupy an elevated position. Only from such a position is it possible to take an extensive view of affairs—to see every-thing. This is out of the question for him who from below merely gets a glimpse of the great world through a miserable cranny.

(2) The second kind of history we may call the reflective. It is

history whose mode of representation is not really confined by the limits of the time to which it relates, but whose spirit transcends the present. Of this second order, strongly marked varieties may be distinguished.

(a) It is the aim of the investigator to gain a view of the entire history of a people or a country, or of the world, in short, what we call *Universal History*. In this case the working up of the historical material is the main point. The workman approaches his task with his own spirit—a spirit distinct from that of the elements he is to manipulate. Here a very important consideration will be the principles to which the author refers, the bearing and motives of the actions and events which he describes, and those which determine the form of his narrative. Among us Germans, this reflective treatment and the display of ingenuity which it occasions assume a manifold variety of phases. Every writer of history proposes to himself an original method. The English and French confess to general principles of historical composition. Their standpoint is more that of cosmopolitan or of national culture. Among us each labors to invent a purely individual point of view. Instead of writing history, we are always beating our brains to discover how history ought to be written. This first kind of Reflective History is most nearly akin to the preceding, when it has no farther aim than to present the annals of a country complete. Such compilations (among which may be reckoned the works of Livy and Diodorus Siculus, and Johannes von Müller's *History of Switzerland*) are, if well performed, highly meritorious. Among the best of the kind may be reckoned such annalists as approach those of the first class; who give so vivid a transcript of events that the reader may well fancy himself listening to contemporaries and eye-witnesses. But it often happens that the individuality of attitude that must characterize a writer belonging to a different culture is not in accord with the period; the spirit of the writer is quite other than that of the times of which he treats. Thus Livy puts into the mouths of the old Roman kings, consuls, and generals, such orations as would be delivered by an accomplished advocate of the Livian era, which strikingly contrast with the genuine traditions of Roman antiquity (*e.g.* the fable of Menenius Agrippa). Similarly, he gives us descriptions of battles as if he had been an actual spectator—but whose features would serve well enough for battles in any period, and whose distinctness contrasts on the other hand with the disconnectedness and inconsistency that prevail elsewhere, even in his treatment of chief points of interest. The difference between such a compiler and an original historian may be best seen by comparing Polybius himself with the style in which Livy uses, expands, and abridges his annals in those periods of which Polybius's account has been preserved. Johannes von Müller has given a stiff, formal, pedantic air to his history, in an endeavor to remain faithful to the times he describes. We much prefer the narratives we find in old Tschudi: all is more naïve and natural than it appears in the garb of a fictitious and affected archaism.

A history that aspires to traverse long periods of time, or to be universal, must indeed forego the attempt to give individual representations of the past as it actually existed. It must foreshorten its pictures by abstractions; and this involves not merely the omission of events and deeds, but whatever is implied in the fact that Thought is, after all, the most trenchant epitomist. A battle, a great victory, a siege, no longer maintains its original proportions, but is put off with a bare mention. When Livy, for example, tells us of the wars with the Volsci, we sometimes have the brief announcement: "This year war was carried on with the Volsci."

(b) A second species of Reflective History is what we may call the Pragmatic. When we have to deal with the Past, and occupy ourselves with a remote world, a Present rises into being for the mind—produced by its own activity, as the reward of its labor. The occurrences are, indeed, various; but the idea which pervades them—their deeper import and connection—is *one*. This takes the occurrence out of the category of the Past and makes it virtually Present. Pragmatic (didactic) reflections, though in their nature decidedly abstract, are truly and indefeasibly of the Present, and quicken the annals of the dead Past with the life of to-day. Whether, indeed, such reflections are truly interesting and enlivening, depends on the writer's own spirit. Moral reflections must here be specially noticed—the moral teaching expected from history, which has not infrequently been treated with a direct view to morality. It may be allowed that examples of virtue elevate the soul, and are applicable in the moral instructions of children for impressing excellence upon their minds. But the destinies of peoples and states, their interests, relations, and the complicated tissue of their affairs, present quite another field. Rulers, Statesmen, Nations, are wont to be emphatically commended to the teaching that experience offers in history. But what experience and history teach is this: that peoples and governments never have learned anything from history or acted on principles deduced from it. Each period is involved in such peculiar circumstances, exhibits a condition of things so strictly idiosyncratic, that its conduct must be regulated by

considerations connected with itself, and itself alone. Amid the
pressure of great events, a general principle gives no help. It is useless to revert to similar circumstances in the Past. The pallid shades
of memory struggle in vain with the life and freedom of the Present.
Looked at in this light, nothing can be shallower than the oft-repeated
appeal to Greek and Roman examples during the French Revolution.
Nothing is more diverse than the genius of those nations and that of
our times. Johannes von Müller, in his *Universal History,* as also in
his *History of Switzerland,* had such moral aims in view. He aimed
to prepare a body of political doctrines for the instruction of princes,
governments and peoples (he formed a special collection of doctrines
and reflections, frequently giving us in his correspondence the exact
number of apophthegms he had compiled in a week); but he cannot reckon this part of his labor as among the best that he accomplished. It is only a thorough, liberal, comprehensive view of historical
relations (such as we find in Montesquieu's *Spirit of the Laws*)
that can give truth and interest to reflections of this order. One Reflective History therefore, supersedes another. The materials are
patent to every writer: each is likely enough to believe himself capable
of arranging and manipulating them; and we may expect that each
will insist upon his own spirit as that of the age in question. Disgusted
by such reflective histories, readers have often returned with pleasure
to a narrative adopting no particular point of view. These certainly
have their value; but for the most part they offer only material for
history. We Germans are not content with such. The French, on the
other hand, display great genius in reanimating bygone times, and in
bringing the past to bear upon the present conditions of things.

(c) The third kind of Reflective History is the Critical. This deserves mention as preëminently the mode of treating history now
current in Germany. It is not history itself that is here presented. We
might more properly designate it as a History of History; a criticism
of historical narratives and an investigation of their truth and credibility. Its peculiarity in point of fact and of intention, consists in the
acuteness with which the writer extorts something from the records
that was not in the matters recorded. The French have given us
much that is profound and judicious in this kind of composition. But
they have not endeavored to pass off a merely critical procedure for
substantial history. They have duly presented their judgments in the
form of critical treatises. Among us, the so-called "higher criticism,"
which reigns supreme in the domain of philology, has also taken
possession of our historical literature. This "higher criticism" has

been the pretext for introducing all the anti-historical monstrosities that a vain imagination could suggest. Here we have the other method of making the past a living reality: putting subjective fancies in the place of historical data; fancies whose merit is measured by their boldness, that is, the scantiness of the particulars on which they are based, and the peremptoriness with which they contravene the best established facts of history.

(d) The last kind of Reflective History announces its fragmentary character on the very face of it. It adopts an abstract position; yet, since it takes general points of view (e.g. as the History of Art, of Law, of Religion), it forms a transition to the Philosophical History of the World. In our time, especially, this form of the history of ideas has been developed and brought to notice. Such branches of national life stand in close relation to the entire complex of a people's annals; and the question of chief importance in relation to our subject is whether the connection of the whole is exhibited in its truth and reality or referred to merely external relations. In the latter case, these important phenomena (Art, Law, Religion, etc.) appear as purely accidental national peculiarities. It must be remarked that, when Reflective History has advanced to the adoption of general points of view, if the position taken is a true one, these are found to constitute, not a merely external thread, a superficial series, but the inward guiding soul of the occurrences and actions that occupy a nation's annals. For, like the soul-conductor Mercury, the Idea is in truth the leader of peoples and of the World; and Spirit, the rational and necessitated will of that conductor, is and has been the director of the events of the World's History. To become acquainted with Spirit in this its office of guidance, is the object of our present undertaking. This brings us to

(3) The third kind of history, the Philosophical. No explanation was needed of the two previous kinds; their nature was self-evident. It is otherwise with this last, which certainly seems to require an exposition or justification. The most general definition that can be given is that the Philosophy of History means nothing but the thoughtful consideration of it. Thought is, indeed, essential to humanity. It is this that distinguishes us from the brutes. In sensation, cognition and intellection, in our instincts and volitions, as far as they are truly human, Thought is an invariable element. To insist upon Thought in this connection with history, may, however, appear unsatisfactory. In this science it would seem as if Thought must be subordinate to what is given, to the realities of fact; that this is its basis and guide:

while Philosophy dwells in the region of self-produced ideas, without reference to actuality. Approaching history with such a presupposition, Speculation might be expected to treat it as a mere passive material; and, so far from leaving it in its native truth, to force it into conformity with a tyrannous idea, and to construe it, as the phrase is, *a priori*. But as it is the business of history simply to adopt into its records what is and has been, actual occurrences and transactions, and since it remains true to its character in proportion as it strictly adheres to its data, we seem to have in Philosophy a process diametrically opposed to that of the historian. This contradiction, and the charge consequently brought against Speculation, shall be explained and confuted. We do not, however, propose to correct the innumerable special misrepresentations, trite or novel, that are current respecting the aims, the interests, and the modes of treating history, and its relation to Philosophy.

II. Reason in History

The only Thought that Philosophy brings with it to the contemplation of History, is the simple conception of Reason; that Reason is the Sovereign of the World; that the history of the world, therefore, presents us with a rational process. This conviction and intuition is a hypothesis in the domain of history as such. In that of Philosophy it is no hypothesis. It is there proved by speculative cognition, that Reason—and this term may here suffice us, without investigating the relation sustained by the Universe to the Divine Being—is Substance, as well as Infinite Power, its own Infinite Material underlying all the natural and spiritual life which it originates, as also the Infinite Form—that which sets this Material in motion. On the one hand, Reason is the substance of the Universe, viz. that by which and in which all reality has its being and subsistence. On the other hand, it is the Infinite Energy of the Universe; since Reason is not so powerless as to be incapable of producing anything but a mere ideal, a mere intention—having its place outside reality, nobody knows where; something separate and abstract, in the heads of certain human beings. It is the infinite complex of things, their entire Essence and Truth. It is its own material which it commits to its own Active Energy to work up; not needing, as finite action does, the conditions of an external material of given means from which it may obtain its support and the objects of its activity. It supplies its own nourishment, and is the object of its own operations. While it is exclusively its own basis of existence, and absolute final aim, it is also the energizing power realizing this aim; developing it not only in the phenomena of the Natural, but also of the Spiritual, Universe—the History of the World. That this "Idea" or "Reason" is the True, the Eternal, the absolutely powerful essence, that it reveals itself in the World, and that in that World nothing else is revealed but this and its honor and glory— is the thesis which, as we have said, has been proved in Philosophy, and is here regarded as demonstrated.

In those of my hearers who are not acquainted with Philosophy, I may fairly presume, at least, the existence of a belief in Reason, a desire, a thirst for acquaintance with it, in entering upon this course of Lectures. It is, in fact, the wish for rational insight, not the ambition to amass a mere heap of acquirements, that should be presupposed in every case as possessing the mind of the learner in the study of science. If the clear idea of Reason is not already developed in our minds, in beginning the study of Universal History, we should at least have the firm, unconquerable faith that Reason *does* exist there; and that the World of intelligence and conscious volition is not abandoned to chance, but must shew itself in the light of the self-cognizant Idea. Yet I am not obliged to make any such preliminary demand upon your faith. What I have said thus provisionally, and what I shall have further to say, is, even in reference to our branch of science, not to be regarded as hypothetical, but as a summary view of the whole; the result of the investigation we are about to pursue; a result which happens to be known to *me,* because I have traversed the entire field. It is only an inference from the history of the World that its development has been a rational process; that the history in question has constituted the rational necessary course of the World-Spirit—that Spirit whose nature is always one and the same, but which unfolds this one nature in the phenomena of the World's existence. This must, as before stated, present itself as the ultimate result of History. But we have to take the latter as it is. We must proceed historically—empirically. Among other precautions we must take care not to be misled by professed historians who (especially among the Germans, and enjoying a considerable authority) are chargeable with the very procedure of which they accuse the Philosopher—introducing *a priori* inventions of their own into the records of the Past. It is, for example, a widely current fiction that there was an original primeval people, taught immediately by God, endowed with perfect insight and wisdom, possessing a thorough knowledge of all natural laws and spiritual truth; that there have been such or such sacerdotal peoples; or, to mention a more specific assertion, that there was a Roman Epos, from which the Roman historians derived the early annals of their city, etc. *A priorities* of this kind we leave to those talented historians by profession, among whom (in Germany at least) their use is not uncommon. We might then announce it as the first condition to be observed, that we should faithfully adopt all that is historical. But in such general expressions as "faithfully" and "adopt" lies the ambiguity. Even the ordinary, the "impartial" historian, who believes and professes that he maintains a simply receptive attitude, surrendering himself only to the data supplied him, is by no means passive as regards the exercise of his thinking powers. He brings his categories with him, and sees the phenomena presented to his mental vision exclusively through these media. And, especially in all that pretends to the name of science, it is indispensable that Reason should not sleep, that reflection should be in full play. To him who looks upon the world rationally, the world in its turn, presents a rational aspect. The relation is mutual. But the various exercises of reflection—the different points of view—the modes of deciding the simple question of the relative importance of events (the first category that occupies the attention of the historian), do not belong to this place.

I will only mention two phases and points of view that concern the generally diffused conviction that Reason has ruled, and is still ruling in the world, and consequently in the world's history, because they give us, at the same time, an opportunity for more closely investigating the question that presents the greatest difficulty, and for indicating a branch of the subject that will have to be enlarged on in the sequel.

(1) One of these points is the historical fact that the Greek Anaxagoras was the first to enunciate the doctrine that νοῦς, Understanding in general, or Reason, governs the world. It is not intelligence as self-conscious Reason, not a spirit as such, that is meant; and we must clearly distinguish these from each other. The movement of the solar system takes place according to unchangeable laws. These laws are Reason, implicit in the phenomena in question. But neither the sun nor the planets that revolve around it according to these laws can be said to have any consciousness of them.

A thought of this kind—that Nature is an embodiment of Reason; that it is unchangeably subordinate to universal laws—appears nowise striking or strange to us. We are accustomed to such conceptions, and find nothing extraordinary in them. And I have mentioned this extraordinary occurrence partly to show how history teaches that ideas of this kind, which may seem trivial to us, have not always been in the world; that on the contrary, such a thought marks an epoch in the annals of human intelligence. Aristotle says of Anaxagoras, as the originator of the thought in question, that he appeared as a sober man among the drunken. Socrates adopted the doctrine from Anaxagoras, and it forthwith became the ruling idea in Philosophy —except in the school of Epicurus, who ascribed all events to chance. "I was delighted with the sentiment," Plato makes Socrates say, "and hoped I had found a teacher who would show me Nature in harmony with Reason, who would demonstrate in each particular phenomenon its specific aim, and in the whole, the grand object of the Universe. I would not have surrendered this hope for a great deal. But how very much was I disappointed, when, having zealously applied myself to the writings of Anaxagoras, I found that he adduces only external causes, such as Atmosphere, Ether, Water, and the like." [1] It is evident that the defect Socrates complains of respecting Anaxagoras' doctrine does not concern the principle itself but the shortcoming of the propounder in applying it to Nature in the concrete. Nature is not deduced from that principle: the latter remains in fact a mere abstraction, inasmuch as the former is not comprehended and exhibited as a development of it—an organization produced by and from Reason. I wish, at the very outset, to call your attention to the important difference between a conception, a principle, a truth limited to an *abstract* form and its determinate application and concrete development. This distinction affects the whole fabric of philosophy; and among other bearings of it there is one to which we shall have to revert at the close of our view of Universal History, in investigating the aspect of political affairs in the most recent period.

(2) We have next to notice the rise of this idea—that Reason directs the world—in connection with a further application of it, well known to us: in the form, viz. of the religious truth that the world is not abandoned to chance and external contingent causes, but that a Providence controls it. I stated above that I would not make a demand on your faith in regard to the principle announced. Yet I might appeal to your belief in it, in this religious aspect, if, as a general rule, the nature of philosophical science allowed it to attach authority to presuppositions. To put it in another form, this appeal is forbidden, because the science of which we have to treat

---

[1] [A paraphrase of a passage in Plato's *Phaedo*, 97-98.—M.C.B.]

proposes itself to furnish the proof (not indeed of the abstract Truth of the doctrine, but) of its correctness as compared with facts. The truth, then, that a Providence (that of God) presides over the events of the World, consorts with the proposition in question; for Divine Providence is Wisdom endowed with an infinite Power, which realizes its aim, viz. the absolute rational design of the World. Reason is Thought conditioning itself with perfect freedom. But a difference—rather a contradiction—will manifest itself, between this belief and our principle, just as was the case in reference to the demand made by Socrates in the case of Anaxagoras' dictum. For that belief is similarly indefinite; it is what is called a belief in a general Providence, and is not followed out into definite application, or displayed in its bearing on the grand total—the entire course of human history. But to *explain* History is to depict the passions of mankind, the genius, the active powers, that play their part on the great stage; and the providentially determined process that these exhibit constitutes what is generally called the "plan" of Providence. Yet it is this very plan which is supposed to be concealed from our view: which it is deemed presumption even to wish to recognize. The ignorance of Anaxagoras as to how intelligence reveals itself in actual existence was ingenuous. Neither in his consciousness nor in that of Greece at large had that thought been further expanded. He had not attained the power to apply his general principle to the concrete, so as to deduce the latter from the former. It was Socrates who took the first step in comprehending the union of the Concrete with the Universal. Anaxagoras, then, did not take up a hostile position towards such an application. The common belief in Providence *does;* at least it opposes the use of the principle on the large scale, and denies the possibility of discerning the plan of Providence. In isolated cases this plan is supposed to be manifest. Pious persons are encouraged to recognize in particular circumstances something more than mere chance, to acknowledge the guiding hand of God—*e.g.* when help has unexpectedly come to an individual in great perplexity and need. But these instances of providential design are of a limited kind, and concern the accomplishment of nothing more than the desires of the individual in question. But in the history of the World, the Individuals we have to do with are Peoples, totalities that are States. We cannot, therefore, be satisfied with what we may call this "peddling" view of Providence, to which the belief alluded to limits itself. Equally unsatisfactory is the merely abstract, undefined belief in a Providence, when that belief is not brought to bear upon the details of the process which it conducts. On the contrary our earnest endeavor must be directed to the recognition of the ways of Providence, the means it uses, and the historical phenomena in which is manifests itself; and we must show their connection with the general principle above mentioned. But in noticing the recognition of the plan of Divine Providence generally, I have implicitly touched upon a prominent question of the day, viz. that of the possibility of knowing God: or rather—since public opinion has ceased to allow it to be a matter of question—the doctrine that it is impossible to know God. In direct contravention of what is commanded in holy Scripture as the highest duty—that we should not merely love, but know God—the prevalent dogma involves the denial of what is there said, viz. that it is the Spirit that leads into Truth, knows all things, penetrates even into the deep things of the Godhead. While the Divine Being is thus placed beyond our knowledge, and outside the limit of all human things, we have the convenient licence of wandering as far as we list in the direction of our own fancies. We are freed from the obligation to refer our knowledge to the Divine and True. On the other hand, the vanity and egotism that characterize it find, in this false position, ample justification; and the pious modesty which puts far from it the knowledge of God can well estimate how much furtherance thereby accrues to its own wayward and vain strivings. I have been unwilling to leave out of sight the connection between our thesis—that Reason governs and has governed the World—and the question of the possibility of a knowledge of God, chiefly that I might not lose the opportunity of mentioning the imputation against Philosophy that it is, or must be, shy of noticing religious truths, in which is insinuated the suspicion that it has anything but a clear conscience in the presence of these truths. So far from this being the case, the fact is that in recent times Philosophy has been obliged to defend the domain of religion against the attacks of several theological systems. In the Christian religion God has revealed Himself—that is, he has given us to understand what He is, so that He is no longer a concealed or secret existence. And this possibility of knowing Him, thus afforded us, renders such knowledge a duty. God wishes no narrow-hearted souls or empty heads for his children, but those whose spirit is of itself indeed poor, but rich in the knowledge of Him, and who regard this knowledge of God as the only valuable possession. That development of the thinking spirit which has resulted from the revelation of the Divine Being as its original basis, must ultimately advance to the intellectual comprehension of what was presented in the first instance to feeling and imagination. The time must eventually come for understanding that rich product of active Reason which the History of the World offers to us. It was for a while the fashion to profess admiration for the wisdom of God as displayed in animals, plants, and isolated occurrences. But, if it be allowed that Providence manifests itself in such objects and forms of existence, why not also in Universal History? This is deemed too great a matter to be thus regarded. But Divine Wisdom, *i.e.* Reason, is one and the same in the great as in the little; and we must not imagine God to be too weak to exercise his wisdom on the grand scale. Our intellectual striving aims at realizing the conviction that what was intended by eternal wisdom is actually accomplished in the domain of existent, active Spirit, as well as in that of mere Nature. Our mode of treating the subject is, in this aspect, a theodicy—a justification of the ways of God—which Leibniz attempted metaphysically, in his method, *i.e.* in indefinite abstract categories, so that the ill that is found in the World might be comprehended, and the thinking Spirit reconciled with the fact of the existence of evil. Indeed, nowhere is such a harmonizing view more pressingly demanded than in Universal History; and it can be attained only by recognizing the *positive* aspect, in which that negative element is a subordinate and vanquished nullity. On the one hand, the ultimate design of the World must be perceived, and, on the other hand, the fact that this design has been actually realized in it, and that evil has not been able permanently to assert a competing position. But this conviction involves much more than the mere belief in a superintending νοῦς or in "Providence." "Reason," whose sovereignty over the World has been maintained, is as indefinite a term as "Providence," supposing the term to be used by those who are unable to characterize it distinctly —to show wherein it consists, so as to enable us to decide whether a thing is rational or irrational. An adequate definition of Reason is the first desideratum; and whatever boast may be made of strict adherence to it in explaining phenomena, without such a definition we get no farther than mere words. With these observations we may proceed to the second point of view that has to be considered in this Introduction.

III. The Realm of Spirit

The enquiry into the essential destiny of Reason—as far as it is considered in reference to the World—is identical with the question, what is the ultimate design of the World? And the expression implies that that design is destined to be realized. Two points of consideration suggest themselves: first, the import of this design, its abstract definition, and second, its realization.

It must be observed at the outset that the phenomenon we investigate—Universal History—belongs to the realm of Spirit. The term "World" includes both physical and psychical Nature. Physical Nature also plays its part in the World's History, and attention will have to be paid to the fundamental natural relations thus involved. But Spirit, and the course of its development, is our substantial object. Our task does not require us to contemplate Nature as a Rational System in itself—though in its own proper domain it proves itself such—but simply in its relation to Spirit. On the stage on which we are observing it—Universal History—Spirit displays itself in its most concrete reality. Notwithstanding this (or rather for the very purpose of comprehending the general principles which this, its form of concrete reality, embodies) we must premise some abstract characteristics of the nature of spirit. Such an explanation, however, cannot be given here under any other form than that of bare assertion. The present is not the occasion for unfolding the idea of Spirit speculatively; for whatever has a place in an Introduction must, as already observed, be taken as simply historical, something assumed as having been explained and proved elsewhere, or whose demonstration awaits the sequel of the Science of History itself.

We have therefore to mention here:

(1) The abstract characteristics of the nature of Spirit.
(2) The means Spirit uses in order to realize its Idea.
(3) The form that the perfect embodiment of Spirit assumes: the State.

1. Freedom as the Goal of Spirit

The nature of Spirit may be understood by a glance at its direct opposite—Matter. As the essence of Matter is Gravity, so, on the other hand, we may affirm that the essence, the substance, of Spirit is Freedom. All will readily assent to the doctrine that, among other properties, Spirit is also endowed with Freedom; but philosophy teaches that all the qualities of Spirit exist only through Freedom, that all are but means for attaining Freedom, that all seek and produce this and this alone. It is a finding of speculative Philosophy that Freedom is the sole truth of Spirit. Matter possesses gravity in virtue of its tendency towards a central point. It is essentially composite, consisting of parts that exclude each other. It seeks its Unity, and therefore exhibits itself as self-destructive, as verging towards its opposite [an indivisible point]. If it could attain this, it would be Matter no longer, it would have perished. It strives after the realization of its Idea, for in Unity it exists ideally. Spirit, on the contrary, may be defined as that which has its center in itself. It has not a unity outside itself, but has already found it; it exists *in* and with itself. Matter has its essence outside itself; Spirit is self-contained existence. Now this is Freedom, exactly. For if I am dependent, my being is referred to something else which I am not; I cannot exist independently of something external. I am free, on the contrary, when my existence depends upon myself. This self-contained existence of Spirit is none other than self-consciousness—consciousness of one's own being. Two things must be distinguished in consciousness: first, the fact that I know; second, what I know. In self-consciousness these are merged in one; for Spirit knows itself. It involves an appreciation of its own nature, as also an energy enabling it to realize itself, to make itself actually that which it is potentially. According to this abstract definition it may be said of Universal History that it is the exhibition of Spirit in the process of working out the knowledge of that which it is potentially. And as the germ bears in itself the whole nature of the tree, and the taste and form of its fruits, so do the first traces of Spirit virtually contain the whole of that History. The Orientals have not attained the knowledge that Spirit—Man as such—is free; and because they do not know this they are not free. They only know that one is free. But on this very account, the freedom of that one is only caprice: ferocity, brutal recklessness or passion, or a mildness and tameness of the desires, which is itself only an accident of Nature, mere caprice like the former. That one is therefore only a Despot, not a free man. The consciousness of Freedom first arose among the Greeks, and therefore they were free; but they, and the Romans likewise, knew only that some are free—not man as such. Even Plato and Aristotle did not know this. The Greeks, therefore, had slaves, and their whole life and the maintenance of their splendid liberty, was implicated with the institution of slavery: a fact, moreover, which on the one hand made that liberty only an accidental, transient and limited growth, on the other hand, made it a rigorous thraldom of our common human nature. The German nations, under the influence of Christianity, were the first to attain the consciousness that man, as man, is free: that it is the freedom of Spirit which constitutes its essence. This consciousness arose first in religion, the inmost region of Spirit; but to introduce the principle into the various relations of the actual world, involves a more extensive problem than its simple implantation—a problem whose solution and application require a severe and lengthened process of culture. In proof of this, we may note that slavery did not cease immediately on the reception of Christianity. Still less did liberty predominate in States, or Governments and Constitutions adopt a rational organization, or recognize freedom as their basis. That application of the principle to political relations; the thorough moulding and interpenetration of the constitution of society by it, is a process identical with history itself. I have already directed attention to the distinction here involved, between a principle as such, and its application, *i.e.* its introduction and carrying out in the actual phenomena of Spirit and Life. This is a point of fundamental importance in our science, and one which must be constantly respected as essential. And in the same way as this distinction has attracted attention in view of the Christian principle of self-consciousness, Freedom, it also shows itself as an essential one, in view of the principle of Freedom generally. The History of the world is none other than the progress of the consciousness of Freedom; a progress whose development according to the necessity of its nature it is our business to investigate.

The general statement given above of the various grades in the consciousness of Freedom—that the Eastern nations knew only that one is free, the Greek and Roman world only that some are free, whilst we know that all men absolutely (man as man) are free—supplies us with the natural division of Universal History, and suggests the mode of its discussion. This is remarked, however, only incidentally and anticipatively; some other ideas must be first explained.

The destiny of the spiritual World, and—since this is the substantial World, while the physical remains subordinate to it, or, in the language of speculation, has no truth as against the spiritual—the final cause of the World at large, we allege to be the consciousness of its own freedom on the part of Spirit, and *ipso facto* the reality of that freedom. But that this term "Freedom," without further qualification, is an indefinite and incalculably ambiguous term, and that, while what it represents is the *ne plus ultra* of attainment, it is liable to an infinity of misunderstandings, confusions and errors, and can become the occasion for all imaginable excesses—has never been more clearly known and felt than in modern times. Yet, for the present, we must content ourselves with the term itself without further definition. Attention was also directed to the importance of the infinite difference between a principle in the abstract and its realization in the concrete. In the process before us, the essential nature of freedom—which involves in it absolute necessity—is to be displayed as coming to a consciousness of itself (for it is in its very nature self-consciousness) and thereby realizing its existence. It is its own object of attainment. and the sole aim of Spirit. This is the result at which the process of the World's History has been continually aiming, and to which the sacrifices that have ever and anon been laid on the vast altar of the earth, through the long lapse of ages, have been offered. This is the only aim that sees itself realized and fulfilled, the only pole of repose amid the ceaseless change of events and conditions, and the sole efficient principle that pervades them. This final aim is God's purpose with the world; but God is the absolute perfect Being, and can, therefore, will nothing other than himself—his own Will. The Nature of His Will—that is, His Nature itself—is what we here call the Idea of Freedom, translating the language of Religion into that of Thought. The question, then, which we may next put, is: What means does this principle of Freedom use for its realization? This is the second point we have to consider.

2. The Role of the Individual

The question of the means by which Freedom develops itself into a World conducts us to the phenomenon of History itself. Although Freedom is, primarily, an inward idea, the means it uses are external and phenomenal, presenting themselves in History to our sensuous vision. The first glance at History convinces us that the actions of men proceed from their needs, their passions, their characters and talents, and impresses us with the belief that such needs, passions and interests are the sole springs of action—the efficient agents in this scene of activity. Among these may, perhaps, be found aims of a liberal or universal kind, benevolence it may be, or noble patriotism; but such virtues and general views are but insignificant as compared with the World and its doings. We may perhaps see the Ideal of Reason actualized in those who adopt such aims, and within the sphere of their influence; but they bear only a trifling proportion to the mass of the human race, and the extent of that influence is limited accordingly. Passions, private aims, and the satisfaction of selfish desires, are on the other hand most effective springs of action. Their power lies in the fact that they respect none of the limitations that justice and morality would impose on them, and that these natural impulses have a more direct influence over man than the artificial and tedious discipline that tends to order and self-restraint, law and morality. When we look at this display of passions and the consequences of their violence, the Unreason which is associated not only with them, but even (rather we might say especially) with good designs and righteous aims—when we see the evil, the vice, the ruin that has befallen the most flourishing kingdoms which the mind of man ever created, we can scarce avoid being filled with sorrow at this universal taint of corruption: and, since this decay is not the work of mere Nature, but of the Human Will—a moral embitterment—a revolt of the Good Spirit (if it have a place within us) may well be the result of our reflections. Without rhetorical exaggeration, a simply truthful account of the miseries that have overwhelmed the noblest of nations and polities, and the finest exemplars of private virtue, forms a picture of most fearful aspect, and excites emotions of the profoundest and most hopeless sadness, counter-balanced by no consolatory result. We endure in beholding it a mental torture, allowing no defense or escape but the consideration that what has happened could not be otherwise, that it is a fatality no intervention could alter. And at last we draw back from the intolerable disgust with which these sorrowful reflections threaten us, into the more agreeable environment of our individual life—the Present formed by our private aims and interests. In short we retreat into the selfishness that stands on the quiet shore, and thence enjoy in safety the distant spectacle of "wrecks confusedly hurled." But even regarding History as the slaughter-bench at which the happiness of peoples, the wisdom of States, and the virtue of individuals have been made victims, the question involuntarily arises: to what principle, to what final aim these enormous sacrifices have been offered. From this point the investigation usually proceeds to what we have made the beginning of our enquiry. At the start we pointed out those phenomena which made up a picture so suggestive of gloomy emotions and thoughtful reflections as the very field which we, for our part, regard as exhibiting only the means for realizing what we assert to be the essential destiny, the absolute aim, or—which comes to the same thing—the true result of the World's History. We have all along purposely eschewed "moral reflections" as a method of rising from the scene of historical particularities to the general principles which they embody. Besides, it is not the interest of such sentimentalities really to rise above those depressing emotions, and to solve the enigmas of Providence which the considerations that occasioned them present. It is essential to their character to find a gloomy satisfaction in the empty and fruitless sublimities of that negative result. We return then to the point of view which we have adopted, observing that the successive steps of the analysis to which it will lead us will also evolve the conditions requisite for answering the enquiries suggested by the panorama of sin and suffering that history unfolds.

The first remark we have to make, one which—though already presented more than once—cannot be too often repeated when the occasion seems to call for it, is that what we call principle, aim, destiny, or the nature and idea of Spirit, is something merely general and abstract. Principle, Plan of Existence, Law, is a hidden, undeveloped essence, which as such—however true in itself—is not completely real. Aims, principles, etc., have a place in our thoughts, in our subjective design only, but not yet in the sphere of reality. What exists only for itself is a possibility, a potentiality, but has not yet emerged into Existence. A second element must be introduced in order to produce actuality—viz. realization, activity whose motive power is the Will, the activity of man in the widest sense. It is only by this activity that that Idea, or abstract characteristics generally, can be realized, actualized; for of themselves they are powerless. The motive power that puts them in operation, and gives them determinate existence, is the need, instinct, inclination, and passion of man. That some conception of mine should be developed into act and existence is my earnest desire: I wish to assert my personality in connection with it; I wish to be satisfied by its execution. If I am to exert myself for any object, it must in some way or other be my object. In the accomplishment of such-and-such designs I must at the same time find my satisfaction, although the purpose for which I exert myself includes a complication of results, many of which have no interest for me. This is the absolute right of personal existence—to find itself satisfied in its activity and labor. If men are to interest themselves for anything, they must (so to speak) have part of their existence involved in it, find their individuality gratified by its attainment. Here a mistake must be avoided. We intend blame, and justly impute it as a fault, when we say of an individual, that he is "interested" (in taking part in such or such transactions) that is, seeks only his private advantage. In reprehending this we find fault with him for furthering his personal aims without any regard to a more comprehensive design, of which he takes advantage to promote his own interest, or which he even sacrifices with this view. But he who is active in promoting an object is not simply "interested," but interested in that object itself. Language faithfully expresses this distinction. Nothing therefore happens, nothing is accomplished, unless the individuals concerned seek their own satisfaction in the issue. They are particular units of society, *i.e.* they have special needs, instincts, and interests generally, peculiar to themselves. Among these needs are not only such as we usually call necessities—the stimuli of individual desire and volition—but also those connected with individual views and convictions, or—to use a term expressing less deliberation—leanings of opinion, supposing the impulses of reflection, understanding, and reason, to have been awakened. In these cases people demand, if they are to exert themselves in any direction, that the object should commend itself to them, that in point of opinion—whether as to its goodness, justice, advantage, profit—they should be able to "enter into it." This is a consideration of especial importance in our age, when people are less than formerly influenced by reliance on others, and by authority —when, on the contrary, they devote their activities to a cause on the ground of their own understanding, their independent conviction and opinion.

We assert then that nothing has been accomplished without interest on the part of the actors; and—if interest be called passion, inasmuch as the whole individuality, to the neglect of all other actual or possible interests and claims, is devoted to an object with every fibre of volition, concentrating all its desires and powers upon it—we may affirm absolutely that nothing great in the World has been accomplished without passion. Two elements, therefore, enter into the object of our investigation: the first the Idea, the second the complex of human passions; the one the warp, the other the woof, of the vast tapestry of Universal History. The concrete mean and union of the two is Liberty, under the conditions of morality in a State. We have spoken of the Idea of Freedom as the nature of Spirit and the absolute goal of History. Passion is regarded as a thing of sinister aspect, as more or less immoral. Man is required to have no passions. "Passion," it is true, is not quite the suitable word for what I wish to express. I mean here nothing more than human activity as resulting from private interests—special, or if you will, self-seeking designs— with this qualification, that the whole energy of will and character is devoted to their attainment, that other interests (which would in themselves constitute tempting goals), indeed everything else, are sacrificed to them. The object in question is so bound up with the man's will that it entirely and alone determines the "hue of resolution," and is inseparable from it. It has become the very essence of his volition. For a person is a specific existence, not man in general (a term to which no real existence corresponds), but a particular human being. The term "character" likewise expresses this idiosyncrasy of Will and Intelligence. But Character comprehends all peculiarities whatever, the way in which a person conducts himself in private relations, etc., and is not limited to his idiosyncrasy in its practical and active phase. I shall, therefore, use the term "passion," understanding thereby the particular bent of character, as far as the peculiarities of volition are not limited to private interest, but supply the impelling and actuating force for accomplishing deeds shared in by the community at large. Passion is in the first instance the subjective, and therefore the formal side of energy, will, and activity— leaving the object or aim still undetermined. And there is a similar relation of formality to reality in merely individual conviction, individual views, individual conscience. It is always a question of essential importance, what is the purport of my conviction, what the object of my passion, in deciding whether the one or the other is of a true and substantial nature. Conversely, if it is so, it will inevitably attain actual existence, be realized.

From this comment on the second essential element in the historical embodiment of an aim, we infer—glancing at the institution of the State in passing—that a State is then well constituted and internally powerful when the private interest of its citizens is one with the common interest of the State, when the one finds its gratification and realization in the other—a proposition in itself very important. But in a State many institutions must be adopted, much political machinery invented, accompanied by appropriate political arrangements, necessitating long struggles of the understanding before what is really appropriate can be discovered—involving, moreover, contentions with private interest and passions, and a tedious discipline of these latter, in order to bring about the desired harmony. The epoch when a State attains this harmonious condition marks the period of its blossoming, its virtue, its vigor, and its prosperity. But the history of mankind does not begin with a conscious aim of any kind, as it is the case with the particular circles into which men form themselves of set purpose. The mere social instinct implies a conscious purpose of security for life and property, and when society has been constituted this purpose becomes more comprehensive. The History of the World begins with its general aim—the realization of the Idea of Spirit—only in an *implicit* form that is, as Nature, a hidden (most profoundly hidden) unconscious instinct; and the whole process of History (as already observed) is directed to rendering this unconscious impulse a conscious one. Thus appearing in the form of merely natural existence, natural will—what has been called the subjective side—physical craving, instinct, passion, private interest, as also opinion and subjective conception, spontaneously present themselves at the very start. This vast congeries of volitions, interests and activities, constitutes the instruments and means of the World-Spirit for attaining its object, bringing it to consciousness, and realizing it. And this aim is none other than finding itself—coming to itself—and contemplating itself in concrete actuality. But that those manifestations of vitality on the part of individuals and peoples, in which they seek and fulfill their own purposes, are, at the same time, the means and instruments of a higher and broader purpose of which they know nothing, which they realize unconsciously, might be made a matter of question—indeed has been questioned, and in every variety of form denied, decried and condemned as mere dreaming and "Philosophy." But on this point I announced my view at the very outset, and asserted our hypothesis—which, however, will appear finally in the form of a legitimate inference—and our belief that Reason governs the world and has consequently governed its history. In relation to this independently universal and substantial existence, all else is subordinate, subservient to it, and the means for its development. The Union of Universal Abstract Existence generally with the Individual, the Subjective, and the fact that this alone is Truth, belong to the department of speculation, and are treated in this general form in Logic. But in the process of the World's History itself, as still incomplete, the abstract final aim of history is not yet made the distinct object of desire and interest. While these limited sentiments are still unconscious of the purpose they are fulfilling, the universal principle is implicit in them, and is realizing itself through them. The question also assumes the form of the union of Freedom and Necessity, the latent abstract process of Spirit being regarded as Necessity, while that which exhibits itself in the conscious will of men as their interest, belongs to the domain of Freedom. As the metaphysical connection (*i.e.* the connection in the Idea) of these forms of thought belongs to Logic, it would be out of place to analyze it here. The chief and cardinal points only shall be mentioned.

Philosophy shows that the Idea advances to an infinite antithesis,

that between the Idea in its free, universal form—in which it exists
for itself—and the contrasted form of abstract introversion, reflection
on itself, which is formal existence-for-self, personality, formal freedom, such as belongs to Spirit only. The universal Idea exists thus as
the substantial totality of things on the one side, and as the abstract
essence of free volition on the other side. This reflection of the mind
on itself is individual self-consciousness—the polar opposite of the
Idea in its general form, and therefore existing in absolute Limitation. This polar opposite is consequently limitation, particularization,
for the universal absolute being; it is the side of its definite existence,
the sphere of its formal reality, the sphere of the reverence paid to
God. To comprehend the absolute connection of this antithesis is the
profound task of metaphysics. This Limitation originates all forms
of particularity of whatever kind. The formal volition [of which we
have spoken] wills itself, desires to make its own personality valid
in all that it purposes and does: even the pious individual wishes to
be saved and happy. This pole of the antithesis, existing for itself,
is—in contrast with the Absolute Universal Being—a special separate
existence, taking cognizance of particularity only, and willing that
alone. In short, it plays its part in the region of mere phenomena.
This is the sphere of particular purposes, in effecting which individuals
exert themselves on behalf of their individuality, give it full play and
objective realization. This is also the sphere of happiness and its
opposite. He is happy who finds his condition suited to his special
character, will, and fancy, and so enjoys himself in that condition.
The History of the World is not the theatre of happiness. Periods of
happiness are blank pages in it, for they are periods of harmony,
periods when the antithesis is in abeyance. Reflection on self—the
Freedom above described—is abstractly defined as the formal element
of the activity of the absolute Idea. The realizing *activity* of which
we have spoken is the middle term of the Syllogism, one of whose
extremes is the Universal essence, the *Idea,* which reposes in the
penetralia of Spirit, and the other, the complex of external things,
objective matter. That activity is the medium by which the universal
latent principle is translated into the domain of objectivity.

I will endeavor to make what has been said more vivid and clear
by examples.

The building of a house is, in the first instance, a subjective aim
and design. On the other hand we have, as means, the several substances required for the work—Iron, Wood, Stones. The elements
are made use of in working up this material: fire to melt the iron,

wind to blow the fire, water to set wheels in motion, in order to cut the wood, etc. The result is that the wind, which has helped to build the house, is shut out by the house; so also are the violence of rains and floods, and the destructive powers of fire, so far as the house is made fire-proof. The stones and beams obey the law of gravity, press downwards, and so high walls are carried up. Thus the elements are made use of in accordance with their nature, and yet are made to cooperate for a product by which their operation is limited. Thus the passions of men are gratified; they develop themselves and their aims in accordance with their natural tendencies, and build up the edifice of human society, thus fortifying a position for Right and Order against themselves.

The connection of events above indicated, involves also the fact that in history an additional result is commonly produced by human actions beyond what they aim at and obtain, what they immediately recognize and desire. They gratify their own interest; but something further is thereby accomplished, latent in the actions in question, though not present to their consciousness and not included in their design. An analogous example is the case of a man who, from a feeling of revenge—perhaps not an unjust one, but produced by injury on the other's part—burns that other man's house. A connection is immediately established between the deed itself and a train of circumstances not directly included in it, considered in abstraction. In itself it consisted in merely presenting a small flame to a small portion of a beam. Events not involved in that simple act follow of themselves. The part of the beam that was set fire to is connected with its remote portions; the beam itself is united with the woodwork of the house generally, and this with other houses, so that a wide conflagration ensues, which destroys the goods and chattels of many others besides the man against whom the act of revenge was first directed—perhaps even costs not a few men their lives. This lay neither in the deed considered in itself, nor in the design of the man who committed it. But the action has a further general bearing. In the design of the doer it was only revenge executed against an individual in the destruction of his property, but it is moreover a crime, and that involves punishment also. This may not have been present to the mind of the perpetrator, still less in his intention; but his deed itself—the general principles it calls into play, its substantial content—entails it. By this example I wish only to impress on you the point that in a simple act something further may be implicated than lies in the intention and consciousness of the agent. The example before us involves, however, this additional consideration, that the substance of the act, consequently we may say the act itself, recoils upon the perpetrator—reacts upon him with destructive tendency. This union of the two extremes—the embodiment of a general idea in the form of direct reality, and the elevation of a particularity into connection with universal truth—is brought to pass, at first sight, under the conditions of an utter diversity of nature between the two, and an indifference of the one extreme towards the other. The aims that the agents set before themselves are limited and special; but it must be remarked that the agents themselves are intelligent thinking beings. The purport of their desires is interwoven with general, essential considerations of justice, good, duty, etc.; for mere desire—volition in its rough and savage forms—falls not within the scene and sphere of Universal History. Those general considerations, which form at the same time a norm for directing aims and actions, have a determinate purport; for such an abstraction as "good for its own sake" has no place in living reality. If men are to act, they must not only intend the Good, but must have decided for themselves whether this or that particular thing is a Good. What special course of action, however, is good or not is determined, as regards the ordinary contingencies of private life, by the laws and customs of a State; and here no great difficulty is presented. Each individual has his position; he knows on the whole what a just, honorable course of conduct is. As to ordinary, private relations, the assertion that it is difficult to choose the right and good—regarding it as the mark of an exalted morality to find difficulties and raise scruples on that score—may be set down to an evil or perverse will that seeks to evade duties not in themselves of a perplexing nature, or, at any rate, to an idly reflective habit of mind, where a feeble will affords no sufficient exercise to the faculties, leaving them therefore to find occupation within themselves, and to expend themselves on moral self-adulation.

It is quite otherwise with the comprehensive relations that History has to do with. In this sphere are presented those momentous collisions between existing, acknowledged duties, laws, and rights, and those contingencies which are adverse to this fixed system, which assail and even destroy its foundations and existence, whose tenor may nevertheless seem good, on the whole advantageous—yes, even indispensable and necessary. These contingencies realize themselves in History: they involve a general principle of a different order from that on which depends the permanence of a people or a State. This principle is an essential phase in the development of the creating

Idea, of Truth striving and urging towards [consciousness of] itself. Historical men—World-Historical Individuals—are those in whose aims such a general principle lies.

Caesar—in danger of losing a position, not perhaps at that time of superiority, yet at least of equality with the others who were at the head of the State, and of succumbing to those who were just on the point of becoming his enemies—belongs essentially to this category. These enemies, who were at the same time pursuing *their* personal aims, had the form of the constitution, and the power conferred by an appearance of justice, on their side. Caesar was contending for the maintenance of his position, honor, and safety; and, since the power of his opponents included the sovereignty over the provinces of the Roman Empire, his victory secured for him the conquest of that entire Empire, and he thus became—though leaving the form of the constitution—the Autocrat of the State. What secured for him the execution of a design, which in the first instance was of negative import—the Autocracy of Rome—was, however, at the same time an independently necessary feature in the history of Rome and of the world. It was not, then, his private gain merely, but an unconscious impulse that occasioned the accomplishment of that for which the time was ripe. Such are all great historical men, whose own particular aims involve those large issues which are the will of the World-Spirit. They may be called Heroes, inasmuch as they have derived their purposes and their vocation, not from the calm, regular course of things, sanctioned by the existing order, but from a concealed fount—one that has not attained to phenomenal, present existence—from that inner Spirit, still hidden beneath the surface, which, impinging on the outer world as on a shell, bursts it in pieces, because it is a different kernel from that which belongs to that shell. They are men, therefore, who appear to draw the impulse of their life from themselves, and whose deeds have produced a condition of things and a complex of historical relations that appear to be only their interest and their work.

Such individuals had no consciousness of the general Idea they were unfolding, while prosecuting those aims of theirs; on the contrary, they were practical, political men. But at the same time they were thinking men, who had an insight into the requirements of the time—what was ripe for development. This was the very Truth for their age, for their world, the genus next in order, so to speak, and which was already formed in the womb of time. It was theirs to know this nascent principle, the necessary, directly sequent step in progress that their world was to take, to make this their aim, and to expend their energy in promoting it. World-historical men—the Heroes of an epoch—must, therefore, be recognized as its clear-sighted ones; their deeds, their words are the best of that time. Great men have formed purposes to satisfy themselves, not others. Whatever prudent designs and counsels they might have learned from others would be the more limited and inconsistent features in their career, for it was they who best understood affairs, from whom others learned, and whose policy was approved, or at least acquiesced in. For that Spirit which had taken this fresh step in history is the inmost soul of all individuals, but in a state of unconsciousness which the great men in question awoke. Their fellows therefore follow these soul-leaders, for they feel the irresistible power of their own inner Spirit thus embodied. If we go on to cast a look at the fate of these World-Historical persons whose vocation it was to be the agents of the World-Spirit, we shall find it to have been no happy one. They attained no calm enjoyment; their whole life was labor and trouble; their whole nature was nothing but their master-passion. When their object is attained they fall off like empty hulls from the kernel. They die early, like Alexander; they are murdered, like Caesar; transported to St. Helena, like Napoleon. This fearful consolation—that historical men have not enjoyed what is called happiness, of which only private life (and this may be passed under very various external circumstances) is capable—this consolation those may draw from history who stand in need of it; and it is craved by Envy, vexed at what is great and transcendent, striving, therefore, to belittle it and to find some flaw in it. Thus in modern times it has been demonstrated *ad nauseam* that princes are generally unhappy on their thrones; in consideration of which the possession of a throne is tolerated, and men acquiesce in the fact that not themselves but the personages in question are its occupants. The Free Man, we may observe, is not envious, but gladly recognizes what is great and exalted, and rejoices that it exists.

It is in the light of those common elements which constitute the interest and therefore the passions of individuals that these historical men are to be regarded. They are great men, because they willed and accomplished something great, not a mere fancy, a mere intention, but what met the case and fell in with the needs of the age. This mode of considering them also excludes the so-called "psychological" view, which—serving the purpose of envy most effectually—contrives to refer all actions to the heart, to bring them under a subjective aspect—so that they appear to have done everything under the impulse of some passion, mean, or grand—some morbid craving— and on account of these passions and cravings to have been not moral men. Alexander of Macedon partly subdued Greece, and then Asia; therefore he was possessed by a morbid craving for conquest. He is alleged to have acted from greed of fame and conquest; and the proof that these were the impelling motives is that what he did resulted in fame. What pedagogue has not demonstrated of Alexander the Great, of Julius Caesar, that they were moved by such passions, and were consequently immoral men? By which it is implied that he, the pedagogue, is a better man than they, because he has not such passions; a proof of which lies in the fact that he does not conquer Asia, vanquish Darius and Porus, but while he enjoys life himself lets others enjoy it too. These psychologists are particularly fond of contemplating those peculiarities of great historical figures which appertain to them as private persons. Man must eat and drink; he sustains relations to friends and acquaintances; he has passing impulses and ebullitions of temper. "No man is a hero to his *valet de chambre*," is a well-known proverb; I have added—and Goethe repeated it two years later—"but not because the former is no hero, but because the latter is a valet." He takes off the hero's boots, assists him to bed, knows that he prefers champagne, etc. Historical person- ages waited upon in historical literature by such psychological valets do not make out well; they are brought down by their attendants to a level with—or rather a few degrees below the level of—the morality of such exquisite discerners of spirits. Homer's Thersites, who abuses the kings, is a standing figure for all times. Blows—that is beat- ing with a solid cudgel—he does not get in every age, as in the Homeric one; but his envy, his egotism, is the thorn he has to carry in his flesh; and the undying worm that gnaws him is the tormenting consideration that his excellent views and vituperations remain abso- lutely without effect in the world. But our satisfaction at the fate of Thersitism also may have its sinister side.

A World-historical individual is not so unwise as to indulge a variety of wishes to divide his regards. He is devoted to the One Aim, regardless of all else. It is even possible that such men may treat other great, even sacred, interests inconsiderately—conduct which is indeed obnoxious to moral reprehension. But so mighty a form must trample down many an innocent flower, crush to pieces many an object in its path.

The special interest of passion is thus inseparable from the active

development of a general principle: for it is from the special and
determinate, and from its negation, that the Universal results. Particularity contends with its like, and some loss is involved in the
issue. It is not the general Idea that is implicated in opposition and
combat and that is exposed to danger. It remains in the background,
untouched and uninjured. This may be called the cunning of Reason
—that it sets the passions to work for itself, while what develops its
existence through such impulsion pays the penalty, and suffers loss.
For it is *phenomenal* being that is so treated, of which part is of no
value, part is positive and real. The particular is for the most part of
too trifling value as compared with the general: individuals are sacrificed and abandoned. The Idea pays the penalty of determinate
existence and of corruptibility, not from itself, but from the passions
of individuals.

But though we might tolerate the thought that individuals, their
desires and the gratification of them, are thus sacrificed, and their
happiness given up to the empire of chance, to which it belongs, and
that as a general rule, individuals come under the category of means
to an ulterior end, there is one aspect of human individuality which
we should hesitate to regard in that subordinate light, even in relation to the highest, since it is absolutely no subordinate element, but
exists in those individuals as inherently eternal and divine. I mean
morality, ethics, religion. Even when speaking of the realization of
the great ideal aim by means of individuals, the subjective element
in them—their interest and that of their cravings and impulses, their
views and judgments, though exhibited as the merely formal side of
their existence—was spoken of as having an infinite right to be considered. The first idea that presents itself in speaking of means is
that of something external to the object, having no share in the
object itself. But merely natural things—even the commonest lifeless
objects—used as means must be of such a kind as adapts them to their
purpose; they must possess something in common with it. Human
beings least of all sustain the bare external relation of mere means to
the great ideal aim. Not only do they, in the very act of realizing it,
make it the occasion of satisfying personal desires whose purport is
divergent from that aim; but they share in that ideal aim itself, and are
for that very reason objects of their own existence, not formally
merely, as the world of living beings generally is—whose individual
life is essentially subordinate to that of man, and is properly used *up*
as an instrument. Men, on the contrary, are objects of existence to
themselves, as regards the intrinsic import of the aim in question

To this order belongs that in them which we would exclude from the category of mere means—Morality, Ethics, Religion. That is to say, man is an object of existence in himself only in virtue of the Divine that is in him—what was designated at the outset as Reason, which, in view of its activity and power of self-determination, was called Freedom. And we affirm—without entering at present on the proof of the assertion—that Religion, Morality, etc. have their foundation and source in that principle, and so are essentially elevated above all alien necessity and chance. And here we must remark that individuals, to the extent of their freedom, are responsible for the depravation and enfeeblement of morals and religion. This is the seal of the absolute and sublime destiny of man, that he knows what is good and what is evil; that his destiny is his very ability to will either good or evil—in one word, that he is the subject of moral imputation, imputation not only of evil, but of good, and not only concerning this or that particular matter, and all that happens *ab extra,* but also the good and evil attaching to his individual freedom. The brute alone is simply innocent. It would, however, demand an extensive explanation —as extensive as the analysis of moral freedom itself—to preclude or obviate all the misunderstandings that are usually occasioned by the statement that innocence is just the entire unconsciousness of evil.

In contemplating the fate that virtue, morality, even piety, experience in history, we must not fall into the Litany of Lamentations that the good and pious often—or for the most part—fare ill in the world, while the evil-disposed and wicked prosper. The term "prosperity" is used in a variety of meanings: riches, outward honor, and the like. But in speaking of something that in and for itself constitutes an aim of existence, the so-called well- or ill-faring of these or those isolated individuals cannot be regarded as an essential element in the rational order of the universe. With more justification than happiness, or a fortunate environment for individuals, it is demanded of the grand aim of the world's existence that it should foster, nay involve the execution and ratification of, good, moral, righteous purposes. What makes men morally discontented (a discontent, by the way, on which they somewhat pride themselves) is that they do not find the present adapted to the realization of aims that they hold to be right and just (more especially in modern times, ideals of political institutions); they contrast unfavorably things as they are with their idea of things as they ought to be. In this case it is not private interest or passion that desires gratification, but Reason, Justice, Liberty; and, equipped with this title, the demand in question assumes a lofty bearing and readily

adopts a position not merely of discontent, but of open revolt against
the actual condition of the world. To estimate such a feeling and such
views aright, the demands insisted upon, and the very dogmatic opinions asserted, must be examined. At no time so much as in our own,
have such general principles and notions been advanced, or with
greater assurance. If in days gone by history seems to present itself
as a struggle of passions, in our time—though displays of passion are
not wanting—it exhibits partly a predominance of the struggle of
notions assuming the authority of principles, partly that of passions
and interests essentially subjective, but under the mask of such higher
sanctions. The pretensions thus contended for as legitimate in the
name of that which has been stated as the ultimate aim of Reason pass
accordingly for absolute aims—to the same extent as Religion, Morals,
Ethics. Nothing, as before remarked, is now more common than the
complaint that the ideals that imagination sets up are not realized—
that these glorious dreams are destroyed by cold actuality. These
Ideals—which in the voyage of life founder on the rocks of hard
reality—may be in the first instance only subjective, and belong to
the idiosyncrasy of the individual, imagining himself the highest and
wisest. Such do not properly belong to this category. For the fancies
that the individual in his isolation indulges cannot be the model
for universal reality; just as universal law is not designed for the
units of the mass. These as such may, in fact, find their interests decidedly thrust into the background. But by the term "Ideal" we also
understand the ideal of Reason, of the Good, of the True. Poets, *e.g.*
Schiller, have painted such ideals touchingly and with strong emotion,
and with the deeply melancholy conviction that they could not be
realized. In affirming, on the contrary, that the Universal Reason does
realize itself, we have indeed nothing to do with the individual empirically regarded. That admits of degrees of better and worse, since
here chance and particularity have received authority from the Idea
to exercise their monstrous power. Much, therefore, in particular aspects of the grand phenomenon might be found fault with. This subjective fault-finding—which, however, only keeps in view the individual and its deficiency, without taking notice of Reason pervading
the whole—is easy; and inasmuch as it asserts an excellent intention
with regard to the good of the whole, and seems to result from a
kindly heart, it feels authorized to give itself airs and assume great
consequence. It is easier to discover a deficiency in individuals, in
states, and in Providence, than to see their real import and value.
For in this merely negative fault-finding a proud position is taken—

one that overlooks the object, without having entered into it, without having comprehended its positive aspect. Age generally makes men more tolerant; youth is always discontented. The tolerance of age is the result of the ripeness of judgment which, not merely out of indifference, is satisfied even with what is inferior, but, more deeply taught by the grave experience of life, has been led to perceive the substantial, solid worth of the object in question. The insight then to which—in contradistinction from those ideals—philosophy is to lead us, is that the real world is as it ought to be, that the truly good, the universal divine reason, is not a mere abstraction, but a vital principle capable of realizing itself. This Good, this Reason, in its most concrete form, is God. God governs the world; the actual working of his government—the carrying out of his plan—is the History of the World. This plan philosophy strives to comprehend; for only what has been developed as the result of it possesses *bona fide* reality. What does not accord with it is negative, worthless existence. Before the pure light of this divine Idea—which is no mere Ideal—the phantom of a world whose events are an incoherent concourse of fortuitous circumstances utterly vanishes. Philosophy wishes to discover the substantial purport, the real aspect, of the divine idea, and to justify the so much despised Reality of things; for Reason is the comprehension of the Divine work. But as to what concerns the perversion, corruption, and ruin of religious, ethical and moral purposes, and states of society generally, it must be affirmed, that in their essence these are infinite and eternal, but that the forms they assume may be of a limited order and consequently belong to the domain of mere nature, and may be subject to the sway of chance. They are therefore perishable, and exposed to decay and corruption. Religion and morality—in the same way as inherently universal essences—have the peculiarity of being present in the individual soul, in the full extent of their Idea, and therefore truly and really, although they may not manifest themselves in it *in extenso,* and are not applied to fully developed conditions. The religion, the morality of a limited sphere of life—*e.g.,* that of a shepherd or a peasant—in its intensive concentration and limitation to a few perfectly simple relations of life—has infinite worth, the same worth as the religion and morality of extensive knowledge, or of an existence rich in the compass of its relations and actions. This inner focus, this simple region of the claims of subjective freedom, the home of volition, resolution, and action, the abstract sphere of conscience—what comprises the responsibility and moral value of the individual—remains untouched, and is

quite shut out from the noisy din of World History—including
not merely external and temporal changes, but also those entailed
by the absolute necessity inseparable from the realization of
the Idea of Freedom itself. But as a general truth this must be
regarded as settled, that whatever in the world possesses claims
as noble and glorious has nevertheless a higher existence above
it. The claim of the World-Spirit rises above all special claims.

These observations may suffice in reference to the means the
World-Spirit uses for realizing its Idea. Stated simply and abstractly,
this mediation involves the activity of personal existences in whom
Reason is present as their absolute, substantial being, but a basis, in
the first instance, still obscure and unknown to them. But the subject
becomes more complicated and difficult when we regard individuals
not merely in their aspect of activity, but more concretely, in conjunction with a particular manifestation of that activity in their religion
and morality—forms of existence that are intimately connected with
Reason and share in its absolute claims. Here the relation of mere
means of an end disappears, and the chief bearings of this seeming
difficulty in reference to the absolute aim of Spirit have been briefly
considered.

3. The Role of the State

The third point to be analyzed is, therefore: what object is to be
realized by these means, *i.e.* what form it assumes in the realm of
reality. We have spoken of means; but in the carrying out of a subjective, limited aim, we have also to take into consideration the
material that either is already present or has to be procured. Thus the
question would arise: What is the material in which the Ideal of
Reason is wrought out? The primary answer would be: Personality
itself, human desires, Subjectivity generally. In human knowledge and
volition, as its material element, Reason attains positive existence.
We have considered subjective volition where it has an object that
is the truth and essence of a reality, viz. where it constitutes a great
World-Historical passion. As a subjective will, occupied with limited
passions, it is dependent, and can gratify its desires only within the
limits of this dependence. But the subjective will has also a substantial
life, a reality, in which it moves in the region of essential being and has
the essential itself as the object of its existence. This essential being
is the union of the subjective with the rational Will: it is the moral
Whole, the State, which is that form of reality in which the individual

has and enjoys his freedom, but on the condition of his recognizing, believing in, and willing what is common to the Whole. And this must not be understood as if the subjective will of the social unit attained its gratification and enjoyment through that common Will, as if this were a means provided for its benefit, as if the individual, in his relations to other individuals, thus limited his freedom, in order that this universal limitation—the mutual constraint of all—might secure a small space of liberty for each. Rather, we affirm that Law, Morality, Government, and they alone, are the positive reality and completion of Freedom. Freedom of a low and limited order is mere caprice, which finds its exercise in the sphere of particular and limited desires.

Subjective volition, Passion, is what sets men in activity, and effects "practical" realization. The Idea is the inner spring of action; the State is the actually existing, realized moral life. For it is the Unity of the universal essential Will with that of the individual; and this is "Morality." The Individual living in this unity has a moral life, possesses a value that consists in this substantiality alone. Sophocles in his *Antigone,* says, "The divine commands are not of yesterday, nor of today; no, they have an infinite existence, and no one could say whence they came." The laws of morality are not accidental, but are the essentially Rational. It is the very purpose of the State that what is essential in the practical activity of men, and in their dispositions, should be duly recognized, that it should have a manifest existence, and maintain its position. It is the absolute interest of Reason that this moral Whole should exist; and herein lies the justification and merit of heroes who have founded states, however rude these may have been. In the history of the World, only those peoples that form a State can come under our notice. For it must be understood that this latter is the realization of Freedom, *i.e.* of the absolute final aim, and that it exists for its own sake. It must further be understood that all the worth the human being possesses, all spiritual reality, he possesses only through the State. For his spiritual reality consists in this, that his own essence—Reason—is objectively present to him, that it possesses objective immediate existence for him. Thus only is he fully conscious; thus only is he a partaker of morality, of a just and moral social and political life. For Truth is the Unity of the universal and subjective Will; and the Universal is to be found in the State, in its laws, its universal and rational arrangements. The State is the Divine Idea as it exists on Earth. We have in it, therefore, the object of History in a more definite shape than before—that in which Freedom obtains objectivity, and lives in the enjoyment of this objectivity. For Law is the objectivity of Spirit; volition in its true form. Only that will which obeys law is free, for it obeys itself—it is independent and so free. When the State, our country, constitutes a community of existence, when the subjective will of man submits to laws, the contradiction between Liberty and Necessity vanishes. The Rational has necessary existence, as being the reality and substance of things, and we are free in recognizing it as law, and following it as the substance of our own being. The objective and the subjective will are then reconciled, and present one identical homogeneous whole. For the morality of the State is not of that ethical reflective kind, in which one's own conviction bears sway; this latter is rather the peculiarity of modern times, while the true ancient morality is based on the principle of abiding by one's duty [to the state at large]. An Athenian citizen did what was required of him, as it were from instinct; but if I reflect on the object of my activity, I must have the consciousness that my will has been called into exercise. But morality is Duty—substantial Right—a "second nature," as it has been justly called; for the first nature of man is his merely animal existence.

a. Freedom and the State

The development *in extenso* of the Idea of the State belongs to the Philosophy of Jurisprudence; but it must be observed that in the theories of our time various errors are current respecting it, which pass for established truths and have become fixed prejudices. We will mention only a few of them, giving prominence to such as have a reference to the subject of history.

The error that first meets us is the direct contradictory of our principle that the state presents the realization of Freedom—the opinion, viz., that man is free by nature, but that in society, in the State—to which nevertheless he is irresistibly impelled—he must limit this natural freedom. That man is free by Nature is quite correct in one sense, viz., that he is so according to the Idea of Humanity; but we imply thereby that he is such only in virtue of his destiny— that he has an undeveloped power to become such, for the "Nature" of an object is exactly synonymous with its "Idea." But the view in question imports more than this. When man is spoken of as "free by Nature," the mode of his existence as well as his destiny is implied. His merely natural and primary condition is intended. In this sense a "state of Nature" is assumed in which mankind at large are in the possession of their natural rights with the unconstrained exercise and enjoyment of their freedom. This assumption is not indeed raised to the dignity of the historical fact; it would indeed be difficult, were the attempt seriously made, to point out any such condition as actually existing, or as having ever occurred. Examples of a savage state of life can be pointed out, but they are marked by brutal passions and deeds of violence, while, however rude and simple their conditions, they involve social arrangements which (to use the common phrase) restrain freedom. That assumption is one of those nebulous images that theory produces, an idea which it cannot avoid originating, but which it fathers upon real existence, without sufficient historical justification.

What we find such a state of Nature to be in actual experience, answers exactly to the Idea of a merely natural condition. Freedom as the ideal of that which is original and natural does not exist as original and natural. Rather must it be first sought out and won; and that by an incalculable discipline of the intellectual and moral powers. The State of Nature is, therefore, predominantly that of injustice and violence, of untamed natural impulses, of inhuman deeds and feelings. Limitation is certainly produced by Society and the State, but it is a limitation of the mere brute emotions and rude instincts, as also, in a more advanced stage of culture, of the premeditated self-will of caprice and passion. This kind of constraint is part of the instrumentality by which the consciousness of Freedom and the desire for its attainment in its true—that is Rational and Ideal—form can be obtained. To the Ideal of Freedom, Law and Morality are indispensably requisite; and they are in and for themselves universal existences, objects and aims, which are discovered only by the activity of thought, separating itself from the merely sensuous, and developing itself in opposition thereto, and which must on the other hand be introduced into and incorporated with the originally sensuous will, contrary to its natural inclination. The perpetually recurring misapprehension of Freedom consists in regarding that term only in its formal, subjective sense, abstracted from its essential objects and aims; thus a constraint put upon impulse, desire, passion—pertaining to the particular individual as such—a limitation of caprice and self-will is regarded as a fettering of Freedom. We should, on the contrary, look upon such limitation as the indispensable proviso of emancipation. Society and the State are the very conditions in which Freedom is realized.

We must notice a second view that denies the principle of the development of moral relations into a legal form. The patriarchal condition is regarded—either in reference to the entire race of man or to some branches of it—as exclusively that condition of things in which the legal element is combined with a due recognition of the moral and emotional parts of our nature, and in which justice, as united with these, truly and really influences the intercourse of the social units. The basis of the patriarchal condition is the family relation, which develops the primary form of conscious morality, succeeded by that of the State as its second phase. The patriarchal condition is one of transition, in which the family has already advanced to the position of a race or people, where the union, therefore, has already ceased to be simply a bond of love and confidence, and has become one of plighted service. We must first examine the ethical principle of the Family. The Family may be reckoned as virtually a single person, since its members have either mutually surrendered their individual personality (and consequently their legal position towards each other, with the rest of their particular interests and desires), as in the case of the parents, or have not yet attained such an independent personality, as in the case of the children, who are at first in that merely natural condition already mentioned. They live, therefore, in a unity of feeling, love, confidence, and faith in each other. And in a relation of mutual love the one individual has the consciousness of himself in the consciousness of the other; he lives out of self, and in this mutual self-renunciation each regains the life that had been virtually transferred to the other—gains, in fact, that other's existence and his own as involved with that other. The further interests connected with the necessities and external concerns of life, as well as the development that has to take place within their circle, *i.e.* of the children, constitute a common object for the members of the Family. The Spirit of the Family—the Penates—forms one substantial being, as much as the Spirit of a People in the State; and morality in both cases consists in a feeling, a consciousness, and a will, not limited to individual personality and interest, but embracing the common interests of the members generally. But this unity is in the case of the Family essentially one of feeling, not advancing beyond the limits of the merely natural. The piety of the Family relation should be respected in the highest degree by the State; by its means the State obtains as its members individuals who are already moral (for as mere persons they are not) and who in uniting to form a state bring with them that sound basis of a political edifice—the capacity of feeling one with a Whole. But the expansion of the Family to a patriarchal unity carries us beyond the ties of blood-relationship, the simply natural elements of that basis; and outside of these limits the members of the community must enter upon the position of independent personality. A review of the patriarchal condition, *in extenso,* would lead us to give special attention to the Theocratic Constitution. The head of the patriarchal clan is also its priest. If the Family in its general relations is not yet separated from civic society and the state, the separation of religion from it has also not yet taken place; and so much the less since the piety of the hearth is itself a profoundly subjective state of feeling.

We have considered two aspects of Freedom, the objective and the subjective; if, therefore, Freedom is asserted to consist in the individuals of a State all agreeing in its arrangements, it is evident that only the subjective aspect is regarded. The natural inference from this principle is that no law can be valid without the approval of all. This difficulty is supposed to be obviated by the decision that the minority must yield to the majority; the majority therefore bear the sway. But long ago J. J. Rousseau remarked that in that case there would be no longer freedom, for the will of the minority would cease to be respected. At the Polish Diet each single member had to give his consent before any political step could be taken; and this kind of freedom it was that ruined the State. Besides, it is a dangerous and false prejudice that the People alone have reason and insight, and know what justice is; for each popular faction may represent itself as the People, and the question as to what constitutes the State is one of advanced science, and not of popular decision.

If the principle of regard for the individual will is recognized as the only basis of political liberty, viz., that nothing should be done by or for the State to which not all the members of the body politic have given their sanction, we have, properly speaking, no Constitution. The only arrangement necessary would be, first, a central office, with no will of its own that would consider what appeared to be the needs of the State, and, second, a contrivance for calling the members of the State together, for taking the votes, and for performing the arithmetical operations of reckoning and comparing the number of votes for the different propositions, and thereby deciding upon them. The State is an abstraction, having its generic existence in its citizens; but it is an actuality, and its simple generic existence must embody itself in individual will and activity. The want of government and political administration in general is felt; this necessitates the selection, and separation from the rest, of those who have to take the helm in political affairs, to decide concerning them, and to give orders to other citizens, with a view to the execution of their plans. If, *e.g.,* even the people in a Democracy resolve on a war, a general must head the army. It is only by a Constitution that the abstraction—the State—attains life and reality; but this involves the distinction between those who command and those who obey. Yet obedience seems inconsistent with liberty, and those who command appear to do the very opposite of what the fundamental idea of the State, viz., that of Freedom, requires. It is, however, urged that—though the distinction between commanding and obeying is absolutely necessary, because affairs could not go on without it (and indeed this seems only a compulsory limitation, external to and contravening freedom in the abstract)—the constitution should be at least so framed that the citizens may obey as little as possible, and the smallest modicum of free volition be left to the commands of the superiors; that the substance of what requires subordination, even in its most important bearings, should be decided and resolved on by the People, by the will of many or of all the citizens, though it is supposed to be thereby provided that the State should be possessed of vigor and strength as a reality, an individual unity. The primary consideration is, then, the distinction between the governing and the governed, and political constitutions in the abstract have been rightly divided into Monarchy, Aristocracy, and Democracy; which gives occasion, however, to the remark that Monarchy itself must be further divided into Despotism and Monarchy proper, that in all the divisions to which the leading Idea gives rise, only the generic character is made prominent, it being not intended thereby that the particular category under review should be exhausted as a Form, Order, or Kind in its concrete development. But especially it must be observed that the above-mentioned divisions admit of a multitude of particular modifications—not only those that lie within the limits of those classes themselves, but also those that are mixtures of several classes and are consequently misshapen, unstable, and inconsistent forms. In such a collision, the troublesome question is what is the best constitution; that is, by what arrangement, organization, or mechanism of the power of the State its object can be most surely attained. This object may indeed be variously understood, for instance, as the calm enjoyment of life on the part of the citizens, or as Universal Happiness. Such aims have suggested the so-called Ideals of Government, such as the Ideal of the education of princes (Fenelon), and of the rulers, or aristocracy (Plato); for the chief point they treat of is the condition of those subjects who stand at the head of affairs, and in these Ideals the concrete details of political organization are not at all considered. The enquiry into the best constitution is frequently treated as if it were not only in theory an affair of subjective independent conviction, but as if the introduction of a constitution recognized as the best, or as superior to others, could be the result of a theoretical decision—as if the form of a constitution were a matter of free choice, determined by nothing else but reflection. In this ingenuous fashion, not indeed the Persian people, but the Persian grandees, deliberated as to what constitution they should introduce into Persia after their conspiracy to overthrow the pseudo-Smerdis and the Magi had succeeded and there was no scion of the royal family living—and Herodotus gives an equally naïve account of this deliberation.

At present, the Constitution of a country and people is not represented as so entirely dependent on free and deliberate choice. The fundamental but abstractly (and therefore imperfectly) entertained conception of Freedom has resulted in the Republic's being very generally regarded—in theory—as the only just and true political constitution. Many who even occupy elevated official positions under monarchical constitutions, so far from being opposed to this idea, are actually its supporters; only they see that such a constitution, though the best, cannot be realized under all circumstances, and that—while men are what they are—we must be satisfied with less freedom, the monarchical constitution, under the given circumstances and the present moral condition of the people, being regarded as the most advantageous. In this view also, the condition on which the necessity of a particular constitution is thought to depend is regarded as nonessential and accidental. This view is based on the distinction that the reflective understanding makes between an idea and the corresponding reality, holding to an abstract and consequently untrue idea, not grasping it in its completeness, or—which is virtually, though not in form, the same—not taking a concrete view of a people and a state. We shall have to show further on that the constitution adopted by a people makes one substance, one spirit, with its religion, its art and its philosophy, or, at least, with its conceptions and thoughts, its culture generally, not to expatiate upon the additional influences, *ab extra,* of climate, of neighbors, of its place in the world. A State is an individual totality, of which you cannot select any particular aspect, even a supremely important one, such as its political constitution, and deliberate and decide about it in isolation. Not only is that constitution most intimately connected with and dependent on those other spiritual forces, but the form of the entire moral and intellectual individuality—comprising all the forces it embodies—is only a step in the development of the grand Whole, with its place preappointed in the process—a fact that gives the highest sanction to the constitution in question, and establishes its absolute necessity. The origin of a State involves imperious lordship on the one hand, instinctive submission on the other. But even obedience—lordly power, and the fear inspired by a ruler—in itself implies some degree of voluntary connection. Even in barbarous states this is the case; it is not the isolated will of individuals that prevail: individual pretensions are relinquished, and the general will is the essential bond of political union. This unity of the general and the particular is the Idea itself, manifesting itself as a State, and subsequently undergoing further development within itself. The abstract yet necessitated process in the development of truly independent states is as follows: They begin with regal power, whether of patriarchal or military origin. In the next phase, particularity and individuality assert themselves in the form of Aristocracy and Democracy. Finally, we have the subjection of these separate interests to a single power, but one that is absolutely such that those spheres have an independent position outside it—it is necessarily Monarchical. Two phases of royalty, therefore, must be distinguished, a primary and a secondary one. This process is necessitated, so that the form of government assigned to a particular stage of development must present itself: it is therefore no matter of choice, but is the form that is adapted to the spirit of the people.

In a Constitution the main feature of interest is the self-development of the rational, that is, the political, condition of a people, the setting free of the successive elements of the Idea, so that the several powers in the State manifest themselves as separate—attain their appropriate and special perfection—and yet in this independent condition work together for one object, and are held together by it—*i.e.,* form an organic whole. The State is thus the embodiment of Rational Freedom, realizing and recognizing itself in an objective form. For its objectivity consists in this, that its successive stages are not merely ideal, but are present in an appropriate reality, and that in their separate and several working they are absolutely merged in that agency by which the totality, the soul, the individual unity, is produced.

The State is the Idea of Spirit in the external manifestation of human will and its freedom. It is in the State, therefore, that historical change is essentially embodied; and the successive phases of the Idea manifest themselves in it as distinct political principles. The Constitutions under which World-Historical peoples have reached their culmination are peculiar to them, and therefore do not present a generally applicable political basis. Were it otherwise, the differences of similar constitutions would consist only in a peculiar method of expanding and developing that generic basis, whereas they really originate in diversity of principle. It follows that from the comparison of the political institutions of the ancient World-Historical peoples, nothing (or practically nothing) can be learned for the Constitutional principle of our own times. In science and art it is quite otherwise; *e.g.*, the ancient philosophy is so decidedly the basis of the modern that it is inevitably contained in the latter, and constitutes its basis. In this case the relation is that of a continuous development of the same structure, whose foundation-stone, walls, and roof have remained what they were. In art, the Greek itself, in its original form, furnishes us the best models. But in regard to political constitutions it is quite otherwise: here the ancient and the modern have not their essential principle in common. Abstract definitions and dogmas respecting just government, implying that intelligence and virtue ought to bear sway are, indeed, common to both. But nothing is so absurd as to look to Greeks, Romans, or Orientals, for models for the political arrangements of our time. From the East may be derived beautiful pictures of a patriarchal condition, of paternal government, and of devotion to it on the part of peoples; from Greeks and Romans, descriptions of popular liberty. Among the latter we find the idea of a Free Constitution admitting all the citizens to a share in deliberations and decisions about the affairs and laws of the Commonwealth. In our times, too, this is generally accepted, only with this modification, that, since our States are so large, and there are so many of "the Many," the latter—direct action being impossible—should by the indirect method of elective substitution express their concurrence with decisions about the general welfare; in other words, for most legislative purposes the people should be represented by deputies. The so-called Representative Constitution is that form of government with which we connect the idea of a free constitution, and this notion has become a rooted prejudice. On this theory People and Government are separated. But there is a perversity in this antithesis, an ill-intentioned *ruse* designed to insinuate that the People are the totality of the State. Besides, the basis of this view is the principle of isolated individuality—the absolute validity of the subjective will—a dogma we have already investigated. The great point is that Freedom in its Ideal conception does not have subjective will and caprice for its principle, but the recognition of the universal Will, and that the process by which Freedom is realized is the free development of its successive stages. The subjective will is a merely formal determination—a *carte blanche*—not including what it is that is willed. Only the rational will is that universal principle which independently determines and unfolds its own being and develops its successive elemental phases as organic members. Of this Gothic-cathedral architecture the ancients knew nothing.

b. Culture: Religion, Art, and Philosophy

At an earlier stage of the discussion, we established the two basic considerations: first, the idea of freedom as the absolute and final aim, second, the means for realizing it, *i.e.* the subjective side of knowledge and will, with its life, movement, and activity. We then recognized the State as the moral Whole and the Reality of Freedom, and consequently as the objective unity of these two elements. For although we make this distinction into two aspects for the sake of discussion, it must be remarked that they are intimately connected, and that their connection is involved in the idea of each when examined separately. We have, on the one hand, recognized the Idea in the definite form of Freedom conscious of and willing itself, having itself alone as its object, involving at the same time the pure and simple Idea of Reason, and likewise what we have called subject, self-consciousness, Spirit actually existing in the World. If, on the other hand, we consider Subjectivity we find that subjective knowledge and will is Thought. But by the very act of thoughtful cognition and volition, I will the universal object—the substance of absolute Reason. We observe, therefore, an essential union between the objective side (the Idea) and the subjective side (the personality that conceives and wills it). The objective existence of this union is the State, which is therefore the basis and center of the other concrete elements of the life of a people—of Art, of Law, of Morals, of Religion, of Science. All the activity of Spirit has only this object—the becoming conscious of this union, *i.e.,* of its own Freedom. Among the forms of this conscious union Religion occupies the highest position. In it, Spirit, rising above the limitations of temporal and secular existence, becomes conscious of the Absolute Spirit, and in this consciousness of the self-existent Being renounces its individual interest; it lays this aside in Devotion—a state of mind in which it refuses to occupy itself any longer with the limited and particular. By Sacrifice man expresses his renunciation of his property, his will, his individual feelings. The religious concentration of the soul appears in the form of feeling; it nevertheless passes also into reflection, of which a form of worship is a result. The second form of the union of the objective and subjective in the human spirit is Art. This advances further into the realm of the actual and sensuous than Religion. In its noblest walk it is occupied with representing, not indeed the Spirit of God, but certainly the Form of God; and in its secondary aims, whatever is divine and spiritual generally. Its office is to render the Divine visible, presenting it to the imaginative and intuitive faculty. But the True is the object not only of conception and feeling, as in Religion, and of intuition, as in Art, but also of the thinking faculty; and this gives us the third form of the union in question, Philosophy. This is consequently the highest, freest, and wisest phase. Of course we do not intend to investigate these three phases here; they have only suggested themselves in virtue of their occupying the same general ground as the object here considered, the State.

The general principle that manifests itself and becomes an object of consciousness in the State—the form under which all that the State includes is brought—is the whole of that cycle of phenomena that constitutes the culture of a nation. But the definite substance that receives the form of universality, and exists in that concrete reality which is the State, is the Spirit of the People itself. The actual State is animated by this spirit, in all its particular affairs—its Wars, Institutions, etc. But man must also attain a conscious realization of this his Spirit and essential nature, and of his original identity with it. For we said that morality is the identity of the subjective or personal with the universal will. Now the mind must give itself an express consciousness of this; and the focus of this knowledge is Religion. Art and Science are only distinct aspects and forms of the same substantial being. In considering Religion, the chief point of enquiry is whether it recognizes the True—the Idea—only in its separate, abstract form, or in its true unity: in separation—God being represented in an abstract form as the Highest Being, Lord of Heaven and Earth, living in a remote region far from human actualities—or in its unity—God, as Unity of the Universal and Individual, the Individual itself assuming the aspect of positive and real existence in the idea of the Incarnation. Religion is the sphere in which a nation gives itself the definition of that which it regards as the True. A definition contains everything that belongs to the essence of an object, reducing its nature to its simple characteristic predicate, as a mirror for every predicate, the generic soul pervading all its details. The conception of God, therefore, constitutes the general basis of a people's character.

In this aspect, religion stands in the closest connection with the political principle. Freedom can exist only where Individuality is recognized as having its positive and real existence in the Divine Being. The connection may be further explained thus: Secular existence, as merely temporal—occupied with particular interests—is consequently only relative and unauthorized, and receives its validity only in as far as the universal soul that pervades it—its principle—receives absolute validity, which it cannot have unless it is recognized as the definite manifestation, the phenomenal existence, of the Divine Essence. This is why the State rests on Religion. We hear this often repeated in our times, though for the most part nothing further is meant than that individual subjects as God-fearing men would be more disposed and ready to perform their duty, since obedience to King and Law so naturally follows in the train of reverence for God. This reverence, indeed, since it exalts the general over the special, may even turn upon the latter, become fanatical, and work with incendiary and destructive violence against the State, its institutions, and arrangements. Religious feeling, therefore, it is thought, should be sober—kept in a certain degree of coolness—that it may not storm against and pull down that which should be defended and preserved by it. The possibility of such a catastrophe is at least latent in it.

While, however, the correct sentiment is adopted, that the State is based on Religion, the position thus assigned to Religion supposes that the State already exists, and that subsequently, in order to maintain it, Religion must be brought into it—in buckets and bushels as it were—and impressed upon people's hearts. It is quite true that men must be trained to religion, but not as to something whose existence has yet to begin. For in affirming that the State is based on Religion—that it has its roots in it—we virtually assert that the former has proceeded from the latter; and that this derivation is going on now and will always continue; i.e., the principles of the State must be regarded as valid in and for themselves, which they can only be in so far as they are recognized as determinate manifestations of the Divine Nature. The form of Religion, therefore, decides that of the State and its constitution. The latter actually originated in the particular religion adopted by the nation, so that, in fact, the Athenian or the Roman State was possible only in connection with the specific form of Heathenism existing among the respective peoples, just as a Catholic State has a spirit and constitution different from that of a Protestant one.

If that outcry—that urging and striving for the implantation of Religion in the community—were an utterance of anguish and a call for help, as it often seems to be, expressing a danger that religion has vanished, or is about to vanish from the State—that would be fearful indeed—worse, in fact, than this outcry supposes, for it implies the belief in a resource against the evil, viz., the implantation and inculcation of religion, whereas religion is by no means a thing to be so produced; its self-production (and there can be no other) lies much deeper.

Another and opposite folly we meet with in our time, is that of pretending to invent and carry out political constitutions independently of religion. The Catholic confession, although sharing the Christian name with the Protestant, does not concede to the State an inherent Justice and Morality—a concession which in the Protestant principle is fundamental. This tearing away of the political morality of the Constitution from its natural connection is necessary to the genius of that religion, inasmuch as it does not recognize Justice and Morality as independent and substantial. But thus excluded from intrinsic worth—torn away from their last refuge, the sanctuary of conscience, the calm retreat where religion has its abode—the principles and institutions of political legislation are destitute of a real center, to the same degree as they are compelled to remain abstract and indefinite.

Summing up what has been said of the State, we find that we have been led to call its vital principle, as actuating the individuals who compose it, Morality. The State, its laws, its arrangements, constitute the rights of its members; its natural features, its mountains, air, and waters, are their country, their fatherland, their outward material property; the history of this State, their deeds; what their ancestors have produced belongs to them and lives in their memory. All is their possession, just as they are possessed by it, for it constitutes their existence, their being.

Their imagination is occupied with the ideas thus presented, while the adoption of these laws and of a fatherland so conditioned is the expression of their will. It is this matured totality that thus constitutes one Being, the spirit of one People. To it the individual members belong; each unit is the Son of his Nation and at the same time— in as far as the State to which he belongs is undergoing development —the Son of his Age. None remains behind it, still less advances beyond it. This spiritual Being (the Spirit of his Time) is his; he is a representative of it; it is that in which he originated and in which he lives. Among the Athenians the word "Athens" had a double import, suggesting primarily a complex of political institutions, but no less, in the second place, that Goddess who represented the Spirit of the People and its unity.

This Spirit of a People is a determinate and particular Spirit, and is, as just stated, further modified by the degree of its historical development. This Spirit, then, constitutes the basis and substance of those other forms of a nation's consciousness that have been noticed. For Spirit in its self-consciousness must become an object of contemplation to itself, and objectivity involves, in the first instance, the rise of differences that make up a total of distinct spheres of objective spirit, in the same way as the Soul exists only as the complex of its faculties, which in their form of concentration in a simple unity produce that Soul. It is thus One Individuality which, presented in its essence as God, is honored and enjoyed in *Religion,* which is exhibited as an object of sensuous contemplation in *Art,* and is apprehended as an intellectual conception in *Philosophy.* In virtue of the original identity of their essence, purport, and object, these various forms are inseparably united with the Spirit of the State. Only in connection with this particular religion, can this particular political constitution exist, just as in such or such a State, such or such a Philosophy or order of Art.

The remark next in order is, that each particular National genius is to be treated as only One Individual in the process of Universal History. For that history is the exhibition of the divine, absolute development of Spirit in its highest forms—that gradation by which it attains its truth and consciousness of itself. The forms that these grades of progress assume are the characteristic "National Spirits" of History, the peculiar tenor of their moral life, of their Government, their Art, Religion, and Science. To realize these grades is the boundless impulse of the World-Spirit, the goal of its irresistible urging; for this division into organic members, and the full development of each, is its Idea. Universal History is exclusively occupied with showing how Spirit comes to a recognition and adoption of the Truth: the dawn of knowledge appears; it begins to discover salient principles, and at last it arrives at full consciousness.

Having, therefore, learned the abstract characteristics of the nature of Spirit, the means which it uses to realize its Idea, and the shape assumed by it in its complete realization in phenomenal existence— namely, the State—nothing further remains for this introductory section to contemplate but

IV. The Course of World-History

The mutations that history presents have long been characterized in general as an advance to something better, more perfect. The changes that take place in Nature—however infinitely varied they may be—exhibit only a perpetually self-repeating cycle; in Nature there happens "nothing new under the sun," and the multiform play of its phenomena so far induces a feeling of *ennui*; only in those changes that take place in the region of Spirit does anything new arise. This peculiarity in the world of mind has indicated in the case of man an altogether different destiny from that of merely natural objects—in which we find always one and the same stable character, to which all change reverts—namely, a real capacity for change, and that for the better, an impulse of perfectibility. This principle, which subsumes change itself under a law, has met with an unfavorable reception from religions—such as the Catholic—and from States claiming as their just right a static, or at least a stable, condition. If the mutability of worldly things in general—political constitutions, for instance—is conceded, either Religion (as the Religion of Truth) is absolutely excepted, or the difficulty is avoided by ascribing changes, revolutions, and abrogations of immaculate theories and institutions, to accident or imprudence, but principally to the levity and evil passions of man. The principle of Perfectibility indeed is almost as indefinite a notion as mutability in general; it is without scope or goal, and has no standard by which to estimate the changes in question: the improved, more perfect, state of things towards which it professedly tends is altogether undetermined.

The principle of Development involves also the existence of a latent germ of being—a capacity or potentiality striving to realize itself. This formal conception finds actual existence in Spirit, which has the History of the World for its theater, its possession, and the sphere of its realization. It is not of such a nature as to be tossed to and fro amid the superficial play of accidents, but is rather the absolute arbiter of things, entirely unmoved by contingencies, which, indeed, it applies and manages for its own purposes. Development, however, is also a property of organized natural objects. Their existence presents itself, not as an exclusively dependent one, subject to external changes, but as one that expands itself in virtue of an internal unchangeable principle, a simple essence whose existence, *i.e.*, as a germ, is at first simple, but subsequently develops a variety of parts that become involved with other objects and consequently live through a continuous process of changes—a process, nevertheless, that results in the very opposite of change, and is even transformed into a *vis conservatrix* of the organic principle and the form embodying it. Thus the organized *individuum* produces itself; it expands itself actually to what it was always *potentially*. So Spirit is only that which it attains by its own efforts; it makes itself actually what it always was potentially. That development (of natural organisms) takes place in a direct, unopposed, unhindered manner. Between the Idea and its realization—the essential constitution of the original germ and the conformity to it of the existence derived from it—no disturbing influence can intrude. But in relation to Spirit it is quite otherwise. The realization of *its* Idea is mediated by consciousness and will; these very faculties are, in the first instance, sunk in their primary merely natural life; the first object and goal of their striving is the realization of their merely natural destiny, which, since it is Spirit that animates it, is possessed of vast attractions and displays great power and [moral] richness. Thus Spirit is at war with itself; it has to overcome itself as its most formidable obstacle. That development, which in the sphere of Nature is a peaceful growth, is in that of Spirit a severe, a mighty conflict with itself. What Spirit really strives for is the realization of its Ideal being; but in doing so, it hides that goal from its own vision, and is proud and well satisfied in this alienation.

Its expansion, therefore, does not present the harmless tranquillity of mere growth, as does that of organic life, but a stern reluctant working against itself. It exhibits, moreover, not the mere formal conception of development, but the attainment of a definite result. The goal of attainment we determined at the outset: it is Spirit in its completeness, in its essential nature, *i.e.,* Freedom. This is the fundamental object, and therefore also the leading principle of the development, that from which it receives meaning and importance (as in Roman history Rome is the object and is consequently what directs our consideration of the facts related); as, conversely, the phenomena of the process have resulted from this principle alone, and possess a sense and value only as referred to it. There are many considerable periods in History in which this development seems to have been intermitted, in which, we might say, the whole enormous gain of previous culture appears to have been entirely lost, after which, unhappily, a new commencement has been necessary, made in the hope of recovering—by the assistance of some remains saved from the wreck of a former civilization, and by dint of a renewed incalculable expenditure of strength and time—one of the regions that had been an ancient possession of that civilization. We behold also continued processes of growth, structures and systems of culture in particular spheres, rich in kind, and well developed in every direction. The merely formal and indeterminate view of development in general can neither assign to one form of expansion superiority over the other, nor render comprehensible the object of that decay of older periods of growth, but must regard such occurrences—or, to speak more particularly, the retrocessions they exhibit—as external contingencies, and can only judge of particular modes of development from indeterminate points of view, which—since the development as such is all in all—are relative and not absolute goals of attainment.

Universal History exhibits the gradation in the development of that principle whose substantial purport is the consciousness of Freedom. The analysis of the successive grades, in their abstract form, belongs to Logic; in their concrete aspect, to the Philosophy of Spirit. Here it is sufficient to state that the first step in the process presents that immersion of Spirit in Nature which has been already referred to; the second shows it as advancing to the consciousness of its freedom. But this initial separation from Nature is imperfect and partial, since it is derived immediately from the merely natural state, is consequently related to it, and is still encumbered with it as an essentially connected element. The third step is the elevation of the soul from this still limited and special form of freedom to its pure universal form, that state in which the spiritual essence attains the consciousness and feeling of itself. These grades are the ground-principles of the general process; but how each of them on the other hand involves within itself a process of formation, constituting the links in a dialectic of transition—to particularize this may be reserved for the sequel.

Here we have only to indicate that Spirit begins with a germ of infinite possibility, but only possibility, containing its substantial existence in an undeveloped form, as the object and goal which it reaches only in its resultant—full reality. In actual existence Progress appears as an advancing from the imperfect to the more perfect; but the former must not be understood abstractly as only the imperfect, but as something which involves the very opposite of itself—the so-called perfect—as a germ or impulse. So—reflectively, at least—possibility points to something destined to become actual; the Aristotelian δύναμις is also *potentia,* power and might. Thus the Im-

perfect, as involving its opposite, is a contradiction that certainly
exists, but that is continually annulled and solved; the instinctive
movement—the inherent impulse in the life of the soul—to break
through the rind of mere nature, sensuousness, and that which is
alien to it, and to attain to the light of consciousness, *i.e.* to itself.

1. The Beginning of History

We have already remarked how the beginning of the history of
Spirit must be conceived so as to be in harmony with its Idea,
when we were speaking of the hypotheses that have been proposed
about a primitive "natural condition" in which freedom and justice
are supposed to exist, or to have existed. This was, however, nothing
more than an assumption of historical existence, conceived in the
twilight of theorizing reflection. A pretension of quite another order—
not a mere inference of reasoning, but making the claim of historical fact, and that supernaturally confirmed—is put forth in connection with a different view that is now widely promulgated by a
certain group of theorizers. This view takes up the idea of the primitive paradisical condition of man, which had been previously expanded by the Theologians after their fashion—involving, *e.g.,* the
supposition that God spoke with Adam in Hebrew—but remodelled
to suit other requirements. The high authority appealed to in the first
instance is the biblical narrative. But this depicts the primitive condition, partly only in the few well-known traits, but partly either as
in man generically—human nature at large—or, so far as Adam is
to be taken as an individual, and consequently one person—as
existing and completed in this one, or only in one human pair. The
biblical account by no means justifies us in imagining a *people,* and
an historical condition of such people, existing in that primitive form;
still less does it warrant us in attributing to them the possession of
a perfectly developed knowledge of God and Nature. "Nature," so
the fiction runs, "like a clear mirror of God's creation, had originally
lain revealed and transparent to the unclouded eye of man." [1] Divine
Truth is imagined to have been equally manifest. It is even hinted,
though left in some degree of obscurity, that in this primary condition
men were in possession of an indefinitely extended and already expanded body of religious truths immediately revealed by God. This
theory affirms that all religions had their historical beginning in this

---

[1] Friedrich von Schlegel, *Philosophy of History.*

primitive knowledge, and that they polluted and obscured the original Truth by the monstrous creations of error and depravity, though in all the mythologies invented by Error traces of that origin and of those primitive true dogmas are supposed to be present and recognizable. An important interest, therefore, accrues to the investigation of the history of ancient peoples, that, viz., of the endeavor to trace their annals up to the point where such fragments of the primary revelation are to be met with in greater purity than lower down.[1]

We owe to the interest that has occasioned these investigations very much that is valuable; but this investigation bears direct testimony against itself, for it would seem to be awaiting the issue of an historical demonstration of that which is presupposed by it as historically established. That advanced condition of the knowledge of God, and of other scientific, *e.g.,* astronomical knowledge (such as has been falsely attributed to the Hindus), and the assertion that such a condition occurred at the very beginning of History—or that the religions of various nations were traditionally derived from it,

---

[1] We have to thank this interest for many valuable discoveries in Oriental literature, and for a renewed study of treasures previously known, in the department of ancient Asiatic Culture, Mythology, Religions, and History. In Catholic countries, where a refined literary taste prevails, Governments have yielded to the requirements of speculative inquiry, and have felt the necessity of allying themselves with learning and philosophy. Eloquently and impressively has the Abbé Lamennais reckoned it among the criteria of the true religion that it must be the universal—that is, catholic—and the oldest in date; and the Congregation has labored zealously and diligently in France towards rendering such assertions no longer mere pulpit tirades and authoritative dicta, such as were deemed sufficient formerly. The religion of Buddha—a god man— which has prevailed to such an enormous extent, has especially attracted attention. The Indian Trimûrtis, as also the Chinese abstraction of the Trinity, has furnished clearer evidence in point of subject matter. The savants, M. Abel Remusat and M. Saint Martin, on the one hand, have undertaken the most meritorious investigations in the Chinese literature, with a view to making this also a base of operations for researches in the Mongolian and, if such were possible, in the Tibetan; on the other hand, Baron von Eckstein, in his way (*i.e.,* adopting from Germany superficial physical conceptions and mannerisms, in the style of Friedrich von Schlegel, though with more geniality than the latter) in his periodical, *Le Catholique,* has furthered the cause of that primitive Catholicism generally, and in particular has gained for the savants of the Congregation the support of the Government; so that it has even set on foot expeditions to the East, in order to discover there treasures still concealed (from which further disclosures have been anticipated, respecting profound theological questions, particularly on the higher antiquity and sources of Buddhism), and with a view to promote the interest of Catholicism by this circuitous but scientifically interesting method.

and have developed themselves in degeneracy and depravity (as is represented in the rudely-conceived so-called "Emanation System") —all these are suppositions that neither have attained, nor (if we may contrast with their arbitrary subjective origin the true conception of History) can attain historical confirmation.

The only consistent and worthy method that philosophical investigation can adopt is to take up History where Rationality begins to manifest itself in the actual conduct of the World's affairs (not where it is merely an undeveloped potentiality)—where a condition of things is present in which it realizes itself in consciousness, will and action. The inorganic existence of Spirit—that of abstract Freedom,—unconscious torpidity in respect to good and evil (and consequently to laws), or, if we please to term it so, "blessed ignorance," is itself not a subject of History. *Natural,* and at the same time religious morality, is the piety of the family. In this social relation, morality consists in the members behaving towards each other not as individuals possessing an independent will, not as persons. The Family therefore, is excluded from that process of development in which History takes its rise. But when this self-involved spiritual Unity steps beyond this circle of feeling and natural love, and first attains the consciousness of personality, we have that dark, dull center of indifference in which neither Nature nor Spirit is open and transparent, and for which Nature and Spirit can become open and transparent only by means of a further process—a very lengthened culture of that Will at length become self-conscious. Consciousness alone is clearness, and is that alone for which God (or any other existence) can be revealed. In its true form—in absolute universality —nothing can be manifested except to consciousness made percipient of it. Freedom is nothing but the recognition and adoption of such universal substantial objects as Right and Law and the production of a reality that is accordant with them—the State. Nations may have passed a long life before arriving at this their destination, and during this period they may have attained considerable culture in some directions. This pre-historical period—consistently with what has been said—lies outside our plan, whether a real history followed it, or the peoples in question never attained a political constitution. It is a great discovery in history—as of a new world—that has been made within rather more than the last twenty years, respecting the Sanskrit and the connection of the European languages with it. In particular, the connection of the German and Indian peoples has been demonstrated with as much certainty as such subjects allow of. Even at the present time we know of peoples that scarcely form a society, much less a State, but that have been long known to exist, while with regard to others, which in their advanced condition excite our especial interest, tradition reaches beyond the record of the founding of the State, and they experienced many changes prior to that epoch. In the connection just referred to, between the languages of nations so widely separated, we have a result before us that proves the diffusion of those nations from Asia as a center, and the so dissimilar development of what had been originally related, as an incontestable fact—not as an inference deduced by that favorite method of combining, and reasoning from, circumstances grave and trivial, which has already enriched and will continue to enrich history with so many fictions given out as facts. But this apparently so extensive range of events lies beyond the pale of history, in fact preceded it.

In our language the term "History" unites the objective with the subjective side, and denotes quite as much the *historia rerum gestarum* as the *res gestae* themselves, both what has happened and the narration of what has happened. This union of the two meanings we must regard as more significant than mere accident; we must suppose historical narrations to have appeared contemporaneously with historical deeds and events. It is an internal vital principle common to both that produces them simultaneously. Family memorials, patriarchal traditions, have an interest confined to the family and the clan. The uniform course of events that such a condition implies is no subject of serious remembrance, though special transactions or turns of fortune may rouse Mnemosyne to form conceptions of them, in the same way as love and the religious emotions provoke imagination to give shape to a previously formless impulse. But it is the State that first presents subject-matter that is not only adapted to the prose of History but involves the production of such history in the very progress of its own being. Instead of merely subjective mandates on the part of government—sufficing for the needs of the moment—a community that is acquiring a stable existence and exalting itself into a State requires formal commands and laws, comprehensive and universally binding prescriptions, and thus produces a record as well as an interest concerned with intelligent, definite—and, in their results, lasting—transactions and occurrences, on which Mnemosyne, with its perennial purpose, the formation and constitution of the State, is impelled to confer perpetuity. Profound sentiments generally, such as that of love, as also religious intuition and its conceptions, are in themselves complete, constantly present and satisfying; but that outward existence of a political constitution which is enshrined in its rational laws and customs, is an imperfect Present, and cannot be thoroughly understood without a knowledge of the past.

The periods—whether we suppose them to be centuries or millennia—that were passed by nations before history was written among them, and that may have been filled with revolutions, nomadic wanderings, and the strangest mutations, are on that very account destitute of objective history, because they present no subjective history, no annals. We need not suppose that the records of such periods have accidentally perished; rather, we find them lacking because they were not possible. Only in a State cognizant of Laws can distinct transactions take place, accompanied by such a clear consciousness of them as supplies the ability and suggests the necessity of an enduring record. It strikes every one who forms an acquaintance with the treasures of Indian literature that a land so rich in intellectual products, and those of the profoundest order of thought, has no History, and in this respect contrasts most strongly with China—an empire possessing one so remarkable, one going back to the most ancient times. India has not only ancient books relating to religion, and splendid poetical productions, but also ancient codes, the existence of which latter kind of literature has been mentioned as a condition necessary to the origination of History—and yet History itself is not found. But in that country the impulse of organization, in beginning to develop social distinctions, was immediately petrified in the merely natural classification according to castes, so that, although the laws concern themselves with civil rights, they make even these dependent on natural distinctions, and are especially occupied with determining the relations (Wrongs rather than Rights) of those classes towards each other, *i.e.*, the privileges of the higher over the lower. Consequently, the element of morality is banished from the pomp of Indian life and from its political institutions. Where that iron bondage of distinctions derived from nature prevails, the connection of society is nothing but wild arbitrariness—transient activity—or rather the play of violent emotion without any goal of advancement or development. Therefore no intelligent reminiscence, no object for Mnemosyne presents itself; and imagination—confused though profound—expatiates in a region, which, to be capable of History, must have had an aim within the domain of Reality, and, at the same time, of substantial Freedom.

Since such are the conditions indispensable to a history, it has happened that the growth of Families to Clans, of Clans to Peoples, and their local diffusion consequent upon this numerical increase—a series of facts that itself suggests so many instances of social complication, war, revolution, and ruin, a process rich in interest and comprehensive in extent—has occurred without giving rise to History: moreover, that the extension and organic growth of the empire of articulate sounds has itself remained voiceless and dumb, a stealthy, unnoticed advance. It is a fact revealed by philological monuments that languages, during a rude condition of the nations that have spoken them, have been very highly developed, that the human understanding occupied this theoretical region with great ingenuity and completeness. For Grammar, in its extended and consistent form, is the work of thought, which makes its categories distinctly visible therein. It is, moreover, a fact, that with advancing social and political civilization, this systematic completeness of intelligence suffers attrition, and language thereupon becomes poorer and ruder—a singular phenomenon: that the progress towards a more highly intellectual condition, while expanding and cultivating rationality, should disregard that intelligent amplitude and expressiveness, should find it an obstruction and contrive to do without it. Speech is the act of theoretical intelligence in a special sense; it is its external manifestation. Exercises of memory and imagination without language are direct, [non-speculative] manifestations. But this act of theoretical intelligence itself, as also its subsequent development, and the more concrete class of facts connected with it—viz. the spreading of peoples over the earth, their separation from each other, their comminglings and wanderings—remain involved in the obscurity of a voiceless past. They are not acts of Will becoming self-conscious, of Freedom mirroring itself in a phenomenal form and creating for itself a proper reality. Not partaking of this element of substantial, veritable existence, those nations—notwithstanding the development of language among them—never advanced to the possession of a history. The rapid growth of language, and the progress and dispersion of Nations, assume importance and interest for concrete Reason, only when they have come in contact with States, or begin to form political constitutions themselves.

2. The Direction of History

After these remarks, relating to the form of the origin of the World's History, and to that ante-historical period which must be excluded from it, we have to state the direction of its course: though here only formally. The further definition of the subject in the concrete comes under the head of arrangement.

Universal history, as already demonstrated, shows the development of the consciousness of Freedom on the part of Spirit, and of the consequent realization of that Freedom. This development implies a gradation—a series of increasingly adequate expressions or manifestations of Freedom, which result from its Idea. The logical, and—as still more prominent—the dialectical nature of the Idea in general, viz. that it is self-determined, that it assumes successive forms which it successively transcends, and by this very process of transcending its earlier stages, gains an affirmative and, in fact, a richer and more concrete shape—this necessity of its nature, and the necessary series of pure abstract forms which the Idea successively assumes, is exhibited in the department of Logic. Here we need adopt only one of its results, viz. that every step in the process, as differing from any other, has its determinate peculiar principle. In history this principle is idiosyncrasy of Spirit—peculiar National Genius. It is within the limitations of this idiosyncrasy that the spirit of the nation, concretely manifested, expresses every aspect of its consciousness and will—the whole cycle of its realization. Its religion, its polity, its ethics, its legislation, and even its science, art, and mechanical skill, all bear its stamp. These special peculiarities find their key in that common peculiarity, the particular principle that characterizes a people, as, on the other hand, in the facts that History presents in detail, that common characteristic principle may be detected. That such or such a specific quality constitutes the peculiar genius of a people is the element of our inquiry that must be derived from experience and historically proved. To accomplish this presupposes not only a disciplined faculty of abstraction but an intimate acquaintance with the Idea. The investigator must be familiar *a priori* (if we like to call it so) with the whole circle of concepts to which the principles in question belong—just as Kepler (to name the most illustrious example in this mode of philosophizing) must have been familiar *a priori* with ellipses, with cubes and squares, and with ideas of their relations, before he could discover, from the empirical data, those immortal "Laws" of his, which are none other than forms of thought embodying those concepts. He who is unfamiliar with the science that embraces these abstract elementary concepts is as little capable—though he may have gazed on the firmament and the motions of the celestial bodies for a lifetime—of understanding those Laws as of discovering them. From this want of acquaintance with the ideas that relate to the development of Freedom proceed a part of those objections that are brought against the philosophical consideration of a science usually regarded as one of mere experience, the so-called *a priori* method, and the attempt to insinuate ideas into the empirical data of history, being the chief points in the indictment. Where this deficiency exists, such conceptions appear alien—not lying within the object of investigation. To minds whose training has been narrow and merely subjective, who have not an acquaintance and familiarity with ideas, they are something strange—not embraced in the notion and conception of the subject which their limited intellect forms. Hence the statement that Philosophy does not understand such sciences. It must, indeed, allow that it has not that kind of Understanding which is the prevailing one in the domain of those sciences, that it does not proceed according to the categories of such Understanding, but according to the categories of Reason—though at the same time recognizing that Understanding and its true value and position. It must be observed that in this very process of scientific Understanding, it is of importance that the essential should be distinguished and brought into relief in contrast with the so-called non-essential. But in order to render this possible, we must know what *is* essential; and that is—in view of the World-History in general—the Consciousness of Freedom, and the phases this consciousness assumes in developing itself. The bearing of historical facts on this category is their bearing on the truly Essential. Of the difficulties stated, and the opposition exhibited to comprehensive conceptions in science, part must be referred to the inability to grasp and understand Ideas. If in Natural History some monstrous hybrid growth is alleged as an objection to the recognition of clear and indubitable classes or species, a sufficient reply is furnished by a sentiment often vaguely urged, that "the exception proves the rule;" *i.e.,* that it is the part of a well-defined rule to show the conditions in which it applies, or the deficiency or hybridism of cases that are abnormal. Mere Nature is too weak to keep its genera and species pure, when conflicting with alien elementary influences. If, *e.g.,* on considering the human organization in its con-

crete aspect, we assert that brain, heart, and so forth are essential
to its organic life, some miserable abortion may be adduced, which
has on the whole the human form, or parts of it, which has been conceived in a human body and has breathed after birth therefrom, but
in which no brain and no heart is found. If such an instance is cited
against the general concept of a human being—the objector persisting
in using the name, coupled with a superficial idea respecting it—it
can be proved that a real, concrete human being is a truly different
object, that such a being must have a brain in its head, and a heart in
its breast.

A similar process of reasoning is adopted in reference to the
correct assertion that genius, talent, moral virtues, and sentiments,
and piety, may be found in every zone, under all political constitutions
and conditions—in confirmation of which examples are forthcoming
in abundance. If in this assertion, the accompanying distinctions are
intended to be repudiated as unimportant or non-essential, reflection
evidently limits itself to abstract categories, and ignores the specialties
of the object in question, which certainly fall under no principle
recognized by such categories. That intellectual position which adopts
such merely formal points of view presents a vast field for ingenious
questions, erudite views, and striking comparisons, for profound-
seeming reflections and declamations, which may be rendered so much
the more brilliant in proportion as the subject they refer to is indefinite, and are susceptible of new and varied forms in inverse proportion
to the importance of the results that can be gained from them, and the
certainty and rationality of their results. Under such an aspect the well-
known Indian epics may be compared with the Homeric, perhaps—
since it is the vastness of the imagination by which poetical genius
proves itself—preferred to them, just as, on account of the similarity
of single strokes of imagination in the attributes of the divinities, it
has been contended that Greek mythological forms may be recognized
in those of India. Similarly the Chinese philosophy, as adopting the
One [the Tao] as its basis, has been alleged to be the same that later
appeared as Eleatic philosophy [τὸ ἕν] and as the Spinozistic system;
while in virtue of its expressing itself also in abstract numbers and
lines Pythagorean and Christian principles have been supposed to be
detected in it. Instances of bravery and indomitable courage, traits of
magnanimity, of self-denial, and self-sacrifice, that are found among
the most savage and the most pusillanimous nations, are regarded as
sufficient to support the view that in these nations as much of social
virtue and morality may be found as in the most civilized Christian

states, or even more. And on this ground a doubt has been suggested whether in the progress of history and of general culture mankind have become better; whether their morality has been increased— morality being regarded in a subjective aspect and view, as founded on what the agent holds to be right and wrong, good and evil, not on a principle that is considered to be in and for itself right and good, or a crime and evil, or on a particular religion believed to be the true one.

We may fairly decline on this occasion the task of tracing the formalism and error of such a view, and establishing the true principles of morality, or rather of social virtue in opposition to false morality. For World-History occupies a higher ground than that on which morality properly has its position, which is personal character, the conscience of individuals, their particular will and mode of action; these have their own value, reward, responsibility, and punishment. What the absolute aim of Spirit requires and accomplishes—what Providence does—transcends the obligations and the liability to blame and the ascription of good or bad motives that attach to individuality in virtue of its social relations. They who on moral grounds, and consequently with noble intention, have resisted what the advance of the Spiritual Idea makes necessary, stand higher in moral worth than those whose crimes have been turned into the means—under the direction of a superior principle—of realizing the purposes of that principle. But in such revolutions both parties generally stand within the limits of the same circle of transient and corruptible existence. Consequently it is only a formal rectitude—deserted by the living Spirit and by God—which those who stand upon ancient right and order maintain. The deeds of great men, who are the Individuals of World-History, thus appear justified not only in view of that intrinsic result of which they were not conscious, but also from the point of view occupied by the secular moralist. But looked at from this point of view, moral claims that are irrelevant must not be brought into collision with world-historical deeds and their accomplishment. The Litany of private virtues—modesty, humility, philanthropy, and forbearance—must not be raised against them. World-History might, on principle, entirely ignore the circle within which morality and the so much talked of distinction between the moral and the politic lies, not only in abstaining from judgments—for the principles involved, and the necessary reference of the deeds in question to those principles, are a sufficient judgment of them—but in leaving Individuals quite out of view and unmentioned. What it has to record is the activity of the Spirit of Peoples, so that the individual forms that Spirit has assumed in the sphere of outward reality might be left to the delineation of special histories.

The same sort of formalism takes advantage of the prevailing lack of precision about the concepts of genius, poetry, and even philosophy and thinks that it finds these, too, everywhere. We have here products of reflective thought; and it is familiarity with those general concepts that single out and name real distinctions without fathoming the true depth of the matter, what is called Culture. It is something merely formal, inasmuch as it aims at nothing more than the analysis of the subject, whatever it be, into its constituent parts, and the comprehension of these in their logical definitions and forms. It is not the free universality of concept necessary for making an abstract principle the object of consciousness. Such a consciousness of Thought itself, and of its forms isolated from a particular object, is Philosophy. This has, indeed, the condition of its existence in Culture, that condition being the taking up of the object of thought, and at the same time clothing it with the form of universality in such a way that the material content and the form given by the intellect are held in an inseparable state—inseparable to such a degree that the object in question, which, by the analysis of one concept into a multitude of concepts, is enlarged to an incalculable treasure of thought, is regarded as a merely empirical datum in whose formation thought has had no share.

But it is quite as much an act of Thought—of the Understanding in particular—to embrace in one simple concept of an object, and designate by one name, a large and concrete significance (such as Earth, Man, Alexander or Caesar), as it is to resolve such a concept—correctly to distinguish the concepts it contains and to give them particular names. And in reference to the view that gave occasion to what has just been said, this much will be clear, that as reflection produces what we include under the general terms "Genius," "Talent," "Art," "Science," formal Culture on every grade of intellectual development, not only can, but must grow, and attain a mature bloom, while the grade in question is developing itself to a State, and on this basis of civilization is advancing to intelligent reflection and to general forms of thought—as in laws, so in regard to all else. In the very association of men in a state lies the necessity of formal culture—consequently of the rise of the sciences and of a cultivated poetry and art generally. The "plastic" arts require besides, even in their technical aspect, the civilized association of men. The poetic art—which has less need of external requirements and means, and which has the element of immediate existence, the voice, as its material—steps forth with great boldness and with matured expression, even under the conditions presented by a people not yet united in a political combination, since, as remarked above, language attains on its own particular ground a high intellectual development, prior to the commencement of civilization.

Philosophy also must make its appearance where political life exists, since that in virtue of which any series of phenomena is reduced within the sphere of culture, as above stated, is the Form strictly proper to Thought, and thus for philosophy, which is nothing other than the consciousness of this form itself—the Thinking of Thinking—the material of which its edifice is to be constructed is already prepared by general culture. If, in the development of the State itself, periods are necessitated that impel the soul of nobler natures to seek refuge from the present in ideal regions—in order to find in them that harmony with itself which it can no longer enjoy in the discordant real world, where the reflective intelligence attacks all that is holy and deep, all that had been spontaneously inwrought into the religion, laws and manners of nations, and brings them down and attenuates them to abstract godless generalities—Thought will be compelled to become Thinking Reason, with the view of effecting in its own element the restoration of its principles from the ruin to which they had been brought.

We find then, it is true, among all world-historical peoples, poetry, plastic art, science, even philosophy; but not only is there a diversity in style and bearing generally, but still more remarkably in subject-matter; and this is a diversity of the most important kind, affecting the rationality of that subject-matter. It is useless for a pretentious aesthetic criticism to demand that our good pleasure should not be made the rule for the matter—the substantial part of their contents—and to maintain that it is the beautiful form as such, the grandeur of the fancy, and so forth, which fine art aims at, and which must be considered and enjoyed by a liberal taste and cultivated mind. A healthy intellect does not tolerate such abstractions, and cannot assimilate productions of the kind referred to. Granted that the Indian epics might be placed on a level with the Homeric, on account of a number of those qualities of form—grandeur of invention and imaginative power, liveliness of images and emotions, and beauty of diction; yet the infinite difference of matter remains, a difference that is consequently of substantial importance and involves the interest of Reason, which is immediately concerned with the consciousness of the Idea of Freedom and its expression in individuals. There is not only a classical form, but a classical order of subject-matter; and in a work of art, form and subject-matter are so closely united that the former can only be classical to the extent to which the latter is. With a fantastical, indeterminate material—the Rule is the essence of Reason—the form becomes measureless and formless, or mean and contracted. In the same way, in that comparison of the various systems of philosophy of which we have already spoken, the only point of importance is overlooked, namely, the character of that Unity which is found alike in the Chinese, the Eleatic, and the Spinozistic philosophy—the distinction between the recognition of that Unity as abstract and as concrete, concrete to the extent of being a unity in and by itself, a unity synonymous with Spirit. But that coordination proves that it recognizes only such an abstract unity, so that while it gives judgment respecting philosophy, it is ignorant of that very point which constitutes the interest of philosophy.

But there are also spheres that, amid all the variety that is presented in the substantial content of a particular form of culture, remain the same. The difference mentioned above in Art, Science, Philosophy, concerns the thinking Reason and Freedom, which is the self-consciousness of the former, and which has the same root as Thought. As it is not the brute, but only the man, that thinks, only he—and only because he is a thinking being—has Freedom. His consciousness involves this, that the individual comprehends itself as a person, that is, recognizes itself in its single existence as possessing universality—as capable of abstraction from, and of surrending all particularity, and therefore as inherently infinite. Consequently those spheres of intelligence which lie beyond the limits of this consciousness are a common ground among those cultural variations. Even morality, which is so intimately connected with the consciousness of Freedom, can be very pure while that consciousness is still lacking, as far, that is to say, as it expresses duties and rights only as objective commands, or even as far as it remains satisfied with the merely formal improvement of the soul—the surrender of the sensual, and of all sensual motives—in a purely negative, self-denying fashion. The Chinese morality—since Europeans have become acquainted with it and with the writings of Confucius—has obtained the highest praise and proportionate attention from those who are familiar with the Christian morality. There is a similar acknowledgment of the sublimity with which the Indian religion and poetry—the highest form of it—but especially the Indian philosophy, expatiate upon and demand the removal and sacrifice of sensuality. Yet both these nations are, it must be confessed, entirely lacking in the essential consciousness of the Idea of Freedom. To the Chinese their moral laws are just like natural laws—external, positive commands, claims established by force, compulsory duties or rules of courtesy towards each other. Freedom, through which alone the essential determinations of Reason become moral sentiments, is absent. Morality is a political affair, and its laws are administered by officers of government and legal tribunals. Their treatises upon it (which are not law books, but are certainly addressed to the subjective will and individual disposition) read—as do the moral writings of the Stoics—like a string of commands stated as necessary for realizing the goal of happiness; so that it seems to be left free to men, on their part, to adopt such commands, to observe them or not; while the conception of an abstract subject, the "wise man" forms the culminating point among the Chinese, as also among the Stoic, moralists. Also in the Indian doctrine of the renunciation of sensual desires and earthly interests, positive moral freedom is not the object and end, but the annihilation of consciousness—the spiritual and even physical privation of life.

It is the concrete spirit of a people which we have distinctly to recognize, and since it is Spirit it can only be comprehended spiritually, that is, by thought. It is this alone which takes the lead in all the deeds and tendencies of that people, and which is occupied in realizing itself —in satisfying its ideal and becoming self-conscious—for its great business is self-production. But for spirit the highest attainment is self-knowledge, an advance not only to intuition, but to thought—the clear conception of itself. This it must, and is also destined to, accomplish; but the accomplishment is at the same time its dissolution, and the rise of another spirit, another world-historical people, another epoch of Universal History. This transition and connection leads us to the connection of the whole, the idea of World-History as such, which we have now to consider more closely, and of which we have to give a representation.

3. Historical Death and Rebirth

History in general is therefore the development of Spirit in Time, as Nature is the development of the Idea in Space.

If then we cast a glance over World History in general, we see a vast picture of changes and transactions of infinitely various forms

of peoples, states, individuals, in unresting succession. Everything that
can enter into and interest the soul of man—all our sensibility to goodness, beauty, and greatness—is called into play. On every hand aims
are adopted and pursued, which we recognize, whose accomplishment
we desire—we hope and fear for them. In all these occurrences and
changes we behold human action and suffering predominant, everywhere something akin to ourselves, and therefore everywhere something that excites our interest for or against. Sometimes it attracts
us by beauty, freedom, and rich variety, sometimes by energy such
as enables even vice to make itself interesting. Sometimes we see the
more comprehensive mass of some general interest advancing with
comparative slowness, and subsequently sacrificed to an infinite complication of trifling circumstances, and so pulverized into atoms. Then,
again, with a vast expenditure of power a trivial result is produced;
while from what appears unimportant a tremendous consequence
proceeds. On every hand there is the motleyest throng of events drawing us within the circle of its interest, and when one combination
vanishes another immediately appears in its place.

The general thought—the category that first presents itself in this
restless mutation of individuals and peoples, existing for a time and
then vanishing—is that of change in general. The sight of the ruins of
some ancient sovereignty directly leads us to contemplate this thought
of change in its negative aspect. What traveller among the ruins of
Carthage, of Palmyra, Persepolis, or Rome, has not been stimulated
to reflection on the transience of kingdoms and men, and to sadness
at the thought of a vigorous and rich life now departed—a sadness that
does not expend itself on personal losses and the uncertainty of one's
own undertakings, but is a disinterested sorrow at the decay of a
splendid and highly cultured national life! But the next consideration
that allies itself with that of change is that change, while it imports
dissolution, involves at the same time the rise of a new life—that
while death is the issue of life, life is also the issue of death. This
is a grand conception, one that the Oriental thinkers attained and
that is perhaps the highest in their metaphysics. In the Idea of Metempsychosis we find it evolved in its relation to individual existence, but
a myth more generally known is that of the Phoenix as a type of the
Life of Nature, eternally preparing for itself its funeral pile, and
consuming itself upon it, but so that from its ashes is produced the
new, fresh, renovated life. But this image is only Asiatic—oriental,
not occidental. Spirit—consuming the envelope of its existence—does
not merely pass into another envelope, nor rise rejuvenescent from the

ashes of its previous form; it comes forth exalted, glorified, a purer spirit. It certainly makes war upon itself, consumes its own existence; but in this very destruction it works up its existence into a new form, and each successive phase becomes in its turn a material, by working on which it exalts itself to something new.

If we consider Spirit in this aspect—regarding its changes not merely as rejuvenescent transitions, *i.e.,* returns to the same form, but rather as manipulations of itself, by which it multiplies the material for future endeavors—we see it exerting itself in a variety of modes and directions, developing its powers and gratifying its desires in a variety that is inexhaustible, because every one of the creations in which it has already found gratification meets it anew as material and is a new stimulus to plastic activity. The abstract conception of mere change gives place to the thought of Spirit manifesting, developing, and perfecting its powers in every direction its manifold nature can follow. What powers it inherently possesses we learn from the variety of products and formations it originates. In this pleasurable activity, it has to do only with itself. As involved with the conditions of mere nature—internal and external—it will indeed meet in these not only opposition and hindrance, but will often see its endeavors thereby fail, often sink under the complications in which it is entangled either by Nature or by itself. But in such a case it perishes in fulfilling its own destiny and proper function, and even thus exhibits the spectacles of proving itself to be spiritual activity.

The very essence of Spirit is activity; it realizes its potentiality—makes itself its own deed, its own work—and thus it becomes an object to itself, contemplates itself as an objective existence. Thus it is with the Spirit of a people: it is a Spirit with strictly defined characteristics, which erects itself into an objective world that exists and persists in a particular religious form of worship, customs, constitution and political laws—in the whole complex of its institutions, in the events and transactions that make up its history. That is its work —that is what this particular Nation is. Nations are what their deeds are. Every Englishman will say: We are the men who navigate the seas, and have the commerce of the world, to whom the East Indies belong and their riches, who have a parliament, juries, etc. The relation of the individual to that Spirit is that he appropriates to himself this substantial existence, that it becomes his character and capability, enabling him to have a definite place in the world—to be *something.* For he finds the being of the people to which he belongs an already established, firm world—objectively present to him—with which he has to incorporate himself. In this its work, this its world, therefore, the Spirit of the people enjoys its existence and finds its satisfaction. A Nation is moral, virtuous, vigorous while it is engaged in realizing its grand objects, and defends its work against external violence during the process of giving to its purposes an objective existence. The contradiction between its potential, subjective being—its inner aim and life—and its actual being is removed; it has attained full reality, has itself objectively present to it. But this having been attained, the activity displayed by the Spirit of the people in question is no longer needed; its desire is satisfied. The Nation can still accomplish much in war and peace at home and abroad, but the living substantial soul itself may be said to have ceased its activity. The essential, supreme interest has consequently vanished from its life, for interest is present only where there is opposition. The nation lives the same kind of life as the individual when passing from maturity to old age, in the enjoyment of itself, in the satisfaction of being exactly what it desired and was able to be. Although its imagination might have transcended that limit, it nevertheless abandoned any such aspirations as objects of actual endeavor, if the real world was less than favorable to their attainment, and restricted its aim by the conditions thus imposed. This mere customary life (the watch wound up and going on of itself) is what brings on natural death. Custom is activity without opposition, for which there remains only a formal duration, in which the fulness and zest that originally characterized the aim of life is out of the question—a merely external sensuous existence that has ceased to throw itself enthusiastically into its aim. Thus perish individuals, thus perish peoples by a natural death; and though the latter may continue in being, it is an existence without intellect or vitality, having no need of its institutions, because the need for them is satisfied—a political nullity and tedium. In order that a truly universal interest may arise, the Spirit of a People must advance to the adoption of some new purpose: but whence can this new purpose originate? It would be a higher, more comprehensive concept of itself—a transcending of its principle—but this very act would involve a principle of a new order, a new National Spirit.

Such a new principle does in fact enter into the Spirit of a people that has arrived at full development and self-realization; it does not die a simple natural death, for it is not a mere single individual, but a spiritual, generic life; in its case natural death appears to imply destruction through its own agency. The reason for this difference from the single natural individual is that the Spirit of a people exists as a genus, and consequently carries within it its own negation, in the very generality that characterizes it. A people can only die a violent death when it has become naturally dead in itself, as *e.g.,* the German Imperial Cities, the German Imperial Constitution.

It is not in the nature of the all-pervading Spirit to die this merely natural death; it does not simply sink into the senile life of mere custom, but—as being a National Spirit belonging to universal History —attains to the consciousness of what its work is; it attains to a conception of itself. In fact it is world-historical only in so far as a universal principle has lain in its fundamental element, in its grand aim: only so far does the work that such a spirit produces become a moral, political organization. If it be mere desires that impel nations to activity, such deeds pass over without leaving a trace, or their traces are only ruin and destruction. Thus it was first Chronos—Time —that ruled; the Golden Age, without moral products; and what was produced—the offspring of that Chronos—was devoured by it. It was Jupiter—from whose head Minerva sprang, and to whose circle of divinities belong Apollo and the Muses—that first put a constraint upon Time, and set a bound to its principle of decadence. He is the Political god, who produced a moral work—the State.

In the very element of an achievement the quality of generality, of thought, is contained; without thought it has no objectivity; that is its basis. The highest point in the development of a people is this: to have gained a conception of its life and condition, to have reduced its laws, its ideas of justice and morality to a science; for in this unity [of the objective and subjective] lies the most intimate unity that Spirit can attain to in and with itself. In its work it is employed in rendering itself an object of its own contemplation; but it cannot develop itself objectively in its essential nature except by thinking itself.

At this point, then, Spirit is acquainted with its principles—the general character of its acts. But at the same time, in virtue of its very generality, this work of thought is different in form from the actual achievements of the national genius, and from the vital agency by which those achievements have been performed. We have then before us a real and an ideal existence of the Spirit of the Nation. If we wish to gain the general idea and concept of what the Greeks were, we find it in Sophocles and Aristophanes, in Thucydides and Plato. In these individuals the Greek spirit conceived and thought itself. This is the profounder kind of satisfaction the Spirit of a people attains; but it is "ideal," and distinct from its "real" activity.

At such a time, therefore, we are sure to see a people finding satisfaction in the idea of virtue, putting *talk* about virtue partly side by side with actual virtue, but partly in the place of it. On the other hand pure, universal thought, since its nature is universality, is apt to bring the particular and spontaneous—Belief, Trust, Customary Morality—to reflect upon itself and its primitive simplicity; to show up the limitation with which it is fettered—partly suggesting reasons for renouncing duties, partly itself demanding reasons and the connection of such requirements with Universal Thought, and, not finding that connection, seeking to impeach the authority of duty generally, as destitute of a sound foundation.

At the same time, the isolation of individuals from each other and from the Whole makes its appearance—their aggressive selfishness and vanity, their seeking personal advantage and consulting this at the expense of the State at large. That inward principle in transcending its outward manifestations is subjective also in form—viz., selfishness and corruption in the unbound passions and egoistic interests of men.

Zeus, therefore, who is represented as having put a limit to the devouring agency of Time, and stayed this transiency by having established something inherently and independently durable—Zeus and his race are themselves swallowed up, and that by the very power that produced them—the principle of thought, perception, reasoning, insight derived from rational grounds, and the requirement of such grounds.

Time is the negative element in the sensuous world. Thought is the same negativity, but it is the deepest, the infinite form of it, in which therefore all existence generally is dissolved; first finite existence, determinate, limited form. But existence generally, in its objective character, is limited; it appears therefore as a mere datum, something immediate, authority; and it is either intrinsically finite and limited, or presents itself as a limit for the thinking subject, and its infinite reflection on itself [unlimited abstraction].

But first we must observe how the life that proceeds from death is itself, on the other hand, only individual life; so that, regarding the species as the real and substantial in this vicissitude, the perishing of the individual is a regress of the species into individuality. The perpetuation of the race is, therefore, none other than the monotonous repetition of the same kind of existence. Further, we must remark how perception—the comprehension of being by thought—is the source and birthplace of a new, and in fact higher, form, in a principle that, while it preserves, dignifies its material. For Thought is that Universal, that Species which is immortal, which preserves identity with itself. The particular form of Spirit does not merely pass away in the world by natural causes in Time, but is annulled in the automatic self-mirroring activity of consciousness. Because this annulling is an activity of Thought, it is at the same time conservative and elevating in its operation. While then, on the one hand, Spirit annuls the reality, the permanence, of that which it *is,* it gains on the other side, the essence, the Thought, the Universal element, of that which it only was [its transient conditions]. Its principle is no longer that immediate import and aim which it was previously, but the essence of that import and aim.

The result of this process is then that Spirit, in rendering itself objective and making its own being an object of thought, on the one hand destroys the determinate form of its being, on the other hand gains a comprehension of the universal element that it involves, and thereby gives a new form to its inherent principle. In virtue of this, the substantial character of the National Spirit has been altered—that is, its principle has risen into another, and in fact a higher principle.

It is of the highest importance in apprehending and comprehending History to have and to understand the thought involved in this transition. The individual traverses as a unity various grades of development, and remains the same individual; in a similar manner does a people, till the Spirit it embodies reaches the grade of universality. In this point lies the fundamental, the Ideal necessity of change. This is the soul—the essential consideration—of the philosophical comprehension of History.

Spirit is essentially the result of its own activity; its activity is the transcending of immediate, simple, unreflected existence, the negation of that existence, and the returning into itself. We may compare it with the seed; for with this the plant begins, yet it is also the result of the plant's entire life. But the weak side of life is exhibited in the fact that the beginning and the end are disjoined from each other. Thus also is it in the life of individuals and peoples. The life of a people ripens a certain fruit; its activity aims at the complete manifestation of the principle which it embodies. But this fruit does not fall back into the bosom of the people that produced and matured it; on the contrary, it becomes a poison-draught to it. That poison-draught it cannot let alone, for it has an insatiable thirst for it: the taste of the draught is its annihilation, though at the same time the rise of a new principle.

We have already discussed the final aim of progression. The principles of the successive phases of Spirit that animate the Nations in a necessary gradation are themselves only steps in the development of the one universal Spirit, which through them elevates and completes itself to a self-comprehending totality.

While we are thus concerned exclusively with the Idea of Spirit, and in the History of the World regard everything as only its manifestation, we have, in traversing the past—however extensive its periods—only to do with what is present; for philosophy, as occupying itself with the True, has to do with the eternally present. Nothing in the past is lost for it, for the Idea is ever present; Spirit is immortal; with it there is no past, no future, but an essential *now*. This necessarily implies that the present form of Spirit comprehends within it all earlier steps. These have indeed unfolded themselves in succession independently; but what Spirit is, it has always been essentially; distinctions are only the development of this essential nature. The life of the ever-present Spirit is a circle of progressive embodiments, which looked at in one respect still exist beside each other, and only as looked at from another point of view appear as past. The grades that Spirit seems to have left behind it, it still possesses in the depths of its present.

Logic (Part I of the Encyclopedia of the Philosophical Sciences) *

[Hegel's *Encyclopedia of the Philosophical Sciences in Outline* was designed as a systematic sketch of his whole philosophical system, a manual for his students. At the end of Chapter I, he explains that Philosophy is the science, or study, of the "Idea," that is, of thought in all its fullness and ramifications. Part I, Logic, is "the science of the Idea in and for itself"; Part II, the Philosophy of Nature, is "the science of the Idea in its otherness"; Part III, the Philosophy of Spirit (or Mind), is "the science of the Idea come back to itself out of that otherness." In Chapter II he explains his conception of Logic and of its method more fully; the following passage from §24 will be helpful in approaching the longer passage from Chapter VII that follows.]

It will now be understood that Logic is the all-animating spirit of all the sciences, and its categories the spiritual hierarchy. They are the heart and center of things; and yet at the same time they are always on our lips, and, apparently at least, perfectly familiar objects. But things thus familiar are usually the greatest strangers. Being, for example, is a category of pure thought; but to make "Is" an object of investigation never occurs to us. Common fancy puts the Absolute far away in a world beyond. The Absolute is rather directly before us, so present that so long as we think, we must, though without express consciousness of it, always carry it with us and always use it. Language is the main depository of these types of thought; and one use of the grammatical instruction which children receive is unconsciously to turn their attention to distinctions of thought.

Logic is usually said to be concerned with forms *only* and to derive the material for them from elsewhere. But this "only," which assumes that the logical thoughts are nothing in comparison with the rest of the contents, is not the word to use about forms which are the absolutely real ground of everything. Everything else rather is an "only" compared with these thoughts. To make such abstract forms a problem presupposes in the enquirer a higher level of culture than ordinary;

---

* Translated by William Wallace, *The Logic of Hegel*, London, 2d ed., 1892. By permission of the Clarendon Press, Oxford. The *Encyclopedia* appeared first in 1816; the second edition, 1827, was much enlarged; the third edition, 1830, was again enlarged.

and to study them in themselves and for their own sake signifies in addition that these thought-types must be deduced out of thought itself, and their truth or reality examined by the light of their own laws. We do not assume them as data from without, and then define them or exhibit their value and authority by comparing them with the shape they take in our minds. If we thus acted, we should proceed from observation and experience, and should, for instance, say we habitually employ the term "force" in such a case, and such a meaning. A definition like that would be called correct, if it agreed with the conception of its object present in our ordinary state of mind. The defect of this empirical method is that a notion is not defined as it is in and for itself, but in terms of something assumed, which is then used as a criterion and standard of correctness. No such test need be applied: we have merely to let the thought-forms follow the impulse of their own organic life.

To ask if a category is true or not, must sound strange to the ordinary mind: for a category apparently becomes true only when it is applied to a given object, and apart from this application it would seem meaningless to enquire into its truth. But this is the very question on which everything turns. We must however in the first place understand clearly what we mean by Truth. In common life truth means the agreement of an object with our conception of it. We thus presuppose an object to which our conception must conform. In the philosophical sense of the word, on the other hand, truth may be described, in general abstract terms, as the agreement of a thought-content with itself. This meaning is quite different from the one given above. At the same time the deeper and philosophical meaning of truth can be partially traced even in the ordinary usage of language. Thus we speak of a true friend; by which we mean a friend whose manner of conduct accords with the notion of friendship. In the same way we speak of a true work of Art. Untrue in this sense means the same as bad, or self-discordant. In this sense a bad state is an untrue state; and evil and untruth may be said to consist in the contradiction subsisting between the function or notion and the existence of the object. Of such a bad object we may form a correct representation, but the import of such representation is inherently false. Of these correctnesses, which are at the same time untruths, we may have many in our heads. God alone is the thorough harmony of notion and reality. All finite things involve an untruth: they have a notion and an existence, but their existence does not meet the requirements of the notion. For this reason they must perish, and then the incompatibility between their notion and their existence becomes manifest. It is in the kind that the individual animal has its notion: and the kind liberates itself from this individuality by death.

The study of truth, or, as it is here explained to mean, consistency, constitutes the proper problem of logic. In our everyday mind we are never troubled with questions about the truth of the forms of thought. We may also express the problem of logic by saying that it examines the forms of thought touching their capability to hold truth. And the question comes to this: What are the forms of the infinite, and what are the forms of the finite? Usually no suspicion attaches to the finite forms of thought; they are allowed to pass unquestioned. But it is from conforming to finite categories in thought and action that all deception originates.

[At the end of Chapter VI, Hegel divides Logic into three parts: Part I is the Doctrine of Being: the theory of Thought "in its immediacy; the Notion implicit and in germ." Part II is the Doctrine of Essence: the theory of Thought "in its reflection and mediation; the being-for-itself and show of the Notion." Part III is the Doctrine of Notion and Idea: the theory of Thought "in its return into itself, and its developed abiding by itself; the Notion in and for itself." The Doctrine of Being itself has three divisions, dealing with (A) Quality, (B) Quantity, and (C) Measure. (A) is given here in full, because it is a good example of Hegel's dialectical method of argument, and it contains his explications of some of the categories that are most fundamental in his system.]

Chapter VII
First Subdivision of Logic: The Doctrine of Being

84. Being is the notion implicit only: its special forms have the predicate "is"; when they are distinguished they are each of them an "other": and the shape which dialectic takes in them, *i.e.* their further specialization, is a passing over into another. This further determination, or specialization, is at once a forth-putting and in that way a disengaging of the notion implicit in being; and at the same time the withdrawing of being inwards, its sinking deeper into itself. Thus the explication of the notion in the sphere of being does two things: it brings out the totality of being, and it abolishes the immediacy of being, or the form of being as such.

85. Being itself and the special sub-categories of it which follow, as well as those of logic in general, may be looked upon as definitions of the Absolute, or metaphysical definitions of God: at least the first and third category in every triad may—the first, where the thought-form of the triad is formulated in its simplicity, and the third, being the return from differentiation to a simple self-reference. For a metaphysical definition of God is the expression of His nature in thoughts as such: and logic embraces all thoughts so long as they continue in the thought-form. The second sub-category in each triad, where the grade of thought is in its differentiation, gives, on the other hand, a definition of the finite. The objection to the form of definition is that it implies a something in the mind's eye on which these predicates may fasten. Thus even the Absolute (though it purports to express God in the style and character of thought) in comparison with its predicate (which really and distinctly expresses in thought what the subject does not) is as yet only an inchoate pretended thought—the indeterminate subject of predicates yet to come. The thought, which is here the matter of sole importance, is contained only in the predicate: and hence the propositional form, like the said subject, viz. the Absolute, is a mere superfluity (cf. § 31, and below, on the Judgment).

Each of the three spheres of the logical idea proves to be a systematic whole of thought-terms, and a phase of the Absolute. This is the case with Being, containing the three grades of quality, quantity, and measure. Quality is, in the first place, the character identical with being: so identical, that a thing ceases to be what it is, if it loses its quality. Quantity, on the contrary, is the character external to being, and does not affect the being at all. Thus, e.g., a house remains what it is, whether it be greater or smaller; and red remains red, whether it be brighter or darker. Measure, the third grade of being, which is the unity of the first two, is a qualitative quantity. All things have their measure: i.e., the quantitative terms of their existence, their being so or so great, does not matter within certain limits; but when these limits are exceeded by an additional more or less, the things cease to be what they were. From measure follows the advance to the second sub-division of the idea, Essence.

The three forms of being here mentioned, just because they are the first, are also the poorest, i.e. the most abstract. Immediate (sensible) consciousness, in so far as it simultaneously includes an intellectual element, is especially restricted to the abstract categories of quality and quantity. The sensuous consciousness is in ordinary estimation the most concrete and thus also the richest; but that is only true as regards materials, whereas, in reference to the thought it contains, it is really the poorest and most abstract.

A. Quality.

(a) Being

86. Pure **Being** makes the beginning: because it is on one hand pure thought, and on the other immediacy itself, simple and indeterminate; and the first beginning cannot be mediated by anything, or be further determined.

All doubts and admonitions which might be brought against beginning the science with abstract empty being will disappear, if we only perceive what a beginning naturally implies. It is possible to define being as "I = I," as "Absolute Indifference" or Identity, and so on. Where it is felt necessary to begin either with what is absolutely certain, *i.e.* the certainty of oneself, or with a definition or intuition of the absolute truth, these and other forms of the kind may be looked on as if they must be the first. But each of these forms contains a mediation, and hence cannot be the real first: for all mediation implies advance made from a first on to a second, and proceeding from something different. If I = I, or even the intellectual intuition, are really taken to mean no more than the first, they are in this mere immediacy identical with being: while conversely, pure being, if abstract no longer, but including in it mediation, is pure thought or intuition.

If we enunciate Being as a predicate of the Absolute, we get the first definition of the latter. The Absolute is Being. This is (in thought) the absolutely initial definition, the most abstract and stinted. It is the definition given by the Eleatics, but at the same time is also the well-known definition of God as the sum of all realities. It means, in short, that we are to set aside that limitation which is in every reality, so that God shall be only the real in all reality, the superlatively real. Or, if we reject reality, as implying a reflection, we get a more immediate or unreflected statement of the same thing, when Jacobi says that the God of Spinoza is the *principium* of being in all existence.

(1) When thinking is to begin, we have nothing but thought in its merest indeterminateness: for we cannot determine unless there is both one and another, and in the beginning there is yet no other. The indeterminate, as we here have it, is the blank we begin with, not a featurelessness reached by abstraction, not the elimination of all character, but the original featurelessness which precedes all definite character and is the very first of all. And this we call Being. It is not to be felt, or perceived by sense, or pictured in imagination: it is only and merely thought, and as such it forms the beginning. Essence also is indeterminate, but in

another sense: it has traversed the process of mediation and contains implicit the determination it has absorbed.

(2) In the history of philosophy the different stages of the logical Idea assume the shape of successive systems, each based on a particular definition of the Absolute. As the logical Idea is seen to unfold itself in a process from the abstract to the concrete, so in the history of philosophy the earliest systems are the most abstract, and thus at the same time the poorest. The relation too of the earlier to the later systems of philosophy is much like the relation of the corresponding stages of the logical Idea: in other words, the earlier are preserved in the later, but subordinated and submerged. This is the true meaning of a much misunderstood phenomenon in the history of philosophy—the refutation of one system by another, of an earlier by a later. Most commonly the refutation is taken in a purely negative sense to mean that the system refuted has ceased to count for anything, has been set aside and done for. Were it so, the history of philosophy would be of all studies most saddening, displaying, as it does, the refutation of every system which time has brought forth. Now, although it may be admitted that every philosophy has been refuted, it must be in an equal degree maintained that no philosophy has been refuted, nay, or can be refuted. And that in two ways. For first, every philosophy that deserves the name always embodies the Idea: and secondly, every system represents one particular factor or particular stage in the evolution of the Idea. The refutation of a philosophy, therefore, only means that its barriers are crossed, and its special principle reduced to a factor in the completer principle that follows. Thus the history of philosophy, in its true meaning, deals not with a past, but with an eternal and veritable present: and, in its results, resembles not a museum of the aberrations of the human intellect, but a Pantheon of Godlike figures. These figures of Gods are the various stages of the Idea, as they come forward one after another in dialectical development. To the historian of philosophy it belongs to point out more precisely how far the gradual evolution of his theme coincides with, or swerves from, the dialectical unfolding of the pure logical Idea. It is sufficient to mention here that logic begins where the proper history of philosophy begins. Philosophy began in the Eleatic school, especially with Parmenides. Parmenides, who conceives the absolute as Being, says that "Being alone is and Nothing is not." Such was the true starting point of philosophy, which is always knowledge by thought: and here for the first time we find pure thought seized and made an object to itself.

Men indeed thought from the beginning (for thus only were they distinguished from the animals). But thousands of years had to elapse before they came to apprehend thought in its purity, and to see in it the truly objective. The Eleatics are celebrated as daring thinkers. But this nominal admiration is often accompanied by the remark that they went too far when they made Being alone true, and denied the truth of every other object of consciousness. We must go further than mere Being, it is true: and yet it is absurd to speak of the other contents of our consciousness as somewhat, as it were, outside and beside Being, or to say that there are other things, as well as Being. The true state of the case is rather as follows. Being, as Being, is nothing fixed or ultimate: it yields to dialectic and sinks into its opposite, which, also taken immediately, is Nothing. After all, the point is that Being is the first pure Thought: whatever else you may begin with (the I = I, the absolute indifference, or God Himself), you begin with a figure of materialized conception, not a product of thought; and that, so far as its thought-content is concerned, such beginning is merely Being.

87. But this mere Being, as it is mere abstraction, is therefore the absolutely negative: which, in a similarly immediate aspect, is just **Nothing.**

(1) Hence was derived the second definition of the Absolute; the Absolute is the Nought. In fact this definition is implied in saying that the thing-in-itself is the indeterminate, utterly without form and so without content—or in saying that God is only the supreme Being and nothing more; for this is really declaring Him to be the same negativity as above. The Nothing which the Buddhists make the universal principle, as well as the final aim and goal of everything, is the same abstraction.

(2) If the opposition in thought is stated in this immediacy as Being and Nothing, the shock of its nullity is too great not to stimulate the attempt to fix Being and secure it against the transition into Nothing. With this intent, reflection has recourse to the plan of discovering some fixed predicate for Being, to mark it off from Nothing. Thus we find Being identified with what persists amid all change, with matter, susceptible of innumerable determinations—or even, unreflectingly, with a single existence, any chance object of the senses or of the mind. But every additional and more concrete characterization causes Being to lose that integrity and simplicity it has in the beginning. Only in, and by virtue of, this mere generality is it Nothing, something inexpressible, whereof the distinction from Nothing is a mere intention or meaning.

All that is wanted is to realize that these beginnings are nothing but these empty abstractions, one as empty as the other. The instinct that induces us to attach a settled import to Being, or to both, is the very necessity which leads to the onward movement of Being and Nothing, and gives them a true or concrete significance. This advance is the logical deduction and the movement of thought exhibited in the.

sequel. The reflection which finds a profounder connotation for Being and Nothing is nothing but logical thought, through which such connotation is evolved, not, however, in an accidental, but a necessary way. Every signification, therefore, in which they afterwards appear, is only a more precise specification and truer definition of the Absolute. And when that is done, the mere abstract Being and Nothing are replaced by a concrete in which both these elements form an organic part. The supreme form of Nought as a separate principle would be Freedom: but Freedom is negativity in that stage, when it sinks self-absorbed to supreme intensity, and is itself an affirmation, and even absolute affirmation.

The distinction between Being and Nought is, in the first place, only implicit, and not yet actually made: they only ought to be distinguished. A distinction of course implies two things, and that one of them possesses an attribute which is not found in the other. Being however is an absolute absence of attributes, and so is Nought. Hence the distinction between the two is only meant to be; it is a quite nominal distinction, which is at the same time no distinction. In all other cases of difference there is some common point which comprehends both things. Suppose, *e.g.*, we speak of two different species: the genus forms a common ground for both. But in the case of mere Being and Nothing, distinction is without a bottom to stand upon: hence there can be no distinction, both determinations being the same bottomlessness. If it be replied that Being and Nothing are both of them thoughts, so that thought may be reckoned common ground, the objector forgets that Being is not a particular or definite thought, and hence, being quite indeterminate, is a thought not to be distinguished from Nothing. It is natural too for us to represent Being as absolute riches, and Nothing as absolute poverty. But if when we view the whole world we can only say that everything *is*, and nothing more, we are neglecting all speciality and, instead of absolute plenitude, we have absolute emptiness. The same stricture is applicable to those who define God to be mere Being; a definition not a whit better than that of the Buddhists, who make God to be Nought, and who from that principle draw the further conclusion that self-annihilation is the means by which man becomes God.

88. Nothing, if it be thus immediate and equal to itself, is also conversely the same as Being is. The truth of Being and of Nothing is accordingly the unity of the two: and this unity is **Becoming.**

(1) The proposition that Being and Nothing are the same seems so paradoxical to the imagination or understanding, that it is perhaps taken for a joke. And indeed it is one of the hardest things thought expects itself to do: for Being and Nothing exhibit the fundamental

contrast in all its immediacy—that is, without the one term being invested with any attribute which would involve its connection with the other. This attribute however, as the above paragraph points out, is implicit in them—the attribute which is just the same in both. So far the deduction of their unity is completely analytical: indeed the whole progress of philosophizing in every case, if it be a methodical, that is to say a necessary, progress, merely renders explicit what is implicit in a notion. It is as correct however to say that Being and Nothing are altogether different, as to assert their unity. The one is not what the other is. But since the distinction has not at this point assumed definite shape (Being and Nothing are still the immediate), it is, in the way that they have it, something unutterable, which we merely mean.

(2) No great expenditure of wit is needed to make fun of the maxim that Being and Nothing are the same, or rather to adduce absurdities which, it is erroneously asserted, are the consequences and illustrations of that maxim.

If Being and Nought are identical, say these objectors, it follows that it makes no difference whether my home, my property, the air I breathe, this city, the sun, the law, mind, God, are or are not. Now in some of these cases, the objectors foist in private aims, the utility a thing has for me, and then ask, whether it be all the same to me if the thing exist and if it do not. For that matter indeed, the teaching of philosophy is precisely what frees man from the endless crowd of finite aims and intentions, by making him so insensible to them that their existence or non-existence is to him a matter of indifference. But it is never to be forgotten that, once mention something substantial, and you thereby create a connection with other existences and other purposes which are *ex hypothesi* worth having: and on such hypothesis it comes to depend whether the Being and not-Being of a determinate subject are the same or not. A substantial distinction is in these cases secretly substituted for the empty distinction of Being and Nought. In others of the cases referred to, it is virtually absolute existences and vital ideas and aims, which are placed under the mere category of Being or not-Being. But there is more to be said of these concrete objects than that they merely are or are not. Barren abstractions, like Being and Nothing—the initial categories which, for that reason, are the scantiest anywhere to be found—are utterly inadequate to the nature of these objects. Substantial truth is something far above these abstractions and their oppositions. And always when a concrete existence is disguised under the name of Being and not-Being, empty-headedness makes its usual mistake of speaking about, and having in the mind an image of, something else than what is in question: and in this place the question is about abstract Being and Nothing.

(3) It may perhaps be said that nobody can form a notion of the unity of Being and Nought. As for that, the notion of the unity is stated in the sections preceding, and that is all: apprehend that, and you have comprehended this unity. What the objector really means by comprehension—by a notion—is more than his language properly implies: he wants a richer and more complex state of mind, a pictorial conception which will propound the notion as a concrete case and one more familiar to the ordinary operations of thought. And so long as incomprehensibility means only the want of habituation for the effort needed to grasp an abstract thought, free from all sensuous admixture, and to seize a speculative truth, the reply to the criticism is that philosophical knowledge is undoubtedly distinct in kind from the mode of knowledge best known in common life, as well as from that which reigns in the other sciences. But if to have no notion merely means that we cannot represent in imagination the oneness of Being and Nought, the statement is far from being true; for every one has count-less ways of envisaging this unity. To say that we have no such con-ception can only mean that in none of these images do we recognize the notion in question, and that we are not aware that they exemplify it. The readiest example of it is Becoming. Every one has a mental idea of Becoming, and will even allow that it is *one* idea: he will further allow that, when it is analyzed, it involves the attribute of Being, and also what is the very reverse of Being, viz. Nothing: and that these two attributes lie undivided in the one idea: so that Be-coming is the unity of Being and Nothing. Another tolerably plain example is a Beginning. In its beginning, the thing is not yet, but it is more than merely nothing, for its Being is already in the beginning. Beginning is itself a case of Becoming; only the former term is em-ployed with an eye to the further advance. If we were to adapt logic to the more usual method of the sciences, we might start with the representation of a Beginning as abstractly thought, or with Begin-ning as such, and then analyze this representation; and perhaps people would more readily admit, as a result of this analysis, that Being and Nothing present themselves as undivided in unity.

(4) It remains to note that such phrases as "Being and Nothing are the same," or "The unity of Being and Nothing"—like all other such unities, that of subject and object, and others—give rise to

reasonable objection. They misrepresent the facts, by giving an exclusive prominence to the unity, and leaving the difference which undoubtedly exists in it (because it is Being and Nothing, for example, the unity of which is declared) without any express mention or notice. It accordingly seems as if the diversity had been unduly put out of court and neglected. The fact is, no speculative principle can be correctly expressed by any such propositional form, for the unity has to be conceived *in* the diversity, which is all the while present and explicit. "To become" is the true expression for the resultant of "To be" and "Not to be"; it is the unity of the two; but not only is it the unity, it is also inherent unrest—the unity, which is no mere reference-to-self and therefore without movement, but which, through the diversity of Being and Nothing that is in it, is at war within itself. Determinate being, on the other hand, is this unity, or Becoming in this form of unity: hence all that "is there and so" is one-sided and finite. The opposition between the two factors seems to have vanished; it is only implied in the unity, it is not explicitly put in it.

(5) The maxim of Becoming, that Being is the passage into Nought, and Nought the passage into Being, is controverted by the maxim of Pantheism, the doctrine of the eternity of matter, that from nothing comes nothing, and that something can only come out of something. The ancients saw plainly that the maxim, "From nothing comes nothing, from something something," really abolishes Becoming: for what it comes from and what it becomes are one and the same. Thus explained, the proposition is the maxim of abstract identity as upheld by the understanding. It cannot but seem strange, therefore, to hear such maxims as, "Out of nothing comes nothing; out of something comes something," calmly taught in these days, without the teacher being in the least aware that they are the basis of Pantheism, and even without his knowing that the ancients have exhausted all that is to be said about them.

Becoming is the first concrete thought, and therefore the first notion: whereas Being and Nought are empty abstractions. The notion of Being, therefore, of which we sometimes speak, must mean Becoming; not the mere point of Being, which is empty Nothing, any more than Nothing, which is empty Being. In Being then we have Nothing, and in Nothing Being: but this Being which does not lose itself in Nothing is Becoming. Nor must we omit the distinction, while we emphasize the unity of Becoming: without that distinction we should once more return to abstract

Being. Becoming is only the explicit statement of what Being is in its truth.

We often hear it maintained that thought is opposed to being. Now in the face of such a statement, our first question ought to be, what is meant by "being." If we understand being as it is defined by reflection, all that we can say of it is that it is what is wholly identical and affirmative. And if we then look at thought, it cannot escape us that thought also is at least what is absolutely identical with itself. Both therefore, being as well as thought, have the same attribute. This identity of being and thought is not however to be taken in a concrete sense, as if we could say that a stone, so far as it has being, is the same as a thinking man. A concrete thing is always very different from the abstract category as such. And in the case of being, we are speaking of nothing concrete: for being is the utterly abstract. So far then the question regarding the being of God—a being which is in itself concrete above all measure—is of slight importance.

As the first concrete thought-term, Becoming is the first adequate vehicle of truth. In the history of philosophy, this stage of the logical Idea finds its analogue in the system of Heraclitus. When Heraclitus says "All is flowing" (πάντα ῥεῖ), he enunciates Becoming as the fundamental feature of all existence, whereas the Eleatics, as already remarked, saw the only truth in Being, rigid processless Being. Glancing at the principle of the Eleatics, Heraclitus then goes on to say: "Being is no more than not-Being" (οὐδὲν μᾶλλον τὸ ὂν τοῦ μὴ ὄντος ἐστί); a statement expressing the negativity of abstract Being, and its identity with not-Being, as made explicit in Becoming; both abstractions being alike untenable. This may be looked at as an instance of the real refutation of one system by another. To refute a philosophy is to exhibit the dialectical movement in its principle, and thus reduce it to a constituent member of a higher concrete form of the Idea. Even Becoming however, taken at its best on its own ground, is an extremely poor term: it needs to grow in depth and weight of meaning. Such deepened force we find, e.g., in Life. Life is a Becoming; but that is not enough to exhaust the notion of Life. A still higher form is found in Mind. Here too is Becoming, but richer and more intensive than mere logical Becoming. The elements whose unity constitutes mind are not the bare abstracts of Being and of Nought, but the system of the logical Idea and of Nature.

(b) Being Determinate

89. In Becoming the Being which is one with Nothing, and the Nothing which is one with Being, are only vanishing factors; they are and they are not. Thus by its inherent contradiction Becoming collapses into the unity in which the two elements are absorbed. This result is accordingly **Being Determinate** (Being there and so).

In this first example we must call to mind, once for all, what was stated in § 82 and in the note there: the only way to secure any growth and progress in knowledge is to hold results fast in their truth. There is absolutely nothing whatever in which we cannot and must not point to contradictions or opposite attributes; and the abstraction made by understanding therefore means a forcible insistance on a single aspect, and a real effort to obscure and remove all consciousness of the other attribute which is involved. Whenever such contradiction, then, is discovered in any object or notion, the usual inference is, Hence this object is nothing. Thus Zeno, who first showed the contradiction native to motion, concluded that there is no motion: and the ancients, who recognized origin and decease, the two species of Becoming, as untrue categories, made use of the expression that the One or Absolute neither arises nor perishes. Such a style of dialectic looks only at the negative aspect of its result, and fails to notice, what is at the same time really present, the definite result, in the present case a pure nothing, but a Nothing which includes Being, and, in like manner, a Being which includes Nothing. Hence Being Determinate is (1) the unity of Being and Nothing, in which we get rid of the immediacy in these determinations, and their contradiction vanishes in their mutual connection— the unity in which they are only constituent elements. And (2) since the result is the abolition of the contradiction, it comes in the shape of a simple unity with itself: that is to say, it also is Being, but Being with negation or determinateness: it is Becoming expressly put in the form of one of its elements, viz. Being.

Even our ordinary conception of Becoming implies that somewhat comes out of it, and that Becoming therefore has a result. But this conception gives rise to the question, how Becoming does not remain mere Becoming, but has a result. The answer to this question follows from what Becoming has already shown itself to be. Becoming always contains Being and Nothing in such a way that these two are always changing into each other, and reciprocally canceling each other. Thus Becoming stands before us in utter restlessness—unable however to maintain itself in this abstract restlessness: for since Being and Nothing vanish in Becoming (and that is the very notion of Becoming), the latter must vanish also. Becoming is as it were a fire which dies out in itself when it consumes its material. The result of this process however is not an empty Nothing, but Being identical with the negation—what we call Being Determinate (being then and there): the primary import of which evidently is that it has become.

90. (α) Determinate Being is Being with a character or mode—which simply *is*; and such unmediated character is **Quality.** And as reflected into itself in this its character or mode, Determinate Being is a somewhat, an existent. The categories which issue by a closer analysis of Determinate Being need only be mentioned briefly.

Quality may be described as the determinate mode immediate and identical with Being—as distinguished from Quantity (to come afterwards), which, although a mode of Being, is no longer immediately identical with Being, but a mode indifferent and external to it. A Something is what it is in virtue of its quality, and losing its quality it ceases to be what it is. Quality, moreover, is completely a category only of the finite, and for that reason too it has its proper place in Nature, not in the world of Mind. Thus, for example, in Nature what are styled the elementary bodies, oxygen, nitrogen, etc., should be regarded as existing qualities. But in the sphere of mind, Quality appears in a subordinate way only, and not as if its qualitativeness could exhaust any specific aspect of mind. If, for example, we consider the subjective mind, which forms the object of psychology, we may describe what is called (moral and mental) character, as in logical language identical with Quality. This however does not mean that character is a mode of being which pervades the soul and is immediately identical with it, as is the case in the natural world with the elementary bodies before mentioned. Yet a more distinct manifestation of Quality as such, in mind even, is found in the case of besotted or morbid conditions, especially in states of passion and when the passion rises to derangement. The state of mind of a deranged person, being one mass of jealousy, fear, etc., may suitably be described as Quality.

91. Quality, as determinateness which *is,* contrasted with the **Negation** which is involved in it but distinguished from it, is **Reality.** Negation is no longer an abstract nothing, but, as a determinate being and somewhat, is only a form on such being—it is as Otherness. Since this otherness, though a determination of Quality itself, is in the first instance distinct from it, Quality is **Being-for-another**—an expansion of the mere point of Determinate Being, or of Somewhat. The Being as such of Quality, contrasted with this reference to somewhat else, is **Being-by-self.**

The foundation of all determinateness is negation (as Spinoza says, *Omnis determinatio est negatio*). The unreflecting observer supposes that determinate things are merely positive, and pins them down under the form of being. Mere being however is not the end of the matter: it is, as we have already seen, utter emptiness and instability besides. Still, when abstract being is confused in this way with being modified and determinate, it implies some perception of the fact that, though in determinate being there is involved an element of negation, this element is at first wrapped up, as it were, and only comes to the front and receives its due in Being-for-self. If we go on to consider determinate Being as a determinateness which is, we get in this way what is called Reality. We speak, for example, of the reality of a plan or a purpose, meaning thereby that they are no longer inner and subjective, but have passed into being-there-and-then. In the same sense the body may be called the reality of the soul, and the law the reality of freedom, and the world altogether the reality of the divine idea. The word "reality" is however used in another acceptation to mean that something behaves conformably to its essential characteristic or notion. For example, we use the expression: This is a real occupation: This is a real man. Here the term does not merely mean outward and immediate existence: but rather that some existence agrees with its notion. In which sense, be it added, reality is not distinct from the ideality which we shall in the first instance become acquainted with in the shape of Being-for-self.

92. (β) Being, if kept distinct and apart from its determinate mode, as it is in Being-by-self (Being implicit), would be only the vacant abstraction of Being. In Being (determinate there and then) the determinateness is one with Being; yet at the same time, when explicitly made a negation, it is a Limit, a Barrier. Hence the otherness is not something indifferent and outside it, but a function proper to it. Somewhat is by its quality—firstly **finite,** secondly **alterable;** so that finitude and variability appertain to its being.

In Being-there-and-then, the negation is still directly one with the Being, and this negation is what we call a Limit (Boundary). A thing is what it is, only in and by reason of its limit. We cannot therefore regard the limit as only external to being which is then and there. It rather goes through and through the whole of such existence. The view of limit as merely an external characteristic of being-there-and-then, arises from a confusion of quantitative with qualitative limit. Here we are speaking primarily of the qualitative limit. If, for example, we observe a piece of ground three acres large, that circumstance is its quantitative limit. But, in addition, the ground is, it may be, a meadow, not a wood or a pond. This is its qualitative limit. Man, if he wishes to be actual, must be-there-and-then, and to this end he must set a limit to himself. People who are too fastidious towards the finite never reach actuality, but linger lost in abstraction, and their light dies away.

If we take a closer look at what a limit implies, we see it involving a contradiction in itself, and thus evincing its dialectical nature. On the one side the limit makes the reality of a thing; on the other it is its negation. But, again, the limit, as the negation of something, is not an abstract nothing but a nothing which is—what we call an "other." Given something, and up starts an other to us: we know that there is not something only, but an other as well. Nor, again, is the other of such a nature that we can think something apart from it; a something is implicitly the other of itself, and the somewhat sees its limit become objective to it in the other. If we now ask for the difference between something and another, it turns out that they are the same: which sameness is expressed in Latin by calling the pair *aliud—aliud*. The other, as opposed to the something, is itself a something, and hence we say some other, or something else; and so on the other hand the first something when opposed to the other, also defined as something, is itself an other. When we say "something else" our first impression is that something taken separately is only something, and that the quality of being another attaches to it only from outside considerations. Thus we suppose that the moon, being something else than the sun, might very well exist without the sun. But really the moon, as a something, has its other implicit in it: Plato says God made the world out of the nature of the "one" and the "other" (τοῦ ἑτέρου): having brought these together, he formed from them a third, which is of the nature of the "one" and the "other." In these words we have in general terms a statement of the nature of the finite, which, as something, does not meet the nature of the other as if it had no affinity to it, but, being implicitly the other of itself, thus undergoes alteration. Alteration thus exhibits the inherent contradiction which originally attaches to determinate being, and which forces it out of its own bounds. To materialized conception existence stands in the character of something solely positive, and quietly abiding within its own limits: though we also know, it is true, that everything finite (such as existence) is subject to change. Such changeableness in existence is to the superficial eye a mere possibility, the realization of which is not a consequence of its own nature. But the fact is, mutability lies in the notion of existence, and change is only the manifestation of what it implicitly is. The living die, simply because as living they bear in themselves the germ of death.

93. Something becomes an other: this other is itself somewhat: therefore it likewise becomes an other, and so on *ad infinitum*.

94. This **Infinity** is the wrong or negative infinity: it is only a negation of a finite: but the finite rises again the same as ever, and is never got rid of and absorbed. In other words, this infinite only expresses the ought-to-be elimination of the finite. The progression to infinity never gets further than a statement of the contradiction involved in the finite, viz. that it is somewhat as well as somewhat else. It sets up with endless iteration the alternation between these two terms, each of which calls up the other.

If we let somewhat and another, the elements of determinate Being, fall asunder, the result is that some becomes other, and this other is itself a somewhat, which then as such changes likewise, and so on *ad infinitum*. This result seems to superficial reflection something very grand, the grandest possible. But such a progression to infinity is not the real infinite. That consists in being at home with itself in its other, or, if enunciated as a process, in coming to itself in its other. Much depends on rightly apprehending the notion of infinity, and not stopping short at the wrong infinity of endless progression. When time and space, for example, are spoken of as infinite, it is in the first place the infinite progression on which our thoughts fasten. We say, "Now; this time," and then we keep continually going forwards and backwards beyond this limit. The case is the same with space, the infinity of which has formed the theme of barren declamation to astronomers with a talent for edification. In the attempt to contemplate such an infinite, our thought, we are commonly informed, must sink exhausted. It is true indeed that we must abandon the unending contemplation, not however because the occupation is too sublime, but because it is too tedious. It is tedious to expatiate in the contemplation of this infinite progression, because the same thing is constantly recurring. We lay down a limit: then we pass it: next we have a limit once more, and so on for ever. All this is but superficial alternation, which never leaves the region of the finite behind. To suppose that by stepping out and away into that infinity we release ourselves from the finite, is in truth but to seek the release which comes by flight. But the man who flees is not yet free: in fleeing he is still conditioned by that from which he flees. If it be also said that the infinite is unattainable, the statement is true, but only because to the idea of infinity has been attached the circumstance of being simply and solely negative. With such empty and other-world stuff philosophy has nothing to do. What philosophy has to do with is always something concrete and in the highest sense present.

No doubt philosophy has also sometimes been set the task of finding an answer to the question, how the infinite comes to the resolution of issuing out of itself. This question, founded as it is upon the assumption of a rigid opposition between finite and infinite, may be answered by saying that the opposition is false, and that in point of fact the infinite eternally proceeds out of itself, and yet does not proceed out of itself. If we further say that the infinite is the not-finite, we have in point of fact virtually expressed the truth: for as the finite itself is the first negative, the not-finite is the negative of that negation, the negation which is identical with itself and thus at the same time a true affirmation.

The infinity of reflection here discussed is only an *attempt* to reach the true infinity, a wretched neither-one-thing-nor-another. Generally speaking, it is the point of view which has in recent times been emphasized in Germany. The finite, this theory tells us, ought to be absorbed; the infinite ought not to be a negative merely, but also a positive. That "ought to be" betrays the incapacity of actually making good a claim which is at the same time recognized to be right. This stage was never passed by the systems of Kant and Fichte, so far as ethics are concerned. The utmost to which this way brings us is only the postulate of a never-ending approximation to the law of Reason: which postulate has been made an argument for the immortality of the soul.

95. (γ) What we now in point of fact have before us, is that somewhat comes to be an other, and that the other generally comes to be an other. Thus essentially relative to another, somewhat is virtually an other against it: and since what is passed into is quite the same as what passes over, since both have one and the same attribute, viz. to be an other, it follows that something in its passage into other only joins with itself. To be thus self-related in the passage, and in the other, is the genuine Infinity. Or, under a negative aspect: what is altered is the other, it becomes the other of the other. Thus Being, but as negation of the negation, is restored again: it is now **Being-for-self.**

Dualism, in putting an insuperable opposition between finite and infinite, fails to note the simple circumstance that the infinite is thereby only one of two, and is reduced to a particular, to which the finite forms the other particular. Such an infinite, which is only a particular, is co-terminous with the finite which makes for it a limit and a barrier: it is not what it ought to be, that is, the infinite, but is only finite. In such circumstances, where the finite is on this side, and the infinite on that—this world as the finite and the other world as the infinite—an equal dignity of permanence and independence is ascribed to finite and to infinite. The being of the finite is made an absolute being, and by this dualism gets independence and stability. Touched, so to speak, by the infinite, it would be annihilated. But it must not be touched by the infinite. There must be an abyss, an impassable gulf between the two, with the infinite abiding on yonder side and the finite steadfast on this. Those who attribute to the finite this inflexible persistence in comparison with the infinite are not, as they imagine, far above metaphysic: they are still on the level of the most ordinary metaphysic of understanding. For the same thing occurs here as in the infinite progression. At one time it is admitted that the finite has no independent actuality, no absolute being, no root and development of its own, but is only a transient. But next moment this is straightway forgotten; the finite, made a mere counterpart to the infinite, wholly separated from it, and rescued from annihilation, is conceived to be persistent in its independence. While thought thus imagines itself elevated to the infinite, it meets with the opposite fate: it comes to an infinite which is only a finite, and the finite, which it had left behind, has always to be retained and made into an absolute.

After this examination (with which it were well to compare Plato's *Philebus*) tending to show the nullity of the distinction made by understanding between the finite and the infinite, we are liable to glide into the statement that the infinite and the finite are therefore one, and that the genuine infinity, the truth, must be defined and enunciated as the unity of the finite and infinite. Such a statement would be to some extent correct; but is just as open to perversion and falsehood as the unity of Being and Nothing already noticed. Besides it may very fairly be charged with reducing the infinite to finitude and making a finite infinite. For, so far as the expression goes, the finite seems left in its place—it is not expressly stated to be absorbed. Or, if we reflect that the finite, when identified with the infinite, certainly cannot remain what it was out of such unity, and will at least suffer some change in its characteristics (as an alkali, when combined with an acid, loses some of its properties), we must see that the same fate awaits the infinite, which, as the negative, will on its part likewise have its edge, as it were, taken off on the other. And this does really happen with the abstract one-sided infinite of understanding. The genuine infinite, however, is not merely in the position of the one-sided acid, and so does not lose itself. The negation of negation is not a neutralization: the infinite is the affirmative, and it is only the finite which is absorbed.

In Being-for-self enters the category of **Ideality**. Being-there-and-then, as in the first instance apprehended in its being or affirmation, has reality (§ 91): and thus even finitude in the first instance is in the category of reality. But the truth of the finite is rather its ideality. Similarly, the infinite of understanding, which is coordinated with the finite, is itself only one of two finites, no whole truth, but a non-substantial element. This ideality of the finite is the chief maxim of philosophy; and for that reason every genuine philosophy is idealism. But everything depends upon not taking for the infinite what, in the very terms of its characterization, is at the same time made a particular and finite. For this reason we have bestowed a greater amount of attention on this distinction. The fundamental notion of philosophy, the genuine infinite, depends upon it. The distinction is cleared up by the simple, and for that reason seemingly insignificant, but incontrovertible, reflections contained in the first paragraph of this section.

(c) Being-for-self

96. (α) Being-for-self, as reference to itself, is immediacy, and as reference of the negative to itself, is a self-subsistent, the **One**. This unit, being without distinction in itself, thus excludes the other from itself.

To be for self—to be one—is completed Quality, and, as such, contains abstract Being and Being modified as non-substantial elements. As simple Being, the One is simple self-reference; as Being modified it is determinate: but the determinateness is not in this case a finite determinateness—a somewhat in distinction from an other—but infinite, because it contains distinction absorbed and annulled in itself.

The readiest instance of Being-for-self is found in the "I." We know ourselves as existents, distinguished in the first place from other existents, and with certain relations thereto. But we also come to know this expan-sion of existence (in these relations) reduced, as it were, to a point in the simple form of being-for-self. When we say "I," we express the reference-to-self which is infinite, and at the same time negative. Man, it may be said, is distinguished from the animal world, and in that way from nature altogether, by knowing himself as "I": which amounts to saying that natural things never attain a free Being-for-self, but as limited to Being-there-and-then, are always and only Being for an other. Again, Being-for-self may be described as ideality, just as Being-there-and-then was de-scribed as reality. It is said that besides reality there is *also* an ideality. Thus the two categories are made equal and parallel. Properly speaking, ideality is not somewhat outside of and beside reality: the notion of ideal-ity just lies in its being the truth of reality. That is to say, when reality is explicitly put as what it implicitly is, it is at once seen to be ideality. Hence ideality has not received its proper estimation, when you allow that reality is not all in all, but that an ideality must be recognized outside of it. Such an ideality, external to, or it may be even beyond, reality, would be no better than an empty name. Ideality only has a meaning when it is the ideality of something: but this something is not a mere indefinite this or that, but existence characterized as reality, which, if retained in isola-tion, possesses no truth. The distinction between Nature and Mind is not improperly conceived, when the former is traced back to reality, and the latter to ideality as a fundamental category. Nature however is far from being so fixed and complete as to subsist even without Mind: in Mind it first, as it were, attains its goal and its truth. And similarly, Mind on its part is not merely a world beyond Nature and nothing more: it is really, and with full proof, seen to be mind only when it involves Nature as absorbed in itself. *A propos* of this, we should note the double meaning of the German word *aufheben* (to put by, or set aside). We mean by it (1) to clear away, or annul: thus, we say, a law or a regulation is set aside; (2) to keep, or preserve: in which sense we use it when we say something is well put by. This double usage of language, which gives to the same word a positive and negative meaning, is not an accident, and gives no ground for reproaching language as a cause of confusion. We should rather recognize in it the speculative spirit of our language rising above the mere "Either—or" of understanding.

97. (β) The relation of the negative to itself is a negative relation, and so a distinguishing of the One from itself, the repulsion of the One; that is, it makes **Many** Ones. So far as regards the immediacy of the self-existents, these Many are: and the repulsion of every One of them becomes to that extent their repulsion against each other as existing units, in other words, their reciprocal exclusion.

Whenever we speak of the One, the Many usually come into our mind at the same time. Whence, then, are we forced to ask, do the Many come? This question is unanswerable by the consciousness which pictures the Many as a primary datum, and treats the One as only one among the Many. But the philosophic notion teaches, contrariwise, that the One forms the presupposition of the Many: and in the thought of the One is implied that it explicitly make itself Many. The self-existing unit is not, like Being, void of all connective reference: it is a reference, as well as Being-there-and-then was, not however a reference connecting somewhat with an other, but, as unity of the some and the other, it is a connection with itself, and this connection, be it noted, is a negative connection. Hereby the One manifests an utter incompatibility with itself, a self-repulsion: and what it makes itself explicitly be, is the Many. We may denote this side in the process of Being-for-self by the figurative term Repulsion. Repulsion is a term originally employed in the study of matter, to mean that matter, as a Many, in each of these many Ones, behaves as exclusive to all the others. It would be wrong however to view the process of repulsion, as if the One were the repellent and the Many the repelled. The One, as already remarked, just is self-exclusion and explicit putting itself as the Many. Each of the Many however is itself a One, and in virtue of its so behaving, this all-round repulsion is by one stroke converted into its opposite, Attraction.

98. (γ) But the Many are one the same as another: each is One, or even one of the Many; they are consequently one and the same. Or when we study all that **Repulsion** involves, we see that as a negative attitude of many Ones to one another, it is just as essentially a connective reference of them to each other; and as

those to which the One is related in its act of repulsion are ones, it is in them thrown into relation with itself. The repulsion therefore has an equal right to be called **Attraction;** and the exclusive One, or Being-for-self, suppresses itself. The qualitative character, which in the One or unit has reached the extreme point of its characterization, has thus passed over into determinateness (quality) suppressed, *i.e.* into Being as Quantity.

The philosophy of the Atomists is the doctrine in which the Absolute is formulated as Being-for-self, as One, and many ones. And it is the repulsion, which shows itself in the notion of the One, which is assumed as the fundamental force in these atoms. But instead of attraction, it is Accident, that is, mere unintelligence, which is expected to bring them together. So long as the One is fixed as one, it is certainly impossible to regard its congression with others as anything but external and mechanical. The Void, which is assumed as the complementary principle to the atoms, is repulsion and nothing else, presented under the image of the nothing existing between the atoms. Modern Atomism—and physics is still in principle atomistic —has surrendered the atoms so far as to pin its faith on molecules or particles. In so doing, science has come closer to sensuous conception, at the cost of losing the precision of thought. To put an attractive by the side of a repulsive force, as the moderns have done, certainly gives completeness to the contrast: and the discovery of this natural force, as it is called, has been a source of much pride. But the mutual implication of the two, which makes what is true and concrete in them, would have to be wrested from the obscurity and confusion in which they were left even in Kant's Metaphysical Rudiments of Natural Science. In modern times the importance of the atomic theory is even more evident in political than in physical science. According to it, the will of individuals as such is the creative principle of the State: the attracting force is the special wants and inclinations of individuals; and the Universal, or the State itself, is the external nexus of a compact.

(1) The Atomic philosophy forms a vital stage in the historical evolution of the Idea. The principle of that system may be described as Being-for-self in the shape of the Many. At present, students of nature who are anxious to avoid metaphysics turn a favorable ear to Atomism. But it is not possible to escape metaphysics and cease to trace nature back to terms of thought, by throwing ourselves into the arms of Atomism. The atom, in fact, is itself a thought; and hence the theory which holds matter to consist of atoms is a metaphysical theory. Newton gave physics an

express warning to beware of metaphysics, it is true; but, to his honor be it said, he did not by any means obey his own warning. The only mere physicists are the animals: they alone do not think: while man is a thinking being and a born metaphysician. The real question is not whether we shall apply metaphysics, but whether our metaphysics are of the right kind: in other words, whether we are not, instead of the concrete logical Idea, adopting one-sided forms of thought, rigidly fixed by understanding, and making these the basis of our theoretical as well as our practical work. It is on this ground that one objects to the Atomic philosophy. The old Atomists viewed the world as a many, as their successors often do to this day. On chance they laid the task of collecting the atoms which float about in the void. But, after all, the nexus binding the many with one another is by no means a mere accident: as we have already remarked, the nexus is founded on their very nature. To Kant we owe the completed theory of matter as the unity of repulsion and attraction. The theory is correct, so far as it recognizes attraction to be the other of the two elements involved in the notion of Being-for-self: and to be an element no less essential than repulsion to constitute matter. Still this dynamical construction of matter, as it is termed, has the fault of taking for granted, instead of deducing, attraction and repulsion. Had they been deduced, we should then have seen the How and the Why of a unity which is merely asserted. Kant indeed was careful to inculcate that Matter must not be taken to be in existence *per se,* and then as it were incidentally to be provided with the two forces mentioned, but must be regarded as consisting solely in their unity. German physicists for some time accepted this pure dynamic. But in spite of this, the majority of these physicists in modern times have found it more convenient to return to the Atomic point of view, and in spite of the warnings of Kästner, one of their number, have begun to regard Matter as consisting of infinitesimally small particles, termed "atoms"—which atoms have then to be brought into relation with one another by the play of forces attaching to them, attractive, repulsive, or whatever they may be. This too is metaphysics; and metaphysics which, for its utter unintelligence, there would be sufficient reason to guard against.

(2) The transition from Quality to Quantity, indicated in the paragraph before us, is not found in our ordinary way of thinking, which deems each of these categories to exist independently beside the other. We are in the habit of saying that things are not merely qualitatively, but also quantitatively defined; but whence these categories originate, and how they are related to each other, are questions not further examined. The fact is, quantity just means quality superseded and absorbed: and it is by the dialectic of quality here examined that this supersession is effected. First of all, we had Being; as the truth of Being, came Becoming, which formed the passage to Being Determinate; and the truth of that we found to be Alteration. And in its result Alteration showed itself to be Being-for-

self, exempt from implication of another and from passage into another—which Being-for-self, finally, in the two sides of its process, Repulsion and Attraction, was clearly seen to annul itself, and thereby to annul quality in the totality of its stages. Still this superseded and absorbed quality is neither an abstract nothing nor an equally abstract and featureless being: it is only being as indifferent to determinateness or character. This aspect of being is also what appears as quantity in our ordinary conceptions. We observe things, first of all, with an eye to their quality—which we take to be the character identical with the being of the thing. If we proceed to consider their quantity, we get the conception of an indifferent and external character or mode, of such a kind that a thing remains what it is, though its quantity is altered, and the thing becomes greater or less.

Supplementary Passages

1

Philosophy and the Actual World

Philosophy is, because it is the exploration of the rational, by that very fact the prehension of the present and the actual, and not the construction of something otherworldly that might be God knows where. . . .

> The rational is actual;
> And the actual is rational.

Upon this conviction rests all naïve consciousness, as does philosophy, and philosophy starts from it in considering the spiritual universe as well as the natural one. If reflections, sentiment or whatever form subjective consciousness may have, looks upon the present as something vain, transcends it and knows it better, such subjective consciousness is itself vanity, since it has reality only in the present. If correspondingly the idea is seen as merely just an idea, an opinionated notion, philosophy by contrast offers the insight that nothing is actual but the idea. Hence what matters is to recognize and know the substance which is immanent and the eternal which is present beneath the temporal and passing which appears. For the rational which is synonymous with the idea appears (by entering through its actuality into an outward existence) in a limitless wealth of forms, appearances and configurations, and thus encloses its kernel with a variegated rind. Consciousness at the outset lives in this rind, but the conception permeates it in search of the inner pulse which beats in the outer configurations. These endlessly manifold relations, this endless material and its regularities are not the subject of philosophy. It would mix in matters which do not concern it; it may save itself the trouble to offer good counsel in such matters. Plato could have omitted recommending to the nurses not to stand still with their children, always to rock them in their arms, likewise Fichte could have omitted perfecting the passport police to the point of suggesting that not only the description of suspects be entered in their passport, but a picture. In such elaborations there is no longer any philosophy and philosophy may omit such matters the more readily as it ought to be most liberal (tolerant) in all such endless details. . . .

Therefore, this treatise in so far as it contains political science is intended to be nothing else but an attempt to understand the state as something rational in itself and so to describe it. As a philosophical study it ought to be furthest from constructing a state as it ought to be. The instruction which it may be able to impart cannot be directed toward telling the state how it ought to be but rather how the state is to be recognized and known as the ethical universe. *Hic Rhodus, hic salta.* . . .

To understand that which exists is the task of philosophy; for what exists is reason. As to the individual, everyone is the son of his time, and therefore philosophy is its time comprehended in thought. It is as silly to imagine that any philosophy could transcend its own time as that an individual could jump out of his time, jump beyond Rhodes. If a man's theory goes beyond its time, if it builds a world as it ought to be, it may exist, but only in his opinion. . . .

With a little change, that saying might be: here is the rose, dance here. Whatever lies between reason as self-conscious spirit and reason as existing actuality, whatever separates that reason from this one and prevents it from being satisfied with it, is the fetter of some kind of abstraction which has not been set free as a conception. To recognize and know reason as the rose within the cross of the present and thus to enjoy this present, this sort of rational insight is the reconciliation with actuality which philosophy provides for those who have received the inner demand to understand.

To say one more word about preaching what the world ought to be like, philosophy arrives always too late for that. As *thought* of the world it appears at a time when actuality has completed its developmental process and is finished. What the conception teaches, history also shows as necessary, namely, that only in a maturing actuality the ideal appears and confronts the real. It is then that the ideal rebuilds for itself this same world in the shape of an intellectual realm, comprehending this world in its substance. When philosophy paints its gray in gray, a form of life has become old, and this gray in gray cannot rejuvenate it, only understand it. The owl of Minerva begins its flight when dusk is falling. . . .

[FROM the Preface to *The Philosophy of Right and Law,* trans. Carl J. Friedrich in *The Philosophy of Hegel,* N. Y.: Modern Library, 1953. Reprinted by permission of Random House, Inc. Copyright, 1953, 1954, by Random House, Inc.]

2

Dialectic

That by means of which the concept forges ahead is the above-mentioned negative which it carries within itself; it is this that constitutes the genuine dialectical procedure. *Dialectic*—which has been regarded as an isolated part of logic, and which as regards its purpose and standpoint has, one may aver, been entirely misunderstood—is thus put in quite a different position. The Platonic dialectic too, even in the *Parmenides* (and still more directly in other places), is sometimes intended merely to dispose of and to refute through themselves limited assertions, and sometimes again has nullity for its result. Dialectic is generally regarded as an external and negative procedure, that does not pertain to the subject matter, that is based on a mere idle subjective craving to disturb and unsettle what is fixed and true, or that at best leads to nothing except the futility of the dialectically treated matter.

Kant set dialectic higher, and this part of his work is among the greatest of his merits, for he freed dialectic from the semblance of arbitrariness attributed to it in ordinary thought, and set it forth as a necessary procedure of reason. Since dialectic was regarded merely as the art of producing deceptions and bringing about illusions, it was straightway assumed that it played a cheating game, and that its whole power depended solely on concealment of the fraud; that its results were reached surreptitiously, and were a mere subjective illusion. When Kant's dialectical expositions in the Antinomies of Pure Reason are looked at closely (as they will be more at large in the course of this work) it will be seen that they are not indeed deserving of any great praise; but the general idea upon which he builds and which he has vindicated is the objectivity of appearance and the necessity of contradiction which belong to the very nature of thought-determinations; primarily indeed in so far as these determinations are applied by reason to things in themselves; but further, just what these determinations are in reason and in respect of that which is self-existent—just this it is which is their own nature. This result, grasped on its positive side, is nothing other than the inherent negativity of these thought-determinations, their self-moving soul, the principle of all physical and spiritual life. But if people stop short at the abstract-negative aspect of the dialectic, they reach only the familiar result that reason is incapable of cognition of the

infinite; a strange result, for—since the infinite is the reasonable—
it amounts to saying that reason is incapable of cognizing that which
is reasonable.

It is in this dialectic (as here understood) and in the comprehension of the unity of opposites, or of the positive in the negative, that
speculative knowledge consists. This is the most important aspect of
the dialectic, but for thought that is as yet unpracticed and unfree, it
is the most difficult. If thought is still in the process of cutting itself
loose from concrete sense-presentation and from syllogizing, it must
first practice abstract thinking, and learn to hold fast concepts in
their definiteness and to recognize by means of them.

> [FROM *The Science of Logic*, trans. W. H. Johnston and L. G.
> Struthers, London: Allen and Unwin, 1929. Reprinted by per-
> mission of George Allen and Unwin, Ltd., London, and the
> Macmillan Company, New York.]

3

Spirit

Reason is spirit, when its certainty of being all reality has been
raised to the level of truth, and reason is consciously aware of itself
as its own world, and of the world as itself. The development of
spirit was indicated in the immediately preceding movement of mind,
where the object of consciousness, the category pure and simple,
rose to be the notion of reason. When reason "observes" this pure
unity of ego and existence, the unity of subjectivity and objectivity,
of for-itself-ness and in-itself-ness this unity is immanent, has the
character of implicitness or of being; and consciousness of reason
finds itself. But the true nature of "observation" is rather the tran-
scendence of this instinct of finding its object lying directly at hand,
and passing beyond this unconscious state of existence. The directly
perceived category, the thing simply "found," enters consciousness
as the self-existence of the ego—an ego which now knows itself in
the objective reality, and knows itself there as the self. But this
feature of the category, viz., of being for-itself as opposed to being
immanent within itself, is equally one-sided, and a moment that
cancels itself. The category therefore gets for consciousness the
character which it possesses in its universal truth—it is self-contained
essential reality. This character, still abstract, which constitutes the
nature of absolute fact, of "fact itself," is to begin with "spiritual
reality"; and its mode of consciousness is here a formal knowledge

of that reality, a knowledge which is occupied with the varied and manifold content thereof. This consciousness is still, in point of fact, a particular individual distinct from the general substance, and either prescribes arbitrary laws or pretends to possess within its own knowledge as such the laws as they absolutely are, and takes itself to be the power that passes judgment on them. Or again, looked at from the side of the substance, this is seen to be the self-contained and self-sufficient spiritual reality, which is not yet a consciousness of its own self. The self-contained and self-sufficient reality, however, which is at once aware of being actual in the form of consciousness and presents itself to itself, is Spirit.

Its essential spiritual being has been above designated as the ethical substance; spirit, however, is concrete ethical actuality. Spirit is the self of the actual consciousness, to which spirit stands opposed, or rather which appears over against itself, as an objective actual world that has lost, however, all sense of strangeness for the self, just as the self has lost all sense of having a dependent or independent existence by itself, cut off and separated from that world. Being substance and universal self-identical permanent essence, spirit is the immovable irreducible basis and the starting point for the action of all and every one; it is their purpose and their goal, because the ideally implicit nature of all self-consciousnesses. This substance is likewise the universal product, wrought and created by the action of each and all, and giving them unity and likeness and identity of meaning; for it is being-by-itself, the self, action. When considered as substance, spirit is unbending righteous self-sameness, self-identity; but when considered as being-by-itself, its continuity is resolved into discrete elements, it is the self-sacrificing soul of goodness, the benevolent essential nature, in which each fulfills his own special work, rends the continuum of the universal substance, and takes his own share of it. This resolution of the essence into individual forms is just the aspect of the separate action and the separate self of all the several individuals; it is the moving soul of the ethical substance, the resultant universal spiritual being. Just because this substance is a being resolved in the self, it is not a lifeless essence, but real and alive.

Spirit is thus the self-supporting absolutely real ultimate being. All the previous modes of consciousness are abstractions from it: they are constituted by the fact that spirit analyzes itself, distinguishes its moments, and halts at each individual mode in turn. The isolating of such moments presupposes spirit itself and requires spirit for its subsistence; in other words, this isolation of modes only exists within spirit, which is existence. Taken in isolation they appear as if they existed as they stand. But their advance and return upon their real ground and essential being showed that they are merely moments or vanishing quantities; and this essential being is precisely this movement and resolution of these moments. Here, where spirit, the reflection of these moments into itself, has become established, our reflection may briefly recall them in this connection: they were consciousness, self-consciousness, and reason. Spirit is thus Consciousness in general, which contains sense-experience, perception, and understanding, so far as in analyzing its own self it holds fast by the moment of being a reality objective to itself, and by abstraction eliminates the fact that this reality is its own self objectified, its own self-existence. When again it holds fast by the other abstract moment produced by analysis, the fact that its object is its own self become objective to itself, is its self-existence, and thus is Self-consciousness. But as immediate consciousness of its inherent and its explicit being, of its immanent self and its objective self, as the unity of consciousness and self-consciousness, it is that type of consciousness which has Reason: it is the consciousness which, as the word "have" indicates, has the object in a form which is implicitly and inherently rational, or is categorized, but in such a way that the object is not yet taken by the consciousness in question to have the value of a category. Spirit here is that consciousness from the immediately preceding consideration of which we have arrived at the present stage. Finally, when this reason, which spirit "has," is seen by spirit to be reason which actually is, that is, to be reason which is actual in spirit and is its world, then spirit has come to its truth; it is spirit, the essential nature of ethical life actually existent.

Spirit, so far as it is the immediate truth, is the ethical life of a nation—the individual, which is a world. It has to advance to the consciousness of what it is immediately; it has to abandon and transcend the beautiful simplicity of ethical life, and get to a knowledge of itself by passing through a series of stages and forms. The distinction between these and those that have gone before consists in their being real spiritual individualities, actualities proper, and instead of being forms of consciousness, they are forms of a world.

The living ethical world is spirit in its truth. As it first comes to an abstract knowledge of its essential nature, ethical life vanishes into the formal generality of right and law. Spirit, being now divided against itself, traces one of its worlds in the element of its objectivity as in a hard reality; this is the realm of culture and civilization; while

over against this in the element of thought is traced the world of
faith, the realm of essence. Both worlds, however, when in the grip
of the conception—when grasped by the spirit, which, after this loss
of its self reflects upon itself—are thrown into confusion and revolu-
tionized through insight and its general diffusion, known as the
"Enlightenment."And the realm which had thus been divided and
expanded into the "present" and the "beyond," into the "here" and
the "hereafter," turns back into self-consciousness. This self-consciousness, again, taking now the form of morality (the inner moral
life) apprehends itself as the essential truth, and the real essence as
its actual self: no longer puts its world and its ground and basis
outside itself, but lets everything fade into itself, and in the form of
conscience is spirit sure and certain of itself.

> [FROM *The Phenomenology of Spirit,* trans. J. B. Baillie, Lon-
> don: Allen and Unwin, 1910; rev. 1931; revised by Carl J.
> Friedrich in *op. cit.* Reprinted by permission of Random House,
> George Allen and Unwin, London, and The Macmillan Com-
> pany, New York.]

4

Art

The modern moralistic view starts from the fixed antithesis of the
will in its spiritual universality to its sensuous natural particularity,
and consists not in the completed reconciliation of these contrasted
sides, but in their conflict with one another, which involves the
requirement that the impulses that conflict with duty ought to yield
to it.

This antithesis does not merely display itself for our consciousness
in the limited region of moral action, but also emerges as a fundamental distinction and antagonism between what is real essentially
and in its own right and what is external reality and existence.
Formulated in the abstract, it is the contrast of the universal and the
particular, when the former is explicitly set over against the latter,
just as the latter is over against the former; more concretely, it
appears in nature as the opposition of the abstract law against the
abundance of individual phenomena, each having its own character;
in the mind, as the sensuous and spiritual in man . . . ; further,
as the contradiction of the dead concept—empty in itself—compared
with full concrete vitality, or of theory and subjective thought contrasted with objective existence and experience. . . .

We . . . lay aside the false position, which has already been remarked upon, that art has to serve as a means for moral ends, and
to conduce to the moral end of the world, as such, by instruction
and moral improvement, and thereby has its substantive aim, not in
itself, but in something else. If, therefore, we now continue to speak
of an aim or purpose, we must, in the first place, get rid of the
perverse idea that, in asking "What is the aim?" we retain the
accessory meaning of the question, "What is the *use*?" The perverse-
ness of this lies in the point that the work of art would then be
regarded as aspiring to something else that is set before consciousness as the essential and as what ought to be, so that then the work
of art would only have value as a useful instrument in the realization
of an end having substantive importance *outside* the sphere of art.
Against this it is necessary to maintain that art has the vocation of
revealing the *truth* in the form of sensuous artistic shape, of representing the reconciled antithesis just described, and, therefore, has
its purpose in itself, in this representation and revelation. . . .

It has already been said that the content of art is the Idea, and
that its form lies in the plastic use of images accessible to sense.
These two sides art has to reconcile into a full and united totality.
The first attribution which this involves is the requirement that the
content, which is to be offered to artistic representation, shall show
itself to be in its nature worthy of such representation. Otherwise we
only obtain a bad combination, whereby a content that will not submit to plasticity and to external presentation, is forced into that
form, and a matter which is in its nature prosaic is expected to find
an appropriate mode of manifestation in the form antagonistic to its
nature.

The second requirement, which is derivable from this first, demands of the content of art that it should not be anything abstract in
itself. This does not mean that it must be concrete as the sensuous is
concrete in contrast to everything spiritual and intellectual, these
being taken as in themselves simple and abstract. For everything
that has genuine truth in the mind as well as in nature is concrete in
itself, and has, in spite of its universality, nevertheless, both subjectivity and particularity within it. If we say, e.g., of God that he is
simply One, the supreme Being as such, we have only enunciated a
lifeless abstraction of the irrational understanding. Such a God, as
he himself is not apprehended in his concrete truth, can afford no
material for art, least of all for plastic art. Hence the Jews and the
Turks have not been able to represent their God, who does not even

amount to such an abstraction of the understanding, in the positive way in which Christians have done so. For God in Christianity is conceived in His truth, and therefore as in Himself thoroughly concrete, as a person, as a subject, and more closely determined, as mind or spirit. What He is as spirit unfolds itself to the religious apprehension as the Trinity of Persons, which at the same time in relation with itself is *One*. Here is essentiality, universality, and particularity, together with their reconciled unity; and it is only such unity that constitutes the concrete. Now, as a content in order to possess truth at all must be of this concrete nature, art demands the same concreteness, because a mere abstract universal has not in itself the vocation to advance to particularity and phenomenal manifestation and to unity with itself therein.

If a true and therefore concrete content is to have corresponding to it a sensuous form and modeling, this sensuous form must, in the third place, be no less emphatically something individual, wholly concrete in itself, and one. The character of concreteness as belonging to both elements of art, to the content as to the representation, is precisely the point in which both may coincide and correspond to one another; as, for instance, the natural shape of the human body is such a sensuous concrete as is capable of representing spirit, which is concrete in itself, and of displaying itself in conformity therewith. Therefore we ought to abandon the idea that it is a mere matter of accident that an actual phenomenon of the external world is chosen to furnish a shape thus conformable to truth. Art does not appropriate this form either because it simply finds it existing or because there is no other. The concrete content itself involves the element of external and actual, we may say indeed of sensible manifestation. But in compensation this sensuous concrete, in which a content essentially belonging to mind expresses itself, is in its own nature addressed to the inward being; its external element of shape, whereby the content is made perceptible and imaginable, has the aim of existing purely for the heart and mind. This is the only reason for which content and artistic shape are fashioned in conformity with each other. . . .

But inasmuch as the task of art is to represent the idea to direct perception in sensuous shape, and not in the form of thought or of pure spirituality as such, and seeing that this work of representation has its value and dignity in the correspondence and the unity of the two sides, i.e., of the Idea and its plastic embodiment, it follows that the level and excellency of art in attaining a realization adequate to its idea, must depend upon the grade of inwardness and unity with which Idea and Shape display themselves as fused into one.

> [FROM the Introduction to Hegel's *Philosophy of Fine Art*, trans. Bernard Bosanquet, London: Routledge and Kegan Paul, 1905, the end of Chapter 3 and the beginning of Chapter 5.]

5

Religion

In the forms of experience hitherto dealt with—which are distinguished broadly as consciousness, self-consciousness, reason, spirit, and religion—the consciousness of absolute being in general has also made its appearance. But that was from the point of view only of consciousness, when it is conscious of the absolute being. Absolute being, however, in its own distinctive nature, the self-consciousness of spirit, has not appeared in those forms.

Even at the plane of consciousness, when it is mere intellect, there is a consciousness of the supersensuous, of the inner aspect of objective existence. But the supersensuous, the eternal, or whatever we care to call it, is devoid of selfhood. It is merely, to begin with, something universal, which is still a long way from being spirit knowing itself as spirit.

Then there was self-consciousness, which came to its final shape in the "unhappy consciousness"; that was merely the pain and sorrow of spirit wrestling to become objectified once more, but not succeeding. The unity of the individual self-consciousness with its unchangeable essence, which is what this stage arrives at, remains, in consequence, a "beyond."

The immediate existence of reason, which we found arising out of that state of sorrow, and the special forms which reason assumes, have no religion because the self-consciousness in these forms knows itself or looks for itself in the direct and immediate present.

On the other hand, in the world of ethics, we met with a type of religion, the religion of the nether world. This is belief in the fearful and unknown darkness of Fate, and in the Eumenides of the spirit of the departed: the former being pure negation taking the form of universality, the latter the same negation but in the form of particularity. The absolute being is, then, in the latter shape no doubt the self and is present, as there is no other way for the self to be except present. But the particular self is the particular shadow, which keeps the universal element, Fate, separated from itself. It is indeed a shadow, a superseded particular, and so a general self. But that negative meaning has not yet turned into this latter positive significance, and hence the superseded self still means specifically this particular being, this unsubstantial reality. Fate, however, without the self remains the darkness of night without consciousness, which never comes to draw distinctions within itself, and never attains the clearness of self-knowledge.

This belief in a necessity that produces nothingness, this belief in the nether world, becomes belief in Heaven, because the self which has departed must be united with its universal nature, must unfold what it contains in terms of this universality, and thus become clear to itself. This kingdom of belief, however, we saw unfold its content merely in the element of reflective thought, without a true conception; and we saw it, on that account, perish in its final fate, that in the religion of enlightenment. Here in this type of religion, the supersensuous beyond, which we found in the intellect, is reinstated again, but in such a way that self-consciousness rests and feels satisfied in the mundane present, not in the "beyond," and thinks of the supersensuous beyond, void and empty, unknowable, and free of all terrors, neither as a self nor as power and might.

In the religion of morality this much is reconstructed, that absolute being has a positive content; but that content is bound up with the negative characteristic of the enlightenment. The content is an objective being, which is at the same time taken back into the self, and remains there enclosed, and is a content with internal distinctions, while its parts are just as immediately negated as they are posited. The final destiny, however, which absorbs this contradictory process, is the self conscious of itself as the controlling necessity or fate of what is essential and actual.

The spirit knowing itself is in religion primarily and immediately its own pure self-consciousness. Those modes of it above considered —"objective spirit," "spirit estranged from itself" and "spirit certain of itself"—together constitute what the spirit is in its condition of consciousness, the state in which, being objectively opposed to its own world, it does not therein apprehend and consciously possess itself. But in conscience it brings itself as well as its objective world as a whole into subjection, as also its idea and its various specific conceptions; it is now self-consciousness at home with itself. Here spirit, represented as an object, has the significance for itself of being universal spirit which contains within itself all that is ultimate and essential and all that is concrete and actual; yet is not in the form of freely subsisting actuality, or of the detached independence of external nature. It has a shape, no doubt, the form of objective being, in that it is the object of its own consciousness; but because this being is put forward in religion with the essential character of being self-consciousness, the form or shape assumed is one perfectly transparent to itself; and the reality which the spirit contains is enclosed in it, or suspended in it, just in the same way as when we speak of "all reality"; it is the universal reality in the sense of a product of thought.

Since, then, in religion, the peculiar characteristic of what is properly consciousness of spirit does not have the form of detached and external otherness, the existence of spirit is distinct from its self-consciousness, and its actual reality proper falls outside religion. There is no doubt one spirit in both, but its consciousness does not embrace both together; and religion appears as a part of existence, of acting, and of striving, whose other part is the life within its own actual world. As we now know that spirit in its own world is the same as spirit conscious of itself as spirit, i.e., spirit in the sphere of religion, the perfection of religion consists in the two forms becoming identical with one another; not merely in its reality being grasped and embraced by religion, but conversely; it, as spirit conscious of itself, becomes actual to itself, and real object of its own consciousness. . . .

While, therefore, religion is the completion of the life of spirit, its final and complete expression, into which, as being their ground, its individual phases, consciousness, self-consciousness, reason, and spirit, return and have returned, they, at the same time, together constitute the objectively existing realization of spirit in its totality; as such spirit is real only as the moving process of these aspects which it possesses, a process of distinguishing them and returning back into itself. In the process of these general phases is contained the development of religion generally. Since, however, each of these attributes was set forth and presented, not only in the way it in general determines itself, but as it is in and for itself, i.e., as within its own being, running its course as a distinct whole, there has thus been presented not merely the development of religion generally; those independently complete processes pursued by the individual phases and stages of spirit contain at the same time the determinate forms of religion itself. Spirit in its entirety, spirit in religion, is once more the process from its immediacy to the attainment of a knowledge of what it implicitly or immediately is; it is the process of attaining the state where the shape and form, in which it appears as an object for its own consciousness, will be perfectly identical with and adequate to its essential nature, and where it will behold itself as it is.

[FROM *The Phenomenology of Spirit,* in Carl J. Friedrich, *op. cit.*]

ARTHUR SCHOPENHAUER

The World as Will and Idea (*abridged*)

ARTHUR SCHOPENHAUER

ARTHUR SCHOPENHAUER (1788–1860) was the son of a successful and independent-minded merchant in the Free City of Danzig, who moved his family to Hamburg after Danzig was taken over by Prussia in 1793. Schopenhauer was brought up to enter the family business and tried it for a time, but after his father's death in 1805 his mother allowed him to become what he wanted to be, a scholar. He studied at Weimar, Göttingen, and Berlin; he received his doctor's degree from Jena. Schopenhauer lived for a time at Weimar with his mother, but became estranged from her. His attempt to compete with Hegel as a philosophical lecturer at Berlin was a failure. The remainder of his long, lonely life of reflection and writing was spent in Dresden, in Italy, and at Frankfurt, where he died. During the final years of his life, fame and reputation arrived at last, after his works had been ignored for many years.

Schopenhauer's masterpiece, *The World as Will and Idea* (trans. E. S. Haldane and J. Kemp, London, 1948–50; reprinted in R. Stern and E. Robison, *Changing Concepts in Art,* New York: Haven Publications, 1983; trans. E. F. J. Payne, 2 vols, 1958; reprinted, New York: Dover, 1966), gives a systematic exposition of his philosophy. It was preceded by his doctoral dissertation, "On the Fourfold Root of the Principle of Sufficient Reason" (1813; trans. Mme. Karl Hillebrand, London: Bell, 1891; and trans. E. F. J. Payne, LaSalle, Ill.: Open Court, 1974), which he refers to frequently in his later works; and it was followed by an essay, *On the Will to Nature* (1836; also trans. Hillebrand, *ibid.*), and *The Two Main Problems in Ethics* (1841). There is also much of philosophical interest in his essays, published as *Parerga and Paralipomena* (1851; see the trans. by T. Bailey Saunders, New York: Wiley, 1942; and the trans. by E. F. J. Payne, 2 vols., Oxford: Clarendon Press, 1974).

Apart from his extensive and intensive effect upon poets, composers, and men in the street, Schopenhauer's contributions to the development of philosophy are noteworthy. He explored one of the important possible ways of extending the philosophy of Kant, and long before Bergson formulated his influential metaphysics of the *élan vital,* Schopenhauer worked out the details of a metaphysics in which process is ultimate, reality is known inwardly by a kind of feeling, and intellect is a mere instrument of the biological will to life. His system of pessimism—a profound rejection of life that has affinities with the Buddhist thought that he was the first Western philosopher to assimilate—stands as one of the world outlooks that everyone must come to terms with. Schopenhauer posed the important question of the function of art, of the value of the arts for human life, in a more profound way than any of his predecessors, and proposed an answer that must contain at least part of the truth. Moreover, his expansive method of exposition, with its detours and frequently sharp and penetrating observations on human nature and human conduct, provides a number of stimulating discussions of particular philosophical problems, for example, on the difference between knowing *that* and knowing *how,* on reductionism, on the "expressive" qualities of music.

The World as Will and Idea*

FIRST BOOK: THE WORLD AS IDEA

FIRST ASPECT: *The Idea Subordinated to the Principle of Sufficient Reason: The Object of Experience and Science*

§ 1. "The world is my idea": this is a truth which holds good for everything that lives and knows, though man alone can bring it into reflective and abstract consciousness. If he really does this, he has attained to philosophical wisdom. It then becomes clear and certain to him that what he knows is not a sun and an earth, but only an eye that sees a sun, a hand that feels an earth; that the world which surrounds him is there only as idea, *i.e.,* only in relation to something else, the consciousness, which is himself. If any truth can be asserted *a priori,* it is this, for it is the expression of the most general form of all possible and thinkable experience: a form which is more general than time, or space, or causality, for they all presuppose it; and each of these, which we have seen to be just so many modes of the principle of sufficient reason, is valid only for a particular class of ideas; whereas the antithesis of object and subject is the common form of all these classes, is that form under which alone any idea of whatever kind it may be, abstract or intuitive, pure or empirical, is possible and thinkable. No truth therefore is more certain, more independent of all others, and less in need of proof than this, that all that exists for knowledge, and therefore this whole world, is only object in relation to subject, perception of a perceiver, in a word, idea. This is obviously true of the past and the future, as well as of the present, of what is farthest off, as of what is near; for it is true of time and space themselves, in which alone these distinctions arise. All that in any way belongs or can belong to the world is inevitably thus conditioned through the subject, and exists only for the subject. The world is idea.

---

* Translated by R. B. Haldane and J. Kemp. Reprinted from *The Philosophy of Schopenhauer,* ed. Irwin Edman, N. Y.: Modern Library, 1928. *Die Welt als Wille und Vorstellung* was first published in 1818; to the second edition (1844) Schopenhauer added an appendix of fifty chapters, expanding and clarifying many of his principles. The present abridgment consists of approximately one-fifth of the original work.

This truth is by no means new. It was implicitly involved in the skeptical reflections from which Descartes started. Berkeley, however, was the first who distinctly enunciated it, and by this he has rendered a permanent service to philosophy, even though the rest of his teaching should not endure. Kant's primary mistake was the neglect of this principle, as is shown in the appendix. How early again this truth was recognized by the wise men of India, appearing indeed as the fundamental tenet of the Vedânta philosophy ascribed to Vyasa, is pointed out by Sir William Jones in the last of his essays: "On the philosophy of the Asiatics" (*Asiatic Researches,* Vol. IV., p. 164), where he says, "The fundamental tenet of the Vedânta school consisted not in denying the existence of matter, that is, of solidity, impenetrability, and extended figure (to deny which would be lunacy), but in correcting the popular notion of it, and in contending that it has no essence independent of mental perception; that existence and perceptibility are convertible terms." These words adequately express the compatibility of empirical reality and transcendental ideality

In this first book, then, we consider the world only from this side, only so far as it is idea. The inward reluctance with which any one accepts the world as merely his idea, warns him that this view of it, however true it may be, is nevertheless one-sided, adopted in consequence of some arbitrary abstraction. And yet it is a conception from which he can never free himself. The defectiveness of this view will be corrected in the next book by means of a truth which is not so immediately certain as that from which we start here; a truth at which we can arrive only by deeper research and more severe abstraction, by the separation of what is different and the union of what is identical. This truth, which must be very serious and impressive if not awful to every one, is that a man can also say and must say, "the world is my will." . . .

§ 2. That which knows all things and is known by none is the subject. Thus it is the supporter of the world, that condition of all phenomena, of all objects, which is always presupposed throughout experience; for all that exists, exists only for the subject. Every one finds himself to be subject, yet only in so far as he knows, not in so far as he is an object of knowledge. But his body is object, and therefore from this point of view we call it idea. For the body is an object among objects, and is conditioned by the laws of objects, although it is an immediate object. Like all objects of perception, it lies within the universal forms of knowledge, time and space, which are the conditions of multiplicity. The subject, on the contrary, which is always the knower, never the known, does not come under these forms, but is presupposed by them; it has therefore neither multiplicity nor its opposite unity. We never know it, but it is always the knower wherever there is knowledge.

So then the world as idea, the only aspect in which we consider it at present, has two fundamental, necessary, and inseparable halves. The one half is the object, the forms of which are space and time, and through these multiplicity. The other half is the subject, which is not in space and time, for it is present, entire and undivided, in every percipient being. So that any one percipient being, with the object, constitutes the whole world as idea just as fully as the existing millions could do; but if this one were to disappear, then the whole world as idea would cease to be. These halves are therefore inseparable even for thought, for each of the two has meaning and existence only through and for the other, each appears with the other and vanishes with it. They limit each other immediately; where the object begins the subject ends. The universality of this limitation is shown by the fact that the essential and hence universal forms of all objects, space, time, and causality, may, without knowledge of the object, be discovered and fully known from a consideration of the subject, *i.e.,* in Kantian language, they lie *a priori* in our consciousness. That he discovered this, is one of Kant's principal merits, and it is a great one. I however go beyond this, and maintain that the principle of sufficient reason is the general expression for all these forms of the object of which we are *a priori* conscious; and that therefore all that we know purely *a priori* is merely the content of that principle and what follows from it; in it all our certain *a priori* knowledge is expressed. . . .

§ 3. The chief distinction among our ideas is that between ideas of perception and abstract ideas. The latter form just one class of ideas, namely concepts, and these are the possession of man alone of all creatures upon earth. The capacity for these, which distinguishes him from all the lower animals, has always been called reason. We shall consider these abstract ideas by themselves later, but, in the first place, we shall speak exclusively of the *ideas of perception.* These comprehend the whole visible world, or the sum total of experience, with the conditions of its possibility. . . .

This quality of the universal forms of intuition, which was discovered by Kant, that they may be perceived in themselves and apart from experience, and that they may be known as exhibiting those laws on which is founded the infallible science of mathematics, is certainly very important. Not less worthy of remark, however, is this other quality of time and space, that the principle of sufficient reason, which conditions experience as the law of causation and of motive, and thought as the law of the basis of judgment, appears here in quite a special form, to which I have given the name of the ground of being. In time, this is the succession of its moments, and in space the position of its parts, which reciprocally determine each other *ad infinitum*.

Anyone who has fully understood from the introductory essay (*On the Fourfold Root of the Principle of Sufficient Reason*) the complete identity of the content of the principle of sufficient reason in all its different forms, must also be convinced of the importance of the knowledge of the simplest of these forms, as affording him insight into his own inmost nature. This simplest form of the principle we have found to be time. In it each instant is, only in so far as it has effaced the preceding one, its generator, to be itself in turn as quickly effaced. The past and the future (considered apart from the consequences of their content) are empty as a dream, and the present is only the indivisible and unenduring boundary between them. And in all the other forms of the principle of sufficient reason, we shall find the same emptiness, and shall see that not time only but also space, and the whole content of both of them, *i.e.*, all that proceeds from causes and motives, has a merely relative existence, is only through and for another like to itself, *i.e.*, not more enduring. The substance of this doctrine is old: it appears in Heraclitus when he laments the eternal flux of things; in Plato when he degrades the object to that which is ever becoming, but never being; in Spinoza as the doctrine of the mere accidents of the one substance which is and endures. Kant opposes what is thus known as the mere phenomenon to the thing in itself. Lastly, the ancient wisdom of the Indian philosophers declares, "It is Mâyâ, the veil of deception, which blinds the eyes of mortals, and makes them behold a world of which they cannot say either that it is or that it is not: for it is like a dream; it is like the sunshine on the sand which the traveller takes from afar for water, or the stray piece of rope he mistakes for a snake." (These similes are repeated in innumerable passages of the Vedas and the Puranas.) But what all these mean, and that of which they all speak, is nothing more than what we have just considered—the world as idea subject to the principle of sufficient reason.

§ 4. Whoever has recognized the form of the principle of sufficient reason, which appears in pure time as such, and on which all counting and arithmetical calculation rests, has completely mastered the nature of time. Time is nothing more than that form of the principle of sufficient reason, and has no further significance. Succession is the form of the principle of sufficient reason in time, and succession is the whole nature of time. Further, whoever has recognized the principle of sufficient reason as it appears in the presentation of pure space, has exhausted the whole nature of space, which is absolutely nothing more than that possibility of the reciprocal determination of its parts by each other, which is called position. The detailed treatment of this, and the formulation in abstract conceptions of the results which flow from it, so that they may be more conveniently used, is the subject of the science of geometry. Thus also, whoever has recognized the law of causation, the aspect of the principle of sufficient reason which appears in what fills these forms (space and time) as objects of perception, that is to say, matter, has completely mastered the nature of matter as such, for matter is nothing more than causation, as any one will see at once if he reflects. Its true being is its action, nor can we possibly conceive it as having any other meaning. Only as active does it fill space and time; its action upon the immediate object (which is itself matter) determines that perception in which alone it exists. The consequence of the action of any material object upon any other, is known only in so far as the latter acts upon the immediate object in a different way from that in which it acted before; it consists only of this. Cause and effect thus constitute the whole nature of matter; its true being is its action. (A fuller treatment of this will be found in the essay on the Principle of Sufficient Reason, § 21.) The nature of all material things is therefore very appropriately called in German, "Wirklichkeit," a word which is far more expressive than "Realität." Again, that which is acted upon is always matter, and thus the whole being and essence of matter consists in the orderly change which one part of it brings about in another part. The existence of matter is therefore entirely relative, according to a relation which is valid only within its limits, as in the case of time and space. . . .

§ 5. It is needful to guard against the grave error of supposing that because perception arises through the knowledge of causality, the relation of subject and object is that of cause and effect. For this relation subsists only between the immediate object and objects known indirectly, thus always between objects alone. It is this false supposition that has given rise to the foolish controversy about the reality of the outer world; a controversy in which dogmatism and skepticism oppose each other, and the former appears, now as realism, now as idealism. Realism treats the object as cause, and the subject as its effect. The idealism of Fichte reduces the object to the effect of the subject. Since however, and this cannot be too much emphasized, there is absolutely no relation according to the principle of sufficient reason between subject and object, neither of these views could be proved, and therefore skepticism attacked them both with success. Now, just as the law of causality precedes perception and experience as their condition, and therefore cannot (as Hume thought) be derived from them, so object and subject precede all knowledge, and hence the principle of sufficient reason in general, as its first condition; for this principle is merely the form of all objects, the whole nature and possibility of their existence as phenomena: but the object always presupposes the subject; and therefore between these two there can be no relation of reason and consequent. My essay on the principle of sufficient reason accomplishes just this: it explains the content of that principle as the essential form of every object—that is to say, as the universal nature of all objective existence, as something which pertains to the object as such; but the object as such always presupposes the subject as its necessary correlative; and therefore the subject remains always outside the province in which the principle of sufficient reason is valid. The controversy as to the reality of the outer world rests upon this false extension of the validity of the principle of sufficient reason to the subject also, and starting with this mistake it can never understand itself. On the one side realistic dogmatism, looking upon the idea as the effect of the object, desires to separate these two, idea and object, which are really one, and to assume a cause quite different from the idea, an object in itself, independent of the subject, a thing which is quite inconceivable; for even as object it presupposes subject, and so remains its idea. Opposed to this doctrine is skepticism, which makes the same false presupposition that in the idea we have only the effect, never the cause, therefore never real being; that we always know merely the action of the object. But this object, it supposes, may perhaps have no resemblance whatever to its effect, may indeed have been quite erroneously received as the cause, for the law of causality is first to be gathered from experience, and the reality of experience is then made to rest upon it. Thus both of these views are open to the correction, firstly, that object and idea are the same; secondly, that the true being of the object of perception is its action, that the reality of the thing consists in this, and the demand for an existence of the object outside the idea of the subject, and also for an essence of the actual thing different from its action, has absolutely no meaning, and is a contradiction: and that the knowledge of the nature of the effect of any perceived object, exhausts such an object itself, so far as it is object, *i.e.*, idea, for beyond this there is nothing more to be known. So far then, the perceived world in space and time, which makes itself known as causation alone, is entirely real, and is throughout simply what it appears to be, and it appears wholly and without reserve as idea, bound together according to the law of causality. This is its empirical reality. On the other hand, all causality is in the understanding alone, and for the understanding. The whole actual, that is, active world is determined as such through the understanding, and apart from it is nothing. This, however, is not the only reason for altogether denying such a reality of the outer world as is taught by the dogmatist, who explains its reality as its independence of the subject. We also deny it, because no object apart from a subject can be conceived without contradiction. The whole world of objects is and remains idea, and therefore wholly and for ever determined by the subject; that is to say, it has transcendental ideality. But it is not therefore illusion or mere appearance; it presents itself as that which it is, idea, and indeed as a series of ideas of which the common bond is the principle of sufficient reason. . . .

§ 6. For the present, however, in this first book we consider everything merely as idea, as object for the subject. And our own body, which is the starting point for each of us in our perception of the world, we consider, like all other real objects, from the side of its knowableness, and in this regard it is simply an idea. Now the consciousness of every one is in general opposed to the explanation of objects as mere ideas, and more especially to the explanation of our bodies as such; for the thing in itself is known to each of us immediately in so far as it appears as our own body; but in so far as it objectifies itself in the other objects of perception, it is known only indirectly. But this abstraction, this one-sided treatment, this forcible separation of what is essentially and necessarily united, is only adopted to meet the demands of our argument; and therefore the disinclination to it must, in the meantime, be suppressed and silenced by the expectation that the subsequent treatment will correct the one-sidedness of the present one, and complete our knowledge of the nature of the world.

At present therefore the body is for us immediate object; that is to say, that idea which forms the starting point of the subject's knowledge; because the body, with its immediately known changes, precedes the application of the law of causality, and thus supplies it with its first data. The whole nature of matter consists, as we have seen, in its causal action. But cause and effect exist only for the understanding, which is nothing but their subjective correlative. The understanding, however, could never come into operation if there were not something else from which it starts. This is simple sensation —the immediate consciousness of the changes of the body, by virtue of which it is immediate object. Thus the possibility of knowing the world of perception depends upon two conditions; the first, *objectively expressed,* is the power of material things to act upon each other, to produce changes in each other, without which common quality of all bodies no perception would be possible, even by means of the sensibility of the animal body. And if we wish to express this condition *subjectively* we say: The understanding first makes perception possible; for the law of causality, the possibility of effect and cause, springs only from the understanding, and is valid only for it, and therefore the world of perception exists only through and for it. The second condition is the sensibility of animal bodies, or the quality of being immediate objects of the subject which certain bodies possess. The mere modification which the organs of sense sustain from without through their specific affections, may here be called ideas, so far as these affections produce neither pain nor pleasure, that is, have no immediate significance for the will, and are yet perceived, exist therefore only for *knowledge.* Thus far, then, I say that the body is immediately *known,* is *immediate object.* But the conception of object is not to be taken here in its fullest sense, for through this immediate knowledge of the body, which precedes the operation of the understanding, and is mere sensation, our own body does not exist specifically as *object,* but first the material things which affect it: for all knowledge of an object proper, of an idea perceived in space, exists only through and for the understanding; therefore not before, but only subsequently to its operation. Therefore the body as object proper, that is, an idea perceived in space, is first known indirectly, like all other objects, through the application of the law of causality to the action of one of its parts upon another, as, for example, when the eye sees the body or the hand touches it. Consequently the form of our body does not become known to us through mere feeling, but only through knowledge, only in idea; that is to say, only in the brain does our own body first come to appear as extended, articulate, organic. A man born blind receives this idea only little by little from the data afforded by touch. A blind man without hands could never come to know his own form; or at the most could infer and construct it little by little from the effects of other bodies upon him. If, then, we call the body an immediate object, we are to be understood with these reservations. . . .

§ 7. With reference to our exposition up to this point, it must be observed that we did not start either from the object or the subject, but from the idea, which contains and presupposes them both; for the antithesis of object and subject is its primary, universal, and essential form. We have therefore first considered this form as such; then (though in this respect reference has for the most part been made to the introductory essay) the subordinate forms of time, space, and causality. The latter belong exclusively to the *object,* and yet, as they are essential to the object *as such,* and as the object again is essential to the subject *as such,* they may be discovered from the subject, *i.e.,* they may be known *a priori,* and so far they are to be regarded as the common limits of both. But all these forms may be referred to one general expression, the principle of sufficient reason, as we have explained in the introductory essay.

This procedure distinguishes our philosophical method from that of all former systems. For they all start either from the object or from the subject, and therefore seek to explain the one from the other, and this according to the principle of sufficient reason. We, on the contrary, deny the validity of this principle with reference to the relation of subject and object, and confine it to the object. It may be thought that the philosophy of identity, which has appeared and become generally known in our own day, does not come under either of the alternatives we have named, for it does not start either from the subject or from the object, but from the absolute, known through "intellectual intuition," which is neither object nor subject, but the identity of the two. I will not venture to speak of this revered identity, and this absolute, for I find myself entirely devoid of all "intellectual intuition." But as I take my stand merely on those manifestoes of the "intellectual intuiter" which are open to all, even to profane persons like myself, I must yet observe that this philosophy is not to be excepted from the alternative errors mentioned above. For it does not escape these two opposite errors in spite of its identity of subject and object, which is not thinkable, but only "intellectually intuitable," or to be experienced by a losing of oneself in it. On the contrary, it combines them both in itself; for it is divided into two parts, firstly, transcendental idealism, which is just Fichte's doctrine of the *ego,* and therefore teaches that the object is produced by the subject, or evolved out of it in accordance with the principle of sufficient reason; secondly, the philosophy of nature, which teaches that the subject is produced little by little from the object, by means of a method called construction, about which I understand very little, yet enough to know that it is a process according to various forms of the principle of sufficient reason. The deep wisdom itself which that construction contains, I renounce; for as I entirely lack "intellectual intuition," all those expositions which presuppose it must for me remain as a book sealed with seven seals. This is so truly the case that, strange to say, I have always been unable to find anything at all in this doctrine of profound wisdom but atrocious and wearisome bombast. . . .

Of all systems of philosophy which start from the object, the most consistent, and that which may be carried furthest, is simple materialism. It regards matter, and with it time and space, as existing absolutely, and ignores the relation to the subject in which alone all this really exists. It then lays hold of the law of causality as a guiding principle or clue, regarding it as a self-existent order (or arrangement) of things, *veritas æterna,* and so fails to take account of the understanding, in which and for which alone causality is. It seeks the primary and most simple state of matter, and then tries to develop all the others from it; ascending from mere mechanism to chemism, to polarity, to the vegetable and to the animal kingdom. And if we suppose this to have been done, the last link in the chain would be animal sensibility—that is, knowledge—which would consequently now appear as a mere modification or state of matter produced by causality. Now if we had followed materialism thus far with clear ideas, when we reached its highest point we would suddenly be seized with a fit of the inextinguishable laughter of the Olympians. As if waking from a dream, we would all at once become aware that its final result, knowledge, which it reached so laboriously, was presupposed as the indispensable condition of its very starting-point, mere matter; and when we imagined that we thought matter, we really thought only the subject that perceives matter; the eye that sees it, the hand that feels it, the understanding that knows it. Thus the tremendous *petitio principii* reveals itself unexpectedly; for suddenly the last link is seen to be the starting-point, the chain a circle, and the materialist is like Baron Münchausen who, when swimming in water on horseback, drew the horse into the air with his legs, and himself also by his cue. . . .

"No object without a subject" is the principle which renders all materialism forever impossible. Suns and planets without an eye that sees them, and an understanding that knows them, may indeed be spoken of in words, but for the idea, these words are absolutely meaningless. On the other hand, the law of causality and the treatment and investigation of nature which is based upon it, lead us necessarily to the conclusion that, in time, each more highly organized state of matter has succeeded a cruder state: so that the lower animals existed before men, fishes before land animals, plants before fishes, and the unorganized before all that is organized; that, consequently, the original mass had to pass through a long series of changes before the first eye could be opened. And yet, the existence of this whole world remains ever dependent upon the first eye that opened, even if it were that of an insect. For such an eye is a necessary condition of the possibility of knowledge, and the whole world exists only in and for knowledge, and without it is not even thinkable. The world is entirely idea, and as such demands the knowing subject as the supporter of its existence. This long course of time itself, filled with innumerable changes, through which matter rose from form to form till at last the first percipient creature appeared—this whole time itself is only thinkable in the identity of a consciousness whose succession of ideas, whose form of knowing it is, and apart from which it loses all meaning and is nothing at all. Thus we see, on the one hand, the existence of the whole world necessarily dependent upon the first conscious being, however undeveloped it may be; on the other hand, this conscious being just as necessarily entirely dependent upon a long chain of causes and effects which have preceded it, and in which it itself appears as a small link. These two contradictory points of view, to each of which we are led with the same necessity, we might again call an *antinomy* in our faculty of knowledge, and set it up as the counterpart of that which we found in the first extreme of natural science. The objective world, the world as idea, is not the only side of the world, but merely its outward side; and it has an entirely different side—the side of its inmost nature—its kernel—the thing-in-itself. This we shall consider in the second book, calling it after the most immediate of its objective manifestations—will. But the world as idea, with which alone we are here concerned, only appears with the opening of the first eye. Without this medium of knowledge it cannot be, and therefore it was not before it. . . .

Opposed to the system we have explained, which starts from the object in order to derive the subject from it, is the system which starts from the subject and tries to derive the object from it. The first of these has been of frequent and common occurrence throughout the history of philosophy, but of the second we find only one example, and that a very recent one: the "philosophy of appearance" of J. G. Fichte. . . . This philosophy of Fichte, otherwise not worth mentioning, is interesting to us only as the tardy expression of the converse of the old materialism. For materialism was the most consistent system starting from the object, as this is the most consistent system starting from the subject. Materialism overlooked the fact that, with the simplest object, it assumed the subject also; and Fichte overlooked the fact that with the subject (whatever he may call it) he assumed the object also, for no subject is thinkable without an object. . . .

§ 8. As from the direct light of the sun to the borrowed light of the moon, we pass from the immediate idea of perception, which stands by itself and is its own warrant, to reflection, to the abstract, discursive concepts of the reason, which obtain their whole content from knowledge of perception, and in relation to it. As long as we continue simply to perceive, all is clear, firm, and certain. There are neither questions nor doubts nor errors; we desire to go no further, can go no further; we find rest in perceiving, and satisfaction in the present. Perception suffices for itself, and therefore what springs purely from it, and remains true to it, for example, a genuine work of art, can never be false, nor can it be discredited through the lapse of time, for it does not present an opinion but the thing itself. But with abstract knowledge, with reason, doubt and error appear in the theoretical, care and sorrow in the practical. In the idea of perception, illusion may at moments take the place of the real; but in the sphere of abstract thought, error may reign for a thousand years, impose its yoke upon whole nations, extend to the noblest impulses of humanity, and, by the help of its slaves and its dupes, may chain and fetter those whom it cannot deceive. It is the enemy against which the wisest men of all times have waged unequal war, and only what they have won from it has become the possession of mankind. Therefore it is well to draw attention to it at once, as we already tread the ground to which its province belongs. It has often been said that we ought to follow truth even although no utility can be seen in it, because it may have indirect utility which may appear when it is least expected; and I would add to this, that we ought to be just as anxious to discover and to root out all error even when no harm is anticipated from it, because its mischief may be very indirect, and may suddenly appear when we do not expect it, for all error has poison at its heart. If it is mind, if it is knowledge, that makes man the lord of creation, there can be no such thing as harmless error, still less venerable and holy error. And for the consolation of those who in any way and at any time may have devoted strength and life to the noble and hard battle against error, I cannot refrain from adding that, so long as truth is absent, error will have free play, as owls and bats in the night; but sooner would we expect to see the owls and the bats drive back the sun in the eastern heavens, than that any truth which has once been known and distinctly and fully expressed can ever again be so utterly vanquished and overcome that the old error shall once more reign undisturbed over its wide kingdom. This is the power of truth; its conquest is slow and laborious, but if once the victory be gained it can never be wrested back again. . . .

§ 9. . . . Although concepts are fundamentally different from ideas of perception, they stand in a necessary relation to them, without which they would be nothing. This relation therefore constitutes the whole nature and existence of concepts. Reflection is the necessary copy or repetition of the originally presented world of perception, but it is a special kind of copy in an entirely different material. Thus concepts may quite properly be called ideas of ideas. . . .

§ 10. . . . Reason is feminine in nature; it can only give after it has received. Of itself it has nothing but the empty forms of its operation. There is no absolutely pure rational knowledge except the four principles to which I have attributed metalogical truth; the principles of identity, contradiction, excluded middle, and sufficient reason of knowledge. For even the rest of logic is not absolutely pure rational knowledge. It presupposes the relations and the combinations of the spheres of concepts. But concepts in general only exist after experience of ideas of perception, and as their whole nature consists in their relation to these, it is clear that they presuppose them. No special content, however, is presupposed, but merely the existence of a content generally, and so logic as a whole may fairly pass for pure rational science. In all other sciences reason has received its content from ideas of perception; in mathematics from the relations of space and time, presented in intuition or perception prior to all experience; in pure natural science, that is, in what we know of the course of nature prior to any experience, the content of the science proceeds from the pure understanding, *i.e.,* from the *a priori* knowledge of the law of causality and its connection with those pure intuitions or perceptions of space and time. In all other sciences everything that is not derived from the sources we have just referred to belongs to experience. Speaking generally, *to know rationally* (*wissen*) means to have in the power of the mind, and capable of being reproduced at will, such judgments as have their sufficient ground of knowledge in something outside themselves, *i.e.,* are true. . . .

§ 12. *Rational knowledge* is then all abstract knowledge—that is, the knowledge which is peculiar to the reason as distinguished from the understanding. Now, as reason only reproduces, for knowledge, what has been received in another way, it does not actually extend our knowledge, but only gives it another form. It enables us to know in the abstract and generally, what first became known in sense-perception, in the concrete. But this is much more important than it appears at first sight when so expressed. For it depends entirely upon the fact that knowledge has become rational or abstract knowledge, that it can be safely preserved, that it is communicable and susceptible of certain and wide-reaching application to practice. Knowledge in the form of sense-perception is valid only of the particular case, extends only to what is nearest, and ends with it, for sensibility and understanding can only comprehend one object at a time. Every enduring, arranged, and planned activity must therefore proceed from principles (that is, from abstract knowledge) and it must be conducted in accordance with them. Thus, for example, the knowledge of the relation of cause and effect arrived at by the understanding, is in itself far completer, deeper and more exhaustive than anything that can be thought about it in the abstract; the understanding alone knows in perception directly and completely the nature of the effect of a lever, of a pulley, or a cog-wheel, the stability of an arch, and so forth. But on account of the peculiarity of the knowledge of perception just referred to, that it only extends to what is immediately present, the mere understanding can never enable us to construct machines and buildings. Here reason must come in; it must substitute abstract concepts for ideas of perception, and take them as the guide of action; and if they are right, the anticipated result will happen. In the same way we have perfect knowledge in pure perception of the nature and constitution of the parabola, hyperbola, and spiral; but if we are to make trustworthy application of this knowledge to the real, it must first become abstract knowledge, and by this it certainly loses its character of intuition or perception, but on the other hand it gains the certainty and preciseness of abstract knowledge. The differential calculus does not really extend our knowledge of the curve, it contains nothing that was not already in the mere pure perception of the curve; but it alters the kind of knowledge, it changes the intuitive into an abstract knowledge, which is so valuable for application. . . .

The greatest value of rational or abstract knowledge is that it can be communicated and permanently retained. It is principally on this account that it is so inestimably important for practice. Anyone may have a direct perceptive knowledge through the understanding alone, of the causal connection, of the changes and motions of natural bodies, and he may find entire satisfaction in it; but he cannot communicate this knowledge to others until it has been made permanent for thought in concepts. Knowledge of the first kind is even sufficient for practice, if a man puts his knowledge into practice himself, in an action which can be accomplished while the perception is still vivid; but it is not sufficient if the help of others is required, or even if the action is his own but must be carried out at different times, and therefore requires a preconceived plan. Thus, for example, a practiced billiard player may have a perfect knowledge of the laws of the impact of elastic bodies upon each other, merely in the understanding, merely for direct perception; and for him it is quite sufficient; but on the other hand it is only the man who has studied the science of mechanics who has, properly speaking, a rational knowledge of these laws, that is, a knowledge of them in the abstract. . . . It is, however, remarkable that in the first kind of activity—in which we have supposed that one man alone, in an uninterrupted course of action, accomplishes something—abstract knowledge, the application of reason or reflection, may often be a hindrance to him; for example in the case of billiard playing, of fighting, of tuning an instrument, or in the case of singing. Here perceptive knowledge must directly guide action; its passage through reflection makes it uncertain, for it divides the attention and confuses the man. . . . In the same way it is of no use to me to know in the abstract the exact angle in degrees and minutes at which I must apply a razor if I do not know it intuitively, that is, if I have not got it in my touch. The knowledge of physiognomy, also, is interfered with by the application of reason. This knowledge must be gained directly through the understanding. We say that the expression, the meaning of the features, can only be *felt,* that is, it cannot be put into abstract concepts. Every man has his direct intuitive method of physiognomy and pathognomy, yet one man understands more clearly than another these *signatura rerum*. But an abstract science of physiognomy to be taught and learned is not possible; for the distinctions of difference are here so fine that concepts cannot reach them; therefore abstract knowledge is related to them as a mosaic is to a painting by a Van der Werft or a Denner. In mosaics, however fine they may be, the limits of the stones are always there, and therefore no continuous passage from one color to another is possible, and this is also the case with regard to concepts, with their rigidity and sharp delineation; however finely we may divide them by exact definition they are still incapable of reaching the finer modifications of the perceptible, and this is just what happens in the example we have taken, knowledge of physiognomy.

This quality of concepts by which they resemble the stones of a mosaic, and on account of which perception always remains their asymptote, is the reason why nothing good is produced in art by their means. If the singer or the virtuoso attempts to guide his execution by reflection he remains silent. And this is equally true of the composer, the painter, and the poet. The concept always remains unfruitful in art; it can only direct the technical part of it, its sphere is science. . . .

Lastly, virtue and holiness do not proceed from reflection, but from the inner depths of the will, and its relation to knowledge. The exposition of this belongs to another part of our work; this, however, I may remark here, that the dogmas relating to ethics may be the same in the reason of whole nations, but the action of every individual different; and the converse also holds good; action, we say, is guided by *feelings*—that is, simply not by concepts, but as a matter of fact by the ethical character. Dogmas occupy the idle reason; but action in the end pursues its own course independently of them, generally not according to abstract rules, but according to unspoken maxims, the expression of which is the whole man himself. Therefore, however different the religious dogmas of nations may be, yet in the case of all of them, a good action is accompanied by unspeakable satisfaction, and a bad action by endless remorse. No mockery can shake the former; no priest's absolution can deliver from the latter. Notwithstanding this, we must allow that for the pursuit of a virtuous life, the application of reason is needful; only it is not its source, but has the subordinate function of preserving resolutions which have been made, of providing maxims to withstand the weakness of the moment, and give consistency to action. It plays the same part ultimately in art also, where it has just as little to do with the essential matter, but assists in carrying it out, for genius is not always at call, and yet the work must be completed in all its parts and rounded off to a whole.

As regards the *content* of the sciences generally, it is, in fact, always the relation of the phenomena of the world to each other, according to the principle of sufficient reason, under the guidance of the *why,* which has validity and meaning only though this principle. *Explanation* is the establishment of this relation. Therefore explanation can never go further than to show two ideas standing to each other in the relation peculiar to that form of the principle of sufficient reason which reigns in the class to which they belong. If this is done we cannot further be asked the question, *why:* for the relation proved is that one which absolutely cannot be imagined as other than it is, *i.e.,* it is the form of all knowledge. Therefore we do not ask why $2 + 2 = 4$; or why the equality of the angles of a triangle determines the equality of the sides; or why its effect follows any given cause; or why the truth of the conclusion is evident from the truth of the premises. Every explanation which does not ultimately lead to a relation of which no "why" can further be demanded, stops at an accepted *qualitas occulta;* but this is the character of every original force of nature. Every explanation in natural science must ultimately end with such a *qualitas occulta,* and thus with complete obscurity. It must leave the inner nature of a stone just as much unexplained as that of a human being; it can give as little account of the weight, the cohesion, the chemical qualities, &c., of the former, as of the knowing and acting of the latter. . . . Philosophy is the most general rational knowledge, the first principles of which cannot therefore be derived from another principle still more general. The principle of contradiction establishes merely the agreement of concepts, but does not itself produce concepts. The principle of sufficient reason explains the connections of phenomena, but not the phenomena themselves; therefore philosophy cannot proceed upon these principles to seek a *causa efficiens* or a *causa finalis* of the whole world. My philosophy, at least, does not by any means seek to know *whence* or *wherefore* the world exists, but merely *what* the world is. But the *why* is here subordinated to the *what,* for it already belongs to the world, as it arises and has meaning and validity only through the form of its phenomena, the principle of sufficient reason. We might indeed say that every one knows what the world is without help, for he is himself that subject of knowledge of which the world is the idea; and so far this would be true. But that knowledge is empirical, is in the concrete; the task of philosophy is to reproduce this in the abstract, to raise to permanent rational knowledge the successive changing perceptions, and in general, all that is contained under the wide concept of feeling and merely negatively defined as not abstract, distinct, rational knowledge. It must therefore consist of a statement in the abstract, of the nature of the whole world, of the whole and of all the parts. . . .

SECOND BOOK: THE WORLD AS WILL

FIRST ASPECT: *The Objectification of the Will*

§ 17. . . . But what now impels us to inquiry is just that we are not satisfied with knowing that we have ideas, that they are such and such, and that they are connected according to certain laws, the general expression of which is the principle of sufficient reason. We wish to know the significance of these ideas; we ask whether this world is merely idea; in which case it would pass by us like an empty dream or a baseless vision, not worth our notice; or whether it is also something else, something more than idea, and if so, what. This much is certain, that this something we seek for must be completely and in its whole nature different from the idea; that the forms and laws of the idea must therefore be completely foreign to it; further, that we cannot arrive at it from the idea under the guidance of the laws which merely combine objects, ideas, among themselves, and which are the forms of the principle of sufficient reason.

Thus we see already that we can never arrive at the real nature of things from without. However much we investigate, we can never reach anything but images and names. We are like a man who goes round a castle seeking in vain for an entrance, and sometimes sketching the façades. And yet this is the method that has been followed by all philosophers before me.

§ 18. In fact, the meaning for which we seek of that world which is present to us only as our idea, or the transition from the world as mere idea of the knowing subject to whatever it may be besides this, would never be found if the investigator himself were nothing more than the pure knowing subject (a winged cherub without a body). But he is himself rooted in that world; he finds himself in it as an *individual,* that is to say, his knowledge, which is the necessary supporter of the whole world as idea, is yet always given through the medium of a body, whose affections are, as we have shown, the starting-point for the understanding in the perception of that world. His body is, for the pure knowing subject, an idea like every other idea, an object among objects. Its movements and actions are so far known to him in precisely the same way as the changes of all other perceived objects, and would be just as strange and incomprehensible to him if their meaning were not explained for him in an entirely different way. Otherwise he would see his actions follow upon given motives with the constancy of a law of nature, just as the changes of other objects follow upon causes, stimuli, or motives. But he would not understand the influence of the motives any more than the connection between every other effect which he sees and its cause. He would then call the inner nature of these manifestations and actions of his body which he did not understand a force, a quality, or a character, as he pleased, but he would have no further insight into it. But all this is not the case; indeed the answer to the riddle is given to the subject of knowledge who appears as an individual, and the answer is *will.* This and this alone gives him the key to his own existence, reveals to him the significance, shows him the inner mechanism of his being, of his action, of his movements. The body is given in two entirely different ways to the subject of knowledge, who becomes an individual only through his identity with it. It is given as an idea in intelligent perception, as an object among objects and subject to the laws of objects. And it is also given in quite a different way as that which is immediately known to every one, and is signified by the word *will*. Every true act of his will is also at once and without exception a movement of his body. The act of will and the movement of the body are not two different things objectively known, which the bond of causality unites; they do not stand in the relation of cause and effect; they are one and the same, but they are given in entirely different ways—immediately, and again in perception for the understanding. The action of the body is nothing but the act of the will objectified, *i.e.,* passed into perception. . . . Thus in a certain sense we may also say that will is the knowledge *a priori* of the body, and the body is the knowledge *a posteriori* of the will. Resolutions of the will which relate to the future are merely deliberations of the reason about what we shall will at a particular time, not real acts of will. Only the carrying out of the resolve stamps it as will, for till then it is never more than an intention that may be changed, and that exists only in the reason *in abstracto*. It is only in reflection that to will and to act are different; in reality they are one. Every true, genuine, immediate act of will is also, at once and immediately, a visible act of the body. And, corresponding to this, every impression upon the body is also, on the other hand, at once and immediately an impression upon the will. As such it is called pain when it is opposed to the will, gratification or pleasure when it is in accordance with it. The degrees of both are widely different. It is quite wrong, how-ever, to call pain and pleasure ideas, for they are by no means ideas but immediately affections of the will in its manifestation, the body; compulsory, instantaneous willing or not-willing of the impression which the body sustains. . . .

§ 19. In the first book we were reluctantly driven to explain the human body as merely idea of the subject which knows it, like all the other objects of this world of perception. But it has now become clear that what enables us consciously to distinguish our own body from all other objects which in other respects are precisely the same, is that our body appears in consciousness in quite another way *toto genere* different from idea, and this we denote by the word *will;* and that it is just this double knowledge which we have of our own body that affords us information about it, about its action and movement following on motives, and also about what it experiences by means of external impressions; in a word, about what it is, not as idea, but as more than idea; that is to say, what it is *in itself*. None of this information have we got directly with regard to the nature, action, and experience of other real objects.

It is just because of this special relation to one body that the knowing subject is an individual. For regarded apart from this relation, his body is for him only an idea like all other ideas. But the relation through which the knowing subject is an *individual,* is just on that account a relation which subsists only between him and one particular idea of all those which he has. Therefore he is conscious of this one idea, not merely as an idea, but in quite a different way as a will. . . . But whether the objects known to the individual only as ideas are yet, like his own body, manifestations of a will, is, as was said in the First Book, the proper meaning of the question as to the reality of the external world. To deny this is *theoretical egoism,* which on that account regards all phenomena that are outside its own will as phantoms, just as in a practical reference exactly the same thing is done by practical egoism. For in it a man regards and treats himself alone as a person, and all other persons as mere phantoms. Theoretical egoism can never be demonstrably refuted, yet in philosophy it has never been used otherwise than as a sceptical sophism, *i.e.,* a pretence. As a serious conviction, on the other hand, it could only be found in a madhouse, and as such it stands in need of a cure rather than a refutation. We do not therefore combat it any further in this regard, but treat it as merely the last stronghold of scepticism, which is always polemical. Thus our knowledge, which is always bound to individuality and is limited by this circumstance, brings with it the necessity that each of us can only *be one,* while, on the other hand, each of us can *know all;* and it is this limitation that creates the need for philosophy. We therefore who, for this very reason, are striving to extend the limits of our knowledge through philosophy, will treat this sceptical argument of theoretical egoism which meets us, as an army would treat a small frontier fortress. The fortress cannot indeed be taken, but the garrison can never sally forth from it, and therefore we pass it by without danger, and are not afraid to have it in our rear.

The double knowledge which each of us has of the nature and activity of his own body, and which is given in two completely different ways, has now been clearly brought out. We shall accordingly make further use of it as a key to the nature of every phenomenon in nature, and shall judge of all objects which are not our own bodies, and are consequently not given to our consciousness in a double way but only as ideas, according to the analogy of our own bodies, and shall therefore assume that as in one aspect they are idea, just like our bodies, and in this respect are analogous to them, so in another aspect, what remains of objects when we set aside their existence as idea of the subject, must in its inner nature be the same as that in us which we call *will*. For what other kind of existence or reality should we attribute to the rest of the material world? Whence should we take the elements out of which we construct such a world? Besides will and idea nothing is known to us or thinkable. If we wish to attribute the greatest known reality to the material world which exists immediately only in our idea, we give it the reality which our own body has for each of us; for that is the most real thing for everyone. But if we now analyze the reality of this body and its actions, beyond the fact that it is idea, we find nothing in it except the will; with this its reality is exhausted. Therefore we can nowhere find another kind of reality which we can attribute to the material world. Thus if we hold that the material world is something more than merely our idea, we must say that besides being idea, that is, in itself and according to its inmost nature, it is that which we find immediately in ourselves as *will*. I say according to its inmost nature; but we must first come to know more accurately this real nature of the will, in order that we may be able to distinguish from it what does not belong to itself, but to its manifestation, which has many grades. . . .

§ 20. As we have said, the will proclaims itself primarily in the voluntary movements of our own body, as the inmost nature of this body, as that which it is besides being object of perception, idea. For these voluntary movements are nothing else but the visible aspect of the individual acts of will, with which they are directly coincident and identical, and only distinguished through the form of knowledge into which they have passed, and in which alone they can be known, the form of idea.

But these acts of will have always a ground or reason outside themselves in motives. Yet these motives never determine more than what I will at *this* time, in *this* place, and under *these* circumstances, not *that* I will in general, or *what* I will in general, that is, the maxims which characterise my volition generally. Therefore the inner nature of my volition cannot be explained from these motives; but they merely determine its manifestation at a given point of time: they are merely the occasion of my will showing itself; but the will itself lies outside the province of the law of motivation, which determines nothing but its appearance at each point of time. It is only under the presupposition of my empirical character that the motive is a sufficient ground of explanation of my action. But if I abstract from my character, and then ask why, in general, I will this and not that, no answer is possible, because it is only the manifestation of the will that is subject to the principle of sufficient reason, and not the will itself, which in this respect is to be called *groundless*. . . .

Thus, although every particular action, under the presupposition of the definite character, necessarily follows from the given motive, and although growth, the process of nourishment, and all the changes of the animal body take place according to necessarily acting causes (stimuli), yet the whole series of actions, and consequently every individual act, and also its condition, the whole body itself which accomplishes it, and therefore also the process through which and in which it exists, are nothing but the manifestation of the will, the becoming visible, *the objectification of the will*. Upon this rests the perfect suitableness of the human and animal body to the human and animal will in general, resembling, though far surpassing, the correspondence between an instrument made for a purpose and the will of the maker, and on this account appearing as design, *i.e.*, the teleological explanation of the body. The parts of the body must, therefore, completely correspond to the principal desires through which the will manifests itself; they must be the visible expression of these desires. Teeth, throat, and bowels are objectified hunger; the organs of generation are objectified sexual desire; the grasping hand, the hurrying feet, correspond to the more indirect desires of the will which they express. As the human form generally corresponds to the human will generally, so the individual bodily structure corresponds to the individually modified will, the character of the individual, and therefore it is throughout and in all parts characteristic and full of expression. . . .

§ 21. Whoever has now gained from all these expositions a knowledge *in abstracto,* and therefore clear and certain, of what every one knows directly *in concreto, i.e.,* as feeling, . . . will find that of itself it affords him the key to the knowledge of the inmost being of the whole of nature; for he now transfers it to all those phenomena which are not given to him, like his own phenomenal existence, both in direct and indirect knowledge, but only in the latter, thus merely one-sidedly as *idea* alone. He will recognize this will of which we are speaking not only in those phenomenal existences which exactly resemble his own, in men and animals as their inmost nature, but the course of reflection will lead him to recognise the force which germinates and vegetates in the plant, and indeed the force through which the crystal is formed, that by which the magnet turns to the north pole, the force whose shock he experiences from the contact of two different kinds of metals, the force which appears in the elective affinities of matter as repulsion and attraction, decomposition and combination, and, lastly, even gravitation, which acts so powerfully throughout matter, draws the stone to the earth and the earth to the sun—all these, I say, he will recognise as different only in their phenomenal existence, but in their inner nature as identical, as that which is directly known to him so intimately and so much better than anything else, and which in its most distinct manifestation is called *will*. It is this application of reflection alone that prevents us from remaining any longer at the phenomenon, and leads us to the *thing-in-itself*. Phenomenal existence is idea and nothing more. All idea, of whatever kind it may be, all *object,* is *phenomenal* existence, but the *will* alone is a *thing-in-itself*. As such, it is throughout not idea, but *toto genere* different from it; it is that of which all idea, all object, is the phenomenal appearance, the visibility, the objectification. It is the inmost nature, the kernel, of every particular thing, and also of the whole. It appears in every blind force of nature and also in the preconsidered action of man; and the great difference between these two is merely in the degree of the manifestation, not in the nature of what manifests itself.

§ 22. Now, if we are to think as an object this thing-in-itself (we wish to retain the Kantian expression as a standing formula), which, as such, is never object, because all object is its mere manifestation, and therefore cannot be it itself, we must borrow for it the name and concept of an object, of something in some way objectively given, consequently of one of its own manifestations. But in order to serve as a clue for the understanding, this can be no other than the most complete of all its manifestations, *i.e.,* the most distinct, the most developed, and directly enlightened by knowledge. Now this is the human will. It is, however, well to observe that here, at any rate, we only make use of a *denominatio a potiori,* through which, therefore, the concept of will receives a greater extension than it has hitherto had. Knowledge of the identical in different phenomena, and of difference in similar phenomena, is, as Plato so often remarks, a *sine qua non* of philosophy. But hitherto it was not recognized that every kind of active and operating force in nature is essentially identical with will, and therefore the multifarious kinds of phenomena were not seen to be merely different species of the same genus, but were treated as heterogeneous. Consequently there could be no word to denote the concept of this genus. I therefore name the genus after its most important species, the direct knowledge of which lies nearer to us and guides us to the indirect knowledge of all other species. But whoever is incapable of carrying out the required extension of the concept will remain involved in a permanent misunderstanding. For by the word *will* he understands only that species of it which has hitherto been exclusively denoted by it, the will which is guided by knowledge, and whose manifestation follows only upon motives, and indeed merely abstract motives, and thus takes place under the guidance of the reason. This, we have said, is only the most prominent example of the manifestation of will. We must now distinctly separate in thought the inmost essence of this manifestation which is known to us directly, and then transfer it to all the weaker, less distinct manifestations of the same nature, and thus we shall accomplish the desired extension of the concept of will. From another point of view I should be equally misunderstood by any one who should think that it is all the same in the end whether we denote this inner nature of all phenomena by the word *will* or by any other. This would be the case if the thing-in-itself were something whose existence we merely *inferred,* and thus knew indirectly and only in the abstract. Then, indeed, we might call it what we pleased; the name would stand merely as the symbol of an unknown quantity. But the world *will,* which, like a magic spell, discloses to us the inmost being of everything in nature, is by no means an unknown quantity, something arrived at only by inference, but is fully and immediately comprehended, and is so familiar to us that we know and understand what will is far better than anything else whatever. The concept of will has hitherto commonly been subordinated to that of force, but I reverse the matter entirely, and desire that every force in nature should be thought as will. It must not be supposed that this is mere verbal quibbling or of no consequence; rather, it is of the greatest significance and importance. For at the foundation of the concept of force, as of all other concepts, there ultimately lies the knowledge in sense-perception of the objective world, that is to say, the phenomenon, the idea; and the concept is constructed out of this. It is an abstraction from the province in which cause and effect reign, *i.e.,* from ideas of perception, and means just the causal nature of causes at the point at which this causal nature is no further etiologically explicable, but is the necessary presupposition of all etiological explanation. The concept will, on the other hand, is of all possible concepts the only one which has its source *not* in the phenomenal, *not* in the mere idea of perception, but comes from within, and proceeds from the most immediate consciousness of each of us, in which each of us knows his own individuality, according to its nature, immediately, apart from all form, even that of subject and object, and which at the same time is this individuality, for here the subject and the object of knowledge are one. If, therefore, we refer the concept of *force* to that of *will,* we have in fact referred the less known to what is infinitely better known; indeed, to the one thing that is really immediately and fully known to us, and have very greatly extended our knowledge. If, on the contrary, we subsume the concept of will under that of force, as has hitherto always been done, we renounce the only immediate knowledge which we have of the inner nature of the world, for we allow it to disappear in a concept which is abstracted from the phenomenal, and with which we can therefore never go beyond the phenomenal. . . .

§ 23. Only those changes which have no other ground than a motive, *i.e.,* an idea, have hitherto been regarded as manifestations of will. Therefore in nature a will has only been attributed to man, or at the most to animals; for knowledge, the idea, is of course, as I have said elsewhere, the true and exclusive characteristic of animal life. But that the will is also active where no knowledge guides it, we see at once in the instinct and the mechanical skill of animals. . . . The bird of a year old has no idea of the eggs for which it builds a nest; the young spider has no idea of the prey for which it spins a web; nor has the ant-lion any idea of the ants for which he digs a trench for the first time. The larva of the stag-beetle makes the hole in the wood, in which it is to await its metamorphosis, twice as big if it is going to be a male beetle as if it is going to be a female, so that if it is a male there may be room for the horns, of which, however, it has no idea. In such actions of these creatures the will is clearly operative as in their other actions, but it is in blind activity, which is indeed accompanied by knowledge but not guided by it. If now we have once gained insight into the fact, that idea as motive is not a necessary and essential condition of the activity of the will, we shall more easily recognise the activity of will where it is less apparent. For example, we shall see that the house of the snail is no more made by a will which is foreign to the snail itself, than the house which we build is produced through another will than our own; but we shall recognise in both houses the work of a will which objectifies itself in both the phenomena—a will which works in us according to motives, but in the snail still blindly as formative impulse directed outwards. In us also the same will is in many ways only blindly active: in all the functions of our body which are not guided by knowledge, in all its vital and vegetative processes, digestion, circulation, secretion, growth, reproduction. Not only the actions of the body, but the whole body itself is, as we have shown above, phenomenon of the will, objectified will, concrete will. All that goes on in it must therefore proceed through will, although here this will is not guided by knowledge, but acts blindly according to causes, which in this case are called *stimuli*. . . .

It only remains for us to take the final step, the extension of our way of looking at things to all those forces which act in nature in accordance with universal, unchangeable laws, in conformity with which the movements of all those bodies take place, which are wholly without organs, and have therefore no susceptibility for stimuli, and have no knowledge, which is the necessary condition of motives. Thus we must also apply the key to the understanding of the inner nature of things, which the immediate knowledge of our own existence alone can give us, to those phenomena of the unorganised world which are most remote from us. And if we consider them attentively, if we observe the strong and unceasing impulse with which the waters hurry to the ocean, the persistency with which the magnet turns ever to the north pole, the readiness with which iron flies to the magnet, the eagerness with which the electric poles seek to be reunited, and which, just like human desire, is increased by obstacles; if we see the crystal quickly and suddenly take form with such wonderful regularity of construction, which is clearly only a perfectly definite and accurately determined impulse in different directions, seized and retained by crystallisation; if we observe the choice with which bodies repel and attract each other, combine and separate, when they are set free in a fluid state, and emancipated from the bonds of rigidity; lastly, if we feel directly how a burden which hampers our body by its gravitation towards the earth, unceasingly presses and strains upon it in pursuit of its one tendency; if we observe all this, I say, it will require no great effort of the imagination to recognize, even at so great a distance, our own nature. That which in us pursues its ends by the light of knowledge, but here, in the weakest of its manifestations, only strives blindly and dumbly in a one-sided and unchangeable manner, must yet in both cases come under the name of will, as it is everywhere one and the same—just as the first dim light of dawn must share the name of sunlight with the rays of the full mid-day. For the name *will* denotes that which is the inner nature of everything in the world, and the one kernel of every phenomenon. . . .

§ 24. . . . Spinoza (Letter 62) says that if a stone which has been projected through the air had consciousness, it would believe that it was moving of its own will. I add to this only that the stone would be right. The impulse given it is for the stone what the motive is for me, and what in the case of the stone appears as cohesion, gravitation, rigidity, is in its inner nature the same as that which I recognize in myself as well, and what the stone also, if knowledge were given to it, would recognize as will. In the passage referred to, Spinoza had in view the necessity with which the stone flies, and he rightly desires to transfer this necessity to that of the particular act of will of a person. I, on the other hand, consider the inner being, which alone imparts meaning and validity to all real necessity (*i.e.,* effect following upon a cause) as its presupposition. In the case of men this is called character; in the case of a stone it is called quality, but it is the same in both. When it is immediately known it is called will. In the stone it has the weakest, and in man the strongest degree of visibility, of objectivity.

§ 26. The lowest grades of the objectification of will are to be found in those most universal forces of nature which partly appear in all matter without exception, as gravity and impenetrability, and partly have shared the given matter among them, so that certain of them reign in one species of matter and others in another species, constituting its specific difference, as rigidity, fluidity, elasticity, electricity, magnetism, chemical properties and qualities of every kind. They are in themselves immediate manifestations of will, just as much as human action; and as such they are groundless, like human character. . . . It is therefore senseless to demand a cause of gravity or electricity, for they are original forces. . . . It is therefore a mistake to say "gravity is the cause of a stone falling"; for the cause in this case is rather the nearness of the earth, because it attracts the stone. Take the earth away and the stone will not fall, although gravity remains. The force itself lies quite outside the chain of causes and effects, which presupposes time, because it only has meaning in relation to it; but the force lies outside time. . . .

In the higher grades of the objectivity of will we see individuality occupy a prominent position, especially in the case of man, where it appears as the great difference of individual characters, *i.e.,* as complete personality, outwardly expressed in strongly marked individual physiognomy, which influences the whole bodily form. None of the brutes have this individuality in anything like so high a degree, though the higher species of them have a trace of it; but the character of the species completely predominates over it, and therefore they have little individual physiognomy. . . .

Thus every universal, original force of nature is nothing but a low grade of the objectification of will, and we call every such grade an eternal *Idea* in Plato's sense. But a *Law of Nature* is the relation of the Idea to the form of its manifestation. This form is time, space, and causality, which are necessarily and inseparably connected and related to each other. Through time and space the Idea multiplies itself in innumerable phenomena, but the order according to which it enters these forms of multiplicity is definitely determined by the law of causality; this law is as it were the norm of the limit of these phenomena of different Ideas, in accordance with which time, space, and matter are assigned to them. This norm is therefore necessarily related to the identity of the aggregate of existing matter, which is the common substratum of all those different phenomena. If all these were not directed to that common matter in the possession of which they must be divided, there would be no need for such a law to decide their claims. They might all at once and together fill a boundless space throughout an endless time. Therefore, because all these phenomena of the eternal Ideas are directed to one and the same matter, must there be a rule for their appearance and disappearance; for if there were not, they would not make way for each other. Thus the law of causality is essentially bound up with that of the permanence of substance; they reciprocally derive significance from each other. Time and space, again, are related to them in the same way. For time is merely the possibility of conflicting states of the same matter, and space is merely the possibility of the permanence of the same matter under all sorts of conflicting states. . . .

§ 27. . . . It follows from all that has been said that it is certainly an error on the part of natural science to seek to refer the higher grades of the objectification of will to the lower; for the failure to recognize, or the denial of, original and self-existing forces of nature is just as wrong as the groundless assumption of special forces when what occurs is merely a peculiar kind of manifestation of what is already known. Thus Kant rightly says that it would be absurd to hope for a blade of grass from a Newton, that is, from one who reduced the blade of grass to the manifestations of physical and chemical forces, of which it was the chance product, and therefore a mere freak of nature, in which no special Idea appeared, *i.e.,* the will did not directly reveal itself in it in a higher and specific grade, but just as in the phenomena of unorganized nature and by chance in this form. On the other hand, it is not to be overlooked that in all Ideas, that is, in all forces of unorganized, and all forms of organized nature, it is *one and the same* will that reveals itself, that is to say, which enters the form of the idea and passes into *objectivity*. Its unity must therefore be also recognizable through an inner relationship between all its phenomena. Now this reveals itself in the higher grades of the objectification of will, where the whole phenomenon is more distinct, thus in the vegetable and animal kingdoms, through the universally prevailing analogy of all forms, the fundamental type which recurs in all phenomena. . . . To discover this fundamental type has been the chief concern, or at any rate the praiseworthy endeavor, of the natural philosophers of the school of Schelling, who have in this respect considerable merit, although in many cases their hunt after analogies in nature degenerated into mere conceits. They have, however, rightly shown that that general relationship and family likeness exists also in the ideas of unorganized nature; for example, between electricity and magnetism, the identity of which was afterwards established; between chemical attraction and gravitation, and so forth. They specially called attention to the fact that *polarity,* that is, the sundering of a force into two qualitatively different and opposed activities striving after reunion, which also shows itself for the most part in space as a dispersion in opposite directions, is a fundamental type of almost all the phenomena of nature, from the magnet and the crystal to man himself. Yet this knowledge has been current in China from the earliest times, in the doctrine of opposition of Yin and Yang. . . .

According to the view I have expressed, the traces of chemical and physical modes of operation will indeed be found in the organism, but it can never be explained from them; because it is by no means a phenomenon even accidentally brought about through the united actions of such forces, but a higher Idea which has overcome these lower Ideas by *subduing assimilation;* for the *one* will which objectifies itself in all Ideas always seeks the highest possible objectification, and has therefore in this case given up the lower grades of its manifestation after a conflict, in order to appear in a higher grade, and one so much the more powerful. No victory without conflict: since the higher Idea or objectification of will can only appear through the conquest of the lower, it endures the opposition of these lower Ideas, which, although brought into subjection, still constantly strive to obtain an independent and complete expression of their being. The magnet that has attracted a piece of iron carries on a perpetual conflict with gravitation, which, as the lower objectification of will, has a prior right to the matter of the iron; and in this constant battle the magnet indeed grows stronger, for the opposition excites it, as it were, to greater effort. In the same way every manifestation of the will, including that which expresses itself in the human organism, wages a constant war against the many physical and chemical forces which, as lower Ideas, have a prior right to that matter. Thus the arm falls which for a while, overcoming gravity, we have held stretched out; thus the pleasing sensation of health, which proclaims the victory of the Idea of the self-conscious organism over the physical and chemical laws, which originally governed the humors of the body, is so often interrupted, and is indeed always accompanied by greater or less discomfort, which arises from the resistance of these forces, and on account of which the vegetative part of our life is constantly attended by slight pain. Thus also digestion weakens all the animal functions, because it requires the whole vital force to overcome the chemical forces of nature by assimilation. Hence also in general the burden of physical life, the necessity of sleep, and, finally, of death; for at last these subdued forces of nature, assisted by circumstances, win back from the organism, wearied even by the constant victory, the matter it took from them, and attain to an unimpeded expression of their being. We may therefore say that every organism expresses the Idea of which it is the image, only after we have subtracted the part of its force which is expended in subduing the lower Ideas that strive with it for matter. This seems to have been running in the mind of Jacob Böhme when he says somewhere that all the bodies of men and animals, and even all plants, are really half dead. According as the subjection in the organism of these forces of nature, which express the lower grades of the objectification of will, is more or less successful, the more or the less completely does it attain to the expression of its Idea; that is to say, the nearer it is to the *ideal* or the further from it— the *ideal* of beauty in its species.

Thus everywhere in nature we see strife, conflict, and alternation of victory, and in it we shall come to recognize more distinctly that variance with itself which is essential to the will. . . . Thus the will to live everywhere preys upon itself, and in different forms is its own nourishment, till finally the human race, because it subdues all the others, regards nature as a manufactory for its use. Yet even the human race, as we shall see in the Fourth Book, reveals in itself with most terrible distinctness this conflict, this variance with itself of the will, and we find *homo homini lupus*. Meanwhile we can recognise this strife, this subjugation, just as well in the lower grades of the objectification of will. Many insects (especially ichneumon-flies) lay their eggs on the skin, and even in the body of the larvæ of other insects, whose slow destruction is the first work of the newly hatched brood. . . . But the bulldog-ant of Australia affords us the most extraordinary example of this kind; for if it is cut in two, a battle begins between the head and the tail. The head seizes the tail with its teeth and the tail defends itself bravely by stinging the head: the battle may last for half an hour, until they die or are dragged away by other ants. This contest takes place every time the experiment is tried. On the banks of the Missouri one sometimes sees a mighty oak the stem and branches of which are so encircled, fettered, and interlaced by a gigantic wild vine, that it withers as if choked. . . .

Thus knowledge generally, rational as well as merely sensuous, proceeds originally from the will itself, belongs to the inner being of the higher grades of its objectification as a mere μηχανη, a means of supporting the individual and the species, just like any organ of the body. Originally destined for the service of the will for the accomplishment of its aims, it remains almost throughout entirely subjected to its service: it is so in all brutes and in almost all men. . . .

§ 28. We have considered the great multiplicity and diversity of the phenomena in which the will objectifies itself, and we have seen their endless and implacable strife with each other. Yet, according to the whole discussion up to this point, the will itself, as thing-in-itself, is by no means included in that multiplicity and change. The diversity of the (Platonic) Ideas, *i.e.,* grades of objectification, the multitude of individuals in which each of these expresses itself, the struggle of forms for matter—all this does not concern it, but is only the manner of its objectification, and only through this has an indirect relation to it, by virtue of which it belongs to the expression of the nature of will for the idea. . . . Although in man, as (Platonic) Idea, the will finds its clearest and fullest objectification, yet man alone could not express its being. In order to manifest the full significance of the will, the Idea of man would need to appear, not alone and sundered from everything else, but accompanied by the whole series of grades, down through all the forms of animals, through the vegetable kingdom to unorganized nature. All these supplement each other in the complete objectification of will; they are as much presupposed by the Idea of man as the blossoms of a tree presuppose leaves, branches, stem, and root; they form a pyramid, of which man is the apex. If fond of similes, one might also say that their manifestations accompany that of man as necessarily as the full daylight is accompanied by all the gradations of twilight, through which, little by little, it loses itself in darkness; or one might call them the echo of man, and say: Animal and plant are the descending fifth and third of man, the inorganic kingdom is the lower octave. . . .

It is only the knowledge of the unity of will as thing-in-itself, in the endless diversity and multiplicity of the phenomena, that can afford us the true explanation of that wonderful, unmistakable analogy of all the productions of nature, that family likeness on account of which we may regard them as variations on the same ungiven theme. So in like measure, through the distinct and thoroughly comprehended knowledge of that harmony, that essential connection of all the parts of the world, that necessity of their gradation which we have just been considering, we shall obtain a true and sufficient insight into the inner nature and meaning of the undeniable *teleology* of all organised productions of nature, which, indeed, we presupposed *a priori,* when considering and investigating them.

This *teleology* is of a twofold description; sometimes an *inner teleology,* that is, an agreement of all the parts of a particular organism, so ordered that the sustenance of the individual and the species results from it, and therefore presents itself as the end of that disposition or arrangement. Sometimes, however, there is an *outward teleology,* a relation of unorganized to organized nature in general, or of particular parts of organized nature to each other, which makes the maintenance of the whole of organized nature, or of the particular animal species, possible, and therefore presents itself to our judgment as the means to this end. . . .

In the beast we see the will to live more naked, as it were, than in the man, in whom it is clothed with so much knowledge, and is, moreover, so veiled through the capacity for dissimulation, that it is almost only by chance, and here and there, that its true nature becomes apparent. In the plant it shows itself quite naked, but also much weaker, as mere blind striving for existence without end or aim. For the plant reveals its whole being at the first glance, and with complete innocence, which does not suffer from the fact that it carries its organs of generation exposed to view on its upper surface, though in all animals they have been assigned to the most hidden part. This innocence of the plant results from its complete want of knowledge. Guilt does not lie in willing, but in willing with knowledge. Every plant speaks to us first of all of its home, of the climate, and the nature of the ground in which it has grown. Therefore, even those who have had little practice easily tell whether an exotic plant belongs to the tropical or the temperate zone, and whether it grows in water, in marshes, on mountain, or on moorland. Besides this, however, every plant expresses the special will of its species, and says something that cannot be uttered in any other tongue. . . .

We must assume that between all these manifestations of the one will there existed a universal and reciprocal adaptation and accommodation of themselves to each other, by which, however, as we shall soon see more clearly, all time-determination is to be excluded, for the Idea lies outside time. In accordance with this, every manifestation must have adapted itself to the surroundings into which it entered, and these again must have adapted themselves to it, although it occupied a much later position in time; and we see this *consensus naturæ* everywhere. Every plant is therefore adapted to its soil and climate, every animal to its element and the prey that will be its food, and is also in some way protected, to a certain extent, against its natural enemy; the eye is adapted to the light and its refrangibility, the lungs and the blood to the air, the air-bladder of fish to water, the eye of the seal to the change of the medium in which it must see, the water-pouch in the stomach of the camel to the drought of the African deserts, the sail of the nautilus to the wind that is to drive its little bark, and so on down to the most special and astonishing outward adaptations.[1] We must abstract however here from all temporal relations, for these can only concern the manifestation of the Idea, not the Idea itself. Accordingly this kind of explanation must also be used retrospectively, and we must not merely admit that every species accommodated itself to the given environment, but also that this environment itself, which preceded it in time, had just as much regard for the being that would some time come into it. For it is one and the same will that objectifies itself in the whole world; it knows no time, for this form of the principle of sufficient reason does not belong to it, nor to its original objectivity, the Ideas, but only to the way in which these are known by the individuals who themselves are transitory, *i.e.,* to the manifestation of the Ideas. . . . The instinct of animals in general gives us the best illustration of what remains of teleology in nature. For as instinct is an action, like that which is guided by the conception of an end, and yet is entirely without this; so all construction of nature resembles that which is guided by the conception of an end, and yet is entirely without it. For in the outer as in the inner teleology of nature, what we are obliged to think as means and end is, in every case, *the manifestation of the unity of the one will so thoroughly agreeing with itself,* which has assumed multiplicity in space and time for our manner of knowing.

The reciprocal adaptation and self-accommodation of phenomena that springs from this unity cannot, however, annul the inner contradiction which appears in the universal conflict of nature described above, and which is essential to the will. That harmony goes only so far as to render possible the duration of the world and the different kinds of existences in it, which without it would long since have

---

[1] See my essay *On the Will in Nature,* the section on comparative anatomy.

perished. Therefore it only extends to the continuance of the species, and the general conditions of life, but not to that of the individual. If, then, by reason of that harmony and accommodation, the *species* in organized nature and the *universal forces* in unorganized nature continue to exist beside each other, and indeed support each other reciprocally, on the other hand, the inner contradiction of the will which objectifies itself in all these ideas shows itself in the ceaseless internecine war of the *individuals* of these species, and in the constant struggle of the *manifestations* of these natural forces with each other, as we pointed out above. The scene and the object of this conflict is matter, which they try to wrest from each other, and also space and time, the combination of which through the form of causality is, in fact, matter, as was explained in the First Book. . . .

§ 29. . . . Every will is a will towards something, has an object, an end of its willing; what then is the final end, or towards what is that will striving that is exhibited to us as the thing-in-itself of the world? This question rests, like so many others, upon the confusion of the thing-in-itself with the manifestation. . . .

In fact, freedom from all aim, from all limits, belongs to the nature of the will, which is an endless striving. This was already touched on above in the reference to centrifugal force. It also discloses itself in its simplest form in the lowest grade of the objectification of will, in gravitation, which we see constantly exerting itself, though a final goal is obviously impossible for it. For if, according to its will, all existing matter were collected in one mass, yet within this mass gravity, ever striving towards the centre, would still wage war with impenetrability as rigidity or elasticity. The tendency of matter can therefore only be confined, never completed or appeased. But this is precisely the case with all tendencies of all phenomena of will. Every attained end is also the beginning of a new course, and so on *ad infinitum*. The plant raises its manifestation from the seed through the stem and the leaf to the blossom and the fruit, which again is the beginning of a new seed, a new individual, that runs through the old course, and so on through endless time. . . . Eternal becoming, endless flux, characterizes the revelation of the inner nature of will. Finally, the same thing shows itself in human endeavors and desires, which always delude us by presenting their satisfaction as the final end of will. As soon as we attain to them they no longer appear the same, and therefore they soon grow stale, are forgotten, and though not openly disowned, are yet always thrown aside as vanished illusions. We are fortunate enough if there still remains something to wish for and to strive after, that the game may be kept up of constant transition from desire to satisfaction, and from satisfaction to a new desire, the rapid course of which is called happiness, and the slow course sorrow, and does not sink into that stagnation that shows itself in fearful ennui that paralyzes life, vain yearning without a definite object, deadening languor. According to all this, when the will is enlightened by knowledge, it always knows what it wills now and here, never what it wills in general; every particular act of will has its end, the whole will has none; just as every particular phenomenon of nature is determined by a sufficient cause so far as concerns its appearance in this place at this time, but the force which manifests itself in it has no general cause, for it belongs to the thing-in-itself, to the groundless will. The single example of self-knowledge of the will as a whole is the idea as a whole, the whole world of perception. It is the objectification, the revelation, the mirror of the will. What the will expresses in it will be the subject of our further consideration.

THIRD BOOK: THE WORLD AS IDEA

SECOND ASPECT: *The Idea Independent of the Principle of Sufficient Reason: The Platonic Idea: The Object of Art*

§ 33. Since now, as individuals, we have no other knowledge than that which is subject to the principle of sufficient reason, and this form of knowledge excludes the Ideas, it is certain that if it is possible for us to raise ourselves from the knowledge of particular things to that of the Ideas, this can only happen by an alteration taking place in the subject which is analogous and corresponds to the great change of the whole nature of the object, and by virtue of which the subject, so far as it knows an Idea, is no more individual.

It will be remembered from the preceding book that knowledge in general belongs to the objectification of will at its higher grades, and sensibility, nerves, and brain, just like the other parts of the organised being, are the expression of the will at this stage of its objectivity, and therefore the idea which appears through them is also in the same way bound to the service of will as a means for the attainment of its now complicated aims for sustaining a being of manifold requirements. Thus originally, and according to its nature, knowledge is completely subject to the will, and, like the immediate object which, by means of the application of the law of causality, is its starting-point, all knowledge which proceeds in accordance with the principle of sufficient reason remains in a closer or more distant relation to the will. For the individual finds his body as an object among objects, to all of which it is related and connected according to the principle of sufficient reason. Thus all investigations of these relations and connections lead back to his body, and consequently to his will. Since it is the principle of sufficient reason which places the objects in this relation to the body, and, through it, to the will, the one endeavor of the knowledge which is subject to this principle will be to find out the relations in which objects are placed to each other through this principle, and thus to trace their innumerable connections in space, time, and causality. For only through these is the object *interesting* to the individual, *i.e.,* related to the will. Therefore the knowledge which is subject to the will knows nothing further of objects than their relations, knows the objects only so far as they exist at this time, in this place, under these circumstances, from these causes, and with these effects—in a word, as particular things; and if all these relations were to be taken away, the objects would also have disappeared for it, because it knew nothing more about them. We must not disguise the fact that what the sciences consider in things is also in reality nothing more than this; their relations, the connections of time and space, the causes of natural changes, the resemblance of forms, the motives of actions—thus merely relations. What distinguishes science from ordinary knowledge is merely its systematic form, the facilitating of knowledge by the comprehension of all particulars in the universal, by means of the subordination of concepts, and the completeness of knowledge which is thereby attained. . . .

Knowledge now, as a rule, remains always subordinate to the service of the will, as indeed it originated for this service, and grew, so to speak, to the will, as the head to the body. In the case of the brutes this subjection of knowledge to the will can never be abolished. In the case of men it can be abolished only in exceptional cases, which we shall presently consider more closely. This distinction between man and brute is outwardly expressed by the difference of the relation of the head to the body. In the case of the lower brutes both are deformed: in all brutes the head is directed towards the earth, where the objects of its will lie: even in the higher species the head and the body are still far more one than in the case of man, whose head seems freely set upon his body, as if only carried by and not serving it. This human excellence is exhibited in the highest degree by the Apollo of Belvedere; the head of the god of the Muses, with eyes fixed on the far distance, stands so freely on his shoulders that it seems wholly delivered from the body, and no more subject to its cares.

§ 34. The transition which we have referred to as possible, but yet to be regarded as only exceptional, from the common knowledge of particular things to the knowledge of the Idea, takes place suddenly; for knowledge breaks free from the service of the will, by the subject ceasing to be merely individual, and thus becoming the pure will-less subject of knowledge, which no longer traces relations in accordance with the principle of sufficient reason, but rests in fixed contemplation of the object presented to it, out of its connection with all others, and rises into it. . . .

If, raised by the power of the mind, a man relinquishes the common way of looking at things, gives up tracing, under the guidance of the forms of the principle of sufficient reason, their relations to each other, the final goal of which is always a relation to his own will; if he thus ceases to consider the where, the when, the why, and the whither of things, and looks simply and solely at the *what;* if, further, he does not allow abstract thought, the concepts of the reason, to take possession of his consciousness, but, instead of all this, gives the whole power of his mind to perception, sinks himself entirely in this, and lets his whole consciousness be filled with the quiet contemplation of the natural object actually present, whether a landscape, a tree, a mountain, a building, or whatever it may be; inasmuch as he *loses* himself in this object (to use a pregnant German idiom), *i.e.,* forgets even his individuality, his will, and only continues to exist as the pure subject, the clear mirror of the object, so that it is as if the object alone were there, without any one to perceive it, and he can no longer separate the perceiver from the perception, but both have become one, because the whole consciousness is filled and occupied with one single sensuous picture; if thus the object has to such an extent passed out of all relation to something outside it, and the subject out of all relation to the will, then that which is so known is no longer the particular thing as such; but it is the *Idea,* the eternal form, the immediate objectivity of the will at this grade; and, therefore, he who is sunk in this perception is no longer individual, for in such perception the individual has lost himself; but he is *pure,* will-less, painless, timeless *subject of knowledge.* This, which in itself is so remarkable (which I well know confirms the saying that originated with Thomas Paine, *Du sublime au ridicule il n'y a qu'un pas*[1]), will by degrees become clearer and less surprising from what follows. It was this that was running in Spinoza's mind when he wrote: *Mens æterna est, quatenus res sub æternitatis specie concipit*[2] (*Ethics* V, Prop. 31, Note). In such contemplation the particular thing becomes at once the *Idea* of its species, and the perceiving individual becomes *pure subject of knowledge*. The individual, as such, knows only particular things; the pure subject of knowledge knows only Ideas. . . . When an individual knower has raised himself in the manner described to be pure subject of knowledge, and at the same time has raised the observed object to the Platonic Idea, the *world as idea* appears complete and pure, and the full objectification of the will takes place, for the Platonic Idea alone is its *adequate objectivity*. . . . When the Platonic Idea appears, in it subject and object are no longer to be distinguished, for the Platonic Idea, the adequate objectivity of will, the true world as idea, arises only when the subject and object reciprocally fill and penetrate each other completely; and in the same way the knowing and the known individuals, as things in themselves, are not to be distinguished. . . .

§ 35. . . . When the clouds move, the figures which they form are not essential, but indifferent to them; but that as elastic vapor they are pressed together, drifted along, spread out, or torn asunder by the force of the wind: this is their nature, the essence of the forces which objectify themselves in them, the Idea; their actual forms are only for the individual observer. To the brook that flows over stones, the eddies, the waves, the foam-flakes which it forms are indifferent and unessential; but that it follows the attraction of gravity, and behaves as inelastic, perfectly mobile, formless, transparent fluid: this is its nature; this, *if known through perception,* is its Idea; these accidental forms are only for us so long as we know as individuals. The ice on the window-pane forms itself into crystals according to the laws of crystallization, which reveal the essence of the force of nature that appears here, exhibit the Idea; but the trees and flowers which it traces on the pane are unessential, and are only there for us. What appears in the clouds, the brook, and the crystal is the weakest echo of that will which appears more fully in the plant, more fully still in the beast, and most fully in man. But only the essential in all these grades of its objectification constitutes the Idea; on the

---

[1] [From the sublime to the ridiculous is but a step.—M.C.B.]

[2] [The mind is eternal in so far as it conceives things under the aspect of eternity.—M.C.B.]

other hand, its unfolding or development, because broken up in the forms of the principle of sufficient reason into a multiplicity of many-sided phenomena, is unessential to the Idea, lies merely in the kind of knowledge that belongs to the individual and has reality only for this. The same thing necessarily holds good of the unfolding of that Idea which is the completest objectivity of will. Therefore, the history of the human race, the throng of events, the change of times, the multifarious forms of human life in different lands and countries, all this is only the accidental form of the manifestation of the Idea, does not belong to the Idea itself, in which alone lies the adequate objectivity of the will, but only to the phenomenon which appears in the knowledge of the individual, and is just as foreign, unessential, and indifferent to the Idea itself as the figures which they assume are to the clouds, the form of its eddies and foam-flakes to the brook, or its trees and flowers to the ice.

To him who has thoroughly grasped this, and can distinguish between the will and the Idea, and between the Idea and its manifestation, the events of the world will have significance only so far as they are the letters out of which we may read the Idea of man, but not in and for themselves. He will not believe with the vulgar that time may produce something actually new and significant; that through it, or in it, something absolutely real may attain to existence, or indeed that it itself as a whole has beginning and end, plan and development, and in some way has for its final aim the highest perfection (according to their conception) of the last generation of man, whose life is a brief thirty years. . . .

§ 36. History follows the thread of events; it is pragmatic so far as it deduces them in accordance with the law of motivation, a law that determines the self-manifesting will wherever it is enlightened by knowledge. At the lowest grades of its objectivity, where it still acts without knowledge, natural science, in the form of etiology, treats of the laws of the changes of its phenomena, and, in the form of morphology, of what is permanent in them. This almost endless task is lightened by the aid of concepts, which comprehend what is general in order that we may deduce what is particular from it. Lastly, mathematics treats of the mere forms, time and space, in which the Ideas, broken up into multiplicity, appear for the knowledge of the subject as individual. All these, of which the common name is science, proceed according to the principle of sufficient reason in its different forms, and their theme is always the phenomenon, its laws, connections, and the relations which result from them. But what kind of knowledge is concerned with that which is outside and independent of all relations, that which alone is really essential to the world, the true content of its phenomena, that which is subject to no change, and therefore is known with equal truth for all time, in a word, the *Ideas,* which are the direct and adequate objectivity of the thing-in-itself, the will? We answer, *Art,* the work of genius. It repeats or reproduces the eternal Ideas grasped through pure contemplation, the essential and abiding in all the phenomena of the world; and according to what the material is in which it reproduces, it is sculpture or painting, poetry or music. Its one source is the knowledge of Ideas; its one aim the communication of this knowledge. While science, following the unresting and inconstant stream of the fourfold forms of reason and consequent, with each end attained sees further, and can never reach a final goal nor attain full satisfaction, any more than by running we can reach the place where the clouds touch the horizon; art, on the contrary, is everywhere at its goal. For it plucks the object of its contemplation out of the stream of the world's course, and has it isolated before it. And this particular thing, which in that stream was a small perishing part, becomes to art the representative of the whole, an equivalent of the endless multitude in space and time. It therefore pauses at this particular thing; the course of time stops; the relations vanish for it; only the essential, the Idea, is its object. We may, therefore, accurately define it as the *way of viewing things independent of the principle of sufficient reason,* in opposition to the way of viewing them which proceeds in accordance with that principle, and which is the method of experience and of science. This last method of considering things may be compared to a line infinitely extended in a horizontal direction, and the former to a vertical line which cuts it at any point. The method of viewing things which proceeds in accordance with the principle of sufficient reason is the rational method, and it alone is valid and of use in practical life and in science. The method which looks away from the content of this principle is the method of genius, which is only valid and of use in art. . . . Only through the pure contemplation described above, which ends entirely in the object, can Ideas be comprehended; and the nature of *genius* consists in pre-eminent capacity for such contemplation. Now, as this requires that a man should entirely forget himself and the relations in which he stands, *genius* is simply the completest *objectivity, i.e.,* the objective tendency of the mind, as opposed to the subjective, which is directed to one's own self—in other words, to the will. Thus genius is the faculty of continuing in the state of pure perception, of losing oneself in perception, and of enlisting in this service the knowledge which originally existed only for the service of the will; that is to say, genius is the power of leaving one's own interests, wishes, and aims entirely out of sight, thus of entirely renouncing one's own personality for a time, so as to remain *pure knowing subject,* clear vision of the world; and this not merely at moments, but for a sufficient length of time, and with sufficient consciousness, to enable one to reproduce by deliberate art what has thus been apprehended, and "to fix in lasting thoughts the wavering images that float before the mind." It is as if, when genius appears in an individual, a far larger measure of the power of knowledge falls to his lot than is necessary for the service of an individual will; and this superfluity of knowledge, being free, now becomes subject purified from will, a clear mirror of the inner nature of the world. . . .

The common mortal, that manufacture of Nature which she produces by the thousand every day, is, as we have said, not capable, at least not continuously so, of observation that in every sense is wholly disinterested, as sensuous contemplation, strictly so called, is. He can turn his attention to things only so far as they have some relation to his will, however indirect it may be. Since in this respect, which never demands anything but the knowledge of relations, the abstract conception of the thing is sufficient, and for the most part even better adapted for use, the ordinary man does not linger long over the mere perception, does not fix his attention long on one object, but in all that is presented to him hastily seeks merely the concept under which it is to be brought, as the lazy man seeks a chair, and then it interests him no further. . . .

§ 37. Genius, then, consists, according to our explanation, in the capacity for knowing, independently of the principle of sufficient reason, not individual things, which have their existence only in their relations, but the Ideas of such things, and of being oneself the correlative of the Idea, and thus no longer an individual, but the pure subject of knowledge. Yet this faculty must exist in all men in a smaller and different degree; for if not, they would be just as incapable of enjoying works of art as of producing them; they would have no susceptibility for the beautiful or the sublime; indeed, these words could have no meaning for them. We must therefore assume that there exists in all men this power of knowing the Ideas in things, and consequently of transcending their personality for the moment, unless indeed there are some men who are capable of no æsthetic pleasure at all. The man of genius excels ordinary men only by possessing this kind of knowledge in a far higher degree and more continuously. Thus, while under its influence he retains the presence of mind which is necessary to enable him to repeat in a voluntary and intentional work what he has learned in this manner; and this repetition is the work of art. Through this he communicates to others the Idea he has grasped. This Idea remains unchanged and the same, so that æsthetic pleasure is one and the same whether it is called forth by a work of art or directly by the contemplation of nature and life. The work of art is only a means of facilitating the knowledge in which this pleasure consists. That the Idea comes to us more easily from the work of art than directly from nature and the real world, arises from the fact that the artist, who knew only the Idea, no longer the actual, has reproduced in his work the pure Idea, has abstracted it from the actual, omitting all disturbing accidents. The artist lets us see the world through his eyes. . . .

All *willing* arises from want, therefore from deficiency, and therefore from suffering. The satisfaction of a wish ends it; yet for one wish that is satisfied there remain at least ten which are denied. Further, the desire lasts long, the demands are infinite; the satisfaction is short and scantily measured out. But even the final satisfaction is itself only apparent; every satisfied wish at once makes room for a new one; both are illusions; the one is known to be so, the other not yet. No attained object of desire can give lasting satisfaction, but merely a fleeting gratification; it is like the alms thrown to the beggar, that keeps him alive to-day that his misery may be prolonged till the morrow. Therefore, so long as our consciousness is filled by our will, so long as we are given up to the throng of desires with their constant hopes and fears, so long as we are the subject of willing, we can never have lasting happiness nor peace. It is essentially all the same whether we pursue or flee, fear injury or seek enjoyment; the care for the constant demands of the will, in whatever form it may be, continually occupies and sways the consciousness; but without peace no true well-being is possible. The subject of willing is thus constantly stretched on the revolving wheel of Ixion, pours water into the sieve of the Danaides, is the ever-longing Tantalus.

But when some external cause or inward disposition lifts us suddenly out of the endless stream of willing, delivers knowledge from the slavery of the will, the attention is no longer directed to the motives of willing, but comprehends things free from their relation to the will, and thus observes them without personal interest, without subjectivity, purely objectively, gives itself entirely up to them so far as they are ideas, but not in so far as they are motives. Then all at once the peace which we were always seeking, but which always fled from us on the former path of the desires, comes to us of its own accord, and it is well with us. It is the painless state which Epicurus prized as the highest good and as the state of the gods; for we are for the moment set free from the miserable striving of the will; we keep the Sabbath of the penal servitude of willing; the wheel of Ixion stands still.

But this is just the state which I described above as necessary for the knowledge of the Idea, as pure contemplation, as sinking oneself in perception, losing oneself in the object, forgetting all individuality, surrendering that kind of knowledge which follows the principle of sufficient reason, and comprehends only relations; the state by means of which at once and inseparably the perceived particular thing is raised to the Idea of its whole species, and the knowing individual to the pure subject of will-less knowledge, and as such they are both taken out of the stream of time and all other relations. It is then all one whether we see the sun set from the prison or from the palace.

Inward disposition, the predominance of knowing over willing, can produce this state under any circumstances. This is shown by those admirable Dutch artists who directed this purely objective perception to the most insignificant objects, and established a lasting monument of their objectivity and spiritual peace in their pictures of *still life,* which the æsthetic beholder does not look on without emotion; for they present to him the peaceful, still, frame of mind of the artist, free from will, which was needed to contemplate such insignificant things so objectively, to observe them so attentively, and to repeat this perception so intelligently . . .

§ 39. All these reflections are intended to bring out the subjective part of æsthetic pleasure; that is to say, that pleasure so far as it consists simply of delight in perceptive knowledge as such, in opposition to will. And as directly connected with this, there naturally follows the explanation of that disposition or frame of mind which has been called the sense of the *sublime.*

We have already remarked above that the transition to the state of pure perception takes place most easily when the objects bend themselves to it, that is, when by their manifold and yet definite and distinct form they easily become representatives of their Ideas, in which beauty, in the objective sense, consists. . . . But if these very objects whose significant forms invite us to pure contemplation, have a hostile relation to the human will in general, as it exhibits itself in its objectivity, the human body; if they are opposed to it, so that it is menaced by the irresistible predominance of their power, or sinks into insignificance before their immeasurable greatness; if, nevertheless, the beholder does not direct his attention to this eminently hostile relation to his will, but, although perceiving and recognizing it, turns consciously away from it, forcibly detaches himself from his will and its relations, and, giving himself up entirely to knowledge, quietly contemplates those very objects that are so terrible to the will, comprehends only their Idea, which is foreign to all relation, so that he lingers gladly over its contemplation, and is thereby raised above himself, his person, his will, and all will—in that case he is filled with the sense of the *sublime*, he is in the state of spiritual exaltation, and therefore the object producing such a state is called *sublime*. Thus what distinguishes the sense of the sublime from that of the beautiful is this: in the case of the beautiful, pure knowledge has gained the upper hand without a struggle, for the beauty of the object, *i.e.*, that property which facilitates the knowledge of its Idea, has removed from consciousness without resistance, and therefore imperceptibly, the will and the knowledge of relations which is subject to it, so that what is left is the pure subject of knowledge without even a remembrance of will. On the other hand, in the case of the sublime that state of pure knowledge is only attained by a conscious and forcible breaking away from the relations of the same object to the will, which are recognized as unfavorable, by a free and conscious transcending of the will and the knowledge related to it. . . .

A few examples will help very much to elucidate this theory of the æsthetic sublime and remove all doubt with regard to it; at the same time they will bring out the different degrees of this sense of the sublime. . . .

If, in the dead of winter, when all nature is frozen and stiff, we see the rays of the setting sun reflected by masses of stone, illuminating without warming, and thus favorable only to the purest kind of knowledge, not to the will; the contemplation of the beautiful effect of the light upon these masses lifts us, as does all beauty, into a state of pure knowing. But, in this case, a certain transcending of the interests of the will is needed to enable us to rise into the state of pure knowing, because there is a faint recollection of the lack of warmth from these rays, that is, an absence of the principle of life; there is a slight challenge to persist in pure knowing, and to refrain from all willing, and therefore it is an example of a transition from the sense of the beautiful to that of the sublime. It is the faintest trace of the sublime in the beautiful; and beauty itself is indeed present only in a slight degree. The following is almost as weak an example.

Let us imagine ourselves transported to a very lonely place, with unbroken horizon, under a cloudless sky, trees and plants in the perfectly motionless air, no animals, no men, no running water, the deepest silence. Such surroundings are, as it were, a call to seriousness and contemplation, apart from all will and its cravings; but this is just what imparts to such a scene of desolate stillness a touch of the sublime. For, because it affords no object, either favorable or unfavorable, for the will which is constantly in need of striving and attaining, there only remains the state of pure contemplation, and whoever is incapable of this, is ignominiously abandoned to the vacancy of unoccupied will, and the misery of ennui. So far it is a test of our intellectual worth, of which, generally speaking, the degree of our power of enduring solitude, or our love of it, is a good criterion. The scene we have sketched affords us, then, an example of the sublime in a low degree, for in it, with the state of pure knowing in its peace and all-sufficiency, there is mingled, by way of contrast, the recollection of the dependence and poverty of the will which stands in need of constant action. This is the species of the sublime for which the sight of the boundless prairies of the interior of North America is celebrated. . . .

The following situation may occasion this feeling in a still higher degree: Nature convulsed by a storm; the sky darkened by black threatening thunder-clouds; stupendous, naked, overhanging cliffs, completely shutting out the view; rushing, foaming torrents; absolute desert; the wail of the wind sweeping through the clefts of the rocks. Our dependence, our strife with hostile nature, our will broken in the conflict, now appears visibly before our eyes. Yet, so long as the personal pressure does not gain the upper hand, but we continue in æsthetic contemplation, the pure subject of knowing gazes unshaken and unconcerned through that strife of nature, through that picture of the broken will, and quietly comprehends the Ideas even of those objects which are threatening and terrible to the will. In this contrast lies the sense of the sublime.

But the impression becomes still stronger, if, when we have before our eyes, on a large scale, the battle of the raging elements, in such a scene we are prevented from hearing the sound of our own voice by the noise of a falling stream; or, if we are abroad in the storm of tempestuous seas, where the mountainous waves rise and fall, dash themselves furiously against steep cliffs, and toss their spray high into the air; the storm howls, the sea boils, the lightning flashes from black clouds, and the peals of thunder drown the voice of storm and sea. Then, in the undismayed beholder, the two-fold nature of his consciousness reaches the highest degree of distinctness. He perceives himself, on the one hand, as an individual, as the frail phenomenon of will, which the slightest touch of these forces can utterly destroy, helpless against powerful nature, dependent, the victim of chance, a vanishing nothing in the presence of stupendous might; and, on the other hand, as the eternal, peaceful, knowing subject, the condition of the object, and, therefore, the supporter of this whole world; the terrific strife of nature only his idea; the subject itself free and apart from all desires and necessities, in the quiet comprehension of the Ideas. This is the complete impression of the sublime. . . .

§ 41. . . . When we say that a thing is *beautiful,* we thereby assert that it is an object of our æsthetic contemplation, and this has a double meaning; on the one hand, it means that the sight of the thing makes us *objective,* that is to say, that in contemplating it we are no longer conscious of ourselves as individuals, but as pure will-less subjects of knowledge; and, on the other hand, it means that we recognize in the object, not the particular thing, but an Idea; and this can only happen so far as our contemplation of it is not subordinated to the principle of sufficient reason, does not follow the relation of the object to anything outside it (which is always ultimately connected with relations to our own will), but rests in the object itself. For the Idea and the pure subject of knowledge always appear at once in consciousness as necessary correlatives, and on their appearance all distinction of time vanishes, for they are both entirely foreign to the principle of sufficient reason in all its forms, and lie outside the relations which are imposed by it; they may be compared to the rainbow and the sun, which have no part in the constant movement and succession of the falling drops. Therefore, if, for example, I contemplate a tree æsthetically, *i.e.,* with artistic eyes, and thus recognize, not it, but its Idea, it becomes at once of no consequence whether it is this tree or its predecessor which flourished a thousand years ago, and whether the observer is this individual or any other that lived anywhere and at any time . . .

Since, on the one hand, every given thing may be observed in a purely objective manner and apart from all relations; and since, on the other hand, the will manifests itself in everything at some grade of its objectivity, so that everything is the expression of an Idea—it follows that everything is also *beautiful.* . . . But one thing is more beautiful than another, because it makes this pure objective contemplation easier, it lends itself to it, and, so to speak, even compels it, and then we call it very beautiful. This is the case sometimes because, as an individual thing, it expresses in its purity the Idea of its species by the very distinct, clearly defined, and significant relation of its parts, and also fully reveals that Idea through the completeness of all the possible expressions of its species united in it, so that it makes the transition from the individual thing to the Idea, and therefore also the condition of pure contemplation, very easy for the beholder. Sometimes this possession of special beauty in an object lies in the fact that the Idea itself which appeals to us in it is a high grade of the objectivity of will, and therefore very significant and expressive. Therefore it is that man is more beautiful than all other objects, and the revelation of his nature is the highest aim of art. Human form and expression are the most important objects of plastic art, and human action the most important object of poetry. Yet each thing has its own peculiar beauty, not only every organism which expresses itself in the unity of an individual being, but also everything unorganized and formless, and even every manufactured article . . . Manufactured articles also serve to express Ideas, only it is not the Idea of the manufactured article which speaks in them, but the Idea of the material to which this artificial form has been given. . . .

§ 42. I return to the exposition of the æsthetic impression. The knowledge of the beautiful always supposes at once and inseparably the pure knowing subject and the known Idea as object. Yet the source of æsthetic satisfaction will sometimes lie more in the comprehension of the known idea, sometimes more in the blessedness and spiritual peace of the pure knowing subject freed from all willing, and therefore from all individuality, and the pain that proceeds from it. And, indeed, this predominance of one or the other constituent part of æsthetic feeling will depend upon whether the intuitively grasped Idea is a higher or a lower grade of the objectivity of will. Thus in æsthetic contemplation (in the real, or through the medium of art) of the beauty of nature in the inorganic and vegetable worlds, or in works of architecture, the pleasure of pure will-less knowing will predominate, because the Ideas which are here apprehended are only low grades of the objectivity of will, and are therefore not manifestations of deep significance and rich content. On the other hand, if animals and man are the objects of æsthetic contemplation or representation, the pleasure will consist rather in the comprehension of these Ideas, which are the most distinct revelation of will; for they exhibit the greatest multiplicity of forms, the greatest richness and deep significance of phenomena, and reveal to us most completely the nature of will, whether in its violence, its terribleness, its satisfaction or its aberration (the latter in tragic situations), or finally in its change and self-surrender, which is the peculiar theme of Christian painting; as the Idea of the will enlightened by full knowledge is the object of historical painting in general, and of the drama. We shall now go through the fine arts one by one, and this will give completeness and distinctness to the theory of the beautiful which we have advanced.

If now we consider *architecture* simply as a fine art and apart from its application to useful ends, in which it serves the will and not pure knowledge, and therefore ceases to be art in our sense; we can assign to it no other aim than that of bringing to greater distinctness some of those ideas which are the lowest grades of the objectivity of will; such as gravity, cohesion, rigidity, hardness, those universal qualities of stone, those first, simplest, most inarticulate manifestations of will; the bass notes of nature; and after these light, which in many respects is their opposite. Even at these low grades of the objectivity of will we see its nature revealing itself in discord; for properly speaking the conflict between gravity and rigidity is the sole æsthetic material of architecture; its problem is to make this conflict appear with perfect distinctness in a multitude of different ways. It solves it by depriving these indestructible forces of the shortest way to their satisfaction, and conducting them to it by a circuitous route, so that the conflict is lengthened and the inexhaustible efforts of both forces become visible in many different ways. . . . Therefore the beauty, at any rate, of a building lies in the obvious adaptation of every part, not to the outward arbitrary end of man (so far the work belongs to practical architecture), but directly to the stability of the whole, to which the position, dimensions, and form of every part must have so necessary a relation that, where it is possible, if any one part were taken away, the whole would fall to pieces. For just because each part bears just as much as it conveniently can, and each is supported just where it requires to be and just to the necessary extent, this opposition unfolds itself, this conflict between rigidity and gravity, which constitutes the life, the manifestation of will, in the stone, becomes completely visible, and these lowest grades of the objectivity of will reveal themselves distinctly. . . .

§ 45. The great problem of historical painting and sculpture is to express directly and for perception the Idea in which the will reaches the highest grade of its objectification. The objective side of the pleasure afforded by the beautiful is here always predominant, and the subjective side has retired into the background. . . .

Human beauty is an objective expression, which means the fullest objectification of will at the highest grade at which it is knowable, the Idea of man in general, completely expressed in the sensible form. . . . That we all recognize human beauty when we see it, but that in the true artist this takes place with such clearness that he shows it as he has never seen it, and surpasses nature in his representation; this is only possible because *we ourselves are* the will whose adequate objectification at its highest grade is here to be judged and discovered. Thus alone have we in fact an anticipation of that which nature (which is just the will that constitutes our own being) strives to express. And in the true genius this anticipation is accompanied by so great a degree of intelligence that he recognises the Idea in the particular thing, and thus, as it were, *understands the half-uttered speech of nature,* and articulates clearly what she only stammered forth. He expresses in the hard marble that beauty of form which in a thousand attempts she failed to produce, he presents it to Nature, saying, as it were, to her, "That is what you wanted to say!" And whoever is able to judge replies, "Yes, that is it. . . ."

§ 51. If now, with the exposition which has been given of art in general, we turn from plastic and pictorial art to poetry, we shall have no doubt that its aim also is the revelation of the Ideas, the grades of the objectification of will, and the communication of them to the hearer with the distinctness and vividness with which the poetical sense comprehends them. . . . As the chemist obtains solid precipitates by combining perfectly clear and transparent fluids; the poet understands how to precipitate, as it were, the concrete, the individual, the perceptible idea, out of the abstract and transparent universality of the concepts by the manner in which he combines them. For the Idea can only be known by perception; and knowledge of the Idea is the end of art. The skill of a master, in poetry as in Chemistry, enables us always to obtain the precise precipitate we intended. This end is assisted by the numerous epithets in poetry, by means of which the universality of every concept is narrowed more and more till we reach the perceptible. . . .

From the general nature of the material, that is, the concepts, which poetry uses to communicate the Ideas, the extent of its province is very great. The whole of nature, the Ideas of all grades, can be represented by means of it, for it proceeds according to the Idea it has to impart, so that its representations are sometimes descriptive, sometimes narrative, and sometimes directly dramatic. If, in the representation of the lower grades of the objectivity of will, plastic and pictorial art generally surpass it, because lifeless nature and even brute nature, reveals almost its whole being in a single well-chosen moment; man, on the contrary, so far as he does not express himself by the mere form and expression of his person, but through a series of actions and the accompanying thoughts and emotions, is the principal object of poetry, in which no other art can compete with it, for here the progress or movement which cannot be represented in plastic or pictorial art just suits its purpose. . . .

In the more objective kinds of poetry, especially in the romance, the epic, and the drama, the end, the revelation of the Idea of man, is principally attained by two means, by true and profound representation of significant characters, and by the invention of pregnant situations in which they disclose themselves. For as it is incumbent upon the chemist not only to exhibit the simple elements, pure and genuine, and their principal compounds, but also to expose them to the influence of such reagents as will clearly and strikingly bring out their peculiar qualities, so is it incumbent on the poet not only to present to us significant characters truly and faithfully as nature itself; but, in order that we may get to know them, he must place them in those situations in which their peculiar qualities will fully unfold themselves, and appear distinctly in sharp outline; situations which are therefore called significant. In real life, and in history, situations of this kind are rarely brought about by chance, and they stand alone, lost and concealed in the multitude of those which are insignificant. . . .

Tragedy is to be regarded, and is recognized, as the summit of poetical art, both on account of the greatness of its effect and the difficulty of its achievement. It is very significant for our whole system, and well worthy of observation, that the end of this highest poetical achievement is the representation of the terrible side of life. The unspeakable pain, the wail of humanity, the triumph of evil, the scornful mastery of chance, and the irretrievable fall of the just and innocent, is here presented to us; and in this lies a significant hint of the nature of the world and of existence. It is the strife of will with itself, which here, completely unfolded at the highest grade of its objectivity, comes into fearful prominence. It becomes visible in the suffering of men, which is now introduced, partly through chance and error, which appear as the rulers of the world, personified as fate, on account of their insidiousness, which even reaches the appearance of design; partly it proceeds from man himself, through the self-mortifying efforts of a few, through the wickedness and perversity of most. It is one and the same will that lives and appears in them all, but whose phenomena fight against each other and destroy each other. In one individual it appears powerfully, in another more weakly; in one more subject to reason, and softened by the light of knowledge, in another less so, till at last, in some single case, this knowledge, purified and heightened by suffering itself, reaches the point at which the phenomenon, the veil of Mâyâ, no longer deceives it. It sees through the form of the phenomenon, the *principium individuationis*. The egoism which rests on this perishes with it, so that now the *motives* that were so powerful before have lost their might, and instead of them the complete knowledge of the nature of the world, which has a *quieting* effect on the will, produces resignation, the surrender not merely of life, but of the very will to live. Thus we see in tragedies the noblest men, after long conflict and suffering, at last renounce the ends they have so keenly followed, and all the pleasures of life forever, or else freely and joyfully surrender life itself. So it is with the steadfast prince of Calderon; with Gretchen in *Faust;* with Hamlet, whom his friend Horatio would willingly follow, but is bade remain a while, and in this harsh world draw his breath in pain, to tell the story of Hamlet, and clear his memory; so also is it with the Maid of Orleans, the Bride of Messina; they all die purified by suffering, *i.e.*, after the will to live which was formerly in them is dead. In the *Mohammed* of Voltaire this is actually expressed in the concluding words which the dying Palmira addresses to Mohammed: "The world is for tyrants: live!" On the other hand, the demand for so-called poetical justice rests on entire misconception of the nature of tragedy, and, indeed, of the nature of the world itself. It boldly appears in all its dulness in the criticisms which Dr. Samuel Johnson made on particular plays of Shakespeare, for he very naïvely laments its entire absence. And its absence is certainly obvious, for in what has Ophelia, Desdemona, or Cordelia offended? But only the dull, optimistic, Protestant-rationalistic, or peculiarly Jewish view of life will make the demand for poetical justice, and find satisfaction in it. The true sense of tragedy is the deeper insight, that it is not his own individual sins that the hero atones for, but original sin, *i.e.*, the crime of existence itself:

> Pues el delito mayor
> Del hombre es haber nacido

> (For the greatest crime of man
> Is that he was born),

as Calderon exactly expresses it.

§ 52. Now that we have considered all the fine arts in the general way that is suitable to our point of view . . . there is still another fine art which has been excluded from our consideration, and had to be excluded, for in the systematic connection of our exposition there was no fitting place for it—I mean *music*. It stands alone, quite cut off from all the other arts. In it we do not recognize the copy or repetition of any Idea of existence in the world. Yet it is such a great and exceedingly noble art, its effect on the inmost nature of man is so powerful, and it is so entirely and deeply understood by him in his inmost consciousness as a perfectly universal language, the distinctness of which surpasses even that of the perceptible world itself, that we certainly have more to look for in it than an *exercitium arithmeticæ occultum nescientis se numerare animi,*[1] which Leibniz called it. Yet he was perfectly right, as he considered only its immediate external significance, its form. But if it were nothing more, the satisfaction which it affords would be like that which we feel when a sum in arithmetic comes out right, and could not be that intense pleasure with which we see the deepest recesses of our nature find utterance. From our standpoint, therefore, at which the æsthetic effect is the criterion, we must attribute to music a far more serious and deep significance, connected with the inmost nature of the world and our own self, and in reference to which the arithmetical proportions, to which it may be reduced, are related, not as the thing signified, but merely as the sign. That in some sense music must be related to the world as the representation to the thing represented, as the copy to the original, we may conclude from the analogy of the other arts, all of which possess this character, and affect us on the whole in the same way as it does, only that the effect of music is stronger, quicker, more necessary and infallible. Further, its representative relation to the world must be very deep, absolutely true, and strikingly accurate, because it is instantly understood by every one, and has the appearance of a certain infallibility, because its form may be reduced to perfectly definite rules expressed in numbers, from which it cannot free itself without entirely ceasing to be music. Yet the point of comparison between music and the world, the respect in which it stands to the world in the relation of a copy or repetition, is very obscure. Men have practised music in all ages without being able to account for this; content to understand it directly, they renounce all claim to an abstract conception of this direct understanding itself. . . .

Music is as *direct* an objectification and copy of the whole *will* as the world itself, nay, even as the Ideas, whose multiplied manifesta-

---

[1] [The secret practice of arithmetic on the part of a mind that does not know it is counting.—M.C.B.]

tion constitutes the world of individual things. Music is thus by no means like the other arts, the copy of the Ideas, but the *copy of the will itself,* whose objectivity the Ideas are. This is why the effect of music is so much more powerful and penetrating than that of the other arts, for they speak only of shadows, but it speaks of the thing itself. Since, however, it is the same will which objectifies itself both in the Ideas and in music, though in quite different ways, there must be, not indeed a direct likeness, but yet a parallel, an analogy, between music and the Ideas whose manifestation in multiplicity and incompleteness is the visible world. The establishing of this analogy will facilitate, as an illustration, the understanding of this exposition, which is so difficult on account of the obscurity of the subject.

I recognize in the deepest tones of harmony, in the bass, the lowest grades of the objectification of will, unorganized nature, the mass of the planet. It is well known that all the high notes which are easily sounded, and die away more quickly, are produced by the vibration in their vicinity of the deep bass note. When, also, the low notes sound, the high notes always sound faintly, and it is the law of harmony that only those high notes may accompany a bass note which actually already sound along with it of themselves (its *sons harmoniques*) on account of its vibration. This is analogous to the fact that the whole of the bodies and organizations of nature must be regarded as having come into existence through gradual development out of the mass of the planet; this is both their supporter and their source, and the same relation subsists between the high notes and the bass. . . . Bass is thus, for us, in harmony what unorganized nature, the crudest mass, upon which all rests, and from which everything originates and develops, is in the world. Now, further, in the whole of the comple- mented parts which make up the harmony between the bass and the leading voice singing the melody, I recognise the whole gradation of the Ideas in which the will objectifies itself. Those nearer to the bass are the lower of these grades, the still unorganized, but yet manifold, phenomenal things; the higher represent to me the world of plants and beasts. . . . Lastly, in the *melody,* in the high, singing, principal voice leading the whole and progressing with unrestrained freedom, in the unbroken significant connection of *one* thought from beginning to end representing a whole, I recognize the highest grade of the objec- tification of will, the intellectual life and effort of man. As he alone, because endowed with reason, constantly looks before and after on the path of his actual life and its innumerable possibilities, and so achieves a course of life which is intellectual, and therefore connected as a whole; corresponding to this, I say, the *melody* has significant intentional connection from beginning to end. It records, therefore, the history of the intellectually-enlightened will. This will expresses itself in the actual world as the series of its deeds; but melody says more, it records the most secret history of this intellectually-enlightened will, pictures every excitement, every effort, every movement of it, all that which the reason collects under the wide and negative concept of feeling, and which it cannot apprehend further through its abstract concepts. Therefore it has always been said that music is the language of feeling and of passion, as words are the language of reason. . . .

Now the nature of man consists in this, that his will strives, is satisfied and strives anew, and so on for ever. Indeed, his happiness and well-being consist simply in the quick transition from wish to satisfaction, and from satisfaction to a new wish. For the absence of satisfaction is suffering, the empty longing for a new wish, languor, *ennui*. And corresponding to this the nature of melody is a constant digression and deviation from the keynote in a thousand ways, not only to the harmonious intervals to the third and dominant, but to every tone, to the dissonant sevenths and to the superfluous degrees; yet there always follows a constant return to the keynote. In all these deviations melody expresses the multifarious efforts of will, but always its satisfaction also by the final return to an harmonious interval, and still more, to the keynote. The composition of melody, the disclosure in it of all the deepest secrets of human willing and feeling, is the work of genius, whose action, which is more apparent here than anywhere else, lies far from all reflection and conscious intention, and may be called an inspiration. The conception is here, as everywhere in art, unfruitful. The composer reveals the inner nature of the world, and expresses the deepest wisdom in a language which his reason does not understand; as a person under the influence of mesmerism tells things of which he has no conception when he awakes. Therefore in the composer, more than in any other artist, the man is entirely separated and distinct from the artist. Even in the explanation of this wonderful art, the concept shows its poverty and limitation. I shall try, however, to complete our analogy. As quick transition from wish to satisfaction, and from satisfaction to a new wish, is happiness and well-being, so quick melodies without great deviations are cheerful; slow melodies, striking painful discords, and only winding back through many bars to the keynote are, as analogous to the delayed and hardly won satisfaction, sad. The delay of the new excitement of will, languor, could have no other expression than the sustained keynote, the effect of which would soon be unbearable; very monotonous and unmeaning melodies approach this effect. The short intelligible subjects of quick dance-music seem to speak only of easily attained common pleasure. On the other hand, the *Allegro maestoso,* in elaborate movements, long passages, and wide deviations, signifies a greater, nobler effort towards a more distant end, and its final attainment. The *Adagio* speaks of the pain of a great and noble effort which despises all trifling happiness. But how wonderful is the effect of the *minor* and *major!* How astounding that the change of half a tone, the entrance of a minor third instead of a major, at once and inevitably forces upon us an anxious painful feeling, from which again we are just as instantaneously delivered by the major. . . .

But it must never be forgotten, in the investigation of all these analogies I have pointed out, that music has no direct, but merely an indirect relation to them, for it never expresses the phenomenon, but only the inner nature, the in-itself of all phenomena, the will itself. It does not therefore express this or that particular and definite joy, this or that sorrow, or pain, or horror, or delight, or merriment, or peace of mind; but joy, sorrow, pain, horror, delight, merriment, peace of mind *themselves,* to a certain extent in the abstract, their essential nature, without accessories, and therefore without their motives. Yet we completely understand them in this extracted quintessence. . . .

All possible efforts, excitements, and manifestations of will, all that goes on in the heart of man and that reason includes in the wide, negative concept of feeling, may be expressed by the infinite number of possible melodies, but always in the universal, in the mere form, without the material, always according to the thing-in-itself, not the phenomenon, the inmost soul, as it were, of the phenomenon, without the body. This deep relation which music has to the true nature of all things also explains the fact that suitable music played to any scene, action, event, or surrounding seems to disclose to us its most secret meaning, and appears as the most accurate and distinct commentary upon it. This is so truly the case, that whoever gives himself up entirely to the impression of a symphony, seems to see all the possible events of life and the world take place in himself, yet if he reflects, he can find no likeness between the music and the things that passed before his mind. For, as we have said, music is distinguished from all the other arts by the fact that it is not a copy of the phenomenon, or, more accurately, the adequate objectivity of will, but is the direct copy of the will itself, and therefore exhibits itself as the metaphysical to everything physical in the world, and as the thing-in-itself to every phenomenon. We might, therefore, just as well call the world embodied music as embodied will; and this is the reason why music makes every picture, and indeed every scene of real life and of the world, at once appear with higher significance, certainly all the more in proportion as its melody is analogous to the inner spirit of the given phenomenon. . . .

FOURTH BOOK: THE WORLD AS WILL

SECOND ASPECT: *The Assertion and Denial of the Will to Live, When Self-Consciousness Has Been Attained*

§ 54. . . . The will, which, considered purely in itself, is without knowledge, and is merely a blind incessant impulse, as we see it appear in unorganized and vegetable nature and their laws, and also in the vegetative part of our own life, receives through the addition of the world as idea, which is developed in subjection to it, the knowledge of its own willing and of what it is that it wills. And this is nothing else but the world as idea, life, precisely as it exists. Therefore we called the phenomenal world the mirror of the will, its objectivity. And since what the will wills is always life, just because life is nothing but the representation of that willing for the idea, it is all one and a mere pleonasm if, instead of simply saying "the will," we say "the will to live." . . .

Above all things, we must distinctly recognize that the form of the phenomenon of will, the form of life or reality, is really only the *present,* not the future nor the past. The latter are only in the conception, exist only in the connection of knowledge, so far as it follows the principle of sufficient reason. No man has ever lived in the past, and none will live in the future; the *present* alone is the form of all life, and is its sure possession which can never be taken from it. . . . The present is the form essential to the objectification of the will. It cuts time, which extends infinitely in both directions, as a mathematical point, and stands immovably fixed, like an everlasting mid-day with no cool evening, as the actual sun burns without intermission, while it only seems to sink into the bosom of night. Therefore, if a man fears death as his annihilation, it is just as if he were to think that the sun cries out at evening, "Woe is me! for I go down into eternal night." And conversely, whoever is oppressed with the burden of life, whoever desires life and affirms it, but abhors its torments, and especially can no longer endure the hard lot that has fallen to himself, such a man has no deliverance to hope for from death, and cannot right himself by suicide. The cool shades of Orcus allure him only with the false appearance of a haven of rest. The earth rolls from day into night, the individual dies, but the sun itself shines without intermission, an eternal noon. Life is assured to the will to live; the form of life is an endless present, no matter how the individuals, the phenomena of the Idea, arise and pass away in time, like fleeting dreams. . . .

But this that we have brought to clearest consciousness, that although the particular phenomenon of the will has a temporal beginning and end, the will itself as thing-in-itself is not affected by it, nor yet the correlative of all object, the knowing but never known subject, and that life is always assured to the will to live—this is not to be numbered with the doctrines of immortality. For permanence has no more to do with the will or with the pure subject of knowing, the eternal eye of the world, than transitoriness, for both are predicates that are only valid in time, and the will and the pure subject of knowing lie outside time. Therefore the egoism of the individual (this particular phenomenon of will enlightened by the subject of knowing) can extract as little nourishment and consolation for his wish to endure through endless time from the view we have expressed, as he could from the knowledge that after his death the rest of the eternal world would continue to exist, which is just the expression of the same view considered objectively, and therefore temporally. For every individual is transitory only as phenomenon, but as thing-in-itself is timeless, and therefore endless. But it is also only as phenomenon that an individual is distinguished from the other things of the world; as thing-in-itself he is the will which appears in all, and death destroys the illusion which separates his consciousness from that of the rest: this is immortality. . . . What we fear in death is the end of the individual which it openly professes itself to be, and since the individual is a particular objectification of the will to live itself, its whole nature struggles against death. Now when feeling thus exposes us helpless, reason can yet step in and for the most part overcome its adverse influence, for it places us upon a higher standpoint, from which we no longer contemplate the particular but the whole. Therefore a philosophical knowledge of the nature of the world, which extended to the point we have now reached in this work but went no farther, could even at this point of view overcome the terror of death in the measure in which reflection had power over direct feeling in the given individual. A man who had thoroughly assimilated the truths we have already advanced, but had not come to know, either from his own experience or from a deeper insight, that constant suffering is essential to life, who found satisfaction and all that he wished in life, and could calmly and deliberately desire that his life, as he had hitherto known it, should endure for ever or repeat itself ever anew, and whose love of life was so great that he willingly and gladly accepted all the hardships and miseries to which it is exposed for the sake of its pleasures—such a man would stand "with firm-knit bones on the well-rounded, enduring earth," and would have nothing to fear. Armed with the knowledge we have given him, he would await with indifference the death that hastens towards him on the wings of time. He would regard it as a false illusion, an impotent spectre, which frightens the weak but has no power over him who knows that he is himself the will of which the whole world is the objectification or copy, and that therefore he is always certain of life, and also of the present, the peculiar and only form of the phenomenon of the will. He could not be terrified by an endless past or future in which he would not be, for this he would regard as the empty delusion of the web of Mâyâ. Thus he would no more fear death than the sun fears the night. In the *Bhagavad-Gita,* Krishna thus raises the mind of his young pupil Arjuna, when, seized with compunction at the sight of the arrayed hosts (somewhat as Xerxes was), he loses heart and desires to give up the battle in order to avert the death of so many thousands. Krishna leads him to this point of view, and the death of those thousands can no longer restrain him; he gives the sign for battle. . . .

§ 55. That the will as such is *free,* follows from the fact that, according to our view, it is the thing-in-itself, the content of all phenomena. The phenomena, on the other hand, we recognize as absolutely subordinate to the principle of sufficient reason in its four forms. And since we know that necessity is throughout identical with following from given grounds, and that these are convertible conceptions, all that belongs to the phenomenon, *i.e.,* all that is object for the knowing subject as individual, is in one aspect reason, and in another aspect consequent; and in this last capacity is determined with absolute necessity, and can, therefore, in no respect be other than it is. The whole content of Nature, the collective sum of its phenomena, is thus throughout necessary, and the necessity of every part, of every phenomenon, of every event, can always be proved, because it must be possible to find the reason from which it follows as a consequent. This admits of no exception: it follows from the unrestricted validity of the principle of sufficient reason. In another aspect, however, the same world is for us, in all its phenomena, objectivity of will. And the will, since it is not phenomenon, is not idea or object, but thing-in-itself, and is not subordinate to the principle of sufficient reason, the form of all object; thus is not determined as a consequent through any reason, knows no necessity, *i.e.,* is free. . . . But man is the most complete phenomenon of will, and, as we explained in the Second Book, he had to be enlightened with so high a degree of knowledge in order to maintain himself in existence, that in it a perfectly adequate copy or repetition of the nature of the world under the form of the idea became possible: this is the comprehension of the Ideas, the pure mirror of the world, as we learnt in the Third Book. Thus in man the will can attain to full self-consciousness, to distinct and exhaustive knowledge of its own nature, as it mirrors itself in the whole world. . . . What has just been said merely affords a preliminary and general indication of how man is distinguished from all the other phenomena of will by the fact that freedom, *i.e.,* independence of the principle of sufficient reason, which only belongs to the will as thing-in-itself, and contradicts the phenomenon, may yet possibly, in his case, appeal in the phenomenon also, where, however, it necessarily exhibits itself as a contradiction of the phenomenon with itself. In this sense, not only the will in itself, but man also may certainly be called free, and thus distinguished from all other beings. . . .

Apart from the fact that the will as the true thing-in-itself is actually original and independent, and that the feeling of its originality and absoluteness must accompany its acts in self-consciousness, though here they are already determined, there arises the illusion of an empirical freedom of the will (instead of the transcendental freedom which alone is to be attributed to it), and thus a freedom of its particular actions, from the attitude of the intellect towards the will. The intellect knows the conclusions of the will only *a posteriori* and empirically; therefore when a choice is presented, it has no data as to how the will is to decide. For the intelligible character, by virtue of which, when motives are given, only *one* decision is possible and is therefore necessary, does not come within the knowledge of the intellect, but merely the empirical character is known to it through the succession of its particular acts. Therefore it seems to the intellect that in a given case two opposite decisions are possible for the will. But this is just the same thing as if we were to say of a perpendicular beam that has lost its balance, and is hesitating which way to fall, "It can fall either to the right hand or the left." This *can* has merely a subjective significance, and really means "as far as the data known to us are concerned." Objectively, the direction of the fall is necessarily determined as soon as the equilibrium is lost. . . .

The assertion of an empirical freedom of the will, a *liberum arbitrium indifferentiæ*, agrees precisely with the doctrine that places the inner nature of man in a *soul,* which is originally a *knowing,* and indeed really an abstract *thinking,* nature, and only in consequence of this a *willing* nature—a doctrine which thus regards the will as of a secondary or derivative nature, instead of knowledge which is really so. The will indeed came to be regarded as an act of thought, and to be identified with the judgment, especially by Descartes and Spinoza. According to this doctrine every man must become what he is only through his knowledge; he must enter the world as a moral cipher, come to know the things in it, and thereupon determine to be this or that, to act thus or thus, and may also through new knowledge achieve a new course of action, that is to say, become another person. Further, he must first know a thing to be *good,* and in consequence of this will it, instead of first *willing* it, and in consequence of this calling it *good.* According to my fundamental point of view, all this is a reversal of the true relation. Will is first and original; knowledge is merely added to it as an instrument belonging to the phenomenon of will. Therefore every man is what he is through his will, and his character is original, for willing is the basis of his nature. Through the knowledge which is added to it he comes to know in the course of experience *what he is, i.e.,* he learns his character. Thus he knows himself in consequence of and in accordance with the nature of his will, instead of *willing* in consequence of and in accordance with his knowing. . . .

§ 56. . . . We have long since recognized this striving, which constitutes the kernel and in-itself of everything, as identical with that which in us, where it manifests itself most distinctly in the light of the fullest consciousness, is called *will.* Its hindrance through an obstacle which places itself between it and its temporary aim we call *suffering,* and, on the other hand, its attainment of the end, satisfaction, well-being, happiness. We may also transfer this terminology to the phenomena of the unconscious world, for though weaker in degree, they are identical in nature. Then we see them involved in constant suffering, and without any continuing happiness. For all effort springs from defect—from discontent with one's estate—is thus suffering so long as it is not satisfied; but no satisfaction is lasting, rather it is always merely the starting-point of a new effort. The striving we see everywhere hindered in many ways, everywhere in conflict, and therefore always under the form of suffering. Thus, if there is no final end of striving, there is no measure and end of suffering.

But what we only discover in unconscious Nature by sharpened observation, and with an effort, presents itself distinctly to us in the intelligent world in the life of animals, whose constant suffering is easily proved. But without lingering over these intermediate grades, we shall turn to the life of man, in which all this appears with the greatest distinctness, illuminated by the clearest knowledge; for as the phenomenon of will becomes more complete, the suffering also becomes more and more apparent. In the plant there is as yet no sensibility, and therefore no pain. A certain very small degree of suffering is experienced by the lowest species of animal life—infusoria and radiata; even in insects the capacity to feel and suffer is still limited. It first appears in a high degree with the complete nervous system of vertebrate animals, and always in a higher degree the more intelligence develops. Thus, in proportion as knowledge attains to distinctness, as consciousness ascends, pain also increases, and therefore reaches its highest degree in man. And then, again, the more distinctly a man knows, the more intelligent he is, the more pain he has; the man who is gifted with genius suffers most of all. In this sense, that is, with reference to the degree of knowledge in general, not mere abstract rational knowledge, I understand and use here that saying of the Preacher: *Qui auget scientiam, auget et dolorem*.[1] . . .

§ 57. At every grade that is enlightened by knowledge, the will appears as an individual. The human individual finds himself as finite in infinite space and time, and consequently as a vanishing quantity compared with them. He is projected into them, and, on account of their unlimited nature, he has always a merely relative, never absolute *when* and *where* of his existence; for his place and duration are finite parts of what is infinite and boundless. His real existence is only in the present, whose unchecked flight into the past is a constant transition into death, a constant dying. For his past life, apart from its possible consequences for the present, and the testimony regarding the will that is expressed in it, is now entirely done with, dead, and no longer anything; and, therefore, it must be, as a matter of reason, indifferent to him whether the content of that past was pain or pleasure. But the present is always passing through his hands into the past; the future is quite uncertain and always short. Thus his existence, even when we consider only its formal side, is a constant hurrying of the present into the dead past, a constant dying. But if we look at it from the physical side; it is clear that, as our walking is admittedly merely a constantly prevented falling, the life of our body is only a constantly prevented dying, an ever-postponed death: finally, in the same way, the activity of our mind is a constantly deferred ennui. Every breath we draw wards off the death that is constantly intruding upon us. In this way we fight with it every moment, and again,

---

[1] [He who increases his knowledge increases also his sorrow.—M.C.B.]

at longer intervals, through every meal we eat, every sleep we take, every time we warm ourselves, and so forth. In the end, death must conquer, for we became subject to him through birth, and he only plays for a little while with his prey before he swallows it up. We pursue our life, however, with great interest and much solicitude as long as possible, as we blow out a soap-bubble as long and as large as possible, although we know perfectly well that it will burst.

We saw that the inner being of unconscious nature is a constant striving without end and without rest. And this appears to us much more distinctly when we consider the nature of brutes and man. Willing and striving is its whole being, which may be very well compared to an unquenchable thirst. But the basis of all willing is need, deficiency, and thus pain. Consequently, the nature of brutes and man is subject to pain originally and through its very being. If, on the other hand, it lacks objects of desire, because it is at once deprived of them by a too easy satisfaction, a terrible void and ennui comes over it, *i.e.,* its being and existence itself becomes an unbearable burden to it. Thus its life swings like a pendulum backwards and forwards between pain and ennui. This has also had to express itself very oddly in this way; after man had transferred all pain and torments to hell, there then remained nothing over for heaven but ennui. . . .

Ennui is by no means an evil to be lightly esteemed; in the end it depicts on the countenance real despair. It makes beings who love each other so little as men do, seek each other eagerly, and thus becomes the source of social intercourse. Moreover, even from motives of policy, public precautions are everywhere taken against it, as against other universal calamities. For this evil may drive men to the greatest excesses, just as much as its opposite extreme, famine: the people require *panem et circenses*. The strict penitentiary system of Philadelphia makes use of ennui alone as a means of punishment, through solitary confinement and idleness, and it is found so terrible that it has even led prisoners to commit suicide. As want is the constant scourge of the people, so ennui is that of the fashionable world. In middle-class life ennui is represented by the Sunday, and want by the six week-days.

Thus between desiring and attaining all human life flows on throughout. The wish is, in its nature, pain; the attainment soon begets satiety: the end was only apparent; possession takes away the charm; the wish, the need, presents itself under a new form; when it does not, then follows desolateness, emptiness, ennui, against which the conflict is just as painful as against want. . . .

§ 58. . . . It is really incredible how meaningless and void of significance when looked at from without, how dull and unenlightened by intellect when felt from within, is the course of the life of the great majority of men. It is a weary longing and complaining, a dream-like staggering through the four ages of life to death, accompanied by a series of trivial thoughts. Such men are like clockwork, which is wound up, and goes it knows not why; and every time a man is begotten and born, the clock of human life is wound up anew, to repeat the same old piece it has played innumerable times before, passage after passage, measure after measure, with insignificant variations. Every individual, every human being and his course of life, is but another short dream of the endless spirit of nature, of the persistent will to live; is only another fleeting form, which it carelessly sketches on its infinite page, space and time, allows to remain for a time so short that it vanishes into nothing in comparison with these, and then obliterates to make new room. And yet, and here lies the serious side of life, every one of these fleeting forms, these empty fancies, must be paid for by the whole will to live, in all its activity, with many and deep sufferings, and finally with a bitter death, long feared and coming at last. This is why the sight of a corpse makes us suddenly so serious.

The life of every individual, if we survey it as a whole and in general, and only lay stress upon its most significant features, is really always a tragedy, but gone through in detail, it has the character of a comedy. For the deeds and vexations of the day, the restless irritation of the moment, the desires and fears of the week, the mishaps of every hour, are all through chance, which is ever bent upon some jest, scenes of a comedy. But the never-satisfied wishes, the frustrated efforts, the hopes unmercifully crushed by fate, the unfortunate errors of the whole life, with increasing suffering and death at the end, are always a tragedy. Thus, as if fate would add derision to the misery of our existence, our life must contain all the woes of tragedy, and yet we cannot even assert the dignity of tragic characters, but in the broad detail of life must inevitably be the foolish characters of a comedy. . . .

§ 59. If we have so far convinced ourselves *a priori,* by the most general consideration, by investigation of the primary and elemental features of human life, that in its whole plan it is capable of no true blessedness, but is in its very nature suffering in various forms, and throughout a state of misery, we might now awaken this conviction much more vividly within us if, proceeding more *a posteriori,* we were to turn to more definite instances, call up pictures to the fancy, and illustrate by examples the unspeakable misery which experience and history present, wherever one may look and in whatever direction one may seek. . . . Every one who has awakened from the first dream of youth, who has considered his own experience and that of others, who has studied himself in life, in the history of the past and of his own time, and finally in the works of the great poets, will, if his judgment is not paralyzed by some indelibly imprinted prejudice, certainly arrive at the conclusion that this human world is the kingdom of chance and error, which rule without mercy in great things and in small, and along with which folly and wickedness also wield the scourge. Hence it arises that everything better only struggles through with difficulty; what is noble and wise seldom attains to expression, becomes effective and claims attention, but the absurd and the perverse in the sphere of thought, the dull and tasteless in the sphere of art, the wicked and deceitful in the sphere of action, really assert a supremacy, only disturbed by short interruptions. . . . If, finally, we should bring clearly to a man's sight the terrible sufferings and miseries to which his life is constantly exposed, he would be seized with horror; and if we were to conduct the confirmed optimist through the hospitals, infirmaries, and surgical operating-rooms, through the prisons, torture-chambers, and slave-kennels, over battle-fields and places of execution; if we were to open to him all the dark abodes of misery, where it hides itself from the glance of cold curiosity, and, finally, allow him to glance into the starving dungeon of Ugolino, he, too, would understand at last the nature of this "best of possible worlds." For whence did Dante take the materials for his hell but from this our actual world? And yet he made a very proper hell of it. And when, on the other hand, he came to the task of describing heaven and its delights, he had an insurmountable difficulty before him, for our world affords no materials at all for this. . . .

§ 60. . . . The *assertion of the will* is the continuous willing itself, undisturbed by any knowledge, as it fills the life of man in general. For even the body of a man is the objectivity of the will, as it appears at this grade and in this individual. And thus his willing which develops itself in time is, as it were, a paraphrase of his body, an elucidation of the significance of the whole and its parts; it is another way of exhibiting the same thing-in-itself, of which the body is already the phenomenon. Therefore, instead of saying assertion of the will, we may say assertion of the body. . . .

The maintenance of the body through its own powers is so small a degree of the assertion of will, that if it voluntarily remains at this degree, we might assume that, with the death of this body, the will also which appeared in it would be extinguished. But even the satisfaction of the sexual passions goes beyond the assertion of one's own existence, which fills so short a time, and asserts life for an indefinite time after the death of the individual. Nature, always true and consistent, here even naïve, exhibits to us openly the inner significance of the act of generation. Our own consciousness, the intensity of the impulse, teaches us that in this act the most decided *assertion* of the will to live expresses itself, pure and without further addition (any denial of other individuals); and now, as the consequence of this act, a new life appears in time and the causal series, *i.e.,* in nature; the begotten appears before the begetter, different as regards the phenomenon, but in himself, *i.e.* according to the Idea, identical with him. . . .

§ 63. We have recognized *temporal justice,* which has its seat in the state, as requiting and punishing, and have seen that this only becomes justice through a reference to the *future.* For without this reference all punishing and requiting would be an outrage without justification, and indeed merely the addition of another evil to that which has already occurred, without meaning or significance. But it is quite otherwise with *eternal justice,* which was referred to before, and which rules not the state but the world, is not dependent upon human institutions, is not subject to chance and deception, is not uncertain, wavering, and erring, but infallible, fixed, and sure. The conception of requital implies that of time; therefore *eternal justice* cannot be requital. Thus it cannot, like temporal justice, admit of respite and delay, and require time in order to triumph, equalizing the evil deed by the evil consequences only by means of time. The punishment must here be so bound up with the offence that both are one.

Now that such an eternal justice really lies in the nature of the world will soon become completely evident to whoever has grasped the whole of the thought which we have hitherto been developing. . . .

Certainly, however, the world does not exhibit itself to the knowledge of the individual as such, developed for the service of the will, as it finally reveals itself to the inquirer as the objectivity of the one and only will to live, which he himself is. But the sight of the uncultured individual is clouded, as the Hindus say, by the veil of Mâyâ. He sees not the thing-in-itself but the phenomenon in time and space, the *principium individuationis,* and in the other forms of the principle of sufficient reason. And in this form of his limited knowledge he sees not the inner nature of things, which is one, but its phenomena as separated, disunited, innumerable, very different, and indeed opposed. For to him pleasure appears as one thing and pain as quite another thing: one man as a tormentor and a murderer, another as a martyr and a victim; wickedness as one thing and evil as another. He sees one man live in joy, abundance, and pleasure, and even at his door another die miserably of want and cold. Then he asks, Where is the retribution? And he himself, in the vehement pressure of will which is his origin and his nature, seizes upon the pleasures and enjoyments of life, firmly embraces them, and knows not that by this very act of his will he seizes and hugs all those pains and sorrows at the sight of which he shudders. He sees the ills and he sees the wickedness in the world, but far from knowing that both of these are but different sides of the manifestation of the one will to live, he regards them as very different, and indeed quite opposed, and often seeks to escape by wickedness, *i.e.,* by causing the suffering of another, from ills, from the suffering of his own individuality, for he is involved in the *principium individuationis,* deluded by the veil of Mâyâ. . . .

But that man only will grasp and comprehend eternal justice who raises himself above the knowledge that proceeds under the guidance of the principle of sufficient reason, bound to the particular thing, and recognises the Ideas, sees through the *principium individuationis,* and becomes conscious that the forms of the phenomenon do not apply to the thing-in-itself. Moreover, he alone, by virtue of the same knowledge, can understand the true nature of virtue, as it will soon disclose itself to us in connection with the present inquiry, although for the practice of virtue this knowledge in the abstract is by no means demanded. Thus it becomes clear to whoever has attained to the knowledge referred to, that because the will is the in-itself of all phenomena, the misery which is awarded to others and that which he experiences himself, the bad and the evil, always concerns only that one inner being which is everywhere the same, although the phenomena in which the one and the other exhibits itself exist as quite different individuals, and are widely separated by time and space. He sees that the difference between him who inflicts the suffering and him who must bear it is only the phenomenon, and does not concern the thing-in-itself, for this is the will living in both, which here, deceived by the knowledge which is bound to its service, does not recognize itself, and seeking an increased happiness in *one* of its phenomena, produces great suffering in *another,* and thus, in the pressure of excitement, buries its teeth in its own flesh, not knowing that it always injures only itself, revealing in this form, through the medium of individuality, the conflict with itself which it bears in its inner nature. The inflicter of suffering and the sufferer are one. The former errs in that he believes he is not a partaker in the suffering; the latter, in that he believes he is not a partaker in the guilt. If the eyes of both were opened, the inflicter of suffering would see that he lives in all that suffers pain in the wide world, and which, if endowed with reason, in vain asks why it was called into existence for such great suffering, its desert of which it does not understand. And the sufferer would see that all the wickedness which is or ever was committed in the world proceeds from that will which constitutes *his* own nature also, appears also in *him,* and that through this phenomenon and its assertion he has taken upon himself all the sufferings which proceed from such a will and bears them as his due, so long as he is this will. . . .

The living knowledge of eternal justice, of the balance that inseparably binds together the *malum culpæ* with the *malum pœnæ,* demands the complete transcending of individuality and the principle of its possibility. Therefore it will always remain unattainable to the majority of men, as will also be the case with the pure and distinct knowledge of the nature of all virtue, which is akin to it, and which we are about to explain. Accordingly the wise ancestors of the Hindu people have directly expressed it in the Vedas, which are only allowed to the three regenerate castes, or in their esoteric teaching, so far at any rate as conception and language comprehend it, and their method of exposition, which always remains pictorial and even rhapsodical, admits; but in the religion of the people, or esoteric teaching, they only communicate it by means of myths. The direct exposition we find in the Vedas, the fruit of the highest human knowledge and wisdom, the kernel of which has at last reached us in the Upanishads as the greatest gift of this century. It is expressed in various ways, but especially by making all the beings in the world, living and lifeless, pass successively before the view of the student, and pronouncing over every one of them that word which has become a formula, and as such has been called the *Mahavakya: Tatoumes*—more correctly, *Tat twam asi*—which means, "This thou art." But for the people, that great truth, so far as in their limited condition they could comprehend it, was translated into the form of knowledge which follows the principle of sufficient reason. This form of knowledge is indeed, from its nature, quite incapable of apprehending that truth pure and in itself, and even stands in contradiction to it, yet in the form of a myth it received a substitute for it which was sufficient as a guide for conduct. For the myth enables the method of knowledge, in accordance with the principle of sufficient reason, to comprehend by figurative representation the ethical significance of conduct, which itself is ever foreign to it. . . . What is here referred to is the myth of the transmigration of souls. It teaches that all sufferings which in life one inflicts upon other beings must be expiated in a subsequent life in this world, through precisely the same sufferings; and this extends so far, that he who only kills a brute must, some time in endless time, be born as the same kind of brute and suffer the same death. It teaches that wicked conduct involves a future life in this world in suffering and despised creatures, and, accordingly, that one will then be born again in lower castes, or as a woman, or as a brute, as Pariah or Chandala, as a leper, or as a crocodile, and so forth. All the pains which the myth threatens it supports with perceptions from actual life, through suffering creatures which do not know how they have merited their misery, and it does not require to call in the assistance of any other hell. As a reward, on the other hand, it promises rebirth, in better, nobler forms, as Brahmans, wise men or saints. The highest reward, which awaits the noblest deeds and the completest resignation, which is also given to the woman who in seven successive lives has voluntarily died on the funeral pile of her husband, and not less to the man whose pure mouth has never uttered a single lie—this reward the myth can only express negatively in the language of this world by the promise, which is so often repeated, that they shall never be born again, *Non adsumes iterum existentiam apparentem*[1]; or, as the Buddhists, who recognize neither Vedas nor castes, express it, "Thou shalt attain to Nirvâna," *i.e.*, to a state in which four things no longer exist— birth, age, sickness, and death.

Never has a myth entered, and never will one enter, more closely into the philosophical truth which is attainable to so few than this primitive doctrine of the noblest and most ancient nation. Broken up as this nation now is into many parts, this myth yet reigns as the universal belief of the people, and has the most decided influence upon life to-day, as four thousand years ago. Therefore Pythagoras and Plato have seized with admiration on that *ne plus ultra* of mythical representation, received it from India or Egypt, honored it, made use of it, and, we know not how far, even believed it. We, on the contrary, now send the Brahmans English clergymen and evangelical linen-weavers to set them right out of sympathy, and to show them that they are created out of nothing, and ought thankfully to rejoice in the fact. But it is just the same

---

[1] [You will not again take on phenomenal existence.—M.C.B.]

as if we fired a bullet against a cliff. In India our religions will never take root. The ancient wisdom of the human race will not be displaced by what happened in Galilee. On the contrary, Indian philosophy streams back to Europe, and will produce a fundamental change in our knowledge and thought.

§ 65. In all the preceding investigations of human action, we have been leading up to the final investigation, and have to a considerable extent lightened the task of raising to abstract and philosophical clearness, and exhibiting as a branch of our central thought, that special ethical significance of action which in life is with perfect understanding denoted by the words *good* and *bad*.

First, however, I wish to trace back to their real meaning those conceptions of *good* and *bad* which have been treated by the philosophical writers of the day, very extraordinarily, as simple conceptions, and thus incapable of analysis; so that the reader may not remain involved in the senseless delusion that they contain more than is actually the case, and express in and for themselves all that is here necessary. I am in a position to do this because in ethics I am no more disposed to take refuge behind the word *good* than formerly behind the words *beautiful* and *true,* in order that by the adding a "ness," which at the present day is supposed to have a special σεμνοτης[1] and therefore to be of assistance in various cases, and by assuming an air of solemnity, I might induce the belief that by uttering three such words I had done more than denote three very wide and abstract, and consequently empty conceptions, of very different origin and significance. Who is there, indeed, who has made himself acquainted with the books of our own day to whom these three words, admirable as are the things to which they originally refer, have not become an aversion after he has seen for the thousandth time how those who are least capable of thinking believe that they have only to utter these three words with open mouth and the air of an intelligent sheep, in order to have spoken the greatest wisdom?

The explanation of the concept *true* has already been given in the essay on the principle of sufficient reason, Ch. V, § 29, *et seq.* The content of the concept *beautiful* found for the first time its proper explanation through the whole of the Third Book of the present work. We now wish to discover the significance of the concept *good,* which can be done with very little trouble. This concept is essentially relative, and signifies *the conformity of an object to any definite effort of the will.* Accordingly everything that corresponds to the will

---

[1] [Dignity.—M.C.B.]

in any of its expressions and fulfils its end is thought through the concept *good,* however different such things may be in other respects. Thus we speak of good eating, good roads, good weather, good weapons, good omens, and so on; in short, we call everything good that is just as we wish it to be; and therefore that may be good in the eyes of one man which is just the reverse in those of another. The conception of the good divides itself into two sub-species—that of the direct and present satisfaction of any volition, and that of its indirect satisfaction, which has reference to the future, *i.e.,* the agreeable, and the useful. The conception of the opposite, so long as we are speaking of unconscious existence, is expressed by the word *bad,* more rarely and abstractly by the word *evil,* which thus denotes everything that does not correspond to any effort of the will. Like all other things that can come into relation to the will, men who are favorable to the ends which happen to be desired, who further and befriend them, are called good in the same sense, and always with that relative limitation, which shows itself, for example, in the expression, "I find this good, but you don't." Those, however, who are naturally disposed not to hinder the endeavors of others, but rather to assist them, and who are thus consistently helpful, benevolent, friendly, and charitable, are called good men, on account of this relation of their conduct to the will of others in general. In the case of conscious beings (brutes and men) the contrary conception is denoted in German, and, within the last hundred years or so, in French also, by a different word from that which is used in speaking of unconscious existence; in German, *böse;* in French, *méchant;* while in almost all other languages this distinction does not exist; and χαχος, *malus, cattivo, bad,* are used of men, as of lifeless things, which are opposed to the ends of a definite individual will. Thus, having started entirely from the passive element in the good, the inquiry could only proceed later to the active element, and investigate the conduct of the man who is called good, no longer with reference to others, but to himself; specially setting itself the task of explaining both the purely objective respect which such conduct produces in others, and the peculiar contentment with himself which it clearly produces in the man himself, since he purchases it with sacrifices of another kind; and also, on the other hand, the inner pain which accompanies the bad disposition, whatever outward advantages it brings to him who entertains it. It was from this source that the ethical systems, both the philosophical and those which are supported by systems of religion, took their rise. Both seek constantly in some way or other to connect happiness with virtue, the former either by means of the principle of contradiction or that of sufficient reason, and thus to make happiness either identical with or the consequence of virtue, always sophistically; the latter, by asserting the existence of other worlds than that which alone can be known to experience. In our system, on the contrary, virtue will show itself, not as a striving after happiness, that is, well-being and life, but as an effort in quite an opposite direction.

It follows from what has been said above, that the *good* is, according to its concept, των προς τι[1]; thus every good is essentially relative, for its being consists in its relation to a desiring will. *Absolute good* is, therefore, a contradiction in terms; highest good, *summum bonum,* really signifies the same thing—a final satisfaction of the will, after which no new desire could arise—a last motive, the attainment of which would afford enduring satisfaction of the will. But, according to the investigations which have already been conducted in this Fourth Book, such a consummation is not even thinkable. The will can just as little cease from willing altogether on account of some particular satisfaction, as time can end or begin; for it there is no such thing as a permanent fulfilment which shall completely and for ever satisfy its craving. It is the vessel of the Danaides; for it there is no highest good, no absolute good, but always a merely temporary good. If, however, we wish to give an honorary position, as it were emeritus, to an old expression, which from custom we do not like to discard altogether, we may, metaphorically and figuratively, call the complete self-effacement and denial of the will, the true absence of will, which alone for ever stills and silences its struggle, alone gives that contentment which can never again be disturbed, alone redeems the world, and which we shall now soon consider at the close of our whole investigation—the absolute good, the *summum bonum*—and regard it as the only radical cure of the disease of which all other means are only palliations or anodynes. . . .

§ 66. A theory of morals without proof, that is, mere moralizing, can effect nothing, because it does not act as a motive. A theory of morals which does act as a motive can do so only by working on self-love. But what springs from this source has no moral worth. It follows from this that no genuine virtue can be produced through moral theory or abstract knowledge in general, but that such virtue must spring from that intuitive knowledge which recognises in the individuality of others the same nature as in our own.

---

[1] [What is conducive to something.—M.C.B.]

For virtue certainly proceeds from knowledge, but not from the abstract knowledge that can be communicated through words. If it were so, virtue could be taught, and by here expressing in abstract language its nature and the knowledge which lies at its foundation, we should make every one who comprehends this even ethically better. But this is by no means the case. On the contrary, ethical discourses and preaching will just as little produce a virtuous man as all the systems of æsthetics from Aristotle downwards have succeeded in producing a poet. For the real inner nature of virtue the concept is unfruitful, just as it is in art, and it is only in a completely subordinate position that it can be of use as a tool in the elaboration and preserving of what has been ascertained and inferred by other means. . . .

§ 67. We have seen how justice proceeds from the penetration of the *principium individuationis* in a less degree, and how from its penetration in a higher degree there arises goodness of disposition proper, which shows itself as pure, *i.e.*, disinterested love towards others. When now the latter becomes perfect, it places other individuals and their fate completely on the level with itself and its own fate. Further than this it cannot go, for there exists no reason for preferring the individuality of another to its own. Yet the number of other individuals whose whole happiness or life is in danger may outweigh the regard for one's own particular well-being. In such a case, the character that has attained to the highest goodness and perfect nobility will entirely sacrifice its own well-being, and even its life, for the well-being of many others. So died Codrus, and Leonidas, and Regulus, and Decius Mus, and Arnold von Winkelried; so dies every one who voluntarily and consciously faces certain death for his friends or his country. And they also stand on the same level who voluntarily submit to suffering and death for maintaining what conduces and rightly belongs to the welfare of all mankind; that is, for maintaining universal and important truths and destroying great errors. So died Socrates and Giordano Bruno, and so many a hero of the truth suffered death at the stake at the hands of the priests.

Now, however, I must remind the reader, with reference to the paradox stated above, that we found before that suffering is essential to life as a whole, and inseparable from it. And that we saw that every wish proceeds from a need, from a want, from suffering, and that therefore every satisfaction is only the removal of a pain, and brings no positive happiness; that the joys certainly lie to the wish, presenting themselves as a positive good, but in truth they have only a negative nature, and are only the end of an evil. Therefore what goodness, love, and nobleness do for others, is always merely an alleviation of their suffering, and consequently all that can influence them to good deeds and works of love, is simply the *knowledge of the suffering of others,* which is directly understood from their own suffering and placed on a level with it. But it follows from this that pure love (αγαπη, *caritas*) is in its nature sympathy; whether the suffering it mitigates, to which every unsatisfied wish belongs, be great or small. Therefore we shall have no hesitation, in direct contradiction to Kant, who will only recognize all true goodness and all virtue to be such if it has proceeded from abstract reflection, and indeed from the conception of duty and of the categorical imperative, and explains felt sympathy as weakness, and by no means virtue, we shall have no hesitation, I say, in direct contradiction to Kant, in saying: the mere concept is for genuine virtue just as unfruitful as it is for genuine art: all true and pure love is sympathy, and all love which is not sympathy is selfishness. . . .

§ 68. . . . Thus he who is still involved in the *principium individuationis,* in egoism, only knows particular things and their relation to his own person, and these constantly become new *motives* of his volition. But, on the other hand, that knowledge of the whole, of the nature of the thing-in-itself which has been described, becomes a *quieter* of all and every volition. The will now turns away from life; it now shudders at the pleasures in which it recognizes the assertion of life. Man now attains to the state of voluntary renunciation, resignation, true indifference, and perfect will-lessness. If at times, in the hard experience of our own suffering, or in the vivid recognition of that of others, the knowledge of the vanity and bitterness of life draws nigh to us also who are still wrapt in the veil of Mâyâ, and we would like to destroy the sting of the desires, close the entrance against all suffering, and purify and sanctify ourselves by complete and final renunciation; yet the illusion of the phenomenon soon entangles us again, and its motives influence the will anew; we cannot tear ourselves free. The allurement of hope, the flattery of the present, the sweetness of pleasure, the well-being which falls to our lot, amid the lamentations of a suffering world governed by chance and error, draws us back to it and rivets our bonds anew. Therefore Jesus says: "It is easier for a camel to go through the eye of a needle, than for a rich man to enter into the kingdom of God."

If we compare life to a course or path through which we must unceasingly run—a path of red-hot coals, with a few cool places here and there; then he who is entangled in delusion is consoled by the cool places, on which he now stands, or which he sees near him. and sets out to run through the course. But he who sees through the *principium individuationis,* and recognizes the real nature of the thing-in-itself, and thus the whole, is no longer susceptible of such consolation; he sees himself in all places at once, and withdraws. His will turns round, no longer asserts its own nature, which is reflected in the phenomenon, but denies it. The phenomenon by which this change is marked, is the transition from virtue to asceticism. That is to say, it no longer suffices for such a man to love others as himself, and to do as much for them as for himself; but there arises within him a horror of the nature of which his own phenomenal existence is an expression, the will to live, the kernel and inner nature of that world which is recognized as full of misery. He therefore disowns this nature which appears in him, and is already expressed through his body, and his action gives the lie to his phenomenal existence, and appears in open contradiction to it. Essentially nothing else but a manifestation of will, he ceases to will anything, guards against attaching his will to anything, and seeks to confirm in himself the greatest indifference to everything. His body, healthy and strong, expresses through the genitals the sexual impulse; but he denies the will and gives the lie to the body; he desires no sensual gratification under any condition. Voluntary and complete chastity is the first step in asceticism or the denial of the will to live. It thereby denies the assertion of the will which extends beyond the individual life, and gives the assurance that with the life of this body, the will, whose manifestation it is, ceases. Nature, always true and naïve, declares that if this maxim became universal, the human race would die out; and I think I may assume, in accordance with what was said in the Second Book about the connection of all manifestations of will, that with its highest manifestation, the weaker reflection of it would also pass away, as the twilight vanishes along with the full light. With the entire abolition of knowledge, the rest of the world would of itself vanish into nothing; for without a subject there is no object. . . .

And what I have here described with feeble tongue and only in, general terms, is no philosophical fable, invented by myself, and only of to-day; no, it was the enviable life of so many saints and beautiful souls among Christians, and still more among Hindus and Buddhists, and also among the believers of other religions. However different were the dogmas impressed on their reason, the same inward, direct, intuitive knowledge from which alone all virtue and holiness proceed, expressed itself in precisely the same way in the conduct of life. For here also the great distinction between intuitive and abstract knowledge shows itself; a distinction which is of such importance and universal application in our whole investigation, and which has hitherto been too little attended to. There is a wide gulf between the two, which can only be crossed by the aid of philosophy, as regards the knowledge of the nature of the world. Intuitively or *in concreto,* every man is really conscious of all philosophical truths, but to bring them to abstract knowledge, to reflection, is the work of philosophy, which neither ought nor is able to do more than this.

Thus it may be that the inner nature of holiness, self-renunciation. mortification of our own will, asceticism, is here for the first time expressed abstractly, and free from all mythical elements, as *denial of the will to live,* appearing after the complete knowledge of its own nature has become a quieter of all volition. On the other hand, it has been known directly and realised in practice by saints and ascetics, who had all the same inward knowledge, though they used very different language with regard to it, according to the dogmas which their reason had accepted, and in consequence of which an Indian, a Christian, or a Lama saint must each give a very different account of his conduct, which is, however, of no importance as regards the fact. A saint may be full of the absurdest superstition, or, on the contrary, he may be a philosopher, it is all the same. His conduct alone certifies that he is a saint, for, in a moral regard, it proceeds from knowledge of the world and its nature, which is not abstractly but intuitively and directly apprehended, and is only expressed by him in any dogma for the satisfaction of his reason. It is therefore just as little needful that a saint should be a philosopher as that a philosopher should be a saint; just as it is not necessary that a perfectly beautiful man should be a great sculptor, or that a great sculptor should himself be a beautiful man. In general, it is a strange demand upon a moralist that he should teach no other virtue than that which he himself possesses. To repeat the whole nature of the world abstractly, universally, and distinctly in concepts, and thus to store up, as it were, a reflected image of it in permanent concepts always at the command of the reason; this and nothing else is philosophy.

But the description I have given above of the denial of the will to live, of the conduct of a beautiful soul, of a resigned and voluntarily expiating saint, is merely abstract and general, and therefore cold. As the knowledge from which the denial of the will proceeds is intuitive and not abstract, it finds its most perfect expression, not in abstract conceptions, but in deeds and conduct. Therefore, in order to understand fully what we philosophically express as denial of the will to live, one must come to know examples of it in experience and actual life. Certainly they are not to be met with in daily experience: *Nam omnia præclara tam difficilia quam rara sunt,*[1] Spinoza admirably says. Therefore, unless by a specially happy fate we are made eye-witnesses, we have to content ourselves with descriptions of the lives of such men. Indian literature, as we see from the little that we as yet know through translations, is very rich in descriptions of the lives of saints, penitents, Samanas or ascetics, Sannyâsis or mendicants, and whatever else they may be called. The history of the world will, and indeed must, keep silence about the man whose conduct is the best and only adequate illustration of this important point of our investigation, for the material of the history of the world is quite different, and indeed opposed to this. It is not the denial of the will to live, but its assertion and its manifestation in innumerable individuals in which its conflict with itself at the highest grade of its objectification appears with perfect distinctness, and brings before our eyes, now the ascendancy of the individual through prudence, now the might of the many through their mass, now the might of chance personified as fate, always the vanity and emptiness of the whole effort. We, however, do not follow here the course of phenomena in time, but, as philosophers, we seek to investigate the ethical significance of action, and take this as the only criterion of what for us is significant and important. Thus we will not be with-held by any fear of the constant numerical superiority of vulgarity and dulness from acknowledging that the greatest, most important, and most significant phenomenon that the world can show is not the conqueror of the world, but the subduer of it—is nothing but the quiet, unobserved life of a man who has attained to the knowledge in consequence of which he surrenders and denies that will to live which fills everything and strives and strains in all, and which first gains freedom here in him alone, so that his conduct becomes the exact opposite of that of other men. In this respect, therefore, for the philosopher, these accounts of the lives of holy, self-denying men, badly as they are generally written, and mixed as they are with superstition and nonsense, are, because of the significance of the material, immeasurably more instructive and important than even Plutarch and Livy. . . .

---

[1] [For all noble things are as difficult as they are rare; the last sentence in Spinoza's *Ethics.*—M.C.B.]

§ 69. Suicide, the actual doing away with the individual manifestation of will, differs most widely from the denial of the will to live, which is the single outstanding act of free will in the manifestation, and is therefore, as Asmus calls it, the transcendental change. This last has been fully considered in the course of our work. Far from being denial of the will, suicide is a phenomenon of strong assertion of will; for the essence of negation lies in this, that the joys of life are shunned, not its sorrows. The suicide wills life, and is only dissatisfied with the conditions under which it has presented itself to him. He therefore by no means surrenders the will to live, but only life, in that he destroys the individual manifestation. He wills life— wills the unrestricted existence and assertion of the body; but the complication of circumstances does not allow this, and there results for him great suffering. The very will to live finds itself so much hampered in this particular manifestation that it cannot put forth its energies. It therefore comes to such a determination as is in conformity with its own nature, which lies outside the conditions of the principle of sufficient reason, and to which, therefore, all particular manifestations are alike indifferent, inasmuch as it itself remains unaffected by all appearing and passing away, and is the inner life of all things; for that firm inward assurance by reason of which we all live free from the constant dread of death, the assurance that a phenomenal existence can never be wanting to the will, supports our action even in the case of suicide. Thus the will to live appears just as much in suicide (Siva) as in the satisfaction of self-preservation (Vishnu) and in the sensual pleasure of procreation (Brahma). This is the inner meaning of the unity of the Trimurtis, which is embodied in its entirety in every human being, though in time it raises now one, now another, of its three heads. Suicide stands in the same relation to the denial of the will as the individual thing does to the Idea. The suicide denies only the individual, not the species. We have already seen that as life is always assured to the will to live, and as sorrow is inseparable from life, suicide, the wilful destruction of the single phenomenal existence, is a vain and foolish act; for the thing-in-itself remains unaffected by it, even as the rainbow endures however fast the drops which support it for the moment may change. But, more than this, it is also the masterpiece of Mâyâ, as the most flagrant example of the contradiction of the will to live with itself. As we found this contradiction in the case of the lowest manifestations of will, in the permanent struggle of all the forces of nature, and of all organic individuals for matter and time and space;

and as we saw this antagonism come ever more to the front with terrible distinctness in the ascending grades of the objectification of the will, so at last in the highest grade, the Idea of man, it reaches the point at which, not only the individuals which express the same Idea extirpate each other, but even the same individual declares war against itself. . . .

§ 70. It might be supposed that the entire exposition (now terminated) of that which I call the denial of the will is irreconcilable with the earlier explanation of necessity, which belongs just as much to motivation as to every other form of the principle of sufficient reason, and according to which, motives, like all causes, are only occasional causes, upon which the character unfolds its nature and reveals it with the necessity of a natural law, on account of which we absolutely denied freedom as *liberum arbitrium indifferentiæ*. . . . But the key to the solution of these contradictions lies in the fact that the state in which the character is withdrawn from the power of motives does not proceed directly from the will, but from a changed form of knowledge. So long as the knowledge is merely that which is involved in the *principium individuationis* and exclusively follows the principle of sufficient reason, the strength of the motives is irresistible. But when the *principium individuationis* is seen through, when the Ideas, and indeed the inner nature of the thing-in-itself, as the same will in all, are directly recognised, and from this knowledge a universal quieter of volition arises, then the particular motives become ineffective, because the kind of knowledge which corresponds to them is obscured and thrown into the background by quite another kind. . . .

Now because, as we have seen, that *self-suppression of the will* proceeds from knowledge, and all knowledge is involuntary, that denial of will also, that entrance into freedom, cannot be forcibly attained to by intention or design, but proceeds from the inmost relation of knowing and volition in the man, and therefore comes suddenly, as if spontaneously from without. This is why the Church has called it *the work of grace;* and that it still regards it as independent of the acceptance of grace corresponds to the fact that the effect of the quieter is finally a free act of will. And because, in consequence of such a work of grace, the whole nature of man is changed and reversed from its foundation, so that he no longer wills anything of all that he previously willed so intensely, so that it is as if a new man actually took the place of the old, the Church has called this consequence of the work of grace the *new birth*. For what it calls the *natural man,* to which it denies all capacity for good, is just the will to live, which must be denied if deliverance from an existence such as ours is to be attained. Behind our existence lies something else, which is only accessible to us if we have shaken off this world. . . .

§ 71. I now end the general account of ethics, and with it the whole development of that one thought which it has been my object to impart; and I by no means desire to conceal here an objection which concerns this last part of my exposition, but rather to point out that it lies in the nature of the question, and that it is quite impossible to remove it. It is this, that after our investigation has brought us to the point at which we have before our eyes perfect holiness, the denial and surrender of all volition, and thus the deliverance from a world whose whole existence we have found to be suffering, this appears to us as a passing away into empty nothingness. . . .

That which is generally received as positive, which we call the real, and the negation of which the concept *nothing* in its most general significance expresses, is just the world as idea, which I have shown to be the objectivity and mirror of the will. Moreover, we ourselves are just this will and this world, and to them belongs the idea in general, as one aspect of them. The form of the idea is space and time, therefore for this point of view all that is real must be in some place and at some time. Denial, abolition, conversion of the will, is also the abolition and the vanishing of the world, its mirror. If we no longer perceive it in this mirror, we ask in vain where it has gone, and then, because it has no longer any where and when, complain that it has vanished into nothing.

A reversed point of view, if it were possible for us, would reverse the signs and show the real for us as *nothing,* and that nothing as the real. But as long as we ourselves are the will to live, this last— nothing as the real—can only be known and signified by us negatively, because the old saying of Empedocles, that like can only be known by like, deprives us here of all knowledge, as, conversely, upon it finally rests the possibility of all our actual knowledge, *i.e.,* the world as idea; for the world is the self-knowledge of the will.

If, however, it should be absolutely insisted upon that in some way or other a positive knowledge should be attained of that which philosophy can only express negatively as the denial of the will, there would be nothing for it but to refer to that state which all those who have attained to complete denial of the will have experienced, and which has been variously denoted by the names ecstasy, rapture, illumination, union with God, and so forth; a state, however, which cannot properly be called knowledge, because it has not the form of subject and object, and is, moreover, only attainable in one's own experience and cannot be further communicated.

We, however, who consistently occupy the standpoint of philosophy, must be satisfied here with negative knowledge, content to have reached the utmost limit of the positive. We have recognized the inmost nature of the world as will, and all its phenomena as only the objectivity of will; and we have followed this objectivity from the unconscious working of obscure forces of Nature up to the completely conscious action of man. Therefore we shall by no means evade the consequence that with the free denial, the surrender of the will, all those phenomena are also abolished; that constant strain and effort without end and without rest at all the grades of objectivity, in which and through which the world consists; the multifarious forms succeeding each other in gradation; the whole manifestation of the will; and, finally, also the universal forms of this manifestation, time and space, and also its last fundamental form, subject and object; all are abolished. No will: no idea, no world.

Before us there is certainly only nothingness. But that which resists this passing into nothing, our nature, is indeed just the will to live, which we ourselves are, as it is our world. That we abhor annihilation so greatly, is simply another expression of the fact that we so strenuously will life, and are nothing but this will, and know nothing besides it. But if we turn our glance from our own needy and embarrassed condition to those who have overcome the world, in whom the will, having attained to perfect self-knowledge, found itself again in all, and then freely denied itself, and who then merely wait to see the last trace of it vanish with the body which it animates; then, instead of the restless striving and effort, instead of the constant transition from wish to fruition, and from joy to sorrow, instead of the never-satisfied and never-dying hope which constitutes the life of the man who wills, we shall see that peace which is above all reason, that perfect calm of the spirit, that deep rest, that inviolable confidence and serenity, the mere reflection of which in the countenance, as Raphael and Correggio have represented it, is an entire and certain gospel; only knowledge remains, the will has vanished. We look with deep and painful longing upon this state, beside which the misery and wretchedness of our own is brought out clearly by the contrast. Yet this is the only consideration which can afford us lasting consolation, when, on the one hand, we have recognized incurable suffering and endless misery as essential to the manifestation of will, the world; and, on the other hand, see the world pass away with the abolition of will, and retain before us only empty nothingness. Thus, in this way, by contemplation of the life and conduct of saints, whom it is certainly rarely granted us to meet with in our own experience, but who are brought before our eyes by their written history, and, with the stamp of inner truth, by art, we must banish the dark impression of that nothingness which we discern behind all virtue and holiness as their final goal, and which we fear as children fear the dark; we must not even evade it like the Indians, through myths and meaningless words, such as reabsorption in Brahma or the Nirvâna of the Buddhists. Rather do we freely acknowledge that what remains after the entire abolition of will is for all those who are still full of will certainly nothing; but, conversely, to those in whom the will has turned and has denied itself, this our world, which is so real, with all its suns and milky ways—is nothing.

AUGUSTE COMTE

A General View of Positivism
CHAPTERS I AND VI (*abridged*)

AUGUSTE COMTE

ISIDORE AUGUSTE MARIE FRANÇOIS COMTE (1798–1857) was born at Montpellier, the son of a tax-collector. He attended the École Polytechnique, but after two years the school was broken up by a student rebellion against one of the instructors, in which he had taken an active part. He went to Paris in 1816 and there he earned a precarious living by giving lessons in mathematics. For a time he became a disciple of the social theorist and reformer Saint-Simon, whose views stimulated his already strong social consciousness, but there was a breach in 1824. In 1825 he married, but he and his wife were not happy together and they separated in 1842. The following year he began a course of lectures that were the first exposition of his philosophy; these were resumed after an interruption for a year by mental illness. In 1833 he was appointed an entrance examiner for the reopened École Polytechnique; after he lost this job, he was supported in large part by contributions from friends and admirers—John Stuart Mill and others. There was a celebrated friendship with Madame Clothilde de Vaux in 1845, which changed the course of his thinking, or perhaps accelerated certain tendencies in it. He founded the Positive Society in 1848.

Comte's lectures were published as the *Course in Positive Philosophy,* 1830–42, 6 vols. (condensed and freely translated by Harriet Martineau, London: J. Chapman, 1853, 2 vols., under the title *The Positive Philosophy of Auguste Comte*). The later development of his system was presented in the *System of Positive Politics,* or *Treatise on Sociology,* 1851–54, 4 vols. (translated by several hands as the *System of Positive Polity,* London: Longmans, Green, 1875–77), of which the *General View of Positivism* was a part. His *Positivist Catechism,* 1852 (translated by Richard Congreve as *The Catechism of Positive Religion,* 3d ed., London: Kegan Paul, 1891) expounds some of the details of his later religious views. See also his *Letters,* selected and translated by J. K. Ingram, London: A. and C. Black, 1901.

Nothing less than a complete reconstruction of the European social and political order, Comte believed, was called for by the emerging of mankind into the "third stage" of human cultural history, the stage of positive science. To this end he bent his broadest philosophical speculations, and he spared no pains to work out the smallest details of the new organization he proposed. What can still seem to us the living and lasting contributions of Comte to our own philosophical development are only a few, yet a significant few, of his ideas. He had a passionate conviction that scientific method could be applied to the study of societies (he coined the term "sociology"), and that the social behavior of man is subject to law and rationally comprehensible. He urged men to be prepared to consider with critical reasonableness the foundations of their society, taken for granted by custom and tradition; he saw that philosophical study could be an important help in this project. Probably no previous philosopher realized so fully the capacity of the concept of humanity as a whole to serve as a basic ethical concern for each person, and as a religious object. In some ethical aspects, as in his sense of the rights of animals, Comte was ahead of his time. (He also gave us the word "altruism.") And for all the fantastic and idiosyncratic elements that he came to attach to his original idea of a "religion of humanity" (his Catholic training led him to think that his humanistic religion must be furnished with a priesthood, a "positivist calendar" of secular saints' days, a catechism, devotional gestures, and prayers), his essential idea of man's obligation to all his fellow men, and each man's oneness of destiny with the whole of the human race, past and future, has, in considerable part by the efforts of Comte himself, become a vital and effective religious ideal in many parts of the world.

A General View of Positivism, Chapters I and VI* (abridged)

Chapter I

The Intellectual Character of Positivism

The object of all true Philosophy is to frame a system which shall comprehend human life under every aspect, social as well as individual. It embraces, therefore, the three kinds of phenomena of which our life consists, Thoughts, Feelings, and Actions. Under all these aspects, the growth of Humanity is primarily spontaneous; and the basis upon which all wise attempts to modify it should proceed, can only be furnished by an exact acquaintance with the natural process. We are, however, able to modify this process systematically; and the importance of this is extreme, since we can thereby greatly diminish the partial deviations, the disastrous delays, and the grave inconsistencies to which so complex a growth would be liable were it left entirely to itself. To effect this necessary intervention is the proper sphere of politics. But a right conception cannot be formed of it without the aid of the philosopher, whose business it is to define and amend the principles on which it is conducted. With this object in view the philosopher endeavors to co-ordinate the various elements of man's existence, so that it may be conceived of theoretically as an integral whole. His synthesis can only be valid in so far as it is an exact and complete representation of the relations naturally existing. The first condition is therefore that these relations be carefully studied. When the philosopher, instead of forming such a synthesis, attempts to interfere more directly with the course of practical life, he commits the error of usurping the province of the statesman, to whom all practical measures exclusively belong. Philosophy and Politics are the two principal functions of the great social organism. Morality, systematically considered, forms the connecting link and at the same time the line of demarcation between them. It is the most important application of philosophy, and it gives a general direction to polity. Natural morality, that is to say the various emotions of our moral nature, will, as I have shown in my previous

* Translated by J. H. Bridges, 1865 (2d ed., London: Reeves and Turner, 1880), from the *Discours sur l'ensemble du Positivisme,* which was first published in 1848 and later became Vol. I of the *Système de Politique Positive,* 1851-54.

work, always govern the speculations of the one and the operations of the other. This I shall explain more fully.

But the synthesis, which it is the social function of Philosophy to construct, will neither be real nor permanent, unless it embraces every department of human nature, whether speculative, affective, or practical. These three orders of phenomena react upon each other so intimately that any system which does not include all of them must inevitably be unreal and inadequate. Yet it is only in the present day, when Philosophy is reaching the positive stage, that this which is her highest and most essential mission can be fully apprehended.

The theological synthesis depended exclusively upon our affective nature; and to this is owing its original supremacy and its ultimate decline. For a long time its influence over all our highest speculations was paramount. This was especially the case during the Polytheistic period, when Imagination and Feeling still retained their sway under very slight restraint from the reasoning faculties. Yet even during the time of its highest development, intellectually and socially, theology exercised no real control over practical life. It reacted, of course, upon it to some extent, but the effects of this were in most cases far more apparent than real. There was a natural antagonism between them, which though at first hardly perceived, went on increasing till at last it brought about the entire destruction of the theological fabric. A system so purely subjective could not harmonize with the necessarily objective tendencies and stubborn realities of practical life. Theology asserted all phenomena to be under the dominion of Wills more or less arbitrary: whereas in practical life men were led more and more clearly to the conception of invariable Laws. For without laws human action would have admitted of no rule or plan. In consequence of this utter inability of theology to deal with practical life, its treatment of speculative and even of moral problems was exceedingly imperfect, such problems being all more or less dependent on the practical necessities of life. To present a perfectly synthetic view of human nature was, then, impossible as long as the influence of theology lasted; because the Intellect was impelled by Feeling and by the Active powers in two totally different directions. The failure of all metaphysical attempts to form a synthesis need not be dwelt upon here. Metaphysicians, in spite of their claims to absolute truth, have never been able to supersede theology in questions of feeling, and have proved still more inadequate in practical questions. Ontology, even when it was most triumphant in the schools, was always limited to subjects of a purely intellectual nature; and even here its abstractions, useless in themselves, dealt only with the case of individual development, the metaphysical spirit being thoroughly incompatible with the social point of view. In my work on Positive Philosophy I have clearly proved that it constitutes only a transitory phase of mind, and is totally inadequate for any constructive purpose. For a time it was supreme; but its utility lay simply in its revolutionary tendencies. It aided the preliminary development of Humanity by its gradual inroads upon Theology, which, though in ancient times entrusted with the sole direction of society, had long since become in every respect utterly retrograde.

But all Positive speculations owe their first origin to the occupations of practical life; and, consequently, they have always given some indication of their capacity for regulating our active powers, which had been omitted from every former synthesis. Their value in this respect has been and still is materially impaired by their want of breadth, and their isolated and incoherent character; but it has always been instinctively felt. The importance that we attach to theories which teach the laws of phenomena, and give us the power of prevision, is chiefly due to the fact that they alone can regulate our otherwise blind action upon the external world. Hence it is that while the Positive spirit has been growing more and more theoretical, and has gradually extended to every department of speculation, it has never lost the practical tendencies which it derived from its source; and this even in the case of researches useless in themselves, and only to be justified as logical exercises. From its first origin in mathematics and astronomy, it has always shown its tendency to systematize the whole of our conceptions in every new subject which has been brought within the scope of its fundamental principle. It exercised for a long time a modifying influence upon theological and metaphysical principles, which has gone on increasing; and since the time of Descartes and Bacon it has become evident that it is destined to supersede them altogether. Positivism has gradually taken possession of the preliminary sciences of Physics and Biology, and in these the old system no longer prevails. All that remained was to complete the range of its influence by including the study of social phenomena. For this study metaphysics had proved incompetent; by theological thinkers it had only been pursued indirectly and empirically as a condition of government. I believe that my work on Positive Philosophy has so far supplied what was wanting. I think it must now be clear to all that the Positive spirit can embrace the entire range of thought without lessening, or rather with the effect of strengthening, its original tendency to regulate practical life. And it is a further guarantee for the stability of the new intellectual synthesis that Social science, which is the final result of our researches, gives them that systematic character in which they had hitherto been wanting, by supplying the only connecting link of which they all admit.

This conception is already adopted by all true thinkers. All must now acknowledge that the Positive spirit tends necessarily towards the formation of a comprehensive and durable system, in which every practical as well as speculative subject shall be included. But such a system would still be far from realizing that universal character without which Positivism would be incompetent to supersede Theology in the spiritual government of Humanity. For the element which really preponderates in every human being, that is to say, Affection, would still be left untouched. This element it is, and this only, which gives a stimulus and direction to the other two parts of our nature: without it the one would waste its force in ill-conceived, or, at least, useless studies, and the other in barren or even dangerous contention. With this immense deficiency the combination of our theoretical and active powers would be fruitless, because it would lack the only principle which could ensure its real and permanent stability. The failure would be even greater than the failure of Theology in dealing with practical questions; for the unity of human nature cannot really be made to depend either on the rational or the active faculties. In the life of the individual, and, still more, in the life of the race, the basis of unity, as I shall show in the fourth chapter, must always be feeling. It is to the fact that theology arose spontaneously from feeling that its influence is for the most part due. And although theology is now palpably on the decline, yet it will still retain, in principle at least, some legitimate claims to the direction of society so long as the new philosophy fails to occupy this important vantage-ground. We come then to the final conditions with which the modern synthesis must comply. Without neglecting the spheres of Thought and Action it must also comprehend the moral sphere; and the very principle on which its claim to universality rests must be derived from Feeling. Then, and not till then, can the claims of theology be finally set aside. For then the new system will have surpassed the old in that which is the one essential purpose of all general doctrines. It will have shown itself able to effect what no other doctrine has done, that is, to bring the three primary elements of our nature into harmony. If Positivism were to prove incapable of satisfying this condition, we must give up all hope of systematization of any kind. For while Positive principles are now sufficiently developed to neutralize those of Theology, yet, on the other hand, the influence of theology would continue to be far greater. Hence it is that many conscientious thinkers in the present day are so inclined to despair for the future of society. They see that the old principles on which society has been governed must finally become powerless. What they do not see is that a new basis for morality is being gradually laid down. Their theories are too imperfect and incoherent to show them the direction towards which the present time is ultimately tending. It must be owned, too, that their view seems borne out by the present character of the Positive method. While all allow its utility in the treatment of practical, and even of speculative, problems, it seems to most men, and very naturally, quite unfit to deal with questions of morality.

But on closer examination they will see reason to rectify their judgment. They will see that the hardness with which Positive science has been justly reproached, is due to the speciality and want of purpose with which it has hitherto been pursued, and is not at all inherent in its nature. Originating as it did in the necessities of our material nature, which for a long time restricted it to the study of the inorganic world, it has not till now become sufficiently complete or systematic to harmonize well with our moral nature. But now that it is brought to bear upon social questions, which for the future will form its most important field, it loses all the defects peculiar to its long period of infancy. The very attribute of reality which is claimed by the new philosophy, leads it to treat all subjects from the moral still more than from the intellectual side. The necessity of assigning with exact truth the place occupied by the intellect and by the heart in the organization of human nature and of society, leads to the decision that Affection must be the central point of the synthesis. In the treatment of social questions Positive science will be found utterly to discard those proud illusions of the supremacy of reason to which it had been liable during its preliminary stages. Ratifying, in this respect, the common experience of men even more forcibly than Catholicism, it teaches us that individual happiness and public welfare are far more dependent upon the heart than upon the intellect. But, independently of this, the question of co-ordinating the faculties of our nature will convince us that the only basis on which they can be brought into harmonious union, is the preponderance of Affection over Reason, and even over Activity.

The fact that intellect, as well as social sympathy, is a distinctive attribute of our nature, might lead us to suppose that either of these two might be supreme, and therefore that there might be more than one method of establishing unity. The fact, however, is that there is only one; because these two elements are by no means equal in their fitness for assuming the first place. Whether we look at the distinctive qualities of each, or at the degree of force which they possess, it is easy to see that the only position for which the intellect is permanently adapted is to be the servant of the social sympathies. If, instead of being content with this honorable post, it aspires to become supreme, its ambitious aims, which are never realized, result simply in the most deplorable disorder.

Even with the individual, it is impossible to establish permanent harmony between our various impulses, except by giving complete supremacy to the feeling which prompts the sincere and habitual desire of doing good. This feeling is, no doubt, like the rest, in itself blind; it has to learn from reason the right means of obtaining satisfaction; and our active faculties are then called into requisition to apply those means. But common experience proves that after all the principal condition of right action is the benevolent impulse; with the ordinary amount of intellect and activity that is found in men, this stimulus, if well sustained, is enough to direct our thoughts and energies to a good result. Without this habitual spring of action they would inevitably waste themselves in barren or incoherent efforts, and speedily relapse into their original torpor. Unity in our moral nature is, then, impossible, except so far as affection preponderates over intellect and activity.

True as this fundamental principle is for the individual, it is in public life that its necessity can be demonstrated most irrefutably. The Problem is in reality the same, nor is any different solution of it required; only it assumes such increased dimensions, that less uncertainty is felt as to the method to be adopted. The various beings whom it is sought to harmonize have in this case each a separate existence; it is clear, therefore, that the first condition of co-operation must be sought in their own inherent tendency to universal love. No calculations of self-interest can rival this social instinct, whether in promptitude and breadth of intuition, or in boldness and tenacity of purpose. True it is that the benevolent emotions have in most cases less intrinsic energy than the selfish. But they have this beautiful quality, that social life not only permits their growth, but stimulates it to an almost unlimited extent, while it holds their antagonists in constant check. Indeed the increasing tendency in the former to prevail over the latter is the best measure by which to judge of the progress of Humanity. But the intellect may do much to confirm their influence. It may strengthen social feeling by diffusing juster views of the relations in which the various parts of society stand to each other; or it may guide its application by dwelling on the lessons which the past offers to the future. It is to this honorable service that the new philosophy would direct our intellectual powers. Here the highest sanction is given to their operations, and an exhaustless field is opened out for them, from which far deeper satisfaction may be gained than from the approbation of the learned societies, or from the puerile specialities with which they are at present occupied.

In fact, the ambitious claims which, ever since the hopeless decline of the theological synthesis, have been advanced by the intellect, never were or could be realized. Their only value lay in their solvent action on the theological system when it had become hostile to progress. The intellect is intended for service, not for empire; when it imagines itself supreme, it is really only obeying the personal instead of the social instincts. It never acts independently of feeling, be that feeling good or bad. The first condition of command is force; now reason has but light; the impulse that moves it must come from elsewhere. The metaphysical Utopias, in which a life of pure contemplation is held out as the highest ideal, attract the notice of our men of science; but are really nothing but illusions of pride, or veils for dishonest schemes. True there is a genuine satisfaction in the act of discovering truth; but it is not sufficiently intense to be an habitual guide of conduct. Indeed, so feeble is our intellect, that the impulse of some passion is necessary to direct and sustain it in almost every effort. When the impulse comes from kindly feeling it attracts attention on account of its rarity or value; when it springs from the selfish motives of glory, ambition, or gain, it is too common to be remarked. This is usually the only difference between the two cases. It does indeed occasionally happen that the intellect is actuated by a sort of passion for truth in itself, without any mixture of pride or vanity. Yet, in this case, as in every other, there is intense egotism in exercising the mental powers irrespectively of all social objects. Positivism, as I shall afterwards explain, is even more severe than Catholicism in its condemnation of this type of character, whether in metaphysicians or in men of science. The true philosopher would consider it a most culpable abuse of the opportunities which civilization affords him for the sake of the welfare of society, in leading a speculative life. . . .

Thus it is that an intellectual synthesis, or systematic study of the laws of nature, is needed on far higher grounds than those of satisfying our theoretical faculties, which are, for the most part, very feeble, even in men who devote themselves to a life of thought. It is needed, because it solves at once the most difficult problem of the moral synthesis. The higher impulses within us are brought under the influence of a powerful stimulus from without. By its means they are enabled to control our discordant impulses, and to maintain a state of harmony towards which they have always tended, but which, without such aid, could never be realized. Moreover, this conception of the order of nature evidently supplies the basis for a synthesis of human action; for the efficacy of our actions depends entirely upon their conformity to this order. But this part of the subject has been fully explained in my previous work, and I need not enlarge upon it further. As soon as the synthesis of mental conceptions enables us to form a synthesis of feelings, it is clear that there will be no very serious difficulties in constructing a synthesis of actions. Unity of action depends upon unity of impulse, and unity of design; and thus we find that the co-ordination of human nature as a whole depends ultimately upon the co-ordination of mental conceptions, a subject which seemed at first of comparatively slight importance.

The subjective principle of Positivism, that is, the subordination of the intellect to the heart is thus fortified by an objective basis, the immutable Necessity of the external world; and by this means it becomes possible to bring human life within the influence of social sympathy. The superiority of the new synthesis to the old is even more evident under this second aspect than under the first. In theological systems the objective basis was supplied by spontaneous belief in a supernatural Will. Now, whatever the degree of reality attributed to these fictions, they all proceeded from a subjective source; and therefore their influence in most cases must have been very confused and fluctuating. In respect of moral discipline they cannot be compared either for precision, for force, or for stability, to the conception of an invariable Order, actually existing without us, and attested, whether we will or no, by every act of our existence.

This fundamental doctrine of Positivism is not to be attributed in the full breadth of its meanings to any single thinker. It is the slow result of a vast process carried out in separate departments, which began with the first use of our intellectual powers, and which is only just completed in those who exhibit those powers in their highest form. During the long period of her infancy Humanity has been preparing this the most precious of her intellectual attainments, as the basis for the only system of life which is permanently adapted to our nature. The doctrine has to be demonstrated in all the more essential cases from observation only, except so far as we admit argument from analogy. Deductive argument is not admissible, except in such cases as are evidently compounded of others in which the proof given has been sufficient. Thus, for instance, we are authorized by sound logic to assert the existence of laws of weather; though most of these are still, and, perhaps, always will be, unknown. For it is clear that meteorological phenomena result from a combination of astronomical, physical, and chemical influences, each of which has been proved to be subject to invariable laws. But in all phenomena which are not thus reducible, we must have recourse to inductive reasoning; for a principle which is the basis of all deduction cannot be itself deduced. Hence it is that the doctrine, being so entirely foreign as it is to our primitive mental state, requires such a long course of preparation. Without such preparation even the greatest thinkers could not anticipate it. It is true that in some cases metaphysical conceptions of a law have been formed before the proof really required had been furnished. But they were never of much service, except so far as they generalized in a more or less confused way the analogies naturally suggested by the laws which had actually been discovered in simpler phenomena. Besides, such assertions always remained very doubtful and very barren in result, until they were based upon some outline of a really Positive theory. Thus, in spite of the apparent potency of this metaphysical method, to which modern intellects are so addicted, the conception of an External Order is still extremely imperfect in many of the most cultivated minds, because they have not verified it sufficiently in the most intricate and important class of phenomena, the phenomena of society. I am not, of course, speaking of the few thinkers who accept my discovery of the principal laws of Sociology. Such uncertainty in a subject so closely related to all others, produces great confusion in men's minds, and affects their perception of an invariable order, even in the simplest subjects. . . .

I have now described the fundamental condition of the Positive Synthesis. Deriving its subjective principle from the affections, it is dependent ultimately on the intellect for its objective basis. This basis connects it with the Economy of the external world, the dominion of which Humanity accepts, and at the same time modifies. I have left many points unexplained; but enough has been said for the purpose of this work, which is only the introduction to a larger treatise. We now come to the essential difficulty that presented itself in the construction of the Synthesis. That difficulty was to discover the true Theory of human and social Development. The first decisive step in this discovery renders the conception of the Order of Nature complete. It stands out then as the fundamental doctrine of an universal system, for which the whole course of modern progress has been preparing the way. For three centuries men of science have been unconsciously co-operating in the work. They have left no gap of any importance, except in the region of Moral and Social phenomena. And now that man's history has been for the first time systematically considered as a whole, and has been found to be, like all other phenomena, subject to invariable laws, the preparatory labors of modern Science are ended. Her remaining task is to construct that synthesis which will place her at the only point of view from which every department of knowledge can be embraced.

In my *System of Positive Philosophy* both these objects were aimed at. I attempted, and in the opinion of the principal thinkers of our time successfully, to complete and at the same time co-ordinate Natural Philosophy, by establishing the general law of human development, social as well as intellectual. I shall not now enter into the discussion of this law, since its truth is no longer contested. Fuller consideration of it is reserved for the third volume of my new treatise. It lays down, as is generally known, that our speculations upon all subjects whatsoever pass necessarily through three successive stages: a Theological stage, in which free play is given to spontaneous fictions admitting of no proof; the Metaphysical stage, characterized by the prevalence of personified abstractions or entities; lastly, the Positive stage, based upon an exact view of the real facts of the case. The first, though purely provisional, is invariably the point from which we start; the third is the only permanent or normal state; the second has but a modifying or rather a solvent influence, which qualifies it for regulating the transition from the first stage to the third. We begin with theological Imagination, thence we pass through metaphysical Discussion, and we end at last with positive Demonstration. Thus by means of this one general law we are enabled to take a comprehensive and simultaneous view of the past, present, and future of Humanity.

In my *System of Positive Philosophy,* this law of Filiation has always been associated with the law of Classification, the application of which to Social Dynamics furnishes the second element requisite for the theory of development. It fixes the order in which our different conceptions pass through each of these phases. That order, as is generally known, is determined by the decreasing generality, or what comes to the same thing, by the increasing complexity, of the phenomena; the more complex being naturally dependent upon those that are more simple and less special. Arranging the sciences according to this mutual relation, we find them grouped naturally in six primary divisions: Mathematics, Astronomy, Physics, Chemistry, Biology, and Sociology. Each passes through the three phases of development before the one succeeding it. Without continuous reference to this classification the theory of development would be confused and vague.

The theory thus derived from the combination of this second or statical law with the dynamical law of the three stages, seems at first sight to include nothing but the intellectual movement. But my previous remarks will have shown that this is enough to guarantee its applicability to social progress also; since social progress has invariably depended on the growth of our fundamental beliefs with regard to the economy that surrounds us. The historical portion of my *Positive Philosophy* has proved an unbroken connection between the development of Activity and that of Speculation; on the combined influence of these depends the development of Affection. The theory therefore requires no alteration: what is wanted is merely an additional statement explaining the phases of active, that is to say, of political development. Human activity, as I have long since shown, passes successively through the stages of Offensive warfare, Defensive warfare, and Industry. The respective connection of these states with the preponderance of the theological, the metaphysical, or the positive spirit leads at once to a complete explanation of history. It reproduces in a systematic form the only historical conception which has become adopted by universal consent; the division, namely, of history into Ancient, Mediæval, and Modern.

Thus the foundation of Social science depends simply upon establishing the truth of this theory of development. We do this by combining the dynamic law, which is its distinctive feature, with the statical principle which renders it coherent; we then complete the theory by extending it to practical life. All knowledge is now brought within the sphere of Natural Philosophy; and the provisional distinction by which, since Aristotle and Plato, it has been so sharply demarcated from Moral Philosophy, ceases to exist. The Positive spirit, so long confined to the simpler inorganic phenomena, has now passed through its difficult course of probation. It extends to a more important and more intricate class of speculations, and disengages them for ever from all theological or metaphysical influence. All our notions of truth are thus rendered homogeneous, and begin at once to converge towards a central principle. A firm objective basis is consequently laid down for that complete co-ordination of human existence towards which all sound Philosophy has ever tended, but which the want of adequate materials has hitherto made impossible.

It will be felt, I think, that the principal difficulty of the Positive Synthesis was met by my discovery of the laws of development, if we bear in mind that while that theory completes and co-ordinates the objective basis of the system, it at the same time holds it in subordination to the subjective principle. It is under the influence of this moral principle that the whole philosophical construction should be carried on. The enquiry into the Order of the Universe is an indispensable task, and it comes necessarily within the province of the intellect; but the intellect is too apt to aim in its pride at something beyond its proper function, which consists in unremitting service of the social sympathies. It would willingly escape from all control and follow its own bent towards speculative digressions; a tendency which is at present favored by the undisciplined habits of thought naturally due to the first rise of Positivism in its special departments. The influence of the moral principle is necessary to recall it to its true function; since if its investigations were allowed to assume an absolute character, and to recognize no limit, we should only be repeating in a scientific form many of the worst results of theological and metaphysical belief. The Universe is to be studied not for its own sake, but for the sake of Man or rather of Humanity. To study it in any other spirit would not only be immoral, but also highly irrational. For, as statements of pure objective truth, our scientific theories can never be really satisfactory. They can only satisfy us from the subjective point of view; that is, by limiting themselves to the treatment of such questions as have some direct or indirect influence over human life. It is for social feeling to determine these limits, outside which our knowledge will always remain imperfect as well as useless; and this even in the case of the simplest phenomena, as astronomy testifies. Were the influence of social feeling to be slackened, the Positive spirit would soon fall back to the subjects which were preferred during the period of its infancy; subjects the most remote from human interest, and therefore also the easiest. While its probationary period lasted, it was natural to investigate all accessible problems without distinction; and this was often justified by the logical value of many problems that, scientifically speaking, were useless. But now that the Positive method has been sufficiently developed to be applied exclusively to the purpose for which it was intended, there is no use whatever in prolonging the period of probation by these idle exercises. Indeed the want of purpose and discipline in our researches is rapidly assuming a retrograde character. Its tendency is to undo the chief results obtained by the spirit of detail during the time when that spirit was really essential to progress.

Here, then, we are met by a serious difficulty. The construction of the objective basis for the Positive synthesis imposes two conditions which seem at first sight incompatible. On the one hand we must allow the intellect to be free, or else we shall not have the full benefit of its services; and, on the other, we must control its natural tendency to unlimited digressions. The problem was insoluble, so long as the study of the natural economy did not include Sociology. But as soon as the Positive spirit extends to the treatment of social questions, these at once take precedence of all others, and thus the moral point of view becomes paramount. Objective science, proceeding from without inwards, falls at last into natural harmony with the subjective or moral principle, the superiority of which it had for so long a time resisted. As a mere speculative question it may be considered as proved to the satisfaction of every true thinker, that the social point of view is logically and scientifically supreme over all others, being the only point from which all our scientific conceptions can be regarded as a whole. Yet its influence can never be injurious to the progress of other Positive studies; for these, whether for the sake of their method or of their subject matter, will always continue to be necessary as an introduction to the final science. Indeed the Positive system gives the highest sanction and the most powerful stimulus to all preliminary sciences, by insisting on the relation which each of them bears to the great whole, Humanity.

Thus the foundation of social science bears out the statement made at the beginning of this work, that the intellect would, under Positivism, accept its proper position of subordination to the heart. The recognition of this, which is the subjective principle of Positivism, renders the construction of a complete system of human life possible. The antagonism which, since the close of the Middle Ages, has arisen between Reason and Feeling, was an anomalous though inevitable condition. It is now for ever at an end; and the only system which can really satisfy the wants of our nature, individually or collectively, is therefore ready for our acceptance. As long as the antagonism existed, it was hopeless to expect that Social Sympathy could do much to modify the preponderance of self-love in the affairs of life. But the case is different as soon as reason and sympathy are brought into active co-operation. Separately, their influence in our imperfect organization is very feeble; but combined it may extend indefinitely. It will never, indeed, be able to do away with the fact that practical life must, to a large extent, be regulated by interested motives; yet it may introduce a standard of morality inconceivably higher than any that has existed in the past, before these two modifying forces could be made to combine their action upon our stronger and lower instincts. . . .

I have now described the general spirit of Positivism. But there are two or three points on which some further explanation is necessary, as they are the source of misapprehensions too common and too serious to be disregarded. Of course I only concern myself with such objections as are made in good faith.

The fact that entire freedom from theological belief is necessary before the Positive state can be perfectly attained, has induced superficial observers to confound Positivism with a state of pure negation. Now this state was at one time, and that even so recently as the last century, favorable to progress; but at present in those who unfortunately still remain in it, it is a radical obstacle to all sound social and even intellectual organization. I have long ago repudiated all philosophical or historical connection between Positivism and what is called Atheism. But it is desirable to expose the error somewhat more clearly.

Atheism, even from the intellectual point of view, is a very imperfect form of emancipation; for its tendency is to prolong the metaphysical stage indefinitely, by continuing to seek for new solutions of Theological problems, instead of setting aside all inaccessible researches on the ground of their utter inutility. The true Positive spirit consists in substituting the study of the invariable Laws of phenomena for that of their so-called Causes, whether proximate or primary; in a word, in studying the *How* instead of the *Why*. Now this is wholly incompatible with the ambitious and visionary attempts of Atheism to explain the formation of the Universe, the origin of animal life, etc. The Positivist comparing the various phases of human speculation, looks upon these scientific chimeras as far less valuable even from the intellectual point of view than the first spontaneous inspirations of primeval times. The principle of Theology is to explain everything by super-natural *Wills*. That principle can never be set aside until we acknowl-edge the search for *Causes* to be beyond our reach, and limit our-selves to the knowledge of *Laws*. As long as men persist in attempting to answer the insoluble questions which occupied the attention of the childhood of our race, by far the more rational plan is to do as was done then, that is, simply to give free play to the imagination. These spontaneous beliefs have gradually fallen into disuse, not because they have been disproved, but because mankind has become more en-lightened as to its wants and the scope of its powers, and has grad-ually given an entirely new direction to its speculative efforts. If we insist upon penetrating the unattainable mystery of the essential Cause that produces phenomena, there is no hypothesis more satisfactory than that they proceed from Wills dwelling in them or outside them; an hypothesis which assimilates them to the effect produced by the desires which exist within ourselves. Were it not for the pride induced by metaphysical and scientific studies, it would be inconceivable that any atheist, modern or ancient, should have believed that his vague hypotheses on such a subject were preferable to this direct mode of explanation. And it was the only mode which really satisfied the reason, until men began to see the utter inanity and inutility of all search for absolute truth. The Order of Nature is doubtless very imperfect in every respect; but its production is far more compatible with the hypothesis of an intelligent Will than with that of a blind mechanism. Persistent atheists therefore would seem to be the most illogical of theologists: because they occupy themselves with theo-logical problems, and yet reject the only appropriate method of handling them. But the fact is that pure Atheism even in the present day is very rare. What is called Atheism is usually a phase of Pantheism, which is really nothing but a relapse, disguised under learned terms, into a vague and abstract form of Fetichism. And it is not impossible that it may lead to the reproduction in one form or other of every theological phase, as soon as the check which modern society still imposes on metaphysical extravagence has become some-what weakened. The adoption of such theories as a satisfactory system of belief, indicates a very exaggerated or rather false view of intel-lectual requirements, and a very insufficient recognition of moral and social wants. It is generally connected with the visionary but mischievous tendencies of ambitious thinkers to uphold what they call the empire of Reason. In the moral sphere it forms a sort of basis for the degrading fallacies of modern metaphysicians as to the absolute preponderance of self-interest. Politically, its tendency is to unlimited prolongation of the revolutionary position: its spirit is that of blind hatred to the past: and it resists all attempts to explain it on Positive principles, with the view of disclosing the future. Atheism, therefore, is not likely to lead to Positivism except in those who pass through it rapidly as the last and most short-lived of metaphysical phases. And the wide diffusion of the scientific spirit in the present day makes this passage so easy that to arrive at maturity without accomplishing it, is a symptom of a certain mental weakness, which is often connected with moral insufficiency, and is very incompatible with Positivism. Negation offers but a feeble and precarious basis for union: and disbelief in Monotheism is of itself no better proof of a mind fit to grapple with the questions of the day than disbelief in Polytheism or Fetichism, which no one would maintain to be an adequate ground for claiming intellectual sympathy. The atheistic phase indeed was not really necessary, except for the revolutionists of the last century who took the lead in the movement towards radical regeneration of society. The necessity has already ceased; for the decayed condition of the old system makes the need of regeneration palpable to all. Persistence in anarchy, and Atheism is the most characteristic symptom of anarchy, is a temper of mind more unfavorable to the organic spirit, which ought by this time to have established its influence, than sincere adhesion to the old forms. This latter is of course obstructive: but at least it does not hinder us from fixing our attention upon the great social problem. Indeed it helps us to do so: because it forces the new philosophy to throw aside every weapon of attack against the older faith except its own higher capacity of satisfying our moral and social wants. But in the Atheism maintained by many metaphysicians and scientific men of the present day, Positivism, instead of wholesome rivalry of this kind, will meet with nothing but barren resistance. Anti-theological as such men may be, they feel unmixed repugnance for any attempts at social regeneration, although their efforts in the last century had to some extent prepared the way for it. Far, then, from counting upon their support, Positivists must expect to find them hostile: although from the incoherence of their opinions it will not be difficult to reclaim those of them whose errors are not essentially due to pride.

The charge of Materialism which is often made against Positive philosophy is of more importance. It originates in the course of scientific study upon which the Positive System is based. In answering the charge, I need not enter into any discussion of impenetrable mysteries.

Our theory of development will enable us to see distinctly the real ground of the confusion that exists upon the subject.

Positive science was for a long time limited to the simplest subjects: it could not reach the highest except by a natural series of intermediate steps. As each of these steps is taken, the student is apt to be influenced too strongly by the methods and results of the preceding stage. Here, as it seems to me, lies the real source of that scientific error which men have instinctively blamed as *materialism*. The name is just, because the tendency indicated is one which degrades the higher subjects of thought by confounding them with the lower. It was hardly possible that this usurpation by one science of the domain of another should have been wholly avoided. For since the more special phenomena do really depend upon the more general, it is perfectly legitimate for each science to exercise a certain deductive influence upon that which follows it in the scale. By such influence the special inductions of that science were rendered more coherent. The result, however, is that each of the sciences has to undergo a long struggle against the encroachments of the one preceding it; a struggle which, even in the case of the subjects which have been studied longest, is not yet over. Nor can it entirely cease until the controlling influence of sound philosophy be established over the whole scale, introducing juster views of the relations of its several parts, about which at present there is such irrational confusion. Thus it appears that Materialism is a danger inherent in the mode in which the scientific studies necessary as a preparation for Positivism were pursued. Each science tended to absorb the one next to it, on the ground of having reached the Positive stage earlier and more thoroughly. The evil then is really deeper and more extensive than is imagined by most of those who deplore it. It passes generally unnoticed except in the highest class of subjects. These doubtless are more seriously affected, inasmuch as they undergo the encroaching process from all the rest; but we find the same thing in different degrees, in every step of the scientific scale. Even the lowest step, Mathematics, is no exception, though its position would seem at first sight to exempt it. To a philosophic eye there is Materialism in the common tendency of mathematicians at the present day to absorb Geometry or Mechanics into the Calculus, as well as in the more evident encroachments of Mathematics upon Physics, of Physics upon Chemistry, of Chemistry, which is more frequent, upon Biology, or lastly in the common tendency of the best biologists to look upon Sociology as a mere corollary of their own science. In these cases it is the same fundamental error: that is, an exaggerated use of deductive reasoning; and in all it is attended with the same result, that the higher studies are in constant danger of being disorganized by the indiscriminate application of the lower. All scientific specialists at the present time are more or less materialists, according as the phenomena studied by them are more or less simple and general. Geometricians, therefore, are more liable to the error than any others; they all aim consciously or otherwise at a synthesis in which the most elementary studies, those of Number, Space, and Motion, are made to regulate all the rest. But the biologists who resist this encroachment most energetically are often guilty of the same mistake. They not unfrequently attempt, for instance, to explain all sociological facts by the influence of climate and race, which are purely secondary; thus showing their ignorance of the fundamental laws of Sociology, which can only be discovered by a series of direct inductions from history.

This philosophical estimate of Materialism explains how it is that it has been brought as a charge against Positivism, and at the same time proves the deep injustice of the charge. Positivism, far from countenancing so dangerous an error, is, as we have seen, the only philosophy which can completely remove it. The error arises from certain tendencies which are in themselves legitimate, but which have been carried too far; and Positivism satisfies these tendencies in their due measure. Hitherto the evil has remained unchecked, except by the theologico-metaphysical spirit, which, by giving rise to what is called Spiritualism, has rendered a very valuable service. But useful as it has been, it could not arrest the active growth of Materialism, which has assumed in the eyes of modern thinkers something of a progressive character, from having been so long connected with the cause of resistance to a retrograde system. Notwithstanding all the protests of the spiritualists, the lower sciences have encroached upon the higher to an extent that seriously impairs their independence and their value. But Positivism meets the difficulty far more effectually. It satisfies and reconciles all that is really tenable in the rival claims of both Materialism and Spiritualsm; and, having done this, it discards them both. It holds the one to be as dangerous to Order as the other to Progress. This result is an immediate consequence of the establishment of the encyclopædic scale, in which each science retains its own proper sphere of induction, while deductively it remains subordinate to the science which precedes it. But what really decides the matter is the fact that such paramount importance, both logically and scientifically, is given by Positive Philosophy to social questions. For these are the questions in which the influence of Materialism is most mischievous, and also in which it is most easily introduced. A system therefore which gives them the precedence over all other questions must hold Materialism to be quite as obstructive as Spiritualism, since both are alike an obstacle to the progress of that science for the sake of which all other sciences are studied. Further advance in the work of social regeneration implies the elimination of both of them, because it cannot proceed without exact knowledge of the laws of moral and social phenomena. In the next chapter I shall have to speak of the mischievous effects of Materialism upon the Art or practice of social life. It leads to a misconception of the most fundamental principle of that Art, namely, the systematic separation of spiritual and temporal power. To maintain that separation, to carry out on a more satisfactory basis the admirable attempt made in the Middle Ages by the Catholic Church, is the most important of political questions. Thus the antagonism of Positivism to Materialism rests upon political no less than upon philosophical grounds. . . .

On reviewing this brief sketch of the intellectual character of Positivism, it will be seen that all its essential attributes are summed up in the word *Positive,* which I applied to the new philosophy at its outset. All the languages of Western Europe agree in understanding by this word and its derivatives the two qualities of *reality* and *usefulness.* Combining these, we get at once an adequate definition of the true philosophic spirit, which, after all, is nothing but good sense generalized and put into a systematic form. The term also implies in all European languages, *certainty* and *precision,* qualities by which the intellect of modern nations is markedly distinguished from that of antiquity. Again, the ordinary acceptation of the term implies a directly *organic* tendency. Now the metaphysical spirit is incapable of organizing; it can only criticise. This distinguishes it from the Positive spirit, although for a time they had a common sphere of action. By speaking of Positivism as organic, we imply that it has a social purpose; that purpose being to supersede Theology in the spiritual direction of the human race.

But the word will bear yet a further meaning. The organic character of the system leads us naturally to another of its attributes, namely, its invariable *relativity.* Modern thinkers will never rise above that critical position which they have hitherto taken up towards the past, except by repudiating all absolute principles. This last meaning is more latent than the others, but is really contained in the term. It will soon become generally accepted, and the word *Positive* will be understood to mean *relative* as much as it now means *organic, precise, certain, useful,* and *real.* Thus the highest attributes of human wisdom have, with one exception, been gradually condensed into a single expressive term. All that is now wanting is that the word should denote what at first could form no part of the meaning, the union of moral with intellectual qualities. At present, only the latter are included; but the course of modern progress makes it certain that the conception implied by the word Positive, will ultimately have a more direct reference to the heart than to the understanding. For it will soon be felt by all that the tendency of Positivism, and that by virtue of its primary characteristic, reality, is to make Feeling systematically supreme over Reason as well as over Activity. After all, the change consists simply in realising the full etymological value of the word *Philosophy.* For it was impossible to realize it until moral and mental conditions had been reconciled; and this has been now done by the foundation of a Positive science of society.

Chapter VI

Conclusion. The Religion of Humanity

. . . All essential phases in the evolution of society answer to corresponding phases in the growth of the individual, whether it has proceeded spontaneously or under systematic guidance, supposing always that his development be complete. But it is not enough to prove the close connection which exists between all modes and degrees of human regeneration. We have yet to find a central point round which all will naturally meet. In this point consists the unity of Positivism as a system of life. Unless it can be thus condensed round one single principle, it will never wholly supersede the synthesis of Theology, notwithstanding its superiority in the reality and stability of its component parts, and in their homogeneity and coherence as a whole. There should be a central point in the system, towards which Feeling, Reason, and Activity alike converge. The proof that Positivism possesses such a central point will remove the last obstacle to its complete acceptance as the guide of private or public life.

Such a center we find in the great conception of Humanity, towards which every aspect of Positivism naturally converges. By it the conception of God will be entirely superseded, and a synthesis be formed, more complete and permanent than that provisionally established by the old religions. Through it the new doctrine becomes at once accessible to men's hearts in its full extent and application. From their hearts it will penetrate their minds, and thus the immediate necessity of beginning with a long and difficult course of study is avoided, though this must of course be always indispensable to its systematic teachers.

This central point of Positivism is even more moral than intellectual in character; it represents the principle of Love upon which the whole system rests. It is the peculiar characteristic of the Great Being who is here set forth, to be compounded of separable elements. Its existence depends therefore entirely upon mutual Love knitting together its various parts. The calculations of self-interest can never be substituted as a combining influence for the sympathetic instincts.

Yet the belief in Humanity, while stimulating Sympathy, at the same time enlarges the scope and vigor of the Intellect. For it requires high powers of generalization to conceive clearly of this vast organism, as the result of spontaneous co-operation, abstraction made of all partial antagonisms. Reason, then, has its part in this central dogma as well as Love. It enlarges and completes our conception of the Supreme Being, by revealing to us the external and internal conditions of its existence.

Lastly, our active powers are stimulated by it no less than our feelings and our reason. For since Humanity is so far more complex than any other organism, it will react more strongly and more continuously on its environment, submitting to its influence and so modifying it. Hence results Progress which is simply the development of Order under the influence of Love.

Thus, in the conception of Humanity, the three essential aspects of Positivism, its subjective principle, its objective dogma, and its practical object, are united. Towards Humanity, who is for us the only true Great Being, we, the conscious elements of whom she is composed, shall henceforth direct every aspect of our life, individual or collective. Our thoughts will be devoted to the knowledge of Humanity, our affections to her love, our actions to her service.

Positivists then may, more truly than theological believers of whatever creed, regard life as a continuous and earnest act of worship; worship which will elevate and purify our feelings, enlarge and enlighten our thoughts, ennoble and invigorate our actions. It supplies a direct solution, so far as a solution is possible, of the great problem of the Middle Ages, the subordination of Politics to Morals. For this follows at once from the consecration now given to the principle that social sympathy should preponderate over self-love

Thus Positivism becomes, in the true sense of the word, a Religion; the only religion which is real and complete; destined therefore to replace all imperfect and provisional systems resting on the primitive basis of theology.

For even the synthesis established by the old theocracies of Egypt and India was insufficient, because, being based on purely subjective principles, it could never embrace practical life, which must always be subordinated to the objective realities of the external world. Theocracy was thus limited at the outset to the sphere of thought and of feeling; and part even of this field was soon lost when Art became emancipated from theocratical control, showing a spontaneous tendency to its natural vocation of idealizing real life. Of science and of morality the priests were still left sole arbiters; but here, too, their influence materially diminished as soon as the discovery of the simpler abstract truths of Positive science gave birth to Greek Philosophy. Philosophy, though as yet necessarily restricted to the metaphysical stage, yet already stood forward as the rival of the sacerdotal system. Its attempts to construct were in themselves fruitless; but they overthrew Polytheism, and ultimately transformed it into Monotheism. In this the last phase of theology, the intellectual authority of the priests was undermined no less deeply than the principle of their doctrine. They lost their hold upon Science, as long ago they had lost their hold upon Art. All that remained to them was the moral guidance of society; and even this was soon compromised by the progress of free thought; progress really due to the Positive spirit, although its systematic exponents still belong to the metaphysical school.

When Science had expanded sufficiently to exist apart from Philosophy, it showed a rapid tendency towards a synthesis of its own, alike incompatible with metaphysics and with theology. It was late in appearing, because it required a long series of preliminary efforts: but as it approached completion, it gradually brought the Positive spirit to bear upon the organization of practical life, from which that spirit had originally emanated. But thoroughly to effect this result was impossible until the science of Sociology had been formed; and this was done by my discovery of the law of historical development. Henceforth all true men of science will rise to the higher dignity of philosophers, and by so doing will necessarily assume something of the sacerdotal character, because the final result to which their researches tend is the subordination of every subject of thought to the moral principle; a result which leads us at once to the acceptance of a complete and homogeneous synthesis. Thus the philosophers of the future become priests of Humanity, and their moral and intellectual influence will be far wider and more deeply rooted than that of any former priesthood. The primary condition of their spiritual authority is exclusion from political power, as a guarantee that theory and practice shall be systematically kept apart. A system in which the organs of counsel and those of command are never identical cannot possibly degenerate into any of the evils of theocracy.

By entirely renouncing wealth and worldly position, and that not as individuals merely, but as a body, the priests of Humanity will occupy a position of unparalleled dignity. For with their moral influence they will combine what since the downfall of the old theocracies has always been separated from it, the influence of superiority in art and science. Reason, Imagination, and Feeling will be brought into unison: and so united will react strongly on the imperious conditions of practical life; bringing it into closer accordance with the laws of universal morality, from which it is so prone to deviate. And the influence of this new modifying power will be the greater that the synthesis on which it rests will have preceded and prepared the way for the social system of the future; whereas theology could not arrive at its central principle, until the time of its decline was approaching. All functions, then, that co-operate in the elevation of man will be regenerated by the Positive priesthood. Science, Poetry, Morality, will be devoted to the study, the praise, and the love of Humanity, in order that under their combined influence, our political action may be more unremittingly given to her service.

With such a mission, Science acquires a position of unparalleled importance, as the sole means through which we come to know the nature and conditions of this great Being, the worship of whom should be the distinctive feature of our whole life. For this all-important knowledge, the study of Sociology would seem to suffice: but Sociology itself depends upon preliminary study, first of the outer world, in which the actions of Humanity take place; and secondly, of Man, the individual agent.

The object of Positivist worship is not like that of theological believers, an absolute, isolated, incomprehensible Being, whose existence admits of no demonstration, or comparison with anything real. The evidence of the Being here set forward is spontaneous, and is shrouded in no mystery. Before we can praise, love, and serve Humanity as we ought, we must know something of the laws which govern her existence, an existence more complicated than any other of which we are cognizant.

And by virtue of this complexity, Humanity possesses the attributes of vitality in a higher degree than any other organization; that is to say, there is at once more intimate harmony of the component elements, and more complete subordination to the external world. Immense as is the magnitude of this organism measured both in Time and Space, yet each of its parts carefully examined will show the general consensus of the whole. At the same time it is more dependent than any other upon the conditions of the outer world; in other words, upon the sum of the laws that regulate inferior phenomena. Like other vital organisms, it submits to mathematical, astronomical, physical, chemical, and biological conditions; and, in addition to these, is subject to special laws of Sociology with which lower organisms are not concerned. But as a further result of its higher complexity it reacts upon the world more powerfully; and is indeed in a true sense its chief. Scientifically defined, then, it is truly the Supreme Being: the Being who manifests to the fullest extent all the highest attributes of life.

But there is yet another feature peculiar to Humanity, and one of primary importance. That feature is, that the elements of which she is composed must always have an independent existence. In other organisms the parts have no existence when severed from the whole; but this, the greatest of all organisms, is made up of lives which can really be separated. There is, as we have seen, harmony of parts as well as independence, but the last of these conditions is as indispensable as the first. Humanity would cease to be superior to other beings were it possible for her elements to become inseparable. The two conditions are equally necessary: but the difficulty of reconciling them is so great as to account at once for the slowness with which this highest of all organisms has been developed. It must not, however, be supposed that the new Supreme Being is, like the old, merely a subjective result of our powers of abstraction. Its existence is revealed to us, on the contrary, by close investigation of objective fact. Man indeed, as an individual, cannot properly be said to exist, except in the exaggerated abstractions of modern metaphysicians. Existence in the true sense can only be predicated of Humanity; although the complexity of her nature prevented men from forming a systematic conception of it until the necessary stages of scientific initiation had been passed. Bearing this conclusion in mind, we shall be able now to distinguish in Humanity two distinct orders of functions: those by which she acts upon the world, and those which bind together her component parts. Humanity cannot herself act otherwise than by her separable members; but the efficiency of these members depends upon their working in co-operation, whether instinctively or with design. We find, then, external functions relating principally to the material existence of this organism; and internal functions by which its moveable elements are combined. This distinction is but an application of the great theory, due to Bichat's genius, of the distinction between the life of nutrition and the life of relation which we find in the individual organism. Philosophically it is the source from which we derive the great social principle of separation of spiritual from temporal power. The temporal power governs: it originates in the personal instincts, and it stimulates activity. On it depends social Order. The spiritual power can only moderate: it is the exponent of our social instincts, and it promotes co-operation, which is the guarantee of Progress. Of these functions of Humanity the first corresponds to the function of nutrition, the second to that of innervation in the individual organism.

Having now viewed our subject statically, we may come to its dynamical aspect; reserving more detailed discussion for the third volume of this treatise, which deals with my fundamental theory of human development. The Great Being whom we worship is not immutable any more than it is absolute. Its nature is relative, and, as such, is eminently capable of growth. In a word it is the most vital of all living beings known to us. It extends and becomes more complex by the continuous successions of generations. But in its progressive changes, as well as in its permanent functions, it is subject to invariable laws. And these laws, considered, as we may now consider them, as a whole, form a more sublime object of contemplation than the solemn inaction of the old Supreme Being, whose existence was passive except when interrupted by acts of arbitrary and unintelligible volition. Thus it is only by Positive science that we can appreciate this highest of all destinies to which all the fatalities of individual life are subordinate. It is with this as with subjects of minor importance: systematic study of the Past is necessary in order to determine the Future, and so explain the tendencies of the Present. Let us then pass from the conception of Humanity as fully developed, to the history of its rise and progress; a history in which all other modes of progress are included. In ancient times the conception was incompatible with the theological spirit and also with the military character of society, which involved the slavery of the productive classes. The feeling of Patriotism, restricted as it was at first, was the only prelude then possible to the recognition of Humanity. From this narrow nationality there arose in the Middle Ages the feeling of universal brotherhood, as soon as military life had entered on its defensive phase, and all supernatural creeds had spontaneously merged into a monotheistic form common to the whole West. The growth of Chivalry, and the attempt made to effect a permanent separation of the two social powers, announced already the subordination of Politics to Morals, and thus showed that the conception of Humanity was in direct course of preparation. But the unreal and anti-social nature of the mediæval creed, and the military and aristocratic character of feudal society, made it impossible to go very far in this direction. The abolition of personal slavery was the most essential result of this important period. Society could now assume its industrial character; and feelings of fraternity were encouraged by modes of life in which all classes alike participated. Meanwhile, the growth of the Positive spirit was proceeding, and preparing the way for the establishment of Social Science, by which alone all other Positive studies could be systematized. This being done, the conception of the Great Being became possible. It was with reference to subjects of a speculative and scientific nature that the conception first arose in a distinct shape. As early as two centuries ago, Pascal spoke of the human race as one Man. Amidst the inevitable decline of the theological and military system, men became conscious of the movement of society, which had now advanced through so many phases; and the notion of Progress as a distinctive feature of Humanity became admitted. Still the conception of Humanity as the basis for a new synthesis was impossible until the crisis of the French Revolution. That crisis on the one hand proved the urgent necessity for social regeneration, and on the other gave birth to the only philosophy capable of effecting it. Thus our consciousness of the new Great Being has advanced coextensively with its growth. Our present conception of it is as much the measure of our social progress as it is the summary of Positive knowledge. . . .

The study of Humanity therefore, directly or indirectly, is for the future the permanent aim of Science; and Science is now in a true sense consecrated, as the source from which the universal religion receives its principles. It reveals to us not merely the nature and conditions of the Great Being, but also its destiny and the successive phases of its growth. The aim is high and arduous; it requires continuous and combined exertion of all our faculties; but it ennobles the simplest processes of scientific investigation by connecting them permanently with subjects of the deepest interest. The scrupulous exactness and rigorous caution of the Positive method, which when applied to unimportant subjects seem almost puerile, will be valued and insisted on when seen to be necessary for the efficacy of efforts relating to our most essential wants. Rationalism, in the true sense of the word, so far from being incompatible with right feeling, strengthens and develops it, by placing all the facts of the case, in social questions especially, in their true light.

But, however honorable the rank which Science when regenerated will hold in the new religion, the sanction given to Poetry will be even more direct and unqualified, because the function assigned to it is one which is more practical and which touches us more nearly. Its function will be the praise of humanity. All previous efforts of Art have been but the prelude to this, its natural mission; a prelude often impatiently performed, since Art threw off the yoke of theocracy at an earlier period than Science. Polytheism was the only religion under which it had free scope: there it could idealize all the passions of our nature, no attempt being made to conceal the similarity of the gods to the human type. The change from Polytheism to Monotheism was unacceptable to Art, because it narrowed its field; but towards the close of the Middle Ages it began to shake off the influence of obscure and chimerical beliefs, and take possession of its proper sphere. The field that now lies before it in the religion of Humanity is inexhaustible. It is called upon to idealize the social life of Man, which, in the time of the nations of antiquity, had not been sufficiently developed to inspire the highest order of poetry.

In the first place it will be of the greatest service in enabling men to realize the conception of Humanity, subject only to the condition of not overstepping the fundamental truths of Science. Science cannot define the nature and destinies of this Great Being with sufficient clearness. In our religion the object of worship must be conceived distinctly, in order to be ardently loved and zealously served. Science, especially in subjects of this nature, is confined within narrow limits; it leaves inevitable deficiencies which esthetic genius must supply. And there are certain qualities in Art, as opposed to Science, which specially qualify it for the representation of Humanity. For Humanity is distinguished from other forms of life by the combination of independence with co-operation, attributes which also are natural to Poetry. For while Poetry is more sympathetic than Science, its productions have far more individuality; the genius of their author is more strongly marked in them, and the debt to his predecessors and contemporaries is less apparent. Thus the synthesis on which the inauguration of the final religion depends, is one in which Art will participate more than Science, Science furnishing merely the necessary basis. Its influence will be even greater than in the times of Polytheism; for powerful as Art appeared to be in those times, it could in reality do nothing but embellish the fables to which the confused ideas of theocracy had given rise. By its aid we shall for the first time rise at last to a really human point of view, and be enabled distinctly to understand the essential attributes of the Great Being of whom we are members. The material power of Humanity, and the successive phases of her physical, her intellectual, and above all, her moral progress, will each in turn be depicted. Without the difficulties of analytical study, we shall gain a clear knowledge of her nature and her conditions, by the poet's description of her future destiny, of her constant struggle against painful fatalities, which have at last become a source of happiness and greatness, of the slow growth of her infancy, of her lofty hopes now so near fulfilment. The history of universal Love, the soul by which this Great Being is animated; the history, that is, of the marvellous advance of man, individually or socially, from brutish appetite to pure unselfish sympathy, is of itself an endless theme for the poetry of the future.

Comparisons, too, may be instituted, in which the poet, without specially attacking the old religion, will indicate the superiority of the new. The attributes of the new Great Being may be forcibly illustrated, especially during the time of transition, by contrast with the inferiority of her various predecessors. All theological types are absolute, indefinite, and immutable; consequently in none of them has it been possible to combine to a satisfactory extent the attributes of goodness, wisdom, and power. Nor can we conceive of their combination, except in a Being whose existence is a matter of certainty, and who is subject to invariable laws. The gods of Polytheism were endowed with energy and sympathy, but possessed neither dignity nor morality. They were superseded by the sublime deity of Monotheism, who was sometimes represented as inert and passionless, sometimes as impenetrable and inflexible. But the new Supreme Being, having a real existence, an existence relative and modifiable, admits of being more distinctly conceived than the old; and the influence of the conception will be equally strong and far more elevating. Each one of us will recognise in it a power superior to his own, a power on which the whole destiny of his life depends, since the life of the individual is in

every respect subordinate to the evolution of the race. But the knowledge of this power has not the crushing effect of the old conception of
omnipotence. For every great or good man will feel that his own life
is an indispensable element in the great organism. The supremacy of
Humanity is but the result of individual co-operation; her power is not
supreme, it is only superior to that of all beings whom we know. Our
love for her is tainted by no degrading fears, yet it is always coupled
with the most sincere reverence. Perfection is in no wise claimed for
her; we study her natural defects with care, in order to remedy them
as far as possible. The love we bear to her is a feeling as noble as it
is strong; it calls for no degrading expressions of adulation, but it
inspires us with unremitting zeal for moral improvement. But these
and other advantages of the new religion, though they can be indicated
by the philosopher, need the poet to display them in their full light.
The moral grandeur of man when freed from the chimeras that op-
press him, was foreseen by Goethe, and still more clearly by Byron.
But the work of these men was one of destruction; and their types
could only embody the spirit of revolt. Poetry must rise above the
negative stage in which, owing to the circumstances of the time, their
genius was arrested, and must embrace in the Positive spirit the
system of sociological and other laws to which human development
is subject, before it can adequately portray the new Man in his relation to the new God. . . .

To live in others is, in the truest sense of the word, life. Indeed
the best part of our own life is passed thus. As yet this truth has not
been grasped firmly, because the social point of view has never yet
been brought systematically before us. But the religion of Humanity,
by giving an esthetic form to the Positivist synthesis, will make it intelligible to minds of every class: and will enable us to enjoy the
untold charm springing from the sympathies of union and of continuity when allowed free play. To prolong our life indefinitely in the
Past and Future, so as to make it more perfect in the Present, is
abundant compensation for the illusions of our youth which have now
passed away for ever. Science, which deprived us of these imaginary
comforts, itself in its maturity supplies the solid basis for consolation
of a kind unknown before: the hope of becoming incorporate into the
Great Being whose static and dynamic laws it has revealed. On this
firm foundation Poetry raises the structure of public and private
worship; and thus all are made active partakers of this universal life,
which minds still fettered by theology cannot understand. Thus
imagination, while accepting the guidance of reason, will exercise a

far more efficient and extensive influence than in the days of Polytheism. For the priests of Humanity the sole purpose of Science is to prepare the field for Art, whether esthetic or industrial. This object once attained, poetic study or composition will form the chief occupation of our speculative faculties. The poet is now called to his true mission, which is to give beauty and grandeur to human life, by inspiring a deeper sense of our relation to Humanity. Poetry will form the basis of the ceremonies in which the new priesthood will solemnize, more efficiently than the old, the most important events of private life: especially Birth, Marriage, and Death; so as to impress the family as well as the state with the sense of this relation. Forced as we are henceforth to concentrate all our hopes and efforts upon the real life around us, we shall feel more strongly than ever that all the powers of Imagination as well as those of Reason, Feeling, and Activity, are required in its service.

Poetry once raised to its proper place, the arts of sound and form, which render in a more vivid way the subjects which Poetry has suggested, will soon follow. Their sphere, like that of Poetry, will be the celebration of Humanity; an exhaustless field, leaving no cause to regret the chimeras which, in the present empirical condition of these arts, are still considered indispensable. Music in modern times has been limited almost entirely to the expression of individual emotions. Its full power has never been felt in public life, except in the solitary instance of the *Marseillaise,* in which the whole spirit of our great Revolution stands recorded. But in the worship of Humanity, based as it is on Positive education, and animated by the spirit of Poetry, Music, as the most social of the special arts, will aid in the representation of the attributes and destinies of Humanity, and in the glorification of great historical types. Painting and Sculpture will have the same object; they will enable us to realise the conception of Humanity with greater clearness and precision than would be possible for Poetry, even with the aid of Music. The beautiful attempts of the artists of the sixteenth century, men who had very little theological belief, to embody the Christian ideal of Woman, may be regarded as an unconscious prelude to the representation of Humanity, in the form which of all others is most suitable. Under the impulse of these feelings, the sculptor will overcome the technical difficulties of representing figures in groups, and will adopt such subjects by preference. Hitherto this has only been effected in bas-reliefs, works which stand midway between painting and sculpture. There are, however, some splendid exceptions from which we can imagine the scope and grandeur of the latter art, when raised to its true position. Statuesque groups, whether the figures are joined or, as is preferable, separate, will enable the sculptor to undertake many great subjects from which he has been hitherto debarred.

In Architecture the influence of Positivism will be felt less rapidly; but ultimately this art like the rest will be made available for the new religion. The buildings erected for the service of God may for a time suffice for the worship of Humanity, in the same way that Christian worship was carried on at first in Pagan temples as they were gradually vacated. But ultimately buildings will be required more specially adapted to a religion in which all the functions connected with education and worship are so entirely different. What these buildings will be it would be useless at present to enquire. It is less easy to foresee the Positivist ideal in Architecture than in any other arts. And it must remain uncertain until the new principles of education have been generally spread, and until the Positivist religion, having received all the aid that Poetry, Music, and the arts of Form can give, has become the accepted faith of Western Europe. When the more advanced nations are heartily engaged in the cause, the true temples of Humanity will soon arise. By that time mental and moral regeneration will have advanced far enough to commence the reconstruction of all political institutions. Until then the new religion will avail itself of Christian churches as these gradually become vacant. . . .

Inspired as it is by sincere gratitude, which increases the more carefully the grounds for it are examined, the worship of Humanity raises Prayer for the first time above the degrading influence of self-interest. We pray to the Supreme Being; but only to express our deep thankfulness for her present and past benefits, which are an earnest of still greater blessings in the future. Doubtless it is a fact of human nature, that habitual expression of such feelings reacts beneficially on our moral nature; and so far we, too, find in Prayer a noble recompense. But it is one that can suggest to us no selfish thoughts, since it cannot come at all unless it come spontaneously. Our highest happiness consists in Love; and we know that more than any other feeling love may be strengthened by exercise; that alone of all feelings it admits of, and increases with, simultaneous expansion in all. Humanity will become more familiar to us than the old gods were to the Polytheists, yet without the loss of dignity which, in their case, resulted from familiarity. Her nature has in it nothing arbitrary, yet she co-operates with us in the worship that we render, since in honoring her we receive back "grace for grace." Homage accepted by the Deity of former times laid him open to the charge of puerile vanity. But the new Deity will accept praise only where it is deserved, and will derive from it equal benefit with ourselves. This perfect reciprocity of affection and of influence is peculiar to Positive religion, because in it alone the object of worship is a Being whose nature is relative, modifiable, and perfectible; a Being of whom her own worshipers form a part, and the laws of whose existence, being more clearly known than theirs, allow her desires and her tendencies to be more distinctly foreseen.

The morality of Positive religion combines all the advantages of spontaneousness with those of demonstration. It is so thoroughly human in all its parts, as to preclude all the subterfuges by which repentance for transgression is so often stifled or evaded. By pointing out distinctly the way in which each individual action reacts upon society, it forces us to judge our own conduct without lowering our standard. Some might think it too gentle, and not sufficiently vigorous; yet the love by which it is inspired is no passive feeling, but a principle which strongly stimulates our energies to the full extent compatible with the attainment of that highest good to which it is ever tending. Accepting the truths of science, it teaches that we must look to our own unremitting activity for the only providence by which the rigor of our destiny can be alleviated. We know well that the great Organism, superior though it be to all beings known to us, is yet under the dominion of inscrutable laws, and is in no respect either absolutely perfect or absolutely secure from danger. Every condition of our existence, whether those of the external world or those of our own nature, might at some time be compromised. Even our moral and intellectual faculties, on which our highest interests depend, are no exception to this truth. Such contingencies are always possible, and yet they are not to prevent us from living nobly; they must not lessen our love, our thought, or our efforts for Humanity; they must not overwhelm us with anxiety, nor urge us to useless complaint. But the very principles which demand this high standard of courage and resignation, are themselves well calculated to maintain it. For by making us fully conscious of the greatness of man, and by setting us free from the degrading influences of fear, they inspire us with keen interest in our efforts, inadequate though they be, against the pressure of fatalities which are not always beyond our power to modify. And thus the reaction of these fatalities upon our character is turned at last to a most beneficial use. It prevents alike overweening anxiety for our own interests and dull indifference to them; whereas, in theological and metaphysical systems, even when inculcating self-denial, there is always a dangerous tendency to concentrate thought on personal considerations. Dignified resignation to evils which cannot be resisted, wise and energetic action where modification of them is possible; such is the moral standard which Positivism puts forward for individuals and for society. . . .

ERNST MACH

The Analysis of Sensations and the Relation of the Physical to the Psychical

CHAPTERS I AND XV

ERNST MACH

BORN and brought up in the country, in Moravia, Ernst Mach (1836–1916) was largely educated by his father until he went to the University of Vienna. As a boy, he spent part of his time learning the trade of cabinetmaker, with the idea of emigrating to America if the liberal politics of his family should make it difficult for him to earn a living in the reactionary period that followed the revolutionary stirrings of 1848. But by the time he received his doctor's degree in 1860 he had found himself, and was ready to begin his long and distinguished scientific and academic career. After working as a tutor for a time he was appointed to the faculty of Gratz in 1864, as a professor first of mathematics, and later of physics. He went to Prague in 1867, married and produced five children, and finally returned to Vienna, where for six years (1895–1901) he held the post of Professor of Philosophy. In 1901 he became a member of the Austrian House of Peers.

To the history of physics Mach is known as a pioneer worker in optics and acoustics. His name has been given to a fundamental quantity in the science of supersonic jets and rockets. To the history of philosophy he is known as an important contributor to the development of the view now often called "scientific empiricism." His careful work on the nature of our concepts of space, physical objects, and natural laws, was the bridge between the early positivism of Comte and the later "logical positivism" of Rudolf Carnap and the Vienna Circle. Besides his most often cited philosophical work, *The Analysis of Sensations* (see below), these others are of philosophic interest: *The Science of Mechanics* (1883; trans. T. J. McCormack, 2d ed., Chicago: Open Court, 1902), which is a fundamental reformulation of Newtonian mechanics in harmony with his conception of science and scientific method; *Knowledge and Error*, 1905 (Dordrecht: D Reidel, 1976); *Space and Geometry in the Light of Physiological, Psychological, and Physical Inquiry* (trans. T. J. McCormack, Chicago: Open Court, 1906), *Inquiry* (trans. T. J. McCormack, Chicago: Open Court, 1906), which brought together three essays published in the *The Monist,* 1901–1903; and *Popular Scientific Lectures* (1896; trans. T. J. McCormack, Chicago: Open Court, 3d ed. rev. 1898).

Mach's attempt to provide a final resolution of the mind-body problem, and to eliminate from philosophical concern all metaphysical questions, by showing how all knowledge can be reduced to relations among sense elements, was more programmatic than conclusive; yet the vigor and persuasiveness, in some quarters, of his view gave strong impetus to lines of thought that turned up important discoveries later on, when the more subtle and powerful tools of symbolic logic and linguistic analysis had become available. Among his other fruitful ideas were the central role of the principle of simplicity or economy in scientific explanation, and even in our concepts of physical objects; his proposal to replace the concept of causality, in physical science, by that of functional dependence; and his idea of the unity of science on a physicalistic basis.

The Analysis of Sensations and the Relation of the Physical to the Psychical, Chapters I and XV *

I. INTRODUCTORY REMARKS: ANTIMETAPHYSICAL

1. The great results achieved by physical science in modern times —results not restricted to its own sphere but embracing that of other sciences which employ its help—have brought it about that physical ways of thinking and physical modes of procedure enjoy on all hands unwonted prominence, and that the greatest expectations are associated with their application. In keeping with this drift of modern inquiry, the physiology of the senses, gradually abandoning the method of investigating sensations in themselves followed by men like Goethe, Schopenhauer, and others, but with greatest success by Johannes Müller, has also assumed an almost exclusively physical character. This tendency must appear to us as not altogether appropriate, when we reflect that physics, despite its considerable development, nevertheless constitutes but a portion of a *larger* collective body of knowledge, and that it is unable, with its limited intellectual implements, created for limited and special purposes, to exhaust all the subject-matter in question. Without renouncing the support of physics, it is possible for the physiology of the senses, not only to pursue its own course of development, but also to afford to physical science itself powerful assistance. The following simple considerations will serve to illustrate this relation between the two.

2. Colors, sounds, temperatures, pressures, spaces, times, and so forth, are connected with one another in manifold ways; and with them are associated dispositions of mind, feelings, and volitions.

---

* Translated from the first German edition (1886) by C. M. Williams, revised and supplemented from the fifth German edition (1906) by Sydney Waterlow, Chicago: Open Court, 1914. *Die Analyse der Empfindungen und das Verhältniss des Physischen zum Psychischen* was, in the first edition, entitled *Beiträge zur Analyse der Empfindungen*. Some footnote references have been omitted.

Out of this fabric, that which is relatively more fixed and permanent stands prominently forth, engraves itself on the memory, and expresses itself in language. Relatively greater permanency is exhibited, first, by certain complexes of colors, sounds, pressures, and so forth, functionally connected in time and space, which therefore receive special names, and are called bodies. Absolutely permanent such complexes are not.

My table is now brightly, now dimly lighted. Its temperature varies. It may receive an ink stain. One of its legs may be broken. It may be repaired, polished, and replaced part by part. But, for me, it remains the table at which I daily write.

My friend may put on a different coat. His countenance may assume a serious or a cheerful expression. His complexion, under the effects of light or emotion, may change. His shape may be altered by motion, or be definitely changed. Yet the number of the permanent features presented, compared with the number of the gradual alterations, is always so great, that the latter may be overlooked. It is the same friend with whom I take my daily walk.

My coat may receive a stain, a tear. My very manner of expressing this shows that we are concerned here with a sum-total of permanency, to which the new element is added and from which that which is lacking is subsequently taken away.

Our greater intimacy with this sum-total of permanency, and the preponderance of its importance for me as contrasted with the changeable element, impel us to the partly instinctive, partly voluntary and conscious economy of mental presentation and designation, as expressed in ordinary thought and speech. That which is presented in a single image receives a single designation, a single name.

Further, that complex of memories, moods, and feelings, joined to a particular body (the human body), which is called the "I" or "Ego," manifests itself as relatively permanent. I may be engaged upon this or that subject, I may be quiet and cheerful, excited and ill-humored. Yet, pathological cases apart, enough durable features remain to identify the ego. Of course, the ego also is only of relative permanency.

The apparent permanency of the ego consists chiefly in the single fact of its continuity, in the slowness of its changes. The many thoughts and plans of yesterday that are continued to-day, and of which our environment in waking hours incessantly reminds us (whence in dreams the ego can be very indistinct, doubled, or entirely wanting), and the little habits that are unconsciously and involuntarily kept up for long periods of time, constitute the ground-work of the ego. There can hardly be greater differences in the egos of different people, than occur in the course of years in one person. When I recall to-day my early youth, I should take the boy that I then was, with the exception of a few individual features, for a different person, were it not for the existence of the chain of memories. Many an article that I myself penned twenty years ago impresses me now as something quite foreign to myself. The very gradual character of the changes of the body also contributes to the stability of the ego, but in a much less degree than people imagine. Such things are much less analyzed and noticed than the intellectual and the moral ego. Personally, people know themselves very poorly.[1] When I wrote these lines in 1886, Ribot's admirable little book, *The Diseases of Personality,* was unknown to me. Ribot ascribes the principal rôle in preserving the continuity of the ego to the general sensibility. Generally, I am in perfect accord with his views.

The ego is as little absolutely permanent as are bodies. That which we so much dread in death, the annihilation of our permanency, actually occurs in life in abundant measure. That which is most valued by us, remains preserved in countless copies, or, in cases of exceptional excellence, is even preserved of itself. In the best human being, however, there are individual traits, the loss of which neither he himself nor others need regret. Indeed, at times, death, viewed as a liberation from individuality, may even become a pleasant thought. Such reflections of course do not make physiological death any the easier to bear.

After a first survey has been obtained, by the formation of the substance-concepts "body" and "ego" (matter and soul), the will is impelled to a more exact examination of the changes that take place in these relatively permanent existences. The element of change in bodies and the ego, is in fact, exactly what moves the will [2] to this

---

[1] Once, when a young man, I noticed in the street the profile of a face that was very displeasing and repulsive to me. I was not a little taken aback when a moment afterwards I found that it was my own face which, in passing by a shop where mirrors were sold, I had perceived reflected from two mirrors that were inclined at the proper angle to each other.

Not long ago, after a trying railway journey by night, when I was very tired, I got into an omnibus, just as another man appeared at the other end. "What a shabby pedagogue that is, that has just entered," thought I. It was myself: opposite me hung a large mirror. The physiognomy of my class, accordingly, was better known to me than my own.

[2] Not to be taken in the metaphysical sense.

examination. Here the component parts of the complex are first exhibited as its properties. A fruit is sweet; but it can also be bitter. Also, other fruits may be sweet. The red color we are seeking is found in many bodies. The neighborhood of some bodies is pleasant; that of others, unpleasant. Thus, gradually, different complexes are found to be made up of common elements. The visible, the audible, the tangible, are separated from bodies. The visible is analyzed into colors and into form. In the manifoldness of the colors, again, though here fewer in number, other component parts are discerned— such as the primary colors, and so forth. The complexes are disintegrated into elements, that is to say, into their ultimate component parts, which hitherto we have been unable to subdivide any further. The nature of these elements need not be discussed at present; it is possible that future investigations may throw light on it. We need not here be disturbed by the fact that it is easier for the scientist to study relations of relations of these elements than the direct relations between them.

3. The useful habit of designating such relatively permanent compounds by single names, and of apprehending them by single thoughts, without going to the trouble each time of an analysis of their component parts, is apt to come into strange conflict with the tendency to isolate the component parts. The vague image which we have of a given permanent complex, being an image which does not perceptibly change when one or another of the component parts is taken away, seems to be something which exists in itself. Inasmuch as it is possible to take away singly every constituent part without destroying the capacity of the image to stand for the totality and to be recognized again, it is imagined that it is possible to subtract all the parts and to have something still remaining. Thus naturally arises the philosophical notion, at first impressive, but subsequently recognized as monstrous, of a "thing-in-itself," different from its "appearance," and unknowable.

Thing, body, matter, are nothing apart from the combinations of the elements—the colors, sounds, and so forth—nothing apart from their so-called attributes. That protean pseudo-philosophical problem of the single thing with its many attributes, arises wholly from a misinterpretation of the fact that summary comprehension and precise analysis, although both are provisionally justifiable and for many purposes profitable, cannot be carried on simultaneously. A body is one and unchangeable only so long as it is unnecessary to consider its details. Thus both the earth and a billiard-ball are spheres, if we are willing to neglect all deviations from the spherical form, and if greater precision is not necessary. But when we are obliged to carry on investigations in orography or microscopy, both bodies cease to be spheres.

4. Man is pre-eminently endowed with the power of voluntarily and consciously determining his own point of view. He can at one time disregard the most salient features of an object, and immediately thereafter give attention to its smallest details; now consider a stationary current, without a thought of its contents (whether heat, electricity, or fluidity), and then measure the width of a Fraunhofer line in the spectrum; he can rise at will to the most general abstractions or bury himself in the minutest particulars. Animals possess this capacity in a far less degree. They do not assume a point of view, but are usually forced to it by their sense-impressions. The baby that does not know its father with his hat on, the dog that is perplexed at the new coat of its master, have both succumbed in this conflict of points of view. Who has not been worsted in similar plights? Even the man of philosophy at times succumbs, as the grotesque problem, above referred to, shows.

In this last case, the circumstances appear to furnish a real ground of justification. Colors, sounds, and the odors of bodies are evanescent. But their tangibility, as a sort of constant nucleus, not readily susceptible of annihilation, remains behind, appearing as the vehicle of the more fugitive properties attached to it. Habit thus keeps our thought firmly attached to this central nucleus, even when we have begun to recognize that seeing, hearing, smelling, and touching are intimately akin in character. A further consideration is that, owing to the singularly extensive development of mechanical physics, a kind of higher reality is ascribed to the spatial and to the temporal than to colors, sounds, and odors; agreeably to which, the temporal and spatial links of colors, sounds, and odors appear to be more real than the colors, sounds, and odors themselves. The physiology of the senses, however, demonstrates that spaces and times may just as appropriately be called sensations as colors and sounds. But of this later.

5. Not only the relation of bodies to the ego, but the ego itself also, gives rise to similar pseudo-problems, the character of which may be briefly indicated as follows:

Let us denote the above-mentioned elements by the letters A B C . . . , K L M . . . , α β γ . . . . Let those complexes of colors, sounds, and so forth, commonly called bodies, be denoted, for the sake of clearness, by A B C . . . ; the complex, known as our own body, which is a part of the former complexes distinguished by certain peculiarities, may be called K L M . . . ; the complex composed of volitions, memory-images, and the rest, we shall represent by α β γ . . . . Usually, now, the complex α β γ . . . K L M . . . , as making up the ego, is opposed to the complex A B C . . . , as making up the world of physical objects; sometimes also, α β γ . . . is viewed as ego, and K L M . . . A B C . . . as world of physical objects. Now, at first blush, A B C . . . appears independent of the ego, and opposed to it as a separate existence. But this independence is only relative, and gives way upon closer inspection. Much, it is true, *may* change in the complex α β γ . . . without much perceptible change being induced in A B C . . . ; and vice versa. But many changes in α β γ . . . do pass, by way of changes in K L M . . . , to A B C . . . ; and vice versa. (As, for example, when powerful ideas burst forth into acts, or when our environment induces noticeable changes in our body.) At the same time the group K L M . . . appears to be more intimately connected with α β γ . . . and with A B C . . . , than the latter with one another; and their relations find their expression in common thought and speech.

Precisely viewed, however, it appears that the group A B C . . . is always codetermined by K L M . . . . A cube when seen close at hand, looks large; when seen at a distance, small; its appearance to the right eye differs from its appearance to the left; sometimes it appears double; with closed eyes it is invisible. The properties of one and the same body, therefore, appear modified by our own body; they appear conditioned by it. But where, now, is that *same* body, which appears so *different*? All that can be said is, that with different K L M . . . different A B C . . . are associated.

A common and popular way of thinking and speaking is to contrast "appearance" with "reality." A pencil held in front of us in the air is seen by us as straight; dip it into the water, and we see it crooked. In the latter case we say that the pencil *appears* crooked, but is in *reality* straight. But what justifies us in declaring one fact rather than another to be the reality, and degrading the other to the level of appearance? In both cases we have to do with facts which present us with different combinations of the elements, combinations which in the two cases are differently conditioned. Precisely because of its environment, the pencil dipped in water is optically crooked; but it is tactually and metrically straight. An image in a concave or flat mirror is *only* visible, whereas under other and ordinary circumstances a tangible body as well corresponds to the visible image. A bright surface is brighter beside a dark surface than beside one brighter than itself. To be sure, our expectation is deceived when, not paying sufficient attention to the conditions, and substituting for one another different cases of the combination, we fall into the natural error of expecting what we are accustomed to, although the case may be an unusual one. The facts are not to blame for that. In these cases, to speak of "appearance" may have a practical meaning, but cannot have a scientific meaning. Similarly, the question which is often asked, whether the world is real or whether we merely dream it, is devoid of all scientific meaning. Even the wildest dream is a fact as much as any other. If our dreams were more regular, more connected, more stable, they would also have more practical importance for us. In our waking hours the relations of the elements to one another are immensely amplified in comparison with what they were in our dreams. We recognize the dream for what it is. When the process is reversed, the field of psychic vision is narrowed; the contrast is almost entirely lacking. Where there is no contrast, the distinction between dream and waking, between appearance and reality, is quite otiose and worthless.

The popular notion of an antithesis between appearance and reality has exercised a very powerful influence on scientific and philosophical thought. We see this, for example, in Plato's pregnant and poetical fiction of the Cave, in which, with our backs turned towards the fire, we observe merely the shadows of what passes (*Republic,* Book VII). But this conception was not thought out to its final consequences, with the result that it has had an unfortunate influence on our ideas about the universe. The universe, of which nevertheless we are a part, became completely separated from us, and was removed an infinite distance away. Similarly, many a young man, hearing for the first time of the refraction of stellar light, has thought that doubt was cast on the whole of astronomy, whereas nothing is required but an easily effected and unimportant correction to put everything right again.

6. We see an object having a point S. If we touch S, that is, bring it into connection with our body, we receive a prick. We can see S, without feeling the prick. But as soon as we feel the prick

we find S on the skin. The visible point, therefore, is a permanent nucleus, to which the prick is annexed, according to circumstances, as something accidental. From the frequency of analogous occurrences we ultimately accustom ourselves to regard all properties of bodies as "effects" proceeding from permanent nuclei and conveyed to the ego through the medium of the body; which effects we call sensations. By this operation, however, these nuclei are deprived of their entire sensory content, and converted into mere mental symbols. The assertion, then, is correct that the world consists only of our sensations. In which case we have knowledge *only* of sensations, and the assumption of the nuclei referred to, or of a reciprocal action between them, from which sensations proceed, turns out to be quite idle and superfluous. Such a view can only suit with a half-hearted realism or a half-hearted philosophical criticism.

7. Ordinarily the complex $\alpha\ \beta\ \gamma\ .\ .\ .\ K\ L\ M\ .\ .\ .$ is contrasted as ego with the complex $A\ B\ C\ .\ .\ .\ .$ At first only those elements of $A\ B\ C\ .\ .\ .$ that more strongly alter $\alpha\ \beta\ \gamma\ .\ .\ .$, as a prick, a pain, are wont to be thought of as comprised in the ego. Afterwards, however, through observations of the kind just referred to, it appears that the right to annex $A\ B\ C\ .\ .\ .$ to the ego nowhere ceases. In conformity with this view, the ego can be so extended as ultimately to embrace the entire world.[1] The ego is not sharply marked off, its limits are very indefinite and arbitrarily displaceable. Only by failing to observe this fact, and by unconsciously narrowing those limits, while at the same time we enlarge them, arise, in the conflict of points of view, the metaphysical difficulties met with in this connection.

As soon as we have perceived that the supposed unities "body" and "ego" are only makeshifts, designed for provisional orientation and for definite practical ends (so that we may take hold of bodies, protect ourselves against pain, and so forth), we find ourselves

---

[1] When I say that the table, the tree, and so forth, are my sensations, the statement, as contrasted with the mode of representation of the ordinary man, involves a real extension of my ego. On the emotional side also such extensions occur, as in the case of the virtuoso, who possesses as perfect a mastery of his instrument as he does of his own body; or in the case of the skillful orator, on whom the eyes of the audience are all converged, and who is controlling the thoughts of all; or in that of the able politician who is deftly guiding his party; and so on. In conditions of depression, on the other hand, such as nervous people often endure, the ego contracts and shrinks. A wall seems to separate it from the world.

obliged, in many more advanced scientific investigations, to abandon
them as insufficient and inappropriate. The antithesis between ego
and world, between sensation (appearance) and thing, then vanishes,
and we have simply to deal with the connection of the elements α β γ
. . . A B C . . . K L M . . . , of which this antithesis was only
a partially appropriate and imperfect expression. This connection is
nothing more or less than the combination of the above-mentioned
elements with other similar elements (time and space). Science has
simply to accept this connection, and to get its bearings in it, without
at once wanting to explain its existence.

On a superficial examination the complex α β γ . . . appears to
be made up of much more evanescent elements than A B C . . .
and K L M . . . , in which last the elements seem to be connected
with greater stability and in a more permanent manner (being joined
to solid nuclei as it were). Although on closer inspection the elements
of all complexes prove to be homogeneous, yet even when this has
been recognized, the earlier notion of an antithesis of body and spirit
easily slips in again. The philosophical spiritualist is often sensible of
the difficulty of imparting the needed solidity to his mind-created
world of bodies; the materialist is at a loss when required to endow
the world of matter with sensation. The monistic point of view,
which reflection has evolved, is easily clouded by our older and
more powerful instinctive notions.

8. The difficulty referred to is particularly felt when we consider the following case. In the complex A B C . . . , which we
have called the world of matter, we find as parts, not only our own
body K L M . . . , but also the bodies of other persons (or animals)
K' L' M' . . . , K'' L'' M'' . . . , to which, by analogy, we imagine
other α' β' γ' . . . , α'' β'' γ'' . . . , annexed, similar to α β γ . . . .
So long as we deal with K' L' M' . . . , we find ourselves in a thor-
oughly familiar province which is at every point accessible to our
senses. When, however, we inquire after the sensations or feelings
belonging to the body K' L' M' . . . , we no longer find these in the
province of sense: we add them in thought. Not only is the domain
which we now enter far less familiar to us, but the transition into it is
also relatively unsafe. We have the feeling as if we were plunging
into an abyss.[1] Persons who adopt this way of thinking only, will

---

[1] When I first came to Vienna from the country, as a boy of four or five
years, and was taken by my father upon the walls of the city's fortifications,
I was very much surprised to see people below in the moat, and could not

never thoroughly rid themselves of that sense of insecurity, which is a very fertile source of illusory problems.

But we are not restricted to this course. Let us consider, first, the reciprocal relations of the elements of the complex $A\ B\ C\ .\ .\ .$, without regarding $K\ L\ M\ .\ .\ .$ (our body). All physical investigations are of this sort. A white ball falls upon a bell; a sound is heard. The ball turns yellow before a sodium lamp, red before a lithium lamp. Here the elements ($A\ B\ C\ .\ .\ .$) appear to be connected only with one another and to be independent of our body ($K\ L\ M\ .\ .\ .$). But if we take santonine, the ball again turns yellow. If we press one eye to the side, we see two balls. If we close our eyes entirely, there is no ball there at all. If we sever the auditory nerve, no sound is heard. The elements $A\ B\ C\ .\ .\ .$, therefore, are not only connected with one another, but also with $K\ L\ M\ .\ .\ .$. To this extent, and to this extent only, do we call $A\ B\ C\ .\ .$ *sensations,* and regard $A\ B\ C\ .\ .\ .$ as belonging to the ego. In what follows, wherever the reader finds the terms "sensation," "sensation-complex," used alongside of or instead of the expressions "element," "complex of elements," it must be borne in mind that it is *only* in the connection and relation in question, *only* in their functional dependence, that the elements are sensations. In another functional relation they are at the same time physical objects. We only use the additional term "sensations" to describe the elements, because most people are much more familiar with the elements in question *as* sensations (colors, sounds, pressures, spaces, times, etc.), while according to the popular conception it is particles of mass that are considered as physical elements, to which the elements, in the sense here used, are attached as "properties" or "effects."

In this way, accordingly, we do not find the gap between bodies and sensations above described, between what is without and what is within, between the material world and the spiritual world. All

---

understand how, from my point of view, they could have got there; for the thought of another way of descent never occurred to me. I remarked the same astonishment, once afterwards, in the case of a three-year-old boy of my own, while walking on the walls of Prague. I recall this feeling every time I occupy myself with the reflection of the text, and I frankly confess that this accidental experience of mine helped to confirm my opinion upon this point, which I have now long held. Our habit of always following the same path, whether materially or psychically, tends greatly to confuse our field of survey. A child, on the piercing of the wall of a house in which he has long dwelt, may experience a veritable enlargement of his world-view, and in the same manner a slight scientific hint may often afford great enlightenment.

elements $A\ B\ C\ .\ .\ .\ ,\ K\ L\ M\ .\ .\ .$, constitute a *single* coherent mass only, in which, when any one element is disturbed, *all* is put in motion; except that a disturbance in $K\ L\ M\ .\ .\ .$ has a more extensive and profound action than one in $A\ B\ C\ .\ .\ .\ .$ A magnet in our neighborhood disturbs the particles of iron near it; a falling boulder shakes the earth; but the severing of a nerve sets in motion the *whole* system of elements. Quite involuntarily does this relation of things suggest the picture of a viscous mass, at certain places (as in the ego) more firmly coherent than in others. I have often made use of this image in lectures.

9. Thus the great gulf between physical and psychological research persists only when we acquiesce in our habitual stereotyped conceptions. A color is a physical object as soon as we consider its dependence, for instance, upon its luminous source, upon other colors, upon temperatures, upon spaces, and so forth. When we consider, however, its dependence upon the retina (the elements $K\ L\ M\ .\ .\ .$), it is a psychological object, a sensation. Not the subject-matter, but the direction of our investigation, is different in the two domains.

Both in reasoning from the observation of the bodies of other men or animals, to the sensations which they possess, as well as in investigating the influence of our own body upon our own sensations, we have to complete observed facts by analogy. This is accomplished with much greater ease and certainty, when it relates, say, only to nervous processes, which cannot be fully observed in our own bodies—that is, when it is carried out in the more familiar physical domain—than when it is extended to the psychical domain, to the sensations and thoughts of other people. Otherwise there is no essential difference.

10. The considerations just advanced, expressed as they have been in an abstract form, will gain in strength and vividness if we consider the concrete facts from which they flow. Thus, I lie upon my sofa. If I close my right eye, the picture represented in the accompanying cut [1] is presented to my left eye. In a frame formed by the ridge of my eyebrow, by my nose, and by my moustache, appears a part of my body, so far as visible, with its environment. My body differs from other human bodies—beyond the fact that every intense motor idea is immediately expressed by a movement of it, and that,

---

[1] [Omitted here—M.C.B.]

if it is touched, more striking changes are determined than if other bodies are touched—by the circumstance that it is only seen piece-meal, and, especially, is seen without a head. If I observe an element *A* within my field of vision, and investigate its connection with another element *B* within the same field, I step out of the domain of physics into that of physiology or psychology, provided *B*, to use the apposite expression of a friend of mine made upon seeing this drawing, passes through my skin. Reflections like that for the field of vision may be made with regard to the province of touch and the perceptual domains of the other senses.

11. Reference has already been made to the different character of the groups of elements denoted by $A\ B\ C\ \ldots$ and $\alpha\ \beta\ \gamma\ \ldots$. As a matter of fact, when we see a green tree before us, or remember a green tree, that is, represent a green tree to ourselves, we are per-fectly aware of the difference of the two cases. The represented tree has a much less determinate, a much more changeable form; its green is much paler and more evanescent; and, what is of especial note, it plainly appears in a different domain. A movement that we will execute is never more than a represented movement, and appears in a different domain from that of the executed movement, which always takes place when the image is vivid enough. Now the statement that the elements A and α appear in different domains, means, if we go to the bottom of it, simply this, that these elements are united with different other elements. Thus far, therefore, the fundamental con-stituents of $A\ B\ C\ \ldots,\ \alpha\ \beta\ \gamma\ \ldots$ would seem to be *the same* (colors, sounds, spaces, times, motor sensations . . .), and only the character of their connection different.

Ordinarily pleasure and pain are regarded as different from sen-sations. Yet not only tactual sensations, but all other kinds of sensa-tions, may pass gradually into pleasure and pain. Pleasure and pain also may be justly termed sensations. Only they are not so well analyzed or so familiar, nor, perhaps, limited to so few organs as the common sensations. In fact, sensations of pleasure and pain, however faint they may be, really constitute an essential part of the content of all so-called emotions. Any additional element that emerges into consciousness when we are under the influence of emotions may be described as more or less diffused and not sharply localized sensations. William James, and after him Théodule Ribot, have investigated the physiological mechanism of the emotions: they hold that what is essential is purposive tendencies of the body to action—tendencies which correspond to circumstances and are expressed in the organism. Only a part of these emerges into consciousness. We are sad because we shed tears, and not vice versa, says James. And Ribot justly observes that a cause of the backward state of our knowledge of the emotions is that we have always confined our observation to so much of these physiological processes as emerges into consciousness. At the same time, he goes too far when he maintains that everything psychical is merely "surajouté" to the physical, and that it is only the physical that produces effects. For us this distinction is non-existent.

Thus, perceptions, presentations, volitions, and emotions, in short the whole inner and outer world, are put together, in combinations of varying evanescence and permanence, out of a small number of homogeneous elements. Usually, these elements are called sensations. But as vestiges of a one-sided theory inhere in that term, we prefer to speak simply of elements, as we have already done. The aim of all research is to ascertain the mode of connection of these elements. If it proves impossible to solve the problem by assuming *one* set of such elements, then more than one will have to be assumed. But for the questions under discussion it would be improper to begin by making complicated assumptions in advance.

12. That in this complex of elements, which fundamentally is only one, the boundaries of bodies and of the ego do not admit of being established in a manner definite and sufficient for all cases, has already been remarked. To bring together elements that are most intimately connected with pleasure and pain into one ideal mental-economical unity, the ego; this is a task of the highest importance for the intellect working in the service of the pain-avoiding, pleasure-seeking will. The delimitation of the ego, therefore, is instinctively effected, is rendered familiar, and possibly becomes fixed through heredity. Owing to their high practical importance, not only for the individual, but for the entire species, the composites "ego" and "body" instinctively make good their claims, and assert themselves with elementary force. In special cases, however, in which practical ends are not concerned, but where knowledge is an end in itself, the delimitation in question may prove to be insufficient, obstructive, and untenable.[1]

---

[1] Similarly, class-consciousness, class-prejudice, the feeling of nationality, and even the narrowest-minded local patriotism may have a high importance, *for certain purposes*. But such attitudes will not be shared by the broad-

The primary fact is not the ego, but the elements (sensations). What was said just above as to the term "sensation" must be borne in mind. The elements constitute the I. "*I* have the sensation green," signifies that the element green occurs in a given complex of other elements (sensations, memories). When *I* cease to have the sensation green, when *I* die, then the elements no longer occur in the ordinary, familiar association. That is all. Only an ideal mental-economical unity, not a real unity, has ceased to exist. The ego is not a definite, unalterable, sharply-bounded unity. None of these attributes are important, for all vary even within the sphere of individual life; in fact their alteration is even sought after by the individual. *Continuity* alone is important. This view accords admirably with the position which Weismann has reached by biological investigations. But continuity is only a means of preparing and conserving what is contained in the ego. This content, and not the ego, is the principal thing. This content, however, is not confined to the individual. With the exception of some insignificant and valueless personal memories, it remains preserved in others even after the death of the individual. The elements that make up the consciousness of a given individual are firmly connected with one another, but with those of another individual they are only feebly connected, and the connection is only casually apparent. Contents of consciousness, however, that are of universal significance, break through these limits of the individual, and, attached of course to individuals again, can enjoy a continued existence of an impersonal, superpersonal kind, independently of the personality by means of which they were developed. To contribute to this is the greatest happiness of the artist, the scientist, the inventor, the social reformer, etc.

The ego must be given up. It is partly the perception of this fact, partly the fear of it, that has given rise to the many extravagances of pessimism and optimism, and to numerous religious, ascetic, and philosophical absurdities. In the long run we shall not be able to

---

minded investigator, at least not in moments of research. All such egoistic views are adequate only for practical purposes. Of course, even the investigator may succumb to habit. Trifling pedantries and nonsensical discussions; the cunning appropriation of others' thoughts, with perfidious silence as to the sources; when the word of recognition must be given, the difficulty of swallowing one's defeat, and the too common eagerness at the same time to set the opponent's achievement in a false light: all this abundantly shows that the scientist and scholar have also the battle of existence to fight, that the ways even of science still lead to the mouth, and that the pure impulse towards knowledge is still an ideal in our present social conditions.

close our eyes to this simple truth, which is the immediate outcome of psychological analysis. We shall then no longer place so high a value upon the ego, which even during the individual life greatly changes, and which, in sleep or during absorption in some idea, just in our very happiest moments, may be partially or wholly absent. We shall then be willing to renounce individual immortality,[1] and not place more value upon the subsidiary elements than upon the principal ones. In this way, we shall arrive at a freer and more enlightened view of life, which will preclude the disregard of other egos and the overestimation of our own. The ethical ideal founded on this view of life will be equally far removed from the ideal of the ascetic, which is not biologically tenable for whoever practises it, and vanishes at once with his disappearance, and from the ideal of an overweening Nietzschean "superman," who cannot, and I hope will not be tolerated by his fellow-men.

If a knowledge of the connection of the elements (sensations) does not suffice us, and we ask, "*Who* possesses this connection of sensations, *Who* experiences it?" then we have succumbed to the old habit of subsuming every element (every sensation) under some unanalyzed complex, and we are falling back imperceptibly upon an older, lower, and more limited point of view. It is often pointed out, that a psychical experience which is not the experience of a determinate subject is unthinkable, and it is held that in this way the essential part played by the unity of consciousness has been demonstrated. But the Ego-consciousness can be of many different degrees and composed of a multiplicity of chance memories. One might just as well say that a physical process which does not take place in some environment or other, or at least somewhere in the universe, is unthinkable. In both cases, in order to make a beginning with our investigation, we must be allowed to abstract from the environment, which, as regards its influence, may be very different in different cases, and in special cases may shrink to a minimum. Consider the sensations of the lower animals, to which a subject with definite features can hardly be ascribed. It is out of sensations that the subject is built up, and, once built up, no doubt the subject reacts in turn on the sensations.

The habit of treating the unanalyzed ego-complex as an indiscerp-

---

[1] In wishing to preserve our personal memories beyond death, we are behaving like the astute Eskimo, who refused with thanks the gift of immortality without his seals and walruses.

tible unity frequently assumes in science remarkable forms. First, the nervous system is separated from the body as the seat of the sensations. In the nervous system again, the brain is selected as the organ best fitted for this end, and finally, to save the supposed psychical unity, a *point* is sought in the brain as the seat of the soul. But such crude conceptions are hardly fit even to foreshadow the roughest outlines of what future research will do for the connection of the physical and the psychical. The fact that the different organs and parts of the nervous system are physically connected with, and can be readily excited by, one another, is probably at the bottom of the notion of "psychical unity."

I once heard the question seriously discussed, how the perception of a large tree could find room in the little head of a man. Now, although this "problem" is no problem, yet it renders us vividly sensible of the absurdity that can be committed by thinking sensations spatially into the brain. When I speak of the sensations of another person, those sensations are, of course, not exhibited in any optical or physical space; they are mentally added, and I conceive them causally, not spatially, attached to the brain observed, or rather, functionally presented. When I speak of my own sensations, these sensations do not exist spatially in my head, but rather my "head" shares with them the same spatial field, as was explained above.[1]

The unity of consciousness is not an argument in point. Since the apparent antithesis between the real world and the world given

---

[1] As early as the writings of Johannes Müller, we can already find a tendency towards views of this kind, although his metaphysical bias prevents him from carrying them to their logical conclusion. But Hering has the following characteristic passage: "The material of which visual objects consists is the visual sensations. The setting sun, as a visual object, is a flat, circular disk, which consists of yellowish-red color, that is to say of a visual sensation. We may therefore describe it directly as a circular, yellowish-red sensation. This sensation we have in the very place where the sun appears to us." I must confess that, so far as the experiments go which I have had occasion to make in conversation, most people, who have not come to close quarters with these questions by serious thinking, will pronounce this way of looking at the matter to be mere hair-splitting. Of course, what is chiefly responsible for their indignation is the common confusion between sensible and conceptual space. But anyone who takes his stand as I do on the *economic* function of science, according to which nothing is important except what can be observed or is a datum for us, and everything hypothetical, metaphysical and superfluous is to be eliminated, must reach the same conclusion.

through the senses lies entirely in our mode of view, and no actual gulf exists between them, a complicated and variously interconnected content of consciousness is no more difficult to understand than is the complicated interconnection of the world.

If we regard the ego as a real unity, we become involved in the following dilemma: either we must set over against the ego a world of unknowable entities (which would be quite idle and purposeless), or we must regard the whole world, the egos of other people included, as comprised in our own ego (a proposition to which it is difficult to yield serious assent).

But if we take the ego simply as a practical unity, put together for purposes of provisional survey, or as a more strongly cohering group of elements, less strongly connected with other groups of this kind, questions like those above discussed will not arise, and research will have an unobstructed future.

In his philosophical notes Lichtenberg says: "We become conscious of certain presentations that are not dependent upon us; of others that we at least think are dependent upon us. Where is the border-line? We know only the existence of our sensations, presentations, and thoughts. We should say, '*It thinks,*' just as we say '*It lightens.*' It is going too far to say *Cogito,* if we translate *Cogito* by '*I think.*' The assumption, or postulation, of the ego is a mere practical necessity." Though the method by which Lichtenberg arrived at this result is somewhat different from ours, we must nevertheless give our full assent to his conclusion.

13. Bodies do not produce sensations, but complexes of elements (complexes of sensations) make up bodies. If, to the physicist, bodies appear the real, abiding existences, whilst the "elements" are regarded merely as their evanescent, transitory appearance, the physicist forgets, in the assumption of such a view, that all bodies are but thought-symbols for complexes of elements (complexes of sensations). Here, too, the elements in question form the real, immediate, and ultimate foundation, which it is the task of physiologico-physical research to investigate. By the recognition of this fact, many points of physiology and physics assume more distinct and more economical forms, and many spurious problems are disposed of.

For us, therefore, the world does not consist of mysterious entities, which by their interaction with another, equally mysterious entity, the ego, produce sensations, which alone are accessible. For us, colors, sounds, spaces, times, . . . are provisionally the ultimate elements, whose given connection it is our business to investigate.[1] It is precisely in this that the exploration of reality consists. In this investigation we must not allow ourselves to be impeded by such abridgments and delimitations as body, ego, matter, spirit, etc., which have been formed for special, practical purposes and with wholly provisional and limited ends in view. On the contrary, the fittest forms of thought must be created in and by that research itself, just as is done in every special science. In place of the traditional, instinctive ways of thought, a freer, fresher view, conforming to developed experience, and reaching out beyond the requirements of practical life, must be substituted throughout.

14. Science always has its origin in the adaptation of thought to some definite field of experience. The results of the adaptation are thought-elements, which are able to represent the whole field. The outcome, of course, is different, according to the character and extent of the field. If the field of experience is enlarged, or if several fields

---

[1] I have always felt it as a stroke of special good fortune, that early in life, at about the age of fifteen, I lighted, in the library of my father, on a copy of Kant's *Prolegomena to Any Future Metaphysics*. The book made at the time a powerful and ineffaceable impression upon me, the like of which I never afterwards experienced in any of my philosophical reading. Some two or three years later the superfluity of the role played by "the thing-in-itself" abruptly dawned upon me. On a bright summer day in the open air, the world with my ego suddenly appeared to me as *one* coherent mass of sensations, only more strongly coherent in the ego. Although the actual working out of this thought did not occur until a later period, yet this moment was decisive for my whole view. I had still to struggle long and hard before I was able to retain the new conception in my special subject. With the valuable parts of physical theories we necessarily absorb a good dose of false metaphysics, which it is very difficult to sift out from what deserves to be preserved, especially when those theories have become very familiar to us. At times, too, the traditional, instinctive views would arise with great power and place impediments in my way. Only by alternate studies in physics and in physiology of the senses, and by historico-physical investigations (since about 1863), and after having endeavored in vain to settle the conflict by a physico-psychological monadology, have I attained to any considerable stability in my views. I make no pretensions to the title of philosopher. I only seek to adopt in physics a point of view that need not be changed the moment our glance is carried over into the domain of another science; for, ultimately, all must form one whole. The molecular physics of to-day certainly does not meet this requirement. What I say I have probably not been the *first* to say. I also do not wish to offer this exposition of mine as a special achievement. It is rather my belief that everyone will be led to a similar view, who makes a careful survey of any extensive body of knowledge.

heretofore disconnected are united, the traditional, familiar thought-elements no longer suffice for the extended field. In the struggle of acquired habit with the effort after adaptation, problems arise, which disappear when the adaptation is perfected, to make room for others which have arisen meanwhile.

To the physicist, *quâ* physicist, the idea of "body" is productive of a real facilitation of view, and is not the cause of disturbance. So, also, the person with purely practical aims is materially supported by the idea of the *I* or ego. For, unquestionably, every form of thought that has been designedly or undesignedly constructed for a given purpose, possesses for that purpose a *permanent* value. When, however, physics and psychology meet, the ideas held in the one domain prove to be untenable in the other. From the attempt at mutual adaptation arise the various atomic and monadistic theories —which, however, never attain their end. If we regard sensations, in the sense above defined, as the elements of the world, the problems referred to appear to be disposed of in all essentials, and the first and most important adaptation to be consequently effected. This fundamental view (without any pretension to being a philosophy for all eternity) can at present be adhered to in all fields of experience; it is consequently the one that accommodates itself with the least expenditure of energy, that is, more economically than any other, to the present temporary collective state of knowledge. Furthermore, in the consciousness of its purely economical function, this fundamental view is eminently tolerant. It does not obtrude itself into fields in which the current conceptions are still adequate. It is also ever ready, upon subsequent extensions of the field of experience, to give way before a better conception.

The presentations and conceptions of the average man of the world are formed and dominated, not by the full and pure desire for knowledge as an end in itself, but by the struggle to adapt himself favorably to the conditions of life. Consequently they are less exact, but at the same time also they are preserved from the monstrosities which easily result from a one-sided and impassioned pursuit of a scientific or philosophical point of view. The unprejudiced man of normal psychological development takes the elements which we have called *A B C* . . . to be spatially contiguous and external to the elements *K L M* . . . , and he holds this view *immediately,* and not by any process of psychological projection or logical inference or construction; even were such a process to exist, he would certainly not be conscious of it. He sees, then, an "external world" *A B C* . . . different from his body *K L M* . . . and existing outside it. As he does not observe at first the dependence of the *A B C*'s . . . on the *K L M*'s . . . (which are always repeating themselves in the same way and consequently receive little attention), but is always dwelling upon the fixed connection of the *A B C*'s . . . with one another, there appears to him a world of things independent of his Ego. This Ego is formed by the observation of the special properties of the particular thing *K L M* . . . with which pain, pleasure, feeling, will, etc., are intimately connected. Further, he notices things *K' L' M'* . . . , *K" L" M"* . . . , which behave in a manner perfectly analogous to *K L M* . . . , and whose behavior he thoroughly understands as soon as he has thought of analogous feelings, sensations, etc., as attached to them in the same way as he observed these feelings, sensations, etc., to be attached to himself. The analogy impelling him to this result is the same as determines him, when he has observed that a wire possesses *all* the properties of a conductor charged with an electric current, except *one* which has not yet been directly demonstrated, to conclude that the wire possesses this one property as well. Thus, since he does not perceive the sensations of his fellow-men or of animals but only supplies them by analogy, while he infers from the behavior of his fellow-men that they are in the same position over against himself, he is led to ascribe to the sensations, memories, etc., a particular *A B C* . . . *K L M* . . of a different nature, always differently conceived according to the degree of civilization he has reached; but this process, as was shown above, is unnecessary, and in science leads into a maze of error, although the falsification is of small significance for practical life.

These factors, determining as they do the intellectual outlook of the plain man, make their appearance alternately in him according to the requirements of practical life for the time being, and persist in a state of nearly stable equilibrium. The scientific conception of the world, however, puts the emphasis now upon one, now upon the other factor, makes sometimes one and sometimes the other its starting-point, and, in its struggle for greater precision, unity, and consistency, tries, so far as seems possible, to thrust into the background all but the most indispensable conceptions. In this way dualistic and monistic systems arise.

The plain man is familiar with blindness and deafness, and knows from his everyday experience that the look of things is influenced by his senses; but it never occurs to him to regard the whole world as the creation of his senses. He would find an idealistic system, or such a monstrosity as solipsism, intolerable in practice.

It may easily become a disturbing element in unprejudiced scientific theorizing when a conception which is adapted to a particular and strictly limited purpose is promoted in advance to be the foundation of *all* investigation. This happens, for example, when all experiences are regarded as "effects" of an external world extending into consciousness. This conception gives us a tangle of metaphysical difficulties which it seems impossible to unravel. But the specter vanishes at once when we look at the matter as it were in a mathematical light, and make it clear to ourselves that all that is valuable to us is the discovery of *functional relations,* and that what we want to know is merely the dependence of experiences on one another. It then becomes obvious that the reference to unknown fundamental variables which are not given (things-in-themselves) is purely fictitious and superfluous. But even when we allow this fiction, uneconomical though it be, to stand at first, we can still easily distinguish different classes of the mutual dependence of the elements of "the facts of consciousness"; and this alone is important for us.

$$
\begin{array}{ll}
\begin{array}{lll} A\ B\ C\ .\ .\ .\ K\ L\ M\ .\ .\ . \\ K'\ L'\ M'\ .\ .\ . \\ K''\ L''\ M''\ .\ .\ . \end{array} &
\begin{array}{lll} \alpha\ \beta\ \gamma\ .\ .\ . \\ \alpha'\ \beta'\ \gamma'\ .\ .\ . \\ \alpha''\ \beta''\ \gamma''\ .\ .\ . \end{array}
\end{array}
$$

The system of the elements is indicated in the above scheme. Within the space surrounded by a single line lie the elements which belong to the sensible world—the elements whose regular connection and peculiar dependence on one another represent both physical (lifeless) bodies and the bodies of men, animals, and plants. All these elements, again, stand in a relation of quite peculiar dependence to certain of the elements $K\ L\ M\ .\ .\ .$ —the nerves of our body, namely —by which the facts of sense-physiology are expressed. The space surrounded by a double line contains the elements belonging to the higher psychic life, memory-images and presentations, including those which we form of the psychic life of our fellow-men. These may be distinguished by accents. These presentations, again, are connected with one another in a different way (association, fancy) from the sensational elements $A\ B\ C\ .\ .\ .\ K\ L\ M\ .\ .\ .\ $, but it cannot be doubted that they are very closely allied to the latter, and that in the last resort their behavior is determined by $A\ B\ C\ .\ .\ .\ K\ L\ M\ .\ .\ .$ (the totality of the physical world), and especially by our body and nervous system. The presentations $\alpha'\ \beta'\ \gamma'\ .\ .\ .$ of the contents of the consciousness of our fellow-men play for us the part of *intermediate substitutions,* by means of which the behavior of our fellow-men— the functional relation of $K'\ L'\ M'\ .\ .\ .$ to $A\ B\ C\ .\ .\ .$ —becomes intelligible, in so far as in and for itself (physically) it would remain unexplained.

It is therefore important for us to recognize that in all questions in this connection that can be asked intelligibly and that can interest us, everything turns on taking into consideration different *ultimate variables* and different *relations of dependence.* That is the main point. Nothing will be changed in the actual facts or in the functional relations, whether we regard all the data as contents of consciousness, or as partially so, or as completely physical.

The biological task of science is to provide the fully developed human individual with as perfect a means of orientating himself as possible. No other scientific ideal can be realized, and any other must be meaningless.

The philosophical point of view of the average man—if that term may be applied to his naïve realism—has a claim to the highest consideration. It has arisen in the process of immeasurable time without the intentional assistance of man. It is a product of nature, and is preserved by nature. Everything that philosophy has accomplished—though we may admit the biological justification of every advance, nay, of every error—is, as compared with it, but an insignificant and ephemeral product of art. The fact is, every thinker, every philosopher, the moment he is forced to abandon his one-sided intellectual occupation by practical necessity, immediately returns to the general point of view of mankind. Professor X., who theoretically believes himself to be a solipsist, is certainly not one in practice when he has to thank a Minister of State for a decoration conferred upon him, or when he lectures to an audience. The Pyrrhonist who is cudgeled in Molière's *Le Mariage Forcé* does not go on saying *"Il me semble que vous me battez,"* [1] but takes his beating as really received.

---

[1] ["It seems to me that you are hitting me."—M.C.B.]

Nor is it the purpose of these "introductory remarks" to discredit the standpoint of the plain man. The task which we have set ourselves is simply to show why and for what purpose we hold that standpoint during most of our lives, and why and for what purpose we are provisionally obliged to abandon it. No point of view has absolute, permanent validity. Each has importance only for some given end.

XV. HOW MY VIEWS HAVE
BEEN RECEIVED

When the first edition of this book was published, opinions about it were greatly divided. But in the great majority of cases it was points of detail that found acceptance, in so far as the reception was favorable, while the fundamental views which had led to the details were for the most part rejected. All the public criticism that I have seen has preserved a tone of moderation, even when it has been hostile, and, in its outspokenness, has been extremely instructive to me.

There is no mistaking the favorable influence which the later publications of Richard Avenarius have exercised on the estimation of my book. It surely gives much food for thought when we find a professional philosopher establishing in an elaborate systematic treatise a position which, when taken up by a scientist, there has been a disposition to explain away as the aberration of a dilettante. To-day Avenarius' pupils, and many younger inquirers who have drawn near to my position by paths of their own, are standing at my side as allies. Nevertheless, all the critics, with few exceptions, including those who reproduce my fundamental ideas quite correctly and have certainly understood them, cannot help feeling serious objections to them. There is nothing surprising in this; for I make great demands on the plasticity of my readers. It is one thing to understand an idea logically, and another to take it up in a sympathetic spirit. The ordering and simplifying function of logic can, indeed, only begin when psychical life is in an advanced stage of development and can already boast a rich store of instinctive acquisitions. Now it is scarcely possible to attain to this instinctive pre-logical nucleus of acquisitions by logical means. It is much more a question of a process of psychical transformation, which, as I found in my own case, is difficult enough even in youth. It would therefore be too much to count on immediate agreement here. On the contrary, I am satisfied to be merely allowed a hearing at all, and to be listened to without prepossessions. I will now, following the impressions I have received from my critics, once more bring out and illustrate those points of which the reception has been most strenuously opposed. In doing this, I shall treat the objections that have been urged as typical objections, with nothing captious or personal about them, and I shall therefore not mention any names.

2. Unless we subject ourselves to a certain compulsion, we see the earth as standing still, and the sun and the fixed stars in motion. This way of looking at the matter is not merely sufficient for ordinary practical purposes, but is also the simplest and most advantageous. But the opposite view has established itself as the more convenient for certain intellectual purposes. Although both are equally correct and equally well adapted to their special purpose, the second view only succeeded in gaining acceptance after a severe combat with a power hostile to science—a power which in this case was in alliance with the instinctive conceptions of ordinary people. But to ask that the observer should imagine himself as standing upon the sun instead of upon the earth, is a mere trifle in comparison with the demand that he should consider the Ego to be nothing at all, and should resolve it into a transitory connection of changing elements. It is true that on various sides, the way has long been prepared for this conception.[1] We see such unities as we call "I" produced by generation and vanishing in death. Unless we indulge ourselves in the fiction, so fantastic nowadays, that these unities existed before birth in a latent state, and will similarly continue to exist after death, we can only suppose that they are just temporary unities. Psychology and psycho-pathology teach us that the Ego can grow and be enriched, can be impoverished and shrink, can become alien to itself, and can split up—in a word, can change in important respects in the course of its life. In spite of all this, the Ego is what is most important and most constant for my instinctive conceptions. It is the bond that holds all my experiences together, and the source of all my activity. In just the same way, again, a rigid body is something very constant for our crude instinctive conceptions. If it is divided, dissolved, or chemically combined with another body, the number of these constancies increases and diminishes. Then, in order to hold fast at any price to the notion that has become so

---

[1] Cp. the standpoint of Hume and Lichtenberg. For thousands of years past, Buddhism has been approaching this conception from the practical side.

dear to us, we assume latent constancies, and take refuge in atomism. Inasmuch as we are often able to restore again the body which has disappeared or changed, this procedure rests upon somewhat better grounds than in the case of the Ego.

Now in practice we can as little do without the Ego-presentation when we act, as we can do without the presentation of a body when we grasp at a thing. Physiologically we remain egoists and materialists, just as we always see the sun rise again. But theoretically this way of looking at the matter cannot be maintained. Let us change it by way of experiment. If in doing so we obtain a glimpse of the truth, it will in the long run bear practical fruits as well.

3. Anyone who has at some time or another been influenced by Kant—anyone who has adopted an idealistic standpoint, and has been unable to get rid of the last traces of the notion of the "thing-in-itself," retains a certain inclination towards solipsism, which will appear more or less clearly. Having been through it in my early youth, I know this condition of mind well, and can easily understand it. The philosophical thinker proceeds to make the single problem of the Ego—a problem which is in principle insoluble—the starting-point for everything else. The Ego is something given to us, we cannot transcend it and get away from it. When, therefore, speculative philosophers say "Solipsism is the only logically consistent standpoint," their utterance is quite intelligible in view of their struggle to reach a closed, all-inclusive, complete system of the universe. To be sure, we ought to add that materialism also is equally consistent for anyone who believes that matter is the only thing that is immediately given, and that cannot be further explained. This, indeed, is true of all systems. But when a man of science tells me that solipsism is the only consistent standpoint, he excites my astonishment. I will not emphasize the fact that this standpoint is better suited to a fakir who dreams his life away in contemplation than to a serious, thoughtful and active man. But what I do believe is that the man of science who inclines this way is making a confusion between philosophical and scientific methods. The man of science is not looking for a completed vision of the universe; he knows beforehand that all his labor can only go to broaden and deepen his insight. For him there is no problem of which the solution would not still require to be carried deeper; but there is also no problem which he can regard as absolutely insoluble. If it is impossible for the time being to make any impression on a problem, he solves in the mean-

while others that are more accessible. If he then returns to the original problem, it has generally lost much of its terrifying appearance.

No doubt the Ego is not exhausted if we say, quite provisionally, that it consists in a peculiar connection of the elements, as long as the nature of this connection is not investigated in detail. But the special problems that are relevant here will not be solved by speculation; their solution will be found by the psychologists, physiologists, and psychiatrists, to whom we already owe many important elucidations of such problems. The physical substratum of the Ego, the body,[1] will afford many points of reference which introspective psychology can only handle in a very imperfect manner. A man of science who should be a solipsist would be like a physicist for whom the thermometer was the fundamental problem of the universe, because on any particular day he did not happen to have a perfectly clear understanding of the influence of temperature on expansion. On the other hand, the philosopher who is a solipsist seems to me to be like the man who gave up turning round because whatever he saw was always in front of him. As to the instinctive, but untenable, splitting up of the Ego into an object experienced and an active or observing subject—a problem which has tormented everybody long enough—anyone who wishes to think out these questions may compare Chapter I above.

4. Whoever cannot get rid of the conception of the Ego as a reality which underlies everything, will also not be able to avoid drawing a fundamental distinction between my sensations and your sensations. In the same way, whoever believes in the absolute constancy of a body, thinks of this body as the single vehicle of all its properties. But when this silvery-white piece of sodium is melted, and dissolves in steam which looks absolutely different from the original thing; when the sodium is divided into different parts and transferred to different chemical combinations, so that more, or even fewer, bodies are present than before; then our habitual manner of thought can only be preserved by extremely artificial devices. It then becomes more advantageous to regard the particular properties as belonging sometimes to one and sometimes to another complex,

---

[1] But what is in question here is not a transcendental, unknowable Ego, which many philosophers perhaps still think it impossible to eliminate as a last remnant of the thing-in-itself, although, generally speaking, they have risen superior to that notion by now.

or body, and to substitute, for the bodies that are not constant, the law which is constant and which survives the change of the properties and of their connections. Here again, it is making no small demand, to ask that this new habit of thought should be adopted. How the thinkers of antiquity would have protested, if someone had said to them, "Earth, water, and air are not constant bodies at all; what are constant are the modern chemical elements of which they are composed, many of which elements cannot be seen, while others can only be isolated or fixed with great difficulty. Fire is not a body at all, but a process," and so on. We are scarcely able to estimate correctly nowadays the magnitude of the change which lies in this step. Yet in modern chemistry a further transformation in this direction is being prepared, and the same methods of abstraction lead in due course to the standpoint which is adopted here. From the standpoint which I here take up for purposes of general orientation, I no more draw an essential distinction between my sensations and the sensations of another person, than I regard red or green as belonging to an individual body. The same elements are connected at different points of attachment, namely the Ego's. But these points of attachment are not anything constant. They arise, they perish, and are incessantly being modified. But where there is no connection at a given moment, there is also no perceptible reciprocal influence. Whether it may or may not prove possible to transfer someone else's sensations to me by means of nervous connections, my view is not affected one way or the other. The most familiar facts provide a sufficient basis for this view.

5. Perhaps even more than in my fundamental ideas, many readers have found a stumbling-block in what they took, erroneously indeed, to be the general character of my conception of the universe. And, to begin with, I must say that anyone who, in spite of repeated protests from myself and from other quarters, identifies my view with that of Berkeley, is undoubtedly very far removed from a proper appreciation of my position.[1] This misconception is no doubt partly

---

[1] Shall I once again state the difference in a word? Berkeley regards the "elements" as conditioned by an unknown cause external to them (God); accordingly Kant, in order to appear as a sober realist, invents the "thing-in-itself"; whereas, on the view which I advocate, a dependence of the "elements" on one another is theoretically and practically all that is required. It seems to me that, in the interpretation of Kant, his very natural and psychologically intelligible fear of being considered fantastic, has not been sufficiently taken

due to the fact that my view was developed from an earlier idealistic phase, which has left on my language traces which are probably not even yet entirely obliterated. For, of all the approaches to my standpoint the one by way of idealism seems to me the easiest and most natural. And connected with this is the fear of panpsychism, which at the same time seizes my readers. Many are the victims that fall a prey to panpsychism, in the desperate struggle between a monistic conception of the universe and instinctive dualistic prejudices. In my early youth I had to work through these tendencies myself, and Avenarius was still laboring at them in his book of 1876. As regards these two points, I feel it to be a piece of particularly good fortune that Avenarius has developed the same conception of the relation between the physical and psychical on an entirely realistic, or, if the phrase be preferred, a materialistic foundation, so that I need do no more than refer to his discussions.

6. My world of elements, or sensations, strikes not only men of science, but also professional philosophers, as too unsubstantial. When I treat matter as a mental symbol standing for a relatively stable complex of sensational elements, this is described as a conception which does not make enough of the material world. The external world, it is felt, is not adequately expressed as a sum of sensations; in addition to the actual sensations, we ought at least to bring in Mill's possibilities of sensation. In reply to this, I must observe that for me also the world is not a mere sum of sensations. Indeed, I speak expressly of functional relations of the elements. But this conception not only makes Mill's "possibilities" superfluous, but replaces them by something much more solid, namely the mathematical concept of function. Had I ever dreamt that a short, precise expression would be so easily overlooked, and that a popular exposition on broad lines would have been more useful, some such exposition as that which H. Cornelius has so admirably given "on the concept of objective existence," would have served my purpose. In

into account. It is only from this point of view that we can understand how, while holding that only those concepts had meaning and value which were applicable to a possible experience, he could posit a thing in itself, of which no experience is conceivable. Over against the particular sensation, the plain man and the man of science both set the thing as a presentational complex of all the experiences, whether remembered or still expected, which are connected with the sensation in question; and this procedure is extremely shrewd. But for anyone who has assimilated Kant's way of thinking, it becomes meaningless at the limits of experience.

any case, even here I should have avoided the expression "possibility," and should have substituted for it the concept of function.

From expressions used in other quarters, it would appear that the true explanation of my position is to be sought in an exaggerated sensationalism, and in a correspondingly inadequate understanding of the value of abstraction and conceptual thought. Now, without a fairly well-marked sensationalism a man of science cannot accomplish much. But this does not prevent him from forming clear and precise concepts. On the contrary. The concepts of modern physics will stand comparison, in point of precision and height of abstraction, with those of any other science, but they offer at the same time the advantage that they can always be traced back with ease and certainty to the sensational elements on which they are built up. For science, the gulf between intuitional presentation and conceptual thought is not so great, and is not unbridgeable. I may remark in passing that I am far from thinking meanly of the concepts of physics; for nearly forty years I have been occupied with the criticism of them in various ways, and with greater thoroughness than they have received before. And since my results are gradually, after long resistance, finding acceptance with physicists, it will perhaps be allowed that this is no cheap and facile agreement. When the physicist, whose training has accustomed him to having a kilogram weight pressed into his hand with every definition, gradually expresses himself as satisfied with definitions which reduce everything to a functional relation of sensational elements, the philosopher will surely not want to be even more of a physicist than the physicist. Naturally, however, there is no room for the necessary working out of details in this sketch, which is intended to be merely a program for the closer connection of the exact sciences with one another; for further information the reader must be referred to my works on physics. It would, indeed, be highly presumptuous of me to assume even that all physicists are acquainted with these works, much more that they are familiar to people who are not professional physicists; yet it is partly want of familiarity with my works which has made it possible for me to be accused, for instance, of having entirely overlooked the "spontaneity" and "autonomy" of thought. Even towards bare sensations our attitude is not one of mere passivity; for sensations disengage a biological reaction, of which the natural continuation is precisely the adaptation of thought to facts. If this adaptation were immediately and perfectly successful, the process would *ipso facto* come to an end. But since different imperfectly adapted thoughts come into conflict with one another, the biological process continues. What I have called the adaptation of thoughts to one another takes place. Now I should really like to know what process of scientific development, the logical process included, is not covered by this statement? Here I may be permitted to break off for the present these controversial remarks, in which I have only been forced to repeat what I have frequently said and have long been saying.

7. To many readers the universe, as conceived by me, seems to be a chaos, a hopelessly tangled web of elements. They feel the want of leading and unifying points of view. But this depends on a misinterpretation of the task that I have set myself. All points of view which are of value for the special sciences and for the philosophical consideration of the world, remain capable of further application, and indeed, are so applied by me. The apparently destructive tendency of the work is merely directed against superfluous, and therefore misleading, additions to our concepts. Thus I believe that the contrasts between the psychical and the physical, and between subjective and objective, have been correctly reduced by me to what is essential in them, and at the same time have been purged of traditional and superstitious conceptions. And this has been done in such a way that scientifically established points of view are not altered, and at the same time room is made for new points of view. I have no desire to set up, in the place of the lamentations of a piously whining "Ignorabimus," an obstinately self-sufficient attitude of rejection of everything that is worth knowing and that can be known. For to refuse to attempt answers to questions that have been recognized as meaningless, is in no sense an act of resignation; in view of the mass of material that can really be investigated, it is the only reasonable course open to a man of science. The physicist who refrains from seeking for the secret of perpetual motion, need not nowadays regard this as an act of resignation, any more than the mathematician who no longer troubles himself about the squaring of the circle or the solution of equations of the fifth degree in closed algebraical form. So, too, with more general philosophical questions: the problems are either solved, or are recognized as pointless.

"In what exactly does the fallacy, or the bias, of Mach's philosophical views consist?" This question, which one of my critics asks, strikes me as very harmless. For I am convinced that my exposition is full of defects in more than one direction. This, indeed, can scarcely be avoided when a writer's views are undergoing a radical process of revolution, for even a single head cannot work out such a process completely to its conclusion. Hence, though I can feel these faults, I cannot put my finger on them. If I could, I should be a long way further advanced towards my goal. But neither have I been able to obtain a clear view of my faults from the writings of my critics. Let us, therefore, wait a little longer.

Against my views, arguments have been brought which have been fully discussed both in this book and in other writings of mine; but I do not state this fact with a desire to reproach anybody. It must be a real torture to have to read everything that is published, and, what is more, to have to pass judgment conscientiously and deliberately in a brief allotted time. I have never discovered in myself any taste for this important vocation, and consequently I have only written three reviews, all told, in a period of forty years. So I do not grudge it to the reviewers, that they should have saved themselves a certain amount of trouble, even though it has been partly at my expense. I hope they will not take it ill on my part, if I do not react to every sally and to every sarcasm which they fancy has hit its mark.

Hönigswald, however, has subsequently devoted a book to my standpoint. I must admit that he has taken the trouble to read my books; nor have I the least objection to make to a criticism which decides that my position is incompatible with Kant's. Not all philosophers will draw the inference that my position must therefore be untenable. My relations to Kant have been peculiar. His critical idealism was, as I recognize with the greatest gratitude, the starting-point of all my critical thought; but it was impossible for me to retain my allegiance to it. I very soon began to gravitate again towards the views of Berkeley, which are contained, in a more or less latent form, in Kant's writings. By studying the physiology of the senses, and by reading Herbart, I then arrived at views akin to those of Hume, though at that time I was still unacquainted with Hume himself. To this very day I cannot help regarding Berkeley and Hume as far more logically consistent thinkers than Kant. It is not the business of a man of science to criticize or refute a philosopher like Kant, though it may be observed in passing that it would no longer be a particularly heroic achievement to show the inadequacy of Kant's philosophy as a guide to modern scientific research. This has long since been effected by the progress that has been made in all departments, including philosophy itself. When Hönigswald enunciates a number of general points of view, and proceeds to elicit from them a closed philosophical system, he completely misapprehends the cautiously tentative methods of approximation employed by science. The constants of the man of science are not absolutely constant, nor, on the other hand, do the changes which he investigates correspond to the limitless flux of Herakleitos. I call biological aims "practical" when they are not directed to pure knowledge as an end in itself. Only consider what the position of the man of science would be if, before he began to think, he had to refute all the philosophical systems one by one. Once more, there is no such thing as "the philosophy of Mach."

8. Whether I shall ever succeed in making my fundamental ideas plausible to the philosophers, I must leave to time to decide. I do not attach much importance to this at present, though I have a deep reverence for the gigantic intellectual labors of the great philosophers of all ages. But I have an honest and lively desire for an understanding with the natural scientists, and I consider that such an understanding is attainable. I should like the scientists to realize that my view eliminates all metaphysical questions indifferently, whether they be only regarded as insoluble at the present moment, or whether they be regarded as meaningless for all time. I should like them, further, to reflect that everything that we can know about the world is necessarily expressed in the sensations, which can be set free from the individual influence of the observer in a precisely definable manner. Everything that we can want to know is given by the solution of a problem in mathematical form, by the ascertainment of the functional dependence of the sensational elements on one another. This knowledge exhausts the knowledge of "reality." The bridge between physics, in the widest sense, and scientific psychology, is formed of these very elements, which are physical and psychical objects according to the kind of combination that is being investigated.

9. Probably a good many physiologists have taken objection to a point of detail in my position, as to which I should like to say something more. I have a great value for researches such as those of S. Exner, and I believe that many important problems as to psychical phenomena can be solved merely by the investigation of the nervous connections of the central organs, and by observation of the way in which stimuli are arranged in a quantitative scale. Indeed Exner's book itself is evidence of this. But I feel that the main problems still remain unsolved. For, from my point of view, I cannot conceive, any more than I could nearly forty years ago, how the qualitative

variety of sensations can arise from the variation of the connections and from mere quantitative differences. Fechner's psychophysics, which have had so important an influence, did not fail to stimulate me exceedingly at the time. Inspired by Fechner's book, I delivered some very bad lectures on the subject, the value of my lectures being still further diminished by the fact that I soon came to see that Fechner's theory of formulæ of measurement was erroneous. In this connection, after explaining Helmholtz's "telegraph-wire" theory of sensation, I said: "But will the electric processes in the nerves prove to be too simple to explain adequately the difference of quality in sensations? Will it be necessary to thrust the explanation further back into regions that are still unknown? What if, after investigating the whole brain, we find everywhere nothing but electric currents? My personal opinion is this. The electrical researches that have been made on the nerves are no doubt of a very delicate nature, but in one respect they are very rough. An electric current of given intensity tells us nothing, except that a definite quantity of living force passes in the time-unit through a cross-section of the current. By what processes and by what molecular movements that living force is assisted, we do not know. It is possible that the most diverse processes underlie one and the same intensity of current." Even today I have not succeeded in getting rid of this idea, and I cannot refrain from bringing forward evidence that confirms it in essentially the same form, as for instance by referring to the presence of an identical current in different electrolytes. The progress of physiological chemistry, and the experiments that have been made in the transplantation of different organs, seem to me today to be still more decisively in favor of my view.

FRIEDRICH NIETZSCHE

Beyond Good and Evil (*abridged*)

SUPPLEMENTARY PASSAGES
The Will to Power
Eternal Recurrence
The Superman
Good and Evil
Christianity
Conscience
Art

FRIEDRICH NIETZSCHE

FRIEDRICH NIETZSCHE (1844–1900), the grandson of two Lutheran ministers, and the son of a Lutheran minister who died when he was five years old, was brought up with his sister by his mother, grandmother, and two maiden aunts. He studied at Bonn, received his doctor's degree from Leipzig, and was appointed professor of classical philology at Basel, where he taught for ten years. Poor health, with which he had to contend during much of his life, forced him to retire in 1879. He served for a time as medical orderly in the Franco-Prussian War of 1870, and during this period he was a friend and admirer of Richard Wagner, from whom he later made a celebrated break. During the next ten years he stayed alternately in Germany and Italy, writing prolifically; in 1889 he sank into the mental illness that put an end to his work, though he still had eleven years to live.

In the thirteen books that Nietzsche published during his lifetime, his philosophical theories are mingled with his convictions about history, contemporary Europe, human nature, women, literature, and music; nor is it possible to draw a sharp line in his thinking between philosophy and these other subjects. All his works throw some light upon his philosophy, but, besides *Beyond Good and Evil* (on which see below), the following are of particular relevance: *Thus Spake Zarathustra* (published in three installments, 1883, 1884, 1885), his most famous book, a brilliant literary work in which Nietzsche's philosophy is expressed poetically and symbolically through the voice of the Persian religious teacher Zoroaster (trans. Walter Kaufmann in *The Portable Nietzsche,* New York: Viking Press, 1954); his early essay on *The Use and Abuse of History* (1874; part of *Thoughts Out of Season;* trans. Adrian Collins, New York: Modern Library, 1927); *The Birth of Tragedy* (1872; trans. Clifton P. Fadiman in *The Philosophy of Nietzsche,* New York: Modern Library, 1927; also trans. Walter Kaufmann, New York: Vintage Books, 1967), a theory of tragedy as the affirmation of life, in opposition to Schopenhauer, and a defense of Wagner; he published the first of two parts of *Human, All Too Human* (1878–79;

the third part appeared in 1880; trans. R. J. Hollingdale, Cambridge: Cambridge University Press, 1986); *The Dawn* (1888; trans. Walter Kaufmann in *The Portable Nietzsche*); *The Gay Science* (1882); *Daybreak: Thoughts on the Prejudices of Morality* (1881; trans. R. J. Hollingdale, Cambridge: Cambridge University Press, 1982); *The Geneology of Morals* (1887; trans. Horace B. Samuel, *ibid.;* also trans. Walter Kaufmann and R. J. Hollingdale, 1967), three essays on the foundations of ethics, drawing on Nietzsche's knowledge of philology and his remarkable psychological insight; *The Antichrist* (1888; trans. Kaufmann, *op. cit.*), the final statement, full of challenging ideas despite its overheated manner, of his rejection of Christianity. His last two books were *Ecce Homo* (1888; trans. Kaufmann, *op. cit.*), an autobiography, and *Nietzsche Contra Wagner* (1888; trans. Kaufmann, *op. cit.*). The fragments known as *The Will to Power* (1883–88; trans. Anthony M. Ludovici, Edinburgh: Foulis, 1910; also trans. Walter Kaufmann and R. J. Hollingdale, New York: Random House, 1967) is a two-volume collection of Nietzsche's notes and sketches published (1910) after his death by his sister Elizabeth Förster-Nietzsche; these notes include many that had already been used for earlier books and others that, though incomplete and sketchy, throw important light on directions in which his later thought was moving.

The meaning and significance of Nietzsche's work has been much obscured, first by the somewhat puzzling form in which he chose to present it—a subtle, varied, allusive style, in short passages he called "aphorisms"—and second by the manner in which it has been distorted and exploited for various ideological purposes by his sister (who secured all his papers) and by Nazi and anti-Nazi interpreters. Even now there is disagreement about how he is to be interpreted and judged, both as a philosopher and as a phenomenon. But it seems fair to say that in certain ways our present-day philosophy would have been much poorer without him. Like Socrates, whom he so much admired, Nietzsche's contribution lay principally in the searching and original questions he asked. His unusual temperament gave him a very special vantage point from which to look upon the tendencies of his own age, in the light of history as he knew it, and to see with more clarity than others a few selected but important aspects of it. He issued the greatest of challenges to the whole democratic outlook—a challenge that cannot be ignored—and pointed out with sharpness and vigor the dangers of uncritical forms of it: the equalitarianism of conformity, the tendency to resent gifted men. His philosophy of human nature, his grasp of the complexities of conscious and unconscious drives, paved the way not only for the twentieth-century psychology of Freud and others but for a more adequate conception of man than was possible before Nietzsche and Dostoyevsky. He addressed himself to a mankind just becoming aware, through the theory of evolution, of its own origin and past road and of its power to be far greater. And he spoke—in a rhapsodic, sometimes wildly ranting voice, but with a passionate affirmation of life—of man's obligation to think and work for the future greatness of his descendants.

Beyond Good and Evil * (*abridged*)

First Article

Prejudices of Philosophers

1.   The Will to Truth, which is to tempt us to many a hazardous
enterprise, the famous Truthfulness of which all philosophers have
hitherto spoken with respect—what questions has this Will to Truth
not laid before us! What strange, perplexing, questionable questions! It
is already a long story; yet it seems as if it were hardly commenced.
Is it any wonder if we at last grow distrustful, lose patience, and
turn impatiently away? That this Sphinx teaches us at last to ask
questions ourselves? *Who* is it really that puts questions to us here?
What really is this "Will to Truth" in us? In fact we made a long halt
at the question as to the origin of this Will—until at last we came to
an absolute standstill before a yet more fundamental question. We
inquired about the *value* of this Will. Granted that we want the
truth: *why not rather* untruth? And uncertainty? Even ignorance?
The problem of the value of truth presented itself before us—or was
it we who presented ourselves before the problem? Which of us is
the Œdipus here? Which the Sphinx? It would seem to be a rendezvous
of questions and notes of interrogation. And, perhaps incredibly, it
at last seems to us as if the problem had never been propounded
before, as if we were the first to discern it, get a sight of it, and *risk
raising* it. For there is risk in raising it; perhaps there is no greater
risk.

2.   *"How could* anything originate out of its opposite? For example, truth out of error? or the Will to Truth out of the will to
deception? or the generous deed out of selfishness? or the pure sun-
bright vision of the wise man out of covetousness? Such genesis is
impossible; whoever dreams of it is a fool, nay, worse than a fool;
things of the highest value must have a different origin, an origin of
their own—in this transitory, seductive, illusory, paltry world, in
this turmoil of delusion and cupidity, they cannot have their source.
Rather in the lap of Being, in the intransitory, in the concealed God,

---

* Translated by Helen Zimmern. Reprinted from *The Philosophy of
Nietzsche*, N. Y.: Modern Library, 1927, with revisions by the present editor,
by arrangement with George Allen & Unwin Ltd. *Jenseits von Gut und Böse*
was first published in 1886. The present abridgment includes about one-third
of the original, the parts of greatest philosophical importance.

in the 'Thing-in-itself'—*there* must be their source, and nowhere else!"—This mode of reasoning discloses the typical prejudice by which metaphysicians of all times can be recognized; this mode of valuation is at the back of all their logical procedure; through this "belief" of theirs, they exert themselves for their "knowledge," for something that is in the end solemnly christened "the Truth." The fundamental belief of metaphysicians is *the belief in the antithetical character of values*. It never occurred even to the wariest of them to doubt here on the very threshold (where doubt, however, was most necessary); though they had made a solemn vow *"de omnibus dubitandum."* [1] For it may be doubted, first, whether antitheses exist at all; and second, whether the popular valuations and antitheses of value upon which metaphysicians have set their seal are not perhaps merely superficial estimates, merely provisional perspectives, besides being probably made from some corner, perhaps from below—"frog perspectives," as it were, to borrow an expression current among painters. In spite of all the value that may belong to the true, the positive, and the unselfish, it might be possible that a higher and more fundamental value for life generally should be assigned to pretence, to the will to delusion, to selfishness, and cupidity. It might even be possible that *what* constitutes the value of those good and respected things, consists precisely in their being insidiously related, knotted, and crocheted to these evil and apparently opposed things—perhaps even in being essentially identical with them. Perhaps! But who wishes to concern himself with such dangerous "Perhapses"! For that investigation one must await the advent of a new order of philosophers, such as will have other tastes and inclinations, the reverse of those hitherto prevalent—philosophers of the dangerous "Perhaps" in every sense of the term. And to speak in all seriousness, I see such new philosophers beginning to appear.

3. Having kept a sharp eye on philosophers, and having read between their lines long enough, I now say to myself that the greater part of conscious thinking must be counted amongst the instinctive functions, and it is so even in the case of philosophical thinking; one has here to learn anew, as one learned anew about heredity and "innateness." As little as the act of birth counts in the whole process and procedure of heredity, just as little is "being-conscious" *opposed* to the instinctive in any decisive sense; the greater part of the conscious thinking of a philosopher is secretly influenced by his instincts, and forced into definite channels. And behind all logic and its seeming

---

[1] [To doubt everything.—M.C.B.]

sovereignty of movement, there are valuations, or to speak more plainly, physiological demands, for the maintenance of a definite mode of life. For example, that the certain is worth more than the uncertain, that illusion is less valuable than "truth": such valuations, in spite of their regulative importance can for *us* be only superficial valuations, special kinds of *niaiserie,* such as may be necessary for the maintenance of beings such as ourselves. Supposing, in effect, that man is not just the "measure of things". . .

4.   The falseness of an opinion is not for us any objection to it: it is here, perhaps, that our new language sounds strangest. The question is, how far an opinion is life-furthering, life-preserving, species-preserving, perhaps species-rearing; and we are fundamentally inclined to maintain that the falsest opinions (to which synthetic *a priori* judgments belong) are the most indispensable to us; that without the acceptance of logical fictions, without a comparison of reality with the purely *imagined* world of the absolute and immutable, without a constant counterfeiting of the world by means of numbers, man could not live—that the renunciation of false opinions would be a renunciation of life, a negation of life. *To recognise untruth as a condition of life:* that is certainly to impugn the traditional ideas of value in a dangerous manner, and a philosophy that ventures to do so, has by this alone placed itself beyond good and evil.

5.   What causes philosophers to be regarded half-distrustfully and half-mockingly, is not the oft-repeated discovery how innocent they are—how often and easily they make mistakes and lose their way, in short, how childish and childlike they are—but that there is not enough candor in them, though they all raise a loud and virtuous outcry when the problem of truthfulness is even hinted at in the remotest manner. They all pose as though their real opinions had been discovered and attained through the self-evolving of a cold, pure, divinely indifferent dialectic (in contrast to all sorts of mystics, who, fairer and foolisher, talk of "inspiration"); whereas, in fact, a prejudiced proposition, idea, or "suggestion," which is generally their heart's desire abstracted and refined, is defended by them with arguments sought out after the event. They are all lawyers who do not wish to be regarded as such, generally astute defenders, also, of their prejudices, which they dub "truths"—and *very* far from having the conscience that bravely admits this to itself; very far from having the good taste or the courage that goes so far as to let this be understood, perhaps to warn friend or foe, or in cheerful confidence and self-mockery. The spectacle of the Tartuffery of old Kant, equally

stiff and decent, with which he entices us into the dialectic by-ways that lead (more correctly mislead) to his "categorical imperative"— makes us fastidious ones smile, we who find no small amusement in spying out the subtle tricks of old moralists and ethical preachers. Or, still more so, the hocus-pocus in mathematical form, by means of which Spinoza has, as it were, clad his philosophy in mail and mask— in fact, the "love of *his* wisdom," to translate the term fairly and squarely—in order thereby to strike terror at once into the heart of the assailant who should dare to cast a glance on that invincible maiden, that Pallas Athene:—how much of personal timidity and vulnerability does this masquerade of a sickly recluse betray!

6.   It has gradually become clear to me what every great philosophy up till now has consisted of—namely, the confession of its originator, and a species of involuntary and unconscious autobiography; and moreover that the moral (or immoral) purpose in every philosophy has constituted the true vital germ out of which the entire plant has always grown. Indeed, to understand how the abstrusest metaphysical assertions of a philosopher have been arrived at, it is always well (and wise) to first ask oneself: "What morality do they (or does he) aim at?" Accordingly, I do not believe that an "impulse to knowledge" is the father of philosophy; but that another impulse, here as elsewhere, has only made use of knowledge (and mistaken knowledge!) as an instrument. But whoever considers the fundamental impulses of man with a view to determining how far they may have here acted as *inspiring* genii (or as demons and cobolds), will find that they have all practiced philosophy at one time or another, and that each one of them would have been only too glad to look upon itself as the ultimate end of existence and the legitimate *lord* over all the other impulses. For every impulse is imperious, and as *such* attempts to philosophize. To be sure, in the case of scholars, in the case of really scientific men, it may be otherwise—"better," if you will; there there may really be such a thing as an "impulse to knowledge," some kind of small, independent clock-work, which, when well wound up, works away industriously to that end, *without* the rest of the scholarly impulses taking any material part therein. The actual "interests" of the scholar, therefore, are generally in quite another direction— in the family, perhaps, or in money-making, or in politics; it is, in fact, almost indifferent at what point of research his little machine is placed, and whether the hopeful young worker becomes a good philologist, a mushroom specialist, or a chemist; he is not *character- ized* by becoming this or that. In the philosopher, on the contrary,

there is absolutely nothing impersonal; and above all, his morality furnishes a decided and decisive testimony as to *who he is*—that is to say, in what order the deepest impulses of his nature stand to each other. . . .

9. You desire to *live* "according to Nature"? Oh, you noble Stoics, what fraud of words! Imagine to yourselves a being like Nature, boundlessly extravagant, boundlessly indifferent, without purpose or consideration, without pity or justice, at once fruitful and barren and uncertain: imagine to yourselves *indifference* as a power—how *could* you live in accordance with such indifference? To live—is not that just endeavoring to be different from this Nature? Is not living valuing, preferring, being unjust, being limited, endeavoring to be different? And granted that your imperative, "living according to Nature," actually means the same as "living according to life"—how could you do *otherwise?* Why should you make a principle out of what you yourselves are, and must be? The fact, however, is the other way around: while you pretend to read with rapture the canon of your law in Nature, you want something quite the contrary, you extraordinary stage-players and self-deluders! In your pride you wish to dictate your morals and ideals to Nature, to Nature herself, and to incorporate them therein; you insist that it shall be Nature "according to the Stoa," and would like everything to be made after your own image, as a vast, eternal glorification of Stoicism! With all your love of truth, you have forced yourselves so long, so persistently, and with such hypnotic rigidity to see Nature *falsely,* that is to say, Stoically, that you are no longer able to see it otherwise—and to crown all, some unfathomable arrogance gives you the Bedlamite hope that *because* you are able to tyrannize over yourselves—Stoicism is self-tyranny—Nature will also allow herself to be tyrannized over: is not the Stoic a *part* of Nature? . . . But this is an old and everlasting story: what happened in old times with the Stoics still happens today, as soon as a philosophy begins to believe in itself. It always creates the world in its own image; it cannot do otherwise; philosophy is this tyrannical impulse itself, the most spiritual Will to Power, the will to "creation of the world," the will to the *causa prima.*

10. The eagerness and subtlety (I should even say craftiness) with which the problem of "the real and the apparent world" is dealt with at present throughout Europe, furnishes food for thought and attention; and he who hears only a "Will to Truth" in the background certainly cannot boast of the sharpest ears. In rare and isolated cases, it may really have happened that such a Will to Truth—a

certain extravagent and adventurous pluck, a metaphysician's ambition of the forlorn hope—has been involved: that which in the end always prefers a handful of "certainty" to a whole cartload of beautiful possibilities; there may even be puritanical fanatics of conscience, who prefer to put their last trust in a certain nothing, rather than in an uncertain something. But that is Nihilism, and the sign of a despairing, mortally wearied soul, notwithstanding the courageous bearing such a virtue may display. It seems, however, to be otherwise with stronger and livelier thinkers who are still eager for life. In that they side *against* appearance, and speak superciliously of "perspective," in that they rank the credibility of their own bodies about as low as the credibility of the ocular evidence that "the earth stands still," and thus, apparently, allowing with complacency their securest possession to escape (for what does one at present believe in more firmly than in one's body?)—who knows if they are not really trying to win back something that was formerly an even *securer* possession, something of the old domain of the faith of former times, perhaps the "immortal soul," perhaps the "old God," in short, ideas by which they could live better, that is to say, more vigorously and more joyously, than by "modern ideas"? There is *distrust* of these modern ideas in this mode of looking at things, a disbelief in all that has been constructed yesterday and today; there is perhaps some slight admixture of satiety and scorn, which can no longer endure the *bric-a-brac* of ideas of the most varied origin, such as so-called Positivism at present throws on the market; a disgust of the more refined taste at the village-fair motleyness and patchiness of all these reality-philosophasters, in whom there is nothing either new or true, except this motleyness. Therein it seems to me that we should agree with those sceptical anti-realists and knowledge-microscopists of the present day; their instinct, which repels them from *modern* reality, is unrefuted . . . what do their retrograde by-paths concern us! The main thing about them is *not* that they wish to go "back," but that they wish to get *away* therefrom. A little *more* strength, swing, courage, and artistic power, and they would be *off*—and not back!

11. It seems to me that there is everywhere an attempt at present to divert attention from the actual influence which Kant exercised on German philosophy, and especially to ignore prudently the value which he set upon himself. Kant was first and foremost proud of his Table of Categories; with it in his hand he said: "This is the most difficult thing that could ever be undertaken on behalf of metaphysics." Let us only understand this "could be"! He was proud of having *dis-*

covered a new faculty in man, the faculty of synthetic *a priori* judgment. Granting that he deceived himself in this matter; the development and rapid flourishing of German philosophy depended nevertheless on his pride, and on the eager rivalry of the younger generation to discover if possible something—at all events "new faculties"—
of which to be still prouder! But let us reflect for a moment—it is
high time to do so. "How are synthetic *a priori* judgments *possible?*"
Kant asks himself—and what is really his answer? *"By means of a
means* (faculty)"—but unfortunately not in five words, but so circum-
stantially, imposingly, and with such display of German profundity
and verbal flourishes, that one altogether loses sight of the comical
niaiserie allemande involved in such an answer. People were beside
themselves with delight over this new faculty, and the jubilation
reached its climax when Kant further discovered a moral faculty in
man—for at that time Germans were still moral, not yet dabbling in
the "Politics of hard fact." Then came the honeymoon of German
philosophy. All the young theologians of the Tübingen institution went
immediately into the groves—all seeking for "faculties." And what
did they not find—in that innocent, rich, and still youthful period of
the German spirit, to which Romanticism, the malicious fairy, piped
and sang, when one could not yet distinguish between "finding" and
"inventing"! Above all a faculty for the "transcendental"; Schelling
christened it "intellectual intuition" and thereby gratified the most
earnest longings of the naturally pious-inclined Germans. One can do
no greater wrong to the whole of this exuberant and eccentric movement (which was really youthfulness, notwithstanding that it disguised
itself so boldly in hoary and senile conceptions) than to take it
seriously, or even treat it with moral indigation. Enough, however—
the world grew older, and the dream vanished. A time came when
people rubbed their foreheads, and they still rub them to-day. People
had been dreaming, and first and foremost—old Kant. "By means of
a means (faculty)"—he had said, or at least meant to say. But, is
that—an answer? An explanation? Or is it not merely begging the
question? How does opium induce sleep? "By means of a means
(faculty)," namely the *virtus dormitiva,* replies the doctor in Molière,

> *Quia est in eo virtus dormitiva,*
> *Cujus est natura sensus assoupire.*[1]

---

[1] [Because it contains a soporific power,
Whose nature is to dull the senses.—M.C.B.]

But such replies belong to the realm of comedy, and it is high time to replace the Kantian question, "How are synthetic *a priori* judgments possible?" by another question, "Why is belief in such judgments *necessary?*"—in effect, it is high time that we should understand that such judgments must be *believed* to be true, for the sake of preserving creatures like ourselves; though they may still be *false* judgments! Or, more plainly spoken, and roughly and readily —synthetic *a priori* judgments should not "be possible" at all; we have no right to them; in our mouths they are nothing but false judgments. Only, of course, the belief in their truth is necessary, as plausible belief and ocular evidence belonging to the perspective view of life. And finally, to call to mind the enormous influence that "German philosophy"—I hope you understand its right to inverted commas (goosefeet)?—has exercised throughout the whole of Europe, there is no doubt that a certain *virtus dormitiva* had a share in it; thanks to German philosophy, it was a delight to the noble idlers, the virtuous, the mystics, the artists, the three-fourths Christians, and the political obscurantists of all nations, to find an antidote to the still overwhelming sensualism which overflowed from the last century into this, in short— *"sensus assoupire"* . . .

12.   As regards materialistic atomism, it is one of the best refuted theories that have been advanced, and in Europe there is now perhaps no one in the learned world so unscholarly as to attach serious significance to it, except for convenient everyday use (as an abbreviation of the means of expression)—thanks chiefly to the Pole Boscovich: he and the Pole Copernicus have hitherto been the greatest and most successful opponents of ocular evidence. For whilst Copernicus has persuaded us to believe, contrary to all the senses, that the earth does *not* stand fast, Boscovich has taught us to abjure the belief in the last thing that "stood fast" of the earth—the belief in "substance," in "matter," in the earth-residuum, and particle-atom: it is the greatest triumph over the senses that has hitherto been gained on earth. One must, however, go still further, and also declare war, relentless war to the knife, against the "atomistic requirements" which still lead a dangerous after-life in places where no one suspects them, like the more celebrated "metaphysical requirements": one must also above all give the finishing stroke to that other and more portentous atomism that Christianity has taught best and longest, the *soul-atomism*. Let it be permitted to designate by this expression the belief that the soul is something indestructible, eternal, indivisible, as a monad, as an *atomon: this* belief ought to be expelled from

science! Between ourselves, it is not at all necessary to get rid of "the soul" thereby, and thus renounce one of the oldest and most venerated hypotheses—as happens frequently to the clumsiness of naturalists, who can hardly touch on the soul without immediately losing it. But the way is open for new acceptations and refinements of the soul-hypothesis; and such conceptions as "mortal soul," and "soul of subjective multiplicity," and "soul as social structure of the instincts and passions," want henceforce to have legitimate rights in science. In that the *new* psychologist is about to put an end to the superstitions that have hitherto flourished with almost tropical luxuriance around the idea of the soul, he is really, as it were, thrusting himself into a new desert and a new distrust (it is possible that the older psychologists had a merrier and more comfortable time of it); eventually, however, he finds that precisely thereby he is also condemned to *invent*—and, who knows? perhaps to *discover* the new.

13. Physiologists should stop to think before putting down self-preservation as the cardinal instinct of an organic being. A living thing seeks above all to *discharge* its strength—life itself is *Will to Power;* self-preservation is only one of the indirect and most frequent *results* thereof. In short, here, as everywhere else, let us beware of *superfluous* teleological principles!—one of which is the instinct of self-preservation (we owe it to Spinoza's inconsistency). It is thus, in effect, that method ordains, of which the essence is economy of principles.

14. It is perhaps just dawning on five or six minds that natural philosophy is only a world-exposition and world-arrangement (an arrangement to suit us, if I may say so!) and *not* a world-explanation; but in so far as it is based on belief in the senses, it is regarded as more, and for a long time to come must be regarded as more—namely, as an explanation. It has eyes and fingers to support it, it has ocular evidence and palpableness of its own: this operates fascinatingly, persuasively, and *convincingly* upon an age with fundamentally plebeian tastes—in fact, it follows instinctively the canon of truth of eternally popular sensualism. What is clear, what is "explained"? Only what can be seen and felt—one must pursue every problem thus far. Conversely, however, the charm of the Platonic mode of thought, which was an *aristocratic* mode, consisted precisely in *resistance to* obvious sense-evidence—perhaps among men who enjoyed even stronger and more fastidious senses than our contemporaries, but who knew how to find a higher triumph in remaining masters of them: and this by means of pale, cold, grey conceptual networks which they threw over the motley whirl of the senses—the mob of the

senses, as Plato said. In this overcoming of the world, and interpreting of the world in the manner of Plato, there was an *enjoyment* different from that which the physicists of today offer us—and likewise the Darwinians and antiteleologists among the physiological workers, with their principle of the "least possible effort," and the greatest possible blunder. "Where there is nothing more to see or to grasp, there is also nothing more for men to do"—that is certainly an imperative different from the Platonic one, but it may notwithstanding be the right imperative for a hardy, laborious race of machinists and bridge-builders of the future, who have nothing but *rough* work to perform.

15.   To study physiology with a clear conscience, one must insist on the fact that the sense-organs are *not* phenomena in the sense of the idealistic philosophy; as such they certainly could not be causes! Sensualism, therefore, at least as regulative hypothesis, if not as heuristic principle. What? And others say even that the external world is the work of our organs? But then our body, as a part of this external world, would be the work of our organs! But then our organs themselves would be the work of—our organs! It seems to me that this is a complete *reductio ad absurdum,* if the conception *causa sui* is something fundamentally absurd. Consequently, the external world is *not* the work of our organs—?

16.   There are still harmless self-observers who believe that there are "immediate certainties"; for instance, "I think," or as the superstition of Schopenhauer puts it, "I will"; as though cognition here got hold of its object purely and simply as "the thing in itself," without any falsification taking place either on the part of the subject or the object. I would repeat it, however, a hundred times, that "immediate certainty," as well as "absolute knowledge" and the "thing in itself," involve a contradiction in terms; we really ought to free ourselves from the misleading significance of words! The people on their part may think that cognition is knowing all about things, but the philosopher must say to himself: "When I analyze the process that is expressed in the sentence, 'I think,' I find a whole series of daring assertions, the proof of which would be difficult, perhaps impossible: for instance, that it is *I* who think, that there must necessarily be something that thinks, that thinking is an activity and operation on the part of a being who is thought of as a cause, that there is an 'ego,' and finally, that it is already determined what is to be designated by thinking—that I *know* what thinking is. For if I had not already decided within myself what it is, by what standard could I determine

whether what is happening now is not perhaps 'willing' or 'feeling'? in short, the assertion 'I think' assumes that I *compare* my state at the present moment with other states of myself that I already know, in order to determine what it is; on account of this retrospective connection with other 'knowledge,' it has, at any rate, no immediate certainty for me."—In place of the "immediate certainty" in which the people may believe in the special case, the philosopher thus finds a series of metaphysical questions presented to him, veritable conscience-questions of the intellect, to wit: "How did I get the notion of 'thinking'? Why do I believe in cause and effect? What gives me the right to speak of an 'ego,' and even of an 'ego' as cause, and finally of an 'ego' as cause of thought?" He who ventures to answer these metaphysical questions at once by an appeal to a sort of *intuitive* perception, like the person who says, "I think, and know that this, at least, is true, actual, and certain"—will encounter a smile and two notes of interrogation in a philosopher nowadays. "Sir," the philosopher will perhaps give him to understand, "it is improbable that you are not mistaken, but why must we have the truth?"

17.   With regard to the superstitions of logicians, I shall never tire of emphasizing a small, terse fact, which these credulous minds are unwilling to recognize—namely, that a thought comes when "it" wishes and, not when "I" wish; so that it is a *perversion* of the facts of the case to say that the subject "I" is the condition of the predicate "think." *Something* thinks; but that this "something" is precisely the famous old "ego," is, to put it mildly, only a supposition, an assertion, and assuredly not an "immediate certainty." After all, one has even gone too far with this "something thinks"—even the "something" contains an *interpretation* of the process, and does not belong to the process itself. One infers here according to the usual grammatical formula—"To think is an activity; every activity requires an agency that is active; consequently . . ." It was pretty much on the same lines that the older atomism sought, besides the operating "power," the material particle wherein it resides and out of which it operates—the atom. More rigorous minds, however, learned at last to get along without this "earth-residuum," and perhaps some day we shall accustom ourselves, even from the logician's point of view, to get along without the little "something" (to which the worthy old "ego" has refined itself).

18.   It is certainly not the least charm of a theory that it is refutable; it is precisely thereby that it attracts the more subtle minds. It seems that the hundred-times-refuted theory of the "free will" owes

its persistence to this charm alone; some one is always turning up who feels himself strong enough to refute it again.

19.   Philosophers are accustomed to speak of the will as though it were the best-known thing in the world; indeed, Schopenhauer has given us to understand that the will alone is really known to us, absolutely and completely known, without deduction or addition. But it seems to me again that in this case Schopenhauer also only did what philosophers are in the habit of doing—he seems to have adopted a *popular prejudice* and exaggerated it. Willing—seems to me to be above all something *complicated,* something that is a unity only in name—and it is precisely in a name that popular prejudice lurks, which has got the mastery over the inadequate precautions of philosophers in all ages. So let us for once be more cautious, let us be "unphilosophical": let us say that in all willing there is firstly a plurality of sensations, namely, the sensation of the condition *"away from which* we go," the sensation of the condition *"towards which* we go," the sensation of this *"from"* and *"towards"* itself, and then, besides, an accompanying muscular sensation, which, even without our putting in motion "arms and legs," commences its action by force of habit, directly we "will" anything. Therefore, just as sensations (and indeed many kinds of sensation) are to be recognized as ingredients of the will, so, in the second place, thinking is also to be recognized; in every act of the will there is a ruling thought—and let us not imagine it possible to subtract this thought from the "willing," as if the will would remain! In the third place, the will is not only a complex of sensation and thinking, but it is above all an *emotion,* and in fact the emotion of commanding. What is termed "freedom of the will" is essentially the emotion of supremacy in respect to him who must obey: "I am free, 'he' must obey"—this consciousness is inherent in every will; and equally so the straining of the attention, the straight look which fixes itself exclusively on one thing, the unconditional judgment that "this and nothing else is necessary now," the inward certainty that obedience will be rendered—and whatever else pertains to the position of the commander. A man who *wills* commands something within himself which renders obedience, or which he believes renders obedience. But now let us notice what is the strangest thing about the will—this affair so extremely complex, for which the people have only one name. Because, in the given circumstances, we are at the same time the commanding *and* the obeying parties, and as the obeying party we know the sensations of constraint, impulsion, pressure, resistance, and motion, which usually commence immediately after the act of

will; because, on the other hand, we are accustomed to disregard this duality, and to deceive ourselves about it by means of the synthetic term "I": a whole series of erroneous conclusions, and consequently of false judgments about the will itself, has become attached to the act of willing—to such a degree that he who wills believes firmly that willing *suffices* for action. Since in the majority of cases there has only been exercise of will when the effect of the command—consequently obedience, and therefore action—was to be *expected,* the *appearance* has translated itself into the feeling that there was a *necessity of effect;* in a word, he who wills believes with some degree of certainty that will and action are somehow one; he ascribes the success, the carrying out of the willing, to the will itself, and thereby enjoys an increase of the sensation of power which accompanies all success. "Freedom of Will"—that is the expression for the complex state of delight of the person exercising volition, who commands and at the same time identifies himself with the executor of the order— who, as such, enjoys also the triumph over obstacles, but thinks within himself that it was really his own will that overcame them. In this way the person exercising volition adds the feelings of delight of his successful executive instruments, the useful "under-wills" or under-souls—indeed, our body is but a social structure composed of many souls—to his feelings of delight as commander. *L'effet c'est moi:* what happens here is what happens in every well-constructed and happy commonwealth, namely, that the governing class identifies itself with the successes of the commonwealth. In all willing it is absolutely a question of commanding and obeying, on the basis, as already said, of a social structure composed of many "souls"; on which account a philosopher should claim the right to include willing-as-such within the sphere of morals—regarded as the doctrine of the relations of supremacy under which the phenomenon of "life" manifests itself.

20. That the various philosophical ideas do not evolve randomly or autonomously, but in connection and relationship with each other; that, however suddenly and arbitrarily they seem to appear in the history of thought, they nevertheless belong just as much to a system as the members of the fauna of a continent—is betrayed in the end by this circumstance: how unfailingly the most diverse philosophers always fill in again a definite fundamental scheme of *possible* philosophies. Under an invisible spell, they always revolve once more in the same orbit; however independent of each other they may feel themselves with their critical or systematic wills, something within them leads them, something impels them in definite order, the one after

the other—to wit, the innate methodology and relationship of their ideas. Their thinking is, in fact, far less a discovery than a recognizing, a remembering, a return and a home-coming to a far-off, ancient common-household of the soul, out of which those ideas formerly grew: philosophizing is in this respect a kind of atavism of the highest order. The wonderful family resemblance of all Indian, Greek, and German philosophizing is easily enough explained. In fact, where there is affinity of language, owing to the common philosophy of grammar— I mean owing to the unconscious domination and guidance of similar grammatical functions—it cannot but be that everything is prepared at the outset for a similar development and succession of philosophical systems; just as the way seems barred against certain other possibilities of world-interpretation. It is highly probable that philosophers within the domain of the Ural-Altaic languages (where the conception of the subject is least developed) look otherwise "into the world," and will be found on paths of thought different from those of the Indo-Europeans and Moslems; the spell of certain grammatical functions is ultimately also the spell of *physiological* valuations and racial conditions.—So much by way of rejecting Locke's superficiality with regard to the origin of ideas.

21.   The *causa sui* is the best self-contradiction that has yet been conceived, it is a sort of logical rape and perversion, but the extravagant pride of man has managed to entangle itself profoundly and frightfully with this very folly. The desire for "freedom of will" in the superlative, metaphysical sense, such as still holds sway, unfortunately, in the minds of the half-educated, the desire to bear the entire and ultimate responsibility for one's actions oneself, and to absolve God, the world, ancestors, chance, and society, involves nothing less than to be precisely this *causa sui,* and, with more than Munchausen daring, to pull oneself up into existence by the hair, out of the slough of nothingness. If any one should find out in this manner the crass stupidity of the celebrated conception of "free will" and put it out of his head altogether, I beg of him to carry his "enlightenment" a step further, and also put out of his head the contrary of this monstrous conception of "free will": I mean "non-free will," which is tantamount to a misuse of cause and effect. One should not wrongly *materialize* "cause" and "effect," as the natural philosophers do (and whoever like them naturalizes in his thinking at present), according to the prevailing mechanical doltishness that makes the cause press and push until it "effects" its end; one should use "cause" and "effect" only as pure *concepts,* that is to say, as conventional fictions for the

purpose of designation and mutual understanding—*not* for explanation. In "being-in-itself" there is nothing of "causal connection," of "necessity," or of "psychological non-freedom"; there the effect does *not* follow the cause, there "law" does not obtain. It is *we* alone who have devised cause, sequence, reciprocity, relativity, constraint, number, law, freedom, motive, and purpose; and when we interpret and intermix this symbol-world, as "being in itself," with things, we think once more as we have always thought—mythologically. The "non-free will" is mythology; in real life it is only a question of *strong* and *weak* wills.—It is almost always a symptom of what is lacking in himself, when a thinker, in every "causal connection" and "psychological necessity," manifests something of compulsion, indigence, obsequiousness, oppression, and non-freedom; it is suspicious to have such feelings—the person betrays himself. And in general, if I have observed correctly, the "non-freedom of the will" is regarded as a problem from two entirely opposite standpoints. but always in a profoundly *personal* manner: some will not give up their "responsibility," their belief in *themselves,* the personal right to *their* merits, at any price (the vain races belong to this class); others on the contrary, do not wish to be answerable for anything, or blamed for anything, and owing to an inward self-contempt, seek *to get out of the business,* no matter how. The latter, when they write books, are in the habit at present of taking the side of criminals; a sort of socialistic sympathy is their favorite disguise. And as a matter of fact, the fatalism of the weak-willed embellishes itself surprisingly when it can pose as *"la religion de la souffrance humaine";* that is *its* "good taste."

22.   Let me be pardoned, as an old philologist who cannot desist from the mischief of putting his finger on bad modes of interpretation, but "Nature's conformity to law," of which you physicists talk so proudly, as though—why, it exists only owing to your explication and bad "philology." It is no matter of fact, no "text," but rather just a naïvely humanitarian adjustment and perversion of meaning, with which you make abundant concessions to the democratic instincts of the modern soul! "Everywhere equality before the law—Nature is not different in that respect, nor better than we": a fine instance of secret motive, in which the vulgar antagonism to everything privileged and autocratic—likewise a very refined atheism—is once more disguised. *"Ni Dieu, ni maître"*—that, also, is what you want; and therefore "Cheers for natural law!"—is it not so? But, as has been said, that is explication, not text; and somebody might come along, who, with opposite intentions and modes of interpretation, could read out of

the same "Nature," and the same phenomena, just the tyrannically inconsiderate and relentless enforcement of the claims of power—an interpreter who should so place the unexceptionalness and uncon- ditionalness of all "Will to Power" before your eyes, that almost every word, and the word "tyranny" itself, would eventually seem unsuitable, or like a weakening and softening metaphor—as being too human; and who should, nevertheless, end by asserting the same about this world as you do, namely, that it has a "necessary" and "calculable" course, *not,* however, because laws obtain in it, but because they are absolutely *lacking,* and every power effects its ultimate consequences every moment. Granted that this also is only explication—and you will be eager enough to make this objection?— well, so much the better.

23.　All psychology hitherto has run aground on moral prejudices and timidities, it has not dared to launch out into the depths. In so far as it is allowable to recognize in what has so far been written evidence of what has so far been kept silent, it seems as if nobody had yet harbored the notion of psychology as the Morphology and *Theory of Evolution of the Will to Power,* as I conceive of it. The power of moral prejudices has penetrated deeply into the most intel- lectual world, the world apparently most indifferent and unprejudiced, and has obviously operated in an injurious, obstructive, blinding, and distorting manner. A proper physio-psychology has to contend with unconscious antagonism in the heart of the investigator, it has "the heart" against it: even a doctrine of the reciprocal conditionalness of the "good" and the "bad" impulses, causes (as refined immorality) distress and aversion in a still strong and manly conscience—still more so, a doctrine of the derivation of all good impulses from bad ones. If, however, a person should regard even the emotions of hatred, envy, covetousness, and imperiousness as life-conditioning emotions, as factors which must be present, fundamentally and essentially, in the general economy of life (which must, therefore, be further de- veloped if life is to be further developed), he will suffer from such a view of things as from sea-sickness. And yet this hypothesis is far from being the strangest and most painful in this immense and almost unexplored domain of dangerous knowledge; and there are in fact a hundred good reaons why every one should keep away from it who *can* do so! On the other hand, if one has once drifted hither with one's bark, well! very good! now let us set our teeth firmly! let us open our eyes and keep our hand fast on the helm! We sail away right *over* morality, we crush out, we destroy perhaps the remains of our own

morality by daring to make our voyage thither—but what do *we*
matter! Never yet did a *profounder* world of insight reveal itself to daring travellers and adventurers, and the psychologist who thus "makes
a sacrifice" (it is *not* the *sacrifizio dell' intelletto*—on the contrary!)
will at least be entitled to demand in return that psychology shall
once more be recognized as the queen of the sciences, for whose service and equipment the other sciences exist. For psychology is once
more the path to the fundamental problems.

Second Article
The Free Spirit

33. It cannot be helped: the sentiment of surrender, of sacrifice
for one's neighbor, and all self-renunciation-morality, must be
mercilessly called to account, and brought to judgment; just as the
æsthetics of "disinterested contemplation," under which the emascula-
tion of art nowadays seeks insidiously to create for itself a good
conscience. There is far too much witchery and sugar in the sentiments "for others" and "*not* for myself" for one not to need to be
doubly distrustful here, and to ask promptly: "Are they not perhaps
—*deceptions?*"—That they *please*—him who has them, and him who
enjoys their fruit, and also the mere spectator—is still no argument in
their *favor,* but just calls for caution. Let us therefore be cautious!
34. At whatever standpoint of philosophy one may place oneself
nowadays, seen from every position, the *erroneousness* of the world
in which we think we live is the surest and most certain thing our
eyes can light upon: of this we find proof after proof, which would
lure us into surmising a deceptive principle in the "nature of things."
He, however, who makes thinking itself, and consequently "the spirit,"
responsible for the falseness of the world—an honorable exit, which
every conscious or unconscious *advocatus dei* avails himself of—he
who regards this world, including space, time, form, and movement,
as falsely *inferred,* would have good reason in the end to become
distrustful of all thinking; has it not hitherto been playing upon us the
meanest tricks? and what guarantee would it give that it would not
continue to do what it has always been doing? In all seriousness, the
innocence of thinkers has something touching and respect-inspiring
in it, which even nowadays permits them to wait upon consciousness
with the request that it will give them *honest* answers: for example
whether it be "real" or not, and why it keeps the outer world so

resolutely at a distance, and other questions of the same description. The belief in "immediate certainties" is a *moral naïveté* which does honor to us philosophers; but—we have now to cease being *"merely* moral" men! Apart from morality, such belief is a folly which does little honor to us! If in middle-class life an ever-ready distrust is regarded as the sign of a "bad character," and consequently as an imprudence, here amongst us, beyond the middle-class world and its Yeas and Nays, what should prevent our being imprudent and saying: the philosopher has at length a *right* to "bad character," as the being who has hitherto been most fooled on earth—he is now under *obligation* to distrustfulness, to the wickedest squinting out of every abyss of suspicion.—Forgive me the joke of this gloomy grimace and turn of expression; for I myself have long ago learned to think and estimate differently with regard to deceiving and being deceived, and I keep at least a couple of pokes in the ribs ready for the blind rage with which philosophers struggle against being deceived. Why *not?* It is nothing more than a moral prejudice that truth is worth more than semblance; it is, in fact, the worst proved supposition in the world. *So* much must be conceded: there could have been no life at all except upon the basis of perspective estimates and semblances; and if, with the virtuous enthusiasm and stupidity of many philosophers, one wished to do away altogether with the "seeming world"—well, granted that *you* could do that, at least nothing of your "truth" would remain! Indeed, what is it that forces us in general to the supposition that there is an essential opposition of "true" and "false"? Is it not enough to suppose degrees of seemingness, and as it were lighter and darker shades and tones of semblance—different *valeurs,* as the painters say? Why might not the world *which concerns us*—be a fiction? And to any one who suggested: "But to a fiction belongs an originator?"—might it not be bluntly replied: *Why?* May not this "belong" also belong to the fiction? Is it not permitted to be a little ironical towards the subject, just as towards the predicate and object? May not the philosopher elevate himself above faith in grammar? All due respect to governesses, but is it not time that philosophy should renounce governess-faith?

35.   O Voltaire! O humanity! O idiocy! There is something ticklish in "the truth," and in the *search* for the truth; and if man goes about it too humanely—*"il ne cherche le vrai que pour faire le bien"* [1]—I wager he finds nothing!

---

[1] [He seeks the truth only in order to do good.—M.C.B.]

36. Supposing that nothing else is "given" as real but our world of desires and passions, that we cannot sink or rise to any other "reality" but just that of our impulses—for thinking is only a relation of these impulses to one another:—are we not permitted to make the experiment and to ask the question whether what is "given" does not *suffice*, by means of our counterparts, for the understanding even of the so-called mechanical (or "material") world? I do not mean as an illusion, a "semblance," an "idea" (in the Berkeleyan and Schopenhauerian sense), but as possessing the same degree of reality as our emotions themselves—as a more primitive form of the world of emotions, in which everything still lies locked in a mighty unity, which afterwards branches off and develops itself in organic processes (naturally also, refines and debilitates)—as a kind of instinctive life in which all organic functions, including self-regulation, assimilation, nutrition, secretion, and metabolism, are still synthetically united with one another—as a *primary form* of life?—In the end, it is not only permitted to make this attempt, it is commanded by the conscience of *logical method*. Not to assume several kinds of causality, so long as the attempt to get along with a single one has not been pushed to its furtherest extent (to absurdity, if I may be allowed to say so): that is a morality of method which one may not repudiate nowadays—it follows "from its definition," as mathematicians say. The question is ultimately whether we really recognize the will as *operating,* whether we believe in the causality of the will; if we do so —and fundamentally our belief *in this* is precisely our belief in causality itself—we *must* make the attempt to posit hypothetically the causality of the will as the only causality. "Will" can naturally only operate on "will"—and not on "matter" (not on "nerves," for instance): in short, the hypothesis must be hazarded, whether will does not operate on will wherever "effects" are recognized—and whether all mechanical action, insofar as a power operates therein, is not just the power of will, the effect of will. Granted, finally, that we succeeded in explaining our entire instinctive life as the development and ramification of one fundamental form of will—namely, the Will to Power, as *my* thesis puts it; granted that all organic functions could be traced back to this Will to Power, and that the solution of the problem of generation and nutrition—it is one problem—could also be found therein: one would thus have acquired the right to define *all* active force unequivocally as *Will to Power*. The world seen from within, the world defined and designated according to its

"intelligible character"—it would simply be "Will to Power," and nothing else.

37.   "What? Does not that mean in popular language: God is disproved, but not the devil?"—On the contrary! On the contrary, my friends! And who the devil also compels you to speak popularly!

42.   A new order of philosophers is appearing; I shall venture to baptize them by a name not without danger. As far as I understand them, as far as they allow themselves to be understood—for it is their nature to *wish* to remain something of a puzzle—these philosophers of the future might rightly (perhaps also wrongly!) claim to be called *experimenters*. This name itself is after all only an experiment, or, if it be preferred, a temptation.

43.   Will they be new friends of "truth," these coming philosophers? Very probably, for all philosophers hitherto have loved their truths. But assuredly they will not be dogmatists. It must be contrary to their pride, and also contrary to their taste, that their truth should be truth for every one—which has hitherto been the secret wish and ultimate purpose of all dogmatic efforts. "My opinion is *my* opinion: another person has not easily a right to it"—this the philosopher of the future will say, perhaps. One must renounce the bad taste of wishing to agree with many people. "Good" is no longer good when one's neighbor takes it into his mouth. And how could there be a "common good"! The expression contradicts itself; what can be common is always of small value. In the end things must be as they are and have always been—the great things remain for the great, the abysses for the profound, the delicacies and thrills for the refined, and, to sum up shortly, everything rare for the rare.

44.   Need I say expressly after all this that they will be free, *very* free spirits, these philosophers of the future—as certainly also they will not be merely free spirits, but something more, higher, greater, and fundamentally different, which does not wish to be misunderstood and mistaken? But while I say this, I feel under *obligation* almost as much to them as to ourselves (we free spirits who are their heralds and forerunners), to sweep away from ourselves altogether a stupid old prejudice and misunderstanding, which, like a fog, has too long made the conception of "free spirit" obscure. In every country of Europe, and the same in America, there is at present something that makes an abuse of this name: a very narrow, prepossessed, enchained group of thinkers who desire almost the opposite of what our intentions and instincts prompt—not to mention that in respect to the *new* philosophers who are appearing, they must still more be closed

windows and bolted doors. Briefly and regrettably, they belong to the *levellers,* these wrongly named "free spirits"—as glib-tongued and scribe-fingered slaves of the democratic taste and its "modern ideas": all of them men without solitude, without personal solitude, blunt, honest fellows to whom neither courage nor honorable conduct ought to be denied; only, they are not free, and are ludicrously superficial, especially in their innate partiality for seeing the cause of almost *all* human misery and failure in the old forms in which society has hitherto existed—a notion which happily inverts the truth entirely! What they would strive for with all their strength is the universal, green-meadow happiness of the herd, together with security, safety, comfort, and alleviation of life for every one; their two most frequently chanted songs and doctrines are called "Equality of Rights" and "Sympathy with all Sufferers"—and suffering itself is looked upon by them as something that must be *done away with.* We opposite ones, however, who have opened our eye and conscience to the question how and where the plant "man" has hitherto grown most vigorously, believe that this has always taken place under the opposite conditions, that for this end the dangerousness of his situation had to be increased enormously, his inventive faculty and dissembling power (his "spirit") had to develop subtlety and daring under long oppression and compulsion, and his Will to Life had to be increased to the unconditioned Will to Power:—we believe that severity, violence, slavery, danger in the street and in the heart, secrecy, stoicism, tempter's art and devilry of every kind—that everything wicked, terrible, tyrannical, predatory, and serpentine in man, serves as well for the elevation of the human species as its opposite:—we do not even say enough when we only say *this much;* and in any case we find ourselves here, both with our speech and our silence, at the *other* extreme of all modern ideology and gregarious desires, as their antipodes perhaps? What wonder that we "free spirits" are not exactly the most communicative spirits? that we do not wish to betray in every respect *what* a spirit can free itself from, and *where* perhaps it will then be driven? And as to the import of the dangerous formula, "Beyond Good and Evil," by which we at least avoid confusion with others, we *are* something other than *"libres-penseurs," "liberi pensatori,"* "free-thinkers," and whatever these honest advocates of "modern ideas" like to call themselves. Having been at home, or at least guests, in many realms of the spirit; having escaped again and again from the stuffy, agreeable nooks in which preferences and prejudices, youth, origin, the accident of men and books, or even

the weariness of travel seemed to confine us; full of malice against
the seductions of dependency that lie concealed in honors, money,
positions, or exaltation of the senses; grateful even for distress and
the vicissitudes of illness, because they always free us from some
rule, and its "prejudice," grateful to the God, devil, sheep, and worm
in us; inquisitive to a fault, investigators to the point of cruelty, with
unhesitating fingers for the intangible, with teeth and stomachs for
the most indigestible, ready for any business that requires sagacity
and acute senses, ready for every adventure, owing to an excess of
"free will"; with anterior and posterior souls, into the ultimate intentions of which it is difficult to pry, with foregrounds and back-
grounds to the end of which no foot may run; hidden under mantles
of light, appropriators, although we resemble heirs and spendthrifts,
arrangers and collectors from morning till night, misers of our wealth
and our full-crammed drawers, economical in learning and forgetting,
inventive in scheming; sometimes proud of tables of categories, sometimes pedants, sometimes night-owls of work even in full day; yea, if
necessary, even scarecrows—and it is necessary nowadays, that is
to say, inasmuch as we are the born, sworn, jealous friends of
solitude, of our own profoundest midnight and mid-day solitude:—
such kind of men are we, we free spirits! And perhaps you are also
something of the same kind, you coming ones, you *new* philosophers?'

Fifth Article

The Natural History of Morals

186. The moral sentiment in Europe at present is perhaps as subtle,
belated, diverse, sensitive, and refined, as its accompanying "Science
of Morals" is recent, immature, awkward, and coarse-fingered—an
interesting contrast, which sometimes becomes incarnate and obvious
in the very person of a moralist. Indeed, the expression "Science of
Morals" is far too presumptuous and counter to *good* taste for what
it designates—which is always a foretaste of more modest expressions. One ought to avow with the utmost fairness *what* is still
necessary here for a long time, *what* is alone proper for the present:
namely, the collection of material, the comprehensive survey and
classification of an immense domain of delicate sentiments of worth,
and distinctions of worth, which live, grow, propagate, and perish—
and perhaps experiments to give a clear idea of the recurring and
more common forms of these living crystallizations—as preparation

for a *theory of types* of morality. To be sure, people have not hitherto been so modest. All the philosophers, with a pedantic and ridiculous seriousness, demanded of themselves something very much higher, more pretentious, and ceremonious, when they concerned themselves with morality as a science: they wanted to *give a basis* to morality—and every philosopher hitherto has believed that he has given it a basis; morality itself, however, has been regarded as something "given." How far from their ambitious pride was the seemingly insignificant problem—left in dust and decay—of a description of forms of morality, notwithstanding that the finest hands and senses could hardly be fine enough for it! It was precisely because moral philosophers knew the moral facts imperfectly, in an arbitrary epitome, or an accidental abridgement—perhaps as the morality of their environment, their position, their church, their *Zeitgeist,* their climate and zone—it was precisely because they were badly instructed with regard to nations, eras, and past ages, and were by no means eager to know about these matters, that they did not even come in sight of the real problems of morals—problems which only disclose themselves by a comparison of *many* kinds of morality. In every "Science of Morals" hitherto, strange as it may sound, the problem of morality itself has been *omitted;* there has been no suspicion that there was anything problematic there! What philosophers called "giving a basis to morality," and endeavored to realize, has, when seen in a right light, proved merely a learned form of good *faith* in prevailing morality, a new means of its *expression,* consequently just another symptom of a given morality, indeed, in its ultimate motive, a sort of denial that it is *lawful* for this morality to be called in question—and in any case the reverse of the testing, analyzing, doubting, and vivisecting of this very faith. Hear, for instance with what innocence—almost worthy of honor—Schopenhauer represents his own task, and draw your conclusions concerning the scientificalness of a "Science" whose latest master still talks in the strain of children and old wives: "The principle," he says, in his *Grundprobleme der Ethik,* "the axiom about the purport of which all moralists are *practically* agreed: *neminem laede, immo omnes quantum potes juva*[1]—is *really* the proposition which all moral teachers strive to establish, . . . the *real* basis of ethics which has been sought, like the philosopher's stone, for centuries."—The difficulty of establishing the proposition referred to may indeed be great—it is

---

[1] [Injure no one, but help every one, so far as you are able.—M.C.B.]

well known that Schopenhauer also was unsuccessful in his efforts; and whoever has thoroughly realized how absurdly false and sentimental this proposition is, in a world whose essence is Will to Power, may be reminded that Schopenhauer, although a pessimist, *actually*— played the flute . . . daily after dinner: one may read about it in his biography. A question by the way: a pessimist, a repudiator of God and of the world, who *makes a halt* at morality—who assents to morality, and plays the flute to *laede-neminem* morals, what? Is he really—a pessimist?

187.   Apart from the value of such assertions as "there is a categorical imperative in us," one can always ask: What does such an assertion indicate about him who makes it? There are systems of morals that are meant to justify their author in the eyes of other people; other systems of morals are meant to tranquillize him, and make him self-satisfied; with other systems he wants to crucify and humble himself; with others he wishes to take revenge; with others to conceal himself; with others to glorify himself and gain superiority and distinction—this system of morals helps its author to forget, that system makes him, or something of him, forgotten; many a moralist would like to exercise power and creative arbitrariness over mankind; many another, perhaps Kant especially, gives us to understand by his system that "what is estimable in me is that I know how to obey—and with you it *shall* not be otherwise than with me!" In short, systems of morals are only a *sign-language of the emotions*.

188.   In contrast to *laisser aller,* every system of morals is a sort of tyranny against "nature" and also against "reason"; that is, however, no objection, unless one should again decree (on the basis of some system of morals) that all kinds of tyranny and unreasonableness are unlawful. What is essential and invaluable in every system of morals is that it is a long constraint. In order to understand Stoicism, or Port-Royal, or Puritanism, one should remember the constraint under which every language has attained to strength and freedom—the metrical constraint, the tyranny of rhyme and rhythm. How much trouble have the poets and orators of every nation given themselves!—not excepting some of the prose writers of today, in whose ear dwells an inexorable conscientiousness—"for the sake of a folly," as utilitarian bunglers say, and thereby deem themselves wise— "from submission to arbitrary laws," as the anarchists say, and thereby fancy themselves "free," even free-spirited. The singular fact remains, however, that everything of the nature of freedom, elegance, boldness, dance, and masterly certainty, that exists or has existed,

whether it be in thought itself, or in administration, or in speaking and persuading, in art just as in conduct, has only developed by means of the "tyranny of such arbitrary law"; and in all seriousness, it is not at all improbable that precisely this is "nature" and "natural" —and *not laisser aller!* Every artist knows how different from the state of letting himself go is his "most natural" condition, the free arranging, locating, disposing, and constructing in the moments of "inspiration"—and how strictly and delicately he then obeys a thousand laws, which, by their very rigidness and precision, defy all formulation in concepts (even the most stable concept has, in comparison therewith, something floating, manifold, and ambiguous in it). The essential thing "in heaven and earth" is, apparently (to repeat it once more), that there should be long *obedience* in the same direction; from this there results, and has always resulted in the long run, something that has made life worth living; for instance, virtue, art, music, dancing, reason, spirituality—anything whatever that is transfiguring, refined, foolish, or divine. The long bondage of the spirit, the distrustful constraint in the communicability of ideas, the discipline that the thinker imposed on himself to think in conformity to the rules of a church or a court, or to Aristotelian premises, the persistent spiritual will to interpret everything that happened according to a Christian scheme, and in every occurrence to rediscover and justify the Christian God:—all this violence, arbitrariness, severity, dreadfulness, and unreasonableness, has proved itself the disciplinary means whereby the European spirit has attained its strength, its remorseless curiosity and subtle mobility; granted also that much irrecoverable strength and spirit had to be stifled, suffocated, and spoiled in the process (for here, as everywhere, "nature" shows herself as she is, in all her extravagant and *indifferent* magnificence, which is shocking, but nevertheless noble). That for centuries European thinkers thought only in order to prove something—nowadays, on the contrary, we are suspicious of every thinker who "wishes to prove something"—that it was always settled beforehand what *was to be* the result of their strictest thinking, as it was perhaps in the Asiatic astrology of former times, or as it is still at the present day in the innocent, Christian-moral explanation of immediate personal events "for the glory of God," or "for the good of the soul":—this tyranny, this arbitrariness, this severe and magnificent stupidity, has *educated* the spirit; slavery, both in the coarser and the finer sense, is apparently an indispensable means even of spiritual education and discipline. One may look at every system of morals in this light: it is "nature" in it that teaches hatred of the *laisser aller,* the too great freedom, and implants the need for limited horizons, for immediate duties—it teaches the *narrowing of perspectives,* and thus, in a certain sense, stupidity as a condition of life and development. "Thou must obey some one, and for a long time; *otherwise* thou wilt come to grief, and lose all respect for thyself"—this seems to me to be the moral imperative of nature, which is certainly neither "categorical," as old Kant wished (consequently the "otherwise"), nor does it address itself to the individual (what does nature care for the individual!), but to nations, races, ages, and ranks, above all, how- ever, to the animal "man" generally, to *mankind.*

202.   Let us at once say again what we have already said a hun- dred times, for people's ears nowadays are unwilling to hear such truths —*our* truths. We know well enough how offensive it sounds when any one plainly, and without metaphor, counts man amongst the animals; but it will be accounted to us almost a *crime,* that it is precisely to men of "modern ideas" that we have constantly applied the terms "herd," "herd-instincts," and such expressions. What avail is it? We cannot do otherwise, for this is precisely our new insight. We have found that in all the principal moral judgments Europe has become unanimous, including likewise the countries where European influence prevails: in Europe people evidently *know* what Socrates thought he did not know, and what the famous serpent of old once promised to teach—they "know" to-day what is good and evil. It must then sound hard and be distasteful to the ear, when we always insist that what thinks it knows, what glorifies itself with praise and blame, and calls itself good, is the instinct of the herding human animal: the instinct that has come and is ever coming more and more to the front, to preponderance and supremacy over other instincts, accord- ing to the increasing physiological approximation and resemblance of which it is the symptom. *Morality in Europe at present is herd-animal morality;* and therefore, as we understand the matter, only one kind of human morality, besides which, before which, and after which many other moralities, and above all *higher* moralities, are or should be possible. Against such a "possibility," against such a "should be," however, this morality defends itself with all its strength; it says obstinately and inexorably: "I am morality itself and nothing else is morality!" Indeed, with the help of a religion that has humored and flattered the sublimest desires of the herd-animal, things have reached such a point that we always find a more visible expression of this morality even in political and social arrangements: the *demo-*

cratic movement is the inheritance of the Christian movement. That its *tempo,* however, is much too slow and sleepy for the more impatient ones, for those who are sick and distracted by the herd-instinct, is indicated by the increasingly furious howling, and increasingly less concealed teeth-gnashing of the anarchist dogs, who are now roving through the highways of European culture. Apparently in opposition to the peacefully industrious democrats and Revolution-ideologues, and still more so to the awkward philosophasters and fraternity-visionaries who call themselves Socialists and want a "free society," those are really at one with them all in their thorough and instinctive hostility to every form of society other than that of the *autonomous* herd (to the extent even of repudiating the notions "master" and "servant"—*ni Dieu ni maître,* says a socialist slogan); at one in their tenacious opposition to every special claim, every special right and privilege (this means ultimately opposition to *every* right, for when all are equal, no one needs "rights" any longer); at one in their distrust of punitive justice (as though it were a violation of the weak, unfair to the *necessary* consequences of all former society); but equally at one in their religion of sympathy, in their compassion for all that feels, lives, and suffers (down to the very animals, even up to "God"—the extravagance of "sympathy for God" belongs to a democratic age); altogether at one in the cry and impatience of their sympathy, in their deadly hatred of suffering generally, in their almost feminine incapacity for witnessing it or *allowing* it; at one in their involuntary beglooming and heart-softening, under the spell of which Europe seems to be threatened with a new Buddhism; at one in their belief in the morality of *mutual* sympathy, as though it were morality in itself, the climax, the *attained* climax of mankind, the sole hope of the future, the consolation of the present, the great discharge from all the obligations of the past; altogether at one in their belief in the community as the *deliverer,* in the herd, and therefore in "themselves."

203. We, who hold a different belief—we, who regard the democratic movement, not only as a degenerate form of political organization, but as equivalent to a degenerating, a waning type of man, as involving his mediocritizing and depreciation: where have *we* to fix our hopes? In *new philosophers*—there is no other alternative: in minds strong and original enough to initiate opposite estimates of value, to transvalue and invert "eternal valuations"; in forerunners, in men of the future, who in the present shall fix the constraints and fasten the knots that will compel millenniums to take *new* paths. To

teach man the future of humanity as his *will,* as depending on human will, and to make preparation for vast hazardous enterprises and collective experiments in rearing and educating, in order to put an end to the frightful rule of folly and chance that has hitherto gone by the name of "history" (the folly of the "greatest number" is only its last form)—for that purpose a new type of philosophers and commanders will some time or other be needed, at the very idea of which everything that has existed in the way of occult, terrible, and benevolent beings might look pale and dwarfed. The image of such leaders hovers before *our* eyes—is it lawful for me to say it aloud, you free spirits? The conditions one would partly have to create and partly utilize for their genesis; the presumptive methods and tests by virtue of which a soul should grow up to such an elevation and power as to feel a *constraint* to these tasks; a transvaluation of values, under the new pressure and hammer of which a conscience should be forged and a heart transformed into brass, so as to bear the weight of such responsibility; and on the other hand the necessity for such leaders, the dreadful danger that they might be lacking, or miscarry and degenerate—these are *our* real anxieties and glooms, you know it well, you free spirits! these are the heavy distant thoughts and storms that sweep across the heaven of *our* life. There are few pains so grievous as to have seen, divined, or experienced how an exceptional man has missed his way and deteriorated; but he who has the rare eye for the universal danger of "man" himself *deteriorating,* he who like us has recognized the extraordinary fortuitousness that has hitherto played its game in respect to the future of mankind—a game in which neither the hand nor even a "finger of God" has participated!—he who divines the fate that is hidden under the idiotic obtuseness and blind confidence of "modern ideas," and still more under the whole of Christian-European morality—suffers from an anguish with which no other is to be compared. He sees at a glance all that could still *be made out of man* through a favorable accumulation and augmentation of human powers and arrangements; he knows with all the knowledge of his conviction how unexhausted man still is for the greatest possibilities, and how often in the past the type man has stood in presence of mysterious decisions and new paths—he knows still better from his painfulest recollections on what wretched obstacles promising developments of the highest rank have hitherto usually gone to pieces, broken down, sunk, and become contemptible. The *universal degeneracy of mankind* to the level of the "man of the future"—as idealized by the socialistic fools and shallow-pates—this degeneracy and dwarfing of man to an absolutely gregarious animal (or, as they call it, to a man of "free society"), this brutalizing of man into a pigmy with equal rights and claims, is undoubtedly *possible!* He who has thought out this possibility to its ultimate conclusion knows *another* loathing unknown to the rest of mankind—and perhaps also a new *mission!*

Sixth Article
We Men of Learning

204.　At the risk that moralizing may also reveal itself here as that which it has always been—namely, resolutely *montrer ses plaies*,[1] according to Balzac—I would venture to protest against an improper and injurious alteration of rank that, quite unnoticed, and as if with the best conscience, threatens nowadays to establish itself in the relations of science and philosophy. I mean to say that one must have the right out of one's own *experience*—experience, as it seems to me, always implies unfortunate experience?—to treat of such an important question of rank, so as not to speak of color like the blind, or *against* science like women and artists ("Ah! this dreadful science!" sigh their instinct and their shame, "it always *finds things out!*"). The declaration of independence of the scientific man, his emancipation from philosophy, is one of the subtler after-effects of democratic organization and disorganization: the self-glorification and self-conceit of the learned man is now everywhere in full bloom, and in its best springtime—which does not imply that in this case self-praise smells sweetly. Here also the instinct of the populace cries, "Freedom from all masters!" and after science has, with the happiest results, resisted theology, whose "handmaid" it had been too long, it now proposes in its wantonness and indiscretion to lay down laws for philosophy, and in its turn to play the "master"—what am I saying! to play the *philosopher* on its own account. My memory —the memory of a scientific man, if you please!—teems with the naïvetés of insolence which I have heard about philosophy and philosophers from young naturalists and old physicians (not to mention the most cultured and most conceited of all learned men, the philologists and academics, who are both the one and the other by profession). On one occasion it was the specialist and the Jack

---

[1] [Showing one's wounds.—M.C.B.]

Horner who instinctively stood on the defensive against all synthetic tasks and capabilities; at another time it was the industrious
worker who had got a scent of *otium* and refined luxuriousness in
the internal economy of the philosopher, and felt himself aggrieved
and belittled thereby. On another occasion it was the color-blindness
of the Utilitarian, who sees nothing in philosophy but a series of
refuted systems, and an extravagant expenditure that "does nobody
any good." At another time the fear of disguised mysticism and of
the boundary-adjustment of knowledge became conspicuous, at another time a disesteem for individual philosophers, which had involuntarily spread to a disesteem for philosophy generally. In fine,
I found most frequently, behind the proud disdain of philosophy in
young scholars, the evil after-effect of some particular philosopher,
to whom on the whole obedience had been foresworn, without,
however, the spell of his scornful estimates of other philosophers
having been got rid of—the result being a general ill-will to all
philosophy. (Such seems to me, for instance, the recent after-effect
of Schopenhauer on Germany: by his unintelligent rage against
Hegel, he has succeeded in severing the whole last generation of
Germans from their connection with German culture, which culture,
all things considered, has been an elevation and an insightful refinement of the *historical sense;* but precisely at this point Schopenhauer himself was poor, unreceptive, and un-German to the point of
genius.) On the whole, speaking generally, it may just have been
the humanness, all-too-humanness of the modern philosophers themselves, in short, their contemptibleness, that has injured most radically
the reverence for philosophy and opened the doors to the instinct of
the populace. . . . It is especially the sight of those hotch-potch
philosophers who call themselves "realists," or "positivists" that is
calculated to implant a dangerous distrust in the soul of a young and
ambitious scholar: those philosophers, at best, are themselves but
scholars and specialists, that is very evident! All of them are persons
who have been vanquished and *brought back again* under the
dominion of science, who at one time or another claimed more from
themselves, without having a right to the "more" and its responsibility
—and who now, creditably, rancorously and vindictively, represent
in word and deed, *disbelief* in the master-task and supremacy of
philosophy. After all, how could it be otherwise? Science flourishes
nowadays and has a good conscience clearly visible on its countenance; while that to which the entire modern philosophy has
gradually sunk, the remnant of philosophy of the present day, excites

distrust and displeasure, if not scorn and pity. Philosophy reduced to a "theory of knowledge," is no more in fact than a diffident science of epochs and doctrine of forbearance: a philosophy that never even gets beyond the threshold, and rigorously *denies* itself the right to enter—that is philosophy in its last throes, an end, an agony, something that awakens pity. How could such a philosophy—*rule!*

205. The dangers that beset the evolution of the philosopher are, in fact, so manifold nowadays, that one might doubt whether this fruit could still come to maturity. . . . In fact, the philosopher has long been mistaken by the multitude, and confused either with the scientific man and ideal scholar, or with the religiously elevated, desensualized, desecularized visionary and God-intoxicated man; and even yet when one hears anybody praised because he lives "wisely" or "philosophically," it hardly means anything more than "prudently and apart." Wisdom: that seems to the populace to be a kind of flight, a way of withdrawing successfully from a bad game; but the *genuine* philosopher—does it not seem so to *us,* my friends?—lives "unphilosophically" and "unwisely," above all, *imprudently,* and feels the obligation and burden of a hundred experiments and temptations of life—he risks *himself* constantly, he plays *this* bad game.

207. However gratefully one may welcome the *objective* spirit—and who has not been sick to death of all subjectivity and its confounded *ipsisimosity!*—in the end, however, one must learn caution even with regard to one's gratitude, and put a stop to the exaggeration with which the unselfing and depersonalizing of the spirit has recently been celebrated, as if it were the goal in itself, as if it were salvation and glorification—as is especially accustomed to happen in the Pessimist school, which has also in its turn good reasons for paying the highest honors to "disinterested knowledge." The objective man, who no longer curses and scolds like the Pessimist, the *ideal* man of learning in whom the scientific instinct blossoms forth fully after a thousand complete and partial failures, is assuredly one of the most costly instruments that exist, but his place is in the hand of one who is more powerful. He is only an instrument; we may say, he is a *mirror*—he is no "purpose in himself." The objective man is in truth a mirror: accustomed to prostration before everything that wants to be known, with such desires only as knowing or "reflecting" imply—he waits until something comes, and then expands himself sensitively, so that even the light footsteps and gliding past of spiritual beings may not be lost on his surface and film. Whatever "personality" he still possesses seems to him accidental, arbitrary, or still oftener,

disturbing; so much has he come to regard himself as the passage and reflection of outside forms and events. . . . His mirroring and eternally self-polishing soul no longer knows how to affirm, no longer how to deny; he does not command; neither does he destroy. *"Je ne méprise presque rien"* [1]—he says, with Leibniz: let us not overlook nor under-value the *presque!* Neither is he a model man; he does not go in advance of any one, nor after, either; he places himself generally too far off to have any reason for espousing the cause of either good or evil. If he has been so long confounded with the *philosopher,* with the Cæsarian trainer and dictator of civilization, he has had far too much honor, and what is more essential in him has been overlooked —he is an instrument, something of a slave, though certainly the sublimest sort of slave, but nothing in himself—*presque rien!* The objective man is an instrument, a costly, easily injured, easily tarnished, measuring instrument and mirroring apparatus, which is to be taken care of and respected; but he is no goal, no outgoing nor upgoing, no complementary man in whom the *rest* of existence justifies itself, no termination—and still less a commencement, an engendering, or primary cause, nothing hardy, powerful, self-centered, that wants to be master; but rather only a soft, inflated, delicate, movable potter's-form that must wait for some kind of content and frame to "shape" itself thereto—for the most part a man without frame and content, a "selfless" man. Consequently, also, nothing for women, *in parenthesi.*

208.   When a philosopher nowadays makes known that he is not a sceptic—I hope that has been gathered from the foregoing description of the objective spirit?—people all hear it impatiently; they regard him on that account with some apprehension, they would like to ask so many, many questions . . . indeed among timid hearers, of whom there are now so many, he is henceforth said to be dangerous. With his repudiation of skepticism, it seems to them as if they heard some evil-threatening sound in the distance, as if a new kind of explosive were being tested somewhere, a dynamite of the spirit, perhaps a newly discovered Russian *nihilin,* a pessimism *bonae voluntatis,* that not only denies, and means denial, but—dreadful thought!—*practices* denial. Against this kind of "good will" —a will to the veritable, actual negation of life—there is, as is generally acknowledged nowadays, no better soporific and sedative than scepticism, the mild, pleasing, lulling poppy of scepticism; and Hamlet himself is now prescribed by the doctors of the day as an antidote to

---

[1] [There is hardly anything that I despise.—M.C.B.]

the "spirit" and its underground noises. "Are not our ears already
full of bad sounds?" say the sceptics, as lovers of repose and as a
kind of safety police, "this subterranean Nay is terrible! Be still, ye
pessimistic moles!" . . . For scepticism is the spiritual expression
of a certain many-sided physiological temperament, which in
ordinary language is called nervous debility and sickliness; it arises
whenever races or classes that have been long separated decisively
and suddenly blend with one another. . . .

209. As to how far the new warlike age on which we Europeans
have evidently entered may perhaps favor the growth of another
and stronger kind of scepticism, I should like to express myself
preliminarily merely by a parable, which the lovers of German history
will readily understand. That unscrupulous enthusiast for big, hand-
some grenadiers (who, as King of Prussia, brought into being a
military and sceptical genius—and therewith, in reality, the new and
now triumphantly emerged type of German), the problematic, crazy
father of Frederick the Great, had at one point the very knack and
lucky grasp of the genius: he knew what was then lacking in Germany, the want of which was a hundred times more alarming and
serious than any lack of culture and social form—his ill-will to the
young Frederick resulted from the anxiety of a profound instinct.
Men were lacking; and he suspected, to his bitterest regret, that his
own son was not man enough. There he deceived himself; but who
would not have deceived himself in his place? He saw his son lapsed
into atheism, to *esprit,* to the pleasant frivolity of clever Frenchmen
—he saw in the background the great bloodsucker, the spider scepticism; he suspected the incurable wretchedness of a heart no longer
hard enough either for evil or good, and of a broken will that no
longer commands, is no longer *able* to command. Meanwhile, however, there grew up in his son that new kind of harder and more
dangerous scepticism—who knows *to what extent* it was encouraged
just by his father's hatred and the icy melancholy of a will condemned
to solitude?—the scepticism of daring manliness, which is closely
related to the genius for war and conquest, and made its first entrance
into Germany in the person of the great Frederick. This scepticism
despises and nevertheless grasps; it undermines and takes possession;
it does not believe, but it does not thereby lose itself; it gives the
spirit a dangerous liberty, but it keeps strict guard over the heart.
It is the *German* form of scepticism, which, as a continued Frederi-
cianism, risen to the highest spirituality, has kept Europe for a considerable time under the dominion of the German spirit and its

critical and historical distrust. Owing to the insuperably strong and tough masculine character of the great German philologists and historical critics (who, rightly estimated, were also all of them artists of destruction and dissolution), a *new* conception of the German spirit gradually established itself—in spite of all Romanticism in music and philosophy—in which the leaning towards masculine scepticism was decidedly prominent: whether, for instance, as fearlessness of gaze, as courage and sternness of the dissecting hand, or as resolute will to dangerous voyages of discovery, to spiritualized North Pole expeditions under barren and dangerous skies. There may be good grounds for it when warm-blooded and superficial humanitarians cross themselves before this spirit, *cet esprit fataliste, ironique, méphistophélique,* as Michelet calls it, not without a shudder. But if one would realize how characteristic is this fear of the "man" in the German spirit which awakened Europe out of its "dogmatic slumber," let us call to mind the former conception that had to be overcome by this new one—and that it is not so very long ago that a masculinized woman could dare, with unbridled presumption, to commend the Germans to the interest of Europe as gentle, goodhearted, weak-willed, and poetical fools. Finally, let us only understand profoundly enough Napoleon's astonishment when he saw Goethe: it reveals what had been regarded for centuries as the "German spirit." *"Voilà un homme!"*—that was as much as to say: "But this is a *man!* And I only expected to see a German!"

210. Supposing, then, that in the picture of the philosophers of the future, some trait suggests the question whether they must not perhaps be sceptics in the last-mentioned sense, yet only something in them would be designated thereby—and *not* they themselves. With equal right they might call themselves critics; and assuredly they will be men of experiments. By the name with which I ventured to baptize them, I have already expressly emphasized their experimenting and their love of experimentation: is this because, as critics in body and soul, they will love to experiment in a new, and perhaps wider and more dangerous, sense? In their passion for knowledge, will they have to go further in daring and painful experiments than the sensitive and pampered taste of a democratic century can approve of?— There is no doubt: these coming ones will be least able to dispense with the serious and not unscrupulous qualities that distinguish the critic from the sceptic: I mean the certainty as to standards of worth, the conscious employment of a unity of method, the wary courage, the standing-alone, and the capacity for self-responsibility; indeed,

they will avow among themselves a *delight* in denial and dissection, and a certain considerate cruelty that knows how to handle the knife surely and deftly, even when the heart bleeds. They will be *sterner* (and perhaps not only towards themselves) than humane people may desire, they will not deal with the "truth" in order that it may "please" them, or "elevate" and "inspire" them—they will rather have little faith in *"truth"* bringing with it such revels for the feelings. They will smile, those rigorous spirits, when any one says in their presence: "That thought elevates me, how could it not be true?" or: "That work enchants me, how could it not be beautiful?" or: "That artist enlarges me, how could he not be great?" Perhaps they will not only have a smile, but a genuine disgust, for all that is thus rapturous, idealistic, feminine, and hermaphroditic; and if any one could look into their inmost hearts, he would not easily find therein the intention to reconcile "Christian sentiments" with "antique taste," or even with "modern parliamentarism" (the kind of reconciliation necessarily found even amongst philosophers in our very uncertain and consequently very conciliatory century). Critical discipline, and every habit that conduces to purity and rigor in intellectual matters, will not only be demanded from themselves by these philosophers of the future; they may even make a display thereof as their special adornment—nevertheless they will not want to be called critics on that account. It will seem to them no small indignity to philosophy to have it decreed, as is so welcome nowadays, that "philosophy itself is criticism and critical science—and nothing else whatever!" Though this estimate of philosophy may enjoy the approval of all the Positivists of France and Germany (and possibly it even flattered the heart and taste of *Kant:* let us call to mind the titles of his principal works), our new philosophers will say, notwithstanding, that critics are instruments of the philosopher, and just on that account, as instruments, they are far from being philosophers themselves! Even the great Chinaman of Königsberg was only a great critic.

211. I insist upon it that people finally cease confounding philosophical workers, and in general scientific men, with philosophers—that precisely here one should strictly give "to each his own," and not give those far too much, these far too little. It may be necessary for the education of the real philosopher that he himself should have once stood upon all those steps upon which his servants, the scientific workers of philosophy, remain standing, and *must* remain standing: he himself must perhaps have been critic, and dogmatist,

and historian, and moreover poet, and collector, and traveller, and riddle-reader, and moralist, and seer, and "free spirit," and almost everything, in order to traverse the whole range of human values and preferences, and that he may *be able,* with a variety of eyes and consciences, to look from a height to any distance, from a depth up to any height, from a nook into any expanse. But all these are only preliminary conditions for his task; this task itself demands something else—it requires him *to create values.* The philosophical workers, after the excellent pattern of Kant and Hegel, have to fix and formalize some great existing body of valuations—that is to say, former *determinations of value,* creations of value, that have become prevalent, and are for a time called "truths"—whether in the domain of the *logical,* the *political* (moral), or the *artistic.* It is for these investigators to make whatever has happened and been esteemed hitherto, conspicuous, conceivable, intelligible, and manageable, to shorten everything long, even "time" itself, and to *subjugate* the entire past: an immense and wonderful task, in the carrying out of which all refined pride, all tenacious will, can surely find satisfaction. *The real philosophers, however, are commanders and law-givers;* they say: "Thus *shall* it be!" They determine first the Whither and the Why of mankind, and thereby go beyond the previous labor of all philosophical workers and all subjugators of the past—they grasp at the future with a creative hand, and whatever is and was becomes for them thereby a means, an instrument, and a hammer. Their "knowing" is *creating,* their creating is a law-giving, their will to truth is—*Will to Power.*—Are there at present such philosophers? Have there ever been such philosophers? *Must* there not be such philosophers some day? . . .

212. It grows more obvious to me that the philosopher, as a man *indispensable* for the morrow and the day after the morrow, has always found himself, and *has been obliged* to find himself, in contradiction to the day in which he lives; his enemy has always been the ideal of his day. Hitherto all those extraordinary furtherers of humanity whom one calls philosophers—who rarely regarded themselves as lovers of wisdom, but rather as disagreeable fools and dangerous interrogators—have found their mission, their hard, involuntary, imperative mission (in the end, however, the greatness of their mission), in being the bad conscience of their age. In putting the vivisector's knife to the breast of the very *virtues of their age,* they have given away their own secret; it has been for the sake of a *new* greatness of man, a new untrodden path to his aggrandizement.

They have always disclosed how much hypocrisy, indolence, self-indulgence, and self-neglect, how much falsehood was concealed under the most venerated types of contemporary morality, how much virtue was *outlived;* they have always said: "We must remove hence to where *you* are least at home." In face of a world of "modern ideas," which would like to confine every one in a corner, in a "specialty," a philosopher (if there could be philosophers nowadays) would be compelled to place the greatness of man and the ideal of "greatness" itself, precisely in his comprehensiveness and multifariousness, in his all-roundness; he would even determine worth and rank according to the amount and variety of what a man could bear and take upon himself, according to the *extent* to which a man could stretch his responsibility. Nowadays the taste and virtue of the age weaken and attenuate the will; nothing is so adapted to the spirit of the age as weakness of will: consequently, in the ideal of the philosopher, strength of will, sternness and capacity for prolonged resolution, must specially be included in the ideal of "greatness"; with as good a right as the opposite doctrine, with its ideal of a silly, renouncing, humble, selfless humanity, was suited to an opposite age—such as the sixteenth century, which suffered from its accumulated energy of will, and from the wildest torrents and floods of selfishness. In the time of Socrates, among men only of worn-out instincts, old conservative Athenians who let themselves go—"for the sake of happiness," as they said; for the sake of pleasure, as their conduct indicated—and who had continually on their lips the old pompous words, their right to which they had long forfeited by the life they led, *irony* was perhaps necessary for greatness of soul, the wicked Socratic assurance of the old physician and plebeian, who cut ruthlessly into his own flesh, as into the flesh and heart of the "noble," with a look that said plainly enough: "Do not dissemble before me! here—we are equal!" At present, on the contrary, when throughout Europe the herd animal alone attains to honors, and dispenses honors, when "equality of right" can too readily be transformed into equality in wrong: I mean to say into general war against everything rare, strange, and privileged, against the higher man, the higher soul, the higher duty, the higher responsibility, the creative plenipotence and lordliness—at present it must be part of the ideal of "greatness" to be noble, to wish to be apart, to be capable of being different, to stand alone, to have to live by personal initiative; and the philosopher will betray something of his own ideal when he asserts: "He shall be the greatest who can be the most solitary, the most concealed, the most non-conformist, the man beyond good and evil, the master of his virtues, and of superabundance of will; precisely this shall be called *greatness:* as diversified as whole, as ample as full." And to ask once more the question: Is greatness *possible*—nowadays?

Ninth Article
What Is Noble?

257. Every elevation of the type "man," has hitherto been the work of an aristocratic society and so it will always be—a society believing in a long scale of gradations of rank and differences of worth among human beings, and requiring slavery in some form or other. Without the *pathos of distance,* such as grows out of the incarnated difference of classes, out of the constant outlooking and downlooking of the ruling caste on subordinates and instruments, and out of their equally constant practice of obeying and commanding, of keeping down and keeping at a distance—that other more mysterious pathos could never have arisen, the longing for an ever new widening of distance within the soul itself, the formation of ever higher, rarer, further, more extended, more comprehensive states, in short, just the elevation of the type "man," the continued "self-surmounting of man," to use a moral formula in a supermoral sense. To be sure, one must not resign oneself to any humanitarian illusions about the history of the origin of an aristocratic society (that is to say, of the preliminary condition for the elevation of the type "man") : the truth is hard. Let us acknowledge unprejudicedly how every higher civilization hitherto has *originated!* Men with a still natural nature, barbarians in every terrible sense of the word, men of prey, still in possession of unbroken strength of will and desire for power, threw themselves upon weaker, more moral, more peaceful races (perhaps trading or cattle-rearing communities), or upon old mellow civilizations in which the final vital force was flickering out in brillant fireworks of wit and depravity. At the commencement, the noble caste was always the barbarian caste: their superiority did not consist first of all in their physical, but in their psychical power—they were more *complete* men (which at every point also implies the same as "more complete beasts").

258. Corruption—as the indication that anarchy threatens to break out among the instincts, and that the foundation of the emotions, called "life," is convulsed—is something radically different accord-

ing to the organization in which it manifests itself. When, for instance, an aristocracy like that of France at the beginning of the Revolution flung away its privileges with sublime disgust and sacrificed itself to an excess of its moral sentiments, it was corruption—it was really only the closing act of the corruption that had existed for centuries, by virtue of which that artistocracy had abdicated step by step its lordly prerogatives and lowered itself to a *function* of royalty (in the end even to its decoration and parade-dress). The essential thing, however, in a good and healthy artisocracy is that it should *not* regard itself as a function either of the kingship or the commonwealth, but as the *significance* and highest justification thereof—that it should therefore accept with a good conscience the sacrifice of a legion of individuals, who, *for its sake,* must be suppressed and reduced to imperfect men, to slaves and instruments. Its fundamental belief must be precisely that society is *not* allowed to exist for its own sake, but only as a foundation and scaffolding by means of which a select class of beings may be able to elevate themselves to their higher duties, and in general to a higher *existence:* like those sun-seeking climbing plants in Java—they are called *Sipo Matador* —which encircle an oak so long and so often with their arms, until at last, high above it, but supported by it, they can unfold their tops in the open light, and exhibit their happiness.

259. To refrain mutually from injury, from violence, from exploitation, and put one's will on a par with that of others: this may result in a certain rough sense in good conduct among individuals when the necessary conditions are given (namely, the actual similarity of the individuals in amount of force and degree of worth, and their co-existence within one organization). As soon, however, as one wished to take this principle more generally, and if possible even as *the fundamental principle of society,* it would immediately disclose what it really is—namely, a Will to the *denial* of life, a principle of dissolution and decay. Here one must think profoundly to the very basis and resist all sentimental weakness: life itself is *essentially* appropriation, injury, conquest of the alien and weak, suppression, severity, obtrusion of one form upon another, incorporation, and at the least, putting it mildest, exploitation;—but why should one for ever use precisely these words, on which for ages a disparaging purpose has been stamped? Even the organization within which, as was previously supposed, the individuals treat each other as equal— it takes place in every healthy aristocracy—must itself, if it be a living and not a dying organization, do to other bodies what the

individuals within it refrain from doing to each other: it will have to be the incarnate Will to Power, it will endeavor to grow, to gain ground, attract to itself and acquire ascendency—not owing to any morality or immorality, but because it *lives,* and because life *is* percisely Will to Power. On no point, however, is the ordinary consciousness of Europeans more unwilling to be corrected than on this matter; people now rave everywhere, even under the guise of science, about coming conditions of society from which "the exploiting character" is to be absent—that sounds to my ears as if they promised to invent a mode of life that would refrain from all organic functions. "Exploitation" does not belong to a depraved or imperfect and primitive society: it belongs to the *nature* of the living being as a primary organic function; it is a consequence of the intrinsic Will to Power, which is precisely the Will to Life.—Granted that as a theory this is a novelty—as a reality it is the *fundamental fact* of all history: let us be so far honest towards ourselves!

260. In a tour through the many finer and coarser moralities that have hitherto prevailed or still prevail on the earth, I found certain traits regularly recurring together, and connected with one another, until finally two primary types revealed themselves to me, and a radical distinction was brought to light. There is *master-morality* and *slave-morality*—I would at once add, however, that in all higher and mixed civilizations there are also attempts at the reconciliation of the two moralities; but one finds still oftener the confusion and mutual misunderstanding of them, indeed, sometimes their close juxtaposition—even in the same man, within one soul. The distinctions of moral values have either originated in a ruling caste, pleasantly conscious of being different from the ruled—or among the ruled class, the slaves and dependents of all sorts. In the first case, when it is the rulers who determine the concept "good," the exalted, proud disposition is regarded as the distinguishing feature, and that which determines the order of rank. The noble type of man separates from himself the beings in whom the opposite of this exalted, proud disposition displays itself: he despises them. Let it at once be noted that in this first kind of morality the antithesis "good" and "bad" means practically the same as "noble" and "despicable";—the antithesis "good" and *"evil"* has a different origin. The cowardly, the timid, the insignificant, and those thinking merely of narrow utility are despised; moreover, also, the distrustful, with their constrained glances, the self-abasing, the dog-like kind of men who let themselves be abused, the mendicant flatterers, and above all the liars—

it is a fundamental belief of all aristocrats that the common people are untruthful. "We truthful ones"—the nobility in ancient Greece called themselves. It is obvious that everywhere the designations of moral value were at first applied to *men,* and were only derivatively and at a later period applied to *actions;* it is a gross mistake, therefore, when historians of morals start questions like, "Why have sympathetic actions been praised?" The noble type of man regards *himself* as a determiner of values; he does not require to be approved; he passes the judgment: "What is injurious to me is injurious in itself"; he knows that it is he himself only who confers honor on things; he is a *creator of values.* He honors whatever he recognizes in himself: such morality is self-glorification. In the foreground there is the feeling of plenitude, of power that seeks to overflow, the happiness of high tension, the consciousness of a wealth that would give and bestow—the noble man also helps the unfortunate, but not—or scarcely—out of pity, but rather from an impulse generated by the superabundance of power. The noble man honors in himself the powerful one, him also who has power over himself, who knows how to speak and how to keep silence, who takes pleasure in subjecting himself to severity and hardness, and has reverence for all that is severe and hard. "Wotan placed a hard heart in my breast," says an old Scandinavian Saga: it is thus rightly expressed from the soul of a proud Viking. Such a type of man is even proud of *not* being made for sympathy; the hero of the Saga therefore adds warningly: "He who has not a hard heart when young, will never have one." The noble and brave who think thus are the furthest removed from the morality that sees precisely in sympathy, or in acting for the good of others, or in *désintéresse-ment,* the characteristic of the moral; faith in oneself, pride in oneself, a radical enmity and irony towards "selflessness," belong as definitely to noble morality, as do a careless scorn and precaution in presence of sympathy and the "warm heart."—It is the powerful who *know* how to honor; it is their art, their domain for invention. The profound reverence for age and for tradition—all law rests on this double reverence—the belief and prejudice in favor of ancestors and unfavorable to newcomers, is typical in the morality of the powerful; and when, conversely, men of "modern ideas" believe almost instinctively in "progress" and the "future," and are more and more lacking in respect for old age, they betray the ignoble origin of these "ideas." A morality of the ruling class, however, is more especially foreign and irritating to present-day taste in the sternness of its principle that one has duties only to one's equals; that one may act towards beings of a lower rank, towards all that is foreign, just as seems good to one, or "as the heart desires," and in any case "beyond good and evil": it is here that sympathy and similar sentiments can have a place. The ability and obligation to exercise prolonged gratitude and prolonged revenge—both only within the circle of equals—artfulness in retaliation, *raffinement* of the idea in friendship, a certain necessity to have enemies (as outlets for the emotions of envy, quarrelsomeness, arrogance—in fact, in order to be a good *friend*): all these are typical characteristics of the noble morality, which, as has been pointed out, is not the morality of "modern ideas," and is therefore at present difficult to realize, and also to unearth and disclose.—It is otherwise with the second type of morality, *slave-morality*. Supposing that the abused, the oppressed, the suffering, the unemancipated, the weary, and those uncertain of themselves, should moralize, what will be the common element in their moral estimates? Probably a pessimistic suspicion with regard to the entire situation of man will find expression, perhaps a condemnation of man, together with his situation. The slave has an unfavorable eye for the virtues of the powerful; he has a scepticism and distrust, a *refinement* of distrust of everything "good" that is there honored—he would persuade himself that the very happiness there is not genuine. On the other hand, *those* qualities which serve to alleviate the existence of sufferers are brought into prominence and flooded with light; it is here that sympathy, the kind, helping hand, the warm heart, patience, diligence, humility, and friendliness attain to honor; for here these are the most useful qualities, and almost the only means of enduring the burden of existence. Slave-morality is essentially the morality of utility. Here is the seat of the origin of the famous antithesis "good" and "evil"—power and dangerousness are assumed to reside in the evil, a certain dreadfulness, subtlety, and strength, which do not admit of being despised. According to slave-morality, therefore, the "evil" man arouses fear; according to master-morality, it is precisely the "good" man who arouses fear and seeks to arouse it, while the bad man is regarded as the despicable being. The contrast attains its maximum when, in accordance with the logical consequences of slave-morality, a shade of depreciation—it may be slight and well-intentioned—at last attaches itself to the "good" man of this morality; because, according to the servile mode of thought, the good man must in any case be the *safe* man: he is good-natured, easily deceived, perhaps a little stupid, *un bonhomme*.

Everywhere that slave-morality gains the ascendency, language shows a tendency to approximate the significations of the words "good" and "stupid."—A last fundamental difference; the desire for *freedom,* the instinct for happiness and the refinements of the feeling of liberty belong as necessarily to slave-morals and morality, as skill and enthusiasm in reverence and devotion are the regular symptoms of an aristocratic mode of thinking and evaluating. . . .

263. There is an *instinct for rank,* which more than anything else is the sign of a *high* rank; there is a *delight* in the *nuances* of reverence that leads one to infer noble origin and habits. The refinement, goodness, and loftiness of a soul are put to a perilous test when something passes by that is of the highest rank, but is not yet protected by the awe of authority from obtrusive touches and incivilities: something that goes its way like a living touchstone, unlabelled, undiscovered, and tentative, perhaps voluntarily veiled and disguised. He whose task and practice it is to investigate souls, will avail himself of many varieties of this very art to determine the ultimate value of a soul, the unalterable, innate order of rank to which it belongs: he will test it by its *instinct for reverence. Différence engendre haine:* the vulgarity of many a nature spurts up suddenly like dirty water, when any holy vessel, any jewel from closed shrines, any book bearing the marks of great destiny, is brought before it; while on the other hand, there is an involuntary silence, a hesitation of the eye, a cessation of all gestures, by which it is indicated that a soul *feels* the nearness of what is worthiest of respect. The way in which, on the whole, the reverence for the *Bible* has hitherto been maintained in Europe, is perhaps the best example of discipline and refinement of manners that Europe owes to Christianity: books of such profoundness and supreme significance required for their protection an external tyranny of authority, in order to acquire the *period* of thousands of years that is necessary to exhaust and unriddle them. Much has been achieved when the sentiment has been at last instilled into the masses (the shallow-pates and the boobies of every kind) that they are not allowed to touch everything, that there are holy experiences before which they must take off their shoes and keep away the unclean hand—it is almost their highest advance towards humanity. On the contrary, in the so-called cultured classes, the believers in "modern ideas," nothing is perhaps so repulsive as their lack of shame, the easy insolence of eye and hand with which they touch, taste, and finger everything; and it is possible that even yet there is more *relative* nobility of taste,

and more tact for reverence among the people, among the lower classes of the people, especially among peasants, than among the newspaper-reading *demimonde* of intellect, the cultured class.

265. At the risk of displeasing innocent ears, I submit that egoism belongs to the essence of a noble soul, I mean the unalterable belief that to a being such as "we," other beings must naturally be in subjection, and have to sacrifice themselves. The noble soul accepts the fact of his egoism without question, and also without consciousness of harshness, constraint, or arbitrariness therein, but rather as something that may have its basis in the primary law of things—if he sought a designation for it he would say: "It is justice itself." He acknowledges under certain circumstances, which made him hesitate at first, that there are other equally privileged ones; as soon as he has settled this question of rank, he moves among those equals and equally privileged ones with the same assurance, as regards modesty and delicate respect, that he enjoys in intercourse with himself—in accordance with an innate heavenly mechanism that all the stars understand. It is an *additional* instance of his egoism, this artfulness and self-limitation in intercourse with his equals—every star is a similar egoist. He honors *himself* in them, and in the rights which he concedes to them, he has no doubt that the exchange of honors and rights, as the *essence* of all intercourse, belongs also the natural condition of things. The noble soul gives as he takes, prompted by the passionate and sensitive instinct of requital that is at the root of his nature. The notion of "favor" has, *inter pares,* neither significance nor good repute; there may be a sublime way of letting gifts as it were light upon one from above, and of drinking them thirstily like dew-drops; but for those arts and displays the noble soul has no aptitude. His egoism hinders him here: in general, he looks "aloft" unwillingly— he looks either *forward,* horizontally and deliberately, or downwards —*he knows that he is on a height.*

287. What is noble? What does the word "noble" still mean for us nowadays? How does the noble man betray himself, how is he recognized under this heavy overcast sky of the growing plebeianism, by which everything is rendered opaque and leaden?—It is not his actions that establish his claim—actions are always ambiguous, always inscrutable; neither is it his "works." One finds nowadays among artists and scholars plenty of those who betray by their works that a profound longing for nobleness impels them; but this very *need* of nobleness is radically different from the needs of the noble soul itself, and is in fact the eloquent and dangerous sign of the lack of it. It is not

the works, but the *faith* that is here decisive and determines the order of rank—to employ once more an old religious formula with a new and deeper meaning—it is some fundamental certainty that a noble soul has about itself, something that is not to be sought, is not to be found, and perhaps, also, is not to be lost.—*The noble soul has reverence for itself.*—

290. Every deep thinker is more afraid of being understood than of being misunderstood. The latter perhaps wounds his vanity; but the former wounds his heart, his sympathy, which always says: "Ah, why would *you* also have as hard a time of it as I have?"

292. A philosopher: that is a man who constantly experiences, sees, hears, suspects, hopes, and dreams extraordinary things; who is struck by his own thoughts as if they came from the outside, from above and below, as a species of events and lightning-flashes *peculiar to him;* who is perhaps himself a storm pregnant with new lightnings; a portentous man, around whom there is always rumbling and mumbling and gaping and something uncanny going on. A philosopher: alas, a being who often runs away from himself, is often afraid of himself—but whose curiosity always makes him "come to himself" again.

293. A man who says: "I like that, I take it for my own, and mean to guard and protect it from every one"; a man who can conduct a case, carry out a resolution, remain true to an opinion, keep hold of a woman, punish and overthrow insolence; a man who has his indignation and his sword, and to whom the weak, the suffering, the oppressed, and even the animals willingly submit and naturally belong; in short, a man who is a *master* by nature—when such a man has sympathy, well! *that* sympathy has value! But of what account is the sympathy of those who suffer! Or of those even who preach sympathy! There is nowadays, throughout almost the whole of Europe, a sickly irritability and sensitiveness towards pain, and also a repulsive irrestrainableness in complaining, an effeminizing which, with the aid of religion and philosophical nonsense, seeks to deck itself out as something superior—there is a regular cult of suffering. The *unmanliness* of what is called "sympathy" by such groups of visionaries, is always, I believe, the first thing that strikes the eye.—One must resolutely and radically taboo this latest form of bad taste; and finally I wish people to put the good amulet, *"gai saber"* ("gay science," in ordinary language), on heart and neck, as a protection against it.

294. *The Olympian Vice.*—Despite the philosopher who, as a genuine Englishman, tried to bring laughter into bad repute in all

thinking minds—"Laughing is a bad infirmity of human nature, which every thinking mind will strive to overcome" (Hobbes)—I would even allow myself to rank philosophers according to the quality of their laughing—up to those who are capable of *golden* laughter. And supposing that gods also philosophize—which I am strongly inclined to believe for many reasons—I have no doubt that they also know how to laugh in a Supermanlike and new fashion—and at the expense of all serious things! Gods are fond of ridicule: it seems that they cannot refrain from laughter even in holy matters.

295.   The *genius of the heart,* as that great mysterious one possesses it, the tempter-god and born rat-catcher of consciences, whose voice can descend into the nether-world of every soul, who neither speaks a word nor casts a glance in which there may not be some motive or touch of allurement, to whose perfection it pertains that he knows how to appear—not as he is, but in a guise that acts as an *additional* constraint on his followers to press ever closer to him, to follow him more cordially and thoroughly;—the genius of the heart, which imposes silence and attention on everything loud and self-conceited, which smooths rough souls and makes them taste a new longing—to lie placid as a mirror, that the deep heavens may be reflected in them;—the genius of the heart, which teaches the clumsy and too hasty hand to hesitate, and to grasp more delicately; which scents the hidden and forgotten treasure, the drop of goodness and sweet spirituality under thick dark ice, and is a divining-rod for every grain of gold, long buried and imprisoned in mud and sand; the genius of the heart, from contact with which every one goes away richer; not favored or surprised, not as though gratified and oppressed by the good things of others; but richer in himself, newer than before, broken up, blown upon, and sounded by a thawing wind; more uncertain, perhaps, more delicate, more fragile, more bruised, but full of hopes that as yet lack names, full of a new will and current, full of a new ill-will and counter-current . . . but what am I doing, my friends? Of whom am I talking to you? Have I forgotten myself so far that I have not even told you his name? Unless it be that you have already divined of your own accord who this questionable God and spirit is, that wishes to be *praised* in such a manner? For, as it happens to every one who from childhood onward has always been on the move, and in foreign lands, I have also encountered on my path many strange and dangerous spirits; above all, however, and again and again, the one of whom I have just spoken: in fact, no less a personage than the god *Dionysus,* the great equivocator and tempter,

to whom, as you know, I once offered in all secrecy and reverence my first-fruits—the last, as it seems to me, who has offered a *sacrifice* to him, for I have found no one who could understand what I was then doing. In the meantime, however, I have learned much, far too much, about the philosophy of this god, and, as I said, from mouth to mouth—I, the last disciple and initiate of the god Dionysus: and perhaps I might at last begin to give you, my friends, as far as I am allowed, a little taste of this philosophy? In a hushed voice, as is but seemly: for it has to do with much that is secret, new, strange, wonderful, and uncanny. The very fact that Dionysus is a philosopher, and that therefore gods also philosophize, seems to me a novelty that is not unensnaring, and might perhaps arouse suspicion precisely amongst philosophers—amongst you, my friends, there is less to be said against it, except that it comes too late and not at the right time; for, as it has been disclosed to me, you are loth nowadays to believe in God and gods. It may happen, too, that in the frankness of my story I must go further than is agreeable to the strict usages of your ears? Certainly the god in question went further, very much further, in such dialogues, and was always many paces ahead of me. . . . Indeed, if it were allowed, I should have to give him, according to human usage, fine ceremonious titles of lustre and merit, I should have to extol his courage as investigator and discoverer, his fearless honesty, truthfulness, and love of wisdom. But such a God does not know what to do with all that respectable trumpery and pomp. "Keep that," he would say, "for yourself and those like you, and whoever else requires it! I—have no reason to cover my nakedness!" One suspects that this kind of divinity and philosopher perhaps lacks modesty?— He once said: "Under certain circumstances I love mankind"—and referred to Ariadne, who was present; "in my opinion man is an agreeable, brave, inventive animal, that has not his equal upon earth, he makes his way even through all labyrinths. I like man, and often think how I can still further advance him, and make him stronger, more evil, and more profound."—"Stronger, more evil, and more profound?" I asked in horror. "Yes," he said again, "stronger, more evil, and more profound; also more beautiful"—and the tempter-god smiled his halcyon smile, as though he had just paid some charming compliment. One here sees at once that it is not only modesty that this divinity lacks—and in general there are good grounds for supposing that in some things the gods could all of them come to us human beings for instruction. We human beings are—more humane.

Supplementary Passages

1

618. Of all the interpretations of the world attempted heretofore, the *mechanical* one seems to-day to be most prominent. Apparently it has a clean conscience on its side; for no science believes inwardly in progress and success unless it be with the help of mechanical procedures. Everyone knows these procedures: "reason" and "purpose" are kept out of consideration as far as possible; it is shown that, provided a sufficient amount of time be allowed to elapse, everything can evolve out of everything else, and no one attempts to suppress his malicious satisfaction, when the "apparent design in the fate" of a plant or of the yolk of an egg, may be traced to stress and thrust—in short, people are heartily glad to pay respect to this principle of profoundest stupidity, if I may be allowed to pass a playful remark concerning these serious matters. Meanwhile, among the most select intellects to be found in this movement, some presentiment of evil, some anxiety is noticeable, as if the theory had a rent in it that sooner or later might be its last: I mean the sort of rent that denotes the end of all balloons inflated with such theories.

Stress and thrust themselves cannot be "explained," one cannot get rid of the *actio in distans.* The belief even in the ability to explain is now lost, and people peevishly admit that one can only describe, not explain, that the dynamic interpretation of the world, with its denial of "empty space" and its little agglomerations of atoms, will soon get the better of physicists: although in this way *Dynamis* is certainly granted an inner quality.

619. The triumphant concept *energy,* with which our physicists created God and the world, needs yet to be completed: it must be given an inner will which I characterize as the *"Will to Power"*—that is to say, as an insatiable desire to manifest power; or the application and exercise of power as a creative instinct, etc. Physicists cannot get rid of the *"actio in distans"* in their principles; any more than they can a repelling force (or an attracting one). There is no help for it, all movements, all "appearances," all "laws" must be understood as *symptoms* of an *inner* phenomenon, and the analogy of man must be used for this purpose. It is possible to trace all the instincts of an animal to the will to power; as also all the functions of organic life to this one source.

852

692. Is the "Will to Power" a kind of will, or is it identical with the concept will? Is it equivalent to desiring or commanding; is it the Will that Schopenhauer says is the essence of things?

My proposition is that the will of psychologists hitherto has been an unjustifiable generalization, and there there is no such thing as this sort of will, that instead of the development of one will into several forms being taken as a fact, the character of will has been cancelled owing to the fact that its content, its "whither," was subtracted from it. In Schopenhauer this is so in the highest degree; what he calls "Will" is merely an empty word. There is even less plausibility in the Will to Live, for life is simply one of the manifestations of the Will to Power; it is quite arbitrary and ridiculous to suggest that everything is striving to enter into this particular form of the Will to Power.

704. How is it that the fundamental article of faith in all psychologies is a piece of most outrageous contortion and fabrication? "Man strives after happiness," for instance—how much of this is true? In order to understand what life is, and what kind of striving and tenseness life contains, the formula should hold good not only of trees and plants, but of animals also. "What does the plant strive after?"—But here we have already invented a false entity that does not exist—concealing and denying the fact of an infinitely variegated growth, with individual and semi-individual starting-points—when we give it the clumsy title "plant" as if it were a unit. It is very obvious that the ultimate and smallest "individuals" cannot be understood in the sense of metaphysical individuals or atoms; their sphere of power is continually shifting its ground: but with all these changes, can it be said that any of them strives after happiness?—All this expanding, this incorporation and growth, is a search for resistance; movement is essentially related to states of pain: the driving power here must represent some other desire if it leads to such continual willing and seeking of pain.—To what end do the trees of a virgin forest contend with each other? "For happiness"?—For power! . . .

Man is now master of the forces of nature, and master too of his own wild and unbridled feelings (the passions have followed suit, and have learned to become useful)—in comparison with primeval man, the man of to-day represents an enormous quantum of power, but not an increase in happiness! How can one maintain, then, that he has striven after happiness? . . .

[FROM *The Will to Power,* trans. Anthony M. Ludovici in vols. 14 and 15 of *The Complete Works of Friedrich Nietzsche,* ed. Oscar Levy, Edinburgh: Foulis, 1910; translation slightly modified.]

2

Eternal Recurrence

1066.   *The new concept of the universe.* The universe exists; it
is nothing that grows into existence and that passes out of existence.
Or, better still, it develops, it passes away, but it never began to
develop, and has never ceased from passing away; it *maintains* itself
in both states. . . . It lives on itself, its excrements are its nourishment.

We need not concern ourselves for one instant with the hypothesis
of a *created* world. The concept "create" is today utterly indefinable
and unrealizable; it is but a word that hails from superstitious ages;
nothing can be explained with a word. The last attempt to conceive
of a world that *began* was recently made in diverse ways, with the
help of logical reasoning chiefly, as you will guess, with an ulterior
theological motive.

Several attempts have been made lately to show that the concept
that "the universe has an infinite past" (*regressus in infinitum*) is
contradictory: in fact, it was even demonstrated, at the price of
confounding the head with the tail. Nothing can prevent me from
calculating backward from this moment of time, and of saying: "I
shall never reach the end"; just as I can calculate without end in a
forward direction, from the same moment. It is only when I wish to
commit the error—I shall be careful to avoid it—of reconciling this
correct concept of a *regressus in infinitum* with the absolutely unrealizable concept of an infinite *progressus* up to the present; only when I
consider the direction (forward or backward) as logically indifferent,
that I take hold of the head—this very moment—and think I hold the
tail: this pleasure I leave to you, Mr. Dühring! . . .

I have come across this thought in other thinkers before me, and
every time I found that it was determined by other ulterior motives
(chiefly theological, in favor of a *creator spiritus*). If the universe
were in any way able to congeal, to dry up, to perish; or if it were
capable of attaining to a state of equilibrium; or if it had any kind of
goal at all which a long lapse of time, immutability, and finality
reserved for it (in short, to speak metaphysically, if becoming could
resolve itself into being or into nonentity), this state ought already
to have been reached. But it has not been reached: it therefore
follows. . . . This is the only certainty we can grasp, which can serve
as a corrective to a host of cosmic hypotheses possible in themselves.

If, for instance, materialism cannot consistently escape the conclusion of a final state, which William Thomson has traced out for it, then materialism is thereby refuted.

If the universe may be conceived as a definite quantity of energy, as a definite number of centres of energy—and every other concept remains indefinite and therefore useless—it follows that the universe must go through a calculable number of combinations in the great game of chance that constitutes its existence. In infinity at some moment or other, every possible combination must have been realized; not only this, but it must have been realized an infinite number of times. And inasmuch as between every one of these combinations and its next recurrence every other possible combination would necessarily have been undergone, and since every one of these combinations would determine the whole series in the same order, a circular movement of absolutely identical series is thus demonstrated: the universe is shown to be a circular movement that has already repeated itself an infinite number of times, and that plays its game for all eternity.— This conception is not simply materialistic; for if it were this, it would not involve an infinite recurrence of identical cases, but a final state. Owing to the fact that the universe has not reached this final state, materialism shows itself to be but an imperfect and provisional hypothesis.

1067. And do you know what "the universe" is to my mind? Shall I show it to you in my mirror? This universe is a monster of energy, without beginning or end; a fixed and brazen quantity of energy that grows neither bigger nor smaller, does not consume itself, but only alters its face; as a whole its bulk is immutable, it is a household without either losses or gains, but likewise without increase and without sources of revenue, surrounded by nonentity as by a frontier. It is nothing vague or wasteful, it does not stretch into infinity; but is a definite quantum of energy located in limited space, and not in space that would be anywhere empty. It is rather energy everywhere, the play of forces and force-waves, at the same time one and many, agglomerating here and diminishing there, a sea of forces storming and raging in itself, forever changing, forever rolling back over incalculable ages to recurrence, with an ebb and flow of its forms, producing the most complicated things out of the most simple structures; producing the most ardent, most savage, and most contradictory things out of the quietest, most rigid, and most frozen material, and then returning from multifariousness to uniformity, from the play of contradictions back into the delight of consonance, saying Yea unto itself, even in this homogeneity of its courses and ages; forever blessing itself as something which recurs for all eternity—a becoming that knows not satiety, or disgust, or weariness—this, my Dionysian world of eternal self-creation, of eternal self-destruction, this mysterious world of twofold voluptuousness; this, my "Beyond Good and Evil," without aim, unless there is an aim in the bliss of the circle, without will, unless a ring must by nature keep good will to itself—would you have a name for my world? A *solution* of all your riddles? Do you also want a light, you most concealed, strongest and most undaunted men of the blackest midnight?—*This world is the Will to Power—and nothing else!* And even you yourselves are this Will to Power—and nothing else!

[FROM *The Will to Power,* trans. Anthony M. Ludovici, *ibid.*]

3

The Superman (see *Beyond Good and Evil,* Aphorisms 44, 263, 265, 287, 293)

[A] 957. . . . He, however, who has reflected deeply concerning the question, how and where the plant man has hitherto grown most vigorously, is forced to believe that this has always taken place under the opposite conditions; that to this end the danger of the situation has to increase enormously, his inventive faculty and dissembling powers have to fight their way up under long oppression and compulsion, and his Will to Life has to be increased to the unconditioned Will to Power, to *over-power:* he believes that danger, severity, violence, peril in the street and in the heart, inequality of rights, secrecy, stoicism, seductive art, and devilry of every kind—in short, the opposite of all gregarious desiderata—are necessary for the elevation of man. Such a morality with opposite designs, which would rear man upwards instead of to comfort and mediocrity; such a morality, with the intention of producing a ruling caste—the future lords of the earth—must, in order to be taught at all, introduce itself as if it were in some way correlated to the prevailing moral law, and must come forward under the cover of the latter's words and forms. But seeing that, to this end, a host of transitionary and deceptive measures must be discovered, and that the life of a single individual stands for almost nothing compared to the accomplishment of such lengthy tasks and aims, the first thing that must be done is to rear *a new kind* of man in whom the duration of the necessary will and the necessary instincts is guaranteed for many generations. This must be a new kind of ruling species and caste—this ought to be quite as clear as the somewhat lengthy and not easily expressed consequences of this thought. The aim should be to prepare a *transvaluation of values* for a particularly strong kind of man, most highly gifted in intellect and will, and, to this end, slowly and cautiously to liberate in him a whole host of slandered instincts hitherto held in check: whoever meditates about this problem belongs to us, the free spirits. . . .

960. From now henceforward there will be such favorable first conditions for greater ruling powers as have never yet been found on earth. And this is by no means the most important point. The establishment has been made possible of international race unions which will set themselves the task of rearing a ruling race, the future "lords of the earth"—a new, vast aristocracy based upon the most severe self-discipline, in which the will of philosophical men of power and artist-tyrants will be stamped upon thousands of years: a higher species of men who, thanks to their preponderance of will, knowledge, riches, and influence, will avail themselves of democratic Europe as the most suitable and supple instrument they can have for taking the fate of the earth into their own hands, and working as artists upon man himself. Enough! The time is coming for us to transform all our views on politics.

1000. I fancy I have divined some of the things that lie hidden in the soul of the highest man; perhaps every man who has divined so much must go to ruin. But he who has seen the highest man must do all he can to make him *possible*.

Fundamental thought: we must make the future the standard of all our valuations—and not seek the laws for our conduct behind us.

1001. Not "mankind," but *Superman,* is the goal.

[FROM *The Will to Power,* trans. Anthony M. Ludovici, *ibid.*]

[B] Let us take an extreme case: suppose a book speaks only of experiences that lie entirely outside the range of general or even exceptional knowledge—suppose it to be the *first* expression of an entirely new series of experiences. In this case nothing it contains will really be heard at all, and, by an acoustic delusion, people will assume that where nothing is heard there is nothing to hear. . . . This, at any rate, has been my ordinary experience, and indicates, if you will, its originality. He who thought he understood something in my work had interpreted something in it according to his own image —not infrequently the very opposite of myself, an "idealist," for instance. He who understood nothing in my work denied me any consideration at all. The word "Superman" [1] designating a type of man whose appearance would be a piece of the greatest good fortune, a type opposed to "modern" men, to "good" men, to Christians and other nihilists—a word which in the mouth of *Zarathustra,* the destroyer of morality, becomes profoundly significant—this word is understood almost everywhere, and with perfect innocence, to correspond to those values of which *Zarathustra* is a flat repudiation—he was considered as an "idealistic" type, a higher kind of man, half "saint," half "genius." . . . Other learned cattle have suspected me of Darwinism on account of this word: even the "hero worship" of that great unconscious and involuntary swindler, Carlyle—a worship I viciously repudiated —was recognized in my doctrine. If I had intimated to some one that he would do better to seek for the Superman in a Cæsar Borgia than in a Parsifal, he would not have believed his ears. I will have to be forgiven my complete lack of curiosity with regard to criticisms of my books, more particularly newspaper criticisms. My friends and publishers know this, and never speak to me of things like this. In one particular case, I once saw all the sins that had been committed against a single book—it was *Beyond Good and Evil;* I could tell you a nice story about it. Is it possible that the *National-Zeitung*—a Prussian paper (I mention this for the sake of my foreign readers—for my own part, I beg to state, I read only the *Journal des Débats*)—should seriously regard the book as a "sign of the times," as a genuine example of Junkerism, for which the *Kreuz-Zeitung* had not sufficient courage?

> [FROM *Ecce Homo,* trans. Clifton Fadiman, in *The Philosophy of Nietzsche,* N. Y.: Modern Library, 1927, Third Essay, Aphorism 1.]

4

Good and Evil (see *Beyond Good and Evil,* Aphorism 260)

4.   The guide-post that first put me on the *right* track was this question—what is the true etymological significance of the various symbols for the idea "good" that have been coined in the various languages? I then found that they all led back to *the same evolution of the same idea*—that everywhere "aristocrat," "noble" (in the social sense), is the root idea, out of which have necessarily developed

---

[1] [*"Übermensch"*—M.C.B.]

"good" in the sense of "with aristocratic soul," "noble," in the sense of "with a soul of high calibre," "with a privileged soul"—a development that invariably runs parallel with that other evolution by which "vulgar," "plebeian," "low," are made to change finally into "bad." The most eloquent proof of this last contention is the German word *"schlecht"* itself: this word is identical with *"schlicht"* (compare *"schlechtweg"* and *"schlechterdings"*), which, originally and as yet without any sinister innuendo, simply denoted the plebeian man in contrast to the aristocratic man. It is at the sufficiently late period of the Thirty Years' War that this sense becomes changed to the sense now current. From the standpoint of the Genealogy of Morals this discovery seems to be substantial: the lateness of it is to be attributed to the retarding influence exercised in the modern world by democratic prejudice in the sphere of all questions of origin. . . .

7. . . . Human history would be too fatuous for anything were it not for the cleverness imported into it by the weak—take at once the most important instance. All the world's efforts against the "aristocrats," the "mighty," the "masters," the "holders of power," are negligible by comparison with what has been accomplished against those classes by *the Jews*—the Jews, that priestly nation which eventually realized that the one method of effecting satisfaction on its enemies and tyrants was by means of a radical transvaluation of values, which was at the same time an act of the *cleverest revenge*. Yet the method was only appropriate to a nation of priests, to a nation of the most jealously nursed priestly vengefulness. It was the Jews who, in opposition to the aristocratic equation (good = aristocratic = beautiful = happy = loved by the gods), dared with a terrifying logic to suggest the contrary equation, and indeed to maintain with the teeth of the most profound hatred (the hatred of weakness) this contrary equation, namely, "the wretched are alone the good; the poor, the weak, the lowly, are alone the good; the suffering, the needy, the sick, the loathsome, are the only ones who are pious, the only ones who are blessed, for them alone is salvation—but you, on the other hand, you aristocrats, you men of power, you are to all eternity the evil, the horrible, the covetous, the insatiate, the godless: eternally also shall you be the unblessed, the cursed, the damned!" We know who it was who reaped the heritage of this Jewish transvaluation. . . .

10. The revolt of the slaves in morals begins in the very principle of *resentment* becoming creative and giving birth to values—a resentment experienced by creatures who, deprived as they are of the proper outlet of action, are forced to find their compensation in an imaginary

revenge. While every aristocratic morality springs from a triumphant affirmation of its own demands, the slave morality says "no" from the very outset to what is "outside itself," "different from itself," and "not itself": and this "no" is its creative deed. This volte-face of the valuing standpoint—this *inevitable* gravitation to the objective instead of back to the subjective—is typical of "resentment": the slave-morality requires as the condition of its existence an external and objective world; to employ physiological terminology, it requires objective stimuli to be capable of action at all—its action is fundamentally a reaction. The contrary is the case when we come to the aristocrat's system of values: it acts and grows spontaneously, it merely seeks its antithesis in order to pronounce a more grateful and exultant "yes" to its own self—its negative conception, "low," "vulgar," "bad," is merely a pale late-born foil in comparison with its positive and fundamental conception (saturated as it is with life and passion) of "we aristocrats, we good ones, we beautiful ones, we happy ones." . . .

11. . . . Granted the truth of the theory now believed to be true, that the very *essence of all civilization* is to *train* out of man, the beast of prey, a tame and civilized animal, a domesticated animal, it follows indubitably that we must regard as the real *tools of civilization* all those instincts of reaction and resentment, by the help of which the aristocratic races, together with their ideals, were finally degraded and overpowered; though that has not yet come to be synonymous with saying that the bearers of those tools also *represented* the civilization. It is rather the contrary that is not only probable—nay, it is *palpable* today; these bearers of vindictive instincts that have to be bottled up, these descendants of all European and non-European slavery, especially of the pre-Aryan population—these people, I say, represent the *decline* of humanity! These "tools of civilization" are a disgrace to humanity, and constitute in reality more of an argument against civilization, more of a reason why civilization should be suspected. One may be perfectly justified in being always afraid of the blonde beast that lies at the core of all aristocratic races, and in being on one's guard: but who would not a hundred times prefer to be afraid, when one at the same time admires, than to be immune from fear, at the cost of being perpetually obsessed with the loathsome spectacle of the distorted, the dwarfed, the stunted, the envenomed? And is that not our fate? What produces today our repulsion towards "man"? —for we *suffer* from "man," there is no doubt about it. It is not fear; it is rather that we have nothing more to fear from men; it is that

the worm "man" is in the foreground and pullulates; it is that the "tame man," the wretched mediocre and unedifying creature, has learned to consider himself a goal and a pinnacle, an inner meaning, an historic principle, a "higher man"; yes, it is that he has a certain right so to consider himself, in so far as he feels that in contrast to that excess of deformity, disease, exhaustion, and effeteness whose odor is beginning to pollute present-day Europe, he at any rate has achieved a relative success, he at any rate still says "yes" to life.

14. Will any one look a little into—right into—the mystery of how *ideals* are *manufactured* in this world? Who has the courage to do it? Come!

Here we have a vista opened into these grimy workshops. Wait just a moment, dear Mr. Inquisitive and Foolhardy; your eye must first grow accustomed to this false changing light—Yes! Enough! Now speak! What is happening below down yonder? Speak out! Tell what you see, man of the most dangerous curiosity—for now *I* am the listener.

"I see nothing, I hear the more. It is a cautious, spiteful, gentle whispering and muttering together in all the corners and crannies. it seems to me that they are lying; a sugary softness adheres to every sound. Weakness is turned to *merit,* there is no doubt about it—it is just as you say."

Further!

"And the impotence which requites not, is turned to 'goodness,' craven baseness to meekness, submission to those whom one hates, to obedience (namely, obedience to one of whom they say that he ordered this submission—they call him God). The inoffensive character of the weak, the very cowardice in which he is rich, his standing at the door, his forced necessity of waiting, gain here fine names, such as 'patience,' which is also called 'virtue'; not being able to avenge one's self, is called not wishing to avenge one's self, perhaps even forgiveness (for *they* know not what they do—we alone know what they do). They also talk of the 'love of their enemies' and sweat thereby."

Further!

"They are miserable, there is no doubt about it, all these whisperers and counterfeiters in the corners, although they try to get warm by crouching close to each other, but they tell me that their misery is a favor and distinction given to them by God, just as one beats the dog one likes best; that perhaps this misery is also a preparation, a proba tion, a training; that perhaps it is still more something that will one day be compensated and paid back with a tremendous interest in gold, nay in happiness. This they call 'Blessedness.' "

Further!

"They are now giving me to understand, that not only are they better men than the mighty, the lords of the earth, whose spittle they have got to lick (*not* out of fear, not at all out of fear! But because God ordains that one should honor all authority)—not only are they better men, but that they also have a 'better time,' at any rate, will one day have a 'better time.' But enough! Enough! I can endure it no longer. Bad air! Bad air! These workshops *where ideals are manufactured*—verily they reek with the crassest lies."

Nay. Just one minute! You are saying nothing about the masterpieces of these virtuosos of black magic, who can produce whiteness, milk, and innocence out of any black you like: have you not noticed what a pitch of refinement is attained by their *chef d'œuvre,* their most audacious, subtle, ingenious, and lying artist-trick? Take care! These cellar-beasts, full of revenge and hate—what do they make, forsooth, out of their revenge and hate? Do you hear these words? Would you suspect, if you trusted only their words, that you are among men of resentment and nothing else?

"I understand, I prick my ears up again (ah! ah! ah! and I hold my nose). Now do I hear for the first time what they have said so often: 'We good, *we are the righteous*'—what they demand they call not revenge but 'the triumph of *righteousness*'; what they hate is not their enemy, no, they hate 'unrighteousness,' 'godlessness'; what they believe in and hope is not the hope of revenge, the intoxication of sweet revenge (—'sweeter than honey,' did Homer call it?), but the victory of God, of the *righteous God,* over the 'godless'; what is left for them to love in this world is not their brothers in hate, but their 'brothers in love,' as they say, all the good and righteous on the earth."

And how do they name that which serves them as a solace against all the troubles of life—the phantasmagoria of their anticipated future blessedness?

"How? Do I hear right? They call it 'the last judgment,' the advent of *their* kingdom, 'the kingdom of God'—but *in the meanwhile* they live 'in faith,' 'in love,' 'in hope.' "

Enough! Enough!

[FROM the First Essay in *The Genealogy of Morals,* trans. Horace B. Samuel, in *The Philosophy of Nietzsche,* N. Y.: Modern Library, 1927; slightly modified. Reprinted by permission of George Allen & Unwin Ltd. and The Macmillan Company.]

5

Christianity (see *Beyond Good and Evil,* Aphorisms 202, 203)

43. When one places life's center of gravity not in life but in the "beyond"—*in nothingness*—one deprives life of its center of gravity altogether. The great lie of personal immortality destroys all reason, everything natural in the instincts—whatever in the instincts is beneficient and life-promoting or guarantees a future now arouses mistrust. To live so that there is no longer any *sense* in living, that now becomes the "sense" of life. Why communal sense, why any further gratitude for descent and ancestors, why cooperate, trust, promote, and envisage any common welfare? Just as many "temptations," just as many distractions from the "right path"—*"one* thing is needful."

That everyone as an "immortal soul" has equal rank with everyone else, that in the totality of living beings the "salvation" of *every* single individual may claim eternal significance, that little prigs and three-quarter-mad men may have the conceit that the laws of nature are constantly broken for their sakes—such an intensification of every kind of selfishness into the infinite, into the *impertinent,* cannot be branded with too much contempt. And yet Christianity owes its triumph to this miserable flattery of personal vanity: it was precisely all the failures, all the rebellious-minded, all the less favored, the whole scum and refuse of humanity who were thus won over to it. The "salvation of the soul"—in plain language: "the world revolves around *me."*

The poison of the doctrine of "equal rights for all"—it was Christianity that spread it most fundamentally. Out of the most secret nooks of bad instincts, Christianity has waged war unto death against all sense of respect and feeling of distance between man and man, that is to say, against the *presupposition* of every elevation, of every growth of culture; out of the *ressentiment* of the masses it forged its chief weapon against *us,* against all that is noble, gay, high-minded on earth, against our happiness on earth. "Immortality" conceded to every Peter and Paul has so far been the greatest, the most malignant, attempt to assassinate *noble* humanity.

And let us not underestimate the calamity which crept out of Christianity into politics. Today nobody has the courage any longer for privileges, for masters' rights, for a sense of respect for oneself and one's peers—for a *pathos of distance*. Our politics is sick from this lack of courage.

The aristocratic outlook was undermined from the deepest under-world through the lie of the equality of souls; and if faith in the "prerogative of the majority" makes and *will make* revolutions—it is Christianity, beyond a doubt, it is *Christian* value judgments, that every revolution simply translates into blood and crime. Christianity is a rebellion of everything that crawls on the ground against that which has *height:* the evangel of the "lowly" makes low.

51.   That faith makes blessed under certain circumstances, that blessedness does not make of a fixed idea a *true* idea, that faith moves no mountains but *puts* mountains where there are none—a quick walk through a madhouse enlightens one sufficiently about this. *Not,* to be sure, a priest, for he denies instinctively that sickness is sickness, that madhouse is madhouse. Christianity *needs* sickness just as Greek culture needs a superabundance of health—to *make* sick is the true, secret purpose of the whole system of redemptive procedures constructed by the church. And the church itself—is it not the catholic madhouse as the ultimate ideal? The earth altogether as a madhouse?

The religious man, as the church wants him, is a typical decadent; the moment when a religious crisis overcomes a people is invariably marked by epidemics of the nerves; the "inner world" of the religious man looks exactly like the "inner world" of the overexcited and the exhausted; the "highest" states that Christianity has hung over man-kind as the value of all values are epileptoid forms—only madmen or great impostors have been pronounced holy by the church *in maiorem dei honorem*. I once permitted myself to designate the whole Christian repentance and redemption training (which today is best studied in England) as a methodically produced *folie circulaire*, as is proper, on soil prepared for it, that is to say, thoroughly morbid soil. Nobody is free to become a Christian: one is not "converted" to Christianity—one has to be sick enough for it.

We others who have the *courage* to be healthy and also to despise —how may we despise a religion which taught men to misunderstand the body! which does not want to get rid of superstitious belief in souls! which turns insufficient nourishment into something "meritori-ous"! which fights health as a kind of enemy, devil, temptation! which fancies that one can carry around a "perfect soul" in a cadaver of a body, and which therefore found it necessary to concoct a new con-ception of "perfection"—a pale, sickly, idiotic-enthusiastic character, so-called "holiness." Holiness—merely a series of symptoms of an impoverished, unnerved, incurably corrupted body.

The Christian movement, as a European movement, has been

from the start a collective movement of the dross and refuse elements of every kind (these want to get power through Christianity). It does *not* express the decline of a race, it is an aggregate of forms of decadence flocking together and seeking each other out from everywhere. It is *not,* as is supposed, the corruption of antiquity itself, of *noble* antiquity, that made Christianity possible. The scholarly idiocy which upholds such ideas even today cannot be contradicted harshly enough. At the very time when the sick, corrupt chandala strata in the whole *imperium* adopted Christianity, the *opposite type,* nobility, was present in its most beautiful and most mature form. The great number became master; the democratism of the Christian instincts *triumphed*. Christianity was not "national," not a function of a race—it turned to every kind of man who was disinherited by life, it had its allies everywhere. At the bottom of Christianity is the rancor of the sick, instinct directed *against* the healthy, *against* health itself. Everything that has turned out well, everything that is proud and prankish, beauty above all, hurts its ears and eyes. Once more I recall the inestimable words of Paul: "The *weak* things of the world, the *foolish* things of the world, the *base* and *despised* things of the world hath God chosen." This was the formula; *in hoc signo* decadence triumphed.

God on the cross—are the horrible secret thoughts behind this symbol not understood yet? All that suffers, all that is nailed to the cross, is *divine*. All of us are nailed to the cross, consequently *we* are divine. We alone are divine. Christianity was a victory, a nobler outlook perished of it—Christianity has been the greatest misfortune of mankind so far.

[FROM "The Antichrist" from *The Portable Nietzsche*, by Friedrich Nietzsche, edited by Walter Kaufmann, translated by Walter Kaufmann, copyright ©1954 by The Viking Press, copyright renewed ©1982 by Viking Penguin Inc. Used by permission of Viking Penguin, a division of Penguin Putnam Inc.]

6

Conscience

1.   The breeding of an animal that *can promise*—is not this just that very paradox of a task which nature has set itself in regard to man? Is not this the very problem of man? The fact that this problem has been to a great extent solved, must appear all the more phenomenal to one who can estimate at its full value that force of *forgetfulness* which works in opposition to it. . . . This very animal who finds it necessary to be forgetful, in whom, in fact, forgetfulness

represents a force and a form of *robust* health, has reared for himself an opposition-power, a memory, with whose help forgetfulness is, in certain instances, kept in check—in the cases, namely, where promises have to be made. How thoroughly, in order to be able to regulate the future in this way, . . . how thoroughly must man have first become *calculable, disciplined, necessitated* even for himself and his own conception of himself, that, like a man entering a promise, he could guarantee himself *as a future.*

2. This is simply the long history of the origin of *responsibility.* . . .

The proud knowledge of the extraordinary privilege of *responsibility,* the consciousness of this rare freedom, of this power over himself and over fate, has sunk right down to his innermost depths, and has become an instinct, a dominating instinct—what name will he give to it, to this dominating instinct, if he needs to have a word for it? But there is no doubt about it—the sovereign man calls it his *conscience.*

3. His conscience?—One apprehends at once that the idea "conscience," which is here seen in its supreme manifestation, supreme in fact to almost the point of strangeness, should already have behind it a long history and evolution. . . . As one may imagine, this primeval problem was not solved by exactly gentle answers and gentle means; perhaps there is nothing more awful and more sinister in the early history of man than his *system of mnemonics.* "Something is burnt in so as to remain in his memory: only that which never stops *hurting* remains in his memory." This is an axiom of the oldest (unfortunately also the longest) psychology in the world. . . . We Germans do certainly not regard ourselves as an especially cruel and hard-hearted nation, still less as an especially casual and happy-go-lucky one; but one has only to look at our old penal ordinances in order to realize what a lot of trouble it takes in the world to evolve a "nation of thinkers" (I mean: *the* European nation which exhibits at this very day the maximum of reliability, seriousness, bad taste, and positiveness, which has on the strength of these qualities a right to train every kind of European mandarin). These Germans employed terrible means to make for themselves a memory, to enable them to master their rooted plebeian instincts and the brutal crudity of those instincts: think of the old German punishments. . . .

4. But how is it that that other melancholy object, the consciousness of sin, the whole "bad conscience," came into the world? And it is here that we turn back to our genealogists of morals. For the

second time I say—or have I not said it yet?—that they are worth nothing. . . .

Have these current genealogists of morals ever allowed themselves to have even the vaguest notion, for instance, that the cardinal moral idea of "ought" originates from the very material idea of "owe"? Or that punishment developed as a *retaliation* absolutely independently of any preliminary hypothesis of the freedom or determination of the will?—And this to such an extent, that a *high* degree of civilization was always first necessary for the animal man to begin to make those much more primitive distinctions of "intentional," "negligent," "accidental," "responsible," and their contraries, and apply them in the assessing of punishment. . . . Throughout the longest period of human history punishment was *never* based on the responsibility of the evil-doer for his action, and was consequently *not* based on the hypothesis that only the guilty should be punished—on the contrary, punishment was inflicted in those days for the same reason that parents punish their children even nowadays, out of anger at an injury that they have suffered, an anger that vents itself mechanically on the author of the injury—but this anger is kept in bounds and modified through the idea that every injury has somewhere or other its *equivalent* price, and can really be paid off, even though it be by means of pain to the author. Whence is it that this ancient deep-rooted and now perhaps ineradicable idea has drawn its strength, this idea of an equivalency between injury and pain? I have already revealed its origin, in the contractual relationship between *creditor* and *ower,* that is as old as the existence of legal right at all, and in its turn points back to the primary forms of purchase, sale, barter, and trade.

5. The realization of these contractual relations excites, of course (as would be already expected from our previous observations), a great deal of suspicion and opposition towards the primitive society that made or sanctioned them. In this society promises will be made; in this society the object is to provide the promiser with a memory; in this society, so may we suspect, there will be full scope for hardness, cruelty, and pain: the "ower," in order to induce credit in his promise of repayment, in order to give a guarantee of the earnestness and sanctity of his promise, in order to drill into his own conscience the duty, the solemn duty, of repayment, will, by virtue of a contract with his creditor to meet the contingency of his not paying, pledge something that he still possesses, something that he still has in his power, for instance, his life or his wife, or his freedom or his body.

. . . But especially has the creditor the power of inflicting on the body of the owner all kinds of pain and torture—the power, for instance, of cutting off from it an amount that appeared proportionate to the greatness of the debt—this point of view resulted in the universal prevalence at an early date of precise schemes of valuation, frequently horrible in the minuteness and meticulosity of their application, *legally* sanctioned schemes of valuation for individual limbs and parts of the body. . . . Thanks to the punishment of the "ower," the creditor participates in the rights of the masters. At last he too, for once in a way, attains the edifying consciousness of being able to despise and ill-treat a creature—as an "inferior"—or at any rate of *seeing* him being despised and ill-treated, in case actual power of punishment, the administration of punishment, has already become transferred to the "authorities." The compensation consequently consists in a claim on cruelty and a right to draw thereon.

6.   It is then in *this* sphere of the law of contract that we find the cradle of the whole moral world of the ideas of "guilt," "conscience," "duty," the "sacredness of duty"—their commencement, like the commencement of all great things in the world, is thoroughly and continuously saturated with blood. And should we not add that this world has never really lost a certain savor of blood and torture (not even in old Kant: the categorical imperative reeks of cruelty). It was in this sphere likewise that there was first formed that sinister and perhaps now indissoluble association of the ideas of "guilt" and "suffering." To put the question yet again, why can suffering be a compensation for "owing"?—Because the *infliction* of suffering produces the highest degree of happiness, because the injured party will get in exchange for his loss (including his vexation at his loss) an extraordinary counter-pleasure: the *infliction* of suffering—a real *feast,* something that, as I have said, was all the more appreciated the greater the paradox created by the rank and social status of the creditor. . . . In my opinion it is repugnant to the delicacy, and still more to the hypocrisy of tame domestic animals (that is, modern men; that is, ourselves) to realise with all their energy the extent to which *cruelty* constituted the great joy and delight of ancient man, was an ingredient which seasoned nearly all his pleasures, and conversely the extent of the naïveté and innocence with which he manifested his need for cruelty, when he actually made as a matter of principle "disinterested malice" (or, to us Spinoza's expression, the *sympathia malevolens*) into a *normal* characteristic of man—as consequently something to which the conscience says a hearty *yes.* . . .

The sight of suffering does one good, the infliction of suffering does one more good—this is a hard maxim, but none the less a fundamental maxim, old, powerful, and "human, all-too-human" . . .

[FROM the Second Essay in *The Genealogy of Morals,* trans. Horace B. Samuel, in *The Philosophy of Nietzsche,* slightly modified.]

7

Art

821. *Pessimism in art?*—The artist gradually learns to like for their own sake those means that bring about the state of aesthetic elation; extreme delicacy and glory of color, definite delineation, quality of tone; distinctness where in normal conditions distinctness is absent. All distinct things, all nuances, in so far as they recall extreme degrees of power that give rise to intoxication, kindle this feeling of intoxication by association—the effect of works of art is the excitation of the state that creates art, of aesthetic intoxication.

The essential feature of art is its power of perfecting existence, its production of perfection and plenitude; art is essentially the affirmation, the blessing, and the deification of existence. . . . What does a pessimistic art signify? Is it not a contradiction?—Yes.—Schopenhauer is in error when he makes certain works of art serve the purpose of pessimism. Tragedy does not teach "resignation." . . . To represent terrible and questionable things is, in itself, the sign of an instinct of power and magnificence in the artist; he doesn't fear them. . . . There is no such thing as a pessimistic art. . . . Art affirms. Job affirms. But Zola? and the Goncourts?—the things they show us are ugly; their reason, however, for showing them to us is their love of ugliness. . . . I don't care what you say! You simply deceive yourselves if you think otherwise.—What a relief Dostoyevsky is!

851. What is tragic?—Again and again I have pointed to the great misunderstanding of Aristotle in maintaining that the tragic emotions were the two depressing emotions—fear and pity. Had he been right, tragedy would be an art unfriendly to life: it would have been necessary to caution people against it as against something generally harmful and suspicious. Art, otherwise the great stimulus of life, the great intoxicant of life, the great will to life, here became a tool of decadence, the handmaiden of pessimism and ill-health (for to suppose, as Aristotle supposed, that by exciting these emotions we thereby purge people of them, is simply an error). Something

that habitually excites fear or pity, disorganizes, weakens, and discourages: and supposing Schopenhauer were right in thinking that tragedy taught resignation (*i.e.* a meek renunciation of happiness, hope, and of the will to live), this would presuppose an art in which art itself was denied. Tragedy would then constitute a process of dissolution; the instinct of life would destroy itself in the instinct of art. Christianity, Nihilism, tragic art, physiological decadence; these things were supposed to be linked, they were supposed to preponderate together and to assist each other onwards—downwards. . . . Tragedy would thus be a symptom of decline.

This theory may be refuted in the most cold-blooded way, namely, by measuring the effect of tragic emotion by means of a dynamometer. The result would be a fact that only the bottomless falsity of a doctrinaire could misunderstand: that tragedy is a tonic. If Schopenhauer refuses to see the truth here, if he regards general depression as a tragic condition, if he would have informed the Greeks that they did not firmly possess the highest principles of life: it is only owing to his *parti pris,* to the need of consistency in his system, to the dishonesty of the doctrinaire—that dreadful dishonesty which step for step corrupted the whole psychology of Schopenhauer (he who had arbitrarily and almost violently misunderstood genius, art itself. morality, pagan religion, beauty, knowledge, and almost everything).

[FROM *The Will to Power,* trans. Anthony M. Ludovici, *op cit.*]

FURTHER READING

DESCARTES

For further study of Descartes' philosophy, see Leon Roth, *Descartes' Discourse on Method*, Oxford, U.K.: Clarendon Press, 1937; Albert G. A. Balz, *Descartes and the Modern Mind*, New Haven, Conn.: Yale University Press, 1952; L. J. Beck, *The Method of Descartes*, Oxford, U.K.: Clarendon Press, 1952; Willis Doney, ed., *Descartes: A Collection of Critical Essays*, Garden City, N.Y.: Anchor Books, 1967; Anthony Kenny, *Descartes: A Study of His Philosophy*, New York: Random House, 1968; Harry Frankfurt, *Demons, Dreamers, and Madmen: The Defense of Reason in Descartes' Meditations*, Indianapolis: Bobbs-Merrill, 1970; Hiram Caton, *The Origin of Subjectivity*, New Haven, Conn.: Yale University Press, 1973; Brian E. O'Neil, *Epistemological Direct Realism in Descartes' Philosophy*, Albuquerque: University of New Mexico Press, 1974; E. M. Curley, *Descartes Against the Skeptics*, Cambridge, Mass.: Harvard University Press, 1978; Michael Hooker, *Descartes: Critical and Interpretative Essays*, Baltimore: The Johns Hopkins University Press, 1978; Bernard Williams, *Descartes: The Project of Pure Inquiry*, Harmondsworth, U.K.: Penguin, 1978; Margaret Dauler Wilson, *Descartes*, London: Routledge and Kegan Paul, 1978; Richard H. Popkin, *The History of Skepticism from Erasmus to Spinoza*, Berkeley: University of California Press, 1979; Stephen Gaukroger, *Descartes: Philosophy, Mathematics and Physics*, Totowa, N.J.: Barnes and Noble, 1980; Desmond M. Clarke, *Descartes' Philosophy of Science*, University Park: Pennsylvania State University Press, 1982; Martial Gueroult, *Descartes' Philosophy Interpreted According to the Order of Reasons*, trans. Roger Ariew, Minneapolis: University of Minnesota Press, 1984–85; Marjorie Grene, *Descartes*, Minneapolis: University of Minnesota Press, 1985; Philip J. Davis and Reuben Hersh, *Descartes' Dream: The World According to Mathematics*, New York: Harcourt, Brace, Jovanovich, 1986; Amélie Oksenberg Rorty, *Essays on Descartes' Meditations*, Berkeley: University of California Press, 1986; Stephen Gaukroger, *Cartesian Logic: An Essay on Descartes's Conception of Inference*, Oxford, U.K.: Oxford University Press, 1989; Steven M. Nadler, *Arnauld and the Cartesian Philosophy of Ideas*, Princeton, N.J.: Princeton University

Press, 1989; John P. Carriero, *Descartes and the Autonomy of Human Under-standing*, New York: Garland, 1990; Nicholas Jolley, *The Light of the Soul: Theories of Ideas in Leibniz, Malebranche, and Descartes*, Oxford, U.K.: Claren-don Press, 1990; Emily R. Grosholz, *Cartesian Method and the Problem of Re-duction*, Oxford, U.K.: Clarendon Press, 1991; John Foster, *The Immaterial Self: A Defense of the Cartesian Dualist Conception of the Mind*, London: Rout-ledge, 1991; Daniel Garber, *Descartes' Metaphysical Physics*, Chicago: Uni-versity of Chicago Press, 1992; George Dicker, *Descartes: An Analytical and Historical Introduction*, New York: Oxford University Press, 1993; Stephen Voss, ed., *Essays on the Philosophy and Science of René Descartes*, New York: Oxford University Press, 1993; John Cottingham, ed., *Reason, Will, and Sensation: Studies in Descartes's Metaphysics*, Oxford, U.K.: Clarendon Press, 1994; Margaret J. Osler, *Divine Will and the Mechanical Philosophy: Gassendi and Descartes on Contingency and Necessity in the Created World*, Cambridge, U.K.: Cambridge University Press, 1994; Roger Ariew and Marjorie Grene, eds., *Descartes and His Contemporaries: Meditations, Objections, and Replies*, Chicago: University of Chicago Press, 1995; Stephen Gaukroger, *Descartes: An Intellectual Biography*, Oxford, U.K.: Clarendon Press, 1995; Dennis L. Sepper, *Descartes's Imagination: Proportion, Images, and the Activity of Thinking*, Berkeley: University of California Press, 1996; John W. Yolton, *Perception and Reality: A History from Descartes to Kant*, Ithaca, N.Y.: Cornell University Press, 1996; Genevieve Rodis-Lewis, *Descartes: His Life and Thought*, trans. Jane Marie Todd, Ithaca, N.Y.: Cornell University Press, 1998; Marleen Rozemond, *Descartes's Dualism*, Cambridge, Mass.: Harvard University Press, 1998; Thomas C. Vinci, *Cartesian Truth*, New York: Oxford University Press, 1998; Jean-Luc Marion, *On Descartes' Metaphysical Prism: The Constitution and the Limits of Onto-Theo-logy in Cartesian Thought*, trans. Jeffrey L. Kosky, Chicago: University of Chicago Press, 1999; Jorge Secada, *Cartesian Metaphysics: The Late Scholastic Origins of Modern Philosophy*, Cambridge, U.K.: Cambridge University Press, 2000; Denis Des Chene, *Spirits and Clocks: Machine and Organism in Descartes*, Ithaca, N.Y.: Cornell University Press, 2001; Daniel Garber, *Descartes Em-bodied: Reading Cartesian Philosophy through Cartesian Science*, Cambridge, U.K.: Cambridge University Press, 2001.

PASCAL

For further discussion of Pascal's philosophy, see the essay by Henry Rogers on the "Genius and Writings of Pascal" in O. W. Wright's transla-tion of *The Thoughts, Letters, and Opuscules*, Boston: Houghton Mifflin, 1888;

Clement C. J. Webb, *Pascal's Philosophy of Religion,* Oxford: Clarendon Press, 1929; Morris Bishop, *Pascal: The Life of Genius,* New York: Reynal and Hitchcock, 1936 (a very illuminating biography); Emile Cailliet, *The Clue to Pascal,* Philadelphia: Westminster Press, 1943; Henri Lefebvre, *Pascal,* 2 vols., Paris: Nagel, 1949, 1954; Ernest Mortimer, *Blaise Pascal: The Life and Work of a Realist,* London: Methuen, 1959; John Broome, *Pascal,* London: Edward Arnold, 1965; Patricia Topliss, *The Rhetoric of Pascal,* Leicester: Leicester University Press, 1966; J. Cruickshank, "Knowledge and Belief in Pascal's Apology," in *Studies Presented to H. W. Lawton,* J. C. Ireson et al., eds., Manchester: Manchester University Press, 1968; Jan Miel, *Pascal and Theology,* Baltimore: The Johns Hopkins University Press, 1969; Maria Vamos, *Pascal's Pensées and the Enlightenment: The Roots of a Misunderstanding,* Geneva: Studies in Voltaire and the Eighteenth Century, 1972; Charles S. MacKenzie, *Pascal's Anguish and Joy,* New York: Philosophical Library, 1973; Roger Hazelton, *Blaise Pascal: The Genius of His Thought,* Philadelphia: Westminster Press, 1974; A.W.S. Baird, *Studies in Pascal's Ethics,* The Hague: M. Nijhoff, 1975; John Barker, *Strange Contrarieties: Pascal in England During the Age of Reason,* Montreal: McGill-Queen's University Press, 1975; Hugh M. Davidson, *The Origins of Certainty: Means and Meanings in Pascal's Pensées,* Chicago: University of Chicago Press, 1979; Robert Nelson, *Pascal: Adversary and Advocate,* Cambridge, Mass.: Harvard University Press, 1981; Hugh M. Davidson, *Blaise Pascal,* Twayne's World Author Series, Boston: G. K. Hall, 1983; Nicholas Rescher, *Pascal's Wager: A Study of Practical Reasoning in Philosophical Theology,* Notre Dame, Ind.: University of Notre Dame Press, 1985; Francis X. J. Coleman, *Neither Angel nor Beast: The Life and Work of Blaise Pascal,* New York: Routledge and Kegan Paul, 1986; Sara Melzer, *Discourses of the Fall: A Study of Pascal's Pensées,* Berkeley: University of California Press, 1986; Norman Buford, *Portraits of Thought: Knowledge, Methods, and Styles in Pascal,* Columbus: Ohio State University Press, 1988; Richard Paris, *Pascal's Letters Provinciales: A Study in Polemic Persuasion,* Oxford, U.K.: Clarendon Press, 1989; Martin Warner, *Philosophical Finesse: Studies in the Art of Rational Persuasion,* Oxford, U.K.: Clarendon Press, 1989; Thomas V. Morris, *Making Sense of It All: Pascal and the Meaning of Life,* Grand Rapids, Mich.: W. B. Eerdmans, 1992; Charles Ruhla, *The Physics of Chance: from Blaise Pascal to Niels Bohr,* trans. G. Barton, Oxford, U.K.: Oxford University Press, 1992; Hugh M. Davidson, *Pascal and the Arts of the Mind,* Cambridge, U.K.: Cambridge University Press, 1993; Nicholas Hammond, *Playing with Truth: Language and the Human Condition in Pascal's Pensées,* Oxford, U.K.: Clarendon Press, 1994; Jeff Jordan, *Gambling on God: Essays on Pascal's Wager,* Lanham, Md.: Rowman and Littlefield, 1994; David Wetsel, *Pascal and Disbelief: Catechesis and Conversion in the Pensées,* Washington, D.C.: Catholic University of America Press, 1994; Donald Adamson, *Blaise Pascal: Mathematician, Physicist, and Thinker about God,* Basingstoke, U.K.: Macmillan Press, 1995; John R. Cole, *Pascal: The Man and His Two Loves,* New York: New York University Press, 1995; Leszek Kolakowski, *God Owes Us Nothing: A Brief Remark on Pascal's Religion and on the Spirit of Jansenism,* Chicago: University of Chicago Press, 1995; José R. Maia Neto, *The Christianization of Pyrrhonism: Scepticism and Faith in Pascal, Kierkegaard, and Shestov,* Dordrecht, Neth.: Kluwer Academic Publishers, 1995; Stephen C. Bold, *Pascal Geometer: Discovery and Invention in Seventeenth-Century France,* Geneva: Librairie Droz, 1996; Richard Lockwood, *The Reader's Figure: Epideictic Rhetoric in Plato, Aristotle, Bossuet, Racine and Pascal,* Geneva: Librairie Droz, 1996; Marvin R. O'Connell, *Blaise Pascal: Reasons of the Heart,* Grand Rapids, Mich.: W. B. Eerdmans, 1997; Ben Rogers, *Pascal,* New York: Routledge, 1999.

SPINOZA

For general studies of Spinoza's philosophy, see Sir Frederick Pollock, *Spinoza,* London: C. Kegan Paul, 1880; Richard P. McKeon, *The Philosophy of Spinoza: The Unity of His Thought,* New York: Longmans, Green and Co., 1928; Leon Roth, *Spinoza,* London: Allyn & Unwin, 1929; Harry Austryn Wolfson, *The Philosophy of Spinoza: Unfolding the Latent Processes of His Reasoning,* Cambridge, Mass., Harvard University Press, 1934; H. F. Hallett, *Benedict de Spinoza: The Elements of His Philosophy,* London: University of London, Athlone Press, 1957; Stuart Hampshire, *Spinoza,* rev. ed., Baltimore: Penguin, 1962; S. Paul Kashap, *Studies in Spinoza: Critical and Interpretive Essays,* Berkeley: University of California Press, 1972; Errol E. Harris, *Salvation from Despair: A Reappraisal of Spinoza's Philosophy,* The Hague: M. Nijhoff, 1973; Marjorie Grene, ed., *Spinoza: A Collection of Essays,* Garden City, N.Y.: Anchor Books, 1973; Eugene Freeman and Maurice Mandelbaum, eds., *Spinoza: Essays in Interpretation,* La Salle, Ill.: Open Court, 1975; Robert W. Shahan and J. I. Biro, *Spinoza: New Perspectives,* Norman: University of Oklahoma, 1978; Richard Kennington, ed., *The Philosophy of Baruch Spinoza,* Washington, D.C.: Catholic University of America Press, 1980; R. J. Delahunty, *Spinoza,* London: Routledge and Kegan Paul, 1985; Roger Scruton, *Spinoza,* Oxford, U.K.: Oxford University Press, 1986; Henry E. Allison, *Benedict de Spinoza: An Introduction,* rev. ed., New Haven, Conn.: Yale University Press, 1987; Gilles Deleuze, *Spinoza, Practical Philosophy,* trans. Robert Hurley, San Francisco: City Lights Books,

1988; Alan Donagan, *Spinoza,* New York: Harvester Wheatsheaf, 1988; Yirmiyahu Yovel, *Spinoza and Other Heretics,* Princeton, N.J.: Princeton University Press, 1989; Gilles Deleuze, *Expressionism in Philosophy: Spinoza,* trans. Martin Joughin, New York: Zone Books, 1990; Errol E. Harris, *Spinoza's Philosophy: An Outline,* Atlantic Highlands, N.J.: Humanities Press International, 1992; Graeme Hunter, ed., *Spinoza: The Enduring Questions,* Toronto: University of Toronto Press, 1994; Errol E. Harris, *The Substance of Spinoza,* Atlantic Highlands, N.J.: Humanities Press International, 1995; Don Garrett, ed., *The Cambridge Companion to Spinoza,* Cambridge, U.K.: Cambridge University Press, 1996; Genevieve Lloyd, *Routledge Philosophy Guidebook to Spinoza and* The Ethics, London: Routledge, 1996; Tom Rubens, *Spinozan Power in a Naturalistic Perspective and Other Essays,* London: Janus, 1996; Warren Montag and Ted Stolze, eds., *The New Spinoza,* Minneapolis: University of Minnesota Press, 1997; Paul Strathern, *Spinoza in 90 Minutes,* Chicago: Ivan Dee, 1998; Moira Gatens and Genevieve Lloyd, *Collective Imaginings: Spinoza, Past and Present,* London: Routledge, 1999.

For studies of Spinoza's metaphysics, see H. F. Hallett, *Aeternitas: A Spinozistic Study,* Oxford, U.K.: Clarendon Press, 1930; Elmer E. Powell, *Spinoza and Religion: A Study of Spinoza's Metaphysics and of His Particular Utterances in regard to Religion, with a View to Determining the Significance of His Thought for Religion and Incidentally His Personal Attitude toward It,* Boston: Chapman and Grimes, 1941; Henry Alonzo Myers, *The Spinoza-Hegel Paradox: A Study of the Choice between Traditional Idealism and Systematic Pluralism,* Ithaca, N.Y.: Cornell University Press, 1944; Ruth Lydia Saw, *The Vindication of Metaphysics: A Study in the Philosophy of Spinoza,* London: Macmillan, 1951; H. F. Hallett, *Creation, Emanation and Salvation: A Spinozistic Study,* The Hague: M. Nijhoff, 1962; Edwin M. Curley, *Spinoza's Metaphysics: An Essay in Interpretation,* Cambridge, Mass.: Harvard University Press, 1969; Antonio Negri, *The Savage Anomaly: The Power of Spinoza's Metaphysics and Politics,* trans. Michael Hardt, Minneapolis: University of Minnesota Press, 1991; Etienne Balibar, *Spinoza and Politics,* trans. Peter Snowdon, London: Verso, 1998; James Thomas, *Intuition and Reality: A Study of the Attributes of Substance in the Absolute Idealism of Spinoza,* Aldershot, Hants, U.K.: Ashgate, 1999.

For studies of Spinoza's ethics, see Harold H. Joachim, *A Study of the Ethics of Spinoza,* Oxford, U.K.: Clarendon Press, 1901; Alexander Shanks, *An Introduction to Spinoza's Ethic,* London: Macmillan, 1938; David Bidney, *The Psychology and Ethics of Spinoza: A Study in the History and Logic of Ideas,* New Haven, Conn.: Yale University Press, 1940; Celestine J. Sullivan, Jr., *Critical and Historical Reflections on Spinoza's "Ethics,"* Berkeley: University of California Press, 1958; Stuart Hampshire, *Two Theories of Morality,* Oxford, U.K.: Published for the British Academy by Oxford University Press, 1977; Alan Hart, *Spinoza's Ethics, Part I and II: A Platonic Commentary,* Leiden, Neth.: E. J. Brill, 1983; Jonathan Bennett, *A Study of Spinoza's Ethics,* Indianapolis, Ind.: Hackett Pub. Co., 1984; Edwin M. Curley, *Behind the Geometrical Method: A Reading of Spinoza's Ethics,* Princeton, N.J.: Princeton University Press, 1988; Lucia Lermond, *The Form of Man: Human Essence in Spinoza's Ethic,* Leiden, Neth.: E. J. Brill, 1988; Genevieve Lloyd, *Part of Nature: Self-Knowledge in Spinoza's* Ethics, Ithaca, N.Y.: Cornell University Press, 1994.

For studies of Spinoza's epistemology, see G.H.R. Parkinson, *Spinoza's Theory of Knowledge,* Oxford, U.K.: Clarendon Press, 1954; Thomas Carson Mark, *Spinoza's Theory of Truth,* New York: Columbia University Press, 1972; Paul Wienpahl, *The Radical Spinoza,* New York: New York University Press, 1979; Herman De Djin, *Spinoza: The Way to Wisdom,* West Lafayette, Ind.: Purdue University Press, 1996.

For studies of Spinoza and religion, see Joseph Ratner, *Spinoza on God,* New York: Holt, 1930; S. M. Melamed, *Spinoza and Buddha: Visions of a Dead God,* Chicago: University of Chicago Press, 1933; Leo Strauss, *Spinoza's Critique of Religion,* trans. E. M. Sinclair, New York: Schocken Books, 1965; Richard Mason, *The God of Spinoza: A Philosophy,* Cambridge, U.K.: Cambridge University Press, 1997; Steven M. Nadler, *Spinoza's Heresy: Immortality and the Jewish Mind,* New York: Oxford University Press, 2002.

See also Lewis Browne, *Blessèd Spinoza: A Biography of the Philosopher,* New York: Macmillan, 1932 (an interesting biography). Other biographies include Rudolf Kayser, *Spinoza, Portrait of a Spiritual Hero,* intro. Albert Einstein, trans. Amy Allen and Maxim Newmark, New York: Philosophical Library, 1946; Abraham Wolfson, *Spinoza: A Life of Reason,* 2d. ed., enl., New York: Philosophical Library, 1969; Dan Levin, *Spinoza, the Young Thinker Who Destroyed the Past,* New York: Weybright and Talley, 1970; Margaret Gullan-Whur, *Within Reason: A Life of Spinoza,* London: Jonathan Cape, 1998; Steven M. Nadler, *Spinoza: A Life,* Cambridge, U.K.: Cambridge University Press, 1999. See Lewis Samuel Feuer, *Spinoza and the Rise of Liberalism,* Boston: Beacon Press, 1958 (a challenging treatment of Spinoza's political significance).

For other studies of Spinoza and political thought, see George L. Kline, ed. and trans., *Spinoza in Soviet Philosophy: A Series of Essays,* London: Routledge and Kegan Paul, 1952; Robert J. McShea, *The Political Philosophy of Spinoza,* New York: Columbia University Press, 1968; Steven B. Smith, *Spinoza, Liberalism, and the Question of Jewish Identity,* New Haven, Conn.: Yale University Press, 1997; Pierre Macherey, *In a Materialist Way: Selected Essays,* ed. Warren Montag, trans. Ted Stolze, London: Verso, 1998.

Other studies on miscellaneous subjects include Gail Belaief, *Spinoza's Philosophy of Law,* The Hague: Mouton, 1971; Jerome Neu, *Emotion, Thought, and Therapy: A Study of Hume and Spinoza and the Relationship of Philosophical Theories of the Emotions to Psychological Theories of Therapy,* Berkeley: University of California Press, 1977; James Collins, *Spinoza on Nature,* Carbondale: Southern Illinois University Press, 1984; Marjorie Grene and Debra Nails, eds., *Spinoza and the Sciences,* Dordrecht, Neth.: Kluwer Academic Publishers, 1986; Christopher Norris, *Spinoza and the Origins of Modern Critical Theory,* Oxford, U.K.: Blackwell, 1991; Michael Della Rocca, *Representation and the Mind-Body Problem in Spinoza,* New York: Oxford University Press, 1996; Warren Montag, *Bodies, Masses, Power: Spinoza and His Contemporaries,* London: Verso, 1999; Jonathan I. Israel, *Radical Enlightenment: Philosophy and the Making of Modernity, 1650–1750,* Oxford, U.K.: Oxford University Press, 2001.

LEIBNIZ

For works about Leibniz's philosophy, see Bertrand Russell, *A Critical Exposition of the Philosophy of Leibniz,* London: G. Allen, 1900, 2d. ed., 1937; H.W.B. Joseph, *Lectures on the Philosophy of Leibniz,* Oxford, U.K.: Clarendon Press, 1949; R. W. Meyer, *Leibniz and the Seventeenth-Century Revolution,* trans. J. P. Stern, Cambridge, U.K.: Bowes and Bowes, 1952; Ruth Lydia Saw, *Leibniz,* Baltimore: Penguin, 1954; R. M. Yost, *Leibniz and Philosophical Analysis,* Berkeley: University of California Press, 1954; Harry Frankfurt, ed., *Leibniz: A Collection of Critical Essays,* Garden City, N.Y: Anchor Books, 1972; Hidé Ishiguro, *Leibniz's Philosophy of Logic and Language,* Ithaca, N.Y.: Cornell University Press, 1972; C. D. Broad, *Leibniz: An Introduction,* Cambridge, U.K.: Cambridge University Press, 1975; Mark Kulstad, ed., *Essays on the Philosophy of Leibniz,* Houston: Rice University Series 63, 1978; Nicholas Rescher, *Leibniz: An Introduction to His Philosophy,* Totowa, N.J.: Rowman and Littlefield, 1979; R. S. Woolhouse, ed., *Leibniz, Metaphysics, and the Philosophy of Science,* New York: Oxford University Press, 1981; Michael Hooker, ed., *Leibniz: Critical and Interpretative Essays,* Minneapolis: University of Minnesota Press, 1982; Diogenes Allen, *Mechanical Explanations and the Ultimate Origin of the Universe according to Leibniz,* Wiesbaden, Ger.: Steiner, 1983; Stuart C. Brown, *Leibniz,* Brighton, Sussex, U.K.: Harvester Press, 1984; George MacDonald Ross, *Leibniz,* Oxford, U.K.: Oxford University Press, 1984; G.H.R. Parkinson, *Logic and Reality in Leibniz's Metaphysics,* New York: Garland, 1985; E. J. Aiton, *Leibniz: A Biography,* Bristol, U.K.: Hilger,

1985; Kathleen Okruhlik and James Brown, eds., *The Natural Philosophy of Leibniz*, Dordrecht, Neth.: Kluwer Academic Publishers, 1985; Marcel Dascal, *Leibniz, Language, Signs, and Thought: A Collection of Essays*, Amsterdam: J. Benjamins, 1986; Benson Mates, *The Philosophy of Leibniz: Metaphysics and Language*, New York: Oxford University Press, 1986; Olga Pombo, *Leibniz and the Problem of a Universal Language*, Münster: Nodus Publikationen, 1987; Nicholas Rescher, ed., *Leibnizian Inquiries: A Group of Essays*, Lanham, Md.: University Press of America, 1988; Catherine Wilson, *Leibniz's Metaphysics: A Historical and Comparative Study*, Manchester, U.K.: Manchester University Press, 1989; François Duchesneau, *Leibniz on the Principle of Continuity*, Montréal: Université de Montréal, Faculté des arts et des sciences, 1989; Clifford Brown, *Leibniz and Strawson: A New Essay in Descriptive Metaphysics*, Munich: Philosophia, 1990; Nicholas Jolley, *The Light of the Soul: Theories of Ideas in Leibniz, Malebranche, and Descartes*, Oxford, U.K.: Clarendon Press, 1990; R. C. Sleigh, *Leibniz and Arnauld: A Commentary on Their Correspondence*, New Haven, Conn.: Yale University Press, 1990; Margaret Dauler Wilson, *Leibniz' Doctrine of Necessary Truth*, New York: Garland, 1990; Mark Kulstad, *Leibniz on Apperception, Consciousness and Reflection*, Munich: Philosophia, 1991; Massimo Mugnai, *Leibniz's Theory of Relations*, Stuttgart: F. Steiner, 1992; Gilles Deleuze, *The Fold: Leibniz and the Baroque*, trans. Tom Conley, Minneapolis: University of Minnesota Press, 1993; R. S. Woolhouse, *Descartes, Spinoza, Leibniz: The Concept of Substance in Seventeenth-Century Metaphysics*, London: Routledge, 1993; Robert Merrihew Adams, *Leibniz: Determinist, Theist, Idealist*, New York: Oxford University Press, 1994; R. S. Woolhouse, *Gottfried Wilhelm Leibniz: Critical Assessments*, London: Routledge, 1994; Allison P. Coudert, *Leibniz and the Kabbalah*, Dordrecht, Neth.: Kluwer Academic Publishers, 1995; Nicholas Jolley, ed., *The Cambridge Companion to Leibniz*, Cambridge, U.K.: Cambridge University Press, 1995; Donald Rutherford, *Leibniz and the Rational Order of Nature*, New York: Cambridge University Press, 1995; Laurence B. McCullough, *Leibniz on Individuals and Individuation: The Persistence of Premodern Ideas in Modern Philosophy*, Dordrecht, Neth.: Kluwer Academic Publishers, 1996; Ezio Vailati, *Leibniz and Clarke: A Study of Their Correspondence*, New York: Oxford University Press, 1997; Allison P. Coudert, Richard H. Popkin, and Gordon M. Weiner, *Leibniz, Mysticism, and Religion*, Dordrecht, Neth.: Kluwer Academic Publishers, 1998; Renato Cristin, *Heidegger and Leibniz: Reason and the Path*, trans. Gerald Parks, Boston: Kluwer Academic Publishers, 1998; Reginald Osburn Savage, *Real Alternatives, Leibniz's Metaphysics of Choice*, Dordrecht, Neth.: Kluwer Academic Publishers, 1998; Dionysios

A. Anapolitanos, *Leibniz: Representation, Continuity, and the Spatiotemporal,* Dordrecht, Neth.: Kluwer Academic Publishers, 1999; Stuart Brown, ed., *The Young Leibniz and His Philosophy, 1646–76,* Dordrecht, Neth.: Kluwer Academic Publishers, 1999; J. A. Cover and John O'Leary-Hawthorne, *Substance and Individuation in Leibniz,* Cambridge, U.K.: Cambridge University Press, 1999; Brandon Look, *Leibniz and the "Vinculum Substantiale,"* Stuttgart: F. Steiner, 1999; Martin Davis, *The Universal Computer: The Road from Leibniz to Turing,* New York: Norton, 2000; Catherine Wilson, ed., *Leibniz,* Aldershot, Hants, U.K.: Ashgate, 2001.

ROUSSEAU

An enormous amount has been written about Rousseau, and even the English bibliography is very large. Works to consult for further study of his thought include: Irving Babbitt, *Rousseau and Romanticism,* Boston: Houghton Mifflin Company, 1919; Alfred Cobban, *Rousseau and the Modern State,* London: G. Allen and Unwin, 1934; Leo Strauss, *Natural Right and History,* Chicago: University of Chicago Press, 1953; John W. Chapman, *Rousseau, Totalitarian or Liberal?,* New York: Columbia University Press, 1956; Ernst Cassirer, *The Question of Jean-Jacques Rousseau,* trans. Peter Gay, Bloomington: Indiana University Press, 1963; Bernard Bosanquet, *The Philosophical Theory of the State,* 4th ed., London: Macmillan, 1965; Roger D. Masters, *The Political Philosophy of Rousseau,* Princeton, N.J.: Princeton University Press, 1968; Joan McDonald, *Rousseau and the French Revolution, 1762–1791,* London: Athlone Press, 1968; Judith N. Shklar, *Men and Citizens: A Study of Rousseau's Social Theory,* Cambridge, U.K.: Cambridge University Press, 1969; Paul de Man, *Blindness and Insight,* New York: Oxford University Press, 1971; J. H. Huizinga, *Rousseau: The Self-made Saint,* New York: Grossman, 1976; Ramon M. Lemos, *Rousseau's Political Philosophy: An Exposition and Interpretation,* Athens: University of Georgia Press, 1977; Edward Duffy, *Rousseau in England,* Berkeley: University of California Press, 1979; Huntington Williams, *Rousseau and Romantic Autobiography,* Oxford, U.K.: Oxford University Press, 1983; James Miller, *Rousseau: Dreamer of Democracy,* New Haven, Conn.: Yale University Press, 1984; Joel Schwartz, *The Sexual Politics of Jean-Jacques Rousseau,* Chicago: University of Chicago Press, 1984; Carol Blum, *Rousseau and the Republic of Virtue: The Language of Politics in the French Revolution,* Ithaca, N.Y.: Cornell University Press, 1986; Christine Jane Carter, *Rousseau and the Problem of War,* New York: Garland, 1987; Asher Horowitz, *Rousseau, Nature, and History,* Toronto: University of Toronto Press, 1987; Thomas

M. Kavanagh, *Writing the Truth: Authority and Desire in Rousseau*, Berkeley: University of California Press, 1987; Christopher Kelly, *Rousseau's Exemplary Life: The Confessions as Political Philosophy*, Ithaca, N.Y.: Cornell University Press, 1987; Andrzej Rapaczynski, *Nature and Politics: Liberalism in the Philosophies of Hobbes, Locke, and Rousseau*, Ithaca, N.Y.: Cornell University Press, 1987; F. M. Barnard, *Self-direction and Political Legitimacy: Rousseau and Herder*, Oxford, U.K.: Clarendon Press, 1988; Peggy Kamuf, *Signature Pieces: On the Institution of Authorship*, Ithaca, N.Y.: Cornell University Press, 1988; Jean Starobinski, *Jean-Jacques Rousseau: Transparency and Obstruction*, trans. Arthur Goldhammer, Chicago: University of Chicago Press, 1988; Maurizio Viroli, *Jean-Jacques Rousseau and the "Well-ordered Society,"* trans. Derek Hanson, Chicago: University of Chicago Press, 1988; N.J.H. Dent, *Rousseau: An Introduction to His Psychological, Social, and Political Theory*, Oxford, U.K.: Blackwell, 1989; Arthur M. Melzer, *The Natural Goodness of Man: On the System of Rousseau's Thought*, Chicago: University of Chicago Press, 1990; Grace G. Roosevelt, *Reading Rousseau in the Nuclear Age*, Philadelphia: Temple University Press, 1990; Stanley Hoffmann and David P. Fidler, eds., *Rousseau on International Relations*, Oxford, U.K.: Clarendon Press, 1991; James F. Jones, *Rousseau's Dialogues: An Interpretive Essay*, Geneva: Droz, 1991; Richard Noble, *Language, Subjectivity, and Freedom in Rousseau's Moral Philosophy*, New York: Garland, 1991; Susan K. Jackson, *Rousseau's Occasional Autobiographies*, Columbus: Ohio State University Press, 1992; Daniel E. Cullen, *Freedom in Rousseau's Political Philosophy*, De Kalb: Northern Illinois University Press, 1993; Alessandro Ferrara, *Modernity and Authenticity: A Study in the Social and Ethical Thought of Jean-Jacques Rousseau*, Albany: State University of New York, 1993; Andrew Levine, *The General Will: Rousseau, Marx, Communism*, Cambridge, U.K.: Cambridge University Press, 1993; Joshua Mitchell, *Not by Reason Alone: Religion, History, and Identity in Early Modern Political Thought*, Chicago: University of Chicago Press, 1993; Zev M. Trachtenberg, *Making Citizens: Rousseau's Political Theory of Culture*, London: Routledge, 1993; Penny A. Weiss, *Gendered Community: Rousseau, Sex, and Politics*, New York: New York University Press, 1993; Mark Hulliung, *The Autocritique of Enlightenment: Rousseau and the Philosophes*, Cambridge, Mass.: Harvard University Press, 1994; Tracy B. Strong, *Jean-Jacques Rousseau: The Politics of the Ordinary*, Thousand Oaks, Calif.: Sage Publications, 1994; Linda M. G. Zerilli, *Signifying Woman: Culture and Chaos in Rousseau, Burke, and Mill*, Ithaca, N.Y.: Cornell University Press, 1994; Thomas McFarland, *Romanticism and the Heritage of Rousseau*, Oxford, U.K.: Clarendon Press, 1995; Michael O'Dea, *Jean-Jacques Rousseau: Music, Illusion, and Desire*, Basingstoke, U.K.: Macmillan, 1995; Dennis Porter, *Rousseau's Legacy: Emer-*

gence and Eclipse of the Writer in France, New York: Oxford University Press, 1995; Robert Wokler, *Rousseau,* Oxford, U.K.: Oxford University Press, 1995; Robert Wokler, ed., *Rousseau and Liberty,* Manchester, U.K.: Manchester University Press, 1995; Naaman Kessous, *Two French Precursors of Marxism: Rousseau and Fourier,* Aldershot, Hants, U.K.: Avebury, 1996; Mira Morgenstern, *Rousseau and the Politics of Ambiguity: Self, Culture, and Society,* University Park: Pennsylvania State University Press, 1996; Nicole Ferman, *Domesticating Passions: Rousseau, Woman, and Nation,* Hanover, N.H.: University Press of New England for Wesleyan University Press, 1997; Ruth W. Grant, *Hypocrisy and Integrity: Machiavelli, Rousseau, and the Ethics of Politics,* Chicago: University of Chicago Press, 1997; Timothy O'Hagan, *Jean-Jacques Rousseau and the Sources of the Self,* Aldershot, Hants, U.K.: Avebury, 1997; Clifford Orwin and Nathan Tarcov, eds., *The Legacy of Rousseau,* Chicago: University of Chicago Press, 1997; Peter V. Conroy, *Jean-Jacques Rousseau,* New York: Twayne Publishers, 1998; Bertil Friden, *Rousseau's Economic Philosophy: Beyond the Market of Innocents,* Dordrecht, Neth.: Kluwer Academic Publishers, 1998; Laurence D. Cooper, *Rousseau, Nature, and the Problem of the Good Life,* University Park: Pennsylvania State University Press, 1999; Gregory Dart, *Rousseau, Robespierre, and English Romanticism,* Cambridge, U.K.: Cambridge University Press, 1999; Michael Davis, *The Autobiography of Philosophy: Rousseau's* The Reveries of the Solitary Walker, Lanham, Md.: Rowman and Littlefield, 1999; Steven Johnston, *Encountering Tragedy: Rousseau and the Project of Democratic Order,* Ithaca, N.Y.: Cornell University Press, 1999; Christopher W. Morris, ed., *The Social Contract Theorists: Critical Essays on Hobbes, Locke, and Rousseau,* Lanham, Md.: Rowman and Littlefield, 1999; Margaret Ogrodnick, *Instinct and Intimacy: Political Philosophy and Autobiography in Rousseau,* Toronto: University of Toronto Press, 1999; Timothy O'Hagan, *Rousseau,* London: Routledge, 1999; Eugene Stelzig, *The Romantic Subject in Autobiography: Rousseau and Goethe,* Charlottesville: University Press of Virginia, 2000; James Swenson, *On Jean-Jacques Rousseau: Considered as One of the First Authors of the Revolution,* Stanford, Calif.: Stanford University Press, 2000; Elizabeth Rose Wingrove, *Rousseau's Republican Romance,* Princeton, N.J.: Princeton University Press, 2000; Tzvetan Todorov, *Frail Happiness: An Essay on Rousseau,* trans. John T. Scott and Robert D. Zaretsky, University Park: Pennsylvania State University Press, 2001.

The vexed and tangled question of Rousseau's personality, and the responsibility for the quarrels that alienated him from his distinguished contemporaries, is not of central importance here, but it is a hard subject to avoid in any consideration of his work. There seems no doubt that he was hypersensitive and developed a paranoid strain in his later life; it also appears that his close associates, such as Diderot and Grim, betrayed his confidence and attacked him viciously behind his back. The classic research on these personal relations, and defense of Rousseau, is Frederika Macdonald, *Jean-Jacques Rousseau: A New Criticism,* 2 vols., New York: Putnam, 1906 (cf. C. E. Vaughan on "Rousseau and His Enemies" in *Studies in the History of Political Philosophy before and after Rousseau,* A. G. Little, ed., Manchester, U.K.: The University Press, 1925). But on the Hume episode, see also Ernest C. Mossner, *The Forgotten Hume,* ch. 6, New York: Columbia University Press, 1954; and *The Life of David Hume,* ch. 35, London: Nelson, 1954. A full and interesting biography is Matthew Josephson, *Jean-Jacques Rousseau,* New York: Harcourt, Brace, 1931. Other biographies include F. C. Green, *Jean-Jacques Rousseau: A Critical Study of His Life and Writings,* Cambridge, U.K.: Cambridge University Press, 1955; Lester G. Crocker, *Jean-Jacques Rousseau,* 2 vols., New York: Macmillan, 1968–73; Maurice Cranston, *Jean-Jacques: The Early Life of Jean-Jacques Rousseau, 1712–1754,* London: A. Lane, 1983; *The Noble Savage: Jean-Jacques Rousseau, 1754–1762,* London: Penguin, 1993; and *The Solitary Self: Jean-Jacques Rousseau in Exile and Adversity,* Chicago: University of Chicago Press, 1997.

KANT

For introductions to Kant's thought, see Josiah Royce, *The Spirit of Modern Philosophy,* Lecture IV and Appendix B, Boston: Houghton Mifflin, 1892; H. J. Paton, *Kant's Metaphysic of Experience,* 2 vols., London: Macmillan, 1936; A. C. Ewing, *A Short Commentary on Kant's Critique of Pure Reason,* London: Methuen, 1938; T. D. Weldon, *Introduction to Kant's* Critique of Pure Reason, Oxford, U.K.: Clarendon Press, 1945; L. W. Beck, *Studies in the Philosophy of Kant,* Indianapolis, Ind.: Bobbs-Merrill, 1965; Jonathan Bennet, *Kant's Analytic,* Cambridge, U.K., Cambridge University Press, 1966; Robert Paul Wolff, ed., *Kant: A Collection of Critical Essays,* South Bend, Ind.: University of Notre Dame Press, 1967; Jonathan Bennet, *Kant's Dialectic,* Cambridge, U.K.: Cambridge University Press, 1974; T. E. Wilkerson, *Kant's* Critique of Pure Reason: *A Commentary for Students,* Oxford, U.K.: Oxford University Press, 1976; Ralph Walker, ed., *Kant on Pure Reason,* Oxford, U.K.: Oxford University Press, 1982; Henry Allison, *Kant's Transcendental Idealism: An Introduction and Defense,* New Haven, Conn.: Yale University Press, 1983; Hubert Schwyzer, *The Unity of Understanding: A Study in Kantian Problems,* Oxford, U.K.: Clarendon Press, 1990; Ruth F. Chadwick, *Kant Criticism from His Own to the Present Time,* London: Routledge, 1992; Robert Howell, *Kant's Transcendental Deduction: An Analysis of*

Main Themes in His Critical Philosophy, Dordrecht, Neth.: Kluwer Academic Publishers, 1992; R. M. Dancy, ed., *Kant and Critique: New Essays in Honor of W. H. Werkmeister,* Dordrecht, Neth.: Kluwer Academic Publishers, 1993; Dieter Henrich, *The Unity of Reason: Essays on Kant's Philosophy,* ed. Richard L. Velkley, trans. Jeffrey Edward, Cambridge, Mass.: Harvard University Press, 1994; Christopher Want and Andrzej Klimowski, *Kant for Beginners,* ed. Richard Appignanesi, Trumpington, U.K., Icon Books, 1996; Robin May Schott, ed., *Feminist Interpretations of Immanuel Kant,* University Park: Pennsylvania State University Press, 1997; Patricia Kitcher, ed., *Kant's* Critique of Pure Reason: *Critical Essays,* Lanham, Md.: Rowman and Littlefield, 1998; Ralph Walker, *Kant,* London: Routledge, 1999; Karl Ameriks, *Kant and the Fate of Autonomy: Problems in the Appropriation of the Critical Philosophy,* Cambridge, U.K.: Cambridge University Press, 2000; John Kemp, *The Philosophy of Kant,* South Bend, Ind.: St. Augustine's Press, 2000; Paul Abela, *Kant's Empirical Realism,* Oxford, U.K.: Oxford University Press, 2001; Predrag Cicovacki, *Kant's Legacy: Essays in Honor of Lewis White Beck,* Rochester, N.Y.: University of Rochester Press, 2001; Michelle Grier, *Kant's Doctrine of Transcendental Illusion,* Cambridge, U.K.: Cambridge University Press, 2001; Robert Hanna, *Kant and the Foundations of Analytic Philosophy,* Oxford, U.K.: Clarendon Press, 2001.

More advanced interpretations of the *First Critique* include Norman Kemp-Smith, *A Commentary to Kant's* Critique of Pure Reason, 2d. rev. ed., London: Macmillan, 1918, 1923; H. W. Cassirer, *Kant's First Critique,* London: Allen and Unwin, 1954; Robert Paul Wolff, *Kant's Theory of Mental Activity,* Cambridge, Mass., Harvard University Press, 1963; P. F. Strawson, *The Bounds of Sense: An Essay on Kant's* Critique of Pure Reason, London: Methuen, 1966; H. J. Paton, *Kant's Metaphysic of Experience: A Commentary on the First Half of the* Kritik der reinen Vernunft, New York: Humanities Press, 1970; Arthur Melnick, *Kant's Analogies of Experience,* Chicago: University of Chicago Press, 1973; L. W. Beck, ed., *Kant's Theory of Knowledge:* Selected Papers from the Third International Kant Congress, Dordrecht, Neth.: D. Reidel, 1974; John Sallis, *The Gathering of Reason,* Athens: Ohio University Press, 1980; J. N. Mohanty and Robert W. Shahan, eds., *Essays on Kant's* Critique of Pure Reason, Norman: University of Oklahoma Press, 1982; Robert B. Pippin, *Kant's Theory of Form: An Essay on the* Critique of Pure Reason, New Haven, Conn.: Yale University Press, 1982; Karl Aschenbrenner, *A Companion to Kant's* Critique of Pure Reason: *Transcendental Aesthetic and Analytic,* Lanham, Md.: University Press of America, 1983; Gordon Nagel, *The Structure of Experience: Kant's System of Principles,* Chicago: University of Chicago Press, 1983; Gilles Deleuze, *Kant's Critical Philosophy,* Minneapolis: University of Minnesota Press,

1984; Ermanno Bencivenga, *Kant's Copernican Revolution,* New York: Oxford University Press, 1987; Richard E. Aquila, *Matter in Mind: A Study of Kant's Transcendental Deduction,* Bloomington: Indiana University Press, 1989; Patricia Kitcher, *Kant's Transcendental Psychology,* New York: Oxford University Press, 1990; Wayne Waxman, *Kant's Model of the Mind: A New Interpretation of Transcendental Idealism,* Oxford, U.K.: Oxford University Press, 1991; Ruth F. Chadwick and Clive Cazeaux, eds., *Kant's* Critique of Pure Reason, London: Routledge, 1992; Klaus Reich, *The Completeness of Kant's Table of Judgments,* trans. Jane Kneller and Michael Losonsky, Stanford, Calif.: Stanford University Press, 1992; Susan Neiman, *The Unity of Reason: Rereading Kant,* New York: Oxford University Press, 1994; F. C. White, *Kant's First Critique and the Transcendental Deduction,* Aldershot, Hants, U.K.: Avebury, 1996; Predrag Cicovacki, *Anamorphosis: Kant on Knowledge and Ignorance,* Lanham, Md.: University Press of America, 1997; Andrew Cutrofello, *Imagining Otherwise: Metapsychology and the Analytic* A Posteriori, Evanston, Ill.: Northwestern University Press, 1997; J. Everet Green, *Kant's Copernican Revolution: The Transcendental Horizon,* Lanham, Md.: University Press of America, 1997; Martin Heidegger, *Phenomenological Interpretation of Kant's* Critique of Pure Reason, trans. Parvis Emad and Kenneth Maly, Bloomington: Indiana University Press, 1997; Rae Langton, *Kantian Humility,* Oxford, U.K.: Clarendon Press, 1998; Beatrice Longuesse, *Kant and the Capacity to Judge: Sensibility and Discursivity in the Transcendental Analytic of the* Critique of Pure Reason, trans. Charles T. Wolfe, Princeton, N.J.: Princeton University Press, 1998; Karl Ameriks, *Kant's Theory of Mind: An Analysis of the Paralogisms of Pure Reason,* Oxford, U.K.: Clarendon Press, 1999; James Van Cleve, *Problems from Kant,* New York: Oxford University Press, 1999; Arthur W. Collins, *Possible Experience: Understanding Kant's* Critique of Pure Reason, Berkeley: University of California Press, 1999; Nicholas Rescher, *Kant and the Reach of Reason: Studies in Kant's Theory of Rational Systematization,* Cambridge, U.K.: Cambridge University Press, 2000; Theodor Adorno, *Kant's Critique of Pure Reason,* ed. Rolf Tiedemann, trans. Rodney Livingstone, Cambridge, U.K.: Polity, 2001; Robert Greenberg, *Kant's Theory of A Priori Knowledge,* University Park: Pennsylvania State University Press, 2001; Samuel Todes, *Body and World,* Cambridge, Mass.: MIT Press, 2001.

On Kant's moral philosophy, see W. T. Jones, *Morality and Freedom in the Philosophy of Immanuel Kant,* Oxford, U.K.: H. Milford, 1940; H. J. Paton, *The Categorical Imperative,* Chicago: University of Chicago Press, 1948; L. W. Beck, *A Commentary on Kant's Critique of Practical Reason,* Chicago: University of Chicago Press, 1960; Mary J. Gregor, *Laws of Freedom,* New York: Barnes and Noble, 1963; Keith Ward, *The Development of Kant's Views of Ethics,* Oxford, U.K.: Blackwell, 1972; Robert Paul Wolff, *The Autonomy of Reason: A Commentary on Kant's* Groundwork of the Metaphysics of Morals, New York: Harper & Row, 1973; Onora Nell, *Acting on Principle: An Essay on Kantian Ethics,* New York: Columbia University Press, 1975; Robert J. Benton, *Kant's Second Critique and the Problem of Transcendental Arguments,* The Hague: M. Nijhoff, 1977; Bruce Aune, *Kant's Theory of Morals,* Princeton, N.J.: Princeton University Press, 1979; Rex Patrick Stevens, *Kant on Moral Practice: A Study of Moral Success and Failure,* Macon, Ga.: Mercer University Press, 1981; Thomas Auxter, *Kant's Moral Teleology,* Macon, Ga.: Mercer University Press, 1982; Gary M. Hochberg, *Kant, Moral Legislation and Two Senses of "Will,"* Washington, D.C.: University Press of America, 1982; J. Gray Cox, *The Will at the Crossroads: A Reconstruction of Kant's Moral Philosophy,* Lanham, Md: University Press of America, 1984; John E. Atwell, *Ends and Principles in Kant's Moral Thought,* Dordrecht, Neth.: M. Nijhoff, 1986; Victor J. Seidler, *Kant, Respect and Injustice: The Limits of Liberal Moral Theory,* London: Routledge and Kegan Paul, 1986; P. C. Lo, *Treating Persons as Ends: An Essay on Kant's Moral Philosophy,* Lanham, Md.: University Press of America, 1987; Harry van der Linden, *Kantian Ethics and Socialism,* Indianapolis: Hackett Pub. Co., 1988; Onora O'Neill, *Constructions of Reason: Explorations of Kant's Practical Philosophy,* Cambridge, U.K.: Cambridge University Press, 1989; Leslie Arthur Mulholland, *Kant's System of Rights,* New York: Columbia University Press, 1990; Ruth F. Chadwick, ed., *Kant's Moral and Political Philosophy,* London: Routledge, 1992; Thomas E. Hill, Jr., *Dignity and Practical Reason in Kant's Moral Theory,* Ithaca, N.Y.: Cornell University Press, 1992; Michael Slote, *From Morality to Virtue,* New York: Oxford University Press, 1992; Barbara Herman, *The Practice of Moral Judgment,* Cambridge, Mass.: Harvard University Press, 1993; Roger J. Sullivan, *An Introduction to Kant's Ethics,* Cambridge, U.K.: Cambridge University Press, 1994; Victoria S. Wike, *Kant on Happiness in Ethics,* Albany: State University of New York Press, 1994; Marcia W. Baron, *Kantian Ethics Almost without Apology,* Ithaca, N.Y.: Cornell University Press, 1995; Henry E. Allison, ed., *Idealism and Freedom: Essays on Kant's Theoretical and Practical Philosophy,* Cambridge, U.K.: Cambridge University Press, 1996; David Cummiskey, *Kantian Consequentialism,* New York: Oxford University Press, 1996; John E. Hare, *The Moral Gap: Kantian Ethics, Human Limits, and God's Assistance,* Oxford, U.K.: Clarendon Press, 1996; Christine Korsgaard, *Creating the Kingdom of Ends,* Cambridge, U.K.: Cambridge University Press, 1996; Nancy Sherman, *Making a Necessity of Virtue: Aristotle and Kant on Virtue,* Cambridge, U.K.: Cambridge University Press, 1997; Paul Guyer, ed., *Kant's* Groundwork of the Metaphysics of Morals: *Critical Essays,* Lanham, Md.: Rowman and

Littlefield, 1998; Jeffrie G. Murphy, *Character, Liberty, and Law: Kantian Essays in Theory and Practice,* Dordrecht, Neth.: Kluwer Academic Publishers, 1998; G. Felicitas Munzel, *Kant's Conception of Moral Character: The "Critical" Link of Morality, Anthropology, and Reflective Judgment,* Chicago: University of Chicago Press, 1999; Allen W. Wood, *Kant's Ethical Thought,* Cambridge, U.K.: Cambridge University Press, 1999; Paul Guyer, *Kant on Freedom, Law, and Happiness,* Cambridge, U.K.: Cambridge University Press, 2000; Thomas E. Hill, Jr., *Respect, Pluralism, and Justice: Kantian Perspectives,* Oxford, U.K.: Oxford University Press, 2000; Robert B. Loudon, *Kant's Impure Ethics: From Rational Beings to Human Beings,* New York: Oxford University Press, 2000; Phillip Stratton-Lake, *Kant, Duty, and Moral Worth,* London: Routledge, 2000; Alenka Zupancic, *Ethics of the Real: Kant, Lacan,* London: Verso, 2000; Sharon Anderson-Gold, *Unnecessary Evil: History and Moral Progress in the Philosophy of Immanuel Kant,* Albany: State University of New York Press, 2001; David M. Sussman, *The Idea of Humanity: Anthropology and Anthroponomy in Kant's Ethics,* New York: Routledge, 2001; Carol W. Voeller, *The Metaphysics of the Moral Law: Kant's Deduction of Freedom,* New York: Garland, 2001.

On Kant's philosophies of art and religion in the *Critique of Judgment,* see H. W. Cassirer, *A Commentary on Kant's* Critique of Judgment, London: Methuen, 1938; Allen W. Wood, *Kant's Moral Religion,* Ithaca, N.Y.: Cornell University Press, 1970; Donald W. Crawford, *Kant's Aesthetic Theory,* Madison: University of Wisconsin Press, 1974; Francis Coleman, *The Harmony of Reason: A Study in Kant's Aesthetics,* Pittsburgh: University of Pittsburgh Press, 1974; Allen W. Wood, *Kant's Rational Theology,* Ithaca, N.Y.: Cornell University Press, 1978; G. E. Michaelson, Jr., *The Historical Dimensions of a Rational Faith: The Role of History in Kant's Religious Thought,* Washington, D.C.: University Press of America, 1979; Eva Shaper, *Studies in Kant's Aesthetics,* Edinburgh: Edinburgh University Press, 1979; Ted Cohen and Paul Guyer, eds., *Essays in Kant's Aesthetics,* Chicago: University of Chicago Press, 1982; Salim Kemal, *Kant and Fine Art: An Essay on Kant and the Philosophy of Fine Art and Culture,* Oxford, U.K.: Oxford University Press, 1986; Kenneth F. Rogerson, *Kant's Aesthetics: The Roles of Form and Expression,* Lanham, Md.: University Press of America, 1986; Mary A. McCloskey, *Kant's Aesthetic,* Basingstoke, U.K.: Macmillan, 1987; Howard Caygill, *Art of Judgement,* Oxford, U.K.: Blackwell, 1989; Paul Crowther, *The Kantian Sublime: From Morality to Art,* Oxford, U.K.: Clarendon Press, 1989; Rudolph A. Makkreel, *Imagination and Interpretation in Kant: The Hermeneutical Import of the* Critique of Judgment, Chicago: University of Chicago Press, 1990; Gordon E. Michalson, Jr., *Fallen Freedom: Kant on Radical Evil and Moral Regeneration,* Cambridge, U.K.: Cambridge University Press, 1990; Philip J.

Rossi and Michael Wreen, eds., *Kant's Philosophy of Religion Reconsidered,* Bloomington: Indiana University Press, 1991; Ruth F. Chadwick and Clive Cazeaux, eds., *Kant's* Critique of Judgement, London: Routledge, 1992; Dieter Henrich, *Aesthetic Judgment and the Moral Image of the World: Studies in Kant,* Stanford, Calif.: Stanford University Press, 1992; John H. Zammito, *The Genesis of Kant's* Critique of Judgment, Chicago: University of Chicago Press, 1992; Adina Davidovich, *Religion as a Province of Meaning: The Kantian Foundations of Modern Theology,* Minneapolis: Augsburg Fortress, 1993; Anthony Savile, *Kantian Aesthetics Pursued,* Edinburgh: Edinburgh University Press, 1993; Sidney Axinn, *The Logic of Hope: Extensions of Kant's View of Religion,* Amsterdam: Rodopi, 1994; Jean-François Lyotard, *Lessons on the Analytic of the Sublime: Kant's* Critique of Judgment, [*sections*] *23–29,* trans. Elizabeth Rottenberg, Stanford, Calif.: Stanford University Press, 1994; Lorne Falkenstein, *Kant's Intuitionism: A Commentary on the Transcendental Aesthetic,* Toronto: University of Toronto Press, 1995; Paul Guyer, *Kant and the Claims of Taste,* 2d. ed., Cambridge, Mass.: Harvard University Press, 1997; Salim Kemal, *Kant's Aesthetic Theory: An Introduction,* 2d. ed., New York: St. Martin's Press, 1997; Patricia M. Matthews, *The Significance of Beauty: Kant on Feeling and the System of the Mind,* Dordrecht, Neth.: Kluwer Academic Publishers, 1997; Winifred Menninghaus, *In Praise of Nonsense: Kant and Bluebeard,* trans. Henry Pickford, Stanford, Calif.: Stanford University Press, 1999; Gordon E. Michalson, Jr., *Kant and the Problem of God,* Oxford, U.K.: Blackwell, 1999; Gary Banham, *Kant and the Ends of Aesthetics,* Basingstoke, U.K.: Macmillan, 2000; Edward Eugene Kleist, *Judging Appearances: A Phenomenological Study of the Kantian* Sensus Communis, Dordrecht, Neth.: Kluwer Academic Publishers, 2000; Henry E. Allison, *Kant's Theory of Taste: A Reading of the Critique of Aesthetic Judgment,* Cambridge, U.K.: Cambridge University Press, 2001.

For studies on free will and determinism in Kant's work, see Bernard Carnois, *The Coherence of Kant's Doctrine of Freedom,* trans. David Booth, Chicago: University of Chicago Press, 1987; Henry E. Allison, *Kant's Theory of Freedom,* Cambridge, U.K.: Cambridge University Press, 1990; Paul Guyer, *Kant and the Experience of Freedom: Essays on Aesthetics and Morality,* Cambridge, U.K.: Cambridge University Press, 1993; Hud Hudson, *Kant's Compatibilism,* Ithaca: N.Y.: Cornell University Press, 1994.

For studies on Kant and politics/law, see Alan W. Norrie, *Law, Ideology and Punishment: Retrieval and Critique of the Liberal Ideal of Criminal Justice,* Dordrecht, Neth.: Kluwer Academic Publishers, 1991; Howard Williams, ed., *Essays on Kant's Political Philosophy,* Cardiff: University of Wales Press, 1992; Ronald Beiner and William James Booth, eds., *Kant and Political Phi-*

losophy: The Contemporary Legacy, New Haven, Conn.: Yale University Press, 1993; Allen D. Rosen, *Kant's Theory of Justice,* Ithaca, N.Y.: Cornell University Press, 1993; Slavoj Zizek, *Tarrying with the Negative: Kant, Hegel, and the Critique of Ideology,* Durham, N.C.: Duke University Press, 1993; Jeffrie G. Murphy, *Kant: The Philosophy of Right,* Macon, Ga.: Mercer University Press, 1994; T. K. Seung, *Kant's Platonic Revolution in Moral and Political Philosophy,* Baltimore: The Johns Hopkins University Press, 1994; Kimberly Hutchings, *Kant, Critique, and Politics,* London: Routledge, 1996; James Bohman and Matthias Lutz-Bachmann, eds., *Perpetual Peace: Essays on Kant's Cosmopolitan Ideal,* Cambridge, Mass.: MIT Press, 1997; Charles Covell, *Kant and the Law of Peace: A Study in the Philosophy of International Law and International Relations,* Basingstoke, U.K.: Macmillan, 1998; Georg Cavallar, *Kant and the Theory and Practice of International Right,* Cardiff: University of Wales Press, 1999; Alexander Kaufman, *Welfare in the Kantian State,* Oxford, U.K.: Oxford University Press, 1999; Katrin Flikschuh, *Kant and Modern Political Philosophy,* Cambridge, U.K.: Cambridge University Press, 2000; John Martin Gilroy, *Justice and Nature: Kantian Philosophy, Environmental Policy, and the Law,* Washington, D.C.: Georgetown University Press, 2000.

Some miscellaneous studies include: Robert Hahn, *Kant's Newtonian Revolution in Philosophy,* Carbondale: Southern Illinois University Press, 1988; Arthur Melnick, *Space, Time, and Thought in Kant,* Dordrecht, Neth.: Kluwer Academic Publishers, 1989; Richard L. Velkley, *Freedom and the End of Reason: On the Moral Foundation of Kant's Critical Philosophy,* Chicago: University of Chicago Press, 1989; Thomas C. Powell, *Kant's Theory of Self-Consciousness,* Oxford, U.K.: Clarendon Press, 1990; Peter D. Fenves, *A Peculiar Fate: Metaphysics and World-History in Kant,* Ithaca, N.Y.: Cornell University Press, 1991; Gerd Buchdahl, *Kant and the Dynamics of Reason: Essays on the Structure of Kant's Philosophy,* Oxford, U.K.: Blackwell, 1992; Michael Friedman, *Kant and the Exact Sciences,* Cambridge, Mass.: Harvard University Press, 1992; Carl J. Posy, ed., *Kant's Philosophy of Mathematics: Modern Essays,* Dordrecht, Neth.: Kluwer Academic Publishers, 1992; Stephen R. Palmquist, *Kant's System of Perspectives: An Architectonic Interpretation of the Critical Philosophy,* Lanham, Md.: University Press of America, 1993; Andrew Brook, *Kant and the Mind,* Cambridge, U.K.: Cambridge University Press, 1994; Sarah L. Gibbons, *Kant's Theory of Imagination: Bridging Gaps in Judgement and Experience,* Oxford, U.K.: Clarendon Press, 1994; Willi Goetschel, *Constituting Critique: Kant's Writing as Critical Praxi,* trans. Eric Schwab, Durham, N.C.: Duke University Press, 1994; Paolo Parrini, ed., *Kant and Contemporary Epistemology,* Dordrecht, Neth.: Kluwer Academic Publishers, 1994; Peter Plaas, *Kant's Theory of Natural Science,* trans. Alfred E. and Maria G. Miller, Dordrecht, Neth.: Kluwer Academic Publishers, 1994; Charles P. Bigger, *Kant's Methodology: An Essay in Philosophical Archeology*, Athens: Ohio University Press, 1996; Frederick C. Doepke, *The Kinds of Things: A Theory of Personal Identity Based on Transcendental Argument*, Chicago: Open Court, 1996; Beryl Logan, ed., *Immanuel Kant's* Prolegomena to Any Future Metaphysics: *In Focus*, London: Routledge, 1996; Susan Meld Shell, *The Embodiment of Reason: Kant on Spirit, Generation, and Community*, Chicago: University of Chicago Press, 1996; Martin Heidegger, *Kant and the Problem of Metaphysics*, 5th. ed., trans. Richard Taft, Bloomington: Indiana University Press, 1997; P. F. Strawson, *Entity and Identity: And Other Essays*, Oxford, U.K.: Clarendon Press, 1997; Pierre Keller, *Kant and the Demands of Self-Consciousness*, Cambridge, U.K.: Cambridge University Press, 1998; Alphonso Lingis, *The Imperative*, Bloomington: Indiana University Press, 1998; Jeffrey Edwards, *Substance, Force, and the Possibility of Knowledge: On Kant's Philosophy of Nature*, Berkeley: University of California Press, 2000; Eckhart Forster, *Kant's Final Synthesis: An Essay on the* Opus Postumum, Cambridge, Mass.: Harvard University Press, 2000; John Llewelyn, *The Hypocritical Imagination: Between Kant and Levinas*, London: Routledge, 2000; Martin Schonfeld, *The Philosophy of the Young Kant: The Precritical Project*, New York: Oxford University Press, 2000; Daniel Warren, *Reality and Impenetrability in Kant's Philosophy of Nature*, New York: Routledge, 2001; Eric Watson, ed., *Kant and the Sciences*, Oxford, U.K.: Oxford University Press, 2001; John H. Zammito, *Kant, Herder, and the Birth of Anthropology*, Chicago: University of Chicago Press, 2002.

For a biography of Kant, see Manfred Kuehn, *Kant: A Biography*, New York: Cambridge University Press, 2001.

FICHTE

For discussions of Fichte's philosophy, see Josiah Royce, *The Spirit of Modern Philosophy*, Lecture V, Boston: Houghton Mifflin, 1892; Anna Boynton-Thompson, *The Unity of Fichte's Doctrine of Knowledge*, Boston: Ginn and Co., 1895; H. C. Engelbrecht, *Johann Gottlieb Fichte: A Study of His Political Writings with Special Reference to His Nationalism*, New York: Columbia University Press, 1933; Russell W. Stine, *The Doctrine of God in the Philosophy of Fichte*, Philadelphia: privately printed, 1945; Robert Benson, "Fichte's Original Argument," Ph.D thesis, Columbia University, 1974; Tom Rockmore, *Fichte, Marx, and the German Philosophical Tradition*, Carbondale: Southern Illinois University Press, 1980; Dieter Henrich,

"Fichte's Original Insight," trans. David R. Lachterman, in *Contemporary German Philosophy I*, University Park: Pennsylvania State University Press, 1982; Frederick C. Beiser, *The Fate of Reason: German Philosophy from Kant to Fichte*, Cambridge, Mass.: Harvard University Press, 1987; John Sallis, *Spacings of Reason and Imagination in Texts of Kant, Fichte, Hegel*, Chicago: University of Chicago Press, 1987; Frederick Neuhouser, *Fichte's Theory of Subjectivity*, Cambridge, U.K.: Cambridge University Press, 1990; Tom Rockmore and Daniel Breazeale, eds., *Fichte: Historical Contexts/Contemporary Controversies*, Atlantic Highlands, N.J.: Humanities Press, 1994; and *New Perspectives on Fichte*, Atlantic Highlands, N.J.: Humanities Press, 1996; Jere Paul Surber, *Language and German Idealism: Fichte's Linguistic Philosophy*, Atlantic Highlands, N.J.: Humanities Press, 1996; Wayne M. Martin, *Idealism and Objectivity: Understanding Fichte's Jena Project*, Stanford, Calif.: Stanford University Press, 1997; Günter Zöller, *Fichte's Transcendental Philosophy: The Original Duplicity of Intelligence and Will*, Cambridge, U.K.: Cambridge University Press, 1998; Anthony O'Hear, ed., *German Philosophy since Kant*, Cambridge, U.K.: Cambridge University Press, 1999; Sally Sedgwick, ed., *The Reception of Kant's Critical Philosophy: Fichte, Schelling, and Hegel*, Cambridge, U.K.: Cambridge University Press, 2000.

For a biography of Fichte, see Anthony J. La Vopa, *Fichte: The Self and the Calling of Philosophy, 1762–1799*, Cambridge, U.K.: Cambridge University Press, 2001.

HEGEL

For general studies of Hegel's philosophy, see Josiah Royce, *The Spirit of Modern Philosophy*, Lecture VII and Appendix C, Boston: Houghton Mifflin, 1982; William Wallace, *Prolegomena to the Study of Hegel's Philosophy*, Oxford, U.K.: Clarendon Press, 1894; Benedetto Croce, *What Is Living and What Is Dead in the Philosophy of Hegel*, trans. Douglas Ainslie, London: Macmillan, 1915; J.M.E. McTaggart, *Studies in the Hegelian Cosmology*, 2d. ed., Cambridge, U.K.: Cambridge University Press, 1918; J.M.E. McTaggart, *Studies in the Hegelian Dialectic*, 2d. ed., Cambridge, U.K.: Cambridge University Press, 1922; Martin Heidegger, *Hegel's Concept of Experience*, trans. Kenley Royce Dove, New York: Harper & Row, 1970; Alasdair MacIntyre, ed., *Hegel: A Collection of Critical Essays*, Garden City, N.Y.: Anchor Books, 1972; Charles Taylor, *Hegel*, Cambridge, U.K.: Cambridge University Press, 1975; Michael J. Inwood, *Hegel*, London: Kegan Paul, 1983; Stephen Houlgate, *Freedom, Truth and History: An Introduction to Hegel's Philosophy*, London: Routledge, 1991; Michael J. Inwood, *A Hegel Dictionary*,

Cambridge, Mass.: Blackwell, 1992; Alan M. Olson, *Hegel and the Spirit: Philosophy as Pneumatology,* Princeton, N.J.: Princeton University Press, 1992; Menahem Rosen, *Problems of the Hegelian Dialectic: Dialectic Reconstructed as a Logic of Human Reality,* Dordrecht, Neth.: Kluwer Academic Publishers, 1992; Theodor Adorno, *Hegel: Three Studies,* trans. Shierry Weber Nicholsen, Cambridge, Mass.: MIT Press, 1993; Frederick C. Beiser, ed., *The Cambridge Companion to Hegel,* Cambridge, U.K.: Cambridge University Press, 1993; Errol E. Harris, *The Spirit of Hegel,* Atlantic Highlands, N.J.: Humanities Press, 1993; Tom Rockmore, *Before and After Hegel: A Historical Introduction to Hegel's Thought,* Berkeley: University of California Press, 1993; Lawrence S. Stepelevich, ed., *Selected Essays on G.W.F. Hegel,* Atlantic Highlands, N.J.: Humanities Press, 1993; Robert Stern, *G.W.F. Hegel: Critical Assessments,* London: Routledge, 1993; William Maker, *Philosophy without Foundations: Rethinking Hegel,* Albany: State University of New York Press, 1994; Howard Kainz, *G.W.F. Hegel,* New York: Twayne Publishers, 1996; Lloyd Spencer and Andrzej Krause, *Hegel for Beginners,* ed. Richard Appignanesi, Trumpington, U.K.: Icon Books, 1996; Jon Stewart, ed., *The Hegel Myths and Legends,* Evanston, Ill.: Northwestern University Press, 1996; Michael Baur and John Russon, eds., *Hegel and the Tradition: Essays in Honour of H. S. Harris,* Toronto: University of Toronto Press, 1997; Raymond Plant, *Hegel,* New York: Routledge, 1999; Peter Singer, *Hegel: A Very Short Introduction,* Oxford, U.K.: Oxford University Press, 2001.

For works on Hegel and social and political philosophy, see Herbert Marcuse, *Reason and Revelation: Hegel and the Rise of Social Theory,* London: Oxford University Press, 1941; Georg Lukács, *The Young Hegel,* trans. Rodney Livingstone, Cambridge, Mass.: MIT Press, 1966; Jürgen Habermas, *Knowledge and Human Interests,* trans. Jeremy J. Shapiro, Boston: Beacon Press, 1968; Alexandre Kojève, *Introduction to the Reading of Hegel,* trans. James H. Nichols, Jr., Ithaca, N.Y.: Cornell University Press, 1969; Judith N. Shklar, *Freedom and Independence: A Study of the Political Ideas of Hegel's Phenomenology of Mind,* Cambridge, U.K.: Cambridge University Press, 1976; Charles Taylor, *Hegel and Modern Society,* Cambridge, U.K.: Cambridge University Press, 1979; Harry Brod, *Hegel's Philosophy of Politics: Idealism, Identity, and Modernity,* Boulder, Colo.: Westview Press, 1992; Mark Tunick, *Hegel's Political Philosophy: Interpreting the Practice of Legal Punishment,* Princeton, N.J.: Princeton University Press, 1992; Fred R. Dallmayr, *G.W.F. Hegel: Modernity and Politics,* Newbury Park, Calif.: Sage Publications, 1993; Slavoj Zizek, *Tarrying with the Negative: Kant, Hegel, and the Critique of Ideology,* Durham, N.C.: Duke University Press, 1993; H. Tristram Engelhardt, Jr., and Terry Pinkard, eds., *Hegel Reconsidered: Beyond Metaphysics and the Authoritarian State,* Dordrecht, Neth.: Kluwer Academic

Publishers, 1994; Michael O. Hardimon, *Hegel's Social Philosophy: The Project of Reconciliation*, Cambridge, U.K.: Cambridge University Press, 1994; Kevin Anderson, *Lenin, Hegel, and Western Marxism: A Critical Study*, Urbana: University of Illinois Press, 1995; Elie Kedourie, *Hegel and Marx: Introductory Lectures*, ed. Sylvia Kedourie and Helen Kedourie, Oxford, U.K.: Blackwell, 1995; John Rosenthal, *The Myth of Dialectics: Reinterpreting the Marx-Hegel Relation*, Basingstoke, U.K.: Macmillan, 1998; Eric Weil, *Hegel and the State*, trans. Mark A. Cohen, Baltimore, Md.: Johns Hopkins University Press, 1998; Gary K. Browning, *Hegel and the History of Political Philosophy*, Basingstoke, U.K.: Macmillan, 1999; Tony Burns and Ian Fraser, eds., *The Hegel-Marx Connection*, Basingstoke, U.K.: Macmillan, 2000; Frederick Neuhouser, *Foundations of Hegel's Social Theory: Actualizing Freedom*, Cambridge, Mass.: Harvard University Press, 2000; Robert Fine, *Political Investigations: Hegel, Marx, Arendt*, London: Routledge, 2001; Adriaan T. Peperzak, *Modern Freedom: Hegel's Legal, Moral, and Political Philosophy*, Dordrecht, Neth.: Kluwer Academic Publishers, 2001; Robert R. Williams, ed., *Beyond Liberalism and Communitarianism: Studies in Hegel's* Philosophy of Right, Albany: State University of New York Press, 2001.

For works on the concept of freedom in Hegel's philosophy, see Merold Westphal, *Hegel, Freedom, and Modernity*, Albany: State University of New York Press, 1992; Paul Franco, *Hegel's Philosophy of Freedom*, New Haven, Conn.: Yale University Press, 1999; Alan Patten, *Hegel's Idea of Freedom*, Oxford, U.K.: Oxford University Press, 1999; Robert Bruce Ware, *Hegel: The Logic of Self-Consciousness and the Legacy of Subjective Freedom*, Edinburgh: Edinburgh University Press, 1999.

For works on Hegel and religion, see Walter Jaeschke, *Reason in Religion: The Foundations of Hegel's Philosophy of Religion*, trans. J. Michael Stewart and Peter C. Hodgson, Berkeley: University of California Press, 1990; Dale M. Schlitt, *Divine Subjectivity: Understanding Hegel's Philosophy of Religion*, London: University of Scranton Press, 1990; Andrew Shanks, *Hegel's Political Theology*, Cambridge, U.K.: Cambridge University Press, 1991; John Walker, ed., *Thought and Faith in the Philosophy of Hegel*, Dordrecht, Neth.: Kluwer Academic Publishers, 1991; David Kolb, ed., *New Perspectives on Hegel's Philosophy of Religion*, Albany: State University of New York Press, 1992; Stephen Crites, *Dialectic and Gospel in the Development of Hegel's Thinking*, University Park: Pennsylvania State University Press, 1998; Yirmiyahu Yovel, *Dark Riddle: Hegel, Nietzsche, and the Jews*, University Park: Pennsylvania State University Press, 1998.

For studies of Hegel's ethical theory, see Allen W. Wood, *Hegel's Ethical Thought*, Cambridge, U.K.: Cambridge University Press, 1990; Robert R.

Williams, *Hegel's Ethics of Recognition,* Berkeley: University of California Press, 1997.

For studies on Hegel and art, see Jack Kamisky, *Hegel on Art: An Interpretation of Hegel's Aesthetics,* Albany: State University of New York Press, 1962; Warren E. Steinkraus and Kenneth Schmitz, eds., *Art and Logic in Hegel's Philosophy,* Atlantic Highlands, N.J.: Humanities Press, 1980; William Desmond, *Art and the Absolute: A Study of Hegel's Aesthetics,* Albany: State University of New York Press, 1986; Beat Wyss, *Hegel's Art History and the Critique of Modernity,* trans. Caroline Dobson Saltzwedel, Cambridge, U.K.: Cambridge University Press, 1999; William Maker, ed., *Hegel and Aesthetics,* Albany: State University of New York Press, 2000.

For discussions of Hegel's philosophy of nature, see Michael John Petry, ed., *Hegel and Newtonianism,* Dordrecht, Neth.: Kluwer Academic Publishers, 1993; John Burbidge, *Real Process: How Logic and Chemistry Combine in Hegel's Philosophy of Nature,* Toronto: University of Toronto Press, 1996; Stephen Houlgate, ed., *Hegel and the Philosophy of Nature,* Albany: State University of New York Press, 1998.

For works on Hegel's philosophy of history, see Jean Hyppolite, *Introduction to Hegel's Philosophy of History,* trans. Bond Harris and Jacqueline Bouchard Spurlock, Gainesville: University Press of Florida, 1996; Shaun Gallagher, ed., *Hegel, History, and Interpretation,* Albany: State University of New York Press, 1997; Joe McCarney, *Routledge Philosophy Guidebook to Hegel on History,* London: Routledge, 2000.

For discussions of Hegel's logic, see J.M.E. McTaggart, *A Commentary on Hegel's* Logic, Cambridge, U.K.: Cambridge University Press, 1910; George di Giovanni, ed., *Essays on Hegel's* Logic, Albany: State University of New York Press, 1990; John F. Hoffmeyer, *The Advent of Freedom: The Presence of the Future in Hegel's* Logic, Rutherford, N.J.: Fairleigh Dickinson University Press, 1994; Clark Butler, *Hegel's Logic: Between Dialectic and History,* Evanston, Ill.: Northwestern University Press, 1996; Jean Hyppolite, *Logic and Existence,* trans. Leonard Lawlor and Amit Sen, Albany: State University of New York Press, 1997; Justus Hartnack, *An Introduction to Hegel's* Logic, ed. Kenneth R. Westphal, trans. Lars Aagaard-Mogensen, Indianapolis, Ind: Hackett Pub. Co., 1998; Peter Simpson, *Hegel's Transcendental Induction,* Albany: State University of New York Press, 1998; Ermanno Bencivenga, *Hegel's Dialectical Logic,* New York: Oxford University Press, 2000.

For studies of Hegel's *Phenomenology of Spirit,* see Jean Hyppolite, *Genesis and Structure of Hegel's* Phenomenology of Spirit, trans. Samuel Cherniak and John Heckman, Evanston, Ill: Northwestern University Press,

1974; Martin Heidegger, *Hegel's* Phenomenology of Spirit, trans. Parvis Emad and Kenneth Maly, Bloomington: Indiana University Press, 1980; Quentin Lauer, *A Reading of Hegel's* Phenomenology of Spirit, New York: Fordham University Press, 1993; Daniel P. Jamros, *The Human Shape of God: Religion in Hegel's* Phenomenology of Spirit, New York: Paragon House, 1994; Terry Pinkard, *Hegel's* Phenomenology: *The Sociality of Reason,* Cambridge, U.K.: Cambridge University Press, 1994; H. S. Harris, *Hegel: Phenomenology and System,* Indianapolis, Ind: Hackett Pub. Co., 1995; Gary K. Browning, ed., *Hegel's* Phenomenology of Spirit: *A Reappraisal,* Dordrecht, Neth.: Kluwer Academic Publishing, 1997; H. S. Harris, *Hegel's Ladder,* Indianapolis, Ind: Hackett Pub. Co., 1997; Tom Rockmore, *Cognition: An Introduction to Hegel's* Phenomenology of Spirit, Berkeley: University of California Press, 1997; Michael N. Forster, *Hegel's Idea of a Phenomenology of Spirit,* Chicago: University of Chicago Press, 1998; Jon Stewart, *The* Phenomenology of Spirit *Reader: Critical and Interpretive Essays,* Albany: State University of New York Press, 1998; Merold Westphal, *History and Truth in Hegel's* Phenomenology, 3d. ed., Bloomington: Indiana University Press, 1998; Jon Stewart, *The Unity of Hegel's* Phenomenology of Spirit: *A Systematic Interpretation,* Evanston, Ill.: Northwestern University Press, 2000; Robert Stern, *Routledge Philosophy Guidebook to Hegel and the* Phenomenology of Spirit, London: Routledge, 2002.

Works on Hegel and miscellaneous topics include Michael N. Forster, *Hegel and Skepticism,* Cambridge, Mass.: Harvard University Press, 1989; Robert Stern, *Hegel, Kant, and the Structure of the Object,* London: Routledge, 1990; Robert R. Williams, *Recognition: Fichte and Hegel on the Other,* Albany: State University of New York Press, 1992; John McCumber, *The Company of Words: Hegel, Language, and Systematic Philosophy,* Evanston, Ill.: Northwestern University Press, 1993; Arkady Plotnitsky, *In the Shadow of Hegel: Complementarity, History, and the Unconscious,* Gainesville: University Press of Florida, 1993; Daniel Berthold-Bond, *Hegel's Theory of Madness,* Albany: State University of New York Press, 1995; Patricia Jagentowicz Mills, ed., *Feminist Interpretations of G.W.F. Hegel,* University Park: Pennsylvania State University Press, 1996; Paul Redding, *Hegel's Hermeneutics,* Ithaca, N.Y.: Cornell University Press, 1996; Tom Rockmore, *On Hegel's Epistemology and Contemporary Philosophy,* Atlantic Highlands, N.J.: Humanities Press, 1996; Robert B. Pippin, *Idealism as Modernism: Hegelian Variations,* Cambridge, U.K.: Cambridge University Press, 1997; Stuart Barnett, ed., *Hegel after Derrida,* London: Routledge, 1998; Andrew Haas, *Hegel and the Problem of Multiplicity,* Evanston, Ill.: Northwestern University Press, 2000; Sally Sedgwick, ed., *The Reception of Kant's Critical Philosophy: Fichte, Schelling, and Hegel,* Cambridge, U.K.: Cambridge University Press, 2000;

Alfredo Ferrarin, *Hegel and Aristotle,* Cambridge, U.K.: Cambridge University Press, 2001; Glenn Alexander Magee, *Hegel and the Hermetic Tradition,* Ithaca, N.Y.: Cornell University Press, 2001; Kathleen Dow Magnus, *Hegel and the Symbolic Mediation of Spirit,* Albany: State University of New York Press, 2001; Jean-Luc Nancy, *The Speculative Remark: One of Hegel's Bons Mots,* trans. Céline Surprenant, Stanford, Calif.: Stanford University Press, 2001; Allen Speight, *Hegel, Literature, and the Problem of Agency,* New York: Cambridge University Press, 2001.

For biographies of Hegel, see Horst Althaus, *Hegel: An Intellectual Biography,* trans. Michael Tarsh, Cambridge, U.K.: Polity Press, 2000; Terry Pinkard, *Hegel: A Biography,* Cambridge, U.K.: Cambridge University Press, 2000.

SCHOPENHAUER

For further discussion of Schopenhauer's philosophy, see Josiah Royce, *The Spirit of Modern Philosophy,* Lecture VIII, Boston: Houghton Mifflin, 1892; William Caldwell, *Schopenhauer's System in Its Philosophical Significance,* Edinburgh: Blackwood, 1899; Israel Knox, *The Aesthetic Theories of Kant, Hegel, and Schopenhauer,* New York: Columbia University Press, 1936; Thomas Mann's essay on Schopenhauer (1938) in *Essays of Three Decades,* trans. H. T. Lowe-Porter, New York: Knopf, 1947; Patrick Gardiner, *Schopenhauer,* Harmondsworth, U.K.: Penguin, 1963; J. P. Stern, "The Aesthetic Re-Interpretation: Schopenhauer," in *Re-Interpretation: Seven Studies in Nineteenth-Century German Literature,* London: Thames and Hudson, 1964; Richard Taylor, "Schopenhauer," in D. J. O'Connor, ed., *A Critical History of Western Philosophy,* New York: Free Press, 1964; George Santayana, "Schopenhauer and Nietzsche," in *The German Mind: A Philosophical Diagnosis,* New York: Thomas Y. Crowell, 1968; Friedrich Nietzsche, *Schopenhauer as Educator,* trans. James W. Hillesheim and Malcolm R. Simpson, Chicago: Henry Regnery, 1965; Frederick Copleston, *Arthur Schopenhauer, Philosopher of Pessimism,* 2d. ed., London: Search Press, 1975; Hans Barth, "Schopenhauer's 'True Critique of Reason,' " in *Truth and Ideology,* trans. Frederick Lilge, Berkeley: University of California Press, 1976; Michael Fox, ed., *Schopenhauer, His Philosophical Achievement,* Brighton, U.K.: Harvester Press, 1980; D. W. Hamlyn, *Schopenhauer,* London: Routledge and Kegan Paul, 1980; Bernard Bykhovsky, *Schopenhauer and the Ground of Existence,* trans. Philip Moran, Amsterdam: B. R. Gruner, 1984; Georg Simmel, *Schopenhauer and Nietzsche,* trans. Helmut Loiskandl, Deena Weinstein, and Michael Weinstein, Amherst, Mass.: University of

Massachusetts Press, 1986; Julian Young, *Willing and Unwilling: A Study in the Philosophy of Arthur Schopenhauer,* Dordrecht, Neth.: Kluwer Academic Publishers, 1987; Patrick Bridgwater, *Arthur Schopenhauer's English Schooling,* London: Routledge, 1988; Christopher Janaway, *Self and World in Schopenhauer's Philosophy,* Oxford, U.K., Clarendon Press, 1989; Rudiger Sanfranski, *Schopenhauer and the Wild Years of Philosophy,* trans. Ewald Osers, London: Weidenfeld and Nicolson, 1989; John E. Atwell, *Schopenhauer, The Human Character,* Philadelphia: Temple University Press, 1990; David Avraham Weiner, *Genius and Talent: Schopenhauer's Influence on Wittgenstein's Early Philosophy,* Rutherford, N.J.: Fairleigh Dickinson University Press, 1992; F. C. White, *On Schopenhauer's* Fourfold Root of the Principle of Sufficient Reason, Leiden, Neth.: E. J. Brill, 1992; Christopher Janaway, *Schopenhauer,* Oxford, U.K.: Oxford University Press, 1994; John E. Atwell, *Schopenhauer on the Character of the World: The Metaphysics of Will,* Berkeley: University of California Press, 1995; Dale Jacquette, ed., *Schopenhauer, Philosophy, and the Arts,* Cambridge, U.K.: Cambridge University Press, 1996; Bryan Magee, *The Philosophy of Schopenhauer,* rev. ed., Oxford, U.K.: Clarendon Press, 1997; Christopher Janaway, ed., *Willing and Nothingness: Schopenhauer as Nietzsche's Educator,* Oxford, U.K.: Oxford University Press, 1998; and *The Cambridge Companion to Schopenhauer,* Cambridge, U.K.: Cambridge University Press, 1999; Michael Tanner, *Schopenhauer,* London: Routledge, 1999; Alain de Bouton, *The Consolations of Philosophy,* New York: Pantheon Books, 2000.

COMTE

A good deal was written about Comte by his nineteenth-century followers and critics. Perhaps the most interesting and balanced discussion (and in itself a fine philosophical essay) is that of John Stuart Mill, *Auguste Comte and Positivism,* Ann Arbor: University of Michigan Press, 1965. Other studies include Lucien Levy-Bruhl, *The Philosophy of Auguste Comte,* London: S. Sonnenschein, 1903; Richard Laurin Hawkins, *Positivism in the United States (1853–1861),* Cambridge, Mass.: Harvard University Press, 1936; F. S. Marvin, *Comte, the Founder of Sociology,* London: Chapman and Hall, 1936; Emile Durkheim, *Socialism and Saint-Simon,* ed. Alvin W. Goulder, trans. Charlotte Sattler, Yellow Springs, Ohio: Antioch Press, 1958; Walter Michael Simon, *European Positivism in the Nineteenth Century, an Essay in Intellectual History,* Ithaca, N.Y.: Cornell University Press, 1963; Raymond Aron, *Main Currents in Sociological Thought,* ch. 1, trans. Richard Howard and Helen Weaver, New York: Anchor Books, 1968; Herbert Spencer, *Reasons for Dis-*

senting from the Philosophy of M. Comte, and Other Essays, Berkeley, Calif.: Glendessary Press, 1968; Kenneth Thompson, *Auguste Comte: The Foundation of Sociology,* New York: Wiley, 1975; Eric Voegelin, *From Enlightenment to Revolution,* ed. John H. Hallowell, Durham, N.C.: Duke University Press, 1975; Christopher Kent, *Brains and Numbers: Elitism, Comtism, and Democracy in Mid-Victorian England,* Toronto: University of Toronto Press, 1978; Arline Reilein Standley, *Auguste Comte,* Boston: Twayne Publishers, 1981; Christopher G. A. Bryant, *Positivism in Social Theory and Research,* Basingstoke, U.K.: Macmillan, 1985; Mary Pickering, *Auguste Comte: An Intellectual Biography,* Cambridge, U.K.: Cambridge University Press, 1993; Gillis J. Harp, *Positivist Republic: Auguste Comte and the Reconstruction of American Liberalism, 1865–1920,* University Park: Pennsylvania State University Press, 1995; Robert C. Scharff, *Comte after Positivism,* Cambridge, U.K.: Cambridge University Press, 1995; Andrew Wernick, *Auguste Comte and the Religion of Humanity: The Post-theistic Program of French Social Theory,* Cambridge, U.K.: Cambridge University Press, 2001.

MACH

Further discussion of Mach's philosophy is to be found in Oswald Külpe, *The Philosophy of the Present in German,* trans. M. L. and G.T.W. Patrick, London: George Allen, 1913; W. Tudor Jones, *Contemporary Thought of Germany,* vol. 1, New York: Knopf, 1931; Carlton Berenda Weinberg, *Mach's Empiro-Pragmatism in Physical Science,* New York: Albee Press, 1937; Philipp Frank, *Between Physics and Philosophy,* Cambridge, Mass.: Harvard University Press, 1941; John Passmore, *A Hundred Years of Philosophy,* pp. 322–25, London: Duckworth, 1957; Erwin N. Hiebert, *The Conception of Thermodynamics in the Scientific Thought of Mach and Planck,* Freiburg/Br.: Ernst-Mach-Institut, 1968; Robert S. Cohen and Raymond J. Seeger, eds., *Ernst Mach, Physicist and Philosopher,* Dordrecht, Neth.: Reidel, 1970; J. Bradley, *Mach's Philosophy of Science,* London: Athlone Press, 1971; John T. Blackmore, *Ernst Mach: His Work, Life, and Influence,* Berkeley: University of California Press, 1972; Robert Musil, *On Mach's Theories,* trans. Kevin Mulligan, Washington, D.C.: Catholic University of America Press, 1982; John T. Blackmore, ed., *Ernst Mach—A Deeper Look: Documents and New Perspectives,* Dordrecht, Neth.: Kluwer Academic Publishers, 1992; Gerald Holton, *Science and Anti-Science,* Cambridge, Mass.: Harvard University Press, 1993, chaps. 1 and 2; Jurgen Renn, *The Third Way to General Relativity: Einstein and Mach in Context,* Berlin: Max-Planck-Institut fur Wissenschaftsgeschichte, 1994; John T. Blackmore, R. Itagaki, and S.

Tanaka, *Ernst Mach's Vienna, 1895–1930, or, Phenomenalism as Philosophy of Science,* Dordrecht, Neth.: Kluwer Academic Publishers, 2001.

NIETZSCHE

General studies about Nietzsche include Walter Kaufmann, *Nietzsche: Philosopher, Psychologist, Antichrist,* Princeton, N.J.: Princeton University Press, 1974 (a 4th reprint of the 1st edition published by Princeton University Press, 1947); Thomas Mann's address at the Library of Congress, April 29, 1947, "Nietzsche's Philosophy in Light of Contemporary Events," published Washington, D.C.: Library of Congress, 1947; Arthur C. Danto, *Nietzsche as Philosopher,* New York: Macmillan, 1965; R. J. Hollingdale, *Nietzsche, the Man and His Philosophy,* Baton Rouge: Louisiana State University Press, 1965; Karl Jaspers, *Nietzsche: An Introduction to the Understanding of His Philosophical Activity,* trans. Charles F. Wallraff and Frederick J. Schmitz, Tucson: University of Arizona Press, 1965; R. J. Hollingdale, *Nietzsche,* London: Routledge and Kegan Paul, 1973; Robert C. Solomon, ed., *Nietzsche: A Collection of Critical Essays,* New York: Doubleday, 1973; J. P. Stern, *Nietzsche,* Glasgow: William Collins Sons, 1978; Martin Heidegger, *Nietzsche,* vol. 1, *The Will to Power as Art,* trans. David Farrell Krell, New York: Harper & Row, 1979; vol. 2, *The Eternal Recurrence of the Same,* trans. David Farrell Krell, San Francisco: Harper & Row, 1984; vol. 3, *The Will to Power as Knowledge and as Metaphysics,* trans. Joan Stambaugh and Frank Capuzzi, San Francisco: Harper & Row, 1984; vol. 4, *Nihilism,* trans. David Farrell Krell, New York: Harper & Row, 1982; J. P. Stern, *A Study of Nietzsche,* Cambridge, U.K.: Cambridge University Press, 1979; Roger Hollinrake, *Nietzsche, Wagner and the Philosophy of Pessimism,* London: George Allen & Unwin, 1982; Richard Schacht, *Nietzsche,* London: Routledge and Kegan Paul, 1983; Keith Ansell-Pearson, *Nietzsche and Modern German Thought,* New York: Routledge, 1991; Ernst Behler, *Confrontations,* trans. Steven Taubeneck, Stanford, Calif.: Stanford University Press, 1991; David E. Cooper, *Authenticity and Learning: Nietzsche's Educational Philosophy,* Aldershot, U.K.: Avebury, 1991; Georg Simmel, *Schopenhauer and Nietzsche,* trans. Helmut Loiskandle, Deena Weinstein, and Michael Weinstein, Urbana: University of Illinois Press, 1991; George J. Stack, *Nietzsche: Man, Knowledge, and Will to Power,* Wolfeboro, N.H.: Longwood Press, 1991; George J. Stack, *Nietzsche and Emerson: An Elective Affinity,* Athens: Ohio University Press, 1992; Michael Tanner, *Nietzsche,* Oxford, U.K.: Oxford University Press, 1994; Irving Zeitlin, *Nietzsche: A Re-examination,* Cambridge, U.K.: Polity, 1994; Daniel R.

Ahern, *Nietzsche as Cultural Physician,* University Park: Pennsylvania State University Press, 1995; Richard Schacht, *Making Sense of Nietzsche: Reflections Timely and Untimely,* Urbana: University of Illinois Press, 1995; Peter R. Sedgwick, ed., *Nietzsche: A Critical Reader,* Oxford, U.K.: Blackwell, 1995; Bernd Magnus and Kathleen M. Higgins, *The Cambridge Companion to Nietzsche,* Cambridge, U.K.: Cambridge University Press, 1996; Laurence Gane and Kitty Chan, *Nietzsche for Beginners,* ed. Richard Appignanesi, Trumpington, U.K.: Icon Books, 1997; Quentin P. Taylor, *The Republic of Genius: A Reconstruction of Nietzsche's Early Thought,* Rochester: University of Rochester Press, 1997; Daniel W. Conway, ed., *Nietzsche: Critical Assessments,* London: Routledge, 1998; Eugen Fink, *Nietzsche's Philosophy,* London: Athlone Press, 1999; Wolfgang Müller-Lauter, *Nietzsche: His Philosophy of Contradictions and the Contradictions of His Philosophy,* trans. David J. Parent, Urbana: University of Illinois Press, 1999; Gianni Vattimo, *Friedrich Nietzsche: An Introduction,* London: Athlone Press, 1999; Robert C. Solomon and Kathleen M. Higgins, *What Nietzsche Really Said,* New York: Schocken Books, 2000; Michael Tanner, *Nietzsche: A Very Short Introduction,* Oxford, U.K.: Oxford University Press, 2000; Paul J. M. van Tongeren, *Reinterpreting Modern Culture: An Introduction to Friedrich Nietzsche's Philosophy,* West Lafayette, Ind.: Purdue University Press, 2000.

For studies about Nietzsche and classical literature and philosophy, see Werner J. Dannhauser, *Nietzsche's View of Socrates,* Ithaca, N.Y.: Cornell University Press, 1974; George Grant, "Nietzsche and the Ancients: Philosophy and Scholarship," *Dionysius* 3 (1979): 5–16; James O'Flaherty, Timothy F. Sellner, and Robert M. Helm, *Studies in Nietzsche and the Classical Tradition,* 2d. ed., Chapel Hill: University of North Carolina Press, 1979; M. S. Silk and J. P. Stern, *Nietzsche on Tragedy,* Cambridge, U.K.: Cambridge University Press, 1981; Robin Small, "Nietzsche and the Platonist Tradition of the Cosmos: Center Everywhere and Circumference Nowhere," *Journal of the History of Ideas* 44 (January–March 1983): 89–104; V. Tejera, *Nietzsche and Greek Thought,* Dordrecht, Neth.: M. Nijhoff, 1987; Robert John Ackermann, *Nietzsche: A Frenzied Look,* Amherst: University of Massachusetts Press, 1990; John Sallis, *Crossings: Nietzsche and the Space of Tragedy,* Chicago: University of Chicago Press, 1991; Laurence Lampert, *Leo Strauss and Nietzsche,* Chicago: University of Chicago Press, 1996; Douglas Thompson, *Reading Nietzsche Rhetorically,* New York: Guilford Press, 1999; James I. Porter, *Nietzsche and the Philology of the Future,* Stanford, Calif.: Stanford University Press, 2000.

For discussions of Nietzsche and epistemology, metaphysics, and the philosophy of science, see John Wilcox, *Truth and Value in Nietzsche: A Study of His Metaethics and Epistemology,* Ann Arbor: University of Michigan Press, 1974; Ruediger Hermann Grimm, *Nietzsche's Theory of Knowledge,* Berlin: Walter de Gruyter, 1977; Stephen Houlgate, *Hegel, Nietzsche, and the Criticism of Metaphysics,* Cambridge, U.K.: Cambridge University Press, 1986; Daniel Breazeale, "Lange, Nietzsche, and Stack: The Question of 'Influence,' " *International Studies in Philosophy* 21, 2 (1989): 91–103; John Wilcox, "The Birth of Nietzsche Out of the Spirit of Lange," *International Studies in Philosophy* 21, 2 (1989): 81–89; Maudmarie Clark, *Nietzsche on Truth and Philosophy,* Cambridge, U.K.: Cambridge University Press, 1990; Beverly E. Gallo, "On the Question of Nietzsche's 'Scientism,' " *International Studies in Philosophy* 22, 2 (1990): 111–19; Keith M. May, *Nietzsche on the Struggle between Knowledge and Wisdom,* Basingstoke, U.K.: Macmillan, 1993; Peter Poellner, *Nietzsche and Metaphysics,* Oxford, U.K: Oxford University Press, 1995; Ted Sadler, *Nietzsche: Truth and Redemption: Critique of the Postmodernist Nietzsche,* London: Athlone Press, 1995; Michel Haar, *Nietzsche and Metaphysics,* Albany: State University of New York Press, 1996; John Richardson, *Nietzsche's System,* Oxford, U.K.: Oxford University Press, 1996; Paul Miklowitz, *Metaphysics to Metafictions: Hegel, Nietzsche, and the End of Philosophy,* Albany: State University of New York Press, 1998; Babette E. Babich, ed., *Nietzsche, Epistemology, and Philosophy of Science,* Dordrecht, Neth.: Kluwer Academic Publishing, 1999; and *Nietzsche and the Sciences,* Dordrecht, Neth.: Kluwer Academic Publishing, 1999; and ed., *Nietzsche, Theories of Knowledge and Critical Theory,* Dordrecht, Neth.: Kluwer Academic Publishing, 1999; Christoph Cos, *Nietzsche: Naturalism and Interpretation,* Berkeley: University of California Press, 1999; Steven D. Hales and Rex Welshon, *Nietzsche's Perspectivism,* Urbana: University of Illinois Press, 2000.

For studies of Nietzsche and ethics, see Alisdair MacIntyre, *After Virtue: A Study of Moral Theory,* Notre Dame: Notre Dame University Press, 1981; Jeffrey Minson, *Genealogies of Morals: Nietzsche, Foucault, Donzelot, and the Eccentricity of Ethics,* Basingstoke, U.K.: Macmillan, 1985; Yirmiyahu Yovel, ed., *Nietzsche as Affirmative Thinker: Papers Presented at the Fifth Jerusalem Philosophical Encounter,* April 1983, Dordrecht, Neth.: M. Nijhoff, 1986; Daniel W. Conway, "A Moral Ideal for Everyone and No One," *International Studies in Philosophy* 22, 2 (1990): 17–29; Charles E. Scott, *The Question of Ethics: Nietzsche, Foucault, Heidegger,* Bloomington: Indiana University Press, 1990; Alan White, *Within Nietzsche's Labyrinth,* New York: Routledge, 1990; Keith Ansell-Pearson, *Nietzsche Contra Rousseau: A Study of Nietzsche's Moral and Political Thought,* Cambridge, U.K.: Cambridge University Press, 1991; Robert Henri Cosineau, *Zarathustra and the Ethical Ideal: Timely Meditations on Philosophy,* Amsterdam, Neth.: J. Benjamins, 1991; Lester H. Hunt, *Nietzsche and the Origin of Virtue,* London: Routledge, 1991; Hans Seigfried, "Nietzsche's Natural Morality," *Journal of Value Inquiry* 26 (1992): 423–31; E. E. Sleinis, *Nietzsche's Revaluation of Values: A Study in Strategies,* Urbana: University of Illinois Press, 1994; Peter Berkowitz, *Nietzsche: The Ethics of an Immoralist,* Cambridge, Mass.: Harvard University Press, 1995; Thomas H. Brobjer, *Nietzsche's Ethics of Character: A Study of Nietzsche's Ethics and Its Place in the History of Moral Thinking,* Uppsala, Swed.: Uppsala University, 1995; Brian Leiter, "Nietzsche and the Morality Critics," *Ethics* 107 (January 1997): 250–85; Simon May, *Nietzsche's Ethics and his War on 'Morality',* Oxford, U.K.: Clarendon Press, 1999; Peter Durno Murray, *Nietzsche's Affirmative Morality: A Revaluation Based in the Dionysian World-view,* Berlin: Walter de Gruyter, 1999; Richard Schacht, ed., *Nietzsche's Postmoralism: Essays on Nietzsche's Prelude to Philosophy's Future,* Cambridge, U.K.: Cambridge University Press, 2001.

For works on Nietzsche and aesthetics and the philosophy of art, see Anthony Ludovici, *Nietzsche and Art,* London: Constable, 1911; Stephen Donadio, *Nietzsche, Henry James, and the Artistic Will,* New York: Oxford University Press, 1978; Richard Schacht, "Nietzsche's Second Thoughts about Art," *Monist* 64 (April 1981): 241–46; Michael Allen Gillespie and Tracy B. Strong, eds, *Nietzsche's New Seas: Explorations in Philosophy, Aesthetics, and Politics,* Chicago: University of Chicago Press, 1988; Adrian Del Caro, *Nietzsche contra Nietzsche: Creativity and the Anti-Romantic,* Baton Rouge: Louisiana State University Press, 1989; Terry Eagleton, *The Ideology of the Aesthetic,* Oxford, U.K.: Blackwell, 1990; Julian Young, *Nietzsche's Philosophy of Art,* Cambridge, U.K.: Cambridge University Press, 1992; Stephen Barker, *Autoaesthetics: Strategies of the Self after Nietzsche,* Atlantic Highlands, N.J.: Humanities Press, 1993; Joan Stambaugh, *The Other Nietzsche,* Albany: State University of New York Press, 1993; Robert McGahey, *The Orphic Moment: Shaman to Poet-Thinker in Plato, Nietzsche, and Mallarmé,* Albany: State University of New York Press, 1994; Edward G. Andrew, *The Genealogy of Values: The Aesthetic Economy of Nietzsche and Proust,* Lanham, Md.: Rowman and Littlefield Publishers, 1995; Nicholas Martin, *Nietzsche and Schiller: Untimely Aesthetics,* Oxford, U.K.: Clarendon Press, 1996; Geoff Waite, *Nietzsche's Corps/e: Aesthetics, Politics, Prophecy, or, The Spectacular Technoculture of Everyday Life,* Durham, N.C.: Duke University Press, 1996; Thomas Heilke, *Nietzsche's Tragic Regime: Culture, Aesthetics, and Political Education,* De Kalb: Northern Illinois University Press, 1998; Salim Kemal, Ivan Gaskell, and Daniel W. Conway, eds., *Nietzsche, Philosophy and the Arts,* Cambridge, U.K.: Cambridge University Press, 1998; Alexandre Kostka and Irving Wohlfarth, eds., *Nietzsche and "An Architecture of Our Minds,"* Los Angeles: Getty Research Institute for the History of Art and the Humanities, 1999; Caroline Joan Picart, *Resentment and "the Feminine" in Nietzsche's Politico-Aesthetics,* University Park: Pennsylvania State University Press, 1999; Matthew Rampley, *Nietzsche, Aesthetics, and Modernity,* Cambridge, U.K.: Cambridge University Press, 2000.

For studies on Nietzsche and religion, see George Wilson Knight, *Christ and Nietzsche, an Essay in Poetic Wisdom,* London: Staples Press, 1948; Conrad Bonifazi, *Christendom Attacked: A Comparison of Kierkegaard and Nietzsche,* London: Rockliff, 1953; Karl Jaspers, *Nietzsche and Christianity,* trans. E. B. Ashton, Chicago: Regnery, 1961; Claude Geffre and Jean-Pierre Jossua, eds., *Nietzsche and Christianity,* Edinburgh: T. & T. Clark, 1981; James C. O'Flaherty, Timothy F. Sellner, and Robert M. Helm, eds., *Studies in Nietzsche and the Judaeo-Christian Tradition,* Chapel Hill: University of North Carolina Press, 1985; William Lloyd Newell, *The Secular Magi: Marx, Freud, and Nietzsche on Religion,* New York: Pilgrim Press, 1986; Irene S. M. Makarushka, *Religious Imagination and Language in Emerson and Nietzsche,* Basingstoke, U.K., Macmillan, 1994; Weaver Santaniello, *Nietzsche, God, and the Jews: His Critique of Judeo-Christianity in Relation to the Nazi Myth,* Albany: State University of New York Press, 1994; Richard Elliott Friedman, *The Disappearance of God: A Divine Mystery,* Boston: Little, Brown, 1995; James Kellenberger, *Kierkegaard and Nietzsche: Faith and Eternal Acceptance,* Basingstoke, U.K.: Macmillan, 1997; Robert G. Morrison, *Nietzsche and Buddhism: A Study in Nihilism and Ironic Affinities,* Oxford, U.K.: Oxford University Press, 1997; Siegfried Mandel, *Nietzsche and the Jews: Exaltation and Denigration,* Amherst, N.Y.: Prometheus Books, 1998; Tyler T. Roberts, *Contesting Spirit: Nietzsche, Affirmation, Religion,* Princeton, N.J.: Princeton University Press, 1998; Yirmiyahu Yovel, *Dark Riddle: Hegel, Nietzsche, and the Jews,* University Park: Pennsylvania State University Press, 1998; Alistair Kee, *Nietzsche against the Crucified,* London: SCM, 1999; Jan-Olav Henriksen, *The Reconstruction of Religion: Lessing, Kierkegaard, and Nietzsche,* Grand Rapids, Mich.: William B. Eerdmans, 2001; Tim Murphy, *Nietzsche, Metaphor, Religion,* Albany: State University of New York Press, 2001; Weaver Santaniello, ed., *Nietzsche and the Gods,* Albany: State University of New York Press, 2001; Giles Fraser, *Redeeming Nietzsche: On the Piety of Unbelief,* London: Routledge, 2002.

For studies of Nietzsche and politics, see Tracy Strong, *Friedrich Nietzsche and the Politics of Transfiguration,* Berkeley: University of California Press, 1975; György Lukács, *The Destruction of Reason,* trans. Peter Palmer, Atlantic Highlands, N.J.: Humanities Press, 1981; Rudolf E. Kuenzli, "The Nazi Appropriation of Nietzsche," *Nietzsche-Studien* 12 (1983): 428–35; R. Hinton Thomas, *Nietzsche in German Politics and Society 1890–1918,* Manchester, U.K.: Manchester University Press, 1983; Ofelia

Schutte, *Beyond Nihilism: Nietzsche without Masks,* Chicago: University of Chicago Press, 1984; Bernard Yack, *The Longing for Total Revolution: Philosophic Sources of Social Discontent from Rousseau to Marx and Nietzsche,* Princeton, N.J.: Princeton University Press, 1986; Peter Bergmann, *Nietzsche: The Last Antipolitical German,* Bloomington: Indiana University Press, 1987; Georg Stauth and Bryan S. Turner, *Nietzsche's Dance: Resentment, Reciprocity, and Resistance in Social Life,* Oxford, U.K.: Blackwell, 1988; Mark Warren, *Nietzsche and Political Thought,* Cambridge, Mass.: MIT Press, 1988; Tom Darby, Béla Egyed, and Ben Jones, eds., *Nietzsche and the Rhetoric of Nihilism: Essays on Interpretation, Language, and Politics,* Ottawa: Carleton University Press, 1989; Debra B. Bergoffen, "Posthumous Popularity: Reading, Privileging, Politicizing Nietzsche," *Soundings* 73, 1 (spring 1990): 37–60; Bruce Detwiler, *Nietzsche and the Politics of Aristocratic Radicalism,* Chicago: University of Chicago Press, 1990; Leslie Paul Thiele, *Friedrich Nietzsche and the Politics of the Soul: A Study of Heroic Individualism,* Princeton, N.J.: Princeton University Press, 1990; Keith Ansell-Pearson, *An Introduction to Nietzsche as Political Thinker: The Perfect Nihilist,* Cambridge, U.K.: Cambridge University Press, 1994; Lawrence J. Hatab, *A Nietzschean Defense of Democracy: An Experiment in Postmodern Politics,* Chicago: Open Court, 1995; David Owen, *Nietzsche, Politics, and Modernity: A Critique of Liberal Reason,* Thousand Oaks, Calif.: Sage Publications, 1995; Daniel W. Conway, *Nietzsche and the Political,* London: Routledge, 1997; Alex McIntyre, *The Sovereignty of Joy: Nietzsche's Vision of Grand Politics,* Toronto: University of Toronto Press, 1997; Frederick Appel, *Nietzsche contra Democracy,* Ithaca, N.Y.: Cornell University Press, 1999; Alan D. Schrift, *Why Nietzsche Still? Reflections on Drama, Culture, and Politics,* Berkeley: University of California Press, 2000.

For studies on Nietzsche and psychology and psychoanalysis, see F. G. Crookshank, *Individual Psychology and Nietzsche,* London: The C. W. Daniel Company, 1933; Antonio Moreno, *Jung, Gods, and Modern Man,* Notre Dame, Ind.: University of Notre Dame Press, 1970; Jacob Golomb, *Nietzsche's Enticing Psychology of Power,* Ames: Iowa State University Press, 1989; Daniel Chapelle, *Nietzsche and Psychoanalysis,* Albany: State University of New York Press, 1993; Graham Parkes, *Composing the Soul: Reaches of Nietzsche's Psychology,* Chicago: University of Chicago Press, 1994; Paul Bishop, *The Dionysian Self: C. G. Jung's Reception of Friedrich Nietzsche,* Berlin: Walter de Gruyter, 1995; Ronald Lehrer, *Nietzsche's Presence in Freud's Life and Thought: On the Origins of a Psychology of Dynamic Unconscious Mental Functioning,* Albany: State University of New York Press, 1995; Jacob Golomb, Weaver Santaniello, and Ronald Lehrer, eds., *Nietzsche and Depth Psychology,* Albany: State University of New York Press, 1999; Paul-

Laurent Assoun, *Freud and Nietzsche,* trans. Richard L. Collier, Jr., New Brunswick, N.J.: Athlone Press, 2000; Eugene Victor Wolfenstein, *Inside/Outside Nietzsche: Psychoanalytic Explorations,* Ithaca, N.Y.: Cornell University Press, 2000.

For studies of Nietzsche and literary criticism and theory, see Gilles Deleuze, *Nietzsche and Philosophy,* trans. Hugh Tomlinson, New York: Columbia University Press, 1961; Peter Heller, *Dialectics and Nihilism: Essays on Lessing, Nietzsche, Mann, and Kafka,* Amherst: University of Massachusetts Press, 1966; Herbert W. Reichert, *Friedrich Nietzsche's Impact on Modern German Literature,* Chapel Hill: University of North Carolina Press, 1975; Sander L. Gilman, *Nietzschean Parody,* Bonn: Bouvier, 1976; Harold Alderman, *Nietzsche's Gift,* Athens: Ohio University Press, 1977; David B. Allison, ed., *The New Nietzsche: Contemporary Styles of Interpretation,* New York: Dell, 1977; Malcolm Pasley, ed. *Nietzsche: Imagery and Thought,* Berkeley: University of California Press, 1978; Paul de Man, *Allegories of Reading: Figural Language in Rousseau, Nietzsche, Rilke, and Proust,* New Haven, Conn.: Yale University Press, 1979; Jacques Derrida, *Spurs: Nietzsche's Styles,* trans. Barbara Harlow, Chicago: University of Chicago Press, 1979; Peter Heller, *Studies in Nietzsche,* Bonn: Bouvier, 1980; Stanley Rosen, "Nietzsche's Image of Chaos," *International Philosophical Quarterly* 20 (1980): 3–23; J. Hillis Miller, "The Disarticulation of the Self in Nietzsche," *Monist* 64 (April 1981): 247–61; Avital Ronell, "Queens of the Night: Nietzsche's Antibodies," *Genre* 16 (1983): 404–22; Michel Foucault, "Ecce Homo or the Written Body," trans. Judith Still, *Oxford Literary Review* 7, 1–2 (1985): 3–24; Michel Foucault, "Nietzsche, Freud, Marx," trans. Jon Anderson and Gary Hentzi, *Critical Texts* 3, 2 (1986): 1–5; Karsten Harries, "Boundary Disputes," *The Journal of Philosophy* 83 (November 1986): 676–77; Robert J. Williams, "Literary Fiction as Philosophy: The Case of Nietzsche's Zarathustra," *The Journal of Philosophy* 83 (November 1986): 667–75; Harold Bloom, ed., *Friedrich Nietzsche,* New York: Chelsea House, 1987; Claudia Crawford, *The Beginnings of Nietzsche's Theory of Language,* Berlin: Walter de Gruyter, 1988; Erich Heller, *The Importance of Nietzsche,* Chicago: University of Chicago Press, 1988; David Farrell Krell and David Wood, eds., *Exceedingly Nietzsche: Aspects of Contemporary Nietzsche Interpretation,* London: Routledge, 1988; Adrian Del Caro, *Nietzsche Contra Nietzsche: Creativity and the Anti-Romantic,* Baton Rouge: Louisiana State University Press, 1989; Bernd Magnus, "Nietzsche and Postmodern Criticism," *Nietzsche-Studien* 18 (1989): 301–16; Gary Shapiro, *Nietzschean Narratives,* Bloomington: Indiana University Press, 1989; Babette E. Babich, "On Nietzsche's Concinnity: An Analysis of Style," *Nietzsche-Studien* 19 (1990): 59–80; and "Self-Deconstruction: Nietzsche's Philosophy as Style," *Soundings* 73, 1 (spring

1990): 107–16; Alan D. Schrift, *Nietzsche and the Question of Interpretation: Between Hermeneutics and Deconstruction*, London: Routledge, 1990; Henry Staten, *Nietzsche's Voice*, Ithaca, N.Y.: Cornell University Press, 1990; Ernst Behler, *Confrontations: Derrida, Heidegger, Nietzsche*, trans. Steven Taubeneck, Stanford, Calif.: Stanford University Press, 1991; Eric Blondel, *Nietzsche, the Body and Culture: Philosophy as a Philological Genealogy*, trans. Sean Hand, Stanford, Calif.: Stanford University Press, 1991; Gary Shapiro, *Alcyone: Nietzsche on Gifts, Noise and Women*, Albany: State University of New York Press, 1991; Georges Bataille, *On Nietzsche*, trans. Bruce Boone, London: Athlone Press, 1992; Daniel W. Conway, "Nietzsche's Art of This-Worldly Comfort: Self-Reference and Strategic Self-Parody," *History of Philosophy Quarterly* 9 (July 1992): 343–57; Keith Ansell-Pearson, ed., *The Fate of the New Nietzsche*, Aldershot, U.K.: Avebury, 1993; Pierre Klossowski, *Nietzsche and the Vicious Circle*, London: Athlone Press, 1993; Sarah Kofman, *Nietzsche and Metaphor*, ed. and trans. Duncan Large, London: Athlone Press, 1993; Bernd Magnus, Stanley Stewart, and Jean-Pierre Mileur, *Nietzsche's Case: Philosophy as/and Literature*, London: Routledge, 1993.

For works on Nietzsche and feminism, see Sandy Frisby. "Woman and the Will to Power," *Gnosis* 1 (spring 1975): 1–10; Hinton R. Tomas, "Nietzsche, Women and the Whip," *German Life and Letters: Special Number for L. W. Forester* 34 (1980): 117–25; Maryanne J. Bertram, "God's Second Blunder—Serpent Woman and the Gestalt in Nietzsche's Thought," *Southern Journal of Philosophy* 19 (fall 1981): 252–78; Lawrence J. Hatab, "Nietzsche on Woman," *Southern Journal of Philosophy* 19 (fall 1981): 333–46; Michael Platt, "Woman, Nietzsche, and Nature," *Maieutics* 2 (winter 1981): 27–42; David Farrell Krell, *Postponements: Woman, Sensuality, and Death in Nietzsche*, Bloomington: Indiana University Press, 1986; Ellen Kennedy and Susan Mendus, eds., *Women in Western Philosophy: Kant to Nietzsche*, Brighton, U.K.: Wheatsheaf Press, 1987; Kelly A. Oliver, "Nietzsche's 'Women': The Poststructuralist Attempt to Do Away with Women," *Radical Philosophy* 48 (spring 1988): 25–29; Carol Diethe, "Nietzsche and the Woman Question," *History of European Ideas* (1989): 865–76; Jean Graybeal, *Language and "The Feminine" in Nietzsche and Heidegger*, Bloomington: Indiana University Press, 1990; Luce Irigaray, *Marine Lover of Friedrich Nietzsche*, trans. Gilliam C. Gill, New York: Columbia University Press, 1991; Paul Patton, ed., *Nietzsche, Feminism, and Political Theory*, London: Routledge, 1993; Peter J. Burgard, *Nietzsche and the Feminine*, Charlottesville: University Press of Virginia, 1994; Carol Diethe, *Nietzsche's Women: Beyond the Whip*, Berlin: Walter de Gruyter, 1996; Jacqueline R. Scott, "Nietzsche and the Problem of Women's Bodies," *International Studies in Philosophy* 21/3 (1999): 65–76.

For discussions of the reception of Nietzsche's work and his influence, see David S. Thatcher, *Nietzsche in England 1900–1914: The Growth of a Reputation,* Toronto: University of Toronto Press, 1970; John Burt Foster, Jr., *Heirs to Dionysus: A Nietzschean Current in Literary Modernism,* Princeton, N.J.: Princeton University Press, 1981; Freny Mistry, *Nietzsche and Buddhism,* Berlin: Walter de Gruyter, 1981; R. Hinton Thomas, *Nietzsche in German Politics and Society, 1890–1918,* Manchester, U.K.: Manchester University Press, 1983; Daniel O'Hara, ed., *Why Nietzsche Now?* Bloomington: Indiana University Press, 1985; Bernice Glatzer Rosenthal, ed., *Nietzsche in Russia,* Princeton, N.J.: Princeton University Press, 1986; Kathryn V. Lindberg, *Reading Pound Reading: Modernism after Nietzsche,* New York: Oxford University Press, 1987; Edith W. Clowes, *The Revolution of Moral Consciousness: Nietzsche in Russian Literature, 1890–1914,* De Kalb: Northern Illinois University Press, 1988; Thomas Harrison, ed., *Nietzsche in Italy,* Saratoga, Calif.: ANMA Libri, 1988; Keiji Nishitani, *The Self-Overcoming of Nihilism,* trans. Graham Parkes with Setsuko Aihara, Albany: State University of New York Press, 1990; Laurence A. Rickels, ed., *Looking After Nietzsche,* Albany: State University of New York Press, 1990; Ezra and Sascha Talmor, eds., *Nietzsche's Influence on Contemporary Thought,* part 3 of *History of European Ideas,* vol. 2 (1989), special issue, *Turning Points in History,* Oxford: Pergamon Press, 1990; Seth Taylor, *Left-wing Nietzscheans: The Politics of German Expressionism, 1910–1920,* Berlin: Walter de Gruyter, 1990; Graham Parkes, ed., *Nietzsche and Asian Thought,* Chicago: University of Chicago Press, 1991; Steven E. Aschheim, *The Nietzsche Legacy in Germany, 1890–1990,* Berkeley: University of California Press, 1993; Bernice Glatzer Rosenthal, ed., *Nietzsche and Soviet Culture: Ally and Adversary,* Cambridge, U.K.: Cambridge University Press, 1994; James Winchester, *Nietzsche's Aesthetic Turn: Reading Nietzsche after Heidegger, Deleuze and Derrida,* Albany: State University of New York Press, 1994; Manfred Putz, ed., *Nietzsche in American Literature and Thought,* Columbia, S.C.: Camden House, 1995; Ted Sadler, *Nietzsche: Truth and Redemption. Critique of the Postmodernist Nietzsche,* London: Athlone Press, 1995; Alan D. Schrift, *Nietzsche's French Legacy: A Genealogy of Poststructuralism,* New York: Routledge, 1995; David Farrell Krell, *Infectious Nietzsche,* Bloomington: Indiana University Press, 1996; Douglas Smith, *Transvaluations: Nietzsche in France, 1872–1972,* Oxford, U.K.: Clarendon Press, 1996; Jacob Golomb, *Nietzsche and Jewish Culture,* New York: Routledge, 1997; Dragan Kujundzic, *The Returns of History: Russian Nietzscheans after Modernity,* Albany: State University of New York Press, 1997; Alice Freifeld, Peter Bergmann, and Bernice Glatzer Rosenthal, eds., *East Europe Reads Nietzsche,* Boulder,

Colo.: East European Monographs, 1998; Raymond Furness, *Zarathustra's Children: A Study of a Lost Generation of German Writers,* Rochester, N.Y.: Camden House, 2000.

For studies of individual works, see Martin Heidegger, "Who is Nietzsche's Zarathustra?," trans. Bernd Magnus, in *The New Nietzsche: Contemporary Styles of Interpretation,* ed. David B. Allison, New York: Dell, 1977; Richard Schacht, "Nietzsche on Art in *The Birth of Tragedy,*" in *Aesthetics: A Critical Anthology,* ed. George Dickie and Richard Sclafani, New York: St. Martin's Press, 1977; David Goicoechea, *The Great Year of Zarathustra (1881–1981),* Lanham, Md.: University Press of America, 1983; Maudemarie Clark, "Deconstructing The Birth of Tragedy," *International Studies in Philosophy* 19, 2 (1987): 67–75; Kathleen Marie Higgins, *Nietzsche's Zarathustra,* Philadelphia: Temple University Press, 1987; Laurence Lambert, *Nietzsche's Teaching: An Interpretation of* Thus Spoke Zarathustra, New Haven, Conn.: Yale University Press, 1987; David Lenson, The Birth of Tragedy: *A Commentary,* Boston: Twayne Publishers, 1987; Carl G. Jung, *Nietzsche's Zarathustra,* ed. James L. Jarrett, Princeton, N.J.: Princeton University Press, 1988; Robert A. Rethy, "The Tragic Affirmation of *The Birth of Tragedy,*" *Nietzsche-Studien* 17 (1988): 1–44; Robert C. Solomon and Kathleen Marie Higgins, eds., *Reading Nietzsche,* New York: Oxford University Press, 1988; Keith M. May, *Nietzsche and the Spirit of Tragedy,* Basingstoke, U.K.: Macmillan, 1990; John C. Sallis, *Crossings: Nietzsche and the Space of Tragedy,* Chicago: University of Chicago Press, 1991; Richard Schacht, *Nietzsche, Genealogy, Morality: Essays on Nietzsche's* On the Genealogy of Morals, Berkeley: University of California Press, 1994; Thomas Steinbok, *A Commentary on Nietzsche's* Ecce Homo, Lanham, Md.: University Press of America, 1994; Daniel W. Conway, *Nietzsche's Dangerous Game: Philosophy in the Twilight of the Idols,* Cambridge, U.K.: Cambridge University Press, 1997; John Wilcox, "What Aphorism Does Nietzsche Explicate in *Genealogy of Morals,* Essay III?" in *Journal of the History of Philosophy* 35, 4 (October 1997): 593–610; Francesca Cauchi, *Zarathustra contra Zarathustra: The Tragic Buffoon,* Aldershot, U.K.: Ashgate, 1998; Sarah Kofman, *Explosion I: Of Nietzsche's* Ecce Homo, trans. Jessica George, David Blacker, and Judith Rowan, London: Athlone Press, 1999; Ruth Abbey, *Nietzsche's Middle Period,* Oxford, U.K.: Oxford University Press, 2000; Kathleen Marie Higgins, *Comic Relief: Nietzsche's* Gay Science, New York: Oxford University Press, 2000; James I. Porter, *The Invention of Dionysus: An Essay on* The Birth of Tragedy, Stanford, Calif.: Stanford University Press, 2000; David B. Allison, *Reading the New Nietzsche,* Lanham, Md: Rowman and Littlefield, 2001; Robert Gooding-Williams, *Zarathus-*

tra's Dionysian Modernism, Stanford, Calif.: Stanford University Press, 2001; Laurence Lampert, *Nietzsche's Task: An Interpretation of* Beyond Good and Evil, New Haven, Conn.: Yale University Press, 2001.

For works on the superman, see Bernd Magnus, *Nietzsche's Existential Imperative,* Bloomington: Indiana University Press, 1978; Bruce Detwiler, *Nietzsche and the Politics of Aristocratic Radicalism,* Chicago: University of Chicago Press, 1990; Keith Ansell-Pearson, *Viroid Life: Perspectives on Nietzsche and the Transhuman Condition,* London: Routledge, 1997; Sheridan Hough, *Nietzsche's Noontide Friend: The Self as Metaphoric Double,* University Park: Pennsylvania State University Press, 1997.

For discussions of the concept of eternal recurrence, see Joan Stambaugh, *Nietzsche's Thought of Eternal Return,* Baltimore: The Johns Hopkins University Press, 1972; Michael E. Zimmerman, "Heidegger and Nietzsche on Authentic Time," *Cultural Hermeneutics* 4 (July 1977): 239–64; Lawrence J. Hatab, *Nietzsche and Eternal Recurrence: The Redemption of Time and Becoming,* Washington, D.C.: University Press of America, 1978; Bernd Magnus, "Eternal Recurrence," *Nietzsche-Studien* 8 (1979): 362–77; Debra B. Bergoffen, "The Eternal Recurrence Again," *International Studies in Philosophy* 15, 2 (1983): 35–46; Robin Small, "Three Interpretations of Eternal Recurrence," *Dialogue, Canadian Philosophical Review* 22 (1983): 21–112; Joan Stambaugh, *The Problem of Time in Nietzsche,* Lewisberg, Pa.: Bucknell University Press, 1987; Karl Löwith, *Nietzsche's Philosophy of the Eternal Recurrence of the Same,* trans. J. Harvey Lomax, Berkeley: University of California Press, 1997.

Works on the concept of genealogy include Michel Foucault, "Nietzsche, Genealogy, History," in *Language, Counter-Memory, Practice,* trans. Donald F. Bouchard and Sherry Simon, Ithaca, N.Y.: Cornell University Press, 1977; Michael Mahon, *Foucault's Nietzschean Genealogy: Truth, Power, and the Subject,* Albany: State University Press of New York, 1992; David Owen, *Maturity and Modernity: Nietzsche, Weber, Foucault and the Ambivalence of Reason,* London: Routledge, 1994; Randall Havas, *Nietzsche's Genealogy: Nihilism and the Will to Knowledge,* Ithaca, N.Y.: Cornell University Press, 1995.

For studies of the will to power, see Jacob Golomb, *Nietzsche's Enticing Philosophy of Power,* Ames: Iowa State University Press, 1989; Bernd Magnus, "Author, Writer, Text: The Will to Power," *International Studies in Philosophy* 22, 2 (1990): 49–57; Stephen P. Schwartz, *Nietzsche's Doctrine of Will to Power,* Cuxhaven, Del.: T. Junghans, 1998; Linda L. Williams, *Nietzsche's Mirror: The World as Will to Power,* Lanham, Md.: Rowman and Littlefield, 2001.

Biographies of Nietzsche include Ronald Hayman, *Nietzsche, a Critical Life,* New York: Oxford University Press, 1980; Alexander Nehamas, *Nietzsche: Life as Literature,* Cambridge, Mass.: Harvard University Press, 1985; Gary Elsner, *Nietzsche: A Philosophical Biography,* Lanham, Md.: University Press of America, 1992; Lesley Chamberlain, *Nietzsche in Turin: An Intimate Biography,* New York: Picador, 1996; Rudiger Safranski, *Nietzsche: A Philosophical Biography,* trans. Shelley Frisch, New York: Norton, 2002.

MODERN LIBRARY IS ONLINE AT
WWW.MODERNLIBRARY.COM

MODERN LIBRARY ONLINE IS YOUR GUIDE
TO CLASSIC LITERATURE ON THE WEB

THE MODERN LIBRARY E-NEWSLETTER

Our free e-mail newsletter is sent to subscribers, and features sample chapters, interviews with and essays by our authors, upcoming books, special promotions, announcements, and news.

To subscribe to the Modern Library e-newsletter, send a blank e-mail to: **join-modernlibrary@list.randomhouse.com** or visit **www.modernlibrary.com**

THE MODERN LIBRARY WEBSITE

Check out the Modern Library website at
www.modernlibrary.com for:

- The Modern Library e-newsletter
- A list of our current and upcoming titles and series
- Reading Group Guides and exclusive author spotlights
- Special features with information on the classics and other paperback series
- Excerpts from new releases and other titles
- A list of our e-books and information on where to buy them
- The Modern Library Editorial Board's 100 Best Novels and 100 Best Nonfiction Books of the Twentieth Century written in the English language
- News and announcements

Questions? E-mail us at **modernlibrary@randomhouse.com**
For questions about examination or desk copies, please visit
the Random House Academic Resources site at
www.randomhouse.com/academic